The CRB Commodity Yearbook 2011

Commodity Research Bureau

www.crbyearbook.com

Published by Commodity Research Bureau, Chicago, Illinois

For general information on our other products and services or for technical support, please contact our Customer Support Department within the United States at (800) 621-5271, outside the United States at (312) 554-8456 or fax (312) 939-4135.

ISBN 978-0-910418-99-7

Printed in the United States of America

10   9   8   7   6   5   4   3   2   1

Commodity Research Bureau
330 South Wells Street, Sixth Floor
Chicago, Illinois 60606-7110 USA
800.621.5271 or +1.312.554.8456
Fax: +1.312.939.4135
Website: www.crbyearbook.com
Email: info@crbyearbook.com

Contents

The Commodity Price Trend

The CRB Continuous Commodity Index (CCI) rallied sharply in 2010 by 30.0%, adding to the 33.4% rally seen in 2008 and easily overcoming the 23.7% downward correction seen in 2008. The CCI index in early 2011 extended the 2010 rally and posted a new record high, bringing the overall 2001-11 commodity bull market to a total of 268%. The rally in commodity prices in 2010 was driven mainly by strong demand across the board for most commodities. The global economy in 2010 showed a solid economic recovery that helped produce stronger demand for nearly all raw materials. Commodity prices in 2010 were also pushed higher by supply disruptions in various markets tied to the weather such as the drought during the summer of 2010 in Russia and eastern Europe that drove wheat prices higher.

All of the six CCI futures sub-sectors closed higher in 2010: Industrials +62.5%, Metals +45.0%, Grains +44.2%, Softs +31.8%, Meats +23.7%, and Energy +8.4%. The sub-sector changes noted above are calculated by taking the average of the percentage changes of the constituents in each sub-sector.

Energy

The CCI Energy sub-sector, which is composed of Crude Oil, Heating Oil, and Natural Gas, accounts for 18% of the overall CCI Index. The constituents in the Energy sub-sector on average in 2010 closed up +8.4%, adding to the 2009 gain of 57.8%. On a nearest-futures basis, crude oil in 2010 closed up +15.1%, gasoline closed up +19.5%, heating oil closed up +20.1%, and natural gas closed down −20.9%. Crude oil prices during 2010 traded in a sideways range mostly between $70-85 per barrel because OPEC maintained a lower production level and was successful in keeping oil prices near its intended target. Crude oil prices in late 2010 and early 2011 started to rally in response to the pickup in the economy and in global fuel demand. Natural gas prices fell sharply in 2010 in response to an oversupply situation.

Grains

The CCI Grains and Oilseeds sub-sector, which is composed of Corn, Soybeans, and Wheat, accounts for 18% of the overall CCI Index. The constituents in the Grains and Oilseeds sub-sector on average closed up 44.2%, more than reversing the loss of -0.9% seen in 2009 and -20.2% in 2008. On a nearest-futures basis, corn in 2010 rose +51.7%, soybeans rose +34.0%, and wheat closed +46.7%. Corn was the leader in 2010 on a smaller-than-expected crop and on very strong demand that led to a very low U.S. stocks-to-use ratio of 5.0%, which matched the post-war record low of 5.0% posted in 1995/96. The supply situation was a little better for soybeans and wheat, but the strong rally in

corn prices set up strong competition for planting acres for spring 2011. Soybean prices were supported by large-scale purchases by China. Wheat prices were supported in 2010 by a drought in Russia and Eastern Europe that slashed supplies from that important wheat growing area.

Industrials

The CCI Industrials sub-sector, which is composed of Copper and Cotton, accounts for 12% of the overall Index. The constituents in the Industrials sub-sector on average showed a +62.5% rise in 2010, adding to the 96.4% increase seen in 2009. Copper closed higher by +33.4%, adding to the +138.5% increase seen in 2009, mainly due to continued strong demand from China. Cotton prices rallied by 91.5% in 2010, adding to the +54.2% rally seen in 2009. The main bullish factor for cotton was large-scale cotton demand from China.

Livestock

The CCI Livestock sub-sector, which is composed of Live Cattle and Lean Hogs, accounts for 12% of the CCI Index. The constituents in the Livestock sub-sector on average closed up +23.7% in 2010, adding to the 4.0% rally in 2009. On a nearest-futures basis, cattle closed +25.7% while lean hogs closed +21.6%. Livestock prices in 2010 were supported by strong demand and limited supply as the sharp increase in feed costs caused livestock producers to minimize their herd sizes.

Precious Metals

The CCI Precious Metals sub-sector, which is composed of Gold, Platinum, and Silver, accounts for 17% of the overall Index. The constituents in the Precious Metals sub-sector on average closed up +45.0% in 2010, adding to the +43.1% rally in 2009. Bullish factors in 2010 centered on general weakness in the dollar, safe-haven demand with the European debt crisis, and fears of an eventual inflation breakout with quantitative easing programs in the U.S., U.K. and Japan.

Softs

The CCI Softs sub-sector, which is composed of Cocoa, Coffee, Orange Juice, and Sugar #11, accounts for 23% of the CCI Index. The constituents in the Softs sub-sector on average in 2010 closed up +31.8%, adding to the +63.5% rally seen in 2009. Three of the four soft commodities rose in 2010 with gains of 76.9% in coffee, +39.0% in orange juice, and +19.2% in sugar. Cocoa closed -7.7% lower in 2010. The softs complex saw strength in 2010 mainly because of improved demand and also because of supply disruptions in specific markets.

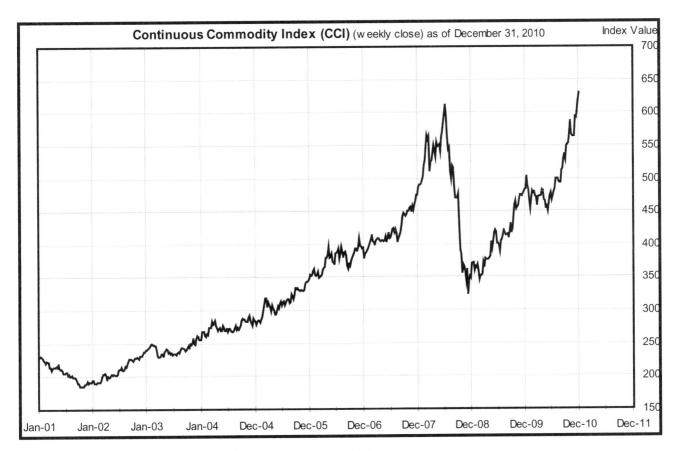

Continuous Commodity Index (CCI) (weekly close) as of December 31, 2010

Index Value

Continuous Commodity Index (CCI)   (High, Low and Close 1967 = 100)

Year		Jan.	Feb.	Mar.	Apr.	May	June	July	Aug.	Sept.	Oct.	Nov.	Dec.	Range
2001	High	232.58	228.34	225.75	216.39	219.29	212.39	209.27	202.90	202.34	191.09	192.74	193.94	232.58
	Low	223.02	219.68	210.24	208.87	208.43	203.86	201.84	197.02	188.24	182.83	181.83	187.73	181.83
	Settle	224.12	221.78	210.26	214.50	209.00	205.56	202.70	199.63	190.49	185.66	192.66	190.61	----
2002	High	195.97	193.53	205.45	208.39	205.33	209.33	215.10	219.24	229.62	231.67	231.83	238.39	238.39
	Low	186.38	187.19	192.26	195.21	197.42	199.56	207.24	208.46	217.60	223.82	223.29	230.17	186.38
	Settle	187.29	192.33	204.92	201.16	204.20	209.29	210.97	219.20	226.53	228.91	230.64	234.52	----
2003	High	248.92	251.59	247.23	236.62	242.16	238.25	237.20	243.74	246.07	250.67	257.54	263.60	263.60
	Low	234.58	245.39	228.10	228.77	231.26	231.39	230.36	233.96	236.79	241.68	244.79	249.60	228.10
	Settle	248.45	247.25	232.15	232.53	235.55	233.78	234.21	243.70	243.66	247.58	248.44	255.29	----
2004	High	271.08	275.02	285.28	284.42	277.94	282.03	275.38	278.10	285.37	289.29	292.49	291.02	292.49
	Low	257.49	258.94	270.52	268.53	266.80	264.34	265.50	265.20	269.12	280.53	280.20	276.15	257.49
	Settle	262.57	274.73	283.77	272.54	277.25	265.94	267.78	276.50	284.98	283.70	290.94	283.90	----
2005	High	288.38	305.00	323.33	313.23	304.25	315.79	316.46	321.60	333.58	338.19	332.58	349.20	349.20
	Low	277.07	280.19	304.22	297.47	292.06	300.76	302.71	309.21	317.05	326.36	326.09	332.62	277.07
	Settle	284.75	305.00	313.57	303.74	300.83	306.91	315.24	318.99	333.33	326.68	332.49	347.89	----
2006	High	363.70	364.28	365.66	382.46	399.66	387.52	396.16	399.90	393.51	389.24	408.91	409.65	409.65
	Low	348.57	345.49	346.56	360.85	376.35	363.63	375.73	380.15	359.07	361.19	385.23	391.77	345.49
	Settle	363.30	353.27	361.91	379.53	379.80	385.63	391.49	390.95	370.10	383.92	408.79	394.89	----
2007	High	396.93	414.62	411.26	411.97	408.05	418.59	426.79	424.78	450.36	454.40	461.06	477.48	477.48
	Low	377.59	390.76	395.75	401.53	401.16	402.80	409.78	395.03	412.70	436.88	446.46	450.94	377.59
	Settle	394.37	410.64	407.45	403.54	407.58	410.36	424.52	413.49	447.56	454.29	451.26	476.08	----
2008	High	503.45	567.84	577.64	556.09	556.84	599.36	615.04	553.81	517.81	457.69	388.82	364.82	615.04
	Low	475.91	501.42	509.00	507.82	523.37	539.42	538.86	498.36	449.70	350.53	341.55	322.53	322.53
	Settle	503.27	565.65	516.38	536.23	541.30	595.98	548.86	516.47	452.42	369.56	361.74	363.06	----
2009	High	382.99	372.28	378.55	379.59	418.80	430.20	413.47	430.19	436.06	473.86	479.70	489.61	489.61
	Low	348.96	342.97	341.44	363.16	372.57	391.97	381.65	403.08	408.80	420.83	454.64	466.83	341.44
	Settle	364.50	352.45	368.83	371.55	417.04	398.76	413.41	415.49	430.67	452.69	479.22	484.42	----
2010	High	504.76	480.49	482.57	483.24	483.27	480.22	499.05	510.69	540.01	566.54	604.30	630.45	630.45
	Low	464.91	451.79	459.65	466.90	447.39	447.89	464.97	486.39	497.50	523.93	553.65	565.80	447.39
	Settle	465.29	478.32	467.25	481.11	458.70	471.37	499.05	496.73	536.12	566.28	565.96	629.53	----

Source: Thomson-Reuters

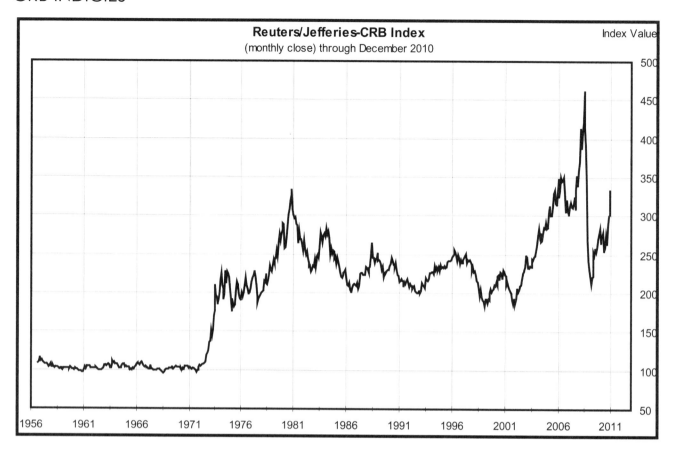

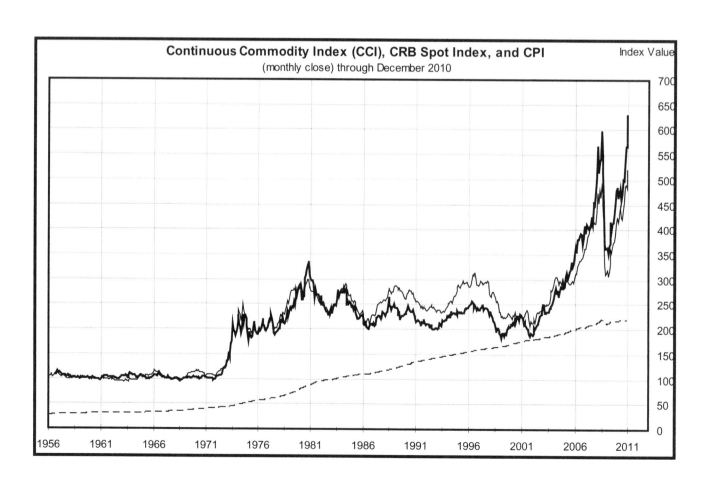

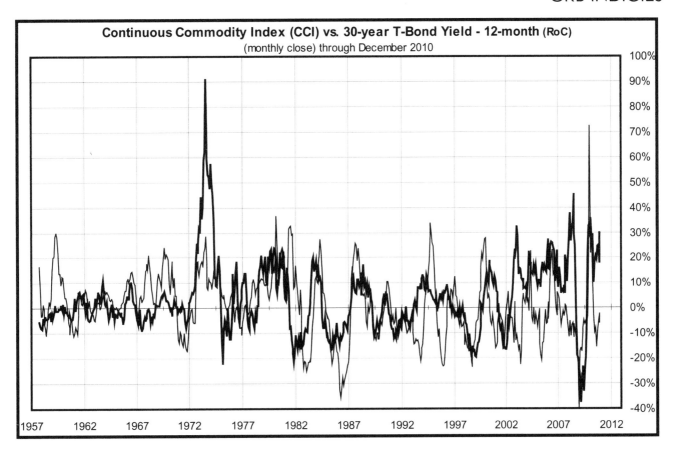

Continuous Commodity Index (CCI) vs. 30-year T-Bond Yield - 12-month (RoC)
(monthly close) through December 2010

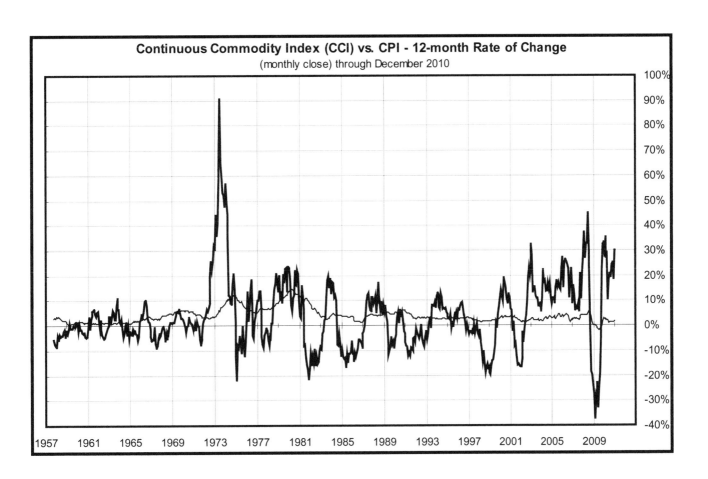

Continuous Commodity Index (CCI) vs. CPI - 12-month Rate of Change
(monthly close) through December 2010

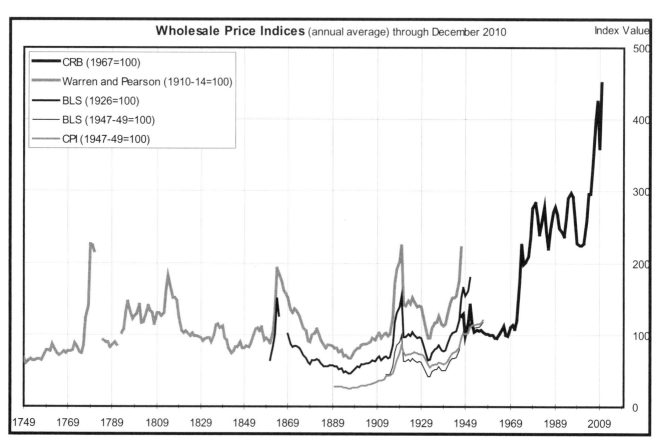

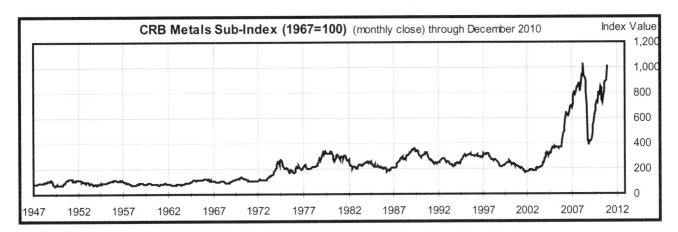

CRB Metals Sub-Index (1967=100) (monthly close) through December 2010

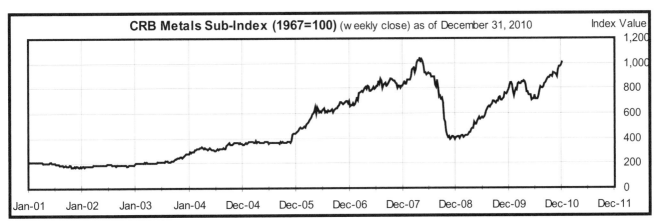

CRB Metals Sub-Index (1967=100) (weekly close) as of December 31, 2010

CRB Textiles Sub-Index (1967=100) (monthly close) through December 2010

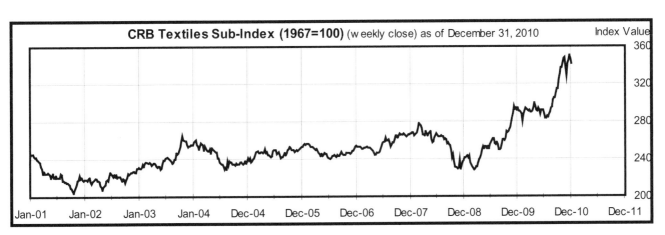

CRB Textiles Sub-Index (1967=100) (weekly close) as of December 31, 2010

CRB INDICIES

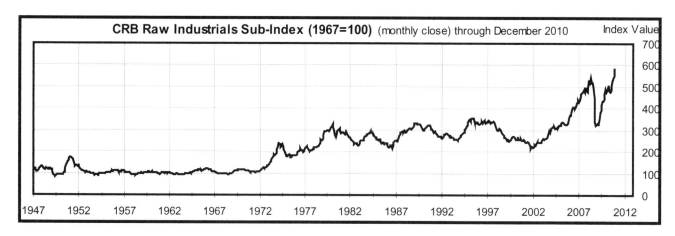

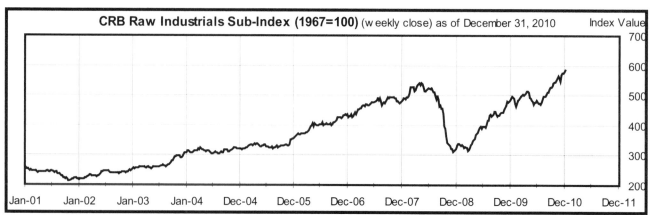

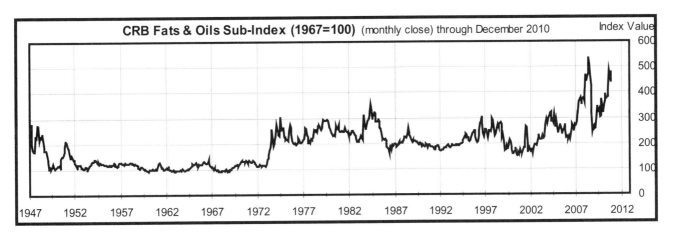

CRB INDICIES

CRB Spot Index (monthly close) through December 2010

Index Value

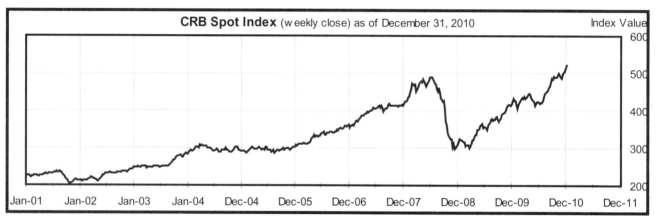

CRB Spot Index (weekly close) as of December 31, 2010

Index Value

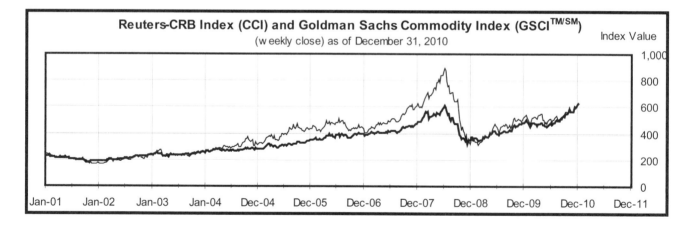

Reuters-CRB Index (CCI) and Goldman Sachs Commodity Index (GSCI$^{TM/SM}$)
(weekly close) as of December 31, 2010

Index Value

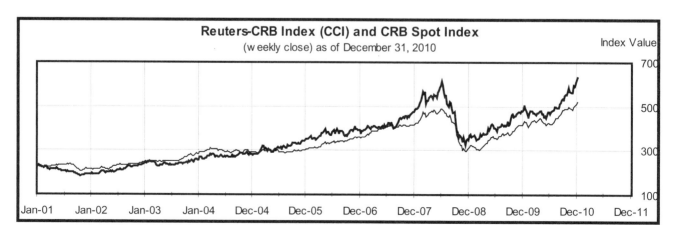

Reuters-CRB Index (CCI) and CRB Spot Index
(weekly close) as of December 31, 2010

Index Value

Continuous Commodity Index (CCI)   (1967=100)

Year	Jan.	Feb.	Mar.	Apr.	May	June	July	Aug.	Sept.	Oct.	Nov.	Dec.	Average
2001	228.30	223.42	218.06	213.43	214.69	208.37	204.98	200.18	195.34	186.20	188.42	190.42	205.98
2002	191.44	190.91	201.86	200.74	201.69	203.92	211.42	214.01	226.00	227.52	228.54	234.62	211.06
2003	242.04	247.89	237.81	231.73	237.38	235.11	234.05	238.13	241.44	246.15	250.66	258.44	241.74
2004	266.65	264.93	278.19	276.48	272.78	270.78	270.41	271.18	276.47	285.36	286.02	283.28	275.21
2005	282.96	289.01	312.70	305.26	298.11	308.07	311.47	315.00	324.05	333.46	330.39	343.83	312.86
2006	354.56	354.30	353.74	371.33	385.81	374.50	386.50	389.11	372.98	376.70	395.21	397.28	376.00
2007	386.38	400.96	403.41	405.99	404.24	410.22	418.88	411.65	432.37	446.95	453.23	467.28	420.13
2008	490.38	531.00	547.16	538.62	544.56	572.19	573.12	517.71	475.59	392.21	360.19	346.15	490.74
2009	364.14	356.43	358.81	372.81	399.62	410.96	400.35	417.38	421.88	450.93	466.10	479.51	408.24
2010	488.95	470.99	472.21	476.18	464.23	465.76	478.19	495.62	523.97	549.42	572.44	604.78	505.23

Average.   *Source: Thomson-Reuters*

Reuters/Jefferies-CRB Futures Index[1]   (1967=100)

Year	Jan.	Feb.	Mar.	Apr.	May	June	July	Aug.	Sept.	Oct.	Nov.	Dec.	Average
2001	228.30	223.42	218.06	213.43	214.69	208.37	204.98	200.18	195.34	186.20	188.42	190.42	205.98
2002	191.44	190.91	201.86	200.74	201.69	203.92	234.05	238.13	226.00	227.52	250.66	258.44	211.06
2003	242.04	247.89	237.81	231.73	237.38	235.11	234.05	238.13	241.44	246.15	250.66	283.28	275.21
2004	266.65	264.93	278.19	276.48	272.78	270.78	270.41	271.18	276.47	285.36	286.02	283.28	275.21
2005	282.96	289.01	312.70	305.26	298.11	306.97	308.04	318.76	326.19	326.44	315.27	327.58	309.77
2006	340.95	331.30	325.98	345.84	351.22	339.21	346.86	340.18	310.28	304.36	310.84	311.60	329.89
2007	292.18	305.63	309.03	314.35	310.77	314.32	320.89	308.89	323.89	336.20	349.82	349.36	319.61
2008	363.88	386.31	403.95	409.23	422.29	445.14	438.75	394.23	360.98	288.86	249.29	221.26	365.35
2009	224.69	212.16	215.45	222.70	241.36	255.94	244.10	260.66	253.92	269.88	274.27	276.58	245.98
2010	281.42	270.35	273.37	276.86	259.57	258.08	262.43	269.78	278.38	295.45	305.25	321.54	279.37

Average.   [1] New Calculation begins June 20, 2005.   *Source: Thomson-Reuters*

Reuters/Jefferies-CRB Total Return Index[1]   (01/02/1982=100)

Year	Jan.	Feb.	Mar.	Apr.	May	June	July	Aug.	Sept.	Oct.	Nov.	Dec.	Average
2001	159.32	160.43	154.34	153.31	154.96	148.13	143.62	143.81	137.50	127.30	124.39	123.48	144.22
2002	123.82	124.53	135.70	138.03	138.93	138.66	143.23	145.91	153.53	153.91	151.63	161.51	142.45
2003	171.83	182.79	178.17	171.17	175.28	178.21	178.96	184.60	182.27	191.06	194.53	204.73	182.80
2004	213.15	215.30	226.72	227.21	234.19	230.03	232.57	236.76	238.75	254.24	248.91	241.10	233.24
2005	244.84	250.48	273.57	267.03	254.14	267.60	271.16	281.23	288.68	289.74	280.70	292.65	271.82
2006	305.70	298.05	294.39	313.52	319.76	310.00	318.32	313.52	287.18	282.84	290.08	291.98	302.11
2007	275.02	288.82	293.24	299.54	297.32	301.96	309.52	299.14	314.90	327.82	342.08	342.69	307.67
2008	357.92	380.80	398.78	404.43	417.85	441.16	435.51	391.90	359.36	287.82	248.68	220.56	362.06
2009	224.05	211.60	214.92	222.20	240.85	255.44	243.66	260.22	253.80	269.50	273.89	276.21	245.53
2010	281.07	270.02	273.08	276.59	259.36	257.89	262.29	269.66	278.28	295.38	305.20	321.54	279.20

Average.   [1] Theoretical data prior to June 20, 2005.   *Source: Thomson-Reuters*

CRB INDICIES

CRB Spot Metals Sub-Index (1967=100)

Year	Jan.	Feb.	Mar.	Apr.	May	June	July	Aug.	Sept.	Oct.	Nov.	Dec.	Average
2001	212.47	212.90	210.59	204.94	205.14	205.60	197.04	188.09	181.32	179.50	172.96	173.80	195.36
2002	174.76	176.41	181.22	186.31	189.12	189.38	192.66	184.51	184.03	185.61	183.21	186.27	184.46
2003	199.71	204.17	206.72	202.78	205.57	207.77	212.24	214.09	220.24	240.20	248.49	266.70	219.06
2004	287.40	306.07	320.96	321.90	314.73	308.28	312.29	318.21	333.97	350.45	359.77	361.92	324.66
2005	355.95	364.50	371.99	371.31	365.83	369.32	361.39	363.75	364.70	369.68	370.47	425.84	371.23
2006	458.64	485.21	504.91	571.37	623.28	616.35	621.31	617.86	623.05	660.11	681.87	693.51	596.46
2007	668.94	691.71	761.81	798.96	798.65	803.29	834.00	840.13	835.06	868.19	828.50	812.12	795.11
2008	843.66	883.22	947.21	1,011.63	1,006.52	914.50	901.61	837.56	728.05	545.95	404.38	400.04	785.36
2009	409.17	416.80	421.44	455.21	410.21	552.61	591.59	651.17	688.67	704.55	716.43	767.81	565.47
2010	830.98	773.24	833.04	850.73	765.47	717.04	728.15	804.22	853.40	896.08	905.01	971.85	827.43

Average.   *Source: Commodity Research Bureau*

CRB Spot Textiles Sub-Index (1967=100)

Year	Jan.	Feb.	Mar.	Apr.	May	June	July	Aug.	Sept.	Oct.	Nov.	Dec.	Average
2001	244.74	241.84	233.40	225.97	224.47	222.12	222.44	218.55	214.74	207.79	215.86	218.99	224.24
2002	218.08	216.84	218.40	214.72	211.21	220.16	222.95	221.74	219.02	220.10	225.85	227.76	219.74
2003	231.25	235.31	235.04	234.64	231.66	235.24	240.88	237.50	244.30	256.99	257.59	254.25	241.22
2004	257.58	253.15	252.37	247.97	249.74	242.65	233.48	233.58	237.31	235.03	235.88	236.39	242.93
2005	239.93	240.36	247.12	247.73	246.60	244.69	247.21	243.08	246.64	251.24	248.96	250.83	246.20
2006	255.02	255.52	251.74	248.26	244.26	244.16	242.03	243.89	245.78	244.89	246.37	251.15	247.76
2007	252.50	251.35	251.91	248.99	245.40	250.72	260.09	256.51	261.58	264.79	265.79	265.28	256.24
2008	267.18	269.60	271.76	267.02	264.71	262.29	263.92	261.98	255.47	241.15	231.28	235.84	257.68
2009	241.13	237.01	229.83	240.05	252.00	253.03	258.94	253.52	257.42	265.67	280.85	293.96	255.28
2010	290.62	287.34	291.16	294.69	292.22	290.03	284.28	295.19	310.18	329.04	341.31	344.99	304.25

Average.   *Source: Commodity Research Bureau*

CRB Spot Raw Industrials Sub-Index (1967=100)

Year	Jan.	Feb.	Mar.	Apr.	May	June	July	Aug.	Sept.	Oct.	Nov.	Dec.	Average
2001	254.54	248.53	246.35	244.03	244.29	245.92	244.22	238.10	228.30	220.52	218.94	221.57	237.94
2002	219.05	222.33	231.03	230.38	231.81	243.72	245.38	240.53	240.77	240.68	243.04	248.21	236.41
2003	255.85	258.59	260.97	258.79	257.65	260.47	263.77	263.99	273.24	291.18	295.88	302.30	270.22
2004	312.24	309.54	316.77	318.52	312.98	308.40	308.84	307.54	315.25	315.13	320.52	322.65	314.03
2005	320.94	324.57	333.31	336.68	331.99	331.88	325.29	324.52	329.36	332.79	332.83	349.53	331.14
2006	363.05	371.00	372.08	385.69	400.62	399.97	403.50	403.90	403.19	415.76	426.67	434.25	398.31
2007	430.87	434.54	452.81	465.37	468.44	475.75	485.36	478.47	483.09	492.43	486.68	475.95	469.15
2008	487.92	502.29	522.98	534.29	532.30	517.02	517.29	495.17	460.96	392.49	329.86	317.83	467.53
2009	335.09	331.50	321.35	343.49	370.17	391.18	403.99	431.59	439.72	435.97	455.27	480.02	394.95
2010	492.93	476.13	499.63	510.22	489.56	476.07	474.97	498.86	518.04	539.43	555.01	574.70	508.80

Average.   *Source: Commodity Research Bureau*

CRB Spot Foodstuffs Sub-Index (1967=100)

Year	Jan.	Feb.	Mar.	Apr.	May	June	July	Aug.	Sept.	Oct.	Nov.	Dec.	Average
2001	189.68	192.93	200.48	203.57	210.24	213.09	222.61	232.42	224.06	199.51	200.24	203.40	207.69
2002	203.33	202.39	204.04	197.88	195.85	207.11	218.25	222.32	226.98	230.63	230.76	237.99	214.79
2003	238.60	237.01	234.16	234.55	239.15	239.53	232.81	234.30	244.69	251.04	255.36	257.99	241.60
2004	263.90	275.85	287.49	287.41	285.33	278.05	273.83	270.42	272.10	257.76	268.47	261.77	273.53
2005	252.84	246.44	253.58	252.19	254.21	255.43	251.31	247.65	249.22	253.37	252.74	242.54	250.96
2006	243.31	241.95	239.60	243.17	250.70	253.86	261.17	267.04	269.14	267.52	271.19	273.16	256.82
2007	275.31	286.30	297.37	299.85	311.98	320.79	322.44	319.95	325.01	322.19	325.40	337.97	312.05
2008	346.56	383.11	390.10	391.07	405.44	421.87	427.47	405.89	385.15	334.27	303.48	284.65	373.26
2009	299.83	286.21	284.71	302.35	316.81	318.81	301.83	304.44	305.01	314.86	338.56	339.54	309.41
2010	349.28	344.48	352.89	357.94	359.11	352.01	361.74	385.62	415.09	424.20	411.58	423.33	378.11

Average.   *Source: Commodity Research Bureau*

CRB Spot Fats and Oils Sub-Index   (1967=100)

Year	Jan.	Feb.	Mar.	Apr.	May	June	July	Aug.	Sept.	Oct.	Nov.	Dec.	Average
2001	170.49	158.27	165.77	177.63	177.95	196.02	232.89	259.60	237.33	177.05	174.66	184.78	192.70
2002	169.64	165.91	177.34	167.61	164.38	193.38	193.29	192.85	193.20	193.90	211.97	230.05	187.79
2003	222.39	209.89	215.72	216.91	219.56	229.01	225.83	223.36	251.40	285.47	288.08	292.22	239.99
2004	305.30	300.47	318.53	330.54	302.31	295.32	304.60	290.52	302.51	267.12	279.42	271.36	297.33
2005	248.45	238.13	252.70	263.98	262.93	266.01	245.81	243.51	259.50	268.43	269.77	231.17	254.20
2006	231.10	221.46	217.14	214.75	222.03	221.97	247.09	271.97	267.18	257.29	264.75	270.94	242.31
2007	274.74	274.35	300.01	313.08	339.65	366.31	376.09	357.79	365.74	365.51	381.69	364.06	339.92
2008	381.95	418.92	459.52	457.65	467.23	498.89	526.26	467.08	443.38	366.91	283.76	238.42	417.50
2009	283.42	254.79	243.41	285.09	321.74	335.76	308.54	340.28	324.64	298.33	343.85	344.85	307.06
2010	337.27	329.26	366.69	378.35	381.68	374.59	379.27	399.57	444.83	471.40	463.11	458.65	398.72

Average.   *Source: Commodity Research Bureau*

CRB Spot Livestock Sub-Index   (1967=100)

Year	Jan.	Feb.	Mar.	Apr.	May	June	July	Aug.	Sept.	Oct.	Nov.	Dec.	Average
2001	267.57	250.14	261.05	273.14	288.88	306.84	329.73	341.78	313.84	260.77	252.97	264.23	284.25
2002	251.61	260.32	274.95	257.32	256.33	289.40	288.22	279.03	274.13	276.94	288.86	313.14	275.85
2003	316.67	308.65	310.49	311.25	320.03	333.29	324.58	327.63	361.30	386.60	385.63	372.48	338.22
2004	372.16	353.19	362.41	369.65	369.31	374.28	395.48	392.33	395.40	365.68	373.69	370.63	374.52
2005	359.25	341.74	353.05	373.63	377.41	361.10	330.39	331.75	349.24	358.04	369.98	337.97	353.63
2006	331.93	328.72	320.09	314.72	327.28	340.29	359.18	388.13	384.78	366.35	364.05	372.08	349.80
2007	379.93	388.03	407.19	425.25	449.92	462.39	459.18	445.81	444.91	434.88	425.72	412.45	427.97
2008	417.36	451.42	468.41	483.09	510.01	522.82	556.10	526.98	492.24	426.75	342.41	288.42	457.17
2009	333.60	310.58	288.18	321.58	347.01	368.85	362.91	393.37	389.53	350.90	386.75	403.06	354.69
2010	411.55	408.71	450.01	478.92	488.46	470.53	465.13	475.55	498.82	495.89	485.02	505.23	469.49

Average.   *Source: Commodity Research Bureau*

CRB Spot Sub-Index   (1967=100)

Year	Jan.	Feb.	Mar.	Apr.	May	June	July	Aug.	Sept.	Oct.	Nov.	Dec.	Average
2001	225.75	224.13	226.51	226.66	229.81	231.98	235.20	235.83	226.62	211.72	211.15	214.01	224.95
2002	212.55	214.02	219.65	216.54	216.43	228.09	233.96	232.98	235.10	236.59	238.01	244.06	227.33
2003	248.72	249.60	249.73	248.66	250.00	251.77	250.71	251.49	261.25	274.11	278.66	283.38	258.17
2004	291.55	295.38	304.54	305.49	301.44	295.70	294.10	291.86	296.90	290.35	298.19	296.26	296.81
2005	291.19	290.08	298.13	299.24	297.73	298.26	292.80	290.63	293.94	297.75	297.48	301.05	295.69
2006	308.31	311.58	310.86	319.47	330.81	332.19	337.82	341.11	341.85	347.18	354.58	359.35	332.93
2007	358.84	366.47	381.36	388.90	396.79	405.08	410.71	405.97	410.96	414.11	412.79	413.88	397.16
2008	424.32	449.73	464.01	470.41	476.34	475.87	478.60	456.61	428.42	367.61	318.88	303.90	426.23
2009	320.03	312.26	305.91	326.11	347.44	359.84	358.67	374.28	378.72	381.73	403.44	416.74	357.10
2010	428.27	417.21	433.51	441.48	431.40	420.89	425.03	449.12	473.29	489.05	491.25	507.30	450.65

Average.   *Source: Commodity Research Bureau*

S&P Goldman Sachs Commodity Index (GSCI)   (12/31/1969=100)

Year	Jan.	Feb.	Mar.	Apr.	May	June	July	Aug.	Sept.	Oct.	Nov.	Dec.	Average
2001	239.18	231.54	220.13	222.86	222.32	213.26	202.89	203.76	197.04	178.07	169.63	167.74	205.70
2002	168.97	172.75	193.58	199.87	200.65	197.07	203.12	208.76	223.69	222.70	212.18	230.03	202.78
2003	241.74	264.19	246.70	221.68	228.18	235.01	233.18	241.35	228.54	242.22	246.24	261.23	240.86
2004	269.18	266.23	280.10	284.06	303.19	292.63	298.97	308.01	315.29	356.70	341.12	314.25	302.48
2005	324.47	332.80	374.05	371.68	350.65	382.96	396.64	431.85	455.28	444.90	418.56	435.45	393.27
2006	442.12	422.49	427.47	469.73	477.93	471.65	490.32	485.65	434.56	431.13	442.05	444.62	453.31
2007	406.98	435.26	446.69	469.60	470.72	485.26	504.65	490.16	528.83	559.36	600.37	593.12	499.25
2008	606.71	638.88	689.26	717.94	778.15	832.31	818.90	716.84	644.00	496.05	405.96	338.27	640.27
2009	346.03	327.48	350.86	367.12	410.82	458.22	429.21	466.68	453.77	492.51	509.71	505.07	426.46
2010	520.05	503.83	523.07	543.90	499.87	497.00	503.57	517.41	526.98	561.66	579.86	614.79	532.67

Average.   *Source: Goldman Sachs*

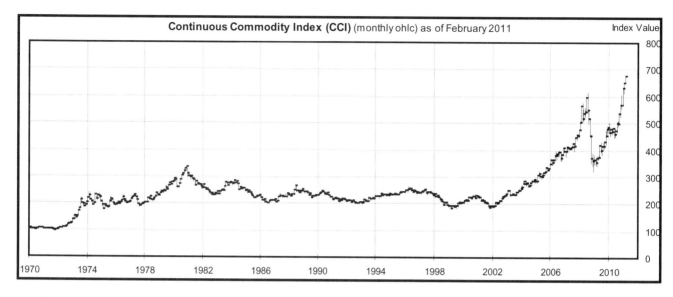

The Continuous Commodity Index (CCI) moved sideways in the early part of 2010 as the European debt crisis weighed down sentiment and threatened to start another global recession. However, the CCI index took off again in the second half of the year and rallied to a new record high, thus reviving the bull market that began in 2001.

The plunge in the CCI index in the latter half of 2008 was in response to the recession and financial crisis but turned out to be simply a technical correction of the massive bull market that started in 2001. The CCI index on its December 2008 low plunged by a total of 48% from the record high of 615.04 posted in July 2008. However, the CCI index in 2010 and 2011 rallied to a new high, confirming that the long-term bull trend remains intact.

The massive bull market that began in 2001 has now shown a total rise of 268%, making it the largest and longest bull market in post-war history, even exceeding the rallies seen in the 1970s. The 1971-74 and 1977-80 commodity bull markets were separated by two years of consolidation in 1975-76. Even if those two rallies are counted as one large bull market, that bull market of 250% is less than the current 2001-2011 bull market of 268%.

The Continuous Commodity Index (CCI) in 2010 outperformed the Reuters/Jefferies CRB index, as illustrated in the chart on the next page. The RJ/CRB index was reformulated in June 2005 with a much heavier 33% weighting on petroleum products versus the 12% weighting in the old CCI index. The strength in grain and softs prices in 2010 allowed the CCI index to rise by 30% in 2010, thus outperforming the RJ/CRB index rise of 17% by a wide margin.

The 2001-11 commodity bull market has been driven mainly by strong demand from the fast-growing emerging markets such as China, India and others. The fact that the rally is being driven by demand, as opposed to a temporary supply disruption, accounts for its size and longevity. The commodity rally in the 1970s, by contrast, was driven mainly by supply disruptions and inflation, not by demand. A rally caused by demand is a much more durable rally, unlike a rally driven by inflation, by a weak dollar, or by supply disruptions, which are usually reversed after a period of time.

Along with strong demand, the weak dollar has also been an important driver of the current commodity rally. As the nearby chart illustrates, the dollar index fell very sharply during 2002-07 and that helped drive commodity prices higher. As the value of the dollar falls, the price of hard assets tends to rise to account for the lower value of the currency in which the hard assets are priced. However, the CCI index in 2009-10 rallied sharply from strong demand and did not need help from the dollar, which moved basically sideways in a volatile range during 2009-10.

The commodity price rally during 2001-11 has occurred

Commodity Bull Markets Ranked by Percentage Gain of Continuous Commodity Index (CCI) (1960-2011[1])							
	-------- Low --------		------- High -------		Percent Rally	Rally Duration Months	Avg CPI (yr-yr%)
2001-11	Oct-01	182.83	Feb-11	672.99	268.1%	112	2.3%
1971-74	Oct-71	96.40	Feb-74	237.80	146.7%	28	4.9%
1977-80	Aug-77	184.70	Nov-80	337.60	82.8%	39	10.2%
1986-88	Jul-86	196.16	Jun-88	272.19	38.8%	23	3.2%
1992-96	Aug-92	198.17	Apr-96	263.79	33.1%	44	2.8%

[1] Data as of February 18, 2011.   Source: Commodity Research Bureau

during a period of low inflation, which attests to the strong fundamentals of demand that underpin the rally. Inflation during the 2001-11 rally has averaged only 2.3% per year, which is only modestly above the upper 2% limit of the Fed's inflation target. However, commodities in 2009-10 did receive some support from fears that inflation may rise substantially in coming years in response to the Federal Reserve's extraordinarily easy monetary policy seen since the financial crisis in 2008. Thus, commodities as an asset class saw a boost from their status as an inflation hedge.

Investment demand for commodities has been an important component in the commodity bull market as well. The total amount of commodity assets under management reached a massive $390 billion as of November 2010, according to a report by Barclays Capital. The academic literature has concluded that the commodity sector is a separate asset class relative to equities or other asset classes. Many institutional and individual investors now devote at least a small percentage of their portfolio to commodities.

Investing in commodities used to be limited to large institutional investors and high net worth investors who could afford to invest directly in large commodity funds. The advent of exchange-traded products funds (ETPs), however, has opened the commodity field to smaller individual investors as well. There are now nearly 100 ETPs that are linked to the price movement of various commodity indexes or individual commodities. ETPs trade on an exchange just like a stock and are very easy for an individual investor to buy and sell.

The outlook for commodity prices continues to look bullish based on the view that global demand for basic commodities will remain strong in coming years and that commodity suppliers will continue to lag in investing in new production capacity. The commodity demand story is mainly tied to the developing world. The need is enormous for food, shelter and infrastructure, which are all sectors that utilize raw commodities.

The depressing fact is that 80% of the world's population lives on less than $10 per day, according to the World Bank's Development Indicators (2008). As these people

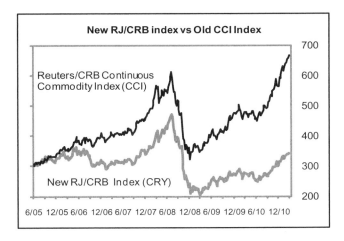

are slowly integrated into the global economy, their food, shelter and transportation needs will expand and they will use more commodities. The best example is China, which has been growing at a breakneck speed near 10% annually in the past decade as the Chinese government tries to satisfy the basic economic needs of its people and indeed foster a middle class that can afford higher end products.

Furthermore, the global population continues to expand at a steady pace. The United Nations forecasts that there will be 2.2 billion more people on earth by 2050, bringing the world's population to 9 billion from its current level near 6.8 billion. These people will need more food, shelter and infrastructure. The need for more food and shelter is obvious. However, there is also a big need for more infrastructure, which requires various construction materials and industrial metals. Global spending on infrastructure will be $25-30 trillion over the next 20 years, according to a recent report by CIBC World Markets.

Individual commodity markets obviously have their own specific drivers. Moreover, the dollar also has a significant influence on commodity prices. However, the big picture is that the world is consuming more food, energy, and metals every day and suppliers are having a hard time keeping up. While there will obviously be periodic market corrections, we look for the 2001-11 bull market in commodities to continue.

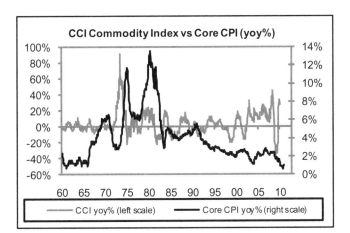

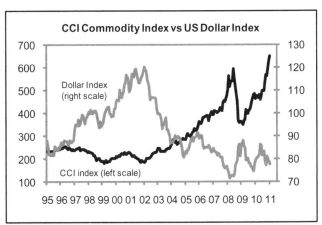

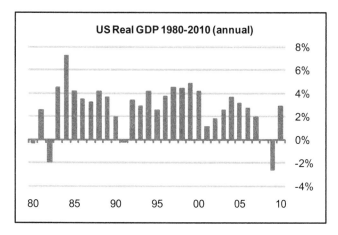

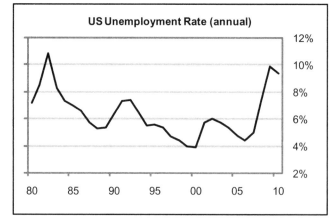

The U.S. economy showed six consecutive quarters of positive GDP growth from the second half of 2009 through 2010, clearly proving that the recession ended. The National Bureau of Economic Research (NBER), the official arbiter of recessions, declared that the U.S. recession lasted from December 2007 through June 2009. The recession was the worst since the Great Depression. U.S. GDP growth in 2007/09 fell by a total of -4.1% from peak to trough, making it worse than the 1957-58 recession of -3.7% and the 1973-75 recession of -3.2%. Yet despite six quarters of consecutive growth, the U.S. economy is still not firing on all cylinders and still needs to be nursed back to heath. The two biggest problems continue to be the labor and housing markets.

The U.S. labor market remains remarkably weak. There was a massive 8.3 million number of jobs lost during the recession, the most jobs lost during a recession since the Great Depression. Even though the economy has been in a recovery mode for more than 1-1/2 years, the U.S. economy has generated only a net 1.11 million new jobs, meaning that only 13% of the jobs lost have been recovered so far. The reality is that many of those jobs were lost forever. It will take the U.S. economy at least another 3-4 years to produce enough jobs just to get the labor market back to where it was before the recession.

Meanwhile, the U.S. unemployment rate currently remains very high at 8.9%, down by only 1.2 percentage points from the 27-year high of 10.1% posted in October

2009. The U.S. "under-employment rate," which includes discouraged workers, is currently extremely high at 15.9%.

The weak labor market has an impact on the economy by reducing consumer income, confidence, and spending. Consumer spending accounts for more than three quarters of the U.S. economy, which basically means that as consumer spending goes, so goes the economy. U.S. personal spending in Q4-2010 showed a nice pickup to 4.2%, which was a step in the right direction, but U.S. consumer confidence remains well below pre-recession levels and U.S. consumers are likely to remain cautious in their spending over the next 1-2 years.

The other main area of weakness for the U.S. economy is the housing market, which continues to wallow in a disaster mode. U.S. home prices fell during the second half of 2010 with the FHFA U.S. home price index in December 2010 posting a new 6-1/2 year low, having fallen by 16% from the record high posted in April 2007. The Case-Schiller Composite-20 Home Price index fell for six consecutive months in the latter half of 2010 and in January 2011 was down by 31% from its record high posted in April 2006.

Home prices in the latter half of 2010 fell mainly because of a fresh bust in home sales following the expiration of the federal home buyers tax credits in April 2010. Home prices were also hurt in late 2010 by a 60 basis point surge in mortgage rates tied to higher T-note yields. The U.S. housing market remains hampered by distressed

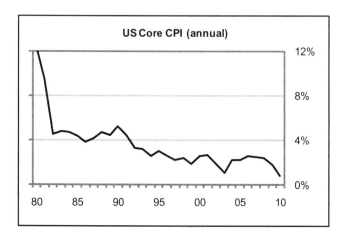

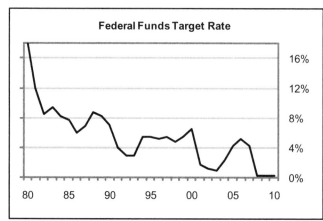

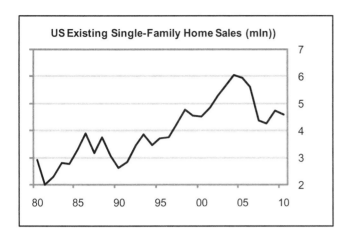

US Existing Single-Family Home Sales (mln))

US Existing Home Median Price ($'000)

sales through foreclosures and short sales, which account for about one-third of home sales. The supply of homes that are currently for sale also remains very high at roughly double pre-recession levels. The fact that the U.S. housing market has not yet hit a confirmed bottom continues to be a major negative factor for the economic outlook.

Despite the ongoing weakness in the labor and housing markets, the consensus is that the U.S. economic expansion will continue. The consensus is that U.S. GDP in 2011 will show a decent growth rate of +3.5%, which is slightly above the post-war average of +3.3%. Economic growth in 2011 will receive a boost from the Obama administration's surprise stimulus move of cutting the payroll tax by 2 percentage points for 2011, which should provide a GDP boost of about 0.5 percentage points for 2011. In addition, exports should continue to recover and U.S. corporations should continue to step up their investment spending to expand capacity.

Short-term U.S. interest rates have been extraordinarily low since the financial crisis emerged in September 2008. The 3-month Libor rate is currently at only 0.31%, where it has been virtually unchanged for the past 1-1/2 years. The market consensus is that the Fed will leave its federal funds rate target unchanged at the current range of zero to 0.25% for at least another year, until spring 2012. The market is then expecting three 25 bp rate hikes in 2012, bringing the funds rate target to 1.25% by late 2012. The low funds rate through the remainder of 2011 should keep other short-term rates low as well such

as the 3-month Libor rate and the Treasury security yields of 2 years and shorter.

The longer end of the yield curve, on the other hand, has normalized to some extent. The 10-year T-note yield is currently trading at 3.40%, which still abnormally low but well above the record low of 2.04% posted in January 2009. T-note yields fell as low as 2.33% during the middle of 2010 in response to the fallout from the European debt crisis and the soft spot in the U.S. economy. However, T-note yields in late 2010 and early 2011 rose sharply by a full percentage point in response to the improvement in the U.S. economy. In addition, the market remains concerned about the Fed's extraordinarily easy monetary policy and whether the Fed will drag its feet in exiting its easy monetary policy and unleash an unintended bout of inflation.

The S&P 500 index in 2010 and early 2011 extended its post-crisis rally to a total of 93% from the post-crisis low in March 2009. The S&P 500 index has now retraced 68.4% of its 2007/09 bear market. The S&P 500 index showed a downside correction of 17% in April-July 2010 due to the European debt crisis, but then resumed its rally in August 2010 as the U.S. economy got back on track in part due to optimism about the Federal Reserve's $600 billion quantitative easing program that was first hinted at in late August 2010. Earnings growth was very strong in 2009 and 2010, which helped drive stocks higher. In addition, the forward price/earnings ratio as of February 2011 remained low at 13.7, which suggested that stocks have room to move higher as earnings growth continues.

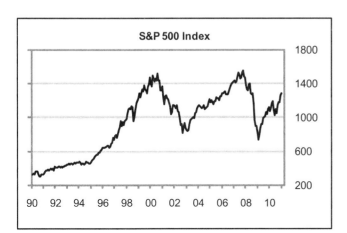

S&P 500 Index

10-year T-Note Yield

TWO-SPEED GLOBAL RECOVERY FAVORS DEVELOPING WORLD

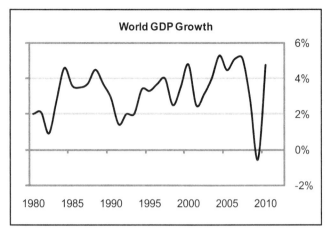

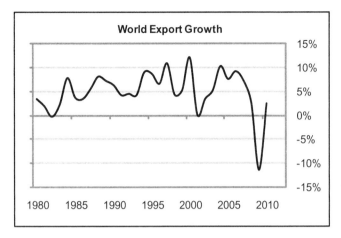

The global economy in 2010 extended the recovery that began in the second half of 2009. The World Bank estimates that the global economy in 2010 grew by +3.9%. That followed the 1.1% decline in GDP growth in 2009, which was the first decline in the overall global economy in post-war history. The World Bank expects global economic growth to be steady at +3.3% in 2011 and +3.6% in 2012.

However, the global economy is on a two-speed path. The developing world is showing strong growth while the developed world is mired in a host of problems including high debt, poor consumer confidence and spending, and ongoing housing market problems. The World Bank is forecasting real GDP growth of only 2.4% in 2011 for the developed countries after +2.8% growth in 2010. By contrast, the World Bank is forecasting 6.0% real GDP growth for the developing world in 2011 after 7.0% growth in 2010.

China's economy is expected to show strong growth of +9.5% in 2011 and +8.8% in 2012, according to the market consensus. India is expected to show GDP growth near +8.5% in both 2011 and 2012. Brazil is expected to show growth near +4.5% in both 2011 and 2012. The developing world saw just a modest downturn in response to the global recession that was caused by housing and banking problems in the U.S. and Europe. The developing world is now back on track with the main drivers being exports and domestic demand from the mass of people being lifted from poverty.

The two main risks for the global economy are currently oil prices and inflation. The Middle East and North Africa in early 2011 saw an extraordinary outpouring of dissent caused by decades of living under autocratic regimes that ruled by intimidation and fear. In the long-term, this is a potentially bullish development for the global economy because the over-arching goal of the movement appears to be democracy and economic opportunity. If these countries can move from the current autocratic kleptocracies to democratic, capitalistic economies, the world economy will see a big boost. However, it will take years for this process to play out and in the meantime the rest of the world may have to deal with a big surge in oil prices.

The other main risk to the global economy is inflation, which is being driven by strong economic growth in the developing world, overly-easy monetary policies by most of the world's central banks, and the surge in energy and commodity prices seen in 2010 and early 2011. Central banks in the developing world have already started raising interest rates in response to inflation risks. China's central bank, for example, raised its key 1-year lending rate by a total of 75 basis points from October 2010 through February 2011. However, there are doubts about whether the European Central Bank and particularly the Federal Reserve will tighten monetary policy fast enough to prevent an inflation outbreak. An inflation outbreak would be very bad news for the global economy since it would take even larger rate hikes later and a possible recession to bring inflation back down to acceptable levels.

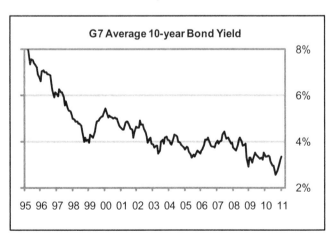

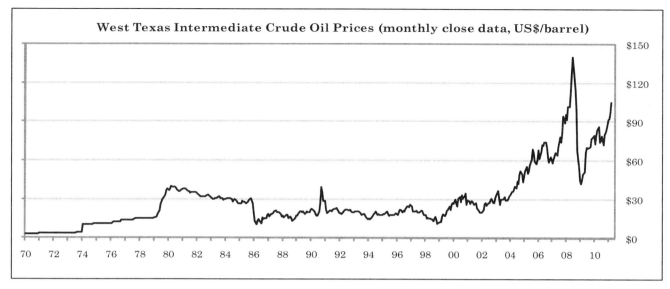

The petroleum market has been on a wild ride in the past several years. Nymex West Texas Intermediate (WTI) crude oil futures prices from 2002 through 2008 more than quadrupled due to a combination of strong developing country demand, lagging capacity and production, the weak dollar, and speculative fervor. That rally culminated in mid-2008 at a record high of $147 per barrel.

Oil prices then plunged in the latter half of 2008 to a 7-year low of $32.40 per barrel in December 2008 in response to the global financial crisis and heavy long liquidation pressure by speculators and hedge funds. The global recession caused world oil demand to fall by 4.7% from the peak of 86.9 million bpd in November 2007 to the 4-year low of 82.8 million bpd posted in May 2009.

Oil prices in 2009 were then able to recover after OPEC (ex-Iraq) slashed production by 16.5% to 25.320 million bpd in March 2009 from the peak of 30.315 million bpd in July 2008. Crude oil prices in the latter half of 2009 and through most of 2010 then traded sideways in the relatively narrow range of about $60-85 per barrel. During that time, oil prices traded near OPEC's target as OPEC maintained its subdued level of production and as demand remained on the weak side.

Oil prices in late 2010, however, started to rally as

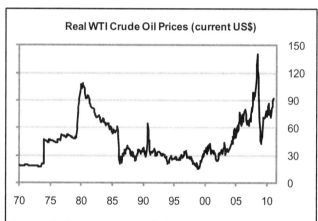

the global economy picked up steam and demand started to increase. OPEC kept its production unchanged but was pleased with the rally in oil prices above its former target range since OPEC members were looking to increase their revenues, which had been depressed by the weak dollar and by the low production levels in 2008-2010. OPEC's general strategy was to keep production low during the recession and early recovery period until excess global inventories slowly declined in response to an improvement in the global economy and higher fuel demand.

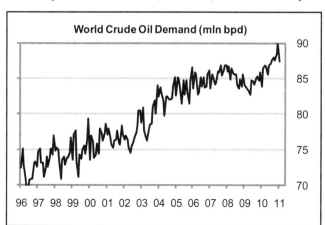

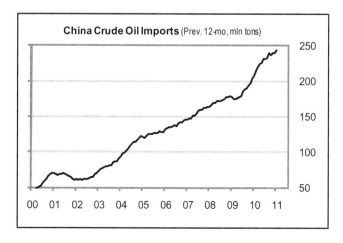

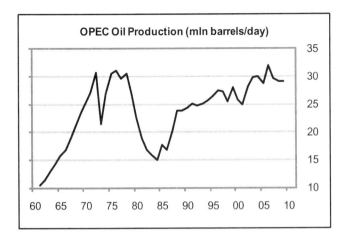

OPEC Oil Production (mln barrels/day)

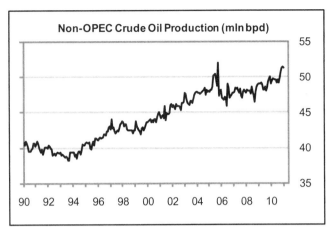

Non-OPEC Crude Oil Production (mln bpd)

The situation in the oil market then changed dramatically in early 2011 when the Arab world erupted in protest. The initial revolutions in Tunisia and Egypt did not have much impact on the oil market. However, oil prices then rose sharply above $100 per barrel after an armed rebellion emerged in Libya against the Qaddafi regime. The Qaddafi regime lost control to the rebels of the eastern part of the country where most of the country's oil facilities are located. The result was that over half of Iraq's normal oil production level of 1.6 million barrels per day was shut down by late February 2011. Saudi Arabia and other OPEC members promised to boost production to offset the lost Libyan oil, but lagged in bringing that production on line.

OPEC as a whole has some 5 million barrels per day of excess capacity, which is more than enough to offset Libya's entire production of 1.6 million bpd. However, the market remains uncertain which country might be hit next with unrest and possible oil supply disruptions. The markets are most concerned about Saudi Arabia because Saudi Arabia is the chief moderate in the OPEC cartel and has the most excess capacity to ramp up if the supply disruptions worsen. While there have been only minor protests in Saudi Arabia thus far, the market is nevertheless nervous that those protests could grow among the Shiite minority in western Saudi Arabia. In neighboring Bahrain, the Shiite majority has engaged in large-scale and persistent protests against the Sunni monarchy, which is a potentially ominous sign for Saudi Arabia.

Looking ahead, crude oil prices are likely to see continued upward pressure in coming months and indeed years. Oil prices were already rising in late 2010 before the Arab unrest emerged because of stronger fuel demand and flat supply. As long as the world economy stays strong, then fuel demand is likely to continue to slowly rise, particularly because of strong demand from the developing world. This expanding demand is likely to put continued upward pressure on oil prices.

Meanwhile, the unrest in the Middle East and North Africa has the potential to eventually create another big upward spike in oil prices. Past oil crises have created huge upward spikes in oil prices such as the 1973 Arab Oil Embargo (+130%), the 1979 Iranian revolution against the Shah (+120%), and Iraq's 1990 invasion of Kuwait (+90%). Even a 90% rally in oil prices would produce an oil price of about $180 per barrel. Such an oil spike, however, would likely be short-lived since it would likely produce a global recession and reduced fuel demand. Moreover, oil production would eventually come back on line after the revolutions end, regardless of what types of governments end up in power after the revolutions.

Aside from Middle East supply distortions, oil prices are still likely to see upward pressure over the long-term The reality is that most of the cheap oil has already been found in the earth's crust. Major new sources of oil can usually be found only in very remote places or under miles of ocean, or have to be extracted from oil shale or tar sands, which is an expensive process. The marginal cost of developing new oil supplies is in the neighborhood of $75-80 per barrel and is rising. Oil producers will only invest the huge sums of capital that are necessary to find new oil supplies if oil prices stay consistently above the cost of extracting new reserves plus a reasonable profit margin. Lagging production and reserves will be an increasingly important factor in coming years as the global economic expansion continues and as fuel demand grows. This is likely to keep upward pressure on oil prices.

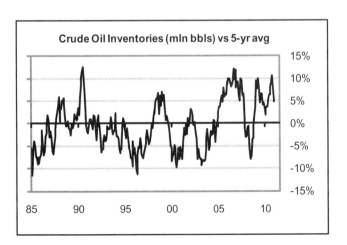

Crude Oil Inventories (mln bbls) vs 5-yr avg

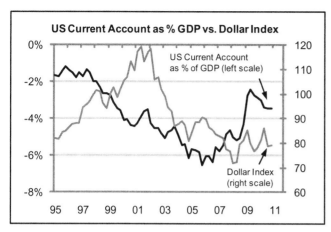

US Current Account as % GDP vs. Dollar Index

US Ex-Petroleum Trade Deficit (US$ bln)

The U.S. dollar index from 2008 through early 2011 moved sideways in a wide consolidation range near the bottom of the 2002-08 sell-off. The dollar during 2008-10 saw two major rallies, but both were based on flight-to quality and were reversed once the panic wore off. The first rally in late 2008 and early 2009 was due to the global financial crisis that erupted in September 2008 with the Lehman bankruptcy. That crisis caused a rush to dollar liquidity by global financial institutions.

The second dollar rally occurred in early 2010 because of the European debt crisis. That crisis caused flight to quality in the dollar and caused a sharp sell-off in the euro due to doubts about the ability of the Eurozone to hold together. However, the Eurozone survived the worst of the crisis. No countries exited the Eurozone and there was virtually no chance of a complete breakup in the euro. The Eurozone nations managed to cobble together a bailout package that helped get Greece and Ireland through the initial stages of the panic.

The European debt crisis exposed a major flaw in the Eurozone system of not enforcing fiscal discipline. Still, the Eurozone has been able to muddle through the crisis and there is now optimism that the Eurozone will be able to grow its way out of the debt problems and that any sovereign debt restructuring or default will be taken in stride by the markets. In any case, the euro in the latter half of 2010 was able to rally as worries about the European debt crisis faded.

The fact that the dollar quickly gave back its rallies on the 2008/09 financial crisis and the 2010 European debt crisis suggests that the dollar has little long-term support. Indeed, the dollar will continue to face two major long-term bearish factors in coming years: the U.S. current account deficit and the slow movement of the global financial system away from a dollar-centric reserve system.

The U.S. trade and current account deficits have improved substantially from their worst levels but remain large and continue to put downward pressure on the dollar. The U.S. current account deficit as a percentage of GDP improved sharply to 2.4% of GDP by Q3-2009 from the worst level of 6.4% of GDP in Q4-2005. The current account deficit has since settled near 3.4% of GDP. The current account deficit at its present quarterly level of $127 billion means that a net $1.4 billion in dollars is flowing out of the U.S. every calendar day to pay for goods and services. That dollar outflow puts downward pressure on the dollar since the recipients of those dollars sell them into the foreign exchange market if they do not want to hang onto them and invest them in dollar-denominated investments.

The good news is that the U.S. trade deficit excluding petroleum has shown a major improvement in the past four years, narrowing to the current deficit of $15 billion from the $44 billion deficit seen in 2006. This improvement is due to the low value of the dollar and the improved competitiveness of U.S. exports in the global economy. The problem regarding the U.S. trade deficit, however, is that the U.S. appetite for imported petroleum will continue for

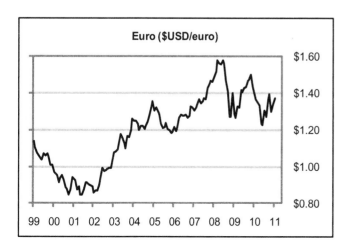

Euro ($USD/euro)

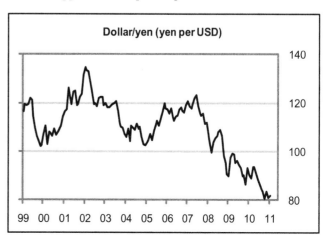

Dollar/yen (yen per USD)

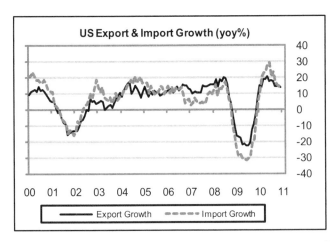

US Export & Import Growth (yoy%)

Export Growth — Import Growth

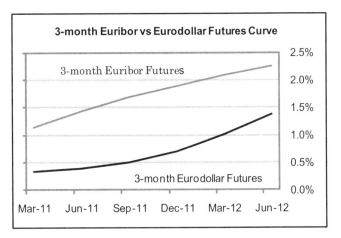

3-month Euribor vs Eurodollar Futures Curve

3-month Euribor Futures

3-month Eurodollar Futures

at least the next several decades regardless of the price of oil or the level of the dollar, thus keeping the overall U.S. trade deficit high.

The second major long-term bearish factor for the dollar is that central banks would like to reduce their dollar risks by reducing the percentage of reserves that are held in dollars. In fact, the data shows that the euro has already gained substantial ground as a reserve currency. The percentage of world reserves held in dollars fell to a record low of 61.3% in Q3-2010, down by 9.7 percentage points from 71.0% in 1999. Meanwhile, the percentage of reserves held in euros was at 26.9% in Q3-2010, just below the record of 27.9% in Q3-2009 and up by 9.0 percentage points from 17.9% in 1999.

The dollar will remain the primary global reserve currency in coming decades and its primacy was proven by the flight into dollars seen during the global financial crisis. Nevertheless, central banks are likely to slowly diversify their reserves away from dollars in coming years, thus providing a mildly bearish factor for the dollar over the long term.

The dollar is currently laboring under a third, shorterterm bearish factor, which is the fact that the Federal Reserve's monetary policy is substantially more expansive than the European Central Bank's policy and that shortterm U.S. interest rates are substantially below European rates. The ECB during the financial crisis did not ease by as much as the Fed, halting its rate cut at 1.00%, as

opposed to the Fed's cut to the range of zero to 0.25%. The Federal Reserve also engaged in two separate quantitative easing programs of buying government bonds, whereas the ECB engaged in virtually no quantitative easing. The ECB did buy bonds of countries such as Greece, Ireland, Portugal and Spain during the European debt crisis but offset the bulk of the reserve effect of those bond purchases with money market operations.

The ECB in fact has already begun to exit its extraordinary liquidity measures by eliminating its longerterm 6 and 12 month bank lending operations. The Fed, by contrast, is expected to keep its funds rate near zero until 2012 and plans to continue its $600 billion second quantitative easing program (QE2) until June 2011. The divergence in monetary policy between the Fed and the ECB is a major bearish factor for the dollar. The 3-month Euribor is currently about 80 bp higher than the U.S. 3-month dollar Libor rate and the market expects that spread to remain wide for at least the next year.

While there are several major bearish factors impacting the dollar, it should be recognized that the dollar has already fallen sharply and is only moderately above the lowest levels seen since currencies began floating in 1973. Thus, while the fundamentals are generally bearish for the dollar, it remains to be seen whether the fundamentals are bearish enough to push the dollar to new lows. Instead, the dollar may simply continue to bump along sideways near those lows, with periodic upside rallies on any new crisis that might emerge.

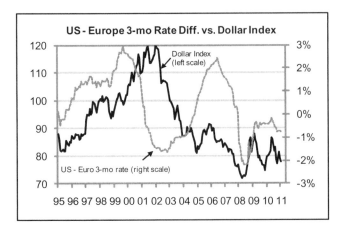

US - Europe 3-mo Rate Diff. vs. Dollar Index

Dollar Index (left scale)

US - Euro 3-mo rate (right scale)

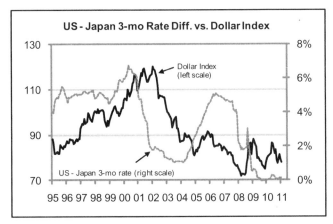

US - Japan 3-mo Rate Diff. vs. Dollar Index

Dollar Index (left scale)

US - Japan 3-mo rate (right scale)

Five years have passed since the U.S. housing bubble started deflating in 2006 and more than three years have passed since the U.S. officially entered a recession in December 2007, according to the National Bureau of Economic Research (NBER). The U.S. recession officially ended almost two years ago in June 2009. Nevertheless, the Federal Reserve is still in the process of pumping reserves into the banking system and still has its federal funds rate target near zero.

The Fed responded aggressively to the financial crisis in 2008 with a wide range of measures. The Fed started cutting its federal funds rate target in October 2007 from 5.25% when the housing crisis started causing strains. By February 2008 the Fed had cut the funds rate to 3.00% and by early 2009 the Fed had cut the funds rate to the current range of zero to 0.25%.

After the financial crisis blew up into global proportions in September 2008 with the bankruptcy of Lehman Brothers, the Fed began a broad range of liquidity programs to lend money not only to banks, but also to securities firms and directly into the commercial paper and mortgage markets. The Fed, in its first quantitative easing move, also purchased $300 billion in Treasury securities from March through September 2009, directly monetizing U.S. government debt and permanently injecting reserves into the banking system. The Fed from January 2009 through March 2010 also conducted a program of buying $1.25 trillion in agency mortgage-backed securities and about $175 billion of agency debt securities. That program kept mortgage rates down and helped to revive the mortgage securitization market.

The Fed in 2010 then began two new programs. In August 2010, the Fed began a program to buy enough Treasury securities to prevent the Fed's balance sheet from declining as mortgage securities in its portfolio matured. This program resulted in the purchase of about $35 billion in Treasury securities per month and that program was still in effect as of February 2011.

Fed Chairman Ben Bernanke began hinting at a second quantitative easing program at the Federal Reserve's annual conference in Jackson Hole, Wyoming in late August 2010. The U.S. economy had hit a soft spot during spring and summer 2010 in response to the fallout from the European debt crisis and the Fed felt that the U.S. economy needed another jolt of liquidity to prevent a new recession from developing.

The Fed on November 3, 2010 finally officially announced a second quantitative easing program, dubbed QE2, to buy $600 billion worth of Treasury securities from November 2010 through June 2011, resulting in the monthly purchase of about $75 billion in Treasury securities. Thus, from November 2010 through June 2011, the Fed was on tracking for buying a total of about $110 billion in Treasury securities per month. This Treasury purchase program will cause the Fed's balance sheet asset level to rise to $2.9 trillion by June 2011. That will represent a massive $2 trillion in excess liquidity above the $900 billion level seen before the financial crisis began.

The purpose of the Fed's QE2 program was two-fold: (1) to keep banks fully supplied with excess reserves to reduce the chances of any liquidity squeeze and to provide plenty of reserves as a base for expanded lending, and (2) to keep long-term Treasury yields relatively low in order to hold down private rates such as corporate bond yields and mortgage rates. The Fed also intended for the QE2 program to change market psychology to one of expecting some inflation versus fears of deflation. The Fed's measures were intended to prevent the U.S. economy from slipping into a deflationary trap such as the one seen in Japan for most of the last two decades.

QE2 turned out to be very effective in helping to improve consumer, business and market confidence and gave the stock market a big boost, thus expanding household wealth. The U.S. economy by late 2010 and early 2011 showed a substantial pickup in growth. The labor market by February 2011 was even showing some signs of life with a decline in the unemployment rate to a 2-year low of 8.9%. The U.S. economy in early 2011 was facing uncertainty from a surge in oil prices on the Middle East unrest, but the economy was at least in much better shape than when the oil price surge started.

Assuming the U.S. economic expansion continues

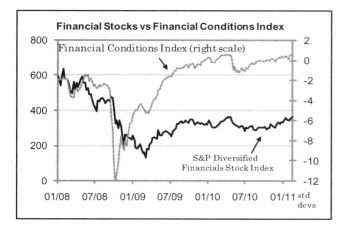

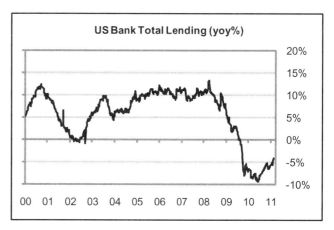

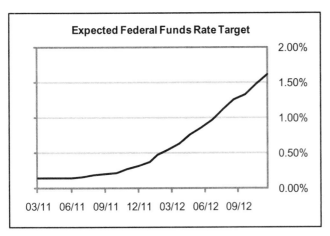

Expected Federal Funds Rate Target

U.S. Inflation Expectations (10yr)

10-yr T-note minus TIPS

through 2011 and is not derailed by oil prices, the question becomes whether the Fed will be successful in exiting its $2 trillion worth of excess liquidity without producing a big surge in inflation. If the Fed does not start draining reserves and raising interest rates on a timely basis, then the Treasury bond market may show an upward spike in yields on inflation fears, thus threatening the economy. If the Fed lets inflation get out of control, then it will take a big increase in interest rates and a possible second recession in order to get inflation back under control. In fact, by early March 2011, the market was already showing some inflation fears with 10-year inflation expectations rising to a 2-2/3 year high of 2.54%.

Fed Chairman Ben Bernanke has already outlined the tools at the Fed's disposal to start exiting its excess liquidity when the time comes. These tools include allowing the Fed's balance sheet asset level to decline naturally as securities mature, selling Treasury and mortgage securities, conducting large reserve repurchase operations, and raising the interest rate on the Fed's reserve deposit facility to soak up reserves. However, the market currently does not expect the Fed to start raising interest rates until spring 2012. The question thus remains whether the Fed will be able to smoothly exit its excess liquidity over the next 1-3 years, or whether the road is going to get rocky with a burst of inflation expectations, a possible sharp rise in bond yields, and a possible recession.

The European Central Bank (ECB) has conducted a significantly tighter monetary policy than the Fed since the financial crisis began in 2008. The ECB wanted to start

exiting its liquidity measures in 2010 but was constrained by the European debt crisis. The European debt crisis had a big impact on the European and U.S. financial markets in spring and summer 2010 because of fears that a sovereign debt default could cause a new European banking crisis by causing big losses among European banks that typically hold large amounts of European sovereign bonds. In addition, there were worries that Greece or Ireland could be forced out of the Eurozone or that the euro might break apart altogether. The ECB was forced to calm the markets by extending its promise of unlimited liquidity into 2011 and by buying bonds to dampen yield spreads for Greece, Ireland, Portugal, Italy and other countries. Unlike the Fed, however, the ECB never engaged in any significant amount of quantitative easing because it offset the reserve effects of those bond purchases.

ECB President Jean-Claude Trichet in early March 2011 surprised the markets with his warning that the inflation situation required "strong vigilance" and that an interest rate hike was possible as soon as the April 2011 meeting. To an extent, Mr. Trichet was simply firing a warning shot at Eurozone officials who in March were working on a strengthened bailout facility for financially troubled Eurozone countries. Nevertheless, the ECB clearly put the markets on notice that it plans to start tightening monetary policy before long. The ECB, with its lineage from the Bundesbank, is well known to have a short fuse on inflation and the Eurozone CPI in January rose to +2.3%, above the ECB's target of just under 2%. The ECB's hawkish stance was a major bullish factor for the euro in early 2011.

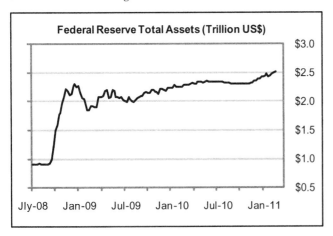

Federal Reserve Total Assets (Trillion US$)

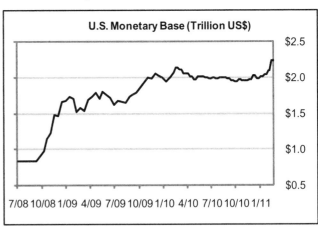

U.S. Monetary Base (Trillion US$)

FOOD PRICES POST RECORD HIGH WITH NO END IN SIGHT

World food prices in early 2011 posted a new record high, with implications for inflation as well as for social stability in some countries. The Food and Agriculture Organization (FAO) of the United Nations reported that its index of 55 food commodities in February 2011 rose by 2.2% from January to post a new record high, exceeding the previous peak in June 2008.

Food prices fell sharply in 2008 in response to the financial crisis and the global recession. However, food then roared back starting in 2009, rising by 20% in 2009 and by another 25% in 2010.

The rally in the UN's food price index is due to a broad rise in most of its 55 individual food components. The chart below illustrates that all of the food commodities that have futures markets, except for cocoa, showed substantial increases of between 20% and 80% in 2010.

The main drivers for the sharp rise in food commodity prices include strong demand, lagging production, and various weather-related supply disruptions in some markets. Wheat rose nearly 50% in 2010, for example, mainly because of the drought in Russia and Eastern Europe.

The biggest bullish factor for food prices, however, is simply strong demand. Food demand is growing, not only because of a rising global population but also because of the improvement in living standards in the developing world where people can afford to buy a higher quantity of better quality food. As people gain more household income, they typically move up the protein scale and eat more meat and dairy products, which in turn requires more grain and feed to support higher livestock production. The UN says that three-quarters of the growth in food demand in the past decade has come from the emerging markets.

The problem of high food prices is not going away anytime soon. The UN predicts that food output will have to increase by an extraordinary 70% by 2050 as the world population grows to 9 billion people from 6.6 billion at present. That increased food supply will materialize only if prices are high enough to bring more producers and land into the production cycle. However, the UN says it will take a matter of years, not months, in order to bring sufficient

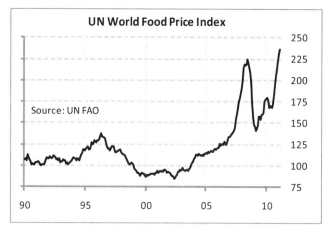

production resources into play.

The bad news is that there is not much more arable land in the U.S. and Europe that can be brought into food production. But the good news is that there is plenty of arable land available in developing countries in South America, Africa, and Asia. The problem will be the logistics and the capital investment needed to bring this land into farm production. However, higher grain and livestock prices will at least provide a strong financial incentive for more farmland in the developing world to be brought into production, thus easing the supply crunch. Food production in the developed world will continue to rise mainly through biotechnology, which significantly boosts crop yields by using seeds that are resistant to drought and pestilence.

The food price crunch has implications in the developed world by pushing the inflation statistics higher and by increasing the amount of disposable income that consumers must spend on food. As spending on food rises, consumers have less money to spend on other consumer goods.

The biggest impact from the food price crunch, however, will be in the developing world. There are as many as 1 billion people in the world that go to sleep each night without enough to eat, according to a recent speech by former President Bill Clinton. Higher prices make food even harder for these impoverished people to obtain.

People in low income countries spend a high portion of their household income on food. A rise in food prices therefore has a very quick and negative impact on their families. There have already been protests and unrest stemming from high food prices in various parts of the world. This unrest is likely to continue and even get worse if food prices continue to climb.

Food prices in coming years are likely to push even higher in response to strong demand and lagging supply. Markets, of course, periodically have downside corrections, but the general trend for food prices is likely to be upward as the world's population rises and as demand for higher quality food increases.

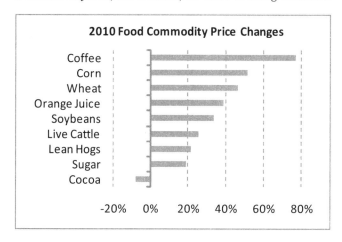

Volume - U.S.

U.S. Futures Volume Highlights
2010 in Comparison with 2009

2010 Rank	Top 50 Contracts Traded in 2009	2010 Contracts	%	2009 Contracts	%	2009 Rank
1	E-Mini S&P 500 Index, CME	556,314,143	23.90%	556,314,143	23.90%	1
2	Eurodollars (3-month), CME	437,585,193	18.80%	437,585,193	18.80%	2
3	T-Notes (10-year), CBT	189,852,019	8.15%	189,852,019	8.15%	3
4	Crude Oil, NYMEX	137,428,494	5.90%	137,428,494	5.90%	4
5	T-Notes (5-year), CBT	98,391,120	4.23%	98,391,120	4.23%	5
6	Euro FX, CME	54,393,644	2.34%	54,393,644	2.34%	8
7	T-Bonds (30-year), CBT	62,232,671	2.67%	62,232,671	2.67%	7
8	E-Mini NASDAQ 100, CME	77,972,143	3.35%	77,972,143	3.35%	6
9	Corn, CBT	50,948,804	2.19%	50,948,804	2.19%	9
10	T-Notes (2-year), CBT	48,158,948	2.07%	48,158,948	2.07%	10
11	Natural Gas, NYMEX	47,951,353	2.06%	47,951,353	2.06%	11
12	Gold (100 oz.), NYMEX	35,139,541	1.51%	35,139,541	1.51%	15
13	E-Mini Russell 2000 Index, ICE	38,686,673	1.66%	38,686,673	1.66%	13
14	Soybeans, CBT	35,758,855	1.54%	35,758,855	1.54%	14
15	Mini ($5) Dow Jones Industrial Index, CBT	39,889,836	1.71%	39,889,836	1.71%	12
16	Japanese Yen, CME	22,749,569	0.98%	22,749,569	0.98%	19
17	British Pound, CME	24,853,787	1.07%	24,853,787	1.07%	18
18	Sugar #11, NYBOT	27,300,259	1.17%	27,300,259	1.17%	16
19	Gasoline, RBOB, NYMEX	21,159,516	0.91%	21,159,516	0.91%	21
20	Heating Oil #2, NYMEX	21,426,015	0.92%	21,426,015	0.92%	20
21	Australian Dollar, CME	16,732,682	0.72%	16,732,682	0.72%	24
22	Wheat, CBT	17,677,547	0.76%	17,677,547	0.76%	22
23	Canadian Dollar, CME	15,481,166	0.66%	15,481,166	0.66%	25
24	Soybean Oil, CBT	17,132,082	0.74%	17,132,082	0.74%	23
25	Henry Hub Swap, NYMEX	25,670,240	1.10%	25,670,240	1.10%	17
26	Soybean Meal, CBT	12,880,767	0.55%	12,880,767	0.55%	26
27	Federal Funds (30-day), CBT	10,349,071	0.44%	10,349,071	0.44%	30
28	Swiss Franc, CME	10,618,630	0.46%	10,618,630	0.46%	28
29	Live Cattle, CME	8,797,033	0.38%	8,797,033	0.38%	32
30	High Grade Copper, NYMEX	6,398,967	0.27%	6,398,967	0.27%	36
31	Natural Gas Penultimate Swap, NYMEX	11,038,692	0.47%	11,038,692	0.47%	27
32	Lean Hogs, CME	6,819,061	0.29%	6,819,061	0.29%	34
33	Ultra T-Bond, CBT	7,713,395	0.33%			
34	S&P 500 Index, CME	10,435,912	0.45%	10,435,912	0.45%	29
35	E-mini S&P MidCap 400 Index	9,133,223	0.39%	9,133,223	0.39%	31
36	Mexican Peso, CME	4,298,939	0.18%	4,298,939	0.18%	37
37	US Dollar Index	2,523,927	0.11%	2,523,927	0.11%	47
38	Cotton #2, NYBOT	3,574,995	0.15%	3,574,995	0.15%	42
39	Wheat, KCBT	3,660,343	0.16%	3,660,343	0.16%	41
40	Coffee "C", NYBOT	4,235,349	0.18%	4,235,349	0.18%	38
41	PJM Western Hub Day Ahead Off-Peak	6,810,613	0.29%	6,810,613	0.29%	35
42	Single Stock Futures	2,012,132	0.09%	2,624,496	0.11%	50
43	Cocoa, NYBOT	3,086,966	0.13%	3,086,966	0.13%	44
44	10-Year Treasury Note (ZNE)	3,600,261	0.15%	1,322,429	0.06%	
45	2-Year Treasury Note (ZTE)	3,424,750	0.15%	1,075,171	0.05%	
46	Nikkei 225 Index (USD), CME	2,935,616	0.13%	2,935,616	0.13%	45
47	New Zealand Dollar	2,235,390	0.10%	1,220,227	0.05%	
48	Mini New York Gold	2,122,569	0.09%	2,122,569	0.09%	49
49	Rogers International TRAKRS, CME	3,686,161	0.16%	3,686,161	0.16%	40
50	Spring Wheat	1,687,228	0.07%	1,198,013	0.05%	
	Top 50 Contracts	2,264,966,290	97.29%	2,251,733,470	96.72%	
	Contracts Below the Top 50	63,148,238	2.71%	76,381,058	3.28%	
	TOTAL	2,328,114,528	100.00%	2,328,114,528	100.00%	

* For 2009 Top 50 contracts totaled 2,267,067,047 including 5 contracts that are not among 2010's Top 50.

U.S. Futures Volume Highlights
2010 in Comparison with 2009

2010 Rank	EXCHANGE	2010 Contracts	%	2009 Contracts	%	2009 Rank
1	Chicago Mercantile Exchange (CME Group)	1,418,240,658	51.30%	1,276,264,462	54.82%	1
2	Chicago Board of Trade (CME Group)	799,926,808	28.93%	587,984,965	25.26%	2
3	New York Mercantile Exchange (CME Group)	419,908,616	15.19%	362,428,100	15.57%	3
4	ICE Futures U.S.	92,520,026	3.35%	81,715,275	3.51%	4
5	ELX Futures	13,142,541	0.48%	5,003,983	0.21%	5
6	Kansas City Board of Trade (KCBT)	5,549,842	0.20%	3,660,343	0.16%	7
7	OneChicago	4,971,160	0.18%	2,983,148	0.13%	8
8	CBOE Futures Exchange (CFE)	4,402,616	0.16%	1,155,969	0.05%	11
9	NYSE Liffe U.S.	4,064,780	0.15%	4,474,734	0.19%	6
10	Minneapolis Grain Exchange (MGE)	1,690,207	0.06%	1,206,824	0.05%	10
11	Chicago Climate Exchange (CCFE)	361,650	0.01%	1,246,123	0.05%	9
	Total Futures	2,764,778,904	100.00%	2,328,123,926	100.00%	

Chicago Climate Futures Exchange (CCFE)

FUTURE	2010	2009	2008	2007	2006
CA Climate Action Registry-Climate Res Tons (CCAR)	193	684			
Carbon Financial Instrument (CFI)	1,707	13,973	29,405	3,566	
Carbon Financial Instrument (CFI-US)	522	891			
Carbon Financial Instrument Offsets (CFI-US-O)	60	50			
Event Linked (IFEX)	2,148	4,499	10,373	2,321	
Event Linked (IFEX) ESW	800				
Event Linked (IFEX) FLW	1,000	1,860	2		
Event Linked (IFEX) GCW	1,000				
Event Linked (IFEX) NEW	1,000				
Nitrogen Financial Instrument - Annual (NFI-A)	100,491	209,223	21,730	205	
Nitrogen Financial Instrument (NFI-OS)	1,220	808	1,348	3,465	
Renewable Energy Certificate Funds-Connecticut	2,172	261			
Renewable Energy Certificate Funds-Massachusetts	4,805				
Renewable Energy Certificate Funds-New Jersey	7,401	2,262			
Regional Greenhouse Gas Initiatives (RGGI)	52,494	693,863	17,043		
Sulfur Financial Instrument (SFI)	184,637	317,749	289,398	181,030	28,924
Total Futures	361,650	1,246,123	370,505	191,899	28,924

CBOE Futures Exchange (CFE)

FUTURE	2010	2009	2008	2007	2006
CBOE Volatility Index (VIX)	4,392,796	1,144,858	1,088,105	1,046,475	434,478
CBOE Mini-Volatility Index (VM)	9,429	9,268			
CBOE S&P 500 12-Month Variance (VA)	3	31	940	56	210
S&P 500 3-Month Variance (VTI)	388	123	2,078	9,302	3,787
Total Futures	4,402,616	1,155,969	1,161,397	1,136,295	478,424

Chicago Board of Trade (CBT)

FUTURE	2010	2009	2008	2007	2006
Wheat	23,090,255	17,677,547	19,011,928	19,582,706	16,224,871
Mini Wheat	91,560	61,355	70,971	79,282	67,637
Corn	69,841,420	50,948,804	59,957,118	54,520,152	47,239,893
Mini Corn	237,394	203,474	219,562	156,210	162,545
Oats	344,587	314,305	441,588	432,741	427,315
Soybeans	36,933,960	35,758,855	36,373,096	31,726,316	22,647,784
Mini Soybeans	412,732	466,367	475,231	540,940	581,047
Soybean Oil	20,791,164	17,132,082	16,928,361	13,170,914	9,488,524
Soybean Meal	14,052,845	12,880,767	13,354,174	12,213,315	9,350,043
Distillers Dried Grain	16				
Grain Bais Swap	57,423	7,918			
Rough Rice	448,724	277,065	362,565	358,905	321,330
T-Bonds (30-year)	83,509,754	62,232,671	89,464,546	107,630,211	93,754,895
T-Notes (10-year)	293,718,907	189,852,019	256,770,689	349,229,371	255,571,869
T-Notes (5-year)	132,149,948	98,391,120	168,127,469	166,207,391	124,870,313
T-Notes (3-year)	6,788	268,622			
T-Notes (2-year)	66,977,168	48,158,948	79,311,002	68,610,392	37,966,797
Interest Rate Swap (30-year)	31,564	55,228	80,169	12,555	
Interest Rate Swap (10-year)	444,751	871,074	1,004,309	848,372	520,090
Interest Rate Swap (7-year)	33,036	21,957	320		
Interest Rate Swap (5-year)	1,039,064	1,331,017	1,147,170	551,505	272,749
OTR 2-Year T-Note	14,853				
OTR 5-Year T-Note	27,570				
OTR 10-Year T-Note	70,067				
Ultra T-Bond	7,713,395				
30-Day Federal Funds	12,753,228	10,349,071	19,434,295	16,597,188	17,833,331
Ethanol	162,725	67,168	29,451	12,516	5,564
OTC Ethanol Forward Swap	636,444	270,596	249,147	60,729	42
Dow Jones Industrial Index ($25)	1,907	3,867	12,392	14,301	18,686
Dow Jones Industrial Index ($10)	188,109	395,584	1,147,657	1,483,817	1,919,847
Mini Dow Jones Industrial Index ($5)	34,059,544	39,889,836	55,348,312	40,098,882	26,792,373
Dow-UBS Commodity Index	84,314	97,223	73,445	51,651	5,990
Dow-UBS Commodity Index Swap	1,592				
Total Futures	799,926,808	587,984,965	825,257,796	895,521,149	678,262,052

Chicago Mercantile Exchange (CME Group)

FUTURE	2010	2009	2008	2007	2006
Live Cattle	11,332,739	8,797,033	9,801,360	8,587,973	8,209,698
Feeder Cattle	1,330,421	1,059,109	1,250,324	1,099,863	1,286,395
Lean Hogs	8,076,535	6,819,061	8,505,138	7,264,832	6,481,001
Pork Bellies, Frozen	4,722	27,852	56,705	68,409	107,564
Class III Milk	277,860	280,636	304,754	311,459	225,137
Class IV Milk	968	332	624	314	113
Nonfat Dry Milk	5,696	1,480	2,239	1,072	954
Deliverable Nonfat Dry Milk	5	2			
International Skimmed Milk Powder	1				
Butter	1	59	135	1,222	3,800

Chicago Mercantile Exchange (CME Group) (continued)

FUTURE	2010	2009	2008	2007	2006
Cash Butter	14,197	16,983	17,495	20,067	18,673
Cash Settled Cheese	3,189				
Dry Whey	7,490	5,246	4,141	6,378	
USD Crude Palm Oil	572				
Hard Wood Pulp	3,750				
Wood Pulp	1,263	3,364	8,740	1,038	
Random Lumber	311,902	317,227	437,613	334,689	271,024
One Month LIBOR	385,821	452,340	571,710	1,194,200	852,119
Eurodollar (3-month)	510,955,113	437,585,193	596,974,081	621,470,328	502,077,391
Euroyen	22,833	40,879	122,917	561,220	662,653
3M Overnight Index Swaps (OIS)	1,650	16,159	15,358		
Australian Dollar	25,903,355	16,732,682	11,212,985	10,785,897	6,567,650
British Pound	30,220,239	24,853,787	20,497,378	20,799,827	16,099,540
Brazilian Real	50,020	30,398	67,168	127,879	94,514
Canadian Dollar	22,083,807	15,481,166	11,378,024	12,224,845	10,279,576
Czech Koruna	727	224	787	496	461
DJ CME FX$ Index	1,694				
Euro FX	86,232,358	54,393,644	53,652,590	43,063,060	40,790,379
E-Mini Euro FX	1,245,374	664,350	774,078	491,401	386,850
Hungarian Forint	2,080	975	901	148	620
Israeli Shekel	6,329	7,495	3,014	3,070	113
Japanese Yen	31,862,793	22,749,569	32,844,404	30,820,442	19,677,365
E-Mini Japanese Yen	67,354	28,906	24,657	19,116	9,203
Korean Won	5,271	1,411	268	2,312	5,867
Mexican Peso	6,763,808	4,298,939	5,302,297	5,154,636	3,795,538
New Zealand Dollar	2,235,390	1,220,227	808,296	928,816	529,782
Norwegian Krone	11,241	11,652	7,327	10,289	6,461
Polish Zloty	20,318	19,848	20,554	25,977	23,899
Russian Ruble	238,490	162,314	213,341	173,613	125,762
South African Rand	138,144	77,848	99,413	84,376	70,491
Swedish Krona	6,972	5,396	2,436	12,374	4,618
Swiss Franc	12,011,173	10,618,630	14,814,153	14,478,658	11,470,031
Turkish Lira	26,521	12,011			
Australian Dollar / Canadian Dollar	4,079	3,582	2,762	1,749	6,708
Australian Dollar / Japanese Yen	26,094	3,493	1,088	44	19
Australian Dollar / New Zealand Dollar	167	281	1,346	903	39
British Pound / Japanese Yen	28,977	6,395	3,430	332	173
British Pound / Swiss Franc	8,762	2,610	702	3,031	6,151
Canadian Dollar / Japanese Yen	838	301	14	236	24
Chinese Renimibi / US Dollar	4,937	7,024	16,790	8,179	5,407
Swiss Franc / Japanese Yen	3,323	302	1,968	2,754	55
Euro / Australian Dollar	9,290	531	246	210	205
Euro / British Pound	275,335	125,657	73,554	80,232	42,053
Euro / Canadian Dollar	1,213	277	85	180	109
Euro / Czech Koruna	177	90	196	65	
Euro / Hungarian Forint	450	189	193	78	1,050
Euro / Japanese Yen	295,766	219,109	320,060	365,895	272,182
Euro / Norwegian Krone	104	356	3,760	6,605	328
Euro / Polish Zloty	46,514	35,455	14,693	18,349	15,194
Euro / Swedish Krona	174	110	50	48	151
Euro / Swiss Franc	152,038	85,059	50,923	97,478	49,475
Euro / Turkish Lira	39,549	22,280			
Micro JPY/USD	29				
Micro CHF/USD	78				
Micro CAD/USD	13				
E-micro EUR/USD	1,063,133	424,726			
E-micro GBP/USD	240,081	170,411			
E-micro USD/CAD	48,573	39,809			
E-micro USD/CHF	27,384	15,182			
E-micro USD/JPY	34,453	94,508			
E-micro AUD/USD	89,358	65,031			
S&P 500 Index	7,689,961	10,435,912	16,763,071	15,837,593	14,844,858
E-mini S&P 500 Index	555,328,670	556,314,143	633,889,466	415,348,228	257,926,673
E-mini S&P European	4,652	65	2,567		
E-mini S&P SmallCap 600 Index	32,168	66,471	107,039	28,894	
E-mini S&P MidCap 400 Index	7,657,372	9,133,223	8,580,467	7,352,427	5,528,263
S&P MidCap 400 Index	38,467	59,360	97,224	118,140	153,268
E-micro S&P CNX Nifty Index	143,753				
E-mini S&P CNX Nifty Index	5,888				
S&P Citigroup Growth	1,463	1,351	8,163	25,132	5,473
S&P Citigroup Value	4,971	5,437	6,450	6,418	7,289
E-Mini NASDAQ 100 Index	79,637,745	77,972,143	108,734,456	95,309,053	79,940,222
NASDAQ 100 Index	507,824	756,919	1,407,413	1,683,378	2,269,870
Nikkei 225 Index (USD)	2,951,246	2,935,616	4,399,966	3,421,085	2,809,839
Nikkei 225 Index (JPY)	5,108,015	4,167,340	4,769,567	3,290,909	2,126,654

Chicago Mercantile Exchange (CME Group) (continued)

FUTURE	2010	2009	2008	2007	2006
S&P 500 Financial Sector	555	5,866	9,032	4,202	
E-Mini MSCI EAFE	1,068,082	602,104	450,138	172,371	17,461
E-mini MSCI Emerging Markets Index	715,849	324,722	171,064	26,793	
TRAKRS PIMCO	306,642	792,148	3,668,906	8,712,135	24,471,474
TRAKRS PIMCO SPTR	104,344	134,141	451,858	2,324,128	2,349,055
Rogers International TRAKRS	1,937,363	3,686,161	11,621,869	17,651,395	26,486,999
HDD Weather	64,388	70,619	119,533	135,702	115,763
HDD Seasonal Weather Strips	6,257	3,550	6,600	12,350	13,675
CDD Weather	57,993	53,398	117,729	114,044	65,258
CDD Seasonal Weather Strips	250	2,900	3,610	7,300	8,450
Euro HDD Weather	8,275	16,950	4,625	3,625	3,435
Euro CAT Weather	1,025	775	350	750	950
Euro HDD Seasonal Strip Weather	5,435	300	2,850	1,750	1,225
Euro CAT Seasonal Strip Weather	100	150			
CSI Housing Index	88	295	1,178	2,995	3,632
Goldman Sachs Commodity Index	521,886	520,462	526,036	644,761	615,260
GSCI Excess Return Index	16,085	55,178	27,206	15,136	13,141
OTC SP GSCI ER 2-Month Swap	14,174				
OTC SP GSCI ER 3-Month Swap	14,967				
OTC SP GSCI ER Swap	12,216				
S&P 500 ETF	977	1,809	1,109	1,165	2,009
Russell 2000 ETF	145	71	550	470	785
Nasdaq 100 ETF	292	328	833	1,470	1,849
Total Futures	1,418,240,658	1,276,264,462	1,612,884,857	1,415,423,615	1,101,712,533

ELX Futures Exchange (ELX)

FUTURE	2010	2009	2008	2007	2006
2-Year Treasury Note (ZTE)	3,424,750	1,075,171			
5-Year Treasury Note (ZFE)	3,565,576	2,012,132			
10-Year Treasury Note (ZNE)	3,600,261	1,322,429			
Ultra Long-Term US T-Bond (ZUE)	20,989				
30-Year Treasury Bond (ZBE)	1,243,715	594,251			
Eurodollar (GEE)	1,287,250				
Total Futures	13,142,541	5,003,983			

ICE Futures U.S. (ICE)

FUTURE	2010	2009	2008	2007	2006
Coffee 'C'	5,488,196	4,235,349	5,446,516	5,128,623	4,407,512
Sugar #11	29,052,539	27,300,259	27,019,704	21,263,799	15,100,721
Sugar #16	99,049	66,719	250		
Cocoa	3,797,679	3,086,966	3,592,268	3,335,283	3,169,202
Cotton #2	5,732,906	3,574,995	6,162,963	6,334,979	4,490,407
Orange Juice, Frozen Concentrate	691,583	656,995	710,512	845,792	923,696
US Dollar / Swedish Krona (Half Size)	35,785	42,749	50,858		
US Dollar / Norwegian Krone (Half Size)	58,091	30,359	48,976		
US Dollar / Czech Koruna (Half Size)	17,901	31,581	12,711		
US Dollar / Hungarian Forint (Half Size)	18,500	21,426	29,945		
US Dollar / South African Rand	123,105	149,046	81,401	88,260	54,756
Canadian Dollar / Japanese Yen	16,147	6,719	13,078	20,463	13,215
Australian Dollar / US Dollar	2,520	2,858	4,920	17,666	29,069
Australian Dollar / Canadian Dollar	18,378	6,671	26,637	25,922	21,291
Australian Dolar / New Zealand Dollar	18,768	9,326	12,307	32,262	15,790
Australian Dollar / Japanese Yen	16,593	17,871	39,382	53,049	57,667
New Zealand Dollar / Japanese Yen	19,141	2,461	558	1,502	20
New Zealand Dollar / US Dollar	4,870	8,156	45,134	61,657	53,413
Norwegian Krone / Japanese Yen	83	1,333			
Norwegian Krone / Swedish Koruna	22,460	29,257	38,021	20,866	15,172
Swiss Franc / Japanese Yen	17,356	15,721	76,734	74,148	65,275
Euro / US Dollar, Small	10,251	61,953	112,675	24,382	116,029
Euro / Australian Dollar	99,371	43,084	62,986	73,821	58,144
Euro / Canadian Dollar	23,478	12,746	21,972	43,266	26,477
Euro / Czech Koruna	39,172	25,233	16,204	49,442	17,533
Euro / Hungarian Forint	49,112	40,094	18,525	31,105	11,615
Euro / Japanese Yen	149,485	182,157	346,417	418,725	586,129
Euro / Swedish Krona	51,498	37,438	55,039	64,617	54,571
Euro / British Pound	80,847	105,056	169,921	241,409	304,382
Euro / Norwegian	42,275	18,857	52,084	58,664	44,635
Euro / South African Rand	113	117	244	318	163
Euro / Swiss Franc	41,269	65,200	159,849	215,173	183,446
Million Euro / US Dollar	1,198	3,062	4,804		
Million US Dollar / Swedish Krona	49				
Million British Pound / US Dollar	54	250	327		
Million US Dollar / Canadian Dollar	46				
British Pound / Australian Dollar	18,216	6,271	8,104	5,994	10
British Pound / Canadian Dollar	12,598	1,033	3,204	5,195	2

VOLUME - U.S.

ICE Futures U.S. (ICE) (continued)

FUTURE	2010	2009	2008	2007	2006
British Pound / New Zealand Dollar	6,535	2,245	16		
British Pound / Norwegian Krone	10,717	383			
British Pound / Swiss franc	13,911	16,317	43,558	66,586	84,210
British Pound / Japanese Yen	48,674	25,686	46,231	111,274	148,696
Small British Pound / US Dollar	12,402	31,175	55,127	14,279	17,437
Small US Dollar / Canadian Dollar	7,621	3,587	6,572	14,672	18,910
Small US Dollar / Japanese Yen	25,061	8,842	26,973	28,251	142,751
Small US Dollar / Swiss Franc	4,414	5,853	9,462	17,866	64,417
US Dollar Index	6,369,517	2,523,927	1,825,326	1,099,800	1,168,486
Revised NYSE Composite Index	252	209	698	4,605	3,213
Russell 1000 Mini Index	326,645	445,752	177,768	81,432	
Russell 1000 Growth Index Mini	35,031				
Russell 1000 Value Index Mini	31,506				
Russell 2000 Mini Index	39,747,503	38,686,673	16,526,331	57,540	
Reuters-CRB Futures Index (CCI)	9,500	15,973	19,185	19,973	14,312
RJ/CRB Futures Index	55	354	44	3	150
Total Futures	92,520,026	81,715,275	63,433,647	40,658,718	32,746,692

Kansas City Board of Trade (KCBT)

FUTURE	2010	2009	2008	2007	2006
Wheat	5,549,842	3,660,343	3,778,266	4,318,007	4,763,168
Total Futures	5,549,842	3,660,343	3,778,266	4,318,007	4,771,711

Minneapolis Grain Exchange (MGE)

FUTURE	2010	2009	2008	2007	2006
Spring Wheat	1,687,228	1,198,013	1,361,042	1,792,310	1,613,239
Soft Red Winter Wheat Index	2,979	8,654			
Total Futures	1,690,207	1,206,824	1,361,067	1,792,453	1,614,543

New York Mercantile Exchange (NYMEX)

FUTURE	2010	2009	2008	2007	2006
Gold	44,730,345	35,139,541	38,377,367	25,060,440	15,917,584
Platinum	1,486,507	802,884	675,543	501,545	373,119
Palladium	901,584	400,821	483,828	400,993	378,116
Silver	12,826,666	7,990,528	8,917,183	6,817,137	5,433,063
Gold, E-mini	11,008	13,341			
Gold, miNY	105,236	59,900	20,034	10,988	313
E-micro Gold	23,534				
Silver, E-mini	1,975	660			
Silver, miNY	24,722	13,367	8,115	5,120	40
Copper	10,305,670	6,398,967	4,618,068	3,753,168	3,281,312
Copper, miNY	10,566	5,987	4,890	4,927	77
Hot-Rolled Steel	21,613	13,494	23		
Uranium	26,097	6,149	13,291	1,268	
Crude Oil, Physical	168,652,141	137,428,494	134,674,264	121,525,967	71,053,203
Crude Oil	453,557	1,139,308	1,360,899	625,839	820,579
Crude Oil, miNY	3,157,814	3,368,983	5,641,145	5,185,214	9,323,467
Brent Crude Oil, Last Day	144,625	31,708	465,056	506,075	
No. 2 Heating Oil, NY	26,970,106	21,426,015	19,583,052	18,078,976	13,990,589
Heating Oil Financial	50,834	91,152	70,561	46,828	19,231
Heating Oil, miNY	411	415	637	21,296	422,248
NY Harbor RBOB Gasoline	27,898,698	21,159,516	20,522,571	19,791,439	3,883,261
RBOB Gasoline, miNY	205	84	307	563	872
LTD Natural Gas	1,540				
Natural Gas, miNY	670,266	1,030,118	1,058,665	1,403,525	2,035,824
Singapore 380 Fuel Oil	50	300	650	150	
PJM Financially Settled Monthly - Peak	115,132	126,778	77,287	84,154	171,655
NYMEX Crude Oil MACI Index	10,651	539	23,742		
Natural Gas	64,323,068	47,951,353	38,730,519	29,786,318	23,029,988
RBOB Gas	48,088	9,800			
3.5% Fuel Oil (Platts) CIF MED Swap	34	278			
AER-Dayton Hub Daily	260			400	590
AER-Dayton Hub Monthly - Peak	5,718	4,000	12,258	4,262	8,026
AER Dayton Hub Monthly - Off-Peak	5,892	11,716	35,148	14,604	12,710
Algonquin City - Gates Natural Gas Index Swap	3,454				
Algonquin City - Gates Natural Gas Basis Swap	3,243	1,924	214		
ANR - LA Natural Gas Index Swap	1,518				
ANR - Louisiana Basis Swap	15,887	46,530	34,499	13,127	24,476
ANR - Oklahoma Basis	28,380	70,712	124,501	99,106	47,516
ANR OK Swing Swap	26				
Central Appalachian Coal	162,020	139,732	108,887	127,529	52,305
Argus Biodiesel RME FOB Rdam Swap	15,765	8,457			
Argus Gasoline Crack Spread SW	332	89,673	40,030	26,156	9,052
Argus LLS vs WTI (Arg) T	7,187	843			

New York Mercantile Exchange (NYMEX) (continued)

FUTURE	2010	2009	2008	2007	2006
Argus Propane Far East Index Swap	4,583	2,220			
Argus Propane (Saudi Aramco) Swap	2,792	433	20		
Brent (ICE) Crude Oil BALMO Swap	3,145	4,619			
Brent (ICE) Calendar Swap	157,237	313,572	335,640	71,534	38,305
Brent CFD (Platts) vs Front Month Swap	7,639	12,357			
Brent (CFD) Swap	25,585	61,632			
Brent Bullet Swap	176,357	276,532	114,701	42,053	20,432
Carbon RGGI Emmissions	400	1,817			
Centerpoint Basis Swap	79,471	188,819	319,716	159,048	68,895
Centerpoint East Index	10,476	9,617	4,644	1,671	1,378
Centerpoint Natural Gas Swing Swap	124		278	240	58
Chicago Basis Swap	428	73,011	575,663	486,313	555,309
Chicago Ethanol Swap	55,779	15,169	15,617	4,590	
Chicago ULSD PL vs HO SPR	110				
CIG Basis Swap	28,833	42,065	117,473	100,525	245,305
CIG Rockies Natural Gas Index Swap	3,664	5,364	1,041		
CIG Rockies Natural Gas Swing Swap	236	726	62		
Cinergy Hub Off-Peak LMP Swap	12,348	32,146	27,524	10,202	24,076
Cinergy Hub Daily Peak Swap	1,040		200	1,358	440
Cinergy Hub LMP Swap-Peak	23,962	43,856	17,280	10,586	13,728
Cinergy Hub 5mw Day Ahead Off-Peak	680,344	604,840			
Cinergy Hub 5mw Day Ahead Peak	42,043	46,939			
Cinergy Hub 5mw Real-Time Off-Peak	185,328	236,576			
Cinergy Hub 5mw Real-Time Peak	19,088	15,321			
CO2 Vintage (76)	450				
CO2 Vintage (98)	450				
Columbia Gulf Mainline Basis Swap	71,361	99,036			
Columbia Gulf Mainline Natural Gas	20,880	556			
Columbia Gulf Louisiana Natural Gas Index Swap	4,520				
Columbia Gulf Onshore Basis	34,980	105,653	211,645	80,422	68,181
Conway Natural Gas (OPIS) Swap	1,575	220			
Conway Normal Butane (OPIS) Swap	490	362			
Conway Propane 5 decimals Swap	18,067	4,129			
Crude Oil Last Day Financial Futures	347	130			
Crude Oil Outrights	1,883				
Canadian Heavy Crude Oil (Net Energy) Index	2,040				
RME Biodiesel (Argus) FOB Rdam vs ICE Gasoil	4,850				
Fame 0 Biodiesel FOB Rdam vs ICE Gasoil Spread	5,170				
Dated Brent (Platts) Daily Swap	35,626	1,802			
Dated-to-Frontline Brent Swap	48,303	141,760	183,262	90,783	21,394
Dawn Basis (Platts IFERC) Swap	40	100			
Demarc Natural Gas Index Swap	7,906	3,461	13,913	3,460	2,218
Demarc Natural Gas Swing Swap	662	1,356	3,169	1,423	1,073
Diesel 10ppm Barge FOB Rdam vs ICE Gasoil BALMO	335	254			
Diesel 10ppm NEW Le Harve CIF Swap	198	5			
Diesel 10ppm NEW Le Harve vs ICE Gas BALMO	40	195			
Diesel 10ppm NEW Le Harve vs ICE Swap	65	25			
Dominion Transmission - Appalachian Basis Index	2,816	46,703	34,100	18,657	10,120
Dominion Transmission - Appalachian Basis	46,950	102,937	229,043	458,950	433,304
Dubai Crude Oil BALMO Swap	6,847	3,774	2,276		
Dubai Crude Oil Calendar Swap	413,157	923,539	325,802	107,329	88,601
Eastern Rail CSX Coal Swap	40,325	29,060	30,488	4,815	
East-West Fuel Oil Spread Swap	13,850	18,589	11,622	2,532	2,069
EIA Flat Tax On-Highway Diesel Swap	4,986	6,974			
ERCOT West Zone MCPE 5MW Peak Swap	210				
Electric Ercot Off-Peak	2,040				
Electric Financially Settled	9,495				
PJM PENELEC Zone Peak Cal Mth Day Ahead LMP	7,172				
PJM DOM Zone Peak Cal mth Day Ahead LMP Swap	210				
Electric MISO Peak	8,225	800			
Electric MISO Peak	255				
Electric NYISO Off-Peak	117,598	15,520			
Electric NYISO Off-Peak	4,680				
PJM Meted Zone Off-Peak Cal Mth Day Ahead LMP	173,870				
PJM PECO Zone Off-Peak Cal Mth Day Ahead LMP	598,550				
PJM PENELEC Zone Off-Peak Cal Mth Day Ahead	131,411				
El Paso/Permian Index Swap	6,919	42,447	46,469	34,194	16,710
El Paso/Permian Swing Swap	248	4,613	12,934	17,639	5,092
ERCOT HOU MCPE 50mw Off-Peak	148	22			
ERCOT HOU MCPE 50mw Peak	1,200	11,024			
ERCOT Houston ZMCPE 5mw Peak	105	1,275			
ERCOT North MCPE 50mw Off-Peak	3,616	33,558			
ERCOT North MCPE 50mw Peak	875	797			
ERCOT North ZMCPE 5mw Off-Peak	3,880	11,690			
ERCOT North ZMCPE 5mw Peak	745	4,285			

New York Mercantile Exchange (NYMEX) (continued)

FUTURE	2010	2009	2008	2007	2006
ERCOT South MCPE 50mw Peak	43	86			
Ethanol T1 FOB Rdam Ex Duty Swap	3,831	2,427			
Ethanol T2 FOB Rdam Incl Duty Swap	2,338	300			
European 1% Fuel Oil BALMO Swap	532	1,886	815	15	
European 3.5% Fuel Oil MED Crack Spread Swap	202				
European 3.5% Fuel Oil Rdam BALMO Swap	2,295	5,121	2,300	20	
European 3.5% Fuel Oil Spread Swap	1,540	740	282	53	5
European Gasoil 10ppm Rdam Barges Swap	379	42	116		
European Gasoil 10ppm Rdam Barges vs Gasoil	6,228	4,789	2,850	436	27
Europe 1% Fuel Oil Calendar Swap	18,943	24,162	24,565	8,048	3,047
Europe 1% Fuel Oil Rdam Calendar Swap	4,517	9,115	18,743	2,872	681
European 6.5% Fuel Oil MED Calendar Swap	541	533	244	15	105
Europe 3.5% Fuel Oil Rotterdam Calendar Swap	76,245	126,496	77,769	20,075	14,699
European Gasoil (ICE)	5,871	1,644			
European Naptha BALMO Swap	1,804	936	139	9	
European Naptha Crack Spread	126,917	110,560	34,053	13,268	2,332
European Dated Brent Crude Oil Calendar Swap	94,187	91,481	34,610	7,815	1,425
European Jet Kero NWE Calendar Swap	969	782	250	71	
European Naptha Calendar Swap	30,006	25,031	5,430	1,143	811
European Propane CIF ARA Swap	6,016	3,555	389		
FAME 0 Biodiesel FOB Rdam Swap	21,840	7,198			
Florida Gas, Zone 3 Natural Gas Index Swap	1,150	668			
Florida Gas, Zone 3 Natural Gas Swing Swap	88				
Florida Gas Transmission Zone 3 Basis Swap	12,779	38,300	87,760	28,098	13,785
Capesize Time Charter Average (Baltic) Swap	1,206				
Freight Routet TC2 (Baltic) Forward	30				
Freight Routet TC5 (Platts) Forward	20				
Freight Routet TD3 (Baltic) Forward	65				
Freight Routet TD5 (Baltic) Forward	40				
Mini Handysize Time Charter Average (Baltic) Swap	20				
Panamax Time Charter Average (Baltic) Swap	750				
3.5% Fuel Oil Rdam Crack Swap	80,788	78,398	39,551	921	152
1% Fuel Oil NWE Crack Spread Swap	3,469	9,042	5,322	1,385	95
Fuel Oil (Platts) CAR CM	116	785			
1% Fuel Oil (Platts) Cargoes CIF NEW Swap	856	210			
High-Low Sulfur Fuel Oil Spread Swap	7,328	21,931	14,528	2,860	1,701
Gas EuroBob OXY NWE Barges	70,147	12,549			
Gas EuroBob OXY NWE Barges Crack	78,732	15,321			
Gasoil 0.1 Barges FOB Rdam vs ICE Gasoil BALMO	134	137			
Gasoil 0.1 Cargoes CIF NEW Swap	195	104			
Gasoil 0.1 CIF BALMO	5				
Gasoil 0.1 CIF MED	243	110			
Gasoil 0.1 CIF MED vs ICE Gasoil Swap	1,589	3,233	124		
Gasoil 0.1 Cargoes CIF NWE vs ICE Gasoil Swap	609	1,294	773		
Gasoil 0.1 CIF MED vs ICE Gasoil BALMO Swap	197	230			
Gasoil 0.1 Cargoes NWE vs ICE Gasoil BALMO Swap	75	59			
Gasoil 0.1 Barges FOB Rdam vs ICE Gasoil Swap	4,111	14,180	10,104		
Gasoil 0.1 Barges FOB Rdam Swap	3,790	1,833	965		
Gasoil 10ppm Cargoes CIF NEW vs ICE Gasoil	491	495			
Gasoil 10ppm Cargoes CIF NWE Swap	599	351	42		
Gasoil 10ppm Cargoes CIF NWE vs ICE Gasoil Swap	6,895	9,233	1,968		
Gasoil (ICE) Bullet Swap	4,081	3,488	4,311	676	
Gasoil (ICE) Calendar Swap	17,272	14,669	6,791	220	419
Gasoil Crack Spread Swap	76,952	257,528	190,522	14,287	14,040
Gasoil (ICE) Mini Calendar Swap	22,064				
Gasoline Up-Down (Argus) Swap	3,946	2,992	125		
Gasoline Up-Down BALMO Swap	3,547	697			
Gulf Coast ULSD Argus Calendar Swap	738				
Group Three (Platts) vs Heating Oil Spread Swap	217				
Group Three Unlead Gas (Platts) vs RBOB Gas Spread	124				
Gulf Coast 3.0% Fuel Oil BALMO Swap	22,229	16,852	3,170		
Gulf Coast Gasoline Calendar Swap	8,130	3,473	7,283	6,142	21,921
Gulf Coast Jet Fuel Calendar Swap	522	410	960	1,725	3,052
Gulf Coast Jet vs NY Harbor No 2 HO Spread Swap	113,926	97,772	27,511	6,470	2,427
Gulf Coast No 6 Fuel Oil 3.0% Sulfur Swap	644,907	683,433	180,907	53,150	27,673
Gulf Coast No 6 Fuel Oil Crack Swap	139,544	75,852	30,872	1,400	360
Gulf Coast ULSD Calendar Swap	8,729	7,538	3,506	305	
Gulf Coast ULSD Crack Spread Swap	4,155	106	825	325	
Gulf Coast Heating Oil (Argus) vs Heating Oil Spread	4,020	5,824			
Gulf Coast Unleaded 87 Crack Spread BALMO Swap	150				
Heating Oil BALMO Calendar Swap	139				
Heating Oil Crack Spread BALMO Swap	345				
Heating Oil vs ICE Gasoil	33,564	72,340	16,561		
Henry Hub Basis Swap	98,290	309,092	287,216	264,818	467,158
Henry Hub Index Swap	65,144	187,879	187,463	207,234	332,129

New York Mercantile Exchange (NYMEX) (continued)

FUTURE	2010	2009	2008	2007	2006
Henry Hub Swap	20,417,178	25,670,240	31,401,575	16,207,044	24,157,726
Henry Hub Swing	8,055	19,156	66,875	73,750	37,243
Houston Ship Channel Basis Swap	184,062	595,698	787,312	1,088,654	1,696,435
Houston Ship Channel Index Swap	23,394	69,071	101,690	132,368	131,702
Houston Ship Channel Swing	335	4,903	41,940	19,333	10,247
ICE Brent-Dubai Swap	72,518	207,977	60,009	19,400	15,455
ICE Gasoil BALMO Swap	101	40	114		
In Delivery Month CER	15,245	4,927			
In Delivery Month EUA	47,267	9,029			
ISO New England Off-Peak	18,038	27,468	20,279	11,258	25,445
ISO New England LMP Swap Peak	19,322	38,225	24,971	21,110	44,965
Japan C&F Naptha Swap	40,120	32,132	5,114	195	
Japan Naptha BALMO Swap	500	201			
Jet AV Fuel (P) Car FM ICE Gas Swap	39	290			
European Jet Rotterdam Barges vs Gasoil Swap	392	384	672		
European Jet CIF NWE vs Gasoil Swap	9,156	17,561	11,358	2,832	480
Jet Fuel Barges Rdam BALMO	2				
Jet Fuel Barges FOB Rdam vs ICE Gasoil BALMO	4	5			
Jet Fuel Cargoes CIF NWE BALMO Swap	2	15	48		
Jet Fuel Cargoes CIF NEW vs ICE Gasoil BALMO	397	941			
Jet Fuel Up-Down BALMO CL	1,703	75			
Jet Up-Down (Argus) Swap	14,980	9,125			
Los Angeles CARB Diesel (OPIS) Outright Swap	550	259	25	25	
Los Angeles CARB Diesel (OPIS) Spread Swap	19,997	13,142	5,189	25	
Los Angeles CARBOB (OPIS) Spread Swap	21,024	4,075	1,592		
Los Angeles Jet Fuel vs NYH #2 Heating Oil Spread	1,100	162	39	300	550
Los Angeles Jet (OPIS) Spread Swap	28,818	33,572	6,425	775	
LL Jet (OPIS) Swap	550				
LLS (Argus) vs WTI Spread Calendar Swap	13,250	2,135	5,049		
Los Angeles CARB Gasoline Swap (OPIS)	25	36			
Mars (Argus) vs WTI Spread Calendar Swap	3,180	1,500			
Mars (Argus) vs WTI Spread Trade Month Swap	2,035	3,720	180		
Mars Blend Crude Oil	825	466			
Coal (API2) cis ARA (Argus/McCloskey) Swap	24				
Coal (API4) fob Richards Bay (Argus/McCloskey) Swap	24				
MichCon Natural Gas Index Swap	5,994	5,413	1,414		
MichCon Natural Gas Swing Swap	267	62			
MichCon Basis Swap	73,658	173,256	283,962	289,738	484,925
Michigan Hub LMP Swap-Peak	20	246	28	620	1,040
MISO 5mw Off-Peak	460,896	120,520			
MISO 5mw Peak	25,768	7,732			
Mini European Naptha CIF NEW Swap	78				
Mont Belvieu Ethane 5 Decimals (OPIS) Swap	97,340	38,404			
Mont Belvieu Ethane (OPIS) BALMO	2,938	126			
Mont Belvieu Ethylene	1,190	1,530			
Mont Belvieu LDH Propane 5 Decimal (OPIS) Swap	210,632	66,945			
Mont Belvieu LDH Propane (OPIS) BALMO Swap	6,389	1,059			
Mont Belvieu Natural Gas 5 Decimal (OPIS) Swap	54,771	15,257			
Mont Belvieu Natural Gas (OPIS) BALMO Swap	939	355			
Mont Belvieu Normal Butane 5 Decimal (OPIS) Swap	56,408	28,214			
Mont Belvieu Normal Butane (OPIS) BALMO Swap	3,002	148			
Natural Gas Penultimate Swap	8,995,324	11,038,692	12,352,928	10,117,889	7,973,290
NBP Henry Hub Basis Swap	1	150			
NEPOOL CNCTCT Day Ahead Off-Peak	461,528	1,194,942			
NEPOOL CONECTIC 5mw Day Ahead Peak	27,569	66,666			
NEPOOL INTR HUB 5mw Day Ahead Off-Peak	1,021,109	2,433,442			
NEPOOL INTR HUB 5mw Day Ahead Peak	67,190	140,169			
NE Maine HUB 5mw Day Ahead Off-Peak	46,848	75,404			
NE Maine HUB 5mw Day Ahead Peak	5,928	4,415			
NEPOOL NE Mass 5mw Day Ahead Off-Peak	306,500	204,984			
NEPOOL NE Mass 5mw Day Ahead Peak	16,226	14,849			
NEPOOL New Hamp 5MW Day Ahead Peak	7,073				
NEPOOL New Hamp 5MW Day Ahead Off-Peak	129,365				
NEPOOL Rhode Island 5MW Day Ahead Peak	255				
NEPOOL SE Mass 5mw Day Ahead Off-Peak	52,409	171,464			
NEPOOL SE Mass 5mw Day Ahead Peak	2,849	12,432			
NEPOOL W CNTR Mass 5mw Day Ahead Off-Peak	82,358	277,045			
NEPOOL W CNTR Mass 5mw Day Ahead Peak	4,961	17,055			
New England Hub Daily Peak Swap	996	276	1,060	464	59,270
New York 0.3% Fuel Oil HiPr (Platts) Swap	7,973	3,850	775		
New York Ethanol Swap	16,371	8,215	3,814	1,739	
New York Heating Oil (Platts)	100				
New York Hub Zone G Peak Swap	100	320			
NGPL Mid-Continent Basis Swap	116,520	275,602	355,491	392,899	279,960
NGPL Mid-Continent Natural Gas Index Swap	3,965	14,420	12,004	8,698	1,615

VOLUME - U.S.

New York Mercantile Exchange (NYMEX) (continued)

FUTURE	2010	2009	2008	2007	2006
NGPL Mid-Continent Natural Gas Swing Swap	316	736	2,481	856	202
NGPL STX Natural Gas Basis Swap	17,256	61,843	11,686		
NGPL STX Natural Gas Index Swap	5,596	1,592			
NGPL TEX/OK Basis Swap	184,279	430,388	524,326	675,365	1,119,784
NGPL TEX/OK Natural Gas Index Swap	1,763	33,584	43,322	14,304	3,537
Northern Illinois Hub Daily Peak	260				
Northern Illinois Hub Monthly Peak	12,508	38,455	23,978	19,359	38,220
No 2 Heating Oil Up-Down Spread Calendar Swap	29,118	20,285	8,762	3,735	4,193
Northern Natural Gas Demarcation Basis Swap	59,065	177,130	334,235	278,478	162,381
Northern Natural Gas Ventura Basis Swap	71,867	259,500	361,503	353,186	306,787
Northern Illinois Hub Monthly Off-Peak	5,383	29,433	113,666	63,896	88,724
Northwest Rockies Basis Swap	88,194	293,089	792,219	1,040,846	1,408,279
NW Europe Gasoline Swap (Argus)	6	51,051	18,348	6,328	5,133
New York 0.7% Fuel Oil (Platts)	888	300			
New York 1% Fuel Oil vs Gulf Coast 3% Fuel Oil Swap	103,093	42,976	8,468		
New York 2.2% Fuel Oil (Platts) Swap	1,580	5,770			
New York 3.0% Fuel Oil Swap	3,904	2,293			
NY Harbor Fuel Oil 1.0% Sulfur BALMO Swap	8,425	5,375	1,161		
NY Harbor Heating Oil Calendar Swap	157,545	141,753	115,500	49,074	44,436
NY Harbor Residual Fuel 1.0% Sulfur Swap	209,696	189,772	93,845	67,130	38,366
NY Harbor Residual Fuel Oil Crack Swap	14,622	6,672	5,255	11,464	4,877
NY Harbor No 2 Crack Spread Calendar Swap	102,877	148,936	53,929	42,335	48,323
New York Heating Oil (Platts) vs NYMEX Heating Oil	1,981	1,895	50		
NY Harbor Conv Gasoline vs RBOB Swap	3,225	601	861	2,650	600
NYISO Zone A LBMP Swap Peak	8,401	12,687	24,128	13,950	61,394
NYISO Zone A LBMP Swap Off-Peak	4,164	5,600	16,232	17,784	18,054
NYISO Zone G LBMP Swap Peak	8,224	10,459	15,500	16,990	50,385
NYISO Zone G LBMP Swap Off-Peak	3,780	10,050	22,442	26,608	13,568
NYISO Zone J LBMP Swap Peak	7,361	8,221	5,265	9,767	26,492
NYISO Zone J LBMP Swap Off-Peak	2,834	2,660	4,218	4,510	9,380
NYISO Zone A 5mw Day Ahead Off-Peak	129,788	284,962			
NYISO Zone A 5mw Day Ahead Peak	12,994	18,320			
NYISO Zone C 5mw Day Ahead Off-Peak	82,560	108,840			
NYISO Zone C 5mw Day Ahead Peak	4,780	8,555			
NYISO Zone G 5mw Day Ahead Off-Peak	57,833	154,380			
NYISO Zone G 5mw Day Ahead Peak	21,407	11,162			
NYISO Zone J 5mw Day Ahead Off-Peak	93,738	37,768			
NYISO Zone J 5mw Day Ahead Peak	8,287	7,512			
NY Jet Fuel (Argus) vs Heating Oil Swap	50	50			
NY Jet Fuel (Platts) vs Heating Oil Swap	350	1,150			
NYISO Zone A LBMP Daily Peak Swap	180				
NYMEX Iron Ore	80				
NYMEX ULSD vs NYMEX Heating Oil Spread Swap	517	558	510	100	
NY ULSD (Argus) vs Heating Oil Spread Swap	6,068	530			
OneOk, OK Natural Gas Index Swap	724	1,020			
OneOk, OK Basis Swap	11,179	21,659			
OPIS Physical Ethane	3,010	475			
OPIS Physical LDH Propane	2,866	1,245			
OPIS Physical Natural Gas	4,637	4,535			
OPIS Physical Non-LDH Propane	1,405	1,405			
OPIS Physical Normal Nutane	8,823	5,676			
Panhandle Basis Swap	417,511	1,277,176	2,017,371	1,497,748	1,404,498
Panhandle Index Swap	11,966	24,002	37,250	31,609	9,444
Panhandle Swing Swap	1,797	6,264	21,182	8,493	3,634
El Paso Natural Gas Permian Basin Basis Swap	68,883	152,858	432,177	521,914	520,763
Argus Propane Far East Index BALMO Swap	262				
European Propane CIF ARA (Argus) BALMO Swap	299				
Mont Belvieu Mini LDH Propane	380				
Mont Belvieu Iso-Butane	2,735	90			
Conway Physical Propane In-Well	55				
HDPE High Density Polyethylene In-Well	8				
Mont Belvieu Spot Ethylene In-Well	880				
Petro European Naptha Crack Spread BALMO Swap	4,688				
3.5% Fuel Oil (Platts) Barges FOB Crack Spread Swap	53				
Argus Gasoline Eurobob Oxy Barges NWE Crack	15				
Gasoil (ICE) Crack Spread Swap	23				
Naptha Cargoes CIF NEW vs Gasoil Swap	101				
Diesel 10ppm UK (Platts) CIF NWE vs Gasoil Swap	88				
Singapore Fuel Oil 180 Crack Spread Swap	240				
Mini European 3.5% Fuel Oil Barges FOB Rdam Swap	4,940				
Mini European 3.5% Fuel Oil Barges FOB Rdam	71				
SME Biodiesel FOB Rdam Swap	60	80			
1% Fuel Oil Rdam vs 1% Fuel Oil NWE (Platts) Swap	144				
Mini SingaporeFuel Oil 180 cst (Platts) BALMO SWAP	3				
3.5% Fuel Oil Rdam vs 3.5% FOB MED Spread Balmo	133				

New York Mercantile Exchange (NYMEX) (continued)

FUTURE	2010	2009	2008	2007	2006
Gasoil EuroBob Oxy NWE Barges Crack Spread	2,115				
EuroBob Gasoline 10ppm (Platts) Barges FOB Rdam	39				
Gasoil EuroBob Oxy NWE Barges BALMO Swap	4,976	3			
EuroBob Gasoline 10ppm Barges FOB Rdam BALMO	5				
Northwest Europe Fuel oil High-Low Sulfur Spread	5				
Gulf Coast CBOB Gasoline A1 (Platts) Crack Spread	265				
European 3.5% Fuel Oil Cargoes FOB MED BALMO	50				
European 1% Fuel Oil Cargoes FOB MED Swap	20				
Euro 1% Fuel Oil Cargoes FOB MED vs Euro 1% Fuel	20				
Mont Belvieu Ethylene (PCW) Financial Swap	1,023				
Mini European 1% Fuel Oil Barges FOB Rdam Swap	28				
Singapore Mogas 95 Unleaded Swap	275				
Ethanol (Argus) T1 FOB Rdam Excluding Duty Swap	10				
PG&E Citygate Basis Swap	48	31,019	387,422	328,283	356,769
PJM AD Hub 5mw Real-Time Off-Peak	430,142	72,498			
PJM AD Hub 5mw Real-Time Peak	14,608	9,962			
PJM AECO Day Ahead Off-Peak	87,350	3,920			
PJM AECO Day Ahead Peak	6,095	308			
PJM APS Zone Day Ahead Off-Peak	33,886				
PJM APS Zone Day Ahead Peak	1,876				
PJM BGE Day Ahead Off-Peak	305,027	823,697	3,800		
PJM BGE Day Ahead Peak	21,080	49,163			
PJM ComEd 5mw Day Ahead Off-Peak	4,648	149,456			
PJM ComEd 5mw Day Ahead Peak	515	10,144			
PJM Financially Settled Daily Peak	3,220	350	1,626	26,610	3,530
PJM Dayton Day Ahead Off-Peak	287,026	269,270	32,648		
PJM Dayton Day Ahead Peak	17,026	38,051	9,514		
PJM DPL Day Ahead Off-Peak	67,864	99,290	4,688		
PJM DPL Day Ahead Peak	2,957	5,635	512		
PJM DUQUE SNE 5MW Day Ahead Peak	7,324				
PJM DUQUE SNE 5MW Day Ahead Off-Peak	132,176				
PJM Eastern Day Ahead Off-Peak	230,010	421,819	19,864		
PJM Eastern Day Ahead Peak	15,876	58,876	5,416		
PJM JCPL Zone Hub Off-Peak Cal-Mth Day Ahead	329,176	653,460	4,664		
PJM JCPL Zone Hub Peak Cal-Mth Day Ahead LMP	23,322	44,379	1,516		
PJM Northern IL Hub 5mw Real-Time Off-Peak	26,815	32,478			
PJM Northern IL Hub 5mw Real-Time Peak	440,021	465,914			
PJM Northern IL Hub Day Ahead Off-Peak	402,357	1,683,800	86,888		
PJM Northern IL Hub Day Ahead Peak	27,594	91,606	10,702		
PJM Off-Peak LMP Swap	32,744	61,397	68,172	50,940	83,734
PJM PECO Zone 5mw Peak Calendar Month Day	36,696	3,840			
PJM PEPCO Day Ahead Off-Peak	338,949	1,254,275	147,640		
PJM PEPCO Day Ahead Peak	25,532	97,197	7,690		
PJM PPL Day Ahead Off-Peak	608,959	332,772			
PJM PPL Day Ahead Peak	41,097	37,398			
PJM PSEG Day Ahead Off-Peak	1,249,809	2,801,488	18,240		
PJM PSEG Day Ahead Peak	82,035	203,264	5,690		
PJM WES Hub 50MW Peak Cal Mth Real Time LMP	82				
PJM Western Hub Day Ahead Off-Peak	4,913,517	6,810,613	231,232		
PJM Western Hub Day Ahead Peak	317,505	531,995	23,435		
PJM Western Hub Real-Time Off-Peak	1,565,616	1,727,213	202,312		
PJM Western Hub Real-Time Peak	78,894	98,311	11,905		
Premium Unld Gasoline 10ppm FOB MED	1,736	1,234			
Premium Unld Gasoline 10ppm CARGOE	17	37			
Premium Unld Gasoline 10ppm FOB	442	280			
Premium Unld Gasoline 10ppm Rdam FOB BALMO	94	60			
Premium Unld Gasoline 10ppm FOB Swap	121	234			
Propane Non-LDH Mt Belvieu (OPIS) BALMO Swap	28	315			
Propane Non-LDH Mt Belvieu (OPIS) Swap	1,986	3,390			
RBOB Calendar Swap	156,852	112,652	81,874	30,235	13,562
RBOB Crack Spread Swap	144,319	151,414	83,269	57,793	13,254
RBOB Crack Spread BALMO Swap	1,010				
RBOB Gasoline BALMO Swap	6,262	3,274			
RBOB vs NYMEX RBOB Gasoline Spread Swap	1,500				
RBOB Up-Down Calendar Swap	97,772	93,703	53,431	22,724	6,169
RBOB vs Heating Oil Swap	14,707	2,860	2,638	8,455	2,175
Rockies Natural Gas Index Swap	5,804	29,993	26,500	19,440	29,994
San Juan Basis Swap	28,434	93,864	169,655	246,858	181,765
San Juan Natural Gas Index Swap	20,785	12,700	2,766	3,425	3,702
San Juan Natural Gas Swing Index	4,212	3,033	6,561	2,419	852
Singapore Fuel Oil 180cst BALMO Swap	3,478	5,762	2,085	90	
Singapore Fuel Oil 380cst BALMO Swap	1,169	929	514	15	
Singapore Fuel Oil 380cst Calendar Swap	16,529	5,982	3,662	2,142	461
Singapore Fuel Oil 180cst Calendar Swap	121,756	133,362	79,252	48,516	20,213
Singapore Fuel Oil Spread Swap	11,980	11,276	4,823	1,532	913

New York Mercantile Exchange (NYMEX) (continued)

FUTURE	2010	2009	2008	2007	2006
Singapore Gasoil BALMO Swap	23,926	28,166	15,214	425	
Singapore Gasoil Calendar Swap	260,561	321,662	128,359	52,955	13,484
Singapore Gasoil vs Rdam Gasoil Swap	33,009	69,019	37,975	18,564	5,610
Singapore Jet Kerosene BALMO Swap	3,567	7,740	4,754	150	
Singapore Jet Kerosene vs Gasoil Spread Swap	35,730	64,490	32,980	18,740	3,075
Singapore Jet Kerosene Swap	66,582	81,705	36,688	20,045	4,898
Singapore Jet Kero vs Gasoil BALMO	2,690	255			
Singapore Mogas 92 Unleaded BALMO	1,236	425			
Singapore Mogas 92 Unleaded Swap	31,649	11,224			
Singapore Naptha BALMO Swap	139	550	375		
Singapore Naptha Swap	9,286	13,887	25,374	9,955	2,750
SoCal Basis Swap	15,349	113,568	1,082,052	1,784,378	2,311,008
SoCal Swing Swap	378	6,359	62,728	50,013	19,888
SONAT Basis Swap	27,493	72,505	130,742	36,106	18,722
Southern Star LA Natural Gas Index Swap	10,580	4,354			
Southern Star LA Natural Gas Swing Swap	370				
Southern Star TX,OK,KS Natural Gas Basis Swap	19,049	4,304			
Sumas Basis Swap	6,102	6,652	63,684	83,641	205,978
Sumas Natural Gas Swing Swap	120	2,087	606	165	2,546
TC2 Rotterdam to USAC 37K	2,135	395	449	205	630
TC4 Singapore to Japan 30	629	305	445	10	
TC5 Ras Tanura to Yokohama Freight	3,275	5,256	560	50	
TCO Basis Swap	34,315	110,615	236,679	394,285	333,867
TCO Natural Gas Index Swap	6,180	25,207	2,648		
TD3 Middle Eastern Gulf to Japan 250K MT	2,505	651	460		
TD5 West Africa to USAC 1	1,320	105			
TD7 North Sea to Continent	30	10			
Tennessee 500 Leg Basis Swap	32,620	126,840	79,271	29,621	19,071
Tennessee 500 Leg Natural Gas Index Swap	8,576	11,895	62		
Tennessee 800 Basis Swap	4,560	6,426			
Tennessee Zone 0 Basis Swap	11,083	12,040	23,876	53,705	81,632
Tennesse Zone 0 Natural Gas Index Swap	17,216	7,777	2,804		
Tennesse Zone 0 Natural Gas Swing Swap	548	698			
TETCO ELA Basis	6,229	44,184	43,217	5,382	11,811
TETCO M-3 Natural Gas Index Swap	5,777	120,561	121,290	54,619	44,685
TETCO STX Basis Swap	5,334	12,289	37,702	51,664	69,669
TETCO STX Natural Gas Index Swap	3,816	7,388	2,195		
Texas Eastern ELA Natural Gas Index Swap	310				
Texas Eastern Zone M-3 Basis Swap	94,942	232,939	412,686	765,236	642,301
Texas Eastern West Louisiana Natural Gas Index	9,344	6,878			
Texas Eastern West Louisiana Basis Swap	25,066	19,300			
Texas Gas Zone 1 Natural Gas	112	523			
Texas Gas Zone 1 Basis Swap	6,391	11,113			
Texas Gas Zone SL Basis Swap	18,023	81,101	71,598	46,454	49,163
Texas Gas Zone SL Natural Gas	92	232			
Texas Gas Zone 1 Basis Swap (Platts IFERC)	2,462	124			
Texas Gas Zone 2 Natural Gas Index Swap	2,384	3,772			
Texas Gas Zone 2 Basis Swap	2,988	3,499			
Transco Zone 3 Basis Swap	24,328	73,501	157,593	126,442	58,349
Transco Zone 3 Natural Gas Index Swap	5,370	12,980	9,215		
Transco Zone 3 Natural Gas Swing Swap	158				
Transco Zone 4 Basis Swap	34,684	70,159	107,097	11,004	13,652
Transco Zone 4 Natural Gas Index	14,467	1,611			
Transco Zone 4 Natural Gas Swing Swap	401				
Transco Zone 6 Basis Swap	32,080	94,997	165,105	545,492	313,674
Transco Zone 6 Natural Gas Index Swap	12,764	79,090	42,904	51,709	11,199
Trunkline, LA Basis Swap	950	10,210	31,481	17,364	7,001
Texas Gas Zone SL Natural Gas Index Swap	1,104	465			
ULSD 10ppm CIF MED Swap	238	146			
ULSD 10ppm CIF MED vs ICE Gasoil Swap	4,725	3,057	125		
ULSD 10ppm CIF MED vs ICE Gasoil BALMO Swap	193	334			
ULSD Up-Down (Argus) Swap	16,155	6,620			
ULSD Up-Down BALMO Swap	9,483	1,206			
Up Down GC ULSD vs NYMEX Heating Oil Spread	525,152	228,195	105,423	19,834	
US Gulf Coast Unleaded 87 Crack Spread Calendar	7,805	8,045	10,724	8,517	19,933
Ventura Natural Gas Index Swap	14,731	6,267	17,671	12,748	2,508
Ventura Natural Gas Swing Swap	980	426	3,131	610	434
WAHA Basis Swap	149,767	425,807	624,817	727,707	611,795
WAHA Index Swap	11,996	101,880	71,755	72,219	26,784
Western Rail Powder River Basin Coal Swap	17,580	24,085	28,340	10,680	
WTI-Brent (ICE) Calendar Swap	70,919	107,192	240,916	60,008	35,343
WTI Crude Oil Calendar Swap	1,216,576	1,057,843	847,658	489,274	377,086
WTS (Argus) vs WTI Spread Trade Month Swap	2,646	1,460	3,082		
NYMEX Columbian Peso	17,308	10,405			
Certified Emission Reduction	975	519	25,083		

New York Mercantile Exchange (NYMEX) (continued)

FUTURE	2010	2009	2008	2007	2006
EU Allowance	110	208	5,066		
Polyethylene	806	48			
NYMEX Cocoa	1,338	1,318	2,222	1,769	
NYMEX Coffee	1,847	1,335	9,780	5,784	
NYMEX Cotton	4,964	1,764	8,495	7,407	
NYMEX Sugar #11	9,244	7,197	26,107	10,470	10
Total Futures	419,908,616	362,428,100	338,490,891	277,408,465	216,252,995

NYSE LIFFE U.S.

FUTURE	2010	2009	2008	2007	2006
Gold	471,446	1,467,450	847,778		
Mini New York Gold	2,090,555	2,122,569	675,114		
Silver	108,114	107,941	72,722		
Mini New York Silver	1,060,631	647,314	236,327		
MSCI EAFE	194,080	75,697			
MSCI EM	139,613	49,373			
MSCI USA	335	4,390			
MSCI EAFE NTR	6				
Total Futures	4,064,780	4,474,734	1,831,941		

ONECHICAGO

FUTURE	2010	2009	2008	2007	2006
Single Stock Futures	4,758,640	2,624,496	3,404,201	7,835,289	7,777,241
Exchange Traded Funds	44,842	101,660	299,547	51,034	9,124
Narrow-Based Equity Index	167,678	256,992	308,533	219,640	136,100
Total Futures	4,971,160	2,983,148	4,012,281	8,105,963	7,922,465

Total Volume

	2010	2009	2008	2007	2006
Total Futures	2,764,778,904	2,328,123,926	2,904,518,236	2,680,196,142	2,068,567,250
Precent Change	18.76%	-19.84%	8.37%	29.57%	23.26%

Options Traded on U.S. Securities Exchanges Volume Highlights
2010 in Comparison with 2009

2010 Rank	EXCHANGE	2010 Contracts	%	2009 Contracts	%	2009 Rank
1	Chicago Board of Options Exchange	1,115,491,922	28.61%	1,134,764,209	31.41%	1
2	Nasdaq OMX PHLX	846,895,365	21.72%	606,456,252	16.79%	3
3	International Securities Exchange	745,176,328	19.11%	960,247,551	26.58%	2
4	NYSE-ARCA	488,093,760	12.52%	421,349,395	11.66%	4
5	NYSE-AMEX	440,021,234	11.29%	248,119,861	6.87%	5
6	Nasdaq Options Market	142,922,225	3.67%	103,912,524	2.88%	7
7	Boston Options Exchange	91,754,121	2.35%	137,784,626	3.81%	6
8	BATS Exchange	25,103,245	0.64%			
9	C2 Exchange	3,610,470	0.09%			
	Total Options	3,899,068,670	100.00%	3,612,634,418	100.00%	

Options Traded on U.S. Futures Exchanges Volume Highlights
2010 in Comparison with 2009

2010 Rank	EXCHANGE	2010 Contracts	%	2009 Contracts	%	2009 Rank
1	Chicago Mercantile Exchange (CME Group)	238,174,901	63.61%	199,818,941	38.51%	1
2	Chicago Board of Trade (CME Group)	123,666,496	33.03%	92,848,854	17.89%	2
3	New York Mercantile Exchange (CME Group)	80,574,639	21.52%	70,210,423	13.53%	3
4	ICE Futures U.S.	14,654,805	3.91%	11,309,749	2.18%	4
5	Kansas City Board of Trade (KCBT)	148,032	0.04%	108,317	0.02%	6
6	Chicago Climate Futures Exchange (CCFE)	79,951	0.02%	126,456	0.02%	5
7	Minneapolis Grain Exchange (MGE)	32,290	0.01%	25,137	0.00%	7
8	NYSE Liffe U.S.	5,736	0.00%	9,207	0.00%	8
	Total Options	457,336,850	100.00%	374,457,084	100.00%	

Chicago Climate Futures Exchange (CCFE)

OPTION	2010	2009	2008	2007	2006
Carbon Financial Instrument (CFI)	58	11,732	11,753		
Carbon Financial Instrument (CFI-US)	848	1,212			
Nitrogen Financial Instrument - Annual (NFI-A)	26,800	13,800	6,500		
Regional Greenhouse Gas Initiatives (RGGI)	8,453	74,363	10,373		
Sulfur Financial Instrument (SFI)	43,792	24,934	85,190	91,858	
Total Options	79,951	126,456	113,817	91,859	

VOLUME - U.S.

Chicago Board of Trade (CBT)

OPTION	2010	2009	2008	2007	2006
Wheat	4,495,955	3,635,792	4,060,865	3,893,354	2,597,975
Corn	20,810,260	14,435,687	20,992,582	14,691,277	11,317,388
Oats	18,312	20,830	23,843	16,381	25,738
Soybeans	10,046,345	9,555,840	9,806,935	8,215,582	6,042,797
Soybean Crush	3,044	3,254	2,452	3,267	6,828
Soybean Oil	1,843,307	1,255,304	1,458,568	1,277,884	902,096
Soybean Meal	1,021,831	891,551	884,721	713,821	746,185
Rough Rice	38,317	15,674	26,681	23,374	26,868
Corn Nearby + 2 Calendar Spread	5,946	186			
Soybean Nearby + 2 Calendar Spread	5,106	603			
Wheat Nearby + 2 Calendar Spread	2,618	510			
Soy Meal Nearby + 2 Calendar Spread	300				
Wheat - Corn ICSO	90				
Soy Oil Nearby + 2 Calendar Spread	2,470				
Dec-July Wheat Calendar Spread	255	150			
July-Nov Soybean Calendar Spread	78,669	20,799			
Nov-July Soybean Calendar Spread	1				
July-Dec Soy Meal Calendar Spread	1,040				
July-Dec Soy Oil Calendar Spread	625				
July-Dec Corn Calendar Spread	21,673	50			
Dec-July Corn Calendar Spread	80				
Dec-Dec Corn Calendar Spread	7,340				
July-July Wheat Calendar Spread	5,254	451			
July-Dec Wheat Calendar Spread	669	320			
Ethanol Forward Month Swap	23,639	8,933	42,477	6,048	
T-Bonds (30-year)	14,447,974	11,142,149	18,209,855	17,391,744	20,731,673
T-Notes (10-year)	55,280,257	40,206,023	56,753,688	61,528,219	61,888,144
T-Notes (5-year)	6,064,380	4,803,364	12,752,318	15,392,035	11,585,131
T-Notes (2-year)	2,400,459	2,397,210	2,333,092	1,056,738	804,975
30-Day Federal Funds	6,666,619	4,217,906	7,478,025	8,020,547	9,424,628
Ultra T-Bind	51,022				
10-Year Swap	2				
Flexible US T-Bonds	188,620	117,292	287,136	252,780	392,648
Flexible T-Notes (10-year)	45,404	7,550	12,575	910,609	311,295
Dow Jones Industrial Index	3,188	22,718	75,840	105,860	100,589
Mini ($5) Dow Jones Industrial Index	85,425	85,934	281,062	300,307	450,601
Total Options	123,666,496	92,848,854	135,519,960	134,047,704	127,622,361

Chicago Mercantile Exchange (CME Group)

OPTION	2010	2009	2008	2007	2006
Live Cattle	2,089,701	1,355,251	1,226,704	726,003	930,169
Live Cattle Calendar ISO	94				
Feeder Cattle	119,382	74,777	99,911	106,587	156,292
Lean Hogs	653,785	651,731	512,159	321,258	225,013
Pork Bellies, Frozen	3	44	211	575	1,198
Class III Milk	172,384	153,513	167,779	94,640	85,713
Class IV Milk	48				
Nonfat Dry Milk	2	59	60		116
Mini BFP Milk	1,057	562	367	967	549
Cash Settled Cheese	25				
Dry Whey	468	862	670		
Cash Butter	758	223	322	17	
Random Lumber	8,840	13,883	17,485	18,127	20,909
Eurodollar (3-month)	106,893,369	117,553,569	187,341,383	313,032,284	268,957,052
Eurodollar Mid-Curve	76,490,147	43,369,605	40,883,014		
Treasury Matched Eurodollar Mid-Curve	196,301	107,128	287,662		
Australian Dollar	551,060	273,516	206,649	74,874	36,562
British Pound	1,208,577	465,413	565,050	352,736	158,473
Canadian Dollar	889,708	465,264	380,894	530,023	375,257
Euro FX	6,651,318	2,207,616	2,696,811	1,801,681	1,849,119
Japanese Yen	1,366,149	758,564	850,340	929,733	544,716
Mexican Peso	43	158	768	51	371
Russian Ruble	750				433
Swiss Franc	174,320	112,861	198,694	78,675	47,984
Euro FX European	107,476	94,244	375,621	230,615	190,610
Euro FX / British Pound	42				
Euro FX / Swiss Franc	1,440	400			
Australian Dollar European	1,682	3,800			
British Pound European	23,463	61,434	89,910	98,323	18,191
Canadian Dollar European	21,403	26,775	54,138	50,899	7,256
Japanese Yen European	14,468	40,178	136,921	155,394	53,753
Swiss Franc European	10,226	20,423	37,868	30,079	6,773
Nikkei 225 Index	2,100	4,500	17,750	17,200	59,200
S&P 500 Index	10,719,451	10,350,127	16,378,218	19,458,815	15,785,802
E-Mini S&P 500 Index	22,778,255	18,142,915	22,167,648	16,213,737	9,893,979

Chicago Mercantile Exchange (CME Group) (continued)

OPTION	2010	2009	2008	2007	2006
EOM S&P 500 Index	1,859,912	1,470,660	2,512,846	816,354	80,424
EOM E-Mini S&P 500 Index	1,872,924	845,519	1,028,368	950,829	147,471
EOW1 S&P 500 Index	287,033	153,184			
EOW1 E-mini S&P 500 Index	769,266	88,404			
EOW2 S&P 500 Index	287,542	114,594			
EOW2 E-mini S&P 500 Index	708,912	82,869			
EOW4 E-mini S&P 500 Index	404,518				
E-Mini S&P MidCap 400 Index	3,534	5,272	5,507	235	
NASDAQ 100 Index	607	1,535	13,096	79,900	71,499
E-Mini NASDAQ 100 Index	514,379	440,634	542,497	742,395	317,765
CDD Weather	61,325	27,050	25,100	19,400	18,050
HDD Weather	40,215	40,250	50,850	63,835	75,277
HDD Seasonal Weather Strip	99,150	115,300	139,800	295,450	209,300
CDD Seasonal Weather Strip	84,000	98,950	245,850	258,350	97,200
HDD Weather European	4,500	3,500			
Euro HDD Seasonal Strip Weather	21,300	3,000	4,200		2,000
Binary Seasonal Hurricane	3,000				
Binary Seasonal Hurricane Event 2	1,000	1,000			
Seasonal Binary	42				
Snowfall	287				
Seasonal Snowfall	160				
Pacific Rim Dat SS Weather	1,000	4,400			
Total Options	238,172,901	199,818,941	280,517,713	360,005,823	301,551,501

ICE Futures U.S. (ICE)

OPTION	2010	2009	2008	2007	2006
Coffee 'C'	2,292,800	1,427,032	2,826,331	2,999,648	2,785,053
Coffee Calendar Spread	3,428				
Sugar #11	8,448,556	7,280,380	9,179,779	5,548,668	6,250,162
Sugar #11 Options on Futures Spreads	204,668	109,849	145,368	204,100	54,880
Cocoa	322,121	318,805	376,444	370,429	377,905
Cotton #2	2,911,509	1,709,004	4,468,327	3,451,217	1,820,259
Cotton Calendar Spread	50				
Orange Juice Frozen Concentrate	237,790	243,741	238,616	385,219	426,967
US Dollar Index	22,248	55,822	72,768	50,562	39,299
Russell 1000 Index Mini	4,836	7,798	877		
Russell 2000 Index Mini	206,624	157,126	73,634		
Reuters-CRB Futures Index (CCI)	175	192	892	435	6,320
Total Options	14,654,805	11,309,749	17,521,134	13,124,201	11,920,477

Kansas City Board of Trade (KCBT)

OPTION	2010	2009	2008	2007	2006
Wheat	148,032	108,317	187,658	352,948	515,479
Total Options	148,032	108,317	187,658	352,948	515,479

New York Mercantile Exchange (NYMEX)

OPTION	2010	2009	2008	2007	2006
COMEX Copper	17,509	18,568	22,559	24,467	75,403
COMEX Gold	7,730,488	4,755,427	4,392,737	3,554,858	3,708,573
COMEX Silver	1,640,232	1,066,721	1,700,882	1,257,505	1,646,959
NYMEX Platinum	10,643	20		300	321
Palladium	12,214				
Appalachian Coal	1,200				
Brent Crude Oil Average Price	139,273	137,549	92,549		
Brent Crude Oil 1 M CSO	11,350				
Brent Crude Oil 6 M CSO	50				
Brent Crude Oil European Style Look-Alike	79,143	18,562	31,181		
Brent Crude Oil American Style	29,880	2,410	8,904		
CAPP Coal Calendar Strip	5				
Central Appalachian Coal	585	255			
Cinergy Hub Peak Month	94,552	142,190	14,240	8,930	
Crude Oil 1-month CSO	2,049,582	719,802	1,016,327	1,851,827	1,209,952
Crude Oil APO	4,621,556	3,203,460	2,227,738	1,445,930	838,985
Crude Oil Calendar Strip	775				
Dubai Crude Oil Average Price	100				
Crude Oil Physical	130,902	86,932	132,590	134,537	21,416
Crude Oil European Style	1,195,827	1,507,042	3,580,861	1,879,999	379,250
Crude Oil	32,785,267	28,551,730	35,255,326	28,398,793	21,016,562
Midwest ISO Cinergy Hub Peak Cal-Mth LMP Swap	200				
European Jet Kerosene NEW APO	344	10			
Heating Oil-Crude Oil Spread	24,529	6,238	824	5,783	29,862
Heating Oil Crack Spread Average Price	3,000				
Heating Oil Physical - European	6,261	11,479	112,488	32,438	1,525
Heating Oil	884,849	686,270	781,003	620,761	595,427

New York Mercantile Exchange (NYMEX) (continued)

OPTION	2010	2009	2008	2007	2006
Henry Hub Financial Last Day	28,775	16,892			
Heating Oil 1-month CSO	10,350	16,345	275		10,185
Houston Ship Channel Pipe	3,736	8,800			
In Delivery Month CER	19,550				
In Delivery Month EUA	16,000	1,250			
In Delivery Month EUA Serial	500				
ISO New England Calendar-Month LMP Swap	7,186	17,410	43,082	45,240	
Natural Gas 1-month CSO Financial	258,719	15,874			
Natural Gas 1-month CSO Financial	37,875	43,290	174,940	120,608	246,472
Natural Gas 2-month CSO Financial	1,650				
Natural Gas 3-month CSO Financial	338,267	52,855			
Natural Gas 5-month CSO Financial	850		250		5,500
Natural Gas Houston Ship Channel Basis	43,844				
Natural Gas Calendar Strip	11,801	3,240			
Natural Gas Physical	369,439	213,170	112,303	13,320	795
Natural Gas Physical - European	23,957,725	25,309,214	31,158,326	29,921,068	19,515,968
Natural Gas Physical	1,360,225	1,135,135	2,336,287	5,051,879	9,581,663
Natural Gas Summer Strip	400	1,000			
Natural Gas Winter Strip	5,800				
Natural Gas 3-month CSO	1,301	10,877	26,605	14,233	24,556
Northern Rockies Pipe	51,800	87,840	11,460	1,960	
NW Pipeline Rockies Basis	12,680	9,508			
NY Harbor Heating Oil Swap	858,571	661,036	240,362	60,471	18,868
NYISO Zone G 5mw Peak	26,120	63,960			
NYMEX European Gasoil APO	32,369	9,957	96		
NYMEX European Style Gasoil	590	317			
Panhandle Basis	7,184	4,528			
Panhandle Pipe Swap	65,996	105,368	47,092		
Petrochemicals	9,035	645			
Petrochemicals - Mt Bel Ethane (OPIS) APO	4,735				
Petrochemicals - Mt Bel Normal Butane (OPIS) APO	735				
Gulf Coast No 6 Fuel Oil 3.0% APO	1,071				
PJM Calendar Strip	13,484				
PJM Monthly Financially Settled Electricity	707,300	528,316	365,316	370,108	247,040
RBOB 1-Month CSO	30,517	32,381			
RBOB Calendar Swap	90,392	57,384	27,402	6,219	142
RBOB Crack Spread	7,214	225	13,072	6,362	220
RBOB Gasoline	546,878	680,635	884,839	1,016,963	82,176
RBOB Gasoline European style	10,016	21,007	84,382	44,382	995
Rotterdam 3.5% Fuel Oil CL	6,857	1,881			
San Juan Pipe	5,652	22,118	3,240		
Singapore Fuel Oil 180 CST	1,157	318			
Singapore Gasoil APO	150				
Singapore Jet Fuel Calendar	2,395	3,023			
SoCal Basis	3,240				
SoCal Pipe Swap	46,172	119,320	26,445		
Transco Zone 6 Pipe Swap	1,500				
WTI Crude Oil 12-month CSO	42,570	20,675	70,137	83,126	24,750
WTI Crude Oil 6-month CSO	6,100		5,450	2,300	400
WTI-Brent Bullet Swap	1,000				
WTI Crude Oil 1-month CSO Financial	33,450	5,370			
MichCon Basis	2,000				
Carbon CER European	1,400	600	3,200		
Total Options	80,574,639	70,210,423	85,014,980	75,976,972	59,899,331

NYSE LIFFE U.S.

OPTION	2010	2009	2008	2007	2006
100 oz Gold	5,631	8,702	4,972		
5,000 oz Silver	105	505	630		
Total Options	5,736	9,207	5,602		

Minneapolis Grain Exchange (MGE)

OPTION	2010	2009	2008	2007	2006
American Spring Wheat	27,354	24,937	47,935	34,354	40,468
Hard Red Winter Wheat Index	4,936				
Total Options	32,290	25,137	47,935	34,354	40,491

Total Volume

	2010	2009	2008	2007	2006
Total Options	457,334,850	374,457,084	518,928,799	583,633,862	501,549,640
Percent Change	22.13%	-27.84%	-11.09%	16.37%	36.30%

Volume - Worldwide

Athens Derivatives Exchange S.A. (ADEX), Greece

	2010	2009	2008	2007	2006
FTSE/Athex 20	2,987,458	2,371,733	2,808,788	2,588,908	
FTSE/Athex-CSE Banking Index	4,964				
All Futures on Individual Equities	4,767,973	5,037,065	3,713,266	3,101,602	
Total Futures	**7,760,395**	**7,408,798**	**6,545,423**	**5,843,937**	
FTSE/Athex 20	615,122	383,555	440,650	591,476	
All Options on Individual Equities	105,764	67,590	182,757	106,913	
Total Options	**720,886**	**451,154**	**626,697**	**737,607**	

Australian Stock Exchange (ASX), Australia

	2010	2009	2008	2007	2006
S&P/ASX Index	370,800	396,723	309,499	238,823	110,769
All Futures on Individual Equities	543,676	777,732	971,261	706,656	693,683
Total Futures	**914,476**	**1,174,455**	**1,280,760**	**945,479**	**804,452**
S&P / ASX Index	5,274,603	3,486,914	2,819,582	1,797,754	1,170,793
All Options on Individual Equities	15,455,208	14,465,066	16,070,022	22,226,578	20,477,083
Total Futures	**20,729,811**	**17,951,980**	**18,889,604**	**24,024,332**	**21,647,876**

Bolsa de Mercadorias & Futuros (BM&F), Brazil

	2010	2009	2008	2007	2006
Arabica Coffee	640,754	596,435	760,761	724,319	528,462
Arabica Coffee Rollover	33,252	48,764	22,476		
Live Cattle	1,153,778	834,304	1,633,113	934,422	392,012
Live Cattle Rollover	4	1,418			
Ethanol	20,925	1	16,608	17,234	
Corn Cash Settled	364,045	259,610	7,767		
Corn Cash Rollover	300				
Soybean	95,598	168,168	284,382	188,279	98,112
Soybean Rollover	80				
Gold Forward	1,195	176	520	283	308
Gold	80	640	1,280	2,100	3,180
Gold Spot	9,567	12,403	12,579	9,118	24,369
Pound Sterling	46,600				
Australian Dollar	49,090				
Canadian Dollar	7,725				
Mexican Peso	31,650				
Japanese Yen	7,140				
Bovespa Stock Index Futures	18,039,345	16,350,493	20,226,662	26,550,491	13,232,399
Bovespa Rollover	1,943,040	1,382,060	118,680		
Bovespa Mini Index	16,705,118	12,374,969	9,928,406	10,692,141	3,702,409
Interest Rate	293,065,417	151,958,184	166,983,583	221,627,417	161,654,736
Interest Rate Swap	144,440	71,545	547,146	91,503	192,356
Interest Rate x Stock Basket Swap	1,022				
Interest Rate x Exchange Rate Swap	449,476	368,853	449,784	483,342	398,757
Interest Rate x Reference Rate Swap	3,600	14,000	22,234	20,200	189,796
Interest Rate x Price Index Swap (formerly Inflation)	1,303,131	655,582	1,054,533	1,486,734	2,760,520
Exchange Rate Swap	138,165	27,883	43,007	54,887	26,443
Forward Exchange Rate	79				
Price Index	1,728				
Interest Rate x IBrX-50	1,610	3,901	9,254	10,467	7,448
ID x US Dollar Spread Futures	1,045,712	738,389	1,150,157	396,326	1,016,176
FRA on ID x US Dollar Spread	21,075,685	17,487,272	21,217,283	20,907,906	14,396,347
ID x US Dollar Spread Swap	21,650	256,434	336,560	44,049	145,943
ID x IPCA Spread	39,485	6,240	69,350	111,025	58,840
CDS Brazil 5-Year	50	218	953		
Global 2040	2,070	3,409	48,533	94,845	57,590
US T-Note	13,563	26,291	107,576	73,123	630
US Dollar	82,453,621	66,776,180	87,442,346	84,774,568	52,350,517
US Dollar Rollover	19,223,570	15,280,530	7,179,600		
Mini US Dollar	1,969,427	573,839	147,424	3,460,153	5,053,580
US Dollar forward points	4,337,700	3,157,515	3,488,158	2,850,000	1,648,807
Euro	390,295	75,265	37,550	2,725	70
Total Futures	**464,830,782**	**289,549,270**	**323,770,173**	**375,885,135**	**258,466,105**
Gold on Actuals	361,960	369,564	363,867	193,380	119,378
Gold Exercise	84,482	61,234	47,630	38,115	19,492
US $ Denominated Arabica Coffee	17,453	8,459	48,166	80,523	30,602
US $ Denominated Arabica Coffee Exercise	2,889	3,427	6,687	3,444	2,370
Corn Cash Settled	114,619	17,364	51		
Corn Cash Exercise	11,301	1,856			
Soybeans	47,163	6,611	6,616	7,184	1,345
Soybeans, Exercise	167	296	1,434	741	
Live Cattle	166,319	46,001	75,622	5,108	987
Live Cattle, Exercise	32,368	14,678	4,328	1,147	251
Hydrous Ethanol	1,305				

Bolsa de Mercadorias & Futuros (BM&F), Brazil (continued)

	2010	2009	2008	2007	2006
Hydrous Ethanol Exercise	385				
Bovespa Stock	199,760	1,714,845	1,229,734	727,015	26,625
Bovespa Stock Exercise	104,510	216,930	194,950	112,690	2,072
Interest Rate	12,477,540	4,545,435	7,317,364	1,886,247	945,250
Interest Rate (IDI) Exercise	528,500	962,310	1,511,261	273,500	18,080
Interest Rate (volatility)	3,148,715	1,455,990	3,724,645	2,436,765	933,445
Interest Rate (IDI)	88,014,027	40,174,869	13,915,878	12,316,359	9,279,101
IDI Index (exercise)	6,166,118	2,499,125	1,236,980	366,650	105,410
IDI Index (volatility)	12,415,185	5,894,010	1,823,370	3,068,460	1,848,810
Flexible IBrX-50 Index	17				
Flexible Spot Interest Rate Index	35,192	159,582			
Flexible Bovespa Stock Index	3,584,446	622,374	469,747	323,459	199,557
US Dollar on Actuals	24,170,975	21,631,255	30,588,575	24,682,702	9,766,867
US Dollar Exercise	1,419,602	1,566,983	1,805,319	1,332,280	552,837
US Dollar Volatility	1,395,970	1,485,170	2,887,345	2,241,390	1,042,235
Flexible Currency	732,042	357,381	495,007	339,827	206,128
Total Options	**155,233,010**	**83,836,882**	**67,844,442**	**50,478,357**	**25,104,136**

BOVESPA, Brazil

	2010	2009	2008	2007	2006
Ibovespa Index	281,815	199,147	210,868	384,837	1,818,764
Exchange Traded Funds	959,093	242,863	17,063		
All Options on Individual Equities	802,229,293	546,547,550	350,046,567	367,305,446	285,699,806
Total Options	**803,470,201**	**546,989,560**	**350,274,498**	**367,690,283**	**287,518,570**

Budapest Stock Exchange (BSE), Hungary

	2010	2009	2008	2007	2006
Feed Corn	3,476	5,068	6,879	7,452	5,050
Feed Wheat	220	801	1,213	528	840
Mill Wheat	7				
Euro Wheat	1,021	874	2,819	3,447	126
Feed Wheat II	9				
Feed Barley	290	391	621	260	238
Sunflower Seed	1,070	1,874	1,942	564	1,235
Rapeseed	750	1,785	1,426	428	471
Ammonium Nitrate	1	9	164	10	4
Budapest Stock Index (BUX)	3,635,407	2,881,483	3,082,870	3,950,947	1,879,034
CHF/HUF	254,925	101,249	159,947	91,977	100,200
CZK/HUF	4,930	2,430	1,370	4,730	48,180
EUR/HUF	2,764,599	3,426,699	2,481,943	2,669,580	2,688,100
GBP/HUF	24,080	14,700	22,050	42,750	82,415
JPY/HUF	29,300	17,780	14,350	62,877	29,267
PLN/HUF	4,320	7,040	40	880	33,600
TRY/HUF	3,300	20,400	138,400	131,950	66,500
USD/HUF	1,046,731	700,606	1,446,993	1,152,754	814,635
AUD/CAD	200				
AUD/CHF	400				
AUD/JPY	1,800	5,550	3,300	2,700	
AUD/USD	27,700	29,400	150,650	32,940	46,400
CAD/JPY	500	1,000	1,500	12,700	19,000
CHF/JPY	800	3,750	2,750	5,050	19,050
CHF/PLN	200				
GBP/AUD	4,200				
GBP/CAD	600				
GBP/CHF	11,300	35,200	188,850	102,456	388,770
GBP/JPY	17,800	116,050	328,270	1,353,100	361,450
GBP/SEK	6,200	15,500	32,300	83,050	242,950
GBP/USD	56,900	103,010	146,068	354,640	631,500
EURO/CHF	124,600	44,300	18,700	86,650	86,350
EURO/CZK	600	1,900	10,400	3,200	35,600
EURO/GBP	29,300	17,650	210,150	100,700	227,500
EURO/JPY	199,170	241,440	227,340	306,673	198,151
EURO/NOK	3,300	23,600	29,100	34,200	93,200
EURO/PLN	23,050	51,400	17,600	14,450	110,070
EURO/RON	17,300	35,750	20,300	3,500	16,400
EURO/SEK	3,100	27,000	17,600	79,500	81,630
EURO/TRY	26,625	99,385	352,440	315,540	379,473
EURO/USD	582,380	416,160	999,736	1,555,406	1,117,803
NZD/JPY	200	16,800	5,000		
USD/CAD	12,840	34,120	78,332	251,316	345,405
USD/CHF	23,300	20,400	73,900	183,200	258,422
USD/CZK	117,500	400	2,300	11,500	6,700
USD/JPY	106,500	64,900	176,150	759,300	239,572

Budapest Stock Exchange (BSE), Hungary (continued)

	2010	2009	2008	2007	2006
USD/PLN	21,400	7,800	4,600	52,600	8,600
USD/TRY	7,400	21,625	86,100	48,550	305,634
EUR (1 week)	367,650	493,066	360,950	594,650	910,300
GBP (1 week)	23,900	56,830	7,200	27,300	2,100
USD (1 week)	91,800	140,290	111,920	71,500	24,000
AUD/CAD (1 week)	800				
AUD/CHF (1 week)	600				
AUD/USD (1 week)	27,200	12,800	800	87,000	500
CHF/PLN (1 week)	600				
EUR/CHF (1 week)	2,100				
EUR/GBP (1 week)	3,800	31,100	4,900	17,000	
EUR/JPY (1 week)	158,000	110,550	85,650	522,900	22,350
EUR/PLN (1 week)	2,800	1,100	2,000	2,000	4,000
EUR/USD (1 week)	561,303	429,700	189,250	330,900	100,690
GBP/AUD (1 week)	1,200				
GBP/CAD (1 week)	2,300				
GBP/CHF (1 week)	23,600	33,773	27,300	8,100	13,200
GBP/JPY (1 week)	42,550	189,750	231,400	432,000	25,700
GBP/USD (1 week)	90,100	106,100	57,200	232,400	34,350
USD/CAD (1 week)	36,900	40,850	84,700	362,040	22,100
USD/CHF (1 week)	40,800	51,600	26,200	22,400	4,900
USD/JPY (1 week)	59,150	45,000	23,400	29,500	3,000
USD/PLN (1 week)	8,600				
All Futures on Individual Equities	1,033,190	1,204,849	1,163,252	1,529,194	919,426
Total Futures	**11,780,544**	**11,570,661**	**12,958,135**	**18,221,627**	**13,656,165**
US Dollar	500	4,750	31,450	21,240	2,000
CHF	500	52,830	13,350	10,300	
EUR	20,750	155,350	130,559	126,766	205,000
EUR/USD (HUF settlement)	8,000	6,600	26,958	23,100	514,901
Total Options	**29,750**	**224,345**	**411,290**	**606,601**	**1,026,764**

Central Japan Commodity Exchange (CJCE), Japan

	2010	2009	2008	2007	2006
Gasoline	364,282	984,956	1,745,785	3,635,329	4,953,168
Kerosene	282,728	716,338	1,430,843	2,685,345	4,027,192
Hen Egg	11	486	6,362	7,077	12,275
Rubber (RSS3)	160	996	19,638	90,983	314,914
Rubber Index	57	4,198	30,822	78,198	180,654
Gold	72,038	65,393			
Total Futures	**719,276**	**1,773,603**	**3,272,665**	**6,549,417**	**9,635,688**

China Financial Futures Exchange (CFFE)

	2010	2009	2008	2007	2006
CSI 300 Index	45,873,295				
Total Futures	**45,873,295**				

Dalian Commodity Exchange (DCE), China

	2010	2009	2008	2007	2006
Corn	35,999,573	16,744,088	59,918,460	59,436,742	64,976,076
No 1 Soybeans	37,393,600	42,507,076	113,681,550	47,432,721	8,897,061
No 2 Soybeans	14,709	32,048	42,791	21,107	1,925,226
Palm Oil	41,799,813	44,426,498	6,302,478	339,175	
Soybean Oil	91,406,238	94,836,881	43,695,993	13,283,866	10,333,006
Soybean Meal	125,581,888	155,404,029	81,265,439	64,719,466	31,549,669
Linear Low Density Polyethylene (LLDPE)	62,488,306	44,752,979	13,252,982	381,836	
Polyvinyl Cloride (PVC)	8,483,624	18,078,662			
Total Futures	**403,167,751**	**416,782,261**	**318,159,693**	**185,614,913**	**117,681,038**

Dubai Mercantile Exchange (DME)

	2010	2009	2008	2007	2006
Oman Crude Oil	744,727	553,888	322,294	200,892	
Total Futures	**744,727**	**553,888**	**330,379**	**223,174**	

EDX London

	2010	2009	2008	2007	2006
FTSE Russia IOB Index	10,244	32			
Total Futures	**10,244**	**4,032**			
FTSE Russia IOB Index	71,082	38,441			
All Options on Individual Equities	32,209,677	34,865,057			
Total Options	**32,280,759**	**34,903,498**			

EUREX, Frankfurt, Germany

	2010	2009	2008	2007	2006
DAX	40,994,689	40,101,438	49,237,082	50,413,122	40,425,513
DJ Global Titans 50	130	160	646	10,358	6,481
DivDAX	3,409	1,803	22,679		
Euro Stoxx 50	372,229,766	333,407,299	432,298,342	327,034,149	213,514,918
Euro Stoxx Select Dividend 30 Index	73,762	132,793	103,422	21,118	
Euro Stoxx	190				
Euro Stoxx Large	186				
Euro Stoxx Mid	3,737				
Euro Stoxx Small	5,921				
MDAX	404,815	297,724	595,273	824,809	395,550
MSCI Japan Index	892	426			
MSCI Russia Index	30,861	46,704	94,697		
OMX-Helsinki 25	250,475	148,333	186,127	100,795	33,860
RDXxt USD RDX Extended Index	6,374	3,549	1,217	26	
Swiss Leader index (SLI)	9,007	43,871	122,721	36,577	
Swiss Market Index Mid-Cap (SMIM)	100,531	80,081	99,254	152,977	29,643
Swiss Market Index (SMI)	11,626,179	12,135,437	17,658,178	14,391,903	11,369,444
Stoxx Europe 50 Index	1,417,882	1,300,945	1,607,048	1,387,401	1,064,167
Stoxx Europe 600	93,633				
Stoxx Europe 600 Index	114,567	119,998	104,591	37,400	21,783
Stoxx Europe Large 200	7,657				
Stoxx Europe Large 200 Index	42,959	101,477	140,741	9,866	
Stoxx Europe Mid 200	57,847				
Stoxx Europe Mid 200 Index	149,577	274,941	471,758	279,128	36,901
Stoxx Europe Small 200	38,155				
Stoxx Europe Small 200 Index	129,223	199,440	279,477	21,848	
TecDAX	232,025	245,270	435,556	585,377	515,891
Euro Stoxx Automobiles	54,507	84,664	212,427	142,146	83,868
Euro Stoxx Banks	1,156,447	437,131	651,855	640,667	225,960
Euro Stoxx Basic Resources	44,913	30,634	39,168	22,501	21,200
Euro Stoxx Chemicals	65,913	36,940	39,868	18,750	12,464
Euro Stoxx Construction & Materials	38,599	44,989	34,171	36,663	7,492
Euro Stoxx Financial Services	10,227	22,295	34,470	27,007	15,804
Euro Stoxx Food and Beverage	25,563	22,160	36,888	11,226	9,161
Euro Stoxx Healthcare	42,894	36,312	50,893	40,201	12,982
Euro Stoxx Industrial Goods & Services	46,383	35,546	26,200	29,283	17,537
Euro Stoxx Insurance	204,346	192,823	234,726	153,642	192,065
Euro Stoxx Media	42,233	34,959	39,198	39,462	30,860
Euro Stoxx Oil & Gas	148,169	85,545	182,422	107,664	101,586
Euro Stoxx Personal & Household Goods	18,442	21,120	21,440	15,420	8,326
Euro Stoxx Real Estate	3,508	2,413	2,742		
Euro Stoxx Retail	17,663	28,668	27,085	18,399	2,441
Euro Stoxx Technology	51,565	89,955	171,420	153,129	210,081
Euro Stoxx Telecom	127,420	143,714	257,493	274,843	246,288
Euro Stoxx Travel & Leisure	19,712	32,092	36,451	24,433	17,618
Euro Stoxx Utilities	131,250	109,173	117,898	74,923	107,036
Euro Stoxx 600 Automobiles & Parts	151,258	145,939	377,947	184,908	43,692
Euro Stoxx 600 Banks	1,727,129	1,178,604	1,634,005	541,557	185,682
Euro Stoxx 600 Basic Resources	490,447	491,332	441,871	214,640	90,361
Euro Stoxx 600 Chemicals	74,946	75,880	89,156	72,184	18,340
Euro Stoxx 600 Construction & Materials	67,965	69,729	144,268	85,996	11,482
Euro Stoxx 600 Financial Services	22,647	28,542	69,389	96,472	14,349
Euro Stoxx 600 Food & Beverage	189,505	212,780	175,795	85,753	91,537
Euro Stoxx 600 Healthcare	372,362	366,782	379,849	305,236	171,262
Euro Stoxx 600 Industrial Goods & Services	452,187	306,558	285,522	174,806	81,265
Euro Stoxx 600 Insurance	412,506	333,646	433,779	349,726	120,278
Euro Stoxx 600 Media	271,169	201,928	273,233	74,664	25,242
Euro Stoxx 600 Oil & Gas	425,478	490,611	534,071	387,825	146,585
Euro Stoxx 600 Personal & Household Goods	104,779	101,473	60,153	15,092	21,262
Euro Stoxx 600 Real Estate	32,431	34,407	17,321		
Euro Stoxx 600 Retail	114,683	164,015	221,545	105,297	32,829
Euro Stoxx 600 Technology	177,025	124,442	168,702	199,401	89,405
Euro Stoxx 600 Telecom	414,900	396,821	386,335	268,292	164,519
Euro Stoxx 600 Travel & Leisure	207,146	158,307	113,510	86,329	25,622
Euro Stoxx 600 Utilities	290,852	229,079	266,804	153,117	59,958
KOPSI 200 Index	166,170				
DAX - Kursindex Index Dividend	275	120			
DivDAX Index Dividend	1,530	8,030			
Euro Stoxx 50 Index Dividend	3,585,955	2,534,348	183,058		
Euro Stoxx Select Dividend 30 Index Dividend	1,019	435			
SMI Index Dividend	13,691	2,576			
Mini-Futures auf VStoxx	431,669	14,576			
Swiss Government Bond (CONF)	205,109	279,720	407,583	360,355	334,314
Euro-BTP	1,396,953	327,914			
Euro-BOBL	133,851,275	105,820,542	155,090,861	170,909,055	167,312,119

EUREX, Frankfurt, Germany (continued)

	2010	2009	2008	2007	2006
Euro-BUND	231,484,529	180,755,004	257,827,619	338,319,416	319,889,369
Euro-BUXL	1,360,503	925,627	1,155,127	1,582,859	1,265,079
Euro-SCHATZ	140,923,898	125,607,110	174,226,719	181,101,310	165,318,779
Short-term Euro-BTP	131,195				
3-Month Euribor	267,985	403,243	703,273	792,635	767,458
CER MidDec	175	23		225,960	233,955
EU Allowance	412	22,117	80,084	21,200	31,221
EUA MidDec	125,875	876		12,464	9,464
European Carbon	735			7,492	2,343
Butter	10			15,804	5,111
European Processing Potatoes	49,336	15,575		9,161	22,700
Hogs	2,215	1,367		12,982	9,694
Piglets	579	289		17,537	11,220
Skimmed Milk Powder	16			192,065	169,198
DJ UBS Agriculture Sub-Index	10,298	5,552		30,860	26,035
DJ UBS Commodity Index	57,255	14,177		101,586	118,601
DJ UBS Energy Sub-Index	5,148	2,238		8,326	5,910
DJ UBS Ex-Energy Sub-Index	2,236				
DJ UBS Grains Sub-Index	214			2,441	9,568
DJ UBS Industrial Metals Sub-Index	3,528	308		210,081	218,982
DJ UBS Petroleum Sub-Index	1,263			246,288	177,863
DJ UBS Precious Metals Sub-Index	3,241				
DJ UBS Softs Sub-Index	843				
IPD UK Annual All Property Index	1,652	547			
Gold	777	4,154			
Xetra-Gold	135				
Silver	474	81			
Single Stock Dividend	779,542				
All Futures on Individual Equities	202,195,229	116,771,129	130,210,348	52,460,383	35,589,089
Total Futures	**1,153,336,562**	**928,766,700**	**1,231,646,824**	**1,146,081,579**	**960,631,763**
DAX	75,123,356	95,926,938	104,939,881	91,850,835	61,411,659
DAX 1st Friday Weekly	529,697	180,486	136,941	192,587	148,881
DAX 2nd Friday Weekly	500,470	117,787	99,993	149,972	100,406
DAX 4th Friday Weekly	539,207	193,299	118,099	209,868	122,774
DAX 5th Friday Weekly	251,562	68,591	41,279	74,790	49,821
Euro STOXX 50 Index	284,707,318	300,208,574	400,931,635	251,438,870	150,049,918
Euro STOXX 50 Index - 1st Friday	227,729	72,606	36,992	149,414	90,475
Euro STOXX 50 Index - 2nd Friday	223,769	78,701	16,865	167,282	79,783
Euro STOXX 50 Index - 4th Friday	248,929	73,304	23,379	200,733	76,568
Euro STOXX 50 Index - 5th Friday	95,331	38,518	19,418	50,709	48,623
MDAX	78,895	60,560	187,159	91,140	10,543
MSCI Russia Index	492	28,424	4,057		
HEX 25	1,333	755	20	1,307	1,075
Swiss Leader Index (SLI)	53,685	48,110	49,519	19,599	
Swiss Market Index Mid-Cap (SMIM)	74,286	54,287	49,610	44,920	14,616
Swiss Market Index (SMI)	4,236,899	4,094,103	5,588,591	5,773,269	3,948,593
Stoxx Europe 50 Index	15,701	52,816	103,080	140,197	63,064
Stoxx Europe 600 Index	529	16,113	37,529	30,593	4,208
Stoxx Europe Mid 200	520				
Stoxx Europe Mid 200 Index	23,669	11,251	112,858	172,017	52,899
Stoxx Europe Small 200 Index	29,943	6,470	31,998	7,607	
TecDAX	23,590	53,753	52,968	37,848	33,025
Euro Stoxx Automobiles & Parts	4,790				
Euro Stoxx Banks	389,123	32,571	103,585	644,500	105,512
Euro Stoxx Basic Resources	120	21	50	415	50
Euro Stoxx Chemicals	6,950	12,317	5,899	12,790	1,540
Euro Stoxx Construction & Materials	80				
Euro Stoxx Food and Beverage	8	1,200	104	3,486	2,000
Euro Stoxx Healthcare	157	74	502		2,460
Euro Stoxx Insurance	34,497	5,430	47,709	19,955	36,561
Euro Stoxx Media	1,276	2,000	5,408	16,559	7,300
Euro Stoxx Oil & Gas	1,109	1,652	14,544	17,870	108,053
Euro Stoxx Personal & Household Goods	5,200	10	165		906
Euro Stoxx Technology	3,907	7,600	24,702	10,000	68,125
Euro Stoxx Telecom	5,043	9,741	51,047	40,018	49,856
Euro Stoxx Utilities	7,362	15,989	13,781	62,494	87,546
Euro Stoxx 600 Automobiles & Parts	21,211	8,580	95,635	85,135	3,100
Euro Stoxx 600 Banks	642,558	245,012	535,531	377,343	30,701
Euro Stoxx 600 Basic Resources	180,572	95,564	179,574	95,047	94,486
Euro Stoxx 600 Chemicals	6,395	2,221	31,488	9,684	1,610
Euro Stoxx 600 Construction & Materials	4,550	1,018	60,216	50,582	305
Euro Stoxx 600 Financial Services	741	1,246	6,947	6,115	3,600
Euro Stoxx 600 Food & Beverage	1,462	1,384	29,802	623	568
Euro Stoxx 600 Healthcare	19,709	28,654	46,305	65,188	18,971
Euro Stoxx 600 Industrial Goods & Services	68,363	57,026	111,988	142,189	41,602

EUREX, Frankfurt, Germany (continued)

	2010	2009	2008	2007	2006
Euro Stoxx 600 Insurance	121,461	147,459	525,853	195,790	11,604
Euro Stoxx 600 Media	15,260	5,990	15,632	10,744	5,206
Euro Stoxx 600 Oil & Gas	69,994	39,455	173,140	89,956	55,822
Euro Stoxx 600 Personal & Household Goods	1,714	706	4,587	7,063	320
Euro Stoxx 600 Retail	11,685	19,958	19,431		
Euro Stoxx 600 Technology	382	1,550	11,612	11,539	4,081
Euro Stoxx 600 Telecom	6,941	76,903	46,994	43,478	52,023
Euro Stoxx 600 Travel & Leisure	40,610	9,208	922	9,653	18,761
Euro Stoxx 600 Utilities	11,804	38,748	84,162	106,487	23,308
Euro Stoxx 50 Index Dividend	144,620				
Stoxx	562,745				
Euro-Bobl	7,803,983	6,955,457	15,083,076	15,135,182	17,220,011
Euro-Bund	39,301,301	28,392,790	33,317,879	44,441,961	41,764,550
Euro-Schatz	17,712,470	16,215,924	20,438,378	19,085,515	17,344,245
3-Month Euribor	371,000				
Gold	10,799	13,181			
Xetra-Gold	142				
Silver	426	106			
All Options on Exchange Traded Funds	141,718	5,515	330,944	31,730	15,732
All Options on Austrian Equities	308,428	188,289	113,901	19,025	
All Options on Belgian Equities	244,081	104,865	31,017		
All Options on Dutch Equities	5,646,218	6,813,332	7,243,976	11,811,227	10,420,237
All Options on Scandinavian Equities	28,816,601	19,342,143	18,414,654	17,291,936	16,396,662
All Options on French Equities	13,138,701	10,539,983	9,429,765	7,795,177	6,667,994
All Options on German Equities	178,639,023	186,930,541	234,948,892	214,969,289	180,695,967
All Options on Great Britain Equities	85,034				
All Options on Italian Equities	1,457,602	1,394,120	1,784,585	1,146,488	1,006,419
All Options on Russian Equities	18,119	59,885	179,672	22,398	
All Options on Spanish Equities	1,794,803	1,202,642	1,319,054	860,700	22,988
All Options on Swedish Equities	121,600				
All Options on Individual Swiss Equities	78,588,478	77,977,503	75,864,298	68,122,792	57,323,550
Total Options	**743,579,836**	**758,392,598**	**933,396,359**	**753,780,347**	**566,120,139**

Hong Kong Futures Exchange (HKFE), Hong Kong

	2010	2009	2008	2007	2006
Hang Seng Index	21,031,085	20,728,034	21,716,508	17,160,964	12,718,380
Mini Hang Seng Index	8,300,654	9,279,877	7,961,028	4,325,977	2,140,242
H-Shares Index	12,429,800	12,394,116	14,440,965	10,846,277	4,880,470
Mini H-Shares Index	992,224	799,894	318,395		
HSI Dividend Point Index	2,123				
HSCEI Dividend Point Index	4,667				
1-Month HIBOR	14	204	881	574	155
3-Month HIBOR	1,055	2,573	23,818	31,678	13,888
Gold	5,642	6,773	3,075		
All Futures on Individual Equities	239,259	271,766	257,015	351,514	102,010
Total Futures	**43,006,523**	**43,483,237**	**44,721,743**	**32,723,598**	**19,863,299**
Hang Seng Index	8,515,049	5,367,403	3,820,797	7,480,183	4,095,679
Mini Hang Seng Index	482,691	286,591	156,957	69,512	53,456
Flexible Hang Seng Index	11,222				
H-Shares Index	2,910,713	1,961,131	1,613,988	1,727,847	758,247
Flexible H-Shares Index	2,532				
All Options on Individual Equities	61,125,647	47,439,896	54,692,865	45,982,968	18,127,353
Total Options	**73,047,854**	**55,055,021**	**60,284,993**	**55,262,088**	**23,042,616**

ICE Futures Canada (ICE), Canada

	2010	2009	2008	2007	2006
Canola (Rapeseed)	4,118,428	3,351,793	3,132,188	3,169,182	2,607,354
Western Barley	2,632	54,839	167,381	214,672	195,024
Total Futures	**4,121,060**	**3,406,632**	**3,299,999**	**3,430,324**	**2,868,933**
Canola	87,818	85,115	21,206	17,067	26,523
Total Options	**87,818**	**85,115**	**21,211**	**21,841**	**27,603**

Italian Derivatives Market of the Italian Stock Exchange, Italy

	2010	2009	2008	2007	2006
MIB 30 Index	5,390,256	4,240,026	7,914,300	4,671,557	4,037,973
Mini FIB 30 Index	2,624,269	2,596,645	2,909,366	2,065,878	1,659,649
Electricity	5,947	5,188	634		
All Futures on Individual Equities	12,713,330	10,973,237	4,417,700	6,363,954	7,031,974
Total Futures	**20,733,802**	**17,815,096**	**15,242,000**	**13,101,389**	**12,729,596**
MIB 30 Index	3,375,497	2,821,434	3,630,359	3,658,686	2,819,916
All Options on Individual Equities	20,081,028	21,946,195	20,056,426	20,364,847	16,056,751
Total Options	**23,456,525**	**24,767,629**	**23,686,785**	**24,023,533**	**18,876,667**

ICE Futures Europe (ICE), United Kingdom

	2010	2009	2008	2007	2006
Brent Crude Oil	100,022,169	74,137,750	68,368,145	59,728,941	44,345,927
Gas Oil (Monthly)	52,296,582	36,038,870	28,805,192	24,509,884	18,289,877
UK Natural Gas Monthly (NBP)	2,105,730	1,629,980	879,420	1,058,290	543,550
UK Natural Gas (Quarters)	423,585	255,435	103,440	37,905	16,080
UK Natural Gas (Seasons)	1,638,720	907,470	279,930	136,740	42,660
ECX EUA (Monthly)	4,263,655	3,775,621	1,991,276	980,780	452,359
ECX EUA (Daily)	194,981	38,214			
WTI Crude (Monthly)	52,586,415	46,393,671	51,091,712	51,388,362	28,672,639
NYH (RBOB) Gasoline (Monthly)	2,257	4,965	26,356	14,805	9,692
Heating Oil (Monthly)	118,863	135,265	116,911	205,072	199,187
ECX CER (Monthly)	864,089	766,349	507,779		
ECX CER (Daily)	16,494	3,780			
Rotterdam Coal (Monthly)	39,901	28,735	5,895	465	45
Rotterdam Coal (Quarters)	216,516	135,240	24,720	3,870	630
Rotterdam Coal (Seasons)	5,790	2,190	630		30
Rotterdam Coal (Calendar)	357,336	255,420	70,860	4,500	120
Richards Bay Coal (Monthly)	33,601	14,225	1,900	240	60
Richards Bay Coal (Quarters)	102,915	44,265	8,880	525	15
Richards Bay Coal (Calendar)	159,564	91,680	34,020	480	
Richards Bay Coal (Seasons)	780	210	30		
gCNewcastle Coal (Monthly)	8,295	4,625			
gCNewcastle Coal (Quarters)	52,050	18,210			
gCNewcastle Coal (Calendars)	62,880	39,240			
Dutch TTF Gas (Monthly)	10,860				
Dutch TTF Gas (Seasons)	25,860				
Dutch TTF Gas (Quarter)	4,800				
Dutch TTF Gas (Calendars)	41,040				
German Natural Gas (Seasons)	732				
German Natural Gas (Quarter)	270				
German Natural Gas (Calendars)	240				
ECX ERU (Monthly)	3,045				
UK Base Electricity (Monthly)	1,020	895	370	990	3,155
UK Base Electricity (Quarters)	255	1,140	975	330	930
UK Base Electricity (Seasons)	18,180	16,830	2,790	1,920	3,870
Total Futures	**215,679,470**	**164,741,409**	**152,322,268**	**138,169,680**	**92,582,921**
Brent Crude Oil	165,286	212,341	121,024	74,056	33,249
ECX EUA	740,889	416,567	242,966	57,541	560
ECX CER	77,134	91,130	69,565		
ECX ERU	250				
WTI Crude Oil	198,245	18,200	11,131	10,416	
Gasoil	259,499	213,884	183,179	159,263	104,320
Total Options	**1,441,303**	**952,122**	**627,865**	**301,276**	**138,129**

JSE Securities Exchange of South Africa, Africa

	2010	2009	2008	2007	2006
White Maize (WMAZ)	773,177	687,472	859,920	956,026	865,549
Yellow Maize (YMAZ)	313,899	311,589	337,429	268,780	164,601
Corn	63,997	15,016			
Wheat	441,738	379,365	469,471	378,289	264,925
Sunflower Seeds	89,194	127,807	165,088	64,402	68,882
Soybeans	136,802	116,530	73,111	44,062	36,939
Sorghum	274				
CBOT Soybeans	190				
CBOT Soybean Meal	173				
CBOT Soybean Oil	1				
Grade 2 White Maize	5,539	18,371	80	14,500	18,913
Grade 2 Yellow Maize	724				
Copper	317				
Gold	3,838	1,725			
Silver	395				
Platinum	1,745	1,596			
Crude Oil	3,002	742			
FTSE/JSE Top 40 Index	11,782,186	12,145,844	15,924,693	16,150,010	13,483,033
FTSE/JSE Top 40 Index - Mini	29,253	10,876	450		
FTSE/JSE African Banks Index	754	56			
Top 100 FTSE/JSE All Share Index	100				
FTSE/JSE 25 Index	1,379	3,058	25,723	22,845	20,259
FTSE/JSE General Retailers Index	200				
FTSE/JSE Gold Mining Index	1,219	2,352	1,651	7,893	11,517
FTSE/JSE FINI 15 Index	4,471	17,826	43,660	16,309	6,421
FTSE/JSE FNDI 30 Index	131,351	183,311	217,863	125,960	319,247
FTSE/JSE Capped Top 40 Index	7,585	11,420	47,687	19,977	106,003
FTSE/JSE Shareholder Weighted Top 40 Index (DTOP)	4,603,466	4,361,957	3,037,960	2,359,997	1,321,011
FTSE/JSE RESI 20 Index	360	780	14,528	5,390	8,254

JSE Securities Exchange of South Africa, Africa (continued)

	2010	2009	2008	2007	2006
Can-Do	9,304,664	10,619,562	1,128,772	736,044	219,211
Kruger Rand	55	12	519	9,922	6,654
Dollar / Rand	5,243,573	5,604,875			
Euro / Rand	321,554	370,297			
British Pound / Rand	434,603	328,838			
ZAAD / Rand	178,492	873,552			
Japanese Yen / Rand	18,093				
Canadian Dollar / Rand	9,525				
Swiss Franc / Rand	1,897				
Maxi Dollar / Rand	210				
Dividend Futures	15,266,618	16,364,671	20,097,204	11,891,790	420,266
IDX Futures	15,475,728	4,321,081	28,362		
IDX Dividend Futures	6,764,568	172,914	1,364,561		
All Futures on Individual Equities	78,620,861	88,791,925	431,212,627	265,493,735	69,665,994
Total Futures	**150,037,770**	**145,845,620**	**475,051,729**	**298,567,616**	**87,036,273**
White Maize	191,223	182,400	455,403	471,727	368,404
Yellow Maize	39,934	41,635	69,339	55,695	20,746
Corn	26,304	61			
Wheat	47,078	28,620	176,079	140,545	57,699
Sunflower Seeds	12,343	7,108	21,073	5,983	9,179
Soybeans	10,922	6,914	5,978	1,986	4,971
Sorghum	14				
FTSE/JSE Top 40 Index	3,483,237	5,691,546	9,834,294	9,008,828	9,878,535
FTSE/JSE 25 Index	20				
FTSE/JSE FNDI 30 Index	25,463	71,950	50,987	70,110	219,444
FTSE/JSE Shareholder Weighted Top 40 Index (DTOP)	1,808,511	4,975,451	4,722,544	4,026,943	1,540,221
Can-Do	645,553	1,247,761	3,604,877	2,978,981	73,454
Dollar / Rand	1,136,585	578,442			
Euro / Rand	112,417	68,919			
British Pound / Rand	7,824	87,924			
ZAAD / Rand	200				
All Options on Individual Equities	12,313,211	15,670,869	19,591,351	14,312,446	5,751,833
Total Options	**19,860,839**	**28,659,600**	**38,532,275**	**31,074,787**	**18,011,251**

Kansai Commodities Exchange (KCE), Japan

	2010	2009	2008	2007	2006
Red Beans	10,212	4,750	4,362	4,362	8,491
US Soybeans	8,766	11,816	16,238	19,712	1,497
Corn	14,930	24,336	133,592	101,401	121,135
Raw Sugar	4,912	5,340	4,559	4,380	7,671
Raw Silk	932	504	358		1,446
Frozen Shrimp	5,832	5,789	5,853	6,248	66,651
Corn 75 Index	8,754	8,682	8,754	8,910	11,087
Coffee Index	8,754	8,683	8,903	11,248	59,627
Total Futures	**63,092**	**69,900**	**183,999**	**164,743**	**315,501**

Korea Futures Exchange (KFE), Korea

	2010	2009	2008	2007	2006
3-Year Treasury Bond	26,922,414	20,050,788	15,958,864	13,555,136	10,343,605
10-Year Treasury Bond	33,054		9,686		
KOPSI 200*	86,214,025	83,117,030	64,835,148	47,758,294	46,611,008
STAR Index	59	490	13,325	21,919	107,538
Lean Hogs	13,943	13,703	16,258		
Gold	36	1,731	1,267	399	
US Dollar	64,256,678	41,161,819	6,672,438	5,752,134	3,104,641
Japanese Yen	411,117	272,531	104,012	271,043	
Euro	388,294	310,540	103,762	212,790	
All Futures on Individual Equities	44,711,133	36,971,510	11,293,134		
Total Futures	**222,950,753**	**181,900,142**	**99,007,894**	**67,571,815**	**60,169,114**
*KOPSI 200 Index	3,525,898,562	2,920,990,655	2,766,474,404	2,709,844,077	2,414,422,952
US Dollar	484				
*All Options on Individual Equities	11,602	980	21	206	1,195
Total Options	**3,525,910,648**	**2,920,991,635**	**2,766,474,425**	**2,709,844,283**	**2,414,424,147**

London Metal Exchange (LME), United Kingdom

	2010	2009	2008	2007	2006
High Grade Primary Aluminium	46,537,180	46,988,069	48,307,389	40,229,693	36,418,131
Aluminium Alloy	466,206	427,452	582,398	492,868	444,738
North American Special Aluminium Alloy	588,269	920,336	1,519,811	1,236,484	1,031,411
Copper - Grade A	29,949,765	24,922,949	26,507,242	21,420,450	18,864,246
Standard Lead	7,744,747	5,983,323	6,188,753	4,697,862	4,568,140
Primary Nickel	7,325,219	6,717,299	5,202,609	3,792,788	4,177,557
Special High Grade Zinc	18,065,641	15,901,774	16,120,770	12,556,285	11,706,008
Far East Steel (MS)	42	447	2,760		
Mediterranean Steel (MS)	191,179	30,764	13,206		

London Metal Exchange (LME), United Kingdom (continued)

	2010	2009	2008	2007	2006
Tin	1,554,269	4,567,915	1,410,450	1,293,722	1,283,897
LMEmini Copper Grade A	736	10	45	1,099	1,411
LMEmini Primary Aluminium	4,072		200	729	1,987
LMEmini Special High Grade Zinc	5		7	195	283
Cobalt	6,812				
Molybdenum	510				
PA Asia	6		33	102	
PE Europe	20	8	22	29	
PN North America	1,235	2,713	2,449	401	
LE Europe	27	26	80	16	
LL Global	16		24		
LA Asia	1,292	37	169		
LN North America	1,869	710	1,705	282	
Total Futures	**112,439,117**	**106,463,839**	**105,861,588**	**85,736,480**	**78,527,839**
High Grade Primary Aluminium	3,479,888	2,505,499	3,702,232	3,115,989	4,690,867
Aluminium Alloy	270	216,735	267,722	316,496	315
North American Special Aluminium Alloy	17,428	4,333	24,052	10,052	4,420
Copper - Grade A	3,111,996	1,624,350	1,987,291	2,027,181	1,850,993
Standard Lead	199,884	145,354	346,672	298,965	164,410
Primary Nickel	172,075	142,168	152,744	167,428	158,496
Special High Grade Zinc	732,279	712,526	715,970	1,111,080	1,335,184
Tin	26,009	33,562	67,716	18,407	17,315
Primary Aluminium TAPOS	38,299	55,149	37,748	43,621	93,540
Aluminium Alloy TAPOS	5,360	48	3,022	3,528	2,141
Copper Grade A TAPOS	21,532	15,212	16,146	16,667	45,346
Lead TAPOS	1,622	3,065	9,411	3,210	3,335
Nickel TAPOS	2,547	3,541	11,347	35,220	14,502
Tin TAPOS	25	12	810	48	850
NASAA TAPOS	140	100	2,290	42	1,170
Special High Grade Zinc TAPOS	9,648	5,335	8,538	10,314	29,466
Total Options	**7,819,002**	**5,466,989**	**7,353,711**	**7,178,248**	**8,412,350**

Malaysia Derivatives Exchange, Malaysia

	2010	2009	2008	2007	2006
Crude Palm Oil	4,064,361	4,008,882	3,003,529	2,793,560	2,230,340
3-Month KLIBOR	95,477	126,690	195,203	239,314	272,502
KLSE Composite Index	1,994,907	1,997,955	2,920,728	3,157,341	1,628,043
Total Futures	**6,154,745**	**6,137,827**	**6,120,032**	**6,202,686**	**4,161,024**

MEFF Renta Variable (RV), Spain

	2010	2009	2008	2007	2006
IBEX 35 Plus Index	6,280,999	5,436,989	7,275,299	8,435,258	6,408,961
Mini IBEX 35 Index	3,579,263	3,148,292	3,300,418	2,865,739	1,598,296
All Futures on Individual Equities	19,684,108	44,586,779	46,237,568	21,294,315	21,029,811
Total Futures	**29,544,370**	**53,172,060**	**56,813,285**	**32,595,312**	**29,037,068**
IBEX 35 Plus Index	3,072,418	4,357,260	8,286,224	5,670,773	5,510,621
All Options on Individual Equities	37,607,374	35,527,914	18,317,249	13,593,493	12,425,979
Total Options	**40,679,792**	**39,885,174**	**26,603,473**	**19,264,266**	**17,936,600**

Mexican Derivatives Exchange (MEXDER), Mexico

	2010	2009	2008	2007	2006
US Dollar	5,662,462	1,587,858	3,186,832	3,223,044	6,026,940
Euro FX	36,168	64,327	44,172	2,105	50,469
IPC Stock Index	1,321,686	1,130,528	1,085,663	951,955	620,557
CETE 91	3,802,874	4,877,430	4,087,066	2,812,500	3,290,100
TIIE 28	26,208,542	37,545,841	57,881,101	220,608,024	264,160,131
M3 Bond	1,051,818	216,150	43,000	36,500	28,600
M10 Bond	2,281,187	2,613,021	3,005,307	1,182,069	471,879
M20 Bond	1,377,266	269,904			
10-Year Interest Rate Swap	43,742	67,144	170,949	25,332	
2-Year Interest Rate Swap	9,725	21,910			
10-Year Interest Rate Swap (Centrally Cleared)	5,226				
2-Year Interest Rate Swap (Centrally Cleared)	14,571				
Exchange Traded Funds	10				
All Futures on Individual Equities	12,044		2,000	2	3,000
Total Futures	**41,827,321**	**48,394,113**	**69,506,090**	**228,841,531**	**274,651,676**
MXN / USD	963	145	7	10	2,343
IPC Stock Index	147,411	40,723	52,556	130,410	115,531
Exchange Traded Funds	10		7,585		
All Options on Individual Equities	619,870	345,718	577,452	78	448,120
Total Options	**768,254**	**386,586**	**637,600**	**130,498**	**565,994**

Mercado a Termino de Buenos Aires (MATBA), Argentina

	2010	2009	2008	2007	2006
Wheat	24,496	25,921	37,243	41,781	41,200
Corn	12,549	15,144	22,269	32,012	18,310
Sunflower	30	99	101	135	206
Sorghum	99				
Soybeans	117,440	101,654	82,164	80,016	59,279
Total Futures	**154,614**	**142,818**	**141,873**	**154,069**	**118,995**
Wheat	2,328	2,584	1,449	5,243	7,934
Corn	1,773	356	1,538	4,068	5,021
Soybeans	40,954	35,126	10,831	12,963	15,195
Total Options	**45,055**	**38,066**	**13,882**	**23,495**	**28,150**

Montreal Exchange (ME), Canada

	2010	2009	2008	2007	2006
3-Month Bankers Acceptance	13,698,870	7,668,781	9,958,833	15,237,958	16,702,302
S&P/TSX Composite Index Mini	261	1,151			
2-Year Canadian Gov't Bond	611			6,363	85,301
10-Year Canadian Gov't Bond	6,405,525	5,310,537	7,363,569	9,337,754	7,691,797
Canada Carbon Dioxide Equivalent Units	140	43	1,179		
Canadian Heavy Crude Oil Differential Price	4				
S&P Canada 60 Index	4,070,604	4,157,917	4,575,352	3,885,872	3,064,695
Banking Index	16	94	24,129	9,014	140
Total Futures	**24,176,031**	**17,150,708**	**22,043,015**	**28,493,454**	**27,578,059**
3-Month Bankers Acceptance	349,675	234,861	282,190	748,991	605,806
10-Year Canadian Gov't Bond	9,742	12,531	23,553	13,782	2,275
US Dollar	17,705	29,902	23,795	34,889	31,262
S&P Canada 60 Index	77,820	34,056	38,666	26,484	57,974
i60 Index	2,333,095	1,956,588	661,286	364,924	317,637
Claymore Global Agriculture	1,562	1,460	64		
Horizons BetaPro S&P/TSX Global Gold Bear Plus Fund	2,740	2,728			
Horizons BetaPro S&P/TSX Global Gold Bull Plus Fund	7,658	4,789			
Horizons BetaPro S&P/TSX 60 Bear Plus ETF	8,476	13,137	3,896		
Horizons BetaPro S&P/TSX 60 Bull Plus ETF	2,898	10,109	7,651		
iShares DJ Canada Select Div Index Fund	4,567	3,159			
iShares CDN S&P/TSX Capped Com Index Fund	4,532	3,022			
iShares CDN S&P/TSX Capped REIT Index Fund	2,117	1,978			
Horizons BetaPro NYMEX Crude Oil Bear Plus Fund	12,054	9,491			
Horizons BetaPro NYMEX Crude Oil Bull Plus Fund	68,123	75,439			
Horizons BetaPro S&P/TSX Capped Fin Bear Plus ETF	2,107	2,662			
Horizons BetaPro S&P/TSX Capped Fin Bull Plus ETF	1,169	2,553			
iShares CDN MSCI EAFE 100% Hedged to CAD $ Index	7,768	1,624			
iShares CDN S&P 500 Hedged to CAD $ Index Fund	5,938	1,268			
Horizons BetaPro S&P/TSX Cap Energy Bear ETF	403	634			
Horizons BetaPro S&P/TSX Cap Energy Bull ETF	733	378			
Claymore Natural Gas Commodity ETF	75,100	79,444			
iShares CDN DEX Corporate Bond Index Fund	4,418	1,280			
iShares CDN DEX Short-term Bond Index Fund	1,685	763			
Horizons BetaPro NYMEX Natural Gas Bear Plus Fund	12,806	451			
Horizons BetaPro NYMEX Natural Gas Bull Plus Fund	101,575	2,038			
Claymore Gold Bullion ETF	3,015				
BMO DJ Canada Titans 60 Index	1,906				
Horizon Beta Pro S&P/TSX 60 Inverse ETF	170				
CDN S&P/TSX Capped Gold Index Fund	127,824	114,884	58,438	89,435	144,695
CDN S&P/TSX Capped Financials Index Fund	248,487	356,040	195,820	101,499	130,730
CDN S&P/TSX Capped IT Index Fund	1,339	2,110	3,248	14,989	10,018
CDN S&P/TSX Capped Materials Index Fund	5,711	14,669	5,811	59,371	11,012
CDN S&P/TSX Capped Energy Index Fund	262,674	121,064	80,838	158,178	234,611
All Options on Individual Equities	16,353,284	14,507,261	14,633,599	12,634,060	11,416,758
Total Options	**20,120,876**	**17,602,373**	**16,021,887**	**14,248,756**	**12,962,778**

Moscow Interbank Currency Exchange (MICEX), Russia

	2010	2009	2008	2007	2006
Wheat	149,301	149,249	79,378		
Rice Groats G1	11,299				
Rice Groats T1	11,032				
Raw Rice	10,616				
EUR	264,805	54,369	96,000	2,000	
US Dollar	10,117,886	17,752,959	131,699,407	85,331,934	
EUR/USD	2,556,227	630			
3-Month MosPrime Rate	90	60	3,275	1,271	
MICEX Index	6,237,229	396,289	25,716	49,568	
All Futures on Individual Equities	12,634,797	954,685			
Total Futures	**31,993,282**	**19,308,241**	**131,905,458**	**85,386,473**	

National Stock Exchange of India

	2010	2009	2008	2007	2006
US Dollar/Indian Rupee	705,319,585	226,362,368			
EUR/Indian Rupee	17,326,787				
GBP/Indian Rupee	1,488,555				
JPY/Indian Rupee	1,491,520				
S&P CNX Nifty Index	156,351,505	195,759,414	202,390,223	138,794,235	70,286,227
All Futures on Individual Equities	175,674,069	161,053,345	225,777,205	179,324,970	100,285,737
Total Futures	**1,057,652,021**	**583,175,127**	**428,167,428**	**318,119,205**	**170,571,964**
S&P CNX Nifty Index	529,773,463	321,265,217	150,916,778	52,707,150	18,702,248
All Options on Individual Equities	28,363,426	14,066,778	11,067,082	9,048,495	5,214,191
Total Options	**558,136,889**	**335,331,995**	**161,983,860**	**61,755,645**	**23,916,439**

NYSE-LIFFE

	2010	2009	2008	2007	2006
All Futures on Individual Equities	289,334,111	199,044,957			
Total Futures	**289,334,111**	**199,044,957**	**124,468,809**	**75,266,349**	**29,515,726**
All Options on Individual Equities	175,228,607	170,870,365			
Total Options	**175,228,607**	**170,870,365**	**184,105,407**	**186,152,718**	**155,552,010**

NYSE-LIFFE - Amsterdam, Netherlands

	2010	2009	2008	2007	2006
AEX Stock Index	11,958,934	10,524,741	12,477,916	12,850,137	11,165,258
AEX Dividend Index	880				
Euro/US Dollar	5,206	6,588	5,124	5,087	7,474
US Dollar/Euro	1,404	829	1,394	918	1,333
Total Futures	**11,966,424**	**10,532,158**	**12,484,434**	**12,856,367**	**11,190,181**
Euro / US Dollar (EDX)	266,086	388,488	394,315	439,811	651,810
US Dollar / Euro	30,178	45,603	55,414	52,499	81,229
AEX Stock Index (AEX)	26,158,523	24,660,898	27,534,800	26,292,719	23,694,580
Total Options	**26,454,787**	**25,094,989**	**27,984,529**	**28,932,245**	**26,527,631**

NYSE-LIFFE - Brussels, Belgium

	2010	2009	2008	2007	2006
Bel 20 Index	158,047	296,543	615,088	596,144	654,520
Total Futures	**158,047**	**296,543**	**615,088**	**596,144**	**654,520**
Bel 20 (E2) Index	9,691	10,192	15,404	133,467	127,000
Bel 20 (E10) Index	20				
Total Options	**9,711**	**10,192**	**15,404**	**133,467**	**127,000**

NYSE-LIFFE - Lisbon

	2010	2009	2008	2007	2006
PSI-20 Index	126,127	61,225	75,904	110,485	88,557
Total Futures	**126,127**	**61,225**	**75,904**	**110,485**	**88,557**

NYSE-LIFFE - Paris

	2010	2009	2008	2007	2006
Wheat #2	4,374,323	1,925,916	1,464,484	980,742	407,843
Corn	240,028	149,008	112,408	94,606	72,044
Malted Barley	6,200				
Skimmed Milk Powder	7				
Rapeseed	1,202,153	812,779	680,765	438,849	238,594
CAC 40 Stock Index 10 Euro	44,559,669	41,940,487	49,242,000	44,668,975	33,405,804
CAC 40 Dividend Index	82,139	322			
FTSE EPRA Eurozone	13,592	28,659	12,265	3,742	
FTSE EPRA Europe	78,147	87,274	53,533	4,278	
FTSEurofirst 80	107,837	186,634	473,365	397,110	26,412
FTSEurofirst 100	407	122	501	21,281	990
Total Futures	**50,664,502**	**45,131,201**	**52,039,321**	**46,653,064**	**34,151,687**
Rapeseed	271,993	79,385	134,370	50,962	26,843
Wheat	1,016,600	655,099	325,464	129,365	41,398
Malted Barley	390				
Corn	20,245	5,720	3,738	4,656	1,818
CAC 40 Index, 10 EUR	6,329,140	6,126,542	8,628,618	9,793,350	6,633,635
Total Options	**7,638,368**	**6,866,746**	**9,092,220**	**9,982,198**	**6,705,070**

New Zealand Futures Exchange (NZFOE), New Zealand

	2010	2009	2008	2007	2006
3-Year Government Stock	1,100	2,510		30	
10-Year Government Stock	1,742	4,329	691	664	594
NZ 30-Day OCR Interbank	400	20			
90-Day Bank Bill	1,426,513	1,484,030	1,453,947	1,638,294	1,801,132
NZ Electricity (Otahuhu)	195	6			
NZ Electricity (Benmore)	272	52			
Total Futures	**1,430,222**	**1,490,947**	**1,454,638**	**1,638,988**	**1,801,726**
90-Day Bank Bill	1,200	3,100	1,850	4,450	24,190
Total Options	**1,200**	**3,100**	**4,450**	**12,050**	**24,301**

VOLUME - WORLDWIDE

NYSE-LIFFE, United Kingdom

	2010	2009	2008	2007	2006
3-Month Short Sterling	112,944,490	104,073,092	104,572,875	119,675,947	83,003,622
3-Month Euroswiss	7,179,251	4,768,825	8,572,662	12,219,848	10,743,902
3-Month Eonia	85,181	135,594	31,322		
3-Month Euribor	248,504,960	192,859,090	228,487,462	221,411,485	202,091,612
3-Month Eurodollar	9,103	6,343	26,692	15,926	69,760
Short Gilt	365,824	30,680			
Medium Gilt	166,521	11,455			
Long Gilt	28,525,983	23,977,779	24,717,249	27,367,489	22,009,284
2-Year Swapnote EUR	392,976	452,362	703,608	512,872	274,459
5-Year Swapnote EUR	254,717	251,078	212,746	407,029	401,365
10-Year Swapnote EUR	78,536	76,200	104,460	273,961	405,011
Japanese Government Bond	49,610	50,953	105,584	173,810	140,487
FTSE 100 Index	37,627,230	38,515,933	42,314,080	33,535,934	25,120,880
FTSE 100 Dividend Index	910,456	667,052			
FTSE Eurotop 100 Index	737	9,882	13,907	27,352	32,694
MSCI Euro Index	15	3,684	5,964	6,360	18,036
MSCI Pan-Euro Index	203,263	358,168	641,354	835,603	701,066
FTSE Mid 250 Index	101,194	91,362	163,652	181,735	62,304
TOPIX	363				
Index F Other Bclear	550,503	95,287			
Cocoa #7	3,519,409	3,218,726	3,577,010	3,319,396	3,095,346
Robusta Coffee - 10 Tonne	2,789,953	2,514,457	207,443		
Wheat	147,684	114,133	131,358	128,073	76,239
White Sugar	1,854,156	1,852,702	1,654,446	2,091,654	1,668,674
Total Futures	**446,262,115**	**374,191,252**	**420,340,439**	**426,960,618**	**354,437,011**
3-Month Short Sterling	26,157,563	37,876,416	59,079,440	50,747,710	34,231,229
3-Month Sterling Mid-curve	20,766,671	12,109,210	12,994,233	4,330,981	3,212,817
3-Month Sterling 2-Year Mid-curve	45,000	10,550			
3-Month Euribor	121,077,679	121,612,383	106,730,522	74,276,297	48,176,163
3-Month Euribor Mid Curve	20,425,277	18,498,853	7,955,894	6,188,559	7,355,609
3-Month Euribor 2-Year Mid-curve	134,920	30,402			
Long Gilt	184,618	384,145			
FTSE 100 Index (ESX)	23,440,064	30,155,112	29,261,814	23,700,667	15,717,186
FTSE 100 Index FLEX	1,219,654	2,400,296	1,434,196	1,021,680	1,979,620
Other Bclear	26,662	34,992	57,250	13,697	16,700
Cocoa	730,027	556,860	251,614	177,788	102,819
Robusta Coffee - 10 Tonne	482,483	192,398	48,987		
Wheat	873	656	523	5,284	2,320
White Sugar	22,482	50,195	224,977	254,307	81,647
Total Options	**214,713,973**	**223,912,468**	**218,508,097**	**161,381,797**	**111,353,733**

NASDAQ OMX Oslo, Norway

	2010	2009	2008	2007	2006
CER Spot	40				
CER Forward	4,870	5,113	52,107		
EUA	40				
EUA Spot	9,818				
EUA Forward	16,732	40,850	69,624		
German Power Base (Year)	1,826	2,710	4,225		
German Power Base (Quarter)	554	1,002	1,212		
German Power Base (Month)	706	449	2,387		
German Power Base (Week)	235	100	895		
German Power Peak (Week)	20				
German Power Peak (Week + Day)	50		75		
Nordic Power Base (Year)	82,382	118,404	128,352		
Nordic Power Base (Quarter)	408,218	307,694	422,468		
Nordic Power Base (Month)	192,260	136,195	167,644		
Nordic Power Base (Week + Day)	140,954	214,819	185,966		
Nordic Power Base (Day)	52,380				
Nordic Power Base (CfD Year)	11,561	50,148	46,458		
Nordic Power Base (CfD Month)	27,198				
Nordic Power Base (CfD Quarter)	22,729				
Nordic Power Peak (Year)	10	375	19		
Nordic Power Peak (Quarter)	52	45	27		
Nordic Power Peak (Month)	20		40		
Nordic Power Peak (Week)	30				
Total Futures	**972,685**	**877,992**	**1,081,668**		
Nordic Power Base (Year)	10,531	28,104	33,182		
Nordic Power Base (Quarter)	20,978				
Total Options	**31,509**	**28,104**	**33,182**		

OMX Exchanges, Sweden

	2010	2009	2008	2007	2006
3-Month STIBOR	15,640,119	12,923,736	16,929,736	14,892,134	
Mortgage Bond (MBF)	28,899				
Policy Rate (RIBA)	2,114,300	1,040,006			
NASDAQ OMX Interest Rate Swap (NOIS)	3,648	1,250			
2-Year Swedish Gov't Bond Forward (R2)	2,950,624	2,096,471	4,049,661	3,568,792	
5-Year Swedish Gov't Bond Forward (R5)	1,511,946	1,179,563	1,366,872	1,930,006	
10-Year Swedish Gov't Bond Forward (R10)	1,063,189	885,565	892,169	798,640	
2-Year Nordea Hypotek Bond Forward (NBHYP2)	340,514	345,156	389,973	168,119	
5-Year Nordea Hypotek Bond Forward (NBHYP5)	290,635	202,314	186,936	118,052	
2-Year Spintab Bond Forward (SPA2)	310	176,791	215,937	154,457	
5-Year Spintab Bond Forward (SPA5)	477,440	240,372	226,499	178,072	
2-Year Stadshypotek Bond Forward (ST2)	385,412	257,681	674,731	386,189	
5-Year Stadshypotek Bond Forward (ST5)	352,728	331,842	294,279	328,507	
OMX Index	32,427,696	33,700,054	39,307,915	31,609,782	24,374,765
All Futures on Individual Equities	2,468,839	6,718,987	15,841,312	9,013,489	8,459,165
Total Futures	**60,056,299**	**60,099,788**	**80,376,020**	**63,376,025**	**45,039,885**
Interest Rate	2,043,400	1,170,505	629,000	685,010	
OMX Index	13,761,881	14,225,611	19,654,145	19,715,476	13,613,210
All Options on Individual Equities	32,753,859	28,775,091	42,767,407	59,660,819	64,514,641
Total Options	**48,559,140**	**44,171,207**	**63,050,552**	**80,061,305**	**78,127,851**

Osaka Securities Exchange (OSE), Japan

	2010	2009	2008	2007	2006
Nikkei 225 Index	22,483,722	25,368,919	35,546,016	30,084,781	25,151,924
Nikkei 225 Mini	125,113,769	104,738,309	95,446,729	49,107,059	6,348,382
Nikkei 300 Index	148	405	35,509	81,907	153,439
US Dollar/Japanese Yen	1,813,592	243,611			
Euro/Japanese Yen	929,577	108,118			
British Pound/Japanese Yen	390,457	51,086			
Australian Dollar/Japanese Yen	1,002,638	52,858			
Swiss Franc/Japanese Yen	27,224	4,953			
Canadian Dollar/Japanese Yen	46,340	13,069			
New Zealand/Japanese Yen	118,211	7,567			
Euro/US Dollar	218,219	71,516			
British Pound/US Dollar	24,566	30,241			
Total Futures	**152,168,463**	**130,690,652**	**131,028,334**	**79,291,064**	**31,661,331**
Nikkei 225 Index	43,791,011	34,986,005	32,126,060	29,181,438	28,230,767
All Options on Individual Equities	390,805	408,752	534,954	444,149	753,937
Total Options	**44,181,816**	**35,394,757**	**32,661,014**	**29,625,747**	**28,985,106**

Oslo Stock Exchange (OSE), Norway

	2010	2009	2008	2007	2006
Forwards	1,460,982	1,173,476	1,637,407	2,630,772	3,615,036
OBX	8,001,664	9,041,941	9,195,919	4,755,934	2,429,235
Total Futures	**9,462,646**	**10,215,417**	**10,833,326**	**7,386,706**	**6,044,271**
OBX	734,458	746,589	1,460,422	1,797,651	1,331,023
All Options on Individual Equities	3,363,236	2,549,240	3,754,682	4,783,490	5,781,666
Total Options	**4,097,694**	**3,295,829**	**5,215,104**	**6,581,141**	**7,112,689**

Rosario Futures Exchange (ROFEX), Argentina

	2010	2009	2008	2007	2006
Wheat	1,654	267	106	405	1,039
Corn	2,622	88	208	294	538
Soybeans	72,183	26,047	17,421	40,000	556
Rosafe Soybean Index (ISR)	154,872	133,712	77,766	143,824	101,029
Rosafe Corn Index (IMR)	276	5,168	7,663	6,292	8,714
Government Bond (DICP)	20		12,784	4,657	
BODEN 2012 Government Bond (RG12)	20		55		
Gold	20,869				
US Dollar (DLR)	61,729,396	51,107,696	41,796,793	25,042,919	17,779,242
Euro (EC)	30,023	11,974	151,620	20	157,005
Total Futures	**51,286,802**	**42,092,168**	**25,249,072**	**18,053,184**	**13,051,248**
Wheat	21				
Corn	124				
Soybeans	7,114				
Rosafe Soybean Index (ISR)	23,273	53,114	24,986	36,972	24,229
US Dollar (DLR)	4,353	128,362	95,960	129,601	124,073
Total Options	**34,885**	**196,627**	**124,493**	**174,878**	**158,888**

Russian Trading Systems Stock Exchange (RTS), Russia

	2010	2009	2008	2007	2006
Ruble Overnight Credit (Deposit) Rate MosIBOR	6,055,964	1,000	80,846	47,031	
Ruble 3 Monthly Credit Interbank Mkt Moscow MosPrime	123,375	17,861	6,940	591	
Moscow Money Market MosPrime Overnight	9,673	8,884	10,278		
AUD/USD	73,446				
EUR/USD	39,476,420	13,658,237			
EUR/RUB	1,298,081	479,084			
GBP/USD	124,956				
USD/RUB	81,122,195	8,468,200			
RTS Consumer & Retail Index	1,265	1,246	9,157	100,103	
RTS Index	224,696,733	150,019,917	87,469,405	34,228,973	
RTS Oil & Gas Index	7,289	29,798	316,255	345,439	
RTS Standard Index	2,327,517				
RTS Telecom Index	2,927	6,453	73,265		
Brent Oil	11,127,254	7,471,665	153,438		
Diesel Fuel (Summer grades)	101,628				
Center Base Load Power	73,270				
Center Peak Load Power	39,604				
East Siberia Base Load Power	81,017				
West Siberia Base Load Power	8,962				
URAL Base Load Power	74,391				
URAL Peak Load Power	21,511				
Urals Oil	785	28,070	701,975	357,145	
Copper	18,912				
Gold	5,562,423	2,903,120	5,199,919	1,632,410	
Palladium	1,982	391			
Platinum	275,555	34,570			
Refined Silver	714,645	104,531	169,276	17,731	
Sugar (Cash settled)	80,809				
Sugar (Deliverable)	2,071	12,602	6,684	1,222	
All Futures on Individual Equities	226,711,751	249,278,962	83,652,425	75,393,694	
Total Futures	**454,465,573**	**191,981,604**	**119,622,650**		
RTS Index	13,179,587	5,062,653	11,446,411	7,150,531	
US Dollar	1,280,316	1,863,930	311,990	154,196	
EUR/USD	17,522				
Gold	98,002	84,164	675,707	117,580	
Platinum	13,420				
Refined Silver	21,784	1,336	8,435		
Brent Crude Oil	12,251				
All Options on Individual Equities	9,153,070	12,962,387	33,796,561	16,933,254	
Total Options	**23,775,952**	**19,974,470**	**46,239,104**	**24,355,561**	

Shanghai Metal Exchange, China

	2010	2009	2008	2007	2006
Copper	50,788,568	81,217,436	20,773,258	16,328,011	5,393,419
Aluminum	17,261,995	20,530,548	14,788,920	4,823,552	13,931,476
Zinc	146,589,373	32,253,386	23,538,897	10,215,449	
Steel Rebar	225,612,417	161,574,521			
Wire Rod	151,702	1,092,016			
Gold	3,397,044	3,406,233	3,890,467		
Rubber	167,414,912	89,035,959	46,461,103	42,191,727	26,047,061
Fuel Oil	10,682,204	45,753,969	30,810,540	12,005,094	12,734,045
Total Futures	**621,898,215**	**434,864,068**	**140,263,185**	**85,563,833**	**58,106,001**

Singapore Commodity Exchange (SICOM), Singapore

	2010	2009	2008	2007	2006
RSS3	35,712	20,027			
TSR20 (FOB)	191,160	48,544			
OTC TSR20	395				
Robusta Coffee	2,843				
Gold	645,354				
Total Futures	**875,464**	**68,571**			

Singapore Exchange (SGX), Singapore

	2010	2009	2008	2007	2006
Euro Stoxx 50 Index	200				
Euroyen TIBOR	85,840	161,492	562,063	1,916,702	3,538,237
Mini Japanese Gov't Bond	741,764	694,655	831,196	1,457,309	1,427,458
Nikkei 225 Index	28,785,870	25,353,225	26,149,701	21,937,499	18,017,221
Nikkei 225 Index (USD)	3,010	666	3,154	10,913	871
Mini Nikkei 225 Index	134,449	1,857	31,640	29,378	
Nikkei Stock Average Dividend Point Index	21,216				
Straits Times Index	436	2,916	2,734	22	4
FTSE/China A50 Index	531,865	1	34,232	12,349	8,932
S&P CNX Nifty Index	10,479,168	7,115,255	12,435,118	750,361	134,445

Singapore Exchange (SGX), Singapore

	2010	2009	2008	2007	2006
MSCI Singapore Index	3,718,450	3,947,690	4,635,517	4,012,860	2,214,521
MSCI Taiwan Index	15,576,877	15,718,096	16,913,325	13,611,314	10,824,249
Fuel Oil 380	6,490				
Total Futures	**60,085,635**	**52,996,512**	**61,605,338**	**43,741,573**	**36,201,370**
MSCI Taiwan Index	5,400	9,901	385	16,010	29,642
MSCI Singapore Index	16,953	2,628			
Nikkei 225 Index	610,630	102,142	233,545	397,704	358,031
Total Options	**632,983**	**114,671**	**235,930**	**465,253**	**396,373**

Singapore Commodity Exchange (SICOM), Singapore

	2010	2009	2008	2007	2006
OTC Forward Freight Agreements	82,618	37,889			
OTC Iron Ore Swap	35,382	10,911			
OTC Energy Swap	38,589	8,835			
Total Futures	**156,589**	**57,635**			

Sydney Futures Exchange (SFE), Australia

	2010	2009	2008	2007	2006
SPI 200	10,061,779	9,538,554	10,174,823	8,407,052	6,516,247
30-Day Interbank Cash Rate	5,214,205	2,315,374	2,785,693	3,585,675	2,009,291
90-Day Bank Bills	17,910,061	14,435,474	20,192,284	22,682,851	19,501,781
3-Year Treasury Bonds	34,482,136	24,197,537	26,116,381	33,585,015	31,017,644
10-Year Treasury Bonds	13,454,773	10,072,494	13,188,549	19,169,641	15,051,399
10-Year Interest Rate Swaps	4,799	6,001			
d-cypha NSW Base Load Electricity	52,543	42,330	30,173	39,076	10,707
d-cypha QLD Base Load Electricity	38,211	28,811	30,469	36,357	9,532
d-cypha SA Base Load Electricity	2,733	1,751	2,191	4,372	2,127
d-cypha VIC Base Load Electricity	49,574	34,867	23,870	34,788	13,581
d-cypha NSW Peak Period Electricity	2,883	1,501	1,236	1,491	1,926
d-cypha QLD Peak Period Electricity	2,130	1,436	1,274	1,804	1,981
d-cypha SA Peak Period Electricity	28	105	251	338	110
d-cypha VIC Peak Period Electricity	2,831	1,774	2,538	4,089	5,038
d-cypha NSW Base $300 CAP	12,378	1,728	1,887	1,397	1,276
d-cypha QLD Base $300 CAP	4,537	2,734	1,625	902	986
d-cypha SA Base $300 CAP	768	232	101	260	62
d-cypha VIC Base $300 CAP	12,401	3,085	3,621	2,422	1,590
Fine Wool	128	375	698	1,828	2,686
Greasy Wool	6,377	9,971	21,612	19,629	16,869
MLA/SFE Cattle	5	225	651	1,140	1,860
Total Futures	**81,315,280**	**60,696,359**	**72,580,096**	**87,595,681**	**74,204,335**
SPI 200	382,378	319,735	436,869	564,156	636,033
90-Day Bank Bills	40,840	33,146	287,103	774,472	182,663
3-Year Treasury Bond	205,816	446,182	326,323	466,507	856,723
Overnight 3-Year Treasury Bond	1,740,511	1,136,306	680,333	1,121,860	1,522,000
3-Year Bonds Intra-Day	1,049,240	430,590	288,288	472,047	576,935
10-Year Treasury Bonds	5,475	9,335	5,034	38,217	52,623
Overnight 10-Year Treasury Bond	2,150	2,250	1,200	19,115	76,909
d-cypha VIC Peak Period Electricity	100	160	60	100	5
Total Options	**3,426,510**	**2,377,784**	**2,025,460**	**3,525,481**	**3,915,771**

Taiwan Futures Exchange, Taiwan

	2010	2009	2008	2007	2006
TAIEX (TX)	25,332,827	24,625,062	19,819,775	11,813,150	9,914,999
Mini TAIEX (MTX)	13,893,559	13,926,904	9,058,436	2,964,042	1,760,583
Taiwan Stock Exchange Electronic Sector Index	1,092,763	1,166,622	1,356,290	1,004,603	1,459,821
Taiwan Stock Exchange Bank & Insurance Sector Index	1,257,861	1,482,264	1,285,074	909,383	786,477
Taiwan 50 Index	618	888	602	506	332
MSCI Taiwan Index (MSF)	1,020	466	1,425	1,132	9,894
GreTai Securities Weighted Stock Index (GTF)	43,335	66,610	94,144	21,231	
Taiwan Stock Exch NonFin/NonElec SubIndex (XIF)	106,768	157,613	168,534	37,197	
30-Day Commercial Paper Interest Rate	2	13,149	114,558	36,243	1,022
Gold (GDF)	677	205	40,174	48,925	32,484
NT Dollar Gold (TGF)	75,218	3,342,838	5,314,069		
All Futures on Individual Equities	724,375				
Total Futures	**42,529,023**	**44,886,570**	**37,724,589**	**16,987,659**	**14,006,287**
TAIEX	95,666,916	72,082,548	92,757,254	92,585,637	96,929,940
TSE Electronic Sector Index	382,747	786,132	1,068,755	1,066,141	773,353
TSE Financial Sector Index	797,910	761,886	927,888	1,203,084	937,044
GreTai Securities Weighted Stock Index (GTO)	123,537	688,481	835,892	187,967	
Taiwan Stock Exch NonFin/NonElec SubIndex (XIO)	118,565	741,908	891,575	186,161	
MSCI Taiwan Index (MSO)	27,048	1,116,142	1,640,944	1,634,117	867,597
DTB-demoninated Gold (TGO)	76,873	5,821,638			
All Options on Individual Equities	70,272	8,240,390	872,880	1,299,858	1,089,158
Total Options	**97,263,868**	**90,239,125**	**98,995,188**	**98,162,965**	**100,597,092**

VOLUME - WORLDWIDE

Thailand Futures Exchange, Thailand

	2010	2009	2008	2007	2006
SET 50	2,362,845	2,522,465	2,099,098	1,228,238	
Gold, 50 Baht	792,960	311,591			
Gold, 10 Baht	178,463				
5-Year Government Bond	40				
3-Month BIBOR	1				
All Futures on Individual Equities	804,156	142,837	3,838		
Total Futures	**4,138,465**	**2,976,893**	**2,102,936**	**1,228,238**	
SET 50	107,317	95,504	45,684	2,428	
Total Options	**107,317**	**95,504**	**45,684**	**2,428**	

Tel-Aviv Stock Exchange (TASE), Israel

	2010	2009	2008	2007	2006
TA-25 Index	24,484	43,025	29,694	19,802	32,474
TA-Banks Index	21,524	8,435			
Shekel-Dollar Rate	336,208	51,198	80		
Shekel-Euro Rate	25,290	4,008			
Total Futures	**407,506**	**106,666**	**29,774**	**20,445**	**57,334**
TA-25 Index	70,573,392	62,271,157	81,483,701	94,520,236	75,486,658
TA-Banks Index	75,248	73,937	72,486	87,445	56,273
Shekel-Dollar Rate	7,927,235	8,067,320	10,596,199	9,508,185	7,344,622
Shekel-Euro Rate	484,415	73,937	391,882	235,452	103,095
All Options on Individual Equities	973,129	321,228			
Total Options	**80,033,419**	**70,807,579**	**92,544,268**	**104,351,318**	**82,990,648**

Tokyo Commodity Exchange (TOCOM), Japan

	2010	2009	2008	2007	2006
Gold	12,198,340	11,913,502	15,163,975	18,203,194	22,228,198
Gold Mini	2,477,688	5,010,476	5,736,883	455,212	
Silver	236,296	111,775	301,216	536,583	858,153
Platinum	4,390,452	3,617,988	6,940,348	9,169,890	11,018,069
Platinum Mini	308,711	413,310	119,606		
Palladium	156,946	107,829	684,682	207,867	361,478
Aluminum	280	3,768	36,203	65,507	157,781
Gasoline	2,509,734	2,732,376	4,054,761	7,529,706	12,932,848
Kerosene	1,196,729	1,026,529	1,319,014	2,350,819	4,492,904
Chukyo Gasoline	7,800				
Chukyo Kerosene	3,856				
Gas Oil	4,366				
Crude Oil	943,450	624,307	755,520	1,489,018	1,961,190
Rubber	3,130,073	3,320,088	5,914,747	7,062,252	9,661,388
Nikkei-TOCOM Commodity Index	71,646				
Total Futures	**27,636,367**	**28,881,948**	**41,026,955**	**47,070,048**	**63,672,011**

Tokyo International Financial Futures Exchange (TIFFE), Japan

	2010	2009	2008	2007	2006
3-Month Euroyen TIBOR	11,274,925	13,066,020	22,372,133	38,952,553	31,495,084
US Dollar / Japanese Yen	27,551,634	20,198,781	13,177,698	7,629,879	
Euro / Japanese Yen	19,921,565	9,961,673	5,883,330	4,070,296	
British pound / Japanese Yen	17,108,444	16,266,521	7,634,056	6,041,471	
Australian Dollar / Japanese Yen	34,272,436	17,793,787	9,246,469	6,835,958	
Swiss Franc / Japanese Yen	368,567	183,224	768,754	669,032	
Canadian Dollar / Japanese Yen	927,926	467,812	1,334,653	2,005,416	
New Zealand Dollar / Japanese Yen	2,196,138	2,097,853	4,966,753	6,330,039	
South African Rand / Japanese Yen	1,185,379	860,162	48,086		
Norway Krone / Japanese Yen	36,144	27,956	1,948		
Hong Kong Dollar / Japanese Yen	53,830	21,825	2,014		
Sweden Krona / Japanese Yen	21,591	15,926	592		
Paland Zloty / Japanese Yen	152,485	217,530	22,335		
Euro / US Dollar	3,674,987	1,116,564	141,449		
British Pound / US Dollar	555,891	426,937	19,796		
British Pound / Swiss Franc	79,909	27,895	2,329		
US Dollar / Swiss Franc	145,093	75,115	11,313		
US Dollar / Canadian Dollar	111,927	45,869	3,939		
Australian Dollar / US Dollar	1,003,682	542,598	15,763		
Euro / Swiss Franc	82,892	20,485	1,100		
Euro / British Pound	100,441	88,194	10,453		
New Zealand Dollar / US Dollar	94,114	38,640	5,000		
Euro / Australian Dollar	208,708	24,891	2,351		
British Pound / Australian Dollar	81,296	59,698	1,087		
Total Futures	**121,210,004**	**83,645,956**	**65,675,700**	**72,535,144**	**31,508,764**
3-Month Euroyen	400	32,088	1,251,367	3,660,673	3,976,764
Total Options	**400**	**32,088**	**1,251,367**	**3,660,673**	**3,976,764**

Tokyo Grain Exchange (TGE), Japan

	2010	2009	2008	2007	2006
American Soybeans	1,147,425	2,320,782	910,992	1,247,786	1,259,515
Non-GMO Soybeans	35,749	189,020	2,899,301	12,280,932	9,885,557
Arabic Coffee	50,526	46,281	282,446	595,871	1,669,181
Azuki (Red Beans)	180,591	243,415	346,356	388,643	478,379
Corn	1,084,049	1,867,864	3,645,293	4,645,239	4,656,352
Robusta Coffee	2,981	1,860	11,197	72,971	206,546
Raw Sugar	365,267	157,102	331,976	433,329	928,316
Total Futures	**2,866,588**	**4,829,183**	**8,433,346**	**19,674,560**	**19,116,748**

Tokyo Stock Exchange (TSE), Japan

	2010	2009	2008	2007	2006
10-Year Government Yen Bond	8,021,458	6,765,074	10,639,934	13,545,239	12,049,979
REIT Index	46,696	52,799	89,922		
TOPIX Stock Index	14,541,751	15,190,781	18,375,802	16,578,731	14,907,723
Mini TOPIX Stock Index	1,044,343	681,248	599,692		
Bank Index	5,808				
TOPIX Core 30 Index	242,105	362,882	202,189		
Nikkei 225 Dividend Index	19,553				
Total Futures	**23,052,830**	**29,907,539**	**30,123,970**	**26,957,702**	**22,630,719**
TOPIX	120,040	52,523	62,045	19,555	18,354
10-Year Government Yen Bond	1,999,282	2,433,217	2,442,598	2,804,811	2,060,624
All Options on Individual Equities	834,941	662,813	88,256	145,449	190,876
Total Options	**2,954,263**	**3,148,553**	**2,592,899**	**2,969,815**	**2,269,854**

Turkish Derivatives Exchange (TurkDEX), Turkey

	2010	2009	2008	2007	2006
Cotton	2		11	29	23
Wheat	2	4	5,503		
Gold	144,965	118,347	21,641	81	1,618
US Dollar/Ounce Gold	2,523				
ISE-100 Index	8,066	6,654	2,961	1,561	39,809
ISE-30 Index	56,508,907	65,393,094	40,332,007	17,015,352	2,203,916
ISE 30 - 100 Index Spread	2,331				
US Dollar	7,095,340	13,687,292	13,979,082	7,832,542	4,393,609
Euro	171,375	225,314	131,210	17,067	204,807
Euro/US Dollar Cross Currency	12,906				
Physically Delivered US Dollar	146	54			
Physically Delivered Euro	30	20			
T-Benchmark	5,584	564	420	401	4,104
Total Futures	**63,952,177**	**79,431,343**	**54,472,835**	**24,867,033**	**6,848,087**

Warsaw Stock Exchange, Poland

	2010	2009	2008	2007	2006
WIG 20 Index	13,481,633	12,766,415	11,743,240	8,792,219	6,242,128
WIG 40 Index	32,998	30,182	25,349	15,819	
CHFPLN	7,673	9,418	5,669		
EURPLN	22,625	59,438	28,600	532	650
USDPLN	88,777	93,382	98,219	5,517	2,494
All Futures on Individual Equities	375,496	465,757	331,646	111,457	112,824
Total Futures	**14,009,202**	**13,424,593**	**12,233,935**	**8,936,225**	**6,386,377**
WIG20 Index	675,112	396,208	326,583	405,657	316,840
Total Options	**675,112**	**396,208**	**326,583**	**405,733**	**327,828**

Wiener Borse - Derivatives Market of Vienna, Austria

	2010	2009	2008	2007	2006
ATF Index	42,254	34,664	32,408	35,043	46,517
ATX Index	266,786	219,038	156,376	108,020	108,004
CeCe (5 Eastern European Indices)	22,167	13,362	59,692	89,335	65,953
All Futures on Individual Equities	4,575	6,053	6,981	11,199	12,371
Total Futures	**335,782**	**273,117**	**255,462**	**243,602**	**232,845**
ATF Index	7,588	3,993	3,236	8,117	1,938
ATX Index	26,005	14,821	22,894	28,067	23,462
CeCe (5 Eastern European Indices)	320		6	4	
All Options on Individual Equities	469,216	474,697	848,021	1,036,975	1,053,298
Total Options	**503,129**	**493,511**	**874,157**	**1,073,293**	**1,078,698**

VOLUME - WORLDWIDE

Zhengzhou Commodity Exchange (ZCE), China

	2010	2009	2008	2007	2006
Cotton #1	86,955,310	8,534,688	5,400,835	2,955,235	2,084,541
Early Rice	26,854,086	1,950,083			
Rapeseed Oil	9,527,915	10,956,863	6,429,404	659,612	
White Sugar	305,303,131	146,063,344	165,485,978	45,468,481	29,342,066
Strong Gluten Wheat	5,804,642	13,735,956	27,509,312	38,982,788	14,676,238
Hard White Winter Wheat	35,095	20,170	164,309	25,719	28,052
PTA	61,424,805	45,851,417	17,567,296	4,960,879	167,220
Total Futures	**495,904,984**	**227,112,521**	**222,557,134**	**93,052,714**	**46,298,117**

Total Worldwide Volume

	2010	2009	2008	2007	2006
Total Futures	8,417,749,184	5,859,892,391	5,444,906,611	4,573,165,703	3,236,223,328
Percent Change	43.65%	7.62%	19.06%	41.31%	36.04%
Total Options	6,757,743,751	5,569,496,199	5,259,609,949	4,862,456,753	4,050,032,450
Percent Change	21.33%	5.89%	8.17%	20.06%	-0.41%
Total Futures and Options	15,175,492,935	11,429,388,590	10,704,516,560	9,435,622,456	7,286,255,778
Percent Change	32.78%	6.77%	13.45%	29.50%	13.04%

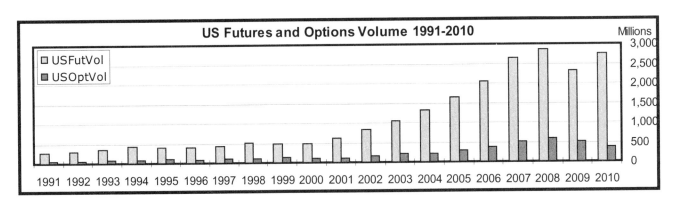

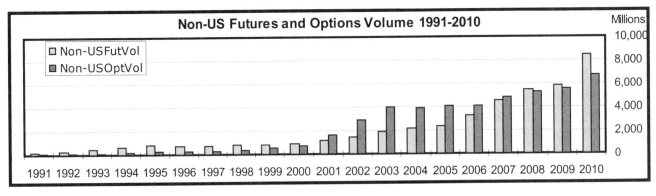

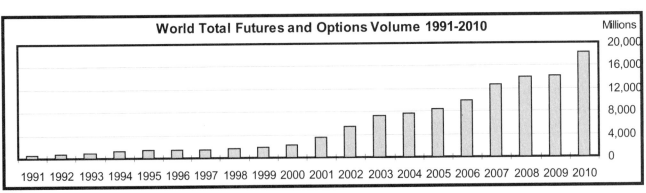

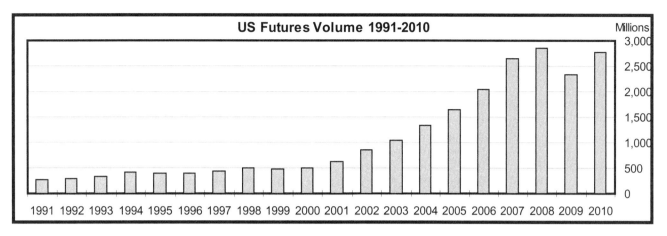

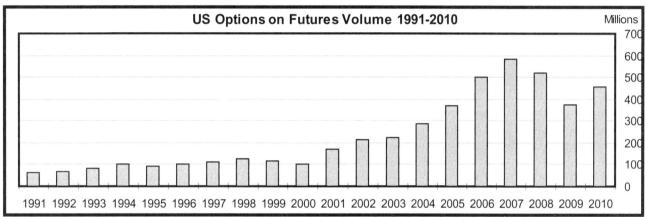

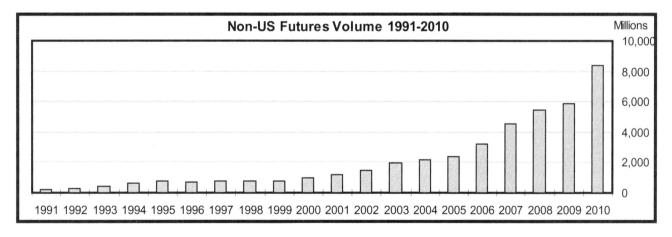

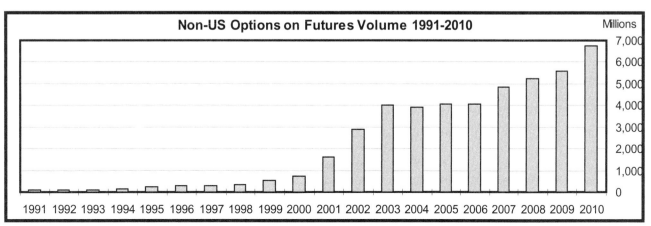

Conversion Factors

Commonly Used Agricultural Weights and Measurements

Bushel Weights:
Corn, Sorghum and Rye = 56 lbs.
Wheat and Soybeans = 60 lbs.
Canola = 50 lbs.
Barley Grain = 48 lbs.
Barley Malt = 34 lbs.
Oats = 32 lbs.

Bushels to tonnes:
Corn, Sorghum and Rye = bushels x 0.0254
Wheat and Soybeans = bushels x 0.027216
Barley Grain = bushels x 0.021772
Oats = bushels x 0.014515

1 tonne (metric ton) equals:
2204.622 lbs.
1,000 kilograms
22.046 hundredweight
10 quintals

Ethanol
1 bushel Corn = 2.75 gallons Ethanol = 18 lbs Dried Distillers Grain
1 tonne Corn = 101.0 gallons Ethanol = 661 lbs Dried Distillers Grain
1 tonne Sugar = 149.3 gallons Ethanol

1 tonne (metric ton) equals:
39.3679 bushels of Corn, Sorghum or Rye
36.7437 bushels of Wheat or Soybeans
22.046 hundredweight
45.9296 bushels of Barley Grain
68.8944 bushels of Oats
4.5929 Cotton bales (the statistical bale used by the USDA and ICAC contains a net weight of 480 pounds of lint)

Area Measurements:
1 acre = 43,560 square feet = 0.040694 hectare
1 hectare = 2.4710 acres = 10,000 square meters
640 acres = 1 square mile = 259 hectares

Yields:
Rye, Corn: bushels per acre x 0.6277 = quintals per hectare
Wheat: bushels per acre x 0.6725 = quintals per hectare
Barley Grain: bushels per acre x 0.538 = quintals per hectare
Oats: bushels per acre x 0.3587 = quintals per hectare

Commonly Used Weights

The troy, avoirdupois and apothecaries' grains are identical in U.S. and British weight systems, equal to 0.0648 gram in the metric system. One avoirdupois ounce equals 437.5 grains. The troy and apothecaries' ounces equal 480 grains, and their pounds contain 12 ounces.

Troy weights and conversions:
24 grains = 1 pennyweigh
20 pennyweights = 1 ounce
12 ounces = 1 pound
1 troy ounce = 31.103 grams
1 troy ounce = 0.0311033 kilogram
1 troy pound = 0.37224 kilogram
1 kilogram = 32.1507 troy ounces
1 tonne = 32,151 troy ounces

Avoirdupois weights and conversions:
27 11/32 grains = 1 dram
16 drams = 1 ounce
16 ounces = 1 lb.
1 lb. = 7,000 grains
14 lbs. = 1 stone (British)
100 lbs. = 1 hundredweight (U.S.)
112 lbs. = 8 stone = 1 hundredweight (British)
2,000 lbs. = 1 short ton (U.S. ton)
2,240 lbs. = 1 long ton (British ton)
160 stone = 1 long ton
20 hundredweight = 1 ton
1 lb. = 0.4536 kilogram
1 hundredweight (cwt.) = 45.359 kilograms
1 short ton = 907.18 kilograms
1 long ton = 1,016.05 kilograms

Metric weights and conversions:
1,000 grams = 1 kilogram
100 kilograms = 1 quintal
1 tonne = 1,000 kilograms = 10 quintals
1 kilogram = 2.204622 lbs.
1 quintal = 220.462 lbs.
1 tonne = 2204.6 lbs.
1 tonne = 1.102 short tons
1 tonne = 0.9842 long ton

U.S. dry volumes and conversions:
1 pint = 33.6 cubic inches = 0.5506 liter
2 pints = 1 quart = 1.1012 liters
8 quarts = 1 peck = 8.8098 liters
4 pecks = 1 bushel = 35.2391 liters
1 cubic foot = 28.3169 liters

U.S. liquid volumes and conversions:
1 ounce = 1.8047 cubic inches = 29.6 milliliters
1 cup = 8 ounces = 0.24 liter = 237 milliliters
1 pint = 16 ounces = 0.48 liter = 473 milliliters
1 quart = 2 pints = 0.946 liter = 946 milliliters
1 gallon = 4 quarts = 231 cubic inches = 3.785 liters
1 milliliter = 0.033815 fluid ounce
1 liter = 1.0567 quarts = 1,000 milliliters
1 liter = 33.815 fluid ounces
1 imperial gallon = 277.42 cubic inches = 1.2 U.S. gallons = 4.546 liters

Energy Conversion Factors

U.S. Crude OIl (average gravity)
1 U.S. barrel = 42 U.S. gallons
1 short ton = 6.65 barrels
1 tonne = 7.33 barrels

Barrels per tonne for various origins

Abu Dhabi	7.624
Algeria	7.661
Angola	7.206
Australia	7.775
Bahrain	7.335
Brunei	7.334
Canada	7.428
Dubai	7.295
Ecuador	7.580
Gabon	7.245
Indonesia	7.348
Iran	7.370
Iraq	7.453
Kuwait	7.261
Libya	7.615
Mexico	7.104
Neutral Zone	6.825
Nigeria	7.410
Norway	7.444
Oman	7.390
Qatar	7.573
Romania	7.453
Saudi Arabia	7.338
Trinidad	6.989
Tunisia	7.709
United Arab Emirates	7.522
United Kingdom	7.279
United States	7.418
Former Soviet Union	7.350
Venezuela	7.005
Zaire	7.206

Barrels per tonne of refined products:

aviation gasoline	8.90
motor gasoline	8.50
kerosene	7.75
jet fuel	8.00
distillate, including diesel	7.46

(continued above)

residual fuel oil	6.45
lubricating oil	7.00
grease	6.30
white spirits	8.50
paraffin oil	7.14
paraffin wax	7.87
petrolatum	7.87
asphalt and road oil	6.06
petroleum coke	5.50
bitumen	6.06
LPG	11.6

Approximate heat content of refined products:

(Million Btu per barrel, 1 British thermal unit is the amount of heat required to raise the temperature of 1 pound of water 1 degree F.)

Petroleum Product	Heat Content
asphalt	6.636
aviation gasoline	5.048
butane	4.326
distillate fuel oil	5.825
ethane	3.082
isobutane	3.974
jet fuel, kerosene	5.670
jet fuel, naptha	5.355
kerosene	5.670
lubricants	6.065
motor gasoline	5.253
natural gasoline	4.620
pentanes plus	4.620

Petrochemical feedstocks:

naptha less than 401*F	5.248
other oils equal to or greater than 401*F	5.825
still gas	6.000
petroleum coke	6.024
plant condensate	5.418
propane	3.836
residual fuel oil	6.287
special napthas	5.248
unfinished oils	5.825
unfractionated steam	5.418
waxes	5.537

Source: U.S. Department of Energy

Natural Gas Conversions

Although there are approximately 1,031 Btu in a cubic foot of gas, for most applications, the following conversions are sufficient:

Cubic Feet			MMBtu		
1,000	(one thousand cubic feet)	=	1 Mcf	=	1
1,000,000	(one million cubic feet)	=	1 MMcf	=	1,000
10,000,000	(ten million cubic feet)	=	10 MMcf	=	10,000
1,000,000,000	(one billion cubic feet)	=	1 Bcf	=	1,000,000
1,000,000,000,000	(one trillion cubic feet)	=	1 Tcf	=	1,000,000,000

Acknowledgments

The editors wish to thank the following for source material:

Agricultural Marketing Service (AMS)

Agricultural Research Service (ARS)

American Bureau of Metal Statistics, Inc. (ABMS)

American Forest & Paper Association (AFPA)

The American Gas Association (AGA)

American Iron and Steel Institute (AISI)

American Metal Market (AMM)

Bureau of the Census

Bureau of Economic Analysis (BEA)

Bureau of Labor Statistics (BLS)

Chicago Board of Trade (CBT)

Chicago Mercantile Exchange (CME / IMM / IOM)

Commodity Credit Corporation (CCC)

Commodity Futures Trading Commision (CFTC)

The Conference Board

Economic Research Service (ERS)

Edison Electric Institute (EEI)

Farm Service Agency (FSA)

Federal Reserve Bank of St. Louis

Fiber Economics Bureau, Inc.

Florida Department of Citrus

Food and Agriculture Organization of the United Nations (FAO)

Foreign Agricultural Service (FAS)

Futures Industry Association (FIA)

ICE Futures U.S, Canada, Europe (ICE)

International Cotton Advisory Committee (ICAC)

International Cocoa Organization (ICCO)

International Rubber Study Group (IRSG)

Johnson Matthey

Kansas City Board of Trade (KCBT)

Leather Industries of America

Minneapolis Grain Exchange (MGEX)

National Agricultural Statistics Service (NASS)

New York Mercantile Exchange (NYMEX)

Oil World

The Organisation for Economic Co-Operation and Development (OECD)

Random Lengths

The Silver Institute

The Society of the Plastics Industry, Inc. (SPI)

United Nations (UN)

United States Department of Agriculture (USDA)

Wall Street Journal (WSJ)

Aluminum

Aluminum (symbol Al) is a silvery, lightweight metal that is the most abundant metallic element in the earth's crust. Aluminum was first isolated in 1825 by a Danish chemist, Hans Christian Oersted, using a chemical process involving a potassium amalgam. A German chemist, Friedrich Woehler, improved Oersted's process by using metallic potassium in 1827. He was the first to show aluminum's lightness. In France, Henri Sainte-Claire Deville isolated the metal by reducing aluminum chloride with sodium and established a large-scale experimental plant in 1854. He displayed pure aluminum at the Paris Exposition of 1855. In 1886, Charles Martin Hall in the U.S. and Paul L.T. Heroult in France simultaneously discovered the first practical method for producing aluminum through electrolytic reduction, which is still the primary method of aluminum production today.

By volume, aluminum weighs less than a third as much as steel. This high strength-to-weight ratio makes aluminum a good choice for construction of aircraft, railroad cars, and automobiles. Aluminum is used in cooking utensils and the pistons of internal-combustion engines because of its high heat conductivity. Aluminum foil, siding, and storm windows make excellent insulators. Because it absorbs relatively few neutrons, aluminum is used in low-temperature nuclear reactors. Aluminum is also useful in boat hulls and various marine devices due to its resistance to corrosion in salt water.

Futures and options on Primary Aluminum and Aluminum Alloy are traded on the London Metal Exchange. Aluminum futures are traded on the Tokyo Commodity Exchange (TOCOM), the Multi Commodity Exchange of India (MCX), and the Shanghai Futures Exchange (SHFE). The London Metals Exchange aluminum futures contracts are priced in terms of dollars were metric tons.

Prices – The London Metals Exchange spot aluminum contract opened 2010 at about $2,302 per metric ton but moved lower to about $1,950 by mid February. Aluminum then rose to about $2,423 in April, fell to about $1,826 in June and then rallied to about $2,492 by the end of the year. The price continued higher into 2011 reaching about $2,590 in March 2011. The 2010 close was below the average of about $2,700 seen from 2006 through mid-2008 but still at a relatively high level, well above the average of about $1500 seen during the 1990-2003 period.

Supply – World production of aluminum in 2009 (latest data) fell by -5.8% to 37.300 million metric tons, down from the 2008 record high of 39.600 million metric tons. The world's largest producers of aluminum are China with 35% of world production in 2009, Russia (10%), Canada (8%), U.S. (5%), and Australia (5%). U.S. production of primary aluminum in 2010 fell -0.64% yr/yr to 1.716 million metric tons. U.S. production of aluminum from secondary sources in 2009 fell -18.6% yr/yr to 2.710 million metric tons.

Demand – World consumption of aluminum in 2001, the latest reporting year for the series, fell -4.8% yr/yr to 23.613 million metric tons, which was moderately below the record high of 24.811 million metric tons consumed in 2000. U.S. consumption of aluminum in 2009 fell -12.6% yr/yr to 4.320 million metric tons which was a three decade low.

Trade – U.S. exports in 2009 fell -17.4% yr/yr to 2.710 million metric tons, down from the 2008 record high of 3.280 million metric tons. U.S. imports of aluminum in 2009 fell -0.8% yr/yr to 3.680 million metric tons, down from the 2005 record high of 4.850 million metric tons. The U.S. was a net exporter in 2008 but in 2010 the U.S. relied on imports for 38% of its consumption.

World Production of Primary Aluminum   In Thousands of Metric Tons

Year	Australia	Brazil	Canada	China	France	Germany	Norway	Russia	Spain	United Kingdom	United States	Venezuela	World Total
2001	1,797	1,140	2,583	3,250	462	652	1,068	3,300	376	341	2,637	571	24,300
2002	1,836	1,318	2,709	4,300	463	653	1,096	3,347	380	344	2,707	605	26,100
2003	1,857	1,381	2,792	5,450	443	661	1,192	3,478	389	343	2,703	601	28,000
2004	1,890	1,460	2,590	6,670	451	668	1,320	3,590	398	360	2,516	624	29,900
2005	1,903	1,499	2,894	7,800	442	648	1,372	3,647	394	369	2,481	615	31,900
2006	1,932	1,605	3,051	9,360	442	516	1,331	3,718	349	360	2,284	610	33,900
2007	1,957	1,655	3,083	12,600	428	551	1,357	3,955	408	365	2,554	610	38,100
2008	1,974	1,661	3,120	13,200	389	606	1,358	4,190	408	326	2,658	610	39,600
2009[1]	1,943	1,536	3,030	12,900	345	292	1,130	3,815	408	253	1,727	610	37,300
2010[2]	1,950	1,550	2,920	16,800		370	800	3,850			1,720	440	41,400

[1] Preliminary.   [2] Estimate.   NA = Not available.   *Source: U.S. Geological Survey (USGS)*

Production of Primary Aluminum (Domestic and Foreign Ores) in the U.S.   In Thousands of Metric Tons

Year	Jan.	Feb.	Mar.	Apr.	May	June	July	Aug.	Sept.	Oct.	Nov.	Dec.	Total
2001	256	220	232	225	229	215	214	212	206	214	208	205	2,637
2002	210	197	220	216	228	225	238	237	227	235	232	241	2,707
2003	242	220	238	225	228	221	226	225	217	224	215	221	2,702
2004	216	202	217	209	217	204	209	210	203	211	207	211	2,516
2005	209	191	214	211	214	206	210	208	199	207	204	208	2,481
2006	197	179	198	190	197	189	192	185	183	190	188	197	2,285
2007	202	185	217	209	210	209	219	220	216	224	220	225	2,556
2008	233	219	234	228	236	224	225	222	214	217	202	204	2,658
2009	193	149	154	145	147	132	135	133	129	137	133	140	1,727
2010[1]	142	130	146	142	148	141	146	145	143	147			1,716

[1] Preliminary.   *Source: U.S. Geological Survey (USGS)*

ALUMINUM

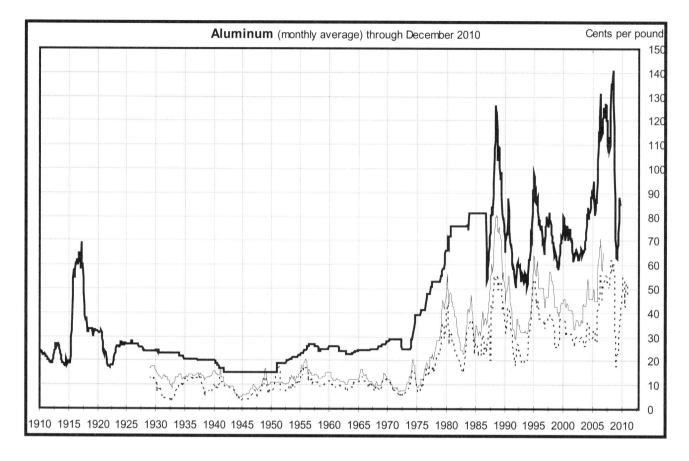

Aluminum (monthly average) through December 2010 — Cents per pound

Salient Statistics of Aluminum in the United States   In Thousands of Metric Tons

	Net Import Reliance as a % of Apparent Consumption	Production Primary	Second-ary	Primary Ship-ments	Recovery from Scrap Old	New	Apparent Con-sumption	Plate, Sheet, Foil	Rolled Structural Shapes[3]	Ex-truded Shapes[4]	All	Perma-nent Mold	Die	Sand	All	Total All Net Ship-ments
Year																
2000	33	3,668	3,450	9,830	1,370	2,080	7,530	4,840	592	1,640	7,240	549	991	152	1,850	9,080
2001	35	2,637	2,970	9,310	1,210	1,760	6,230	4,370	512	1,550	6,580	484	873	251	1,760	8,340
2002	39	2,707	2,930	9,640	1,170	1,750	6,320	4,450	559	1,550	6,710	693	1,280	279	2,450	9,160
2003	38	2,703	2,820	9,760	1,070	1,750	7,120	4,370	531	1,670	6,580	719	1,210	285	2,400	8,970
2004	39	2,516	3,030	10,400	1,160	1,870	6,570	4,750	579	1,810	7,140	735	1,250	221	2,370	9,510
2005	41	2,481	3,030	10,461	1,080	1,950	6,530	5,330	1,080	2,090	8,500	785	1,110	289	2,290	10,790
2006	31	2,284	3,540	10,500	1,260	2,290	5,900	4,690	608	192	5,490	754	1,170	335	2,310	7,800
2007	19	2,554	3,790	9,710	1,540	2,250	5,740	5,000	888	1,580	7,468	615	1,260	315	2,230	9,698
2008	E	2,658	3,330		1,370	1,960	4,940	4,770	789	1,380	6,939	570	1,030	255	1,900	8,839
2009[1]	18	1,727	2,710		1,190	1,520	4,320	4,050	632	1,070	5,752	371	691	160	1,230	6,982

Net Shipments[5] by Producers — Wrought Products — Castings

[1] Preliminary.   [2] To domestic industry.   [3] Also rod, bar & wire.   [4] Also rod, bar, tube, blooms & tubing.   [5] Consists of total shipments less shipments to other mills for further fabrication.   *Source: U.S. Geological Survey (USGS)*

Supply and Distribution of Aluminum in the United States   In Thousands of Metric Tons

Year	Apparent Con-sumption	Production Primary	From Old Scrap	Imports	Exports	Inventories - December 31 - Private	Govern-ment[2]	Year	Apparent Con-sumption	Production Primary	From Old Scrap	Imports	Exports	Inventories - December 31 - Private	Govern-ment[2]
1999	7,770	3,779	1,570	4,000	1,650	1,870	----	2005	6,530	2,481	1,080	4,850	2,370	1,430	----
2000	7,530	3,668	1,370	3,910	1,760	1,550	----	2006	5,900	2,284	1,260	4,660	2,820	1,410	----
2001	6,230	2,637	1,210	3,740	1,590	1,300	----	2007	5,740	2,554	1,540	4,020	2,840	1,400	----
2002	6,320	2,707	1,170	4,060	1,590	1,320	----	2008	4,940	2,658	1,370	3,710	3,280	1,220	----
2003	7,120	2,703	1,070	4,130	1,540	1,400	----	2009[1]	4,320	1,727	1,190	3,680	2,710	937	----
2004	6,570	2,516	1,160	4,720	1,820	1,470	----	2010[2]	4,610	1,720	1,120	3,800	1,900	937	----

[1] Preliminary.   [2] Estimate.   [3] National Defense Stockpile.   [4] Less than 1/2 unit.   *Source: U.S. Geological Survey (USGS)*

Aluminum Products Distribution of End-Use Shipments in the United States   In Thousands of Metric Tons

Year	Building & Construction	Consumer Durables	Containers and Packaging	Electrical	Exports	Machinery and Equipment	Trans-portation	Other	Total
2000	1,450	767	2,260	771	1,280	679	3,600	293	11,100
2001	1,500	681	2,250	686	902	641	3,190	367	10,200
2002	1,560	722	2,260	677	1,070	616	3,410	390	10,700
2003	1,560	689	2,240	653	905	659	3,540	415	10,700
2004	1,680	713	2,310	720	930	730	3,860	416	11,400
2005	1,671	708	2,320	746	1,125	741	3,939	336	11,586
2006	1,650	746	2,320	774	1,270	762	3,930	330	11,800
2007	1,410	664	2,230	762	1,450	736	3,580	359	11,200
2008	1,180	607	2,240	700	1,490	688	2,830	334	10,100
2009[1]	964	458	2,150	593	1,280	475	1,910	254	8,090

[1] Preliminary.   *Source: U.S. Geological Survey (USGS)*

World Consumption of Primary Aluminum   In Thousands of Metric Tons

Year	Brazil	Canada	China	France	Germany	India	Italy	Japan	Rep. of Korea	Russia	United Kingdom	United States	World Total
1992	377.1	420.4	1,253.8	730.5	1,457.1	414.3	660.0	2,271.6	397.0	1,242.0	550.0	4,616.9	18,529.5
1993	378.9	492.5	1,339.9	667.2	1,150.7	475.3	554.0	2,138.3	524.8	657.0	540.0	4,877.1	18,122.6
1994	414.1	559.0	1,500.1	736.3	1,370.3	475.0	660.0	2,344.8	603.9	470.0	570.0	5,407.1	19,670.8
1995	500.6	611.9	1,941.6	743.8	1,491.3	581.0	665.4	2,335.6	675.4	476.0	620.0	5,054.8	20,480.9
1996	497.0	619.9	2,135.3	671.7	1,355.4	584.8	585.1	2,392.6	674.3	443.8	571.0	5,348.0	20,596.4
1997	478.6	628.2	2,260.3	724.2	1,558.4	553.4	671.0	2,434.3	666.3	469.2	583.0	5,390.0	21,721.8
1998	521.4	720.6	2,425.4	733.8	1,519.0	566.5	675.4	2,082.0	505.7	489.2	579.0	5,813.6	21,797.2
1999	463.1	777.2	2,925.9	774.2	1,438.6	569.5	735.3	2,112.3	814.0	562.8	496.8	6,203.3	23,323.0
2000	513.8	798.7	3,499.1	780.4	1,490.3	602.4	780.3	2,224.9	822.6	748.4	575.5	6,079.5	24,811.4
2001[1]	550.8	759.6	3,545.4	772.9	1,590.9	558.0	770.4	2,014.0	849.6	786.2	433.3	5,117.0	23,612.8

[1] Preliminary.   *Source: American Metal Market (AMM)*

Salient Statistics of Recycling Aluminum in the United States

Year	Percent Recycled	New Scrap[1]	Old Scrap[2]	Recycled Metal[3]	Apparent Supply	New Scrap[1]	Old Scrap[2]	Recycled Metal[3]	Apparent Supply
		In Thousands of Metric Tons				Value in Millions of Dollars			
1999	37	2,120	1,570	3,700	9,890	3,070	2,280	5,350	14,300
2000	36	2,080	1,370	3,450	9,610	3,420	2,260	5,670	15,800
2001	37	1,760	1,210	2,970	7,990	2,670	1,830	4,500	12,100
2002	36	1,750	1,170	2,930	8,070	2,510	1,680	4,190	11,500
2003	32	1,750	1,070	2,820	8,870	2,620	1,610	4,230	13,300
2004	33	1,870	1,160	3,030	9,080	3,460	2,140	5,600	16,800
2005	33	1,950	1,080	3,030	9,220	3,910	2,160	6,070	18,500
2006	39	2,290	1,260	3,540	8,190	6,160	3,380	9,540	22,000
2007	47	2,250	1,540	3,790	7,990	6,110	4,170	10,300	21,700
2008	48	1,960	1,370	3,330	6,900	5,240	3,650	8,890	18,500

[1] Scrap that results from the manufacturing process.   [2] Scrap that results from consumer products.   [3] Metal recovered from new plus old scrap.
Source: U.S. Geological Survey (USGS)

Producer Prices for Aluminum Used Beverage Can Scrap   In Cents Per Pound

Year	Jan.	Feb.	Mar.	Apr.	May	June	July	Aug.	Sept.	Oct.	Nov.	Dec.	Average
2001	54.26	55.50	55.45	54.50	54.23	50.79	46.93	45.50	45.50	44.63	44.50	44.50	49.71
2002	44.50	44.66	47.21	49.41	48.68	48.50	46.89	45.06	46.36	47.07	49.76	50.29	47.37
2003	50.50	52.30	52.45	49.43	50.17	49.75	49.22	49.83	47.43	50.17	52.00	53.73	50.58
2004	57.44	61.64	61.65	63.00	57.85	60.00	62.23	60.57	59.48	62.07	61.45	63.81	60.93
2005	64.80	65.79	71.91	71.40	64.75	62.23	60.05	62.96	60.40	61.76	65.25	72.90	65.35
2006	81.03	85.76	85.13	91.08	99.41	83.50	83.40	82.74	80.70	79.66	83.90	85.00	85.11
2007	89.05	89.58	90.18	93.14	93.16	87.86	85.90	80.39	76.37	79.57	82.98	79.68	85.66
2008	82.81	90.35	100.19	100.09	97.52	98.88	98.75	88.83	79.38	63.43	55.67	46.33	83.52
2009	43.70	41.42	41.91	44.00	46.80	50.64	54.27	61.62	58.00	61.43	64.42	71.16	53.28
2010	73.95	68.05	75.48	78.77	69.10	65.77	67.43	72.45	74.76	82.57	79.38	82.26	74.16

Source: American Metal Market (AMM)

ALUMINUM

Average Price of Cast Aluminum Scrap (Crank Cases) in Chicago[1]   In Cents Per Pound

Year	Jan.	Feb.	Mar.	Apr.	May	June	July	Aug.	Sept.	Oct.	Nov.	Dec.	Average
2001	31.00	31.00	31.00	31.00	31.00	31.00	28.29	28.00	28.00	28.00	26.40	26.00	29.25
2002	26.00	27.47	28.95	30.00	30.00	30.00	30.00	29.64	28.00	28.00	28.00	28.00	28.67
2003	28.10	30.00	30.00	29.00	29.00	27.90	26.68	26.00	26.00	26.00	26.00	26.00	27.56
2004	30.00	31.26	36.00	36.00	33.00	29.00	29.00	29.00	29.00	29.00	29.00	29.00	30.77
2005	29.00	29.00	31.61	33.00	31.33	28.00	28.00	28.00	28.00	28.00	28.00	39.71	30.14
2006	42.50	42.50	43.80	47.50	47.50	55.91	46.48	45.46	44.50	46.45	51.15	51.10	47.07
2007	52.50	52.50	54.00	55.50	55.50	53.07	52.50	52.50	51.34	50.50	50.50	50.50	52.58
2008	50.50	52.00	58.50	62.09	60.12	57.50	60.00	60.60	53.69	35.76	26.94	18.45	49.68
2009	17.50	17.50	22.27	22.50	22.50	22.50	24.55	27.50	37.50	37.50	37.50	42.24	27.63
2010	45.39	47.50	48.80	55.23	51.50	43.41	42.50	47.27	47.50	51.31	52.50	47.50	48.37

[1] Dealer buying prices.   Source: American Metal Market (AMM)

Aluminum Exports of Crude Metal and Alloys from the United States   In Thousands of Metric Tons

Year	Jan.	Feb.	Mar.	Apr.	May	June	July	Aug.	Sept.	Oct.	Nov.	Dec.	Total
2001	19.6	16.1	18.9	14.7	16.8	15.6	12.4	14.5	12.6	18.9	16.7	15.1	191.9
2002	17.1	15.2	15.6	16.4	19.4	18.3	15.0	15.5	17.5	19.8	19.4	16.4	205.6
2003	14.3	14.8	14.5	16.9	17.0	17.8	16.5	20.4	18.7	22.9	20.4	19.7	213.9
2004	18.2	20.8	24.3	25.2	25.1	27.6	23.7	23.0	28.3	26.9	28.0	27.4	298.5
2005	26.5	23.4	24.3	27.0	28.9	29.6	25.9	33.1	27.2	29.5	29.6	23.9	328.9
2006	40.0	26.0	30.5	29.4	38.8	25.3	23.7	32.0	26.1	25.8	27.0	22.0	346.6
2007	32.1	27.1	27.0	28.6	33.8	31.1	26.4	30.3	28.5	29.9	29.6	24.5	348.9
2008	30.8	26.8	26.4	30.4	28.4	27.6	25.9	26.4	27.4	25.3	17.3	15.6	308.3
2009	15.9	15.9	12.7	14.8	24.7	24.9	24.6	24.7	24.4	28.0	26.4	25.1	262.1
2010[1]	20.2	22.0	22.4	16.8	20.5	25.6	22.8	24.5	35.2				280.0

[1] Preliminary.   Source: U.S. Geological Survey (USGS)

Aluminum General Imports of Crude Metal and Alloys into the United States   In Thousands of Metric Tons

Year	Jan.	Feb.	Mar.	Apr.	May	June	July	Aug.	Sept.	Oct.	Nov.	Dec.	Total
2001	193.0	200.0	237.0	197.0	209.0	179.0	201.0	198.0	252.0	220.0	248.0	227.0	2,561.0
2002	272.0	205.0	223.0	221.0	221.0	263.0	228.0	279.0	235.0	196.0	264.0	186.0	2,793.0
2003	215.0	246.0	350.0	202.0	265.0	261.0	233.0	194.0	215.0	210.0	233.0	243.0	2,867.0
2004	211.0	288.0	248.0	254.0	282.0	309.0	297.0	225.0	279.0	286.0	272.0	294.0	3,245.0
2005	334.0	289.0	262.0	372.0	372.0	324.0	324.0	264.0	282.0	298.0	240.0	299.0	3,660.0
2006	348.0	247.0	289.0	353.0	315.0	298.0	249.0	315.0	289.0	259.0	233.0	241.0	3,436.0
2007	251.0	258.0	238.0	259.0	220.0	254.0	236.0	266.0	268.0	244.0	238.0	215.0	2,947.0
2008	240.0	208.0	247.0	238.0	237.0	263.0	227.0	204.0	229.0	249.0	219.0	233.0	2,794.0
2009	270.0	204.0	333.0	233.0	292.0	200.0	299.0	216.0	212.0	207.0	211.0	217.0	2,894.0
2010[1]	238.0	209.0	230.0	257.0	233.0	232.0	223.0	207.0	224.0				2,737.3

[1] Preliminary.   Source: U.S. Geological Survey (USGS)

Average Open Interest of Aluminum Futures in New York   In Contracts

Year	Jan.	Feb.	Mar.	Apr.	May	June	July	Aug.	Sept.	Oct.	Nov.	Dec.
2002	3,277	2,744	2,738	2,250	2,397	2,902	3,903	4,618	4,643	5,139	8,057	10,479
2003	9,573	9,163	6,960	7,190	7,686	8,529	8,402	8,445	7,655	7,283	8,434	9,427
2004	8,815	7,384	9,666	10,575	10,363	10,370	9,626	10,287	10,292	10,035	9,706	8,879
2005	8,183	8,487	7,464	6,612	5,654	5,061	4,359	3,223	3,225	2,676	2,232	1,670
2006	1,066	708	482	1,110	948	816	1,068	1,125	1,116	865	994	950
2007	608	614	491	450	415	368	329	276	237	194	156	132
2008	0	0	0	0	0	0	0	0	0	0	0	0

Source: CME Group; New York Mercantile Exchange (NYMEX)

Volume of Trading of Aluminum Futures in New York   In Contracts

Year	Jan.	Feb.	Mar.	Apr.	May	June	July	Aug.	Sept.	Oct.	Nov.	Dec.	Total
2002	2,774	4,635	4,924	2,593	5,388	5,389	8,953	4,194	2,571	7,328	16,185	9,066	74,000
2003	12,565	9,625	8,163	5,440	10,567	8,463	11,797	9,451	5,119	6,222	8,536	11,542	107,490
2004	9,425	9,621	9,548	9,770	5,438	5,453	5,280	2,063	5,533	4,822	2,525	2,691	72,169
2005	5,294	2,829	3,244	2,627	2,613	1,832	1,247	902	1,625	623	3,135	2,520	28,491
2006	633	245	1,343	1,558	210	471	1,046	1,546	662	323	842	270	9,149
2007	94	332	82	28	2	56	84	19	25	0	1	0	723
2008	0	0	0	0	0	0	0	0	0	0	0	0	

Source: CME Group; New York Mercantile Exchange (NYMEX)

Antimony

Antimony (symbol Sb) is a lustrous, extremely brittle and hard crystalline semi-metal that is silvery white in its most common allotropic form. Antimony is a poor conductor of heat and electricity. In nature, antimony has a strong affinity for sulfur and for such metals as lead, silver, and copper. Antimony is primarily a byproduct of the mining, smelting and refining of lead, silver, and copper ores. There is no longer any mine production of antimony in the U.S.

The most common use of antimony is in antimony trioxide, a chemical that is used as a flame retardant in textiles, plastics, adhesives and building materials. Antimony trioxide is also used in battery components, ceramics, bearings, chemicals, glass, and ammunition.

Prices – Antimony prices in 2010 rose by 62.6% to a new record high of 410.5 cents per pound. Antimony prices in 2010 were more than six times the 34-year low price of 66.05 cents per pound posted as recently as 1999. Bullish factors included stronger U.S. and global economic growth in 2010, the weak dollar, and tight supplies. The price continued to rise into 2011 to reach 609.3 cents per pound in January.

Supply – World mine production of antimony in 2010 fell by -12.9% to 135,000 metric tons, farther down from the 2008 record high of 182,000 metric tons. China accounted for 89% of world antimony production in 2010. After China, the only significant producers were Bolivia (2.0% of world production) and South Africa (2.0%). U.S. secondary production of antimony in 2009 fell by -5.0% yr/yr to 3,020 metric tons.

Demand – U.S. industrial consumption of antimony in 2009 (latest data available) fell -16.8% to 6.770 metric tons. Of the consumption in the U.S. in 2008, 36% was used for non-metal products, 35% was used for flame-retardants, and 30% was used for metal products.

Trade –The total U.S. gross weight of imports of antimony ore in 2009 (latest data available) fell by -6.3% to 268 metric tons. The antimony content of that ore rose by +1.8% to 167 metric tons. The gross weight of U.S. imports of antimony oxide in 2009 fell by -30.2% to 18,300 metric tons. U.S. exports of antimony oxide in 2009 fell by -6.4% to 2,060 metric tons.

World Mine Production of Antimony (Content of Ore)　In Metric Tons

Year	Australia	Bolivia	Canada	China[2]	Guatemala	Kyrgyzstan	Mexico[3]	Peru[4]	Russia	South Africa	Thailand	Turkey	World Total
2007	1,010	3,881	162	163,000	1,000	10	----	590	3,500	3,354	----	1,200	180,000
2008	1,500	3,905	97	166,000	----	10	----	531	3,500	3,370	----	1,300	182,000
2009[1]	1,000	3,000	56	140,000	----	10	----	530	3,500	2,800	----	1,700	155,000
2010[2]		3,000		120,000					3,000	3,000			135,000

[1] Preliminary.　[2] Estimate.　[3] Includes antimony content of miscellaneous smelter products.　[4] Recoverable.
Source: U.S. Geological Survey (USGS)

Salient Statistics of Antimony in the United States　In Metric Tons

Year	Avg. Price Cents/lb. C.i.F. U.S. Ports	Production[3] Primary[2] Mine	Primary[2] Smelter	Secondary (Alloys)[2]	Imports for Consumption Ore Gross Weight	Ore Antimony Content	Oxide (Gross Weight)	Exports (Oxide)	Industry Stocks, December 31[3] Metallic	Oxide	Sulfide	Other	Total
2006	238.0	----	W	3,520	205	153	27,700	1,680	421	1,690	W	15	2,120
2007	257.3	W	W	3,480	313	226	26,100	1,980	470	1,410	W	18	1,900
2008[1]	279.5	----	W	3,180	286	164	26,200	2,200	217	916	W	357	1,490
2009[2]	235.6	----	W	3,020	268	167	18,300	2,060	154	899	W	363	1,420

[1] Preliminary.　[2] Estimate.　[3] Antimony content.　[4] Including primary antimony residues & slag.　W = Withheld proprietary data.
Source: U.S. Geological Survey (USGS)

Industrial Consumption of Primary Antimony in the United States　In Metric Tons (Antimony Content)

Year	Metal Products Ammunition	Antimonial Lead[3]	Sheet & Pipe[4]	Bearing Metal & Bearings	Solder	Products	Flame Retardants Plastics	Total	Non-Metal Products Ceramics & Glass	Pigments	Plastics	Total	Grand Total
2006	W	W	W	20	61	3,000	2,810	3,810	258	215	W	3,600	10,400
2007	W	W	W	21	71	2,520	2,710	3,580	231	329	W	3,500	9,590
2008	W	W	W	18	54	1,690	2,290	3,190	259	448	W	2,680	8,140
2009[1]	W	W	W	14	44	2,000	1,830	2,340	W	403	W	2,430	6,770

[1] Preliminary.　[2] Estimated coverage based on 77% of the industry.　W = Withheld proprietary data.　*Source: U.S. Geological Survey (USGS)*

Average Price of Antimony[1] in the United States　In Cents Per Pound

Year	Jan.	Feb.	Mar.	Apr.	May	June	July	Aug.	Sept.	Oct.	Nov.	Dec.	Average
2007	252.88	252.88	252.26	251.75	251.75	250.42	249.74	258.55	254.24	255.39	258.24	258.55	253.89
2008	257.27	275.29	281.23	281.23	287.42	292.57	294.84	294.84	294.84	294.84	294.84	294.84	287.00
2009	294.84	294.84	202.98	198.35	200.77	212.06	235.57	265.46	276.69	278.14	292.57	277.04	252.44
2010	286.41	299.37	303.07	378.70	417.80	392.26	406.90	440.56	470.86	476.28	505.76	547.72	410.47

[1] Prices are for antimony metal (99.65%) merchants, minimum 18-ton containers, c.i.f. U.S. Ports.　*Source: American Metal Market (AMM)*

Apples

The apple tree is the common name of trees from the rose family, Rosaceae, and the fruit that comes from them. The apple tree is a deciduous plant and grows mainly in the temperate areas of the world. The apple tree is believed to have originated in the Caspian and Black Sea area. Apples were the favorite fruit of the ancient Greeks and Romans. The early settlers brought apple seeds with them and introduced them to America. John Champman, also known as Johnny Appleseed, was responsible for extensive planting of apple trees in the Midwestern United States.

Prices – The average monthly price of apples received by growers in the U.S. in 2010 rose by +25.4% yr/yr to 31.2 cents per pound.

Supply – World apple production in the 2010-11 marketing year fell -5.5% yr/yr to 59.207 million metric tons. The world's largest apple producers in 2010-11 were China (with 50.7% of world production), the European Union (18.8%), the U.S. (7.1%), and Turkey (4.2%). U.S. apple production in 2010-11 fell -4.2% to 4.219, down from the 7-year high of 4.686 million metric tons in 2004-05 and far above the 2-decade low of 3.798 million metric tons posted in 2002-03.

Demand – The utilization breakdown of the 2009 apple crop showed that 66.0% of apples were for fresh consumption, 34.0% for canning, 14.7% for juice and cider, 2.5% for frozen apples, and 2.1% for dried apples. U.S. per capita apple consumption in 2009 was 16.4 pounds.

World Production of Apples[3], Fresh (Dessert & Cooking) — In Thousands of Metric Tons

Year	Argentina	Canada	Chile	China	European Union	Japan	Mexico	New Zealand	Russia	South Africa	Turkey	United States	World Total
2005-06	1,051	414	1,240	20,400	----	819	587	400	1,563	638	2,570	4,340	42,409
2006-07	1,047	403	1,250	26,059	11,134	832	510	425	1,250	710	2,000	4,414	54,417
2007-08	980	446	1,350	24,800	10,295	840	505	436	1,300	749	2,458	4,103	53,173
2008-09	933	427	1,280	29,800	12,655	911	512	457	1,115	809	2,600	4,327	60,807
2009-10[1]	830	413	1,370	31,681	12,211	892	561	421	1,230	750	2,750	4,404	62,658
2010-11[2]	990	405	1,315	30,000	11,114	810	540	471	1,000	800	2,500	4,220	59,207

[1] Preliminary. [2] Estimate. NA = Not available. *Source: Foreign Agricultural Service, U.S. Department of Agriculture (FAS-USDA)*

Salient Statistics of Apples[2] in the United States

Year	Production Total	Production Utilized	Growers Prices Fresh Cents/lb.	Growers Prices Processing $/ton	Fresh	Canned	Dried	Frozen	Juice & Cider	Other[3]	Avg. Farm Price Cents/lb.	Farm Value Million $	Exports Fresh	Imports Fresh Dried[5] & Dried[5]	Imports Fresh Dried[5] & Dried[5]	Fresh Per Capita Consumption Lbs.
2004	10,412	10,333	18.2	107.0	6,619	3,714	201	256	1,870	78	13.6	1,405.9	638.9	32.5	155.1	18.8
2005	9,667	9,567	24.2	106.0	6,097	3,470	191	259	1,695	64	17.3	1,675.1	654.1	27.4	198.5	16.7
2006	9,823	9,730	31.6	129.0	6,309	3,422	253	272	1,550	61	22.7	2,213.2	652.8	32.9	255.3	17.7
2007	9,089	9,045	38.3	190.0	6,077	2,968	204	258	1,257	60	28.8	2,608.2	681.1	31.7	238.4	16.4
2008	9,633	9,540	30.1	198.0	6,274	3,266	213	211	1,349	112	23.2	2,599.5	780.9		164.9	15.9
2009[1]	9,915	9,708	31.8	127.0	6,404	3,304	206	241	1,429	65	23.1	2,246.6	808.3		165.3	16.4

[1] Preliminary.   [2] Commercial crop.   [3] Mostly crushed for vinegar, jam, etc.   [4] Year beginning July.   [5] Fresh weight basis.
NA = Not available.   Source: Economic Research Service, U.S. Department of Agriculture (ERS-USDA)

Price of Apples Received by Growers (for Fresh Use) in the United States — In Cents Per Pound

Year	Jan.	Feb.	Mar.	Apr.	May	June	July	Aug.	Sept.	Oct.	Nov.	Dec.	Average
2005	21.6	20.3	18.4	17.3	17.4	16.2	15.7	21.1	30.9	28.8	29.4	25.8	21.9
2006	21.7	20.6	19.8	19.3	18.9	22.9	42.3	35.9	42.0	36.2	36.1	31.0	28.9
2007	29.9	29.7	29.2	28.1	26.9	29.6	30.6	34.4	40.2	37.9	40.3	35.0	32.7
2008	35.5	34.8	34.4	33.8	36.2	41.2	44.6	53.7	50.6	42.5	36.0	29.3	39.4
2009	27.2	23.7	21.5	20.4	18.7	18.1	17.2	23.8	35.7	31.2	33.3	27.5	24.9
2010[1]	29.0	28.9	29.5	30.0	31.8	30.8	30.4	31.7	34.9	34.9	32.1	29.5	31.1

[1] Preliminary.   *Source: Economic Research Service, U.S. Department of Agriculture (ERS-USDA)*

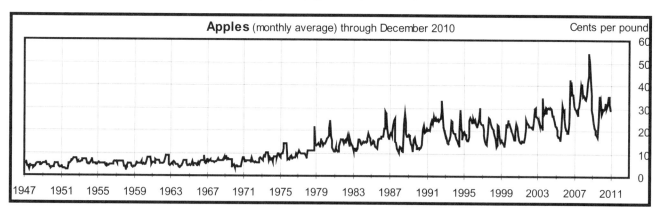

Apples (monthly average) through December 2010 — Cents per pound

Arsenic

Arsenic (symbol As) is a silver-gray, extremely poisonous, semi-metallic element. Arsenic, which is odorless and flavorless, has been known since ancient times, but it wasn't until the Middle Ages that its poisonous characteristics first became known. Metallic arsenic was first produced in the 17th century by heating arsenic with potash and soap. Arsenic is rarely found in nature in its elemental form and is generally recovered as a by-product of ore processing. Recently, small doses of arsenic have been found to put some forms of cancer into remission. It can also help thin blood. Homoeopathists have successfully used undetectable amounts of arsenic to cure stomach cramps.

The U.S. does not produce any arsenic and instead imports all its consumption needs for arsenic metals and compounds. More than 95 percent of the arsenic consumed in the U.S. is in compound form, mostly as arsenic trioxide, which in turn is converted into arsenic acid. Production of chromated copper arsenate, a wood preservative, accounts for about 90% of the domestic consumption of arsenic trioxide. Three companies in the U.S. manufacture chromate copper arsenate. Another company used arsenic acid to produce an arsenical herbicide. Arsenic metal is used to produce nonferrous alloys, primarily for lead-acid batteries.

One area where there is increased consumption of arsenic is in the semiconductor industry. Very high-purity arsenic is used in the production of gallium arsenide. High speed and high frequency integrated circuits that use gallium arsenide have better signal reception and lower power consumption. An estimated 30 metric tons per year of high-purity arsenic is used in the production of semiconductor materials.

In the early 2000's, as much as 88% of U.S. arsenic production was used for wood preservative treatments, so the demand for arsenic was closely tied to new home construction, home renovation, and deck construction. However, the total demand for arsenic in 2004 dropped by 69% from 2003, and due to arsenic's toxicity and tighter environmental regulation; only 65% of that much smaller amount was used for wood preservative treatments. Since then the specific percentage used for wood preservative treatments is no longer available.

Supply –World production of white arsenic (arsenic trioxide) in 2010 rose by 0.2% to 54,500 metric tons. The world's largest producer is China with about 46% of world production, followed by Chile with 21% of world production, Peru with 8%, Russia with 3%, and Mexico with 2%. China's production of arsenic was fairly constant at about 40,000 metric tons per year but that has dropped to about 25,000 to 30,000 in the last five years. The U.S. supply of arsenic in 2010 rose by +15.3% to 5,880 metric tons, up from 3009's 32-year low of 5,098 metric tons.

Demand – U.S. demand for arsenic in 2010 rose by 16.0% to 5,500 metric tons, up from the 2008 record low of 4,130 metric tons. The use for arsenic is no longer available but in 2004 (latest data) about 65% was for wood preservatives, 10% was for non-ferrous alloys and electric usage, 10% was for glass, and 3% was for other uses.

Trade – U.S. imports of trioxide arsenic in 2009 (latest data available) fell by -3.0% to a record low of 6,130 metric tons from 12,400 metric tons in 2006. U.S. exports of trioxide arsenic in 2010 rose by +10.2% to 390 metric tons, but still down from the record high of 3,270 metric tons in 2005.

World Production of White Arsenic (Arsenic Trioxide)   In Metric Tons

Year	Belgium	Bolivia	Canada[4]	Chile	China	France	Germany	Mexico	Namibia[3]	Peru	Philip-pines	Russia	World Total
2003	1,000	276	250	11,600	40,000	----	----	1,729	----	4,640	----	1,500	69,700
2004	1,000	168	250	11,500	30,000	----	----	1,829	----	3,037	----	1,500	57,800
2005	1,000	120	250	11,700	30,000	----	----	1,664	----	3,150	----	1,500	60,000
2006	1,000	90	250	11,700	30,000	----	----	1,595	----	4,399	----	1,500	61,100
2007	1,000	----	250	11,400	25,000	----	----	1,600	----	4,321	----	1,500	55,700
2008	1,000	74	250	10,000	25,000	----	----	513	----	4,822	----	1,500	53,600
2009[1]	1,000	100	250	11,000	25,000	----	----	500	----	4,850	----	1,500	54,400
2010[2]	1,000			11,500	25,000	----	----	1,000	----	4,500	----	1,500	54,500

[1] Preliminary. [2] Estimate. [3] Output of Tsumeb Corp. Ltd. only. [4] Includes low-grade dusts that were exported to the U.S. for further refining.
Source: U.S. Geological Survey (USGS)

Salient Statistics of Arsenic in the United States   (In Metric Tons -- Arsenic Content)

	Supply		Distribution			Estimated Demand Pattern							Average Price			
	Imports		Industry Stocks Jan. 1	Total	Apparent Demand	Industry Stocks Dec. 31	Agricultural Chemicals	Glass	Wood Preservatives	Non-Ferrous Alloys & Electric	Other	Total	Trioxide Mexican -- Cents/Pound --	Metal Chinese	Imports Trioxide[3]	Exports
Year	Metal	Compounds														
2003	990	20,800	----	21,790	21,600	----	----	660	19,200	660	200	21,600	34	87	27,300	173
2004	872	6,150	----	7,022	6,800	----	----	650	4,450	650	200	6,800	32	88	8,090	220
2005	812	8,330	----	9,142	5,870	----	----	NA	NA	NA	NA	5,870	67	95	11,000	3,270
2006	1,070	9,430	----	10,500	7,450	----	----	----	----	----	----	7,450	NA	62	12,400	3,060
2007	759	7,010	----	7,769	5,280	----	----	----	----	----	----	5,280	----	122	9,220	2,490
2008	376	4,810	----	5,186	4,130	----	----	----	----	----	----	4,130	----	125	6,320	1,050
2009[1]	438	4,660	----	5,098	4,740	----	----	----	----	----	----	4,740	----	121	6,130	354
2010[2]	980	4,900	----	5,880	5,500	----	----	----	----	----	----	5,500	----	120		390

[1] Preliminary. [2] Estimate. [3] For Consumption. *Source: U.S. Geological Survey (USGS)*

Barley

Barley is the common name for the genus of cereal grass and is native to Asia and Ethiopia. Barley is an ancient crop and was grown by the Egyptians, Greek, Romans and Chinese. Barley is now the world's fourth largest grain crop, after wheat, rice, and corn. Barley is planted in the spring in most of Europe, Canada and the United States. The U.S. barley crop year begins June 1. It is planted in the autumn in parts of California, Arizona and along the Mediterranean Sea. Barley is hardy and drought resistant and can be grown on marginal cropland. Salt-resistant strains are being developed for use in coastal regions. Barley grain, along with hay, straw, and several by-products are used for animal feed. Barley is used for malt beverages and in cooking. Barley, like other cereals, contains a large proportion of carbohydrate (67%) and protein (12.8%). Barley futures are traded on ICE Futures Canada (ICE), the NYSE-LIFFE – Paris, the Budapest Stock Exchange (BSE), the Multi Commodity Exchange of India (MCX), and the National Commodity & Derivatives Exchange of India.

Prices – The monthly average price for all barley received by U.S. farmers in the 2010-11 marketing year (through January 20010) fell by -17.3% yr/yr to $3.78 per bushel.

Supply – World barley production in the 2010-11 marketing year fell -3.1% yr/yr to 149.183 million metric tons. The world's largest barley crop of 179.038 million metric tons occurred in 1990-91. The world's largest barley producers are the European Union with 42.8% of world production in 2010-11, Australia (7.9), Ukraine (6.8%), Russia (6.7%), Canada (6.1%), Turkey (4.7%), and the U.S. (3.1%).

U.S. barley production in the 2010-11 marketing year fell by -20.7% yr/yr to 180.268 million bushels and that is less than 40% of the record U.S. barley crop of 608.532 million bushels seen in 1986-87. U.S. farmers harvested -20.8% yr/yr fewer acres in 2010-11 at 2.465 million acres, not much less than the 2006-07 level of 2.951 million acres which was the lowest acreage since 1885. Barley yield in 2010-11 rose +0.1% yr/yr to a record high yield of 73.1 bushels per acre. Ending stocks for the 2010-11 marketing year fell -20.9% to 91.00 million bushels which is not below the 11-year high of 128.4 million bushels in 2004-05.

Demand – U.S. total barley disappearance in 2010-11 fell -0.9% yr/yr to 215.0 million bushels. About 74.0% of barley is used for food and alcoholic beverages, 20.9% for animal feed, and 2.9% for seed.

Trade – World exports of barley in 2010-11 fell by -1.8% yr/yr to 16.808 million metric tons. The largest world exporters of barley in 2010-11 were Australia with 28.0% of world exports, the European Union with 27.4%, Canada with 7.7%, and the U.S. with only 1.3%. The single largest importer of barley is Saudi Arabia with 7.300 million metric tons of imports in 2010-11, which is about 44.5% of total world imports.

World Barley Supply and Demand   In Thousands of Metric Tons

Year	Exports						Imports			Utilization			Ending Stocks		
	Australia	Canada	European Union	Total Non-US	United States	Total	Saudi Arabia	Unaccounte	Total	Russia	United States	Total	Canada	United States	Total
2001-02	4,676	1,149	4,188	16,733	575	17,308	6,000	489	16,800	14,250	5,661	136,254	2,047	2,006	29,233
2002-03	1,984	403	5,234	15,583	659	16,242	7,200	225	17,000	15,500	5,179	136,974	1,475	1,510	27,384
2003-04	6,398	1,839	2,641	15,969	409	16,378	7,000	444	15,391	18,600	4,990	145,330	2,102	2,619	23,327
2004-05	4,261	1,167	3,262	14,588	506	15,094	5,800	530	16,115	16,500	5,672	143,603	3,435	2,796	32,961
2005-06	5,267	2,257	3,311	17,678	606	18,284	7,100	660	17,544	15,500	4,570	140,375	3,289	2,350	28,057
2006-07	1,851	1,224	3,476	14,987	441	15,428	6,700	350	14,999	16,400	4,596	142,790	1,491	1,500	21,285
2007-08	3,386	3,046	3,803	14,580	902	15,482	7,400	455	15,766	15,050	4,324	134,308	1,568	1,485	20,132
2008-09	3,234	1,483	3,597	19,748	288	20,036	7,200		19,328	17,100	5,127	143,967	2,843	1,932	31,056
2009-10[1]	3,915	1,309	1,134	16,998	123	17,121	7,500		17,198	16,800	4,604	144,182	2,583	2,515	36,554
2010-11[2]	4,700	1,300	4,600	16,590	218	16,808	7,300		16,415	9,800	4,464	138,792	1,338	1,976	22,030

[1] Preliminary.   [2] Estimate.   *Source: Foreign Agricultural Service, U.S. Department of Agriculture (FAS-USDA)*

World Production of Barley   In Thousands of Metric Tons

Year	Australia	Belarus	Canada	China	European Union	India	Iran	Kazakhstan	Russia	Turkey	Ukraine	United States	World Total
2001-02	8,280	1,700	10,846	2,893	58,767	1,432	2,423	2,244	19,500	6,900	10,186	5,407	143,459
2002-03	3,865	1,681	7,489	3,322	58,168	1,500	3,085	2,209	18,700	7,200	10,364	4,940	134,367
2003-04	10,387	1,800	12,164	2,717	55,818	1,410	2,908	2,154	18,000	6,900	6,850	6,059	142,260
2004-05	7,740	2,000	12,557	3,222	64,085	1,300	2,940	1,388	17,200	7,400	11,100	6,091	152,216
2005-06	9,483	1,800	11,678	3,400	54,752	1,200	2,857	1,528	15,800	7,600	9,000	4,613	136,211
2006-07	4,257	1,350	9,573	3,115	56,220	1,220	2,956	1,953	18,100	7,500	11,350	3,923	136,447
2007-08	7,160	1,700	10,984	2,785	57,545	1,330	3,000	2,441	15,650	6,000	6,000	4,575	132,871
2008-09	7,997	2,200	11,781	2,823	65,509	1,200	2,000	2,059	23,100	5,700	12,600	5,230	155,599
2009-10[1]	7,909	1,650	9,517	2,500	61,980	1,690	2,600	2,519	17,900	6,500	11,800	4,949	149,603
2010-11[2]	9,800	1,400	7,605	2,400	53,398	1,300	3,100	1,300	8,300	5,900	8,500	3,925	124,661

[1] Preliminary.   [2] Estimate.   *Source: Foreign Agricultural Service, U.S. Department of Agriculture (FAS-USDA)*

Barley Acreage and Prices in the United States

Crop Year Beginning June 1	Acreage 1,000 Acres Planted	Acreage 1,000 Acres Harvested for Gain	Yield Per Harvested Acre Bushels	Seasonal Prices — Received by Farmers[3] — Dollars per Bushel — All	Feed[4]	Malting[4]	Portland No. 2 Western	National Average Loan Rate	Target Price	Government Price Support Operations Put Under Support (mil. Bu.)	Percent of Production
2003-04	5,348	4,727	58.9	2.90	2.27	3.07	2.74	1.88	2.21	17.9	6.4
2004-05	4,527	4,021	69.6	2.46	1.76	2.79	2.39	1.85	2.24	8.3	3.0
2005-06	3,875	3,269	64.8	2.54	1.89	2.80	2.44	1.85	2.24	12.0	5.7
2006-07	3,452	2,951	61.0	2.90	2.72	2.98	4.08	1.85	2.24	9.3	5.2
2007-08	4,018	3,502	60.0	4.14	4.42	4.00	5.71	1.85	2.24		
2008-09	4,246	3,779	63.6	5.23	3.61	5.56	5.29				
2009-10[1]	3,567	3,113	73.0	4.57	2.62	4.95	NQ				
2010-11[2]	2,872	2,465	73.1	3.82	3.04	4.08					

[1] Preliminary.   [2] Estimate.   [3] Excludes support payments.   *Source: Economic Research Service, U.S. Department of Agriculture (ERS-USDA)*

Salient Statistics of Barley in the United States   In Millions of Bushels

Crop Year Beginning June 1	Supply Beginning Stocks	Production	Imports	Total Supply	Disappearance — Domestic Use — Food & Alcohol Beverage	Seed	Feed & Residual	Total	Exports	Total Disappearance	Ending Stocks Gov't Owned	Privately Owned	Total Stocks
2003-04	69.3	278.3	20.6	368.3	147.5	7.4	74.3	229.2	18.8	247.9	0	120.3	120.3
2004-05	120.3	279.7	12.1	412.2	151.3	6.4	103.3	260.5	23.3	283.8	0	128.4	128.4
2005-06	128.4	211.9	5.4	345.7	152.2	5.7	52.0	209.9	27.8	237.8	0	107.9	107.9
2006-07	107.9	180.2	12.1	300.2	149.0	6.6	55.5	211.1	20.3	231.3	0	68.9	68.9
2007-08	68.9	210.1	29.2	308.2	161.6	7.0	30.0	198.6	41.4	240.0	0	68.2	68.2
2008-09	68.2	240.2	29.0	337.4	163.0	5.9	66.6	235.5	13.2	248.7	0	88.7	88.7
2009-10[1]	88.7	227.3	17.0	333.0	158.7	6.3	48.0	212.0	6.0	217.0	0	115.0	115.0
2010-11[2]	115.0	180.3	10.0	306.0	159.0	6.3	45.0	205.0	10.0	215.0	0	91.0	91.0

[1] Preliminary.   [2] Estimate.   [3] Uncommitted inventory.   [4] Includes quantity under loan & farmer-owned reserve.   [5] Included in Food & Alcohol.
Source: Economic Research Service, U.S. Department of Agriculture (ERS-USDA)

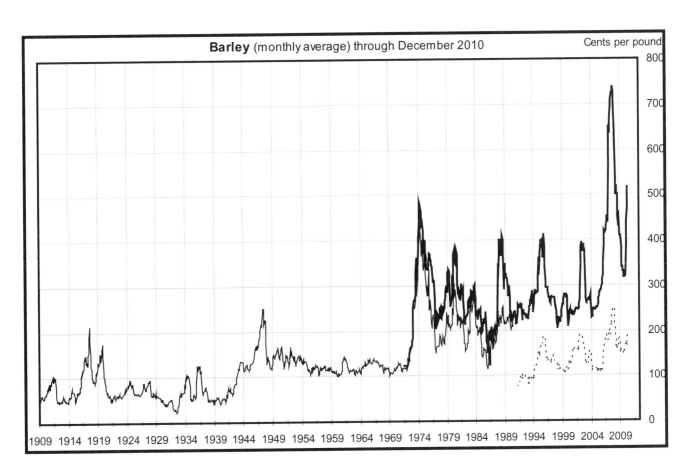

Barley (monthly average) through December 2010 — Cents per pound

BARLEY

Average Price Received by Farmers for All Barley in the United States   In Dollars Per Bushel

Year	June	July	Aug.	Sept.	Oct.	Nov.	Dec.	Jan.	Feb.	Mar.	Apr.	May	Average
2003-04	2.77	2.71	2.70	2.53	2.76	2.92	2.93	3.03	3.09	3.11	3.07	3.12	2.90
2004-05	2.63	2.54	2.77	2.43	2.29	2.45	2.49	2.41	2.31	2.49	2.26	2.46	2.46
2005-06	2.54	2.37	2.50	2.36	2.41	2.58	2.48	2.42	2.55	2.70	2.65	2.97	2.54
2006-07	2.77	2.71	2.70	2.53	2.76	2.92	2.93	3.03	3.09	3.11	3.07	3.12	2.90
2007-08	3.30	3.46	3.55	4.05	4.53	4.31	4.44	4.35	4.38	4.18	4.56	4.52	4.14
2008-09	4.78	5.12	5.46	5.97	5.73	5.44	5.49	5.34	4.99	5.03	4.84	4.59	5.23
2009-10	4.70	5.09	5.17	4.78	4.41	4.46	4.54	4.68	4.53	4.15	4.11	4.25	4.57
2010-11[1]	3.74	3.75	3.68	3.62	3.75	3.82	3.84	3.85	4.36				3.82

[1] Preliminary.   *Source: National Agricultural Statistical Service, U.S. Department of Agriculture (NASS-USDA)*

Average Price Received by Farmers for Feed Barley in the United States   In Dollars Per Bushel

Year	June	July	Aug.	Sept.	Oct.	Nov.	Dec.	Jan.	Feb.	Mar.	Apr.	May	Average
2003-04	2.33	2.22	2.39	2.27	2.24	2.43	2.26	2.15	2.16	2.19	2.17	2.39	2.27
2004-05	2.20	2.21	1.83	1.64	1.58	1.78	1.66	1.65	1.60	1.67	1.56	1.71	1.76
2005-06	1.91	1.88	1.77	1.84	1.81	1.91	1.76	1.94	1.83	1.80	1.81	2.45	1.89
2006-07	2.08	2.04	2.06	2.31	2.68	2.84	2.79	3.11	3.15	3.19	3.20	3.20	2.72
2007-08	3.50	3.27	3.60	4.47	4.89	5.05	4.79	4.89	4.67	4.29	4.67	4.99	4.42
2008-09	5.49	4.72	4.54	4.46	3.82	3.43	3.00	2.90	2.63	2.73	2.65	2.99	3.61
2009-10	3.16	2.94	2.49	2.14	2.29	2.50	2.63	2.63	3.11	2.68	2.40	2.49	2.62
2010-11[1]	2.07	2.50	2.34	2.88	3.35	3.31	3.29	3.43	4.17				3.04

[1] Preliminary.   *Source: National Agricultural Statistical Service, U.S. Department of Agriculture (NASS-USDA)*

Average Open Interest of Western Feed Barley Futures in Winnipeg   In Contracts

Year	Jan.	Feb.	Mar.	Apr.	May	June	July	Aug.	Sept.	Oct.	Nov.	Dec.
2003	8,559	8,203	8,546	9,028	9,631	10,290	10,676	9,580	8,409	7,154	7,524	5,346
2004	6,731	6,881	6,262	9,779	10,497	9,930	9,992	9,743	11,140	11,956	12,786	10,916
2005	9,321	8,164	9,144	9,476	9,475	9,140	6,481	6,880	6,046	5,839	6,538	7,281
2006	8,179	10,505	10,719	12,131	12,543	12,762	12,948	13,680	14,938	16,026	13,803	14,620
2007	16,178	16,769	16,969	15,901	16,351	16,951	13,808	13,941	14,270	15,480	14,337	13,830
2008	14,224	15,626	15,758	14,304	14,394	13,462	12,975	12,052	10,528	9,502	8,462	8,486
2009	7,616	5,100	4,380	3,819	3,216	2,522	3,058	3,398	2,484	1,825	1,478	1,286
2010	973	439	35	21	15	36	22	28	119	74	57	2

Contract size = 20 tonnes.   *Source: ICE Futures Canada (ICE)*

Volume of Trading of Western Feed Barley Futures in Winnipeg   In Contracts

Year	Jan.	Feb.	Mar.	Apr.	May	June	July	Aug.	Sept.	Oct.	Nov.	Dec.	Total
2003	10,555	18,933	13,069	18,879	13,900	15,153	13,293	29,799	19,438	18,937	17,768	10,977	200,701
2004	11,405	16,265	12,784	23,806	13,179	27,081	15,326	14,933	23,072	15,790	22,516	8,478	204,635
2005	15,452	12,171	19,849	9,325	16,469	14,741	4,100	11,815	7,573	12,665	8,452	3,952	136,564
2006	16,241	9,238	23,987	9,361	26,466	8,083	4,294	25,858	14,903	37,489	12,620	6,484	195,024
2007	24,784	10,380	21,229	12,525	21,161	23,044	11,151	20,457	27,030	27,072	11,926	3,913	214,672
2008	20,322	15,642	20,495	13,025	19,547	14,392	5,719	15,473	13,251	14,171	11,529	3,815	167,381
2009	11,518	6,580	5,388	6,579	3,955	3,876	1,887	4,910	3,222	4,064	950	1,910	54,839
2010	1,025	991	104	16	9	62	42	55	141	19	86	32	2,582

Contract size = 20 tonnes.   *Source: ICE Futures Canada (ICE)*

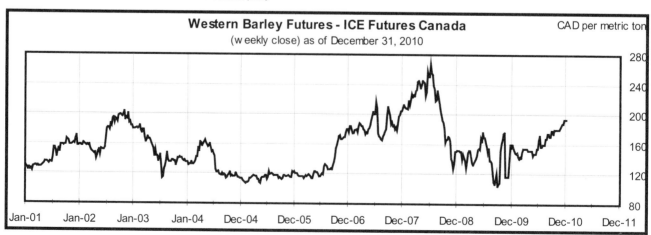

Western Barley Futures - ICE Futures Canada
(weekly close) as of December 31, 2010   CAD per metric ton

Bauxite

Bauxite is a naturally occurring, heterogeneous material comprised of one or more aluminum hydroxide minerals plus various mixtures of silica, iron oxide, titanium, alumina-silicates, and other impurities in trace amounts. Bauxite is an important ore of aluminum and forms by the rapid weathering of granite rocks in warm, humid climates. It is easily purified and can be converted directly into either alum or metallic aluminum. It is a soft mineral with hardness varying from 1 to 3, and specific gravity from 2 to 2.55. Bauxite is dull in appearance and may vary in color from white to brown. It usually occurs in aggregates in pea-sized lumps.

Bauxite is the only raw material used in the production of alumina on a commercial scale in the United States. Bauxite is classified according to the intended commercial application, such as abrasive, cement, chemical, metallurgical, and refractory. Of all the bauxite mined, about 95 percent is converted to alumina for the production of aluminum metal with some smaller amounts going to nonmetal uses as various forms of specialty alumina. Small amounts are used in non-metallurgical bauxite applications. Bauxite is also used to produce aluminum chemicals and is used in the steel industry.

Supply – World production of bauxite in 2010 rose +6.0% yr/yr to 211.000 million metric tons, equaling the 2008 record high. The world's largest producer of bauxite is Australia with 33% of the world's production in 2010, followed by China (19%), Brazil (15%), India (9%), Guinea (8%), and Jamaica (4%). Chinese production of bauxite has quadrupled in the past 10 years. India's bauxite production has also risen rapidly and is more than triple the amount seen 15 years ago.

Demand – U.S. consumption of bauxite in 2009 fell by –30.7% yr/yr to 6.620 million metric tons from 13.600 million metric tons in 2004 which was still well below the record high of 15.962 million metric tons seen in 1980. The alumina industry took 98% of bauxite production in 2009, or 6,480 million metric tons. According to 2004 data (the latest data available) the refractory industry usually takes about 1.4% of the U.S. bauxite supply, the abrasive industry takes about 0.2%, and the chemical industry takes the rest.

Trade – The U.S. relies on imports for almost 100% of its consumption needs. Domestic ore, which provides less than 1 percent of the U.S. requirement for bauxite, is mined by one company from surface mines in the states of Alabama and Georgia. U.S. imports of bauxite fell 33.6% yr/yr to 6.970 million metric tons in 2009, which was well below the record of 14.976 million metric tons seen in 1974. U.S. exports of bauxite in 2009 were negligible at 9,000 metric tons.

World Production of Bauxite   In Thousands of Metric Tons

Year	Australia	Brazil	China	Greece	Guinea	Guyana[3]	Hungary	India	Jamaica[3]	Russia[3]	Sierra Leone	Suriname	Total
2001	53,799	13,032	9,800	2,052	15,100	1,950	1,000	7,864	12,370	4,000	----	4,394	137,000
2002	54,135	13,260	12,000	2,492	15,300	1,690	720	9,647	13,120	4,500	----	4,002	144,000
2003	55,602	17,363	13,000	2,418	15,000	1,846	666	10,414	13,444	5,500	----	4,215	153,000
2004	56,593	20,950	17,000	2,444	15,254	1,506	647	11,285	13,296	6,000	----	4,052	164,000
2005	59,959	22,034	22,000	2,495	16,817	1,694	535	12,385	14,116	5,000	----	4,757	178,000
2006	61,780	23,236	27,000	2,163	18,784	1,479	538	13,940	14,865	6,300	1,071	4,924	193,000
2007	62,398	25,461	30,000	2,126	18,519	2,243	546	20,343	14,568	5,775	1,169	5,054	204,000
2008	61,389	28,098	35,000	2,176	18,400	2,092	511	21,210	14,363	5,675	954	5,200	211,000
2009[1]	65,231	28,200	40,000	2,100	15,600	1,760	317	16,000	7,817	5,775	757	4,000	199,000
2010[2]	70,000	32,100	40,000	2,000	17,400	1,800		18,000	9,200	4,700		3,100	211,000

[1] Preliminary.   [2] Estimate.   [3] Dry Bauxite equivalent of ore processed.   *Source: U.S. Geological Survey (USGS)*

Salient Statistics of Bauxite in the United States   In Thousands of Metric Tons

Year	Net Import Reliance as a % of Apparent Consumption	Average Price F.O.B. Mine $ per Ton	Consumtion by Industry Total	Alumina	Abrasive	Chemical	Re-fractoty	Dry Equivalent Imports[4]	Exports[3]	Consumption	Stocks, December 31 Producers & Consumers	Gov't Owned	Total
2000	100	23	10,800	10,100	111	W	160	8,550	133	10,800	1,300	5,710	7,000
2001	100	23	9,770	9,010	61	W	175	8,300	67	9,770	1,740	2,070	3,810
2002	100	20	9,980	9,290	52	W	115	7,340	27	9,980	1,280	1,770	3,050
2003	100	19	11,300	10,600	53	W	150	8,390	55	11,300	3,830	66	3,830
2004	100	22	13,600	12,500	53	W	260	9,640	42	13,600	3,120	----	3,120
2005	100	26	12,400	11,900	W	W	W	11,800	34	12,400	W	----	W
2006	100	28	12,300	11,800	W	W	W	11,600	20	12,300	W	----	W
2007	100		10,200	9,830	W	W	W	9,840	15	10,200	W	----	W
2008[1]	100		9,550	9,310	W	W	W	10,500	14	9,550	W	----	W
2009[2]	100		6,620	6,480	W	W	W	6,970	9	6,620	W	----	W

[1] Preliminary.   [2] Estimate.   [3] Including concentrates.   [4] For consumption.   W = Withheld.   *Source: U.S. Geological Survey (USGS)*

Bismuth

Bismuth (symbol Bi) is a rare metallic element with a pinkish tinge. Bismuth has been known since ancient times, but it was confused with lead, tin, and zinc until the middle of the 18th century. Among the elements in the earth's crust, bismuth is ranked about 73rd in natural abundance. This makes bismuth about as rare as silver. Most industrial bismuth is obtained as a by-product of ore extraction.

Bismuth is useful for castings because of the unusual way that it expands after solidifying. Some of bismuth's alloys have unusually low melting points. Bismuth is one of the most difficult of all substances to magnetize. It tends to turn at right angles to a magnetic field. Because of this property, it is used in instruments for measuring the strength of magnetic fields.

Bismuth finds a wide variety of uses such as pharmaceutical compounds, ceramic glazes, crystal ware, and chemicals and pigments. Bismuth is found in household pharmaceuticals and is used to treat stomach ulcers. Bismuth is opaque to X-rays and can be used in fluoroscopy. Bismuth has also found new use as a nontoxic substitute for lead in various applications such as brass plumbing fixtures, crystal ware, lubricating greases, pigments, and solders. There has been environmental interest in the use of bismuth as a replacement for lead used in shot for waterfowl hunting and in fishing sinkers. Another use has been for galvanizing to improve drainage characteristics of galvanizing alloys. Zinc-bismuth alloys have the same drainage properties as zinc-lead without being as hazardous.

Prices – The average price of bismuth (99.99% pure) in the U.S. in 2010 rose by 4.6% to $8.63 per pound, but still below the 2007 record high of $13.32 per pound. Up until 2007 the prices were in the $3.00 to $5.00 per pound range.

Supply – World mine production of bismuth in 2010 fell -7.3% to 7,600 metric tons, down from the 2009 record high of 8,200 metric tons. The world's largest producer in 2010 was China with 67% of world production, followed by Peru with 15%, Mexico with 13%, and Canada with 1%. Regarding production of the refined metal in 2009 China had 80% of production, Mexico had 6%, Belgium had 5%, and Peru had 4%. The U.S. does not have any significant domestic refinery production of bismuth.

Demand – U.S. consumption of bismuth in 2010 fell by -11.0% to 1,050 metric tons, further below the record high of 2,420 metric tons in 2004. In 2009 the consumed uses of bismuth were 60% for chemicals, 36% for metallurgical additives, 4% for fusible alloys, and 0.3% for other alloy uses.

Trade – U.S. imports of bismuth in 2010 fell -4.0% to 1,200 metric tons, down from the 2007 record high of 3,070 metric tons. Of U.S. imports in 2009, 36% came from Belgium and 5% came from Mexico. U.S. exports of bismuth and alloys in 2010 fell -11.8% yr/yr to 350 metric tons, further below the 2001 record high of 541 metric tons.

World Production of Bismuth   In Metric Tons (Mine Output=Metal Content)

	Mine Output, Metal Content						Refined Metal						
Year	Canada	China	Japan	Mexico	Peru	Total	Belgium	China	Kazak-hastan[3]	Japan	Mexico	Peru	Total
2004	185	3,000	26	1,064	1,000	5,600	800	11,700	130	522	1,064	600	15,000
2005	185	3,000	23	970	952	5,400	800	10,600	120	463	970	600	14,000
2006	177	3,000	21	1,186	950	5,800	800	11,800	115	425	1,186	600	15,000
2007	137	3,500	20	1,200	950	6,200	800	12,100	120	408	1,200	600	16,000
2008	71	5,000	20	1,170	960	7,600	800	12,000	125	410	1,170	600	15,000
2009[1]	86	6,000	21	854	960	8,200	800	12,000	125	420	854	600	15,000
2010[2]	100	5,100		1,000	1,100	7,600							

[1] Preliminary.   [2] Estimate.   *Source U.S. Geological Survey (USGS)*

Salient Statistics of Bismuth in the United States   In Metric Tons

			Bismuth Consumed, By Uses					Imports from				Dealer Price
	Metal-lurgical	Other Alloys	Fusible	Chem-	Total Con-	Consumer Stocks	Exports of Metal	Metallic Bismuth from				$ Per
Year	Additives	& Uses	Alloys	icals[3]	sumption	Dec. 31	& Alloys	Belgium	Mexico	Preu	Total	Pound
2004	1,110	22	703	584	2,420	167	109	793.0	495.0	39.8	1,990	3.35
2005	1,150	14	685	498	2,340	175	142	1,050.0	480.0	----	2,530	3.91
2006	1,050	12	260	660	1,990	120	311	876.0	552.0	17.6	2,300	5.04
2007	1,130	45	709	744	2,630	139	421	1,020.0	420.0	3.7	3,070	14.07
2008	375	38	75	597	1,090	228	375	509.0	40.0	55.7	1,930	12.73
2009[1]	422	3	52	706	1,180	134	397	450.0	59.4	29.4	1,250	7.84
2010[2]					1,050	125	350				1,200	8.22

[1] Preliminary.   [2] Estimate.   [3] Includes pharmaceuticals.   *Source: U.S. Geological Survey (USGS)*

Average Price of Bismuth (99.99%) in the United States   In Dollars Per Pound

Year	Jan.	Feb.	Mar.	Apr.	May	June	July	Aug.	Sept.	Oct.	Nov.	Dec.	Average
2007	4.63	4.63	8.36	13.00	17.02	18.36	17.64	17.08	15.92	14.89	14.63	13.63	13.32
2008	13.00	12.35	12.00	12.00	14.94	13.70	12.75	12.21	10.50	10.50	10.50	10.50	12.08
2009	10.50	10.50	8.00	7.68	7.44	7.08	6.86	6.85	8.50	8.99	8.56	8.03	8.25
2010	7.72	7.84	8.10	9.36	9.32	8.58	7.94	8.11	8.91	9.38	9.24	9.00	8.63

Source: American Metal Market (AMM)

Broilers

Broiler chickens are raised for meat rather than for eggs. The broiler industry was started in the late 1950's when chickens were selectively bred for meat production. Broiler chickens are housed in massive flocks mainly between 20,000 and 50,000 birds, with some flocks reaching over 100,000 birds. Broiler chicken farmers usually rear five or six batches of chickens per year.

After just six or seven weeks, broiler chickens are slaughtered (a chicken's natural lifespan is around seven years). Chickens marketed as pouissons, or spring chickens, are slaughtered after four weeks. A few are kept longer than seven weeks to be sold as the larger roasting chickens.

Prices – The average monthly price received by farmers for broilers (live weight) rose in 2010 by +7.4% yr/yr to 48.5 cents per pound. The average monthly price for wholesale broilers (ready-to-cook) in 2010 rose +6.9% to 82.92 cents per pound, setting a new record high.

Supply – Total production of broilers in 2010 rose by +1.0% yr/yr to 35.900 billion pounds. The number of broilers raised for commercial production in 2010 was up 1.5% yr/yr to 8.648 billion birds, down from the 2008 record high of 9.009 billion birds. The average live-weight per bird rose by +2.0% to 5.70 pounds, which was a new record high and was about 50% heavier than the average bird weight of 3.62 pounds seen in 1970, attesting to the increased efficiency of the industry.

Demand – U.S. per capita consumption of broilers in 2010 rose by +1.1% to 81.0 pounds (ready-to-cook) per person per year, down very slightly from the 2006 record high of 86.9. U.S. consumption of chicken has nearly doubled in the past two decades, up from 47.0 pounds in 1980, as consumers have increased their consumption of chicken because of the focus on low-carb diets and because chicken is a leaner and healthier meat than either beef or pork.

Broiler Supply and Prices in the United States

Years and Quarters	Number (Million)	Average Weight (Pounds)	Liveweight Pounds (Mil. Lbs.)	Certified RTC[3] Weight (Mil. Lbs.)	Total Production RTC[3] (Mil. Lbs.)	Per Capita Consumption RTC[3] Basis (Mil. Lnbs.)	Farm	Georgia Dock[4]
							Cents per Pound	
2005	8,842	5.38	47,475	35,238	35,365	85.8	43.33	72.83
2006	8,838	5.47	48,333	35,750	35,500	86.5	38.92	68.25
2007	8,889	5.51	48,983	35,964	36,126	85.4	44.92	77.46
2008	8,915	5.51	49,753	35,863	36,906	83.5	46.58	83.11
2009[1]	8,519	5.59	47,604	35,505	35,511	79.6	45.17	84.97
2010[2]	8,649	5.70	49,313	36,909	36,851	82.8	48.50	85.25
I	2,073	5.63	11,678	8,732	8,732	20.0	48.00	82.93
II	2,165	5.67	12,281	9,198	9,198	20.5	50.00	85.65
III	2,254	5.63	12,694	9,496	9,496	21.4	49.33	87.06
IV	2,158	5.87	12,661	9,484	9,425	20.9	46.67	85.37

[1] Preliminary. [2] Estimate. [3] Total production equals federal inspected slaughter plus other slaughter minus cut-up & further processing condemnation. [4] Ready-to-cook basis. *Source: Economic Research Service, U.S. Department of Agriculture (ERS-USDA)*

Salient Statistics of Broilers in the United States

Year	Commercial Production Number (Mil. Lbs.)	Commercial Production Liveweight (Mil. Lbs.)	Average Liveweight Per Bird (Mil. Lbs.)	Average Price (cents Lb.)	Value of Production (Mil. $)	Production Federally Inspected	Production Other Chickens	Total	Storage Stocks January 1	Exports	Broiler Feed Ratio (pounds)	Consumption Total (Mil. Lbs.)	Per Capita[4] (Pounds)
						In Millions of Pounds							
2004	8,741	45,796	5.24	44.6	20,446	33,699	504	34,203	611	4,783	5.9	34,063	84.30
2005	8,872	47,856	5.39	43.6	20,878	35,365	516	35,881	716	5,203	7.0	35,293	85.90
2006	8,868	48,830	5.51	36.3	17,739	35,500	505	36,005	926	5,205	6.2	36,325	86.60
2007	8,907	49,331	5.54	43.6	21,514	36,159	498	36,657	750	5,904	5.1	29,827	85.20
2008	9,009	50,442	5.60	45.8	23,203	36,906	559	37,465	719	6,961	3.7	30,800	83.40
2009[1]	8,520	47,613	5.59		21,811	35,510	500	36,011	745	6,835	4.1		79.60
2010[2]	8,648	49,308	5.70			36,904	504	37,407			4.5		

[1] Preliminary. [2] Estimate. [3] Ready-to-cook. [4] Retail weight basis. *Source: Economic Research Service, U.S. Department of Agriculture (ERS-USDA)*

Average Wholesale Broiler[1] Prices RTC (Ready-to-Cook)   In Cents Per Pound

Year	Jan.	Feb.	Mar.	Apr.	May	June	July	Aug.	Sept.	Oct.	Nov.	Dec.	Average
2004	68.66	74.96	75.94	76.40	79.54	82.00	81.59	75.44	70.07	68.79	68.08	68.01	74.12
2005	71.40	71.43	72.81	73.21	72.54	72.19	72.47	71.45	72.51	69.02	66.95	63.98	70.83
2006	63.13	63.19	61.77	58.91	59.57	64.44	67.10	68.26	68.18	65.16	65.93	66.48	64.34
2007	70.43	75.89	78.66	78.63	81.00	81.34	80.68	78.82	78.19	70.60	71.74	71.06	76.42
2008	75.91	78.79	79.51	77.84	81.58	82.48	84.60	79.34	77.98	77.65	78.51	82.01	79.68
2009	81.90	80.17	77.01	76.39	82.96	86.22	82.95	74.50	72.81	71.00	71.76	73.56	77.60
2010[2]	81.57	81.07	84.00	82.12	86.35	86.63	86.12	83.25	84.04	80.42	81.12	78.38	82.92

[1] 12-city composite wholesale price. [2] Preliminary. *Source: Economic Research Service, U.S. Department of Agriculture (ERS-USDA)*

Butter

Butter is a dairy product produced by churning the fat from milk, usually cow's milk, until it solidifies. In some parts of the world, butter is also made from the milk of goats, sheep, and even horses. Butter has been in use since at least 2,000 BC. Today butter is used principally as a food item, but in ancient times it was used more as an ointment, medicine, or illuminating oil. Butter was first churned in skin pouches thrown back and forth over the backs of trotting horses.

It takes about 10 quarts of milk to produce 1 pound of butter. The manufacture of butter is the third largest use of milk in the U.S. California is generally the largest producing state, followed closely by Wisconsin, with Washington as a distant third. Commercially finished butter is comprised of milk fat (80% to 85%), water (12% to 16%), and salt (about 2%). Although the price of butter is highly correlated with the price of milk, it also has its own supply and demand dynamics.

The consumption of butter has dropped in recent decades because pure butter has a high level of animal fat and cholesterol that have been linked to obesity and heart disease. The primary substitute for butter is margarine, which is produced from vegetable oil rather than milk fat. U.S. per capita consumption of margarine has risen from 2.6 pounds in 1930 to recent levels near 8.3 pounds, much higher than U.S. butter consumption.

Futures on butter are traded at the Chicago Mercantile Exchange (CME). The CME's butter futures contract calls for the delivery of 20,000 pounds of Grade AA butter and is priced in cents per pound.

Prices – The average monthly price of butter at the Chicago Mercantile Exchange in 2010 rose +18.3% yr/yr to 147.02 cents/pound. That is still down from the 2004 record high of 181.66 cents per pound, but higher than the 13-year low of 110.59 cents per pound posted in 2002.

Supply – World production of butter in 2010 rose +2.5% yr/yr to 8.017 million metric tons, down from the record high of 9.594 million metric tons in 2007. The world's largest producers of butter are India with 50.8% of the world production in 2010, the European Union with 24.2%, the United States with 8.5%, New Zealand with 5.5%, and Russia with 2.9%. Production of creamery butter by U.S. factories in 2010 fell -0.4% yr/yr to 1.562 billion pounds. The record high was 1.872 billion pounds in 1941.

Demand – Total commercial use of creamery butter in the U.S fell by -39.9% yr/yr to 9.408 million pounds, down from the 2008 a record high of 1.716 billion pounds. That is about one-third higher that the commercial use of butter back in the 1950's. Cold storage stocks of creamery butter in the U.S. on December 1, 2010 fell -51.0% yr/yr to 69.932 million pounds.

Trade – World imports of butter in 2010 fell -11.6% yr/yr to 297,000 metric tons. U.S. imports of butter in 2010 were unchanged yr/yr at 16,000 metric tons. World exports of butter in 2010 fell -1.1% yr/yr to 788,000 metric tons. U.S exports in 2010 fell -10.7% yr/yr to 50,000 metric tons, down from the 2008 16-year high of 105,000 metric tons.

Supply and Distribution of Butter in the United States   In Millions of Pounds

	----------------- Supply -----------------				----------------------- Distribution -----------------------						------- 93 Score --------
		Cold Storage				-- Domestic Disappearance --			-- Department of Agriculture --			AA Wholesale Price
Year	Pro-duction	Stocks[3] Jan. 1	Imports	Total Supply	Total	Per Capita (Pounds)	Exports	Stocks[4] Jan. 1	Stocks[4] Dec 31	Removed by USDA Programs	Total Use	$ per Pound
2002	1,355	56	34.800	1,446	1,293	4.5	8	0	1		1,288	----	1.1059
2003	1,242	158	32.200	1,432	1,307	4.5	9	1	6	29.1	1,332	----	1.1450
2004	1,250	100	50.600	1,400	1,326	4.5	26	6	0	-6.6	1,356	----	1.8166
2005	1,347	45	31.418	1,424	1,335	4.6	13	0			1,370	----	1.5484
2006	1,448	59	39.683	1,548	1,415	4.7	24				1,548	----	1.2360
2007	1,533	109	37.478	1,678	1,435	5.0	88				1,678	----	1.3680
2008	1,645	154	37.478	1,836	1,521	5.0	196				1,836		
2009[1]	1,574	119	37.478	1,731	1,559		40				1,731		
2010[2]	1,530	132	35.274	1,698	1,488		123				1,698		

[1] Preliminary.   [2] Estimates.   [3] Includes butter-equivalent.   [4] Includes butteroil.   [5] Includes stocks held by USDA.
Source: Economic Research Service, U.S. Department of Agriculture (ERS-USDA)

Quarterly Commercial Disappearance of Creamery Butter in the United States   In Millions of Pounds

Year	First Quarter	Second Quarter	Third Quarter	Fourth Quarter	Total	Year	First Quarter	Second Quarter	Third Quarter	Fourth Quarter	Total
1999	299.3	316.4	318.3	374.8	1,308.8	2005	287.1	304.9	349.6	423.1	1,364.7
2000	300.8	286.9	332.3	380.6	1,300.6	2006	320.2	308.5	333.2	471.6	1,433.5
2001	290.9	278.4	316.1	397.0	1,282.4	2007	344.6	299.2	376.8	498.3	1,518.9
2002	313.5	263.5	317.4	393.4	1,287.8	2008	399.3	381.4	424.9	512.2	1,717.8
2003	304.2	275.4	317.2	411.8	1,308.6	2009	372.9	374.0	352.8	464.4	1,564.1
2004	286.3	303.2	340.8	421.1	1,351.4	2010[1]	382.5	382.7	398.9	475.5	1,639.6

[1] Preliminary.   *Source: Economic Research Service, U.S. Department of Agriculture (ERS-USDA)*

World Production of Butter[3]   In Thousands of Metric Tons

Year	Australia	Brazil	Canada	Egypt	European Union	India	Japan	Mexico	New Zealand	Russia	Ukraine	United States	World Total
2004	132	75	84	12	2,164	2,600	80	88	418	270	138	565	8,834
2005	131	77	84	12	2,155	2,749	84	93	379	275	118	611	8,966
2006	129	79	75	10	2,035	3,050	80	109	390	290	105	657	9,126
2007	117	82	79	10	2,053	3,360	75	214	442	300	100	695	9,649
2008	111	84	85	----	2,040	3,690	72	180	422	305	85	746	7,881
2009	118	76	87	----	2,030	3,910	81	171	482	246	75	714	8,041
2010[1]	110	78	85	----	1,980	4,155	78	173	453	240	76	694	8,174
2011[2]	113	80	85	----	1,975	4,325	78	175	500	252	72	718	8,423

[1] Preliminary.   [2] Forecast.   [3] Factory (including creameries and dairies) & farm.   NA = Not available.
Source: Foreign Agricultural Service, U.S. Department of Agriculture (FAS-USDA)

Production of Creamery Butter in Factories in the United States   In Millions of Pounds

Year	Jan.	Feb.	Mar.	Apr.	May	June	July	Aug.	Sept.	Oct.	Nov.	Dec.	Total
2003	141.9	128.1	126.4	122.8	114.9	84.2	80.1	70.9	73.3	96.8	88.4	114.6	1,242.4
2004	129.3	108.6	100.4	100.3	110.1	99.2	92.6	90.3	94.2	104.4	101.4	118.8	1,249.7
2005	128.0	116.9	122.4	117.1	120.7	106.6	95.9	93.2	100.6	108.9	110.9	126.0	1,347.2
2006	149.8	136.8	141.7	127.7	128.6	101.1	94.7	88.9	104.3	119.1	118.1	137.6	1,448.5
2007	150.6	134.0	138.4	133.0	124.0	110.0	116.5	110.9	112.9	130.4	130.8	141.5	1,532.9
2008	168.8	146.8	151.9	150.1	142.6	119.8	114.2	115.7	121.0	130.0	133.7	156.3	1,651.1
2009	174.7	145.7	147.2	142.5	139.4	125.5	114.3	100.9	94.6	112.9	120.5	150.8	1,568.9
2010[1]	162.1	141.1	138.8	133.2	130.5	117.3	111.0	101.7	113.8	121.6	133.3	158.1	1,562.2

[1] Preliminary.   *Source: Economic Research Service, U.S. Department of Agriculture (ERS-USDA)*

Cold Storage Holdings of Creamery Butter in the United States, on First of Month   In Millions of Pounds

Year	Jan.	Feb.	Mar.	Apr.	May	June	July	Aug.	Sept.	Oct.	Nov.	Dec.
2003	157.8	204.8	239.9	249.0	263.7	298.0	301.4	283.9	253.9	207.2	170.2	122.5
2004	99.6	152.4	159.1	158.1	155.7	178.7	189.2	193.5	161.0	133.0	107.2	57.2
2005	45.0	77.2	110.9	132.4	164.5	178.0	179.6	259.8	215.2	124.1	98.1	60.4
2006	58.6	125.3	169.1	195.3	227.7	261.5	263.0	259.8	215.2	190.6	157.6	108.1
2007	108.6	148.7	185.4	193.1	245.9	270.2	273.0	271.5	260.9	240.3	196.6	143.2
2008	155.2	188.1	210.4	224.8	251.5	269.5	258.4	246.1	213.7	186.9	149.4	119.9
2009	119.0	176.5	204.9	212.5	240.0	253.3	262.9	262.8	259.6	227.9	190.6	142.7
2010[1]	133.0	168.1	202.9	195.9	206.3	212.5	197.6	193.5	155.3	130.0	108.8	69.9

[1] Preliminary.   *Source: Agricultural Statistics Board, U.S. Department of Agriculture (ASB-USDA)*

Average Price of Butter at Chicago Mercantile Exchange   In Cents Per Pound

Year	Jan.	Feb.	Mar.	Apr.	May	June	July	Aug.	Sept.	Oct.	Nov.	Dec.	Average
2003	108.2	104.1	109.2	109.1	109.2	111.4	119.9	117.1	117.3	118.5	120.6	129.7	114.5
2004	143.2	171.3	213.5	222.0	203.6	193.0	174.6	154.1	176.6	164.8	192.4	170.8	181.7
2005	157.8	161.5	155.3	149.3	140.4	153.1	162.1	168.6	169.9	162.0	142.6	135.5	154.8
2006	133.7	119.3	116.6	116.3	117.6	116.4	116.5	130.4	131.7	132.1	129.2	124.1	123.6
2007	122.5	121.9	132.2	137.3	148.3	150.2	149.1	144.6	137.8	130.2	135.9	131.9	136.8
2008	122.5	120.9	134.5	139.1	147.5	150.0	153.9	162.8	169.7	173.2	161.7	120.1	146.3
2009	111.0	111.0	117.7	120.4	125.3	122.4	123.5	120.1	122.0	128.3	150.1	139.7	124.3
2010	139.5	135.6	146.4	154.6	159.0	163.8	177.9	199.0	222.6	219.0	193.0	163.3	172.8

Source: Economic Research Service, U.S. Department of Agriculture (ERS-USDA)

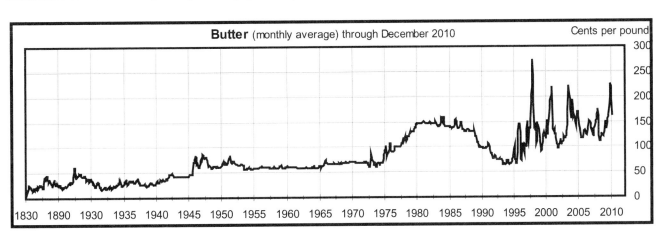

Cadmium

Cadmium (symbol Cd) is a soft, bluish-white, metallic element that can easily be shaped and cut with a knife. Cadmium melts at 321 degrees Celsius and boils at 765 degrees Celsius. Cadmium burns brightly in air when heated, forming the oxide CdO. In 1871, the German chemist Friedrich Stromeyer discovered cadmium in incrustations in zinc furnaces.

Rare greenockite is the only mineral bearing cadmium. Cadmium occurs most often in small quantities associated with zinc ores, such as sphalerite. Electrolysis or fractional distillation is used to separate the cadmium and zinc. About 80% of world cadmium output is a by-product from zinc refining. The remaining 20% comes from secondary sources and recycling of cadmium products. Cadmium recycling is practical only from nickel-cadmium batteries and from some alloys and dust from electric-arc furnaces.

Cadmium is used primarily for metal plating and coating operations in transportation equipment, machinery, baking enamels, photography, and television phosphors. It is also used in pigments and lasers, and in nickel-cadmium and solar batteries.

Prices – Cadmium prices for the 8 years up to 2005 were at severely depressed levels, reflecting the decreased demand for the substance. In 2005, however, cadmium prices rose very sharply by +172.7% to $1.50 cents per pound. In 2007 the price rose further to a 21-year high of $3.45 per pound. In 2010 the price rose by +35.6% yr/yr to

$1.77 per pound. The record high of $7.89 per pound was posted in 1988.

Supply – World cadmium production in 2010 rose by +17.0% yr/yr to a record high of 22,000 metric tons, far above the 30-year low of 17,800 metric tons seen in 2002. The largest producer was China with 25% of total world production followed by Japan with 9% and Kazakhstan with 8%. The U.S. produced only 3% of world. The U.S. production in 2010 rose by +2.7% to 650 metric tons, up from the 2009 lowest level of 633 metric tons since 1932.

Demand – Consumption of cadmium has been declining fairly steeply in the last few years due to environmental concerns. U.S. cadmium consumption in 2009 fell by 62.3% yr/yr to 199 metric tons, which was the lowest since 1926. Of the total apparent consumption, about 75% is used for batteries, 12% for pigments, 8% for coatings and plating, 4% for nonferrous alloys, and 1% for other uses.

Trade – The U.S. in 2004 relied on imports for 20% of its cadmium usage, down from 38% in 1998. U.S. imports of cadmium had plunged over the past 13 years but recovered to post a 10-year high in 2005 at 288 metric tons. That, however, was still far below the 1,110 metric tons seen as recently as 1994. In 2010 the U.S. imported 210 metric tons which was up +80% from 2009. U.S. exports of cadmium in 2010 fell -65% yr/yr to 230 metric tons.

World Refinery Production of Cadmium   In Metric Tons

Year	Australia	Belgium	Canada	China	Finland	Germany	Italy	Japan	Kazakhstan	Mexico	United Kingdom	United States[3]	World Total
2003	560	----	1,759	2,710	----	640	22	2,497	1,351	1,590	529	1,450	18,400
2004	347	----	1,880	2,800	----	640	10	2,233	1,900	1,615	532	1,480	18,600
2005	358	----	1,727	4,080	----	640	10	2,297	2,000	1,653	481	1,470	20,100
2006	329	----	2,090	3,790	----	640	10	2,287	2,000	1,401	416	723	19,900
2007	351	----	1,388	4,210	----	400	10	1,933	2,100	1,617	347	735	19,400
2008	330	----	1,409	4,300	----	400	10	2,116	2,100	1,550	371	777	20,100
2009[1]	370	----	1,300	4,300	----	400	10	1,820	1,800	1,210	----	633	18,800
2010[2]	360	----	1,500	5,600	----	400		1,900	1,700	1,300	----	650	22,000

[1] Preliminary.   [2] Estimate.   [3] Primary and secondary metal.   *Source: U.S. Geological Survey (USGS)*

Salient Statistics of Cadmium in the United States   In Metric Tons of Contained Cadmium

Year	Net import Reliance As a % of Apparent Consumption	Production (Metal)	Producer Shipments	Cadmium Sulfide Production	Production Other Compounds	Imports of Cadmium Metal[3]	Exports[4]	Apparent Consumption	Industry Stocks Dec. 31[5]	New York Dealer Price $ Per Lb.
2003	E	1,450	1,200	----	----	112	615	1,020	1,430	.59
2004	20	1,480	1,410	----	----	263	154	1,840	1,170	.55
2005	E	1,470	1,680	----	----	288	686	2,060	1,540	1.50
2006	E	723	833	----	----	179	483	530	1,400	1.35
2007	E	735	692	----	----	315	424	594	1,440	3.45
2008	E	777	774	----	----	153	421	528	1,460	2.69
2009[1]	E	633	737	----	----	117	661	199	1,450	1.30
2010[2]	E	650		----	----	210	230	572		1.77

[1] Preliminary.   [2] Estimate.   [3] For consumption.   [4] Cadmium metal, alloys, dross, flue dust.   [5] Metallic, Compounds, Distributors.   [6] Sticks & Balls in 1 to 5 short ton lots of metal (99.95%).   E = Net exporter.   *Source: U.S. Geological Survey (USGS)*

Average Price of Cadmium (99.95%) in the United States   In Dollars Per Pound

Year	Jan.	Feb.	Mar.	Apr.	May	June	July	Aug.	Sept.	Oct.	Nov.	Dec.	Average
2008	301.90	315.00	315.00	315.00	315.00	315.00	315.00	306.67	280.00	280.00	280.00	280.00	301.55
2009	280.00	280.00	157.27	141.43	121.38	142.05	141.25	166.67	180.00	189.05	190.00	167.63	179.73
2010	173.42	193.16	238.91	225.34	212.88	203.41	197.50	187.27	185.00	185.00	185.00	180.00	197.24

Source: American Metal Market (AMM)

Canola (Rapeseed)

Canola is a genetic variation of rapeseed that was developed by Canadian plant breeders specifically for its nutritional qualities and its low level of saturated fat. The term *Canola* is a contraction of "Canadian oil." The history of canola oil begins with the rapeseed plant, a member of the mustard family. The rape plant is grown both as feed for livestock and birdfeed. For 4,000 years, the oil from the rapeseed was used in China and India for cooking and as lamp oil. During World War II, rapeseed oil was used as a marine and industrial lubricant. After the war, the market for rapeseed oil plummeted. Rapeseed growers needed other uses for their crop, and that stimulated the research that led to the development of canola. In 1974, Canadian plant breeders from the University of Manitoba produced canola by genetically altering rapeseed. Each canola plant produces yellow flowers, which then produce pods. The tiny round seeds within each pod are crushed to produce canola oil. Each canola seed contains approximately 40% oil. Canola oil is the world's third largest source of vegetable oil accounting for 13% of world vegetable oils, following soybean oil at 32%, and palm oil at 28%. The rest of the seed is processed into canola meal, which is used as high protein livestock feed.

The climate in Canada is especially suitable for canola plant growth. Today, over 13 million acres of Canadian soil are dedicated to canola production. Canola oil is Canada's leading vegetable oil. Due to strong demand from the U.S. for canola oil, approximately 70% of Canada's canola oil is exported to the U.S. Canola oil is used as a salad oil, cooking oil, and for margarine as well as in the manufacture of inks, biodegradable greases, pharmaceuticals, fuel, soap, and cosmetics.

Canola futures and options are traded at the ICE Futures Canada (ICE). The futures contract calls for the delivery of 20 metric tons of canola and 5 contracts are together called a "1 board lot." The futures contract is priced in Canadian dollars per metric ton.

Prices – Canola prices on the ICE nearest-futures chart started 2009 at about CD$437 per metric ton and drifted lower to about CD$407 in February. The price then moved up to the year's high at about CD$477 and then moved lower the rest of the year to end the year at about CD$405 per metric ton. The price continued lower into 2010 to about CD$385 in February.

The average monthly wholesale price of canola oil in the Midwest in 2009 fell -34.5% yr/yr to 40.28 cents per pound. The average monthly wholesale price of canola meal (delivery Pacific Northwest) in the 2010-11 crop year (through November 2010) rose by +16.7% to $262.53 per short ton.

Supply – World canola production in the 2010-11 marketing year fell by -3.7% yr/yr to 58.387, just below last year's record high of 60.624 million metric tons. The world's largest canola producers were the European Union with 34.8% of world production in 2010-11, China (21.9%), Canada (20.3%), and India (12.0%). U.S. production of canola and canola oil in 2010-11 rose +66.5% yr/yr to 1.114 million metric tons. Regarding canola products, world production of canola oil in 2010-11 rose +1.4% to 22.661 million metric tons, which was a new record high. U.S. production of canola oil in 2010-11 rose +10.7% to 526,000 metric tons, which is a new record high. World production of canola meal in 2010-11 rose +1.4% to a record high of 34.134 million metric tons.

Demand – World crush demand for canola in 2010-11 rose +1.4% yr/yr to 57.589 million metric tons, which was a new record high. World consumption of canola oil in 2010-11 rose +4.8% yr/yr to a new record high of 23.286 million metric tons. World consumption of canola meal in 2010-11 fell by -0.2% to 33.779, just below last year's record high of 33.839 million metric tons.

Trade – World canola exports in 2010-11 fell -5.8% to 10.283 million metric tons, world canola oil exports rose +6.2% to a record high of 2.857 million metric tons, and world canola meal exports rose +20.7% yr/yr to a record high of 4.202 million metric tons. World canola imports in 2010-11 fell -4.6% to 10.088 million metric tons, world canola oil imports fell -3.5% to 2.830 million metric tons, and world canola meal imports rose +6.5% to a record high of 3.896 million metric tons. Regarding U.S. canola trade, U.S. canola imports in 2010-11 fell -12.0% to 500,000 metric tons and U.S. exports rose +49.5% to 308,000 metric tons.

World Production of Canola (Rapeseed)   In Thousands of Metric Tons

Year	Australia	Canada	China	Bangla-desh	Belarus	European Union	India	Pakistan	Romania	Russia	Ukraine	United States	World Total
2001-02	1,756	5,017	11,331	238	95	11,585	4,500	221	----	140	135	908	36,010
2002-03	871	4,521	10,552	233	60	11,752	4,050	235	----	115	61	697	33,262
2003-04	1,703	6,771	11,420	218	55	11,185	6,800	238	----	192	51	686	39,436
2004-05	1,542	7,674	13,182	211	143	15,432	6,500	215	----	276	149	613	46,112
2005-06	1,419	9,483	13,052	191	150	15,523	7,000	181	----	303	285	718	48,542
2006-07	573	9,000	10,966	235	115	16,092	5,800	318	----	523	600	633	45,121
2007-08	1,214	9,601	10,573	210	250	18,358	5,450	190	----	630	1,100	650	48,563
2008-09[1]	1,844	12,643	12,100	220	590	19,000	6,700	225	----	752	2,900	656	57,908
2009-10[2]	1,910	12,417	13,657	225	650	21,566	6,400	230	----	667	1,900	669	60,624
2010-11[3]	2,150	11,866	12,800	225	400	20,300	7,000	230	----	500	1,470	1,114	58,387

[1] Preliminary.   [2] Estimate.   [3] Forecast.   *Source: Economic Research Service, U.S. Department of Agriculture (ERS-USDA); The Oil World*

CANOLA

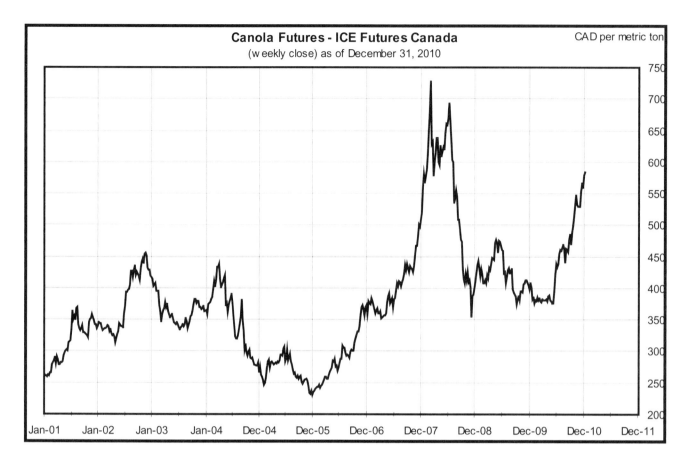

Canola Futures - ICE Futures Canada
(weekly close) as of December 31, 2010

CAD per metric ton

Volume of Trading of Canola Futures in Winnipeg   In 20 Metric Ton Units

Year	Jan.	Feb.	Mar.	Apr.	May	June	July	Aug.	Sept.	Oct.	Nov.	Dec.	Total
2001	196,137	292,226	286,463	247,744	205,798	188,175	163,901	155,531	143,220	205,016	174,910	165,852	2,424,973
2002	164,945	179,753	166,889	159,981	133,202	139,256	132,524	174,527	131,034	170,873	105,661	169,477	1,828,122
2003	129,903	152,738	108,991	153,528	120,178	152,979	90,909	66,768	109,760	217,310	90,950	153,269	1,547,283
2004	145,339	204,567	178,516	192,429	120,218	128,843	73,417	97,483	113,368	175,776	110,922	196,094	1,736,972
2005	116,678	207,198	141,717	124,636	102,424	178,001	87,724	121,749	138,701	200,004	145,231	258,922	1,822,985
2006	195,189	240,070	237,537	229,470	211,688	238,967	129,433	145,133	212,164	284,033	191,676	291,994	2,607,354
2007	204,893	309,278	198,589	273,755	281,240	321,022	160,846	181,145	212,288	396,852	268,743	360,531	3,169,182
2008	368,963	388,180	307,536	318,641	209,631	290,152	172,089	170,596	220,479	293,978	126,273	265,670	3,132,188
2009	265,415	345,108	267,276	358,030	286,069	326,924	161,569	188,651	268,629	340,368	211,160	332,594	3,351,793
2010	221,754	321,429	283,156	415,932	232,711	534,781	200,250	277,736	351,663	500,943	284,703	447,694	4,072,752

Contract size = 20 tonnes.   *Source: ICE Futures Canada (ICE)*

Average Open Interest of Canola Futures in Winnipeg   In 20 Metric Ton Units

Year	Jan.	Feb.	Mar.	Apr.	May	June	July	Aug.	Sept.	Oct.	Nov.	Dec.
2001	57,537	73,539	88,111	78,143	77,425	84,315	72,430	70,137	67,275	71,651	65,580	66,884
2002	57,821	56,443	53,321	56,830	50,924	38,901	48,329	54,286	53,630	50,379	56,896	57,983
2003	52,818	54,749	55,369	53,480	50,549	49,930	47,479	45,314	44,510	49,008	45,423	48,655
2004	54,524	57,944	71,624	77,357	69,783	59,012	50,669	51,009	49,659	53,855	65,215	68,719
2005	64,147	75,090	65,205	63,514	54,341	53,390	57,706	56,305	65,700	68,186	66,117	87,246
2006	82,651	88,576	84,828	88,970	84,710	81,561	81,243	77,356	81,597	80,800	90,694	102,651
2007	103,317	103,250	94,001	102,050	114,244	124,321	117,967	111,470	121,589	122,965	146,879	156,698
2008	164,326	172,229	165,282	135,226	111,687	102,353	91,891	82,272	90,075	90,062	91,459	88,373
2009	88,487	100,072	97,016	104,423	111,922	109,921	94,574	104,426	95,168	99,968	93,108	99,736
2010	112,406	125,895	122,112	133,172	134,768	159,949	154,881	150,209	155,712	181,660	199,487	193,948

Contract size = 20 tonnes.   *Source: ICE Futures Canada (ICE)*

World Supply and Distribution of Canola and Products   In Thousands of Metric Tons

	------------------- Canola ---------------------				------------------ Canola Meal ------------------					------------------ Canola oil -------------------				
Year	Pro-duction	Exports	Imports	Crush	Ending Stocks	Pro-duction	Exports	Imports	Con-sumption	Ending Stocks	Pro-duction	Exports	Imports	Con-sumption	Ending Stocks
2003-04	39,436	5,491	5,148	36,422	2,099	21,783	2,491	2,491	21,613	449	14,109	1,325	1,357	14,303	397
2004-05	46,112	4,900	5,018	40,606	4,746	24,235	2,239	2,297	24,397	345	15,742	1,293	1,202	15,556	492
2005-06	48,542	6,982	6,684	44,656	5,506	26,564	2,505	2,553	26,367	590	17,357	1,648	1,465	16,982	684
2006-07	45,121	6,621	7,013	43,651	4,660	25,926	2,957	3,050	26,362	247	17,134	2,032	2,198	17,524	460
2007-08	48,563	8,152	7,562	46,705	3,512	27,670	3,686	3,556	27,535	252	18,434	1,912	2,021	18,275	728
2008-09[1]	57,908	12,024	12,125	52,120	6,672	30,834	3,560	3,530	30,821	235	20,487	2,420	2,434	20,148	1,081
2009-10[2]	60,624	10,912	10,574	56,768	7,541	33,658	3,482	3,659	33,839	231	22,351	2,689	2,933	22,221	1,455
2010-11[3]	58,387	10,283	10,088	57,589	5,356	34,134	4,202	3,896	33,779	280	22,661	2,857	2,830	23,286	803

[1] Preliminary.   [2] Estimate.   [3] Forecast.   *Source: Economic Research Service, U.S. Department of Agriculture (ERS-USDA); The Oil World*

Salient Statistics of Canola and Canola Oil in the United States   In Thousands of Metric Tons

	--------------------------- Canola ---------------------------							-------------------------------- Canola Oil --------------------------------						
	---------------- Supply ----------------				------ Disappearance ------			---------------- Supply ----------------			------- Disappearance -------		
Year	Stocks June 1	Pro-duction	Imports	Total Supply	Crush	Exports	Total[3]	Stocks Oct. 1	Pro-duction	Imports	Total Supply	Domestic	Exports	Total
2003-04	72	686	244	1,002	640	305	945	35	291	555	881	713	126	839
2004-05	40	613	467	1,120	901	140	1,041	42	378	514	934	754	122	876
2005-06	60	718	518	1,296	1,030	157	1,187	58	421	726	1,205	871	214	1,085
2006-07	87	633	647	1,367	963	246	1,209	120	423	712	1,255	901	286	1,187
2007-08	135	650	874	1,659	1,050	423	1,473	68	460	1,017	1,545	1,327	158	1,485
2008-09	158	656	825	1,639	1,218	191	1,409	60	497	1,050	1,607	1,280	249	1,529
2009-10[1]	203	669	568	1,440	1,087	206	1,293	78	475	1,067	1,620	1,289	251	1,540
2010-11[2]	122	1,114	500	1,736	1,256	308	1,564	80	526	1,156	1,762	1,495	185	1,680

[1] Preliminary.   [2] Forecast.   [3] Includes planting seed and residual.   *Source: Economic Research Service, U.S. Department of Agriculture (ERS-USDA)*

Wholesale Price of Canola Oil in Midwest   In Cents Per Pound

Year	Jan.	Feb.	Mar.	Apr.	May	June	July	Aug.	Sept.	Oct.	Nov.	Dec.	Average
2003	24.30	28.88	27.63	27.44	28.13	27.13	26.56	26.30	28.44	31.88	32.67	33.92	28.61
2004	33.44	37.19	38.19	36.81	35.60	32.88	31.63	29.50	31.38	28.35	31.75	31.75	33.21
2005	29.80	28.88	31.38	31.00	31.25	33.00	31.95	29.75	30.50	31.50	30.88	28.81	30.73
2006	38.63	29.06	30.19	29.70	31.56	31.69	33.95	33.06	32.94	34.50	37.63	37.42	33.36
2007	38.56	40.06	38.95	38.44	40.44	42.56	45.00	44.25	48.00	50.38	57.30	61.50	45.45
2008	64.94	71.80	70.56	71.38	73.05	76.69	74.13	61.05	54.88	42.85	39.81	37.19	61.53
2009	38.80	35.66	35.38	39.75	41.50	42.38	39.80	42.00	39.31	41.55	44.38	42.90	40.28
2010[1]	40.56	41.88	42.50	42.20	40.00	40.00	44.00	47.19	47.38	51.45	53.63	58.25	45.75

[1] Preliminary.   *Source: Economic Research Service, U.S. Department of Agriculture (ERS-USDA)*

Average Price of Canola in Vancouver   In Canadian Dollars Per Metric Ton

Year	Jan.	Feb.	Mar.	Apr.	May	June	July	Aug.	Sept.	Oct.	Nov.	Dec.	Average
2003	396.78	380.81	351.97	362.89	344.59	333.48	322.64	319.37	324.07	338.93	343.65	338.57	346.48
2004	345.51	370.53	402.02	395.92	384.09	378.62	360.93	349.57	341.29	288.64	275.37	265.15	346.47
2005	261.56	250.02	270.29	273.13	275.58	286.78	279.45	259.58	240.30	235.00	233.21	226.39	257.61
2006	230.48	231.43	241.57	248.63	267.11	263.66	277.90	265.70	265.20	295.90	335.39	348.60	272.63
2007	354.09	357.65	350.26	348.36	357.87	368.11	372.55	380.70	401.35	402.61	417.23	453.82	380.38
2008	519.88	608.92	618.85	594.74	578.47	616.27	601.79	517.00	457.86	391.62	399.41	371.48	523.02
2009	413.77	416.13	409.67	428.95	459.08	461.29	422.69	429.38	394.03	377.19	377.74	389.42	414.95
2010	376.26	373.42	374.40	377.22	372.83	400.29	439.34	443.06	453.22	481.16	514.84	542.25	429.02

Source: ICE Futures Canada (ICE)

Average Wholesale Price of Canola Meal, 36% Pacific Northwest   In Dollars Per Short Ton

Year	Oct.	Nov.	Dec.	Jan.	Feb.	Mar.	Apr.	May	June	July	Aug.	Sept.	Average
2003-04	169.65	187.19	181.35	201.07	205.50	228.65	214.40	200.03	189.00	192.09	146.99	145.55	188.46
2004-05	133.39	138.81	135.13	129.21	139.55	146.08	140.85	139.25	153.98	150.48	138.12	132.10	139.75
2005-06	130.13	139.55	158.06	150.05	143.94	134.74	136.04	136.59	139.63	137.83	143.28	136.38	140.52
2006-07	149.77	166.80	163.17	173.30	198.37	195.37	169.01	168.19	189.11	171.14	159.33	176.98	173.38
2007-08	167.24	192.25	226.30	276.78	285.83	276.85	268.14	258.75	293.20	310.19	239.88	220.42	251.32
2008-09	192.55	217.99	228.62	279.23	243.30	217.02	230.06	287.99	325.48	261.55	277.30	224.74	248.82
2009-10	220.90	177.69	NA	248.63	218.18	214.11	226.95	222.28	224.56	245.18	244.44	231.20	224.92
2010-11[1]	251.03	257.73	265.54	275.80									262.53

[1] Preliminary.   *Source: Economic Research Service, U.S. Department of Agriculture (ERS-USDA)*

Cassava

Cassava is a perennial woody shrub with an edible root. Cassava, which is also called manioc, mandioca, or yucca, grows in tropical and subtropical areas of the world. Cassava has been known since the 1500s and originates in Latin America. The cassava's starchy roots are a major source of dietary energy for more than 500 million people. Cassava is the highest producer of carbohydrates among staple crops, and it ranks fourth in food crops in developing countries. The leaves of the cassava plant are also edible and are relatively rich in protein and vitamins A and B.

Cassava is drought-tolerant and needs less soil preparation and weeding than other crops. Because cassava can be stored in the ground for up to 3 years, it also serves as a reserve food when other crops fail. The cassava is propagated by cuttings of the woody stem, thereby resulting in a low multiplication rate compared to crops propagated by true seeds.

One problem with cassava is the poisonous cyanides, which need to be destroyed before consumption. The cyanide content differs with each variety of cassava, but higher cyanide is usually correlated to high yields. The cyanide content can be destroyed through heat and various processing methods such as grating, sun drying, and fermenting.

Cassava is the primary source of tapioca. Cassava is also eaten raw or boiled, and is processed into livestock feed, starch and glucose, flour, and pharmaceuticals. One species of cassava has been successfully grown for its rubber.

Prices – The average price of tapioca (hard pellets, FOB Rotterdam) in 2008 (latest data) fell by -4.4% to $214 per metric ton, down from the record $224 per metric ton posted in 2007. The lower 2008 price is still more than double the record low of $82 in 2001.

Supply – World production of cassava in 2008 (latest data available) rose by +3.9% to a record high of 232.950 million metric tons. The world's largest producers of cassava in 2008 were Nigeria (with 19% of world production), Thailand (12%), Brazil (11%), and Indonesia (9.0%).

Trade – World exports of tapioca in 2008 (latest available) fell -35.7% to 4.092 million metric tons, down from the 2007 fifteen-year high of 6.360 million metric tons. Thailand accounted for 73% of world exports in 2008, followed by Vietnam with 21%, and Indonesia with 3%. The world's two main importers of tapioca in 2008 were China with 52% of world imports, the Republic of Korea with 24%, and the European Union with 16.

World Cassava Production — In Thousands of Metric Tons

Year	Brazil	China	Ghana	India	Indonesia	Mozam-bique	Nigeria	Paraguay	Tanzania	Thailand	Uganda	Congo[2]	World Total
2002	23,066	3,925	9,731	6,516	16,913	5,925	34,120	4,430	5,176	16,868	5,373	862	184,557
2003	21,961	4,015	10,239	5,426	18,524	6,150	36,304	4,669	3,962	19,718	5,450	878	191,322
2004	23,927	3,816	9,739	5,950	19,425	6,413	38,845	5,500	4,441	21,440	5,500	932	203,108
2005	25,872	4,016	9,567	7,463	19,321	6,500	41,565	4,785	5,539	16,938	5,576	935	207,332
2006	26,639	4,313	9,638	7,855	19,987	6,659	45,721	4,800	6,158	22,584	4,926	1,000	222,879
2007	26,541	4,362	10,218	8,232	19,988	5,039	43,410	4,800	6,600	26,916	4,973	950	226,312
2008	26,703	4,412	11,351	9,056	21,593	5,039	44,582	2,219	6,600	25,156	5,072	1,000	232,463
2009[1]	26,031	4,512	12,231	9,623	22,039			2,610		30,088	5,179		240,989

[1] Estimate. [2] Formerly Zaire. *Source: Food and Agriculture Organization of the United Nations (FAO-UN)*

World Trade in Tapioca — In Thousands of Metric Tons

Year	Costa Rica	Indonesia	Thailand	Vietnam	World Total	China	European Union	Japan	Korea	Philippines	Singapore	World Total
	Exports					Imports						
2002	12	130	3,067	308	3,556	1,760	1,560	14	157	10	19	3,580
2003	14	42	3,994	681	4,785	2,368	1,869	21	247	6	19	4,624
2004	17	234	4,579	730	5,626	3,442	2,075	30	460	12	19	6,134
2005	18	230	3,028	545	3,889	3,335	362	23	265	----	21	4,062
2006	22	132	4,361	1,106	5,690	4,950	263	20	268	3	22	5,570
2007	25	210	4,798	1,256	6,360	4,625	1,325	27	302	----	19	6,500
2008	76	130	2,984	846	4,085	1,976	619	37	900	----	20	3,770
2009[1]	82	168	4,357	2,290	6,950	6,107	42	32	552	----	20	6,880

[1] Estimate. [2] Intra-EU trade is excluded. *Source: The Oil World*

Prices of Tapioca, Hard Pellets, F.O.B. Rotterdam — U.S. Dollars Per Tonne

Year	Jan.	Feb.	Mar.	Apr.	May	June	July	Aug.	Sept.	Oct.	Nov.	Dec.	Average
2001	83	80	77	78	80	82	84	84	87	83	84	84	82
2002	86	82	82	84	87	91	96	97	95	93	93	89	90
2003	91	92	95	96	101	101	103	108	114	134	138	143	110
2004	138	132	121	118	117	118	120	122	128	134	139	148	128
2005	147	149	153	145	142	130	----	----	----	----	----	----	144
2006	----	----	----	----	----	----	----	----	----	----	----	----	----
2007	165	169	164	171	185	203	229	273	317	299	265	247	224
2008	255	261	264	257	249	241	247	226	214	212	172	171	214

Source: The Oil World

Castor beans

Castor bean plants are native to the Ethiopian region of tropical east Africa. The seeds of the castor bean are used to produce castor oil. The average castor bean seed contains 35% to 55% oil. The oil is removed from the bean seeds by either pressing or solvent extraction. Castor oil is used in many products. In the U.S., the paint and varnish industry is the single largest market for castor oil. Castor oil is also used for coating fabrics, insulation, cosmetics, skin emollients, hair oils, inks, nylon plastics, greases, and hydraulic fluids.

Ricin is found in all parts of the castor bean plant, but the most concentrated amounts are found in the cake by-product after oil extraction. Ricin is one of the most deadly, naturally occurring poisons known. Ricin received attention when it was used in a subway attack in Japan in 1995 and again when it was sent to a Congressional office in an envelope in February 2004. One non-deadly use for ricin is for medical research where it is being studied for use as a potential treatment for cancer.

Supply – World production of castor-seed beans in the 2009-10 marketing year (the latest data available) fell by -5.5% to 1.328 million metric tons. The world's largest producer of castor-seed beans by far is India with 70.0% of world production in 2009-10 at 930,000 metric tons. The second and third largest producers are China with 14.3% of world production (190,000 metric tons) and Brazil with 7.0% of world production (93,000 metric tons).

Demand – U.S. consumption of castor oil in 2009-10 fell by -35.5% to 39.311 million pounds, down from the 2007-08 record high of 97.769 million pounds. The 2009-10 consumption is estimated to be only about 58 million pounds based on the first three months of the year.

World Production of Castorseed Beans   In Thousands of Metric Tons

Year	Brazil	China	Ecuador	India	Mexico	Paraguay	Pakistan	Philip-pines	Sudan	Tanzania	Thailand	Former U.S.S.R.	Total
2002-03	72	265	4	650	1	7	1	4	1	3	10	2	1,055
2003-04	78	258	4	720	1	10	10	4	1	3	10	2	1,154
2004-05	129	250	2	870	1	11	7	4	1	3	10	2	1,350
2005-06	162	220	2	930	1	12	8	4	1	3	11	2	1,418
2006-07	92	190	3	820	1	9	8	4	1	3	11	2	1,210
2007-08[1]	94	170	3	1,000	1	10	8	4	1	3	11	2	1,376
2008-09[2]	123	190	3	975	1	13	8	4	1	4	11	----	1,405
2009-10[3]	93	190	3	930	1	13	8	4	1	3	11	----	1,328

[1] Preliminary.   [2] Estimate.   [3] Forecast.   *Sources: Foreign Agricultural Service, U.S.Department of Agriculture (FAS-USDA); The Oil World*

Castor Oil Consumption[2] in the United States   In Thousands of Pounds

Year	Oct.	Nov.	Dec.	Jan.	Feb.	Mar.	Apr.	May	June	July	Aug.	Sept.	Total
2004-05	2,155	1,391	1,581	1,365	1,915	1,992	2,175	2,211	1,827	1,689	2,021	1,162	21,484
2005-06	1,389	1,761	1,654	1,602	1,610	1,426	1,457	1,766	1,899	1,516	1,768	1,379	19,227
2006-07	1,583	2,026	1,642	2,021	4,011	6,577	5,105	4,107	5,360	5,123	2,161	3,813	43,529
2007-08	2,616	4,583	W	7,664	7,890	7,942	9,327	9,190	9,101	10,361	11,406	9,542	89,622
2008-09	10,137	7,123	7,775	7,231	5,447	2,994	4,758	4,322	4,718	W	2,109	4,363	60,977
2009-10	4,294	5,658	4,529	4,850	4,590	4,243	W	1,763	3,583	3,696	1,097	1,008	39,311
2010-11[1]	W	W	W										

[1] Preliminary.   [2] In inedible products (Resins, Plastics, etc.).   W = Withheld.   *Source: Bureau of the Census, U.S. Department of Commerce*

Castor Oil Stocks in the United States, on First of Month   In Thousands of Pounds

Year	Oct.	Nov.	Dec.	Jan.	Feb.	Mar.	Apr.	May	June	July	Aug.	Sept.
2004-05	34,525	31,608	24,287	19,476	32,641	25,318	27,876	19,098	31,493	22,919	15,963	35,604
2005-06	38,357	45,720	37,111	29,428	21,047	25,076	15,756	25,543	25,070	22,165	21,329	14,389
2006-07	39,635	24,055	18,780	43,896	30,734	46,850	58,989	50,455	49,276	46,715	37,668	26,019
2007-08	16,945	34,444	23,661	36,046	30,034	20,303	22,240	14,167	39,649	27,285	14,907	W
2008-09	W	W	47,243	38,349	56,845	50,612	38,987	32,208	42,361	34,222	25,908	25,111
2009-10	28,817	21,217	20,504	22,054	19,057	21,675	W	W	W	W	W	W
2010-11[1]	W	W	W									

[1] Preliminary.   W = Withheld proprietary data.   *Source: Bureau of the Census, U.S. Department of Commerce*

Average Wholesale Price of Castor Oil No. 1, Brazilian Tanks in New York   In Cents Per Pound

2003	47.00	47.00	47.00	47.00	47.00	47.00	47.00	47.00	47.00	47.00	47.00	47.00	47.00
2004	47.00	47.00	47.00	47.00	47.00	47.00	47.00	47.00	47.00	47.00	47.00	48.00	47.08
2005	50.00	50.00	50.00	50.00	50.00	50.00	50.00	49.00	49.00	47.00	45.50	45.00	48.79
2006	45.00	45.00	44.00	43.00	43.00	43.00	43.00	43.00	44.00	44.00	44.00	43.50	43.71
2007	46.60	49.75	52.00	54.60	58.00	57.50	56.00	NA	60.00	60.00	60.00	60.29	55.89
2008	63.57	66.11	70.20	72.00	72.00	74.29	78.00	82.00	82.00	80.18	79.21	77.67	74.77
2009	76.00	72.58	70.00	69.00	67.00	64.45	64.09	65.00	65.00	67.00	67.00	70.64	68.15
2010	71.00	71.00	72.04	74.95	80.45	82.00	83.05	84.09	NA	NA	NA	NA	77.32

Source: Foreign Agricultural Service, U.S.Department of Agriculture (FAS-USDA)

Cattle and Calves

The beef cycle begins with the cow-calf operation, which breeds the new calves. Most ranchers breed their herds of cows in summer, thus producing the new crop of calves in spring (the gestation period is about nine months). This allows the calves to be born during the milder weather of spring and provides the calves with ample forage through the summer and early autumn. The calves are weaned from the mother after 6-8 months and most are then moved into the "stocker" operation. The calves usually spend 6-10 months in the stocker operation, growing to near full-sized by foraging for summer grass or winter wheat. When the cattle reach 600-800 pounds, they are typically sent to a feedlot and become "feeder cattle." In the feedlot, the cattle are fed a special food mix to encourage rapid weight gain. The mix includes grain (corn, milo, or wheat), a protein supplement (soybean, cottonseed, or linseed meal), and roughage (alfalfa, silage, prairie hay, or an agricultural by-product such as sugar beet pulp). The animal is considered "finished" when it reaches full weight and is ready for slaughter, typically at around 1,200 pounds, which produces a dressed carcass of around 745 pounds. After reaching full weight, the cattle are sold for slaughter to a meat packing plant. Futures and options on live cattle and feeder cattle are traded at the Chicago Mercantile Exchange. Both the live and feeder cattle futures contracts trade in terms of cents per pound.

Prices – Live cattle futures prices, after posting a 4-1/2 year low of 78.7 cents per pound in December 2009, moved up to a 2-year high of 102.0 cents in April as foreign demand for U.S. beef picked up. The increase in foreign demand cut into supplies with U.S. beef in cold storage falling to a 5-year low of 363 million lbs in May. Live cattle prices then traded sideways in the range of about 89-100 cents into Q4 of 2010 when prices rose into the end of the year, closing the year up 25% at 107.9 cents. Cattle prices in January of 2011 rose to an all-time high of $1.12375 a pound, the highest since cattle futures trading began in 1964. Strong export demand underpinned prices with US beef exports up +18.9% y/y in 2010. The USDA's quarterly cattle report in Jan 2011 showed the US cattle herd as of Jan 1 2011 was 92.582 million head, -1.4% y/y and the smallest since 1958 as high feed costs prompted ranchers to cull herds. Future cattle supplies may be limited after the USDA estimated the number of calves born during 2010 was 35.685 million, down -0.7% y/y and the fewest since 1950.

Supply – The world's number of cattle as of January 1, 2010 rose +0.1% to 992.212 million head, which is just above last year's 3-1/2 decade low. As of January 1, 2010 the number of cattle and calves on farms in the U.S. fell -1.4% to 92.582 million, which is just above last year's lowest level since the 1959 figure of 93.881. World production of beef and veal in 2010 fell -1.2% to 56.763 million metric tons (carcass weight equivalent) and the USDA is forecasting a drop of -0.2% to 56.663 million metric tons in 2011. U.S. commercial production of beef in 2010 rose by 1.3% to 26.311 billion pounds.

Demand – World consumption of beef and veal in 2010 fell -0.5% to 56.742 million metric tons and the USDA is forecasting a further drop of 0.1% in 2011 to 56.371 million metric tons. U.S. consumption of beef and veal in 2010 fell -2.5% to 12.239 million metric tons and the USDA is forecasting a further drop of 1.8% in 2011 to 11.715 million metric tons.

Trade – U.S. imports of live cattle in 2010 rose +14.1% to 2.283 million head, but remained well above the low levels seen when mad cow disease caused the U.S. to close the Canadian border to live cattle in 2003. U.S. exports of live cattle in 2010 rose +53.8% yr/yr to 89.146 head, but still up from the multi-decade low of 21,607 in 2005 caused by cattle trading bans by key U.S. trading partners.

U.S. imports of beef in 2011 are forecasted to rise +9.4% to 2.445 billion pounds. U.S. exports of beef in 2011 are forecasted to be unchanged at 2.300 billion pounds, which would still be below the levels of about 2.5 billion pounds seen before mad cow disease hit in December 2003 and sharply curbed U.S. beef exports.

World Cattle and Buffalo Numbers as of January 1 — In Thousands of Head

Year	Argentina	Australia	Brazil	Canada	China	European Union	India	Mexico	Russia	South Africa	Ukraine	United States	World Total (Mil. Head)
2002	52,369	27,870	156,314	13,752	118,092	93,234	285,124	25,349	24,510	13,505	9,433	96,723	1,017.9
2003	53,069	27,870	161,463	13,466	115,678	91,597	286,079	26,011	23,500	13,635	9,108	96,100	1,015.0
2004	53,968	26,640	165,492	14,555	114,344	90,375	283,103	25,199	22,285	13,540	7,712	94,403	1,008.6
2005	53,767	27,270	169,567	14,925	112,354	89,319	285,000	24,309	21,100	13,510	6,992	95,018	1,010.4
2006	54,266	27,782	172,111	14,655	109,908	89,672	290,000	23,669	19,850	13,790	6,514	96,342	1,016.0
2007	55,664	28,400	173,830	14,155	104,651	88,463	296,500	23,316	19,000	13,934	6,175	96,573	1,018.1
2008	55,662	28,040	175,437	13,895	105,948	89,043	303,000	22,850	18,370	14,082	5,491	96,035	1,020.5
2009	54,260	27,321	179,540	13,180	105,722	88,837	303,500	22,666	17,900	14,195	5,079	94,521	1,010.1
2010[1]	49,057	27,907	185,325	13,013	105,430	88,300	304,000	22,192	17,630	----	4,950	93,701	991.2
2011[2]	48,656	28,280	191,000	12,288	105,060	87,500	304,000	21,697	16,919	----	4,871	92,550	992.2

[1] Preliminary. [2] Forecast. *Source: Foreign Agricultural Service, U.S. Department of Agriculture (FAS-USDA)*

Cattle Supply and Distribution in the United States   In Thousands of Head

Year	Cattle & Calves on Farms Jan. 1	Imports	Calves Born	Total Supply	Livestock Slaughter - Cattle and Calves - Commercial Federally Inspected	Other³	All Commercial	Farm	Total Slaughter	Deaths on Farms	Exports	Total Disappearance
2001	97,277	2,437	38,280	137,994	35,751	625	36,377	200	36,577	4,209	449	41,235
2002	96,704	2,503	38,224	137,431	36,139	641	36,780	190	36,970	4,076	244	41,290
2003	96,100	1,752	37,903	135,755	35,883	611	36,494	192	36,686	4,030	99	40,815
2004	94,888	1,371	37,505	133,764	32,979	592	33,571	189	33,760	4,003	16	37,779
2005	95,438	1,816	37,575	134,829	32,549	573	33,122	189	33,311	4,052	22	37,385
2006	96,342	2,289	37,016	135,646	33,844	566	34,410	187	34,597	4,167	50	38,813
2007	96,573	2,495	36,759	135,827	34,465	557	35,022	187	35,209	4,251	66	39,526
2008	96,035	2,284	36,153	134,471	34,747	574	35,322	186	35,507	4,074	107	39,688
2009¹	94,521	2,002	35,939	132,462	33,696	587	34,282	185	34,468	4,064	58	38,590
2010²	93,881	2,284	35,685	131,850	34,566						89	

¹ Preliminary.   ² Estimate.   ³ Wholesale and retail.   *Source: Economic Research Service, U.S. Department of Agriculture (ERS-USDA)*

Beef Supply and Utilization in the United States

Years and Quarters	Beginning Stocks	Production Commercial	Production Total	Imports	Total Supply	Exports	Ending Stocks	Total Disappearance	Per Capita Disappearance - Carcass Weight	Retail Weight Total
2007	630	26,421	27,051	3,052	30,103	1,434	630	28,141	93.2	65.2
I	630	6,237	6,867	770	7,637	269	559	6,845	22.7	15.9
II	559	6,649	7,208	885	8,093	364	568	7,175	23.8	16.6
III	568	6,802	7,370	774	8,144	425	639	7,095	23.5	16.4
IV	639	6,733	7,372	624	7,996	376	630	7,026	23.2	16.2
2008	630	26,561	27,191	2,537	29,728	1,888	642	27,303	89.6	62.8
I	630	6,372	7,002	637	7,639	360	553	6,764	22.3	15.6
II	553	6,899	7,452	661	8,113	471	559	7,097	23.3	16.3
III	559	6,908	7,467	584	8,051	609	590	6,865	22.5	15.8
IV	590	6,382	6,972	655	7,627	448	642	6,576	21.5	15.1
2009	642	25,963	26,605	2,628	29,233	1,869	565	26,836	87.3	61.2
I	642	6,248	6,890	704	7,594	384	556	6,651	21.7	15.3
II	556	6,602	7,158	751	7,909	471	570	6,855	22.3	15.7
III	570	6,689	7,259	623	7,882	496	560	6,841	22.2	15.6
IV	560	6,524	7,084	550	7,634	518	565	6,489	21.0	14.7
2010¹	----	26,316	26,316	2,271	28,587	2,303	----	----	----	59.5
I	565	6,251	6,816	573	7,389	478	502	6,445	20.9	14.6
II	502	6,549	7,051	690	7,741	585	487	6,684	21.6	15.1
III	487	6,771	7,258	598	7,856	590	514	6,767	21.8	15.3
IV	----	6,746	6,746	410	7,156	650	----	----	----	14.6
2011²	----	25,915	25,915	2,382	28,297	2,345	----	----	----	58.5
I	----	6,420	6,420	525	6,945	580	----	----	----	14.6
II	----	6,610	6,610	630	7,240	610	----	----	----	15.0
III	----	6,575	6,575	640	7,215	590	----	----	----	14.8
IV	----	6,310	6,310	590	6,900	565	----	----	----	14.2

¹ Preliminary.   ² Forecast.   *Source: Economic Research Service, U.S. Department of Agriculture (ERS-USDA)*

United States Cattle on Feed in 13 States   In Thousands of Head

Year	Number on Feed³	Placed on Feed	Marketings	Other Disappearance	Year	Number on Feed³	Placed on Feed	Marketings	Other Disappearance
2007	11,974	23,400	22,461	821	2009¹	11,234	22,187	21,755	746
I	11,974	5,309	5,395	244	I	11,234	5,344	5,243	173
II	11,644	5,384	6,041	250	II	11,162	4,629	5,812	227
III	10,737	6,156	5,761	165	III	9,752	6,370	5,565	146
IV	10,967	6,551	5,264	162	IV	10,474	5,844	5,135	200
2008	12,092	22,299	22,404	753	2010²	10,983	23,366	22,079	787
I	12,092	5,246	5,471	183	I	10,983	5,352	5,395	198
II	11,684	4,954	6,128	215	II	10,767	5,277	5,723	251
III	10,295	5,998	5,733	145	III	10,070	6,486	5,628	149
IV	10,415	6,101	5,072	210	IV	10,779	6,251	5,333	189

¹ Preliminary.   ² Estimate.   ³ Beginning of period.   *Source: Economic Research Service, U.S. Department of Agriculture (ERS-USDA)*

CATTLE AND CALVES

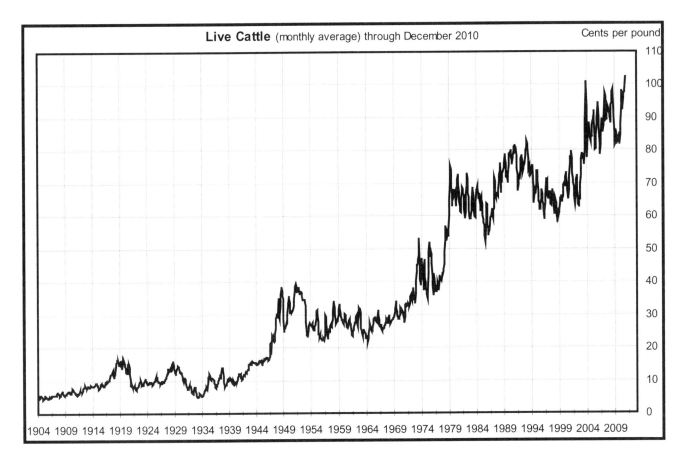

Live Cattle (monthly average) through December 2010   Cents per pound

United States Cattle on Feed, 1000+ Capacity Feedlots, on First of Month In Thousands of Head

Year	Jan.	Feb.	Mar.	Apr.	May	June	July	Aug.	Sept.	Oct.	Nov.	Dec.
2001	11,798	11,941	11,695	11,523	11,170	11,245	11,011	10,891	10,855	11,125	11,863	11,891
2002	11,565	11,572	11,518	11,587	10,971	10,990	10,507	10,109	10,159	10,452	10,785	10,946
2003	10,658	10,700	10,546	10,713	10,535	10,539	9,923	9,590	9,839	10,218	11,043	11,335
2004	11,253	11,138	10,987	10,763	10,375	10,640	10,132	9,868	9,988	10,502	11,334	11,334
2005	11,299	11,342	11,154	10,873	10,641	10,771	10,394	10,093	10,000	10,482	11,473	11,726
2006	11,804	12,110	12,023	11,812	11,559	11,187	10,872	10,822	10,986	11,385	11,969	11,973
2007	11,974	11,726	11,599	11,644	11,297	11,272	10,737	10,299	10,302	10,967	11,769	12,099
2008	12,092	11,966	11,853	11,684	11,135	10,815	10,295	9,869	9,997	10,415	10,972	11,346
2009	11,234	11,288	11,228	11,162	10,822	10,407	9,752	9,637	9,900	10,474	11,134	11,277
2010[1]	10,983	10,959	10,849	10,767	10,443	10,494	10,070	9,873	10,173	10,779	11,487	11,620

[1] Preliminary.   *Source: Economic Research Service, U.S. Department of Agriculture (ERS-USDA)*

United States Cattle Placed on Feed, 1000+ Capacity Feedlots   In Thousands of Head

Year	Jan.	Feb.	Mar.	Apr.	May	June	July	Aug.	Sept.	Oct.	Nov.	Dec.	Total
2001	2,263	1,580	1,842	1,551	2,372	1,965	1,986	2,204	2,141	2,702	1,908	1,578	24,092
2002	2,179	1,810	1,963	1,463	2,267	1,644	1,840	2,228	2,194	2,396	1,982	1,610	23,576
2003	2,089	1,650	2,032	1,870	2,307	1,672	1,997	2,384	2,474	2,781	1,926	1,748	24,930
2004	1,754	1,612	1,810	1,600	2,370	1,647	1,719	2,102	2,375	2,701	1,743	1,834	23,267
2005	1,888	1,523	1,750	1,660	2,223	1,769	1,678	1,993	2,355	2,788	2,045	1,884	23,556
2006	2,199	1,588	1,837	1,619	1,903	1,946	1,958	2,290	2,227	2,430	1,884	1,714	23,595
2007	1,690	1,659	1,960	1,568	2,159	1,657	1,622	2,119	2,415	2,725	2,125	1,701	23,400
2008	1,787	1,723	1,736	1,536	1,900	1,518	1,656	2,061	2,281	2,438	2,016	1,647	22,299
2009	1,858	1,678	1,808	1,600	1,638	1,391	1,863	2,119	2,388	2,474	1,844	1,526	22,187
2010[1]	1,822	1,674	1,856	1,627	2,022	1,628	1,754	2,270	2,462	2,504	1,958	1,789	23,366

[1] Preliminary.   *Source: Economic Research Service, U.S. Department of Agriculture (ERS-USDA)*

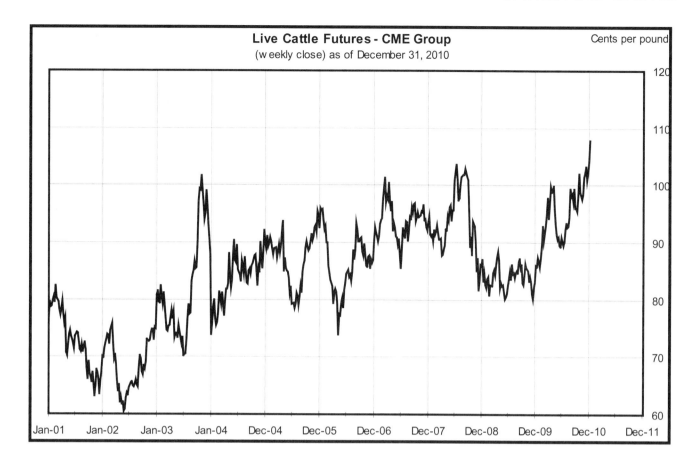

Live Cattle Futures - CME Group
(weekly close) as of December 31, 2010

Cents per pound

United States Cattle Marketings, 1000+ Capacity Feedlots[2]   In Thousands of Head

Year	Jan.	Feb.	Mar.	Apr.	May	June	July	Aug.	Sept.	Oct.	Nov.	Dec.	Total
2001	2,042	1,745	1,916	1,815	2,196	2,122	2,047	2,186	1,825	1,896	1,800	1,811	23,401
2002	2,083	1,801	1,825	1,996	2,171	2,076	2,193	2,135	1,848	1,979	1,731	1,799	23,637
2003	1,972	1,733	1,803	1,985	2,238	2,227	2,270	2,075	2,032	1,855	1,537	1,740	23,467
2004	1,775	1,694	1,967	1,891	2,026	2,085	1,925	1,926	1,800	1,803	1,635	1,777	22,304
2005	1,772	1,634	1,963	1,801	1,997	2,083	1,918	2,033	1,816	1,739	1,701	1,715	22,172
2006	1,810	1,602	1,958	1,785	2,160	2,198	1,950	2,067	1,760	1,765	1,797	1,625	22,477
2007	1,841	1,711	1,843	1,816	2,085	2,140	1,999	2,066	1,696	1,876	1,738	1,650	22,461
2008	1,853	1,776	1,842	2,010	2,140	1,978	2,037	1,884	1,812	1,814	1,575	1,683	22,404
2009	1,737	1,682	1,824	1,871	1,952	1,989	1,935	1,800	1,767	1,755	1,635	1,745	21,692
2010[1]	1,776	1,716	1,903	1,857	1,869	1,997	1,903	1,923	1,802	1,734	1,769	1,830	22,079

[1] Preliminary.   *Source: Economic Research Service, U.S. Department of Agriculture (ERS-USDA)*

Quarterly Trade of Live Cattle in the United States   In Head

Year	Imports First Quarter	Imports Second Quarter	Imports Third Quarter	Imports Fourth Quarter	Imports Total	Exports First Quarter	Exports Second Quarter	Exports Third Quarter	Exports Fourth Quarter	Exports Total
2001	701,347	611,570	444,604	679,194	2,436,715	111,458	75,632	67,042	194,563	448,695
2002	785,559	398,072	474,185	845,157	2,502,973	73,060	62,140	50,859	58,335	244,394
2003	630,381	409,239	142,296	569,980	1,751,896	36,692	34,152	11,114	16,860	98,818
2004	306,555	315,996	280,824	467,236	1,370,611	176	7,208	2,629	5,708	15,721
2005	336,216	348,368	342,661	788,293	1,815,538	5,580	6,446	5,977	3,604	21,607
2006	708,680	470,176	418,117	691,870	2,288,843	8,721	12,473	10,249	18,235	49,678
2007	629,157	518,173	462,359	885,276	2,494,965	13,723	15,112	10,441	27,107	66,383
2008	682,174	562,566	405,199	634,054	2,283,993	38,319	30,575	15,181	23,417	107,492
2009	612,188	423,742	342,988	622,851	2,001,769	6,903	18,152	16,437	16,481	57,973
2010[1]	598,958	596,197	407,068	681,767	2,283,990	15,570	20,693	16,532	36,351	89,146

[1] Preliminary.   *Source: Economic Research Service, U.S. Department of Agriculture (ERS-USDA)*

CATTLE AND CALVES

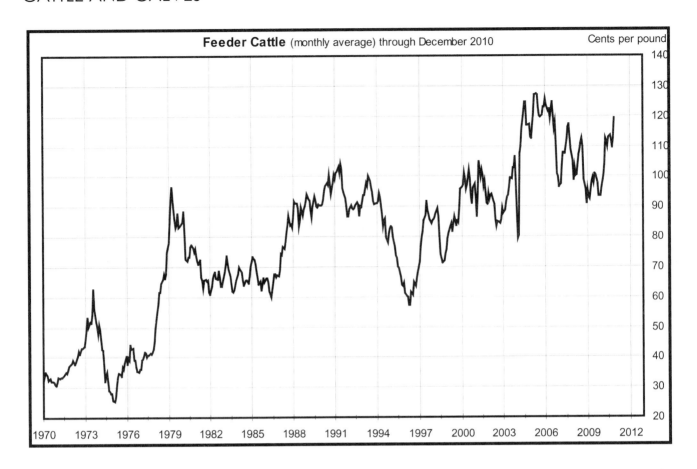

Feeder Cattle (monthly average) through December 2010 — Cents per pound

Average Slaughter Steer Price, Choice 2-4, Nebraska Direct (1100-1300 Lb.) In Dollars Per 100 Pounds

Year	Jan.	Feb.	Mar.	Apr.	May	June	July	Aug.	Sept.	Oct.	Nov.	Dec.	Average
2004	80.36	79.15	86.96	87.04	88.22	89.19	84.27	84.15	82.33	84.03	84.64	86.60	84.75
2005	87.77	87.73	91.78	91.98	88.83	83.06	79.37	80.80	85.19	87.40	90.32	93.08	87.28
2006	92.90	89.09	85.73	81.30	79.02	80.85	81.14	85.87	89.18	87.43	86.56	85.83	85.41
2007	86.75	88.68	96.39	98.04	95.50	86.81	89.09	91.49	93.49	91.69	93.37	90.50	91.82
2008	88.63	90.85	89.28	89.04	93.86	95.55	98.83	99.14	97.37	90.61	90.40	83.66	92.27
2009	81.60	79.68	81.66	87.02	85.27	81.31	82.72	82.48	83.13	83.53	83.43	80.34	82.68
2010	83.46	87.41	92.93	99.58	97.93	92.25	93.12	96.42	97.22	97.85	99.89	102.30	95.03

Source: Economic Research Service, U.S. Department of Agriculture (ERS-USDA)

Average Price of Feeder Steers in Oklahoma City In Dollars Per 100 Pounds

Year	Jan.	Feb.	Mar.	Apr.	May	June	July	Aug.	Sept.	Oct.	Nov.	Dec.	Average
2004	79.35	80.18	107.35	109.99	115.40	121.10	124.63	124.65	116.97	116.96	117.13	113.01	110.56
2005	112.40	116.87	120.48	126.77	127.13	126.91	122.73	119.96	119.61	120.29	122.84	122.75	121.56
2006	125.49	123.56	121.41	122.29	119.35	122.29	124.55	120.35	123.90	114.85	100.78	99.80	118.22
2007	96.54	97.50	103.38	107.97	107.74	107.65	112.29	116.30	117.20	112.79	108.80	105.13	107.77
2008	98.62	102.81	100.17	100.45	107.08	108.90	111.07	112.53	109.69	98.84	95.76	90.76	103.06
2009	95.57	93.19	92.47	98.05	99.58	97.74	100.65	100.39	97.75	93.56	93.33	93.29	96.30
2010	96.25	100.06	103.82	112.43	111.44	109.75	112.68	113.53	111.92	109.65	112.58	119.32	109.45

Source: Economic Research Service, U.S. Department of Agriculture (ERS-USDA)

Federally Inspected Slaughter of Cattle in the United States In Thousands of Head

Year	Jan.	Feb.	Mar.	Apr.	May	June	July	Aug.	Sept.	Oct.	Nov.	Dec.	Total
2004	2,527	2,381	2,818	2,654	2,792	2,949	2,745	2,775	2,689	2,693	2,492	2,642	32,156
2005	2,477	2,297	2,675	2,517	2,751	2,894	2,677	2,948	2,729	2,625	2,623	2,619	31,831
2006	2,591	2,302	2,806	2,566	2,993	3,116	2,795	3,089	2,721	2,803	2,797	2,566	33,145
2007	2,748	2,518	2,747	2,660	3,008	3,035	2,860	3,088	2,621	3,046	2,787	2,603	33,721
2008	2,847	2,598	2,684	2,914	3,095	2,912	3,017	2,866	2,842	2,933	2,475	2,623	33,805
2009	2,668	2,479	2,681	2,724	2,806	2,936	2,878	2,738	2,766	2,829	2,556	2,704	32,765
2010[1]	2,657	2,503	2,864	2,801	2,743	3,004	2,860	2,912	2,851	2,809	2,830	2,868	33,702

[1] Preliminary.   *Source: National Agricultural Statistics Service, U.S. Department of Agriculture (NASS-USDA)*

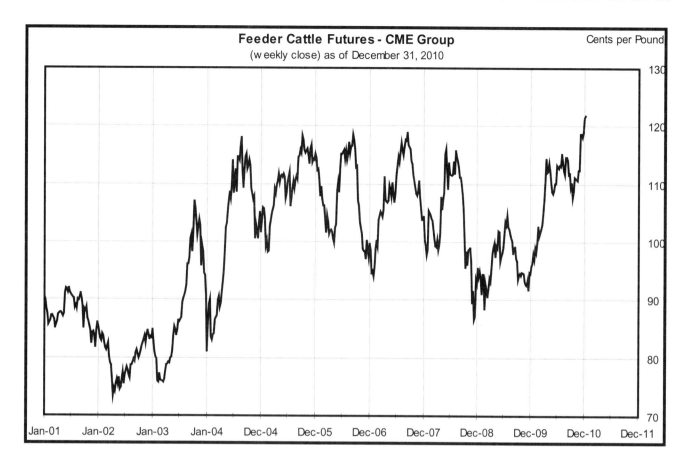

Feeder Cattle Futures - CME Group
(weekly close) as of December 31, 2010

Cents per Pound

Average Open Interest of Live Cattle Futures in Chicago   In Contracts

Year	Jan.	Feb.	Mar.	Apr.	May	June	July	Aug.	Sept.	Oct.	Nov.	Dec.
2001	132,298	132,866	131,312	123,075	112,180	114,970	116,162	105,252	114,214	109,677	108,574	95,182
2002	93,589	91,566	98,176	98,343	98,846	91,129	93,541	92,966	109,651	111,338	121,671	116,588
2003	111,874	105,882	98,943	96,875	107,193	111,397	113,324	115,417	130,836	124,525	113,224	106,522
2004	98,752	99,491	112,449	124,930	128,727	126,481	114,656	109,588	104,928	109,832	112,709	123,483
2005	142,333	140,869	146,062	141,610	145,235	133,768	135,971	134,329	148,094	167,175	174,496	197,090
2006	225,313	220,947	220,042	240,567	261,496	235,783	231,914	213,918	214,583	205,776	211,814	224,501
2007	257,373	273,121	296,235	281,239	261,866	240,526	235,110	212,154	234,754	234,584	240,710	241,614
2008	252,555	273,397	276,043	285,956	298,370	298,937	300,862	278,808	265,436	227,860	215,054	211,836
2009	207,768	203,912	207,221	206,462	204,424	211,978	222,562	233,578	251,083	260,285	266,293	262,738
2010	276,265	294,225	343,951	362,939	362,895	327,910	323,477	339,349	344,298	317,349	321,039	332,858

Contract size = 40,000 lbs.   *Source: CME Group; Chicago Mercantile Exchange (CME)*

Volume of Trading of Live Cattle Futures Chicago   In Thousands of Contracts

Year	Jan.	Feb.	Mar.	Apr.	May	June	July	Aug.	Sept.	Oct.	Nov.	Dec.	Total
2001	511,050	357,474	385,581	302,829	348,294	289,093	318,564	324,614	340,969	403,101	403,009	294,695	4,279,273
2002	331,026	275,699	387,115	448,508	304,900	247,940	286,248	288,525	314,927	352,487	315,658	298,703	3,851,736
2003	378,862	343,931	334,007	306,713	391,477	311,239	449,966	319,677	473,218	469,405	324,732	332,862	4,436,089
2004	362,295	265,370	442,636	353,886	419,888	345,611	381,151	340,973	382,536	344,517	511,516	359,749	4,510,128
2005	519,794	395,847	598,171	377,494	503,753	405,687	506,253	406,010	569,040	438,631	627,585	485,291	5,833,556
2006	783,018	498,779	849,546	570,015	817,491	709,706	718,772	670,410	698,285	631,911	757,795	503,970	8,209,698
2007	907,155	663,121	1,046,653	575,800	814,423	513,667	849,053	634,475	724,467	638,942	761,870	458,347	8,587,973
2008	982,593	596,374	954,198	724,449	936,181	731,340	1,006,398	738,206	998,230	801,087	773,949	558,355	9,801,360
2009	819,482	616,769	789,335	641,323	721,536	617,848	855,383	657,909	854,593	739,683	844,321	638,851	8,797,033
2010	900,995	782,922	1,167,167	863,189	1,204,478	785,824	923,813	868,264	1,158,829	827,133	1,066,253	783,872	11,332,739

Contract size = 40,000 lbs.   *Source: CME Group; Chicago Mercantile Exchange (CME)*

CATTLE AND CALVES

Beef Steer-Corn Price Ratio[1] in the United States

Year	Jan.	Feb.	Mar.	Apr.	May	June	July	Aug.	Sept.	Oct.	Nov.	Dec.	Average
2003	33.4	33.4	32.9	33.7	33.4	33.6	36.4	38.6	40.6	46.1	45.4	41.4	37.4
2004	35.7	31.5	32.0	30.8	32.3	33.6	36.4	38.9	40.7	42.6	44.0	45.0	37.0
2005	44.5	47.7	47.1	49.1	48.5	45.3	41.8	45.0	48.5	52.8	54.9	51.9	48.1
2006	51.0	48.3	45.0	42.3	39.8	41.2	42.1	43.8	43.3	36.7	31.3	29.6	41.2
2007	29.4	26.6	28.5	29.4	28.1	26.4	28.0	29.4	30.0	29.4	27.9	25.3	28.2
2008	23.5	20.8	19.8	17.9	18.2	17.6	19.0	19.0	19.8	21.3	21.3	20.9	19.9
2009	19.7	21.7	21.8	22.9	22.1	21.2	23.7	25.6	26.3	23.4	23.4	23.3	22.9
2010[1]	23.9	25.5	26.9	29.6	28.6	27.8	27.5	26.8	24.3	22.9	22.2	21.6	25.6

[1] Bushels of corn equal in value to 100 pounds of steers and heifers. [2] Preliminary. *Source: Economic Research Service, U.S. Department of Agriculture*

Farm Value, Income and Wholesale Prices of Cattle and Calves in the United States

	January 1 Per Head Dollars	January 1 Total Million $	Gross Income From C & C[2] Million $	At Omaha Steers Choice	At Omaha Steers Select	At Omaha Heifers[4] Select	At Omaha Heifers[4] Choice	Feeder Heifers at Oklahoma City[5]	Cows, Boning Utility Sioux Falls[6]	Cows, Commercial Sioux Falls	Wholesale Prices, Central U.S. Choice 700-850 lb.	Wholesale Prices, Central U.S. Select 700-850 lb.	Cow[6], Canner, Cutter
Year								Dollars per 100 Pounds					
2004	818	77,595	47,935	84.78	----	----	84.40	100.09	55.20	52.35	141.33	132.65	NA
2005	916	87,386	49,668	86.54	----	----	87.35	106.87	55.52	54.36	145.78	136.36	NA
2006	1,009	97,579	49,423	85.55	----	----	86.58	102.00	50.50	47.56	146.82	132.56	NA
2007	922	89,447	50,284					102.06	54.77	52.12	149.80	140.09	NA
2008	987	95,401	48,934					96.85	57.75	54.92	153.17	147.68	NA
2009			44,163					90.49	50.87	47.94	140.77	135.70	NA
2010[1]								104.22	NA	NA	156.91	150.99	NA

[1] Preliminary. [2] Excludes interfarm sales & Gov't. payments. Cash receipts from farm marketings + value of farm home consumption.
[3] 1,000 to 1,100 lb. [4] 1,000 to 1,200 lb. [5] 700 to 750 lb. [6] All weights.
Source: Economic Research Service, U.S. Department of Agriculture (NASS-USDA)

Average Price Received by Farmers for Beef Cattle in the United States   In Dollars Per 100 Pounds

Year	Jan.	Feb.	Mar.	Apr.	May	June	July	Aug.	Sept.	Oct.	Nov.	Dec.	Average
2003	73.20	73.90	72.60	74.50	75.50	74.90	75.80	79.30	84.90	91.50	93.40	90.40	79.99
2004	80.90	78.50	83.70	85.00	88.50	89.80	88.10	87.70	85.90	86.50	85.40	86.80	85.57
2005	89.40	88.80	91.00	93.70	92.10	88.00	85.00	84.40	88.00	90.40	90.80	93.30	89.58
2006	95.10	92.40	87.90	84.80	82.20	84.00	85.80	87.20	90.00	88.20	84.40	83.10	87.09
2007	84.30	86.10	91.60	93.70	92.80	88.80	89.00	91.40	93.10	90.90	89.90	89.20	90.07
2008	87.30	89.00	87.80	86.80	91.30	91.90	95.00	95.80	94.20	87.40	84.30	79.70	89.21
2009	80.10	78.90	79.10	83.80	83.20	80.10	80.90	80.40	80.50	79.20	79.60	78.50	80.36
2010[1]	82.10	85.70	90.50	95.70	94.80	90.30	91.60	93.50	94.20	93.10	94.00	98.10	91.97

[1] Preliminary. *Source: National Agricultural Statistics Service, U.S. Department of Agriculture (NASS-USDA)*

Average Price Received by Farmers for Calves in the United States   In Dollars Per 100 Pounds

Year	Jan.	Feb.	Mar.	Apr.	May	June	July	Aug.	Sept.	Oct.	Nov.	Dec.	Average
2003	96.80	97.20	96.70	98.90	100.00	101.00	102.00	106.00	109.00	112.00	111.00	112.00	103.55
2004	110.00	111.00	115.00	117.00	121.00	125.00	130.00	131.00	128.00	126.00	123.00	122.00	121.58
2005	125.00	129.00	136.00	141.00	143.00	140.00	133.00	133.00	135.00	135.00	137.00	137.00	135.33
2006	141.00	143.00	139.00	137.00	134.00	135.00	137.00	136.00	136.00	128.00	119.00	116.00	133.42
2007	115.00	114.00	122.00	125.00	124.00	124.00	126.00	127.00	126.00	123.00	122.00	120.00	122.33
2008	117.00	120.00	118.00	116.00	120.00	118.00	114.00	117.00	113.00	106.00	105.00	98.90	113.58
2009	106.00	104.00	106.00	109.00	111.00	109.00	108.00	108.00	105.00	103.00	104.00	105.00	106.50
2010[1]	109.00	113.00	115.00	122.00	122.00	121.00	120.00	121.00	117.00	120.00	124.00	128.00	119.33

[1] Preliminary. *Source: National Agricultural Statistics Board, U.S. Department of Agriculture (NASS-USDA)*

Federally Inspected Slaughter of Calves and Vealers in the United States   In Thousands of Head

Year	Jan.	Feb.	Mar.	Apr.	May	June	July	Aug.	Sept.	Oct.	Nov.	Dec.	Total
2003	92	81	83	77	74	72	83	78	80	85	76	95	976
2004	77	70	75	69	63	65	67	71	66	61	66	73	823
2005	66	61	67	60	57	58	57	64	60	54	55	59	718
2006	54	52	58	47	56	58	57	66	57	62	66	67	699
2007	73	66	70	56	58	60	62	65	55	64	58	60	745
2008	70	68	70	72	70	74	87	78	86	94	80	93	942
2009	84	73	79	67	64	76	79	76	80	82	80	91	930
2010[1]	82	73	79	67	59	67	74	75	70	70	72	77	864

[1] Preliminary. *Source: Crop Reporting Board, U.S. Department of Agriculture (CRB-USDA)*

Cement

Cement is made in a wide variety of compositions and is used in many different ways. The best-known cement is *Portland cement*, which is bound with sand and gravel to create concrete. Concrete is used to unite the surfaces of various materials and to coat surfaces to protect them from various chemicals. Portland cement is almost universally used for structural concrete. It is manufactured from lime-bearing materials, usually limestone, together with clays, blast-furnace slag containing alumina and silica or shale. The combination is usually approximately 60 percent lime, 19 percent silica, 8 percent alumina, 5 percent iron, 5 percent magnesia, and 3 percent sulfur trioxide. To slow the hardening process, gypsum is often added. In 1924, the name "Portland cement" was coined by Joseph Aspdin, a British cement maker, because of the resemblance between concrete made from his cement and Portland stone. The United States did not start producing Portland cement in any great quantity until the 20th century. Hydraulic cements are those that set and harden in water. Clinker cement is an intermediate product in cement manufacture. The production and consumption of cement is directly related to the level of activity in the construction industry.

Prices – The average value (F.O.B. mill) of Portland cement in 2010 fell -7.1% yr/yr to $92 per ton, down from the 2008 record high $103.00 per ton.

Supply – World production of hydraulic cement in 2010 rose +7.8% yr/yr to 3.300 billion tons, a new record high. The world's largest hydraulic cement producers were China with 54.5% of world production in 2010, India (6.7%), U.S. (1.9%), and Japan (1.7%).

U.S. production of Portland cement in 2008 (latest data available) fell -8.6% yr/yr to 83,283, further down from the 2005 record high of 93.904 million tons. U.S. shipments of finished Portland cement from mills in the U.S. in 2010 rose +0.1% to 64.450 million metric tons, falling farther below the 2005 record high of 95.588 million metric tons.

Demand – U.S. consumption of cement in 2010 fell -2.8% to 69.500 million metric tons, falling farther below the 2005 record high of 128.260 million metric tons.

Trade – The U.S. relied on imports for 8% of its cement consumption in 2010. The two main suppliers of cement to the U.S. were Canada and a Mexico. U.S. exports of cement in 2010 rose +13.1% yr/yr to 1.000 million metric tons.

World Production of Hydraulic Cement   In Thousands of Short Tons

Year	Brazil	China	France	Germany	India	Italy	Japan	Rep. of Korea	Russia	Spain	Turkey	United States	World Total
2003	34,010	862,080	19,655	32,749	123,000	43,580	68,766	60,725	41,000	44,747	35,077	94,329	2,030,000
2004	34,413	970,000	20,962	31,854	130,000	45,343	67,376	56,955	45,700	45,593	38,796	99,015	2,190,000
2005	36,673	1,068,850	21,277	31,009	145,000	40,284	69,629	51,391	48,500	50,347	42,787	100,903	2,350,000
2006	39,540	1,236,770	22,540	33,630	160,000	47,814	69,942	53,971	54,700	54,033	47,499	99,712	2,610,000
2007	46,406	1,361,170	22,300	33,382	170,000	47,542	67,685	57,042	59,900	54,720	49,553	96,850	2,810,000
2008	51,865	1,388,380	21,700	33,581	177,000	43,030	62,810	53,900	53,600	42,088	51,432	87,610	2,840,000
2009[1]	51,700	1,629,000	21,000	30,400	205,000	36,300	54,800	50,100	44,300	50,000	54,000	72,800	3,060,000
2010[2]	59,000	1,800,000		31,000	220,000	35,000	56,000	46,000	49,000	50,000	60,000	63,500	3,300,000

[1] Preliminary.   [2] Estimate.   *Source: U.S. Geological Survey (USGS)*

Salient Statistics of Cement in the United States

Year	Net Import Reliance as a % of Apparent Consumption	Production Portland	Production Other[3]	Production Total	Capacity Used at Portland Mills %	Shipments From Mills Total (Mil. MT)	Shipments From Mills Value[4] (Mil. $)	Average Value (F.O.B. Mill) $ per MT	Stocks at Mills Dec. 31	Exports	Apparent Consumption	Imports for Consumption[5] by Country Canada	Japan	Mexico	Spain	Total
2003	20	88,106	4,737	92,843	78.5	111,000	8,340	75.00	6,610	837	114,090	6,319	----	891	355	23,959
2004	21	92,434	5,000	97,434	81.6	120,000	9,520	79.50	6,740	749	121,950	5,753	2	1,429	408	27,026
2005	23	93,904	5,415	99,319	82.3	128,000	11,700	91.00	7,450	766	128,260	5,404	4	2,173	236	33,261
2006	27	92,768	5,399	98,167	80.6	129,240	12,900	101.50	9,380	723	127,660	5,059	3	2,264	69	35,566
2007	19	91,144	4,320	95,464	78.2	115,426	11,900	104.00	8,890	886	116,600	5,326	5	1,684	29	22,468
2008	11	83,283	3,027	86,310	70.9	97,322	9,990	103.50	8,360	823	96,800	4,104	6	1,071	1	11,365
2009[1]	8			63,929		71,489		99.00	6,130	884	71,500					6,767
2010[2]	8			62,800		71,100		92.00	4,700	1,000	69,500					6,890

[1] Preliminary.   [2] Estimate.   [3] Masonry, natural & pozzolan (slag-line).   [4] Value received F.O.B. mill, excluding cost of containers.   [5] Hydraulic & clinker cement for consumption.   [6] Less than 1/2 unit.   *Source: U.S. Geological Survey (USGS)*

Shipments of Finished Portland Cement from Mills in the United States   In Thousands of Metric Tons

Year	Jan.	Feb.	Mar.	Apr.	May	June	July	Aug.	Sept.	Oct.	Nov.	Dec.	Total
2004	5,241	5,146	8,059	8,837	8,624	9,103	9,134	9,326	8,883	8,609	7,417	6,528	94,908
2005	5,337	5,732	7,498	8,316	9,102	9,595	8,305	9,604	8,847	8,870	8,065	6,317	95,588
2006	6,542	6,088	7,704	7,763	8,871	9,230	7,917	9,144	8,011	8,539	7,549	6,097	93,456
2007	5,574	5,207	7,241	7,697	9,082	8,869	8,693	9,426	8,218	9,182	7,890	5,189	92,268
2008	5,503	5,323	6,347	7,768	8,064	8,182	8,640	7,974	7,822	8,291	6,021	4,555	84,490
2009	4,022	4,242	4,908	5,539	5,727	6,508	6,615	6,306	6,167	5,624	5,215	3,545	64,418
2010[1]	3,173	3,131	5,028	6,065	5,793	6,471	6,147	6,671	6,224	6,466	5,418	3,864	64,450

[1] Preliminary.   *Source: U.S. Geological Survey (USGS)*

Cheese

Since prehistoric times, humans have been making and eating cheese. Dating back as far as 6,000 BC, archaeologists have discovered that cheese had been made from cow and goat milk and stored in tall jars. The Romans turned cheese making into a culinary art, mixing sheep and goat milk and adding herbs and spices for flavoring. By 300 AD, cheese was being exported regularly to countries along the Mediterranean coast.

Cheese is made from the milk of cows and other mammals such as sheep, goats, buffalo, reindeer, camels, yaks, and mares. More than 400 varieties of cheese exist. There are three basic steps common to all cheese making. First, proteins in milk are transformed into curds, or solid lumps. Second, the curds are separated from the milky liquid (or whey) and shaped or pressed into molds. Finally, the shaped curds are ripened according to a variety of aging and curing techniques. Cheeses are usually grouped according to their moisture content into fresh, soft, semi-soft, hard, and very hard. Many classifications overlap due to texture changes with aging.

Cheese is a multi-billion-dollar a year industry in the U.S. Cheddar cheese is the most common natural cheese produced in the U.S., accounting for 35% of U.S. production. Cheeses originating in America include Colby, cream cheese, and Monterey Jack. Varieties other than American cheeses, mostly Italian, now have had a combined level of production that easily exceeds American cheeses.

Prices – Average monthly cheese prices at the Chicago Mercantile Exchange in 2010 rose by +9.0% yr/yr to 141.28 cents per pound, down from the 2008 record high of 185.58 cents per pound.

Supply – World production of cheese in 2010 rose +1.1% yr/yr to 14.954 million metric tons, well below the 2007 record high of 21.440 million metric tons. The European Union is the world's largest producer of cheese with 47.1% of the total world production in 2010. The U.S. production was the next largest with 31.9% of the total. U.S. production of cheese in 2010 rose +1.0% to 10.445 billion pounds, which was a new record high.

Demand – U.S. consumption of cheese in 2007 (latest data available) rose +2.5% to 10.112 billion pounds. U.S. per capita cheese consumption in 2002 (latest data available) rose +2.0% to 30.60 pounds per person per year which is a new record high.

Trade – U.S. imports of cheese in 2005 (latest data available) fell -2.5% to 460 million pounds. U.S. exports of cheese in 2005 fell 4.9% to 128 million pounds, down from 2004's record high of 134 million pounds.

World Production of Cheese   In Thousands of Metric Tons

Year	Argentina	Australia	Brazil	Canada	Egypt	European Union	Japan	Mexico	New Zealand	Russia	Ukraine	United States	World Total
2002	370	413	470	350	410	6,106	34	138	312	340	129	3,877	19,116
2003	325	368	460	342	450	6,205	35	126	301	335	169	3,882	19,219
2004	370	389	470	345	455	6,481	35	134	305	350	224	4,025	20,019
2005	400	375	495	352	480	6,625	39	143	297	375	274	4,150	20,582
2006	480	362	528	291	408	6,801	40	145	292	405	210	4,320	20,965
2007	520	360	580	308	420	6,760	43	184	350	435	244	4,435	21,440
2008	525	344	607	285	----	6,800	47	188	292	430	249	4,496	14,303
2009	530	321	614	291	----	6,810	45	242	308	400	228	4,586	14,413
2010[1]	540	335	648	297	----	6,970	48	244	303	430	220	4,720	14,792
2011[2]	550	345	675	305	----	7,040	55	247	313	430	205	4,765	14,954

[1] Preliminary.   [2] Forecast.   NA = Not available.   *Source: Foreign Agricultural Service, U.S. Department of Agriculture (FAS-USDA)*

Supply and Distribution of All Cheese in the United States   In Millions of Pounds

	Production		Supply			Cheese 40-lb. Blocks Wisconsin Assembly Points (Cents/Lb.)	Distribution				Domestic Disappearance		
Year	Whole Milk[2]	All Cheese[3]	Commercial Stocks Jan. 1	Imports[4]	Total Supply		Exports & Shipments[5]	Gov't Stocks Dec. 31	American Cheese Removed by USDA Programs	Total Disappearance	American Cheese Donated	Total	Per Capita
2000	3,642	8,258	621	416	9,295	116.15	105	2.3	28.0	8,555	----	8,406	29.80
2001	3,544	8,261	706	445	9,412	144.92	115	4.0	3.9	8,741	----	8,586	30.00
2002	3,691	8,547	659	475	9,681	118.22	119	2.7	15.8	8,933	----	8,819	30.60
2003	3,622	8,557	730	476	9,763	131.24	115	27.4	41.3	9,007			
2004	3,739	8,873	715	472	10,060	164.92	134	9.0	5.9	9,342			
2005	3,808	9,149	701	460	10,310	145.53	128			9,519			
2006	3,913	9,525	758			123.85				9,869			
2007	3,877	9,777	817			175.78				10,112			
2008	4,109	9,913	798			185.58							
2009[1]	4,202	10,109	852			129.61							

[1] Preliminary.   [2] Whole milk American cheddar.   [3] All types of cheese except cottage, pot and baker's cheese.   [4] Imports for consumption.
[5] Commercial.   *Source: Economic Research Service, U.S. Department of Agriculture (ERS-USDA)*

Production of Cheese in the United States   In Millions of Pounds

Year	American Whole Milk	American Part Skim	American Total	Swiss, Including Block	Munster	Brick	Lim-burger	Crean & Neufchatel Cheese	Italian Varieties	Blue Mond	All Other Varieties	Total of All Cheese[2]	Cottage Cheese Lowfat	Cottage Cheese Curd[3]	Cottage Cheese Creamed[4]
2000	3,642	NA	3,642	229.3	85.5	8.6	.6	687.4	3,288.9	5	219.7	8,258	363.7	461.0	371.5
2001	3,544	NA	3,544	245.5	82.2	8.7	.7	645.1	3,425.9	5	199.6	8,261	370.2	453.2	371.6
2002	3,691	NA	3,691	254.1	81.1	10.0	.7	686.2	3,470.0	5	229.8	8,547	374.3	436.6	374.2
2003	3,622	NA	3,622	264.7	79.4	9.8	.7	676.7	3,524.0	5	246.7	8,557	384.4	448.0	385.2
2004	3,739	NA	3,739	281.3	72.8	8.1	.9	699.1	3,661.6	5	268.1	8,873	396.4	464.0	382.4
2005	3,808	NA	3,808	300.1	77.9	8.9	.8	714.8	3,803.0	5	268.3	9,149	407.9	468.6	376.7
2006	3,913	NA	3,913	314.5	95.5	8.6	.8	756.2	3,972.9	5	281.5	9,525	409.2	459.0	368.8
2007	3,877	NA	3,877	313.7	103.6	7.4	.7	772.8	4,198.8	5	311.9	9,777	425.4	458.5	348.6
2008	4,109	NA	4,109	294.0	117.2	6.9	.6	763.6	4,120.8	5	307.5	9,913	389.2	428.1	325.0
2009[1]	4,202	NA	4,202	322.3	115.4	9.4	5	767.0	4,180.3	5	305.9	10,109	387.7	434.8	341.9

[1] Preliminary.   [2] Excludes full-skim cheddar and cottage cheese.   [3] Includes cottage, pot, and baker's cheese with a butterfat content of less than 4%.
[4] Includes cheese with a butterfat content of 4 to 19 %.   [5] Included in All Other Varieties.   NA = Not available.
Source: Economic Research Service, U.S. Department of Agriculture ERS-USDA)

Average Price of Cheese, 40-lb. Blocks, Chicago Mercantile Exchange[2]   In Cents Per Pound

Year	Jan.	Feb.	Mar.	Apr.	May	June	July	Aug.	Sept.	Oct.	Nov.	Dec.	Average
2001	110.3	120.0	131.9	140.5	160.3	166.8	168.5	171.8	173.9	139.7	126.4	129.1	144.9
2002	132.4	120.8	121.3	124.5	120.1	113.0	108.9	115.8	120.4	119.5	108.9	113.1	118.2
2003	109.3	109.2	108.2	112.3	114.2	118.6	151.2	160.0	160.0	158.8	139.3	133.8	131.2
2004	130.6	139.6	182.0	216.9	199.3	171.1	144.9	157.3	157.0	151.7	169.6	159.2	164.9
2005	162.7	149.3	153.2	154.1	147.7	150.7	105.4	142.5	156.4	144.7	137.6	142.2	145.5
2006	133.4	119.9	116.4	116.5	118.6	119.2	116.3	123.5	129.3	123.5	137.5	132.2	123.8
2007	131.8	134.1	138.2	146.3	172.1	201.0	191.4	195.5	199.3	189.6	209.3	200.8	175.8
2008	182.6	200.2	182.3	188.3	209.8	203.5	196.7	174.0	187.6	179.6	171.0	151.3	185.6
2009	108.3	121.7	124.6	120.5	113.9	113.5	115.2	134.7	132.9	147.1	157.9	165.0	129.6
2010[1]	145.4	145.3	129.8	141.8	144.2	139.6	155.5	163.7	173.7	172.5	146.2	138.1	149.6

[1] Preliminary.   [2] Data through December 2001 are for Wholesale Price of Cheese, 40-lb. Blocks, Wisconsin Assembly Points.
Source: Economic Research Service, U.S. Department of Agriculture (ERS-USDA)

Production[2] of Cheese in the United States   In Millions of Pounds

Year	Jan.	Feb.	Mar.	Apr.	May	June	July	Aug.	Sept.	Oct.	Nov.	Dec.	Total
2001	680.3	625.3	713.7	670.2	706.8	678.5	676.0	660.0	641.8	682.1	691.2	703.1	8,129
2002	717.5	667.9	742.8	719.2	748.3	708.3	692.2	714.3	683.9	732.2	725.4	747.2	8,599
2003	714.8	648.6	730.3	718.8	737.0	712.3	718.3	700.1	708.7	740.0	710.0	758.9	8,598
2004	738.0	705.5	785.6	761.0	752.1	715.3	708.7	719.5	714.4	748.0	754.3	773.9	8,876
2005	754.0	704.6	797.5	754.8	783.9	764.5	739.5	757.4	745.5	760.4	766.1	798.9	9,127
2006	782.7	720.5	820.8	793.6	820.0	796.1	775.4	795.1	788.6	812.3	798.1	831.1	9,534
2007	822.9	754.1	840.5	803.8	824.6	792.6	799.5	797.0	777.2	825.8	815.2	847.3	9,700
2008	812.7	784.6	834.7	810.2	831.8	809.4	813.2	820.7	796.5	843.5	824.0	859.0	9,840
2009	826.9	768.0	870.5	847.6	856.1	838.1	842.8	850.7	842.5	862.8	839.5	863.9	10,109
2010[1]	841.6	775.3	891.6	862.0	879.3	880.9	881.6	875.2	878.6	891.9	883.0	907.8	10,449

[1] Preliminary.   [2] Excludes cottage cheese.   *Source: National Agricultural Statistics Service, U.S. Department of Agriculture (NASS-USDA)*

Cold Storage Holdings of All Varieties of Cheese in the United States, on First of Month   In Millions of Pounds

Year	Jan.	Feb.	Mar.	Apr.	May	June	July	Aug.	Sept.	Oct.	Nov.	Dec.
2001	707.8	709.9	723.9	711.6	711.8	712.1	739.2	752.6	721.2	708.7	672.2	631.3
2002	660.0	693.6	720.3	731.7	765.6	789.0	797.6	833.6	801.5	753.9	720.4	697.1
2003	730.1	761.2	770.0	771.3	781.1	791.0	800.1	809.0	794.2	762.2	722.4	695.5
2004	724.4	756.9	766.1	759.5	767.6	804.5	842.0	870.0	811.5	790.7	756.1	704.3
2005	705.8	713.8	723.7	749.2	780.8	815.6	823.4	837.2	812.9	769.0	755.9	720.8
2006	758.2	765.0	782.8	810.7	832.8	863.3	876.0	898.9	862.3	843.1	810.2	784.8
2007	817.4	850.0	875.7	892.9	894.3	898.9	891.2	886.0	846.2	820.4	810.6	805.9
2008	798.3	781.4	801.0	824.3	855.9	881.3	902.5	902.8	880.3	834.2	829.0	818.6
2009	852.0	882.4	892.5	915.2	938.9	970.3	987.4	1,000.2	997.6	983.9	969.2	961.7
2010[1]	966.8	981.6	995.9	994.5	1,008.3	1,016.2	1,025.3	1,053.3	1,040.7	1,042.1	1,035.6	1,003.8

Quantities are given in "net weight."   [1] Preliminary.   *Source: National Agricultural Statistics Service, U.S. Department of Agriculture (NASS-USDA)*

Chromium

Chromium (symbol Cr) is a steel-gray, hard, and brittle, metallic element that can take on a high polish. Chromium and its compounds are toxic. Discovered in 1797 by Louis Vauquelin, chromium is named after the Greek word for color, *khroma*. Vauquelin also discovered that an emerald's green color is due to the presence of chromium. Many precious stones owe their color to the presence of chromium compounds.

Chromium is primarily found in chromite ore. The primary use of chromium is to form alloys with iron, nickel, or cobalt. Chromium improves hardness and resistance to corrosion and oxidation in iron, steel, and nonferrous alloys. It is a critical alloying ingredient in the production of stainless steel, making up 10% or more of the final composition. More than half of the chromium consumed is used in metallic products, and about one-third is used in refractories. Chromium is also used as a lustrous decorative plating agent, in pigments, leather processing, plating of metals, and catalysts.

Supply – World production of chromium in 2010 rose +14.0% yr/yr to 22.000 million metric tons, but still down from the 2008 record high of 23.800 million metric tons. The world's largest producers of chromium in 2010 were South Africa with 39% of world production, India with 17%, and Kazakhstan with 16%. India has emerged as a major producer of chromium in the past two decades. India's 2010 production level of 3.800 million metric tons was more than ten times the level of 360,000 metric tons seen 20 years earlier. South Africa's production in 2010 at 8.5 million metric tons was down only -14% from the 2008 record high of 9.683 million metric tons and that is more than double the levels seen as recently as the early 1990s. Kazakhstan's production in 2010 of 3.400 million metric tons was down from the 2007 record high of 3.687 million metric tons. Zimbabwe's chromium production in 2008 (latest available data) was 484,482 metric tons. U.S. Government stocks of chromium as of Dec 31, 2006 (latest available data) fell 98.4% yr/yr to a record low of 1.160 metric tons.

Demand – Based on the most recently available data from 1994, the metallurgical and chemical industry accounts for about 94% of chromium usage in the U.S., with the remaining 6% used by the refractory industry.

Trade – The U.S. relied on imports for a record low of 56% of its chromium consumption in 2010. That is well below the record high of 91% posted back in the 1970s. U.S. chromium imports in 2008 (latest available data) rose +22.8% yr/yr to 402,400 metric tons. U.S. exports of chromium in 2008 (latest available data) fell -39.7% yr/yr to 36,200 metric tons.

World Mine Production of Chromite   In Thousands of Metric Tons (Gross Weight)

Year	Albania	Brazil	Cuba	Finland	India	Iran	Kazak-hstan	Mada-gascar	philip-pines	South Africa	Turkey	Zim-babwe	Total[1]
2001	130	409	50	575	1,678	145	2,046	24	27	5,502	390	780	12,200
2002	73	284	20	566	2,699	513	2,369	11	22	6,436	314	749	14,600
2003	98	377	33	549	2,210	97	2,928	45	34	7,405	229	637	15,500
2004	160	593	40	580	2,949	139	3,287	77	42	7,677	506	621	17,900
2005	170	617	34	571	3,255	224	3,581	141	38	7,552	688	820	19,200
2006	210	563	28	549	3,600	245	3,366	132	47	7,418	1,060	713	19,700
2007	324	628	25	556	3,320	186	3,687	122	32	9,647	1,679	664	23,000
2008	204	630	25	614	3,900	188	3,629	84	15	9,683	1,886	484	23,800
2009[1]					3,760		3,330			6,870			19,300
2010[2]					3,800		3,400			8,500			22,000

[1] Preliminary.   [2] Estimate.   *Source: U.S. Geological Survey (USGS)*

Salient Statistics of Chromite in the United States   In Thousands of Metric Tons (Gross Weight)

Year	Net Import Reliance as a % of Appearent Consumption	Production of Ferro-chromium	Exports	Imports for Con-sumption	Reexports	Consumption by -- Primary Consumer Group -- Total	Metal-lurgical & Chemical	Refractory	Government[5] Stocks, Dec. 31 - Metal-lurgical & Chemical	Refractory	Total Stocks	--- $/Metric Ton --- South Africa[3]	Turkish[4]
2000	77	W	86	453	----	W	W	W	396	241	637	60-65	140-150
2001	63	W	43	239	----	W	W	W	396	241	637	NA	NA
2002	69	W	29	263	----	W	W	W	78	126	204	NA	NA
2003	57	W	46	317	----	W	W	W	78	156	234	NA	NA
2004	64	W	35	326	----	W	W	W	46	88	135	NA	NA
2005	68	W	57	353	----	W	W	W	4	70	73	NA	NA
2006	70	W	56	342	----	W	W	W	----	1	1	NA	NA
2007	67	W	60	328	----	W	W	W	----	----	----	NA	NA
2008[1]	66	W	36	402	----	W	W	W	----	----	----	NA	NA
2009[2]	12	W			----	W	W	W	----	----	----	NA	NA

[1] Preliminary.   [2] Estimate.   [3] Cr_2O_3, 44% (Transvaal).   [4] 48% Cr_2O_3.   [5] Data through 1999 are for Consumer.   W = Withheld.
Source: U.S. Geological Survey (USGS)

Coal

Coal is a sedimentary rock composed primarily of carbon, hydrogen, and oxygen. Coal is a fossil fuel formed from ancient plants buried deep in the Earth's crust over 300 million years ago. Historians believe coal was first used commercially in China for smelting copper and for casting coins around 1,000 BC. Almost 92% of all coal consumed in the U.S. is burned by electric power plants, and coal accounts for about 55% of total electricity output. Coal is also used in the manufacture of steel. The steel industry first converts coal into coke, then combines the coke with iron ore and limestone, and finally heats the mixture to produce iron. Other industries use coal to make fertilizers, solvents, medicine, pesticides, and synthetic fuels.

There are four types of mined coal: anthracite (used in high-grade steel production), bituminous (used for electricity generation and for making coke), sub-bituminous, and lignite (both used primarily for electricity generation).

Central Appalachian Coal futures trade at the New York Mercantile Exchange (NYMEX). The contract trades in units of 1,550 tons and is priced in terms of dollars and cents per short ton.

Supply – U.S. production of bituminous coal in 2010 (annualized through November) rose +1.2% yr/yr to 1.086 billion tons, down from the 2008 record high of 1.169 billion tons.

Demand – U.S. consumption of coal in 2009 (latest data available) fell by -11.0% to 997,478 billion tons, down from the 2007 record high of 1.128 billion tons.

Trade – U.S. exports of coal in 2009 (latest data available) fell -27.5% yr/yr to 59.096 below last year's 11-year high of 81.519 million tons, and imports fell -33.8% yr/yr to 22.639 million tons, down from the 2007 record high of 36.347 million tons. The major exporting destinations for the U.S. are Canada and Europe.

World Production[3] of Coal (Monthly Average)   In Thousands of Metric Tons

Year	Australia	Canada	China	Czech-Republic	Germany	India	Indonesia	Kazak-hstan	Poland	Russia	Ukraine	United Kingdom	United States
2001	22,018	2,836	80,040	1,261	2,406	26,563	7,554	6,015	8,658	15,507	6,908	2,677	68,666
2002	23,123	2,468	92,339	1,206	2,197	27,938	8,588	6,493	8,642	15,198	5,163	2,499	66,565
2003	30,000	2,215	109,602	1,137	2,396	29,036	9,551	6,734	8,573	16,329	5,354	2,353	81,023
2004	31,250	2,438	130,434	1,109	2,429	31,438	11,021	6,922	8,436	17,495	4,947	2,089	92,953
2005	32,917	2,382	150,891	1,104	2,335	33,129	11,755	6,899	8,159	18,472	5,033	1,667	94,439
2006	33,583	2,492	171,288	1,115	1,980	35,088	12,571	7,631	7,935	19,468	5,135	1,544	96,782
2007	35,167	2,734	192,229	1,074	1,794	37,134	14,569	8,199	7,316	20,178	4,897	1,417	95,550
2008	35,917	2,737	215,472	1,054	1,431	40,289	15,131	8,773	7,020	20,464	4,939	1,504	97,624
2009[1]	35,583	2,330	248,666	917	1,141	43,448	17,445	8,015	6,493	19,193	4,568	1,489	89,577
2010[2]	34,667	2,764	249,629	965	1,091	42,195	19,657		6,353	20,470	4,469	1,498	89,772

[1] Preliminary.   [2] Estimate.   [3] All grades of anthracite and bituminous coal, but excludes recovered slurries, lignite and brown coal.
Source: United Nations

Production of Bituminous & Lignite Coal in the United States   In Thousands of Short Tons

Year	Alabama	Colorado	Illinois	Indiana	Kentucky	Montana	Ohio	Pennsyl-vania	Texas	West Virgina	Virgina	Wyoming	Total
2001	19,513	33,372	33,783	36,738	134,298	39,143	25,400	74,784	45,042	33,060	162,631	368,749	1,125,749
2002	19,062	35,103	33,358	35,513	124,388	37,386	21,157	67,104	45,247	30,126	150,222	373,161	1,092,916
2003	20,207	35,831	31,760	35,512	113,126	36,994	22,009	63,792	47,517	31,771	139,755	376,270	1,071,753
2004	22,329	39,870	31,912	35,206	114,743	39,989	23,222	66,023	45,863	31,647	148,017	396,493	1,110,393
2005	21,453	38,510	32,014	34,457	120,029	40,354	24,718	65,852	45,939	27,964	153,655	404,319	1,129,794
2006	18,830	36,322	32,729	35,119	120,848	41,823	22,722	64,500	45,548	29,740	152,374	446,742	1,162,750
2007	19,522	36,384	32,857	35,003	115,530	43,390	22,575	63,621	41,948	25,462	153,522	453,568	1,145,067
2008	21,157	32,028	33,074	36,040	120,778	44,786	26,251	63,742	39,017	24,748	157,805	467,644	1,170,096
2009[1]	19,171	28,267	34,021	35,850	107,802	39,486	27,651	57,222	35,093	21,019	137,194	431,107	1,073,002
2010[2]	20,842	25,088	33,086	34,847	105,954	44,629	27,116	57,553	39,777	21,526	136,205	440,797	1,082,013

[1] Preliminary.   [2] Estimate.   *Source: Energy Information Administration, U.S. Department of Energy (EIA-DOE)*

Production[2] of Bituminous Coal in the United States   In Thousands of Short Tons

Year	Jan.	Feb.	Mar.	Apr.	May	June	July	Aug.	Sept.	Oct.	Nov.	Dec.	Total
2001	96,721	86,802	99,176	89,954	94,840	92,657	89,037	99,048	88,985	99,529	93,736	88,234	1,118,719
2002	101,939	90,208	90,108	90,039	91,673	85,555	86,190	92,054	92,212	94,033	87,836	91,058	1,092,905
2003	92,649	82,130	88,976	89,202	90,435	88,348	88,301	89,355	90,344	93,928	84,155	94,154	1,071,977
2004	93,182	86,306	94,876	91,739	87,210	94,835	92,260	95,209	93,525	92,618	92,268	95,478	1,109,506
2005	92,804	89,039	102,178	93,296	90,168	95,374	91,930	97,907	95,493	93,532	94,842	92,774	1,129,337
2006	98,385	88,826	101,339	95,288	99,706	97,023	94,861	100,504	94,029	98,674	96,400	95,939	1,160,974
2007	99,221	88,084	97,490	92,923	96,867	95,432	92,884	100,493	92,288	98,691	96,769	93,010	1,144,152
2008	98,488	93,428	96,805	96,991	96,425	90,096	99,014	100,312	99,203	104,222	95,264	99,604	1,169,852
2009	96,418	89,126	95,457	88,797	84,989	88,435	90,435	89,902	87,775	87,898	85,396	86,053	1,070,681
2010[1]	85,458	83,213	97,087	92,509	86,741	90,123	89,776	92,311	92,085	91,232	91,095	92,409	1,084,039

[1] Preliminary.   [2] Includes small amount of lignite.   *Source: Energy Information Administration, U.S. Department of Energy (EIA-DOE)*

COAL

Production[2] of Pennsylvania Anthracite Coal   In Thousands of Short Tons

Year	Jan.	Feb.	Mar.	Apr.	May	June	July	Aug.	Sept.	Oct.	Nov.	Dec.	Total
2001	302	275	323	283	300	297	328	358	318	375	349	173	3,681
2002	131	117	116	121	122	240	116	126	119	130	120	126	1,584
2003	108	98	98	115	114	107	97	95	101	130	111	116	1,290
2004	197	183	147	111	101	214	141	145	150	145	151	127	1,812
2005	133	129	149	137	135	157	125	140	135	156	179	127	1,704
2006	138	121	147	117	128	125	124	140	115	134	126	123	1,538
2007	141	125	139	125	133	134	120	135	116	134	141	128	1,568
2008	131	126	127	160	162	103	147	146	148	168	140	154	1,712
2009	150	141	153	146	132	147	171	167	171	188	168	177	1,911
2010[1]	131	118	144	158	141	152	94	99	98	124	133	136	1,528

[1] Preliminary.   [2] Represents production in Pennsylvania only.   *Source: Energy Information Administration, U.S. Department of Energy (EIA-DOE)*

Salient Statistics of Coal in the United States   In Thousands of Short Tons

Year	Production	Imports	Consumption	Exports Brazil	Canada	Europe	Asia	Total	Total Ending Stocks[2]	Losses & Unaccounted For[3]
2000	1,073,612	12,513	1,084,094	4,536	18,769	24,969	6,702	58,489	140,282	938
2001	1,127,689	19,787	1,060,146	4,574	17,633	20,821	3,246	48,666	181,912	7,120
2002	1,094,283	16,875	1,066,355	3,538	16,686	15,574	1,735	39,601	192,127	4,039
2003	1,071,753	25,044	1,094,861	3,514	20,760	15,148	266	43,014	165,468	-4,403
2004	1,112,099	27,280	1,107,255	4,361	17,760	15,211	7,475	47,998	154,006	6,887
2005	1,131,498	30,460	1,125,978	4,199	19,466	18,825	5,082	49,942	144,304	9,092
2006	1,162,750	36,246	1,112,292	4,534	19,889	20,805	2,008	49,647	186,946	8,824
2007	1,146,635	36,347	1,127,998	6,512	18,389	27,119	1,202	59,163	192,758	4,085
2008	1,171,809	34,208	1,120,548	6,380	22,979	40,306	5,269	81,519	205,112	5,740
2009[1]	1,074,923	22,639	997,478	7,416	10,599	30,073	6,483	59,097	238,823	14,985

[1] Preliminary.   [2] Producer & distributor and consumer stocks, excludes stocks held by retail dealers for consumption by the residential and commercial sector.   [3] Equals production plus imports minus the change in producer & distributor and consumer stocks minus consumption minus exports.
Source: Energy Information Administraion, U.S. Department of Energy (EIA-DOE)

Consumption and Stocks of Coal in the United States   In Thousands of Short Tons

Year	Consumption Electric Utilities Anthracite	Bituminous	Lignite	Total	Industrial Coke Plants	Other Industrial[2]	Residential and Commercial	Total	Stocks, Dec. 31 Consumer Electric Utilities	Coke Plants	Other Industrials	Producers and Distributors
2000	NA	781,821	75,794	985,821	28,939	65,208	4,127	1,084,095	102,296	1,494	4,587	31,905
2001	NA	NA	NA	964,433	26,075	65,268	4,369	1,060,146	138,496	1,510	6,006	35,900
2002	NA	NA	NA	977,507	23,656	60,747	4,445	1,066,355	141,714	1,364	5,792	43,257
2003	NA	NA	NA	1,005,116	24,248	61,261	4,236	1,094,861	121,567	905	4,718	38,277
2004	NA	NA	NA	1,016,268	23,670	62,195	5,122	1,107,255	106,669	1,344	4,842	41,151
2005	NA	NA	NA	1,037,485	23,434	60,340	4,720	1,125,978	101,237	2,615	5,582	34,971
2006	NA	NA	NA	1,026,636	22,957	59,472	3,226	1,112,292	140,964	2,928	6,506	36,548
2007	NA	NA	NA	1,045,141	22,715	56,615	3,526	1,127,998	151,221	1,936	5,624	33,977
2008	NA	NA	NA	1,040,580	22,070	54,393	3,506	1,120,548	161,589	2,331	6,007	34,688
2009[1]	NA	NA	NA	933,627	15,326	45,314	3,210	997,478	189,467	1,957	5,109	47,718

[1] Preliminary.   [2] Including transportation.   [3] Excludes stocks held at retail dealers for consumption by the residential and commercial sector.
Source: Energy Information Administration, U.S. Department of Energy (EIA-DOE)

Average Prices of Coal in the United States   In Dollars Per Short Ton

Year	End-Use Sector Electric Utilities	Coke Plants	Other Industrial[2]	Imports[3]	Exports Steam	Metal-lurgical	Total Average[3]	Year	End-Use Sector Electric Utilities	Coke Plants	Other Industrial[2]	Imports[3]	Exports Steam	Metal-lurgical	Total Average[3]
2000	24.28	44.38	31.46	30.10	29.67	38.99	34.89	2005	31.22	83.79	47.63	46.71	47.64	81.56	67.10
2001	24.68	46.42	32.26	34.00	31.88	41.63	36.97	2006	34.26	92.87	51.67	49.10	46.25	90.81	70.93
2002	24.74	50.67	35.49	35.51	34.51	45.41	40.44	2007	NA	94.97	54.42	47.64	47.90	88.99	70.25
2003	25.29	50.63	34.70	31.45	26.94	44.55	35.98	2008	NA	118.09	63.44	59.83	57.35	134.62	97.68
2004	27.30	61.50	39.30	37.52	42.03	63.63	54.11	2009[1]	NA	143.01	64.87	63.91	73.63	117.73	101.44

[1] Preliminary.   [2] Manufacturing plants only.   [3] Based on the free alongside ship (F.A.S.) value.
Source: Energy Information Administration, U.S. Department of Energy (EIA-DOE)

Trends in Bituminous Coal, Lignite and Pennsylvania Anthracite in the United States   In Thousands of Short Tons

| | Bituminous Coal and Lignite | | | | Labor Productivity | | | Pennsylvania Anthracite | | | | All Mines | |
| | Production | | | | Under-Ground | Surface | Average | | | | | Labor Productivity | Labor Productivity |
Year	Under-Ground	Surface	Total	Miners[1] Employed	Short Tons Per Miner Per Hour			Under-Ground	Surface	Total	Miners[1] Employed	Short Tons Miner/Hr.	Short Tons Miner/Hr.
2000	373,659	699,953	1,073,612	72,748	4.15	11.01	6.99	301	4,271	4,572	1,272	1.89	6.99
2001	380,627	745,308	1,127,689	77,088	4.02	10.60	6.82	341	1,143	1,484	955	.81	6.82
2002	357,385	735,910	1,094,283	75,466	3.98	10.38	6.80	305	998	1,303	872	.78	6.80
2003	352,785	717,870	1,071,753	71,023	4.04	10.76	6.95	282	961	1,243	814	.82	6.95
2004	367,557	743,552	1,112,099	73,912	3.96	10.57	6.80	271	1,408	1,679	890	.97	6.80
2005	368,612	762,190	1,131,498	79,283	3.62	10.04	6.36	264	1,296	1,560	891	.95	6.36
2006	359,022	802,976	1,161,998	82,959	3.37	10.19	6.26	239	1,132	1,371	869	.95	6.26
2007	351,790	793,690	1,145,480	81,278	3.34	10.25	6.27	224	1,199	1,423	910	.89	6.27
2008	357,079	813,322	1,170,401	86,859	3.15	9.82	5.96	227	2,455	2,682	929	.91	5.96
2009	332,062	740,174	1,072,236	87,592	2.99	9.22	5.60	268	2,415	2,683	941	.95	5.61

[1] Excludes miners employed at mines producing less than 10,000 tons.
Source: Energy Information Administration, U.S. Department of Energy (EIA-DOE)

Average Mine Prices of Coal in the United States   In Dollars Per Short Ton

| | Average Mine Prices by Method | | | Average Mine Prices by Rank | | | | Bituminous & Lignite FOB Mines[2] | Anthracite FOB Mines[2] | All Coal CIF[3] Electric Utility Plants |
Year	Under-ground	Surface	Total	Lignite	Sub-bituminous	Bituminous	Anthracite[1]			
2000	23.84	12.26	16.44	11.41	7.12	24.15	40.90	24.15	40.90	24.28
2001	25.37	13.18	17.38	11.52	6.67	25.36	47.67	25.36	47.67	24.68
2002	26.68	13.65	17.98	11.07	7.34	26.57	47.78	26.57	47.78	24.74
2003	26.71	13.42	17.85	11.20	7.73	26.73	49.55	26.73	49.55	25.29
2004	30.36	14.75	19.93	12.27	8.12	30.56	39.77	30.56	39.77	27.30
2005	36.42	17.37	23.59	13.49	8.68	36.80	41.00	36.80	41.00	31.22
2006	38.28	18.88	25.16	14.00	9.95	39.32	43.61	39.32	43.61	34.26
2007	40.29	19.41	26.20	14.89	10.69	40.80	52.24	40.80	52.24	36.06
2008	51.35	22.35	31.25	16.50	12.31	51.40	60.76	51.40	60.76	
2009	55.77	23.24	33.24	17.26	13.35	55.44	57.10	55.44	57.10	

[1] Produced in Pennsylvania.   [2] FOB = free on board.   [3] CIF = cost, insurance and freight.   W = Withheld data.
Source: Energy Information Adminstration, U.S. Department of Energy (EIA-DOE)

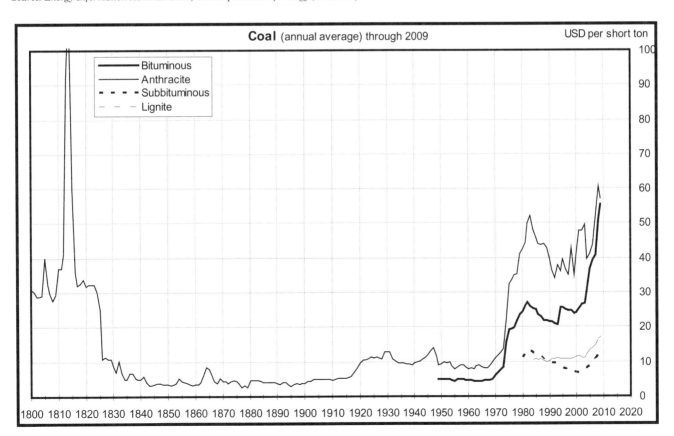

Coal (annual average) through 2009   USD per short ton

Legend: Bituminous, Anthracite, Subbituminous, Lignite

Cobalt

Cobalt (symbol Co) is a lustrous, silvery-white, magnetic, metallic element used chiefly for making alloys. Cobalt was known in ancient times and used by the Persians in 2250 BC to color glass. The name **cobalt** comes from the German word *kobalt* or **kobold**, meaning evil spirit. Miners gave cobalt its name because it was poisonous and troublesome since it polluted and degraded other mined elements, like nickel. In the 1730s, George Brandt first isolated metallic cobalt and was able to show that cobalt was the source of the blue color in glasses. In 1780, it was recognized as an element. Cobalt is generally not found in nature as a free metal and is instead found in ores. Cobalt is generally produced as a by-product of nickel and copper mining.

Cobalt is used in a variety of applications: high temperature steel alloys; fasteners in gas turbine engines; magnets and magnetic recording media; drying agents for paints and pigments; and steel-belted radial tires. Cobalt-60, an important radioactive tracer and cancer-treatment agent, is an artificially produced radioactive isotope of cobalt.

Prices – The price of cobalt in 2010 rose by 17.6% to $21.00 per pound, well below the 2008 record high of $39.01 per pound, but triple the 20-year low of $6.91 per pound in 2002, just eight years ago.

Supply – World production of cobalt in 2010 rose by 21.7% to a record high of 88,000 metric tons. The world's largest cobalt mine producers in 2010 were the Congo with 51% of world production, Zambia (13%), Russia (7%),

Australia (5%), and Canada (3%).

The U.S. does not specifically mine or refine cobalt although some cobalt is produced as a by-product of other mining operations. Imports, stock releases, and secondary materials comprise the U.S. cobalt supply. Secondary production includes extraction from super-alloy scrap, cemented carbide scrap, and spent catalysts. In the U.S. there are two domestic producers of extra-fine cobalt powder. One company produces the powder from imported primary metal and the other from recycled materials. There are only about seven companies that produce cobalt compounds. U.S. secondary production of cobalt in 2010 rose +11.7% yr/yr to 2,000 metric tons but remains well below the record high of 3,080 metric tons seen in 1998.

Demand – U.S. consumption of cobalt in 2010 rose by +33.0% yr/yr to 10,000 metric tons, but still below the 2005 record high of 11,800 metric tons. The largest use of cobalt by far was for super-alloys 43% of consumption in 2008 consumption. Other smaller-scaled applications for cobalt include cutting and wear-resistant materials (8.0%), magnetic alloys (3.6%), and welding materials (2.2%). Demand for some other uses is not available as proprietary information.

Trade – U.S. imports of cobalt in 2010 rose +43.2% to 11,000 metric tons, but still below the 2006 record high of 11,600 metric tons. In 2009 the U.S. relied on imports for 81% of its cobalt consumption, which is down from the 99% level seen in the early 1970s.

World Mine Production of Cobalt In Metric Tons (Cobalt Content)

Year	Australia	Botswana	Canada	Cuba	Finland (Refinery)	France (Refinery)	Japan (Refinery)	New Caledonia	Norway (Refinery)	Russia	Congo[3]	Zambia	World Total
2001	6,300	325	5,326	3,425	8,100	199	350	1,400	3,314	4,600	12,000	8,000	44,800
2002	6,800	269	5,148	3,442	8,240	176	354	2,780	3,994	4,600	14,600	10,000	52,200
2003	6,000	294	4,327	3,274	7,989	181	379	2,602	4,556	6,100	14,800	11,300	52,900
2004	5,600	223	5,060	3,554	7,893	199	429	2,726	4,670	6,000	20,200	10,000	60,300
2005	5,600	326	5,767	4,798	8,171	280	471	1,769	5,021	6,300	24,500	9,300	66,200
2006	6,000	303	7,115	5,602	8,582	256	920	1,629	4,927	6,300	27,100	8,000	69,800
2007	5,900	242	8,692	4,540	9,173	305	1,084	1,620	3,939	6,300	25,300	7,500	72,600
2008	6,100	337	8,644	3,175	8,645	311	1,071	1,600	3,719	6,200	31,000	6,900	75,900
2009[1]	4,600		4,100	3,500				1,000		6,100	35,500	5,000	72,300
2010[2]	4,600		2,500	3,500				1,700		6,100	45,000	11,000	88,000

[1] Preliminary. [2] Estimate. [3] Formerly Zaire. *Source: U.S. Geological Survey (USGS)*

Salient Statistics of Cobalt in the United States In Metric Tons (Cobalt Content)

Year	Net Import Reliance As a % of Apparent Consumption	Cobalt Secondary Production	Processor and Consumer Stocks Dec. 31	Imports for Consumption	Ground Coat Frit	Stainless & Heat Resisting	Catalysts	Super-alloys	Tool Steel	Magnetic Alloys	Pigments	Drier in Paints, etc	Cutting & Wear-Resistant Material	Welding Materials	Total Apparent Uses	Price $ Per Pound[4]
2001	76	2,780	852	9,410	W	W	W	4,850	W	472	W	W	720	661	11,800	10.55
2002	72	2,800	917	8,450	W	W	W	3,700	W	416	W	W	618	634	9,830	6.91
2003	79	2,130	649	8,080	W	W	W	3,400	W	282	W	W	662	632	10,000	10.60
2004	77	2,300	719	8,720	W	W	W	3,650	W	396	W	W	765	627	9,950	23.93
2005	83	2,030	705	11,100	W	W	W	4,140	W	343	W	W	762	227	11,800	15.96
2006	82	2,010	1,180	11,600	W	W	W	4,170	W	386	W	W	808	224	11,000	17.22
2007	80	1,930	1,310	10,300	W	W	W	4,410	W	385	W	W	726	225	9,630	30.55
2008	81	1,930	1,160	10,700	W	W	W	4,320	W	368	W	W	827	226	10,100	39.01
2009[1]	76	1,790	840	7,680											7,520	17.86
2010[2]	81	2,000	880	11,000											10,000	21.00

[1] Preliminary. [2] Estimate. [3] Or related usage. [4] Annual spot for cathodes. W = Withheld. *Source: U.S. Geological Survey (USGS)*

Cocoa

Cocoa is the common name for a powder derived from the fruit seeds of the cacao tree. The Spanish called cocoa "the food of the gods" when they found it in South America 500 years ago. Today, it remains a valued commodity. Dating back to the time of the Aztecs, cocoa was mainly used as a beverage. The processing of the cacao seeds, also known as cocoa beans, begins when the harvested fruit is fermented or cured into a pulpy state for three to nine days. The cocoa beans are then dried in the sun and cleaned in special machines before they are roasted to bring out the chocolate flavor. After roasting, they are put into a crushing machine and ground into cocoa powder. Cocoa has a high food value because it contains as much as 20 percent protein, 40 percent carbohydrate, and 40 percent fat. It is also mildly stimulating because of the presence of theobromine, an alkaloid that is closely related to caffeine. Roughly two-thirds of cocoa bean production is used to make chocolate and one-third to make cocoa powder.

Four major West African cocoa producers, the Ivory Coast, Ghana, Nigeria and Cameroon, together account for about two-thirds of world cocoa production. Outside of West Africa, the major producers of cocoa are Indonesia, Brazil, Malaysia, Ecuador, and the Dominican Republic. Cocoa producers like Ghana and Indonesia have been making efforts to increase cocoa production while producers like Malaysia have been switching to other crops. Ghana has had an ongoing problem with black pod disease and with smuggling of the crop into neighboring Ivory Coast. Brazil was once one of the largest producers of cocoa but has had problems with witches' broom disease. In West Africa, the main crop harvest starts in the September-October period and can be extended into the January-March period. Cocoa trees reach maturity in 5-6 years but can live to be 50 years old or more. During the course of a growing season, the cocoa tree will produce thousands of flowers but only a few will develop into cocoa pods.

Cocoa futures and options are traded at the ICE Futures U.S. (ICE) and on the NYSE-LIFFE in London. The futures contracts call for the delivery of 10 metric tons of cocoa and the contract is priced in US dollars per metric ton.

Prices – After posting a 31-year high of $3,510 per metric ton in December 2009, cocoa prices moved lower to a 1-1/2 year low of $2,562 per metric ton in September of 2010 on the prospects for an abundant Ivory Coast cocoa crop and on the hike by the International Cocoa Organization of its global cocoa surplus estimate for the 2010/11 season to 100,000 MT. Cocoa prices recovered into the end of the year, but still finished 2010 down 13.5% at $3,035 per metric ton. Cocoa prices rallied sharply in early 2011 as the presidential election in the Ivory Coast in November 2010 was disputed and disrupted cocoa exports from the Ivory Coast, a key cocoa supplier. Cocoa prices rallied to a 32-year nearest-futures high of $3,726 per metric ton in February of 2011 when the Ivory Coast's President-elect banned exports for a month starting in January and extended the export ban into March of 2011 as the disputed outcome of the November presidential election continued. The market was also concerned that stockpiled Ivory Coast cocoa beans from the export ban would quickly go bad in hot and humid Ivory Coast warehouses. The record high for cocoa futures is $5379.2 per metric ton posted in July 1977.

Supply – The world production of cocoa beans in the 2010-11 crop year fell -6.8% to 3.938 million metric tons. The world's largest cocoa producer by far is the Ivory Coast with 33.6% of total world production in 2010-11. The Ivory Coast's production in 2010-11, rose +8.3% yr/yr. After the Ivory Coast the major producers are Ghana with 21.0% of total world production in 2010-11, Indonesia with 12.7%, Nigeria with 6.1%, Cameroon with 5.6%, and Brazil with 4.8%. Closing stocks of cocoa in the 2010-11 crop year rose +7.2% yr/yr to 1.763 metric tons.

Demand – World seasonal grindings of cocoa in 2010-11 rose by +2.8% y/y to 3.780 million metric tons, a new record high. European is by far the largest global consumer of cocoa, consuming about 37.1% of the global crop.

Trade – U.S. imports of cocoa and cocoa products in 2010 (annualized through November) rose +4.5% yr/yr to 1.222 million metric tons, but still below the record high of 1.317 million metric tons in 2005.

World Supply and Demand Cocoa   In Thousands of Metric Tons

Crop Year Beginning Oct. 1	Stocks Oct. 1	Net World Production[4]	Total Availability	Seasona Grindings	Closing Stocks	Stock Change	Stock/Consumption Ratio %
2001-02	1,344	2,857	4,201	2,886	1,315	-29	45.6
2002-03	1,315	3,157	4,472	3,078	1,394	79	45.3
2003-04	1,394	3,526	4,920	3,238	1,682	288	51.9
2004-05	1,682	3,347	5,029	3,363	1,666	-16	49.5
2005-06	1,666	3,773	5,439	3,508	1,931	265	55.0
2006-07	1,931	3,399	5,330	3,662	1,668	-263	45.5
2007-08	1,668	3,713	5,381	3,745	1,636	-32	43.7
2008-09[1]	1,636	3,566	5,202	3,492	1,710	74	49.0
2009-10[2]	1,710	3,611	5,321	3,677	1,644	-66	44.7
2010-11[3]	1,644	3,899	5,543	3,780	1,763	119	46.6

[1] Preliminary.   [2] Estimate.   [3] Forecast.   [4] Obtained by adjusting the gross world crop for a one percent loss in weight.

Source: ED&F Man Cocoa Limited

COCOA

World Production of Cocoa Beans   In Thousands of Metric Tons

Crop Year Beginning Oct. 1	Brazil	Came-roon	Colom-bia	Dominican Republic	Ecuador	Ghana	Indo-nesia	Ivory Coast	Malaysia	Mexico	Nigeria	Papau New Guinea	World Total
2001-02	186	122	36	45	76	390	428	1,212	58	47	340	39	3,109
2002-03	175	125	34	45	88	341	571	1,265	48	46	362	42	3,272
2003-04	170	155	42	47	88	497	573	1,352	36	50	385	43	3,580
2004-05	196	167	39	48	90	737	642	1,407	33	44	412	39	4,017
2005-06	209	179	37	31	94	740	643	1,360	28	36	441	48	4,053
2006-07	212	165	35	46	88	734	769	1,372	32	38	485	51	4,272
2007-08	202	179	40	45	86	615	740	1,384	35	30	500	47	4,146
2008-09[1]	202	188	45	55	94	700	793	1,370	28	28	500	49	4,288
2009-10[2]	225	210	49	58	121	632	800	1,223	18	31	240	50	4,224
2010-11[3]	190	220	45	55	150	825	500	1,325	20	30	240	50	3,938

[1] Preliminary.   [2] Estimate.   [3] Forecast.   Source: Food and Agricultural Organization of the United Nations (FAO-UN)

World Consumption of Cocoa[4]   In Thousands of Metric Tons

Crop Year Beginning Oct. 1	Canada	Brazil	European Union	Ghana	Indonesia	Ivory Coast	Japan	Malaysia	Singa-pore	Turkey	United States	Russia	World Total
2001-02	56	173	1,159	80	108	265	50	93	62	39	393	69	2,886
2002-03	57	196	1,190	69	115	290	64	129	71	50	400	60	3,078
2003-04	72	207	1,256	78	122	321	57	200	59	71	401	63	3,238
2004-05	65	209	1,328	76	111	320	53	228	57	58	409	68	3,363
2005-06	76	223	1,328	85	130	336	60	265	70	56	432	70	3,508
2006-07	66	226	1,390	121	140	360	50	301	87	64	418	65	3,662
2007-08	59	232	1,409	123	160	374	42	331	89	60	391	65	3,745
2008-09[1]	55	216	1,320	133	120	419	41	278	80	52	361	54	3,492
2009-10[2]	59	161	1,373	212	120	400	42	298	80	65	382	54	3,677
2010-11[3]		190	1,403	275	130	350	40	315	80	70	390	55	3,780

[1] Preliminary.   [2] Estimate.   [3] Forecast.   [4] Figures represent the "grindings" of cocoa beans in each country.   NA = Not available.
Source: International Cocoa Organization (ICO)

Imports of Cocoa Butter in Selected Countries   In Metric Tons

Year	Australia	Austria	Belgium	Canada	France	Germany	Italy	Japan	Nether-lands	Sweden	Switzer-land	United Kingdom	United States
2000	20,590	4,325	51,826	22,009	54,197	72,014	12,071	21,695	37,261	6,010	19,922	38,770	94,648
2001	20,633	3,945	51,577	23,307	51,145	80,839	11,765	21,665	36,687	6,349	20,604	41,827	80,806
2002	20,800	3,777	48,992	24,397	63,814	82,313	12,099	20,212	47,562	6,401	21,545	46,912	84,788
2003	22,310	3,823	54,621	26,309	58,759	77,880	13,337	22,579	55,523	6,564	21,555	39,092	78,035
2004	23,514	4,536	56,328	27,646	70,386	79,155	13,891	22,166	63,657	6,668	22,960	50,593	94,890
2005	21,527	4,281	61,200	28,382	72,561	82,050	16,114	24,633	70,255	6,276	24,264	70,777	96,876
2006	19,172	4,729	68,173	23,803	75,572	82,726	16,285	25,603	82,864	5,774	25,725	48,447	96,455
2007	15,845	4,367	75,283	31,301	78,858	85,113	20,973	24,417	70,598	3,441	27,265	48,911	86,258
2008	14,970	4,847	64,782	23,516	69,153	85,605	21,706	23,368	72,786	3,993	27,193	42,879	102,868
2009[1]	13,113	4,110	69,990	20,758	64,516	84,942	21,086	22,037	70,262	3,698	24,790	43,244	84,499

[1] Preliminary.   Sources: Food and Agricultural Organization of the United Nations (FAO)

Imports of Cocoa Liquor and Cocoa Powder in Selected Countries   In Metric Tons

Year	Cocoa Liquor						Cocoa Powder						
	France	Germany	Japan	Nether-lands	United Kingdom	United States	Denmark	France	Germany	Italy	Japan	Nether-lands	United States
2000	67,812	14,295	1,618	33,815	8,529	10,902	3,661	37,165	39,498	18,249	11,765	29,044	130,610
2001	67,500	17,548	1,553	41,913	10,289	17,940	3,792	25,631	32,621	19,224	12,004	29,866	113,592
2002	64,820	28,100	1,193	46,369	14,038	22,215	2,895	35,128	39,871	19,642	10,859	54,422	126,443
2003	71,337	31,391	1,764	35,089	20,154	20,018	3,142	43,915	37,065	18,757	12,895	38,713	136,813
2004	72,057	42,975	2,773	40,847	17,753	20,758	3,447	44,213	35,460	19,538	14,973	38,692	147,392
2005	80,194	42,537	3,327	46,409	6,574	33,540	3,996	43,626	33,202	23,085	13,705	45,859	141,044
2006	86,767	43,918	14,684	43,885	6,541	24,359	3,053	39,833	41,050	22,485	15,831	34,770	145,820
2007	58,344	39,985	7,659	48,960	6,725	20,357	3,106	41,030	47,480	28,241	16,218	35,979	158,132
2008	58,469	60,364	8,438	44,435	6,603	20,135	3,046	45,652	47,232	28,576	18,050	24,364	156,028
2009[1]	58,994	64,205	7,513	44,521	6,798	19,369	2,617	42,069	49,685	24,692	15,611	34,518	163,827

[1] Preliminary.   NA = Not available.   Source: Food and Agricultural Organization of the United Nations (FAO)

Imports of Cocoa and Products in the United States   In Thousands of Metric Tons

Year	Jan.	Feb.	Mar.	Apr.	May	June	July	Aug.	Sept.	Oct.	Nov.	Dec.	Total
2001	108	97	77	47	68	61	80	78	76	86	92	118	989
2002	87	74	73	61	76	72	87	98	61	66	90	72	916
2003	115	74	92	71	68	74	95	82	79	95	85	116	1,046
2004	110	82	130	100	101	103	94	94	100	90	80	89	1,171
2005	129	109	156	108	104	93	91	104	84	97	113	129	1,317
2006	114	104	109	94	92	89	108	140	103	91	90	124	1,258
2007	111	121	110	102	82	76	83	83	84	95	76	106	1,130
2008	108	115	109	87	80	65	88	82	79	90	83	129	1,114
2009	114	98	88	95	82	99	80	88	103	103	94	126	1,170
2010[1]	150	103	134	85	94	78	80	84	110	88	100	115	1,223

[1] Preliminary.   *Source: Foreign Agricultural Service, U.S. Department of Agriculture (FAS-USDA)*

Visible Stocks of Cocoa in Port of Hampton Road Warehouses[1], at End of Month   In Thousands of Bags

Year	Jan.	Feb.	Mar.	Apr.	May	June	July	Aug.	Sept.	Oct.	Nov.	Dec.
2001	741.9	657.4	632.0	607.7	577.3	518.8	498.2	487.5	475.2	506.8	509.0	511.4
2002	509.7	462.8	436.7	415.4	383.8	353.4	322.9	273.3	255.1	194.8	181.5	169.9
2003	149.9	121.7	102.6	100.7	80.5	71.8	69.2	67.7	56.9	53.0	48.4	49.3
2004	48.6	47.8	47.5	47.5	45.8	43.9	41.2	40.4	40.1	38.0	38.0	36.8
2005	31.1	30.9	28.6	28.0	28.0	27.4	27.4	27.4	27.4	27.4	27.4	27.4
2006	18.3	17.9	17.3	17.3	17.3	17.3	17.3	17.3	17.1	17.1	17.1	17.1
2007	16.8	16.8	16.8	16.8	16.8	16.8	16.8	15.6	15.6	15.6	15.6	15.6
2008	15.6	15.6	15.6	15.6	15.8	15.8	15.8	15.8	15.8	15.6	15.6	15.6
2009	14.9	14.9	14.9	14.9	14.9	14.9	13.7	13.7	13.7	13.7	13.7	13.7
2010	13.3	12.3	12.3	12.3	12.3	12.3	12.3	12.3	12.3	12.3	12.3	12.3

[1] Licensed warehouses approved by ICE.   *Source: ICE Futures U.S. (ICE)*

Visible Stocks of Cocoa in Philadelphia (Del. River) Warehouses[1], at End of Month   In Thousands of Bags

Year	Jan.	Feb.	Mar.	Apr.	May	June	July	Aug.	Sept.	Oct.	Nov.	Dec.
2001	1,844.0	2,082.3	2,173.3	1,960.0	1,785.9	1,610.4	1,391.6	1,543.0	1,391.3	1,131.4	1,303.2	1,682.1
2002	1,705.4	1,876.7	1,849.3	1,702.0	1,746.4	1,689.5	1,899.2	1,832.7	1,736.2	1,334.5	1,162.7	1,250.6
2003	1,347.2	1,422.0	1,327.9	1,311.7	1,217.2	1,178.5	1,170.9	1,123.7	868.7	798.9	765.0	806.0
2004	1,294.9	1,061.5	1,067.1	1,187.1	1,232.7	1,366.8	1,432.6	1,529.3	1,379.5	1,569.4	1,378.2	1,335.7
2005	1,588.9	1,809.8	2,066.3	2,264.5	2,434.3	2,258.3	2,465.0	2,481.0	2,470.5	2,385.2	2,382.8	2,566.4
2006	2,888.5	2,828.9	3,013.5	3,246.1	3,111.0	2,913.8	2,754.7	3,404.0	3,382.1	3,307.2	3,085.7	3,293.0
2007	3,488.8	4,113.3	4,326.8	4,324.0	4,226.5	3,860.3	3,437.9	3,106.8	2,883.0	2,660.0	2,327.4	2,334.5
2008	2,431.0	2,679.8	2,920.4	2,787.6	2,733.9	2,486.3	2,223.6	2,110.8	1,717.5	1,571.2	1,390.4	1,533.4
2009	2,062.7	2,339.1	2,292.6	2,530.2	2,456.1	2,405.8	2,137.2	2,059.1	1,938.5	1,931.4	2,105.8	2,196.4
2010	2,699.9	3,217.3	3,442.6	3,400.3	3,317.0	3,128.8	2,935.7	2,602.8	2,491.2	2,159.6	1,985.2	2,197.6

[1] Licensed warehouses approved by ICE.   *Source: ICE Futures U.S. (ICE)*

Visible Stocks of Cocoa in New York Warehouses[1], at End of Month   In Thousands of Bags

Year	Jan.	Feb.	Mar.	Apr.	May	June	July	Aug.	Sept.	Oct.	Nov.	Dec.
2001	1,005.6	1,173.8	1,119.6	1,024.9	967.5	906.6	776.2	758.5	657.6	687.4	750.8	1,196.2
2002	1,104.1	870.8	892.0	806.6	739.1	736.0	628.7	553.6	669.2	525.7	473.1	554.8
2003	614.6	625.4	593.5	604.4	515.1	470.3	446.8	388.2	451.7	301.9	260.7	342.9
2004	229.9	415.2	615.4	579.9	711.3	680.1	676.3	596.1	485.9	334.5	210.2	209.6
2005	201.2	446.3	495.9	677.7	813.6	916.5	805.2	625.2	457.2	430.3	388.3	599.2
2006	758.4	971.5	869.7	820.6	758.3	691.8	634.1	685.8	654.2	649.1	532.3	502.8
2007	532.2	460.2	632.6	667.1	611.9	605.4	577.7	530.5	496.8	442.2	394.8	343.2
2008	408.9	411.1	574.4	618.7	614.0	554.4	527.9	434.6	396.1	375.6	323.1	242.5
2009	291.7	413.2	423.9	472.0	501.5	557.3	672.2	664.2	653.9	726.0	714.6	722.3
2010	831.4	1,005.7	1,099.3	1,042.0	954.2	825.2	730.7	662.7	618.4	572.3	524.9	487.3

[1] Licensed warehouses approved by ICE.   *Source: ICE Futures U.S. (ICE)*

COCOA

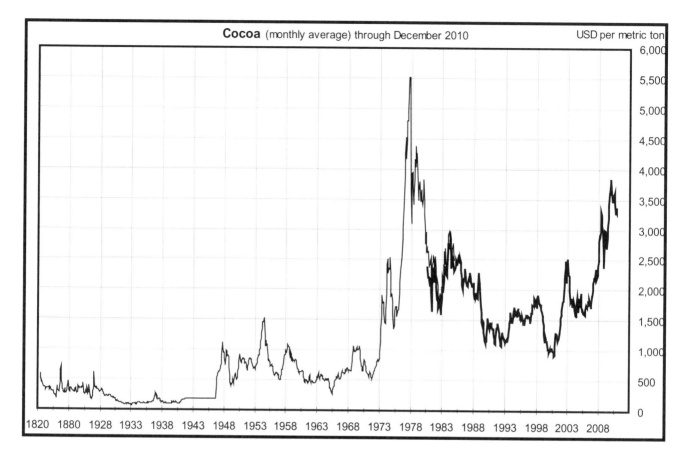

Cocoa (monthly average) through December 2010 — USD per metric ton

Average Cash Price of Cocoa, Ivory Coast in New York   In Dollars Per Metric Ton

Year	Jan.	Feb.	Mar.	Apr.	May	June	July	Aug.	Sept.	Oct.	Nov.	Dec.	Average
2001	1,093	1,299	1,290	1,244	1,281	1,146	1,152	1,200	1,183	1,288	1,439	1,543	1,263
2002	1,586	1,674	1,794	1,800	1,814	1,836	2,081	2,191	2,391	2,471	2,123	2,322	2,007
2003	2,483	2,506	2,258	2,232	1,996	1,818	1,803	1,843	1,877	1,713	1,737	1,832	2,008
2004	1,840	1,763	1,695	1,610	1,588	1,571	1,733	1,889	1,698	1,654	1,867	1,848	1,730
2005	1,740	1,827	1,950	1,744	1,656	1,687	1,625	1,626	1,640	1,598	1,585	1,670	1,696
2006	1,752	1,729	1,739	1,749	1,806	1,794	1,862	1,795	1,764	1,725	1,773	1,897	1,782
2007	1,883	1,996	2,120	2,169	2,214	2,225	2,361	2,185	2,242	2,198	2,251	2,396	2,187
2008	2,486	2,806	2,922	2,867	2,971	3,307	3,248	3,078	2,972	2,533	2,371	2,837	2,867
2009	2,985	2,977	2,781	2,830	2,699	2,892	3,047	3,186	3,427	3,634	3,596	3,782	3,153
2010	3,851	3,611	3,452	3,580	3,535	3,539	3,602	3,455	3,269	3,314	3,279	3,354	3,487

Source: Economic Research Service, U.S. Department of Agriculture (ERS-USDA)

Total Visible Stocks of Cocoa in Warehouses[1], at End of Month   In Thousands of Bags

Year	Jan.	Feb.	Mar.	Apr.	May	June	July	Aug.	Sept.	Oct.	Nov.	Dec.
2001	3,591.5	3,913.4	3,925.0	3,592.5	3,330.7	3,035.8	2,666.1	2,788.9	2,524.1	2,325.6	2,563.0	3,389.7
2002	3,319.2	3,210.2	3,177.9	2,924.0	2,869.4	2,778.9	2,850.8	2,659.6	2,660.4	2,055.0	1,817.3	1,975.3
2003	2,111.7	2,169.1	2,024.1	2,016.8	1,812.7	1,720.6	1,686.9	1,579.6	1,377.3	1,153.8	1,074.1	1,198.1
2004	1,573.5	1,524.4	1,730.0	1,814.5	1,989.8	2,090.9	2,150.1	2,165.8	1,905.5	1,941.9	1,626.4	1,582.0
2005	1,821.1	2,287.0	2,590.8	2,970.3	3,276.0	3,202.2	3,297.5	3,133.6	2,955.1	2,842.9	2,798.5	3,192.9
2006	3,665.1	3,818.4	3,900.5	4,249.5	4,021.8	3,737.7	3,512.1	4,375.5	4,271.5	4,166.7	3,811.4	4,194.0
2007	4,366.4	4,882.4	5,239.0	5,347.3	5,148.4	4,821.1	4,322.9	3,897.1	3,604.0	3,297.4	2,867.8	2,832.9
2008	3,211.7	3,453.9	3,916.2	3,757.7	3,648.4	3,322.8	3,003.3	2,771.8	2,322.7	2,114.2	1,875.9	1,950.5
2009	2,557.4	2,996.2	2,956.0	3,266.2	3,177.1	3,166.2	3,000.9	2,909.0	2,751.1	2,783.3	2,932.8	3,027.8
2010	3,639.8	4,330.1	4,727.3	4,636.9	4,477.2	4,170.8	3,901.1	3,492.1	3,318.1	2,884.6	2,645.7	2,801.8

[1] Licensed warehouses approved by ICE.   *Source: ICE Futures U.S. (ICE)*

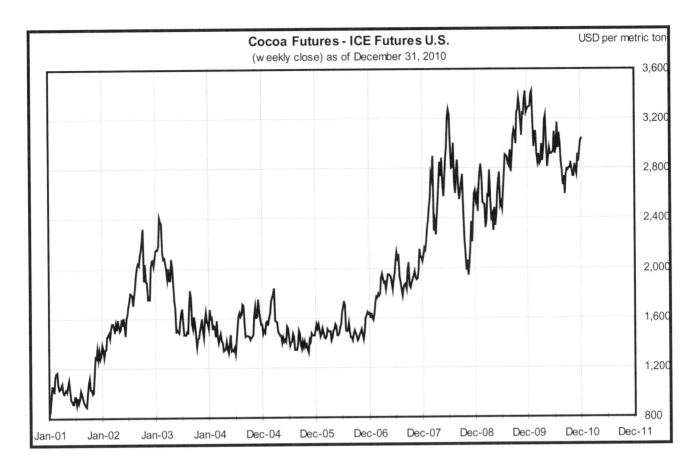

Cocoa Futures - ICE Futures U.S.
(weekly close) as of December 31, 2010

USD per metric ton

Average Open Interest of Cocoa Futures in New York   In Contracts

Year	Jan.	Feb.	Mar.	Apr.	May	June	July	Aug.	Sept.	Oct.	Nov.	Dec.
2001	132,711	119,459	114,036	102,275	107,008	111,224	104,473	99,280	92,235	96,204	93,088	92,326
2002	97,563	98,169	96,336	98,851	103,746	100,701	107,080	102,441	107,294	107,880	82,236	82,844
2003	96,375	91,944	83,625	83,230	95,307	96,813	89,846	78,197	76,468	86,392	99,038	94,010
2004	88,879	84,078	99,918	100,429	108,150	99,476	103,350	111,318	101,998	119,033	117,876	118,769
2005	117,091	115,007	144,055	124,417	124,925	128,203	126,388	129,562	118,468	132,629	131,733	123,302
2006	131,527	127,471	129,426	129,814	131,035	138,004	154,163	134,942	139,544	153,485	136,329	140,099
2007	145,503	152,358	172,846	157,373	154,649	148,608	167,565	134,823	123,171	133,362	137,208	165,522
2008	188,039	182,389	166,939	136,591	146,759	160,366	151,896	134,715	127,674	122,381	113,422	113,240
2009	119,496	118,145	114,051	111,859	117,027	114,792	112,079	112,935	121,226	133,635	129,171	129,296
2010	137,675	127,994	129,562	128,298	130,258	119,074	124,335	119,070	127,315	138,385	136,708	137,345

Source: ICE Futures U.S. (ICE)

Volume of Trading of Cocoa Futures in New York   In Contracts

Year	Jan.	Feb.	Mar.	Apr.	May	June	July	Aug.	Sept.	Oct.	Nov.	Dec.	Total
2001	311,900	168,587	164,131	136,021	154,397	201,299	108,189	207,569	118,428	124,884	202,847	107,565	2,005,817
2002	155,699	187,550	129,833	217,590	160,364	220,289	176,450	209,249	138,394	207,310	162,982	114,270	2,079,980
2003	172,845	215,240	136,564	179,956	176,969	207,255	143,888	206,428	146,113	197,316	209,775	135,857	2,128,206
2004	174,684	180,693	181,667	244,946	174,452	238,201	219,018	260,025	146,090	150,443	290,227	128,604	2,389,050
2005	185,624	239,511	231,917	249,209	134,330	288,809	151,339	252,868	222,122	182,337	283,663	161,198	2,582,927
2006	235,410	264,557	201,604	295,814	244,032	333,275	331,108	313,591	174,246	264,490	308,782	202,293	3,169,202
2007	239,568	338,998	273,605	333,551	212,318	328,646	242,710	378,897	213,143	265,018	273,419	235,410	3,335,283
2008	322,864	434,965	316,509	328,981	293,874	353,593	280,275	345,973	197,765	313,220	228,699	175,550	3,592,268
2009	265,308	282,200	242,110	279,621	214,640	303,030	216,046	292,552	188,138	289,133	338,296	175,892	3,086,966
2010	255,025	361,068	282,222	372,997	290,545	366,645	253,289	425,322	247,749	284,483	404,682	253,652	3,797,679

Source: ICE Futures U.S. (ICE)

Coconut Oil and Copra

Coconut oil and copra come from the fruit of the coconut palm tree, which originated in Southeast Asia. Coconut oil has been used for thousands of years as cooking oil, and is still a staple in the diets of many people living in tropical areas. Until shortages of imported oil developed during WWII, Americans also used coconut oil for cooking.

Copra is the meaty inner lining of the coconut. It is an oil-rich pulp with a light, slightly sweet, nutty flavor. Copra is used mainly as a source of coconut oil and is also used shredded for baking. High-quality copra contains about 65% to 72% oil, and oil made from the copra is called crude coconut oil. Crude coconut oil is processed from copra by expeller press and solvent extraction. It is not considered fit for human consumption until it has been refined, which consists of neutralizing, bleaching and deodorizing it at high heat with a vacuum. The remaining oil cake obtained as a by-product is used for livestock feed.

Premium grade coconut oil, also called virgin coconut oil, is oil made from the first pressing without the addition of any chemicals. Premium grade coconut oil is more expensive than refined or crude oil because the producers use only selected raw materials and there is a lower production yield due to only one pressing.

Coconut oil accounts for approximately 20% of all vegetable oils used worldwide. Coconut oil is used in margarines, vegetable shortening, salad oils, confections, and in sports drinks to boost energy and enhance athletic performance. It is also used in the manufacture of soaps, detergents, shampoos, cosmetics, candles, glycerin and synthetic rubber. Coconut oil is very healthy, unless it is hydrogenated, and is easily digested.

Prices – The average monthly price of coconut oil (crude) in 2009 fell -41.0% yr/yr to 34.65 cents per pound. The record high of 60.21 cents per pound was posted in 1984.

Supply – World production of copra in 2010 rose by +5.2% yr/yr to 5.482 million metric tons, but remains below the record high of 5.662 million metric tons posted in 2001. The world's largest producers of copra are the Philippines with 40.1% of world production, Indonesia with 28.1%, India with 12,6%, and Mexico with 4.2%. World production of coconut oil in the 2009-10 marketing year rose by +12.1% yr/yr to 3.442 million metric tons.

Demand – Virtually all of world production of copra goes for crushing into coconut meal and oil (over 99%). World consumption of coconut oil in 2009-10 rose by +11.2% yr/yr to 3.415 million metric tons, a new record high.

Trade – Copra is generally crushed in the country of origin, meaning that less than 4% of copra itself is exported; the rest is exported in the form of coconut oil. World exports of coconut oil in 2009-10 rose by 20.0% yr/yr to 2.108 million metric tons, and still below the 2005-06 record high of 2.189 million metric tons.

World Production of Copra   In Thousands of Metric Tons

Year	India	Indonesia	Ivory Coast	Malaysia	Mexico	Mozam-bique	Papua New Guinea	Philip-pines	Sri Lanka	Thailand	Vanuatu	Vietnam	World Total
2001	690	1,185	45	47	198	75	95	2,790	113	60	30	41	5,662
2002	713	1,290	45	50	203	50	71	2,010	59	61	25	46	4,920
2003	690	1,260	45	51	185	55	85	2,406	50	68	25	49	5,267
2004	700	1,300	45	51	182	50	90	1,980	60	71	35	49	4,915
2005	690	1,460	45	48	209	50	112	2,100	67	72	30	50	5,252
2006	680	1,370	45	51	187	48	94	2,100	65	65	30	51	5,110
2007	670	1,570	45	49	217	46	97	1,880	69	68	30	54	5,121
2008[1]	680	1,435	46	52	226	48	123	1,910	73	68	32	55	5,076
2009[2]	680	1,520	46	54	228	48	100	1,980	74	69	31	55	5,209
2010[3]	690	1,540	46	55	230	48	110	2,200	75	70	32	57	5,482

[1] Preliminary.   [2] Estimate.   [3] Forecast.   *Source: The Oil World*

World Supply and Distribution of Coconut Oil   In Thousands of Metric Tons

	Production							Consumption						Ending Stocks		
Year	India	Indo-nesia	Malay-sia	Philip-pines	Total	Exports	Imports	European Union	India	Indo-nesia	Philip-pines	United States	Total	Philip-pines	United States	Total
2000-01	419	700	48	1,731	3,496	2,159	2,173	751	439	277	348	437	3,349	60	118	572
2001-02	421	773	45	1,403	3,183	1,846	1,872	712	448	278	332	506	3,274	62	103	507
2002-03	418	758	41	1,425	3,180	1,958	1,991	786	454	273	352	384	3,301	53	98	418
2003-04	419	731	41	1,379	3,104	1,860	1,833	713	428	246	311	399	3,125	58	60	370
2004-05	416	881	42	1,263	3,164	2,116	2,067	814	434	175	253	361	3,083	73	110	402
2005-06	409	789	45	1,450	3,240	2,189	2,175	768	437	180	253	494	3,223	66	101	405
2006-07	402	960	47	1,211	3,176	1,921	1,905	704	417	187	339	435	3,163	108	58	402
2007-08[1]	405	887	44	1,300	3,202	1,998	2,027	685	420	179	387	506	3,238	83	82	396
2008-09[2]	407	851	44	1,199	3,070	1,757	1,780	631	425	160	447	419	3,072	96	83	418
2009-10[3]	411	936	47	1,469	3,442	21,083	2,091	745	430	182	413	490	3,415	72	98	428

[1] Preliminary.   [2] Estimate.   [3] Forecast.   *Source: The Oil World*

Supply and Distribution of Coconut Oil in the United States   In Millions of Pounds

Year	Rotterdam Copra Tonne ($ U.S.)	Coconut Oil, CIF ($ U.S.)	Imports For Consumption	Stocks Oct. 1	Total Supply	Exports	Disappearance Total Domestic	Edible Products	Inedible Products	Production of Coconut Oil (Refined) Total	Oct.-Dec.	Jan.-Mar.	April-June	July-Sept.
2000-01	208	323	1,100	136	1,236	8	968	237	297	534.9	135.7	128.3	146.9	124.0
2001-02	245	388	1,150	260	1,410	11	1,100	294	302	501.8	139.5	126.1	115.4	120.8
2002-03	286	450	866	226	1,092	28	1,205	305	310	546.7	128.8	137.0	155.6	125.2
2003-04	424	630	812	216	1,028	17	1,312	330	274	594.9	160.7	132.8	162.8	138.6
2004-05	431	636	936	131	1,067	29	1,374	341	280	623.3	153.7	157.5	160.8	151.3
2005-06	387	583	1,127	242	1,369	58	1,323	366	270	599.9	141.9	156.2	160.5	141.4
2006-07	537	812	892	222	1,114	26	1,443	339	309	654.6	162.6	152.2	165.4	174.4
2007-08	867	1,306	1,196	128	1,325	28	1,383	373	447	627.4	139.9	165.9	161.1	160.5
2008-09[1]	487	735	961	181	1,143	37	1,293	364	394	586.6	147.6	131.1	122.8	185.2
2009-10[2]	539	807	1,146	182	1,329	33	1,836	441	W	833.0	190.1	214.9	211.2	216.8

[1] Preliminary.   [2] Forecast.   *Source: Bureau of Census, U.S. Department of Commerce*

Consumption of Coconut Oil in End Products (Edible and Inedible) in the United States   In Millions of Pounds

Year	Jan.	Feb.	Mar.	Apr.	May	June	July	Aug.	Sept.	Oct.	Nov.	Dec.	Total
2001	49.3	40.6	45.5	42.5	48.3	43.3	46.5	45.6	48.4	50.3	44.4	45.5	550.2
2002	55.4	41.3	50.8	59.3	53.9	46.4	50.7	51.8	45.9	54.3	56.1	49.4	615.4
2003	51.2	49.3	56.8	50.6	52.3	46.7	48.9	49.6	50.3	47.8	41.8	38.5	583.7
2004	50.0	51.7	58.5	54.6	48.5	55.6	52.9	55.1	48.9	48.2	64.3	51.7	640.0
2005	50.0	51.7	58.5	54.6	48.5	55.5	47.2	58.1	49.2	52.8	53.4	58.1	621.1
2005	46.7	52.0	47.9	48.8	51.4	55.5	47.2	58.1	49.2	52.8	53.4	58.1	621.1
2006	70.4	62.7	50.4	47.5	50.7	51.6	43.1	51.6	43.8	49.6	44.4	40.8	606.4
2007	49.8	48.5	47.0	51.2	53.7	60.3	60.3	74.2	67.5	71.8	71.3	62.7	718.3
2008	63.6	72.1	64.8	74.4	69.7	70.4	65.8	67.6	65.8	63.0	63.6	53.6	794.5
2009	67.9	62.8	60.2	66.9	66.9	27.6	36.5	28.1	29.4	32.8	32.1	30.6	541.8
2010[1]	41.0	36.6	45.3	34.9	39.8	38.6	37.2	40.4	32.1	41.4	39.9	70.8	498.1

[1] Preliminary.   *Source: Bureau of Census, U.S. Department of Commerce*

Stocks of Coconut Oil (Crude and Refined) in the United States, on First of Month   In Millions of Pounds

Year	Jan.	Feb.	Mar.	Apr.	May	June	July	Aug.	Sept.	Oct.	Nov.	Dec.
2001	245.4	280.3	357.8	276.5	286.9	194.3	254.4	260.9	246.4	259.7	234.1	231.3
2002	245.9	238.8	249.6	251.3	233.5	231.6	303.3	301.6	245.8	226.5	273.8	264.1
2003	195.2	194.0	214.3	224.9	223.7	187.8	162.2	202.9	195.6	218.9	184.6	186.1
2004	167.2	160.3	192.6	181.7	131.4	108.7	90.6	132.8	149.2	131.3	147.7	182.5
2005	225.9	163.7	188.4	191.0	170.6	187.7	263.5	250.4	253.7	242.1	252.3	273.3
2006	268.3	236.9	224.5	227.3	260.2	229.1	213.8	214.4	204.7	224.5	179.2	180.2
2007	214.4	228.5	261.5	223.1	191.8	157.9	171.2	154.4	127.7	128.4	142.5	212.6
2008	205.6	192.9	180.9	191.9	223.9	203.9	187.8	181.5	180.4	182.2	163.3	174.6
2009	164.1	183.7	215.6	167.2	143.9	138.0	134.8	133.2	102.3	182.3	159.0	154.7
2010[1]	220.2	204.5	172.1	144.6	119.3	120.3	172.2	179.3	197.1	185.8	166.7	167.2

[1] Preliminary.   *Source: Bureau of Census, U.S. Department of Commerce*

Average Price of Coconut Oil (Crude) Tank Cars in New York   In Cents Per Pound

Year	Jan.	Feb.	Mar.	Apr.	May	June	July	Aug.	Sept.	Oct.	Nov.	Dec.	Average
2001	26.00	24.00	22.75	22.50	21.00	21.00	24.00	26.50	26.50	26.50	24.50	24.50	24.15
2002	16.38	17.38	17.25	18.75	20.05	21.13	21.06	21.35	28.50	28.25	27.13	26.00	21.94
2003	26.00	26.00	24.60	24.50	24.50	25.00	25.00	25.00	25.00	25.00	28.75	31.00	25.86
2004	32.00	33.38	34.56	39.20	45.00	46.00	46.00	46.00	39.25	32.65	31.25	31.25	38.05
2005	31.05	31.00	32.67	35.00	34.67	34.00	33.00	33.00	33.00	35.00	29.13	27.75	32.44
2006	27.75	27.75	27.75	27.75	27.75	27.75	27.75	27.75	29.25	30.75	32.25	34.95	29.10
2007	35.75	36.00	36.00	37.50	40.13	45.75	48.00	NA	42.50	45.16	45.38	46.32	41.68
2008	58.02	62.33	70.98	67.38	67.38	71.73	70.33	59.62	55.82	47.73	37.46	35.51	58.69
2009	35.25	33.14	30.07	31.58	37.84	37.34	32.78	35.00	35.75	35.75	35.75	35.53	34.65
2010[1]	36.20	35.75	37.88	41.99	43.60	44.00	46.49	54.31	55.94	63.65	69.00	79.50	50.69

[1] Preliminary.   *Source: Economic Research Service, U.S. Department of Agriculture (ERS-USDA)*

Coffee

Coffee is one of the world's most important cash commodities. Coffee is the common name for any type of tree in the genus madder family. It is actually a tropical evergreen shrub that has the potential to grow 100 feet tall. The coffee tree grows in tropical regions between the Tropics of Cancer and Capricorn in areas with abundant rainfall, year-round warm temperatures averaging about 70 degrees Fahrenheit, and no frost. In the U.S., the only areas that produce any significant amount of coffee are Puerto Rico and Hawaii. The coffee plant will produce its first full crop of beans at about 5 years old and then be productive for about 15 years. The average coffee tree produces enough beans to make about 1 to 1 ½ pounds of roasted coffee per year. It takes approximately 4,000 handpicked green coffee beans to make a pound of coffee. Wine was actually the first drink made from the coffee tree using the coffee cherries, honey, and water. In the 17th century, the first coffee house, also known as a "penny university" because of the price per cup, opened in London. The London Stock Exchange grew from one of these first coffee houses.

Coffee is generally classified into two types of beans: arabica and robusta. The most widely produced coffee is arabica, which makes up about 70 percent of total production. It grows mostly at high altitudes of 600 to 2,000 meters, with Brazil and Colombia being the largest producers. Arabic coffee is traded on the ICE Futures U.S. (ICE) exchange. The stronger of the two types is robusta. It is grown at lower altitudes with the largest producers being Indonesia, West Africa, Brazil, and Vietnam. Robusta coffee is traded on NYSE-LIFFE exchange in London.

Ninety percent of the world coffee trade is in green (unroasted) coffee beans. Seasonal factors have a significant influence on the price of coffee. There is no extreme peak in world production at any one time of the year, although coffee consumption declines by 12 percent or more below the year's average in the warm summer months. Therefore, coffee imports and roasts both tend to decline in spring and summer and pick up again in fall and winter.

The very low prices for coffee in 2000-03 created serious problems for coffee producers. When prices fall below the costs of production, there is little or no economic incentive to produce coffee. The result is that coffee trees are neglected or completely abandoned. When prices are low, producers cannot afford to hire the labor needed to maintain the trees and pick the crop at harvest. The result is that trees yield less due to reduced use of fertilizer and fewer employed coffee workers. One effect is a decline in the quality of the coffee that is produced. Higher quality Arabica coffee is often produced at higher altitudes, which entails higher costs. It is this coffee that is often abandoned. Although the pressure on producers can be severe, the market eventually comes back into balance as supply declines in response to low prices.

Coffee prices are subject to upward spikes in June, July and August due to possible freeze scares in Brazil during the winter months in the Southern Hemisphere. The Brazilian coffee crop is harvested starting in May and extending for several weeks into what are the winter months in Brazil. A major freeze in Brazil occurs roughly every five years on average.

Coffee futures are traded on the Bolsa de Mercadorias & Futuros (BM&F), the Tokyo Grain Exchange (TGE), the NYSE-LIFFE exchange in London, and the ICE Futures U.S. (ICE) exchange. Options are traded on the BM&F, the LIFFE and the ICE.

Prices – ICE Arabica coffee futures prices traded sideways to lower during the first half of 2010 on the prospects of an abundant Brazilian coffee harvest. Coffee prices then began a steady push higher in June of 2010 that continued through the rest of the year and took prices up to a 13-1/2 year high of 242.25 cents per pound in December of 2010. Prices finished 2010 up sharply by 77% at 240.50 cents per pound. Bullish factors in 2010 included (1) the fall in coffee production after global coffee output in 2009/10 fell -4.5% y/y to 122.9 million bags (ICO), (2) increasingly tight supplies as ICE-monitored coffee stockpiles fell for 27 straight months through February 2011 to a 10-3/4 year low of 1.594 million bags, (3) the prediction by the International Cocoa Organization (ICO) that Brazil's Arabica bean output may will 13% in the year starting July 1, 2011 with plants in the lower-yielding half of their 2-year cycle, and (4) ICO's statement that global coffee supplies will likely be "tight" through the rest of 2011 as stockpiles in producing nations stay near a 40-year low of 13 million bags, which will further extend a "precariousness of the supply/demand balance." Coffee prices continued to advance in early and in Feb 2011 posted a 13-3/4 year high of 277.00 cents per pound.

Supply – World coffee production in the 2010-11 marketing year (July-June) rose 9.6% yr/yr to a new record high of 139.084 million bags (1 bag equals 60 kilograms or 132.3 pounds). The increase in production caused the 2010-11 ending stocks to rise 21.3% to 31.343 million bags.

Brazil is the world's largest coffee producer by far with 54.5 million bags of production in 2010-11, which was 39.2% of total world production. Other key producers include Vietnam with 13.5% of the world's production and with Columbia and Indonesia each with 6.5%. Brazil's coffee production in 2010-11 rose 21.7% y/y to 54.5 million bags. Vietnam has become a major coffee producer in recent years, boosting its production to 18.725 million bags in 2010-11, up from less than a million bags in 1990.

Demand – U.S. coffee consumption in 2010 rose 3.1% to 22.550 million bags, but still not far below the record high of 25.377 million bags seen in 1968.

Trade – World coffee exports in 2010-11 rose 3.7% yr/yr to 104.967 million bags, setting a new record high. The world's largest exporters of coffee in 2010-11 were Brazil with 33.3% of world exports, Vietnam with 16.8%, and Columbia with 7.4%. U.S. coffee imports in 2010 (latest data) rose 3.1% yr/yr from the previous year to 23.163 million bags. The all-time high of 24.549 million bags was posted in 1962. The key countries from which the U.S. imported coffee in 2010 were Brazil (which accounted for 27.2% of U.S. imports), Columbia (13%), Guatemala (5.9%), and Mexico (5.9%).

World Supply and Distribution of Coffee for Producing Countries   In Thousands of 60 Kilogram Bags

Year	Beginning Stocks	Production	Imports	Total Supply	Total Exports	Bean Exports	Rst/Grn Exports	Soluble Exports	Domestic Use	Ending Stocks
2001-02	22,618	111,518	6,974	135,783	88,292	81,739	337	6,216	27,611	25,207
2002-03	39,422	127,102	90,663	150,977	94,108	88,499	293	6,439	115,170	47,909
2003-04	47,909	110,750	90,698	182,140	90,071	83,758	317	7,097	118,941	40,345
2004-05	40,345	121,262	93,011	247,139	93,195	83,778	294	7,070	119,759	41,664
2005-06	41,664	116,721	92,195	242,277	92,829	80,187	350	6,499	125,122	32,629
2006-07	32,629	131,818	97,360	260,501	102,799	93,774	344	7,296	123,900	35,108
2007-08	35,108	121,984	96,819	253,911	96,439	86,086	444	7,544	127,309	30,163
2008-09[1]	30,163	133,623	96,746	260,532	99,452	89,312	460	7,736	124,112	36,968
2009-10[2]	36,968	126,916	98,815	262,699	101,263	89,788			135,598	25,838
2010-11[3]	25,838	139,084	102,413	267,335	104,967	93,298			131,025	31,343

[1] Preliminary.   [2] Estimate.   [3] Forecast.   132.276 Lbs. Per Bag   *Source: Foreign Agricultural Service, U.S. Department of Agriculture (FAS-USDA)*

World Production of Green Coffee   In Thousands of 60 Kilogram Bags

Crop Year	Brazil	Colombia	Costa Rica	El Salvador	Ethiopia	Guate-mala	India	Indo-nesia	Ivory Coast	Mexico	Uganda	Vietnam	World Total
2001-02	35,100	11,950	2,338	1,610	3,756	3,530	5,010	6,160	3,568	4,200	3,158	12,833	111,518
2002-03	53,600	11,712	2,207	1,351	3,693	3,802	4,588	6,140	3,145	4,350	2,890	11,167	127,102
2003-04	33,200	11,053	2,106	1,343	3,875	3,671	4,508	6,000	2,689	4,428	2,599	15,000	110,750
2004-05	43,600	11,532	1,907	1,329	4,575	3,817	4,672	8,450	2,301	3,900	2,593	14,500	121,262
2005-06	36,100	11,953	1,751	1,387	4,000	3,605	4,617	9,450	1,962	4,000	2,159	16,335	116,721
2006-07	46,700	12,164	1,782	1,400	4,036	4,050	4,665	7,500	2,447	4,500	2,300	19,500	131,818
2007-08	39,100	12,515	1,867	1,650	3,906	4,110	4,660	7,600	2,098	4,350	2,500	18,000	121,984
2008-09[1]	53,300	8,664	1,580	1,550	3,650	3,980	4,375	9,300	1,853	4,550	3,200	16,980	133,623
2009-10[2]	44,800	8,100	1,456	1,300	4,000	3,910	4,825	10,175	2,350	4,150	2,800	18,750	126,916
2010-11[3]	54,500	9,000	1,500	1,600	4,400	4,000	5,125	9,000	2,200	4,500	3,200	18,725	139,084

[1] Preliminary.   [2] Estimate.   [3] Forecast.   132.276 Lbs. Per Bag   *Source: Foreign Agricultural Service, U.S. Department of Agriculture (FAS-USDA)*

World Exportable[4] Production of Green Coffee   In Thousands of 60 Kilogram Bags

Crop Year	Brazil	Colombia	Ethiopia	Guate-mala	Honduras	India	Indo-nesia	Ivory Coast	Mexico	Peru	Uganda	Vietnam	World Total
2001-02	24,795	10,665	1,939	3,330	2,617	3,442	4,729	3,058	3,200	2,360	3,153	12,000	88,292
2002-03	29,396	10,478	2,277	3,500	2,438	3,567	4,801	5,166	3,400	2,575	2,810	11,176	94,108
2003-04	24,920	10,154	2,375	3,314	2,794	3,826	4,408	2,622	3,550	2,685	2,523	14,500	90,071
2004-05	27,920	11,032	2,625	3,451	2,450	2,790	4,600	1,984	2,107	3,306	2,489	13,992	93,195
2005-06	24,543	10,752	2,550	3,325	2,978	3,580	5,070	1,645	2,600	2,225	2,002	12,958	92,829
2006-07	29,260	11,237	2,775	3,700	3,248	3,664	4,710	2,691	2,720	4,430	2,700	18,600	102,799
2007-08	21,710	11,378	2,200	3,642	3,594	2,937	5,340	1,201	2,300	3,832	2,440	17,100	96,439
2008-09[1]	33,340	7,464	1,600	3,365	3,295	2,472	6,447	1,085	2,250	3,905	2,500	16,936	99,452
2009-10[2]	24,850	7,900	2,100	3,765	3,661	3,000	6,730	1,690	2,300	3,780	2,700	16,385	101,263
2010-11[3]	35,000	7,800	2,575	3,665	3,300	3,375	7,100	1,900	2,640	3,850	2,775	17,675	104,967

[1] Preliminary.   [2] Estimate.   [3] Forecast.   [4] Marketing year begins in October in some countries and April or July in others. Exportable production represents total harvested production minus estimated domestic consumption.   132.276 Lbs. Per Bag
Source: Foreign Agricultural Service, U.S. Department of Agriculture (FAS-USDA)

Coffee[2] Imports in the United States   In Thousands of 60 Kilogram Bags

Year	Brazil	Colombia	Costa Rica	Republic	Ecuador	El Salvador	Ethiopia	Guate-mala	Indo-nesia	Mexico	Peru	Vene-zuela	World Total
2001	3,007	3,272	915	50	230	507	80	2,040	887	2,057	692	4	20,491
2002	5,060	3,597	987	51	145	470	74	1,626	759	2,034	842	170	20,632
2003	5,321	3,884	914	80	133	569	101	2,023	966	1,510	807	180	21,695
2004	4,475	3,714	957	2	157	524	121	1,624	1,636	1,477	788	103	22,049
2005	4,464	4,090	920	2	74	406	177	1,752	1,599	1,285	587	0	21,791
2006	4,795	3,904	751	60	147	435	250	1,654	1,677	1,528	850	2	22,659
2007	4,968	4,064	823	35	123	565	234	1,815	1,122	1,495	919	25	23,216
2008	4,970	4,245	953	35	40	657	348	1,901	1,351	1,427	963	93	23,217
2009	5,642	3,425	750	56	65	463	202	1,739	1,318	1,642	854	7	22,465
2010[1]	6,302	3,018	715	6	56	366	306	1,310	1,352	1,371	882	7	23,163

[1] Preliminary.   132.276 Lbs. Per Bag   *Source: Bureau of Census, U.S. Department of Commerce*

COFFEE

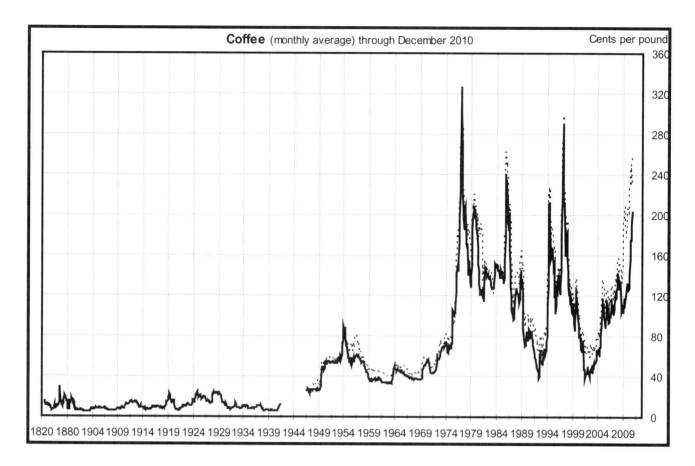

Coffee (monthly average) through December 2010   Cents per pound

Monthly Coffee[2] Imports in the United States   In Thousands of 60 Kilogram Bags (132.276 Lbs. Per Bag)

Year	Jan.	Feb.	Mar.	Apr.	May	June	July	Aug.	Sept.	Oct.	Nov.	Dec.	Total
2001	1,747	1,690	1,906	1,825	1,823	1,685	1,863	1,605	1,430	1,502	1,581	1,833	20,490
2002	1,652	1,364	1,613	1,697	1,672	1,547	1,802	1,794	1,850	1,877	1,807	1,958	20,631
2003	1,994	1,755	2,007	1,916	1,715	1,710	2,015	1,732	1,712	1,750	1,525	1,863	21,694
2004	1,813	1,635	1,967	1,862	2,049	2,034	1,784	1,766	1,708	1,684	1,798	1,947	22,047
2005	1,939	1,942	2,072	1,965	1,893	1,891	1,781	1,606	1,481	1,718	1,699	1,803	21,791
2006	1,852	1,647	2,042	1,672	2,007	1,916	1,780	2,091	2,089	1,894	1,834	1,833	22,657
2007	2,167	1,760	1,992	2,015	1,887	1,743	2,005	2,249	2,037	2,038	1,712	1,608	23,215
2008	1,987	1,867	2,117	2,073	2,002	1,945	1,980	1,851	1,977	1,863	1,542	2,012	23,217
2009	1,872	1,679	1,996	1,980	2,041	2,196	2,357	1,895	1,662	1,604	1,389	1,792	22,463
2010[1]	1,706	1,696	1,989	1,987	2,034	1,990	1,870	2,095	1,860	1,829	2,055	2,052	23,163

[1] Preliminary.   [2] Data through 1999 are for Green Coffee.   *Source: Bureau of the Census, U.S. Department of Commerce*

Average Price of Brazilian[1] Coffee in New York   In Cents Per Pound

Year	Jan.	Feb.	Mar.	Apr.	May	June	July	Aug.	Sept.	Oct.	Nov.	Dec.	Average
2001	62.38	62.50	60.35	55.11	57.19	51.86	46.43	46.49	42.42	38.63	42.28	41.60	50.60
2002	42.56	42.79	48.79	49.90	45.19	42.96	43.58	40.55	44.46	45.28	48.37	46.70	45.09
2003	49.14	48.54	43.77	48.71	51.06	47.11	49.64	52.88	55.19	53.51	54.15	56.92	50.89
2004	64.32	66.08	65.79	62.89	64.31	67.62	59.39	60.25	69.46	68.63	80.20	89.17	68.18
2005	94.00	108.05	117.03	112.82	111.89	105.08	94.66	95.66	87.02	94.54	99.35	96.23	101.36
2006	115.89	109.51	103.52	105.89	99.00	91.26	91.01	98.90	97.36	97.39	109.34	115.60	102.89
2007	111.99	109.78	102.34	100.84	99.66	105.89	105.25	112.47	116.43	120.95	118.99	124.06	110.72
2008	126.26	142.25	130.45	123.15	125.18	130.52	131.10	131.85	126.82	104.57	102.74	95.22	122.51
2009	101.43	100.45	97.48	101.46	113.13	109.81	104.55	114.01	114.12	122.84	126.21	131.23	111.39
2010	128.11	121.61	125.28	124.94	121.66	136.18	146.74	152.91	162.02	163.86	179.16	186.05	145.71

[1] And other Arabicas.   *Source: Foreign Agricultural Service, U.S. Department of Agriculture (FAS-USDA)*

Average Monthly Retail[1] Price of Coffee in the United States   In Cents Per Pound

Year	Jan.	Feb.	Mar.	Apr.	May	June	July	Aug.	Sept.	Oct.	Nov.	Dec.	Average
2003	299.9	292.4	293.3	300.8	293.7	293.1	294.4	292.1	291.9	282.5	277.9	287.5	291.6
2004	289.2	285.6	293.2	290.8	283.1	275.0	287.8	287.8	287.4	284.0	277.8	277.6	284.9
2005	304.9	294.0	300.9	324.0	332.9	341.6	333.4	342.8	337.6	344.7	329.3	323.5	325.8
2006	323.2	317.4	330.1	329.2	334.9	315.8	315.4	319.6	317.3	313.8	315.8	311.3	320.3
2007	328.8	345.6	347.5	343.7	330.8	340.7	352.9	349.7	NA	NA	360.7	368.5	346.9
2008	NA	NA	NA	NA	NA	NA	NA	NA	NA	NA	NA	NA	NA
2009	NA	NA	NA	NA	NA	NA	NA	NA	NA	NA	NA	366.9	366.9
2010	381.1	373.6	356.5	364.1	366.4	369.7	385.7	393.5	417.4	417.5	446.7	414.6	390.6

[1] Roasted in 13.1 to 20 ounce cans.   *Source: Foreign Agricultural Service, U.S. Department of Agriculture (FAS-USDA)*

Average Price of Colombian Mild Arabicas[1] in the United States   In Cents Per Pound

Year	Jan.	Feb.	Mar.	Apr.	May	June	July	Aug.	Sept.	Oct.	Nov.	Dec.	Average
2003	69.68	69.60	61.82	66.12	67.56	65.01	67.84	68.65	68.37	66.59	67.04	69.38	67.31
2004	76.61	79.34	80.12	77.08	80.61	85.62	78.27	78.85	85.71	85.52	95.63	106.48	84.15
2005	110.03	124.34	137.10	129.80	128.36	122.47	112.48	111.21	101.31	108.77	111.66	106.54	117.01
2006	129.64	123.17	117.00	119.87	113.03	106.84	109.45	116.22	112.26	113.73	126.23	132.85	118.36
2007	127.54	125.54	119.92	117.51	116.14	122.35	122.32	126.68	131.51	137.71	133.81	139.87	126.74
2008	143.37	161.30	151.48	142.41	143.51	150.60	151.56	154.23	150.20	133.37	133.40	134.72	145.85
2009	148.88	149.58	162.00	190.94	225.58	195.27	192.11	181.61	169.90	175.16	180.08	199.38	180.87
2010	214.55	208.36	206.37	195.18	197.76	229.06	230.88	241.77	239.26	225.83	239.59	256.52	223.76

[1] ICO monthly and composite indicator prices on the New York Market, 1979 ICA Agreement basis.   *Source: Foreign Agricultural Service, U.S. Department of Agriculture (FAS-USDA)*

Average Price of Other Mild Arabicas[1] in the United States   In Cents Per Pound

Year	Jan.	Feb.	Mar.	Apr.	May	June	July	Aug.	Sept.	Oct.	Nov.	Dec.	Average
2003	65.22	67.60	61.66	65.35	66.47	61.34	62.32	63.60	65.50	62.58	62.36	65.01	64.08
2004	74.25	77.51	77.29	74.24	76.40	82.24	73.64	72.99	81.22	106.09	108.81	102.19	80.15
2005	107.07	122.20	134.81	128.80	126.21	119.87	108.45	108.43	98.17	106.09	108.81	102.68	114.30
2006	124.26	118.46	112.20	114.65	107.96	101.21	102.77	112.13	109.36	110.91	123.57	129.93	113.95
2007	124.40	122.34	116.44	114.59	112.35	118.76	116.80	123.53	128.04	134.43	130.28	136.47	123.20
2008	139.10	158.03	148.07	138.06	139.32	144.90	145.13	146.03	141.50	122.04	120.76	116.87	138.32
2009	128.03	128.63	127.76	134.44	147.34	145.17	137.87	146.87	145.67	151.95	150.23	155.86	141.65
2010	154.40	155.92	162.13	171.32	174.21	193.52	205.25	212.80	222.10	215.84	227.96	237.33	194.40

[1] ICO monthly and composite indicator prices on the New York Market, 1979 ICA Agreement basis.   *Source: Foreign Agricultural Service, U.S. Department of Agriculture (FAS-USDA)*

Average Price of Robustas 1976[1] in the United States   In Cents Per Pound

Year	Jan.	Feb.	Mar.	Apr.	May	June	July	Aug.	Sept.	Oct.	Nov.	Dec.	Average
2003	42.75	42.35	38.26	38.68	38.90	35.33	36.71	37.92	38.76	37.32	36.05	37.59	38.39
2004	41.32	39.10	38.61	38.02	38.04	41.09	36.44	34.81	35.10	31.77	34.07	38.98	37.28
2005	39.63	44.61	50.70	53.32	58.66	64.14	68.66	75.73	77.88	76.26	79.67	77.71	70.28
2006	66.46	65.50	62.92	64.45	63.97	64.14	93.47	88.51	93.61	97.34	92.28	91.37	88.29
2007	80.55	80.97	78.95	81.64	86.06	94.76	115.09	113.48	106.67	89.69	92.81	83.99	106.31
2008	100.68	117.10	122.44	112.06	109.58	112.16	115.09	113.48	106.67	77.31	73.08	74.68	77.16
2009	85.77	81.66	77.48	76.50	77.00	75.88	74.83	75.04	77.31	76.68	73.08	74.68	77.16
2010	75.09	73.49	72.53	76.26	76.21	82.51	89.95	89.06	87.11	90.57	97.94	98.32	84.09

[1] ICO monthly and composite indicator prices on the New York Market, 1979 ICA Agreement basis.   *Source: Foreign Agricultural Service, U.S. Department of Agriculture (FAS-USDA)*

Average Price of Composite 1979[1] in the United States   In Cents Per Pound

Year	Jan.	Feb.	Mar.	Apr.	May	June	July	Aug.	Sept.	Oct.	Nov.	Dec.	Average
2003	54.04	54.07	49.61	51.87	53.19	48.90	50.89	52.22	54.10	51.72	49.81	52.44	51.91
2004	58.69	59.87	60.80	58.80	59.91	64.28	58.46	56.98	61.47	61.10	67.74	77.72	62.15
2005	79.35	89.40	101.44	98.20	99.78	96.29	88.48	85.31	78.79	82.55	85.93	86.85	89.36
2006	101.20	97.39	92.76	94.20	90.00	86.04	101.20	95.78	95.98	95.53	103.48	108.01	96.80
2007	105.81	104.18	100.09	99.30	100.09	107.03	106.20	107.98	113.20	115.71	114.43	118.16	107.68
2008	122.33	138.82	136.17	126.55	126.76	130.51	132.78	131.14	126.69	108.31	107.88	103.07	124.25
2009	108.39	107.60	105.87	111.61	123.05	119.05	112.90	117.45	116.40	121.09	119.67	124.96	115.67
2010	126.85	123.37	125.30	126.89	128.10	142.20	153.41	157.46	163.61	161.56	173.90	184.26	147.24

[1] ICO monthly and composite indicator prices on the New York Market, 1979 ICA Agreement basis.   *Source: Foreign Agricultural Service, U.S. Department of Agriculture (FAS-USDA)*

COFFEE

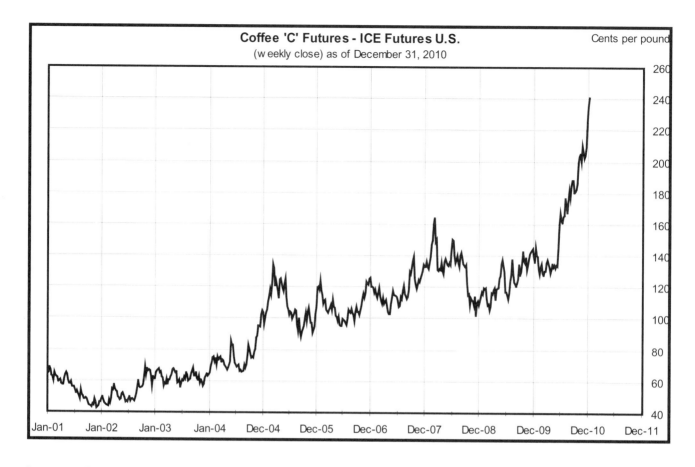

Coffee 'C' Futures - ICE Futures U.S.
(weekly close) as of December 31, 2010

Cents per pound

Average Open Interest of Coffee "C" Futures in New York   In Contracts

Year	Jan.	Feb.	Mar.	Apr.	May	June	July	Aug.	Sept.	Oct.	Nov.	Dec.
2001	48,914	53,050	58,111	57,722	53,481	58,311	57,888	57,243	55,674	58,345	55,317	53,953
2002	57,897	66,825	66,798	66,207	66,289	68,994	69,197	69,635	70,079	73,753	73,431	69,343
2003	69,508	71,682	76,934	77,954	72,716	72,155	72,110	68,259	73,809	79,038	81,253	76,670
2004	92,388	103,966	102,281	98,430	96,738	102,276	89,446	88,021	83,001	78,047	83,360	107,832
2005	102,163	107,715	117,419	105,245	96,063	94,139	93,303	89,662	85,518	86,489	81,525	81,234
2006	102,195	102,614	99,982	102,882	104,230	120,907	120,007	107,928	105,175	111,392	117,469	123,259
2007	128,158	132,849	141,033	146,723	159,011	157,086	168,019	163,288	162,445	173,426	158,146	160,331
2008	176,128	193,555	179,957	160,544	150,017	146,166	147,056	133,178	126,573	132,112	116,643	118,223
2009	129,577	130,101	135,143	134,290	134,827	127,263	107,711	100,880	97,935	114,065	118,016	123,699
2010	129,749	126,850	124,238	133,961	136,711	151,959	169,669	156,086	143,454	139,801	138,738	134,477

Source: ICE Futures U.S. (ICE)

Volume of Trading of Coffee "C" Futures in New York   In Contracts

Year	Jan.	Feb.	Mar.	Apr.	May	June	July	Aug.	Sept.	Oct.	Nov.	Dec.	Total
2001	189,977	221,775	167,466	236,757	182,621	220,708	134,809	250,151	100,443	153,739	229,495	111,430	2,199,371
2002	201,327	279,966	229,764	295,701	159,670	225,177	174,567	254,563	232,255	250,483	236,307	178,728	2,718,508
2003	205,420	283,317	169,611	334,188	255,935	270,424	237,210	278,746	332,473	309,930	314,182	219,595	3,211,031
2004	389,864	397,656	301,270	395,552	324,849	467,887	247,439	366,171	305,196	280,733	424,146	292,540	4,193,303
2005	280,912	469,605	356,855	459,018	240,989	428,227	224,531	404,307	259,177	266,697	376,844	220,616	3,987,778
2006	357,994	416,964	326,256	429,249	322,932	476,542	289,027	481,870	238,953	313,459	492,904	261,362	4,407,512
2007	334,593	468,712	383,506	474,542	373,291	600,122	361,467	596,622	373,925	484,038	468,987	208,818	5,128,623
2008	419,096	729,397	515,528	556,002	354,887	642,074	317,917	512,002	381,241	384,451	383,346	250,575	5,446,516
2009	309,386	406,786	328,940	404,635	305,326	435,239	244,504	388,567	244,371	332,043	535,063	300,489	4,235,349
2010	336,188	544,197	388,468	586,602	372,641	791,873	384,464	601,583	336,930	370,233	519,808	255,209	5,488,196

Source: ICE Futures U.S. (ICE)

Coke

Coke is the hard and porous residue left after certain types of bituminous coals are heated to high temperatures (up to 2,000 degrees Fahrenheit) for about 17 hours. It is blackish-gray and has a metallic luster. The residue is mostly carbon. Coke is used as a reducing agent in the smelting of pig iron and the production of steel. Petroleum coke is made from the heavy tar-like residue of the petroleum refining process. It is used primarily to generate electricity.

Supply – Production of petroleum coke in the U.S. in 2010 (annualized through April) rose +0.8% yr/yr to 294.364 million barrels. That was further down from the 2006 three-decade high of 309.980 and far below the U.S. production record of 369.305 million barrels posted back in 1957. U.S. stocks of coke at coke plants (Dec 31) in 2009 fell by -15.3% yr/yr to 776,000 short tons.

Trade – U.S. coke exports in 2009 fell -33.3% to 1.306 million tons, and over a third of those exports were to Canada. U.S. coke imports in 2009 fell by -90.4% yr/yr to 346,692 short tons. About 13% of the imports were from Japan.

Salient Statistics of Coke in the United States   In Thousands of Short Tons

Year	Middle Atlantic	East North Central	East South Central	Other	Total	Coke Total	Breeze Total	Consumption[2]	Producer and Distributor Stocks Dec. 31	Canada	Total	Japan	Total
2004	W	8,614	2,104	7,356	18,074	16,909	1,165	22,492	351	596	1,319	943	6,873
2005	W	8,448	W	9,456	17,904	16,719	1,184	18,239	614	764	1,747	699	3,529
2006	W	8,439	W	9,112	17,551	16,404	1,147	18,784	685	840	1,616	838	4,068
2007	W	8,009	W	9,409	17,418	16,201	1,217	17,270	632	589	1,444	791	2,460
2008	W	7,578	W	9,153	16,731	15,646	1,085	17,006	916	758	1,959	604	3,603
2009[1]	W	5,972	W	5,796	11,768	11,143	625	10,323	776	419	1,307	46	347

[1] Preliminary.   [2] Equal to production plus imports minus the change in producer and distributor stocks minus exports.
W = Withheld.   *Source: Energy Information Administration, U.S. Department of Energy (EIA-DOE)*

Production of Petroleum Coke in the United States   In Thousands of Barrels

Year	Jan.	Feb.	Mar.	Apr.	May	June	July	Aug.	Sept.	Oct.	Nov.	Dec.	Total
2004	25,640	22,380	24,025	25,086	26,789	25,874	26,263	26,151	24,259	25,899	25,897	27,599	305,862
2005	25,093	23,806	26,896	25,648	27,209	26,950	26,612	26,410	22,209	22,039	24,372	26,575	303,819
2006	26,180	23,706	25,722	24,987	26,690	26,128	26,372	26,395	26,300	25,957	25,048	26,495	309,980
2007	25,883	22,117	25,369	24,592	26,071	24,904	26,345	26,316	24,613	24,143	24,220	26,050	300,623
2008	25,862	22,994	24,616	24,100	25,432	25,801	26,691	25,993	21,350	24,796	25,196	25,875	298,706
2009	25,902	21,991	25,071	24,741	24,402	25,339	25,205	24,862	24,364	23,823	22,490	23,857	292,047
2010[1]	23,127	20,913	24,490	23,911	25,878	25,618	26,761	26,089	23,986				294,364

[1] Preliminary.   *Source: Energy Information Administration, U.S. Department of Energy (EIA-DOE)*

Coal Receipts and Average Prices at Coke Plants in the United States

	Coal Receipts at Coke Plants By Census Division, in Thousands of Short Tons					Average Price of Coal Receipts at Coke Plants By Census Division, In Dollars per Short Ton				
Year	Middle Atlantic	East North Central	East South Central	Other	Total	Middle Atlantic	East North Central	East South Central	Other	Total
2004	W	11,591	2,710	9,795	24,096	W	63.30	59.16	W	61.50
2005	W	11,523	W	12,778	24,301	W	89.97	W	W	83.79
2006	W	11,488	W	11,865	23,353	W	99.48	W	W	92.87
2007	W	9,907	W	11,725	21,632	W	99.20	W	W	94.97
2008	W	10,362	W	12,067	22,429	W	122.18	W	W	118.09
2009[1]	W	7,772	W	7,333	15,105	W	150.93	W	W	143.01

[1] Preliminary.   W = Withheld.   *Source: Energy Information Administration, U.S. Department of Energy (EIA-DOE)*

Coal Carbonized and Coke and Breeze Stocks at Coke Plants in the United States   In Thousands of Short Tons

	Coal Carbonized at Coke Plants By Census Division					Stocks at Coke Plants, Dec. 31 By Census Division						
Year	Middle Atlantic	East North Central	East South Central	Other	Total	Middle Atlantic	East North Central	East South Central	Other	Total	Coke Total	Breeze Total
2004	W	11,322	2,644	9,704	23,670	W	166	154	144	464	351	113
2005	W	11,064	W	12,370	23,434	W	363	W	383	746	614	132
2006	W	11,100	W	11,857	22,957	W	487	W	284	771	685	87
2007	W	10,486	W	12,229	22,715	W	414	W	296	710	632	78
2008	W	10,228	W	11,842	22,070	W	658	W	335	993	916	77
2009[1]	W	7,849	W	7,477	15,326	W	538	W	320	858	776	82

[1] Preliminary.   W = Withheld.   *Source: Energy Information Administration, U.S. Department of Energy (EIA-DOE)*

Copper

The word *copper* comes from name of the Mediterranean island Cyprus that was a primary source of the metal. Dating back more than 10,000 years, copper is the oldest metal used by humans. From the Pyramid of Cheops in Egypt, archeologists recovered a portion of a water plumbing system whose copper tubing was found in serviceable condition after more than 5,000 years.

Copper is one of the most widely used industrial metals because it is an excellent conductor of electricity, has strong corrosion-resistance properties, and is very ductile. It is also used to produce the alloys of brass (a copper-zinc alloy) and bronze (a copper-tin alloy), both of which are far harder and stronger than pure copper. Electrical uses of copper account for about 75% of total copper usage, and building construction is the single largest market (the average U.S. home contains 400 pounds of copper). Copper is biostatic, meaning that bacteria will not grow on its surface, and it is therefore used in air-conditioning systems, food processing surfaces, and doorknobs to prevent the spread of disease.

Copper futures and options are traded on the London Metal Exchange (LME) and the New York Mercantile Exchange (NYMEX). Copper futures are traded on the Shanghai Futures Exchange. The NYMEX copper futures contract calls for the delivery of 25,000 pounds of Grade 1 electrolyte copper and is priced in terms of cents per pound.

Prices – NYMEX copper futures prices in 2010 posted a 1-1/2 year high of $3.68 per pound in April 2010 but then plunged to a 1-1/2 year low of $2.72 per pound in June 2010. Copper prices then began a rally in June 2010 that continued into the end of the year with prices soaring to a record high of $4.44 per pound in December 2010 and closing 2010 up 33% at $4.395 per pound. Copper prices advanced further and in February 2011 posted yet another record high of $4.6495 per pound. Strength in the global economy was the main bullish factor for copper prices along with limited supplies with ICSG data showing the global copper market in deficit throughout 2010.

Supply – World production of copper in 2010 rose by +1.9% yr/yr to 16.200 million metric tons, which was a new record high. The largest producer of copper was Chile with 34.1% of the world's production, followed by the Peru with 7.9%, China with 7.1%, the US with 6.9%, and Australia with 5.6%. U.S. production of refined copper in 2010 fell -4.8% yr/yr to 1.104 million short tons, which was far below the record U.S. production level of 2.490 million short tons seen in 1998.

Demand – U.S. consumption of copper in 2008 (latest data available) fell 5.6% yr/yr to 2.020 million metric tons. The primary users of copper in the U.S. in 2008 by class of consumer were wire rod mills with 73.8% of usage, brass mills with 23.7% of usage, and nominal use of 1.2% or less by each of foundries, ingot makers, and chemical plants.

Trade – U.S. exports of refined copper in 2010 rose by +15.0% to 92,960 metric tons, above the 2008 6-year low of 36,500 metric tons. U.S. imports of copper in 2010 fell by 7.2% yr/yr to 615,733 metric tons.

World Mine Production of Copper (Content of Ore) In Thousands of Metric Tons

Year	Australia	Canada[3]	Chile	China	Indonesia	Mexico	Peru	Poland	Russia	South Africa	United States[3]	Zambia	World Total[2]
2001	871.0	633.5	4,739.0	605	1,081.0	371.1	722.3	474.0	600	141.9	1,340	312.0	13,700
2002	867.8	603.5	4,581.0	593	1,171.7	329.9	844.6	502.8	695	129.6	1,140	330.0	13,600
2003	839.6	557.1	4,904.2	620	1,005.8	355.7	862.6	505.0	675	89.5	1,120	378.0	13,800
2004	854.1	562.8	5,412.5	752	840.3	405.5	1,035.6	531.0	675	87.0	1,160	402.9	14,700
2005	916.3	595.4	5,320.5	777	1,064.2	429.1	1,009.9	512.0	700	88.6	1,140	432.0	15,000
2006	858.8	603.3	5,360.8	889	818.0	327.5	1,048.5	497.0	725	89.5	1,200	474.0	15,000
2007	870.0	596.2	5,557.0	946	796.9	337.5	1,190.3	452.0	740	97.0	1,170	509.0	15,500
2008	886.0	607.0	5,330.3	960	632.6	246.6	1,267.9	429.0	750	109.0	1,310	546.0	15,400
2009[1]	854.0	491.0	5,390.0	995	996.0	238.0	1,275.0	439.0	725		1,180	697.0	15,900
2010[2]	900.0	480.0	5,520.0	1150	840.0	230.0	1,285.0	430.0	750		1,120	770.0	16,200

[1] Preliminary. [2] Estimate. [3] Recoverable. *Source: U.S. Geological Survey (USGS)*

Commodity Exchange Inc. Warehouse Stocks of Copper, on First of Month In Thousands of Short Tons

Year	Jan.	Feb.	Mar.	Apr.	May	June	July	Aug.	Sept.	Oct.	Nov.	Dec.
2001	64.7	79.3	90.0	105.1	126.5	150.9	165.1	176.1	186.8	199.6	211.0	236.5
2002	269.2	284.8	304.0	314.1	326.0	337.4	355.7	374.6	375.9	380.3	381.6	382.8
2003	399.3	395.2	373.7	362.7	351.2	336.7	320.5	310.6	303.9	299.0	294.4	288.1
2004	280.9	262.7	241.9	213.3	171.7	130.7	95.1	79.0	62.3	49.2	45.5	42.4
2005	48.2	45.8	46.8	43.3	30.1	22.0	15.3	11.0	9.3	7.2	3.7	3.7
2006	6.8	11.7	30.4	20.7	16.7	9.5	7.9	6.8	12.4	22.3	23.2	31.3
2007	34.0	36.2	37.0	36.4	33.7	27.2	22.1	21.8	20.7	20.1	19.0	18.0
2008	14.1	14.0	13.1	11.9	10.8	11.1	11.0	5.4	5.4	9.9	9.9	24.5
2009	NA	40.2	45.3	46.5	54.1	56.8	59.8	54.1	53.5	55.0	55.0	70.7
2010	94.5	94.5	94.5	102.0	101.2	101.9	101.9	100.4	95.3	84.9	74.3	70.8

Source: CME Group; New York Mercantile Exchange (NYMEX)

Salient Statistics of Copper in the United States In Thousands of Metric Tons

	--------- New Copper Produced -----------					Secondary Recovery	----- Imports[5] ------		----- Exports -----			Primary Producers (Refined)	Blister & Material in Solution	Apparent Consumption	
	-- From Domestic Ores --			From Foreign Ores	Total New		Unmanu-factured	Refined	Ore, Concen-trate[6]	Refined[7]	COMEX			Refined Copper (Reported)	Primary & Old Copper[8]
Year	Mines	Smelters	Refin-eries												
2001	1,340	919	808	192	1,630	317	1,400	991	45	23	244	952	98	2,620	2,500
2002	1,140	683	725	116	1,440	190	1,230	927	23	27	362	1,030	44	2,370	2,610
2003	1,120	539	532	130	1,250	207	1,140	882	10	93	255	656	57	2,290	2,430
2004	1,160	542	531	140	1,260	191	1,060	807	24	118	44	134	51	2,410	2,550
2005	1,140	523	524	130	1,210	183	1,230	1,000	137	40	6	64	44	2,270	2,420
2006	1,200	501	531	144	1,210	151	1,320	1,070	108	106	31	194	19	2,110	2,200
2007	1,170	617	702	62	1,270	158	1,100	832	134	51	14	130	26	2,140	2,270
2008	1,310	574	603	109	1,220	155	934	721	301	37	31	187	20	2,020	2,000
2009[1]	1,180				1,110	172	788	645	151	81		433		1,650	1,600
2010[2]	1,120				1,050	160	760	620	140	90		440		1,730	1,730

[1] Preliminary. [2] Estimate. [3] Also from matte, etc., refinery reports. [4] From old scrap only. [5] For consumption. [6] Blister (copper content). [7] Ingots, bars, etc. [8] Old scrap only. W = Withheld. *Source: U.S. Geological Survey (USGS)*

Consumption of Refined Copper[3] in the United States In Thousands of Metric Tons

	---------------------------- By-Products ----------------------------						----------------------- By Class of Consumer -----------------------						Total Con-sumption
Year	Cathodes	Wire Bars	Ingots and Ingot Bars	Cakes & Slabs	Billets	Other[4]	Wire Rod Mills	Brass Mills	Chemical Plants	Ingot Makers	Foundries	Miscel-laneous[5]	
1999	2,710.0	W	24.4	79.3	W	166.0	2,230.0	691.0	1.2	4.5	21.2	29.8	2,980.0
2000	2,730.0	W	23.8	101.0	W	175.0	2,240.0	723.0	1.2	4.6	24.3	32.5	3,030.0
2001	2,360.0	W	24.0	95.9	W	140.0	1,940.0	623.0	1.2	4.6	21.6	28.6	2,620.0
2002	2,140.0	W	22.8	72.6	W	126.0	1,710.0	593.0	1.0	4.6	19.8	35.7	2,370.0
2003	2,070.0	W	22.3	41.8	W	153.0	1,640.0	587.0	1.0	4.6	21.9	36.7	2,290.0
2004	2,160.0	W	21.4	57.0	W	173.0	1,780.0	573.0	1.2	4.6	21.0	35.2	2,410.0
2005	2,040.0	W	28.8	35.3	W	167.0	1,680.0	528.0	1.2	4.5	20.2	39.3	2,270.0
2006	1,910.0	W	30.8	37.1	W	135.0	1,570.0	490.0	1.0	4.5	21.4	24.1	2,110.0
2007[1]	1,930.0	W	28.8	42.7	W	135.0	1,610.0	476.0	1.0	4.5	19.4	25.7	2,140.0
2008[2]	1,820.0	W	28.6	45.0	W	130.0	1,490.0	479.0	0.3	4.5	20.4	24.7	2,020.0

[1] Preliminary. [2] Estimate. [3] Primary & secondary. [4] Includes Wirebars and Billets. [5] Includes iron and steel plants, primary smelters producing alloys other than copper, consumers of copper powder and copper shot, and other manufacturers. W = Withheld.
Source: U.S. Geological Survey (USGS)

London Metals Exchange Warehouse Stocks of Copper, at End of Month In Thousands of Metric Tons

Year	Jan.	Feb.	Mar.	Apr.	May	June	July	Aug.	Sept.	Oct.	Nov.	Dec.
2001	349.9	327.9	400.5	445.2	431.3	464.7	651.9	661.2	729.0	737.2	780.4	799.5
2002	855.5	910.9	950.9	973.8	958.3	892.1	893.6	896.6	870.6	863.2	862.8	855.9
2003	833.8	825.9	813.2	768.2	740.8	665.8	612.6	620.3	580.4	516.5	467.0	430.7
2004	358.2	281.6	187.5	151.3	132.3	101.5	87.7	111.3	91.8	77.9	59.8	48.9
2005	46.4	52.5	45.3	61.0	44.4	28.9	31.6	68.0	79.9	65.1	72.6	92.3
2006	96.0	115.3	120.7	117.6	111.2	93.6	100.6	125.4	116.9	135.2	156.8	190.7
2007	216.2	205.4	181.1	156.6	127.5	112.6	103.5	139.1	130.7	167.1	189.6	199.0
2008	177.9	141.4	111.3	110.1	124.0	122.4	144.6	173.8	199.1	238.0	291.3	240.7
2009	491.3	536.8	501.9	398.8	312.1	265.8	282.2	300.0	346.2	372.2	441.1	502.5
2010[1]	543.6	551.4	512.6	497.1	475.7	449.5	413.2	398.9	373.9	367.7	355.0	

[1] Preliminary. *Source: American Bureau of Metal Statistics (ABMS)*

Copper Refined from Scrap in the United States In Thousands of Metric Tons

Year	Jan.	Feb.	Mar.	Apr.	May	June	July	Aug.	Sept.	Oct.	Nov.	Dec.	Total
2001	15.4	14.2	15.2	13.4	12.8	13.2	13.9	13.5	12.3	10.2	6.4	5.7	154.0
2002	7.1	6.2	7.2	7.6	8.2	7.8	7.0	7.6	7.1	6.3	5.1	3.9	81.1
2003	5.8	3.9	5.7	3.9	4.1	4.9	4.9	3.9	4.2	4.5	4.1	4.1	53.8
2004	4.2	3.9	4.3	4.4	4.2	4.1	4.1	3.9	4.7	4.5	4.2	4.0	50.8
2005	4.4	4.4	4.2	4.2	3.8	3.6	3.9	3.6	3.6	3.8	3.8	3.9	47.1
2006	3.8	3.7	3.8	3.7	3.7	3.7	3.7	3.7	3.8	3.7	3.7	3.8	44.8
2007	3.9	3.9	3.4	3.5	3.4	3.4	3.4	3.4	3.5	3.4	3.6	3.5	42.1
2008	4.1	4.2	4.1	4.3	4.6	5.0	4.3	4.5	4.3	4.6	4.6	4.6	53.2
2009	5.4	4.8	4.4	4.4	4.0	4.2	4.1	2.9	3.0	3.0	3.0	3.2	46.4
2010[1]	2.9	3.2	2.8	3.3	3.0	3.3	3.2	3.5	3.3	3.2			38.0

[1] Preliminary. *Source: U.S. Geological Survey (USGS)*

COPPER

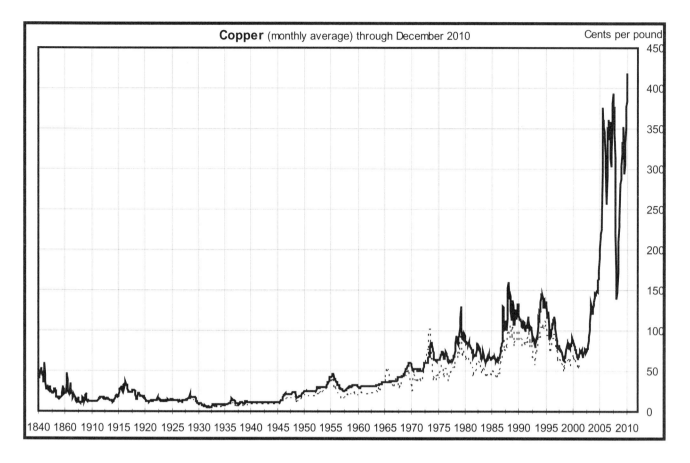

Copper (monthly average) through December 2010 — Cents per pound

Average Open Interest of Copper Futures in New York   In Contracts

Year	Jan.	Feb.	Mar.	Apr.	May	June	July	Aug.	Sept.	Oct.	Nov.	Dec.
2001	77,952	76,721	78,034	83,647	72,970	85,495	83,690	88,782	87,004	88,166	85,809	68,981
2002	72,823	79,806	79,156	75,229	74,350	80,981	82,661	102,056	99,225	99,470	89,213	79,218
2003	81,820	81,499	72,484	85,485	77,704	81,509	82,868	94,517	92,768	106,924	103,218	90,208
2004	91,726	88,136	77,158	71,705	65,531	64,879	65,310	71,096	81,162	85,421	81,928	88,822
2005	85,363	96,537	116,004	120,138	98,240	106,218	109,156	109,481	102,652	106,829	110,972	104,062
2006	102,227	93,813	93,069	97,283	83,758	75,841	74,471	72,158	69,004	72,023	72,517	68,402
2007	69,972	70,373	69,324	78,919	80,834	79,257	88,691	78,113	72,469	86,909	78,385	71,626
2008	81,778	94,021	101,503	105,050	98,787	103,055	109,591	96,254	76,523	80,961	76,869	71,809
2009	82,402	85,831	90,636	103,517	106,511	111,555	111,849	118,935	117,782	127,204	146,612	149,621
2010	147,311	126,659	131,619	151,712	132,069	134,323	132,119	140,543	142,628	160,288	156,869	162,683

Source: CME Group; New York Mercantile Exchange (NYMEX)

Volume of Trading of Copper Futures in New York   In Contracts

Year	Jan.	Feb.	Mar.	Apr.	May	June	July	Aug.	Sept.	Oct.	Nov.	Dec.	Total
2001	240,588	246,052	247,722	279,348	260,697	317,001	159,394	298,639	129,622	190,469	337,589	149,520	2,856,641
2002	217,598	233,704	164,747	254,259	218,091	267,201	263,395	303,642	195,637	232,731	276,492	179,789	2,807,286
2003	232,921	269,806	249,306	274,079	221,364	301,709	252,713	324,175	196,481	230,413	363,865	172,438	3,089,270
2004	213,536	385,848	265,312	340,236	203,906	280,882	208,415	310,299	212,082	245,011	317,220	207,878	3,190,625
2005	199,938	391,949	298,181	469,849	288,399	475,756	227,917	435,848	252,733	265,234	458,258	186,780	3,950,842
2006	234,295	401,404	284,478	406,984	260,422	321,626	182,175	310,023	189,405	216,369	320,780	153,351	3,281,312
2007	241,333	333,967	264,511	402,764	292,359	367,217	272,429	451,599	225,624	289,319	412,949	199,097	3,753,168
2008	345,506	459,539	298,485	466,514	344,500	462,033	382,095	463,234	349,533	403,803	414,380	228,444	4,618,066
2009	343,546	446,018	361,043	592,879	373,551	661,946	499,520	746,223	511,205	599,658	809,343	454,049	6,398,981
2010	645,450	996,343	772,636	1,049,049	894,696	1,051,141	724,928	980,523	604,396	822,346	1,132,320	631,842	10,305,670

Source: CME Group; New York Mercantile Exchange (NYMEX)

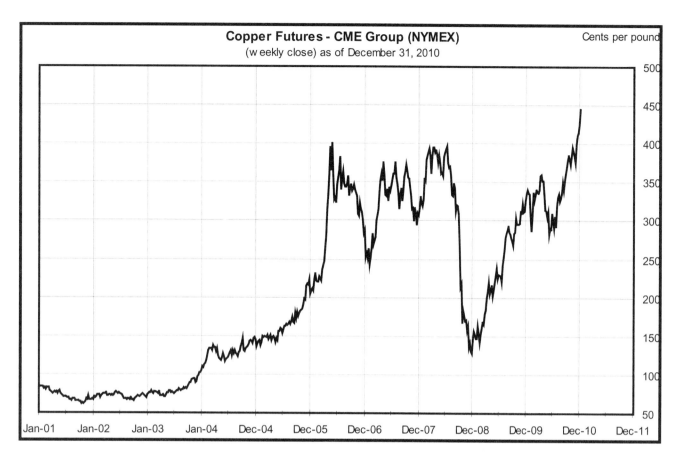

Producers' Price of Electrolytic (Wirebar) Copper, Delivered to U.S. Destinations   In Cents Per Pound

Year	Jan.	Feb.	Mar.	Apr.	May	June	July	Aug.	Sept.	Oct.	Nov.	Dec.	Average
2001	95.70	94.01	92.07	88.27	88.85	84.58	81.44	79.34	77.41	75.21	78.13	79.83	84.57
2002	81.79	84.23	86.60	85.11	85.22	88.23	84.44	79.82	79.71	80.16	84.57	75.56	82.62
2003	78.62	80.21	78.87	75.60	78.56	80.44	81.55	83.51	85.34	91.50	96.47	103.72	84.53
2004	113.93	129.91	139.96	135.82	129.44	129.11	134.34	135.50	138.74	142.01	147.99	151.88	135.72
2005	151.25	152.89	154.68	155.42	154.19	168.31	169.62	178.39	182.00	197.61	208.60	224.25	174.77
2006	225.07	230.74	238.31	302.74	382.65	346.65	368.49	359.91	353.01	345.83	322.45	307.00	315.24
2007	263.89	265.67	298.65	356.76	355.24	346.59	370.42	343.65	351.87	364.48	318.93	306.74	328.57
2008	325.53	364.78	385.98	399.96	383.39	375.08	382.31	349.89	320.54	224.32	174.59	145.09	319.29
2009	153.55	155.38	176.45	209.36	215.36	233.23	243.36	285.81	285.91	292.24	307.45	320.57	239.89
2010	337.71	315.88	343.54	356.46	315.33	299.00	312.18	337.50	357.31	382.81	390.16	419.69	347.30

Source: American Metal Market (AMM)

Dealers' Buying Price of No. 2 Heavy Copper Scrap in Chicago   In Cents Per Pound

Year	Jan.	Feb.	Mar.	Apr.	May	June	July	Aug.	Sept.	Oct.	Nov.	Dec.	Average
2001	51.62	49.16	49.00	49.81	50.00	50.00	49.14	44.00	44.00	43.48	41.45	41.47	46.93
2002	41.00	41.00	41.00	41.00	41.00	41.00	41.00	41.00	41.00	41.00	41.00	41.00	41.00
2003	41.00	41.00	41.00	41.00	41.00	41.00	41.00	41.00	41.00	48.17	56.00	56.00	43.99
2004	56.65	69.00	69.00	69.32	76.00	76.00	76.64	90.00	90.00	90.00	90.00	90.00	78.55
2005	90.00	90.00	90.00	90.00	90.00	94.09	100.00	100.00	100.00	100.00	100.00	129.52	97.80
2006	137.50	137.50	139.46	145.00	145.00	171.36	175.25	185.89	184.10	192.09	192.85	183.30	165.78
2007	155.83	153.92	164.32	197.83	210.09	203.60	216.83	219.89	213.97	224.72	210.20	191.87	196.92
2008	198.21	210.00	238.21	246.82	247.02	237.50	240.00	233.93	226.07	141.85	97.50	87.02	200.34
2009	80.00	92.24	104.32	124.40	134.00	155.23	166.59	182.02	192.50	194.40	203.55	224.61	154.49
2010	245.13	220.92	258.37	275.68	244.50	214.32	214.64	255.68	260.36	273.93	277.50	268.29	250.78

Source: American Metal Market (AMM)

COPPER

Imports of Refined Copper into the United States   In Thousands of Metric Tons

Year	Jan.	Feb.	Mar.	Apr.	May	June	July	Aug.	Sept.	Oct.	Nov.	Dec.	Total
2001	105.0	91.6	90.1	94.4	70.3	72.7	61.7	66.3	83.5	71.0	110.0	74.4	991.0
2002	82.5	87.8	53.0	92.6	59.9	76.2	80.3	90.5	69.9	79.0	82.0	73.0	927.0
2003	60.7	87.8	69.9	78.5	72.7	62.3	74.0	78.1	81.7	82.0	73.2	61.1	882.0
2004	55.4	48.8	70.7	59.3	70.8	51.3	83.9	78.7	91.7	68.4	77.0	51.1	807.1
2005	85.2	66.5	75.8	63.7	107.0	64.7	75.8	79.4	79.4	99.4	101.0	106.0	1,003.9
2006	138.0	108.0	80.1	69.1	100.0	94.1	91.4	101.0	106.0	96.4	58.3	56.5	1,098.9
2007	87.3	76.4	68.4	65.8	80.1	58.9	66.6	77.7	68.5	66.9	54.5	NA	841.2
2008	58.6	57.8	53.6	59.8	63.6	48.9	77.5	86.9	54.5	49.7	51.0	61.7	723.6
2009	76.4	67.7	80.0	53.9	52.6	35.7	54.2	36.4	56.0	39.9	55.2	55.5	663.5
2010[1]	60.3	61.3	46.2	46.7	46.7	61.6	66.0	37.7	35.3				615.7

[1] Preliminary.   *Source: U.S. Geological Survey (USGS)*

Exports of Refined Copper from the United States   In Thousands of Metric Tons

Year	Jan.	Feb.	Mar.	Apr.	May	June	July	Aug.	Sept.	Oct.	Nov.	Dec.	Total
2001	1.2	.9	.8	1.9	1.0	.8	1.7	2.6	1.2	4.6	5.3	.6	22.5
2002	.4	.7	3.2	.7	.8	6.8	7.7	2.6	1.3	.6	.5	1.5	26.6
2003	2.5	.8	1.5	.6	15.9	23.0	5.1	4.1	4.3	4.6	8.5	22.3	93.2
2004	11.0	18.5	23.9	28.4	3.7	2.7	5.5	9.4	.6	3.9	2.5	8.4	118.4
2005	4.5	3.2	2.8	1.9	7.2	4.3	3.0	2.7	1.8	3.3	3.3	3.0	40.9
2006	5.6	7.3	6.8	9.6	6.3	13.1	6.0	9.6	9.3	13.7	6.2	12.6	106.1
2007	3.1	2.7	5.1	3.6	3.9	6.6	3.6	3.4	5.4	7.1	3.0	NA	51.8
2008	6.0	5.7	6.3	3.2	1.9	1.4	2.0	2.0	1.5	3.2	1.7	1.6	36.5
2009	.9	1.7	3.8	6.5	21.4	19.2	8.9	6.3	4.0	2.1	3.0	3.2	80.9
2010[1]	6.2	13.9	13.6	10.4	4.7	4.5	4.2	5.3	7.0				93.0

[1] Preliminary.   *Source: U.S. Geological Survey (USGS)*

Stocks of Refined Copper in the United States, on First of Month   In Thousands of Short Tons

Year	Jan.	Feb.	Mar.	Apr.	May	June	July	Aug.	Sept.	Oct.	Nov.	Dec.
2001	383.8	408.4	416.2	481.9	552.6	585.7	626.7	733.1	767.4	895.6	916.6	985.7
2002	1,045.1	1,096.2	1,132.4	1,155.3	1,175.0	1,158.8	1,126.7	1,132.2	1,123.0	1,123.7	1,110.5	1,109.0
2003	1,119.8	109.7	1,038.8	1,042.1	998.3	959.8	891.8	848.9	855.6	825.5	761.2	768.0
2004	733.8	646.3	566.7	463.9	367.0	311.8	247.8	218.3	194.5	169.2	158.9	147.4
2005	145.8	151.0	143.4	134.4	129.3	116.2	105.3	98.5	83.0	68.2	56.8	59.4
2006	66.8	76.9	103.3	109.0	88.2	84.5	68.3	76.4	80.1	88.4	103.4	152.3
2007	194.9	222.1	216.8	197.7	165.8	130.7	114.3	118.8	114.0	110.3	115.0	123.8
2008	147.2	122.5	106.3	105.9	74.4	81.3	72.8	83.8	106.3	123.6	134.6	165.7
2009	231.1	290.3	321.7	376.8	380.1	355.9	320.8	331.1	336.3	362.9	384.3	431.7
2010[1]	480.2	523.4	544.8	525.4	509.6	486.9	479.9	471.9	454.5	425.6	408.5	

Recoverable Copper Content.   [1] Preliminary.   *Source: American Bureau of Metal Statistics (ABMS)*

Stocks of Refined Copper Outside the United States, on First of Month   In Thousands of Short Tons

Year	Jan.	Feb.	Mar.	Apr.	May	June	July	Aug.	Sept.	Oct.	Nov.	Dec.
2001	795.0	999.5	986.4	971.2	995.7	969.4	1,000.8	1,091.0	1,108.7	1,083.3	1,021.0	1,104.5
2002	1,241.3	1,273.5	1,291.5	1,370.4	1,391.1	1,399.4	1,289.0	1,342.6	1,369.1	1,321.1	1,219.7	1,224.5
2003	1,238.8	2,147.6	1,188.0	1,216.3	1,147.4	1,109.8	1,129.2	1,139.9	1,150.9	1,140.2	1,170.8	1,157.1
2004	1,191.5	1,149.9	1,139.5	995.5	968.4	826.0	807.1	812.4	830.2	825.2	778.0	816.8
2005	833.8	802.2	929.8	848.0	758.2	771.3	822.6	786.4	846.9	774.3	803.4	805.0
2006	871.2	956.8	923.2	797.7	816.4	819.2	789.1	812.9	872.4	830.1	877.6	905.9
2007	1,016.2	969.5	966.6	994.3	973.0	873.8	893.9	845.9	880.9	894.4	884.8	860.7
2008	947.7	920.0	833.9	1,257.0	1,253.4	1,311.1	1,309.1	1,315.5	1,318.0	1,487.6	366.8	957.6
2009	931.3	1,155.7	1,125.6	1,024.3	853.1	788.4	817.5	752.9	864.3	943.4	958.9	1,032.0
2010[1]	1,083.3	1,105.2	1,131.6	1,084.3	1,122.5	1,088.1	1,030.7	933.6	985.4	909.8	973.0	

Recoverable Copper Content.   [1] Preliminary.   *Source: American Bureau of Metal Statistics (ABMS)*

Production of Refined Copper in the United States   In Thousands of Short Tons

Year	Jan.	Feb.	Mar.	Apr.	May	June	July	Aug.	Sept.	Oct.	Nov.	Dec.	Total
2001	155.0	144.0	156.0	145.0	155.0	157.0	146.0	143.0	148.0	149.0	152.0	150.0	1,800
2002	134.0	117.0	124.0	129.0	134.0	128.0	130.0	124.0	120.0	129.0	120.0	119.0	1,508
2003	124.0	110.0	118.0	98.7	98.8	106.0	110.0	110.0	112.0	108.0	101.0	111.0	1,308
2004	104.0	98.9	105.0	111.0	109.0	113.0	104.0	107.0	112.0	111.0	109.0	123.0	1,307
2005	102.0	102.0	104.0	105.0	109.0	101.0	100.0	102.0	103.0	104.0	108.0	115.0	1,255
2006	99.9	101.0	117.0	109.0	113.0	114.0	100.0	101.0	102.0	89.8	94.4	108.0	1,249
2007	101.0	97.1	116.0	113.0	116.0	112.0	116.0	117.0	108.0	120.0	91.5	103.0	1,311
2008	109.0	107.0	108.0	102.0	107.0	102.0	98.7	107.0	108.0	110.0	107.0	113.0	1,279
2009	105.0	96.7	95.9	93.7	91.8	90.3	94.4	97.6	94.3	101.0	98.0	101.0	1,160
2010[1]	96.2	91.3	95.0	89.2	85.1	88.9	95.6	94.4	94.2	90.1			1,104

Recoverable Copper Content.   [1] Preliminary.   *Source: U.S. Geological Survey (USGS)*

Production of Refined Copper Outside North America   In Thousands of Short Tons

Year	Jan.	Feb.	Mar.	Apr.	May	June	July	Aug.	Sept.	Oct.	Nov.	Dec.	Total
2001	1,279.1	1,188.0	1,316.5	1,243.6	1,295.9	1,241.7	1,269.8	1,296.1	1,247.1	1,308.5	1,299.8	1,318.5	15,305
2002	1,310.4	1,190.9	1,307.8	1,268.2	1,294.3	1,257.6	1,254.9	1,272.7	1,242.9	1,293.6	1,263.1	1,282.0	15,238
2003	1,274.4	1,188.2	1,283.9	1,244.3	1,292.2	1,253.9	1,289.6	1,272.9	1,268.6	1,320.6	1,302.4	1,349.4	15,340
2004	1,286.7	1,256.0	1,344.1	1,290.0	1,277.3	1,291.9	1,358.8	1,366.5	1,370.6	1,390.0	1,402.4	1,406.5	16,041
2005	1,407.9	1,252.0	1,388.1	1,343.0	1,390.5	1,389.3	1,402.3	1,409.2	1,407.9	1,429.0	1,444.8	1,493.6	16,758
2006	1,423.7	1,346.1	1,466.0	1,435.9	1,459.1	1,457.0	1,476.2	1,459.2	1,460.0	1,521.8	1,494.8	1,566.7	17,567
2007	1,568.4	1,443.8	1,541.9	1,502.0	1,520.9	1,483.0	1,491.6	1,501.0	1,531.9	1,549.1	1,570.6	1,601.4	18,306
2008	1,554.2	1,475.5	1,612.2	1,577.6	1,569.2	1,610.8	1,642.3	1,640.4	1,605.5	1,606.6	1,567.9	1,579.2	19,041
2009	1,532.9	1,467.7	1,553.8	1,537.4	1,585.6	1,560.6	1,596.1	1,614.7	1,620.6	1,650.2	1,650.2	1,701.2	19,071
2010[1]	1,624.0	1,526.0	1,661.7	1,650.3	1,676.4	1,703.8	1,697.3	1,693.5	1,629.4	1,651.5	1,772.8		19,849

Recoverable Copper Content.   [1] Preliminary.   *Source: American Bureau of Metal Statistics (ABMS)*

Deliveries of Refined Copper to Fabricators in the United States   In Thousands of Short Tons

Year	Jan.	Feb.	Mar.	Apr.	May	June	July	Aug.	Sept.	Oct.	Nov.	Dec.	Total
2001	166.1	150.8	167.4	148.4	167.6	165.2	162.7	154.0	151.6	160.7	154.7	147.5	1,897
2002	152.1	126.0	140.7	149.3	148.6	136.2	147.9	141.1	129.5	141.6	124.5	129.7	1,667
2003	136.4	123.4	124.6	106.6	107.7	117.0	127.1	120.6	125.8	127.9	114.4	133.8	1,465
2004	126.4	131.1	137.6	137.7	130.9	143.5	133.3	132.9	136.8	129.3	128.8	137.5	1,606
2005	120.1	120.0	131.2	125.4	125.7	119.2	106.9	112.8	108.0	110.9	112.6	115.9	1,409
2006	124.8	110.3	131.5	121.9	121.8	132.7	117.5	119.9	112.7	95.5	95.6	100.5	1,385
2007	115.9	118.9	131.9	127.4	128.1	126.2	131.3	132.3	112.2	134.9	113.3	100.9	1,473
2008	134.1	118.8	123.2	114.7	111.6	120.8	105.4	118.3	121.4	129.7	109.4	110.6	1,418
2009	117.6	105.0	104.3	99.4	97.6	105.7	115.3	110.1	100.7	101.6	104.9	117.3	1,280
2010[1]	100.9	102.0	111.1	101.7	102.4	96.7	107.9	105.1	100.7	100.3	92.2		1,223

Recoverable Copper Content.   [1] Preliminary.   *Source: American Bureau of Metal Statistics (ABMS)*

Deliveries of Refined Copper to Fabricators Outside the United States   In Thousands of Short Tons

Year	Jan.	Feb.	Mar.	Apr.	May	June	July	Aug.	Sept.	Oct.	Nov.	Dec.	Total
1990	419.9	466.3	436.7	392.9	408.3	466.7	303.7	373.5	370.8	448.9	469.1	420.7	4,972
1991	405.0	404.4	391.5	361.2	406.3	433.5	368.5	323.4	420.7	499.1	391.4	483.4	4,807
1992	453.7	408.9	441.8	416.4	413.4	432.4	410.4	364.7	432.6	403.5	406.1	461.3	5,045
1993	427.9	392.9	452.3	361.7	422.2	442.6	384.4	347.9	387.5	414.8	463.4	458.5	4,956
1994	399.8	429.5	481.2	466.5	468.9	428.1	387.9	369.2	423.5	448.9	457.1	436.0	5,197
1995[2]	758.5	810.1	892.8	882.2	853.0	867.3	863.7	814.1	803.4	835.1	796.6	726.2	9,903
1996	875.2	859.4	934.3	907.2	816.7	950.7	908.3	817.4	911.5	1,056.0	922.7	918.3	10,878
1997	862.2	889.7	977.9	1,007.1	991.1	982.7	897.8	873.9	886.2	1,009.0	980.4	966.6	11,349
1998	1,091.7	973.8	1,062.0	1,055.5	995.7	1,014.8	986.8	924.8	913.3	987.9	982.1	1,023.0	12,011
1999[1]	314.5	745.5	NA	NA	NA	NA	NA	NA	NA	NA	NA	NA	6,360

Recoverable Copper Content.   [1] Preliminary.   [2] New reporting method beginning January 1995, includes crude copper deliveries.
Source: American Bureau of Metal Statistics (ABMS)

Corn

Corn is a member of the grass family of plants and is a native grain of the American continents. Fossils of corn pollen that are over 80,000 years old have been found in lake sediment under Mexico City. Archaeological discoveries show that cultivated corn existed in the southwestern U.S. for at least 3,000 years, indicating that the indigenous people of the region cultivated corn as a food crop long before the Europeans reached the New World. Corn is a hardy plant that grows in many different areas of the world. It can grow at altitudes as low as sea level and as high as 12,000 feet in the South American Andes Mountains. Corn can also grow in tropical climates that receive up to 400 inches of rainfall per year, or in areas that receive only 12 inches of rainfall per year. Corn is used primarily as livestock feed in the United States and the rest of the world. Other uses for corn are alcohol additives for gasoline, adhesives, corn oil for cooking and margarine, sweeteners, and as food for humans. Corn is the largest crop in the U.S., both in terms of the value of the crop and of the acres planted.

The largest futures market for corn is at the Chicago Board of Trade. Corn futures also trade at the Bolsa de Mercadorias & Futuros (BM&F) in Brazil, the Budapest Commodity Exchange, the Marche a Terme International de France (MATIF), the Mercado a Termino de Buenos Aires in Argentina, the Kanmon Commodity Exchange (KCE) in Korea, and the Tokyo Grain Exchange (TGE). The CBOT futures contract calls for the delivery of 5000 bushels of No. 2 yellow corn at par contract price, No. 1 yellow at 1-1/2 cents per bushel over the contract price, or No. 3 yellow at 1-1/2 cents per bushel below the contract price.

Prices – Corn futures prices in 2010 traded sideways to lower in the first half of the year and fell to a 1-1/2 year low of $3.2450 a bushel in June 2010 on the prospects for a record U.S. corn crop. Corn prices then climbed the rest of the year and posted a 2-1/2 year high of $6.30 a bushel in December 2010 and finished the year up 52% at $6.20 a bushel. Prices advanced further and in February 2011 rose to a 2-1/2 year high of $7.2425 a bushel. Despite the 8.4% y/y increase in U.S. corn production in 2009/10 to 13.1 billion bushels, strong foreign and domestic demand has underpinned prices. U.S. corn demand for ethanol production continued to climb and in February 2011 the USDA raised its corn usage estimate for ethanol production to a record 4.95 billion bushels, which prompted a cut in the USDA's 2010/11 US carry-over estimate to a 2-1/2 year low of 675 million bushels. The other major bullish factor for corn prices was Chinese demand. China in 2010 became a corn importer for the first time in 15 years as its own domestic corn supplies were crimped by a drought and an increase in feed demand due to expanded domestic pork and beef production. With Russia's action to ban grain exports in 2010 due to drought, the U.S., along with Brazil and Argentina, became the world's main source of corn supplies. With global corn supplies continuing to dwindle, the USDA in February 2011 cut its global corn carry-over

estimate to a 4-year low of 122.51 MMT. The corn stocks/use ratios for 2010/11 were extremely tight with the US stocks/use ratio of 5.0% matching the 7-decade low posted in 1995-96 and the world stocks/use ratio at 14.6%. This should support corn prices going forward even though the USDA is predicting US corn acreage in 2011 may rise to a 4-year high of 92 million acres.

Supply – World production of corn in the 2010-11 marketing year rose +0.2% to a new record high of 813.78 million metric tons. The world's largest corn producers are the U.S. with 42% of world production, China (20.6%), and Brazil (6.3%). Corn production in both China and Brazil has nearly tripled since 1980. Production in the U.S. over that same time frame has risen by about 50%. The world area harvested with corn in 2010-11 rose +0.3% yr/yr to 307.9 million hectares, down from the 13-year high of 318.0 million hectares in 2007-08. World ending stocks of corn and coarse grains in 2010-11 fell by –15% to 123 million metric tons.

U.S. corn production for the 2010-11 marketing year (Sep-Aug) fell by -5.1% yr/yr to 12.446 billion bushels. U.S. farmers harvested 81.446 million acres of corn for grain usage in 2010-11, which was up +2.3% yr/yr. U.S. corn yield in 2010-11 fell to 152.8 bushels per acre from 164.7 bushels per acre in 2009-10. U.S. ending stocks for 2010-11 fell 60% to 675 million bushels. The largest corn producing states in the U.S. in 2010 were Iowa with 17.3% of U.S. production, Illinois (15.6%), Nebraska (11.8%), Minnesota (10.4%), and Indiana (7.2%). The value of the U.S. corn crop in 2010-11 was $47.378 billion.

Demand – World consumption of corn and rough grains in 2010-11 rose by +1.6% yr/yr to 1,123.2 million metric tons, which was a new record high. The U.S. distribution tables for corn show that 5.25 billion bushels of corn were used for livestock feed in the marketing year 2009-10 (latest data available) or about 42% of overall utilization. The second largest demand category for corn is for ethanol production (alcohol fuel) with usage of 4.700 billion bushels in 2010-11. That was up +4% y/y and was 75.0% of total non-feed usage. While the U.S. ethanol industry is a big consumer of U.S. corn, about 30% of the corn is returned to the corn market in the form of distiller dried grains that is used as feed for livestock. After ethanol, the next largest non-feed usage categories are for high fructose corn syrup (HFCS) with 9% of U.S. usage, corn starch (5%), glucose and dextrose sugars (5%), cereal and other corn products (4%), and alcoholic beverages (3%).

Trade – U.S. exports of corn in 2010-11 (latest data available) rose +4.6% yr/yr to 49.833 million metric tons, which is farther below the record high of 61.417 million metric tons posted in 1979-80. The largest destination countries for U.S. corn exports are Japan, which accounted for 29.5% of U.S. corn exports in 2010-11, Mexico (16.5%), South Korea (13.6%), Taiwan (6%), Egypt (6%), and Canada (3.9%).

World Production of Corn or Maize   In Thousands of Metric Tons

Crop Year Beginning Oct. 1	Argentina	Brazil	Canada	China	European Union	Egypt	India	Mexico	Romania	South Africa	United States	Ukraine	World Total
2001-02	14,712	35,501	8,389	114,088	58,022	6,160	13,510	20,400	7,000	10,050	3,641	241,377	601,358
2002-03	15,500	44,500	8,999	121,300	57,660	6,000	11,100	19,280	7,300	9,675	4,180	227,767	603,072
2003-04	14,951	42,000	9,587	115,830	47,905	5,740	14,980	21,800	7,020	9,700	6,850	256,229	627,442
2004-05	20,483	35,000	8,837	130,290	66,471	5,840	14,180	22,050	12,000	11,716	8,800	299,876	715,703
2005-06	15,800	41,700	9,332	139,365	60,668	5,932	14,710	19,500	10,300	6,935	7,150	282,263	699,537
2006-07	22,500	51,000	8,990	151,600	53,829	6,149	15,100	22,350	8,500	7,300	6,400	267,503	713,565
2007-08	22,017	58,600	11,649	152,300	47,555	6,174	18,960	23,600	----	13,164	7,400	331,177	793,761
2008-09[1]	15,500	51,000	10,592	165,900	62,321	6,645	19,730	24,226	----	12,567	11,400	307,142	798,414
2009-10[2]	22,800	56,100	9,561	158,000	57,147	6,822	16,680	20,374	----	13,420	10,500	332,549	812,337
2010-11[3]	22,000	51,000	11,714	168,000	55,193	7,000	21,000	24,000	----	12,500	11,900	316,165	814,256

[1] Preliminary.   [2] Estimate.   [3] Forecast.   *Source: Foreign Agricultural Service, U.S. Department of Agriculture (FAS-USDA)*

World Supply and Demand of Coarse Grains   In Millions of Metric Tons/Hectares

Crop Year Beginning Oct. 1	Area Harvested	Yield	Production	World Trade	Total Consumption	Ending Stocks	Stocks as % of Consumption[3]
2001-02	300.9	3.00	896.6	100.5	909.1	199.3	21.9
2002-03	291.5	3.00	873.5	102.8	901.0	171.7	19.1
2003-04	306.1	3.00	916.1	102.6	944.8	143.0	15.1
2004-05	300.3	3.40	1,015.4	101.3	978.6	179.8	18.4
2005-06	300.8	3.30	979.6	108.6	993.7	165.8	16.7
2006-07	304.8	3.20	987.5	114.7	1,012.5	140.8	13.9
2007-08	318.0	3.40	1,079.1	128.9	1,056.2	163.7	15.5
2008-09	313.0	3.50	1,110.1	110.7	1,079.7	194.1	18.0
2009-10[1]	307.0	3.60	1,107.6	119.0	1,106.0	195.8	17.7
2010-11[2]	307.9	3.50	1,081.5	117.1	1,123.2	154.1	13.7

[1] Preliminary.   [2] Estimate.   [3] Represents the ratio of marketing year ending stocks to total consumption.   *Source: Foreign Agricultural Service, U.S. Department of Agriculture (FAS-USDA)*

Acreage and Supply of Corn in the United States   In Millions of Bushels

Crop Year Beginning Sept. 1	Planted	Harvested For Grain	Harvested For Silage	Yield Per Harvested Acre Bushels	Carry-over, Sept. 1 On Farms	Carry-over, Sept. 1 Off Farms	Beginning Stocks	Supply Production	Supply Imports	Total Supply
		In Thousands of Acres								
2001-02	75,752	68,808	6,148	138.2	753.2	1,146.0	1,899	9,507	10	11,412
2002-03	78,894	69,330	7,122	129.3	586.8	1,009.6	1,596	8,967	14	10,578
2003-04	78,603	70,944	6,583	142.2	484.9	601.8	1,087	10,089	14	11,188
2004-05	80,930	73,632	6,103	160.4	438.0	520.1	958	11,807	11	12,775
2005-06	81,759	75,107	5,920	147.9	820.5	1,293.5	2,114	11,112	9	13,235
2006-07	78,327	70,648	6,477	149.1	749.5	1,217.7	1,967	10,531	12	12,510
2007-08	93,527	86,520	6,060	150.7	460.1	843.5	1,304	13,038	20	14,362
2008-09	85,982	78,570	5,965	153.9	500.0	1,124.2	1,624	12,092	14	13,729
2009-10[1]	86,482	79,590	5,605	164.7	607.5	1,065.8	1,673	13,110	8	14,774
2010-11[2]	88,192	81,446	5,567	152.8	485.1	1,222.7	1,708	12,447	20	14,175

[1] Preliminary.   [2] Estimate.   *Source: Economic Research Service, U.S. Department of Agriculture (ERS-USDA)*

Production of Corn (For Grain) in the United States, by State   In Million of Bushels

Year	Illinois	Indiana	Iowa	Kansas	Michigan	Minnesota	Missouri	Nebraska	Ohio	South Dakota	Texas	Wisconsin	Total
2001	1,649.2	884.5	1,664.4	387.4	199.5	806.0	345.8	1,139.3	437.5	370.6	167.6	330.2	9,506.8
2002	1,471.5	631.6	1,931.6	301.6	234.0	1,051.9	283.5	940.8	264.3	308.8	202.3	391.5	8,966.8
2003	1,812.2	786.9	1,868.3	300.0	259.8	970.9	302.4	1,124.2	478.9	427.4	194.7	367.7	10,089.2
2004	2,088.0	929.0	2,244.4	432.0	257.3	1,121.0	466.6	1,319.7	491.4	539.5	233.5	353.6	11,807.2
2005	1,708.9	888.6	2,162.5	465.8	288.9	1,191.9	329.7	1,270.5	464.8	470.1	210.9	429.2	11,112.1
2006	1,817.5	844.7	2,050.1	345.0	286.7	1,102.9	362.9	1,178.0	470.6	312.3	175.5	400.4	10,531.1
2007	2,283.8	981.0	2,376.9	507.8	287.8	1,146.1	457.8	1,472.0	541.5	542.1	291.6	442.8	13,037.9
2008	2,130.1	873.6	2,188.8	486.4	295.3	1,180.8	381.6	1,393.7	421.2	585.2	253.8	394.6	12,091.6
2009	2,053.2	933.7	2,420.6	598.3	309.3	1,244.1	446.8	1,575.3	546.4	706.7	254.8	448.3	13,110.1
2010[1]	1,946.8	898.0	2,153.3	581.3	315.0	1,292.1	369.0	1,469.1	533.0	569.7	301.6	502.2	12,446.9

[1] Preliminary.   *Source: National Agricultural Statistics Service, U.S. Department of Agriculture (NASS-USDA)*

CORN

Quarterly Supply and Disappearance of Corn in the United States   In Millions of Bushels

Crop Year Beginning Sept. 1	Beginning Stocks	Pro-duction	Imports[3]	Total Supply	Food & Alcohol	Seed	Feed & Residual	Total	Exports[3]	Total Disap-pearance	Gov't Owned[4]	Privately Owned[5]	Total Stocks
		— Supply —				— Domestic Use —					— Ending Stocks —		
2006-07	1,967	10,531	12.0	12,510	3,467	23.8	5,591	9,081	2,125	11,207			1,304
Sept.-Nov.	1,967	10,531	1.2	12,499	799	0	2,172	2,971	596	3,567			8,933
Dec.-Feb.	8,933	----	1.7	8,934	821	0	1,533	2,353	513	2,866			6,068
Mar.-May	6,068	----	5.5	6,074	895	23.4	1,127	2,045	495	2,540			3,533
June-Aug.	3,533	----	3.7	3,537	952	.3	760	1,712	521	2,233			1,304
2007-08	1,304	13,038	20.0	14,362	4,342	21.8	5,913	10,277	2,437	12,737			1,624
Sept.-Nov.	1,304	13,038	2.2	14,344	971	0	2,402	3,372	693	4,066			10,278
Dec.-Feb.	10,278	----	2.8	10,281	1,021	0	1,748	2,769	642	3,422			6,859
Mar.-May	6,859	----	9.7	6,868	1,144	20.7	1,082	2,247	583	2,840			4,028
June-Aug.	4,028	----	5.3	4,033	1,206	1.1	681	1,889	519	2,409			1,624
2008-09	1,624	12,092	13.5	13,729	5,003	21.9	5,182	10,207	1,849	12,056			1,673
Sept.-Nov.	1,624	12,092	2.8	13,719	1,219	0	1,978	3,198	449	3,647			10,072
Dec.-Feb.	10,072	----	4.1	10,076	1,178	0	1,573	2,751	371	3,122			6,954
Mar.-May	6,954	----	5.1	6,959	1,238	20.4	947	2,205	493	2,698			4,261
June-Aug.	4,261	----	1.5	4,263	1,368	1.5	684	2,053	536	2,590			1,673
2009-10[1]	1,673	13,092	8.3	14,774	5,916	22.3	5,140	11,079	1,987	13,066			1,708
Sept.-Nov.	1,673	13,092	1.0	14,766	1,379	0	2,018	3,397	467	3,864			10,902
Dec.-Feb.	10,902	----	1.3	10,904	1,433	0	1,354	2,787	423	3,210			7,694
Mar.-May	7,694	----	3.1	7,697	1,530	21.7	1,285	2,837	550	3,387			4,310
June-Aug.	4,310	----	2.9	4,313	1,574	.7	483	2,058	547	2,605			1,708
2010-11[2]	1,708	12,447	20.0	14,175	6,327	22.9	5,200	11,550	1,950	13,500			675
Sept.-Nov.	1,708	12,447	5.3	14,160	1,576	0	2,090	3,666	454	4,120			10,040

[1] Preliminary.   [2] Estimate.   [3] Uncommitted inventory.   [4] Includes quantity under loan and farmer-owned reserve.   Source: Economic Research Service, U.S. Department of Agriculture (ERS-USDA)

Corn Production Estimates and Cash Price in the United States

Year	Aug. 1	Sept. 1	Oct. 1	Nov. 1	Final	St. Louis No. 2 Yellow	Omaha No. 2 Yellow	Gulf Ports No. 2 Yellow	Kansas City No. 2 White	Chicago No. 2 Yellow	Average Farm Price[2]	Value of Pro-duction (Mil. $)
	— Corn for Grain Production Estimates —											
	— In Thousands of Bushels —					— Dollars Per Bushel —						
2001-02	9,266,397	9,238,356	9,429,543	9,545,513	9,506,840	2.15	1.95	2.35	2.20	2.13	1.98	18,888
2002-03	8,886,009	8,848,529	8,969,836	9,003,364	8,966,787	2.49	2.29	2.71	2.94	2.46	2.32	20,882
2003-04	10,064,452	9,944,418	10,207,141	10,277,932	10,089,222	2.49	2.29	2.94	2.66	2.66	2.50	24,477
2004-05	10,923,099	10,960,710	11,613,226	11,740,920	11,807,217	2.73	2.50	2.48	2.01	2.08	2.05	24,381
2005-06	10,349,841	10,638,661	10,857,440	11,032,105	11,112,072	2.13	1.82	2.69	2.11	2.10	2.01	22,198
2006-07	10,975,740	11,113,766	10,905,194	10,744,806	10,531,123	2.19	1.88	3.95	4.18	3.46	3.13	32,083
2007-08	13,053,617	13,307,999	13,318,102	13,167,741	13,037,875	3.60	3.33	5.54	5.19	4.98	4.45	54,667
2008-09	12,287,875	12,072,365	12,199,908	12,019,894	12,091,648	5.05	4.84	4.39	4.13	3.89	4.05	49,313
2009-10	12,760,986	12,954,500	13,018,058	12,920,928	13,110,062	3.88	3.80	4.14	3.71	3.64	3.53	46,734
2010-11[1]	13,365,225	13,159,700	12,663,949	12,539,646	12,446,865	3.69	3.49	6.07	5.60	5.41	4.73	66,650

[1] Preliminary.   [2] Season-average price based on monthly prices weigthed by monthly marketings.
Source: Economic Research Service, U.S. Department of Agriculture (ERS-USDA)

Distribution of Corn in the United States   In Millions of Bushels

Crop Year Beginning Sept. 1	HFCS	Glucose & Dextrose	Starch	Fuel	Bev-rage[3]	Seed	Cereal & Other Products	Total	Livestock Feed[4]	Exports (Including Grain Equiv. of Products)	Domestic Disap-pearance	Total Utilization
	— Food, Seed and Industrial Use —			— Alcohol —								
2001-02	541	217	246	706	131	20.1	186	2,046	5,864	1,904.8	7,911	9,815
2002-03	532	219	256	996	131	20.0	187	2,340	5,563	1,587.9	7,903	9,491
2003-04	530	228	271	1,168	132	20.6	187	2,537	5,793	1,899.8	8,330	10,230
2004-05	521	222	277	1,323	133	20.8	189	2,666	6,155	1,818.1	8,842	10,661
2005-06	529	229	275	1,603	135	19.9	190	2,961	6,152	2,133.8	9,134	11,268
2006-07	510	239	272	2,117	136	23.8	190	3,464	5,591	2,125.4	9,081	11,207
2007-08	490	236	262	3,049	135	21.8	192	4,387	5,858	2,437.4	10,300	12,737
2008-09	489	245	234	3,709	134	22.0	192	5,025	5,182	1,848.9	10,207	12,056
2009-10[1]	513	257	250	4,568	134	22.3	194	5,939	5,140	1,986.6	11,079	13,066
2010-11[2]	530	260	255	4,950	135	22.9	197	6,350	5,200	1,950.0	11,550	13,500

[1] Preliminary.   [2] Estimate.   [3] Also includes nonfuel industrial alcohol.   [4] Feed and waste (residual, mostly feed).
Source: Economic Research Service, U.S. Department of Agriculture (ERS-USDA)

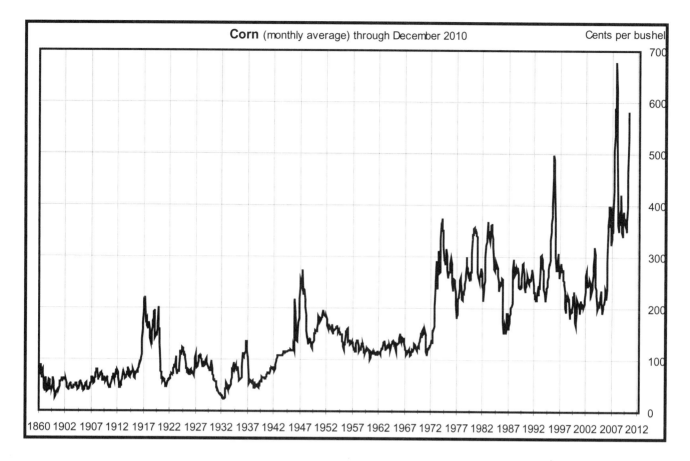

Corn (monthly average) through December 2010 — Cents per bushel

1860 1902 1907 1912 1917 1922 1927 1932 1937 1942 1947 1952 1957 1962 1967 1972 1977 1982 1987 1992 1997 2002 2007 2012

Average Cash Price of Corn, No. 2 Yellow in Central Illinois   In Dollars Per Bushel

Year	Sept.	Oct.	Nov.	Dec.	Jan.	Feb.	Mar.	Apr.	May	June	July	Aug.	Average
2001-02	1.94	1.84	1.90	1.97	1.95	1.92	1.92	1.89	1.96	2.04	2.22	2.50	2.00
2002-03	2.57	2.41	2.36	2.32	2.29	2.33	2.31	2.36	2.40	2.37	2.13	2.26	2.34
2003-04	2.25	2.11	2.26	2.38	2.52	2.73	2.89	3.03	2.90	2.76	2.26	2.17	2.52
2004-05	1.98	1.77	1.79	1.87	1.86	1.86	1.97	1.94	1.93	2.02	2.20	1.98	1.93
2005-06	1.75	1.67	1.75	1.89	1.98	2.07	2.04	2.18	2.22	2.15	2.22	2.07	2.00
2006-07	2.21	2.82	3.43	3.53	3.66	3.90	3.76	3.36	3.52	3.68	3.03	3.08	3.33
2007-08	3.15	3.28	3.66	4.03	4.55	4.91	5.15	5.59	5.58	6.55	5.97	5.04	4.79
2008-09	5.00	3.69	3.42	3.33	3.61	3.46	3.60	3.69	3.98	3.97	3.22	3.21	3.68
2009-10	3.10	3.52	3.62	3.59	3.52	3.39	3.40	3.36	3.43	3.24	3.49	3.77	3.45
2010-11[1]	4.51	5.19	5.33	5.65	6.10								5.36

[1] Preliminary.   *Source: Economic Research Service, U.S. Department of Agriculture (ERS-USDA)*

Average Cash Price of Corn, No. 2 Yellow at Gulf Ports[2]   In Dollars Per Bushel

Year	Sept.	Oct.	Nov.	Dec.	Jan.	Feb.	Mar.	Apr.	May	June	July	Aug.	Average
2001-02	2.27	2.19	2.28	2.35	2.34	2.30	2.28	2.21	2.29	2.37	2.53	2.79	2.35
2002-03	2.89	2.79	2.77	2.71	2.69	2.69	2.67	2.68	2.74	2.72	2.48	2.56	2.70
2003-04	2.63	2.65	2.75	2.85	2.95	3.12	3.27	3.39	3.29	3.13	2.66	2.64	2.94
2004-05	2.49	2.37	2.39	2.43	2.44	2.40	2.54	2.45	2.42	2.49	2.69	2.59	2.48
2005-06	2.47	2.58	2.44	2.61	2.61	2.72	2.67	2.74	2.81	2.78	2.90	2.92	2.69
2006-07	3.05	3.82	4.17	4.08	4.19	4.50	3.81	3.88	4.07	4.20	3.73	3.84	3.95
2007-08	4.05	4.17	4.35	4.58	5.25	5.59	5.99	6.26	6.18	7.29	6.74	5.97	5.54
2008-09	5.94	4.65	4.18	4.02	4.39	4.15	4.18	4.29	4.58	4.56	3.86	3.87	4.39
2009-10	3.82	4.25	4.36	4.18	4.25	4.11	4.04	3.99	4.15	3.88	4.15	4.46	4.14
2010-11[1]	5.23	5.99	6.05	6.36	6.73								6.07

[1] Preliminary.   [2] Barge delivered to Louisiana Gulf.   *Source: Economic Research Service, U.S. Department of Agriculture (ERS-USDA)*

CORN

Weekly Outstanding Export Sales and Cumulative Exports of U.S. Corn — In Thousands of Metric Tons

Marketing Year 2008/2009 Week Ending	Out-standing Sales	Cumu-lative Exports	Marketing Year 2009/2010 Week Ending	Out-standing Sales	Cumu-lative Exports	Marketing Year 2010/2011 Week Ending	Out-standing Sales	Cumu-lative Exports
Sep 04, 2008	11,883.8	199.3	Sep 03, 2009	12,131.4	537.0	Sep 02, 2010	15,102.5	285.8
Sep 11, 2008	11,346.4	1,062.1	Sep 10, 2009	11,934.6	1,699.4	Sep 09, 2010	14,587.5	1,385.0
Sep 18, 2008	10,900.0	2,056.3	Sep 17, 2009	11,569.5	2,737.7	Sep 16, 2010	14,157.5	2,376.8
Sep 25, 2008	10,302.6	3,220.2	Sep 24, 2009	11,827.8	3,702.9	Sep 23, 2010	14,141.6	3,318.6
Oct 02, 2008	10,435.2	4,045.5	Oct 01, 2009	11,205.5	4,847.1	Sep 30, 2010	13,770.2	4,297.1
Oct 09, 2008	10,486.9	4,918.6	Oct 08, 2009	11,167.2	5,516.8	Oct 07, 2010	13,868.4	5,104.9
Oct 16, 2008	10,522.9	5,672.2	Oct 15, 2009	10,584.1	6,334.8	Oct 14, 2010	13,247.4	5,938.4
Oct 23, 2008	10,332.9	6,275.3	Oct 22, 2009	10,284.3	7,001.7	Oct 21, 2010	13,216.5	6,501.5
Oct 30, 2008	10,185.9	6,893.6	Oct 29, 2009	10,140.1	7,709.9	Oct 28, 2010	12,797.8	7,381.0
Nov 06, 2008	9,732.8	7,702.2	Nov 05, 2009	9,870.5	8,468.0	Nov 04, 2010	12,620.4	8,132.8
Nov 13, 2008	9,410.7	8,458.1	Nov 12, 2009	9,540.2	9,151.2	Nov 11, 2010	12,375.4	8,911.6
Nov 20, 2008	9,110.1	9,224.0	Nov 19, 2009	10,135.9	9,779.1	Nov 18, 2010	12,415.5	9,694.5
Nov 27, 2008	8,523.5	10,154.5	Nov 26, 2009	9,915.4	10,658.6	Nov 25, 2010	12,389.1	10,479.0
Dec 04, 2008	8,763.6	10,843.1	Dec 03, 2009	10,056.6	11,365.1	Dec 02, 2010	12,365.0	11,174.2
Dec 11, 2008	8,665.9	11,553.3	Dec 10, 2009	10,507.3	12,141.5	Dec 09, 2010	12,365.3	11,984.7
Dec 18, 2008	8,386.0	12,384.6	Dec 17, 2009	11,684.4	12,556.2	Dec 16, 2010	12,442.6	12,813.5
Dec 25, 2008	8,053.8	12,986.7	Dec 24, 2009	11,593.4	13,419.8	Dec 23, 2010	12,058.9	13,896.3
Jan 01, 2009	7,702.9	13,598.2	Dec 31, 2009	11,160.1	14,217.8	Dec 30, 2010	11,814.2	14,510.1
Jan 08, 2009	7,307.4	14,209.9	Jan 07, 2010	10,829.3	14,875.9	Jan 06, 2011	11,737.7	15,025.8
Jan 15, 2009	7,709.4	14,893.9	Jan 14, 2010	11,603.8	15,711.8	Jan 13, 2011	12,055.4	15,612.9
Jan 22, 2009	8,078.4	15,632.6	Jan 21, 2010	11,974.3	16,243.6	Jan 20, 2011	11,700.0	16,383.0
Jan 29, 2009	8,497.0	16,378.2	Jan 28, 2010	11,774.5	17,366.6	Jan 27, 2011	12,004.9	17,244.8
Feb 05, 2009	9,473.4	16,945.6	Feb 04, 2010	11,913.9	17,970.5	Feb 03, 2011	12,443.1	17,913.9
Feb 12, 2009	9,894.4	17,856.9	Feb 11, 2010	12,236.3	18,598.2	Feb 10, 2011	12,797.6	18,589.8
Feb 19, 2009	9,571.6	18,628.6	Feb 18, 2010	11,397.0	19,838.7	Feb 17, 2011	13,238.3	19,650.4
Feb 26, 2009	9,455.4	19,536.7	Feb 25, 2010	11,103.1	20,894.1	Feb 24, 2011	13,518.7	20,450.5
Mar 05, 2009	9,478.4	20,606.1	Mar 04, 2010	10,476.8	21,858.9	Mar 03, 2011	12,791.0	21,655.4
Mar 12, 2009	8,985.5	21,539.6	Mar 11, 2010	10,269.2	22,814.2	Mar 10, 2011	12,946.7	22,536.0
Mar 19, 2009	9,400.4	22,316.0	Mar 18, 2010	9,715.2	23,975.0	Mar 17, 2011	12,961.9	23,415.8
Mar 26, 2009	9,657.3	23,310.3	Mar 25, 2010	9,326.7	25,189.6	Mar 24, 2011		
Apr 02, 2009	9,663.6	24,366.8	Apr 01, 2010	9,809.1	26,065.0	Mar 31, 2011		
Apr 09, 2009	9,678.6	25,221.5	Apr 08, 2010	9,702.2	27,178.2	Apr 07, 2011		
Apr 16, 2009	9,866.0	26,248.4	Apr 15, 2010	10,027.6	28,333.8	Apr 14, 2011		
Apr 23, 2009	10,253.4	27,086.3	Apr 22, 2010	10,342.5	29,228.2	Apr 21, 2011		
Apr 30, 2009	10,052.0	27,876.3	Apr 29, 2010	11,337.9	30,083.6	Apr 28, 2011		
May 07, 2009	9,716.5	29,148.6	May 06, 2010	11,123.7	31,116.8	May 05, 2011		
May 14, 2009	9,691.7	29,856.9	May 13, 2010	11,498.9	32,095.8	May 12, 2011		
May 21, 2009	9,637.7	30,667.0	May 20, 2010	11,289.9	33,335.6	May 19, 2011		
May 28, 2009	9,386.1	31,523.1	May 27, 2010	10,262.1	34,562.1	May 26, 2011		
Jun 04, 2009	9,475.0	32,147.4	Jun 03, 2010	10,369.0	35,474.1	Jun 02, 2011		
Jun 11, 2009	9,424.4	32,965.2	Jun 10, 2010	10,386.4	36,547.1	Jun 09, 2011		
Jun 18, 2009	9,072.4	34,003.7	Jun 17, 2010	10,691.7	37,365.2	Jun 16, 2011		
Jun 25, 2009	9,485.0	34,746.2	Jun 24, 2010	10,388.9	38,317.6	Jun 23, 2011		
Jul 02, 2009	9,266.2	35,714.0	Jul 01, 2010	9,859.6	39,348.1	Jun 30, 2011		
Jul 09, 2009	8,996.4	36,683.5	Jul 08, 2010	9,495.0	40,390.9	Jul 07, 2011		
Jul 16, 2009	8,832.5	37,605.1	Jul 15, 2010	9,160.7	41,339.3	Jul 14, 2011		
Jul 23, 2009	7,837.1	39,059.1	Jul 22, 2010	8,393.7	42,538.5	Jul 21, 2011		
Jul 30, 2009	7,070.4	40,248.6	Jul 29, 2010	8,032.6	43,371.2	Jul 28, 2011		
Aug 06, 2009	6,653.8	41,206.4	Aug 05, 2010	7,464.1	44,379.4	Aug 04, 2011		
Aug 13, 2009	6,107.2	42,330.0	Aug 12, 2010	7,052.9	45,385.5	Aug 11, 2011		
Aug 20, 2009	5,097.9	43,605.0	Aug 19, 2010	5,923.3	46,557.4	Aug 18, 2011		
Aug 27, 2009	4,397.7	44,650.0	Aug 26, 2010	4,752.6	47,699.6	Aug 25, 2011		

Source: Foreign Agricultural Service, U.S. Department of Agriculture (FAS-USDA)

Average Price Received by Farmers for Corn in the United States   In Dollars Per Bushel

Year	Sept.	Oct.	Nov.	Dec.	Jan.	Feb.	Mar.	Apr.	May	June	July	Aug.	Average
2001-02	1.91	1.84	1.85	1.98	1.97	1.93	1.94	1.91	1.93	1.97	2.13	2.38	1.98
2002-03	2.47	2.34	2.28	2.32	2.33	2.34	2.33	2.34	2.38	2.34	2.17	2.15	2.32
2003-04	2.20	2.12	2.20	2.31	2.39	2.61	2.75	2.89	2.87	2.79	2.51	2.34	2.50
2004-05	2.20	2.14	2.05	2.04	2.12	1.95	2.02	2.00	1.98	2.03	2.11	1.95	2.05
2005-06	1.90	1.82	1.77	1.92	2.00	2.02	2.06	2.11	2.17	2.14	2.14	2.09	2.01
2006-07	2.20	2.55	2.88	3.01	3.05	3.44	3.43	3.39	3.49	3.53	3.32	3.26	3.13
2007-08	3.28	3.29	3.44	3.77	3.98	4.54	4.70	5.14	5.27	5.47	5.25	5.26	4.45
2008-09	5.01	4.37	4.26	4.11	4.36	3.87	3.85	3.85	3.96	4.01	3.60	3.33	4.05
2009-10	3.25	3.61	3.65	3.60	3.66	3.55	3.55	3.41	3.48	3.41	3.49	3.65	3.53
2010-11[1]	4.08	4.32	4.55	4.82	4.94	5.66							4.73

[1] Preliminary.   *Source: Economic Research Service, U.S. Department of Agriculture (ERS-USDA)*

Corn Price Support Data in the United States

Crop Year Beginning Sept. 1	National Average Loan Rate[3] --- Dollars Per Bushel -----	Target Price	Placed Under Loan	% of Production	Acquired by CCC	Owned by CCC Aug. 31	CCC Owned	Under CCC Loan	Quantity Pledged (Thousands of Bushels)	Face Amount (Thousands of Dollars)
							CCC Inventory ----- As of Dec. 31 -----			
2001-02	1.89	NA	1,395	14.7	0	6	24	----	1,394,561	2,557,874
2002-03	1.98	2.60	1,367	15.2	0	4	18	----	1,366,513	2,622,823
2003-04	1.98	2.60	1,327	13.2	1	0	16	----	1,326,884	2,555,183
2004-05	1.95	2.63	1,366	11.6	25	0	12	----	40,814	87,053
2005-06	1.95	2.63	1,064	9.6	2	2	12	----	47,595	99,406
2006-07	1.95	2.63	1,108	10.5	0	0	1	----	31,873	65,968
2007-08	1.95	2.63	1,217	9.3	0	0	1	----	56,674	117,648
2008-09	1.95	2.63	1,074	8.9	0	0	30	----	46,573	91,966
2009-10[1]	1.95	2.63	890	6.8	0	0	9	----	80,876	147,579
2010-11[2]	1.95	2.63								

[1] Preliminary.   [2] Estimate.   [3] Findley or announced loan rate.   NA = Not available.
Source: National Agricultural Statistics Service, U.S. Department of Agriculture (NASS-USDA)

U.S. Exports[1] of Corn (Including Seed), By Country of Destination   In Thousands of Metric Tons

Crop Year Beginning Oct. 1	Algeria	Canada	Egypt	Israel	Japan	Mexico	Rep. of Korea	Russia	Saudi Arabia	Spain	Taiwan	Vene-zuela	Total
2000-01	1,180	2,797	4,116	621	14,091	5,928	3,109	26	1,003	0	4,894	1,152	48,192
2001-02	1,343	3,979	4,283	847	14,817	4,025	1,085	86	670	5	4,599	502	47,058
2002-03	1,009	3,811	2,904	313	14,384	5,220	272	0	222	0	4,139	651	40,780
2003-04	1,158	2,014	3,120	1,154	14,968	5,730	3,942	70	402	5	4,757	669	48,724
2004-05	1,036	2,210	3,738	393	15,036	5,935	2,210	13	126	14	4,446	90	45,262
2005-06	1,255	1,901	4,156	725	16,361	6,755	5,866	15	619	8	4,519	133	56,038
2006-07	940	2,142	3,522	844	14,840	8,886	3,873	9	540	3	4,213	514	54,159
2007-08	898	3,051	2,971	1,207	15,043	9,526	8,380	7	985	10	3,792	1,085	60,593
2008-09	95	1,810	2,445	138	15,491	7,710	5,735	0	440	3	3,713	1,145	47,658
2009-10[2]	64	1,935	3,005	330	14,695	8,246	6,795	0	706	3	3,009	1,121	49,833

[1] Excludes exports of corn by-products.   [2] Preliminary.   *Source: Foreign Agricultural Service, U.S. Department of Agriculture (FAS-USDA)*

Stocks of Corn (Shelled and Ear) in the United States   In Millions of Bushels

Year	On Farms Mar. 1	June 1	Sept. 1	Dec. 1	Off Farms Mar. 1	June 1	Sept. 1	Dec. 1	Total Stocks Mar. 1	June 1	Sept. 1	Dec. 1
2001	3,600.0	2,230.8	753.2	5,275.0	2,443.0	1,693.2	1,146.0	2,989.7	6,043.0	3,924.0	1,899.1	8,264.7
2002	3,355.0	2,020.6	586.8	4,800.0	2,440.3	1,576.3	1,009.6	2,838.0	5,795.3	3,596.9	1,596.4	7,638.0
2003	2,940.0	1,620.2	484.9	5,286.0	2,191.9	1,364.7	601.8	2,667.8	5,131.9	2,984.9	1,086.7	7,953.8
2004	3,030.0	1,540.0	438.0	6,144.0	2,241.5	1,430.1	520.1	3,308.5	5,271.5	2,970.1	958.1	9,452.5
2005	4,137.0	2,462.3	820.5	6,325.0	2,619.3	1,858.5	1,293.5	3,490.0	6,756.3	4,320.8	2,114.0	9,815.0
2006	4,055.0	2,350.5	749.5	5,627.0	2,932.3	2,011.2	1,217.7	3,305.7	6,987.3	4,361.7	1,967.2	8,932.7
2007	3,330.0	1,826.6	460.1	6,530.0	2,738.3	1,706.8	843.5	3,748.1	6,068.3	3,533.4	1,303.6	10,278.1
2008	3,780.0	1,970.9	500.0	6,482.0	3,078.7	2,057.1	1,124.2	3,590.1	6,858.7	4,028.0	1,624.2	10,072.1
2009	4,085.0	2,205.4	607.5	7,405.0	2,869.1	2,056.0	1,065.8	3,497.5	6,954.1	4,261.4	1,673.3	10,902.5
2010[1]	4,548.0	2,131.4	485.1	6,302.0	3,145.8	2,178.7	1,222.7	3,737.9	7,693.8	4,310.1	1,707.8	10,039.9

[1] Preliminary.   *Source: National Agricultural Statistics Service, U.S. Department of Agriculture (NASS-USDA)*

CORN

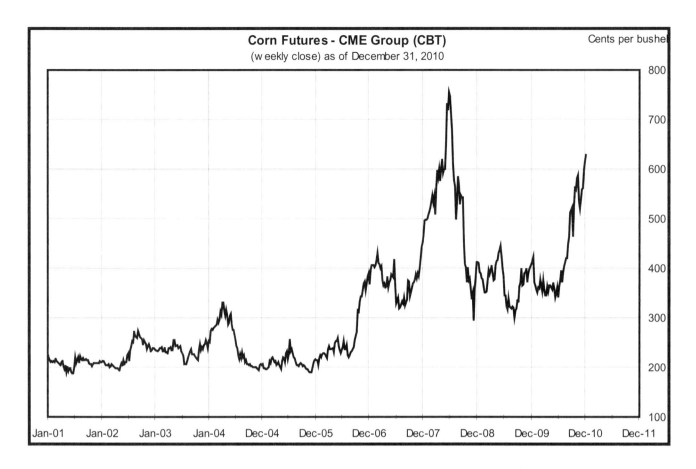

Corn Futures - CME Group (CBT)
(weekly close) as of December 31, 2010

Cents per bushel

Volume of Trading of Corn Futures in Chicago   In Thousands of Contracts

Year	Jan.	Feb.	Mar.	Apr.	May	June	July	Aug.	Sept.	Oct.	Nov.	Dec.	Total
2001	1,397.2	1,197.4	1,329.5	1,518.7	1,173.2	1,612.1	2,023.5	1,549.0	1,072.3	1,223.3	1,741.2	891.4	16,728.7
2002	996.3	1,449.6	944.7	1,498.0	1,434.5	1,851.5	1,958.4	2,158.7	1,635.4	1,523.3	1,801.4	880.5	18,132.4
2003	1,204.0	1,559.1	1,156.9	1,633.1	1,657.0	1,951.2	1,499.3	1,830.6	1,389.7	2,057.7	1,815.9	1,364.3	19,118.7
2004	2,025.7	2,367.0	2,190.9	2,870.9	1,855.3	2,538.6	1,740.5	1,883.0	1,446.9	1,476.4	2,473.3	1,169.6	24,038.2
2005	1,467.8	2,680.8	2,278.1	2,519.1	2,188.3	3,446.1	2,626.0	2,993.6	1,618.5	1,504.2	2,892.2	1,750.3	27,965.1
2006	2,494.6	3,599.1	3,041.0	3,507.5	3,773.1	4,693.4	3,743.6	4,226.9	3,760.5	5,300.2	6,279.4	2,820.6	47,239.9
2007	5,166.5	5,111.6	4,959.0	6,095.4	4,519.9	6,090.9	4,035.7	4,344.1	3,128.9	3,306.5	4,615.6	3,145.9	54,520.2
2008	4,213.2	5,808.2	4,350.8	6,501.1	4,876.9	7,593.8	5,402.2	4,989.1	3,934.7	4,572.5	4,448.6	3,266.2	59,957.1
2009	3,041.3	4,487.1	3,684.9	4,567.6	4,151.8	5,636.8	4,765.8	4,441.8	3,153.8	4,374.0	5,509.1	3,134.9	50,948.8
2010	4,025.9	5,217.5	3,935.4	6,466.0	4,240.6	6,207.8	4,863.8	6,899.6	7,033.7	7,501.1	9,169.7	4,280.4	69,841.4

Contract size = 5,000 bu.   *Source: CME Group; Chicago Board of Trade (CBT)*

Average Open Interest of Corn Futures in Chicago   In Thousands of Contracts

Year	Jan.	Feb.	Mar.	Apr.	May	June	July	Aug.	Sept.	Oct.	Nov.	Dec.
2001	454.3	469.0	440.5	455.7	424.4	423.8	389.9	387.7	370.3	419.4	462.9	416.6
2002	459.3	464.4	431.9	430.7	411.3	430.9	458.1	509.1	501.5	485.9	497.0	450.0
2003	456.0	469.6	445.3	412.0	407.0	385.8	384.6	383.6	356.2	420.7	470.2	447.5
2004	544.0	641.4	678.0	704.9	637.4	621.9	566.5	562.2	548.8	606.3	639.5	588.9
2005	629.3	654.1	659.7	673.8	677.3	702.4	713.1	733.6	714.2	794.4	852.5	774.2
2006	875.3	1,048.8	1,066.0	1,176.0	1,288.2	1,327.8	1,360.2	1,347.2	1,302.1	1,312.6	1,405.7	1,381.5
2007	1,448.2	1,498.8	1,427.3	1,345.9	1,257.6	1,244.1	1,213.4	1,132.8	1,108.5	1,161.7	1,202.6	1,211.5
2008	1,383.2	1,463.1	1,421.8	1,445.3	1,409.2	1,396.1	1,279.9	1,170.4	1,050.9	995.5	967.6	820.5
2009	806.7	801.1	767.8	823.3	860.6	971.7	894.1	862.6	850.1	923.9	1,002.9	969.2
2010	1,105.4	1,149.6	1,124.2	1,169.6	1,196.2	1,204.5	1,161.3	1,324.5	1,405.8	1,509.8	1,629.6	1,511.5

Contract size = 5,000 bu.   *Source: CME Group; Chicago Board of Trade (CBT)*

Corn Oil

Corn oil is a bland, odorless oil produced by refining the crude corn oil that is mechanically extracted from the germ of the plant seed. High-oil corn, the most common type of corn used to make corn oil, typically has an oil content of 7% or higher compared to about 4% for normal corn. Corn oil is widely used as cooking oil, for making margarine and mayonnaise, and for making inedible products such as soap, paints, inks, varnishes, and cosmetics. For humans, studies have shown that no vegetable oil is more effective than corn oil in lowering blood cholesterol levels.

Prices –The average monthly price of corn oil (wet mill price in Chicago) in the 2010-11 marketing year (Oct-Sep) rose +34.9% yr/yr to 52.02 cents per pound, down from 2007-08 record high of 69.37 cents per pound. Seasonally, prices tend to be highest around March/April and lowest late in the calendar year.

Supply – U.S. corn oil production in the 2009-10 marketing year (latest data) rose +0.5% yr/yr to 2.430 billion pounds, down from the 2006-07 high of 2.560 billion pounds. Seasonally, production tends to peak around December and March and reaches a low in July. U.S. stocks in the 2009-10 marketing year (Oct 1) fell -11.1% yr/yr to 182.0 million pounds.

Demand – U.S. usage (domestic disappearance) in 2009-10 rose +1.6% to 1.697 billion pounds.

Exports – U.S. corn oil exports in 2009-10 fell -7.2% to 755 million pounds. U.S. corn oil imports in 2009-10 fell by -8.0% to 40.000 million pounds.

Supply and Disappearance of Corn Oil in the United States   In Millions of Pounds

| | Supply | | | | Disappearance | | | | | | |
Year	Stocks Oct. 1	Pro-duction	Imports	Total Supply	Baking and Frying Fats	Salad and Cooking Oil	Marg-arine	Total Edible Products	Domestic Disap-pearance	Exports	Total Disap-pearance
2003-04	119	2,396	66.0	2,582	W	W	W	1,724	1,662	767	2,429
2004-05	153	2,396	49.1	2,598	W	1,466	W	1,690	1,653	789	2,442
2005-06	156	2,483	45.0	2,683	W	1,407	W	1,607	1,685	799	2,483
2006-07	200	2,560	43.1	2,803	W	1,335	W	1,735	1,832	793	2,625
2007-08	179	2,507	45.2	2,731	W	1,722	W	1,606	1,756	769	2,525
2008-09[1]	205	2,418	43.5	2,667	W	1,722	W	1,591	1,671	814	2,484
2009-10[2]	182	2,430	40.0	2,652	W	1,881	W	1,589	1,697	755	2,452

[1] Preliminary.   [2] Estimate.   W = Withheld.   *Source: Economic Research Service, U.S. Department of Agriculture (ERS-USDA)*

Production[2] of Crude Corn Oil in the United States   In Millions of Pounds

Year	Oct.	Nov.	Dec.	Jan.	Feb.	Mar.	Apr.	May	June	July	Aug.	Sept.	Total
2004-05	208.8	187.1	191.0	205.2	182.5	206.6	217.2	188.2	211.5	206.7	198.5	189.0	2,392
2005-06	207.5	199.9	200.3	209.2	184.8	217.6	191.7	218.7	206.7	215.3	222.0	209.0	2,483
2006-07	228.7	216.0	226.1	224.7	187.9	216.4	194.1	214.4	212.7	219.8	209.5	209.4	2,560
2007-08	213.5	213.0	214.0	205.4	193.7	222.5	190.7	220.9	193.7	214.9	217.3	207.3	2,507
2008-09	206.3	210.6	198.7	200.3	199.8	218.8	189.4	202.5	189.0	186.0	201.4	215.8	2,419
2009-10	212.9	205.2	203.2	197.9	188.1	212.4	214.7	205.4	214.7	216.8	213.6	200.1	2,485
2010-11[1]	205.1	211.2	198.9	234.5									2,549

[1] Preliminary.   [2] Not seasonally adjusted.   *Source: Bureau of the Census, U.S. Department of Commerce*

Consumption Corn Oil, in Refining, in the United States   In Millions of Pounds

Year	Oct.	Nov.	Dec.	Jan.	Feb.	Mar.	Apr.	May	June	July	Aug.	Sept.	Total
2004-05	W	165.4	131.6	140.3	W	147.3	132.2	124.8	149.0	142.9	142.4	132.1	1,690
2005-06	148.4	140.4	140.3	148.4	123.4	128.0	110.8	145.2	138.9	121.6	131.6	130.0	1,607
2006-07	143.6	146.7	153.3	155.3	131.1	137.2	W	W	147.7	142.2	146.0	143.0	1,735
2007-08	155.2	W	133.8	119.5	119.2	143.8	124.2	142.9	109.7	131.8	150.3	141.8	1,606
2008-09	137.8	132.1	130.8	131.4	113.7	134.3	102.7	129.4	121.6	158.2	144.2	154.6	1,591
2009-10	146.8	126.4	133.9	119.1	W	138.2	W	W	W	127.7	130.7	136.5	1,589
2010-11[1]	128.0	135.6	107.1										1,483

[1] Preliminary.   W = Withheld proprietary data.   *Source: Bureau of Census, U.S. Department of Commerce*

Average Corn Oil Price, Wet Mill in Chicago   In Cents Per Pound

Year	Oct.	Nov.	Dec.	Jan.	Feb.	Mar.	Apr.	May	June	July	Aug.	Sept.	Average
2004-05	23.10	24.24	26.67	27.41	27.58	28.08	29.29	30.65	30.73	30.01	28.83	27.75	27.86
2005-06	27.50	27.08	26.08	25.22	23.65	22.61	23.19	25.25	25.70	25.75	25.42	24.71	25.18
2006-07	24.70	26.47	28.05	28.05	28.66	29.08	29.93	31.56	34.71	37.25	39.61	43.61	31.81
2007-08	52.50	56.32	59.47	63.67	74.89	83.55	87.09	87.29	82.33	76.64	60.00	48.71	69.37
2008-09	34.76	31.06	26.88	25.19	29.05	29.64	31.31	37.23	39.57	36.30	35.23	36.83	32.75
2009-10	37.59	38.12	40.02	40.34	37.54	38.37	38.50	38.50	38.93	39.29	41.48	42.85	39.29
2010-11[1]	47.50	51.96	54.71	57.91									53.02

[1] Preliminary.   *Source: Economic Research Service, U.S. Department of Agriculture (ERS-USDA)*

Cotton

Cotton is a natural vegetable fiber that comes from small trees and shrubs of a genus belonging to the mallow family, one of which is the common American Upland cotton plant. Cotton hCotton is a natural vegetable fiber that comes from small trees and shrubs of a genus belonging to the mallow family, one of which is the common American Upland cotton plant. Cotton has been used in India for at least the last 5,000 years and probably much longer, and was also used by the ancient Chinese, Egyptians, and North and South Americans. Cotton was one of the earliest crops grown by European settlers in the U.S.

Cotton requires a long growing season, plenty of sunshine and water during the growing season, and then dry weather for harvesting. In the United States, the Cotton Belt stretches from northern Florida to North Carolina and westward to California. In the U.S., planting time varies from the beginning of February in Southern Texas to the beginning of June in the northern sections of the Cotton Belt. The flower bud of the plant blossoms and develops into an oval boll that splits open at maturity. At maturity, cotton is most vulnerable to damage from wind and rain. Approximately 95% of the cotton in the U.S. is now harvested mechanically with spindle-type pickers or strippers and then sent off to cotton gins for processing. There it is dried, cleaned, separated, and packed into bales.

Cotton is used in a wide range of products from clothing to home furnishings to medical products. The value of cotton is determined according to the staple, grade, and character of each bale. Staple refers to short, medium, long, or extra-long fiber length, with medium staple accounting for about 70% of all U.S. cotton. Grade refers to the color, brightness, and amount of foreign matter and is established by the U.S. Department of Agriculture. Character refers to the fiber's diameter, strength, body, maturity (ratio of mature to immature fibers), uniformity, and smoothness. Cotton is the fifth leading cash crop in the U.S. and is one of the nation's principal agricultural exports. The weight of cotton is typically measured in terms of a "bale," which is deemed to equal 480 pounds.

Cotton futures and options are traded on the ICE Futures U.S. (ICE) exchange. Cotton futures are also traded on the Bolsa de Mercadorias & Futuros (BM&F). Cotton yarn futures are traded on the Central Japan Commodity Exchange (CCOM) and the Osaka Mercantile Exchange (OME). The ICE's futures contract calls for the delivery of 50,000 pounds net weight (approximately 100 bales) of No. 2 cotton with a quality rating of Strict Low Middling and a staple length of 1-and-2/32 inch. Delivery points include Texas (Galveston and Houston), New Orleans, Memphis, and Greenville/Spartanburg in South Carolina.

Prices – Cotton prices in 2010 continued the rally from the 8-1/2 year low of 36.7 cents per pound posted in November 2008, with cotton prices supported by insatiable Chinese demand and limited global cotton supplies. Cotton prices through the first half of 2010 traded sideways at 2-1/2 year highs and then exploded higher the rest of the year as they posted a record high of 159.12 cents per pound in December 2010 and closed the year up 92% at 144.81 cents per pound. Cotton prices extended their parabolic rally into March 2011 and surged to an all-time high of 227.00 cents a pound, the highest price since cotton began recorded-trading 140 years ago. Chinese cotton demand continued to expand with 2010 China cotton imports surging +86% y/y to 2.84 MMT. Adverse weather reduced global cotton supplies in 2010 with China's cotton crop hurt by the worst flooding in a decade while cotton production in Australia, the world's fourth-largest exporter, was decimated after the worst floods there in 50 years. U.S. cotton production in 2009/10 dropped -4.9% y/y to 12.188 million bales and global cotton production in 2009/10 fell -5.2% y/y to 101.54 million bales. The USDA in February 2011 cut its 2010/11 global cotton carry-over estimate to 42.81 million bales, a 15-year low.

Supply – World cotton production in 2010-11 rose +13.5% yr/yr to 115.250 million bales (480 pounds per bale), close the record high of 121.812 million bales seen in 2006-07. The world's largest cotton producers were China with 26.0% of world production in 2010-11, India with 22.6%, the U.S. with 15.9%, and Pakistan with 7.6%. World beginning stocks in 2010-11 fell 27.3% yr/yr to a fourteen year low of 43.994 million bales.

The U.S. cotton crop in 2010-11 rose by +50.3% yr/yr to 18.314 million bales, down from the 2005-06 record high of 23.890 million bales. U.S. farmers harvested 10.706 million acres of cotton in 2010-11, up +42.2% yr/yr. The U.S. cotton yield in 2010-11 rose +5.7% to 821 pounds per acre, not far behind the 2007-08 record high of 879 pounds per acre. The leading U.S. producing states of Upland cotton are Texas with 47.6% of U.S. production in 2010, Georgia (12.7%), Arkansas (7.1%), North Carolina (5.7%), Missouri (4.1%), Mississippi (5.0%), and California (2.2%). U.S. production of cotton cloth has fallen sharply by almost half in the past decade due to the movement of the textile industry out of the U.S. to low-wage foreign countries. Specifically, U.S. production of cotton cloth in 2010 fell –0.3% yr/yr to a record low of 1.316 billion square yards, less than one-fourth of the production level seen in 1950.

Demand – World consumption of cotton in 2010-11 fell by +1.8% yr/yr to 116.415 million bales, but still below the 2006-07 record high of 121.986. Consumption of cotton continues to move toward countries with low wages, where the raw cotton is utilized to produce textiles and other cotton products. The largest consumers of cotton in 2010-11 were China (40.4% of world total), India (18.5%), and Pakistan (8.8%). U.S. consumption of cotton by mills in 2008-09 (latest data) fell –4.5% yr/yr to 4.400 million bales, and accounted for 25% of U.S. production. The remaining 75% of U.S. cotton production went for exports.

Trade – World exports of cotton in 2010-11 rose by +7.2% yr/yr to 38.120 million bales, but still below the 2005-06 record high of 44.854 million bales. The U.S. is the world's largest cotton exporter by far and accounts for 41.3% of world cotton exports. Key world cotton importers include Turkey with 8.1% of total world imports in 2010-11, Indonesia with 5.1%, Mexico with 3.4%, and Russia with 1.4%. U.S. cotton exports in 2010-11 (latest data) fell by -5.0% yr/yr to 12.523 million bales. The main destinations for U.S. exports in 2010-11 were China (31.0%), Mexico (11.9%), Indonesia (5.3%), Taiwan (4.8%), and Thailand (3.4%).

Supply and Distribution of All Cotton in the United States   In Thousands of 480-Pound Bales

Crop Year Beginning Aug. 1	Acre Planted 1,000 Acres	Acre Harvested 1,000 Acres	Yield Lbs./Acre	Beginning Stocks[3]	Supply Pro-duction[4]	Imports	Total	Mill Use	Exports	Total	Unac-counted	Ending Stocks	Farm Price[5]	"A" Index Price[6]	Value of Pro-duction Million USD
2001-02	15,769	13,828	705	6,000	20,303	21	26,324	7,696	11,000	18,696	-180	7,448	32.0	41.88	3,121.8
2002-03	13,958	12,417	665	7,448	17,209	67	24,724	7,273	11,900	19,173	-166	5,385	45.7	55.81	3,777.1
2003-04	13,480	12,003	730	5,385	18,255	45	23,685	6,266	13,758	20,024	-211	3,450	63.0	68.22	5,516.8
2004-05	13,659	13,057	855	3,450	23,251	29	26,730	6,691	14,436	21,127	-108	5,495	44.7	52.22	4,993.6
2005-06	14,245	13,803	831	5,495	23,890	28	29,413	5,871	17,673	23,544	200	6,069	49.7	56.19	5,695.2
2006-07	15,274	12,732	814	6,069	21,588	19	27,676	4,935	12,959	17,894	-303	9,479	48.4	59.22	5,013.2
2007-08	10,827	10,489	879	9,479	19,207	12	28,698	4,584	13,634	18,218	-429	10,051	61.3	73.02	5,652.9
2008-09	9,471	7,569	813	10,051	12,815	0	22,866	3,587	13,261	16,848	319	6,337	49.1	61.10	3,021.5
2009-10[1]	9,150	7,529	777	6,337	12,188	0	18,525	3,461	12,037	15,498	-80	2,947	62.8	78.13	3,788.0
2010-11[2]	10,973	10,707	821	2,947	18,315	0	21,365	3,450	15,750	19,200	35	2,200	75-87		7,317.7

[1] Preliminary.   [2] Estimate.   [3] Excludes preseason ginnings (adjusted to 480-lb. bale net weight basis).   [4] Includes preseason ginnings.   [5] Marketing year average price.   [6] Average of 5 cheapest types of SLM 1 3/32" staple length cotton offered on the European market.
Source: Economic Research Service, U.S. Department of Agriculture (ERS-USDA)

World Production of All Cotton   In Thousands of 480-Pound Bales

Crop Year Beginning Aug. 1	Argentina	Australia	Brazil	Burkina	China	Egypt	Greece	India	Pakistan	Turkey	United States	Uzbek-istan	Total
2001-02	300	3,340	3,519	725	24,400	1,454	2,093	12,300	8,286	3,975	20,303	4,900	98,703
2002-03	290	1,680	3,890	750	25,200	1,331	1,715	10,600	7,972	4,179	17,209	4,600	90,976
2003-04	515	1,700	6,015	965	23,800	920	1,530	14,000	7,845	4,100	18,255	4,100	96,734
2004-05	675	3,000	5,900	1,180	30,300	1,356	1,800	19,000	11,138	4,150	23,251	5,200	121,569
2005-06	625	2,800	4,700	1,367	28,400	938	1,975	19,050	9,850	3,550	23,890	5,550	116,433
2006-07	800	1,350	7,000	1,300	35,500	975	1,400	21,800	9,600	3,800	21,588	5,350	121,812
2007-08	703	640	7,360	675	37,000	970	1,550	24,000	8,600	3,100	19,207	5,350	119,683
2008-09	600	1,500	5,480	850	36,700	483	1,150	22,600	8,700	1,930	12,815	4,600	107,102
2009-10[1]	1,000	1,775	5,450	700	32,000	432	900	23,200	9,600	1,750	12,188	3,900	101,544
2010-11[2]	1,200	4,000	8,200	850	30,000	600	850	26,000	8,800	2,250	18,315	4,650	115,250

[1] Preliminary.   [2] Estimate.   *Source: Foreign Agricultural Service, U.S. Department of Agriculture (FAS-USDA)*

World Stocks and Trade of Cotton   In Thousands of 480-Pound Bales

Crop Year Beginning Aug. 1	Beginning Stocks United States	Beginning Stocks Uzbek-istan	Beginning Stocks China	Beginning Stocks World Total	Imports Indo-nesia	Imports Mexico	Imports Russia	Imports Turkey	Imports World Total	Exports United States	Exports Uzbek-istan	Exports China	Exports World Total
2001-02	6,000	668	19,741	49,408	2,356	2,065	1,800	2,977	29,304	11,000	3,500	342	29,149
2002-03	7,448	918	18,848	54,530	2,228	2,330	1,650	2,265	30,187	11,900	3,400	751	30,457
2003-04	5,385	1,018	17,474	47,625	2,150	1,858	1,475	2,370	34,112	13,758	3,100	173	33,198
2004-05	3,450	923	18,983	48,084	2,200	1,810	1,450	3,414	33,840	14,436	3,950	30	35,014
2005-06	5,495	1,298	18,388	60,575	2,200	1,744	1,375	3,501	44,771	17,673	4,800	36	44,854
2006-07	6,069	1,248	22,536	61,887	2,200	1,353	1,325	4,029	38,029	12,959	4,500	88	37,476
2007-08	9,479	1,198	20,536	62,266	2,300	1,530	1,125	3,267	38,959	13,634	4,200	62	39,005
2008-09	10,051	1,348	20,504	60,728	2,000	1,315	845	2,919	30,143	13,261	3,000	84	30,065
2009-10[1]	6,337	1,948	22,366	60,517	2,100	1,393	600	4,394	35,984	12,037	3,800	75	35,550
2010-11[2]	2,947	948	15,246	43,994	1,925	1,300	550	3,100	38,103	15,750	3,500	76	38,120

[1] Preliminary.   [2] Estimate.   *Source: Foreign Agricultural Service, U.S. Department of Agriculture (FAS-USDA)*

World Consumption of All Cottons in Specified Countries   In Thousands of 480-Pound Bales

Crop Year Beginning Aug. 1	Bangla-desh	Brazil	China	Egypt	India	Indonesia	Mexico	Pakistan	Russia	Thailand	Turkey	United States	Total
2001-02	1,201	3,689	25,400	798	13,275	2,350	2,225	8,525	1,800	1,825	6,150	7,876	93,736
2002-03	1,552	3,585	28,950	913	13,300	2,300	2,125	9,425	1,650	1,975	6,300	7,439	97,611
2003-04	1,802	3,865	30,950	913	13,500	2,200	2,025	9,625	1,500	1,875	6,000	6,477	97,189
2004-05	2,205	4,160	37,250	963	14,800	2,200	2,125	10,525	1,425	2,125	7,100	6,799	107,904
2005-06	2,505	4,302	43,500	1,013	16,700	2,225	2,125	11,525	1,375	2,075	6,900	5,671	115,038
2006-07	3,210	4,423	48,000	1,013	18,100	2,225	2,125	12,025	1,325	1,975	7,204	5,238	121,986
2007-08	3,510	4,450	48,500	963	18,600	2,275	2,025	12,025	1,150	1,975	6,090	5,013	121,175
2008-09	3,760	4,050	41,750	938	17,750	2,050	1,875	11,275	900	1,625	5,013	3,268	107,391
2009-10[1]	3,810	4,250	50,000	863	19,650	2,100	1,925	10,925	650	1,800	5,720	3,541	118,501
2010-11[2]	3,910	4,350	47,000	813	21,500	1,950	1,850	10,225	550	1,625	5,820	3,617	116,415

[1] Preliminary.   [2] Estimate.   *Source: Foreign Agricultural Service, U.S. Department of Agriculture (FAS-USDA)*

COTTON

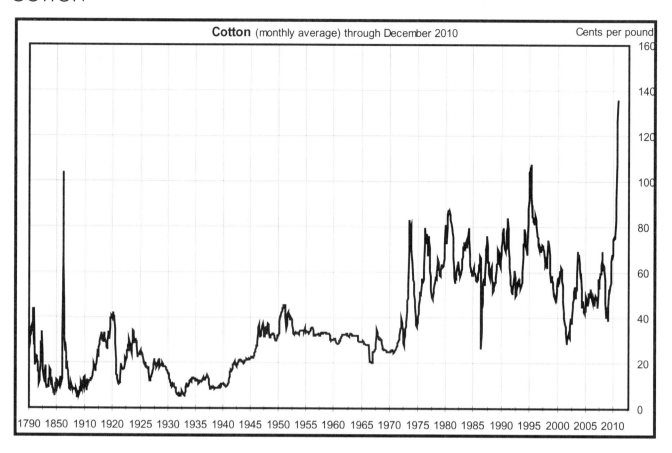

Cotton (monthly average) through December 2010   Cents per pound

Average Spot Cotton Prices[2], C.I.F. Northern Europe   In U.S. Cents Per Pound

Crop Year Beginning Aug. 1	Argentina "C"[3] 1 1/16" M 1 3/32"	Australia M 1 3/32"	Cotlook Index A	Cotlook Index B	Egypt Giza[4] 81	Greece M 1 3/32"	Mexico[5] M 1 3/32"	Pakistan Sind/ Punjab[6]	Tanzania AR[7] Type 3	Turkey Izmir[8] 1 3/32"	U.S. Calif. ACALA SJV[9]	U.S. Memphis Terr.[10] M 1 3/32"	U.S. Orleans/ Texas[11] M 1 1/32"
1990-1	77.06	85.58	82.90	77.80	177.43	84.24	84.46	77.19	89.62	81.32	92.84	88.13	80.35
1991-2	55.08	65.97	63.05	58.50	128.10	65.90	68.19	58.14	68.90	74.66	74.47	66.35	63.41
1992-3	64.31	64.01	57.70	53.70	99.24	56.92	----	52.66	62.24	----	68.37	63.08	58.89
1993-4	80.20	72.81	70.60	67.30	88.35	58.81	----	54.42	69.83	59.80	77.55	72.80	69.78
1994-5	101.88	81.05	92.75	92.40	93.70	88.64	82.65	73.75	----	----	106.40	98.67	95.70
1995-6	82.98	93.75	85.61	81.06	----	84.95	94.94	81.86	96.20	90.38	103.49	94.71	90.37
1996-7	79.71	83.24	78.59	74.80	----	75.85	79.60	73.37	79.22	----	89.55	82.81	79.77
1997-8	69.96	77.49	72.19	70.69	----	72.03	81.70	72.93	84.04	----	85.11	78.12	74.74
1998-9	57.19	66.48	58.94	54.26	----	58.66	65.78	----	72.70	----	78.57	74.20	70.95
1999-00[1]	----	61.97	52.85	49.55	----	51.71	56.43	----	55.67	----	68.76	66.29	55.67

[1] Preliminary.   [2] Generally for prompt shipment.   [3] 1-1/32" prior to January 20, 1984; 1-1/16" since.   [4] Dendera until 1969/70; Giza 67 1969/70 until December 1983; Giza 69/75/81 until November 1990; Giza 81 since.   [5] S. Brazil Type 5, 1-1/32" prior to 1968-69; 1-1/16" until 1987/88; Brazilian Type 5/6, 1-1/16" since.   [6] Punjab until 1979/80; Sind SG until June 1984; Sind/Punjab SG until January 1985; Afzal 1" until January 1986; Afzal 1-1/32" since.   [7] No. 1 until 1978/79; No. 1/2 until February 1986; AR' Mwanza No. 3 until January 1992; AR' Type 3 since.   [8] Izmir ST 1 White 1-1/16" RG prior to 1981/82; 1-3/32" from 1981/82 until January 1987; Izmir/Antalya ST 1 White 1-3/32" RG since.   [9] SM 1-3/32" prior to 1975/76; SM 1-1/8" since.   [10] SM 1-1/16" prior to 1981/82; Middling 1-3/32" since.   [11] Middling 1" prior to 1988/89; Middling 1-1/32" since.
Source: International Cotton Advisory Committee (ICAC)

Average Producer Price Index of Gray Cotton Broadwovens   Index 1982 = 100

Year	Jan.	Feb.	Mar.	Apr.	May	June	July	Aug.	Sept.	Oct.	Nov.	Dec.	Average
2001	112.8	113.1	113.1	112.7	112.8	112.9	113.2	112.9	112.9	112.0	111.2	111.1	112.6
2002	110.7	109.9	110.1	108.1	107.3	108.0	106.9	107.0	106.9	105.9	105.7	106.2	107.7
2003	105.7	105.2	105.0	105.9	106.0	106.7	107.2	109.1	110.1	111.0	110.6	108.9	107.6
2004	109.9	111.2	110.6	111.5	112.3	112.6	113.7	113.2	113.5	113.6	113.3	112.5	112.3
2005	112.6	112.0	111.9	111.8	111.2	111.2	111.1	111.2	111.2	111.3	110.9	111.1	111.5
2006	111.1	110.5	109.9	109.9	110.1	110.1	110.1	110.1	110.1	110.0	110.0	109.9	110.2
2007	110.0	109.9	109.9	110.0	109.8	109.9	109.9	109.9	109.9	110.0	109.9	109.9	109.9
2008	110.1	110.1	110.1	110.1	110.0	109.9	110.2	111.7	111.7	111.7	111.6	111.4	110.7
2009	111.0	111.0	111.0	107.2	107.2	107.2	107.2	107.5	107.5	107.5	108.9	108.9	108.5
2010[1]	109.8	113.7	113.7	113.7	114.9	116.6	119.0	118.8	118.8	118.8	119.1	119.1	116.3

[1] Preliminary.   *Source: Bureau of Labor Statistics (0337-01), U.S. Department of Commerce*

Average Price of SLM 1-1/16", Cotton/5 at Designated U.S. Markets   In Cents Per Pound (Net Weight)

Year	Aug.	Sept.	Oct.	Nov.	Dec.	Jan.	Feb.	Mar.	Apr.	May	June	July	Average
2001-02	36.05	33.22	28.42	31.23	32.21	32.13	31.60	33.23	31.86	31.14	36.36	39.78	33.10
2002-03	39.20	37.91	39.62	44.98	46.38	48.60	51.35	53.82	53.38	48.94	50.92	54.45	47.46
2003-04	51.94	58.02	69.38	68.88	65.09	68.21	63.35	61.78	57.50	60.22	52.35	45.05	60.15
2004-05	44.92	47.48	44.55	42.62	41.68	43.21	42.90	48.19	49.58	48.57	45.92	47.78	45.62
2005-06	45.38	47.43	51.02	48.80	49.53	51.91	52.39	50.04	49.00	47.00	47.90	47.15	48.96
2006-07	48.65	46.80	45.15	46.32	49.85	49.90	48.77	49.21	46.97	44.62	50.35	57.50	48.67
2007-08	53.46	57.08	59.06	59.59	59.44	63.34	65.92	69.27	63.91	60.67	63.34	62.85	61.49
2008-09	60.93	56.72	46.90	39.83	42.07	44.87	41.81	38.53	45.11	52.92	50.80	53.98	47.87
2009-10	53.77	55.78	60.44	64.90	68.11	65.93	68.08	74.54	75.46	74.70	75.19	76.16	67.76
2010-11[1]	81.16	91.53	108.26	126.62	135.46	144.79	177.65						123.64

[1] Preliminary.   [2] Grade 41, leaf 4, staple 34, mike 35-36 and 43-49, strength 23.5-26.4.   *Source: Agricultural Marketing Service, U.S. Department of Agriculture (AMS-USDA)*

Average Spot Cotton, 1-3/32", Price (SLM) at Designated U.S. Markets[2]   In Cents Per Pound (Net Weight)

Year	Aug.	Sept.	Oct.	Nov.	Dec.	Jan.	Feb.	Mar.	Apr.	May	June	July	Average
2001-02	38.88	36.11	31.55	34.03	34.82	34.55	34.08	36.04	34.84	34.03	39.31	42.86	35.93
2002-03	42.31	41.07	43.08	48.78	50.70	52.87	55.34	57.88	57.54	52.96	55.09	58.46	51.34
2003-04	55.87	61.76	73.27	72.63	68.90	71.96	67.34	66.42	63.11	65.97	57.99	51.11	64.69
2004-05	50.45	52.55	49.45	47.23	46.41	48.16	48.17	53.37	54.67	53.76	51.26	52.97	50.70
2005-06	50.59	52.81	56.01	53.78	54.47	56.69	57.16	55.03	54.07	52.02	52.97	52.35	54.00
2006-07	53.80	51.95	50.20	51.13	54.71	54.75	53.66	54.05	51.59	49.12	54.71	61.59	53.44
2007-08	57.53	61.15	63.08	63.71	63.50	67.22	69.73	72.68	67.25	63.99	66.67	66.17	65.22
2008-09	64.25	60.01	50.52	43.76	45.95	48.76	45.67	42.40	49.02	56.81	54.70	57.94	51.65
2009-10	57.77	59.82	64.58	69.23	72.59	70.45	72.47	79.02	79.81	78.99	79.37	80.30	72.03
2010-11[1]	87.38	95.48	112.06	130.62	139.68								113.04

[1] Preliminary.   *Source: Agricultural Marketing Service, U.S. Department of Agriculture (AMS-USDA)*

Average Spot Prices of U.S. Cotton,[2] Base Quality (SLM) at Designated Markets   In Cents Per Pound

Crop Year Beginning Aug. 1	Dallas (EastTex.-Okl.)	Fresno (San Joaquin Valley)	Greenville (Southeast)	Greenwood (South Delta)	Lubbock (West Texas)	Memphis (North Delta)	Phoenix Desert (Southwest)	Average
2000-01	51.03	52.45	52.63	52.32	50.71	52.32	49.47	51.56
2001-02	32.59	34.64	33.02	33.24	32.39	33.24	32.60	33.10
2002-03	46.76	47.52	48.28	48.46	46.51	48.47	46.27	47.46
2003-04	59.95	59.71	60.80	60.85	59.71	60.78	59.23	60.15
2004-05	44.22	47.38	45.91	46.02	44.08	46.02	45.66	45.61
2005-06	47.69	50.06	49.65	49.63	47.78	49.67	48.26	48.96
2006-07	48.17	48.58	49.90	49.46	48.06	49.46	47.08	48.67
2007-08	60.89	60.57	63.95	62.67	60.64	62.67	59.07	61.50
2008-09	47.08	49.10	48.97	47.99	46.93	47.99	47.03	47.87
2009-10[1]	66.57	67.20	70.13	69.30	66.38	69.30	65.40	67.76

[1] Preliminary   [2] Prices are for mixed lots, net weight, uncompressed in warehouse.
Source: Agricultural Marketing Service, U.S. Department of Agriculture (AMS-USDA)

Average Price[1] Received by Farmers for Upland Cotton in the United States   In Cents Per Pound

Year	Aug.	Sept.	Oct.	Nov.	Dec.	Jan.	Feb.	Mar.	Apr.	May	June	July	Average
2001-02	37.3	36.5	30.7	27.8	30.8	27.3	28.0	28.4	27.2	26.7	33.7	35.3	29.8
2002-03	33.0	35.2	39.4	43.0	44.3	45.5	46.5	48.6	45.4	45.9	45.5	46.3	43.2
2003-04	46.3	55.7	67.8	63.0	63.3	62.2	61.9	61.6	60.3	59.7	59.9	53.8	59.6
2004-05	53.7	49.3	50.6	43.2	39.3	38.5	38.3	40.3	41.4	39.6	41.9	41.1	43.1
2005-06	42.1	44.3	48.5	48.5	48.0	48.6	48.9	50.0	48.5	46.4	47.4	46.8	47.3
2006-07	45.8	47.3	45.9	47.4	49.0	49.4	47.4	46.4	46.3	44.0	45.4	45.2	46.6
2007-08	44.9	52.0	55.5	57.4	59.6	61.5	63.0	63.0	65.5	64.6	64.0	66.2	59.8
2008-09	58.5	61.1	58.8	54.8	53.3	46.0	41.2	40.4	44.7	44.9	45.0	43.6	49.4
2009-10	47.7	55.0	58.5	59.5	63.4	60.8	65.0	64.5	66.2	66.0	67.6	67.3	61.8
2010-11[2]	77.2	74.7	78.1	81.2	80.9	82.2	88.3						80.4

[1] Weighted average by sales.   [2] Preliminary.   *Source: Agricultural Marketing Service, U.S. Department of Agriculture (AMS-USDA)*

COTTON

Purchases Reported by Exchanges in Designated U.S. Spot Markets[1]   In Running Bales

Crop Year Beginning Aug. 1	Aug.	Sept.	Oct.	Nov.	Dec.	Jan.	Feb.	Mar.	Apr.	May	June	July	Market Total
2001-02	118,000	94,697	214,785	644,860	225,869	289,778	180,362	278,853	84,259	155,391	143,422	93,489	2,523,765
2002-03	43,047	49,671	194,020	204,564	369,838	481,730	432,055	169,064	170,951	213,679	149,780	86,830	2,565,229
2003-04	125,240	245,295	273,028	167,285	321,083	417,090	267,237	167,357	62,031	70,979	79,061	58,400	2,254,086
2004-05	135,568	46,749	91,390	263,999	369,597	402,504	445,448	424,472	210,285	93,471	95,154	20,398	2,599,035
2005-06	67,318	63,884	138,910	220,961	363,287	434,818	183,744	183,273	62,703	73,726	117,934	60,708	1,971,266
2006-07	87,527	58,849	111,619	112,634	214,384	174,852	140,273	125,562	207,478	310,748	168,730	137,204	1,849,860
2007-08	85,183	133,709	126,008	149,748	197,651	359,180	303,523	95,053	104,513	64,281	119,022	46,555	1,784,426
2008-09	79,487	75,191	89,246	92,960	113,117	149,362	106,701	175,099	265,718	92,969	66,390	77,746	1,383,986
2009-10	34,279	54,457	57,362	179,007	199,006	75,580	175,053	69,900	34,523	9,790	13,412	1,732	904,101
2010-11	1,431	5,498	69,122	126,009	153,780	130,932	59,520						936,501

[1] Seven markets.   *Source: Agricultural Marketing Service, U.S. Department of Agriculture (AMS-USDA)*

Production of Cotton (Upland and American-Pima) in the United States   In Thousands of 480-Pound Bales

	-- Upland --												Total American-Pima
Year	Alabama	Arizona	Arkansas	California	Georgia	Louisiana	sippi	Missouri	Carolina	Carolina	nessee	Texas	
2001	920	690	1,833	1,770	2,220	1,034	2,396	695	1,673	423	978	4,260	700.4
2002	570	613	1,669	1,460	1,578	739	1,935	610	806	131	818	5,040	678.3
2003	820	550	1,804	1,495	2,110	1,027	2,120	700	1,037	326	890	4,330	432.3
2004	814	723	2,089	1,790	1,797	885	2,346	830	1,360	390	984	7,740	745.6
2005	848	622	2,202	1,623	2,140	1,098	2,147	864	1,437	410	1,122	8,484	630.5
2006	675	556	2,525	779	2,334	1,241	2,107	985	1,285	433	1,368	5,800	765.4
2007	416	514	1,896	650	1,660	699	1,318	764	783	160	600	8,250	851.8
2008	469	405	1,296	367	1,600	281	683	698	755	246	530	4,450	430.8
2009[1]	345	443	852	240	1,860	349	415	502	763	207	492	4,620	399.9
2010[2]	490	600	1,200	380	2,150	450	850	700	970	365	695	8,050	497.8

[1] Preliminary.   [2] Forecast.   *Source: Agricultural Statistics Board, U.S. Department of Agriculture (ASB-USDA)*

Cotton Production and Yield Estimates

	-------- Forecasts of Production (1,000 Bales of 480 Lbs.[1]) --------						Actual Crop	---- Forecasts of Yield (Lbs. Per Harvested Acre) ----						Actual Yield
Year	Aug.1	Sept.1	Oct. 1	Nov. 1	Dec. 1	Jan. 1		Aug.1	Sept.1	Oct. 1	Nov. 1	Dec. 1	Jan. 1	
2001	20,003	19,992	20,072	20,175	20,064	----	20,303	670	679	681	685	691	----	705
2002	18,439	18,134	18,070	17,815	17,375	----	17,209	675	675	674	665	648	----	665
2003	17,104	16,939	17,559	18,215	18,215	----	18,255	667	667	696	722	722	----	730
2004	20,183	20,895	21,545	22,545	22,815	----	23,251	727	758	782	818	828	----	855
2005	21,291	22,282	22,717	23,161	23,703	----	23,890	748	782	797	813	832	----	831
2006	20,431	20,345	20,659	21,299	21,297	----	21,588	765	762	774	798	798	----	814
2007	17,346	17,812	18,154	18,862	18,987	----	19,207	783	811	826	859	864	----	879
2008	13,767	13,846	13,711	13,528	13,613	----	12,815	842	849	849	837	843	----	813
2009	13,207	13,438	12,998	12,496	12,592	----	12,188	816	816	807	776	782	----	777
2010	18,534	18,841	18,873	18,418	18,268	----	18,315	837	839	841	821	814	----	821

[1] Net weight bales.   *Source: Agricultural Statistics Board, U.S. Department of Agriculture (ASB-USDA)*

Supply and Distribution of Upland Cotton in the United States   In Thousands of 480-Pound Bales

Crop Year Beginning Aug. 1	-------------- Area --------------			-------------------- Supply --------------------				-------------- Disappearance --------------				Farm Price[5] Cents/ Lb.
	Planted	Harvested	Yield	Beginning	Pro-		Total	Mill			Ending	
	----- 1,000 Acres -----		Lbs./Acre	Stocks[3]	duction	Imports	Supply	Use	Exports	Total	Stocks	
2001-02	15,499	13,560	694	5,879	19,603	6	25,488	7,592	10,603	18,195	7,120	29.8
2002-03	13,714	12,174	652	7,120	16,530	10	23,661	7,170	11,266	18,436	5,140	43.2
2003-04	13,301	11,826	723	5,140	17,823	4	22,967	6,204	13,239	19,443	3,384	59.6
2004-05	13,409	12,809	843	3,384	22,505	8	25,897	6,629	13,683	20,312	5,482	43.1
2005-06	13,975	13,534	825	5,482	23,260	9	28,751	5,820	17,115	22,935	5,991	47.3
2006-07	14,948	12,408	806	5,991	20,822	10	26,824	4,896	12,324	17,220	9,291	46.6
2007-08	10,535	10,201	864	9,291	18,355	6	27,652	4,548	12,801	17,349	9,895	59.8
2008-09	9,297	7,400	803	9,895	12,385	0	22,279	3,558	13,029	16,587	6,032	49.4
2009-10[1]	9,008	7,391	777	6,032	12,188	0	17,820	3,429	11,343	14,772	2,929	61.8
2010-11[2]	10,973	10,707	821	2,929	18,315	0	20,849	3,420	15,275	18,695	2,179	80.4

[1] Preliminary.   [2] Estimate.   [3] Excludes preseason ginnings (adjusted to 480-lb. bale net weight basis).   [4] Includes preseason ginnings.   [5] Marketing year average price.   *Source: Economic Research Service, U.S. Department of Agriculture (ERS-USDA)*

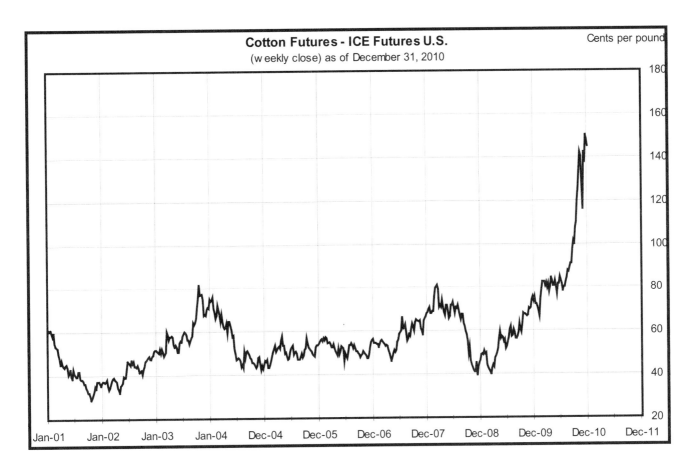

Cotton Futures - ICE Futures U.S.
(weekly close) as of December 31, 2010

Cents per pound

Average Open Interest of Cotton #2 Futures in New York   In Contracts

Year	Jan.	Feb.	Mar.	Apr.	May	June	July	Aug.	Sept.	Oct.	Nov.	Dec.
2001	71,849	73,383	71,389	70,407	66,680	64,032	61,183	65,257	65,496	59,777	56,896	58,156
2002	64,096	64,572	63,451	63,827	67,601	65,848	74,892	72,612	69,554	71,526	82,802	74,685
2003	83,775	89,852	91,336	78,658	73,146	69,137	62,565	62,781	80,348	108,981	97,809	79,627
2004	93,191	81,871	84,600	89,082	81,988	79,310	77,029	75,449	69,514	76,556	86,280	84,409
2005	92,651	94,047	118,183	120,416	103,446	93,818	92,284	99,959	105,874	117,889	103,466	100,660
2006	118,234	129,108	129,728	141,156	165,386	170,190	161,719	166,806	178,539	184,002	170,275	164,797
2007	177,495	199,342	214,628	225,473	223,839	212,296	214,893	206,042	215,820	239,217	229,629	219,185
2008	264,235	279,240	286,505	259,800	258,309	239,935	219,979	216,387	211,933	177,277	146,431	127,380
2009	130,049	120,331	128,054	128,973	134,079	120,861	122,153	127,019	136,585	165,683	180,594	182,489
2010	178,305	166,475	185,608	190,458	184,193	171,459	160,118	201,962	231,513	235,834	217,587	201,510

Contract size = 50,000 lbs.   *Source: ICE Futures U.S. (ICE)*

Volume of Trading of Cotton #2 Futures in New York   In Contracts

Year	Jan.	Feb.	Mar.	Apr.	May	June	July	Aug.	Sept.	Oct.	Nov.	Dec.	Total
2001	267,930	270,876	237,356	215,903	175,808	214,513	132,065	118,685	98,947	152,702	258,847	116,033	2,259,665
2002	156,834	248,299	162,781	237,861	188,340	234,442	170,893	128,185	145,946	199,779	296,859	157,741	2,327,960
2003	202,615	267,234	217,791	325,627	249,314	271,822	164,027	127,080	283,988	422,132	356,052	148,310	3,035,992
2004	272,948	359,105	300,820	376,669	184,869	357,548	159,924	195,886	196,739	224,431	341,709	185,370	3,156,018
2005	356,817	407,277	317,486	465,210	306,971	456,584	171,139	189,584	271,268	290,650	408,580	207,424	3,848,990
2006	311,926	495,729	375,624	515,709	330,785	601,971	184,482	259,259	268,847	308,584	587,710	249,781	4,490,407
2007	366,579	713,894	375,964	765,244	439,838	745,901	428,059	445,099	435,529	520,221	759,829	338,822	6,334,979
2008	684,489	971,319	730,160	651,281	427,731	690,183	281,522	306,004	418,279	401,064	426,785	174,146	6,162,963
2009	276,977	326,853	272,091	373,379	274,983	372,124	187,347	177,989	228,815	347,989	509,375	227,073	3,574,995
2010	321,331	570,117	344,389	567,774	365,998	550,206	327,296	331,579	440,411	600,977	887,594	425,234	5,732,906

Contract size = 50,000 lbs.   *Source: ICE Futures U.S. (ICE)*

COTTON

Daily Rate of Upland Cotton Mill Consumption[2] on Cotton-System Spinning Spindles in the United States
In Thousands of Running Bales

Crop Year Beginning Aug. 1	Aug.	Sept.	Oct.	Nov.	Dec.	Jan.	Feb.	Mar.	Apr.	May	June	July	Average
2001-02	28.8	28.1	27.5	26.3	27.1	27.1	27.5	27.9	27.4	28.4	29.3	30.6	28.0
2002-03	28.0	28.3	27.9	27.4	27.2	26.5	26.8	26.4	26.0	25.0	24.3	24.7	26.5
2003-04	23.0	22.7	22.6	23.0	22.7	22.4	23.1	23.1	22.8	23.1	23.2	24.2	23.0
2004-05	25.1	25.1	24.9	24.4	25.2	24.8	23.7	23.7	24.0	23.6	25.2	24.4	24.5
2005-06	23.2	22.0	22.6	21.2	20.5	22.9	23.1	22.4	20.7	20.2	19.9	19.5	21.5
2006-07	18.9	18.8	18.5	W	W	W	W	W	W	W	W	W	18.7
2007-08	W	W	W	W	W	16.7	17.0	16.0	17.2	16.6	16.9	16.4	16.7
2008-09	17.4	15.9	16.7	14.3	9.4	13.4	11.5	11.7	12.0	12.5	12.0	13.1	13.3
2009-10	13.1	10.8	13.3	13.3	10.7	13.3	12.9	12.5	13.1	13.7	13.5	13.5	12.8
2010-11[1]	14.3	14.0	15.1	13.7	11.9								13.8

[1] Preliminary.   [2] Not seasonally adjusted.   W = Withheld.   *Source: Bureau of the Census: U.S. Department of Commerce*

Consumption of American and Foreign Cotton in the United States   In Thousands of Running Bales

Year	Aug.	Sept.	Oct.	Nov.	Dec.	Jan.	Feb.	Mar.	Apr.	May	June	July	Total
2001-02	616	751	600	521	563	541	580	759	575	594	754	571	7,425
2002-03	574	733	585	545	598	671	556	708	541	523	616	456	7,106
2003-04	476	599	482	468	504	478	475	609	461	473	582	446	6,053
2004-05	484	604	483	460	500	470	472	601	469	463	581	449	6,035
2005-06	454	574	472	415	438	452	476	593	430	422	531	381	5,637
2006-07	385	492	389	357	370	361	363	461	371	371	476	348	4,744
2007-08	358	467	366	343	362	423	341	402	346	333	430	329	4,499
2008-09	349	399	333	285	234	261	230	302	230	251	311	254	3,439
2009-10	263	280	261	266	267	266	259	313	261	275	338	270	3,318
2010-11[1]	286	351	303	274	298								3,628

[1] Preliminary.   *Source: Bureau of the Census, U.S. Department of Commerce*

Exports of All Cotton[2] from the United States   In Thousands of Running Bales

Year	Aug.	Sept.	Oct.	Nov.	Dec.	Jan.	Feb.	Mar.	Apr.	May	June	July	Total
2001-02	612	824	678	649	927	964	1,042	1,225	999	842	1,067	679	10,505
2002-03	472	653	373	626	935	1,206	873	1,597	1,174	1,150	1,273	1,231	11,561
2003-04	810	555	446	758	1,116	1,194	1,238	1,869	1,453	1,117	1,576	1,021	13,154
2004-05	760	374	422	632	1,087	1,179	1,214	1,839	1,461	1,094	1,411	1,828	13,301
2005-06	1,407	742	533	763	1,236	946	1,541	2,195	1,758	1,725	1,906	1,903	16,655
2006-07	688	412	487	599	812	683	824	1,266	1,269	1,385	2,174	1,745	12,342
2007-08	1,116	1,337	883	977	781	981	945	955	1,096	1,360	1,292	1,427	13,150
2008-09	994	983	1,159	923	747	733	813	1,128	1,442	1,475	1,266	1,106	13,179
2009-10	885	809	664	570	778	944	1,173	1,447	1,177	1,362	1,344	1,371	12,523
2010-11[1]	1,020	471	449	1,146	1,699								11,482

[1] Preliminary.   *Source: Foreign Agricultural Service, U.S. Department of Agriculture (FAS-USDA)*

U.S. Exports of American Cotton to Countries of Destination   In Thousands of 480-Pound Bales

Crop Year Beginning Aug. 1	Canada	China	Hong Kong	Indo-nesia	Italy	Japan	Rep. of Korea	Mexico	Philip-pines	Taiwan	Thailand	United Kingdom	Total
2000-01	322	124	287	558	52	355	489	1,760	42	237	367	1	6,740
2001-02	235	306	407	947	58	385	577	1,516	126	693	693	0	10,397
2002-03	303	1,840	364	869	81	380	480	1,777	104	592	556	4	11,607
2003-04	303	4,919	169	889	63	284	469	1,620	100	527	396	20	13,758
2004-05	305	4,085	274	1,138	75	301	643	1,589	110	846	711	60	14,436
2005-06	178	9,095	280	933	33	265	431	1,511	46	530	660	23	18,039
2006-07	101	3,641	238	928	36	265	307	1,200	39	456	429	0	12,219
2007-08	40	4,491	177	1,261	62	376	361	1,432	26	838	390	0	13,972
2008-09[1]	19	3,770	184	1,057	23	158	302	1,320	52	615	436		13,179
2009-10[2]	9	3,888	69	657	21	150	352	1,490	51	607	424		12,523

[1] Preliminary.   [2] Estimate.   *Source: Foreign Agricultural Service, U.S. Department of Agriculture (FAS-USDA)*

Cotton[1] Government Loan Program in the United States

Crop Year Beginning Aug. 1	Support Price	Target Price	Put Under Support	% of Production	Acquired	Owned July 31	Crop Year Beginning Aug. 1	Support Price	Target Price	Put Under Support	% of Production	Acquired	Owned July 31
	--- Cents Per Lb. ---		Ths. Bales		----- Ths. Bales -----			--- Cents Per Lb. ---		Ths. Bales		----- Ths. Bales -----	
2001-02	51.92	NA	13,655	67.3	31	2	2006-07	52.00	72.4	17,839	82.6	79	29
2002-03	52.00	72.4	12,740	74.0	0	106	2007-08	52.00	72.4	14,636	76.2	169	14
2003-04	52.00	72.4	10,466	57.3	16	0	2008-09	52.00	71.3	10,005	78.1	4	13
2004-05	52.00	72.4	17,092	73.5	8	0	2009-10	52.00	71.3	8,233	67.6	0	6
2005-06	52.00	72.4	17,783	74.4	181	11	2010-11[2]	52.00	71.3				

[1] Upland.   [2] Preliminary.   NA = Not applicable.   *Source: Economic Research Service, U.S. Department of Agriculture (ERS-USDA)*

Production of Cotton Cloth[1] in the United States   In Millions of Square Yards

Year	First Quarter	Second Quarter	Third Quarter	Fourth Quarter	Total	Year	First Quarter	Second Quarter	Third Quarter	Fourth Quarter	Total
2001	1,047	976	873	811	3,706	2006	583	609	551	487	2,230
2002	893	912	894	825	3,524	2007	521	507	488	453	1,969
2003	836	780	662	620	2,898	2008	447	460	451	393	1,751
2004	648	644	640	614	2,547	2009	336	357	320	307	1,320
2005	672	640	653	664	2,629	2010[2]	327	321	340		1,316

[1] Cotton broadwoven goods over 12 inches in width.   [2] Preliminary.   *Source: Bureau of Census, U.S. Department of Commerce*

Cotton Ginnings[1] in the United States To: In Thousands of Running Bales

Crop Year	Aug. 1	Sept. 1	Sept. 15	Oct. 1	Oct. 15	Nov. 1	Nov. 15	Dec. 1	Dec. 15	Jan. 1	Jan. 15	Feb. 1	Total Crop
2001-02	99	609	802	2,072	4,616	8,806	12,558	15,564	17,606	18,759	19,268	19,532	19,771
2002-03	56	538	898	1,656	3,520	6,697	9,265	12,368	14,392	15,654	16,285	16,576	16,710
2003-04	29	567	958	2,001	3,819	7,393	10,507	13,466	15,678	16,883	17,409	17,601	17,709
2004-05	48	563	1,157	2,227	4,788	8,758	12,019	14,754	17,072	18,925	20,155	21,249	22,556
2005-06	69	592	976	2,314	4,556	8,691	12,569	15,991	18,401	20,108	21,282	22,255	23,253
2006-07	23	406	996	2,572	5,039	8,604	11,833	15,139	17,657	19,212	20,062	20,559	20,998
2007-08	W	182	375	1,566	3,793	7,072	10,099	12,593	14,341	15,700	16,690	17,585	18,713
2008-09	13	335	476	797	2,027	4,358	6,800	8,928	10,463	11,572	12,094	12,370	12,462
2009-10	5	110	175	234	552	2,189	4,957	7,873	9,728	10,812	11,383	11,706	11,826
2010-11[2]	W	287	747	2,289	4,710	7,972	10,585	13,196	15,132	16,447	17,143	17,529	

[1] Excluding linters.   [2] Preliminary.   W = Withheld.   *Source: National Agricultural Statistics Service, U.S. Department of Agriculture (NASS-USDA)*

Fiber Prices in the United States   In Cents Per Pound

Year	Cotton[1] Actual	Cotton[1] Raw[5] Equivalent	Rayon[2] Actual	Rayon[2] Raw[5] Equivalent	Polyester[3] Actual	Polyester[3] Raw[5] Equivalent	Price Ratios[4] In Percent Cotton/ Rayon	Price Ratios[4] In Percent Cotton/ Polyester
2000	64.06	71.17	97.58	101.65	57.08	59.46	70.0	119.1
2001	47.08	52.32	98.50	102.61	60.42	62.93	52.0	83.0
2002	45.56	50.63	97.83	101.91	61.17	63.72	50.0	79.0
2003	62.54	69.49	90.25	94.01	60.67	63.20	74.1	111.0
2004	60.42	67.13	99.08	103.21	62.67	65.28	66.5	103.5
2005	54.75	60.00	114.58	119.36	67.75	70.57	51.0	86.2
2006	56.70	63.00	113.00	117.71	69.00	71.86	53.5	88.0
2007	61.97	68.86	113.00	117.71	74.00	77.08	58.5	89.3
2008[6]	73.79	82.01	113.00	117.71	74.00	77.08	69.7	121.1
Jan.	73.32	81.47	113.00	117.71	74.00	77.08	69.2	120.3
Feb.	74.25	82.54	113.00	117.71	74.00	77.08	70.1	121.8
Mar.	NA	NA	NA	NA	NA	NA	NA	NA
Apr.	NA	NA	NA	NA	NA	NA	NA	NA
May	NA	NA	NA	NA	NA	NA	NA	NA
June	NA	NA	NA	NA	NA	NA	NA	NA
July	NA	NA	NA	NA	NA	NA	NA	NA
Aug.	NA	NA	NA	NA	NA	NA	NA	NA
Sept.	NA	NA	NA	NA	NA	NA	NA	NA
Oct.	NA	NA	NA	NA	NA	NA	NA	NA
Nov.	NA	NA	NA	NA	NA	NA	NA	NA
Dec.								

[1] SLM-1 1/16" at group B Mill points, net weight.   [2] 1.5 and 3.0 denier, regular rayon staples.   [3] Reported average market price for 1.5 denier polyester staple for cotton blending.   [4] Raw fiber equivalent.   [5] Actual prices converted to estimated raw fiber equivalent as follows: cotton, divided by 0.90, rayon and polyester, divided by 0.96.   [6] Preliminary.
Source: Economic Research Service, U.S. Department of Agriculture (ERS-USDA)

Cottonseed and Products

Cottonseed is crushed to produce both oil and meal. Cottonseed oil is typically used for cooking oil and cottonseed meal is fed to livestock. Before the cottonseed is crushed for oil and meal, it is de-linted of its linters. Linters are used for padding in furniture, absorbent cotton swabs, and for the manufacture of many cellulose products. The sediment left by cottonseed oil refining, called foots, provides fatty acids for industrial products. The value of cottonseeds represents a substantial 18% of a cotton producer's income.

Prices – The average monthly price of cottonseed oil in 2010 rose by +14.6% yr/yr to 55.92 cents per pound, below the 2008 record high of 68.09 cents per pound. The average monthly price of cottonseed meal in 2010 fell by -19.1% yr/yr to $245.63 per short ton, below the 2008 record high of $265.22 per short ton.

Supply – World production of cottonseed in the 2009-10 marketing year fell –4.9% yr/yr to 39.147 million metric tons, down from the record high of 45.136 million metric tons posted in 2004-05. The world's largest cottonseed producers are China with 29.1% of world production, India with 25.5%, the U.S. with 9.6%, and Pakistan with 10.8%. U.S. production of cottonseed in the 2010-11 marketing year rose by +49.2% yr/yr to 6.191 million tons. U.S. production of cottonseed oil in 2010-11 rose by +29.7% yr/yr to 800 million pounds, below the 12-year high of 957 million pounds posted in 2004-05. U.S. annualized production of cottonseed cake and meal for the first five months of the 2010-11 marketing year (Aug-Jul) rose by 25.7% yr/yr to 1.046 million short tons.

Demand – U.S. cottonseed crushed (consumed) in the U.S. annualized for the first five months of the 2010-11 marketing year rose by +21.8% to 2.315 million tons, far below the levels of over 4 million tons seen in the 1970s.

Trade – U.S. exports of cottonseed in 2010-11 rose +20.3% to 350,000 short tons, while imports were zero.

World Production of Cottonseed   In Thousands of Metric Ton

Crop Year Beginning Oct. 1	Argentina	Australia	Brazil	China	Egypt	Greece	India	Mexico	Pakistan	Turkey	United States	Former USSR	World Total
2001-02	102	1,054	1,407	9,476	527	743	5,372	152	3,610	1,354	6,761	2,749	37,365
2002-03	90	470	1,451	8,750	475	718	4,624	68	3,472	1,457	5,610	2,584	33,641
2003-04	159	494	2,390	8,651	338	611	6,018	115	3,416	1,337	6,046	2,442	36,131
2004-05	247	912	2,309	11,257	487	645	8,250	212	4,853	1,402	7,437	2,938	45,226
2005-06	230	770	1,816	10,171	399	677	8,200	221	4,428	1,280	7,414	3,165	42,949
2006-07	300	330	2,498	13,409	372	520	9,300	249	4,294	1,456	6,666	3,100	46,029
2007-08	271	180	2,422	13,571	389	500	10,400	209	3,695	1,297	5,977	3,158	45,719
2008-09[1]	214	466	1,794	13,330	185	420	9,800	201	3,840	1,037	3,901	3,070	41,178
2009-10[2]	340	528	1,832	11,390	175	343	10,000	151	4,220	950	3,764	2,723	39,147

[1] Preliminary.   [2] Estimate.   *Source: The Oil World*

Salient Statistics of Cottonseed in the United States   In Thousands of Short Tons

Crop Year Beginning Aug. 1	Supply			Disappearance				Farm Price USD/Ton	Value of Production Mil. USD	Products Produced	
	Stocks	Production	Total Supply	Crush	Exports	Other	Total				Total
2002-03	400	6,184	6,687	2,495	370	3,477	6,341	101	616.4	725	1,115
2003-04	347	6,665	7,013	2,643	354	3,595	6,592	117	779.0	874	1,244
2004-05	421	8,242	8,664	2,923	379	4,770	8,072	107	872.8	957	1,362
2005-06	592	8,172	8,764	3,010	523	4,630	8,163	96	779.5	951	1,372
2006-07	602	7,348	7,950	2,680	616	4,165	7,461	111	814.2	849	1,241
2007-08	489	6,589	7,080	2,706	599	3,132	6,437	162	1,069.8	856	1,262
2008-09	643	4,300	4,943	2,240	190	1,999	4,429	230	962.7	669	934
2009-10[1]	514	4,149	4,687	1,900	291	2,154	4,345	200-260	670.0	617	895
2010-11[2]	342	6,191	6,533	2,500	350	3,240	6,090		1,003.9		

[1] Preliminary.   [2] Estimate.   *Source: Economic Research Service, U.S. Department of Agriculture (ERS-USDA)*

Average Wholesale Price of Cottonseed Meal (41% Solvent)[2] in Memphis   In Dollars Per Short Ton

Year	Jan.	Feb.	Mar.	Apr.	May	June	July	Aug.	Sept.	Oct.	Nov.	Dec.	Average
2002	133.13	125.00	131.88	124.30	120.88	137.50	151.50	159.75	156.38	150.10	150.00	156.00	141.37
2003	157.38	143.60	142.40	142.40	131.75	131.50	143.00	151.70	153.20	163.50	182.50	185.00	152.33
2004	188.00	193.00	205.10	219.67	203.00	185.40	177.50	156.20	142.75	126.75	119.00	117.00	169.45
2005	112.50	111.25	110.80	108.00	110.40	138.75	151.00	143.00	140.00	133.13	132.50	175.00	130.53
2006	172.50	152.50	148.75	144.38	131.50	135.00	132.50	134.50	139.00	132.40	131.88	152.50	142.28
2007	161.00	174.75	185.50	148.25	137.00	131.25	137.50	144.75	167.50	183.40	176.25	196.67	161.99
2008	273.60	292.00	245.00	230.00	240.50	293.25	333.00	290.00	292.00	238.75	225.00	229.50	265.22
2009	237.50	236.25	213.00	212.50	236.25	306.00	305.00	315.00	308.00	250.00	260.00	283.75	263.60
2010[1]	286.25	253.75	213.00	175.00	171.25	176.00	183.75	198.00	200.00	225.31	235.00	240.63	213.16

[1] Preliminary.   *Source: Economic Research Service, U.S. Department of Agriculture (ERS-USDA)*

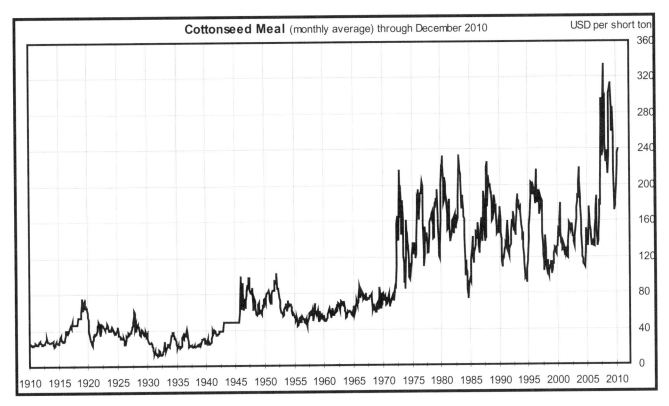

Cottonseed Meal (monthly average) through December 2010   USD per short ton

Supply and Distribution of Cottonseed Oil in the United States   In Millions of Pounds

Crop Year Beginning Oct. 1	Stocks	Pro-duction	Imports	Total Supply	Domestic	Exports	Total	Per Capita Consumption of Salad & Cooking Oils --- In Lbs. ---	Short-ening	Salad & Cooking Oils	Total	U.S.[3] (Crude) --- $/Metric Ton ---	Rott[4] (Cif)
2004-05	109	957	2.0	1,068	935	57	991	40	166	304	470	617	649
2005-06	76	951	1.0	1,028	860	67	927	43	213	389	602	649	669
2006-07	101	849	1.0	951	714	138	852	45	162	547	709	787	804
2007-08	99	856	0	956	623	186	809	50	166	567	733	1,622	1,648
2008-09	147	669	0	815	502	192	694	54	W	638	638	820	822
2009-10[1]	121	617	0	738	559	95	654	48	W	509	509	888	
2010-11[2]	85	800	0	885	675	125	800						

Span headers: ------------------ Supply ------------------ ------- Disappearance ------- / Utilization -------- Food Uses ---------- / ------ Prices ------

[1] Preliminary.   [2] Estimate.   [3] Valley Points FOB; Tank Cars.   [4] Rotterdam; US, PBSY, fob gulf.   W = Withheld.
Source: Economic Research Service, U.S. Department of Agriculture (ERS-USDA)

Consumption of Crude Cottonseed Oil, in Refining[2], in the United States   In Millions of Pound

Year	Oct.	Nov.	Dec.	Jan.	Feb.	Mar.	Apr.	May	June	July	Aug.	Sept.	Total
2004-05	60.0	66.4	67.0	73.7	69.2	66.8	72.6	52.9	64.7	57.0	71.8	55.2	777.1
2005-06	72.7	79.0	75.1	70.9	64.0	71.1	58.2	71.6	61.2	52.6	61.4	52.4	790.2
2006-07	65.7	55.7	61.4	63.9	55.3	63.7	60.1	63.6	54.1	56.3	56.5	55.6	711.9
2007-08	59.6	60.9	61.7	74.0	70.2	68.0	70.9	62.2	52.3	55.3	57.1	52.8	744.8
2008-09	47.2	56.4	63.5	58.3	58.4	57.5	44.0	48.1	50.6	36.9	39.3	37.5	597.6
2009-10	32.6	46.2	51.6	45.0	41.4	43.9	38.5	42.7	39.5	W	45.6	47.4	517.6
2010-11[1]	38.7	60.1	59.0										631.6

[1] Preliminary.   *Source: U.S. Bureau of Census, U.S. Department of Commerce*

Exports of Cottonseed Oil (Crude and Refined) from the United States   In Thousands of Pounds

Year	Jan.	Feb.	Mar.	Apr.	May	June	July	Aug.	Sept.	Oct.	Nov.	Dec.	Total
2004	14,203	8,982	8,321	10,399	9,632	10,720	7,931	9,891	4,617	5,669	7,619	7,507	105,492
2005	3,490	3,161	5,191	3,461	5,873	3,029	3,147	3,763	4,823	3,847	2,926	4,676	47,387
2006	5,084	5,724	5,410	7,738	5,519	6,640	7,539	6,608	5,755	8,827	9,377	14,365	88,586
2007	7,461	17,932	9,732	14,573	10,676	10,647	11,768	10,404	12,055	12,697	17,137	11,420	146,503
2008	11,089	21,546	25,577	11,565	12,436	17,019	17,441	11,300	17,263	22,083	20,819	18,611	206,747
2009	14,423	20,981	15,258	19,313	12,296	14,087	12,070	10,915	11,370	8,506	14,923	8,455	162,597
2010	6,880	9,414	7,075	6,728	6,494	4,399	3,553	5,523	12,740	20,331	16,878	7,038	107,052

[1] Preliminary.   *Source: Economic Research Service, U.S. Department of Agriculture (ERS-USDA)*

COTTONSEED AND PRODUCTS

Cottonseed Crushed (Consumption) in the United States   In Thousands of Short Tons

Year	Aug.	Sept.	Oct.	Nov.	Dec.	Jan.	Feb.	Mar.	Apr.	May	June	July	Total
2002-03	195.1	131.4	207.8	242.5	236.6	274.5	224.5	230.4	241.5	203.6	179.4	127.4	2,495
2003-04	138.7	98.9	251.6	254.8	252.0	265.2	242.3	278.0	217.1	240.2	217.7	182.4	2,639
2004-05	193.8	141.0	247.9	260.3	263.5	283.1	266.3	270.2	287.7	221.0	266.6	221.6	2,923
2005-06	240.7	170.3	272.2	289.4	296.9	291.3	245.0	276.7	235.0	280.3	227.2	203.4	3,028
2006-07	204.8	158.2	252.4	223.3	236.7	251.2	222.5	249.1	230.8	243.2	204.6	203.3	2,680
2007-08	173.4	163.8	242.5	241.2	252.1	267.5	264.1	236.3	245.2	233.4	190.3	193.1	2,703
2008-09	202.3	147.4	175.2	206.5	230.0	234.3	217.6	206.5	170.7	168.1	158.1	133.2	2,250
2009-10	107.1	92.8	131.2	169.2	189.7	202.4	184.6	187.0	180.0	191.3	141.2	124.0	1,900
2010-11[1]	151.0	143.9	172.8	245.7	251.3	245.5							2,421

[1] Preliminary.   Source: Economic Research Service, U.S. Department of Agriculture (ERS-USDA)

Production of Cottonseed Cake and Meal in the United States   In Thousands of Short Tons

Year	Aug.	Sept.	Oct.	Nov.	Dec.	Jan.	Feb.	Mar.	Apr.	May	June	July	Total
2002-03	92.4	79.3	95.5	112.6	108.0	123.0	100.3	96.7	108.9	89.8	81.4	63.0	1,151
2003-04	74.9	59.5	112.3	111.0	112.5	113.9	105.1	123.4	94.2	104.7	97.7	91.0	1,200
2004-05	95.3	82.5	105.4	110.4	118.7	125.7	119.3	120.4	124.4	103.6	121.0	106.2	1,333
2005-06	116.4	91.1	109.6	134.6	129.3	128.8	108.2	119.4	104.5	129.3	107.2	99.0	1,377
2006-07	102.0	83.0	118.8	101.8	102.4	115.3	101.8	114.6	105.9	112.6	97.4	102.3	1,258
2007-08	81.3	87.3	112.5	111.0	111.9	125.6	119.9	116.3	110.4	103.2	86.8	90.7	1,257
2008-09	96.5	76.9	74.8	89.7	103.5	102.7	99.2	90.8	76.6	73.0	75.6	60.7	1,020
2009-10	46.9	40.8	60.9	73.4	82.1	92.2	81.0	78.6	76.8	87.2	59.9	53.0	833
2010-11[1]	63.2	74.9	82.2	103.8	112.0	105.5							1,083

[1] Preliminary.   Source: Bureau of Census, U.S. Department of Commerce

Production of Crude Cottonseed Oil[2] in the United States   In Millions of Pounds

Year	Aug.	Sept.	Oct.	Nov.	Dec.	Jan.	Feb.	Mar.	Apr.	May	June	July	Total
2002-03	60.2	53.7	62.8	72.1	67.9	80.8	65.6	66.7	71.0	59.9	52.8	39.9	753
2003-04	45.0	40.7	77.5	78.2	79.0	82.4	75.7	87.2	67.0	73.8	66.7	59.7	833
2004-05	68.6	58.1	77.1	82.2	81.4	88.7	83.4	84.3	90.7	71.3	81.6	69.5	937
2005-06	84.3	62.0	86.9	95.7	90.9	92.8	77.2	87.8	70.9	90.4	70.4	68.1	977
2006-07	68.4	59.2	77.1	71.7	73.9	78.6	67.1	78.1	72.5	77.2	65.2	66.7	856
2007-08	58.2	62.5	77.5	73.8	76.8	83.5	82.1	77.1	77.1	70.3	58.5	60.3	858
2008-09	64.4	55.0	49.4	64.4	71.2	70.4	68.4	65.9	53.5	57.2	58.7	60.3	718
2009-10	34.5	35.5	38.3	54.1	59.1	59.8	55.9	60.0	51.5	59.8	41.1	36.6	586
2010-11[1]	48.0	52.9	54.3	79.1	79.8	78.0							784

[1] Preliminary.   [2] Not seasonally adjusted.   Source: Bureau of Census, U.S. Department of Commerce

Production of Refined Cottonseed Oil in the United States   In Millions of Pounds

Year	Aug.	Sept.	Oct.	Nov.	Dec.	Jan.	Feb.	Mar.	Apr.	May	June	July	Total
2002-03	52.7	47.1	48.3	59.2	55.7	66.5	55.6	56.8	58.9	49.4	42.4	31.7	624
2003-04	38.5	34.6	59.8	63.5	61.4	64.3	58.4	68.3	55.1	55.1	52.4	43.8	655
2004-05	53.4	52.0	59.7	66.1	66.9	73.4	68.8	66.6	72.3	52.7	64.6	56.6	753
2005-06	71.2	54.7	72.8	78.5	74.7	70.3	63.8	70.8	57.8	71.2	60.8	52.3	799
2006-07	61.0	52.0	65.2	55.3	61.1	63.5	55.3	62.9	58.9	63.5	54.0	56.1	709
2007-08	56.4	55.5	59.6	60.9	61.6	73.8	70.0	67.8	70.5	62.1	52.3	55.2	746
2008-09	56.9	52.6	46.9	56.3	63.2	57.9	58.1	57.2	43.7	47.9	50.3	36.7	628
2009-10	39.2	37.5	32.6	46.2	51.6	44.9	41.4	43.9	38.5	42.7	39.5	W	500
2010-11[1]	45.6	47.3	38.7	60.1	59.0								602

[1] Preliminary.   Source: Bureau of the Census, U.S. Department of Commerce

Stocks of Cottonseed Oil (Crude and Refined) in the U.S., at End of Month   In Millions of Pounds

Year	Aug.	Sept.	Oct.	Nov.	Dec.	Jan.	Feb.	Mar.	Apr.	May	June	July
2002-03	46.1	39.7	32.8	40.2	38.0	46.1	58.8	72.2	83.3	84.2	91.4	64.0
2003-04	50.5	36.0	51.9	56.1	68.7	85.9	100.6	117.6	116.8	125.7	121.0	123.0
2004-05	123.3	109.0	106.6	110.6	111.3	116.6	122.0	112.9	121.2	111.5	90.0	86.2
2005-06	90.6	76.4	69.0	76.1	74.0	84.0	99.0	108.5	103.3	110.8	105.8	95.6
2006-07	98.9	101.1	93.2	92.3	106.8	119.2	117.0	112.2	124.5	126.1	119.5	160.2
2007-08	132.9	105.8	92.8	91.6	94.9	114.3	138.4	143.5	156.1	161.4	158.7	143.1
2008-09	153.8	146.6	139.7	124.7	120.0	126.7	134.1	149.4	151.4	160.9	144.7	150.3
2009-10	141.0	120.6	98.1	85.4	114.2	112.2	122.7	130.4	126.6	128.8	121.2	97.5
2010-11[1]	78.6	84.9	72.1	78.0	103.4							

[1] Preliminary.   Source: Bureau of the Census, U.S. Department of Commerce

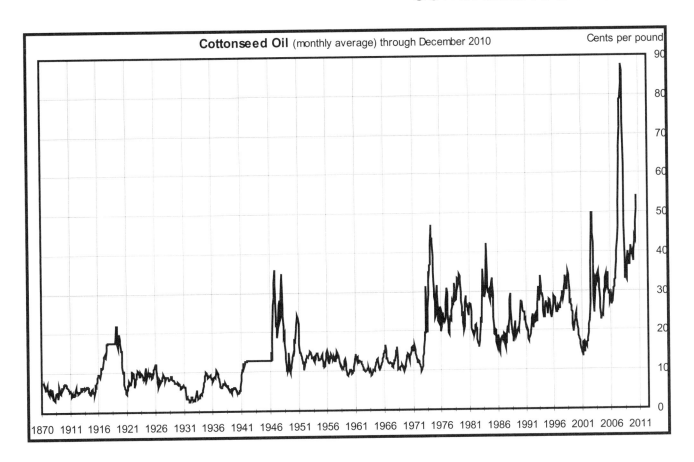

Cottonseed Oil (monthly average) through December 2010

Cents per pound

Source: Economic Research Service, U.S. Department of Agriculture (ERS-USDA)

Average Price of Crude Cottonseed Oil, PBSY, Greenwood, MS.[1] in Tank Cars   In Cents Per Pound

Year	Jan.	Feb.	Mar.	Apr.	May	June	July	Aug.	Sept.	Oct.	Nov.	Dec.	Average
2001	16.24	15.20	15.53	14.03	14.53	13.27	16.78	17.18	15.78	14.44	15.91	16.07	15.41
2002	16.38	15.89	16.77	16.98	17.95	19.48	21.30	22.32	22.32	26.84	36.90	46.89	23.34
2003	49.82	49.90	47.52	44.57	42.33	28.69	24.38	25.51	29.64	32.93	32.24	33.26	36.73
2004	32.76	34.21	34.91	34.47	32.57	30.72	27.83	25.29	23.29	22.74	23.88	23.81	28.87
2005	23.70	24.38	28.19	29.80	30.63	33.13	34.15	30.44	31.25	34.44	34.09	30.50	30.39
2006	29.63	29.50	29.75	27.05	28.06	27.25	29.20	26.69	27.13	27.44	30.25	30.75	28.56
2007	31.00	32.69	33.00	34.38	37.75	40.00	42.44	42.15	46.56	52.20	63.60	66.63	43.53
2008	71.69	78.60	78.94	79.75	82.75	87.56	86.06	72.55	62.44	46.45	37.38	32.88	68.09
2009	35.70	33.19	32.63	37.38	39.90	38.75	36.55	39.13	36.44	37.90	40.69	41.40	37.47
2010	39.00	39.13	39.88	38.75	37.38	40.00	42.45	43.69	43.00	47.20	50.75	54.00	42.94

Source: Economic Research Service, U.S. Department of Agriculture (ERS-USDA)

Exports of Cottonseed Oil to Important Countries from the United States   In Thousands of Metric Tons

Year	Canada	Dominican Republic	Egypt	Guate-mala	Japan	Mexico	Nether-lands	El Salvador	Rep. of Korea	Turkey	Venez-uela	Total
2001	26.0	.0	0	.5	6.5	8.6	3.1	4.8	2.5	0	0	64.6
2002	36.4	0	3.0	0	5.4	6.9	0	1.8	4.7	.3	0	63.2
2003	33.6	0	0	0	3.5	7.2	0	.0	.7	0	0	46.2
2004	26.5	0	0	0	11.6	8.6	0	0	.0	0	0	47.9
2005	12.7	0	0	0	1.0	6.5	0	0	.1	0	0	21.5
2006	10.0	.0	0	.0	1.3	11.2	0	0	14.1	0	.1	40.2
2007	24.0	.1	0	0	7.1	11.6	0	0	17.3	0	.0	66.5
2008	40.8	.1	0	0	9.0	22.3	0	0	14.5	0	0	93.8
2009	37.0	0	0	0	2.6	18.1	.1	.2	8.7	0	0	73.8
2010[1]	17.6	0	0	0	1.5	26.0	0	0	.9	0	0	48.6

[1] Preliminary.   *Source: Foreign Agricultural Service, U.S. Department of Agriculture (FAS-USDA)*

Continuous Commodity Index (CCI)

The Continuous Commodity Index (CCI) was first calculated by Commodity Research Bureau, Inc. in 1957 and made its inaugural appearance in the 1958 CRB Commodity Year Book.

The Index originally consisted of two cash markets and 26 futures markets which were traded on exchanges in the U.S. and Canada. It included barley and flaxseed from the Winnipeg exchange; cocoa, coffee "B", copper, cotton, cottonseed oil, grease wool, hides, lead, potatoes, rubber, sugar #4, sugar #6, wool tops and zinc from New York exchanges; and corn, oats, wheat, rye, soybeans, soybean oil, soybean meal, lard, onions, and eggs from Chicago exchanges. In addition to those 26, the Index also included the spot New Orleans cotton and Minneapolis wheat markets.

Like the Bureau of Labor Statistics spot index, the CCI is calculated to produce an unweighted geometric mean of the individual commodity price relatives. In other words, a ratio of the current price to the base year average price. Currently, 1967 is the base year the Index is calculated against (1967=100).

The formula considers all future delivery contracts that expire on or before the end of the sixth calendar month from the current date, using up to a maximum of five contracts per commodity. However, a minimum of two contracts must be used to calculate the current price, even if the second contract is outside the six-month window. Contracts are excluded when in their delivery period.

The 2010 closing value of 629.53 was 29.96 percent higher than the 2009 close of 484.42. 15 of the 17 component commodities finished higher for the year.

Futures and options on the CCI are traded on the ICE Futures U.S. (ICE) exchange.

Continuous Commodity Index (CCI) Component Commodities by Group

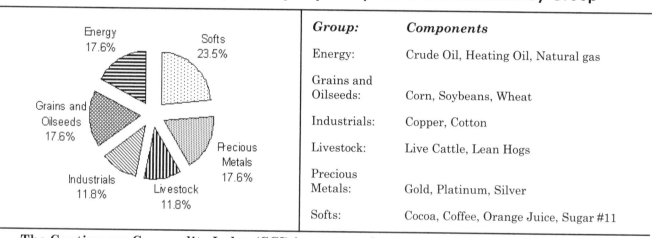

Group:	Components
Energy:	Crude Oil, Heating Oil, Natural gas
Grains and Oilseeds:	Corn, Soybeans, Wheat
Industrials:	Copper, Cotton
Livestock:	Live Cattle, Lean Hogs
Precious Metals:	Gold, Platinum, Silver
Softs:	Cocoa, Coffee, Orange Juice, Sugar #11

The Continuous Commodity Index (CCI) is computed using a three-step process:

1) Each of the Index's 17 component commodities is arithmetically averaged using the prices for all of the designated contract months which expire on or before the end of the sixth calendar month from the current date, except that: a) no contract shall be included in the calculation while in delivery; b) there shall be a minimum of two contract months for each component commodity (adding contracts beyond the six month window if necessary); c) there shall be a maximum of five contract months for each commodity (dropping the most deferred contracts to remain at five, if necessary). The result is that the Index extends six to seven months into the future depending on where one is in the current month. For example, live cattle's average price on October 30, 1995 would be computed as follows:

$$\text{Cattle Average} = \frac{\text{Dec. '96} + \text{Feb. '97}}{2}$$

2) These 17 component averages are then geometrically averaged by multiplying all of the numbers together and taking the 17th root.

$$\text{Geometric Average} = \sqrt[17]{\text{Crude Avg.} * \text{Heating Oil Avg.} * \text{Sugar Avg.} \ldots}$$

3) The resulting average is divided by 30.7766, the 1967 base-year average for these 17 commodities. That result is then multiplied by an adjustment factor of .8486. This adjustment factor is necessitated by the nine revisions to the Index since its inception in 1957. Finally, that result is multiplied by 100 in order to convert the Index into percentage terms:

$$\text{CCI} = \frac{\text{Current Geometric Average}}{\text{1967 Geometric Avg. (30.7766)} * .8486 * 100}$$

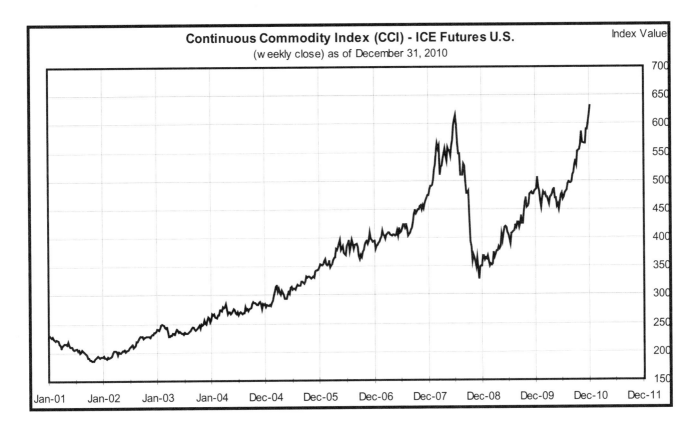

Continuous Commodity Index (CCI) - ICE Futures U.S.
(weekly close) as of December 31, 2010

Average Open Interest of Continuous Commodity Index (CCI) in New York   In Contracts

Year	Jan.	Feb.	Mar.	Apr.	May	June	July	Aug.	Sept.	Oct.	Nov.	Dec.
2001	1,280	1,063	1,032	1,036	969	1,006	1,058	1,048	993	559	354	404
2002	422	514	458	384	400	412	489	399	583	646	684	710
2003	748	877	835	849	939	905	858	917	1,078	1,029	1,013	760
2004	838	870	942	704	357	305	413	412	539	600	581	604
2005	540	561	710	663	644	683	861	1,023	1,016	1,024	1,016	1,035
2006	1,045	1,025	998	1,061	1,045	964	939	919	935	948	955	959
2007	927	914	995	1,251	1,526	1,500	1,409	1,560	1,416	1,603	1,864	1,484
2008	1,349	1,355	1,241	1,159	1,168	1,226	1,329	1,302	1,435	1,677	1,541	1,392
2009	1,540	1,449	1,551	1,634	1,411	1,288	1,247	1,283	1,251	1,422	1,319	1,324
2010	1,306	1,422	1,553	1,550	1,528	1,528	1,465	1,185	1,197	1,204	1,211	867

Contract size = $500.   *Source: ICE Futures U.S. (ICE)*

Volume of Trading of Continuous Commodity Index (CCI) in New York   In Contracts

Year	Jan.	Feb.	Mar.	Apr.	May	June	July	Aug.	Sept.	Oct.	Nov.	Dec.	Total
2001	2,428	1,823	1,310	2,062	930	1,965	880	2,021	625	1,263	843	728	16,878
2002	1,251	1,231	896	1,472	785	1,191	1,217	915	1,100	1,654	1,430	1,141	14,283
2003	2,289	2,154	1,826	1,634	1,514	2,106	1,632	1,350	1,712	2,123	2,502	2,314	23,156
2004	2,477	1,695	3,169	2,672	1,209	1,618	792	1,341	759	813	1,630	979	19,154
2005	1,154	861	2,023	1,891	1,027	2,105	1,623	1,931	605	707	1,258	882	16,067
2006	2,231	1,114	1,017	1,836	1,563	1,323	927	1,020	892	461	1,220	708	14,312
2007	1,156	249	1,698	1,648	885	3,164	1,716	927	802	1,837	5,615	276	19,973
2008	1,888	1,454	2,139	2,186	745	1,758	2,162	1,311	1,408	499	2,692	943	19,185
2009	2,525	124	724	3,213	1,047	2,560	697	938	74	2,856	778	437	15,973
2010	453	1,778	958	143	860	49	1,409	252	68	62	1,277	2,191	9,500

Contract size = $500.   *Source: ICE Futures U.S. (ICE)*

Currencies

A currency rate involves the price of the base currency (e.g., the dollar) quoted in terms of another currency (e.g., the yen), or in terms of a basket of currencies (e.g., the dollar index). The world's major currencies have traded in a floating-rate exchange rate regime ever since the Bretton-Woods international payments system broke down in 1971 when President Nixon broke the dollar's peg to gold. The two key factors affecting a currency's value are central bank monetary policy and the trade balance. An easy monetary policy (low interest rates) is bearish for a currency because the central bank is aggressively pumping new currency reserves into the marketplace and because foreign investors are not attracted to the low interest rate returns available in the country. By contrast, a tight monetary policy (high interest rates) is bullish for a currency because of the tight supply of new currency reserves and attractive interest rate returns for foreign investors.

The other key factor driving currency values is the nation's current account balance. A current account *surplus* is bullish for a currency due to the net inflow of the currency, while a current account *deficit* is bearish for a currency due to the net outflow of the currency. Currency values are also affected by economic growth and investment opportunities in the country. A country with a strong economy and lucrative investment opportunities will typically have a strong currency because global companies and investors want to buy into that country's investment opportunities. Futures on major currencies and on cross-currency rates are traded primarily at the Chicago Mercantile Exchange.

Dollar – The dollar index rallied in the first half of 2010 mainly because of the European debt crisis, which caused safe-haven demand for the dollar and caused weakness in the euro due to concern that the Eurozone might break apart. The European debt crisis emerged when it became obvious that Greece and other Eurozone countries such as Ireland had amassed such large fiscal deficits that they were on the cusp of defaulting on their sovereign debt. This raised the possibility that such countries could be forced to drop out of the Eurozone or that the euro might break apart altogether if Germany refused to foot the bill for a bailout. However, Germany, France and the other stronger members of the Eurozone were able to cobble together a bailout package that at least temporarily kept Greece and Ireland from defaulting on their debts. The bailout reduced worries about the debt crisis and the dollar in the second half of 2010 gave back the rally seen in the first half of the year.

The dollar in the second half of 2010 was pressured by two main long-term bearish factors, i.e., the persistent U.S. current account deficit and the desire of Asian central banks to slowly diversify away from their heavy reserve holdings of dollars. The U.S. current account deficit remained very high at over 3% of GDP in 2010, which meant that about $1.4 billion in dollars flowed out of the country every calendar day. The dollar was also pressured by the fact that the European Central Bank's monetary policy was significant tighter than the monetary policy of the Federal Reserve during 2010.

Euro – The euro showed weakness in the first half of 2010 as the European debt crisis emerged with Greece nearly defaulting on its sovereign debt. The euro fell from $1.50 in December 2009 to a 5-year low of $1.19 in June 2010 as the European debt crisis caused widespread talk that the euro might break completely apart. However, Eurozone leaders were able to cobble together a bailout package for Greece and Ireland that at least kept those countries afloat for the time being. The market continues to suspect that those countries eventually will have to restructure their debt, but the bailout at least pushed that default date out into the future and took the downward pressure off the euro. The euro in the second half of 2010 then recovered much of its losses as the Germany and global economy picked up steam in the latter part of 2010. This encouraged the European Central Bank to exit some of its emergency liquidity measures such as its 6-month and 12-month bank loan programs. The ECB during the financial crisis eased its key policy rate to only 1.00% versus the Fed's policy rate range of zero to 0.25% and the ECB's tighter monetary policy helped to support the euro during 2010.

Yen – The yen strengthened during 2010 with USDJPY falling to a 15-year low of 80.21 yen in November 2010, nearly matching the record low of 79.78 yen posted in 1995. The Bank of Japan during 2010 maintained its extremely easy monetary policy and even expanded its quantitative easing program of buying bonds and other assets. Moreover, Japan's economy was generally weak during 2010 and the country's cumulative debt load continued to rise. Nevertheless, the yen in 2010 rallied on Japan's large current account surplus, which has the effect of reducing the amount of yen available internationally.

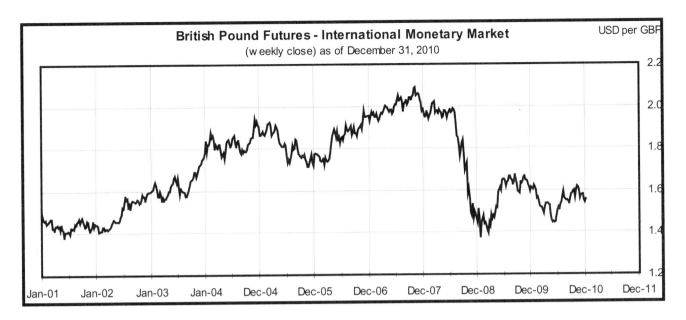

U.S. Dollars per British Pound

Year	Jan.	Feb.	Mar.	Apr.	May	June	July	Aug.	Sept.	Oct.	Nov.	Dec.	Average
2001	1.4767	1.4522	1.4438	1.4350	1.4268	1.4025	1.4149	1.4376	1.4646	1.4520	1.4358	1.4422	1.4403
2002	1.4314	1.4233	1.4233	1.4434	1.4601	1.4849	1.5566	1.5375	1.5562	1.5576	1.5718	1.5882	1.5029
2003	1.6184	1.6077	1.5832	1.5751	1.6230	1.6606	1.6242	1.5942	1.6141	1.6778	1.6899	1.7536	1.6352
2004	1.8223	1.8675	1.8273	1.8050	1.7888	1.8292	1.8433	1.8195	1.7932	1.8069	1.8608	1.9298	1.8328
2005	1.8783	1.8883	1.9034	1.8961	1.8538	1.8179	1.7518	1.7947	1.8078	1.7649	1.7355	1.7454	1.8198
2006	1.7665	1.7478	1.7446	1.7690	1.8693	1.8435	1.8451	1.8934	1.8858	1.8766	1.9124	1.9634	1.8431
2007	1.9585	1.9586	1.9479	1.9874	1.9834	1.9870	2.0344	2.0112	2.0202	2.0453	2.0709	2.0168	2.0018
2008	1.9692	1.9640	2.0012	1.9815	1.9662	1.9675	1.9897	1.8870	1.7997	1.6899	1.5290	1.4869	1.8526
2009	1.4484	1.4417	1.4197	1.4727	1.5460	1.6379	1.6387	1.6532	1.6312	1.6196	1.6610	1.6230	1.5661
2010	1.6160	1.5621	1.5059	1.5337	1.4658	1.4758	1.5302	1.5652	1.5575	1.5858	1.5953	1.5599	1.5461

Average.   *Source: FOREX*

Volume of Trading of British Pound Futures in Chicago   In Thousands of Contracts

Year	Jan.	Feb.	Mar.	Apr.	May	June	July	Aug.	Sept.	Oct.	Nov.	Dec.	Total
2001	125.6	126.2	198.7	127.0	166.3	248.9	164.2	183.6	197.1	178.9	161.4	187.4	2,065.4
2002	182.0	168.2	230.4	168.2	174.1	239.8	133.3	138.3	185.3	177.5	160.9	198.0	2,155.9
2003	158.3	161.8	217.4	158.1	164.7	288.6	214.9	163.5	284.5	212.6	206.2	364.5	2,595.2
2004	310.3	291.6	470.3	293.1	282.5	427.8	373.4	367.1	471.4	405.4	348.4	635.2	4,676.5
2005	376.7	410.5	628.7	453.3	555.5	763.5	640.2	735.3	1,034.5	887.8	1,080.6	1,203.1	8,769.8
2006	1,013.7	1,012.0	1,479.2	1,207.6	1,465.1	1,262.1	963.1	1,262.2	1,486.2	1,387.1	1,563.9	1,997.4	16,099.5
2007	1,639.3	1,485.2	2,151.4	1,330.1	1,705.8	2,066.0	1,946.6	1,964.1	1,668.3	1,729.8	1,793.9	1,319.3	20,799.8
2008	1,541.0	1,442.5	1,886.1	1,979.0	1,633.7	2,058.8	1,896.4	1,805.7	2,151.8	1,584.1	1,240.3	1,278.1	20,497.4
2009	1,446.3	1,457.1	1,721.8	1,509.2	1,736.4	2,609.0	2,127.0	2,126.5	2,644.3	2,864.8	2,389.1	2,222.4	24,853.8
2010	2,258.4	2,538.3	3,253.0	2,367.8	3,139.4	2,906.1	2,170.7	2,349.4	2,541.7	2,305.1	2,299.2	2,091.1	30,220.2

Contract size = 62,500 GBP.   *Source: CME Group; Chicago Mercantile Exchange (CME)*

Average Open Interest of British Pound Futures in Chicago   In Contracts

Year	Jan.	Feb.	Mar.	Apr.	May	June	July	Aug.	Sept.	Oct.	Nov.	Dec.
2001	28,776	30,555	36,532	34,713	39,836	48,310	33,273	40,935	50,083	38,579	40,461	35,424
2002	26,450	31,023	30,474	39,952	46,178	47,355	38,138	31,320	31,513	29,599	40,901	36,671
2003	36,892	33,066	27,042	25,274	36,171	50,118	41,702	46,979	40,183	55,884	66,660	70,197
2004	61,694	68,173	51,968	43,830	45,843	53,615	68,262	71,503	60,274	66,565	87,487	86,572
2005	67,140	70,872	81,799	80,850	88,397	79,278	75,387	73,199	81,479	79,854	84,884	91,497
2006	83,051	97,226	83,641	83,275	106,555	98,417	91,563	129,334	120,737	106,288	145,026	157,837
2007	147,183	152,892	135,618	130,611	130,861	145,405	157,336	124,948	110,905	118,737	128,761	96,974
2008	87,465	94,154	98,154	109,464	158,836	126,688	100,775	105,857	112,717	110,761	113,147	93,313
2009	81,141	84,191	88,354	82,933	91,683	92,365	90,994	98,358	88,658	104,344	96,882	83,847
2010	86,016	116,480	136,357	122,843	145,514	136,099	126,486	138,872	97,056	89,011	95,465	80,042

Contract size = 62,500 GBP.   *Source: CME Group; Chicago Mercantile Exchange (CME)*

Canadian Dollar Futures - International Monetary Market
(weekly close) as of December 31, 2010

USD per CAD

Canadian Dollars per U.S. Dollar

Year	Jan.	Feb.	Mar.	Apr.	May	June	July	Aug.	Sept.	Oct.	Nov.	Dec.	Average
2001	1.5021	1.5227	1.5579	1.5581	1.5403	1.5238	1.5294	1.5384	1.5665	1.5708	1.5934	1.5793	1.5486
2002	1.5996	1.5961	1.5872	1.5814	1.5491	1.5312	1.5447	1.5685	1.5747	1.5783	1.5715	1.5588	1.5701
2003	1.5395	1.5119	1.4752	1.4567	1.3819	1.3520	1.3801	1.3948	1.3638	1.3226	1.3128	1.3121	1.4003
2004	1.2967	1.3292	1.3282	1.3410	1.3774	1.3582	1.3225	1.3127	1.2880	1.2476	1.1958	1.2177	1.3013
2005	1.2248	1.2386	1.2157	1.2368	1.2553	1.2402	1.2239	1.2048	1.1781	1.1777	1.1813	1.1619	1.2116
2006	1.1573	1.1488	1.1571	1.1440	1.1094	1.1139	1.1287	1.1191	1.1161	1.1281	1.1365	1.1531	1.1343
2007	1.1757	1.1708	1.1687	1.1351	1.0948	1.0655	1.0512	1.0585	1.0260	0.9752	0.9680	1.0021	1.0743
2008	1.0114	1.0001	1.0031	1.0130	0.9999	1.0170	1.0133	1.0539	1.0582	1.1797	1.2204	1.2337	1.0670
2009	1.2244	1.2449	1.2638	1.2244	1.1502	1.1274	1.1225	1.0878	1.0812	1.0547	1.0587	1.0558	1.1413
2010	1.0435	1.0561	1.0233	1.0052	1.0415	1.0397	1.0433	1.0408	1.0335	1.0180	1.0128	1.0081	1.0305

Average.   *Source: FOREX*

Volume of Trading of Canadian Dollar Futures in Chicago   In Thousands of Contracts

Year	Jan.	Feb.	Mar.	Apr.	May	June	July	Aug.	Sept.	Oct.	Nov.	Dec.	Total
2001	194.7	201.1	317.9	188.2	228.4	351.0	221.6	235.9	265.1	214.1	218.1	287.3	2,923.3
2002	222.9	191.5	338.3	249.6	222.2	358.7	278.8	204.2	279.1	245.3	207.4	324.4	3,122.3
2003	270.8	256.7	475.5	289.2	353.1	494.2	331.3	266.2	393.3	285.7	294.4	509.3	4,219.6
2004	380.7	328.0	516.3	380.3	337.1	504.0	366.5	419.4	640.8	512.0	499.5	726.8	5,611.3
2005	548.6	483.0	678.0	592.9	555.2	761.5	562.2	566.3	914.2	671.3	736.0	861.0	7,930.2
2006	695.1	648.6	1,040.9	654.9	816.6	1,043.4	658.3	811.0	1,073.7	805.8	960.8	1,070.4	10,279.6
2007	795.9	724.5	1,089.4	749.9	949.9	1,348.4	1,101.2	1,015.5	1,226.6	1,054.0	1,238.3	931.2	12,224.8
2008	960.2	957.8	1,202.2	948.1	958.2	1,151.9	932.0	966.4	1,240.9	812.9	601.8	645.8	11,378.0
2009	625.5	685.7	1,040.2	964.4	1,222.0	1,691.7	1,318.6	1,319.2	1,644.8	1,626.3	1,569.5	1,773.2	15,481.2
2010	1,391.4	1,623.9	1,989.7	1,742.0	2,329.7	2,120.7	1,774.7	1,839.7	1,905.7	1,841.7	1,889.4	1,635.3	22,083.8

Contract size = 100,000 CAD.   *Source: CME Group; Chicago Mercantile Exchange (CME)*

Average Open Interest of Canadian Dollar Futures in Chicago   In Contracts

Year	Jan.	Feb.	Mar.	Apr.	May	June	July	Aug.	Sept.	Oct.	Nov.	Dec.
2001	54,369	58,660	72,051	64,550	65,407	62,489	54,742	54,580	73,647	71,610	82,083	67,578
2002	68,927	72,132	70,484	68,120	81,574	86,250	74,347	63,116	63,605	57,031	60,648	71,852
2003	82,870	105,051	107,507	97,515	96,689	85,665	68,741	63,518	70,261	79,754	82,366	74,271
2004	74,577	64,032	61,981	72,750	84,356	68,458	73,164	83,483	97,486	112,648	110,035	81,976
2005	74,703	84,753	93,986	77,680	95,229	79,464	86,451	101,128	120,542	108,095	106,773	122,584
2006	103,427	118,978	103,066	92,541	114,587	107,605	89,443	91,591	112,788	99,209	121,729	146,474
2007	151,511	144,025	140,775	119,430	163,570	180,961	147,966	132,910	136,952	145,923	120,912	99,261
2008	86,448	99,650	109,567	103,486	115,665	103,145	95,618	120,175	116,163	103,135	94,297	66,313
2009	59,962	70,940	70,863	63,119	83,214	88,873	87,203	98,521	91,989	97,587	89,022	94,758
2010	106,475	92,349	143,969	148,414	125,802	102,117	87,121	100,655	101,319	113,964	116,126	110,800

Contract size = 100,000 CAD.   *Source: CME Group; Chicago Mercantile Exchange (CME)*

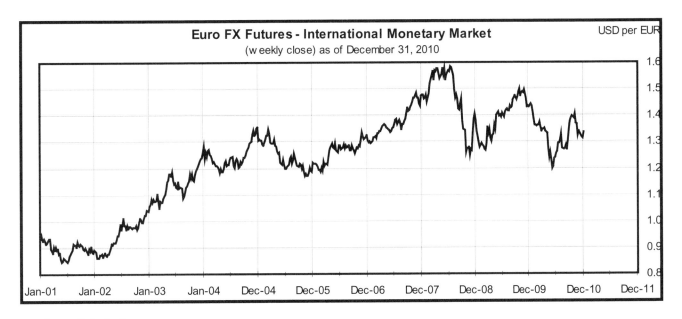

Euro FX Futures - International Monetary Market
(weekly close) as of December 31, 2010

USD per EUR

Euro¹ per U.S. Dollar

Year	Jan.	Feb.	Mar.	Apr.	May	June	July	Aug.	Sept.	Oct.	Nov.	Dec.	Average
2001	.9380	.9208	.9085	.8931	.8747	.8536	.8616	.9023	.9123	.9062	.8882	.8913	.8959
2002	.8828	.8706	.8767	.8866	.9179	.9567	.9924	.9781	.9810	.9818	1.0020	1.0210	.9456
2003	1.0636	1.0778	1.0795	1.0875	1.1580	1.1670	1.1374	1.1154	1.1260	1.1701	1.1714	1.2314	1.1321
2004	1.2604	1.2633	1.2263	1.1999	1.2013	1.2147	1.2265	1.2192	1.2226	1.2504	1.3001	1.3415	1.2439
2005	1.3110	1.3020	1.3178	1.2940	1.2685	1.2156	1.2049	1.2299	1.2246	1.2030	1.1796	1.1861	1.2448
2006	1.2121	1.1940	1.2033	1.2282	1.2773	1.2665	1.2693	1.2811	1.2734	1.2623	1.2893	1.3200	1.2564
2007	1.2989	1.3087	1.3249	1.3512	1.3511	1.3422	1.3720	1.3620	1.3918	1.4234	1.4681	1.4561	1.3709
2008	1.4722	1.4759	1.5527	1.5760	1.5560	1.5569	1.5765	1.4954	1.4367	1.3286	1.2723	1.3518	1.4709
2009	1.3253	1.2805	1.3074	1.3207	1.3675	1.4014	1.4087	1.4267	1.4565	1.4817	1.4926	1.4577	1.3939
2010	1.4270	1.3681	1.3574	1.3427	1.2536	1.2212	1.2803	1.2899	1.3092	1.3899	1.3640	1.3227	1.3272

Average.   Source: FOREX

Volume of Trading of Euro FX Futures in Chicago   In Thousands of Contracts

Year	Jan.	Feb.	Mar.	Apr.	May	June	July	Aug.	Sept.	Oct.	Nov.	Dec.	Total
2001	453.5	373.2	556.4	368.3	407.7	585.3	425.1	494.7	533.9	533.6	545.0	781.1	6,057.8
2002	567.8	582.3	783.3	650.2	611.4	917.7	821.6	525.5	675.3	525.2	426.7	625.4	7,712.3
2003	610.6	749.2	977.9	785.5	902.7	1,103.8	866.2	824.5	1,112.4	1,069.6	958.9	1,232.6	11,193.9
2004	1,487.3	1,469.2	1,837.7	1,326.7	1,328.9	1,682.2	1,491.2	1,518.5	1,798.7	1,786.0	2,138.5	2,591.9	20,456.7
2005	2,646.0	2,266.4	2,772.9	2,992.0	2,771.6	3,656.1	2,732.6	2,765.1	3,206.6	2,613.6	3,164.2	2,943.6	34,530.7
2006	2,956.0	2,563.9	3,411.2	2,984.4	4,496.3	3,765.7	2,789.0	3,229.5	3,364.0	3,123.5	3,790.4	4,316.6	40,790.4
2007	3,701.9	3,032.1	4,427.3	2,979.1	3,337.4	3,877.6	3,560.5	4,074.2	3,286.6	3,831.5	3,793.1	3,161.6	43,063.1
2008	3,669.9	3,327.5	4,709.2	4,596.3	4,537.8	5,312.0	4,661.3	5,009.7	6,216.8	4,556.3	3,607.9	3,447.8	53,652.6
2009	3,574.5	3,903.4	4,564.5	3,155.7	3,758.9	5,261.4	4,675.6	4,220.4	5,123.9	5,429.9	5,419.9	5,305.7	54,393.6
2010	5,407.6	6,439.6	7,562.4	7,157.1	9,578.8	7,913.1	6,006.4	6,418.2	7,294.2	7,476.0	8,241.8	6,737.2	86,232.4

Contract size = 125,000 EUR.   *Source: CME Group; Chicago Mercantile Exchange (CME)*

Average Open Interest of Euro FX Futures in Chicago   In Contracts

Year	Jan.	Feb.	Mar.	Apr.	May	June	July	Aug.	Sept.	Oct.	Nov.	Dec.
2001	89,049	91,130	90,127	78,762	89,390	94,160	84,637	104,437	112,797	108,445	108,999	104,323
2002	100,258	108,955	113,075	112,413	136,660	135,364	112,462	101,992	99,365	85,462	103,156	108,602
2003	105,762	106,905	100,759	85,604	108,619	111,651	96,338	98,671	95,553	102,568	113,601	131,560
2004	125,879	133,690	115,712	112,361	138,193	120,281	140,430	160,315	121,180	136,959	202,074	175,374
2005	135,748	152,110	140,879	130,131	154,751	163,584	142,826	148,309	149,184	142,879	171,035	160,065
2006	133,092	150,085	152,674	166,920	196,057	177,700	155,865	173,151	155,567	152,410	182,079	214,241
2007	173,989	196,963	205,366	217,899	222,019	204,945	218,401	221,095	221,268	207,644	221,736	204,536
2008	179,767	206,661	200,084	178,993	211,068	193,878	170,675	153,423	163,948	180,955	169,315	144,926
2009	127,134	156,321	141,863	110,261	124,438	130,793	129,062	133,469	156,493	168,629	169,331	155,488
2010	169,083	199,832	211,780	216,500	285,206	251,763	226,656	242,448	198,817	203,635	198,138	172,703

Contract size = 125,000 EUR.   *Source: CME Group; Chicago Mercantile Exchange (CME)*

CURRENCIES

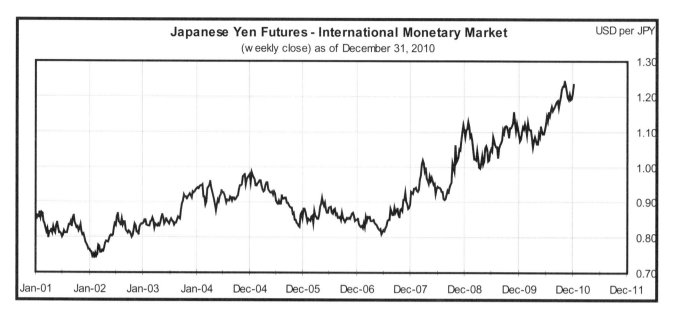

Japanese Yen Futures - International Monetary Market
(weekly close) as of December 31, 2010

USD per JPY

Japanese Yen per U.S. Dollar

Year	Jan.	Feb.	Mar.	Apr.	May	June	July	Aug.	Sept.	Oct.	Nov.	Dec.	Average
2001	116.83	116.17	121.44	123.64	121.66	122.38	124.45	121.29	118.64	121.35	122.39	127.72	121.50
2002	132.77	133.50	131.11	130.75	126.29	123.25	118.02	119.04	120.88	123.92	121.50	121.83	125.24
2003	118.76	119.39	118.76	119.81	117.37	118.31	118.64	118.61	114.94	109.51	109.17	107.70	115.91
2004	106.38	106.70	108.51	107.61	112.05	109.44	109.46	110.24	110.10	108.81	104.71	103.79	108.15
2005	103.29	104.98	105.35	107.19	106.71	108.75	111.92	110.62	111.19	114.84	118.42	118.39	110.14
2006	115.53	117.92	117.31	116.97	111.77	114.65	115.69	115.95	117.14	118.61	117.28	117.43	116.35
2007	120.45	120.40	117.33	118.96	120.82	122.65	121.47	116.78	115.08	115.92	110.92	112.37	117.76
2008	107.71	107.11	100.80	102.69	104.33	106.88	106.87	109.41	106.62	100.15	96.80	91.13	103.37
2009	90.33	92.86	97.74	98.94	96.49	96.67	94.46	94.90	91.40	90.32	89.12	89.99	93.60
2010	91.13	90.17	90.71	93.49	91.88	90.81	87.56	85.38	84.38	81.79	82.58	83.23	87.76

Average.   *Source: FOREX*

Volume of Trading of Japanese Yen Futures in Chicago   In Thousands of Contracts

Year	Jan.	Feb.	Mar.	Apr.	May	June	July	Aug.	Sept.	Oct.	Nov.	Dec.	Total
2001	258.6	223.7	598.4	295.4	351.2	459.4	307.4	369.4	518.6	286.2	350.1	595.9	4,614.1
2002	415.7	417.5	630.8	391.7	318.5	461.7	301.2	234.2	499.2	349.5	255.4	535.8	4,811.1
2003	423.9	388.3	634.4	453.4	495.6	621.0	518.8	427.0	731.0	396.6	353.4	641.8	6,085.2
2004	410.1	484.9	741.8	516.4	415.5	685.8	487.5	490.7	807.6	629.6	650.5	1,074.9	7,395.3
2005	789.9	718.8	1,045.2	915.4	876.2	1,263.0	946.9	1,012.4	1,285.4	963.7	1,001.0	1,653.9	12,471.7
2006	1,221.1	1,128.7	1,950.5	1,385.9	1,890.9	1,905.3	1,317.9	1,395.9	1,965.8	1,525.1	1,852.8	2,137.5	19,677.4
2007	1,602.2	2,006.6	3,286.7	1,771.1	1,802.4	2,777.8	3,083.8	3,954.2	2,860.7	2,493.1	3,125.2	2,056.6	30,820.4
2008	3,013.2	2,558.7	3,384.5	2,632.6	2,502.9	3,193.9	2,898.0	2,428.9	3,446.2	3,117.8	1,937.5	1,730.2	32,844.4
2009	1,644.2	1,802.9	1,796.0	1,469.3	1,600.9	1,932.6	2,061.8	1,924.0	2,260.9	2,157.6	1,916.7	2,182.7	22,749.6
2010	2,321.3	2,382.1	2,664.8	2,397.2	3,481.7	3,094.9	2,712.4	2,591.6	3,065.3	2,171.1	2,484.6	2,495.8	31,862.8

Contract size = 12,500,000 JPY.   *Source: CME Group; Chicago Mercantile Exchange (CME)*

Average Open Interest of Japanese Yen Futures in Chicago   In Contracts

Year	Jan.	Feb.	Mar.	Apr.	May	June	July	Aug.	Sept.	Oct.	Nov.	Dec.
2001	89,680	90,652	109,536	96,244	89,377	82,838	93,430	107,588	102,710	75,096	97,368	137,756
2002	129,917	123,735	95,535	72,358	88,905	88,324	77,168	71,683	79,980	80,104	74,584	99,643
2003	116,574	107,929	101,809	81,168	107,090	102,507	107,450	125,884	149,978	152,368	138,799	147,255
2004	156,929	156,416	120,848	117,483	108,078	105,505	106,280	110,234	93,780	127,644	181,093	172,526
2005	164,708	155,593	132,268	134,802	172,574	164,580	161,763	170,290	159,227	186,631	202,939	191,591
2006	168,309	198,855	203,450	201,459	210,578	197,160	191,480	218,893	239,426	258,509	242,216	265,490
2007	312,252	338,933	246,715	234,352	303,537	347,031	302,278	272,937	227,242	225,047	202,361	195,324
2008	197,886	233,558	224,932	176,577	171,298	171,516	185,657	207,309	168,119	142,938	128,891	130,118
2009	112,194	108,893	90,828	79,142	86,624	81,378	95,456	80,087	119,014	118,478	123,821	110,809
2010	116,578	121,216	117,096	131,315	143,384	111,812	129,460	135,623	130,539	142,646	133,612	111,840

Contract size = 12,500,000 JPY.   *Source: CME Group; Chicago Mercantile Exchange (CME)*

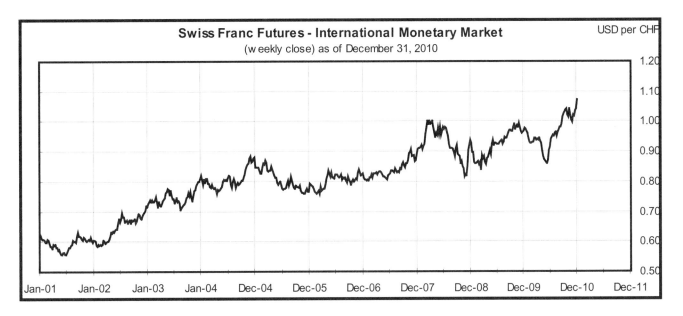

Swiss Franc Futures - International Monetary Market (weekly close) as of December 31, 2010 — USD per CHF

Swiss Francs per U.S. Dollar

Year	Jan.	Feb.	Mar.	Apr.	May	June	July	Aug.	Sept.	Oct.	Nov.	Dec.	Average
2001	1.6296	1.6681	1.6903	1.7115	1.7525	1.7842	1.7564	1.6791	1.6338	1.6337	1.6501	1.6569	1.6872
2002	1.6710	1.6972	1.6741	1.6527	1.5868	1.5389	1.4731	1.4968	1.4929	1.4922	1.4647	1.4360	1.5564
2003	1.3748	1.3609	1.3617	1.3770	1.3091	1.3196	1.3597	1.3813	1.3741	1.3234	1.3314	1.2627	1.3446
2004	1.2425	1.2458	1.2773	1.2954	1.2818	1.2501	1.2458	1.2625	1.2624	1.2338	1.1702	1.1455	1.2428
2005	1.1802	1.1906	1.1763	1.1955	1.2183	1.2663	1.2935	1.2626	1.2657	1.2872	1.3100	1.3056	1.2460
2006	1.2781	1.3056	1.3044	1.2822	1.2185	1.2319	1.2362	1.2319	1.2440	1.2597	1.2351	1.2102	1.2532
2007	1.2438	1.2385	1.2179	1.2128	1.2217	1.2329	1.2076	1.2034	1.1847	1.1743	1.1229	1.1397	1.2000
2008	1.1001	1.0894	1.0116	1.0141	1.0443	1.0363	1.0278	1.0843	1.1091	1.1429	1.1923	1.1393	1.0826
2009	1.1280	1.1635	1.1540	1.1472	1.1057	1.0810	1.0784	1.0677	1.0399	1.0218	1.0117	1.0304	1.0858
2010	1.0341	1.0719	1.0660	1.0682	1.1325	1.1263	1.0531	1.0392	1.0012	.9688	.9852	.9671	1.0428

Average. *Source: FOREX*

Volume of Trading of Swiss Franc Futures in Chicago — In Thousands of Contracts

Year	Jan.	Feb.	Mar.	Apr.	May	June	July	Aug.	Sept.	Oct.	Nov.	Dec.	Total
2001	193.5	203.0	280.3	168.7	191.6	326.0	257.6	229.4	261.8	227.5	238.2	297.3	2,874.8
2002	195.3	183.2	281.3	211.5	208.1	297.0	187.2	218.5	323.1	237.6	207.8	271.6	2,822.1
2003	236.1	289.9	412.7	256.9	277.8	384.9	315.0	252.1	349.9	237.2	283.8	300.5	3,596.7
2004	216.1	230.1	359.6	260.0	255.7	370.9	331.4	313.7	404.5	428.3	329.0	568.4	4,067.8
2005	444.3	389.1	575.5	605.0	521.4	753.4	546.4	596.4	888.8	765.9	797.1	901.2	7,784.5
2006	803.5	745.9	1,129.0	837.5	1,011.3	993.3	771.2	1,014.8	1,046.8	919.6	1,078.1	1,118.9	11,470.0
2007	994.4	998.5	1,418.5	959.4	1,100.0	1,507.0	1,660.0	1,588.2	1,113.7	1,129.8	1,067.3	941.8	14,478.7
2008	1,090.5	1,082.4	1,311.8	1,350.7	1,362.8	1,789.1	1,650.0	1,330.3	1,578.9	1,042.4	574.0	651.3	14,814.2
2009	677.7	624.5	813.9	641.5	731.2	1,094.1	844.8	727.0	1,015.2	1,098.5	1,206.6	1,143.5	10,618.6
2010	1,046.8	954.5	1,218.2	1,105.8	1,299.4	1,066.8	813.5	806.1	997.7	847.7	940.4	914.3	12,011.2

Contract size = 125,000 CHF. *Source: CME Group; Chicago Mercantile Exchange (CME)*

Average Open Interest of Swiss Franc Futures in Chicago — In Contracts

Year	Jan.	Feb.	Mar.	Apr.	May	June	July	Aug.	Sept.	Oct.	Nov.	Dec.
2001	50,121	44,405	46,470	41,641	53,265	60,943	53,687	60,986	61,689	48,962	53,445	46,771
2002	35,116	44,388	45,434	38,248	55,039	54,573	42,060	38,102	37,675	35,796	48,951	50,107
2003	56,268	57,099	50,008	37,451	53,642	49,688	41,489	50,677	52,641	54,259	62,584	60,475
2004	45,259	42,950	41,250	38,563	38,024	48,654	51,116	40,256	33,539	47,200	74,988	70,330
2005	51,858	56,240	50,827	41,322	55,995	78,794	72,596	67,489	66,009	75,088	91,072	98,443
2006	80,904	107,509	101,445	82,280	98,416	89,254	67,127	69,406	83,545	97,034	89,039	74,522
2007	83,176	103,073	70,627	66,246	89,737	121,557	108,394	118,597	100,948	73,433	81,366	73,025
2008	67,993	67,786	71,972	60,528	65,029	58,511	56,337	61,521	53,448	39,448	42,315	31,420
2009	26,083	32,701	33,518	28,613	34,585	40,027	35,918	39,324	49,537	51,736	52,912	41,890
2010	36,523	41,531	36,834	38,093	49,842	48,989	52,203	55,870	58,484	53,703	45,087	44,460

Contract size = 125,000 CHF. *Source: CME Group; Chicago Mercantile Exchange (CME)*

CURRENCIES

United States Merchandise Trade Balance[1]   In Millions of Dollars

Year	Jan.	Feb.	Mar.	Apr.	May	June	July	Aug.	Sept.	Oct.	Nov.	Dec.	Total
2001	-40,659	-35,227	-38,554	-36,056	-32,601	-34,793	-35,148	-33,335	-35,290	-35,118	-34,015	-31,184	-421,980
2002	-33,767	-36,196	-36,163	-38,680	-39,206	-39,657	-38,708	-41,090	-41,163	-39,581	-43,872	-47,262	-475,345
2003	-44,617	-43,394	-47,119	-45,654	-45,096	-43,897	-44,932	-43,591	-45,624	-45,433	-44,065	-48,122	-541,544
2004	-48,870	-49,008	-51,633	-52,189	-52,587	-58,987	-56,160	-57,028	-56,017	-59,769	-63,688	-59,696	-665,632
2005	-61,235	-63,450	-59,064	-62,658	-61,718	-63,603	-63,434	-64,027	-70,632	-73,386	-69,994	-70,601	-783,802
2006	-73,024	-67,569	-68,164	-68,846	-71,406	-69,871	-72,932	-74,507	-71,525	-66,204	-66,027	-69,380	-839,455
2007	-65,989	-66,581	-70,741	-68,734	-68,058	-68,781	-69,317	-67,244	-67,937	-68,597	-72,027	-69,185	-823,191
2008	-71,272	-73,607	-70,721	-74,861	-73,926	-73,879	-78,694	-72,548	-71,055	-69,980	-53,173	-50,937	-834,653
2009	-45,912	-36,684	-38,601	-39,366	-35,900	-38,241	-43,746	-42,105	-46,268	-43,976	-47,063	-49,082	-506,944
2010[1]	-47,109	-51,525	-52,259	-52,598	-54,480	-62,065	-54,875	-58,933	-57,033	-51,134	-51,438	-53,629	-647,078

[1] Not seasonally adjusted.   [2] Preliminary.   *Source: Bureau of Economic Analysis, U.S. Department of Commerce (BEA)*

Index of Real Trade-Weighted Dollar Exchange Rates for Total Agriculture[3]   (2000 = 100)

Year		Jan.	Feb.	Mar.	Apr.	May	June	July	Aug.	Sept.	Oct.	Nov.	Dec.
2004	U.S. Markets	101.5	102.2	103.0	103.6	106.0	105.0	103.9	103.7	103.3	102.0	99.5	98.2
	U.S. Competitors	100.4	100.6	102.8	103.9	105.4	104.9	103.5	103.7	103.2	101.4	98.4	95.9
2005	U.S. Markets	98.5	98.7	98.4	99.8	99.7	100.2	100.7	100.0	100.6	101.6	101.3	100.1
	U.S. Competitors	97.0	97.2	96.7	98.2	98.8	101.1	102.0	100.6	101.3	102.4	102.6	101.7
2006	U.S. Markets	99.2	99.4	99.9	100.0	98.6	100.2	100.1	99.2	98.9	98.6	97.7	97.0
	U.S. Competitors	100.7	101.1	101.1	100.1	97.8	99.3	99.1	98.0	97.9	97.6	95.8	93.9
2007	U.S. Markets	98.2	98.2	98.2	97.6	97.0	96.9	95.7	95.6	94.2	92.3	91.4	91.7
	U.S. Competitors	95.0	94.7	94.3	92.8	92.4	92.7	90.9	91.7	90.2	87.7	86.1	86.3
2008	U.S. Markets	91.3	90.3	89.0	88.9	89.4	89.9	89.4	90.5	92.1	97.1	97.5	95.8
	U.S. Competitors	85.9	85.1	82.6	81.9	82.5	82.8	82.1	84.8	88.3	94.8	97.4	93.8
2009	U.S. Markets	97.1	100.0	101.5	98.5	95.7	95.5	94.9	93.7	93.0	91.6	91.0	90.8
	U.S. Competitors	95.9	98.9	98.4	96.1	92.9	91.2	90.8	89.4	88.1	86.4	85.7	86.6
2010[1]	U.S. Markets	90.8	91.4	90.5	89.9	92.0	92.4	91.0	89.9	89.1	86.6	86.6	87.0
	U.S. Competitors	87.6	89.9	89.6	89.5	93.7	95.4	92.2	91.2	89.9	86.0	86.7	88.1
2011[2]	U.S. Markets	86.0	85.1	84.3	83.5	82.9	82.3	81.6	80.9	80.2	79.5	78.9	78.3
	U.S. Competitors	87.4	85.9	85.0	84.3	84.0	83.5	82.8	82.1	81.4	80.9	80.3	79.7

[1] Not seasonally adjusted.   [2] Preliminary.   *Source: Bureau of Economic Analysis, U.S. Department of Commerce (BEA)*

United States Balance on Current Account[1]   In Millions of Dollars

Year	First Quarter	Second Quarter	Third Quarter	Fourth Quarter	Annual
2001	-95,611	-98,060	-113,840	-89,648	-397,159
2002	-90,735	-115,719	-127,638	-123,982	-458,074
2003	-122,135	-130,844	-141,188	-126,500	-520,667
2004	-123,406	-157,208	-170,581	-179,292	-630,487
2005	-157,944	-181,264	-198,674	-209,708	-747,590
2006	-179,840	-204,387	-229,976	-188,433	-802,636
2007	-179,421	-190,207	-183,965	-164,501	-718,094
2008	-151,718	-175,358	-191,632	-150,145	-668,853
2009	-80,215	-83,149	-111,577	-103,490	-378,431
2010[1]	-91,795	-120,426	-141,083	-116,938	-470,242

[1] Not seasonally adjusted.   [2] Estimate.   *Source: Bureau of Economic Analysis, U.S. Department of Commerce (BEA)*

Merchandise Trade and Current Account Balances[1]   In Billions of Dollars

Year	Merchanise Trade Balance					Current Account Balance				
	Canada	Germany	Japan	Switzerland	United Kingdom	Canada	Germany	Japan	Switzerland	United Kingdom
2002	32.4	93.4	51.2	18.4	-42.2	12.6	40.8	112.6	24.8	-27.9
2003	32.5	98.2	69.3	21.4	-42.7	10.6	47.5	136.2	43.4	-30.0
2004	42.7	137.7	89.0	25.1	-59.5	22.9	125.6	171.6	48.4	-45.6
2005	42.5	147.0	63.3	25.0	-77.7	21.6	141.0	166.0	51.9	-59.2
2006	32.0	168.1	54.5	32.4	-76.7	18.0	187.6	171.5	59.3	-83.1
2007	27.1	239.4	73.3	44.7	-86.1	11.8	256.0	212.8	39.7	-72.8
2008	24.8	234.4	6.1	57.4	-71.3	8.0	247.5	157.4	7.2	-43.1
2009	-23.1	165.4	15.7	54.3	-51.7	-38.6	166.4	142.2	59.7	-27.1
2010[2]	-24.4	172.5	69.3	66.2	-71.4	-42.1	170.4	190.8	66.5	-49.4
2011[3]	-26.9	211.5	76.6	72.2	-72.3	-46.3	213.2	218.8	62.5	-38.1

[1] Not seasonally adjusted.   [2] Estimate.   [3] Projection.   *Source: Organization for Economic Cooperation and Development (OECD)*

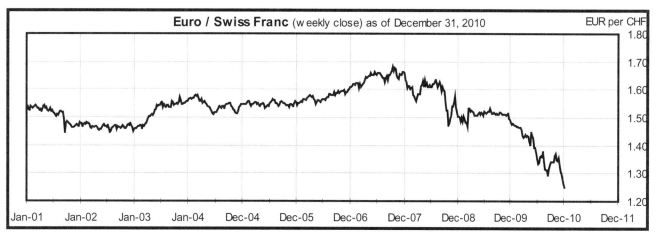

Euro / Swiss Franc (weekly close) as of December 31, 2010 — EUR per CHF

Euro / British Pound (weekly close) as of December 31, 2010 — EUR per GBP

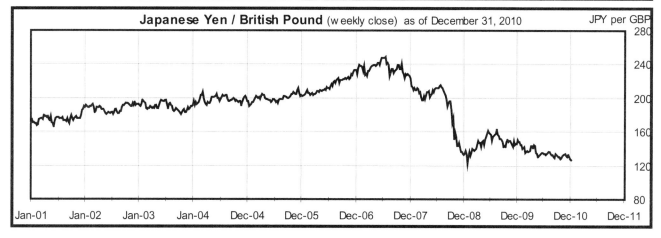

Japanese Yen / British Pound (weekly close) as of December 31, 2010 — JPY per GBP

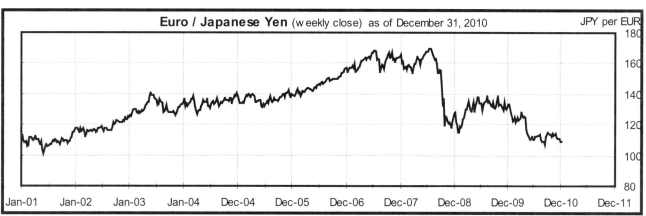

Euro / Japanese Yen (weekly close) as of December 31, 2010 — JPY per EUR

Diamonds

The diamond, which is the mineral form of carbon, is the hardest, strongest natural material known on earth. The name *diamond* is derived from **adamas**, the ancient Greek term meaning "invincible." Diamonds form deep within the Earth's crust and are typically billions of years old. Diamonds have also have been found in and near meteorites and their craters. Diamonds are considered precious gemstones but lower grade diamonds are used for industrial applications such as drilling, cutting, grinding and polishing.

Supply – World production of natural gem diamonds in 2009 (latest data) rose by +4.5% yr/yr to 90.900 million carats, but still down from the 2006 record high of 93.800

million carats (one carat equals 1/5 gram or 200 milligrams). The world's largest producers of natural gem diamonds are Botswana with 35% of world production in 2009, Russia with 24%, Australia with 8%, Angola with 9%, South Africa with 6%, and the Congo with 6%. World production of natural industrial diamonds in 2008 (latest data) was up +0.4% yr/yr to 77.000 million carats. World production of synthetic diamonds in 2008 was up +0.4% yr/yr to 568.000 million carats. The main producer of synthetic diamonds was the U.S. with 46% of world production.

Trade – The U.S. in 2009 (latest data) relied on net imports for 78% of its consumption of natural diamonds.

World Production of Natural Gem Diamonds   In Thousands of Carats

Year	Angola	Australia	Botswana	Brazil	Central African Republic	China	Dem. Rep. of Congo	Ghana	Namibia	Russia	Suerra Leone	South Africa	World Total
2004	5,490	6,058	23,300	300	263	100	5,900	725	2,004	23,700	318	5,800	88,400
2005	6,371	8,577	23,900	208	300	100	7,000	810	1,902	23,000	395	6,400	92,800
2006	8,258	7,305	24,000	181	340	100	5,700	780	2,400	23,400	401	6,100	93,700
2007	8,732	231	25,000	182	370	100	5,300	720	2,200	23,300	360	6,100	91,500
2008[1]	8,100	273	25,000	200	400	100	5,400	520	1,500	21,925	220	5,200	87,000
2009[2]	8,000	260	32,000	200	350	100	5,400	500	2,000	21,900	300	5,200	90,900

[1] Preliminary.   [2] Estimate.   *Source: U.S. Geological Survey (USGS)*

World Production of Natural Industrial Diamonds[4]   In Thousands of Carats

Year	Angola	Australia	Botswana	Brazil	Central African Republic	China	Ghana	Russia	Leone	South Africa	Vene-zuela	Dem. Rep of Congo[3]	World Total
2003	570	17,087	7,600	600	83	955	21,600	180	13,000	274	7,540	24	69,900
2004	610	18,172	7,800	600	88	960	23,600	180	15,200	374	8,500	60	76,700
2005	708	25,730	8,000	600	80	960	28,200	200	15,000	274	9,400	69	90,400
2006	918	21,915	8,000	600	85	965	22,800	190	15,000	252	9,100	70	80,300
2007[1]	970	18,960	8,000	600	93	970	21,300	180	15,000	240	9,100	70	76,300
2008[2]	900	15,400	8,000	600	80	1,000	21,600	120	15,000	150	7,700	70	71,800

[1] Preliminary.   [2] Estimate.   [3] Formerly Zaire.   *Source: U.S. Geological Survey (USGS)*

World Production of Synthetic Diamonds   In Thousands of Carats

Year	Belarus	China	Czech Republic	France	Greece	Ireland	Japan	Russia	South Africa	Sweden	Ukraine	United States	World Total
2003	25,000	17,000	5	3,000	----	60,000	34,000	80,000	60,000	20,000	8,000	236,000	543,000
2004	25,000	3,800,000	5	3,000	----	60,000	34,000	80,000	60,000	20,000	8,000	252,000	4,340,000
2005	25,000	3,800,000	5	3,000	----	60,000	34,000	80,000	60,000	20,000	8,000	256,000	4,350,000
2006	25,000	3,900,000	5	3,000	----	60,000	34,000	80,000	60,000	20,000	8,000	258,000	4,450,000
2007[1]	25,000	4,000,000	5	3,000	----	60,000	34,000	80,000	60,000	20,000	8,000	260,000	4,550,000
2008[2]	25,000	4,000,000	5	3,000	----	60,000	34,000	80,000	60,000	20,000	8,000	261,000	4,550,000

[1] Preliminary.   [2] Estimate.   *Source: U.S. Geological Survey (USGS)*

Salient Statistics of Industrial Diamonds in the United States   In Millions of Carats

	Bort, Grit & Powder & Dust								Stones (Natural)						Net
	--- Production --- Natural and Synthetic		Imports	Exports &	In Manu-factured	Gov't	Apparent Con-	Price Value of Imports	Secon dary Pro-	Imports for Con-	Exports &	Gov't	Apparent Con-	Price Value of Imports	Import Reliance % of Con-
Year	Manu-factured Diamond	Secon-dary	for Con-sumption	Reexports	Products	Sales	sumption	$/Carat	duction	sumption	Reexports	Sales	sumption	$/Carat	sumption
2005	256.0	4.6	284.0	92.0	----	----	453.0	.27	[3]	2.1	[3]	----	2.2	13.91	77
2006	258.0	34.2	371.0	90.0	----	----	362.0	.22	[3]	2.2	[3]	[3]	2.8	12.61	78
2007	260.0	34.4	411.0	107.0	----	----	386.0	.19	[3]	3.1	----	[3]	3.5	11.54	79
2008	261.0	33.9	492.0	116.0	----	----	458.0	.15	----	3.2	[3]	.5	4.1	12.89	82
2009[1]	260.0	33.5	246.0	67.0	----	----	271.0	.17	----	1.4	----	----	3.0	13.31	71
2010[2]		33.0	520.0	100.0	----	----	490.0	.15	----	1.7	----	----	3.0	18.09	85

[1] Preliminary.   [2] Estimate.   [3] Less than 1/2 unit.   *Source: U.S. Geological Survey (USGS)*

Eggs

Eggs are a low-priced protein source and are consumed worldwide. Each commercial chicken lays between 265-280 eggs per year. In the United States, the grade and size of eggs are regulated under the federal Egg Products Inspection Act (1970). The grades of eggs are AA, A, and B, and must have sound, whole shells and must be clean. The difference among the grades of eggs is internal and mostly reflects the freshness of the egg. Table eggs vary in color and can be determined by the color of the chicken's earlobe--white earlobes lay white eggs, reddish--brown earlobes lay brown eggs, etc. In the U.S., egg size is determined by the weight of a dozen eggs, not individual eggs, and range from Peewee to Jumbo. Store-bought eggs in the shell stay fresh for 3 to 5 weeks in a home refrigerator, according to the USDA.

Eggs are primarily used as a source of food, although eggs are also widely used for medical purposes. Fertile eggs, as a source of purified proteins, are used to produce many vaccines. Flu vaccines are produced by growing single strains of the flu virus in eggs, which are then extracted to make the vaccine. Eggs are also used in biotechnology to create new drugs. The hen's genetic make-up can be altered so the whites of the eggs are rich in tailored proteins that form the basis of medicines to fight cancer and other diseases. The U.S. biotech company Viragen and the Roslin Institute in Edinburgh have produced eggs with 100 mg or more of the easily-extracted proteins used in new drugs to treat various illnesses including ovarian and breast cancers.

Prices – The average monthly price of all eggs received

by farmers in the U.S. in 2010 rose by +4.4% yr/yr to 85.0 cents per dozen, which down from the 2008 record high of 106.5 cents per dozen.

Supply – World egg production in 2008, the latest reporting year, was 1,144.0 billion eggs. The world's largest egg producers at that time were China with 40.1% of world production, the U.S. with 8.0%, Japan with 4.0%, Mexico with 4.0%, Russia with 3.0%, and Brazil with 3.0%. U.S. egg production in 2010 rose +0.8% to 91.141 billion eggs, a new record high. The average number of hens and pullets on U.S. farms in 2009 fell by -0.5% yr/yr to 337.376 million, down further from the 2006 record high of 347.880 million.

Demand – U.S. consumption of eggs in 2009 fell -0.3% yr/yr to 6.316 billion dozen eggs. That was down from the 2006 record high of 6.468 billion dozen, but still up about 20% from ten years earlier, reflecting sharply higher egg consumption due to the popularity of a low-carbohydrate diet since eggs are high in protein. U.S. per capita egg consumption in 2010 fell 0.2% yr/yr to 245.8 eggs per year per person. Per capita egg consumption was at a high of 277.2 eggs in 1970, then fell sharply in the 1990s to a low of 174.9 in 1995, and then began rebounding in 1997 to current levels of about 250 eggs per year.

Trade – U.S. imports of eggs in 2010 rose +5.3% yr/yr to 12.0 million dozen eggs. U.S. exports of eggs in 2010 fell -8.1% yr/yr to 220.0 million dozen eggs, still below the record export level of 253.1 million dozen eggs in 1996.

World Production of Eggs   In Millions of Eggs

Year	Brazil	China	France	Germany	Italy	Japan	Mexico	Russia	Spain	Ukraine	United Kingdom	United States	World Total
2001	30,783	383,074	16,940	14,167	12,830	41,985	37,843	35,002	11,928	9,553	10,332	85,884	983,951
2002	30,951	393,179	16,480	14,262	12,855	42,157	38,012	36,106	13,113	11,159	10,272	87,216	1,008,456
2003	31,423	403,660	16,598	12,588	12,838	42,173	37,451	36,296	13,722	11,380	10,116	87,473	1,022,902
2004	32,319	410,015	15,757	12,353	13,054	41,346	40,033	35,562	15,213	11,883	10,704	89,091	1,045,290
2005	33,499	420,951	15,502	12,028	12,896	41,377	40,494	36,691	13,122	12,955	10,608	90,027	1,069,133
2006	35,207	418,718	15,138	12,137	12,123	41,611	45,801	37,651	13,122	14,122	10,166	90,877	1,090,051
2007	35,584	436,664	14,640	11,974	12,929	43,050	45,817	37,889	13,095	13,978	9,920	91,101	1,215,435
2008[1]	36,893	454,955	15,783	12,103	12,929	42,567	46,744	37,830	12,894	14,809	10,277	90,151	1,157,337
2009[2]		477,395	15,305			41,750		39,188	13,050	15,700			1,180,516

[1] Preliminary.   [2] Forecast.   [3] Selected countries.   *Source: Food and Agricultural Organization of the United Nations (FAO)*

Salient Statistics of Eggs in the United States

	Hens & Pullets		Rate of Lay	Eggs								Consumption	
Year	On Farm Dec. 1[3]	Average Number During Year	Per Layer During Year[4]	Total Produced	Price in cents Per Dozen	Value of Production[5] Million USD	Total Egg Production	Imports[6]	Exports[6]	Used for Hatching	Total	Per Capita Eggs[6] Number
	----- Thousands -----		(Number)	----- Millions -----			--------------------- Million Dozen ---------------------					
2002	339,827	339,024	257	87,252	58.9	4,281	7,270	15.0	174.0	961.3	6,150	256.0
2003	340,979	338,393	259	87,473	73.2	5,333	7,299	13.3	146.0	959.4	6,204	255.7
2004	344,278	341,956	261	89,091	71.4	5,299	7,450	12.7	167.6	988.1	6,306	257.3
2005	347,917	343,792	262	90,027	54.0	4,049	7,538	8.5	203.3	996.7	6,345	255.8
2006	348,719	347,880	263	91,328	58.2	4,432	7,650	8.6	202.1	992.2	6,468	257.8
2007	344,492	346,498	263	91,101	88.5	6,719	7,587	13.6	250.3	1,016.3	6,335	250.1
2008	339,643	339,131	266	90,040	109.0	8,216	7,501	14.6	206.3	996.3	6,307	248.9
2009[1]	339,526	337,848	268	90,484	81.7	6,156	7,534	11.0	242.2	955.1	6,347	247.7
2010[2]	340,189	339,961	269	91,398			7,638	12.4	244.3	985.4	6,421	246.2

[1] Preliminary.   [2] Forecast.   [3] All layers of laying age.   [4] Number of eggs produced during the year divided by the average number of all layers of laying age on hand during the year.   [5] Value of sales plus value of eggs consumed in households of producers. 6/ Shell-egg equivalent of eggs and egg products.   *Source: National Agricultural Statistics Service, U.S. Department of Agriculture (NASS-USDA)*

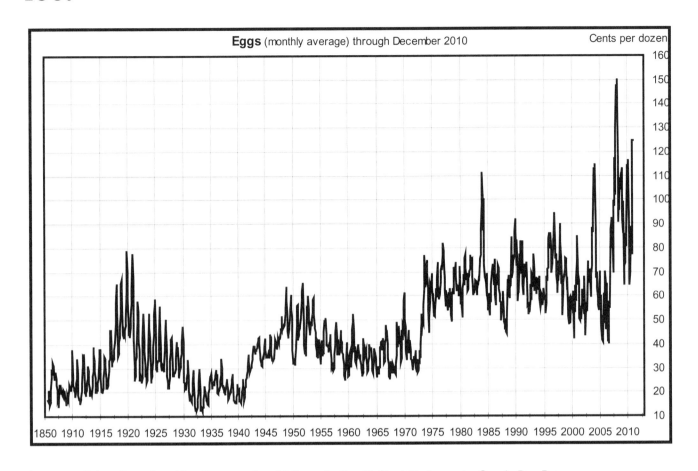

Eggs (monthly average) through December 2010 — Cents per dozen

Average Price Received by Farmers for All Eggs in the United States   In Cents Per Dozen

Year	Jan.	Feb.	Mar.	Apr.	May	June	July	Aug.	Sept.	Oct.	Nov.	Dec.	Average
2001	67.2	68.2	69.1	65.0	55.2	55.0	54.0	56.6	55.5	59.9	64.1	59.0	60.7
2002	62.3	55.9	68.5	52.2	50.5	62.1	60.8	66.4	57.1	56.0	70.7	62.8	60.4
2003	63.6	59.3	68.7	68.6	58.7	67.2	68.7	80.8	77.6	83.8	102.0	86.8	73.8
2004	92.6	87.5	110.0	76.7	62.6	77.3	64.0	52.6	53.8	49.4	60.4	65.4	71.0
2005	55.8	55.1	52.6	47.4	45.6	45.2	52.7	47.1	63.6	51.1	65.0	71.9	54.4
2006	61.0	49.5	67.0	51.2	42.7	54.7	43.5	55.0	53.4	54.1	81.2	80.7	57.8
2007	91.5	78.1	82.8	72.9	78.0	73.4	94.5	86.6	107.0	93.5	126.0	136.0	93.4
2008	129.0	131.0	138.0	103.0	86.8	106.0	84.1	96.3	99.6	102.0	102.0	99.9	106.5
2009	103.0	80.9	81.6	92.0	61.7	59.4	70.8	75.8	74.4	80.0	101.0	105.0	82.1
2010[1]	103.0	91.7	116.0	76.7	63.3	61.9	70.8	79.2	63.6	81.3	113.0	108.0	85.7

[1] Preliminary.   *Source: Economic Research Service, U.S. Department of Agriculture (ERS-USDA)*

Average Wholesale Price of Shell Eggs (Large) Delivered, Chicago   In Cents Per Dozen

Year	Jan.	Feb.	Mar.	Apr.	May	June	July	Aug.	Sept.	Oct.	Nov.	Dec.	Average
2001	68.52	64.45	69.00	66.12	50.61	49.81	52.83	55.46	50.21	57.41	62.50	58.05	58.75
2002	60.43	52.00	68.00	47.23	43.73	56.40	53.02	57.16	53.20	54.43	74.00	66.38	57.17
2003	69.57	65.39	71.05	68.83	59.10	68.76	72.39	88.26	86.21	92.07	113.16	101.09	79.66
2004	105.10	103.89	115.00	86.88	67.28	70.00	63.12	59.45	55.81	53.79	60.36	69.83	75.88
2005	54.78	60.26	48.32	42.00	41.57	40.72	51.38	42.78	61.19	48.38	62.41	70.21	52.00
2006	65.40	46.08	65.11	57.11	41.32	56.14	40.30	57.46	54.97	55.64	84.38	87.65	59.30
2007	91.75	92.71	89.23	80.00	83.55	69.60	99.95	97.37	117.50	101.89	128.93	147.70	100.02
2008	144.55	142.70	150.15	115.23	90.64	107.33	95.43	100.07	108.98	103.85	110.50	109.50	114.91
2009	113.40	92.29	85.64	99.26	64.55	72.41	73.55	85.69	80.17	86.14	110.75	114.41	89.86
2010[1]	111.50	107.55	116.80	84.81	64.15	69.68	73.74	88.73	83.17	76.88	124.79	124.73	93.88

[1] Preliminary.   *Source: National Agricultural Statistics Service, U.S. Department of Agriculture (NASS-USDA)*

Total Egg Production in the United States   In Millions of Eggs

Year	Jan.	Feb.	Mar.	Apr.	May	June	July	Aug.	Sept.	Oct.	Nov.	Dec.	Total
2001	7,226	6,524	7,336	7,099	7,240	6,992	7,195	7,221	7,044	7,347	7,191	7,420	85,835
2002	7,264	6,581	7,417	7,105	7,297	7,126	7,347	7,356	7,147	7,412	7,226	7,451	86,729
2003	7,390	6,665	7,424	7,187	7,327	7,105	7,403	7,367	7,112	7,439	7,326	7,554	87,299
2004	7,386	6,901	7,547	7,358	7,513	7,289	7,557	7,538	7,344	7,659	7,482	7,721	89,295
2005	7,626	6,928	7,738	7,407	7,572	7,346	7,563	7,528	7,348	7,665	7,514	7,793	90,028
2006	7,727	6,980	7,843	7,543	7,637	7,401	7,645	7,647	7,430	7,678	7,549	7,815	90,895
2007	7,675	6,951	7,806	7,472	7,622	7,380	7,599	7,594	7,393	7,726	7,542	7,808	90,568
2008	7,646	7,114	7,675	7,373	7,564	7,367	7,599	7,551	7,339	7,625	7,490	7,778	90,121
2009	7,678	6,903	7,737	7,472	7,607	7,360	7,590	7,593	7,376	7,696	7,569	7,853	90,434
2010[1]	7,724	6,935	7,839	7,578	7,716	7,484	7,719	7,765	7,514	7,698	7,573	7,920	91,465

[1] Preliminary.   Source: National Agricultural Statistics Service, U.S. Department of Agriculture (NASS-USDA)

Per Capita Disappearance of Eggs[4] in the United States   In Number of Eggs

Year	First Quarter	Second Quarter	Third Quarter	Fourth Quarter	Total	Total Consumption (Million Dozen)	Year	First Quarter	Second Quarter	Third Quarter	Fourth Quarter	Total	Total Consumption (Million Dozen)
2000	64.5	64.0	64.2	65.6	252.1	5,955	2006	64.1	63.7	63.9	64.7	257.8	6,468
2001	64.5	64.2	64.7	66.6	252.7	6,043	2007	62.2	61.7	62.4	63.8	250.1	6,335
2002	62.4	62.6	64.0	64.6	256.0	6,150	2008	61.8	61.3	62.0	63.8	248.9	6,307
2003	62.6	63.0	63.8	65.3	255.7	6,204	2009[1]	62.0	61.5	61.4	62.9	247.7	6,347
2004	63.7	63.9	64.1	65.5	257.3	6,306	2010[2]	61.1	61.1	61.8	62.4	246.3	6,421
2005	63.4	63.0	63.5	65.0	255.8	6,345	2011[3]	61.4	61.2	61.7	63.0	247.4	6,400

[1] Preliminary.   [2] Estimate.   [3] Forecast.   Source: Economic Research Service, U.S. Department of Agriculture (ERS-USDA)

Egg-Feed Ratio[1] in the United States

Year	Jan.	Feb.	Mar.	Apr.	May	June	July	Aug.	Sept.	Oct.	Nov.	Dec.	Average
2001	10.9	11.4	11.6	11.3	8.6	8.5	7.9	8.4	8.5	10.3	11.5	9.3	9.9
2002	10.2	8.4	11.6	7.4	6.7	9.5	7.5	7.9	7.1	6.6	10.5	8.9	8.5
2003	9.0	8.0	9.5	9.3	6.9	8.8	9.8	12.7	11.6	12.6	15.7	12.2	10.5
2004	12.9	10.7	13.2	7.8	6.0	6.6	5.9	5.6	6.5	5.8	8.8	9.8	8.3
2005	7.2	7.4	6.3	5.2	4.6	4.4	5.9	5.1	9.3	6.6	10.3	11.3	7.0
2006	8.5	5.9	9.8	6.3	4.2	7.1	4.6	7.5	6.9	6.4	10.6	10.1	7.3
2007	11.7	8.4	9.1	7.6	8.1	6.4	10.7	9.5	12.3	10.2	13.9	13.9	10.2
2008	12.7	11.1	11.8	7.4	5.8	7.3	5.4	6.6	7.7	8.9	9.4	9.2	8.6
2009	9.0	7.0	7.2	8.4	4.3	3.8	5.6	6.5	6.8	7.3	10.0	10.3	7.2
2010[1]	10.1	8.9	12.2	7.0	5.1	5.0	6.0	6.9	4.6	6.5	9.5	8.1	7.5

[1] Pounds of laying feed equivalent in value to one dozen eggs.   [2] Preliminary.   Source: Economic Research Service, U.S. Department of Agriculture (ERS-USDA)

Hens and Pullets of Laying Age (Layers) in the United States, on First of Month   In Thousands

Year	Jan.	Feb.	Mar.	Apr.	May	June	July	Aug.	Sept.	Oct.	Nov.	Dec.
2001	332,107	335,449	336,131	337,472	336,755	333,522	332,274	332,148	333,417	336,573	337,549	338,625
2002	339,423	338,465	337,478	337,376	336,131	335,547	335,236	335,717	336,561	337,923	338,350	339,827
2003	340,752	341,019	340,080	339,645	336,678	335,611	333,925	334,381	334,248	334,103	336,528	339,989
2004	338,272	338,774	340,479	342,879	342,305	343,233	342,392	342,522	343,405	344,794	345,267	344,278
2005	347,273	348,412	349,117	344,759	342,346	341,247	338,424	338,674	339,984	341,803	343,789	347,917
2006	349,763	349,930	350,452	350,453	346,809	343,596	341,733	340,728	342,309	343,946	345,090	348,719
2007	349,192	348,563	349,081	347,280	343,835	341,057	339,373	340,648	340,604	341,322	343,909	344,492
2008	345,535	343,891	342,666	341,320	340,318	339,867	337,416	335,094	335,396	333,534	336,301	339,643
2009	341,373	341,388	340,716	341,067	339,239	334,953	333,064	332,371	332,808	334,917	336,671	339,526
2010[1]	341,411	339,747	341,191	341,757	338,203	337,624	339,256	338,326	339,602	335,659	336,098	340,189

[1] Preliminary.   Source: National Agricultural Statistics Service, U.S. Department of Agriculture (NASS-USDA)

EGGS

Eggs Laid Per Hundred Layers in the United States   In Number of Eggs

Year	Jan.	Feb.	Mar.	Apr.	May	June	July	Aug.	Sept.	Oct.	Nov.	Dec.	Average
2001	2,165	1,943	2,178	2,106	2,160	2,100	2,166	2,170	2,103	2,180	2,130	2,188	2,132
2002	2,143	1,947	2,198	2,110	2,173	2,125	2,190	2,188	2,119	2,192	2,139	2,189	2,143
2003	2,168	1,957	2,184	2,125	2,180	2,122	2,215	2,203	2,128	2,218	2,166	2,223	2,157
2004	2,182	2,032	2,209	2,148	2,192	2,126	2,207	2,198	2,134	2,220	2,170	2,234	2,171
2005	2,192	1,986	2,230	2,156	2,215	2,162	2,234	2,218	2,155	2,236	2,172	2,234	2,183
2006	2,210	1,994	2,238	2,164	2,212	2,160	2,240	2,239	2,165	2,228	2,176	2,234	2,188
2007	2,200	1,993	2,242	2,162	2,226	2,169	2,235	2,229	2,168	2,255	2,191	2,255	2,194
2008	2,218	2,072	2,244	2,163	2,224	2,175	2,260	2,252	2,194	2,277	2,216	2,283	2,215
2009	2,249	2,024	2,269	2,197	2,256	2,203	2,281	2,283	2,209	2,292	2,239	2,303	2,234
2010[1]	2,268	2,037	2,292	2,220	2,274	2,203	2,270	2,283	2,218	2,285	2,233	2,311	2,241

[1] Preliminary.   Source: National Agricultural Statistics Service, U.S. Department of Agriculture (NASS-USDA)

Egg-Type Chicks Hatched by Commercial Hatcheries in the United States   In Thousands

Year	Jan.	Feb.	Mar.	Apr.	May	June	July	Aug.	Sept.	Oct.	Nov.	Dec.	Total
2001	36,728	37,836	41,015	42,789	42,655	40,822	38,651	34,987	37,140	35,825	32,355	31,870	452,673
2002	35,655	34,473	36,985	38,096	38,760	35,144	35,581	35,689	35,742	32,157	31,154	32,113	421,549
2003	33,521	30,474	36,775	37,820	37,630	36,602	35,578	33,199	35,763	34,812	30,241	33,588	416,003
2004	35,155	31,923	37,545	37,466	38,347	37,508	34,919	36,854	36,631	34,866	38,758	37,332	437,304
2005	38,291	34,427	41,701	38,049	38,792	35,034	34,897	38,700	33,623	35,461	32,285	35,917	437,177
2006	35,159	33,409	38,805	35,435	39,744	37,406	32,727	35,611	36,873	36,162	31,554	33,183	426,068
2007	36,195	36,739	38,561	39,254	38,080	40,641	35,952	36,930	35,327	36,332	36,232	35,866	446,109
2008	40,256	38,534	41,954	42,329	41,826	40,928	37,250	35,578	37,111	40,198	34,187	37,091	467,242
2009	37,812	36,795	41,737	42,794	40,758	41,968	36,213	37,945	40,515	37,566	34,512	39,554	468,169
2010[1]	38,794	40,120	45,151	47,503	43,075	42,623	38,053	37,023	40,307	41,263	38,947	37,845	490,704

[1] Preliminary.   Source: National Agricultural Statistics Service, U.S. Department of Agriculture (NASS-USDA)

Cold Storage Holdings of Frozen Eggs in the United States, on First of Month   In Millions of Pounds[2]

Year	Jan.	Feb.	Mar.	Apr.	May	June	July	Aug.	Sept.	Oct.	Nov.	Dec.
2001	15.0	16.9	15.5	14.6	15.9	15.8	14.4	16.7	17.8	17.7	15.5	13.9
2002	13.7	13.1	13.9	11.7	10.2	11.1	12.7	12.9	13.2	13.2	13.1	11.2
2003	13.5	15.3	17.1	17.0	15.7	17.7	18.0	18.6	18.0	16.6	16.9	14.9
2004	18.0	21.3	21.1	19.2	20.9	20.6	18.3	16.7	17.3	18.7	17.9	17.3
2005	19.1	18.6	17.9	18.5	18.9	17.7	19.7	19.6	19.9	18.8	17.6	17.6
2006	21.0	22.5	24.5	20.8	23.3	21.0	22.1	23.6	21.6	19.0	16.3	17.1
2007	16.5	17.2	15.7	14.6	14.3	15.2	17.4	17.5	18.5	17.7	17.6	15.2
2008	14.7	12.0	16.7	16.3	16.0	12.4	16.1	21.1	20.8	21.9	22.4	21.3
2009	22.6	22.6	22.1	20.3	18.2	21.7	21.7	22.6	22.6	21.6	22.9	21.2
2010[1]	23.6	24.3	24.1	21.6	22.4	22.4	25.0	24.7	24.7	26.1	25.6	22.9

[1] Preliminary.   [2] Converted on basis 39.5 pounds frozen eggs equals 1 case.   Source: National Agricultural Statistics Service, U.S. Department of Agriculture (NASS-USDA)

Electric Power

The modern electric utility industry began in the 1800s. In 1807, Humphry Davy constructed a practical battery and demonstrated both incandescent and arc light. In 1831, Michael Faraday built the first electric generator proving that rotary mechanical power could be converted into electric power. In 1879, Thomas Edison perfected a practical incandescent light bulb. The electric utility industry evolved from gas and electric carbon-arc commercial and street lighting systems. In 1882, in New York City, Thomas Edison's Pearl Street electricity generating station established the industry by displaying the four key elements of a modern electric utility system: reliable central generation, efficient distribution, successful end use, and a competitive price.

Electricity is measured in units called watts and watt-hours. Electricity must be used when it is generated and cannot be stored to any significant degree. That means the power utilities must match the level of electricity generation to the level of demand in order to avoid wasteful over-production. The power industry has been deregulated to some degree in the past decade and now major utility companies sell power back and forth across major national grids in order to meet supply and demand needs. The rapid changes in the supply-demand situation mean that the cost of electricity can be very volatile.

Electricity futures trade at the New York Mercantile Exchange (NYMEX). The futures contract is a financially settled contract, which is priced based on electricity prices in the PJM western hub at 111 delivery points, mainly on the utility transmission systems of Pennsylvania Electric Co. and the Potomac Electric Co. The contract is priced in dollars and cents per megawatt hours.

Supply – U.S. electricity production in 2010 (annualized through September) rose +3.1% yr/yr to 2.447 trillion kilowatt-hours. That was well below the record high of 3.212 trillion kilowatt-hours in 1998 and indicated that recent electricity production has been reduced by more efficient production and distribution systems, and to some extent by conservation of electricity by both business and residential consumers.

U.S. electricity generation in 2009 (latest data available) required the use of 2.911 trillion cubic feet of natural gas (+6.6% yr/yr), 695 million tons of coal (8.5% yr/yr), and 45 million barrels of fuel oil (-9.6% yr/yr).

In terms of kilowatt-hours, coal is the most widely used source of electricity production in the U.S. accounting for 45.9% of electricity production in 2009, followed by nuclear (20.9%), hydro (7.1%), natural gas (22.0%), and fuel oil (0.9%). Alternative sources of fuel for electricity generation that are gaining favor include geothermal, biomass, solar, wind, etc. but so far account for only 0.5% of total electricity production in the U.S.

Demand – Residential use of electricity accounts for the largest single category of electricity demand with usage of 1.362 trillion kilowatt hours in 2009 (latest data) accounting for 38.1% of overall usage. Business users in total use more electricity than residential users, but business users are broken into the categories of commercial with 37.0% of usage and industrial with 24.7% of usage.

World Electricity Production (Monthly Average) In Millions of Kilowatt Hours

Year	Australia	Canada	China	Germany	India	Italy	Japan	Rep. of Korea	Russia	South Africa	Ukraine	United Kingdom	United States
2001	15,548	56,576	118,439	47,107	42,434	23,242	77,742	23,768	74,031	17,508	14,414	29,414	311,387
2002	15,646	57,873	133,513	47,211	44,141	23,638	77,139	25,500	74,078	18,142	14,477	29,220	321,538
2003	15,564	56,294	153,229	49,060	52,773	24,386	76,661	26,856	76,158	19,267	15,030	35,006	307,250
2004	16,095	56,844	176,169	44,439	48,968	24,975	71,574	28,472	77,562	20,648	15,180	34,924	316,000
2005	16,870	49,559	199,780	48,840	51,125	25,754	72,667	30,363	79,355	20,673	15,505	33,377	336,499
2006	19,077	48,758	229,119	45,030	54,309	26,037	74,906	31,773	82,619	21,150	16,115	33,272	338,725
2007	18,958	50,265	265,047	43,565	57,933	26,070	82,731	33,594	84,656	21,957	16,272	30,117	346,395
2008	19,793	50,141	282,692	43,565	59,874	26,393	82,573	35,313	86,429	21,524	15,982	29,607	343,282
2009[1]	19,287	47,898	301,774	39,528	63,035	24,160	76,494	36,109	82,681	20,796	14,412	28,456	329,426
2010[2]	19,392	53,316	334,619	39,647	66,111	24,547	77,875	38,886	84,086	21,707	15,229	28,093	349,695

[1] Preliminary.　[2] Estimate.　NA = Not avaliable.　*Source: United Nations*

Installed Capacity, Capability & Peak Load of the U.S. Electric Utility Industry In Thousands of Megawatts (Nameplate)

Year	Total Electric Utility Industry	------ Type of Prime Mover ------ Hydro & Steam	Gas Turbine Nuclear Power	Internal Combustion	------------- Type of Ownership ------------- Investor	Cooper-ative	Sub-total Gov't.	Munic-ipal Utilities	Federal	Power Districts, State Projects	Capa-bility at Winter Peak Load	Non-Coin-cident Winter Peak Load	Capacity Margin Non-Co-incident Peak Load (%)	Total Electric Utility Industry Generation (Mil. kWh)	Annual Peak Load Factor (%)
1990	735.1	87.2	531.1	108.0	8.7	568.8	26.3	139.9	40.1	65.4	34.4	696.8	484.8	20.4	2,901.3	60.4
1991	740.0	88.7	534.1	108.4	8.8	573.0	26.5	140.5	40.4	65.6	34.5	703.2	486.4	20.2	2,935.6	60.9
1992	741.7	89.7	534.5	107.9	9.6	572.9	26.0	142.7	41.6	66.1	35.0	707.8	493.6	21.1	2,934.4	61.1
1993	744.7	90.2	536.9	107.8	9.8	575.2	26.1	143.4	41.8	66.1	35.5	712.0	522.4	17.1	3,043.9	61.0
1994	764.0	90.3	537.9	107.9	9.9	574.8	26.4	144.7	42.0	66.3	36.4	715.1	518.9	16.7	3,088.7	61.2
1995	769.0	91.1	541.6	107.9	9.9	578.7	27.1	144.8	42.2	65.9	36.6	727.7	545.4	13.2	3,194.2	59.8
1996	463.0	91.0	546.6	109.0	9.9	582.2	27.2	147.1	43.0	67.2	36.9	740.5	554.1	27.7	3,284.1	61.0
1997	775.9	92.5	549.7	107.6	10.0	582.5	28.0	149.4	43.8	68.9	36.7	743.8	529.9	26.0	3,329.4	61.3
1998	778.6	91.2	522.1	104.8	10.2	531.3	32.5	164.5	50.5	68.7	45.3	835.3	567.6	25.7	3,457.4	62.0
1999[1]	775.9	89.8	476.3	102.3	9.6	483.7	34.6	159.6	50.2	68.7	40.7	848.9	570.9	26.7	3,530.0	61.2

[1] Preliminary.　*Source: Edison Electric Institute (EEI)*

ELECTRIC POWER

Available Electricity and Energy Sales in the United States — In Billions of Kilowatt Hours

| | Net Generation — Electric Utility Industry | | | | | | | | | Sales to Ultimate Customer | | | | | | | |
Year	Total[2]	Hydro	Natural Gas	Coal	Fuel Oil	Nu-clear	Other Sources[3]	Total	Total Million $	Total	Resi-den-tial	Inter-depart-mental	Com-mercial	Indus-trial	Street & highway Lighting	Other Public Auth.	Rail-ways & Rail-roads
2000	3,638	271.3	518.0	1,943	105.2	753.9	46.0	3,802	233,163	3,421	1,192	[4]	1,055.2	1,064	[4]	109.5	[4]
2001	3,580	213.7	554.9	1,883	119.1	768.8	40.6	3,737	247,343	3,394	1,202	[4]	1,083.1	997	[4]	113.2	[4]
2002	3,698	260.5	607.7	1,911	89.7	780.1	49.9	3,858	249,411	3,465	1,265	[4]	1,104.5	990	[4]	105.6	[4]
2003	3,721	271.5	567.3	1,953	113.7	763.7	52.2	3,883	259,767	3,494	1,276	[4]	1,198.7	1,012	[4]	NA	[4]
2004	3,808	265.1	627.2	1,957	114.7	788.5	55.7	3,971	270,119	3,547	1,292	[4]	1,230.4	1,018	[4]	NA	[4]
2005	3,902	267.0	683.8	1,992	116.5	782.0	60.8	4,055	298,003	3,661	1,359	[4]	1,275.1	1,019	[4]	NA	[4]
2006	3,908	286.3	734.4	1,970	59.7	787.2	70.7	4,065	326,506	3,670	1,352	[4]	1,299.7	1,011	[4]	NA	[4]
2007	4,005	245.8	814.8	1,998	61.3	806.4	78.6	4,157	343,703	3,765	1,392	[4]	1,336.3	1,028	[4]	NA	[4]
2008	3,974	253.1	802.4	1,969	42.9	806.2	101.0	4,119	363,650	3,733	1,380	[4]	1,336.0	1,009	[4]	NA	[4]
2009[1]	3,814	270.2	840.9	1,750	35.8	798.7	119.0	3,953	353,581	3,575	1,362	[4]	1,323.4	882	[4]	NA	[4]

[1] Preliminary.   [2] Includes internal combustion.   [3] Includes electricity produced from geothermal, wood, waste, wind, solar, etc.   [4] Included in Other.
NA = Not available.   *Source: Edison Electric Institute (EEI)*

Electric Power Production by Electric Utilities in the United States — In Millions of Kilowatt Hours

Year	Jan.	Feb.	Mar.	Apr.	May	June	July	Aug.	Sept.	Oct.	Nov.	Dec.	Total
2001	236,467	199,802	211,942	197,499	215,508	233,622	253,400	258,901	214,236	204,307	192,518	211,742	2,629,946
2002	215,684	187,929	200,833	194,038	208,436	227,940	248,962	241,449	215,408	201,705	194,205	212,868	2,549,457
2003	217,338	189,944	193,305	181,914	200,634	212,297	234,888	234,675	201,966	192,198	189,362	213,758	2,462,281
2004	221,782	198,675	193,763	182,744	207,224	219,767	235,266	227,785	209,507	197,320	191,813	219,585	2,505,231
2005	212,654	185,283	196,136	178,408	197,082	221,116	239,381	238,790	211,139	193,687	188,255	212,914	2,474,845
2006	204,976	192,304	197,249	184,803	204,107	223,950	243,526	242,624	200,655	193,321	189,435	206,705	2,483,655
2007	218,288	197,329	197,229	184,017	202,783	218,554	234,728	246,147	209,641	197,285	189,498	208,631	2,504,130
2008	220,229	197,368	194,959	185,415	201,811	225,775	239,383	230,563	201,631	186,930	184,192	207,111	2,475,367
2009	216,218	179,859	184,963	174,130	189,695	213,482	221,545	222,452	193,720	184,019	179,276	213,417	2,372,776
2010[1]	221,058	195,004	187,407	170,973	198,954	227,924	243,277	239,569	202,389	177,956	178,811	216,900	2,460,222

[1] Preliminary.   *Source: Energy Information Administration, U.S. Department of Energy (EIA-DOE)*

Use of Fuels for Electric Generation in the United States

Year	Coal (Thousand ShortTons)	Fuel Oil (Thousand Barrels)	Gas (Million Cubic Feet)	Total Fuel in Coal Equiva-lent[3]	Net Generation by Fuels[4] (Million Kilowatt Hour)	Pounds of Coal Per Kilowatt Hour (Pounds)	Cost of Fossil-Fuel at Elec. Utilities (Cents/MMBTU)	Average Cost of Fuel Per Kilowatt Hour (In Cents)	Heat Rate BTU Per Kilowatt Hour	Cost Per Million BTU Consumed (In Cents)
2000	859,335	125,788	3,043,094				173.8			174.0
2001	806,269	133,456	2,686,287				173.0			173.0
2002	767,803	99,219	2,259,684				151.5			186.0
2003	757,384	118,087	1,763,764							228.0
2004	772,224	124,541	1,809,443							248.0
2005	761,349	118,874	2,134,859							325.0
2006	753,390	71,624	2,478,396							302.0
2007	764,765	70,950	2,736,418							323.0
2008	760,326	50,475	2,730,134							411.0
2009[1]	695,615	45,651	2,911,279							304.0

[1] Preliminary.   [2] 42-gallon barrels.   [3] Coal equivalents are calculated on the basis of Btu instead of generation data.   [4] Excludes wood & waste fuels.
Source: Edison Electric Institute (EEI)

Ethanol

World Production of Ethanol   In Millions of Gallons

Year	Brazil	China	France	Germany	India	Russia	Saudi Arabia	South Africa	Spain	Thailand	United Kingdom	United States	World Total
2004	3,989	964	219	71	462	198	79	110	79	74	106	3,404	10,770
2005	4,227	1,004	240	114	449	198	32	103	93	79	92	3,904	12,150
2006	4,491	1,017	251	202	502	171	52	102	122	93	74	4,885	13,489
2007	5,019	486			53					79		6,519	13,102
2008	6,472	502			66					90		9,307	17,335
2009[1]	6,578	542			92					435		10,939	19,535
2010[2]	6,922	542										13,229	

[1] Preliminary.   [2] Estimate.   *Source: Renewable Fuels Association*

Salient Statistics of Ethanol in the United States

Year	Ethanol Plants	Ethanol Production Capacity (mgy)	Plants Under Con-struction	Capacity Under Construction (mgy)	Farmer Owned Plants	Farmer Owned Capacity (mgy)	Percent of Total Capacity Farmer	Farmer Owned UC Plants	Farmers Owned UC Capacity	Percent of Total UC Capacity	States with Ethanol Plants
2003	68	2,706.8	11	483.0	28	796.6	29	8	318	66	20
2004	72	3,100.8	15	598.0	33	1,041.1	34	12	447	75	19
2005	81	3,643.7	16	754.0	40	1,388.6	38	10	450	60	18
2006	95	4,336.4	31	1,778.0	46	1,677.1	39	4	187	11	20
2007	110	5,493.4	76	5,635.5	46	1,677.1	39	4	187	11	21
2008	139	7,888.4	61	5,536.0	49	1,948.6	28	13	771	12	21
2009[1]	170	12,475.4	24	2,066.0	NA	NA	NA	NA	NA	NA	26
2010[2]	189	13,028.4	15	1,432.0	NA	NA	NA	NA	NA	NA	26

[1] Preliminary.   [2] Estimate.   *Source: Renewable Fuels Association*

Production of Fuel Ethanol in the United States   In Thousands of Barrels Per Day

Year	Jan.	Feb.	Mar.	Apr.	May	June	July	Aug.	Sept.	Oct.	Nov.	Dec.	Average
2003	177	169	175	179	175	181	178	180	190	188	194	207	183
2004	211	212	214	218	221	222	218	225	226	226	232	233	222
2005	241	245	243	238	237	249	258	260	261	269	275	280	255
2006	288	302	301	289	293	318	316	330	336	339	348	362	319
2007	375	386	384	391	406	418	422	438	447	459	486	492	425
2008	518	535	565	572	605	588	614	647	645	647	671	656	605
2009	631	652	649	646	678	704	738	746	741	757	804	811	713
2010[1]	818	833	847	832	847	854	857	870	869	884	925	918	863

[1] Preliminary.   *Source: Energy Information Administration, U.S. Department of Energy (EIA-DOE)*

Production of Fuel Ethanol in the United States   In Thousands of Barrels

Year	Jan.	Feb.	Mar.	Apr.	May	June	July	Aug.	Sept.	Oct.	Nov.	Dec.	Total
2003	5,497	4,734	5,430	5,384	5,426	5,440	5,529	5,589	5,685	5,829	5,806	6,423	66,772
2004	6,551	6,155	6,648	6,525	6,857	6,648	6,749	6,977	6,766	7,007	6,946	7,229	81,058
2005	7,461	6,847	7,530	7,135	7,357	7,463	8,007	8,050	7,841	8,335	8,259	8,676	92,961
2006	8,935	8,463	9,333	8,663	9,086	9,531	9,791	10,235	10,088	10,512	10,442	11,215	116,294
2007	11,621	10,795	11,892	11,716	12,573	12,553	13,083	13,581	13,402	14,221	14,568	15,258	155,263
2008	16,058	15,527	17,527	17,152	18,756	17,651	19,040	20,059	19,338	20,048	20,139	20,342	221,637
2009	19,561	18,255	20,121	19,374	21,024	21,125	22,887	23,136	22,218	23,467	24,122	25,134	260,424
2010[1]	25,366	23,328	26,270	24,962	26,244	25,631	26,581	26,963	26,061	27,410	27,745	28,457	315,018

[1] Preliminary.   *Source: Energy Information Administration, U.S. Department of Energy (EIA-DOE)*

Stocks of Fuel Ethanol in the United States   In Thousands of Barrels

Year	Jan.	Feb.	Mar.	Apr.	May	June	July	Aug.	Sept.	Oct.	Nov.	Dec.
2003	6,933	5,943	6,549	6,528	6,507	6,753	6,975	6,744	7,256	7,201	6,472	5,978
2004	5,830	5,469	5,578	5,433	5,796	5,345	5,971	6,367	6,641	6,664	6,414	6,002
2005	6,142	6,261	6,605	6,861	6,810	6,064	5,926	5,398	5,317	5,591	5,723	5,563
2006	6,099	7,268	8,626	8,990	7,767	6,675	7,706	9,133	9,725	9,723	9,232	8,760
2007	8,656	8,765	8,539	8,807	8,966	9,171	9,866	11,011	11,555	11,449	11,218	10,535
2008	11,383	11,173	12,288	12,572	13,297	13,323	13,448	14,771	16,110	15,214	15,286	14,226
2009	14,514	15,834	16,411	15,322	14,173	13,974	14,223	14,671	15,283	14,933	15,578	16,594
2010[1]	17,800	18,897	19,691	19,682	19,721	18,610	17,784	17,340	17,295			

[1] Preliminary.   *Source: Energy Information Administration, U.S. Department of Energy (EIA-DOE)*

ETHANOL

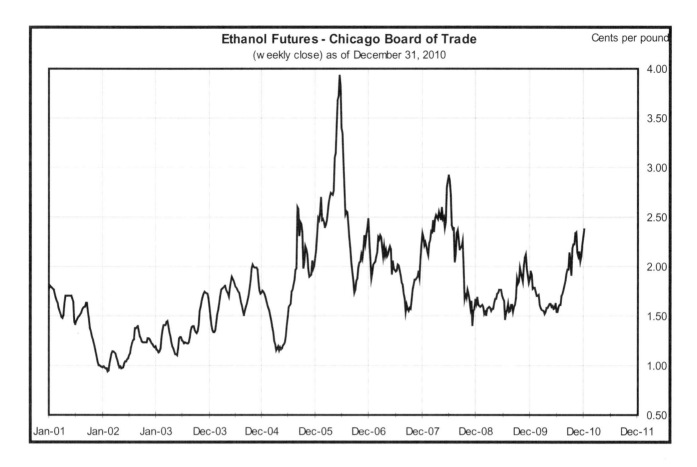

Ethanol Futures - Chicago Board of Trade
(weekly close) as of December 31, 2010

Cents per pound

Average Price of Ethanol in the United States[1]   In Dollars Per Gallon

Year	Jan.	Feb.	Mar.	Apr.	May	June	July	Aug.	Sept.	Oct.	Nov.	Dec.	Average
2003	1.151	1.278	1.427	1.269	1.131	1.242	1.234	1.262	1.388	1.381	1.645	1.716	1.344
2004	1.423	1.398	1.666	1.791	1.753	1.862	1.762	1.624	1.585	1.878	1.995	1.812	1.712
2005	1.733	1.597	1.365	1.237	1.221	1.405	1.786	2.031	2.695	2.511	2.130	1.916	1.802
2006	1.967	2.428	2.450	2.475	2.903	3.597	3.208	2.668	2.148	1.815	2.045	2.234	2.495
2007	2.144	1.899	2.185	2.159	2.169	2.089	1.970	1.849	1.581	1.523	1.739	1.950	1.938
2008	2.188	2.129	2.316	2.455	2.485	2.535	2.642	2.224	2.150	1.846	1.648	1.493	2.176
2009	1.518	1.488	1.461	1.497	1.553	1.673	1.585	1.535	1.540	1.798	1.984	1.962	1.633
2010	1.817	1.689	1.515	1.439	1.508	1.523	1.507	1.692	2.012	2.120	2.331	2.108	1.772

[1] Northeast and Northwest Iowa.   *Source: Agricultural Marketing Service, U.S. Department of Agriculture (AMS-USDA)*

Volume of Trading of Ethanol Futures in Chicago   In Contracts

Year	Jan.	Feb.	Mar.	Apr.	May	June	July	Aug.	Sept.	Oct.	Nov.	Dec.	Total
2005	----	----	350	119	222	61	155	321	227	390	559	272	2,676
2006	443	508	329	421	330	686	1,141	365	779	348	97	117	5,564
2007	191	526	945	1,153	784	1,163	792	969	704	966	1,436	2,887	12,516
2008	1,889	1,045	1,634	2,594	1,956	2,843	2,156	3,556	2,969	2,857	2,327	3,625	29,451
2009	2,969	2,116	7,158	4,673	4,031	5,535	4,707	4,843	7,439	6,530	6,521	10,646	67,168
2010	9,629	9,887	19,404	12,659	12,794	17,809	15,406	15,073	13,694	13,176	11,952	11,242	162,725

Contract size = 29,000 US gallons.   *Source: CME Group; Chicago Board of Trade (CBT)*

Month-End Open Interest of Ethanol Futures in Chicago   In Contracts

Year	Jan.	Feb.	Mar.	Apr.	May	June	July	Aug.	Sept.	Oct.	Nov.	Dec.
2005	----	----	246	215	88	39	61	208	301	461	759	778
2006	774	856	860	900	745	735	829	599	474	442	396	322
2007	402	478	593	623	842	1,227	1,100	1,378	1,326	1,642	1,853	2,141
2008	2,328	2,245	2,257	1,862	2,053	2,659	2,763	2,447	2,641	3,055	3,114	2,935
2009	3,146	3,228	4,644	4,145	4,381	4,174	3,877	4,631	4,940	5,575	5,932	6,904
2010	7,186	8,478	7,827	8,603	10,531	11,833	11,720	10,118	10,013	8,267	7,437	7,209

Contract size = 29,000 US gallons.   *Source: CME Group; Chicago Board of Trade (CBT)*

Fertilizer

Fertilizer is a natural or synthetic chemical substance, or mixture, that enriches soil to promote plant growth. The three primary nutrients that fertilizers provide are nitrogen, potassium, and phosphorus. In ancient times, and still today, many commonly used fertilizers contain one or more of the three primary ingredients: manure (containing nitrogen), bones (containing small amounts of nitrogen and large quantities of phosphorus), and wood ash (containing potassium).

At least fourteen different nutrients have been found essential for crops. These include three organic nutrients (carbon, hydrogen, and oxygen, which are taken directly from air and water), three primary chemical nutrients (nitrogen, phosphorus, and potassium), and three secondary chemical nutrients (magnesium, calcium, and sulfur). The others are micronutrients or trace elements and include iron, manganese, copper, zinc, boron, and molybdenum.

Prices – The average price of ammonia, a key source of ingredients for fertilizers, rose by +55.4% yr/yr in 2010 to $390 per metric ton, below the 2008 record high of $590 per metric ton. The average price of phosphate rock in the U.S. in 2006 (latest data available) rose by +3.1% yr/yr to a record high of $30.52 per metric ton. The average price of potash in the U.S. in 2009 (latest data) rose by +17.1% yr/yr to a record high of $820.00 per metric ton.

Supply – World production of nitrogen (as contained in ammonia) in 2010 rose +0.8% 131.000 million metric tons from the 2008 record high of 133.000 million metric tons. The world's largest producers of nitrogen in 2010 were China with 32.1% of world production, India (8.9%), Russia

(7.9%), and the U.S. (6.3%). U.S. nitrogen production in 2009 fell -1.9% to 7.700 million metric tons.

World production of phosphate rock, basic slag and guano in 2010 rose +6.0% yr/yr to 176.000 million metric tons. The world's largest producers of phosphate rock in 2010 were China (with 36.9% of world production), U.S. (14.8%), Morocco (14.8%), and Russia (5.7%). U.S. production in 2010 fell -1.1% y/y to 26.1 million metric tons.

World production of marketable potash in 2010 rose +32.0% yr/yr to 33.0 million metric tons, down from the 2008 record high of 34.7 million metric tons. The world's largest producers of potash in 2010 were Canada with 28.8% of world production, Russia (20.6%), Belarus (15.2%), and Germany (9.1%). U.S. production of potash in 2010 rose 28.6% yr/yr to 900,000 metric tons.

Demand – U.S. consumption of nitrogen in 2007 (latest data) rose +9.1% yr/yr to a 7-year high of 12.000 million metric tons. U.S. consumption of phosphate rock in 2010 rose +10.5% yr/yr to 30.4 million metric tons. U.S. consumption of potash in 2010 rose +100% yr/yr to 5.2 million metric tons, down from 2004's 12-year high of 6.000 million metric tons.

Trade – U.S. imports of nitrogen in 2010 rose +41.3% yr/yr to 6.400 million metric tons and the U.S. relied on imports for 43% of consumption. U.S. imports of phosphate rock in 2010 rose +5.0% yr/yr to 2.100 million metric tons. U.S. imports of potash in 2010 rose +111.7% to 4.700 million metric tons up from last year's 4-decade low of 2.400 million metric tons, and imports accounted for 83%

World Production of Ammonia — In Thousands of Metric Tons of Contained Nitrogen

Year	Canada	China	France	Germany	India	Indonesia	Japan	Mexico	Nether-lands	Poland	Russia	United States	Total
2002	3,700	30,200	1,172	2,560	9,827	4,200	1,192	559	2,053	1,311	8,600	10,300	109,000
2003	3,662	31,500	1,153	2,803	10,048	4,250	1,061	439	1,750	1,906	9,100	8,450	110,000
2004	4,107	34,770	1,120	2,741	10,718	4,120	1,101	560	1,970	1,984	9,800	8,990	117,000
2005	4,100	37,850	1,206	2,789	10,800	4,400	1,083	423	1,700	2,080	10,000	8,338	122,000
2006	4,100	40,660	616	2,718	10,900	4,300	1,091	487	1,800	2,007	10,500	8,190	126,000
2007	4,498	42,480	800	2,746	11,000	4,400	1,114	487	1,800	1,995	10,500	8,538	131,000
2008	4,781	41,140	800	2,819	11,100	4,500	1,110	625	1,800	1,995	10,425	7,867	130,000
2009[1]	4,000	42,300	800	2,360	11,200	4,600	1,120	624	1,800	1,990	10,400	7,704	130,000
2010[2]	4,000	42,000		2,500	11,700	4,600	1,000		1,800	1,900	10,400	8,300	131,000

[1] Preliminary. [2] Estimate. *Source: U.S. Geological Survey (USGS)*

Salient Statistics of Nitrogen[3] (Ammonia) in the United States — In Thousands of Metric Tons

Year	Net Import Reliance As a % of Apparent Consumption	Production[3] (Fixed) Fertilizer	Production[3] (Fixed) Non-fertilizer	Production[3] (Fixed) Total	Imprts[4] (Fixed)	Exports	Nitrogen[5] Compounds Produced	Nitrogen[5] Compounds Consumption	Stocks, Dec. 31 Ammonia	Stocks, Dec. 31 Fixed Nitrogen Compounds	Ammonia Consumption (Apparent)	Urea FOB Gulf[6] Coast	Urea FOB Corn Belt	Ammonium Nitrate: FOB Corn Belt	Ammonia FOB Gulf Coast
2002	29	9,300	1,030	10,300	4,670	437	9,937	11,000	286	1,140	14,500	128-132	150-160	120-130	137
2003	39	7,490	961	8,450	5,720	400	9,122	11,000	195	476	13,900	192-195	215-225	190-195	245
2004	38	8,470	524	8,990	5,900	381	9,258	11,900	298	590	14,400	225-230	255-270	195-210	274
2005	42	7,450	884	8,340	6,520	525	9,099	11,300	254	605	14,400	260-267	300-325	265-270	304
2006	41	7,270	921	8,190	5,920	194	9,083	11,000	201	485	14,000	265-280	295-305	250-260	302
2007	43	7,610	930	8,540	6,530	145	9,485	12,000	157	407	15,000	435-445	465-490	590-620	307
2008	42	6,730	1,140	7,870	6,020	192	8,605	11,500	302	794	13,600	190-210	270-330	450-650	590
2009[1]	38	6,470	1,240	7,700	4,530	16	8,071	11,600	167	364	12,300	307-315	350-360	340-390	251
2010[2]	43			8,300	6,400	8			151		14,700				390

[1] Preliminary. [2] Estimate. [3] Anhydrous ammonia, synthetic. [4] For consumption. [5] Major downstream nitrogen compounds. [6] Granular.
Source: U.S. Geological Survey (USGS)

FERTILIZER

World Production of Phosphate Rock, Basic Slag & Guano   In Thousands of Metric Tons (Gross Weight)

Year	Brazil	China	Egypt	Israel	Jordan	Morocco	Russia	Senegal	Syria	Togo	Tunisia	United States	World Total
2001	4,805	21,000	972	3,511	5,843	21,983	10,500	1,708	2,043	1,067	8,144	31,900	126,000
2002	5,084	23,000	1,550	4,091	7,179	23,028	10,700	1,551	2,483	1,271	7,461	36,100	136,000
2003	5,584	25,200	2,183	3,708	6,650	23,338	11,000	1,765	2,414	1,471	7,890	35,000	138,000
2004	5,690	25,500	2,219	3,290	6,188	26,675	11,000	1,580	2,883	1,115	8,051	35,800	143,000
2005	5,450	30,400	2,144	3,236	6,375	28,788	11,000	1,455	3,500	1,350	8,220	36,100	150,000
2006	5,930	38,600	2,200	2,949	5,805	27,000	11,000	584	3,664	1,650	7,801	30,100	151,000
2007	6,000	45,400	2,200	3,100	5,540	27,000	11,000	600	3,700	800	7,800	29,700	156,000
2008	6,200	50,700	3,000	3,090	6,270	25,000	10,400	700	3,220	800	8,000	30,200	161,000
2009[1]	6,350	60,200	5,000	2,700	5,280	23,000	10,000	650	2,470	850	7,400	26,400	166,000
2010[2]	5,500	65,000	5,000	3,000	6,000	26,000	10,000	650	2,800	800	7,600	26,100	176,000

[1] Preliminary.   [2] Estimate.   *Source: U.S. Geological Survey (USGS)*

Salient Statistics of Phosphate Rock in the United States   In Thousands of Metric Tons

Year	Mine Production	Marketable Production	Value Million Dollars	Imports for Consumption	Exports	Apparent Consumption	Producer Stocks, Dec. 31	Avg. Price FOB Mine $/Metric Ton	Avg. Price of Florida & N. Carolina - $/Met. Ton - FOB Mine (-60% to +74%) - Domestic	Export	Average
2001	130,000	31,900	856	2,500	9	35,300	7,510	26.82	26.82	W	26.81
2002	154,000	36,100	993	2,700	62	37,400	8,860	27.47	27.69	W	27.69
2003	153,000	35,000	946	2,400	64	38,800	7,540	27.01	26.95	W	26.95
2004	146,000	35,800	995	2,500	----	39,000	7,220	27.79	27.76	NA	27.76
2005	151,000	36,100	1,070	2,630	----	37,800	6,970	29.61	29.67	NA	29.60
2006	111,000	30,100	919	2,420	----	32,600	7,070	30.49	W	NA	30.52
2007	126,000	29,700	1,520	2,670	----	33,800	4,970	51.10	W	NA	51.36
2008	124,000	30,200	2,320	2,750	----	31,600	6,340	76.76	W	NA	76.64
2009[1]		26,400		2,000	----	27,500	8,120	127.19	W	NA	
2010[2]		26,100		2,100	----	30,400	5,800	50.00	W	NA	

[1] Preliminary.   [2] Estimate.   *Source: U.S. Geological Survey (USGS)*

World Production of Marketable Potash   In Thousands of Metric Tons (K_2O Equivalent)

Year	Belarus	Brazil	Canada	China	France	Germany	Israel	Jordan	Russia	Spain	United Kingdom	United States	World Total
2001	3,700	319	8,237	385	244	3,549	1,770	1,180	4,300	471	532	1,200	26,400
2002	3,800	337	8,515	450	130	3,472	1,950	1,191	4,400	481	540	1,200	27,100
2003	4,230	416	9,104	650	----	3,564	1,960	1,194	5,465	594	1,040	1,100	29,900
2004	4,600	403	10,100	770	----	3,627	2,138	1,180	6,405	590	547	1,200	32,200
2005	4,844	405	10,140	1,500	----	3,664	2,224	1,115	7,131	575	439	1,200	33,800
2006	4,605	403	8,518	1,800	----	3,625	2,187	1,036	6,610	435	420	1,100	31,200
2007	4,972	471	11,085	2,600	----	3,637	2,182	1,096	7,275	435	427	1,100	35,800
2008	4,968	471	10,455	2,750	----	3,280	2,300	1,223	6,730	435	427	1,100	34,700
2009[1]	3,850	500	6,500	2,750	----	2,300	2,000	1,100	3,600	400	400	700	25,000
2010[2]	5,000	400	9,500	3,000	----	3,000	2,100	1,200	6,800	400	400	900	33,000

[1] Preliminary.   [2] Estimate.   *Source: U.S. Geological Survey (USGS)*

Salient Statistics of Potash in the United States   In Thousands of Metric Tons (K_2O Equivalent)

Year	Net Import Reliance As a % of Apparent Consumption	Production	Sales by Producers	Value Million Dollars	Imports for Consumption	Exports	Apparent Consumption	Producer Stocks Dec. 31	Avg Value of Product	Avg Value of K_2O Equiv	Avg Price[3] (Metric Ton)
									----------- Dollars per Ton -----------		
2001	80	1,200	1,100	260.0	4,540	366	5,300	----	110.00	230.00	165.00
2002	80	1,200	1,200	280.0	4,620	371	5,400	----	110.00	230.00	155.00
2003	80	1,100	1,200	280.0	4,720	329	5,600	----	110.00	230.00	170.00
2004	80	1,200	1,300	340.0	4,920	233	6,000	----	125.00	270.00	200.00
2005	80	1,200	1,200	410.0	4,920	200	5,900	----	165.00	350.00	280.00
2006	79	1,100	1,100	410.0	4,470	332	5,200	----	170.00	375.00	290.00
2007	81	1,100	1,200	480.0	4,970	199	5,900	----	185.00	400.00	400.00
2008	84	1,100	1,100	740.0	5,800	222	6,700	----	300.00	675.00	700.00
2009[1]	73	700			2,220	303	2,600	----		835.00	820.00
2010[2]	83	900			4,700	380	5,200	----		600.00	

[1] Preliminary.   [2] Estimate.   [3] Unit of K_2O, standard 60% muriate F.O.B. mine.   *Source: U.S. Geological Survey (USGS)*

Fish

Fish are the primary source of protein for a large portion of the world's population. The worldwide yearly harvest of all sea fish (including aquaculture) is between 85 and 130 million metric tons. There are approximately 20,000 species of fish, of which 9,000 are regularly caught. Only 22 fish species are harvested in large amounts. Ground-fish, which are fish that live near or on the ocean floor, account for about 10% of the world's fishery harvest, and include cod, haddock, pollock, flounder, halibut and sole. Large pelagic fish such as tuna, swordfish, marlin, and mahi-mahi, account for about 5% of world harvest. The fish eaten most often in the United States is canned tuna.

Rising global demand for fish has increased the pressure to harvest more fish to the point where all 17 of the world's major fishing areas have either reached or exceeded their limits. Atlantic stocks of cod, haddock and blue-fin tuna are all seriously depleted, while in the Pacific, anchovies, salmon and halibut are all over-fished. Aquaculture, or fish farming, reduces pressure on wild stocks and now accounts for nearly 20% of world harvest.

Supply – The U.S. grand total of fishery products in 2009 fell -2.4% to 18.735 billion pounds, down from a record high of 20.959 billion pounds in 2006. The U.S. total domestic catch in 2009 fell by -5.5% to 7.867 billion pounds, and that comprised 42% of total U.S. supply. Of the U.S. total domestic catch in 2009, 44.2% of the catch was finfish for human consumption, 16.9% of the catch was a variety of fish for industrial use, and 11.4% was shellfish for human consumption. The principal species of U.S. fishery landings in 2008 were Pollock (with 2.298 billion pounds landed), Menhaden (1.341 billion pounds), Pacific Salmon (658 million pounds), Flounder (663 million pounds), and Sea Herring (259 million pounds).

About 30% of the fish harvested in the world are processed directly into fishmeal and fish oil. Fishmeal is used primarily in animal feed. Fish oil is used in both animal feed and human food products. World fishmeal production in the 2009-10 marketing year fell by -10.1% to 4.449 million metric tons. World production of fish oil in 2009-10 fell -17.6% to 837.0 million metric tons. Peru and Chile are by far the world's largest producers of fishmeal and fish oil.

Trade – U.S. imports of fishery products in 2009 (latest data) fell -0.1% yr/yr to 10.868, down from the 2006 record high of 11.476 billion pounds, comprising 58% of total U.S. supply.

					-------------- Domestic Catch ------------------					--------------- Imports -----------------			
	Grand	- **For Human Food** -		For Industrial		Percent of Grand	- **For Human Food** -		For Industrial		Percent of Grand	- **For Human Food** -		For Industrial
Year	Total	Finfish	Shellfish[3]	Use[4]	Total	Total	Finfish	Shellfish[3]	Use[4]	Total	Total	Finfish	Shellfish[3]	Use[4]
2003	19,850	12,617	4,570	2,663	9,507	47.9	6,388	1,133	1,986	10,343	52.1	6,229	3,437	677
2004	20,413	12,959	4,689	2,765	9,683	47.4	6,641	1,153	1,889	10,730	52.6	6,318	3,536	876
2005	20,612	13,567	4,588	2,457	9,707	47.1	6,914	1,084	1,710	10,905	52.9	6,653	3,505	747
2006	20,960	13,484	5,110	2,366	9,483	45.2	6,671	1,171	1,641	11,477	54.8	6,813	3,939	725
2007	20,561	13,339	4,914	2,308	9,309	45.3	6,415	1,075	1,819	11,252	54.7	6,925	3,838	489
2008	19,200	12,295	4,742	2,163	8,326	43.4	5,590	1,043	1,692	10,874	56.6	6,705	3,699	471
2009[1]	18,736	11,571	4,903	2,262	7,867	42.0	4,800	1,235	1,833	10,868	58.0	6,771	3,668	430

[1] Preliminary. [2] Live weight, except percent. [3] For univalue and bivalues mollusks (conchs, clams, oysters, scallops, etc.) the weight of meats, excluding the shell is reported. [4] Fish meal and sea herring. *Source: Fisheries Statistics Division, U.S. Department of Commerce*

Fisheries -- Landings of Principal Species in the United States   In Millions of Pounds

					--------------------------------------- Fish --------------------------------------						--------------------------- Shellfish -----------------------				
	Cod, Atlantic	Flounder	Halibut	Herring, Sea	Man-haden	Pollock	Salmon, Pacific	Tuna	Whiting	Clams (Meats)	Crabs	Lobsters American	Oysters ----- (Meats) -----	Scallops	Shrimp
Year															
2003	24	365	80	287	1,599	3,372	674	62	19	128	332	74	37	56	315
2004	16	360	80	265	1,498	3,365	739	57	19	119	316	88	39	65	309
2005	14	419	76	303	1,244	3,426	899	44	17	106	299	88	34	57	261
2006	13	446	71	290	1,307	3,414	664	50	12	111	340	93	34	59	320
2007	17	483	70	233	1,484	3,085	885	51	14	116	294	81	38	59	281
2008	19	663	67	259	1,341	2,298	658	48	14	108	325	82	30	54	257
2009[1]	20	575	60	313	1,404	1,883	705	49	17	101	326	97	36	58	301

[1] Preliminary. *Source: National Marine Fisheries Service, U.S. Department of Commerce*

U.S. Fisheries: Quantity & Value of Domestic Catch & Consumption & World Fish Oil Production

	-------------------------- Disposition -------------------------					For Human Food	For Industrial Products	Ex-vessel Value[3]	Average Price	Fish Per Capita Consumption	World[2] Fish Oil Production
	Fresh & Frozen	Canned	Cured	For Meal, Oil, etc.	Total						
Year	----------------------------- Millions of Pounds -----------------------------							- Million $ -	- Cents /Lb. -	- - Pounds - -	1,000 Tons -
2003	7,266	498	119	1,624	9,507	7,521	1,986	3,347	35.2	16.3	1,006
2004	7,488	552	137	1,506	9,683	7,794	1,889	3,756	38.8	16.6	1,128
2005	7,776	563	160	1,208	9,707	7,997	1,710	3,942	40.6	16.2	976
2006	7,627	573	117	1,166	9,483	7,842	1,641	4,024	42.4	16.5	973
2007	7,450	514	121	1,224	9,309	7,490	1,819	4,192	45.0	16.3	1,053
2008	6,538	336	138	1,313	8,325	6,633	1,692	4,383	52.6	16.0	1,035
2009[1]	6,040	392	103	1,332	7,867	6,035	1,833	3,882		15.8	999

[1] Preliminary. [2] Crop years on a marketing year basis. [3] At the Dock Prices. Source: Fisheries Statistics Division, U.S. Department of Commerce

FISH

Imports of Seafood Products into the United States   In Thousands of Pounds

Year	Fresh Atlantic Salmon	Fresh Pacific Salmon[2]	Fresh Shrimp	Fresh & Frozen Trout	Frozen Atlantic Salmon	Frozen Pacific Salmon[2]	Frozen Shrimp	Canned & Prepared Salmon[3]	Fresh & Prepared Shrimp[4]	Oysters[5]	Mussels[6]	Clams[7]	Tilapia[8]
2003	9,044	132,801	22,462	8,776	27,309	879,924	272,802	25,312	234,834	198,955	22,283	43,275	34,416
2004	8,580	121,724	22,396	7,917	40,860	871,856	264,586	24,632	271,199	249,167	23,120	50,817	31,111
2005	7,171	142,244	22,514	5,052	42,270	870,595	275,501	25,672	301,534	297,639	22,912	51,662	32,912
2006	10,215	171,848	20,905	5,137	52,161	920,922	257,970	27,456	385,701	348,707	24,599	50,796	34,454
2007	11,717	178,778	17,577	6,619	52,643	912,953	265,078	30,470	317,735	383,153	24,041	53,091	30,618
2008	9,137	182,929	12,843	6,219	52,407	943,989	250,282	28,468	304,907	395,559	20,544	54,261	33,143
2009	12,021	198,260	12,278	7,844	61,750	896,045	220,550	32,444	321,372	404,132	20,503	57,062	37,657
2010[1]	16,337	203,914	18,956	6,058	81,060	914,589	178,874	27,222	321,795	474,827	23,770	56,940	40,132

[1] Preliminary.   [2] Also contains salmon with no specific species noted.   [3] Includes smoked and cured salmon.   [4] Shrimp, canned, breaded, or prepared.   [5] Oysters fresh or prepared.   [6] Mussels fresh or prepared.   [7] Clams, fresh or prepared.   [8] Tilapia, frozen whole fish plus fresh and frozen fillets.
Source: Bureau of the Census, U.S. Department of Commerce

Exports of Seafood Products From the United States   In Thousands of Pounds

Year	Fresh Atlantic Salmon	Fresh Pacific Salmon[2]	Fresh Shrimp	Fresh & Frozen Trout	Frozen Atlantic Salmon	Frozen Pacific Salmon[2]	Frozen Shrimp	Canned & Prepared Salmon[3]	Fresh & Prepared Shrimp[4]	Oysters[5]	Mussels[6]	Clams[7]
2003	2,600	11,388	39,846	99	155,256	16,395	121,038	16,172	5,905	1,340	10,071	13,443
2004	1,180	13,995	34,249	197	187,954	12,730	138,455	14,620	7,688	924	12,506	16,909
2005	972	11,760	18,965	379	261,124	9,105	146,064	13,026	7,852	1,026	10,523	25,591
2006	875	8,759	19,869	106	219,019	7,544	137,538	12,944	6,241	2,525	12,257	29,110
2007	817	7,303	15,778	257	300,386	8,723	139,103	14,153	6,231	1,896	12,470	23,908
2008	1,107	17,705	16,198	247	277,331	7,902	138,048	17,684	7,241	1,855	14,366	24,694
2009	978	14,039	11,661	173	263,564	7,841	115,974	12,842	6,396	1,498	12,907	26,183
2010[1]	658	20,794	17,634	204	316,312	6,056	112,817	11,289	7,625	1,064	11,992	24,597

[1] Preliminary.   [2] Also contains salmon with no specific species noted.   [3] Includes smoked and cured salmon.   [4] Shrimp, canned, breaded, or prepared.   [5] Oysters fresh or prepared.   [6] Mussels fresh or prepared.   [7] Clams, fresh or prepared.   *Source: Bureau of the Census, U.S. Department of Commerce*

World Production of Fish Meal   In Thousands of Metric Tons

Year	Chile	Denmark	European Union	Iceland	Japan	Norway	Peru	Russia	South Africa	Spain	Thailand	United States	World Total
2002-03	858.9	238.9	495.8	268.5	326.0	199.2	1,344.6	71.8	115.3	98.0	398.8	322.4	5,770.4
2003-04	929.7	255.9	520.4	214.6	319.0	234.2	1,842.2	61.3	136.6	83.4	404.3	305.0	6,245.9
2004-05	886.1	231.2	472.8	202.1	318.0	155.6	1,949.2	59.6	121.3	53.2	407.9	269.4	6,129.8
2005-06	857.2	213.7	434.4	137.7	250.0	162.4	1,503.3	64.0	72.7	43.4	430.0	260.7	5,418.3
2006-07	798.5	164.8	386.3	151.6	204.0	173.1	1,400.1	67.3	88.6	40.9	429.0	258.1	5,192.5
2007-08[1]	740.8	161.9	375.6	144.0	202.0	140.9	1,426.9	70.3	80.7	35.0	409.0	223.9	5,031.0
2008-09[2]	685.9	175.8	388.6	125.0	198.9	130.1	1,442.6	75.3	66.7	33.0	400.0	248.7	4,950.1
2009-10[3]	515.0	155.0	360.6	122.0	190.0	126.0	1,160.0	77.3	55.0	29.3	445.0	185.0	4,449.8

[1] Preliminary.   [2] Estimate.   [3] Forecast.   *Source: The Oil World*

World Production of Fish Oil   In Thousands of Metric Tons

Year	Canada	Chile	China	Denmark	Iceland	Japan	Norway	Peru	Africa	Russia	United States	World Total	Fish Oil CIF[4] $ Per Tonne
2002-03	4.5	152.1	18.3	112.9	122.0	65.6	51.6	208.0	5.4	3.5	89.6	1,017.2	560
2003-04	4.8	176.5	14.0	107.4	74.2	68.1	40.5	263.5	7.1	3.6	81.9	1,036.0	648
2004-05	5.2	182.3	12.0	74.7	59.3	65.8	29.7	342.2	7.1	3.7	77.6	1,042.9	716
2005-06	5.0	179.0	12.1	75.0	49.5	68.5	36.1	277.4	7.5	3.8	62.7	979.0	792
2006-07	5.2	179.7	13.0	52.6	55.4	66.9	41.5	307.9	4.5	3.9	71.4	1,005.0	885
2007-08[1]	5.4	166.6	12.5	63.2	74.2	64.3	42.9	284.6	4.0	4.0	81.7	1,042.9	1,612
2008-09[2]	5.5	155.3	14.0	67.3	72.3	59.6	38.0	285.1	4.2	4.0	80.3	1,016.0	855
2009-10[3]	5.6	114.0	15.0	50.0	70.0	63.0	42.0	145.0	4.3	4.1	70.0	837.0	926

[1] Preliminary.   [2] Estimate.   [3] Forecast.   [4] Any origin, N.W. Europe.   *Source: The Oil World*

Monthly Production of Catfish--Round Weight Processed--in the United States   In Thousands of Pounds (Live Weight)

Year	Jan.	Feb.	Mar.	Apr.	May	June	July	Aug.	Sept.	Oct.	Nov.	Dec.	Total
2003	55,523	55,461	65,007	57,105	58,424	52,441	54,089	54,153	51,885	57,652	51,246	48,518	661,504
2004	53,849	54,173	60,272	53,896	52,324	50,155	51,055	53,295	51,329	52,396	49,536	48,170	630,450
2005	53,856	51,720	57,117	50,306	51,552	49,626	47,241	50,686	47,151	49,034	46,674	45,707	600,670
2006	50,703	49,145	56,315	43,126	42,865	41,214	45,528	51,736	47,296	50,788	45,680	41,735	566,131
2007	46,079	44,083	45,477	37,954	38,867	37,275	39,168	42,626	39,519	45,890	40,307	39,001	496,246
2008	45,992	47,634	47,908	45,018	44,326	43,265	42,583	40,985	39,057	43,344	36,869	32,616	509,597
2009	36,406	37,702	44,912	40,768	39,925	39,370	40,966	39,490	36,408	40,191	36,211	33,751	466,100
2010[1]	40,042	40,977	46,650	37,111	38,244	38,656	39,302	39,231	39,494	40,455	36,683	34,838	471,683

[1] Preliminary.   *Source: Economic Research Service, U.S. Department of Agriculture ERS-USDA)*

Average Price Paid to Producers for Farm-Raised Catfish in the United States   In Cents Per Pound (Live Weight)

Year	Jan.	Feb.	Mar.	Apr.	May	June	July	Aug.	Sept.	Oct.	Nov.	Dec.	Average
2003	52.9	54.4	58.5	63.0	61.8	58.6	56.4	55.2	56.0	56.7	61.0	62.9	58.1
2004	66.8	70.3	72.3	72.8	72.0	68.9	68.2	68.3	68.3	69.5	68.9	69.0	69.6
2005	72.5	73.1	73.3	72.5	72.2	72.1	72.3	72.4	72.4	72.4	72.4	72.6	72.5
2006	72.7	72.9	74.5	78.5	79.6	80.7	81.2	81.1	83.2	83.6	83.7	83.8	79.6
2007	83.7	83.8	83.8	84.1	84.0	81.7	76.2	73.1	69.7	68.2	66.6	65.0	76.7
2008	65.8	68.8	74.3	75.7	77.6	79.4	81.8	82.7	82.7	82.5	82.3	82.1	78.0
2009	81.0	77.0	77.3	76.3	76.2	76.3	77.1	76.9	77.2	76.8	76.5	76.3	77.1
2010[1]	76.4	76.5	78.5	80.4	79.6	78.6	78.8	79.0	81.6	83.2	84.1	86.1	80.2

[1] Preliminary.   *Source: Economic Research Service, U.S. Department of Agriculture (ERS-USDA)*

Sales of Fresh Catfish in the United States   In Thousands of Pounds

Year	Jan.	Feb.	Mar.	Apr.	May	June	July	Aug.	Sept.	Oct.	Nov.	Dec.	Total
Whole													
2005	3,111	3,177	3,402	2,938	2,679	2,765	2,686	2,673	2,687	2,546	2,615	2,784	34,063
2006	3,195	3,331	4,024	2,940	2,795	2,464	2,715	2,679	2,594	2,696	2,426	2,543	34,402
2007	2,756	2,824	3,247	2,631	2,715	2,679	2,489	2,737	2,730	2,944	2,541	2,432	32,725
2008	3,338	3,585	3,194	2,908	2,868	2,612	2,552	2,605	2,227	2,830	2,302	2,517	33,538
2009	2,537	2,752	3,137	2,733	2,551	2,546	2,582	2,332	2,321	2,830	2,352	2,461	31,134
2010[1]	2,811	3,156	3,743	3,046	2,844	2,730	2,277	2,582	2,518	2,863	2,297	2,434	33,301
Fillets[2]													
2005	5,274	5,615	5,795	4,979	5,274	4,987	4,714	4,998	4,848	5,072	4,291	4,209	60,056
2006	5,160	5,109	6,090	5,077	4,653	4,446	4,276	4,411	4,075	4,334	3,549	3,579	54,759
2007	4,282	4,405	4,685	4,001	4,280	3,708	4,005	4,045	3,959	4,468	3,473	3,417	48,728
2008	4,489	4,922	4,823	4,145	4,000	4,761	3,943	3,803	3,503	3,723	3,083	3,075	48,270
2009	3,795	3,732	4,196	3,894	3,864	3,621	3,649	3,554	3,444	3,495	2,989	3,038	43,271
2010[1]	3,607	4,221	3,905	3,495	3,720	3,475	3,411	3,606	3,456	3,343	2,791	3,045	42,075
Other[3]													
2005	1,300	1,295	1,370	1,271	1,204	1,130	1,097	1,128	1,084	1,121	965	900	13,865
2006	1,126	1,024	1,214	987	915	807	862	868	811	866	768	816	11,064
2007	812	814	884	809	850	723	753	766	759	816	669	633	9,288
2008	913	819	755	786	736	704	653	665	642	713	717	568	8,671
2009	709	810	797	684	751	783	646	709	644	685	616	611	8,445
2010[1]	695	735	807	668	713	641	631	650	647	621	516	564	7,888

[1] Preliminary.   [2] Includes regular, shank and strip fillets; excludes breaded products.   [3] Includes steaks, nuggets and all other products not reported.
Source: Economic Research Service, U.S. Department of Agriculture (ERS-USDA)

Prices of Fresh Catfish in the United States   In Dollars Per Pound

Year	Jan.	Feb.	Mar.	Apr.	May	June	July	Aug.	Sept.	Oct.	Nov.	Dec.	Average
Whole													
2005	1.64	1.64	1.61	1.61	1.61	1.58	1.58	1.57	1.58	1.63	1.55	1.50	1.59
2006	1.53	1.49	1.54	1.65	1.70	1.74	1.72	1.74	1.78	1.81	1.76	1.80	1.69
2007	1.79	1.77	1.71	1.75	1.71	1.71	1.73	1.70	1.65	1.59	1.56	1.56	1.69
2008	1.49	1.50	1.56	1.59	1.60	1.68	1.68	1.76	1.73	1.71	1.72	1.66	1.64
2009	1.72	1.67	1.65	1.68	1.70	1.64	1.66	1.69	1.66	1.59	1.57	1.57	1.65
2010[1]	1.55	1.49	1.50	1.55	1.55	1.58	1.67	1.58	1.63	1.57	1.61	1.71	1.58
Fillets[2]													
2005	2.81	2.75	2.85	2.87	2.86	2.85	2.84	2.83	2.83	2.84	2.84	2.84	2.83
2006	2.86	2.87	2.89	2.98	3.08	3.14	3.18	3.17	3.22	3.23	3.24	3.25	3.09
2007	3.28	3.24	3.27	3.27	3.27	3.26	3.18	3.08	3.03	2.96	2.93	2.91	3.14
2008	2.90	2.88	2.96	3.03	3.10	3.08	3.25	3.33	3.33	3.31	3.30	3.31	3.15
2009	3.30	3.24	3.24	3.23	3.23	3.22	3.21	3.21	3.20	3.19	3.18	3.19	3.22
2010[1]	3.16	3.10	3.18	3.22	3.25	3.26	3.25	3.22	3.24	3.29	3.32	3.32	3.23
Other[3]													
2005	1.67	1.67	1.74	1.71	1.77	1.78	1.72	1.68	1.64	1.65	1.60	1.65	1.69
2006	1.64	1.63	1.65	1.75	1.73	1.86	1.86	1.83	1.86	1.75	1.74	1.79	1.76
2007	1.71	1.79	1.78	1.80	1.76	1.76	1.72	1.63	1.56	1.53	1.54	1.52	1.68
2008	1.46	1.51	1.57	1.61	1.65	1.80	1.81	1.77	1.76	1.73	1.68	1.62	1.66
2009	1.64	1.52	1.61	1.75	1.60	1.68	1.64	1.64	1.67	1.64	1.66	1.67	1.64
2010[1]	1.66	1.60	1.65	1.81	1.76	1.71	1.72	1.72	1.69	1.68	1.74	1.75	1.71

[1] Preliminary.   [2] Includes regular, shank and strip fillets; excludes breaded products.   [3] Includes steaks, nuggets and all other products not reported.
Source: Economic Research Service, U.S. Department of Agriculture (ERS-USDA)

Flaxseed and Linseed Oil

Flaxseed, also called linseed, is an ancient crop that was cultivated by the Babylonians around 3,000 BC. Flaxseed is used for fiber in textiles and to produce oil. Flaxseeds contain approximately 35% oil, of which 60% is omega-3 fatty acid. Flaxseed or linseed oil is obtained through either the expeller extraction or solvent extraction method. Manufacturers filter the processed oil to remove some impurities and then sell it as unrefined. Unrefined oil retains its full flavor, aroma, color, and naturally occurring nutrients. Flaxseed oil is used for cooking and as a dietary supplement as well as for animal feed. Industrial linseed oil is not for internal consumption due to possible poisonous additives and is used for making putty, sealants, linoleum, wood preservation, varnishes, and oil paints.

Prices – The average monthly price received by U.S. farmers for flaxseed in the 2010-11 marketing year (through January 2011) rose by +45.9% yr/yr to $11.97 per bushel, down from the 2007-08 record high of $13.54 per bushel.

Supply – World production of flaxseed in the 2009-10 marketing year rose by +9.1% yr/yr to 2.380 million metric tons, but still below the 9-year high of 2.864 million metric tons in 2005-06. The world's largest producer of flaxseed is Canada with 43.3% of world production in 2009-10, followed by the China (18.3%), the former USSR (8.5%), the US (7.9%), and India (6.7%). U.S. production of flaxseed in 2010-11 rose +22.0% to 9.056 million bushels, but still well below the record high of 19.695 million bushels in 2005-06. North Dakota is by far the largest producing state of flaxseed and accounted for 94.3% of flaxseed production in 2010, followed by Montana with 2.8% of production and South Dakota with 2.3% of production.

World production of linseed oil in 2008-09 fell by -4.0% yr/yr to 606.5 million metric tons. The world's largest producers of linseed oil are China (with 29.7% of world production in 2009-10), the US (17.7%), Belgium. (12.7%), and India (7.6%). U.S. production of linseed oil in 2008-09 fell by –17.5% yr/yr to 188 million pounds.

Demand – U.S. distribution of flaxseed in 2007-08 fell by –19.4% yr/yr to 14.160 million bushels. The breakdown was 77% for crushing into meal and oil, 14% for exports, 4.7% for seed, and 4.6% for residual. U.S. consumption of linseed oil (inedible products) in the 2009-10 marketing year (through November 2009) fell by -13.9% yr/yr to 120.387 million pounds.

Trade – U.S. exports of flaxseed in 2007-08 rose by +11.8% yr/yr to 2.000 million bushels. U.S. imports of flaxseed in 2007-08 rose by +34.2% yr/yr to a 10-year high of 7.312 million bushels.

World Production of Flaxseed   In Thousands of Metric Tons

Crop Year	Argentina	Australia	Bangladesh	Canada	China	Egypt	France	Hungary	India	Romania	United States	Former USSR	World Total
2000-01	22	9	48	775	520	30	38	1	240	1	273	74	2,361
2001-02	16	9	50	770	273	26	23	1	240	2	291	82	1,980
2002-03	11	9	50	750	409	15	17	1	200	2	301	60	1,974
2003-04	29	9	3	835	450	22	11	1	230	2	265	85	2,169
2004-05	36	10	3	592	460	31	13	2	200	3	263	98	2,008
2005-06	54	10	3	1,150	475	28	25	3	210	----	480	105	2,864
2006-07	38	7	9	1,060	480	27	43	2	200	----	280	140	2,559
2007-08[1]	13	8	8	720	480	12	34	2	190	----	150	135	1,991
2008-09[2]	19	8	8	950	475	12	15	1	150	----	145	145	2,182
2009-10[3]	50	8	8	1,030	435	16	18	2	160	----	189	202	2,380

[1] Preliminary.   [2] Estimate.   [3] Forecast.   *Source: The Oil World*

Supply and Distribution of Flaxseed in the United States   In Thousands of Bushels

Crop Year Beginning June 1	Planted	Harvested	Yield Per Acre (Bushels)	Beginning Stocks	Production	Imports	Total Supply	Seed	Crush	Exports	Residual	Total
	---- 1,000 Acres ----											
2001-02	585	578	19.8	1,308	11,455	1,904	14,667	635	10,000	2,386	753	13,774
2002-03	784	703	16.9	893	11,863	2,901	15,657	482	10,500	3,181	416	14,579
2003-04	595	588	17.9	1,078	10,516	4,580	16,174	424	11,260	2,516	686	14,886
2004-05	523	516	20.3	1,288	10,471	5,413	17,069	796	13,600	1,510	301	16,206
2005-06	983	955	20.6	863	19,695	4,256	24,814	659	16,400	3,780	440	21,279
2006-07	813	767	14.4	3,535	11,019	5,464	20,018	287	14,900	1,788	599	17,574
2007-08	354	349	16.9	2,444	5,896	8,019	16,359	287	11,700	2,221	640	14,847
2008-09[1]	354	340	16.8	1,512	5,716	4,794	12,022	257	8,150	432	631	9,470
2009-10[2]	317	314	23.6	2,552	7,423	6,283	16,258	341	12,000	1,751	609	14,701
2010-11[3]	421	418	21.7	1,557	9,056	5,110	15,723	333	11,200	1,768	672	13,973

[1] Preliminary.   [2] Estimate.   [3] Forecast.   NA = not avaliable.   *Source: Economic Research Service, U.S. Department of Agriculture (ERS-USDA)*

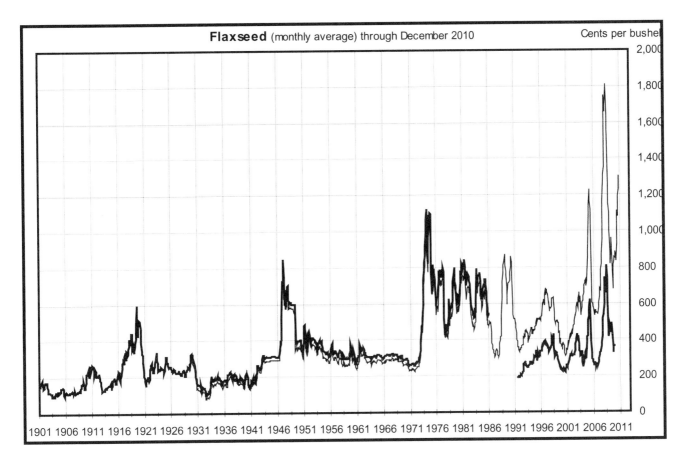

Flaxseed (monthly average) through December 2010 — Cents per bushel

Production of Flaxseed in the United States, by States — In Thousands of Bushels

Year	Minnesota	North Dakota	South Dakota	Montana[2]	Total	Year	Minnesota	North Dakota	South Dakota	Montana[2]	Total
2001	52	10,900	323	180	11,455	2006	126	10,368	228	297	11,019
2002	64	11,560	44	195	11,863	2007	72	5,548	96	180	5,896
2003	161	9,990	144	221	10,516	2008	69	5,491	84	72	5,716
2004	51	9,840	135	342	10,471	2009	63	7,032	168	160	7,423
2005	132	18,165	480	918	19,695	2010[1]	56	8,536	209	255	9,056

[1] Preliminary. [2] Data through 1999 are "Other". *Source: National Agricultural Statistics Service, U.S. Department of Agriculture (NASS-USDA)*

Factory Shipments of Paints, Varnish and Lacquer in the United States — In Millions of Dollars

Year	First Quarter	Second Quarter	Third Quarter	Fourth Quarter	Total	Year	First Quarter	Second Quarter	Third Quarter	Fourth Quarter	Total
2001	3,625.0	4,345.4	4,094.5	3,652.6	15,718	2006	4,626.5	5,408.8	5,050.5	4,305.7	19,392
2002	3,729.9	4,440.7	4,251.4	3,600.7	16,023	2007	4,311.4	5,483.2	5,245.9	4,277.0	19,318
2003	3,981.5	4,671.8	4,374.7	3,905.8	16,934	2008	4,211.2	5,160.9	5,197.9	3,885.7	18,456
2004	4,306.1	5,000.1	4,843.2	4,104.7	18,254	2009	3,713.7	4,582.9	4,510.2	3,413.3	16,220
2005	4,061.1	5,268.4	4,953.6	4,254.9	18,538	2010[1]	3,943.5	5,060.6	4,898.1		18,536

[1] Preliminary. *Source: Bureau of the Census, U.S. Department of Commerce*

Consumption of Linseed Oil (Inedible Products) in the United States — In Millions of Pounds

Year	July	Aug.	Sept.	Oct.	Nov.	Dec.	Jan.	Feb.	Mar.	Apr.	May	June	Average
2003-04	7.9	6.9	6.0	6.8	3.5	5.0	5.6	7.3	6.0	7.7	8.1	8.2	79.1
2004-05	7.3	7.3	6.7	5.6	4.8	5.1	3.7	4.8	4.9	4.0	5.7	4.7	64.6
2005-06	4.8	4.5	4.2	3.7	2.7	2.7	3.9	3.8	4.9	3.3	5.9	6.0	50.5
2006-07	4.4	5.8	5.7	3.5	3.7	2.8	3.6	4.3	4.2	5.0	6.8	7.2	56.8
2007-08	8.6	W	W	W	W	W	5.8	W	W	W	W	W	86.4
2008-09	W	W	W	W	W	W	W	9.7	18.0	10.2	10.3	10.2	139.9
2009-10	10.0	W	10.1	10.1	9.8	W	W	W	W	W	W	W	120.4
2010-11[1]	W	W	W	W	W	W							

[1] Preliminary. W = Withheld. *Source: Bureau of the Census, U.S. Department of Commerce*

FLAXSEED AND LINSEED OIL

Supply and Distribution of Linseed Oil in the United States   In Millions of Pounds

| Crop Year Beginning June 1 | Supply | | | Disappearance | | | Average Price at Minneapolis Cents/Lb. |
	Stocks June 1	Production	Total	Exports	Domestic	Total	
2000-01	49	234	295	73	178	251	36.0
2001-02	45	195	250	50	169	219	38.1
2002-03	31	205	249	70	145	215	39.9
2003-04	34	220	268	76	172	248	42.0
2004-05	20	265	301	107	149	256	59.5
2005-06	45	320	375	98	248	346	54.0
2006-07	29	291	328	76	202	278	44.4
2007-08	51	228	291	74	191	265	70.3
2008-09[1]	26	159	191	66	64	130	86.5
2009-10[2]	60	196	261	90	136	226	68.5-71.5

[1] Preliminary.   [2] Forecast.   *Source: Economic Research Service, U.S. Department of Agriculture (ERS-USDA)*

World Production and Price of Linseed Oil   In Thousands of Metric Tons

Year	Argentina	Bangladesh	Belgium	China	Egypt	Germany	India	Japan	United Kingdom	United States	Former USSR	World Total	Rotterdam Ex-TankUSD $/Tonne
2000-01	6.2	12.9	75.2	133.0	23.0	63.4	74.7	21.1	17.0	114.7	16.4	669.0	378
2001-02	3.8	13.5	95.0	75.3	15.6	57.3	72.4	18.9	9.9	95.7	20.7	584.1	454
2002-03	2.1	7.5	92.1	111.4	15.1	64.4	63.3	8.6	5.9	105.5	15.1	582.4	679
2003-04	2.3	0.6	119.6	124.0	11.3	66.6	67.7	7.5	6.7	103.8	17.1	624.1	757
2004-05	6.9	0.6	97.9	127.0	12.0	37.9	62.7	6.8	3.5	135.5	16.3	625.7	1,191
2005-06	13.1	2.6	97.9	137.6	14.8	65.2	63.7	5.7	3.5	147.7	16.2	691.5	686
2006-07	5.0	4.3	135.9	146.6	16.5	59.3	61.7	6.2	5.3	140.3	15.8	720.4	809
2007-08	2.8	2.8	118.4	148.1	8.6	53.6	58.4	4.6	2.8	98.1	20.5	637.9	1,635
2008-09[1]	2.1	2.3	92.4	158.9	6.4	37.7	46.9	2.6	3.2	83.0	15.6	578.4	975
2009-10[2]	6.1	2.3	79.3	185.1	7.7	35.5	47.7	1.6	2.8	110.1	17.5	623.7	1,087

[1] Preliminary.   [2] Forecast.   *Source: The Oil World*

Average Price Received by Farmers for Flaxseed in the United States   In Dollars Per Bushel

Year	July	Aug.	Sept.	Oct.	Nov.	Dec.	Jan.	Feb.	Mar.	Apr.	May	June	Average
2001-02	4.28	4.09	4.10	4.21	4.33	4.55	4.22	4.75	4.75	4.80	5.02	5.29	4.53
2002-03	5.38	5.27	5.55	5.76	6.04	5.92	5.71	6.25	6.47	6.57	6.05	6.02	5.92
2003-04	6.38	5.30	5.43	5.77	6.02	6.15	6.08	6.39	6.53	7.01	7.10	7.23	6.28
2004-05	7.33	6.90	7.19	7.36	8.62	8.42	8.89	10.90	11.40	12.30	11.60	11.20	9.34
2005-06	10.40	6.28	6.10	6.05	5.94	5.81	5.64	5.59	5.31	5.56	5.59	5.40	6.14
2006-07	5.47	5.50	5.46	5.41	5.38	5.73	6.03	6.39	6.79	6.72	7.08	7.81	6.15
2007-08	8.14	8.64	9.55	11.60	12.90	13.10	13.50	16.00	17.50	16.60	16.90	18.00	13.54
2008-09	18.10	16.50	15.60	12.60	12.60	11.50	11.00	9.98	8.84	8.13	8.96	9.59	11.95
2009-10	8.28	8.14	6.79	6.78	8.12	8.40	8.53	8.57	8.82	8.52	8.31	9.29	8.21
2010-11[1]	10.70	11.10	10.80	11.90	12.30	13.00	13.70	14.70					12.28

[1] Preliminary.   *Source: National Agricultural Statistics Service, U.S. Department of Agriculture (NASS-USDA)*

Stocks of Linseed Oil (Crude and Refined) at Factories and Warehouses in the U.S.   In Millions of Pounds

Year	July 1	Aug. 1	Sept. 1	Oct. 1	Nov. 1	Dec. 1	Jan. 1	Feb. 1	Mar. 1	Apr. 1	May 1	June 1
2001-02	29.1	30.2	22.6	38.4	32.4	29.9	33.4	36.6	26.8	33.4	32.3	31.1
2002-03	27.8	17.7	12.8	21.8	30.5	29.0	31.9	35.9	34.6	36.2	33.7	33.7
2003-04	30.2	27.2	22.3	78.5	42.0	35.0	40.0	43.4	37.6	32.9	24.5	19.9
2004-05	15.1	15.8	8.0	13.0	17.1	26.9	31.3	35.4	35.4	41.0	43.9	47.2
2005-06	38.1	24.8	14.1	33.9	31.1	21.0	29.4	38.4	42.2	32.2	25.5	29.8
2006-07	22.2	27.9	21.6	23.6	28.4	33.5	38.5	41.5	44.9	44.3	49.6	51.6
2007-08	41.5	44.4	49.5	39.4	50.3	49.9	34.3	22.8	37.1	28.0	35.6	26.5
2008-09	22.4	26.1	31.8	28.5	30.3	37.7	37.6	47.5	43.1	39.7	58.3	60.5
2009-10	48.7	49.4	70.3	28.3	41.7	34.9	41.7	33.1	46.2	34.8	36.0	32.1
2010-11[1]	34.4	35.6	39.9	32.7	59.0	50.2	58.8					

[1] Preliminary.   *Source: Bureau of the Census, U.S. Department of Commerce*

Wholesale Price of Raw Linseed Oil at Minneapolis in Tank Cars   In Cents Per Pound

Year	Jan.	Feb.	Mar.	Apr.	May	June	July	Aug.	Sept.	Oct.	Nov.	Dec.	Average
2001-02	35.50	38.00	39.00	39.00	39.00	39.00	39.00	39.00	39.00	39.00	39.65	40.35	38.79
2002-03	40.00	38.00	41.00	31.75	41.00	41.00	41.00	41.00	41.00	41.00	41.19	41.75	39.97
2003-04	41.75	41.75	42.00	42.75	43.13	43.25	42.60	40.00	40.00	40.00	45.00	45.50	42.31
2004-05	48.50	50.00	55.00	57.20	60.00	58.17	60.80	64.00	66.00	73.75	75.00	75.00	61.95
2005-06	75.00	75.00	75.00	48.75	42.75	43.50	42.40	42.00	42.38	42.94	43.10	42.35	51.26
2006-07	43.30	43.25	43.44	43.83	44.00	44.38	44.60	44.67	46.00	46.10	46.50	47.75	44.82
2007-08	49.00	NA	65.67	70.00	72.64	75.00	77.43	77.16	85.55	86.00	86.10	89.14	75.79
2008-09	93.18	95.71	90.00	87.86	87.21	85.82	86.35	83.42	82.59	80.00	77.00	75.36	85.38
2009-10	73.27	70.29	70.00	70.00	70.00	70.00	65.11	62.95	62.00	60.95	60.00	61.82	66.37
2010-11[1]	70.00	70.00	NA	NA	NA	NA							70.00

[1] Preliminary.   *Source: Economic Research Service, U.S. Department of Agriculture (ERS-USDA)*

Average Price of Linseed Meal (34% protein) at Minneapolis   In Dollars Per Ton

Year	Jan.	Feb.	Mar.	Apr.	May	June	July	Aug.	Sept.	Oct.	Nov.	Dec.	Average
2001-02	135.00	135.60	111.30	114.00	122.50	124.40	123.70	119.20	114.50	112.80	112.50	113.50	119.92
2002-03	127.50	143.80	127.10	114.00	113.10	112.50	118.40	120.10	133.00	126.70	125.00	127.30	124.04
2003-04	129.10	130.60	125.20	139.90	178.80	162.30	166.30	174.40	193.60	197.80	181.80	151.80	160.97
2004-05	139.80	112.40	112.40	99.50	114.60	109.10	111.60	109.90	109.80	104.00	96.00	116.00	111.26
2005-06	159.40	157.80	99.00	100.40	113.60	118.00	127.30	130.20	129.00	126.60	119.10	116.90	124.78
2006-07	111.50	101.10	92.80	100.80	118.10	123.30	134.20	156.40	156.30	149.00	135.10	132.00	125.88
2007-08	135.80	123.90	131.40	170.20	184.60	186.80	242.70	250.00	247.10	253.70	240.30	265.40	202.66
2008-09	273.70	231.30	200.00	160.80	164.00	189.60	248.80	270.00	231.90	233.50	263.10	250.00	226.39
2009-10	226.90	217.00	195.20	185.00	220.00	256.50	228.75	222.50	201.50	200.83	202.75	189.50	212.20
2010-11[1]	199.38	204.00	200.00	208.75	237.50	234.38							214.00

[1] Preliminary.   *Source: Economic Research Service, U.S. Department of Agriculture (ERS-USDA)*

Flaxseed Futures - Winnipeg Commodity Exchange
(weekly close) as of October 31, 2005
CAD per metric ton

Fruits

A fruit is any seed-bearing structure produced from a flowering plant. A widely used classification system divides fruit into fleshy or dry types. Fleshy fruits are juicy and include peaches, mangos, apples, and blueberries. Dry fruits include tree nuts such as almonds, walnuts, and pecans. Some foods that are commonly called vegetables, such as tomatoes, squash, peppers and eggplant, are technically fruits because they develop from the ovary of a flower.

Worldwide, over 430 million tons of fruit are produced each year and are grown everywhere except the Arctic and the Antarctic. The tropics, because of their abundant moisture and warm temperatures, produce the most diverse and abundant fruits. Mexico and Chile produce more than half of all the fresh and frozen fruit imported into the U.S. In the U.S., the top three fruits produced are oranges, grapes, and apples. Virtually all U.S. production of almonds, pistachios, and walnuts occurs in California, which leads the U.S. in tree nut production.

Prices – Overall fruit prices were fairly strong in 2009 with the fresh fruit Consumer Price Index (CPI) rising +2.6% to 150.5 and the processed fruit CPI index falling -6.1% to 324.4. Individual fruit prices, however, were mixed in 2009: Red Delicious Apples -10.4% to $1.182 per pound), bananas (+0.3% to 61.1 cents per pound), Anjou pears (-2.0% to $1.305 per pound), Thompson seedless grapes (-4.6% to $2.109 per pound), lemons (-24.2% to $1.520 per pound), grapefruit (-6.5% to $0.903 per pound), navel oranges (-9.0% to $1.050 cents per pound), and Valencia oranges (-5.9% to $0.956 per pound).

Supply – U.S. commercial production of selected fruits in 2009 fell -1.1% to 29.806 million short tons. By weight, oranges accounted for 30.6% of that U.S. fruit production figure, followed by grapes at 24.5%, and apples at 16.6%. The value of U.S. fruit production in 2009 rose +1.9% yr/yr to $18.688 billion.

Demand – U.S. per capita fresh fruit consumption in 2009 rose +0.7% to 100.85 pounds per year, but remained below the 2004 record high of 102.46. The highest per capita consumption categories for non-citrus fruits in 2009 were bananas (24.74 pounds) and apples (16.42 pounds). Per capital consumption of citrus fruits were lemons (3.13 pounds) oranges (9.06 pounds), grapefruit (2.80 pounds), Tangerines & Tangelos (3.15 pounds). The utilization breakdown for 2009 shows that total U.S. non-citrus fruit was used for fresh fruit (41.7%), wine (24.1%), dried fruit (11.9%), canned fruit (7.9%), juice (6.9%), and frozen fruit (4.2%). The value of utilized non-citrus fruit production in 2009 rose +4.6% yr/yr to $11.795 billion.

Commercial Production for Selected Fruits in the United States   In Thousands of Short Tons

Year	Apples	Cherries[2]	Cran-berries	Grapes	Grape-fruit	Lemons	Nect-arines	Oranges	Peaches	Pears	Pine-apple[3]	Prunes & Plums	Straw-berries	Tang-elos	Tang-erines	Total All Fruits
2003	4,390	359	310	6,644	2,063	1,026	273	11,545	1,260	934	300	803	1,078	105	382	31,985
2004	5,206	390	309	6,240	2,165	798	269	12,872	1,307	878	220	325	1,107	45	417	33,012
2005	4,834	386	312	7,814	1,018	870	251	9,251	1,185	823	212	476	1,161	70	335	29,549
2006	4,912	425	345	6,378	1,232	980	232	9,020	1,010	842	185	813	1,202	63	417	28,390
2007	4,545	437	328	7,057	1,627	798	283	7,625	1,127	873	W	405	1,223	56	361	27,145
2008	4,816	355	393	7,319	1,548	619	303	10,076	1,135	870	W	544	1,266	68	527	30,150
2009[1]	4,958	609	346	7,295	1,304	912	220	9,128	1,104	957	W	627	1,401	52	443	29,806

[1] Preliminary.   [2] Sweet and tart.   [3] Utilized production.   *Source: Economic Research Service, U.S. Department of Agriculture (ERS-USDA)*

Utilized Production for Selected Fruits in the United States   In Thousands of Short Tons

	Utilized Production				Value of Production			
Year	Citrus[2]	Noncitrus	Tree nuts[3]	Total	Citrus[2]	Noncitrus	Tree nuts[3]	Total
	In Thousands of Short Tons				In Thousands of Dollars			
2003	15,180	16,848	1,458	33,486	2,259,976	8,434,610	2,472,480	13,167,066
2004	16,360	16,823	1,524	34,706	2,485,052	8,553,060	3,527,904	14,566,016
2005	11,573	18,272	1,467	31,312	2,303,425	9,805,757	4,175,893	16,285,075
2006	11,744	16,816	1,598	30,158	2,738,361	10,510,417	3,680,383	16,929,161
2007	10,467	17,048	2,000	29,515	3,147,755	11,436,449	4,273,279	18,857,483
2008	12,838	17,603	2,139	32,580	3,240,271	11,279,829	3,816,917	18,337,017
2009[1]	11,839	18,129	2,009	31,977	2,742,010	11,795,005	4,151,010	18,688,025

[1] Preliminary.   [2] Year harvest was completed.   [3] Tree nuts on an in-shell equivalent.
Source: Economic Research Service, U.S. Department of Agriculture (ERS-USDA)

Annual Average Retail Prices for Selected Fruits in the United States   In Dollars Per Pound

Year	Red Delicious Apples	Bananas	Anjou Pears	Thompson Seedless Grapes	Lemons	Grapefruit	Oranges Navel	Oranges Valencias
2003	.980	.509	NA	1.899	1.317	.723	.838	.575
2004	1.043	.495	NA	2.059	1.235	.819	.859	.691
2005	.949	.492	1.114	2.078	1.411	.998	.996	.897
2006	1.067	.500	1.133	2.246	1.529	1.114	1.087	1.001
2007	1.115	.510	1.273	2.092	1.857	.964	1.284	1.074
2008	1.319	.609	1.331	2.212	2.004	.965	1.155	1.016
2009[1]	1.182	.611	1.305	2.109	1.520	.903	1.050	.956

[1] Estimate.   *Source: Economic Research Service, U.S. Department of Agriculture (ERS-USDA)*

Utilization of Noncitrus Fruit Production, and Value in the United States   1,000 Short Tons (Fresh Equivalent)

Year	Utilized Production	Fresh	Canned	Dried	Juice	Frozen	Wine	Other Processed	Value of Utilized Production $1,000
2000	18,854	7,015	1,812	3,023	1,712	691	4,130	191	7,883,036
2001	16,740	6,488	1,859	2,290	1,462	665	3,568	169	7,918,636
2002	17,122	6,549	1,727	2,582	1,251	591	3,999	138	8,137,640
2003	16,848	6,672	1,762	2,293	1,295	716	3,582	219	8,434,610
2004	16,823	7,168	1,710	1,425	1,418	685	3,819	290	8,553,060
2005	18,272	7,188	1,575	2,101	1,555	712	4,551	277	9,805,757
2006	16,816	6,930	1,400	2,219	1,256	710	3,726	235	10,510,417
2007	17,048	7,013	1,453	2,030	1,277	748	3,921	278	11,436,449
2008	17,603	7,248	1,406	2,413	1,228	682	3,944	290	11,279,829
2009[1]	18,129	7,555	1,426	2,154	1,254	754	4,373	267	11,795,005

[1] Preliminary.   Source: Economic Research Service, U.S. Department of Agriculture (ERS-USDA)

Average Price Indexes for Fruits in the United States

Year	Index of all Fruit & Nut Prices Received by Growers (1990-92=100)	Producer Price Index Fresh Fruit 1982 = 100	Dried Fruit	Canned Fruits and Juices	Frozen Fruits and Juices	Consumer Price Index Fresh Fruit 1982-84 = 100	Processed Fruit
2000	98	91.4	122.4	139.5	108.9	258.3	106.9
2001	109	97.7	120.3	143.3	111.9	265.1	109.0
2002	105	91.5	120.7	141.7	112.5	270.2	111.6
2003	106	84.1	122.1	142.3	115.7	279.1	113.7
2004	124	104.9	NA	143.1	113.3	286.8	114.0
2005	128	102.8	NA	148.1	112.4	297.4	118.4
2006	154	111.0	NA	153.0	119.7	315.2	121.5
2007	158	123.4	NA	156.9	138.5	329.5	125.2
2008	147	122.9	NA	167.5	146.7	345.4	135.6
2009[1]	135	110.4	NA	181.5	150.5	324.4	142.8

[1] Estimate.   NA = Not availavle.   Source: Economic Research Service, U.S. Department of Agriculture (ERS-USDA)

Fresh Fruit: Per Capita Consumption[1] in the United States   In Pounds

Year	Oranges	Tangerines & Tangelos	Lemons	Grapefruit	Total	Apples	Apricots	Avocados	Bananas	Cherries	Cranberries
2000	11.74	2.86	2.44	5.09	23.52	17.46	.15	2.21	28.45	.60	.14
2001	11.88	2.72	2.96	4.85	23.92	15.61	.08	2.50	26.64	.77	.13
2002	11.74	2.56	3.34	4.63	23.36	16.01	.09	2.34	26.78	.70	.11
2003	11.90	2.72	3.33	4.10	23.81	16.91	.13	2.75	26.18	.92	.10
2004	10.80	2.77	3.12	4.14	22.68	18.81	.12	3.06	25.79	.99	.11
2005	11.42	2.50	2.95	2.65	21.60	16.67	.13	3.48	25.20	.87	.09
2006	10.25	2.69	4.15	2.31	21.64	17.74	.08	3.59	25.13	1.07	.09
2007	7.46	2.56	2.81	2.84	17.93	16.41	.16	3.50	25.98	1.22	.10
2008	9.93	3.09	1.97	3.16	20.62	15.92	.13	3.81	25.06	1.00	.10
2009[2]	9.06	3.15	3.13	2.80	20.68	16.42	.14	4.11	24.74	1.48	.09

Columns under headings: Cutrus Fruit (Oranges, Tangerines & Tangelos, Lemons, Grapefruit, Total); Noncitrus Fruit (Apples, Apricots, Avocados, Bananas, Cherries, Cranberries)

[1] All data on calendar-year basis except for citrus fruits; apples, August; grapes and pears, July; grapefruit, September; lemons, August of prior year; all other citrus, November.   [2] Preliminary.   Source: Economic Research Service, U.S. Department of Agriculture (ERS-USDA)

Fresh Fruit: Per Capita Consumption[1] in the United States   In Pounds

Noncitrus Fruit Continued

Year	Grapes	Kiwifruit	Mangos	& Peaches	Pears	Pineapples	Papaya	Prunes	Strawberries	Total Noncitrus	Total Fruit
2000	7.44	.56	1.75	5.30	3.40	3.22	.68	1.19	4.86	77.68	101.20
2001	7.38	.44	1.79	5.16	3.25	3.16	.78	1.33	4.21	73.58	97.50
2002	8.42	.38	1.97	5.23	3.06	3.82	.79	1.26	4.65	75.99	99.35
2003	7.66	.38	2.06	5.17	3.08	4.40	.87	1.24	5.29	77.53	101.35
2004	7.80	.41	2.02	5.15	2.96	4.43	1.03	1.12	5.48	79.81	102.49
2005	8.60	.45	1.88	4.83	2.91	4.91	.94	1.11	5.83	78.34	99.94
2006	7.60	.47	2.10	4.58	3.19	5.21	1.04	1.02	6.14	79.62	101.26
2007	8.02	.44	2.11	4.47	3.09	5.02	1.08	1.01	6.27	79.45	97.38
2008	8.53	.46	2.11	5.09	3.11	5.08	.98	.92	6.45	79.56	100.18
2009[2]	7.92	.50	2.02	4.41	3.19	5.09	1.20	.74	7.17	80.17	100.85

[1] All data on calendar-year basis except for citrus fruits; apples, August; grapes and pears, July; grapefruit, September; lemons, August of prior year; all other citrus, November.   [2] Preliminary.   Source: Economic Research Service, U.S. Department of Agriculture (ERS-USDA)

Gas

Natural gas is a fossil fuel that is colorless, shapeless, and odorless in its pure form. It is a mixture of hydrocarbon gases formed primarily of methane, but it can also include ethane, propane, butane, and pentane. Natural gas is combustible, clean burning, and gives off a great deal of energy. Around 500 BC, the Chinese discovered that the energy in natural gas could be harnessed. They passed it through crude bamboo-shoot pipes and then burned it to boil sea water to create potable fresh water. Around 1785, Britain became the first country to commercially use natural gas produced from coal for streetlights and indoor lights. In 1821, William Hart dug the first well specifically intended to obtain natural gas and he is generally regarded as the "father of natural gas" in America. There is a vast amount of natural gas estimated to still be in the ground in the U.S. Natural gas as a source of energy is significantly less expensive than electricity per Btu.

Natural gas futures and options are traded on the New York Mercantile Exchange (NYMEX). The NYMEX natural gas futures contract calls for the delivery of natural gas representing 10,000 million British thermal units (mmBtu) at the Henry Hub in Louisiana, which is the nexus of 16 intra-state and inter-state pipelines. The contract is priced in terms of dollars per mmBtu. NYMEX also has basic swap futures contracts available for 30 different natural gas pricing locations versus the benchmark Henry Hub location. Natural gas futures are also listed on the ICE Futures Europe (ICE) exchange in London.

Prices – NYMEX natural gas futures on the nearest-futures chart during 2010 traded mildly lower in a relatively narrow range and finished the year at $4.405 per mmBtu, down 21% from the 2009.

Supply – U.S. recovery of natural gas in 2009 (latest data available) rose +2.2% to a record high of 26.320 billion cubic feet. The top U.S. producing states for natural gas were Texas with 31.4% of U.S. production in 2009, (latest data) Oklahoma with 8.5%, Wyoming with 10.7%, New Mexico with 6.4%, and Louisiana with 7.3%. In 2010 the world's largest natural gas producers were Russia with 1,781,800 terajoules of production and the U.S. with 1,944,907 terajoules.

Demand – U.S.- delivered consumption of natural gas in 2009 (latest data available) fell -1.7% yr/yr to 22.841 billion cubic feet, of which about 30.2% was delivered to electrical utility plants, 26.9% to industrial establishments, 20.9% to residences, and 13.6% to commercial establishments.

Trade – U.S. imports of natural gas (consumed) in 2009 (latest data available) fell -6.8% yr/yr to 3.712 billion cubic feet, down from the 2007 record high of 4,607 billion cubic feet. U.S. exports of natural gas in 2009 rose +4.2% yr/yr to 1,048 billion cubic feet, which is a new record high.

World Production of Natural Gas (Monthly Average Marketed Production[3])   In Terajoule[4]

Year	Australia	Canada	China	Germany	Indonesia	India	Italy	Mexico	Netherlands	Romania	Russia	United Kingdom	United States
2001	96,523	550,463	98,431	60,463	258,122	91,063	48,008	171,940	192,180	40,422	1,887,953	370,237	1,848,810
2002	96,841	553,183	106,720	61,147	280,939	92,568	46,190	168,675	186,206	38,004	1,934,011	361,414	1,792,367
2003	99,771	534,434	111,352	61,441	289,371	89,570	42,812	174,733	178,853	38,831	2,016,895	358,798	1,726,221
2004	104,731	537,643	132,281	55,108	282,364	83,996	39,760	177,650	232,485	41,725	2,055,061	333,492	1,564,674
2005	108,249	547,204	163,802	55,089	267,057	92,451	38,167	187,151	218,699	40,959	2,065,477	307,775	1,636,149
2006	115,535	551,543	193,124	55,557	279,573	101,144	34,670	208,018	191,741	33,977	2,134,095	278,935	1,682,950
2007	115,541	540,070	223,107	49,895	292,656	101,150	30,839	230,885	189,494	34,001	2,116,869	251,428	1,745,050
2008	113,672	507,412	261,162	51,475	266,428	102,793	28,893	264,454	210,393	32,374	1,862,664	242,895	1,861,285
2009[1]	125,739	473,792	277,124	49,268	278,445	130,868	25,778	269,628	195,122	31,328	1,638,043	208,190	1,896,952
2010[2]	131,261		309,161	40,243	290,396	172,055	26,346	269,073	199,219	30,990	1,801,851	199,841	1,919,283

[1] Preliminary.   [2] Estimate.   [3] Compares all gas collected & utilized as fuel or as a chemical industry raw material, including gas used in oilfields and/or gasfields as a fuel by producers.   [4] Terajoule = 10 to the 12th power Joule = approximately 10 to the 9th power BTU.   *Source: United Nations*

Marketed Production of Natural Gas in the United States, by States   In Million Cubic Feet

Year	Alaska	California	Colorado	Kansas	Louisiana[2]	Michigan	Mississippi	Mexico	Oklahoma	Texas[2]	Wyoming	Total
2001	471,440	377,824	817,206	480,145	1,502,086	275,036	107,541	1,689,125	1,615,384	5,282,723	1,363,879	20,570,295
2002	463,301	360,205	937,245	454,901	1,361,751	274,476	112,980	1,632,080	1,581,606	5,141,075	1,453,957	19,884,780
2003	489,757	337,216	1,011,285	418,893	1,350,399	236,987	133,901	1,604,015	1,558,155	5,243,567	1,539,318	19,974,360
2004	471,899	319,919	1,079,235	397,121	1,353,249	259,681	63,353	1,632,539	1,655,769	5,067,315	1,592,203	19,517,491
2005	487,282	317,637	1,133,086	377,229	1,296,048	261,112	52,923	1,645,166	1,670,137	5,276,401	1,639,317	18,927,095
2006	444,724	315,209	1,202,821	371,044	1,361,119	365,294	60,531	1,609,223	1,688,985	5,548,022	1,816,201	19,409,674
2007	433,485	----	----	----	1,365,333	----	----	1,517,922	1,783,682	6,123,180	2,047,882	20,196,346
2008	398,442	----	----	----	1,377,969	----	----	1,446,204	1,886,710	6,960,693	2,274,850	21,112,053
2009	397,077	----	----	----	1,548,607	----	----	1,383,004	1,857,777	6,818,973	2,335,328	21,604,158
2010[1]	376,955	----	----	----	2,246,108	----	----	1,322,137	1,825,513	6,672,171	2,323,223	22,562,633

[1] Preliminary.   *Source: Energy Information Administration, U.S. Department of Energy (EIA-DOE)*

World Production of Natural Gas Plant Liquids — Thousand Barrels per Day

Year	Algeria	Canada	Mexico	Saudi Arabia	Russia	United States	Persian Gulf[2]	OAPEC[3]	OPEC-12[4]	OPEC-11[4]	World
2002	270	698	408	1,095	246	1,880	1,797	2,137	2,326	2,403	6,872
2003	280	724	418	1,220	390	1,719	1,972	2,312	2,473	2,548	7,134
2004	292	658	442	1,310	456	1,809	2,100	2,437	2,634	2,702	7,382
2005	295	645	426	1,460	457	1,717	2,282	2,667	2,874	2,930	7,658
2006	310	685	427	1,427	417	1,739	2,289	2,804	2,955	2,999	7,893
2007	342	726	396	1,440	426	1,783	2,313	2,862	3,031	3,083	7,976
2008	357	677	365	1,434	422	1,784	2,339	2,891	3,088	----	8,103
2009	345	640	370	1,422	423	1,910	2,365	2,896	3,097	----	8,360
2010[1]	350	651	378	1,521	436	1,989	2,528	3,039	3,272	----	

Average. [1] Preliminary. [2] Bahrain, Iran, Iraq, Kuwait, Qatar, Saudi Arabia, and the United Arab Emirates. [3] Organization of Arab Petroleum Exporting Countriess: Algeria, Iraq, Kuwait, Libya, Qatar, Saudi Arabia, and the United Arab Emirates. [4] OPEC-12: Organization of the Petroleum Exporting Countries: Algeria, Angola, Indonesia, Iran, Iraq, Kuwait, Libya, Nigeria, Qatar, Saudi Arabia, the United Arab Emirates, and Venezuela. OPEC-11 does not include Angola. *Source: Energy Information Administration, U.S. Department of Energy (EIA-DOE)*

Recoverable Reserves and Deliveries of Natural Gas in the United States — In Billions of Cubic Feet

Year	Gross Withdrawals	Recoverable Reserves of Natural Gas Dec. 31[2]	Residential	Commercial	Electric Utility Plants[3]	Industrial	Total	Lease & Plant Fuel	Used as Pipline Fuel	Heating Value BTU per Cubic Foot
2002	23,941	186,946	4,889	3,144	5,672	7,507	23,007	1,113	667	1,027
2003	24,119	189,044	5,079	3,179	5,135	7,150	22,277	1,122	591	1,031
2004	23,970	192,513	4,869	3,129	5,464	7,243	22,389	1,098	566	1,026
2005	23,457	204,385	4,827	2,999	5,869	6,597	22,011	1,112	584	1,028
2006	23,535	211,085	4,368	2,832	6,222	6,512	21,685	1,142	584	1,028
2007	24,664	237,726	4,722	3,013	6,841	6,648	23,097	1,226	621	1,029
2008	25,636	244,656	4,892	3,153	6,668	6,661	23,268	1,220	648	1,027
2009	26,013	272,509	4,778	3,119	6,872	6,167	22,839	1,275	598	1,025
2010[1]	26,852		4,952	3,206	7,379	6,600	24,134	1,332	632	

[1] Preliminary. [2] Estimated proved recoverable reserves of dry natural gas. [3] Figures include gas other than natural (impossible to segregate); therefore, shown separately from other consumption. *Source: Energy Information Administration, U.S. Department of Energy (EIA-DOE)*

Gas Utility Sales in the United States by Types and Class of Service — In Trillions of BTUs

Year	Total Utility Sales	Number of Customers (Millions)	Residential	Commercial	Industrial	Electric Generation	Other	Total	Residential	Commercial	Industrial	Electric Generation	Other
2000	9,232	61.3	4,741	2,077	1,698	709	6	59,243	35,828	13,338	7,432	2,612	33
2001	8,667	61.4	4,525	2,053	1,461	620	8	69,150	42,454	16,848	7,513	2,286	49
2002	8,864	62.0	4,589	2,055	1,748	459	13	57,112	35,062	13,512	6,840	1,639	59
2003	8,927	62.6	4,722	2,125	1,672	397	11	72,606	43,664	17,349	9,478	2,048	68
2004	8,766	63.3	4,566	2,075	1,763	351	12	79,929	47,275	18,689	11,230	2,653	83
2005	8,848	64.4	4,516	2,056	1,654	610	12	96,909	55,680	22,653	13,751	4,718	107
2006	8,222	65.0	4,117	1,861	1,576	606	62	91,928	53,961	21,557	12,006	3,921	484
2007[1]	8,565	65.4	4,418	1,943	1,522	626	57	92,131	55,027	21,248	11,323	4,076	457
2008[2]	8,594	65.5	4,541	2,009	1,410	614	21	102,641	60,195	23,592	13,205	5,406	243

[1] Preliminary. [2] Estimate. *Source: American Gas Association (AGA)*

Salient Statistics of Natural Gas in the United States

Year	Marketed Production	Extraction Loss	Dry Production	Storage Withdrawals	Imports (Con sumed)	Total Supply	Consumption	Exports	Added to Storage	Total Disposition	Wellhead Price	Imports	Exports	Residential	Commercial	Industrial	Electric Utilities
2002	19,885	957	18,928	3,138	4,015	26,767	23,007	516	2,670	26,767	2.95	3.14	3.41	7.89	6.63	4.02	3.68
2003	19,974	876	19,099	3,099	3,944	26,963	22,277	680	3,292	26,963	4.88	5.17	5.54	9.63	8.40	5.89	5.57
2004	19,517	927	18,591	3,037	4,259	26,985	22,389	854	3,150	26,985	5.46	5.81	6.09	10.75	9.43	6.53	6.11
2005	18,927	876	18,051	3,057	4,341	26,325	22,011	729	3,002	25,741	7.33	8.12	7.59	12.70	11.34	8.56	8.47
2006	19,410	906	18,504	2,493	4,186	26,089	21,685	724	2,924	25,333	6.39	6.88	6.83	13.73	12.00	7.87	7.11
2007	20,196	930	19,266	3,325	4,608	28,129	23,097	822	3,133	27,053	6.25	6.87	6.92	13.08	11.34	7.68	7.31
2008	21,112	953	20,159	3,374	3,984	28,470	23,268	963	3,340	27,572	7.97	8.70	8.58	13.89	12.23	9.65	9.26
2009[1]	21,604	1,024	20,580	2,966	3,751	28,322	22,839	1,072	3,315	27,227	3.67	4.19	4.47	12.14	10.06	5.33	4.93
2010[2]	22,563	992	21,571	3,303	3,683	29,549	24,134	1,122	3,298	28,554	4.16			11.19	9.15	5.40	

Supply and Disposition figures In Billions of Cubic Feet; Average Price Delivered to Customers in Dollars Per Thousand Cubic Feet.

[1] Preliminary. [2] Estimate. *Source: Energy Information Administration, U.S. Department of Energy (EIA-DOE)*

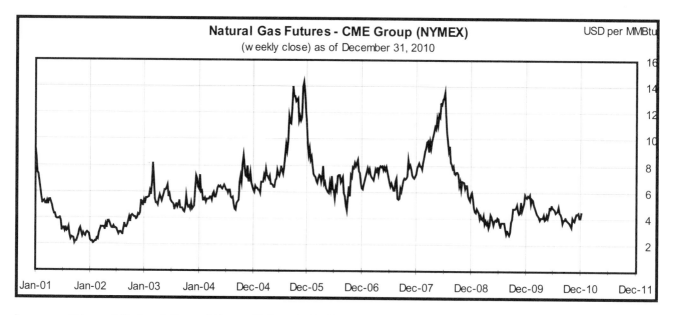

Average Price of Natural Gas at Henry Hub   In Dollars Per MMBtu

Year	Jan.	Feb.	Mar.	Apr.	May	June	July	Aug.	Sept.	Oct.	Nov.	Dec.	Average
2001	8.18	5.62	5.16	5.16	4.21	3.71	3.11	2.95	2.15	2.45	2.35	2.43	3.96
2002	2.25	2.31	3.03	3.42	3.49	3.22	2.98	3.09	3.55	4.12	4.04	4.75	3.35
2003	5.49	7.41	6.08	5.27	5.81	5.83	5.03	4.97	4.61	4.66	4.47	6.13	5.48
2004	6.17	5.39	5.38	5.71	6.30	6.29	5.93	5.44	5.11	6.39	6.15	6.64	5.91
2005	6.13	6.13	6.91	7.22	6.48	7.15	7.63	9.46	11.87	13.42	10.28	13.05	8.81
2006	8.65	7.54	6.90	7.16	6.23	6.19	6.22	7.14	4.90	5.84	7.36	6.73	6.74
2007	6.60	7.92	7.10	7.59	7.63	7.35	6.21	6.23	6.08	6.78	7.15	7.13	6.98
2008	7.98	8.54	9.44	10.13	11.28	12.68	11.06	8.25	7.67	6.73	6.67	5.81	8.85
2009	5.23	4.52	3.95	3.50	3.83	3.81	3.39	3.15	3.01	4.02	3.70	5.33	3.95
2010	5.77	5.33	4.29	4.03	4.15	4.81	4.62	4.31	3.91	3.43	3.73	4.24	4.38

Source: Energy Information Administration, U.S. Department of Energy (EIA-DOE)

Volume of Trading of Natural Gas Futures in New York   In Thousands of Contracts

Year	Jan.	Feb.	Mar.	Apr.	May	June	July	Aug.	Sept.	Oct.	Nov.	Dec.	Total
2001	1,044.4	1,044.6	1,131.7	1,144.8	1,632.5	1,536.9	1,350.3	1,510.9	901.1	1,639.7	1,891.7	1,639.6	16,468.1
2002	1,942.5	1,668.6	2,381.1	2,421.7	2,281.4	1,911.7	2,266.1	2,115.6	1,990.0	2,103.4	1,569.2	1,706.4	24,357.8
2003	2,134.4	1,909.1	1,362.4	1,321.3	1,521.7	1,584.8	1,543.7	1,315.3	1,503.7	1,948.9	1,376.6	1,515.2	19,037.1
2004	1,162.1	1,125.1	1,420.3	1,443.1	1,587.5	1,588.5	1,508.8	1,724.1	1,885.6	1,458.3	1,320.0	1,218.6	17,441.9
2005	1,442.2	1,490.4	1,653.3	1,586.0	1,504.1	1,931.9	1,528.4	2,044.4	1,587.6	1,433.1	1,449.5	1,491.7	19,142.5
2006	1,609.9	1,833.9	1,682.2	1,911.6	2,272.5	1,920.6	1,786.2	2,428.7	2,017.7	1,935.1	1,799.6	1,832.0	23,030.0
2007	2,597.6	2,417.5	1,922.6	2,163.2	2,266.2	2,683.7	2,346.7	3,049.9	2,468.5	3,044.3	2,452.0	2,374.2	29,786.3
2008	2,921.9	3,330.7	2,983.6	3,382.9	3,168.0	3,379.1	4,274.0	3,756.1	3,458.5	3,151.7	2,539.9	2,384.3	38,730.5
2009	2,343.7	2,780.6	2,989.9	2,493.1	3,479.0	4,486.6	3,979.4	4,445.9	5,597.7	5,594.7	4,413.7	5,347.2	47,951.4
2010	4,501.7	4,557.7	4,690.9	5,740.4	4,729.9	5,911.9	5,267.7	5,791.0	5,428.1	5,920.0	5,780.8	6,002.9	64,323.1

Contract size = 10,000 MMBtu.   *Source: CME Group; New York Mercantile Exchange (NYMEX)*

Average Open Interest of Natural Gas Futures in New York   In Contracts

Year	Jan.	Feb.	Mar.	Apr.	May	June	July	Aug.	Sept.	Oct.	Nov.	Dec.
2001	364,532	346,343	360,032	380,632	421,145	456,512	473,675	497,972	494,475	488,187	455,766	415,882
2002	458,924	491,215	527,765	559,413	556,277	526,016	494,133	437,285	419,532	413,312	393,953	391,424
2003	415,642	420,329	367,673	354,154	365,838	366,610	357,299	343,622	354,568	352,685	356,622	340,756
2004	322,762	312,475	322,366	338,786	382,160	366,135	373,853	378,787	393,477	392,626	383,712	387,605
2005	401,829	405,692	458,013	479,880	480,318	472,631	498,440	524,235	544,165	551,121	545,270	551,444
2006	545,165	582,231	634,072	700,588	795,375	851,655	883,492	938,024	940,339	931,949	903,355	889,759
2007	905,449	839,142	761,701	747,721	752,596	787,099	823,127	776,747	778,512	749,480	789,360	843,361
2008	881,812	942,089	906,497	875,484	885,165	946,673	963,953	922,474	915,638	859,278	744,821	702,918
2009	693,269	708,968	652,412	649,925	678,413	709,236	737,506	731,555	713,822	709,965	713,612	719,561
2010	761,998	786,388	839,164	855,385	860,760	817,712	783,921	819,168	812,356	800,760	783,715	774,390

Contract size = 10,000 MMBtu.   *Source: CME Group; New York Mercantile Exchange (NYMEX)*

Gasoline

Gasoline is a complex mixture of hundreds of lighter liquid hydrocarbons and is used chiefly as a fuel for internal-combustion engines. Petroleum crude, or crude oil, is still the most economical source of gasoline with refineries turning more than half of every barrel of crude oil into gasoline. The three basic steps to all refining operations are the separation process (separating crude oil into various chemical components), conversion process (breaking the chemicals down into molecules called hydrocarbons), and treatment process (transforming and combining hydrocarbon molecules and other additives). Another process, called hydro treating, removes a significant amount of sulfur from finished gasoline as is currently required by the state of California.

Octane is a measure of a gasoline's ability to resist pinging or knocking noise from an engine. Most gasoline stations offer three octane grades of unleaded fuel—regular at 87 (R+M)/2, mid-grade at 89 (R+M)/2, and premium at 93 (R+M)/2. Additional refining steps are needed to increase the octane, which increases the retail price. This does not make the gasoline any cleaner or better, but yields a different blend of hydrocarbons that burn more slowly.

In an attempt to improve air quality and reduce harmful emissions from internal combustion engines, Congress in 1990 amended the Clean Air Act to mandate the addition of ethanol to gasoline. Some 2 billion gallons of ethanol are now added to gasoline each year in the U.S. The most common blend is E10, which contains 10% ethanol and 90% gasoline. Auto manufacturers have approved that mixture for use in all U.S. vehicles. Ethanol is an alcohol-based fuel produced by fermenting and distilling crops such as corn, barley, wheat and sugar.

RBOB gasoline futures and options trade at the New York Mercantile Exchange (NYMEX). The NYMEX gasoline futures contract calls for the delivery of 1,000 barrels (42,000 gallons) of RBOB gasoline in the New York harbor and is priced in terms of dollars and cents per gallon.

Price – NYMEX gasoline futures prices rallied in early 2010, traded lower through August, and then showed a sharp rally late in the year, closing 2010 up 18% at $2.43 per gallon.

The average monthly retail price of regular unleaded gasoline in 2010 (through November) rose +18.6% yr/yr to $2.78 per gallon. The average monthly retail price of unleaded premium motor gasoline in the U.S. in 2010 (through November) rose +16.9% to $3.04 per gallon. The average monthly refiner price of finished aviation gasoline to end users in 2010 (through September) rose +22.4% yr/yr to $3.00 per gallon.

Supply – U.S. production of gasoline in 2010 (through November, annualized) rose +2.8% yr/yr to 9.029 million barrels per day. Gasoline stocks in October of 2010 were 65.584 million barrels, down from 84.927 million barrels in December of 2009.

Demand – U.S. consumption of finished motor gasoline in 2010 (through November, annualized) rose +0.7% yr/yr to 9.055 million barrels per day, but still below 2007's record high of 9.284 million barrels per day.

Production of Finished Motor Gasoline in the United States — In Thousand Barrels per Day

Year	Jan.	Feb.	Mar.	Apr.	May	June	July	Aug.	Sept.	Oct.	Nov.	Dec.	Average
2001	7,888	7,822	8,011	8,450	8,651	8,637	8,481	8,277	8,381	8,446	8,366	8,301	8,312
2002	8,160	8,117	8,072	8,626	8,729	8,661	8,665	8,666	8,320	8,190	8,738	8,734	8,475
2003	7,870	7,800	7,724	8,161	8,311	8,293	8,320	8,355	8,228	8,253	8,450	8,540	8,194
2004	7,956	7,979	8,102	8,233	8,447	8,336	8,370	8,357	7,993	8,384	8,346	8,659	8,264
2005	8,157	8,194	8,119	8,549	8,475	8,589	8,352	8,326	8,129	7,953	8,468	8,503	8,318
2006	8,189	7,969	7,765	8,032	8,613	8,957	8,624	8,610	8,465	8,210	8,335	8,567	8,361
2007	8,348	8,012	8,101	8,122	8,491	8,686	8,504	8,547	8,320	8,276	8,353	8,501	8,355
2008	8,516	8,495	8,373	8,560	8,700	8,564	8,523	8,513	7,855	8,889	8,722	8,850	8,547
2009	8,445	8,408	8,646	8,724	8,793	9,068	8,952	8,856	8,829	8,770	8,905	9,006	8,784
2010[1]	8,327	8,489	8,910	9,053	9,059	9,165	9,493	9,417	9,128	9,062	9,043	9,203	9,029

[1] Preliminary.   Source: Energy Information Administration, U.S. Department of Energy (EIA-DOE)

Disposition of Finished Motor Gasoline, Total Product Supplied in the United States — In Thousand Barrels per Day

Year	Jan.	Feb.	Mar.	Apr.	May	June	July	Aug.	Sept.	Oct.	Nov.	Dec.	Average
2001	8,099	8,234	8,532	8,575	8,706	8,690	9,023	8,953	8,557	8,655	8,677	8,585	8,610
2002	8,227	8,607	8,655	8,766	9,078	9,140	9,143	9,313	8,687	8,814	8,829	8,893	8,848
2003	8,414	8,525	8,602	8,838	9,042	9,170	9,192	9,411	8,926	9,108	8,946	9,011	8,935
2004	8,705	8,838	9,024	9,126	9,179	9,322	9,357	9,327	9,015	9,097	9,055	9,206	9,104
2005	8,813	8,861	8,994	9,128	9,278	9,373	9,534	9,537	8,915	9,036	9,115	9,296	9,157
2006	8,839	8,911	9,054	9,154	9,308	9,478	9,607	9,564	9,236	9,267	9,244	9,338	9,250
2007	8,886	9,006	9,178	9,215	9,434	9,491	9,640	9,582	9,254	9,236	9,229	9,251	9,284
2008	8,810	8,866	9,066	9,112	9,251	9,110	9,150	9,134	8,497	9,024	8,904	8,927	8,988
2009	8,623	8,836	8,903	9,029	9,084	9,180	9,260	9,295	8,911	8,986	8,906	8,931	8,995
2010[1]	8,525	8,651	8,787	9,103	9,217	9,284	9,332	9,366	9,163	9,086	8,954	9,189	9,055

[1] Preliminary.   Source: Energy Information Administration, U.S. Department of Energy (EIA-DOE)

GASOLINE

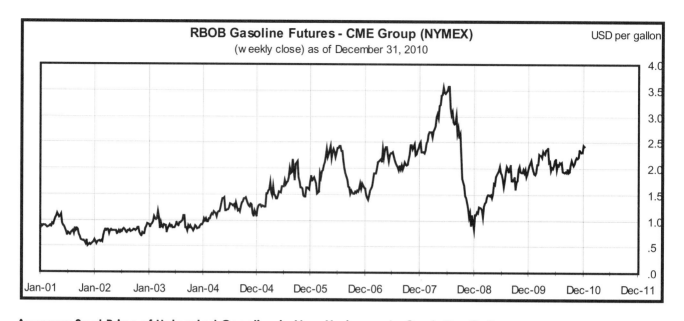

RBOB Gasoline Futures - CME Group (NYMEX)
(weekly close) as of December 31, 2010
USD per gallon

Average Spot Price of Unleaded Gasoline in New York   In Cents Per Gallon

Year	Jan.	Feb.	Mar.	Apr.	May	June	July	Aug.	Sept.	Oct.	Nov.	Dec.	Average
2001	83.32	82.56	78.18	94.95	92.37	71.85	68.31	77.18	75.00	59.79	51.34	51.85	73.89
2002	54.30	55.41	69.64	74.66	70.32	71.65	76.62	76.75	78.36	82.34	76.08	80.56	72.22
2003	87.56	99.62	95.51	80.08	76.16	80.65	87.17	100.42	90.41	87.12	87.33	88.37	88.37
2004	99.66	104.63	109.12	112.02	133.98	115.70	122.65	120.89	126.17	137.75	126.96	106.90	118.04
2005	123.85	122.42	143.90	147.06	137.06	151.02	158.89	191.13	214.78	170.87	147.73	159.88	155.72
2006	173.39	149.98	175.87	214.62	204.68	206.50	223.99	203.23	158.42	152.00	158.71	166.70	182.34
2007	141.63	164.55	193.58	210.05	224.09	218.30	213.51	199.83	209.72	216.93	242.33	232.69	205.60
2008	233.09	238.37	249.09	277.45	309.23	329.79	315.86	290.20	280.69	190.84	129.29	97.18	245.09
2009	115.11	121.66	128.84	137.77	169.79	190.79	174.74	193.01	178.43	192.30	198.63	192.00	166.09
2010	204.28	199.38	214.86	222.10	201.35	201.13	200.38	195.01	197.47	216.07	224.31	238.74	209.59

Source: Energy Information Administration, U.S. Department of Energy (EIA-DOE)

Volume of Trading of Gasoline, RBOB[1] Futures in New York   In Contracts

Year	Jan.	Feb.	Mar.	Apr.	May	June	July	Aug.	Sept.	Oct.	Nov.	Dec.	Total
2001	825.2	701.2	809.2	981.0	1,056.5	895.0	737.3	790.8	581.9	664.9	613.3	567.2	9,223.4
2002	795.0	744.7	942.7	1,019.3	985.2	834.5	967.8	893.6	867.6	1,105.0	865.9	958.4	10,979.7
2003	1,054.1	968.7	1,010.9	909.0	933.7	944.0	987.5	1,021.5	943.0	877.1	760.8	761.6	11,172.1
2004	956.1	998.7	1,169.2	1,169.0	1,203.8	1,194.5	1,027.0	1,177.7	1,052.9	983.7	849.0	995.9	12,777.5
2005	974.6	1,000.9	1,193.5	1,252.5	1,060.2	1,104.7	1,103.2	1,341.3	1,221.3	999.2	928.1	989.0	13,168.4
2006	1,149.6	1,233.0	1,259.1	1,079.6	1,122.7	1,039.8	939.8	1,145.5	891.4	839.6	838.1	966.0	12,504.2
2007	1,172.9	1,272.2	1,722.5	1,826.7	2,134.5	1,811.8	1,770.2	1,872.8	1,627.3	1,706.1	1,531.3	1,343.2	19,791.4
2008	1,660.6	1,887.5	2,111.9	1,986.3	1,917.6	1,854.4	1,621.6	1,667.7	1,862.1	1,452.9	1,193.4	1,306.4	20,522.6
2009	1,597.7	1,592.3	1,594.4	1,612.9	1,841.8	2,060.8	1,748.6	1,773.9	1,600.3	2,082.5	1,908.8	1,746.5	21,160.5
2010	1,979.2	1,978.8	2,318.0	2,829.9	2,537.8	2,186.6	1,946.1	2,402.3	2,325.4	2,614.0	2,529.1	2,251.3	27,898.7

[1] Data thru September 2005 are Unleaded, October 2005 thru December 2006 are Unleaded and RBOB.
Contract size = 42,000 US gallons.   *Source: CME Group; New York Mercantile Exchange (NYMEX)*

Average Open Interest of Gasoline, RBOB[1] Futures in New York   In Contracts

Year	Jan.	Feb.	Mar.	Apr.	May	June	July	Aug.	Sept.	Oct.	Nov.	Dec.
2001	117,540	126,762	124,631	124,162	111,576	103,058	101,249	92,156	87,841	102,414	115,699	126,634
2002	136,795	139,191	133,649	129,274	120,224	114,663	106,463	94,648	95,754	100,427	105,175	109,737
2003	117,558	124,288	113,380	98,627	96,405	93,285	95,433	99,394	85,457	90,007	95,002	105,919
2004	125,207	141,837	150,573	146,375	148,782	138,248	140,691	146,532	147,088	150,643	138,280	153,907
2005	162,432	161,603	172,012	166,620	145,587	148,482	156,730	156,282	140,270	134,833	138,659	144,396
2006	157,562	173,978	168,067	165,233	150,913	138,578	146,173	135,367	131,771	124,963	128,906	135,085
2007	161,557	161,335	166,936	170,675	172,870	183,443	189,084	184,342	188,954	196,730	206,392	208,238
2008	230,032	253,303	241,781	250,852	264,988	256,220	238,170	219,229	198,263	162,480	172,267	194,234
2009	192,691	187,748	199,423	204,956	220,450	215,256	200,537	217,625	205,517	219,883	256,151	238,789
2010	262,247	258,312	304,437	320,529	275,659	245,923	239,242	246,901	241,014	270,830	282,949	273,638

[1] Data thru September 2005 are Unleaded, October 2005 thru December 2006 are Unleaded and RBOB.
Contract size = 42,000 US gallons.   *Source: CME Group; New York Mercantile Exchange (NYMEX)*

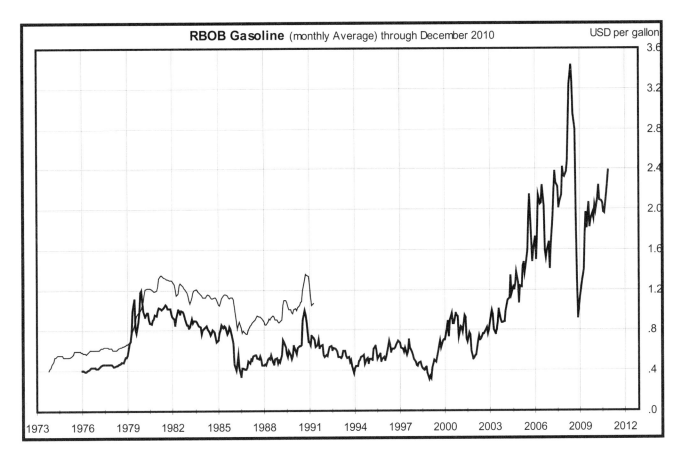

RBOB Gasoline (monthly Average) through December 2010   USD per gallon

Stocks of Finished Gasoline[2] on Hand in the United States, at End of Month   In Millions of Barrels

Year	Jan.	Feb.	Mar.	Apr.	May	June	July	Aug.	Sept.	Oct.	Nov.	Dec.
2001	158.7	154.6	144.7	150.3	160.1	169.4	162.3	150.6	158.0	160.2	161.2	161.5
2002	169.7	165.5	159.8	167.0	168.3	167.6	164.8	157.3	157.4	148.2	158.0	161.9
2003	157.2	151.1	144.7	151.4	155.2	153.0	150.1	145.2	146.1	140.4	146.3	146.9
2004	138.7	133.5	132.1	133.1	137.2	140.2	140.5	137.9	135.7	138.4	141.5	143.2
2005	145.6	146.4	136.4	141.1	140.7	140.9	133.6	122.5	127.3	131.3	135.4	135.8
2006	142.2	137.9	124.2	115.4	121.5	119.1	117.9	116.6	120.5	112.8	113.8	116.1
2007	124.3	116.0	109.2	108.5	114.5	116.6	114.2	110.6	113.2	108.8	110.5	111.4
2008	117.4	119.9	110.6	106.2	106.0	107.3	102.3	97.8	92.6	95.9	96.9	98.3
2009	95.3	86.9	85.9	86.0	83.5	88.6	86.1	86.7	84.7	79.4	83.0	84.9
2010[1]	87.1	83.5	81.9	78.2	75.0	71.8	72.0	72.5	70.2	65.6	65.6	63.4

[1] Preliminary.   [2] Includes oxygenated and other finished.   *Source: Energy Information Administration, U.S. Department of Energy (EIA-DOE)*

Average Refiner Price of Finished Motor Gasoline to End Users[1] in the United States   In Cents Per Gallon

Year	Jan.	Feb.	Mar.	Apr.	May	June	July	Aug.	Sept.	Oct.	Nov.	Dec.	Average
2001	106.8	106.7	103.9	117.7	130.1	120.7	103.2	102.5	1,009.2	89.9	76.9	68.5	103.2
2002	70.6	71.8	87.2	100.4	99.9	99.1	100.3	100.1	100.1	104.0	101.2	98.1	94.7
2003	106.0	122.1	130.0	120.1	110.0	109.3	110.6	123.1	126.5	115.0	109.5	106.5	115.7
2004	117.3	125.6	133.8	139.6	156.9	154.4	148.3	145.1	145.0	158.6	155.1	141.3	143.4
2005	139.5	146.8	163.7	180.3	171.4	172.1	185.0	208.0	241.7	226.2	182.4	173.9	182.6
2006	187.2	183.3	198.3	233.1	245.8	243.6	252.8	248.6	207.6	178.9	178.8	186.8	212.1
2007	179.1	184.2	213.8	240.5	266.9	256.9	248.8	232.0	233.7	235.0	261.4	255.2	234.0
2008	257.1	256.6	278.3	298.4	331.6	358.0	356.8	327.9	320.7	253.7	161.7	121.9	276.9
2009	135.8	146.8	150.3	160.1	185.6	218.7	206.7	215.7	208.6	210.4	217.3	214.4	189.2
2010[2]	224.0	217.3	230.1	237.0	235.3	225.1	224.7	225.0	221.9	231.9			227.2

[1] Excludes aviation and taxes.   [2] Preliminary.   *Source: Energy Information Administration, U.S. Department of Energy (EIA-DOE)*

GASOLINE

Average Retail Price of Unleaded Premium Motor Gasoline[2] in the United States — In Cents per Gallon

Year	Jan.	Feb.	Mar.	Apr.	May	June	July	Aug.	Sept.	Oct.	Nov.	Dec.	Average
2001	165.7	167.1	163.8	174.8	193.4	188.1	169.5	163.6	172.6	156.0	142.7	131.2	165.7
2002	132.3	133.0	145.0	162.2	162.5	160.8	160.7	162.0	161.9	164.3	164.3	158.9	157.8
2003	166.6	182.8	192.4	184.6	172.9	170.0	171.0	180.8	191.1	178.9	172.4	168.6	177.7
2004	177.9	185.8	194.9	201.2	218.6	222.5	213.0	209.1	208.2	221.5	220.3	208.0	206.8
2005	201.7	210.5	225.1	246.8	240.3	236.5	250.2	270.1	313.0	300.1	256.0	239.3	249.1
2006	252.1	251.9	260.3	296.7	316.9	313.9	321.9	320.7	281.9	249.3	245.9	255.0	280.5
2007	250.1	250.9	281.8	309.3	334.8	328.1	320.0	301.8	302.1	303.7	330.7	326.4	303.3
2008	329.1	327.2	350.2	369.0	400.3	431.9	435.0	404.5	394.0	343.2	243.3	195.1	351.9
2009	203.6	218.2	219.7	230.9	251.1	288.3	280.6	288.7	284.5	282.6	291.7	288.2	260.7
2010[1]	298.7	292.2	303.5	311.3	312.4	300.0	299.7	301.5	296.8	305.5	310.9	323.4	304.7

[1] Preliminary. [2] Including taxes. *Source: Energy Information Administration, U.S. Department of Energy (EIA-DOE)*

Average Retail Price of Unleaded Regular Motor Gasoline[2] in the United States — In Cents per Gallon

Year	Jan.	Feb.	Mar.	Apr.	May	June	July	Aug.	Sept.	Oct.	Nov.	Dec.	Average
2001	147.2	148.4	144.7	156.4	172.9	164.0	148.2	142.7	153.1	136.2	126.3	113.1	146.1
2002	113.9	113.0	124.1	140.7	142.1	140.4	141.2	142.3	142.2	144.9	144.8	139.4	135.8
2003	147.3	164.1	174.8	165.9	154.2	151.4	152.4	162.8	172.8	160.3	153.5	149.4	159.1
2004	159.2	167.2	176.6	183.3	200.9	204.1	193.9	189.8	189.1	202.9	201.0	188.2	188.0
2005	182.3	191.8	206.5	228.3	221.6	217.6	231.6	250.3	292.7	278.5	234.3	218.6	229.5
2006	231.5	231.0	240.1	275.7	294.7	291.7	299.9	298.5	258.9	227.2	224.1	233.4	258.9
2007	227.4	228.5	259.2	286.0	313.0	305.2	296.1	278.2	278.9	279.3	306.9	302.0	280.1
2008	304.7	303.3	325.8	344.1	376.4	406.5	409.0	378.6	369.8	317.3	215.1	168.9	326.6
2009	178.7	192.8	194.9	205.6	226.5	263.1	254.3	262.7	257.4	256.1	266.0	262.1	235.0
2010[1]	273.1	265.9	278.0	285.8	286.9	273.6	273.6	274.5	270.4	279.5	285.2	298.5	278.8

[1] Preliminary. [2] Including taxes. *Source: Energy Information Administration, U.S. Department of Energy (EIA-DOE)*

Average Retail Price of All-Types[2] Motor Gasoline[3] in the United States — In Cents per Gallon

Year	Jan.	Feb.	Mar.	Apr.	May	June	July	Aug.	Sept.	Oct.	Nov.	Dec.	Average
2001	152.5	153.8	150.3	161.7	181.2	173.1	156.5	150.9	160.9	144.2	132.4	120.0	153.1
2002	120.9	121.0	132.4	149.3	150.8	148.9	149.6	150.8	150.7	153.5	153.4	147.7	144.1
2003	155.7	168.6	179.1	170.4	158.7	155.8	156.7	167.1	177.1	164.6	157.8	153.8	163.8
2004	163.5	171.5	180.9	187.5	205.0	208.3	198.2	194.1	193.4	207.2	205.3	192.6	192.3
2005	186.6	196.0	210.7	232.5	225.7	221.8	235.7	254.8	296.9	283.0	238.7	223.0	233.8
2006	235.9	235.4	244.4	280.1	299.3	296.3	304.6	303.3	263.7	231.9	228.7	238.0	263.5
2007	232.1	233.3	263.9	290.9	317.6	310.0	301.3	283.3	283.9	284.3	311.8	306.9	284.9
2008	309.6	308.3	330.7	349.1	381.3	411.5	414.2	383.8	374.9	322.5	220.8	174.2	331.7
2009	183.8	197.9	200.0	210.7	231.4	268.1	259.4	267.7	262.6	261.3	270.9	267.1	240.1
2010[1]	277.9	270.9	282.9	290.6	291.5	278.3	278.3	279.5	275.4	284.3	289.9	303.1	283.6

[1] Preliminary. [2] Also includes types of motor oil not shown separately. [3] Including taxes. *Source: Energy Information Administration, U.S. Department of Energy (EIA-DOE)*

Average Refiner Price of Finished Aviation Gasoline to End Users[2] in the United States — In Cents per Gallon

Year	Jan.	Feb.	Mar.	Apr.	May	June	July	Aug.	Sept.	Oct.	Nov.	Dec.	Average
2001	128.5	129.2	124.5	134.9	150.9	145.1	134.6	136.3	142.4	125.3	119.4	115.8	132.3
2002	111.8	110.6	122.6	129.8	128.9	127.3	139.2	136.9	139.1	143.0	141.8	139.8	128.8
2003	139.7	W	W	W	139.8	145.1	151.9	162.2	158.9	150.8	W	146.6	149.4
2004	W	W	W	177.4	194.4	192.3	185.4	184.9	187.8	195.5	187.0	176.7	186.8
2005	173.8	186.7	201.5	221.7	212.1	211.6	223.0	238.6	280.8	270.8	218.6	219.3	221.5
2006	239.1	232.4	247.3	286.9	301.3	305.7	310.3	305.8	253.2	238.5	235.3	234.9	265.9
2007	217.9	228.5	262.7	296.9	309.6	297.8	305.3	282.3	290.0	285.5	306.7	297.5	281.7
2008	298.7	295.4	329.6	335.8	361.5	396.5	392.9	379.2	383.7	297.5	223.0	181.4	322.9
2009	185.7	197.4	197.7	215.0	242.3	270.7	260.7	276.4	268.4	269.3	284.5	279.9	245.7
2010[1]	291.4	285.5	310.3	320.1	312.9	298.1	302.8	296.7	289.3	300.0			300.7

[1] Preliminary. [2] Excluding taxes. NA = Not available. W = Withheld proprietary data. *Source: Energy Information Administration, U.S. Department Energy (EIA-DOE)*

112

Gold

Gold is a dense, bright yellow metallic element with a high luster. Gold is an inactive substance and is unaffected by air, heat, moisture, and most solvents. Gold has been coveted for centuries for its unique blend of rarity, beauty, and near indestructibility. The Egyptians mined gold before 2,000 BC. The first known, pure gold coin was made on the orders of King Croesus of Lydia in the sixth century BC.

Gold is found in nature in quartz veins and secondary alluvial deposits as a free metal. Gold is produced from mines on every continent with the exception of Antarctica, where mining is forbidden. Because it is virtually indestructible, much of the gold that has ever been mined still exists above ground in one form or another. The largest producer of gold in the U.S. by far is the state of Nevada, with Alaska and California running a distant second and third.

Gold is a vital industrial commodity. Pure gold is one of the most malleable and ductile of all the metals. It is a good conductor of heat and electricity. The prime industrial use of gold is in electronics. Another important sector is dental gold where it has been used for almost 3,000 years. Other applications for gold include decorative gold leaf, reflective glass, and jewelry.

In 1792, the United States first assigned a formal monetary role for gold when Congress put the nation's currency on a bimetallic standard, backing it with gold and silver. Under the gold standard, the U.S. government was willing to exchange its paper currency for a set amount of gold, meaning the paper currency was backed by a physical asset with real value. However, President Nixon in 1971 severed the convertibility between the U.S. dollar and gold, which led to the breakdown of the Bretton Woods international payments system. Since then, the prices of gold and of paper currencies have floated freely. U.S. and other central banks now hold physical gold reserves primarily as a store of wealth.

Gold futures and options are traded at the New York Mercantile Exchange (NYMEX). Gold futures are traded on the Bolsa de Mercadorias and Futuros (BM&F) and on the Tokyo Commodity Exchange (TOCOM), the NYSE-LIFFE exchange, the Central Japan Commodity Exchange (CJCE), the Hong Kong Futures Exchange (HKFE) and the Korea Futures Exchange (KOFEX). The NYMEX gold futures contract calls for the delivery of 100 troy ounces of gold (0.995 fineness), and the contract trades in terms of dollars and cents per troy ounce.

Prices – NYMEX gold futures prices on a nearest-futures basis weakened in early 2010 as inflation in the U.S. slipped to a four decade low. Gold prices fell to a 1-1/4 year low of $1,045 in February 2010. Gold prices then began a rally that lasted through most of 2001, posting an all-time high of $1,431 an ounce in December and finishing 2010 up +30% at $1,421. As dollar weakness intensified after June 2010 and the European sovereign-debt crisis expanded from Greece to Ireland, demand for gold surged. Gold prices continued their rally in early 2011 and in March 2011 posted another all-time high of $1445. The markets remain concerned that the Federal Reserve, the Bank of England and Bank of Japan will be slow to end their quantitative easing and run the risk of causing a surge in inflation within the next year or two.

Supply – World mine production of gold rose +2.0% yr/yr to 2.500 million kilograms in 2010, and was still below the record high of 2.570 million kilograms seen in 1999 and 2000 (1 kilogram = 32.1507 troy ounces). The world's largest producers of gold in 2010 were China with 13.8% of world production, followed by Australia (10.2%), the U.S (9.2%), South Africa (7.6%), and Russia (7.6%).

Gold mine production has been moving lower in most major gold-producing countries such as South Africa, Australia, and the U.S. For example, South Africa's production of 190,000 kilograms in 2010 was down -4.0% yr/yr and that was about one-third the production levels of more than 600,000 kilograms seen in the 1980s and early 1990s. On the other hand, China's gold production in 2009 rose +7.8% to a record 345,000 kilograms. U.S. gold mine production in 2010 rose +3.1% yr/yr to 230,000 kilograms, just above last year's production level which was the lowest production since 1988. U.S. refinery production of gold from domestic and foreign ore sources in 2010 rose +5.9% yr/yr to 180,000 kilograms. U.S. refinery production of gold from secondary scrap sources in 2010 rose +8.5% yr/yr to 205,000 kilograms.

Demand – U.S. consumption of gold in 2010 remained unchanged at 150,000 kilograms. The most recent data available from the early 1990s showed that 71% of that gold demand came from jewelry and the arts, 22% from industrial uses, and 7% from dental uses.

Trade – U.S. exports of gold (excluding coinage) in 2010 fell -0.3% yr/yr to 380,000 kilograms, down from the 16-year high of 568,000 kilograms seen in 2008. U.S. imports of gold for consumption in 2010 rose +68.8% yr/yr to 540,000 kilograms, a new record high.

World Mine Production of Gold   In Kilograms (1 Kilogram = 32.1507 Troy Ounces)

Year	Australia	Brazil	Canada	Chile	China	Ghana	Indonesia	Papua New Guinea	Russia	South Africa	United States	Uzebistan	World Total
2002	266,100	41,662	151,904	38,688	192,000	69,271	142,238	61,379	168,411	398,523	298,000	90,000	2,530,000
2003	282,000	40,416	140,861	38,954	205,000	70,749	141,019	67,832	170,068	373,300	277,000	90,000	2,540,000
2004	259,000	47,596	129,478	39,986	215,000	63,139	91,710	73,670	163,148	337,223	258,000	93,000	2,420,000
2005	262,000	38,293	119,549	40,447	225,000	66,852	130,620	68,483	164,186	294,671	256,000	90,000	2,470,000
2006	247,000	43,082	103,513	42,100	245,000	69,817	93,176	58,349	159,340	272,128	252,000	85,000	2,370,000
2007	247,000	49,613	102,211	41,527	275,000	83,558	117,851	65,000	156,975	252,600	238,000	85,000	2,370,000
2008	215,000	49,700	95,004	39,162	285,000	80,503	60,200	68,000	176,347	212,744	233,000	85,000	2,280,000
2009[1]	222,000	60,000	97,000	41,000	320,000	86,000	130,000	66,000	191,000	198,000	223,000	90,000	2,450,000
2010[2]	255,000	65,000	90,000	40,000	345,000	100,000	120,000	60,000	190,000	190,000	230,000	90,000	2,500,000

[1] Preliminary.   [2] Estimate.   Source: U.S. Geological Survey (USGS)

GOLD

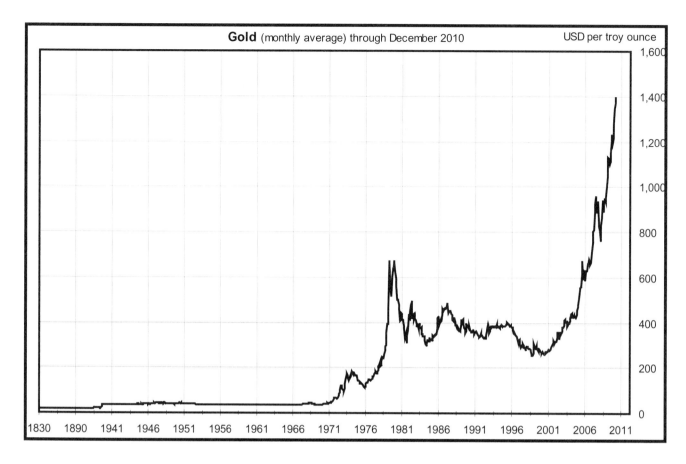

Gold (monthly average) through December 2010 — USD per troy ounce

Salient Statistics of Gold in the United States   In Kilograms (1 Kilogram = 32.1507 Troy Ounces)

Year	Mine Pro- duction	Value Million $	Refinery Production - Domestic & Foreign Ores	Secondary (Old Scrap)	Exports, Excluding Coinage	Imports for Con- sumption	Treasury Depart- ment[3]	Futures Exchange	Industry	Official World Reserves[4]	Dental	Indus- trial[5]	Jewelry & Arts	Total
2001	335,000	2,940.0	191,000	82,700	489,000	194,000	8,120,000	38,000	3,670	33,000	----	----	----	179,000
2002	298,000	2,980.0	196,000	78,100	257,000	217,000	8,140,000	63,900	3,490	32,200	----	----	----	163,000
2003	277,000	3,250.0	194,000	89,100	352,000	249,000	8,140,000	97,100	3,590	31,800	----	----	----	183,000
2004	258,000	3,400.0	222,000	91,700	257,000	283,000	8,140,000	180,000	1,080	31,400	----	----	----	185,000
2005	256,000	3,670.0	195,000	81,300	324,000	341,000	8,140,000	211,000	2,040	30,800	----	----	----	183,000
2006	252,000	4,910.0	181,000	89,100	389,000	263,000	8,140,000	234,000	2,000	30,400	----	----	----	185,000
2007	238,000	5,350.0	176,000	135,000	519,000	170,000	8,140,000	229,000	1,140	29,900	----	----	----	180,000
2008	233,000	6,550.0	168,000	181,000	567,000	231,000	8,140,000	265,000	W	28,700	----	----	----	176,000
2009[1]	223,000		170,000	189,000	381,000	320,000	8,140,000				----	----	----	150,000
2010[2]	230,000		180,000	205,000	380,000	540,000	8,140,000							150,000

[1] Preliminary.   [2] Estimate.   [3] Includes gold in Exchange Stabilization Fund.   [4] Held by market economy country central banks and governments and international monetary orgainzations.   [5] Including space and defense.   NA = Not available.   Source: U.S. Geological Survey (USGS)

Monthly Average Gold Price (Handy & Harman) in New York   Dollars Per Troy Ounce

Year	Jan.	Feb.	Mar.	Apr.	May	June	July	Aug.	Sept.	Oct.	Nov.	Dec.	Average
2001	265.58	261.99	263.03	260.56	272.07	270.23	267.53	272.40	283.78	283.06	276.49	275.98	271.06
2002	281.47	295.40	294.06	302.68	314.08	321.81	313.51	310.18	319.49	316.56	319.14	333.21	310.13
2003	356.91	359.60	340.55	328.25	355.03	356.35	351.01	359.91	379.07	378.92	389.13	407.44	363.51
2004	414.09	404.52	405.99	403.96	383.94	392.73	398.08	400.86	405.45	420.46	438.21	442.20	409.21
2005	424.39	423.15	433.91	429.23	422.53	430.66	424.33	438.03	456.52	469.90	474.87	510.01	444.79
2006	549.27	555.02	557.09	610.41	673.97	596.15	634.89	632.10	596.76	585.78	627.12	629.38	604.00
2007	630.97	664.43	655.30	679.20	667.86	655.40	665.83	665.21	714.79	749.73	806.68	803.20	696.55
2008	890.47	923.25	966.30	909.70	886.29	889.49	940.16	838.30	830.30	806.62	754.95	816.09	870.99
2009	859.98	943.20	924.27	890.50	927.34	945.67	934.31	949.34	996.76	1043.16	1122.03	1212.50	979.09
2010	1116.74	1095.26	1114.36	1147.70	1204.50	1232.92	1192.25	1217.11	1272.02	1342.02	1370.46	1389.70	1224.59

[1] Preliminary.   Source: U.S. Geological Survey (USGS)

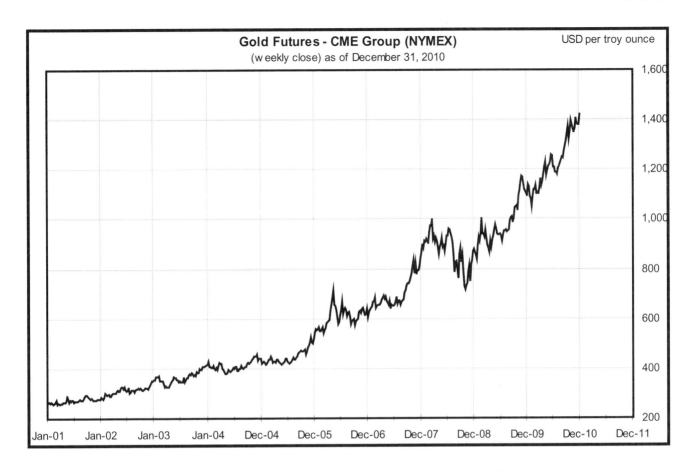

Gold Futures - CME Group (NYMEX)
(weekly close) as of December 31, 2010

USD per troy ounce

Volume of Trading of Gold Futures in New York (COMEX)   In Thousands of Contracts

Year	Jan.	Feb.	Mar.	Apr.	May	June	July	Aug.	Sept.	Oct.	Nov.	Dec.	Total
2001	755.2	483.3	766.6	438.1	971.6	481.4	578.3	547.4	341.0	481.4	573.6	367.4	6,785.3
2002	733.6	613.2	717.7	559.8	1,089.6	775.5	998.9	585.8	621.8	669.0	844.8	808.5	9,018.2
2003	1,260.1	1,007.5	987.6	667.8	1,160.3	824.3	1,191.7	837.5	1,034.0	1,091.3	1,864.7	1,053.2	12,235.5
2004	1,581.3	962.6	1,649.5	1,202.9	1,344.8	960.6	1,405.0	953.0	944.9	1,067.2	1,864.7	1,053.2	14,989.6
2005	1,502.3	944.4	1,599.0	858.1	1,451.7	1,240.0	1,432.4	1,234.4	1,380.2	1,174.0	1,852.7	1,221.5	15,890.6
2006	2,018.8	1,162.7	2,052.7	1,302.9	2,071.0	1,148.6	1,487.2	804.5	884.7	857.1	1,284.7	842.7	15,917.6
2007	1,929.8	1,455.9	2,195.9	1,405.2	2,336.6	1,610.8	2,292.2	1,710.7	2,024.6	2,584.4	3,837.1	1,677.2	25,060.4
2008	4,041.7	2,617.6	3,901.8	2,765.5	3,328.0	2,624.0	4,269.9	3,066.1	4,109.4	3,045.1	2,687.1	1,921.1	38,377.4
2009	3,073.0	2,444.2	3,385.0	1,808.4	2,766.7	2,305.0	2,846.2	1,815.6	2,831.4	3,216.7	4,564.3	4,083.1	35,139.5
2010	4,574.3	3,616.1	4,385.6	2,932.3	4,824.1	3,024.7	4,097.3	2,184.9	2,732.1	3,858.8	5,530.4	2,969.7	44,730.3

Contract size = 100 oz.   *Source: CME Group; New York Mercantile Exchange (NYMEX)*

Average Open Interest of Gold in New York (COMEX)   In Thousands of Contracts

Year	Jan.	Feb.	Mar.	Apr.	May	June	July	Aug.	Sept.	Oct.	Nov.	Dec.
2001	134,401	142,673	126,558	120,111	118,426	116,788	114,098	116,687	125,907	125,639	114,238	111,622
2002	124,222	142,763	142,638	159,892	190,845	174,123	166,042	146,596	167,620	162,456	164,581	191,594
2003	221,495	210,247	186,656	176,033	191,459	198,808	199,741	224,694	284,906	258,238	275,346	277,183
2004	283,813	238,816	256,873	274,898	250,963	225,001	239,579	237,940	259,181	306,522	344,665	329,669
2005	277,112	263,191	301,758	283,546	277,469	275,508	268,068	304,000	339,269	356,526	334,562	331,527
2006	348,949	338,851	331,223	350,380	336,735	288,309	316,969	309,186	320,850	330,152	346,141	335,204
2007	350,958	387,321	372,781	377,094	405,645	401,337	379,066	339,923	394,400	479,735	530,775	500,409
2008	556,302	487,373	471,320	418,693	435,847	401,914	460,178	382,302	378,216	321,545	290,706	280,402
2009	331,891	359,420	376,201	341,491	366,468	382,960	380,301	383,826	454,286	493,909	522,556	504,102
2010	512,723	469,214	489,600	521,976	574,107	579,416	561,781	541,408	595,118	619,536	626,630	589,823

Contract size = 100 oz.   *Source: CME Group; New York Mercantile Exchange (NYMEX)*

GOLD

Commodity Exchange, Inc. (COMEX) Depository Warehouse Stocks of Gold   In Thousands of Troy Ounces

Year	Jan. 1	Feb. 1	Mar. 1	Apr. 1	May 1	June 1	July 1	Aug. 1	Sept. 1	Oct. 1	Nov. 1	Dec. 1
2001	1,701.2	1,775.3	1,653.7	1,302.4	858.3	864.2	891.3	901.1	793.6	824.3	1,164.6	1,425.7
2002	1,220.3	1,186.7	1,285.7	1,322.3	1,372.3	1,764.1	1,850.7	1,835.6	1,915.0	1,892.4	1,994.9	2,046.5
2003	2,056.5	2,159.8	2,262.4	2,383.9	2,460.7	2,474.9	2,675.1	2,743.8	2,729.4	2,822.6	2,912.1	3,058.9
2004	3,122.2	3,324.0	3,476.9	3,677.1	4,142.0	4,391.8	4,399.6	4,657.0	4,880.1	5,122.4	5,334.7	5,374.3
2005	5,795.6	5,962.6	5,913.9	5,960.7	6,156.7	6,036.6	5,751.0	5,713.8	6,008.5	6,737.1	6,351.5	6,614.3
2006	6,657.7	7,320.9	7,518.9	7,426.6	7,334.4	7,796.0	8,031.2	8,199.0	7,980.8	7,695.2	7,565.8	7,491.1
2007	7,534.5	7,459.2	7,487.2	7,302.5	7,624.8	7,633.1	7,276.1	7,130.5	7,077.1	7,211.9	7,346.7	7,366.1
2008	7,492.5	7,588.0	7,371.3	7,623.1	7,760.4	7,588.9	7,611.6	8,266.0	8,442.8	8,594.9	8,171.8	8,540.3
2009	NA	8,556.8	8,635.9	8,508.6	8,322.6	8,725.8	8,893.4	9,144.6	9,173.0	9,316.2	9,316.2	9,508.9
2010	9,679.4	9,679.4	9,679.4	10,022.9	10,184.3	10,736.8	10,923.5	11,112.1	10,816.9	10,896.7	11,311.9	11,488.4

Source: CME Group; New York Mercantile Exchange (NYMEX)

Central Gold Bank Reserves   In Millions of Troy Ounces

	Industrial Countries											Deve- loping Oil	Deve- loping Non-Oil	IMF[2]	Bank for Int'l Settle- ments	World Total
Year	Belgium	Can- ada	France	Ger- many	Italy	Japan	Nether- lands	Switzer- land	United Kingdom	United States	Industrial Total					
2000	8.3	1.2	97.2	111.5	78.8	24.5	29.3	77.8	15.7	261.6	796.5	41.6	112.0	103.4	6.5	1,060.1
2001	8.3	1.1	97.2	111.1	78.8	24.6	28.4	70.7	11.4	262.0	791.3	42.3	111.3	103.4	6.5	1,054.7
2002	8.3	0.6	97.2	110.8	78.8	24.6	27.4	61.6	10.1	262.0						1,042.1
2003	8.3	0.1	97.2	110.6	78.8	24.6	25.0	52.5	10.1	261.5						1,024.3
2004	8.3	0.1	96.0	110.4	78.8	24.6	25.0	43.5	10.0	261.6						1,007.7
2005	7.3	0.1	90.9	110.2	78.8	24.6	22.3	41.5	10.0	261.6						988.4
2006	7.3	0.1	87.4	110.0	78.8	24.6	20.6	41.5	10.0	261.5						976.7
2007	7.3	0.1	83.7	109.9	78.8	24.6	20.0	36.8	10.0	261.5						960.5
2008	7.3	0.1	80.1	109.7	78.8	24.6	19.7	33.4	10.0	261.5						954.6
2009[1]	7.3	0.1	78.3	109.5	78.8	24.6	19.7		10.0	261.5						

[1] Preliminary.   [2] International Monetary Fund.   *Source: American Metal Market (AMM)*

Mine Production of Recoverable Gold in the United States   In Kilograms

Year	Arizona	California	Idaho	Montana	Nevada	Alaska	Colorado	South Dakota	New Mexico	Utah	Other States	Total
2000	442	17,200	W	9,310	268,000	15,600	W	8,230	W	W	34,218	353,000
2001	W	13,800	W	W	253,000	16,700	W	W	W	W	51,500	335,000
2002	W	9,180	W	W	240,000	W	W	W	W	W	48,820	298,000
2003	W	4,270	W	W	227,000	W	W	W	W	W	45,730	277,000
2004	W	3,260	W	W	216,000	W	W	W	W	W	38,740	258,000
2005	W	W	W	W	212,000	W	W	W	W	W	44,200	256,000
2006	W	W	W	W	206,000	W	W	W	W	W	45,800	252,000
2007	W	W	W	W	186,000	W	W	W	W	W	52,400	238,000
2008	W	W	W	W	178,000	W	W	W	W	W	55,400	233,000
2009[1]	W	W	W	W	153,000	W	W	W	W	W	62,000	215,000

[1] Preliminary.   W = Withheld proprietary data, included in "Other States."   *Source: U.S. Geological Survey (USGS)*

Consumption of Gold, By End-Use in the United States   In Kilograms

	Jewelry and the Arts					Industrial					
Year	Gold-Filled & Other	Electro- plating	Karat Gold	Total	Dental	Gold-Filled & Other	Electro- plating	Karat Gold	Total	Grand Total
1986	6,780	2,689	43,916	53,385	7,921	23,050	11,486	1,202	35,738	97,234
1987	9,256	3,133	58,635	71,024	6,944	21,010	12,343	1,892	35,245	113,319
1988	7,598	1,469	57,959	67,027	7,576	21,034	15,088	1,104	37,226	111,836
1989	7,364	1,283	60,877	69,524	7,927	15,723	20,684	1,215	37,621	115,078
1990	8,132	429	69,952	78,514	8,700	12,725	17,251	1,020	30,996	118,216
1991	3,848	373	79,875	84,096	8,485	8,102	12,624	1,068	21,793	114,375
1992	3,546	581	79,381	83,508	6,543	8,802	10,476	1,082	20,360	110,410
1993	3,530	373	61,700	65,600	6,170	9,470	9,090	1,100	19,700	91,400
1994	3,650	369	49,700	53,700	5,430	7,450	9,470	96	17,000	76,100
1995	NA	NA	NA	NA	NA	NA	NA	NA	NA	NA

[1] Preliminary.   NA = Not available.   *Source: U.S. Geological Survey (USGS)*

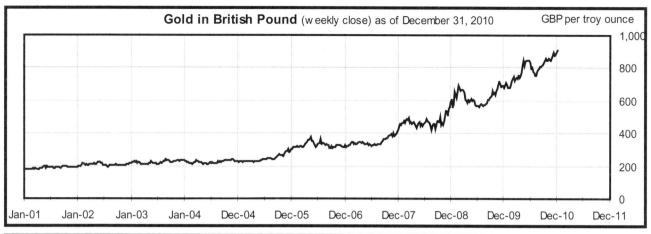

Gold in British Pound (weekly close) as of December 31, 2010 — GBP per troy ounce

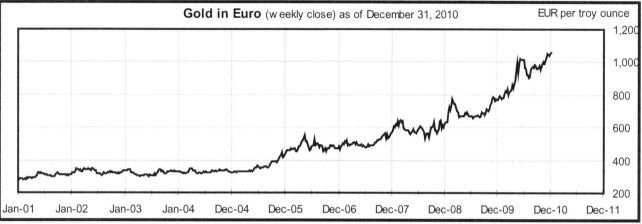

Gold in Euro (weekly close) as of December 31, 2010 — EUR per troy ounce

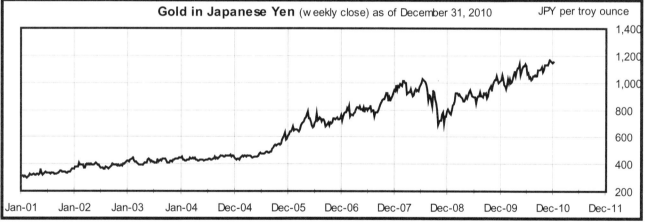

Gold in Japanese Yen (weekly close) as of December 31, 2010 — JPY per troy ounce

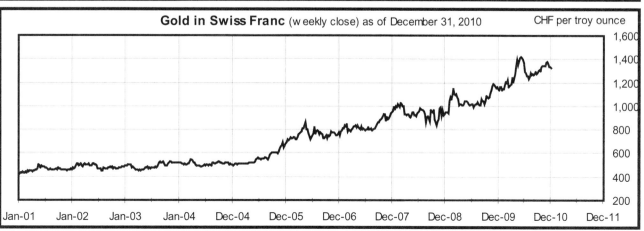

Gold in Swiss Franc (weekly close) as of December 31, 2010 — CHF per troy ounce

Grain Sorghum

Grain sorghums include milo, kafir, durra, feterita, and kaoliang. Grain sorghums are tolerant of drought by going into dormancy during dry and hot conditions and then resuming growth as conditions improve. Grain sorghums are a staple food in China, India, and Africa but in the U.S. they are mainly used as livestock feed. The two key U.S. producing states are Texas and Kansas, each with about one-third of total U.S. production. U.S. sorghum production has become more popular with the breeding of dwarf grain sorghum hybrids which are only about 3 feet tall (versus up to 10 feet tall for wild sorghum) and are easier to harvest with a combine. The U.S. sorghum crop year begins September 1.

Prices – The monthly average price for sorghum grain received by U.S. farmers in the 2010-11 marketing year (Sep-Aug) rose by +48.2% yr/yr to $8.44 per hundred pounds (annualized through January 2011). The value of U.S. grain sorghum production in the 2008-09 marketing year (latest data) fell 12.7% to $1.682 billion.

Supply – World production of sorghum in the 2010-11 marketing year rose +6.3% to 63.006 million metric tons, well below the 13-year high of 66.289 million metric tons

posted in 2007-08. U.S. grain sorghum production in 2010-11 fell -9.8% yr/yr to 345.395 million bushels. Sorghum acreage harvested in 2010-11 is forecasted fell 12.9% to 4,808 million acres, only slightly below the 2006-07 figure of 4.937 acres which was the smallest sorghum acreage since the late 1930s. Yield in 2010-11 was 71.8 bushels per acre, but that was still below the record high of 73.2 bushels per acre in 2007-08.

Demand – World utilization (consumption) of grain sorghum in the 2010-11 marketing year rose +3.5% to 63.081 million metric tons. The biggest consumers are Mexico utilizing 15.1% of the world supply and the U.S. utilizing 8.1% of the world supply.

Trade – World exports of sorghum in the 2010-11 marketing year fell -2.7% to 6.450 million metric tons, well below the 21-year high of 9.730 million metric tons seen in 2007-08. U.S. exports in 2010-11 fell -9.7% yr/yr to 3.810 million metric tons, accounting for 60% of total world exports. Argentina is the world's other major exporter with 1.400 million metric tons of exports in 2010-11, accounting for 17.6% of total world exports. Major world importers are Mexico and Japan.

World Supply and Demand of Grain Sorghum   In Thousands of Metric Tons

	Exports				Imports			Total		Utilization				Ending Stocks		
Crop Year	Argen-tina	Non-U.S.	U.S.	Total	Japan	Mexico	Unac-counted	Total	Pro-duction	China	Mexico	U.S.	Total	Non-U.S.	U.S.	Total
2005-06	197	442	4,936	5,378	1,393	3,029	176	5,335	59,634	2,300	8,600	4,818	59,293	3,753	1,668	5,421
2006-07	1,083	1,587	3,876	5,463	1,276	1,954	406	4,839	57,650	2,050	8,100	4,012	57,911	3,722	814	4,536
2007-08	1,223	2,700	7,030	9,730	1,084	1,156	525	9,679	65,886	2,000	7,200	5,081	64,399	4,632	1,340	5,972
2008-09[1]	1,113	2,352	3,632	5,984	1,629	2,496		6,112	64,809	2,000	8,600	8,319	64,584	4,935	1,390	6,325
2009-10[2]	1,700	2,408	4,221	6,629	1,649	2,528		6,118	59,262	1,900	9,700	5,849	60,954	3,074	1,048	4,122
2010-11[3]	1,400	2,640	3,810	6,450	1,600	2,400		6,415	63,006	1,750	9,500	5,080	63,081	3,081	931	4,012

[1] Preliminary.   [2] Estimate.   [3] Forecast.   Source: Foreign Agricultural Service, U.S. Department of Agriculture (FAS-USDA)

Salient Statistics of Grain Sorghum in the United States

	Acreage Planted[4]		For Grain				For Silage			Sorghum Grain Stocks			
Crop Year Beginning Sept. 1	for All Purposes	Acreage Harvested	Pro-duction (1,000 Bushels)	Yield Per Harvested Acre (Bushels)	Price in Cents Per Bushel	Value of Pro-duction (Million $)	Acreage Harvested (1,000 Acres)	Pro-duction (1,000 Tons)	Yield Per Harvested Acre (Tons)	Dec. 1 On Farms	Dec. 1 Off Farms	June 1 On Farms	June 1 Off Farms
	-- 1,000 Acres --									1,000 Bushels			
2005-06	6,454	5,736	392,933	68.7	186	737.0	311	4,218	13.6	55,000	235,376	12,650	102,213
2006-07	6,522	4,937	277,538	56.2	329	883.2	347	4,642	13.4	38,100	174,094	5,380	69,490
2007-08	7,712	6,792	497,445	73.2	408	1,925.3	392	5,246	13.4	51,400	239,850	7,000	94,019
2008-09[1]	8,284	7,271	472,342	65.0	320	1,631.1	408	5,646	13.8	54,400	243,290	12,000	90,215
2009-10[2]	6,633	5,520	382,983	69.4	322	1,207.1	254	3,680	14.5	48,000	202,759	10,700	77,162
2010-11[3]	5,404	4,808	345,395	71.8	515-585	1,743.0	273	3,420	12.5	30,500	205,023		

[1] Preliminary.   [2] Estimate.   [3] Forecast.   Source: Foreign Agricultural Service, U.S. Department of Agriculture (FAS-USDA)

Production of All Sorghum for Grain in the United States, by States   In Thousands of Bushels

Year	Arkansas	Colo-rado	Illinois	Kansas	Louis-iana	Miss-issippi	Missouri	Nebraska	New Mexico	Okla-homa	South Dakota	Texas	Total
2005	4,960	3,410	7,636	195,000	8,712	----	9,880	21,750	4,365	11,520	4,420	111,000	392,933
2006	5,100	3,380	6,408	145,000	8,352	----	8,075	19,200	2,100	6,800	2,880	62,400	277,538
2007	20,640	5,550	6,237	209,350	23,275	9,775	9,600	22,560	3,000	12,320	7,800	159,250	497,445
2008	10,120	4,500	7,828	214,500	9,570	5,822	7,760	19,110	3,440	13,950	7,360	158,600	472,342
2009	2,923	6,750	2,952	224,400	5,330	770	3,698	13,020	2,300	12,320	7,320	98,400	382,983
2010[1]	2,695	7,520	3,168	171,000	7,410	650	2,574	6,750	4,488	13,000	5,270	119,000	345,395

[1] Preliminary.   Source: National Agricultural Statistics Service, U.S. Department of Agriculture (NASS-USDA)

Quarterly Supply and Disappearance of Grain Sorghum in the United States   In Millions of Bushels

Crop Year Beginning Sept. 1	Beginning Stocks	Pro-duction	Imports[3]	Total Supply	Food & Alcohol	Seed	Feed & Residual	Total	Exports[3]	Total Disap-pearance	Gov't Owned[4]	Privately Owned[5]	Total Stocks
2007-08	32.1	497.4	.0	529.5	34.1	1.1	164.9	200.0	276.7	476.8			52.8
Sept.-Nov.	32.1	497.4	.0	529.5	8.5	0	136.1	144.6	93.7	238.3			291.3
Dec.-Feb.	291.3	----	.0	291.3	8.5	0	5.9	14.4	91.0	105.3			185.9
Mar.-May	185.9	----	.0	185.9	8.7	.6	17.9	27.2	57.7	84.9			101.0
June-Aug.	101.0	----	.0	101.0	8.4	.5	5.1	13.9	34.3	48.3			52.8
2008-09	52.8	472.3	.1	525.2	94.1	.8	232.6	327.5	143.0	470.5			54.7
Sept.-Nov.	52.8	472.3	.1	525.2	27.3	0	156.0	183.4	44.2	227.5			297.7
Dec.-Feb.	297.7	----	.0	297.7	27.3	0	32.4	59.7	32.2	91.9			205.9
Mar.-May	205.9	----	0	205.9	27.8	.5	40.1	68.4	35.2	103.6			102.2
June-Aug.	102.2	----	0	102.2	11.7	.3	4.1	16.1	31.4	47.5			54.7
2009-10[1]	54.7	383.0	.0	437.7	89.3	.7	140.3	230.3	166.2	396.5			41.2
Sept.-Nov.	54.7	383.0	0	437.7	25.0	0	115.7	140.7	46.2	186.9			250.8
Dec.-Feb.	250.8	----	.0	250.8	25.0	0	7.0	32.0	43.2	75.2			175.6
Mar.-May	175.6	----	0	175.6	25.2	.4	14.8	40.4	47.3	87.7			87.9
June-Aug.	87.9	----	0	87.9	14.0	.4	2.7	17.1	29.5	46.6			41.2
2010-11[2]	41.2	345.4	.0	386.6	89.2	.8	110.0	200.0	150.0	350.0			36.6
Sept.-Nov.	41.2	345.4	.0	386.6	23.6		91.7	115.3	35.8	151.1			235.5

[1] Preliminary.   [2] Estimate.   [3] Uncommitted inventory.   [4] Includes quantity under loan and farmer-owned reserve.   *Source: Economic Research Service, U.S. Department of Agriculture (ERS-USDA)*

Average Price of Sorghum Grain, No. 2, Yellow in Kansas City   In Dollars Per Hundred Pounds (Cwt.)

Year	Sept.	Oct.	Nov.	Dec.	Jan.	Feb.	Mar.	Apr.	May	June	July	Aug.	Average
2003-04	4.15	4.18	4.50	4.61	4.71	4.88	5.18	5.37	4.94	4.67	3.92	3.75	4.57
2004-05	3.45	3.21	3.17	3.21	3.13	3.23	3.44	3.30	3.36	3.56	3.90	3.53	3.37
2005-06	3.22	3.08	2.93	3.30	3.46	3.58	3.65	3.79	4.03	3.90	4.15	3.79	3.57
2006-07	3.82	5.07	5.97	6.03	6.36	6.72	6.38	5.69	5.97	6.09	5.33	5.50	5.75
2007-08	5.68	5.60	6.13	7.34	8.36	8.86	9.13	9.70	9.65	11.63	10.10	8.37	8.38
2008-09	8.43	5.92	5.49	5.19	5.67	5.48	5.51	5.76	6.37	6.29	4.66	4.75	5.79
2009-10	4.81	5.49	5.72	6.44	5.81	5.58	5.69	5.64	5.77	5.50	6.03	6.59	5.75
2010-11[1]	8.23	9.10	9.40	9.91	10.62								9.45

[1] Preliminary.   *Source: Economic Research Service, U.S. Department of Agriculture (ERS-USDA)*

Exports of Grain Sorghum, by Country of Destination from the United States   In Metric Tons

Year	Canada	Ecuador	Ethiopia	Israel	Japan	Jordan	Mexico	South Africa	Spain	Sudan	Turkey	World Total
2003-04	8,025	210	54,320	105,170	889,054	0	2,814,386	156	267,691	11,430	0	4,626,171
2004-05	5,270	0	53,540	26,654	1,088,171	0	2,883,335	2,000	167,896	116,577	0	4,474,017
2005-06	4,227	0	31,500	16,177	1,193,039	0	3,004,518	30,398	131,995	211,021	0	4,929,700
2006-07	3,999	0	4,100	54,533	674,824	0	1,914,111	0	1,018,325	299,650	0	4,333,212
2007-08	5,775	0	27,600	137,284	505,919	125	1,150,231	45,498	1,929,955	303,818	0	6,653,444
2008-09[1]	4,987	0	28,170	0	313,179	0	2,476	41,000	0	268,160	0	3,585,632
2009-10[2]	3,928	0	0	20,681	827,748	0	2,518	21,000	0	344,283	0	4,067,832

[1] Preliminary.   [2] Estimate.   *Source: Economic Research Service, U.S. Department of Agriculture (ERS-USDA)*

Grain Sorghum Price Support Program and Market Prices in the United States

Year	Price Support Quantity	% of Pro-duction	Aquired by CCC	Owned by CCC at Year End	Basic Loan Rate	Target Price	Findley Loan Rate	Effective Base[3] (Million Acres)	Partici-pation Rate[4] % of Base	Kansas City	Texas High Plains	Los Angeles	Gulf Ports
	Million Cwt.				Dollars Per Bushel					No. 2 Yellow ($ Per Cwt.)			
2003-04	3.5	1.6	0	0	3.54	4.54	1.98	12.1	----	4.57	5.01	----	5.45
2004-05	5.5	2.2	.2	0	3.48	4.59	1.95	12.0	----	3.37	3.95	----	4.42
2005-06	5.4	2.4	0	0	3.48	4.59	1.95	11.9	----	3.57	3.84	----	5.04
2006-07	1.9	1.2	0	0	3.48	4.59	1.95	11.8	----	5.75	6.09	----	7.39
2007-08	1.8	.7	0	0	3.48	4.59	1.95	11.7	----	8.38	8.49	----	9.81
2008-09[1]	4.5	1.7	0	0	3.48	4.59	1.95	11.6	----	5.79	5.44	----	7.18
2009-10[2]	1.7				3.48	4.59	1.95		----	5.75	5.73	----	7.74

[1] Preliminary.   [2] Estimate.   [3] National effective crop acreage base as determined by ASCS.   [4] Percentage of effective base acres enrolled in acreage reduction programs.   5/ Beginning with the 1996-7 marketing year, target prices are no longer applicable.   *Source: Economic Research Service, U.S. Department of Agriculture (ERS-USDA)*

Hay

Hay is a catchall term for forage plants, typically grasses such as timothy and Sudan-grass, and legumes such as alfalfa and clover. Alfalfa and alfalfa mixtures account for nearly half of all hay production. Hay is generally used to make cured feed for livestock. Curing, which is the proper drying of hay, is necessary to prevent spoilage. Hay, when properly cured, contains about 20% moisture. If hay is dried excessively, however, there is a loss of protein, which makes it less effective as livestock feed. Hay is harvested in virtually all of the lower 48 states.

Prices – The average monthly price of hay received by U.S. farmers in the first nine months of the 2010-11 marketing year (May/April) as of January 2011 rose by +2.0% yr/yr to $112.44 per ton, down from 2008-09 record high of $148.42 per ton. The farm production value of hay produced in 2008-09 (latest data available) was $18.777 million.

Supply – U.S. hay production in 2010-11 fell -1.5% yr/yr to 145,556 million tons. U.S. farmers harvested 59.862 million acres of hay in 2010-11, up +0.1% yr/yr. The yield in 2010-11 was 2.43 tons per acre, below the 2004-05 record high of 2.55. U.S. carryover (May 1) in 2009-10 (latest data) rose +2.22% to 22.065 million tons.

The largest hay producing states in the U.S. for 2010 were Texas, (with 7.4% of U.S. hay production), California (5.7%), Missouri (5.2%), South Dakota (5.0%), Oklahoma (4.1%), Nebraska (4.4%), Idaho (3.8%), and Minnesota (3.7%).

Salient Statistics of All Hay in the United States

Crop Year Beginning May 1	Acres Harvested (1,000 Acres)	Yield Per Acre (Tons)	Pro- duction	Carry- over May 1	Disap- pearance	Supply Per Animal Unit In Tons	Disap- pearance	Animal Units Fed[3] (Millions)	Farm Price ($ Per Ton)	Farm Pro- duction Value Million $	Alfalfa (Certified)	Timothy	Red Clover	Sudan- grass
			-------- Millions of Tons --------								----------- Dollars Per Cwt. -----------			
2005-06	61,637	2.44	150.5	27.8	157.9	2.49	2.19	71.6	98.4	12,585	281.00	105.00	174.00	57.40
2006-07	60,632	2.32	140.8	21.3	147.1	2.26	2.05	71.8	111.1	13,634	286.00	106.00	177.00	50.20
2007-08	61,006	2.41	146.9	15.0	140.3	2.26	1.96	71.5	130.8	16,842	292.00	112.00	202.00	56.70
2008-09	60,152	2.43	146.3	21.6	145.8	2.37	2.06	70.9	148.4	18,639	342.00	133.00	241.00	62.10
2009-10[1]	59,775	2.47	147.7	22.1	148.6	2.41	2.11	69.7	110.0	14,716	379.00	149.00	289.00	72.50
2010-11[2]	59,862	2.43	145.6	20.9		2.41			112.8	14,401				

[1] Preliminary. [2] Estimate. [3] Roughage-consuming animal units fed annually. NA = Not available.
Source: Economic Research Service, U.S. Department of Agriculture (ERS-USDA)

Production of All Hay in the United States, by States   In Thousands of Tons

Year	California	Idaho	Iowa	Minne- sota	Missouri	New York	North Dakota	Ohio	Okla- homa	South Dakota	Texas	Wisconsin	Total
2005	9,206	5,382	5,860	6,055	6,718	6,945	5,646	3,630	5,084	7,560	9,140	4,470	150,461
2006	9,568	5,505	5,189	5,679	6,944	5,588	3,137	3,421	3,556	4,180	8,675	5,264	140,783
2007	9,042	5,345	4,944	4,240	7,528	6,185	5,063	2,804	6,858	7,275	14,740	4,392	146,901
2008	9,414	5,588	5,330	5,265	8,820	6,232	4,118	2,802	5,536	7,840	9,211	4,810	146,270
2009	8,890	5,528	4,002	5,250	8,040	6,235	5,240	2,876	5,278	7,830	8,250	4,430	147,700
2010[1]	8,238	5,460	3,760	5,400	7,512	6,349	5,321	2,871	5,953	7,335	10,800	4,526	145,556

[1] Preliminary.   *Source: Agricultural Statistics Board, U.S. Department of Agriculture (ASB-USDA)*

Hay Production and Farm Stocks in the United States   In Thousands of Short Tons

Year	Alfalfa & Mixtures	All Others	All Hay	Corn for Silage[1]	Sorghum Silage[1]	May 1	Dec. 1
	-- Production --					------------- Farm Stocks -------------	
2005	75,610	74,851	150,461	106,486	4,218	27,758	105,181
2006	70,548	70,235	140,783	105,294	4,612	21,345	96,400
2007	69,880	77,021	146,901	106,229	5,246	14,990	104,089
2008	70,180	76,090	146,270	111,619	5,646	21,585	103,658
2009	71,072	76,628	147,700	108,209	3,680	22,065	107,222
2010[2]	67,903	77,653	145,556	107,314	3,420	20,931	102,134

[1] Not included in all tame hay.   [2] Preliminary.   *Source: Agricultural Statistics Board, U.S. Department of Agriculture (ASB-USDA)*

Mid-Month Price Received by Farmers for All Hay (Baled) in the United States   In Dollars Per Ton

Year	May	June	July	Aug.	Sept.	Oct.	Nov.	Dec.	Jan.	Feb.	Mar.	Apr.	Average
2005-06	107.0	102.0	99.7	99.7	99.0	97.7	91.7	92.0	93.1	95.8	97.5	105.0	98.4
2006-07	113.0	109.0	107.0	106.0	108.0	109.0	106.0	110.0	109.0	113.0	119.0	124.0	111.1
2007-08	138.0	131.0	131.0	124.0	127.0	128.0	129.0	127.0	126.0	129.0	133.0	147.0	130.8
2008-09	168.0	161.0	164.0	163.0	161.0	156.0	149.0	138.0	135.0	131.0	129.0	126.0	148.4
2009-10	130.0	123.0	116.0	104.0	105.0	105.0	105.0	105.0	106.0	104.0	108.0	109.0	110.0
2010-11[1]	116.0	114.0	112.0	111.0	111.0	113.0	111.0	112.0	112.0	116.0			112.8

[1] Preliminary.   [2] Marketing year average.   *Source: Economic Research Service, U.S. Department of Agriculture (ERS-USDA)*

Heating Oil

Heating oil is a heavy fuel oil that is derived from crude oil. Heating oil is also known as No. 2 fuel oil and accounts for about 25% of the yield from a barrel of crude oil. That is the second largest "cut" after gasoline. The price to consumers of home heating oil is generally comprised of 42% for crude oil, 12% for refining costs, and 46% for marketing and distribution costs (Source: EIA's Petroleum Marketing Monthly, 2001). Generally, a $1 increase in the price of crude oil translates into a 2.5-cent per gallon rise in heating oil. Because of this, heating oil prices are highly correlated with crude oil prices, although heating oil prices are also subject to swift supply and demand shifts due to weather changes or refinery shutdowns.

The primary use for heating oil is for residential heating. In the U.S., approximately 8.1 million households use heating oil as their main heating fuel. Most of the demand for heating oil occurs from October through March. The Northeast region, which includes the New England and the Central Atlantic States, is most reliant on heating oil. This region consumes approximately 70% of U.S. heating oil. However, demand for heating oil has been dropping as households switch to a more convenient heating source like natural gas. In fact, demand for heating oil is down by about 10 billion gallons/year from its peak use in 1976 (Source: American Petroleum Institute).

Refineries produce approximately 85% of U.S. heating oil as part of the "distillate fuel oil" product family, which includes heating oil and diesel fuel. The remainder of U.S. heating oil is imported from Canada, the Virgin Islands, and Venezuela.

Recently, a team of Purdue University researchers developed a way to make home heating oil from a mixture of soybean oil and conventional fuel oil. The oil blend is made by replacing 20% of the fuel oil with soybean oil, potentially saving 1.3 billion gallons of fuel oil per year. This soybean heating oil can be used in conventional furnaces without altering existing equipment. The soybean heating oil is relatively easy to produce and creates no sulfur emissions.

The "crack-spread" is the processing margin earned when refiners buy crude oil and refine it into heating oil and gasoline. The crack-spread ratio commonly used in the industry is the 3-2-1, which involves buying 1 heating oil contract and 2 gasoline futures contracts, and then selling 3 crude oil contracts. As long as the crack spread is positive, it is profitable for refiners to buy crude oil and refine it into products. The NYMEX has a crack-spread calculator on their web site at www.NYMEX.com.

Heating oil futures and options trade at the New York Mercantile Exchange (NYMEX). The heating oil futures contract calls for the delivery of 1,000 barrels of fungible No. 2 heating oil in the New York harbor. In London, gas/oil futures and options are traded on the ICE Futures Europe (ICE) exchange.

Prices – NYMEX heating oil futures prices on the nearest-futures chart traded basically sideways in the first half of 2010, but then rallied sharply starting in September and closed the year up 20% at $2.54 per gallon.

Supply – U.S. production of distillate fuel oil in 2010 (through November, annualized) rose by +3.8% yr/yr to 4.204 million barrels per day, down from the record high of 4.292 million barrels per day in 2008. Stocks of distillate fuel oil in November 2010 were 161.9 million barrels. U.S. production of residual fuel in 2010 (through November, annualized) fell by -5.2% yr/yr to an average of 567,000 barrels per day, which less than half the production levels of well over 1 million barrels per day produced in the 1970s. U.S. stocks of residual fuel oil as of January 1, 2010 rose +20.0% to 40.259 million barrels, down from the 2007 record of 42.329 million barrels.

Demand – U.S. usage of distillate fuel oil in 2010 (through November, annualized) rose +3.6% yr/yr to 3.764 million barrels per day, further down from 2007's record high of 4.198 million barrels per day.

Trade – U.S. imports of distillate fuel oil in 2010 (through November, annualized) fell -1.9% to an average of 221,000 barrels per day, down from the 2006 record high of 365,000 barrels per day. U.S. exports of distillate fuel oil in 2007 (latest data) rose by +2.7% yr/yr to a 13-year high average of 221 barrels per day. U.S. imports of residual fuel oil in 2010 rose +15.1% yr/yr to 381,000 barrels per day, which was less than a third of the levels of over 1 million barrels per day seen back in the 1970s. U.S. exports of residual fuel oil in 2007 (latest data) rose +9.2% to 309,000 barrels per day, which was a new record high.

Average Price of Heating Oil #2   In Cents Per Gallon

Year	Jan.	Feb.	Mar.	Apr.	May	June	July	Aug.	Sept.	Oct.	Nov.	Dec.	Average
2001	84.30	78.55	74.17	78.02	77.11	75.74	69.88	73.41	71.65	62.63	54.37	52.60	71.04
2002	53.52	54.03	63.52	66.60	66.54	64.50	67.79	69.81	77.25	76.55	72.14	81.70	67.83
2003	90.09	112.84	99.70	79.75	74.31	75.95	79.03	81.61	73.54	81.97	83.35	89.04	85.10
2004	97.91	91.19	90.88	91.87	101.65	99.41	109.42	116.86	125.73	148.55	138.16	127.32	111.58
2005	132.01	134.26	155.44	152.35	140.89	161.20	163.71	180.75	196.50	188.75	168.67	170.32	162.07
2006	174.99	163.68	177.70	198.27	197.17	191.76	192.30	198.25	169.17	154.53	165.00	167.85	179.22
2007	151.99	169.48	174.05	186.30	188.47	200.31	206.99	198.36	218.06	228.32	258.79	257.54	203.22
2008	255.64	264.17	306.80	322.96	361.64	379.99	375.67	317.16	290.76	222.44	185.15	138.93	285.11
2009	146.43	127.78	128.30	135.95	147.87	174.72	163.18	186.59	173.05	193.34	198.48	197.22	164.41
2010	205.23	197.52	208.47	221.26	203.78	203.44	197.75	202.24	209.48	224.23	231.74	246.43	212.63

Source: Energy Information Administration, U.S. Department of Energy (EIA-DOE)

HEATING OIL

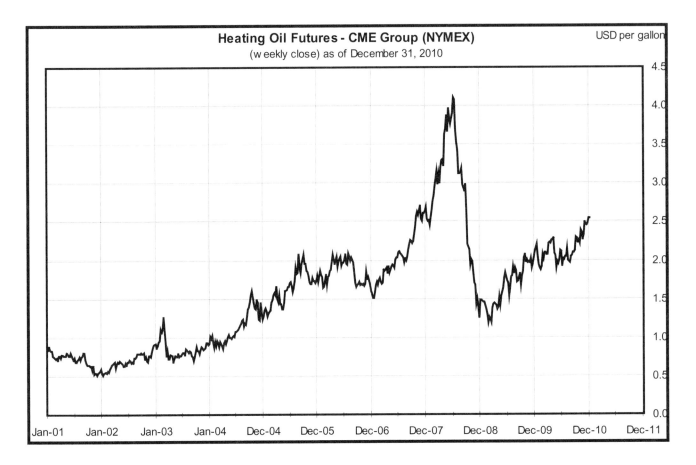

Heating Oil Futures - CME Group (NYMEX)
(weekly close) as of December 31, 2010

USD per gallon

Average Open Interest of Heating Oil #2 Futures in New York   In Contracts

Year	Jan.	Feb.	Mar.	Apr.	May	June	July	Aug.	Sept.	Oct.	Nov.	Dec.
2001	138,980	127,219	120,899	127,395	130,328	141,436	149,577	145,605	145,692	155,540	162,392	153,850
2002	166,824	173,110	160,205	144,936	139,979	136,201	131,742	141,084	147,692	153,739	161,137	156,268
2003	178,932	174,224	134,616	111,706	118,822	124,675	127,273	146,821	150,893	156,142	145,857	145,555
2004	153,794	145,924	161,945	174,618	176,784	167,331	193,291	206,099	197,783	188,843	176,298	163,629
2005	155,528	152,479	174,437	179,923	176,770	185,831	182,710	185,185	174,229	172,772	178,199	178,008
2006	170,094	165,627	168,415	170,955	171,732	169,123	179,773	185,648	208,848	221,942	228,152	216,033
2007	219,690	219,715	209,805	208,829	210,128	224,289	239,109	218,913	235,403	232,165	224,475	209,578
2008	202,976	220,716	230,646	227,140	224,480	218,004	223,645	221,733	212,561	212,981	224,465	224,359
2009	237,894	252,753	261,552	259,008	260,646	283,068	294,270	308,022	311,296	312,653	322,505	309,113
2010	317,506	306,607	319,389	310,085	311,994	313,624	304,866	305,549	325,342	327,588	319,732	308,661

Contract size = 42,000 US gallons.   *Source: CME Group; New York Mercantile Exchange (NYMEX)*

Volume of Trading of Heating Oil #2 Futures in New York   In Thousands of Contracts

Year	Jan.	Feb.	Mar.	Apr.	May	June	July	Aug.	Sept.	Oct.	Nov.	Dec.	Total
2001	914.4	650.7	758.0	728.6	722.8	849.9	712.9	745.8	694.0	853.8	835.5	798.1	9,264.5
2002	998.5	810.8	885.5	844.1	789.8	720.1	798.8	866.0	794.4	1,017.9	1,039.5	1,129.9	10,695.2
2003	1,340.1	1,158.9	965.9	757.7	811.6	802.9	849.9	891.3	1,118.5	1,095.5	817.3	971.8	11,581.7
2004	1,153.8	1,059.7	1,139.9	1,007.8	910.0	1,100.5	920.7	1,105.7	1,060.8	1,148.6	1,112.7	1,164.4	12,884.5
2005	1,090.6	1,046.1	1,204.2	1,062.5	999.7	1,193.5	1,058.5	1,150.4	1,165.1	1,019.5	1,009.5	1,136.0	13,135.6
2006	1,157.5	1,131.2	1,121.7	974.8	1,185.1	1,114.0	1,027.1	1,166.1	1,235.9	1,291.1	1,228.6	1,357.5	13,990.6
2007	1,655.6	1,507.5	1,370.3	1,326.0	1,462.2	1,605.8	1,478.9	1,579.8	1,394.7	1,687.2	1,544.1	1,467.0	18,079.0
2008	1,611.7	1,726.3	1,763.3	1,639.2	1,825.3	1,651.9	1,571.3	1,641.9	1,578.0	1,646.4	1,297.3	1,630.4	19,583.1
2009	1,789.0	1,512.9	1,670.1	1,633.3	1,644.5	1,809.7	2,004.2	1,652.6	1,777.3	1,975.9	1,921.9	2,035.1	21,426.5
2010	2,096.3	1,872.5	2,230.6	2,459.2	2,493.3	2,305.2	1,963.7	2,409.5	2,548.9	2,230.9	2,165.8	2,194.1	26,970.1

Contract size = 42,000 US gallons.   *Source: CME Group; New York Mercantile Exchange (NYMEX)*

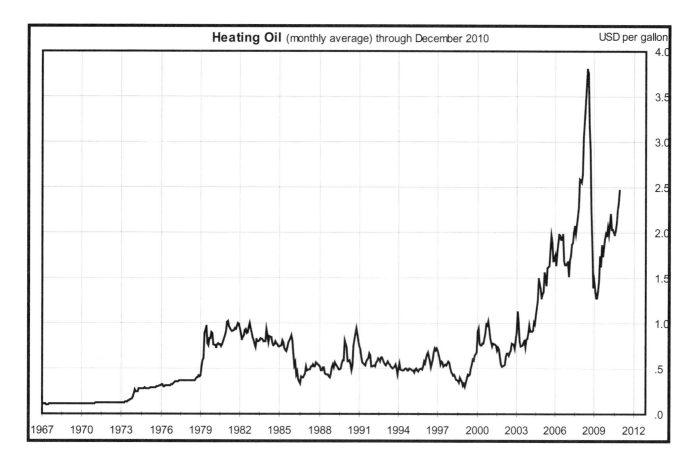

Heating Oil (monthly average) through December 2010 — USD per gallon

Stocks of Distillate and Residual Fuel in the United States, on First of Month   In Millions of Barrels

Year	Jan.	Feb.	Mar.	Apr.	May	June	July	Aug.	Sept.	Oct.	Nov.	Dec.	Residual Fuel --- Oil Stocks --- Jan. 1	July 1
2001	118.2	117.0	105.0	104.9	107.1	113.9	125.2	122.0	127.0	128.9	138.9	144.5	41.0	41.7
2002	136.9	130.0	123.1	122.4	127.0	133.1	133.8	130.6	126.9	121.4	124.4	134.1	31.3	32.7
2003	112.6	97.7	98.6	97.2	106.7	112.2	118.0	126.5	131.3	132.1	136.1	136.5	37.8	35.3
2004	122.8	112.2	104.4	101.5	107.5	114.3	121.9	130.8	123.1	118.3	123.2	126.3	42.4	37.5
2005	121.9	117.3	105.4	105.4	112.4	119.7	133.3	139.1	127.7	124.7	133.7	136.0	37.4	37.7
2006	139.4	135.6	120.5	116.5	124.0	129.9	137.5	145.1	149.3	142.8	140.6	143.7	42.4	42.7
2007	139.6	123.7	120.0	121.3	125.1	123.8	130.3	134.6	134.2	134.4	134.8	133.9	39.3	36.1
2008	131.0	117.6	107.8	107.1	113.9	121.7	130.9	133.0	127.7	127.6	135.9	146.0	36.1	41.2
2009	143.7	148.1	145.3	150.1	156.7	162.7	165.9	168.6	172.7	171.2	171.1	166.0	37.2	36.9
2010[1]	163.0	154.8	146.0	144.8	150.3	157.9	166.2	170.4	166.7	161.6	161.9	164.5	41.3	42.3

[1] Preliminary.   Source: Energy Information Administration; U.S. Department of Energy (EIA-DOE)

Production of Distillate Fuel Oil in the United States   In Thousand Barrels per Day

Year	Jan.	Feb.	Mar.	Apr.	May	June	July	Aug.	Sept.	Oct.	Nov.	Dec.	Average
2001	3,609	3,612	3,483	3,650	3,652	3,702	3,837	3,654	3,625	3,796	3,968	3,744	3,695
2002	3,508	3,498	3,360	3,647	3,709	3,679	3,561	3,538	3,536	3,380	3,768	3,922	3,592
2003	3,403	3,459	3,732	3,796	3,833	3,728	3,673	3,730	3,721	3,750	3,800	3,845	3,707
2004	3,592	3,446	3,550	3,874	3,857	3,956	3,902	3,981	3,625	3,808	4,004	4,159	3,813
2005	3,777	3,797	3,874	4,028	4,179	4,274	4,236	4,108	3,570	3,585	3,966	4,044	3,953
2006	3,840	3,941	3,736	3,833	4,105	4,107	4,065	4,234	4,300	4,090	4,070	4,159	4,040
2007	4,256	4,582	4,334	4,214	4,068	4,114	4,026	4,146	4,161	4,213	4,074	4,193	4,198
2008	4,130	3,980	3,953	4,287	4,459	4,587	4,523	4,466	3,681	4,435	4,489	4,511	4,292
2009	4,284	4,231	3,939	4,132	4,093	4,047	3,929	3,965	4,099	3,984	4,018	3,877	4,050
2010[1]	3,563	3,670	3,833	4,152	4,375	4,416	4,431	4,404	4,341	4,315	4,345	4,602	4,204

[1] Preliminary.   Source: Energy Information Administration; U.S. Department of Energy (EIA-DOE)

HEATING OIL

Imports of Distillate Fuel Oil in the United States   In Thousand of Barrels per Day

Year	Jan.	Feb.	Mar.	Apr.	May	June	July	Aug.	Sept.	Oct.	Nov.	Dec.	Average
2003	325	503	460	246	287	337	299	375	352	281	241	305	333
2004	370	507	449	267	275	324	283	313	272	243	319	292	326
2005	353	344	257	264	281	236	243	263	275	507	486	435	329
2006	552	388	292	297	437	297	361	363	438	307	288	355	365
2007	352	334	360	322	272	273	318	346	261	288	245	241	301
2008	309	249	249	266	188	180	181	109	195	166	203	262	213
2009	368	327	269	166	206	245	191	166	205	177	164	224	226
2010[1]	429	293	179	201	191	237	166	236	189	163	143	229	221

[1] Preliminary.   Source: Energy Information Administration, U.S. Department of Energy (EIA-DOE)

Exports of Distillate Fuel Oil from the United States   In Thousand of Barrels per Day

Year	Jan.	Feb.	Mar.	Apr.	May	June	July	Aug.	Sept.	Oct.	Nov.	Dec.	Average
2003	119	132	161	139	162	101	103	80	43	62	81	100	107
2004	72	86	99	92	100	163	113	120	88	101	102	176	109
2005	49	102	165	192	199	227	189	163	108	109	92	65	138
2006	123	156	120	200	229	187	231	191	456	291	252	149	215
2007	253	202	155	167	227	240	243	311	274	173	188	NA	221
2008	NA	NA	NA	NA	NA	NA	NA	NA	NA	NA	NA	NA	NA
2009	NA	NA	NA	NA	NA	NA	NA	NA	NA	NA	NA	NA	NA
2010[1]	NA	NA	NA	NA	NA	NA	NA	NA	NA	NA	NA	NA	NA

[1] Preliminary.   Source: Energy Information Administration, U.S. Department of Energy (EIA-DOE)

Disposition of Distillate Fuel Oil, Total Product Supplied in the United States   In Thousand of Barrels per Day

Year	Jan.	Feb.	Mar.	Apr.	May	June	July	Aug.	Sept.	Oct.	Nov.	Dec.	Average
2003	4,301	4,362	4,001	3,951	3,651	3,781	3,680	3,752	3,871	3,945	3,824	4,037	3,927
2004	4,334	4,232	4,152	4,145	3,840	3,888	3,827	3,887	4,065	4,104	4,058	4,176	4,059
2005	4,223	4,202	4,349	4,101	4,037	4,038	3,854	4,020	4,116	4,079	4,061	4,339	4,118
2006	4,159	4,308	4,395	4,065	4,072	4,019	3,950	4,162	4,141	4,315	4,180	4,268	4,170
2007	4,256	4,582	4,334	4,214	4,068	4,114	4,026	4,146	4,161	4,213	4,074	4,193	4,198
2008	4,192	4,281	4,161	4,106	3,931	3,763	3,688	3,659	3,740	4,182	3,872	3,783	3,947
2009	4,079	3,864	3,744	3,455	3,436	3,513	3,395	3,426	3,560	3,654	3,596	3,861	3,632
2010[1]	3,656	3,866	3,842	3,707	3,635	3,759	3,561	3,800	3,890	3,769	3,822	3,862	3,764

[1] Preliminary.   Source: Energy Information Administration, U.S. Department of Energy (EIA-DOE)

Production of Residual Fuel Oil in the United States   In Thousands of Barrels per Day

Year	Jan.	Feb.	Mar.	Apr.	May	June	July	Aug.	Sept.	Oct.	Nov.	Dec.	Average
2003	658	683	652	632	729	666	632	663	662	640	616	686	660
2004	656	659	635	701	668	648	618	631	617	610	703	723	656
2005	701	691	619	598	645	673	614	594	555	530	642	674	628
2006	670	635	644	643	580	645	658	652	619	597	624	656	635
2007	667	650	656	658	647	628	708	698	698	689	694	676	672
2008	588	643	662	710	734	695	584	579	485	575	588	597	620
2009	585	571	583	475	605	613	586	631	604	672	624	624	598
2010[1]	625	630	576	593	611	556	570	551	588	528	474	501	567

[1] Preliminary.   Source: Energy Information Administration, U.S. Department of Energy (EIA-DOE)

Supply and Disposition of Residual Fuel Oil in the United States

	Supply		Disposition			Ending Stocks (Million	Average Sales to End Users[3]
Year	Total Production	Imports	Stock Change	Exports	Product Supplied	Barrels)	(Cents per Gallon)
	In Tousands of Barrels Per Day						
2003	660	327	18	197	772	38	69.8
2004	655	426	12	205	865	42	73.9
2005	628	530	-14	251	920	37	104.8
2006	635	350	14	283	689	42	121.8
2007	673	372	-13	309	723	39	137.4
2008	620	349	NA	NA	622	36	196.4
2009	598	331	NA	NA	511	37	134.1
2010[1]	567	381	NA	NA	534	39	

[1] Preliminary.   [2] Less than +500 barrels per day and greater than -500 barrels per day.   [3] Refiner price excluding taxes.
Source: Energy Information Administration, U.S. Department of Energy (EIA-DOE)

Hides and Leather

Hides and leather have been used since ancient times for boots, clothing, shields, armor, tents, bottles, buckets, and cups. Leather is produced through the tanning of hides, pelts, and skins of animals. The remains of leather have been found in the Middle East dating back at least 7,000 years.

Today, most leather is made of cowhide but it is also made from the hides of lamb, deer, ostrich, snakes, crocodiles, and even stingray. Cattle hides are the most valuable byproduct of the meat packing industry. U.S. exports of cowhides bring more than $1 billion in foreign trade, and U.S. finished leather production is worth about $4 billion.

Prices – The average monthly price of wholesale cattle hides (packer heavy native steers FOB Chicago) in 2010 rose +62.5% yr/yr to 88.79 cents per pound, down from 2007's record high of 90.53 cents per pound.

Supply – World production of cattle and buffalo hides in 2009 (latest data available) rose by +0.1% yr/yr to a record high of 8.730 million metric tons. The world's largest producers of cattle and buffalo hides in 2008 were the U.S. with 12.3% of world production, Brazil with 10.5%, and Argentina with 4.6%. U.S. new supply of cattle hides from domestic slaughter in 2004 (latest data available) fell 7.8% yr/yr to 32,728 million hides, which is far below the record high of 43.582 million hides posted in 1976.

U.S. production of leather footwear has been dropping off sharply in recent years due to the movement of production offshore to lower cost producers. U.S. production of leather footwear in 2003 (latest data available) fell -46% yr/yr to 22.3 million pairs and was a mere 4% of the 562.3 million pairs produced in 1970.

Demand – World consumption of cowhides and skins in 2000, the last reporting year for the series, rose +1.4% to 4,774 metric tons, which was a record high for the data series, which goes back to 1984. The world's largest consumers of cowhides and skins in 2000 were the U.S. with 13.0% of world consumption, Italy (10.6%), Brazil (8.9%), Mexico, (6.0%), Argentina (6.0%), and South Korea (5.9%).

Trade – U.S. net exports of cattle hides in 2004 (latest data available) fell –4.3% yr/yr to 17.388 million hides from the 15-year high of 21.750 million hides posted in 2001. The total value of U.S. leather exports in 2004 rose +16.8% yr/yr to $1.344 billion. The largest destinations for U.S. exports in 2008 were South Korea (which took 15% of U.S. exports), Mexico (7%), Taiwan (5%), Thailand (3%), and Italy (2%). World imports of cowhides and skins in 2000 (latest data available) rose +2.8% yr/yr to a record high of 2,058 metric tons. The world's largest importers of cowhides and skins in 2000 were South Korea (with 13% of world imports in 2000), Italy (11%) and Taiwan (7%).

World Production of Cattle and Buffalo Hides   In Thousands of Metric Tons

Year	Argentina	Australia	Brazil	Canada	Colombia	France	Germany	Italy	Mexico	Russia	United Kingdom	United States	World Total
2000	372	238	670	96	82	153	152	143	175	232	68	1,116	8,186
2001	348	254	725	95	76	156	153	130	178	220	61	1,086	8,069
2002	345	243	750	96	72	162	151	132	178	224	65	1,128	8,232
2003	375	248	770	88	72	160	141	130	180	229	63	1,093	8,326
2004	429	243	792	111	80	150	145	128	191	223	66	1,009	8,421
2005	428	245	850	112	86	148	132	126	192	203	68	1,016	8,508
2006	402	233	886	104	85	143	135	124	197	183	74	1,076	8,650
2007	405	252	914	96	88	142	132	122	199	180	75	1,086	8,705
2008[1]	405	252	914	96	94	142	132	121	199	181	75	1,073	8,719
2009[2]	405			96	96	139		121		179			8,730

[1] Preliminary.   [2] Forecast.   Source: Food and Agricultural Organization of the United Nations (FAO-UN)

Salient Statistics of Hides and Leather in the United States   In Thousands of Equivalent Hides

Year	Federally Inspected	Unin-spected[4]	Total Production	Net Exports	Heavy Native Cows[2]	Heavy Native[3] Steers	All U.S. Tanning	Cattle-hide	Value of Leather Exports ($1,000)	Men	Women	Pro-duction[5]	Exports
	----- New Supply of Cattle hides ----- ----- Domestic Slaughter -----				Wholesale Prices - Cents Per Pound -		----- Production -----			Wholesale Leather ------ Indicies ------ -------Upper-------- (1982 = 100)		------ Footwear ------- ----- Million Pairs -----	
	----- Thousands of Equivalent Hides -----						In 1,000 Equiv. Hides						
2000	35,631	615	36,246	19,670	83.41	80.2	17,332	16,746	1,125,957	157.2	133.6	58,870	20,157
2001	34,771	599	35,370	21,750	85.52	85.8	14,212	13,779	1,221,131	158.4	133.8	55,600	19,472
2002	35,120	614	35,735	19,484	85.73	82.3		16,403	1,161,944	158.8	133.5	41,100	21,582
2003	34,907	587	35,493	18,177	88.34	83.8		17,470	1,150,212	161.4	132.1	22,300	21,319
2004	32,156	573	32,728	17,388	57.07	67.1		15,492	1,344,017	161.7	129.2		21,464
2005	31,832	556	32,388		57.89	65.6				163.5	132.1		
2006	33,145	553	33,698		60.30	68.9				164.6	134.2		
2007	33,721	543	34,264		65.70	72.0				167.0	137.0		
2008	33,805	560	34,365		58.35	63.9				173.7	139.7		
2009[1]	32,765	573	33,338		29.22	44.8				177.6	139.9		

[1] Preliminary.   [2] Central U.S., heifers.   [3] F.O.B. Chicago.   [4] Includes farm slaughter; diseased & condemned animals & hides taken off fallen animals.
[5] Other than rubber.   Sources: Leather Industries of America (LIA); Bureau of Labor Statistics, U.S. Department of Commerce (BLS)

HIDES AND LEATHER

Production of All Footwear (Shoes, Sandals, Slippers, Athletic, Etc.) in the United States In Millions of Pairs

Year	First Quarter	Second Quarter	Third Quarter	Fourth Quarter	Total	Year	First Quarter	Second Quarter	Third Quarter	Fourth Quarter	Total
1994	42.5	40.8	40.1	39.5	163.0	1999	26.7	26.1	24.5	21.7	78.5
1995	37.2	38.3	34.8	36.7	147.0	2000	----	----	----	----	58.8
1996	33.2	31.8	29.7	33.2	128.0	2001	----	----	----	----	55.6
1997	31.4	33.1	28.6	30.6	124.4	2002	----	----	----	----	41.1
1998	32.8	31.8	29.3	28.6	108.5	2003[1]	----	----	----	----	22.3

[1] Preliminary.   Source: Bureau of the Census, U.S. Department of Commerce

Average Factory Price[2] of Footwear in the United States   In Dollars Per Pair

Year	First Quarter	Second Quarter	Third Quarter	Fourth Quarter	Total	Year	First Quarter	Second Quarter	Third Quarter	Fourth Quarter	Total
1994	25.77	23.60	21.49	22.44	23.22	1999	23.33	22.70	19.90	19.50	21.19
1995	19.61	21.46	25.37	21.26	21.79	2000	----	----	----	----	24.14
1996	23.65	22.78	22.14	20.38	22.07	2001	----	----	----	----	25.66
1997	22.42	21.56	22.21	22.24	22.11	2002	----	----	----	----	24.12
1998	24.39	24.21	20.27	19.78	21.84	2003[1]	----	----	----	----	45.95

[1] Preliminary.   [2] Average value of factory shipments per pair.   Source: Bureau of the Census, U.S. Department of Commerce

Imports and Exports of All Cattle Hides in the United States   In Thousands of Hides

| | ----- Imports ----- | | -- U.S. Exports - by Country of Destination -- | | | | | | | | | | |
Year	Total	From Canada	Total	Canada	Italy	Japan	Rep of Korea	Mexico	Portugal	Romania	Spain	Taiwan	Thailand
2001	1,721	1,615	23,471	716	920	1,343	7,602	1,647	54	0	159	2,751	888
2002	1,298	1,227	20,784	837	1,099	584	5,812	1,470	14	0	189	2,145	914
2003	4,051	1,921	19,139	530	779	483	4,784	1,257	6	0	63	1,982	788
2004	9,000	6,171	18,795	346	417	468	4,218	1,419	4	0	16	1,842	684
2005	4,517	2,897	19,231	141	568	334	4,048	1,288	2	0	8	1,730	652
2006	2,491	1,786	20,059	57	523	277	3,455	1,225	5	0	41	1,902	441
2007	1,986	1,243	17,687	91	191	234	2,867	1,243	3	0	44	1,260	724
2008	1,863	1,182	16,015	113	265	175	2,346	1,135	0	0	99	795	453
2009	1,475	975	16,661	345	407	189	2,379	1,510	11	0	62	1,249	574
2010[1]	1,388	1,064	15,434	193	1,010	148	2,044	1,422	1	0	90	1,446	460

[1] Preliminary.   Source: Leather Industries of America

Imports of Bovine Hides and Skins by Selected Countries   In Metric Tons

Year	Brazil	Canada	Hong Kong	Italy	Japan	Mexico	Portugal	Rep. of Korea	Spain	Taiwan	Turkey	United States	World Total
1992	11	17	80	131	188	71	32	385	26	91	28	65	1,266
1993	21	26	81	141	188	71	39	372	35	94	37	57	1,426
1994	16	28	95	243	139	60	56	356	29	112	17	49	1,556
1995	33	35	100	250	152	30	43	342	42	112	43	57	1,715
1996	20	34	79	263	123	71	42	341	33	124	50	60	1,692
1997	13	39	64	254	114	96	37	323	44	140	68	60	1,985
1998	10	42	71	249	96	110	39	229	44	142	45	59	1,876
1999[1]	8	34	91	215	95	115	42	254	29	142	55	57	2,002
2000[2]	8	36	93	220	95	115	43	260	30	142	60	57	2,058

[1] Preliminary.   [2] Forecast.   Source: Foreign Agricultural Service, U.S. Department of Agriculture (FAS-USDA)

Exports of Bovine Hides and Skins by Selected Countries   In Metric Tons

Year	Australia	Brazil	Canada	Germany	Hong Kong	Italy	Nether-lands	New Zealand	Poland	Russia	United Kingdom	United States	World Total
1992	144	71	74	38	75	9	66	31	17	28	19	610	1,261
1993	142	76	87	40	76	7	35	21	5	150	25	581	1,374
1994	96	84	79	24	93	10	37	22	2	216	22	455	1,271
1995	85	148	90	34	100	10	47	22	2	195	22	510	1,351
1996	93	174	97	33	72	20	47	28	3	212	24	506	1,423
1997	115	216	97	35	60	16	48	27	3	210	25	473	1,475
1998	111	220	86	31	69	24	32	28	6	202	17	443	1,400
1999[1]	115	230	83	28	90	7	30	30	7	190	15	436	1,389
2000[2]	108	250	85	31	92	8	25	30	7	170	15	427	1,399

[1] Preliminary.   [2] Forecast.   Source: Foreign Agricultural Service, U.S. Department of Agriculture (FAS-USDA)

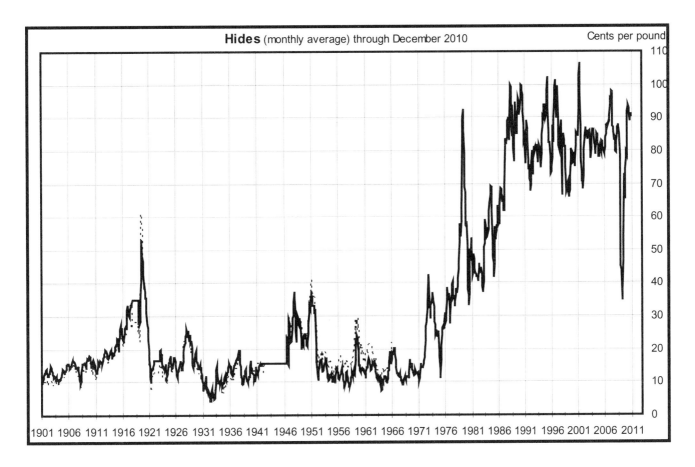

Hides (monthly average) through December 2010   Cents per pound

Utilization of Bovine Hides and Skins by Selected Countries   In Metric Tons

Year	Argentina	Brazil	Colombia	Germany	Italy	Japan	Mexico	Rep. of Korea	Spain	Taiwan	Turkey	United States	World Total
1992	298	382	97	129	435	229	231	400	98	91	90	528	3,977
1993	302	510	94	100	435	226	232	385	98	94	95	554	4,322
1994	304	505	96	83	550	200	226	374	94	112	85	536	4,282
1995	300	493	89	79	570	191	200	355	98	112	100	523	4,365
1996	308	461	91	80	615	165	230	353	95	124	110	548	4,332
1997	332	387	89	101	570	150	251	347	106	140	120	572	4,609
1998	285	412	91	100	540	135	275	265	108	142	100	603	4,584
1999[1]	300	415	89	102	500	130	280	280	104	142	110	623	4,707
2000[2]	285	425	89	103	505	130	285	283	108	142	120	623[2]	4,774

[1] Preliminary.   [2] Forecast.   *Source: Foreign Agricultural Service, U.S. Department of Agriculture (FAS-USDA)*

Wholesale Price of Hides (Packer Heavy Native Steers) F.O.B. Chicago   In Cents Per Pound

Year	Jan.	Feb.	Mar.	Apr.	May	June	July	Aug.	Sept.	Oct.	Nov.	Dec.	Average
2001	85.33	84.12	93.02	102.64	106.19	97.31	87.59	77.28	73.51	70.58	73.30	69.16	85.00
2002	68.23	72.39	80.41	83.21	84.32	86.72	84.43	85.77	85.84	85.75	83.35	85.18	82.13
2003	83.77	85.81	86.04	85.81	79.42	77.64	80.53	84.09	86.78	86.13	85.89	86.05	84.00
2004	85.17	81.79	82.89	79.15	80.16	82.43	85.11	84.54	85.05	82.23	81.42	78.02	82.33
2005	78.14	80.90	79.04	80.45	79.49	83.07	82.70	81.78	80.58	80.44	80.07	79.03	80.47
2006	79.28	81.01	83.86	84.95	87.76	88.07	87.93	87.15	88.29	88.08	88.81	90.50	86.31
2007	93.75	95.85	95.66	98.13	97.68	93.19	87.36	86.95	86.14	83.08	84.72	83.83	90.53
2008	79.55	79.43	82.79	85.58	85.82	87.01	87.55	87.49	85.10	85.31	78.38	44.98	80.75
2009	43.75	43.09	34.55	36.22	38.33	46.84	53.76	73.02	68.86	65.35	74.23	77.51	54.63
2010	79.31	78.31	83.78	91.83	93.38	93.69	92.86	91.36	88.90	90.68	90.44	90.90	88.79

Source: National Agricultural Statistics Service, U.S. Department of Agriculture (NASS-USDA)

Hogs

Hogs are generally bred twice a year in a continuous cycle designed to provide a steady flow of production. The gestation period for hogs is 3-1/2 months and the average litter size is 9 pigs. The pigs are weaned at 3-4 weeks of age. The pigs are then fed so as to maximize weight gain. The feed consists primarily of grains such as corn, barley, milo, oats, and wheat. Protein is added from oilseed meals. Hogs typically gain 3.1 pounds per pound of feed. The time from birth to slaughter is typically 6 months. Hogs are ready for slaughter at about 254 pounds, producing a dressed carcass weight of around 190 pounds and an average 88.6 pounds of lean meat. The lean meat consists of 21% ham, 20% loin, 14% belly, 3% spareribs, 7% Boston butt roast and blade steaks, and 10% picnic, with the remaining 25% going into jowl, lean trim, fat, miscellaneous cuts, and trimmings. Futures on lean hogs are traded at the Chicago Mercantile Exchange. The futures contract is settled in cash based on the CME Lean Hog Index price, meaning that no physical delivery of hogs occurs. The CME Lean Hog Index is based on the 2-day average net price of slaughtered hogs at the average lean percentage level.

Prices – Lean hog futures prices extended their rally in early 2010 from the 8-year low in August 2009, and posted a 14-year high of 90.175 cents per pound in May 2010. Hog prices rallied as U.S. hog producers cut their breeding herd to 5.76 million sows, the lowest since USDA data began in 1988. Prices ratcheted lower into November 2010 and posted a 1-year low of 65.15 cents per pound as carcass weights rose to 8-year highs and pig litters jumped to a record 9.89 pigs per litter in the 3 months ended November 2010. Lean hog prices then strengthened from a surge in feed costs (i.e. corn prices at 2-1/2 year highs), along with increased pork imports from South Korea after Asia's worst outbreak of foot-and-mouth disease in 50 years forced the South Koreans to cull over 25% of their pig herds and remove import tariffs on frozen pork Lean hog futures rallied into year-end and finished 2010 up 22% at 79.79 cents per pound. Lean hog prices continued higher into 2011. In February 2011, lean hog prices posted a record high of 95.00 cents per pound, the highest since hog futures trading began in 1966.

Supply – World pork production in 2010 rose +1.0% yr/yr to 100.507 million metric tons. The USDA is forecasting an increase of +1.9% in 2011 to 103.392 million metric tons. The world's largest pork producers are China with 49% of world production in 2010, the European Union with 22%, and the U.S. with 10%. U.S. pork production in 2010 fell -3.7% to 10.052 million metric tons, but is forecasted by the USDA to rise by +1.5% to 10.204 million metric tons in 2011. The number of hogs and pigs on U.S. farms in 2010 (Dec 1) fell by -0.9% to 64,325 million, well below the more than 6-decade high of 68.117 in 2007. The federally-inspected hog slaughter in the U.S. in 2010 fell -2.9% to 109.315 million head, well below the 2008 record high of 115.421 million head.

Demand – World consumption of pork in 2010 rose by +0.8% yr/yr to 101.126 million metric tons. The USDA is forecasting an increase of +2.0% in 2011 to 103.115 million metric tons. U.S. consumption of pork in 2010 fell by 6.5% to 9.013 million metric tons, but the USDA is forecasting a rise in 2011 of +0.7% in 2011 to 8.485 million metric tons. The U.S. accounted for 8% of world consumption in 2010.

Trade – World pork exports in 2010 rose +7.3% yr/yr to 6.052 million metric tons, and the USDA is forecasting an increase of +0.3% yr/yr to 6.068 million metric tons for 2011. The world's largest pork exporters are the U.S. with 33% of world exports in 2010, the European Union with 28%, Canada with 19%, and Brazil with 10%. U.S. pork exports in 2010 rose by +9.2% yr/yr to 2.207 million metric tons and the USDA is forecasting a rise of +4.6% in 2011 to 2.121 million metric tons.

World pork imports in 2010 rose +2.4% to 5.645 million metric tons, and the USDA is forecasting a rise of +2.8% to 5.805 million metric tons in 2011. The world's largest pork importers are Japan, which accounted for 20% of world imports in 2010, Russia (15%), Mexico (12%), South Korea (7%), and the U.S. (7%).

Salient Statistics of Pigs and Hogs in the United States

	Pig Crop						Value of Hogs on Farms, Dec. 1-		Hog Mar-ketings (1,000 Head)	Quantity Pro-duced (Live Wt.) (Mil. Lbs.)	Value of Pro-duction (Million $)	Hogs Slaughtered, Thousand Head --- Commercial				
	Spring[3]			Fall[4]												
Year	Sows Farrowed --- 1,000 Head ---	Pig Crop	Pigs Per Litter	Sows Farrowed --- 1,000 Head ---	Pig Crop	Pigs Per Litter	$ Per Head	Total Million $				Federally Inspected	Other	Total	Farm	Total
2001	5,619	49,472	8.81	5,767	51,031	8.85	77.0	4,584	119,262	25,884	11,430	96,528	1,434	97,962	120	98,082
2002	5,776	50,858	8.81	5,716	50,820	8.89	71.0	4,231	124,013	26,274	8,691	98,915	1,348	100,263	115	100,378
2003	5,655	50,029	8.85	5,773	51,462	8.91	67.0	4,025	124,383	26,260	9,663	99,685	1,233	100,931	116	101,047
2004	5,706	50,737	8.89	5,793	52,043	8.98	103.0	6,306	127,563	26,689	13,072	102,361	1,103	103,463	114	103,577
2005	5,716	51,330	8.98	5,818	52,635	9.05	95.0	5,834	129,056	27,416	13,607	102,519	1,063	103,582	109	103,690
2006	5,768	52,242	9.06	5,862	53,376	9.11	90.0	5,599	132,262	28,149	12,702	103,689	1,048	104,737	105	104,842
2007	5,935	54,266	9.14	6,312	58,608	9.28	73.0	4,986	137,519	29,606	13,468	108,138	1,034	109,172	106	109,278
2008	6,123	57,019	9.31	6,103	58,011	9.51	89.0	5,958	148,986	31,411	14,457	115,421	1,026	116,446	106	116,553
2009[1]	6,029	57,564	9.55	5,874	56,978	9.70	83.0	5,465	149,065	31,131	12,762	112,612	1,001	113,614	116	113,729
2010[2]	5,801	56,327	9.71	5,754	56,662	9.85						109,315	942	110,257		110,257

[1] Preliminary. [2] Estimate. [3] December-May. [4] June-November. *Source: Economic Research Service, U.S. Department of Agriculture (ERS-USDA)*

World Hog Numbers in Specified Countries as of January 1 In Thousands of Head

Year	Brazil	Canada	China	European Union	Japan	Rep. of Korea	Mexico	Philip-pines	Russia	Taiwan	Ukraine	United States	World Total
2002	32,710	14,375	419,505	158,250	9,612	7,856	9,302	11,816	16,570	7,165	8,317	59,722	781,882
2003	32,655	14,745	417,762	160,486	9,725	8,110	9,284	12,218	17,000	6,794	9,204	59,554	785,949
2004	32,081	14,725	413,818	158,970	9,724	8,367	9,389	12,518	17,200	6,779	7,321	60,453	781,054
2005	32,323	14,810	421,234	156,973	9,600	8,044	9,068	12,139	16,500	6,819	6,466	60,982	785,964
2006	32,938	15,110	433,191	159,115	9,620	8,098	8,911	13,041	16,550	7,172	7,052	61,463	804,599
2007	33,147	14,907	418,504	161,526	9,759	8,518	9,021	13,693	17,180	7,092	8,055	62,516	797,388
2008	32,947	13,810	439,895	159,732	9,745	8,742	9,401		18,187		7,020	68,177	772,659
2009	33,892	12,180	462,913	153,067	9,899	8,223	9,912		19,562		6,526	67,148	785,734
2010[1]	35,122	11,835	469,960	151,961	10,000	8,721	10,485		20,230		7,577	64,887	793,080
2011[2]	37,401	11,357	468,507	151,150	9,700	9,101	10,942		20,325		8,400	64,450	793,783

[1] Preliminary. [2] Forecast. *Source: Foreign Agricultural Service, U.S. Department of Agriculture (FAS-USDA)*

Hogs and Pigs on Farms in the United States on December 1 In Thousands of Head

Year	Georgia	Illinois	Indiana	Iowa	Kansas	Minnesota	Missouri	Nebraska	North Carolina	Ohio	South Dakota	Wisconsin	Total
2001	315	4,250	3,200	15,400	1,570	5,800	3,000	2,900	9,800	1,430	1,290	540	59,804
2002	345	4,150	3,250	15,500	1,530	6,100	2,950	3,000	9,700	1,440	1,330	520	59,554
2003	295	4,000	3,100	15,900	1,650	6,500	2,950	2,900	10,000	1,520	1,280	480	60,444
2004	275	4,100	3,200	16,300	1,710	6,500	2,900	2,850	9,900	1,450	1,340	430	60,975
2005	270	4,000	3,250	16,600	1,790	6,600	2,700	2,850	9,800	1,560	1,490	430	61,449
2006	245	4,200	3,350	17,300	1,840	6,900	2,800	3,050	9,500	1,690	1,270	450	62,490
2007	265	4,350	3,700	19,400	1,880	7,700	3,150	3,350	10,200	1,830	1,460	440	68,177
2008	235	4,350	3,550	19,900	1,740	7,500	3,150	3,350	9,700	1,940	1,280	360	67,148
2009	195	4,250	3,600	19,000	1,810	7,200	3,100	3,100	9,600	2,010	1,190	350	64,887
2010[1]	160	4,300	3,650	18,900	1,810	7,700	2,900	3,100	8,800	2,030	1,290	340	64,325

[1] Preliminary. *Source: National Agricultural Statistics Service, U.S. Department of Agriculture (NASS-USDA)*

Hog-Corn Price Ratio[2] in the United States

Year	Jan.	Feb.	Mar.	Apr.	May	June	July	Aug.	Sept.	Oct.	Nov.	Dec.	Average
2001	18.8	20.0	23.5	25.3	27.7	29.7	27.6	26.6	23.7	21.8	18.9	16.8	23.4
2002	19.1	19.9	18.6	16.6	17.2	18.2	18.4	13.4	10.7	13.2	12.2	13.1	15.9
2003	14.2	14.7	14.9	14.9	17.4	19.2	19.7	18.4	18.0	17.3	15.8	14.8	16.6
2004	15.4	16.3	17.2	16.4	19.7	20.3	22.7	23.6	24.9	24.4	27.1	25.7	21.1
2005	25.1	26.0	25.3	25.6	27.7	24.4	23.6	26.2	26.0	25.8	24.6	23.1	25.3
2006	20.4	21.1	20.8	19.6	22.2	25.1	23.5	24.7	22.2	18.2	15.6	14.5	20.7
2007	14.0	13.8	13.1	14.0	15.2	15.4	15.7	15.7	14.3	12.9	11.0	10.5	13.8
2008	9.3	9.3	8.6	8.6	10.5	9.8	10.3	11.5	10.5	11.1	9.6	10.2	9.9
2009	9.8	11.3	11.4	11.4	11.3	10.8	12.0	11.2	11.6	10.5	11.0	12.5	11.2
2010[1]	13.2	13.8	14.7	16.6	17.8	17.1	16.8	16.8	15.0	12.3	10.5	10.9	14.6

[1] Preliminary. [2] Bushels of corn equal in value to 100 pounds of hog, live weight. *Source: Economic Research Service, U.S. Department of Agriculture (ERS-USDA)*

Cold Storage Holdings of Frozen Pork[2] in the United States, on First of Month In Millions of Pounds

Year	Jan.	Feb.	Mar.	Apr.	May	June	July	Aug.	Sept.	Oct.	Nov.	Dec.
2001	411.5	471.4	468.3	432.3	432.6	421.5	374.1	339.5	332.6	366.9	430.6	432.7
2002	465.0	503.9	510.9	531.5	567.7	548.0	497.8	472.2	464.4	480.2	489.8	463.9
2003	468.5	512.7	519.7	530.5	520.0	499.7	460.0	440.7	430.2	435.2	446.8	438.9
2004	470.7	504.1	477.1	447.3	448.6	412.8	373.0	366.8	382.1	413.8	423.1	436.3
2005	482.9	496.8	538.2	540.2	562.8	511.2	488.6	442.9	408.5	425.6	440.7	431.3
2006	421.3	527.7	528.0	505.0	520.0	477.0	412.6	417.8	415.6	458.4	488.4	468.5
2007	442.5	484.3	483.2	494.8	528.5	492.0	467.9	455.9	458.3	484.9	494.8	474.6
2008	458.7	574.9	611.8	657.3	663.4	579.4	530.1	505.3	502.7	526.2	528.0	526.7
2009	555.6	606.9	624.5	594.1	612.3	584.5	577.9	539.7	530.1	528.7	516.3	482.8
2010[1]	471.1	492.3	515.9	513.1	483.7	446.0	413.0	391.2	388.3	424.3	481.7	468.0

[1] Preliminary. [2] Excludes lard. *Source: Economic Research Service, U.S. Department of Agriculture (ERS-USDA)*

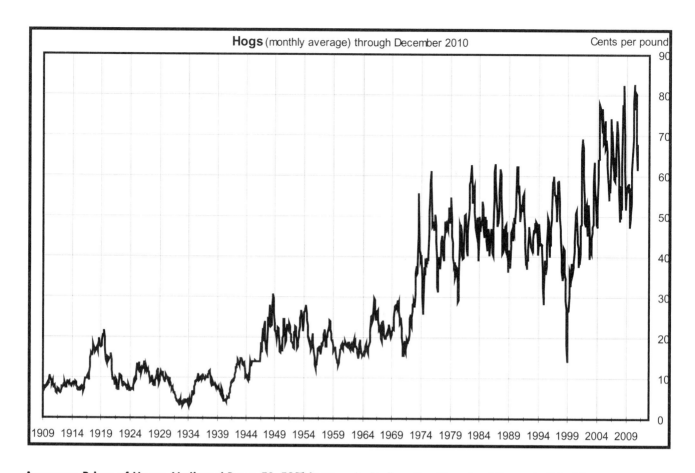

Average Price of Hogs, National Base 51-52% lean   In Dollars Per Hundred Pounds (Cwt.)

Year	Jan.	Feb.	Mar.	Apr.	May	June	July	Aug.	Sept.	Oct.	Nov.	Dec.	Average
2001	38.61	41.47	48.41	49.28	52.34	54.53	53.75	52.47	46.93	41.27	35.49	35.14	45.81
2002	40.16	40.65	37.47	32.97	34.64	37.32	40.53	34.00	26.98	31.69	29.99	32.35	34.90
2003	34.39	35.64	36.11	36.42	43.62	47.88	44.98	41.90	41.82	38.63	36.02	36.02	39.45
2004	39.02	45.21	48.30	48.34	58.45	57.95	58.21	56.19	55.34	53.68	56.23	53.15	52.51
2005	53.36	51.11	51.30	51.00	55.40	49.86	49.96	51.60	49.98	47.49	37.70	44.81	49.46
2006	41.37	43.17	43.34	41.45	49.00	54.90	51.89	53.32	50.28	47.57	45.97	44.84	47.26
2007	44.04	48.60	45.47	48.43	54.40	54.82	52.39	52.01	46.61	41.96	36.95	39.40	47.09
2008	36.77	42.74	39.40	45.06	57.75	54.71	56.48	62.56	52.76	47.06	38.90	39.80	47.83
2009	41.43	42.43	42.47	42.83	43.18	42.21	42.74	36.56	37.41	37.65	40.12	45.82	41.24
2010[1]	49.81	48.98	52.43	57.43	63.13	58.23	58.25	61.49	60.64	52.41	47.00	50.92	55.06

[1] Preliminary.   Source: Economic Research Service, U.S. Department of Agriculture (ERS-USDA)

Average Price Received by Farmers for Hogs in the United States   In Cents Per Pound

Year	Jan.	Feb.	Mar.	Apr.	May	June	July	Aug.	Sept.	Oct.	Nov.	Dec.	Average
2001	37.2	39.2	45.9	47.8	50.4	52.2	51.7	50.8	45.2	40.2	35.0	33.3	44.1
2002	37.7	38.5	36.0	31.7	33.2	35.8	39.2	31.9	26.5	30.8	27.8	30.3	33.3
2003	33.0	34.3	34.7	34.8	41.3	45.0	42.7	39.6	39.7	36.7	34.7	34.2	37.6
2004	36.8	42.6	47.2	47.4	56.6	56.7	57.1	55.3	54.8	52.2	55.6	52.4	51.2
2005	53.2	50.7	51.2	51.1	54.9	49.5	49.8	51.0	49.4	47.0	43.5	44.3	49.6
2006	40.7	42.6	42.8	41.3	48.2	53.8	50.2	51.6	48.9	46.5	44.9	43.5	46.3
2007	42.7	47.5	44.9	47.3	53.1	54.3	52.2	51.3	46.8	42.4	37.9	39.6	46.7
2008	37.2	42.2	40.3	44.4	55.3	53.4	54.3	60.7	52.6	48.5	40.7	41.9	47.6
2009	42.8	43.8	43.9	44.0	44.6	43.3	43.3	37.3	37.7	37.8	40.3	45.0	42.0
2010[1]	48.4	48.9	52.2	56.5	62.1	58.3	58.5	61.3	61.2	53.3	47.8	52.3	55.1

[1] Preliminary.   Source: Economic Research Service, U.S. Department of Agriculture (ERS-USDA)

Quarterly Hogs and Pigs Report in the United States, 10 States   In Thousands of Head

Year[2]	Inventory[3]	Breeding[3]	Market[3]	Farrowings	Pig Crop	Year[2]	Inventory[3]	Breeding[3]	Market[3]	Farrowings	Pig Crop
2001	59,138	6,270	52,868	11,385	100,503	2006	61,449	6,011	55,438	11,629	105,618
I	59,138	6,270	52,868	2,748	23,963	I	61,449	6,011	55,438	2,841	25,662
II	57,524	6,232	51,292	2,870	25,509	II	60,326	6,025	54,301	2,927	26,580
III	58,603	6,186	52,417	2,878	25,539	III	61,687	6,060	55,627	2,912	26,519
IV	59,777	6,158	53,619	2,889	25,492	IV	62,914	6,079	56,835	2,949	26,857
2002	59,804	6,209	53,594	11,492	101,677	2007	62,490	6,087	56,402	12,248	112,873
I	59,804	6,209	53,594	2,835	24,857	I	62,490	6,087	56,402	2,905	26,395
II	59,256	6,230	53,026	2,941	26,001	II	61,896	6,149	55,746	3,030	27,870
III	60,391	6,208	54,183	2,883	25,725	III	63,947	6,169	57,777	3,133	29,095
IV	60,753	6,051	54,702	2,833	25,094	IV	67,275	6,208	66,708	3,180	29,513
2003	59,554	6,058	53,496	11,429	101,491	2008	68,177	6,233	61,944	12,226	115,030
I	59,554	6,058	53,496	2,769	24,400	I	68,177	6,233	61,944	3,071	28,388
II	58,183	6,027	52,156	2,886	25,629	II	67,218	6,200	61,018	3,052	28,631
III	59,602	6,026	53,576	2,918	25,974	III	67,400	6,131	61,269	3,075	29,240
IV	61,009	5,938	55,071	2,856	25,488	IV	68,196	6,061	62,135	3,028	28,771
2004	60,444	6,009	54,434	11,499	102,781	2009	67,148	6,062	61,087	11,903	114,542
I	60,444	6,009	54,434	2,836	25,105	I	67,148	6,062	61,087	3,011	28,552
II	59,520	5,961	53,558	2,870	25,633	II	65,819	5,992	59,828	3,018	29,012
III	60,698	5,937	54,760	2,905	26,162	III	66,809	5,968	60,842	2,959	28,718
IV	61,519	5,962	55,556	2,888	25,881	IV	66,716	5,875	60,842	2,915	28,260
2005	60,975	5,969	55,005	11,535	103,965	2010[1]	64,887	5,850	59,037	11,555	112,990
I	60,975	5,969	55,005	2,835	25,343	I	64,887	5,850	59,037	2,872	27,597
II	59,699	5,941	53,757	2,882	25,986	II	63,568	5,760	57,808	2,929	28,730
III	60,732	5,977	54,754	2,918	26,449	III	64,650	5,788	58,862	2,907	28,512
IV	61,846	5,972	55,873	2,900	26,187	IV	65,311	5,770	59,541	2,847	28,151

[1] Preliminary.   [2] Quarters are Dec. preceding year-Feb.(I), Mar.-May(II), June-Aug.(III) and Sept.-Nov.(IV).
[3] Beginning of period.   Source: National Agricultural Statistics Service, U.S. Department of Agriculture (NASS-USDA)

Federally Inspected Hog Slaughter in the United States   In Thousands of Head

Year	Jan.	Feb.	Mar.	Apr.	May	June	July	Aug.	Sept.	Oct.	Nov.	Dec.	Total
2001	8,521	7,491	8,207	7,722	7,836	7,368	7,333	8,247	7,687	9,210	8,610	8,298	96,528
2002	8,552	7,400	7,879	8,321	8,215	7,425	7,957	8,425	8,384	9,547	8,506	9,254	99,685
2003	8,680	7,587	8,069	8,238	7,715	7,665	8,008	7,951	8,466	9,547	8,506	9,150	99,685
2004	8,704	7,805	8,942	8,567	7,494	8,415	8,008	8,616	8,897	8,883	8,881	9,150	102,361
2005	8,402	8,031	8,858	8,369	7,939	8,470	7,582	8,888	8,778	9,027	9,038	9,138	102,519
2006	8,834	7,978	9,148	7,884	8,450	8,256	7,805	8,991	8,738	9,541	9,276	8,788	103,689
2007	9,281	8,040	9,119	8,389	8,680	8,218	8,312	9,296	8,683	10,555	9,964	9,601	108,138
2008	10,474	9,297	9,579	9,911	8,981	8,801	9,373	9,170	9,878	10,654	9,250	10,053	115,421
2009	9,846	8,840	9,574	9,353	8,379	9,101	9,062	9,250	9,848	10,230	9,385	9,742	112,612
2010[1]	8,838	8,619	9,947	8,980	7,897	8,968	8,396	9,030	9,257	9,651	9,895	9,838	109,315

[1] Preliminary.   Source: National Agricultural Statistics Service, U.S. Department of Agriculture (NASS-USDA)

Average Live Weight of all Hogs Slaughtered Under Federal Inspection   In Pounds Per Head

Year	Jan.	Feb.	Mar.	Apr.	May	June	July	Aug.	Sept.	Oct.	Nov.	Dec.	Average
2001	265	264	264	265	264	264	261	258	262	267	269	268	264
2002	268	267	267	268	267	266	261	259	261	264	268	268	265
2003	268	267	268	268	268	266	263	261	263	268	270	269	267
2004	269	268	268	268	266	265	263	263	266	267	270	270	267
2005	270	270	271	271	270	269	265	263	265	269	272	272	269
2006	273	272	272	272	271	267	264	262	267	269	272	271	269
2007	271	270	271	270	269	267	265	264	267	270	273	272	269
2008	273	271	271	270	268	266	263	261	266	270	271	271	268
2009	272	272	272	272	272	270	268	268	270	272	272	270	271
2010[1]	272	271	272	273	273	271	269	267	271	276	278	278	273

[1] Preliminary.   Source: National Agricultural Statistics Service, U.S. Department of Agriculture (NASS-USDA)

HOGS

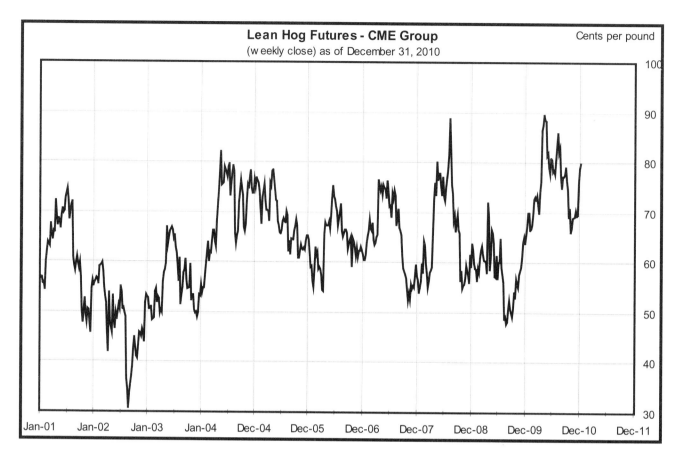

Lean Hog Futures - CME Group
(weekly close) as of December 31, 2010

Cents per pound

Average Open Interest of Lean Hog Futures in Chicago   In Contracts

Year	Jan.	Feb.	Mar.	Apr.	May	June	July	Aug.	Sept.	Oct.	Nov.	Dec.
2001	41,425	41,892	48,381	45,296	41,910	45,715	51,661	47,760	42,072	36,983	32,821	27,687
2002	28,720	31,662	33,056	33,472	33,161	28,719	29,338	32,030	36,136	35,245	42,852	43,974
2003	40,660	39,862	40,446	37,883	43,672	47,338	39,706	37,700	49,469	46,295	43,552	43,352
2004	46,380	55,058	63,889	77,756	80,271	81,370	79,860	84,840	86,092	86,423	94,336	98,328
2005	102,580	97,550	95,841	94,008	96,662	91,871	97,160	95,841	107,617	113,754	116,005	124,492
2006	133,258	144,506	145,020	144,250	157,259	158,276	157,899	165,781	176,336	174,971	188,965	179,057
2007	174,424	182,146	178,296	174,233	176,897	177,274	174,144	176,425	175,093	179,402	204,475	206,458
2008	212,644	227,377	219,938	232,309	252,497	242,588	238,162	231,283	206,602	171,506	168,129	159,600
2009	137,693	122,594	126,377	134,363	143,493	135,606	131,683	130,844	143,952	152,820	164,819	174,739
2010	194,351	179,300	197,407	217,304	217,779	190,933	197,940	214,535	230,240	209,159	198,160	200,932

Contract size = 40,000 lbs.   *Source: Chicago Mercantile Exchange (CME)*

Volume of Trading of Lean Hog Futures in Chicago   In Contracts

Year	Jan.	Feb.	Mar.	Apr.	May	June	July	Aug.	Sept.	Oct.	Nov.	Dec.	Total
2001	183,493	159,020	197,004	142,892	165,220	184,421	198,503	164,712	152,178	177,601	163,798	129,497	2,018,339
2002	145,266	120,994	168,929	196,956	163,816	158,074	166,064	140,154	174,797	167,065	165,039	164,106	1,931,260
2003	186,436	137,479	186,511	156,370	209,740	210,901	199,782	124,677	232,705	207,247	164,190	148,117	2,164,155
2004	212,420	170,270	249,205	211,501	295,271	304,279	315,197	215,233	356,295	242,204	376,823	255,488	3,204,186
2005	347,467	237,079	380,658	287,828	412,655	398,201	354,819	315,949	391,121	295,817	421,714	310,235	4,153,543
2006	561,152	319,827	597,852	356,950	658,973	826,312	578,656	478,837	577,375	533,532	649,293	342,242	6,481,001
2007	687,585	449,649	721,014	423,223	620,985	744,799	865,371	559,139	591,564	485,066	730,036	386,401	7,264,832
2008	800,566	527,093	809,724	736,404	796,703	938,662	968,358	617,855	781,563	506,765	576,326	445,119	8,505,138
2009	614,928	390,054	593,621	503,180	620,260	727,565	644,070	510,721	657,827	540,591	590,062	426,182	6,819,061
2010	672,191	464,868	706,267	567,410	740,462	803,035	763,584	627,870	808,561	683,542	753,457	485,288	8,076,535

Contract size = 40,000 lbs.   *Source: Chicago Mercantile Exchange (CME)*

Honey

Honey is the thick, supersaturated sugar solution produced by bees to feed their larvae. It is composed of fructose, glucose and water in varying proportions and also contains several enzymes and oils. The color of honey varies due to the source of nectar and age of the honey. Light colored honeys are usually of higher quality than darker honeys. The average honeybee colony can produce more than 700 pounds of honey per year but only 10 percent is usually harvested by the beekeeper. The rest of the honey is consumed by the colony during the year. American per capita honey consumption is 1 pound per person per year. Honey is said to be humanity's oldest sweet, and beeswax the first plastic.

Honey is used in many ways, including direct human consumption, baking, and medicine. Honey has several healing properties. Its high sugar content nourishes injured tissues, thus enhancing faster healing time. Honey's phytochemicals create a form of hydrogen peroxide that cleans out the wound, and the thick consistency protects the wound from contact with air. Honey has also proven superior to antibiotic ointments for reducing rates of infection in people with burns.

Prices – U.S. average domestic honey prices in 2009 (latest data) rose by +1.7% to a record high of 144.5 cents per pound. The value of U.S. honey production in 2009 fell -10.5% to $208.23 million, but stayed below the 2003 record high of $253.106 million.

Supply – World production of honey in 2009 (latest data available) fell -0.4% to 1.511 million metric tons, not far below the 2006 record high of 1.512 million metric tons. The major producer of honey by far is China with 367,219 metric tons in 2009 which is 24.3% of total world production. Other major producers in 2009 were Argentina with 81,000 metric tons, the U.S. with 65,366 metric tons, Russia with 53,598 metric tons, and Mexico with 55,271 metric tons.

U.S. production of honey in 2009 (latest data) fell -12.0% to 144.108 million pounds, remaining well below the 14-year high of 220.339 million pounds posted in 2000. Stocks fell by 27.4% to 37.153 million pounds in 2009 (Jan 1), which is a new 26-year. Yield per colony in 2009 fell -16.3% to 58.5 pounds per colony. The number of colonies in 2009 rose +5.1% to 2.462, above last year's record low of 2.301 million.

Trade – U.S. imports of honey in 2008 (latest data) fell by -0.7% to 231.4 million pounds, down from the 2006 record high of 277.7 million pounds. U.S. exports of honey are generally small and in 2008 they totaled only 10.1 million pounds, which was only 6.3% of U.S. production.

World Production of Honey   In Metric Tons

Year	Argentina	Australia	Brazil	Canada	China	Germany	Japan	Mexico	Russia	United States	Total
2003	75,000	16,000	30,022	34,602	294,721	23,691	3,300	57,045	48,048	82,431	1,335,163
2004	80,000	16,000	32,290	34,241	297,987	25,575	3,300	56,917	52,666	83,272	1,368,105
2005	110,000	16,000	33,750	36,109	299,527	21,232	3,300	50,631	52,123	72,927	1,410,448
2006	105,000	17,500	36,194	48,353	337,578	25,199	3,300	55,970	55,678	70,238	1,511,709
2007	81,000	18,000	34,747	31,489	357,220	18,266	3,300	55,459	53,655	67,286	1,463,848
2008	81,000	18,000	37,792	28,112	367,219	15,727	3,300	55,271	57,440	74,293	1,517,747
2009[1]	81,000			29,387	367,219	18,151			53,598	65,366	1,511,257

[1] Preliminary.   NA = Not available.   *Source: Food and Agricultural Organization of the United Nations (FAO)*

Salient Statistics of Honey in the United States   In Millions of Pounds

Year	Number of Colonies (1,000)	Yield Per Colony (Pounds)	Stocks Jan. 1	Total U.S. Production	Imports for Consumption	Domestic Disappearance	Exports	Total Supply	Placed Under Loan	CCC Take Over	Net Gov't. Expenditure[3] (Million $)	Domestic Avg. Price All Honey - Cents Per Pound -	National Avg. Price Support	Per Capita Consumption (Pounds)
2005	2,413	72.4	62.5	174.8	233.0	----	7.6	470.3	----	----	----	91.8	----	----
2006	2,393	64.7	60.5	154.9	277.7	----	7.0	493.1	----	----	----	103.6	----	----
2007	2,443	60.7	52.6	148.3	233.0	----	8.3	434.0	----	----	----	107.7	----	----
2008	2,342	69.9	51.2	163.8	231.4	----	10.1	446.4	----	----	----	142.1	----	----
2009[1]	2,498	58.6	37.5	146.4	210.5	----	9.7	394.4	----	----	----	147.3	----	----
2010[2]	2,684	65.5	45.3	175.9	251.2	----	9.6	472.4	----	----	----	160.3	----	----

[1] Preliminary.   [2] Forecast.   [3] Fiscal year.   *Source: Economic Research Service, U.S. Department of Agriculture (ERS-USDA)*

Production and Yield of Honey in the United States

| | -------------- Production in Thousands of Pounds --------------- | | | | | | Value of | ------------------- Yield Per Colony in Pounds ------------------- | | | | | |
Year	California	Florida	Minnesota	North Dakota	South Dakota	Total	Production ($1,000)	California	Florida	Minnesota	North Dakota	South Dakota	Average
2005	30,000	13,760	8,880	33,670	17,380	174,818	160,428	75	86	74	91	79	72.4
2006	19,760	13,770	10,000	25,900	10,575	154,907	160,484	52	81	80	74	47	64.7
2007	13,600	11,360	8,840	31,080	13,260	148,341	159,763	40	71	68	74	52	60.8
2008	18,360	11,850	9,516	36,000	21,375	163,789	232,744	51	79	78	90	95	69.9
2009	11,715	11,560	7,930	34,650	17,820	146,416	215,671	33	68	65	77	66	58.6
2010[1]	27,470	13,800	8,316	46,410	15,635	175,904	281,974	67	69	66	91	59	65.5

[1] Preliminary.   *Source: National Agricultural Statistics Service, U.S. Department of Agriculture (NASS-USDA)*

Interest Rates - U.S.

U.S. interest rates can be characterized in two main ways, by credit quality and by maturity. Credit quality refers to the level of risk associated with a particular borrower. U.S. Treasury securities, for example, carry the lowest risk. Maturity refers to the time at which the security matures and must be repaid. Treasury securities carry the full spectrum of maturities, from short-term cash management bills, to T-bills (4-weeks, 3-months, and 6-months), T-notes (2-year, 3-year, 5-year and 10-year), and 30-year T-bonds. The most active futures markets are the Treasury note and bond futures traded at the Chicago Board of Trade (CBOT) and the Eurodollar futures traded at the Chicago Mercantile Exchange (CME).

Prices – T-note prices from mid-2009 through early-2010 traded on the defensive in a sideways range due to the U.S. economic recovery that emerged in the second half of 2009. However, T-note prices then rallied starting in April 2010 due to the European debt crisis and the sharp downdraft in stock prices that nearly sent the U.S. economy into a double dip recession. The U.S. economy in Q2-2010 registered growth of only 1.7%.

Federal Reserve Chairman Ben Bernanke during the summer of 2010 became worried that the U.S. economy was stalling and was in danger of slipping into a deflationary trap such as the one seen in Japan for much of the past two decades. As a result, the Fed in August 2010 announced that it would use the incoming cash from principal repayments on its mortgage portfolio to buy Treasury securities, thus preventing its balance sheet asset level from dropping and causing a back-door tightening of monetary policy.

Mr. Bernanke then went further at the Fed's Jackson

Hole conference in late August 2010 and raised the possibility of a new quantitative easing program, dubbed QE2 by the markets. After sending up its trial balloon during September and October, the Fed finally officially announced QE2 on November 3, 2010, saying it would purchase $600 billion worth of Treasury securities from November 2010 through June 2011. The Fed's two Treasury purchase programs meant that the Treasury was buying a total of about $75 billion in Treasury securities per month from November 2010 through June 2011. Those purchase programs should bring the total asset level on the Fed's balance sheet to $2.9 billion by June 2011, representing an extra $2 trillion of liquidity above the Fed's normal asset level of $900 billion.

T-note prices peaked in November 2010 when the Fed announced its QE2 program because it turned out that the QE2 program was successful in improving business and consumer confidence and helping to boost the stock market and the economy. The Fed with QE2 was mainly trying to keep long-term yields down and boost asset prices, thus staving off deflationary fears. After the November peak, T-note prices fell in December 2010 and early 2011 as the U.S. economy strengthened substantially and as the unemployment rate fell to a 2-year low of 8.9% by February 2011. T-note prices also fell due to market concerns that the Fed might not withdraw its emergency liquidity in time to prevent an inflationary outbreak. Inflation in early 2011 started creeping higher with the U.S. CPI in January rising to an 8-month high of +1.6% and the core CPI rising to a 10-month high of +1.0%. As of March 2011, the market consensus was that the Fed would leave its funds rate target range of zero to 0.25% in place through early 2012.

U.S. Producer Price Index[2] for All Commodities   1982 = 100

Year	Jan.	Feb.	Mar.	Apr.	May	June	July	Aug.	Sept.	Oct.	Nov.	Dec.	Average
2001	140.0	137.4	135.9	136.4	136.8	135.5	133.4	133.4	133.3	130.3	129.8	128.1	134.2
2002	128.5	128.4	129.8	130.8	130.8	130.9	131.2	131.5	132.3	133.2	133.1	132.9	131.1
2003	135.3	137.6	141.2	136.8	136.7	138.0	137.7	138.0	138.5	139.3	138.9	139.5	138.1
2004	141.4	142.1	143.1	144.8	146.8	147.2	147.4	148.0	147.7	150.0	151.4	150.2	146.7
2005	150.9	151.6	153.7	155.0	154.3	154.3	156.3	157.6	162.2	166.2	163.7	163.0	157.4
2006	164.3	161.8	162.2	164.3	165.8	166.1	166.8	167.9	165.4	162.2	164.6	165.6	164.8
2007	164.0	166.8	169.3	171.4	173.3	173.8	175.1	172.4	173.5	174.7	179.0	178.6	172.7
2008	181.0	182.7	187.9	190.9	196.6	200.5	205.5	199.0	196.9	186.4	176.8	170.9	189.6
2009	171.2	169.3	168.1	169.1	170.8	174.1	172.5	175.0	174.1	175.2	177.4	178.1	172.9
2010[1]	181.9	181.0	183.3	184.4	184.8	183.5	184.1	184.9	184.9	186.6	188.0	189.9	184.8

[1] Preliminary.   [2] Not seasonally adjusted.   *Source: Bureau of Labor Statistics, U.S. Department of Commerce (BLS)*

U.S. Consumer Price Index[2] for All Urban Consumers   1982-84 = 100

Year	Jan.	Feb.	Mar.	Apr.	May	June	July	Aug.	Sept.	Oct.	Nov.	Dec.	Average
2001	175.1	175.8	176.2	176.9	177.7	178.0	177.5	177.5	178.3	177.7	177.4	176.7	177.1
2002	177.1	177.8	178.8	179.8	179.8	179.9	180.1	180.7	181.0	181.3	181.3	180.9	179.9
2003	181.7	183.1	184.2	183.8	183.5	183.7	183.9	184.6	185.2	185.0	184.5	184.3	184.0
2004	185.2	186.2	187.4	188.0	189.1	189.7	189.4	189.5	189.9	190.9	191.0	190.3	188.9
2005	190.7	191.8	193.3	194.6	194.4	194.5	195.4	196.4	198.8	199.2	197.6	196.8	195.3
2006	198.3	198.7	199.8	201.5	202.5	202.9	203.5	203.9	202.9	201.8	201.5	201.8	201.6
2007	202.4	203.5	205.4	206.7	207.9	208.4	208.3	207.9	208.5	208.9	210.2	210.0	207.3
2008	211.1	211.7	213.5	214.8	216.6	218.8	220.0	219.1	218.8	216.6	212.4	210.2	215.3
2009	211.1	212.2	212.7	213.2	213.9	215.7	215.4	215.8	216.0	216.2	216.3	215.9	214.5
2010[1]	216.7	216.7	217.6	218.0	218.2	218.0	218.0	218.3	218.4	218.7	218.8	219.2	218.1

[1] Preliminary.   [2] Not seasonally adjusted.   *Source: Bureau of Labor Statistics, U.S. Department of Commerce (BLS)*

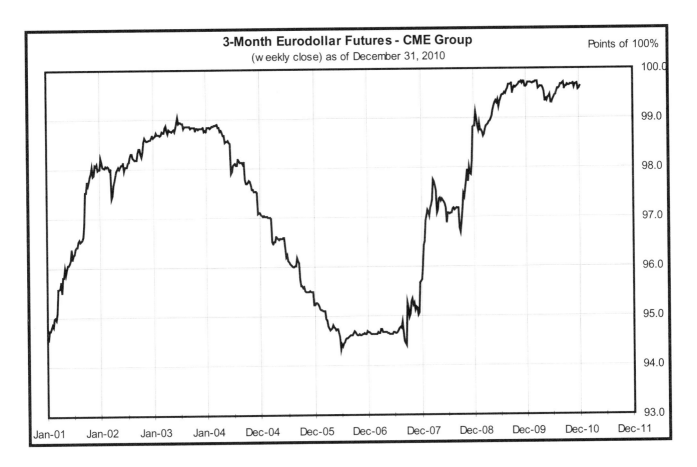

3-Month Eurodollar Futures - CME Group
(weekly close) as of December 31, 2010

Points of 100%

Volume of Trading of 3-month Eurodollar Futures in Chicago   In Thousands of Contracts

Year	Jan.	Feb.	Mar.	Apr.	May	June	July	Aug.	Sept.	Oct.	Nov.	Dec.	Total
2001	17,515.1	12,908.4	15,478.5	15,191.7	15,691.1	14,309.9	12,673.1	14,947.9	16,776.2	14,139.1	21,150.1	13,234.4	184,015
2002	19,487.1	14,491.2	17,986.7	17,946.9	18,717.5	17,931.8	20,366.9	17,757.9	15,309.9	18,495.9	13,348.6	10,240.5	202,081
2003	13,534.2	12,314.9	18,275.3	15,392.9	19,403.0	21,162.6	18,732.5	18,724.3	18,817.0	20,004.3	15,431.9	16,978.2	208,771
2004	20,808.8	16,042.4	22,583.6	26,673.6	25,548.9	28,067.1	25,114.4	24,859.3	32,283.0	25,737.3	27,945.3	21,920.2	297,584
2005	27,793.8	28,549.2	34,472.4	42,437.2	36,599.9	37,997.0	26,794.7	32,920.8	45,483.5	35,148.8	34,775.7	27,382.0	410,355
2006	35,602.4	34,218.0	47,463.8	37,752.2	44,154.6	45,443.4	36,794.1	45,126.7	45,180.3	46,453.5	42,700.7	41,187.7	502,077
2007	43,204.2	46,365.8	63,154.7	39,567.7	50,305.2	58,372.0	53,290.3	77,539.0	49,528.8	45,862.8	53,795.1	40,484.5	621,470
2008	70,787.1	59,378.2	60,956.1	56,371.5	48,683.4	60,086.5	54,178.8	36,521.6	58,497.7	40,508.5	24,515.5	26,489.2	596,974
2009	31,370.9	29,422.6	35,280.3	29,706.3	34,665.5	51,021.4	40,062.0	36,483.1	39,604.4	40,397.6	32,914.4	36,656.6	437,585
2010	36,569.3	37,746.7	47,459.2	52,132.3	57,806.8	36,986.2	32,120.3	34,582.2	38,196.5	34,205.0	55,512.9	47,637.1	510,955

Contract size = $1,000,000.   *Source: CME Group; International Monetary Market (IOM), division of the Chicago Mercantile Exchange (CME)*

Average Open Interest of 3-month Eurodollar Futures in Chicago   In Thousands of Contracts

Year	Jan.	Feb.	Mar.	Apr.	May	June	July	Aug.	Sept.	Oct.	Nov.	Dec.
2001	3,576.4	3,878.6	4,117.4	4,109.3	4,316.3	4,471.7	4,452.4	4,753.5	4,567.8	4,524.0	4,950.8	4,559.1
2002	4,592.0	4,937.0	4,727.9	4,411.6	4,421.0	4,295.5	4,123.7	4,482.4	4,243.4	4,237.9	4,553.7	4,072.5
2003	4,007.1	4,500.1	4,517.3	4,448.6	5,098.7	5,514.2	5,218.4	5,277.9	5,034.1	4,935.4	5,024.2	4,936.1
2004	5,128.0	5,624.1	5,640.5	5,602.2	6,060.0	6,117.3	6,026.7	6,236.3	5,992.8	5,968.9	6,527.8	6,706.7
2005	7,163.3	7,858.5	8,124.1	8,244.1	8,604.5	8,045.7	7,416.0	8,044.7	8,054.2	8,471.9	9,264.8	9,145.1
2006	8,833.5	9,574.0	9,586.0	9,679.6	10,126.2	9,995.4	9,572.4	10,153.9	9,949.4	9,809.8	10,345.5	10,201.1
2007	9,682.3	10,400.5	10,847.9	10,827.1	11,895.5	11,285.2	11,166.9	11,416.3	10,782.6	10,019.4	10,631.2	10,515.5
2008	11,033.0	11,206.7	10,356.6	9,225.3	9,282.5	9,266.0	9,589.0	9,882.1	8,953.0	8,141.7	8,286.9	7,389.1
2009	6,772.8	6,857.6	6,371.3	6,055.5	6,480.5	6,383.2	6,540.1	6,748.5	6,659.5	6,937.8	7,382.3	6,876.4
2010	6,957.6	7,607.2	7,643.6	7,850.9	7,728.4	7,297.3	7,652.9	7,876.1	7,528.6	7,953.2	8,245.8	7,433.0

Contract size = $1,000,000.   *Source: CME Group; International Monetary Market (IOM), division of the Chicago Mercantile Exchange (CME)*

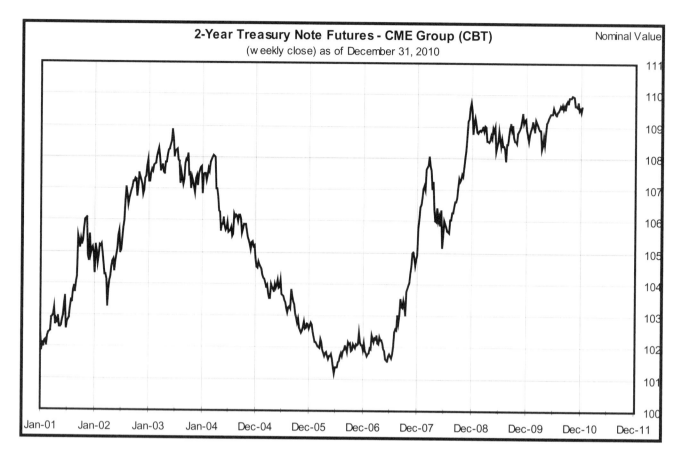

2-Year Treasury Note Futures - CME Group (CBT)
(weekly close) as of December 31, 2010

Nominal Value

Volume of Trading of 2-Year U.S. Treasury Note Futures in Chicago   In Thousands of Contracts

Year	Jan.	Feb.	Mar.	Apr.	May	June	July	Aug.	Sept.	Oct.	Nov.	Dec.	Total
2001	174.6	299.2	160.9	194.8	274.0	163.3	93.4	316.4	198.1	122.9	303.8	160.6	2,462
2002	195.0	332.9	290.4	159.2	377.0	242.9	177.0	377.0	253.0	174.8	387.2	232.3	3,199
2003	146.8	392.9	292.5	153.3	513.9	339.2	274.1	514.0	522.8	281.1	496.7	488.5	4,416
2004	310.4	829.8	630.0	462.4	872.2	788.8	406.7	1,009.9	1,014.5	678.0	1,393.3	1,058.5	9,455
2005	953.7	1,997.5	1,706.1	1,548.3	2,306.3	1,811.4	1,153.0	2,144.2	2,118.0	1,344.1	2,451.5	1,671.3	21,205
2006	2,053.3	3,223.3	3,206.5	2,090.0	4,690.9	2,837.1	2,525.1	4,461.0	2,768.3	2,422.9	4,826.4	2,862.0	37,967
2007	2,892.6	5,666.6	5,321.4	3,128.3	7,197.4	5,495.7	4,793.7	10,567.2	4,788.1	4,771.2	8,849.7	5,138.5	68,610
2008	7,526.1	10,092.8	7,515.4	5,102.6	8,195.6	7,207.2	6,366.1	7,529.6	8,126.5	5,355.3	4,067.9	2,225.8	79,311
2009	2,117.4	3,797.2	2,486.1	2,219.7	4,409.0	3,818.7	3,094.7	5,931.9	3,915.7	5,012.4	7,205.5	4,150.6	48,159
2010	4,487.2	8,143.4	6,164.3	6,164.1	9,494.2	4,398.8	4,083.6	6,491.7	3,189.8	6,849.9	6,849.9	3,791.0	70,108

Contract size = $200,000.   *Source: CME Group; Chicago Board of Trade (CBT)*

Average Open Interest of 2-Year U.S. Treasury Note Futures in Chicago   In Thousands of Contracts

Year	Jan.	Feb.	Mar.	Apr.	May	June	July	Aug.	Sept.	Oct.	Nov.	Dec.
2001	82.2	79.4	81.7	72.5	66.2	63.6	56.6	73.0	74.4	65.4	72.7	71.3
2002	86.5	103.3	103.6	87.9	102.0	105.9	99.4	108.0	110.4	108.1	115.5	113.6
2003	107.1	114.2	123.9	109.0	120.3	118.8	112.1	149.1	151.9	144.6	149.0	156.5
2004	161.9	195.2	186.8	172.4	198.9	210.7	191.7	207.1	216.4	205.5	221.6	248.5
2005	287.3	345.7	329.6	307.0	341.5	372.9	362.3	371.1	364.4	351.3	357.3	363.2
2006	437.8	489.3	469.0	489.5	607.6	541.1	595.1	701.4	683.6	680.7	698.4	716.0
2007	764.5	826.7	896.3	1,003.3	1,125.5	965.1	1,016.8	985.4	902.3	993.1	1,043.6	997.3
2008	1,101.2	1,313.0	1,187.3	1,110.0	1,166.8	972.5	895.4	922.6	783.7	735.0	648.0	503.4
2009	505.7	495.1	473.4	487.5	514.2	535.3	627.8	741.6	772.4	735.0	648.0	503.4
2010	885.7	982.1	891.3	1,001.7	1,022.3	900.3	847.1	805.6	708.2	734.8	710.8	664.9

Contract size = $200,000.   *Source: CME Group; Chicago Board of Trade (CBT)*

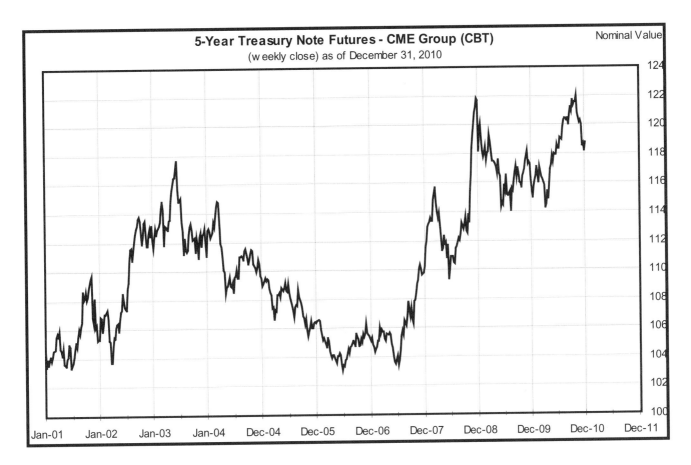

5-Year Treasury Note Futures - CME Group (CBT)
(weekly close) as of December 31, 2010

Nominal Value

Volume of Trading of 5-Year U.S. Treasury Note Futures in Chicago   In Thousands of Contracts

Year	Jan.	Feb.	Mar.	Apr.	May	June	July	Aug.	Sept.	Oct.	Nov.	Dec.	Total
2001	2,422.8	2,591.5	2,281.2	2,062.8	3,221.5	2,264.0	1,702.0	2,697.4	2,617.3	2,525.7	4,052.5	2,683.6	31,122
2002	2,867.9	3,826.0	3,848.2	3,092.4	4,637.6	4,095.7	4,437.4	5,354.4	4,859.3	5,026.7	5,013.2	3,453.2	50,512
2003	4,435.6	5,178.5	5,533.7	4,623.6	7,267.6	6,165.7	6,462.6	7,090.2	7,453.9	6,364.3	6,885.3	6,285.6	73,746
2004	5,856.9	7,388.8	7,775.6	7,793.1	10,979.4	9,458.2	7,109.8	10,656.0	10,311.6	7,686.2	11,036.9	9,416.8	105,469
2005	7,797.7	11,168.4	11,848.9	10,720.3	12,320.4	9,164.3	7,698.0	12,662.9	10,999.9	8,510.5	11,996.4	7,021.1	121,909
2006	9,388.4	12,141.7	11,865.2	7,869.8	12,971.9	9,368.7	8,102.0	13,347.5	9,369.3	8,730.9	13,423.5	8,291.5	124,870
2007	9,208.6	14,410.2	14,156.0	8,372.3	15,673.4	13,243.1	13,001.7	22,354.8	11,376.0	12,495.6	21,271.6	10,644.1	166,207
2008	15,479.7	20,790.4	17,424.0	12,474.7	17,616.2	14,904.3	14,514.1	15,085.6	16,979.1	10,079.8	8,057.9	4,721.7	168,127
2009	4,821.3	8,349.9	7,388.4	5,837.7	9,658.3	8,314.8	8,034.1	10,588.0	8,259.3	9,242.9	10,231.8	7,664.7	98,391
2010	7,434.9	11,815.6	10,096.3	9,631.3	16,093.0	10,212.4	9,662.0	13,062.2	9,404.1	14,828.5	14,828.5	10,282.0	137,351

Contract size = $100,000.   *Source: CME Group; Chicago Board of Trade (CBT)*

Average Open Interest of 5-Year U.S. Treasury Note Futures in Chicago   In Thousands of Contracts

Year	Jan.	Feb.	Mar.	Apr.	May	June	July	Aug.	Sept.	Oct.	Nov.	Dec.
2001	377.7	392.0	374.5	376.9	436.3	422.0	461.0	483.3	451.4	463.2	554.6	491.1
2002	507.2	576.2	585.6	632.2	656.4	594.9	554.9	652.8	655.0	662.5	720.7	692.8
2003	685.1	743.2	777.8	835.5	856.3	827.5	781.7	840.4	737.0	819.4	925.6	880.1
2004	874.2	1,008.1	987.2	1,043.0	1,145.4	1,118.5	1,217.3	1,322.5	1,168.1	1,099.4	1,290.7	1,318.7
2005	1,160.2	1,237.0	1,325.0	1,383.0	1,320.9	1,127.9	1,247.7	1,450.3	1,190.2	1,342.0	1,397.6	1,126.8
2006	1,105.1	1,404.8	1,238.0	1,257.2	1,326.0	1,264.7	1,258.3	1,409.8	1,341.3	1,413.8	1,484.4	1,423.8
2007	1,468.1	1,499.6	1,481.0	1,614.9	1,763.5	1,601.5	1,586.9	1,648.0	1,564.9	1,666.1	1,932.4	1,841.2
2008	1,940.6	2,101.2	1,923.8	1,850.9	1,851.0	1,669.6	1,574.5	1,600.7	1,483.4	1,378.1	1,267.1	1,057.8
2009	965.5	964.7	897.8	812.7	860.8	774.2	761.1	831.9	800.3	770.9	854.0	831.6
2010	805.1	939.1	942.4	937.2	1,045.8	932.2	940.4	1,095.6	925.0	1,012.8	1,136.6	1,010.9

Contract size = $100,000.   *Source: CME Group; Chicago Board of Trade (CBT)*

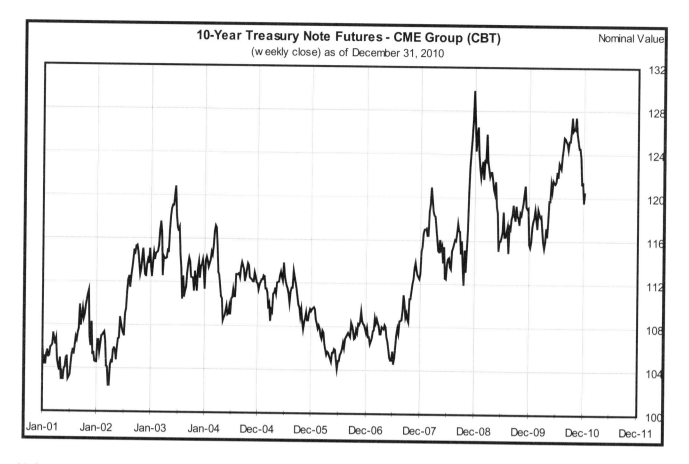

10-Year Treasury Note Futures - CME Group (CBT)
(weekly close) as of December 31, 2010

Nominal Value

Volume of Trading of 10-year U.S. Treasury Note Futures in Chicago   In Thousands of Contracts

Year	Jan.	Feb.	Mar.	Apr.	May	June	July	Aug.	Sept.	Oct.	Nov.	Dec.	Total
2001	4,632.8	4,915.3	4,500.5	4,299.4	5,483.3	4,083.8	3,493.1	5,683.1	4,389.7	4,144.8	7,270.1	4,689.8	57,586
2002	5,539.7	6,407.2	6,520.6	5,463.3	8,309.1	7,547.7	8,980.8	10,590.5	8,529.1	11,198.8	9,679.2	7,020.2	95,786
2003	9,120.6	10,746.5	11,320.5	9,377.2	13,817.0	12,149.5	15,285.0	14,248.7	13,706.7	13,586.9	12,474.5	10,912.2	146,745
2004	13,608.5	14,569.4	16,984.0	16,478.4	17,785.8	15,184.2	12,954.3	17,419.5	18,467.8	16,622.0	21,006.4	15,038.9	196,119
2005	13,901.3	19,565.4	21,132.8	19,487.3	22,688.8	16,778.7	13,894.5	20,120.1	18,348.2	15,357.3	20,705.4	13,144.2	215,124
2006	17,188.6	21,262.7	22,739.9	17,241.5	26,174.6	20,311.2	16,645.2	24,796.6	22,125.2	20,602.6	28,413.8	18,070.1	255,572
2007	21,492.5	30,367.2	30,210.2	18,529.8	34,343.9	37,171.0	32,361.3	38,785.6	24,375.6	25,280.4	36,890.7	18,070.1	349,229
2008	28,924.8	33,426.2	23,331.5	19,043.9	27,414.0	22,591.8	22,903.0	21,069.7	23,265.1	15,101.1	11,826.6	7,873.1	256,771
2009	9,778.0	14,548.1	15,116.1	11,893.7	17,309.8	16,994.6	16,420.7	19,292.8	16,099.0	19,268.8	19,037.2	14,093.3	189,852
2010	16,865.3	23,588.6	19,582.2	22,070.6	35,156.5	24,198.2	22,294.5	30,744.0	22,947.9	29,360.3	29,360.3	20,840.2	297,009

Contract size = $100,000.   *Source: CME Group; Chicago Board of Trade (CBT)*

Average Open Interest of 10-year U.S. Treasury Note Futures in Chicago   In Thousands of Contracts

Year	Jan.	Feb.	Mar.	Apr.	May	June	July	Aug.	Sept.	Oct.	Nov.	Dec.
2001	550.3	541.6	560.0	595.1	628.7	512.1	550.2	627.3	610.4	590.3	662.0	559.9
2002	572.9	643.9	679.6	699.1	806.5	793.0	877.6	958.3	888.7	970.2	938.0	751.6
2003	772.9	896.9	914.9	897.1	968.1	993.6	1,009.5	1,032.5	856.2	985.7	1,140.7	965.0
2004	1,145.9	1,320.6	1,312.9	1,347.7	1,392.4	1,300.3	1,348.2	1,456.6	1,503.6	1,626.9	1,767.4	1,642.0
2005	1,671.3	1,888.6	1,980.2	2,003.5	2,140.8	1,869.0	1,859.3	1,992.8	1,749.4	1,677.7	1,778.6	1,635.6
2006	1,700.0	1,990.4	2,048.7	2,259.7	2,321.0	2,054.2	2,087.1	2,265.3	2,271.5	2,408.2	2,398.2	2,236.0
2007	2,343.6	2,367.3	2,294.0	2,586.9	2,878.3	2,853.9	2,871.5	2,820.5	2,269.5	2,497.2	2,661.6	2,313.2
2008	2,431.2	2,517.6	2,179.8	2,073.7	2,144.6	1,978.8	1,802.6	1,835.2	1,658.2	1,385.2	1,226.4	1,074.2
2009	1,034.9	1,027.6	1,007.0	1,010.0	1,132.3	1,070.9	1,056.2	1,139.7	1,120.2	1,239.1	1,327.5	1,203.9
2010	1,292.9	1,420.4	1,423.8	1,632.0	1,838.8	1,756.8	1,802.2	1,973.0	1,686.3	1,617.2	1,527.4	1,335.3

Contract size = $100,000.   *Source: CME Group; Chicago Board of Trade (CBT)*

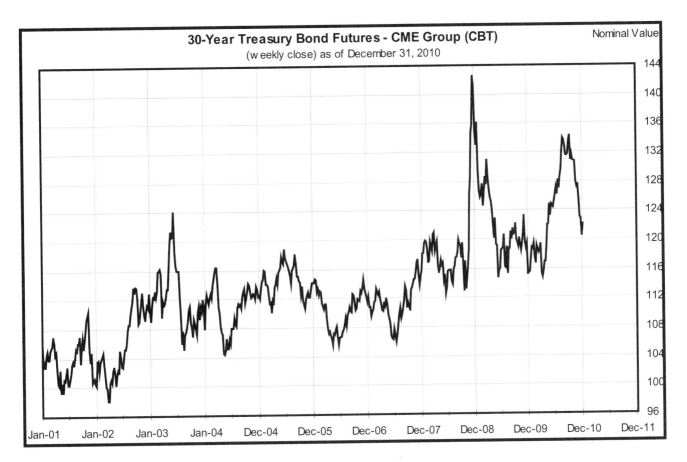

30-Year Treasury Bond Futures - CME Group (CBT)
(weekly close) as of December 31, 2010

Nominal Value

Volume of Trading of 30-year U.S. Treasury Bond Futures in Chicago   In Thousands of Contracts

Year	Jan.	Feb.	Mar.	Apr.	May	June	July	Aug.	Sept.	Oct.	Nov.	Dec.	Total
2001	5,123.0	5,545.9	5,196.3	4,584.0	6,022.2	4,233.2	3,347.0	4,965.6	4,331.0	4,598.6	6,746.4	3,886.0	58,579
2002	4,132.7	4,721.1	4,504.8	3,932.8	5,191.4	4,722.2	5,157.9	5,666.5	4,534.5	5,190.1	4,722.8	3,605.6	56,082
2003	3,625.3	4,840.9	5,106.9	3,795.0	7,188.4	5,896.2	6,352.1	6,198.0	5,738.4	5,121.8	4,823.4	4,835.2	63,522
2004	5,025.4	5,762.8	6,687.9	5,983.2	6,463.8	5,556.9	4,540.1	6,343.5	7,638.7	5,658.6	7,374.2	5,914.0	72,949
2005	6,134.8	8,973.5	8,573.7	7,293.5	8,558.9	7,407.2	5,367.0	7,771.3	7,193.6	6,450.4	7,928.8	5,274.0	86,927
2006	7,044.8	8,511.6	8,980.6	6,969.2	10,354.4	7,564.5	5,854.2	8,736.7	7,553.9	6,375.1	9,461.6	6,348.2	93,755
2007	7,108.8	10,060.2	10,338.3	6,108.4	10,578.5	11,338.4	9,452.1	11,439.3	6,864.4	7,232.1	11,146.2	5,963.6	107,630
2008	9,667.3	11,646.2	8,739.1	5,835.3	9,173.4	7,176.8	7,429.4	7,521.6	7,830.0	5,559.1	5,267.6	3,618.7	89,465
2009	3,805.9	6,062.7	4,525.5	3,224.8	6,465.1	5,192.0	4,995.2	7,238.3	4,297.6	5,133.4	6,978.4	4,313.9	62,233
2010	4,617.8	7,345.1	5,748.7	6,033.7	10,457.5	5,899.4	5,711.8	9,165.6	6,774.8	6,806.7	9,379.5	5,569.2	83,510

Contract size = $100,000.   *Source: CME Group; Chicago Board of Trade (CBT)*

Average Open Interest of 30-year U.S. Treasury Bond Futures in Chicago   In Contracts

Year	Jan.	Feb.	Mar.	Apr.	May	June	July	Aug.	Sept.	Oct.	Nov.	Dec.
2001	413,244	479,165	519,987	509,558	503,194	455,799	458,613	531,098	525,972	567,177	602,647	478,418
2002	468,455	520,573	479,939	463,100	472,778	458,020	427,896	465,971	496,815	467,440	459,877	440,225
2003	420,797	506,910	487,277	488,921	553,721	512,566	517,893	594,905	584,416	594,353	640,026	634,008
2004	488,484	571,445	557,595	557,595	735,910	665,235	579,724	600,565	595,736	586,653	618,647	574,121
2005	674,170	792,247	749,403	710,061	858,812	760,240	760,749	813,905	763,092	737,070	810,426	803,020
2006	601,094	662,314	622,927	739,601	858,812	760,240	760,749	813,905	763,092	737,070	810,426	803,020
2007	816,747	903,121	852,305	875,810	949,173	980,004	891,111	880,157	877,623	756,790	731,186	754,687
2008	1,033,106	1,041,505	979,695	893,308	941,317	879,149	891,111	880,157	749,290	739,723	777,241	704,259
2009	726,062	733,323	712,813	708,243	724,577	706,818	696,641	727,674	749,290	739,723	777,241	704,259
2010	656,438	676,778	648,845	663,991	740,180	663,330	682,310	738,206	669,950	683,476	654,901	563,632

Contract size = $100,000.   *Source: CME Group; Chicago Board of Trade (CBT)*

Municipal Note Futures - Chicago Board of Trade
(weekly close) as of March 22, 2006

Nominal Value

U.S. Federal Funds Rate   In Percent

Year	Jan.	Feb.	Mar.	Apr.	May	June	July	Aug.	Sept.	Oct.	Nov.	Dec.	Average
2001	5.98	5.49	5.31	4.80	4.21	3.97	3.77	3.65	3.07	2.49	2.09	1.82	3.89
2002	1.73	1.74	1.73	1.75	1.75	1.75	1.73	1.74	1.75	1.75	1.34	1.24	1.67
2003	1.24	1.26	1.25	1.26	1.26	1.22	1.01	1.03	1.01	1.01	1.00	0.98	1.13
2004	1.00	1.01	1.00	1.00	1.00	1.03	1.26	1.43	1.61	1.76	1.93	2.16	1.35
2005	2.28	2.50	2.63	2.79	3.00	3.04	3.26	3.50	3.62	3.78	4.00	4.16	3.21
2006	4.29	4.49	4.59	4.79	4.94	4.99	5.24	5.25	5.25	5.25	5.25	5.24	4.96
2007	5.25	5.26	5.26	5.25	5.25	5.25	5.26	5.02	4.94	4.76	4.49	4.24	5.02
2008	3.94	2.98	2.61	2.28	1.98	2.00	2.01	2.00	1.81	0.97	0.39	0.16	1.93
2009	0.15	0.22	0.18	0.15	0.18	0.21	0.16	0.16	0.15	0.12	0.12	0.16	0.16
2010	0.11	0.13	0.16	0.20	0.20	0.18	0.18	0.19	0.19	0.19	0.19	0.18	0.18

Source: Bureau of Economic Analysis, U.S. Department of Commerce (BEA)

U.S. Municipal Bond Yield[1]   In Percent

Year	Jan.	Feb.	Mar.	Apr.	May	June	July	Aug.	Sept.	Oct.	Nov.	Dec.	Average
2001	5.10	5.18	5.13	5.27	5.29	5.20	5.20	5.03	5.09	5.05	5.04	5.25	5.15
2002	5.16	5.11	5.29	5.22	5.19	5.09	5.02	4.95	4.74	4.88	4.95	4.85	5.04
2003	4.90	4.81	4.76	4.74	4.41	4.33	4.74	5.10	4.92	4.89	4.73	4.65	4.75
2004	4.61	4.55	4.41	4.82	5.07	5.05	4.87	4.70	4.56	4.49	4.52	4.48	4.68
2005	4.41	4.35	4.57	4.46	4.31	4.23	4.31	4.32	4.29	4.48	4.57	4.46	4.40
2006	4.37	4.41	4.44	4.58	4.59	4.60	4.61	4.39	4.27	4.30	4.14	4.11	4.40
2007	4.23	4.22	4.15	4.26	4.31	4.60	4.56	4.64	4.51	4.39	4.46	4.42	4.40
2008	4.27	4.64	4.93	4.70	4.58	4.69	4.68	4.69	4.86	5.50	5.23	5.56	4.86
2009	5.07	4.90	4.99	4.78	4.56	4.81	4.72	4.60	4.24	4.20	4.37	4.21	4.62
2010	4.33	4.36	4.36	4.41	4.29	4.36	4.32	4.03	3.87	3.87	4.40	4.92	4.29

[1] 20-bond average.   *Source: Bureau of Economic Analysis, U.S. Department of Commerce (BEA)*

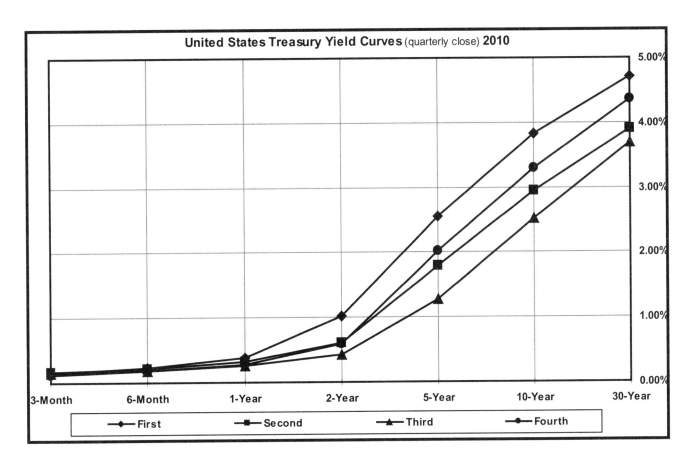

United States Treasury Yield Curves (quarterly close) 2010

Legend: First — Second — Third — Fourth

X-axis: 3-Month, 6-Month, 1-Year, 2-Year, 5-Year, 10-Year, 30-Year

Y-axis: 0.00%, 1.00%, 2.00%, 3.00%, 4.00%, 5.00%

U.S. Industrial Production Index[1]   1997 = 100

Year	Jan.	Feb.	Mar.	Apr.	May	June	July	Aug.	Sept.	Oct.	Nov.	Dec.	Average
2001	91.1	90.6	90.3	90.1	89.5	88.9	88.5	88.2	87.9	87.5	87.0	87.1	88.9
2002	87.6	87.6	88.2	88.6	89.1	89.9	89.6	89.7	89.8	89.5	89.9	89.5	89.1
2003	90.1	90.4	90.3	89.6	89.6	89.6	90.0	89.9	90.4	90.4	91.2	91.1	90.2
2004	91.3	91.8	91.3	91.7	92.4	91.5	92.2	92.4	92.3	93.2	93.4	94.1	92.3
2005	94.5	95.2	95.1	95.2	95.4	95.7	95.6	95.7	93.8	94.8	95.8	96.4	95.3
2006	96.4	96.5	96.7	97.1	97.0	97.4	97.7	97.9	97.8	97.8	97.6	98.7	97.4
2007	98.3	99.4	99.5	100.2	100.2	100.1	100.3	100.3	100.7	100.0	100.4	100.5	100.0
2008	100.1	99.9	99.6	98.8	98.3	98.0	98.0	96.8	93.0	93.9	92.9	91.0	96.7
2009	89.1	88.5	87.2	86.5	85.7	85.5	86.7	87.8	88.4	88.6	89.1	89.6	87.7
2010/1	90.5	90.5	91.0	91.5	92.6	92.6	93.5	93.6	93.9	93.8	94.1	95.2	92.7

[1] Total Index of the Federal Reserve Index of Quantity Output, seasonally adjusted.   [2] Preliminary.   Source: Bureau of Economic Analysis, U.S. Department of Commerce (BEA)

U.S. Gross National Product, National Income, and Personal Income   In Billions of Constant Dollars[1]

	Gross Domestic Product					National Income					Personal Income				
Year	First Quarter	Second Quarter	Third Quarter	Fourth Quarter	Total	First Quarter	Second Quarter	Third Quarter	Fourth Quarter	Total	First Quarter	Second Quarter	Third Quarter	Fourth Quarter	Total
2001	10,165	10,301	10,305	10,373	10,286	9,184	9,210	9,157	9,189	9,185	8,859	8,881	8,881	8,912	8,883
2002	10,499	10,602	10,702	10,767	10,642	9,305	9,381	9,418	9,531	9,409	8,978	9,061	9,075	9,127	9,060
2003	10,888	11,008	11,256	11,417	11,142	9,614	9,757	9,899	10,090	9,840	9,195	9,321	9,419	9,578	9,378
2004	11,597	11,778	11,951	12,145	11,868	10,281	10,445	10,642	10,769	10,534	9,680	9,847	9,999	10,223	9,937
2005	12,380	12,517	12,742	12,916	12,638	11,020	11,157	11,360	11,559	11,274	10,239	10,387	10,578	10,741	10,486
2006	13,184	13,348	13,453	13,612	13,399	11,838	11,966	12,093	12,228	12,031	11,027	11,204	11,337	11,505	11,268
2007	13,790	14,008	14,158	14,291	14,062	12,261	12,361	12,407	12,556	12,396	11,714	11,839	11,954	12,141	11,912
2008	14,328	14,472	14,485	14,191	14,369	12,628	12,620	12,686	12,297	12,558	12,300	12,461	12,447	12,356	12,391
2009	14,050	14,035	14,115	14,277	14,119	12,150	12,130	12,205	12,416	12,225	12,093	12,203	12,164	12,239	12,175
2010[2]	14,446	14,579	14,745		14,590	12,621	12,783	12,878		12,760	12,350	12,517	12,593		12,487

[1] Seasonally adjusted at annual rates.   [2] Preliminary.   Source: Bureau of Economic Analysis, U.S. Department of Commerce (BEA)

INTEREST RATES - U.S.

U.S. Money Supply M1[2]   In Billions of Dollars

Year	Jan.	Feb.	Mar.	Apr.	May	June	July	Aug.	Sept.	Oct.	Nov.	Dec.	Average
2001	1,097.2	1,101.3	1,109.7	1,115.0	1,119.6	1,126.7	1,140.0	1,150.1	1,205.0	1,165.8	1,170.8	1,182.1	1,140.3
2002	1,190.3	1,190.4	1,192.6	1,185.5	1,189.1	1,193.0	1,200.3	1,186.4	1,195.7	1,203.9	1,208.5	1,219.7	1,196.3
2003	1,226.0	1,238.2	1,239.0	1,248.1	1,268.0	1,281.0	1,288.8	1,294.3	1,297.7	1,297.1	1,297.6	1,306.5	1,273.5
2004	1,305.0	1,321.1	1,329.6	1,331.0	1,331.5	1,343.2	1,341.0	1,353.2	1,362.6	1,360.6	1,374.9	1,376.4	1,344.2
2005	1,366.0	1,371.9	1,372.0	1,356.6	1,364.4	1,379.7	1,367.2	1,376.6	1,378.2	1,375.2	1,376.3	1,374.9	1,371.6
2006	1,380.0	1,379.2	1,382.9	1,379.6	1,385.4	1,373.4	1,370.4	1,370.2	1,362.6	1,369.3	1,370.9	1,366.3	1,374.2
2007	1,373.2	1,363.9	1,366.4	1,377.5	1,379.2	1,364.9	1,370.7	1,373.0	1,373.4	1,378.8	1,371.2	1,373.6	1,372.2
2008	1,380.1	1,381.0	1,386.7	1,389.9	1,389.6	1,399.0	1,419.9	1,402.4	1,461.0	1,472.8	1,512.0	1,602.7	1,433.1
2009	1,587.1	1,568.9	1,577.4	1,609.8	1,610.5	1,651.7	1,661.5	1,655.3	1,665.8	1,679.8	1,679.9	1,693.6	1,636.8
2010[1]	1,681.0	1,703.2	1,712.0	1,700.2	1,707.1	1,727.4	1,731.0	1,751.5	1,774.5	1,784.1	1,821.5	1,832.1	1,743.8

[1] Preliminary.   [2] M1 -- The sum of currency held outside the vaults of depository institutions, Federal Reserve Banks, and the U.S. Treasury; travelers checks; and demand and other checkable deposits issued by financial institutions (except demand deposits due to the Treasury and depository institutions), minus cash items in process of collection and Federal Reserve float. Seasonally adjusted.   *Source: Board of Governors of the Federal Reserve System*

U.S. Money Supply M2[2]   In Billions of Dollars

Year	Jan.	Feb.	Mar.	Apr.	May	June	July	Aug.	Sept.	Oct.	Nov.	Dec.	Average
2001	4,968.8	5,005.6	5,065.3	5,126.6	5,130.4	5,168.9	5,202.0	5,234.1	5,343.1	5,335.7	5,379.3	5,428.6	5,199.0
2002	5,459.1	5,485.9	5,493.3	5,498.9	5,521.4	5,543.5	5,592.6	5,630.0	5,653.4	5,706.1	5,749.5	5,775.2	5,592.4
2003	5,804.4	5,839.7	5,854.1	5,898.8	5,953.8	5,991.8	6,046.9	6,090.2	6,071.6	6,058.7	6,057.6	6,064.1	5,977.6
2004	6,068.7	6,105.6	6,144.3	6,187.2	6,253.1	6,265.5	6,274.7	6,296.2	6,334.1	6,355.7	6,392.5	6,407.8	6,257.1
2005	6,407.3	6,422.5	6,436.0	6,444.5	6,459.7	6,496.8	6,521.8	6,555.0	6,591.9	6,621.4	6,646.7	6,673.4	6,523.1
2006	6,713.2	6,739.7	6,751.9	6,784.6	6,797.8	6,834.2	6,868.8	6,900.4	6,926.9	6,983.7	7,023.4	7,065.2	6,865.8
2007	7,104.6	7,122.9	7,152.7	7,221.5	7,245.0	7,269.9	7,305.1	7,369.8	7,401.7	7,432.3	7,462.8	7,493.8	7,298.5
2008	7,528.1	7,616.8	7,674.6	7,723.9	7,732.4	7,744.5	7,802.3	7,790.1	7,890.4	8,002.1	8,051.0	8,245.1	7,816.8
2009	8,307.8	8,347.2	8,399.0	8,390.5	8,431.8	8,452.8	8,452.8	8,428.7	8,452.4	8,482.3	8,511.5	8,528.7	8,432.1
2010[1]	8,469.5	8,537.1	8,515.2	8,527.2	8,568.3	8,599.1	8,615.3	8,660.8	8,708.6	8,748.4	8,785.8	8,816.4	8,629.3

[1] Preliminary.   [2] M2 -- M1 plus savings deposits (including money market deposit accounts) and small-denomination (less than $100,000) time deposits issued by financial institutions; and shares in retail money market mutual funds (funds with initial investments of less than $50,000), net of retirement accounts. Seasonally adjusted.   *Source: Board of Governors of the Federal Reserve System*

U.S. Money Supply M3[2]   In Billions of Dollars

Year	Jan.	Feb.	Mar.	Apr.	May	June	July	Aug.	Sept.	Oct.	Nov.	Dec.	Average
1997	5,013.2	5,041.7	5,080.2	5,119.8	5,147.1	5,177.4	5,235.8	5,291.4	5,332.3	5,376.3	5,417.1	5,460.5	5,224.4
1998	5,508.8	5,541.3	5,611.5	5,647.3	5,686.9	5,728.4	5,750.0	5,815.0	5,882.0	5,953.7	6,010.1	6,051.9	5,765.6
1999	6,080.7	6,129.5	6,133.6	6,172.3	6,201.0	6,237.7	6,269.0	6,299.1	6,323.0	6,378.4	6,464.1	6,551.8	6,270.0
2000	6,605.5	6,642.2	6,704.0	6,767.3	6,776.9	6,823.6	6,875.2	6,945.0	7,003.5	7,027.0	7,038.3	7,117.6	6,860.5
2001	7,237.2	7,308.5	7,372.0	7,507.8	7,564.1	7,644.7	7,691.9	7,696.3	7,853.2	7,897.8	7,973.0	8,035.4	7,648.5
2002	8,063.9	8,109.3	8,117.3	8,142.6	8,175.1	8,190.8	8,244.2	8,298.1	8,331.5	8,368.9	8,498.8	8,568.0	8,259.0
2003	8,588.1	8,628.7	8,648.8	8,686.0	8,741.9	8,791.6	8,888.7	8,918.2	8,906.5	8,896.8	8,880.3	8,872.3	8,787.3
2004	8,930.2	9,000.3	9,080.7	9,149.6	9,243.8	9,275.7	9,282.7	9,314.4	9,351.8	9,359.4	9,395.1	9,433.0	9,234.7
2005	9,487.2	9,531.6	9,565.3	9,620.9	9,665.0	9,725.3	9,762.4	9,864.6	9,950.8	10,032.0	10,078.5	10,154.0	9,786.5
2006[1]	10,242.8	10,298.7	Discontinued										10,270.8

[1] Preliminary.   [2] M3 -- M2 plus large-denomination ($100,000 or more) time deposits; repurchase agreements issued by depository institutions; Eurodollar deposits, specifically, dollar-denominated deposits due to nonbank U.S. addresses held at foreign offices of U.S. banks worldwide and all banking offices in Canada and the United Kingdom; and institutional money market mutual funds (funds with initial investments of $50,000 or more). Seasonally adjusted.   *Source: Board of Governors of the Federal Reserve System*

U.S. Money Supply MZM[2]   In Billions of Dollars

Year	Jan.	Feb.	Mar.	Apr.	May	June	July	Aug.	Sept.	Oct.	Nov.	Dec.	Average
2001	4,778.2	4,875.8	4,962.9	5,061.2	5,115.1	5,193.4	5,249.4	5,274.6	5,438.6	5,516.6	5,598.1	5,678.0	5,228.5
2002	5,717.4	5,762.4	5,779.7	5,803.2	5,833.9	5,855.5	5,906.4	5,935.5	5,947.2	5,985.7	6,106.2	6,158.6	5,899.3
2003	6,173.9	6,204.9	6,208.0	6,236.9	6,279.1	6,325.2	6,431.1	6,449.4	6,434.1	6,416.3	6,403.6	6,384.1	6,328.9
2004	6,394.1	6,430.8	6,478.1	6,525.6	6,599.4	6,606.6	6,603.4	6,612.7	6,634.9	6,637.0	6,666.6	6,668.6	6,571.5
2005	6,651.0	6,648.8	6,643.1	6,642.8	6,639.6	6,671.8	6,696.6	6,722.6	6,761.4	6,791.9	6,809.1	6,838.1	6,709.7
2006	6,875.8	6,887.9	6,889.1	6,916.0	6,925.1	6,964.0	6,994.9	7,020.6	7,045.4	7,108.1	7,157.0	7,225.0	7,000.7
2007	7,249.3	7,271.8	7,320.2	7,411.4	7,467.9	7,523.6	7,601.9	7,738.0	7,857.4	7,970.3	8,070.1	8,137.8	7,635.0
2008	8,184.0	8,398.3	8,539.5	8,638.8	8,678.2	8,725.8	8,787.9	8,766.3	8,795.3	8,836.1	8,955.2	9,191.2	8,708.1
2009	9,318.9	9,399.5	9,483.4	9,520.1	9,602.0	9,633.0	9,637.0	9,586.3	9,589.5	9,582.3	9,579.5	9,563.3	9,541.2
2010[1]	9,484.3	9,508.9	9,437.8	9,402.1	9,419.7	9,443.0	9,473.1	9,538.7	9,611.1	9,664.8	9,718.0	9,746.0	9,537.3

[1] Preliminary.   [2] MZM (money, zero maturity): M2 minus small-denomination time deposits, plus institutional money market mutual funds (that is, those included in M3 but excluded from M2). The label MZM was coined by William Poole (1991); the aggregate itself was proposed earlier by Motley (1988). Seasonally adjusted.   *Source: Board of Governors of the Federal Reserve System*

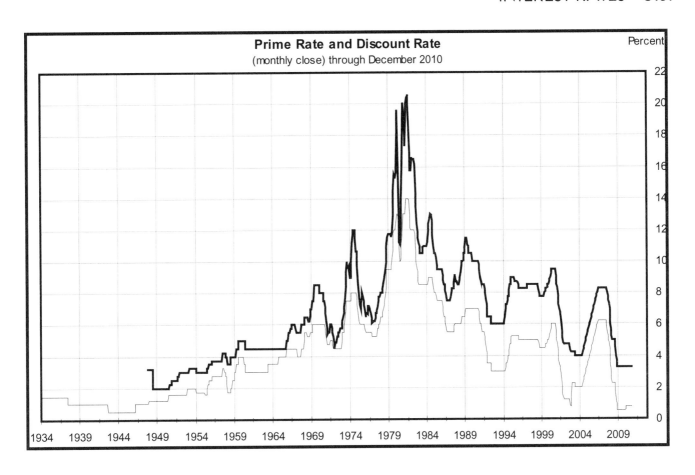

Prime Rate and Discount Rate
(monthly close) through December 2010

Percent

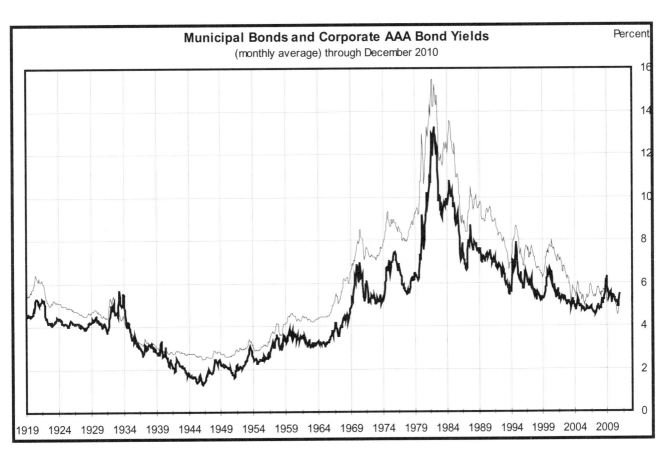

Municipal Bonds and Corporate AAA Bond Yields
(monthly average) through December 2010

Percent

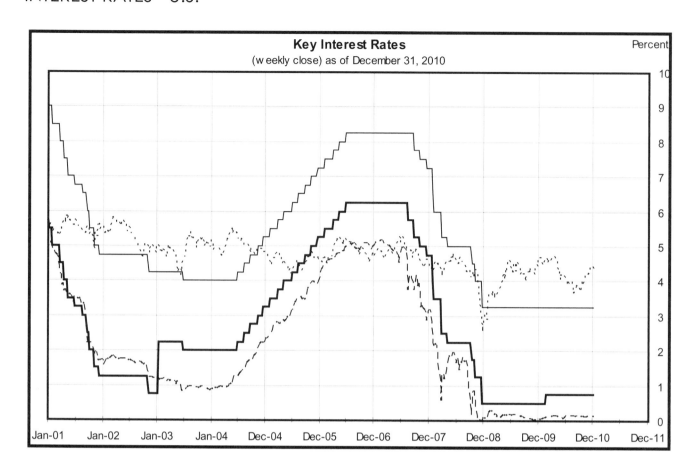

Key Interest Rates
(weekly close) as of December 31, 2010

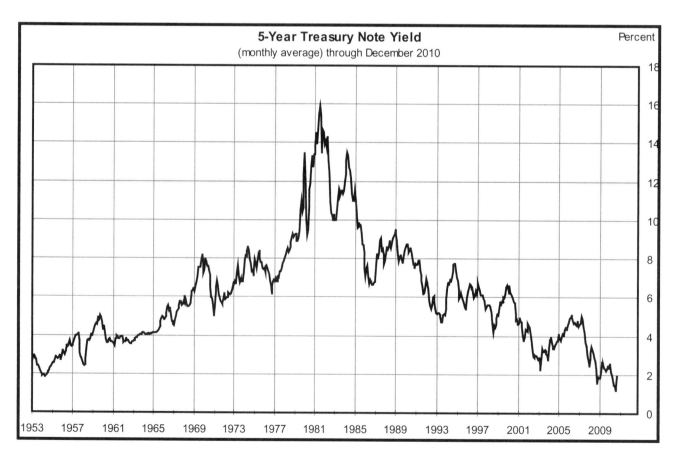

5-Year Treasury Note Yield
(monthly average) through December 2010

Interest Rates - Worldwide

Interest rate futures contracts are widely traded throughout the world. The most popular futures contracts are generally the 10-year government bond and the 3-month interest rate contracts. In Europe, futures on German interest rates are traded at the all-electronic Eurex Exchange in Frankfurt. Futures on UK interest rates are traded at the Liffe Exchange in London. Futures on Canadian interest rates are traded at the Montreal Exchange. Futures on Japanese interest rates are traded at the Singapore Exchange (Simex) and at the Tokyo Stock Exchange. A variety of other interest rate futures contracts are traded throughout the rest of the world (please see the front of this Yearbook for a complete list).

Euro-Zone – The Eurex 10-year Euro Bund futures contract rallied sharply in the first half of 2010 on the European debt crisis but then topped out in August and fell during the remainder of the year, finally closing the year up only 4.12 points at 125.31. The 10-year Bund yield hit a record low of 2.09% in August 2010 but then moved higher the rest of the year to close the year 43 basis points lower at 2.96%. The 3-month Euribor interbank lending rate hit a record low of 0.63% in March 2010 but then steadily rose the rest of the year and closed at 1.01%.

The European debt crisis was the main factor influencing Eurozone interest rates and monetary policy during 2010. The Eurozone economy entered an economic recovery in 2010 following the 2008 financial crisis and recession during 2009, but debt loads in various Eurozone countries emerged as a major problem by early 2010. Greece was the first country to run into trouble with its 2010 budget deficit of more than 10% of its GDP and its cumulative debt load of more than 125% of its GDP. Greek 10-year bond yields in April 2010 soared from 6% at the beginning of the month to a peak of more than 12% by the end of the month as investors dumped Greek bonds on fears of an impending default. However, the IMF and the Eurozone finally stepped in with a bailout package on May 2, 2010. Ireland then ran into progressively worse trouble during 2010 due to its pledge to bail out its banks and Ireland finally required a Eurozone bailout by November 2010. Portugal and Spain also ran into trouble in 2010 but have so far been able to avoid a bailout.

The European debt crisis caused concern about sovereign bond defaults and even about the possibility of the euro breaking apart. The European Central Bank was forced to take the lead on addressing the crisis, keeping its monetary policy easy and even buying the bonds of the troubled Eurozone countries to try to keep yields down to more affordable levels. The ECB during 2010 wanted to exit more of its emergency liquidity measures, but was forced to keep its promise of unlimited liquidity in place into 2011 due to the strains from the European debt crisis. The ECB left its 2-week refinancing rate unchanged at 1.00% all through 2010. By March 2011, the Eurozone had strengthened European Financial Stability Facility (EFSF) and the crisis started to abate, thus allowing the ECB in March to warn of a possible interest rate hike by April 2011 in response to rising inflation.

UK – The Liffe 10-year Gilt futures contract hit a record high in July 2010 but then fell back to close the year up 5.04 points. The 10-year gilt yield hit a record low of 2.79% in August 2010, but then rose to close the year down 61 basis points at 3.40%. The 3-month UK Libor rate during 2010 moved slightly higher during the year to close up 15 basis points at 0.76%. The Bank of England (BOE) during all of 2010 maintained its extremely easy monetary policy with the base rate at 0.50% and with its quantitative easing program intact. The BOE was forced to maintain its easy monetary policy to offset the effects of an aggressive budget deficit cutting program by the Conservative Party that helped to cause negative GDP growth in Q4-2010 of -0.6% q/q. However, the markets were expecting the UK economy to regain its balance in 2011 with an annual GDP gain of 1.7%. Inflation became a problem in early 2011 with the core UK CPI reaching a 10-month high of +3.0% in January, prompting the BOE to seriously consider a rate hike.

Canada – The Montreal Exchange's Canadian 10-year government note futures contract rallied during the middle of 2010 on the European debt crisis and the weakening global economy, but then fell back in the latter part of the year as the global economy regained speed. The Canadian 10-year bond contract closed the year up 4.72 points. The 10-year Canadian bond yield fell to a 2-year low of 2.68% in October 2010 but then moved higher and closed the year down 49 basis points at 3.12%. The 3-month Canadian interbank lending rate was little changed at 0.40% early in the year but then moved higher to 1.20% during the middle of 2010 on a tighter monetary policy tied to an improving Canadian economy and rising inflation. The Bank of Canada implemented three 25 basis point rate hikes from June through September 2010, bringing the overnight rate to 1.00% by September 2010. Canada's GDP moved higher in the first half of 2010 and reached a peak of +4.2% in August 2010, but then faded to +3.2% by year-end.

Japan – The SGX 10-year JGB futures rallied during the middle of 2010 and reached a 7-year high in October 2010 but then faded late in the year to close up 0.88%. The 10-year JGB government bond yield in 2010 fell to a 7-year low of 0.83% in October 2010 but then moved higher to close the year down 17 basis points at 1.13%. Japan's GDP was strong in Q2-201 at +6.1%, but then faded in mid-2010 to the 2-3% area and turned negative to -1.3% in Q4-2010. The Bank of Japan, in response to weaker economic growth, cut its overnight rate to near zero in October 2010 from its previous target of 0.10% and also instituted a larger quantitative easing program. The market consensus was that Japan would show weak growth in 2011 and 2012 as it continues to try to climb out of the deflationary trap it has been in for most of the last two decades.

Long Gilt Futures - Euronext-LIFFE

(weekly close) as of December 31, 2010

Nominal Value

3-Month Sterling Futures - Euronext-LIFFE

(weekly close) as of December 31, 2010

Points of 100%

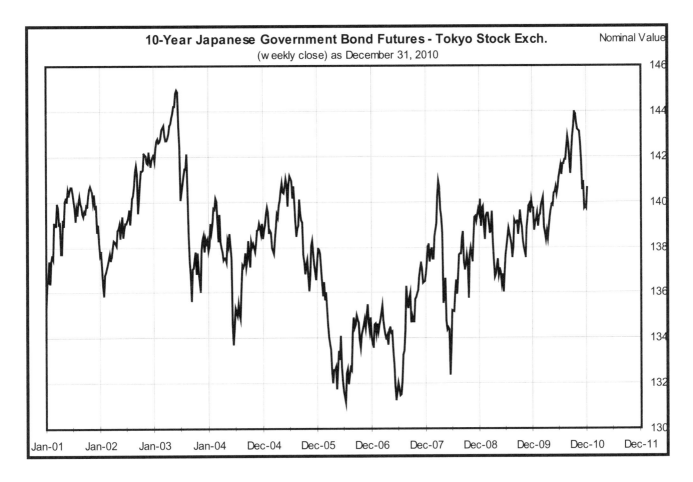

10-Year Japanese Government Bond Futures - Tokyo Stock Exch.
(weekly close) as December 31, 2010

Nominal Value

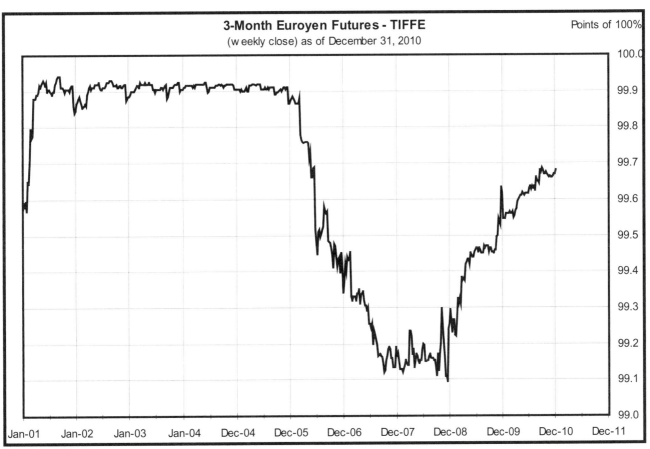

3-Month Euroyen Futures - TIFFE
(weekly close) as of December 31, 2010

Points of 100%

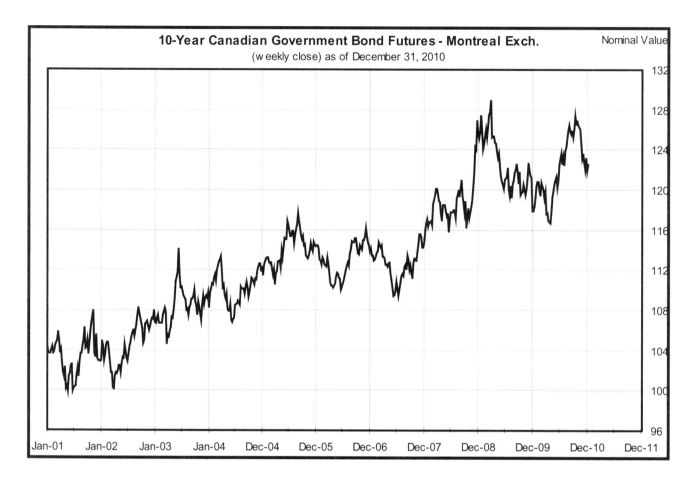

10-Year Canadian Government Bond Futures - Montreal Exch.
(weekly close) as of December 31, 2010

Nominal Value

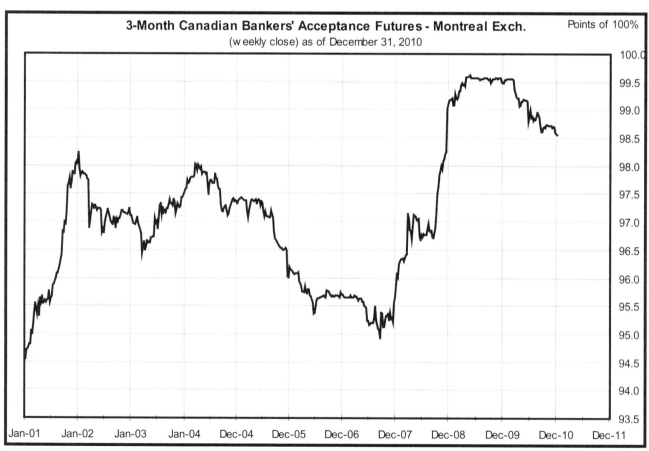

3-Month Canadian Bankers' Acceptance Futures - Montreal Exch.
(weekly close) as of December 31, 2010

Points of 100%

Australia -- Economic Statistics   Percentage Change from Previous Period

Year	Real GDP	Nominal GDP	Real Private Consumption	Real Public Consumption	Grossed Fixed Investment	Real Total Domestic Demand	Real Exports of Goods & Services	Real Imports of Goods & Services	Consumer Prices[3]	Unemployment Rate
2003	3.5	5.9	3.8	3.9	9.7	6.2	-2.2	10.6	2.8	5.9
2004	3.2	7.5	5.3	3.9	6.2	4.9	4.0	15.1	2.3	5.4
2005	3.5	8.1	3.7	2.2	9.6	5.0	2.4	8.6	2.7	5.0
2006	2.4	7.8	3.0	3.6	4.1	2.8	3.4	7.2	3.5	4.8
2007	5.0	9.2	5.2	3.3	9.8	7.0	3.3	12.2	2.3	4.4
2008	2.1	8.6	1.9	3.3	9.0	3.7	3.1	11.1	4.4	4.2
2009	1.2	1.6	1.7	2.8	-1.1	.5	1.0	-8.3	1.8	5.6
2010[1]	3.3	9.3	3.3	5.2	7.0	5.1	4.7	13.3	2.9	5.2
2011[2]	3.6	7.2	3.2	2.1	6.6	4.0	6.1	8.1	2.8	4.9

[1] Estimate.   [2] Projection.   [3] National accounts implicit private consumption deflator.   *Source: Organization for Economic Co-operation and Development (OECD)*

Canada -- Economic Statistics   Percentage Change from Previous Period

Year	Real GDP	Nominal GDP	Real Private Consumption	Real Public Consumption	Grossed Fixed Investment	Real Total Domestic Demand	Real Exports of Goods & Services	Real Imports of Goods & Services	Consumer Prices[3]	Unemployment Rate
2003	1.9	5.2	3.0	3.1	6.2	4.5	-2.3	4.1	2.7	7.6
2004	3.1	6.4	3.3	2.0	7.8	4.1	5.0	8.0	1.8	7.2
2005	3.0	6.4	3.7	1.4	9.3	4.9	1.9	7.1	2.2	6.8
2006	2.8	5.6	4.2	3.0	7.1	4.4	.6	4.9	2.0	6.3
2007	2.2	5.5	4.6	2.7	3.5	3.9	1.2	5.9	2.1	6.0
2008	.5	4.6	2.9	3.9	1.4	2.5	-4.6	1.2	2.4	6.2
2009	-2.5	-4.5	.4	3.5	-11.7	-2.6	-14.2	-13.9	.3	8.3
2010[1]	3.0	5.8	3.2	3.3	6.6	4.8	6.8	12.7	1.6	8.1
2011[2]	2.3	3.9	2.1	.8	4.8	2.5	5.3	5.7	1.7	7.8

[1] Estimate.   [2] Projection.   [3] National accounts implicit private consumption deflator.   *Source: Organization for Economic Co-operation and Development (OECD)*

France -- Economic Statistics   Percentage Change from Previous Period

Year	Real GDP	Nominal GDP	Real Private Consumption	Real Public Consumption	Grossed Fixed Investment	Real Total Domestic Demand	Real Exports of Goods & Services	Real Imports of Goods & Services	Consumer Prices[3]	Unemployment Rate
2003	1.1	3.0	2.1	2.0	2.2	1.7	-1.2	1.2	2.2	8.5
2004	2.3	3.9	2.4	2.2	3.3	3.0	3.5	6.4	2.3	8.8
2005	2.0	4.0	2.5	1.3	4.5	2.7	3.5	6.3	1.9	8.9
2006	2.4	4.9	2.6	1.3	4.5	2.7	5.0	5.9	1.9	8.8
2007	2.3	4.9	2.5	1.5	5.9	3.2	2.5	5.7	1.6	8.0
2008	.1	2.7	.5	1.6	.3	.4	-.8	.3	3.2	7.4
2009	-2.5	-2.0	.6	2.8	-7.0	-2.3	-12.2	-10.6	.1	9.1
2010[1]	1.6	2.0	1.5	1.6	-1.8	1.5	9.9	8.8	1.6	9.3
2011[2]	1.6	2.6	1.6	.6	2.8	2.0	6.4	7.5	1.1	9.1

[1] Estimate.   [2] Projection.   [3] National accounts implicit private consumption deflator.   *Source: Organization for Economic Co-operation and Development (OECD)*

Germany -- Economic Statistics   Percentage Change from Previous Period

Year	Real GDP	Nominal GDP	Real Private Consumption	Real Public Consumption	Grossed Fixed Investment	Real Total Domestic Demand	Real Exports of Goods & Services	Real Imports of Goods & Services	Consumer Prices[3]	Unemployment Rate
2003	-.2	.9	.9	.1	.4	-.3	.6	2.4	5.3	1.0	9.2
2004	.7	1.7	-.2	-.7	-1.3	-.5	9.2	6.5	1.8	9.7
2005	.9	1.6	.4	.4	1.1	.1	8.0	6.9	1.9	10.5
2006	3.6	4.0	1.5	1.0	8.7	2.5	13.5	12.3	1.8	9.8
2007	2.8	4.7	-.2	1.6	4.9	1.3	7.9	5.2	2.3	8.3
2008	.7	1.7	.6	2.3	1.8	1.0	2.0	2.9	2.8	7.3
2009	-4.7	-3.3	-.1	2.9	-10.0	-1.9	-14.3	-9.4	.2	7.4
2010[1]	3.5	4.3	-.1	2.6	4.9	2.3	15.2	13.6	1.0	6.9
2011[2]	2.5	3.6	1.3	.7	2.7	1.5	9.0	7.4	1.2	6.3

[1] Estimate.   [2] Projection.   [3] National accounts implicit private consumption deflator.   *Source: Organization for Economic Co-operation and Development (OECD)*

INTEREST RATES - WORLDWIDE

Italy -- **Economic Statistics**   Percentage Change from Previous Period

Year	Real GDP	Nominal GDP	Real Private Consumption	Real Public Consumption	Grossed Fixed Investment	Real Total Domestic Demand	Real Exports of Goods & Services	Real Imports of Goods & Services	Consumer Prices[3]	Unemployment Rate
2003	.1	3.2	1.0	1.9	-.9	.8	-1.5	1.6	2.8	8.4
2004	1.4	4.0	.8	2.2	1.5	1.3	3.6	3.3	2.3	8.0
2005	.8	2.9	1.2	1.9	1.4	1.0	2.0	2.7	2.2	7.7
2006	2.1	4.0	1.3	.5	3.1	2.0	6.5	6.2	2.2	6.8
2007	1.4	4.0	1.1	.9	1.3	1.2	3.9	3.3	2.0	6.2
2008	-1.3	1.4	-.8	.8	-4.0	-1.4	-3.9	-4.3	3.5	6.7
2009	-5.1	-3.0	-1.7	.6	-12.2	-3.8	-19.1	-14.6	.8	7.8
2010[1]	1.0	1.7	.4	-.3	2.0	.7	7.9	6.6	1.5	8.6
2011[2]	1.3	2.5	.6	.1	1.5	.6	6.7	3.7	1.4	8.5

[1] Estimate.   [2] Projection.   [3] National accounts implicit private consumption deflator.   *Source: Organization for Economic Co-operation and Development (OECD)*

Japan -- **Economic Statistics**   Percentage Change from Previous Period

Year	Real GDP	Nominal GDP	Real Private Consumption	Real Public Consumption	Grossed Fixed Investment	Real Total Domestic Demand	Real Exports of Goods & Services	Real Imports of Goods & Services	Consumer Prices[3]	Unemployment Rate
2003	1.4	-.2	.4	2.3	-.5	.8	9.2	3.9	-.2	5.3
2004	2.7	1.6	1.6	1.9	1.4	1.9	13.9	8.1	.0	4.7
2005	1.9	.7	1.3	1.6	3.1	1.7	7.0	5.8	-.6	4.4
2006	2.0	1.1	1.5	.4	.5	1.2	9.7	4.2	.2	4.1
2007	2.4	1.6	1.6	1.5	-1.2	1.3	8.4	1.6	.1	3.8
2008	-1.2	-2.0	-.7	.3	-2.6	-1.3	1.6	1.2	1.4	4.0
2009	-5.2	-6.1	-1.0	1.5	-14.0	-4.0	-23.9	-16.7	-1.4	5.1
2010[1]	3.7	1.8	2.4	1.6	-.1	1.7	25.4	10.5	-.9	5.1
2011[2]	1.7	.9	1.0	1.7	3.2	1.6	6.7	6.6	-.8	4.9

[1] Estimate.   [2] Projection.   [3] National accounts implicit private consumption deflator.   *Source: Organization for Economic Co-operation and Development (OECD)*

Switzerland -- **Economic Statistics**   Percentage Change from Previous Period

Year	Real GDP	Nominal GDP	Real Private Consumption	Real Public Consumption	Grossed Fixed Investment	Real Total Domestic Demand	Real Exports of Goods & Services	Real Imports of Goods & Services	Consumer Prices[3]	Unemployment Rate
2003	-.2	.8	.9	1.9	-1.2	.5	-.5	1.3	.6	4.3
2004	2.5	3.1	1.6	.8	4.5	1.9	7.9	7.3	.8	4.4
2005	2.6	2.8	1.7	1.2	3.8	1.8	7.8	6.6	1.2	4.4
2006	3.6	5.8	1.6	.3	4.7	1.4	10.3	6.5	1.1	4.0
2007	3.6	6.2	2.3	.3	5.1	1.4	9.6	6.1	.7	3.6
2008	1.9	4.4	1.3	1.7	.5	.2	3.3	.3	2.4	3.5
2009	-1.9	-1.6	1.0	1.6	-4.9	.6	-8.7	-5.4	-.5	4.4
2010[1]	2.7	2.8	1.7	.2	3.7	.7	10.6	8.3	.5	4.4
2011[2]	2.2	2.9	2.0	.4	4.2	2.6	4.8	6.4	.1	4.3

[1] Estimate.   [2] Projection.   [3] National accounts implicit private consumption deflator.   *Source: Organization for Economic Co-operation and Development (OECD)*

United Kingdom -- **Economic Statistics**   Percentage Change from Previous Period

Year	Real GDP	Nominal GDP	Real Private Consumption	Real Public Consumption	Grossed Fixed Investment	Real Total Domestic Demand	Real Exports of Goods & Services	Real Imports of Goods & Services	Consumer Prices[3]	Unemployment Rate
2003	2.8	6.0	3.0	3.4	1.1	3.0	1.8	2.2	1.4	5.0
2004	3.0	5.5	3.1	3.0	5.1	3.5	5.0	6.9	1.3	4.8
2005	2.2	4.2	2.2	2.0	2.4	2.1	7.9	7.1	2.0	4.8
2006	2.8	5.9	1.7	1.4	6.4	2.4	11.1	9.1	2.3	5.4
2007	2.7	5.8	2.2	1.3	7.8	3.1	-2.6	-.8	2.3	5.4
2008	-.1	2.9	.4	1.6	-5.0	-.7	1.0	-1.2	3.6	5.7
2009	-5.0	-3.7	-3.3	1.0	-15.1	-5.5	-11.1	-12.3	2.2	7.6
2010[1]	1.8	5.1	1.2	1.9	2.0	2.7	4.4	7.5	3.1	7.9
2011[2]	1.7	3.7	1.7	-1.1	2.3	1.3	5.0	3.1	2.6	7.8

[1] Estimate.   [2] Projection.   [3] National accounts implicit private consumption deflator.   *Source: Organization for Economic Co-operation and Development (OECD)*

Iron and Steel

Iron (symbol Fe) is a soft, malleable, and ductile metallic element. Next to aluminum, iron is the most abundant of all metals. Pure iron melts at about 1535 degrees Celsius and boils at 2750 degrees Celsius. Archaeologists in Egypt discovered the earliest iron implements dating back to about 3000 BC, and iron ornaments were used even earlier.

Steel is an alloy of iron and carbon, often with an admixture of other elements. The physical properties of various types of steel and steel alloys depend primarily on the amount of carbon present and how it is distributed in the iron. Steel is marketed in a variety of sizes and shapes, such as rods, pipes, railroad rails, tees, channels, and I-beams. Steel mills roll and form heated ingots into the required shapes. The working of steel improves the quality of the steel by refining its crystalline structure and making the metal tougher. There are five classifications of steel: carbon steels, alloy steels, high-strength low-alloy steels, stainless steel, and tool steels.

Prices –In 2010 the average wholesale price for No. 1 heavy-melting steel scrap in Chicago rose +61.9% to $334.13 per metric ton. That was down from the 2008 record high of $354.89. However, in January 2011 the price rose to $429.00 per metric ton.

Supply – World production of iron ore in 2010 rose by +7.1% to 2.400 billion metric tons, which was a new record high. The world's largest producers of iron ore are China (with 38% of world production), Australia (with 18%), and Brazil (with 15%). The U.S. accounted for only 2.0% of world iron ore production in 2010. World production of raw steel (ingots and castings) in 2010 rose +12.9 % yr/yr to 1,400 million metric tons, with the largest producers being China (with 45% of world production), Japan (with 8%), and the U.S. (with 6%).

U.S. production of steel ingots in 2010 rose by 52.5% to 90.000 million short tons, up from the 2009 record low of 59.000 million short tons. U.S. production of pig iron (excluding ferro-alloys) in 2010 (annualized through July) was up +40.6% to 30.617 million short tons.

Demand – U.S. consumption of ferrous scrap and pig iron fell –2.0% yr/yr in 2008 (latest data available) to 102.760 million metric tons which is the lowest level since 1986. The largest consumers of ferrous scrap and pig iron were the manufacturers of pig iron and steel ingots and castings with 90% of consumption at 92.050 million metric tons in 2008. Iron foundries and miscellaneous users accounted for 8.4% of consumption and manufacturers of steel castings (scrap) accounted for 2% of consumption.

Trade – The U.S. imported 3.870 million metric tons of iron ore in 2009, down 58.2% yr/yr from 9.250 million metric tons in 2008. The bulk of U.S. iron ore imports came from Canada (81% with 3.140 million metric tons), Chili (5.2% with 203,000 metric tons), and Brazil (4.9% with 188,000 metric tons).

World Production of Raw Steel (Ingots and Castings)   In Thousands of Metric Tons

Year	Brazil	Canada	China	France	Germany	Italy	Japan	Rep. of Korea	Russia	Ukraine	United Kindom	United States	World Total
2001	26,718	16,300	151,630	19,431	44,775	26,483	102,866	43,852	59,030	33,110	13,610	90,100	853,000
2002	29,605	16,300	182,370	20,524	44,999	25,930	107,745	45,390	59,777	34,538	11,718	91,600	907,000
2003	31,150	15,928	222,340	19,803	44,809	26,832	110,511	46,310	62,710	36,900	13,128	93,700	974,000
2004	32,918	16,305	272,450	20,770	46,374	28,317	112,718	47,521	65,646	38,740	13,766	99,700	1,060,000
2005	31,631	15,327	353,240	19,481	44,524	29,061	112,471	47,820	66,186	38,636	13,210	94,900	1,140,000
2006	30,901	15,493	419,150	19,857	47,224	31,550	116,266	48,455	70,816	40,899	13,931	98,200	1,250,000
2007	33,782	15,569	489,290	19,252	48,550	31,990	120,203	51,517	72,389	42,830	14,300	98,100	1,350,000
2008	33,713	15,100	500,490	17,874	45,833	30,477	118,739	53,322	68,700	37,107	13,538	91,900	1,330,000
2009[1]	34,000		568,000	13,000	33,000	18,000	88,000	53,000	59,000	30,000	10,000	59,000	1,240,000
2010[2]	33,000		630,000	16,000	44,000		110,000	56,000	66,000	31,000	10,000	90,000	1,400,000

[1] Preliminary.   [2] Estimate.   *Source: U.S. Geological Survey (USGS)*

Average Wholesale Prices of Iron and Steel in the United States

| | No. 1 Heavy Melting Steel Scrap | | -- Pittsburg Prices -- | | | | | | | | | |
| | Pittsburg | Chicago | Hot Rolled | Sheet Bars Hot Rolled | Cold Finished | Hot Rolled Strip | Carbon Steel Plates | Cold Rolled Strip | Galvan- ized Sheets | Rail Road Steel Scrap[2] | Used Steel Cans[3] |
Year	----- $ Per Gross Ton -----		--------------------------------- Cents Per Pound ---------------------------------							---- $ Per Gross Ton ----	
2000	103.73	96.07	15.67	----	23.08	----	15.69	----	21.38	150.00	82.23
2001	79.34	74.17	11.71	----	22.76	----	12.94	----	16.41	NA	68.52
2002	101.06	89.92	16.46	----	23.26	----	----	----	22.00	NA	66.71
2003	128.32	113.82	14.80	----	25.15	----	----	----	20.08	----	116.21
2004	221.05	220.13	30.84	----	38.67	----	----	----	36.69	----	192.80
2005	199.10	196.75	27.83	----	44.96	----	----	----	33.77	----	172.00
2006	222.39	225.21	29.78	----	44.02	----	----	----	38.09	----	212.63
2007	250.98	262.80	26.89	----	45.26	----	----	----	38.25	----	244.65
2008	365.62	357.88	44.56	----	61.67	----	----	----	54.91	----	314.63
2009[1]	204.21	206.14	24.60	----	42.10	----	----	----	34.23	----	121.84

[1] Preliminary.   [2] Specialties scrap.   [3] Consumer buying prices.   NA = Not available.   *Source: American Metal Market (AMM)*

IRON AND STEEL

Salient Statistics of Steel in the United States   In Thousands of Short Tons

Year	Pig Iron Production	Producer Price Index for Steel Mill Products (1982=100)	Raw Steel Production By Type of Furnace — Basic Oxygen	Open Hearth	Electric[2]	Stainless	Carbon	Alloy	Total	Net Shipments Steel Mill Products	Total Steel Products — Exports	Imports
2000	52,787	108.4	59,485	----	52,756	2,104	102,141	5,379	111,903	109,050	6,529	37,957
2001	46,424	101.3	52,204	----	47,118	1,836	92,946	4,666	99,322	99,448	6,144	30,080
2002	44,341	104.8	50,114	----	51,564	1,894	92,518	4,779	101,679	99,191	6,009	32,686
2003	43,122	109.5	50,942	----	48,751	1,952	98,772	4,901	99,693	105,625	8,220	23,125
2004	44,731	147.2	50,613	----	58,456	2,073	105,161	4,851	109,069	112,085	7,933	35,808
2005	40,036	159.7	45,231	----	57,599	1,903	96,636	4,935	102,830	103,474	9,393	32,108
2006	37,900	174.1	39,298	----	50,346	1,775	78,846	9,025	89,645	99,300	8,830	41,100
2007	36,300	182.9	36,147	----	53,161	1,713	86,958	8,026	96,697	96,500	10,100	30,200
2008	33,700	220.6	W	W	W	1,511	73,899	9,051	84,461	89,300	12,200	29,000
2009[1]	19,000	165.2	W	W	W	880	33,230	3,726	37,836	56,400	8,400	14,700

[1] Preliminary.   [2] Includes crucible steels.   *Sources: American Iron & Steel Institute (AISI); U.S. Geological Survey (USGS)*

Production of Steel Ingots, Rate of Capability Utilization[1] in the United States   In Percent

Year	Jan.	Feb.	Mar.	Apr.	May	June	July	Aug.	Sept.	Oct.	Nov.	Dec.	Average
2001	77.6	82.3	81.8	82.9	81.5	81.6	79.8	80.4	80.5	77.5	73.5	65.9	78.8
2002	84.5	88.4	86.7	90.3	89.4	92.5	86.8	91.0	94.0	90.8	86.8	83.9	88.8
2003	83.1	87.3	85.0	87.8	81.1	86.2	78.9	78.3	80.7	82.8	82.8	81.9	83.0
2004	88.0	90.9	93.8	93.3	92.9	94.4	93.5	95.0	97.3	97.5	94.8	91.5	93.6
2005	90.9	92.9	88.4	89.2	84.2	79.8	77.1	81.3	86.4	89.3	88.1	85.0	86.1
2006	85.6	89.5	92.8	91.4	92.5	92.1	88.7	88.7	91.2	86.2	81.5	75.0	87.9
2007	78.2	87.8	86.3	85.0	88.4	88.6	87.0	87.7	86.5	88.5	88.5	88.1	86.7
2008	90.3	91.6	89.7	90.3	91.1	90.3	88.8	90.4	84.5	70.5	50.7	40.9	80.8
2009	42.6	45.5	42.9	40.8	42.8	46.9	52.4	57.7	62.1	62.3	61.4	60.9	51.5
2010[2]	64.2	71.1	73.2	74.0	74.8	75.4	69.6	68.1	70.2	67.3	68.3		70.6

[1] Based on tonnage capability to produce raw steel for a full order book.   [2] Preliminary.   *Sources: American Iron and Steel Institute (AISI); U.S. Geological Survey (USGS)*

Production of Steel Ingots in the United States   In Thousands of Short Tons

Year	Jan.	Feb.	Mar.	Apr.	May	June	July	Aug.	Sept.	Oct.	Nov.	Dec.	Total
1997	8,735	8,266	9,175	8,882	9,048	8,662	8,692	8,818	9,006	9,128	9,116	9,071	107,488
1998	9,510	9,087	9,839	9,524	9,483	8,863	8,832	9,194	8,548	8,681	7,710	8,013	107,643
1999	8,422	7,837	8,854	8,643	8,914	8,413	8,619	8,993	8,650	9,574	9,357	9,604	105,882
2000	9,838	9,170	10,009	9,843	10,097	9,592	9,411	9,213	8,830	8,978	8,054	7,982	111,015
2001	8,475	8,122	8,932	8,685	8,832	8,550	8,459	8,525	8,263	8,125	7,226	6,695	98,889
2002	8,050	7,609	8,261	8,214	8,401	8,414	8,510	8,918	8,916	9,015	8,340	8,329	100,976
2003	8,617	8,175	8,817	8,692	8,047	8,534	8,163	8,096	8,026	8,514	8,347	8,414	100,442
2004	8,656	8,400	9,268	8,901	9,163	9,006	9,164	9,314	9,234	9,551	8,989	8,660	108,305
2005	9,123	8,419	9,028	8,757	8,543	7,837	7,896	8,330	8,562	9,032	8,629	8,599	102,754
2006[1]	8,918	8,506	9,770	9,382	9,811	9,458	9,324	9,320	9,282	8,922	8,169	7,760	108,621

[1] Preliminary.   *Source: American Iron and Steel Institute (AISI)*

Shipments of Steel Products[1] by Market Classifications in the United States   In Thousands of Short Tons

Year	Appliances Utensils & Cutlery	Automotive	Containers, Packaging & Shipping Materials	Construction Including Maint. Products	Contractors Products	Electrical Equipment	Export	Machinery, Industrial Equip. & Tools	Oil and Gas	Rail Transportation	Steel for Converting & Processing[2]	Steel Service Center & Distributors	All Other[3]	Total Shipments
1997	1,635	15,251	4,163	15,885	[5]	2,434	2,610	2,355	3,811	1,410	11,263	27,800	17,241	105,858
1998	1,729	15,842	3,829	15,289	[5]	2,255	2,556	2,147	2,649	1,657	9,975	27,751	16,741	102,420
1999	1,712	15,639	3,768	14,685	[5]	2,260	2,292	1,547	1,544	876	7,599	21,439	32,840	106,201
2000	1,530	14,697	3,684	14,763	[5]	2,039	2,752	1,513	2,268	994	7,753	22,537	35,093	109,624
2001	1,675	12,767	3,193	16,339	[5]	1,694	2,281	1,210	2,134	720	7,462	23,887	26,086	99,448
2002	1,734	12,562	3,251	15,729	[5]	1,336	1,844	1,137	1,658	751	7,201	22,828	29,160	99,191
2003	1,891	11,937	2,949	14,403	[5]	1,200	2,572	1,108	1,800	799	6,798	24,266	35,905	105,628
2004	1,919	12,527	2,978	15,114	[5]	1,139	2,426	1,332	2,043	957	7,295	25,385	38,969	112,085
2005	1,895	13,031	2,504	15,858	[5]	1,088	2,592	1,300	2,056	1,019	7,559	23,213	31,359	103,474
2006[4]	1,781	14,003	2,535	17,544	[5]	1,228	3,068	1,360	2,459	1,242	8,531	23,706	31,153	108,609

[1] All grades including carbon, alloy and stainless steel.   [2] Net total after deducting shipments to reporting companies for conversion or resale.
[3] Includes agricultural; bolts, nuts rivets & screws; forgings (other than automotive); shipbuilding & marine equipment; aircraft; mining, quarrying & lumbering; other domestic & commercial equipment machinery; ordnance & other direct military; and shipments of non-reporting companies.
[4] Preliminary.   [5] Included in Construction.   *Source: American Iron and Steel Institute (AISI)*

Net Shipments of Steel Products[2] in the United States   In Thousands of Short Tons

Year	Cold Finished Bars	Rails & Accessories	Wire Drawn	Tin Mill Products	Plates Cut & Coils	Sheet & Strip[3] Galv, Hot Dipped	Hot Rolled Bars	Pipe & Tubing	Structural Shapes & Steel Piling	Reinforcing Bars	Hot Rolled Sheets	Cold Rolled Sheets	Carbon	Alloy	Stainless
1997	1,809	875	619	4,057	8,855	12,439	8,153	6,548	6,029	6,188	18,221	13,322	97,509	6,282	2,067
1998	1,780	938	725	3,714	8,864	13,481	8,189	5,409	5,595	5,909	15,715	13,185	94,536	5,847	2,037
1999	1,775	646	611	3,771	8,200	14,870	8,078	4,772	5,995	6,183	17,740	13,874	98,694	5,421	2,086
2000	1,756	783	579	3,742	8,898	14,917	7,901	5,385	7,402	6,893	19,236	14,802	102,141	5,379	2,104
2001	1,369	630	481	3,202	8,349	14,310	7,032	5,377	6,789	6,976	18,866	12,352	92,314	4,789	1,837
2002	1,404	789	733	3,419	8,769	14,944	6,581	4,809	6,729	6,359	19,243	12,673	92,518	4,779	1,894
2003	1,426	739	684	3,513	9,230	15,221	6,486	4,597	7,437	7,970	22,218	13,485	98,772	4,901	1,952
2004	1,520	843	428	3,247	10,740	16,306	7,181	5,328	7,812	8,274	23,106	14,762	105,161	4,851	2,073
2005	1,495	920	560	2,874	10,274	15,249	6,674	5,096	8,070	7,464	20,569	12,793	97,884	5,183	1,903
2006[1]	1,487	1,016	603	2,880	10,827	16,358	7,595	5,426	8,652	7,419	20,862	13,281	101,572	4,956	2,081

[1] Preliminary.   [2] All grades, including carbon, alloy and stainless steel.   *Source: American Iron and Steel Institute (AISI)*

World Production of Pig Iron (Excludes Ferro-Alloys)   In Thousands of Metric Tons

Year	Belgium	Brazil	China	France	Germany	India	Italy	Japan	Russia	Ukraine	United Kingdom	United States	World Total
2001	7,732	27,623	155,540	12,004	29,184	21,900	10,650	78,836	44,980	26,400	9,861	42,125	624,086
2002	8,053	29,667	170,850	13,217	29,427	24,315	9,736	80,979	46,060	27,560	8,561	40,200	653,000
2003	7,813	32,036	213,660	12,756	29,481	26,550	10,604	82,092	48,368	29,570	10,228	40,600	719,000
2004	8,224	34,558	251,850	13,198	30,018	25,117	10,664	82,974	50,427	31,000	10,180	42,300	773,000
2005	7,254	33,884	343,750	12,705	28,854	27,125	11,423	83,058	49,175	30,747	10,236	37,200	858,000
2006	7,516	32,452	412,450	13,013	30,360	28,300	11,535	84,270	51,683	32,926	10,736	37,900	939,000
2007	6,576	35,571	476,520	12,426	31,149	28,800	11,100	86,771	51,523	35,647	10,960	36,300	1,020,000
2008	6,500	34,969	470,670	12,400	29,111	29,000	11,100	86,171	48,300	30,982	11,000	33,700	998,000
2009[1]		35,000	544,000	8,000	20,000	30,000	5,000	86,000	44,000	26,000	8,000	19,000	935,000
2010[2]		23,000	600,000	10,000	29,000	39,000		82,000	47,000	26,000	7,000	29,000	1,000,000

[1] Preliminary.   [2] Estimate.   *Source: U.S. Geological Survey (USGS)*

Production of Pig Iron (Excludes Ferro-Alloys) in the United States   In Thousands of Short Tons

Year	Jan.	Feb.	Mar.	Apr.	May	June	July	Aug.	Sept.	Oct.	Nov.	Dec.	Total
2001	3,808	3,691	4,255	4,183	4,278	4,143	4,048	4,121	3,920	3,837	3,202	2,965	46,451
2002	3,493	3,308	3,616	3,480	3,584	3,612	3,854	3,983	4,006	4,018	3,710	3,677	44,341
2003	3,832	3,631	3,906	3,810	3,381	3,569	3,395	3,253	3,289	3,527	3,530	3,733	42,856
2004	3,682	3,524	4,018	3,749	3,670	3,633	3,590	3,839	3,818	3,940	3,668	3,389	44,520
2005	3,773	3,592	4,030	3,397	3,395	2,962	2,895	3,183	3,127	3,237	3,310	3,135	40,036
2006	3,519	3,421	3,765	3,612	3,816	3,667	3,540	3,525	3,544	3,403	3,059	2,909	41,780
2007	2,850	2,610	3,040	3,010	3,130	3,120	3,080	3,010	3,010	3,200	2,940	3,160	36,160
2008	2,900	3,110	3,280	3,240	3,210	3,020	3,090	3,290	2,900	2,770	2,040	1,690	34,540
2009	1,450	1,510	1,630	1,410	1,370	1,380	1,840	2,090	1,930	2,510	2,240	2,410	21,770
2010[1]	2,350	2,530	2,870	2,030	2,830	2,800	2,450						30,617

[1] Preliminary.   *Source: American Iron and Steel Institute*

Salient Statistics of Ferrous Scrap and Pig Iron in the United States   In Thousands of Metric Tons

	Consumption: Ferrous Scrap & Pig Iron Charged To												Stocks, Dec. 31 Ferrous Scrap & Pig Iron at Consumers		
	Mfg. of Pig Iron & Steel Ingots & Castings			Iron Foundries & Misc. Users			Mfg. of Steel Castings (Scrap)	All Uses			Imports of Scrap[2]	Exports of Scrap[3]			
Year	Scrap	Pig Iron	Total	Scrap	Pig Iron	Total		Ferrous Scrap	Pig Iron	Grand Total					Total
1999	56,000	48,000	106,200	13,000	1,100	14,113	1,900	71,000	49,000	122,200	3,360	5,000	5,450	724	6,174
2000	59,000	49,000	110,300	13,000	1,200	14,216	2,200	74,000	50,000	126,300	3,040	5,230	5,320	930	6,250
2001	56,700	46,900	105,400	12,000	1,100	13,113	2,200	71,000	48,000	120,800	2,630	7,440	4,880	787	5,667
2002	56,400	42,500	101,100	11,000	1,500	12,513	1,800	69,000	44,000	115,200	3,130	8,950	4,930	754	5,684
2003	55,200	39,700	96,670	4,460	655	5,119	2,680	61,900	41,000	104,670	3,480	10,800	4,410	381	4,791
2004	57,100	38,000	96,590	8,490	1,020	9,514	1,330	66,500	39,100	107,100	4,660	11,800	5,400	721	6,121
2005	54,600	36,900	93,240	9,010	1,090	10,103	1,810	65,400	38,000	105,150	3,840	13,000	4,970	664	5,634
2006	54,500	36,700	92,730	9,370	857	10,232	1,640	65,600	37,600	104,740	4,820	14,900	4,370	700	5,070
2007	54,600	36,500	93,140	9,080	1,290	10,374	1,380	65,000	37,800	104,850	3,700	16,500	4,420	771	5,191
2008[1]	56,600	33,500	92,050	7,760	844	8,608	2,070	66,400	34,400	102,760	3,600	21,500	4,630	884	5,514

[1] Preliminary.   [2] Includes tinplate and terneplate.   [3] Excludes used rails for rerolling and other uses and ships, boats, and other vessels for scrapping.
Source: U.S. Geological Survey (USGS)

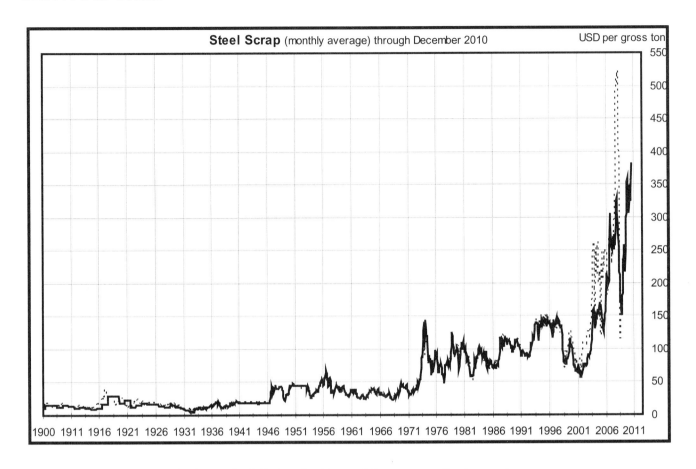

Consumption of Pig Iron in the United States, by Type of Furance or Equipment   In Thousands of Metric Tons

Year	Open Hearth	Electric	Cupola	Basic Oxygen Process	Air & Other Furnace	Direct Casting	Total
1999	----	3,100	520	45,000	W	36	49,000
2000	----	2,900	530	47,000	W	35	50,000
2001	----	2,700	500	45,000	W	36	48,000
2002	----	3,200	520	40,000	W	36	44,000
2003	----	2,310	792	37,900	W	36	41,000
2004	----	3,030	354	35,700	W	36	39,100
2005	----	3,040	528	34,400	W	36	38,000
2006	----	3,380	435	33,800	W	36	37,600
2007[1]	----	3,980	401	33,400	8	36	37,800
2008[2]	----	W	W	30,500	W	W	33,600

[1] Preliminary.   [2] Estimate.   W = Withheld.   *Source: U.S. Geological Survey (USGS)*

Wholesale Price of No. 1 Heavy Melting Steel Scrap in Chicago   In Dollars Per Metric Ton

Year	Jan.	Feb.	Mar.	Apr.	May	June	July	Aug.	Sept.	Oct.	Nov.	Dec.	Average
2001	83.55	74.50	74.50	74.50	73.23	72.50	75.93	76.50	76.50	72.54	67.50	67.50	74.17
2002	70.21	75.03	75.50	85.05	93.09	97.10	97.50	97.50	100.50	98.85	93.50	93.50	89.78
2003	96.93	101.97	105.07	105.50	101.69	96.88	101.05	116.79	122.02	122.50	138.22	159.74	114.03
2004	187.75	219.92	250.85	224.55	181.90	180.00	222.50	249.32	217.38	237.62	248.00	223.57	220.28
2005	203.00	190.00	190.00	217.14	180.95	124.32	135.50	189.78	241.19	204.29	246.25	242.43	197.07
2006	222.70	237.76	237.07	245.00	249.23	249.23	245.25	204.41	207.25	202.55	197.90	203.55	225.16
2007	225.24	252.37	305.00	291.90	255.36	254.71	250.71	257.04	268.74	265.65	252.10	273.42	262.69
2008	334.00	338.70	352.57	482.73	513.10	498.10	510.45	466.43	313.62	188.00	91.67	169.29	354.89
2009	183.00	176.68	157.73	150.00	179.25	185.00	230.00	244.29	257.86	244.76	216.32	251.05	206.33
2010	297.63	305.00	352.83	360.00	338.75	335.00	305.00	325.91	347.14	324.29	338.00	380.00	334.13

Source: American Metal Market (AMM)

World Production of Iron Ore[3]   In Thousands of Metric Tons (Gross Weight)

Year	Australia	Brazil	Canada	China	India	Mauritania	Russia	South Africa	Sweden	Ukraine	United States	Venezuela	World Total
2001	181,553	201,430	27,119	220,000	79,200	10,302	82,500	34,757	19,486	54,650	46,192	16,902	1,046,430
2002	187,198	214,560	30,902	231,000	86,400	9,553	84,236	36,484	20,300	58,900	51,600	16,684	1,100,000
2003	212,981	230,707	33,322	261,000	99,100	10,377	91,760	38,086	21,500	62,498	48,600	17,954	1,210,000
2004	234,000	261,696	28,596	320,000	120,600	10,505	96,980	39,322	22,300	65,550	54,700	19,196	1,360,000
2005	262,000	281,462	30,387	420,000	152,000	11,133	96,764	39,542	23,300	68,570	54,300	21,200	1,550,000
2006	275,000	317,800	33,543	601,000	181,000	10,658	102,000	41,326	23,300	74,000	52,700	22,100	1,840,000
2007	299,000	354,674	32,744	707,000	202,000	11,817	105,000	42,082	24,700	77,900	52,500	20,700	2,040,000
2008	342,000	355,000	31,273	824,000	220,000	10,950	99,900	48,983	23,800	72,700	53,600	20,700	2,220,000
2009[1]	394,000	300,000	32,000	880,000	245,000	10,000	92,000	55,000	18,000	66,000	27,000	15,000	2,240,000
2010[2]	420,000	370,000	35,000	900,000	260,000	11,000	100,000	55,000	25,000	72,000	49,000	16,000	2,400,000

[1] Preliminary.   [2] Estimate.   [3] Iron ore, iron ore concentrates and iron ore agglomerates.   Source: U.S. Geological Survey (USGS)

Salient Statistics of Iron Ore[3] in the United States   In Thousands of Metric Tons

Year	Net Import Reliance As a % of Apparent Consumption	Production Total	Production Lake Superior	Production Other Regions	Shipments	Value Million $ (at Mine)	Average Value $ at Mine Per Ton	Stock, Dec. 31 Mines	Stock, Dec. 31 Consuming Plants	Stock, Dec. 31 Lake Erie Docks	Imports	Exports	Consumption	Total
2001	15	46,200	46,100	NA	50,600	1,210.0	23.87	3,800	12,300	1,960	10,700	5,610	65,700	293.0
2002	11	51,600	51,500	NA	51,500	1,340.0	26.04	4,090	12,400	1,820	12,500	6,750	59,700	313.0
2003	11	48,600	NA	NA	46,100	1,490.0	32.30	4,910	10,900	1,630	12,600	6,770	61,600	328.0
2004	6	54,700	NA	NA	54,900	2,080.0	37.92	3,930	NA	NA	11,800	8,400	64,500	371.0
2005	4	54,300	NA	NA	53,200	2,370.0	44.50	2,040	NA	NA	13,000	11,800	60,100	532.0
2006	8	52,700	NA	NA	52,700	2,840.0	53.88	1,650	NA	NA	11,500	8,270	58,200	611.0
2007	E	52,500	NA	NA	50,900	3,040.0	59.64	2,090	NA	NA	9,400	9,310	54,700	543.0
2008	E	53,600	NA	NA	53,600	3,770.0	70.43	4,070	NA	NA	9,250	11,100	51,900	918.0
2009[1]	E	26,700	NA	NA	27,600		92.80				3,900	3,900	31,000	
2010[2]	E	49,000	NA	NA	50,000		90.00				7,000	11,000	50,000	

[1] Preliminary.   [2] Estimate.   [3] Usable iron ore exclusive of ore containing 5% or more manganese and includes byproduct ore.
NA = Not available.   Source: U.S. Geological Survey (USGS)

U.S. Imports (for Consumption) of Iron Ore[2]   In Thousands of Metric Tons

Year	Australia	Brazil	Canada	Chile	Mauritania	Peru	Sweden	Venezuela	Total
2000	755	6,090	7,990	135	----	40	250	349	15,700
2001	576	4,260	4,530	711	----	71	70	87	10,700
2002	567	5,750	5,540	319	----	86	44	49	12,500
2003	128	4,980	6,970	296	----	77	88	21	12,600
2004	[3]	5,020	5,830	244	----	56	111	262	11,800
2005	1	4,180	7,510	270	----	33	133	148	13,000
2006	8	4,530	6,240	283	----	52	[3]	23	11,500
2007	----	3,210	5,520	279	----	140	141	58	9,400
2008	----	2,620	5,900	215	----	59	88	68	9,250
2009[1]	----	188	3,140	203		34	31	21	3,870

[1] Preliminary.   [2] Including agglomerates.   [3] Less than 1/2 unit.   Source: U.S. Geological Survey (USGS)

Iron Ore Stocks in the United States, at End of Month   In Thousands of Metric Tons

Year	Jan.	Feb.	Mar.	Apr.	May	June	July	Aug.	Sept.	Oct.	Nov.	Dec.
2001	10,712	13,176	14,681	13,839	11,558	9,364	7,433	6,367	6,345	5,659	4,789	3,803
2002	4,980	6,810	8,270	7,740	7,270	6,330	5,020	4,080	3,420	3,290	3,540	3,210
2003	4,640	7,790	10,100	9,500	8,180	7,080	6,550	6,160	5,820	5,640	5,240	3,860
2004	4,220	7,260	8,780	8,360	7,660	7,080	5,670	4,500	3,470	3,850	3,700	2,990
2005	4,060	6,770	8,410	7,690	7,730	7,370	7,420	7,240	6,550	5,840	6,250	5,750
2006	6,750	9,620	11,900	11,100	10,800	10,100	9,353	8,760	8,090	8,120	7,590	5,880
2007	7,330	10,100	11,800	11,000	10,300	9,870	9,340	8,700	7,950	7,660	7,110	6,490
2008	6,930	9,820	12,400	11,300	9,950	9,370	8,170	6,910	6,110	5,800	5,830	6,630
2009	8,680	10,900	12,500	12,300	10,600	9,010	7,410	5,990	5,430	5,130	3,900	3,120
2010[1]	3,760	6,080	7,040	6,030	5,360	4,120	3,730	3,240				

[1] Preliminary.   Source: U.S. Geological Survey (USGS)

Lard

Lard is the layer of fat found along the back and underneath the skin of a hog. The hog's fat is purified by washing it with water, melting it under constant heat, and straining it several times. Lard is an important byproduct of the meatpacking industry. It is valued highly as cooking oil because there is very little smoke when it is heated. However, demand for lard in cooking is declining because of the trend toward healthier eating. Lard is also used for medicinal purposes such as ointments, plasters, liniments, and occasionally as a laxative for children. Lard production is directly proportional to commercial hog production, meaning the largest producers of hogs are the largest producers of lard.

Prices – The average monthly wholesale price of lard in 2010 (through December) rose by +38.1% to 48.50 per pound, a new record high.

Supply – World production of lard in the 2009-10

(latest data) marketing year rose by +2.0% yr/yr to 7.890 million metric tons, which was a new record high. The world's largest lard producers were China (with 43.1% of world production), the U.S (7.4%), Germany (6.8%), Brazil (5.2%), the former USSR (5.2%), Spain (3.6%), and Poland (2.8%). U.S. production of lard in 2009-10 fell -2.1% yr/yr to 1.288 billion pounds.

Demand – U.S. consumption of lard in 2010 rose +19.0% to 359.618 million pounds, down from 2008 record high of 490.602 million pounds. The current level of consumption is less than 20% of the consumption of 1.574 billion pounds in 1971.

Exports – U.S. exports of lard in 2007-08 latest data available) rose by +1.4% to 73.0 million pounds, and accounted for only 6% of U.S. production.

World Production of Lard   In Thousands of Metric Tons

Year	Brazil	Canada	China	France	Germany	Italy	Japan	Poland	Romania	Spain	United States	Ex-USSR	World Total
2001-02	361.4	112.1	2,920.9	157.4	422.3	199.3	61.8	252.0	76.9	263.9	508.1	324.6	6,963.7
2002-03	350.2	124.2	3,040.4	156.2	433.7	204.8	59.3	272.5	60.1	280.9	510.0	346.0	7,166.8
2003-04	337.2	127.0	3,154.3	155.5	439.5	208.3	59.3	257.7	69.4	273.4	531.7	334.1	7,308.2
2004-05	344.2	127.4	3,317.8	153.4	456.9	199.2	59.4	243.8	58.9	278.1	532.4	314.4	7,475.3
2005-06	368.9	126.5	3,371.0	151.3	471.3	200.9	55.9	266.4	66.7	282.1	541.3	324.1	7,647.1
2006-07	382.5	126.1	3,181.3	152.2	501.2	207.7	54.2	270.9	76.2	300.5	552.7	362.1	7,629.3
2007-08[1]	388.4	123.7	3,192.7	153.0	520.1	208.7	54.7	249.9	75.0	308.5	605.3	386.3	7,734.5
2008-09[2]	399.4	120.4	3,280.9	140.6	532.9	207.9	52.9	208.9	72.1	293.0	597.3	389.9	7,736.2
2009-10[3]	407.0	122.7	3,402.7	134.1	540.4	206.5	52.4	219.3	71.9	280.8	584.6	407.1	7,890.0

[1] Preliminary.   [2] Estimate.   [3] Forecast.   *Source: The Oil World*

Supply and Distribution of Lard in the United States   In Millions of Pounds

Year	Production	Stocks Oct. 1	Total Supply	Domestic	Baking or Frying Fats	Margarine[3]	Exports	Total Disappearance	Direct Use	Per Capita (Lbs.)
2001-02	1,058.0	16.2	1,077.0	626.7	W	6.0	103.3	730.0	325.4	1.1
2002-03	1,083.0	13.6	1,105.0	670.9	W	7.0	84.2	755.2	370.3	1.3
2003-04	1,090.0	10.5	1,108.0	639.6	W	16.0	117.3	756.9	368.5	1.3
2004-05	1,117.0	13.3	1,136.0	487.8	W	6.0	289.2	777.0	220.2	0.7
2005-06	1,193.3	13.8	1,207.1	694.8	W	3.0	93.8	788.6	459.7	1.5
2006-07	1,218.5	9.4	1,227.9	718.5	W	W	71.9	790.4	498.6	1.7
2007-08	1,334.4	14.2	1,348.6	756.8	W	W	72.9	829.7	486.7	1.6
2008-09[1]	1,316.8	13.9	1,330.7	800.9	W	W	81.4	882.3	310.3	1.0
2009-10[2]	1,288.8	17.5	1,306.3	784.1	W	W	71.4	855.5	461.6	1.5

[1] Preliminary.   [2] Forecast.   [3] Includes edible tallow.   W = Withheld.
Source: Economic Research Service, U.S. Department of Agriculture (ERS-USDA)

Consumption of Lard (Edible and Inedible) in the United States   In Millions of Pounds

Year	Jan.	Feb.	Mar.	Apr.	May	June	July	Aug.	Sept.	Oct.	Nov.	Dec.	Total
2001	27.8	22.2	28.3	24.5	22.5	23.3	21.8	27.1	23.2	27.9	26.7	24.4	299.8
2002	26.4	26.1	21.8	26.7	24.8	21.2	22.9	26.4	23.6	26.4	28.1	28.7	303.2
2003	22.6	22.3	23.4	21.4	23.3	24.0	23.0	21.4	22.5	24.3	20.2	21.0	269.5
2004	22.9	25.8	25.9	23.9	23.5	22.0	19.1	19.7	21.3	22.4	21.9	19.9	268.1
2005	19.0	15.4	21.4	18.7	19.9	20.4	18.9	19.5	20.1	19.7	22.2	17.9	233.1
2006	15.7	16.4	20.6	21.4	20.2	16.7	14.9	17.7	17.8	18.9	22.3	20.9	223.4
2007	21.6	16.2	22.2	19.7	20.5	20.8	22.8	23.9	22.8	31.1	29.7	31.4	282.8
2008	34.8	32.2	44.6	50.7	50.8	44.4	47.8	39.7	44.0	37.5	31.7	32.2	490.6
2009	23.4	17.3	26.8	26.0	26.3	25.8	21.3	20.5	25.4	32.4	29.9	27.0	302.3
2010[1]	22.2	W	38.8	W	30.4	30.8	30.4	32.4	30.1	31.1	30.4	30.3	360.0

[1] Preliminary.   *Source: Bureau of the Census, U.S. Department of Commerce*

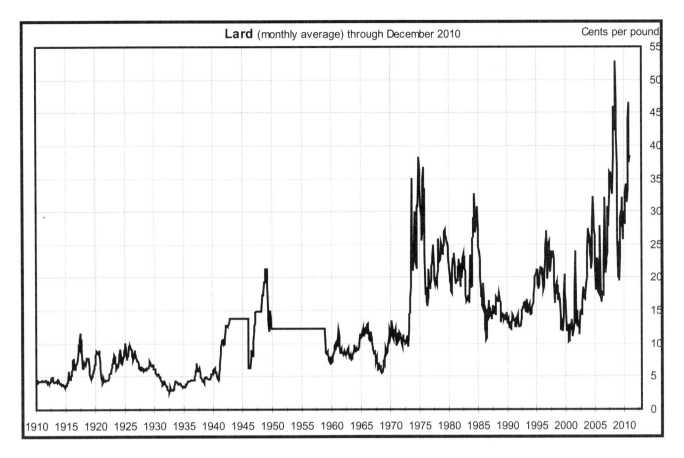

Lard (monthly average) through December 2010 — Cents per pound

Average Wholesale Price of Lard--Loose, Tank Cars, in Chicago   In Cents Per Pound

Year	Jan.	Feb.	Mar.	Apr.	May	June	July	Aug.	Sept.	Oct.	Nov.	Dec.	Average
2001	13.57	11.92	11.07	12.09	11.84	13.38	18.05	24.11	22.00	13.04	13.18	14.92	14.93
2002	12.69	12.50	13.07	12.42	11.38	14.64	14.60	15.00	15.21	14.39	16.28	18.42	14.22
2003	18.61	17.11	16.85	16.72	17.29	18.90	18.93	20.08	23.98	27.50	26.40	25.18	20.63
2004	26.50	25.83	23.77	22.58	21.31	22.50	27.53	32.06	32.38	27.95	27.26	26.50	26.35
2005	22.10	18.30	17.71	20.72	22.95	21.30	18.08	17.75	20.97	27.38	27.76	18.60	21.14
2006	17.16	16.44	16.82	18.00	17.13	17.63	22.21	29.91	31.86	23.55	20.78	22.58	21.17
2007	23.00	23.82	30.75	27.71	28.60	32.64	36.00	35.77	36.00	35.09	33.78	32.66	31.32
2008	33.01	38.33	46.00	43.04	42.27	44.93	52.82	46.50	41.73	37.07	26.40	20.00	39.34
2009	25.36	20.31	19.49	23.36	29.00	30.06	27.63	32.20	29.73	25.75	30.07	28.75	26.81
2010	28.60	28.25	32.95	33.95	34.24	32.98	31.42	33.33	43.59	46.64	37.32	38.30	35.13

Source: Economic Research Service, U.S. Department of Agriculture (ERS-USDA)

Cold Storage Holdings of all Lard[1] in the United States, on First of Month   In Millions of Pounds

Year	Jan.	Feb.	Mar.	Apr.	May	June	July	Aug.	Sept.	Oct.	Nov.	Dec.
2001	16.0	14.9	14.9	17.9	13.7	13.1	10.3	12.4	11.8	13.6	13.0	11.7
2002	13.2	18.0	16.4	16.5	20.3	22.4	18.9	18.3	12.0	10.5	14.6	11.3
2003	10.5	14.0	19.6	18.7	16.5	13.5	11.9	9.7	8.4	9.3	10.1	12.4
2004	13.3	19.8	18.6	20.3	20.5	15.0	12.9	10.8	10.3	11.8	11.4	13.2
2005	13.7	14.6	20.6	19.0	17.8	12.3	12.0	12.3	12.5	13.0	12.2	14.7
2006	9.6	11.5	13.7	13.6	9.3	9.9	13.0	12.4	13.0	11.5	16.1	16.0
2007	16.4	14.9	13.3	18.5	10.9	14.6	11.3	12.8	11.0	9.2	14.6	18.8
2008	14.0	22.4	20.4	22.9	23.0	19.5	22.7	13.6	18.0	17.8	16.1	20.4
2009	12.1	13.6	15.4	16.2	14.5	18.8	17.3	21.6	20.5	26.7	18.5	15.4
2010[2]	13.9	14.5	21.0	22.9	26.1	15.7	19.4	17.9	14.1	13.8	15.6	15.5

[1] Stocks in factories and warehouses (except that in hands of retailers).   [2] Preliminary.   *Source: Bureau of the Census, U.S. Department of Commerce*

Lead

Lead (symbol Pb) is a dense, toxic, bluish-gray metallic element, and is the heaviest stable element. Lead was one of the first known metals. The ancients used lead in face powders, rouges, mascaras, paints, condiments, wine preservatives, and water supply plumbing. The Romans were slowly poisoned from lead because of its diverse daily usage.

Lead is usually found in ore with zinc, silver, and most often copper. The most common lead ore is galena, containing 86.6% lead. Cerussite and angleside are other common varieties of lead. More than half of the lead currently used comes from recycling.

Lead is used in building construction, bullets and shot, tank and pipe lining, storage batteries, and electric cable sheathing. Lead is used extensively as a protective shielding for radioactive material (e.g., X-ray apparatus) because of its high density and nuclear properties. Lead is also part of solder, pewter, and fusible alloys.

Lead futures and options trade at the London Metal Exchange (LME). The LME lead futures contract calls for the delivery of 25 metric tons of at least 99.970% purity lead ingots (pigs). The contract is priced in U.S. dollars per metric ton. Lead first started trading on the LME in 1903.

Prices – The price of lead at the beginning of 2010 was about $2,400 per metric ton. The price then rallied to about $2,600 in February, and then moved lower to about $1,600 in May. From there the price moved higher to close the year at about $2,500. In January of 2011 the price moved higher to about $2,700 per metric ton by March.

Supply – World smelter production of lead (both primary and secondary) in 2009 (the latest data available) rose +1.4% yr/yr to 8.820 million metric tons to post a new record high production level. The world's largest smelter producers of lead (both primary and secondary) are China with 42% of world production in 2009, followed by the U.S. with 14%, Germany with 4%, and with the UK, Australia, Canada, Japan, each with 3%.

U.S. mine production of recoverable lead fell -1.0% yr/yr to a 14-year low of 395,000 metric tons in 2009 (latest data available). Missouri was responsible for 94% of U.S. production, with the remainder produced mainly by Idaho and Montana. Lead recovered from scrap in the U.S. (secondary production) fell -1.1% yr/yr in 2010 (through December, annualized) to 1.138 million metric tons, down from the 2008 record high of 1.220 metric tons. The amount of lead recovered from scrap is almost three times twice the amount of lead produced in the U.S. from mines (primary production). The value of U.S. secondary lead production in 2009 (latest data available) fell by -29.9% to $2.130 billion, down from the 2007 record high of $3.220 billion.

Demand – U.S. lead consumption in 2010 (through December, annualized) fell -1.3% to 1.405 million metric tons, which was a 15-year low. The record level of U.S. lead consumption was 1.680 million metric tons posted in 1999.

Trade – The U.S. relied on imports for 8% of its lead consumption in 2001 but has been a net exporter ever since. U.S. imports of lead pigs and bars in 2009 (latest data available) fell -18.8% yr/yr to 251,000 metric tons. U.S. lead exports in 2009 were comprised of ore concentrate (287,000 metric tons), scrap (140,000 metric tons), unwrought lead (77,600 metric tons), and wrought lead (4,310 metric tons).

World Smelter (Primary and Secondary) Production of Lead   In Thousands of Metric Tons

Year	Australia[3]	Belgium[4]	Canada[3]	China[2]	France	Germany	Italy	Japan	Mexico[3]	Spain	United Kingdom[3]	United States	World Total
2001	303.0	96.0	230.9	1,200.0	238.0	373.4	203.0	302.4	253.5	98.0	366.0	1,390	6,600
2002	304.0	88.0	251.6	1,330.0	204.0	379.9	205.0	285.8	237.2	116.0	374.6	1,360	6,800
2003	295.0	65.0	223.4	1,580.0	96.7	356.9	246.0	295.3	247.5	102.0	364.6	1,380	6,990
2004	268.0	63.0	241.2	1,940.0	105.6	359.2	202.0	282.9	217.4	105.6	245.9	1,280	7,040
2005	263.0	83.4	230.2	2,390.0	105.0	417.7	211.5	274.6	226.5	110.0	304.4	1,300	7,660
2006	233.0	54.0	250.5	2,720.0	104.2	379.0	190.5	279.4	212.5	110.0	307.7	1,310	7,970
2007	229.0	117.0	236.7	2,790.0	104.2	405.1	210.0	276.3	212.0	110.0	300.0	1,300	8,250
2008[1]	248.0	101.0	259.1	3,200.0	92.0	415.1	211.8	279.5	199.8	110.0	294.0	1,280	8,700
2009[2]	229.0	100.0	258.9	3,710.0	92.0	391.0	149.0	275.0	210.4	110.0	294.0	1,210	8,820

[1] Preliminary.   [2] Estimate.   [3] Refinded & bullion.   [4] Includes scrap.   Source: U.S. Geological Survey (USGS)

Consumption of Lead in the United States, by Products   In Metric Tons

Year	Ammunition	Bearing Metals	Pipes, Traps & Bends[2]	Cable Covering	Calking Lead	Casting Metals	Other Metal Products[3]	Total Other Oxides[4]	Sheet Lead	Solder	-- Storage Battery -- Grids, Post, etc.	Oxides	Brass and Bronze	Total Consumption
2001	53,600	837	2,370	W	927	31,800	17,100	43,900	22,400	6,120	655,000	694,000	2,590	1,550,000
2002	57,600	406	2,250	W	1,060	34,800	24,200	51,900	25,600	6,450	554,000	641,000	2,730	1,440,000
2003	48,800	13,500	1,550	W	822	31,700	9,730	35,600	24,400	6,310	523,000	642,000	2,810	1,390,000
2004	61,500	1,300	W	W	W	17,900	W	25,700	31,600	7,440	657,000	630,000	2,390	1,480,000
2005	61,300	1,180	1,220	W	W	30,400	22,200	14,100	29,100	8,370	579,000	705,000	2,100	1,490,000
2006	65,700	1,240	1,440	W	W	29,900	23,400	16,000	28,400	7,280	586,000	710,000	3,130	1,490,000
2007	69,400	1,410	1,230	W	W	31,500	23,600	15,800	28,600	7,220	640,000	738,000	2,870	1,570,000
2008	67,400	1,250	1,190	W	W	20,100	7,670	10,700	26,400	6,610	575,000	715,000	2,460	1,440,000
2009[1]	67,900	1,100	1,130	W	W	15,900	5,790	10,100	25,400	6,450	389,000	750,000	1,370	1,290,000

[1] Preliminary.   [2] Including building.   [3] Including terne metal, type metal, and lead consumed in foil, collapsible tubes, annealing, plating, galvanizing and fishing weights.   [4] Includes paints, glass and ceramic products, and other pigments and chemicals.   W = Withheld.
Source: U.S. Geological Survey (USGS)

Salient Statistics of Lead in the United States   In Thousands of Metric Tons

Year	Net Import Reliance as a % of Apparent Consumption	Production of Refined Lead From Domestic Ores[3]		Foreighn Ores[3]	Total Primary	Total Value of Refined Million $	As Soft Lead	In Anti-monial Lead	In Other Alloys	Total	Total Value of Secondary Million USD	Primary	Con-sumer[4]	New York	London
2001	8	290.0	W	290.0	279.0	734.0	291.0	75.9	1,100.0	1,060.0	W	100.0	43.64	21.58
2002	E	262.0	W	262.0	252.0	754.0	289.0	72.8	1,120.0	1,070.0	W	111.0	43.56	20.52
2003	E	245.0	W	245.0	236.0	829.0	303.0	4.2	1,140.0	1,110.0	W	84.6	43.76	23.34
2004	E	148.0	W	148.0	143.0	841.0	283.0	3.0	1,130.0	1,370.0	W	59.0	55.14	40.19
2005	E	143.0	W	143.0	----	869.0	271.0	4.5	1,150.0	1,550.0	W	46.8	61.03	44.23
2006	E	153.0	W	153.0	----	948.0	200.0	12.4	1,160.0	1,980.0	W	54.8	77.40	58.00
2007	E	123.0	W	123.0	----	1,020.0	160.0	2.4	1,180.0	3,220.0	W	39.0	123.84	117.00
2008	E	135.0	W	135.0	----	1,000.0	140.0	2.4	1,140.0	3,040.0	W	72.5	120.33	94.79
2009[1]	E	103.0	W	103.0	----	960.0	151.0	NA	1,110.0	2,130.0	W	63.0	86.87	77.95
2010[2]	E	115.0	W	115.0	----				1,150.0		W	58.0	106.00	94.00

[1] Preliminary.   [2] Estimate.   [3] And base bullion.   [4] Also at secondary smelters.   W = Withheld.   E = Net exporter.
Source: U.S. Geological Survey (USGS)

U.S. Foreign Trade of Lead   In Thousands of Metric Tons

Year	Ore Con-centrate	Un-wrought Lead[3]	Wrought Lead[4]	Scrap	Ash & Re-sidues[5]	Ores, Flue Dust or Fume & Mattes	Base Bullion	Pigs & Bars	Re-claimed Scrap, Etc.	Value Million $	Aus-tralia	Can-ada	Peru	Can-ada	Mexico	Peru
2000	117.0	21.4	27.2	71.6	11.3	31.2	0.1	356.0	0.0	217.1	----	5	10.8	216.0	18.4	1.8
2001	181.0	17.0	17.7	108.0	14.2	2.2	----	271.0	10.2	166.8	----	----	----	167.0	12.4	2.3
2002	241.0	31.4	11.7	106.0	----	0.0	----	210.0	2.6	124.9	----	----	----	172.0	7.5	----
2003	253.0	92.1	30.5	92.8	----	----	----	175.0	4.2	111.9	----	----	----	167.0	8.3	----
2004	292.0	58.6	23.8	56.3	----	----	----	197.0	4.8	235.3	----	----	----	166.0	8.8	7.3
2005	390.2	45.5	19.0	67.3	----	----	----	298.0	3.3	334.8	----	----	----	190.0	15.2	23.9
2006	297.6	52.7	15.8	120.9	----	----	0.5	331.0	1.6	450.8	----	----	----	222.0	15.8	34.6
2007	300.0	51.8	4.6	129.0	----	----	2.0	263.0	2.4	591.4	----	----	----	208.0	35.6	16.5
2008[1]	277.0	68.1	6.2	175.0	----	----	2.7	309.0	1.3	681.6	----	----	----	219.0	58.1	10.6
2009[2]	287.0	77.6	4.3	140.0	----	----	0.8	251.0	1.3	418.8	----	----	----	205.0	41.1	1.0

[1] Preliminary.   [2] Estimate.   [3] And lead alloys.   [4] Blocks, pigs, etc.   [5] Less than 1/2 unit.   *Source: U.S. Geological Survey (USGS)*

Annual Mine Production of Recoverable Lead in the United States   In Metric Tons

Year	Total	Idaho	Missouri	Montana	Other States	Missouri's % of Total
2000	449,000	W	410,000	W	38,700	91%
2001	454,000	W	423,000	W	30,900	93%
2002	440,000	W	428,000	W	12,300	97%
2003	449,000	W	432,000	W	17,200	96%
2004	430,000	W	407,000	W	23,400	95%
2005	426,000	W	397,000	W	29,500	93%
2006	419,000	W	393,000	W	26,100	94%
2007	434,000	W	400,000	W	34,200	92%
2008[1]	399,000	W	360,000	W	38,600	90%
2009[2]	395,000	W	370,000	W	24,900	94%

[1] Preliminary.   [2] Estimate.   W = Withheld, included in Other States.   *Source: U.S. Geological Survey (USGS)*

Mine Production of Recoverable Lead in the United States   In Thousands of Metric Tons

Year	Jan.	Feb.	Mar.	Apr.	May	June	July	Aug.	Sept.	Oct.	Nov.	Dec.	Total
2001	42.9	37.8	39.4	33.7	35.0	32.2	38.2	39.6	32.4	39.5	32.1	35.4	450.0
2002	39.5	35.5	41.2	36.1	39.3	36.1	35.0	39.6	33.2	34.8	34.1	34.2	438.6
2003	33.7	34.9	38.5	36.2	38.8	39.2	41.3	38.0	38.3	37.2	34.0	33.9	444.0
2004	33.4	32.8	33.5	35.1	31.2	33.1	33.8	36.9	36.9	36.2	35.0	31.8	409.7
2005	31.1	31.1	34.6	35.2	33.4	41.4	39.5	37.4	38.2	37.9	34.6	37.9	432.3
2006	36.7	33.3	38.1	33.6	33.4	33.9	36.6	36.3	37.0	38.0	35.0	29.6	421.5
2007	38.1	33.9	36.7	31.6	36.9	34.5	38.7	41.3	34.6	39.4	31.5	37.1	434.3
2008	38.0	36.9	36.1	33.0	31.0	34.4	37.8	34.2	33.8	29.1	27.8	33.7	405.8
2009	33.8	30.5	32.8	34.7	33.6	33.7	29.9	35.7	35.6	36.9	28.5	32.8	398.5
2010[1]	31.6	28.6	32.7	31.5	29.7	26.5	29.5	26.9	30.1	31.3	27.8	30.0	356.2

[1] Preliminary.   *Source: U.S. Geological Survey (USGS)*

LEAD

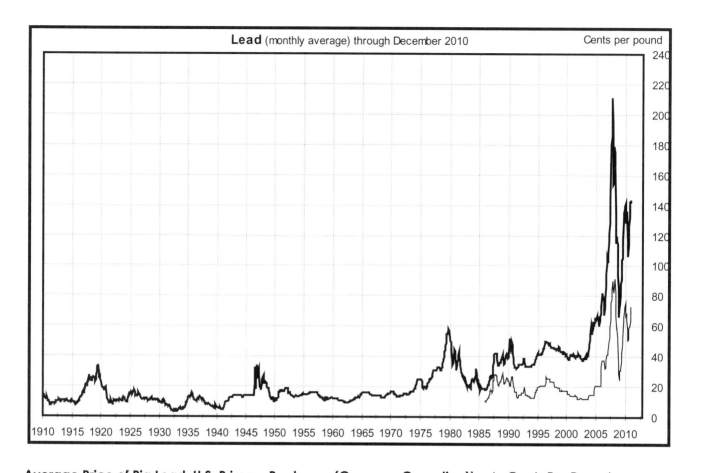

Lead (monthly average) through December 2010 — Cents per pound

Average Price of Pig Lead, U.S. Primary Producers (Common Corroding)[1]   In Cents Per Pound

Year	Jan.	Feb.	Mar.	Apr.	May	June	July	Aug.	Sept.	Oct.	Nov.	Dec.	Average
2001	45.00	45.00	45.00	45.00	45.00	45.00	45.00	45.00	45.00	45.00	45.00	45.00	45.00
2002	45.00	45.00	45.00	45.00	45.00	45.00	45.00	45.00	45.00	45.00	45.00	45.00	45.00
2003	23.14	24.65	23.81	23.13	24.56	24.77	26.93	26.05	27.23	30.16	32.09	35.46	26.83
2004	38.48	44.79	45.30	39.93	42.44	45.16	48.20	47.46	48.08	48.01	49.54	49.75	45.60
2005	50.46	52.20	54.00	53.25	53.41	53.26	47.22	47.53	49.76	54.01	54.68	59.63	52.45
2006	66.16	67.16	63.28	61.58	61.16	51.92	56.07	61.48	69.24	77.64	82.09	86.22	67.00
2007	83.62	88.42	94.72	98.73	103.14	117.95	148.17	148.47	153.50	175.59	159.80	124.81	124.74
2008	125.37	146.72	141.77	134.92	106.42	88.93	93.68	92.49	90.49	73.02	65.52	49.58	100.74
2009	57.27	55.74	61.81	67.86	70.02	80.87	81.05	91.57	104.06	105.75	109.61	110.96	83.05
2010	113.15	102.18	104.73	108.78	92.43	83.23	89.48	99.29	104.31	113.11	113.59	114.22	103.21

[1] New York Delivery.   *Source: American Metal Market*

Refiners Production[1] of Lead in the United States   In Metric Tons

Year	Jan.	Feb.	Mar.	Apr.	May	June	July	Aug.	Sept.	Oct.	Nov.	Dec.	Total
2001	NA	NA	NA	NA	NA	NA	NA	NA	NA	NA	NA	NA	290,000
2002	NA	NA	NA	NA	NA	NA	NA	NA	NA	NA	NA	NA	262,000
2003	NA	NA	NA	NA	NA	NA	NA	NA	NA	NA	NA	NA	245,000
2004	NA	NA	NA	NA	NA	NA	NA	NA	NA	NA	NA	NA	NA
2005	NA	NA	NA	NA	NA	NA	NA	NA	NA	NA	NA	NA	143,000
2006	NA	NA	NA	NA	NA	NA	NA	NA	NA	NA	NA	NA	143,000
2007	NA	NA	NA	NA	NA	NA	NA	NA	NA	NA	NA	NA	NA
2008	NA	NA	NA	NA	NA	NA	NA	NA	NA	NA	NA	NA	NA
2009	NA	NA	NA	NA	NA	NA	NA	NA	NA	NA	NA	NA	NA
2010[2]	NA	NA	NA	NA	NA	NA	NA	NA	NA	NA	NA	NA	NA

[1] Represents refined lead produced from domestic ores by primary smelters plus small amounts of secondary material passing through these smelters. Includes GSA metal purchased for remelt.   [2] Preliminary.   NA = Not available.   *Source: U.S. Geological Survey (USGS)*

Total Stocks of Lead[1] in the United States at Refiners, at End of Month   In Metric Tons

Year	Jan.	Feb.	Mar.	Apr.	May	June	July	Aug.	Sept.	Oct.	Nov.	Dec.
2001	NA	NA	NA	NA	NA	NA	NA	NA	NA	NA	NA	NA
2002	NA	NA	NA	NA	NA	NA	NA	NA	NA	NA	NA	NA
2003	NA	NA	NA	NA	NA	NA	NA	NA	NA	NA	NA	NA
2004	NA	NA	NA	NA	NA	NA	NA	NA	NA	NA	NA	NA
2005	NA	NA	NA	NA	NA	NA	NA	NA	NA	NA	NA	NA
2006	NA	NA	NA	NA	NA	NA	NA	NA	NA	NA	NA	NA
2007	NA	NA	NA	NA	NA	NA	NA	NA	NA	NA	NA	NA
2008	NA	NA	NA	NA	NA	NA	NA	NA	NA	NA	NA	NA
2009	NA	NA	NA	NA	NA	NA	NA	NA	NA	NA	NA	NA
2010[2]	NA	NA	NA	NA	NA	NA	NA	NA	NA	NA	NA	NA

[1] Primary refineries.   [2] Preliminary.   NA = Not available.   *Source: U.S. Geological Survey (USGS)*

Total[1] Lead Consumption in the United States   In Thousands of Metric Tons

Year	Jan.	Feb.	Mar.	Apr.	May	June	July	Aug.	Sept.	Oct.	Nov.	Dec.	Total
2001	145.0	135.0	133.0	130.0	138.0	136.0	135.0	136.0	142.0	146.0	138.0	138.0	1,652
2002	132.0	131.0	133.0	142.0	142.0	144.0	143.0	145.0	141.0	145.0	142.0	133.0	1,673
2003	134.0	129.0	126.0	120.0	121.0	121.0	121.0	122.0	123.0	127.0	122.0	125.0	1,491
2004	119.0	118.0	119.0	119.0	117.0	119.0	118.0	118.0	117.0	117.0	117.0	119.0	1,417
2005	125.0	117.0	109.0	108.0	134.0	130.0	124.0	129.0	126.0	126.0	126.0	126.0	1,480
2006	124.0	130.0	129.0	128.0	128.0	128.0	125.0	126.0	127.0	128.0	126.0	126.0	1,525
2007	130.0	128.0	129.0	128.0	131.0	139.0	131.0	134.0	132.0	137.0	132.0	127.0	1,578
2008	140.0	136.0	130.0	135.0	135.0	141.0	134.0	129.0	134.0	136.0	127.0	126.0	1,603
2009	123.0	119.0	116.0	124.0	116.0	117.0	116.0	115.0	118.0	122.0	121.0	117.0	1,424
2010[2]	119.0	118.0	114.0	115.0	117.0	118.0	116.0	117.0	118.0	117.0	118.0	118.0	1,405

[1] Represents total consumption of primary & secondary lead as metal, in chemicals, or in alloys.   [2] Preliminary.   *Source: U.S. Geological Survey (USGS)*

Lead Recovered from Scrap in the United States   In Thousands of Metric Tons (Lead Content)

Year	Jan.	Feb.	Mar.	Apr.	May	June	July	Aug.	Sept.	Oct.	Nov.	Dec.	Total
2001	90.3	90.4	86.7	92.6	93.7	93.6	90.4	95.1	93.9	96.7	94.6	94.6	1,112.6
2002	89.3	82.3	88.2	93.1	93.9	93.6	88.0	96.1	93.3	97.5	95.0	95.7	1,106.0
2003	95.7	83.6	86.2	85.1	94.0	94.8	95.7	93.9	93.3	102.0	93.7	95.2	1,113.2
2004	94.0	94.2	96.3	97.9	94.4	96.6	97.4	96.3	94.8	96.8	94.9	95.4	1,149.0
2005	94.4	95.1	86.8	86.8	87.1	94.6	94.7	94.8	93.0	95.9	96.4	92.4	1,112.0
2006	90.2	96.7	97.4	98.2	99.5	95.7	94.9	97.0	95.6	98.4	98.4	95.9	1,157.9
2007	99.0	96.5	98.6	93.5	94.5	100.0	103.0	103.0	101.0	104.0	104.0	94.6	1,191.7
2008	104.0	98.2	102.0	100.0	105.0	102.0	92.0	102.0	91.7	100.0	122.0	101.0	1,219.9
2009	97.3	99.0	101.0	90.2	91.6	93.8	97.0	97.2	90.9	96.3	98.0	98.0	1,150.3
2010[1]	96.2	95.2	92.1	86.3	89.8	92.9	94.2	98.0	95.6	101.0	100.0	96.8	1,138.1

[1] Preliminary.   *Source: U.S. Geological Survey (USGS)*

Domestic Shipments[1] of Lead in the United States, by Refiners   In Thousands of Short Tons

Year	Jan.	Feb.	Mar.	Apr.	May	June	July	Aug.	Sept.	Oct.	Nov.	Dec.	Total
1989	29.3	28.5	32.2	35.7	45.1	36.4	32.8	41.5	40.0	44.2	40.2	31.1	437.1
1990	39.3	33.9	39.1	33.5	38.4	32.9	32.6	38.9	36.6	38.9	37.9	31.7	433.7
1991	35.4	33.8	34.3	39.8	33.9	26.0	31.8	37.9	35.1	35.7	28.7	26.7	399.2
1992	31.3	23.9	30.4	26.3	25.6	27.2	27.3	28.7	26.3	28.5	26.3	21.7	323.5
1993	24.6	23.6	32.5	30.0	31.3	35.1	28.9	34.0	35.5	35.5	31.7	33.5	376.2
1994	35.9	32.8	35.2	32.7	34.7	36.7	31.6	33.4	34.8	34.3	34.0	33.3	409.3
1995	36.5	30.3	35.1	31.1	33.7	31.9	28.6	40.3	34.9	40.9	33.2	29.8	406.4
1996	37.2	32.4	29.5	30.2	29.4	26.7	27.7	33.5	30.1	33.5	28.1	27.6	366.0
1997[2]	31.5	27.8	24.7	35.2	39.2	36.1	33.4	29.4	26.4	31.5	30.4	28.1	377.8
1998[2]	Data no longer available.												

[1] Includes GSA metal.   [2] Preliminary.   *Source: American Metal Market (AMM)*

Lumber and Plywood

Humans have utilized lumber for construction for thousands of years, but due to the heaviness of timber and the manual methods of harvesting, large-scale lumbering didn't occur until the mechanical advances of the Industrial Revolution. Lumber is produced from both hardwood and softwood. Hardwood lumber comes from deciduous trees that have broad leaves. Most hardwood lumber is used for miscellaneous industrial applications, primarily wood pallets, and includes oak, gum, maple, and ash. Hardwood species with beautiful colors and patterns are used for such high-grade products as furniture, flooring, paneling, and cabinets and include black walnut, black cherry, and red oak. Wood from cone-bearing trees is called softwood, regardless of its actual hardness. Most lumber from the U.S. is softwood. Softwoods, such as southern yellow pine, Douglas fir, ponderosa pine, and true firs, are primarily used as structural lumber such as 2x4s and 2x6s, poles, paper and cardboard.

Plywood consists of several thin layers of veneer bonded together with adhesives. The veneer sheets are layered so that the grain of one sheet is perpendicular to that of the next, which makes plywood exceptionally strong for its weight. Most plywood has from three to nine layers of wood. Plywood manufacturers use both hard and soft woods, although hardwoods serve primarily for appearance and are not as strong as those made from softwoods. Plywood is primarily used in construction, particularly for floors, roofs, walls, and doors. Homebuilding and remodeling account for two-thirds of U.S. lumber consumption. The price of lumber and plywood is highly correlated with the strength of the U.S. home-building market.

The forest and wood products industry is dominated by Weyerhaeuser Company (ticker symbol WY), which has about $20 billion in annual sales. Weyerhaeuser is a forest products conglomerate that engages not only in growing and harvesting timber, but also in the production and distribution of forest products, real estate development, and construction of single-family homes. Forest products include wood products, pulp and paper, and containerboard. The timberland segment of the business manages 7.2 million acres of company-owned land and 800,000 acres of leased commercial forestlands in North America. The company's Canadian division has renewable, long-term licenses on about 35 million acres of forestland in five Canadian provinces. In order to maximize its long-term yield from its acreage, Weyerhaeuser engages in a number of forest management activities such as extensive planting, suppression of non-merchantable species, thinning, fertilization, and operational pruning.

Lumber futures and options are traded on the Chicago Mercantile Exchange (CME). The CME's lumber futures contract calls for the delivery of 111,000 board feet (one 73 foot rail car) of random length 8 to 12 foot 2 x 4s, the type used in construction. The contract is priced in terms of dollars per thousand board feet.

Prices – CME lumber futures prices rallied early in 2010 and posted a 4-year high of $327 in April, but then fell sharply in May and June. Lumber futures prices then staged a new rally through year-end that led to a close for 2010 of +47% at $302.

Supply – The U.S. led the world in the production of industrial round wood but in 2009 (latest data) production fell -9.6% yr/yr to 304.398 million cubic meters, followed by Canada with 105.108 million cubic meters (-20.5% yr/yr), and Russia with 112.900 million cubic meters (-17.4% yr/yr). The U.S. also led the world in the production of plywood with 10.378.846 million cubic meters of production in 2009 (-14.7% yr/yr), followed by Russia with 2.107 million cubic meters (-18.7% yr/yr), and then Canada with 2.096 million cubic meters (5.8% yr/yr). U.S. softwood lumber production in latest data from the series of 2006 (latest data annualized through November) fell 4.4% yr/yr to 38.503 billion board feet.

Demand – U.S. consumption of softwood lumber in 2006, the last reporting year, fell by 1.9% yr/yr to 63.080 billion board feet.

Trade – U.S. total lumber imports in 2006, the last reporting year, fell 1.8% to 25.285 billion board feet, down from last year's record high. U.S. imports of hardwood in 2006 fell by 3.1% to 1,042 million board feet. U.S. imports of softwood in 2006 fell by 1.7% to 24.214 billion board feet. The leading softwood import was spruce with 1.730 billion board feet of imports in 20065, followed by cedar at 721 million board feet.

Total U.S. exports of lumber in 2006 (latest data) rose +3.6% yr/yr to 2.779 billion board feet, which is a 6-year high. The record high was 4.528 billion board feet in 1988. U.S. exports of hardwood in 2006 rose by +21.7% yr/yr to 1.797 billion board feet. U.S. exports of softwood in 2006 rose by 9.5% yr/yr to 982 million board feet. The largest types of U.S. softwood exports in 2006 were southern pine with 232 million board feet of exports, Ponderosa white pine (114 million board feet), and Douglas Fir (76 million board feet). The world's largest exporter of plywood in 2009 was Russia with 1.334 million cubic meters of exports, followed by Finland with 683 million cubic meters, and Belgium with 379 thousand cubic meters.

World Production of Industrial Roundwood by Selected Countries   In Thousands of Cubic Meters

Year	Austria	Canada	Czech Republic	Finland	France	Germany	Poland	Romania	Russia	Spain	Sweden	Turkey	United States
2000	10,416	198,918	13,501	50,147	39,476	51,088	24,489	10,116	105,800	12,721	57,400	10,429	420,619
2001	10,562	182,945	13,364	47,727	33,792	36,502	23,375	9,806	117,800	13,276	57,300	9,976	403,212
2002	11,810	195,211	13,534	48,529	29,384	37,755	24,995	12,092	118,600	13,850	60,700	11,191	404,958
2003	13,719	176,799	13,960	49,246	27,459	45,415	27,204	12,537	126,600	14,075	61,200	10,729	405,613
2004	12,943	205,273	14,411	49,281	28,187	48,657	29,337	12,794	130,600	14,235	61,400	11,225	418,131
2005	12,786	200,247	14,285	47,116	28,253	50,905	28,531	11,542	138,000	13,351	92,300	11,202	423,456
2006	14,430	181,010	16,333	45,521	28,592	54,000	28,767	9,454	144,600	14,109	58,700	12,253	412,134
2007	16,521	157,609	16,738	51,406	29,817	68,029	32,461	11,572	162,000	12,546	72,300	13,674	378,771
2008[1]	16,772	132,232	14,307	45,965	28,366	46,806	30,470	9,517	136,700	14,427	64,900	14,462	336,895
2009[2]	12,144	105,108	14,307	36,701	29,016	48,073	30,706	9,874	112,900	11,901	59,200	14,382	304,398

[1] Preliminary.   [2] Estimate.   NA = Not available.   *Source: Food and Agriculture Organization of the United Nations (FAO-UN)*

LUMBER AND PLYWOOD

Lumber Production and Consumption in the United States   In Millions of Board Feet

| | Production | | | | | Domestic Consumption | | | | | | |
Year	California Redwood	Inland Region	Southern Pine	West Coast	Other Softwood	Total Softwood	Inland Region	California Redwood	Southern Pine	West Coast	Other Softwood	Softwood Imports	Total Softwood
1998	1,391	7,298	16,151	7,797	2,040	34,677	7,256	1,409	15,788	7,502	1,567	18,686	52,209
1999	1,325	7,580	16,922	8,625	2,153	36,605	7,445	1,358	16,525	8,115	1,641	19,178	54,262
2000	1,320	7,078	16,672	8,782	2,115	35,967	6,926	1,257	16,374	8,300	1,629	19,449	53,934
2001	1,121	6,563	16,094	8,764	2,035	34,577	6,490	1,132	15,937	8,471	1,724	20,075	53,828
2002	1,035	6,759	16,686	9,244	2,106	35,830	6,641	1,056	16,571	8,966	1,832	20,986	56,050
2003	977	6,716	16,841	9,904	2,151	36,591	6,709	976	16,759	9,585	1,751	21,188	56,969
2004	1,049	6,742	18,050	10,934	2,300	39,075	6,600	1,021	17,935	10,705	1,971	23,584	61,819
2005	1,048	21,386	18,986	11,599	2,139	40,458	6,635	1,060	18,829	11,346	1,781	24,626	64,279
I	280	1,789	4,725	2,914	542	10,250	1,712	246	4,615	2,708	455	5,632	15,368
II	265	16,394	4,939	2,928	548	10,374	1,690	283	4,934	2,948	472	6,685	17,014
III	271	1,692	4,731	2,877	535	10,106	1,709	291	4,720	2,844	446	6,297	16,308
IV	232	1,511	4,591	2,880	514	9,728	1,524	240	4,560	2,846	408	6,012	15,589
2006[1]	972	6,404	19,560	11,700	2,156	40,792	6,320	760	18,772	11,332	1,680	24,212	63,080
I	243	1,601	4,890	2,925	539	10,198	1,580	190	4,693	2,833	420	6,053	15,770
II													
III													

[1] Preliminary.   Source: American Forest & Paper Association (AFPA)

U.S. Housing Starts: Seasonally Adjusted Annual Rate   In Thousands

Year	Jan.	Feb.	Mar.	Apr.	May	June	July	Aug.	Sept.	Oct.	Nov.	Dec.	Average
2001	1,600	1,625	1,590	1,649	1,605	1,636	1,670	1,567	1,562	1,540	1,602	1,568	1,601
2002	1,698	1,829	1,642	1,592	1,764	1,717	1,655	1,633	1,804	1,648	1,753	1,788	1,710
2003	1,853	1,629	1,726	1,643	1,751	1,867	1,897	1,833	1,939	1,967	2,083	2,057	1,854
2004	1,911	1,846	1,998	2,003	1,981	1,828	2,002	2,024	1,905	2,072	1,782	2,042	1,950
2005	2,144	2,207	1,864	2,061	2,025	2,068	2,054	2,095	2,151	2,065	2,147	1,994	2,073
2006	2,273	2,119	1,969	1,821	1,942	1,802	1,737	1,650	1,720	1,491	1,570	1,649	1,812
2007	1,409	1,480	1,495	1,490	1,415	1,448	1,354	1,330	1,183	1,264	1,197	1,037	1,342
2008	1,083	1,100	993	1,001	971	1,078	933	849	822	763	655	556	900
2009	488	581	520	477	550	583	587	585	586	529	589	576	554
2010[1]	612	605	634	679	588	539	550	614	601	533	548	520	585

[1] Preliminary.   Total Privately owned.   Source: Bureau of the Census, U.S. Department of Commerce

Stocks (Gross) of Softwood Lumber in the United States, on First of Month   In Millions of Board Feet

Year	Jan.	Feb.	Mar.	Apr.	May	June	July	Aug.	Sept.	Oct.	Nov.	Dec.
1997	3,973	4,019	4,113	4,067	3,963	4,017	3,915	3,871	3,875	3,927	3,925	3,865
1998	3,884	3,970	4,048	4,062	4,158	4,084	NA	NA	NA	NA	NA	NA
1999	3,519	3,595	3,688	3,726	3,698	3,581	3,512	3,485	3,533	3,491	3,562	3,536
2000	3,639	3,704	3,811	3,887	3,960	2,738	3,902	3,936	3,878	3,848	3,957	3,875
2001	3,919	3,864	4,013	3,951	4,095	3,955	NA	3,961	3,938	4,076	4,100	4,248
2002	4,784	3,735	3,826	3,756	3,273	3,316	3,242	3,230	3,136	3,098	3,173	3,127
2003	3,175	3,177	3,202	3,249	3,308	3,211	3,075	3,085	3,081	3,158	3,076	3,055
2004	2,904	2,904	2,904	2,873	2,966	2,966	2,966	2,966	3,030	3,030	3,031	2,450
2005	2,912	2,994	3,076	3,056	2,866	2,687	2,554	2,641	2,497	2,986	3,059	2,913
2006[1]	3,004	3,100	3,111	2,978	2,952	2,925	2,918	2,917	2,956	2,960	2,954	

[1] Preliminary.   NA = Not available.   Source: American Forest & Paper Association (AFPA)

Lumber (Softwood) Production in the United States   In Millions of Board Feet

Year	Jan.	Feb.	Mar.	Apr.	May	June	July	Aug.	Sept.	Oct.	Nov.	Dec.	Total
1997	3,012	2,791	2,866	3,149	2,890	3,027	3,097	2,889	2,905	3,094	2,536	2,487	34,743
1998	2,767	2,760	2,928	3,084	2,647	3,051	3,079	2,930	2,953	3,167	2,667	2,754	34,787
1999	2,783	2,921	3,190	3,227	3,071	3,318	3,115	3,054	2,992	3,096	2,954	2,795	36,516
2000	3,020	3,128	3,474	3,058	3,276	3,249	2,730	2,971	2,839	3,041	2,761	2,342	35,889
2001	2,832	2,457	2,918	2,928	NA	3,032	2,812	3,240	2,743	3,188	2,740	2,372	34,104
2002	3,019	2,761	3,074	3,284	3,126	3,200	3,104	3,128	2,862	3,386	2,599	2,482	36,025
2003	2,971	2,801	2,937	2,994	2,931	3,109	3,088	2,981	3,052	3,335	2,793	2,740	35,732
2004	3,037	2,978	3,380	3,434	3,021	3,329	3,227	3,271	3,147	3,321	3,082	2,931	38,158
2005	3,233	3,169	3,596	3,486	3,339	3,535	3,248	3,490	3,385	3,574	3,180	3,052	40,287
2006[1]	3,511	3,216	3,550	3,294	3,360	3,420	3,195	3,349	2,877	3,154	2,368		38,503

[1] Preliminary.   Source: American Forest & Paper Association (AFPA)

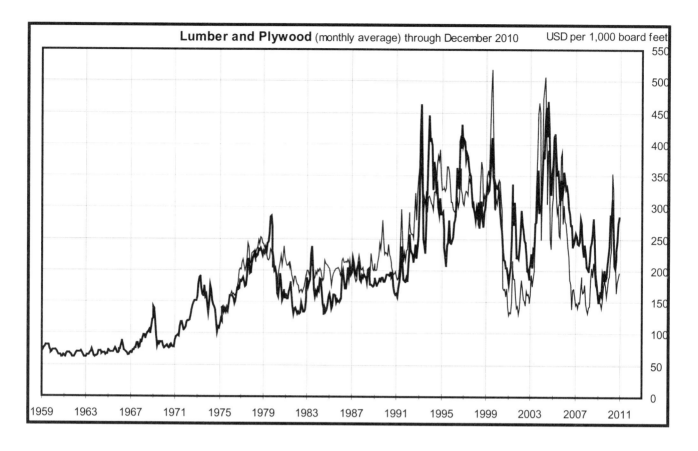

Lumber and Plywood (monthly average) through December 2010   USD per 1,000 board feet

Lumber (Softwood) Shipments in the United States   In Millions of Board Feet

Year	Jan.	Feb.	Mar.	Apr.	May	June	July	Aug.	Sept.	Oct.	Nov.	Dec.	Total
1997	2,966	2,697	2,890	3,253	2,834	3,126	3,139	2,885	2,852	3,096	2,598	2,461	34,797
1998	2,685	2,685	2,863	3,019	2,684	3,175	3,132	2,963	2,948	3,205	2,703	2,865	34,927
1999	2,689	2,829	3,177	3,227	3,071	3,383	3,141	3,004	3,037	3,021	2,944	2,691	36,214
2000	2,953	3,039	3,394	2,974	3,292	3,309	2,686	3,027	2,871	2,931	2,752	2,444	35,672
2001	2,859	2,372	2,981	2,974	NA	2,961	2,936	3,279	2,644	3,166	2,732	2,396	34,145
2002	3,032	2,815	3,049	3,212	3,064	3,260	3,234	3,111	2,858	3,299	2,675	2,501	36,110
2003	3,018	2,742	2,843	3,134	2,969	3,173	3,209	3,137	3,030	3,413	2,787	2,722	36,177
2004	3,067	2,840	3,262	3,582	3,061	3,385	3,485	3,372	3,086	3,345	3,135	2,964	38,584
2005	3,264	3,087	3,506	3,506	3,542	3,696	3,389	3,512	3,413	3,542	3,145	3,196	40,798
2006[1]	3,423	3,122	3,536	3,280	3,386	3,447	3,202	3,349	2,838	3,151	2,374		38,300

[1] Preliminary.   *Source: American Forest & Paper Association (AFPA)*

Imports and Exports of Lumber in the United States, by Type   In Millions of Board Feet

	Imports[2] Softwood						Total Hard-wood	Total Lumber	Exports[2] Softwood		Pond-erosa/ White Pine	South-ern Pine	Total	Total Hard-wood	Total Lumber
Year	Cedar	Douglas Fir	Hem-lock	Pine	Spruce	Total			Douglas Fir	Hem-lock					
1997	586	264	250	314	1,040	18,014	465	18,506	436	105	122	299	1,820	1,281	3,189
1998	514	417	268	363	849	18,686	589	19,306	252	39	113	279	1,265	1,119	2,601
1999	591	426	259	449	803	19,178	708	19,903	249	54	140	326	1,431	1,242	2,867
2000	694	455	184	450	812	19,449	795	20,268	232	46	116	298	1,355	1,319	2,822
2001	667	471	199	365	838	20,075	645	20,737	168	26	86	232	968	1,222	2,351
2002	648	385	69	445	1,046	20,986	739	21,774	111	19	83	205	848	1,219	2,313
2003	536	356	53	472	854	21,188	794	22,023	96	18	100	132	948	1,236	2,368
2004	630	570	67	580	1,183	23,483	995	24,499	88	19	93	156	821	1,496	2,533
2005	637	494	76	439	1,769	24,626	1,075	25,738	93	19	112	235	897	1,477	2,682
2006[1] I	180	88	31	100	432	6,054	261	6,321	19	3	29	58	246	449	695
II															
III															

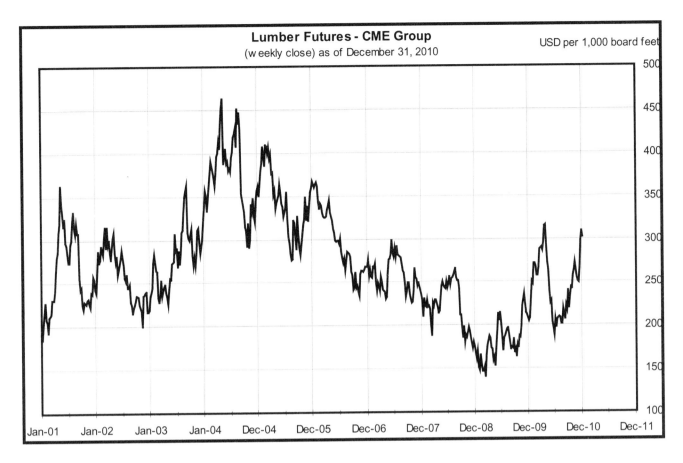

Lumber Futures - CME Group
(weekly close) as of December 31, 2010

USD per 1,000 board feet

Average Open Interest of Random Lumber Futures in Chicago   In Contracts

Year	Jan.	Feb.	Mar.	Apr.	May	June	July	Aug.	Sept.	Oct.	Nov.	Dec.
2001	4,605	4,494	3,654	3,644	3,867	3,733	2,612	2,949	2,148	2,102	2,173	2,416
2002	2,106	2,382	2,441	2,011	1,502	2,136	1,879	2,265	2,654	2,974	3,315	3,249
2003	3,238	3,222	2,521	2,804	2,937	3,188	2,370	2,827	3,492	3,033	1,824	1,887
2004	2,884	3,996	3,790	5,414	5,436	5,042	5,123	6,216	4,667	3,826	3,489	3,540
2005	3,759	5,169	5,040	4,705	3,463	3,576	3,401	4,227	3,913	3,883	4,713	5,202
2006	5,893	5,144	4,084	4,959	4,586	5,449	5,317	6,429	5,912	6,351	6,121	7,018
2007	6,466	7,807	7,684	8,680	7,726	8,206	7,130	7,666	6,493	9,356	8,960	9,731
2008	9,827	13,134	13,385	14,637	14,801	14,275	14,417	14,016	12,110	9,466	7,744	8,084
2009	7,912	7,937	6,852	7,732	7,815	9,039	7,910	8,873	9,248	9,593	10,174	9,557
2010	9,674	10,231	9,538	10,571	8,358	9,402	8,675	9,498	8,812	9,707	9,620	10,018

Contract size = 110,000 board feet.   *Source: CME Group; Chicago Mercantile Exchange (CME)*

Volume of Trading of Random Lumber Futures in Chicago   In Contracts

Year	Jan.	Feb.	Mar.	Apr.	May	June	July	Aug.	Sept.	Oct.	Nov.	Dec.	Total
2001	21,567	15,076	24,561	22,458	23,681	18,878	15,210	16,440	12,882	11,608	11,989	12,490	206,840
2002	15,328	13,239	16,401	13,910	12,427	11,950	12,046	10,154	13,518	13,442	15,828	16,180	164,423
2003	24,241	17,533	17,027	11,573	20,132	21,840	21,097	22,418	22,891	19,387	12,480	13,272	223,891
2004	17,921	17,713	22,544	25,743	19,951	17,190	22,672	20,902	24,238	17,111	17,271	19,617	242,873
2005	20,838	20,257	24,595	20,360	17,338	17,115	16,244	19,590	22,895	15,896	23,404	17,709	236,241
2006	26,803	19,152	18,504	21,358	21,619	23,959	21,568	23,800	22,618	24,804	22,385	24,454	271,024
2007	26,214	28,328	24,741	26,433	31,540	28,545	23,462	28,610	24,841	33,876	29,738	28,361	334,689
2008	31,401	43,338	37,899	50,586	37,909	38,362	41,612	40,693	32,155	36,226	20,277	27,155	437,613
2009	18,478	29,930	22,193	25,349	24,351	34,027	24,340	29,548	22,271	33,768	21,817	31,155	317,227
2010	25,483	26,365	20,928	32,393	24,763	29,446	18,360	24,660	26,107	31,689	23,662	28,046	311,902

Contract size = 110,000 board feet.   *Source: CME Group; Chicago Mercantile Exchange (CME)*

LUMBER AND PLYWOOD

Production of Plywood by Selected Countries   In Thousands of Cubic Meters

Year	Austria	Canada	Finland	France	Germany	Italy	Japan	Poland	Romania	Russia	Spain	Sweden	United States
2002	186	2,176	1,240	459	285	520	2,735	261	90	1,821	360	87	15,307
2003	186	2,206	1,300	415	245	511	3,024	289	94	1,978	370	75	14,870
2004	186	2,344	1,350	435	283	485	3,149	342	117	2,246	375	71	14,833
2005	195	2,322	1,305	415	236	390	3,212	361	126	2,556	557	92	14,449
2006	178	2,252	1,415	431	235	334	3,314	385	188	2,614	468	92	13,651
2007	258	2,639	1,410	378	229	420	3,073	440	107	2,777	450	72	12,402
2008[1]	268	2,225	1,265	360	174	421	2,586	395	152	2,592	250	75	10,376
2009[2]	213	2,096	780	360	176	337	2,586	414	85	2,107	250	75	8,846

[1] Preliminary.   [2] Estimate.   NA = Not available.   *Source: Food and Agricultural Organization of the United Nations (FAO-UN)*

Imports of Plywood by Selected Countries   In Thousands of Cubic Meters

Year	Austria	Belgium	Canada	Denmark	France	Germany	Italy	Japan	Netherlands	Sweden	Switzerland	United Kingdom	United States
2002	156	505	489	254	349	905	558	5,119	541	152	128	1,297	3,890
2003	180	572	509	394	363	1,103	558	4,221	527	161	130	1,253	4,249
2004	144	624	350	413	383	1,214	581	5,122	542	164	140	1,474	5,900
2005	140	521	690	371	411	1,142	532	4,732	526	189	145	1,456	6,181
2006	140	610	685	544	445	1,314	575	5,046	603	197	128	1,497	6,393
2007	172	672	1,827	1,014	459	1,516	588	4,064	608	240	126	1,624	4,397
2008[1]	133	633	2,149	391	503	1,325	530	3,583	635	192	131	1,487	3,059
2009[2]	148	530	904	2,227	954	1,039	417	3,583	428	144	53	1,164	2,441

[1] Preliminary.   [2] Estimate.   NA = Not available.   *Source: Food and Agricultural Organization of the United Nations (FAO-UN)*

Exports of Plywood by Selected Countries   In Thousands of Cubic Meters

Year	Austria	Baltic States	Belgium	Canada	Finland	France	Germany	Italy	Netherlands	Poland	Russia	Spain	United States
2002	240	238	371	1,056	1,117	190	167	204	43	138	1,157	82	523
2003	262	245	436	1,017	1,172	187	200	208	32	149	1,201	88	512
2004	265	255	474	1,027	1,234	192	265	201	46	171	1,438	114	525
2005	287	253	423	1,118	1,173	196	287	146	40	177	1,527	117	503
2006	311	282	470	950	1,250	225	321	239	60	137	1,577	124	492
2007	285	318	386	964	1,229	227	368	295	55	148	1,503	162	443
2008[1]	278	197	470	583	1,083	223	349	184	51	133	1,326	213	506
2009[2]	361	211	379	305	683	335	256	148	49	109	1,334	122	350

[1] Preliminary.   [2] Estimate.   NA = Not available.   *Source: Food and Agricultural Organization of the United Nations (FAO-UN)*

Imports of Industrial Roundwood by Selected Countries   In Thousands of Cubic Meters

Year	Austria	Belgium	Canada	Finland	France	Germany	Italy	Norway	Poland	Portugal	Spain	Sweden	United States
2002	7,289	2,653	6,941	12,586	1,993	2,623	4,703	2,561	726	901	3,374	9,705	2,687
2003	7,498	2,667	6,615	12,869	2,250	2,519	4,323	2,722	663	468	3,191	9,021	2,551
2004	8,812	2,879	5,961	12,961	2,175	2,227	4,614	2,866	943	364	2,973	9,398	2,437
2005	8,629	3,188	6,274	16,031	2,344	3,005	4,755	3,145	2,009	362	3,640	8,686	3,569
2006	9,102	3,284	5,787	14,655	2,601	3,669	4,486	2,333	1,814	335	3,841	6,664	2,922
2007	8,722	4,094	5,100	12,942	3,181	4,692	4,299	2,539	2,088	746	3,965	7,364	2,242
2008[1]	7,550	3,194	4,608	13,371	2,358	5,758	3,478	1,808	1,868	521	2,860	6,781	1,430
2009[2]	8,036	3,031	4,555	3,761	1,453	7,199	2,703	933	1,874	473	1,868	4,175	914

[1] Preliminary.   [2] Estimate.   NA = Not available.   *Source: Food and Agricultural Organization of the United Nations (FAO-UN)*

Exports of Industrial Roundwood by Selected Countries   In Thousands of Cubic Meters

Year	Canada	Czech Republic	Estonia	France	Germany	Hungary	Latvia	Lithuania	Russia	Slovakia	Sweden	Switzerland	United States
2002	4,471	2,302	3,132	4,244	4,907	1,210	4,225	1,420	36,800	1,187	1,755	1,970	11,067
2003	5,004	2,955	3,029	4,111	4,592	1,366	3,922	1,378	37,518	1,034	1,520	1,748	10,288
2004	3,899	2,858	2,297	3,851	5,589	1,137	4,136	1,178	41,553	1,142	1,522	1,741	10,402
2005	5,592	2,942	1,806	3,862	6,819	871	3,919	1,131	48,020	1,691	3,095	1,416	9,815
2006	4,640	2,679	1,606	3,695	7,557	1,095	3,419	1,061	50,900	1,218	3,004	1,727	9,638
2007	3,560	2,384	1,502	3,966	7,674	1,054	3,690	1,671	49,100	1,457	3,808	1,327	9,949
2008[1]	2,839	3,101	1,469	3,547	7,037	661	3,193	1,171	36,784	2,192	2,349	1,155	10,200
2009[2]	2,692	4,074	1,080	4,023	4,205	799	2,500	673	21,700	2,538	1,177	936	9,511

[1] Preliminary.   [2] Estimate.   NA = Not available.   *Source: Food and Agricultural Organization of the United Nations (FAO-UN)*

Magnesium

Magnesium (symbol Mg) is a silvery-white, light, and fairly tough, metallic element and is relatively stable. Magnesium is one of the alkaline earth metals. Magnesium is the eighth most abundant element in the earth's crust and the third most plentiful element found in seawater. Magnesium is ductile and malleable when heated, and with the exception of beryllium, is the lightest metal that remains stable under ordinary conditions. First isolated by the British chemist Sir Humphrey Davy in 1808, magnesium today is obtained mainly by electrolysis of fused magnesium chloride.

Magnesium compounds, primarily magnesium oxide, are used in the refractory material that line the furnaces used to produce iron and steel, nonferrous metals, glass, and cement. Magnesium oxide and other compounds are also used in the chemical, agricultural, and construction industries. Magnesium's principal use is as an alloying addition for aluminum. These aluminum-magnesium alloys are used primarily in beverage cans. Due to their lightness and considerable tensile strength, the alloys are also used in structural components in airplanes and automobiles.

Prices – The average price of magnesium in 2010 rose 1.13% to $2.61 per pound, but still down from 2008's record high of $3.38 per pound.

Supply – World primary production of magnesium in 2009 fell -9.25% yr/yr to 6-9,000 metric tons, down further from 2007's record high of 751,000 metric tons. The current level of magnesium production has more than

doubled since the mid-1970s when 1976's production was 249,367 metric tons.

The world's largest primary producers of magnesium in 2009 were China with 501,000 metric tons, Russia with 37,000 metric tons, and Brazil with 16,000 metric tons. The U.S. production amount is not available because it is considered proprietary data but is probably less than about 50,000 metric tons. China's production has increased over the past 10 years from 70,500 metric tons in 1998 to 501,000 metric tons in 2009 but that was still well below its record high of 625,000 in 2007. By 2006 Canada's production had grown by more than seven-fold from the mid-1980s, but that fell sharply in 2007 by -75% to 16,300 metric tons and down to 2,000 in 2008.

Demand – Total U.S. consumption of primary magnesium in 2009 fell −21.4% to 50,714 from 64,517 metric tons. U.S. consumption of magnesium for structural products in 2009 rose +8.3% yr/yr to 20,714 metric tons. Of the structural product consumption category, 94% was for castings and the remaining 6% was for wrought products. U.S. consumption of magnesium for aluminum alloys fell -34.3% yr/yr in 2009 to 23,000 metric tons. The consumption of magnesium for other uses fell by -30.1% yr/yr in 2009 to 7,200 metric tons.

Trade – U.S. exports of magnesium in 2010 fell -18.4% yr/yr to 16,000 metric tons, but still up from the 2005 record low of 9,650 metric tons. U.S. imports of magnesium in 2010 rose +5.72% yr/yr to 50,000 metric tons.

World Production of Magnesium (Primary and Secondary)   In Metric Tons

| | --------------------------------------- Primary Production -- | | | | | | | ------------------ Secondary Production ----------------- | | | | |
Year	Brazil	Canada	China	France	Norway	Russia	United States	Total	Japan	United Kingdom	United States	Former USSR	Total
2005	6,000	50,000	470,000	----	----	45,000	W	622,000	----	----	----	----	----
2006	6,000	65,000	520,000	----	----	35,000	W	675,000	----	----	----	----	----
2007	18,000	16,300	625,000	----	----	37,000	W	751,000	----	----	----	----	----
2008	15,000	2,000	559,000	----	----	37,000	W	670,000	----	----	----	----	----
2009[1]	16,000	----	501,000	----	----	37,000	W	608,000	----	----	----	----	----
2010[2]	16,000	----	650,000	----	----	40,000	W	760,000	----	----	----	----	----

[1] Preliminary.   [2] Estimate.   W = Withheld.   *Source: U.S. Geological Survey (USGS)*

Salient Statistics of Magnesium in the United States   In Metric Tons

| | --------------- Production --------------- | | | | | | | Price | ------- Domestic Consumption of Primary Magnesium ------- | | | | | |
| | | ---- Secondary ---- | | | | | | | | ----- Structural Products ----- | | | | | |
Year	Primary (Ingot)	New Scrap	Old Scrap	Total	Total Exports[3]	Imports for Consumption	Stocks Dec. 31[4]	Price $ Per Pound[5]	Castings	Wrought	Total Structural Products	Aluminum Alloys	Other Uses	Total
2005	W	53,500	19,400	73,300	9,650	84,700	W	1.23	34,024	2,890	36,914	30,300	14,800	45,100
2006	W	60,500	21,700	81,900	12,300	75,300	W	1.40	26,007	2,410	28,417	33,700	15,400	49,100
2007	W	59,900	23,500	84,100	14,800	71,800	W	2.25	23,727	2,820	26,547	32,000	13,600	45,600
2008	W	61,100	22,600	83,700	14,400	83,300	W	3.15	16,647	2,480	19,127	35,000	10,300	45,300
2009[1]	W	47,100	19,500	66,600	19,600	47,300	W	2.30	19,554	1,160	20,714	23,000	7,200	30,200
2010[2]	W			70,000	16,000	50,000		2.60						

[1] Preliminary.   [2] Estimate.   [3] Metal & alloys in crude form & scrap.   [4] Estimate of Industry Stocks, metal.   [5] Magnesium ingots (99.8%), f.o.b. Valasco, Texas.   [6] Distributive or sacrificial purposes.   W = Withheld proprietary data.   *Source: U.S. Geological Survey (USGS)*

Average Price of Magnesium   In Dollars Per Pound

Year	Jan.	Feb.	Mar.	Apr.	May	June	July	Aug.	Sept.	Oct.	Nov.	Dec.	Average
2006	1.25	1.18	1.18	1.16	1.16	1.16	1.16	1.16	1.20	1.21	1.29	1.33	1.20
2007	1.42	1.56	1.58	1.62	1.65	1.65	1.65	1.65	1.65	1.98	2.09	2.20	1.73
2008	2.89	3.08	3.27	3.39	3.55	3.55	3.55	3.55	3.55	3.50	3.43	3.22	3.38
2009	3.13	2.99	2.83	2.73	2.73	2.73	2.52	2.35	2.30	2.25	2.23	2.23	2.59
2010	2.43	2.65	2.65	2.68	2.65	2.65	2.67	2.66	2.63	2.60	2.55	2.55	2.61

Source: American Metal Market (AMM)

Manganese

Manganese (symbol Mn) is a silvery-white, very brittle, metallic element used primarily in making alloys. Manganese was first distinguished as an element and isolated in 1774 by Johan Gottlieb Gahn. Manganese dissolves in acid and corrodes in moist air.

Manganese is found in the earth's crust in the form of ores such as rhodochrosite, franklinite, psilomelane, and manganite. Pyrolusite is the principal ore of manganese. Pure manganese is produced by igniting pyrolusite with aluminum powder or by electrolyzing manganese sulfate.

Manganese is used primarily in the steel industry for creating alloys, the most important ones being ferromanganese and spiegeleisen. In steel, manganese improves forging and rolling qualities, strength, toughness, stiffness, wear resistance, and hardness. Manganese is also used in plant fertilizers, animal feed, pigments, and dry cell batteries.

Prices – The average monthly price of ferromanganese (high carbon, FOB plant) rose by +8.5% yr/yr in 2010 to $1,391.04 per gross ton, but still below 2008's record high of $2,953.84 per gross ton. The 2010 price, however, is still about three times the 22-year low price of $447.44 per gross ton posted as recently as 2001.

Supply – World production of manganese ore in 2008 (latest data available) rose by +8.19% to 38.3 million metric tons, which was a new record high. That was well above the record low of 17.8 million metric tons posted in 1999. The world's largest producers of manganese ore are China with 29% of world production in 2008, South Africa with 18%, Australia with 13%, Brazil with 8%, and the Ukraine with 4%. China's production in 2008 rose by +10.0% yr/yr to 11.000 million metric tons.

Demand – U.S. consumption of manganese ore in 2010 rose +13.7% to 480,000 metric tons, up further from the 2007 record low of 351,000 metric tons. U.S. consumption of ferromanganese in 2010 rose +18.1% yr/yr to 300,000 metric tons, but still below the 12-year high of 315,000 metric tons posted in 2004. The 2010 figure is about 25% of the U.S. consumption in the early 1970s.

Trade – The U.S. still relies on imports for 100% of its manganese consumption, as it has since 1985. U.S. imports of manganese ore for consumption in 2010 rose +82.2% yr/yr to 490,000 metric tons, up from 2009's 17-year low of 269 metric tons. U.S. imports of ferromanganese for consumption in 2010 rose +109.2% yr/yr to 320,000 metric tons. U.S. imports of silico-manganese in 2010 rose +138.5% yr/yr to 320,000 metric tons, up from 2009's 25-year low of 130,000 metric tons. The primary sources of U.S. imports of manganese ore in 2008 were Gabon with 63% imports, Australia with 18%, and South Africa with 5%.

World Production of Manganese Ore   In Thousands of Metric Tons (Gross Weight)

Year	Aus- tralia[2] 37-53[4]	Brazil 37[4]	China 20-30[4]	Gabon 45-53[4]	Georgia[5] 29-30[4]	Ghana 32-34[4]	India 10-54[4]	Kazak- hstan[5] 29-30[4]	Mexico 27-50[4]	South Africa 30-48+[4]	Ukraine[5] 30-35[4]	Other	World Total
1999	1,892	1,656	3,190	1,908	----	639	1,500	980	459	3,122	1,985	458	17,800
2000	1,614	1,925	3,500	1,743	----	896	1,550	1,136	435	3,635	2,741	433	19,600
2001	2,069	1,970	4,300	1,791	----	1,077	1,600	1,387	277	3,266	2,700	490	20,900
2002	2,189	2,529	4,500	1,856	----	1,136	1,553	1,792	245	3,322	2,470	526	22,100
2003	2,564	2,544	4,600	2,000	----	1,509	1,650	2,361	320	3,501	2,591	547	24,200
2004	3,431	3,143	5,500	2,460	----	1,597	1,776	2,318	377	4,282	2,362	656	27,900
2005	3,136	3,200	7,500	2,859	----	1,715	2,386	2,208	369	4,612	2,260	745	31,000
2006	4,556	3,128	8,000	3,000	----	1,659	2,084	2,531	346	5,213	1,606	772	32,900
2007	5,289	1,866	10,000	3,300	----	1,156	2,300	2,482	423	5,996	1,720	869	35,400
2008[1]	4,837	3,210	11,000	3,460	----	1,150	2,400	2,485	472	6,807	1,447	992	38,300

[1] Preliminary.   [2] Metallurgical Ore.   [3] Concentrate.   [4] Ranges of percentage of manganese.   *Source: U.S. Geological Survey (USGS)*

Salient Statistics of Manganese in the United States   In Thousands of Metric Tons (Gross Weight)

Year	Net Import Reliance As a % of Apparent Consumption	Manganese Ore (35% or More Manganese) — Imports for Con- sumption	Exports	Con- sumption	Stocks Dec. 31[3]	Ferromanganese — Imports for Con- sumption	Exports	Con- sumption	Avg Price Mn. Metal- lurgical Ore $/Lg. Ton Unit[4]	Silicomanganese — Exports	Imports
2001	100	358	9	425	138	251	9	266	2.44	3.6	269.0
2002	100	427	15	360	151	275	9	253	2.30	0.5	247.0
2003	100	347	18	398	156	238	11	248	2.41	0.6	267.0
2004	100	451	123	441	159	429	9	315	2.89	0.5	422.0
2005	100	656	13	368	337	255	14	286	4.39	0.9	327.0
2006	100	572	2	365	153	358	22	297	3.22	0.9	400.0
2007	100	602	29	351	190	315	29	272	3.10	3.3	414.0
2008	100	571	48	464	255	448	23	304	12.15	7.1	365.0
2009[1]	100	269	15	422	115	153	24	254	6.61	7.0	130.0
2010[2]	100	490	18	480	170	320	12	300	8.00	19.0	310.0

[1] Preliminary.   [2] Estimate.   [3] Including bonded warehouses; excludes Gov't stocks; also excludes small tonnages of dealers' stocks.
[4] 46-48% Mn, C.I.F. U.S. Ports.   *Source: U.S. Geological Survey (USGS)*

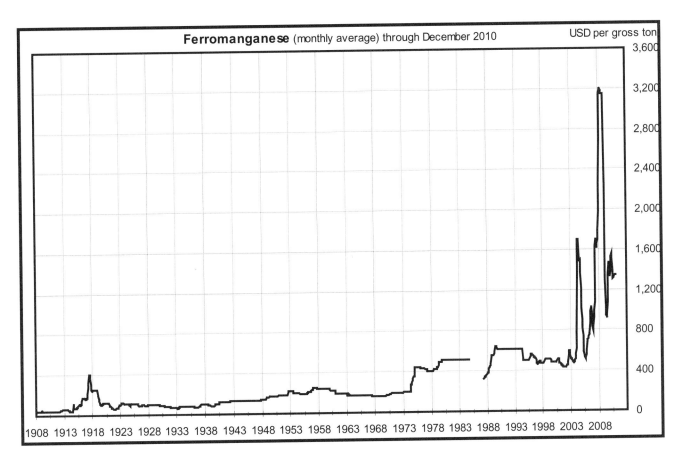

Ferromanganese (monthly average) through December 2010   USD per gross ton

Imports[3] of Manganese Ore (20% or More Mn) in the United States   In Metric Tons (Mn Content)

Year	Australia	Brazil	Gabon	Mexico	Morocco	South Africa	Total	Customs Value ($1,000)
1999	23,500	1	142,000	9,130	----	39,100	224,000	37,200
2000	18,100	3,250	188,000	3,250	----	----	219,000	32,100
2001	18,000	3,480	158,000	1,720	----	17,400	199,000	28,000
2002	18,400	12,900	140,000	1,100	----	41,800	214,000	29,200
2003	12,900	7	123,000	1,520	----	36,900	175,000	27,000
2004	27,700	----	188,000	1,640	----	13,200	234,000	37,700
2005	21,300	7,020	252,000	4,320	----	33,100	334,000	58,200
2006	12,800	5,800	120,000	1,320	----	91,200	270,000	53,900
2007[1]	34,900	20,000	170,000	3,670	----	53,600	298,000	57,600
2008[2]	51,900	34,400	181,000	----	----	14,600	289,000	154,000

[1] Preliminary.   [2] Estimate.   [3] Imports for consumption.   *Source: U.S. Geological Survey (USGS)*

Average Price of Ferromanganese[1]   In Dollars Per Gross Ton -- Carloads

Year	Jan.	Feb.	Mar.	Apr.	May	June	July	Aug.	Sept.	Oct.	Nov.	Dec.	Average
2001	473.93	467.89	460.00	454.29	450.00	450.00	446.90	444.57	430.79	430.00	430.00	430.00	447.44
2002	430.00	430.00	437.14	447.73	449.55	456.75	481.82	556.14	597.00	589.67	552.89	518.93	495.64
2003	509.52	510.00	502.38	497.61	492.50	481.79	477.27	470.00	478.57	497.83	516.67	559.76	499.49
2004	610.00	790.00	1,382.61	1,700.00	1,700.00	1,674.43	1,490.34	1,488.64	1,500.00	1,371.43	1,207.50	1,019.52	1,327.87
2005	904.50	818.68	739.46	651.67	586.19	547.39	528.13	512.07	522.14	550.24	597.75	694.05	637.69
2006	707.25	712.50	737.50	759.00	764.55	870.23	987.50	1,025.00	1,021.25	946.25	836.25	790.00	846.44
2007	834.29	930.00	949.55	1,000.00	1,074.43	1,633.33	1,705.00	1,620.00	1,620.00	1,656.96	1,700.00	1,785.53	1,375.76
2008	1,978.57	2,262.75	2,734.29	3,145.45	3,200.00	3,200.00	3,175.00	3,150.00	3,150.00	3,150.00	3,150.00	3,150.00	2,953.84
2009	2,225.00	1,300.00	1,300.00	1,038.10	950.00	928.18	955.45	1,071.43	1,344.52	1,481.67	1,431.84	1,365.26	1,282.62
2010	1,326.58	1,387.50	1,530.43	1,559.09	1,507.00	1,389.09	1,310.00	1,320.45	1,327.38	1,345.00	1,345.00	1,345.00	1,391.04

[1] Domestic standard, high carbon, FOB plant, carloads.   *Source: American Metal Market (AMM)*

Meats

U.S. commercial red meat includes beef, veal, lamb, and pork. Red meat is a good source of iron, vitamin B12, and protein, and eliminating it from the diet can lead to iron and zinc deficiencies. Today, red meat is far leaner than it was 30 years ago due to newer breeds of livestock that carry less fat. The leanest cuts of beef include tenderloin, sirloin, and flank. The leanest cuts of pork include pork tenderloin, loin chops, and rib chops.

The USDA (United States Department of Agriculture) grades various cuts of meat. "Prime" is the highest USDA grade for beef, veal, and lamb. "Choice" is the grade designation below Prime for beef, veal, and lamb. "Commercial" and "Cutter" grades are two of the lower designations for beef, usually sold as ground meat, sausage, and canned meat. "Canner" is the lowest USDA grade designation for beef and is used primarily in canned meats not sold at retail.

Supply – World meat production in 2010 rose +0.8% to a new record high of 158.288 million metric tons. China was the world's largest meat producer in 2010 with 55.830 million metric tons of production (up +2.9% yr/yr), accounting for 35.3% of world production.

U.S. production of meat in 2008 (latest data) rose by +3.6% yr/yr to 50.567 billion pounds, which was a new record high. U.S. production of beef in 2008 rose 0.6% yr/yr to 26.682 billion pounds, which will be just moderately below the record of 27.192 billion pounds in 2002. Beef accounted for 53.0% of all U.S. meat production. U.S. production of pork in 2008 rose +7.3% yr/yr to a new record high of 23.554 billion pounds. Pork accounts for 47.0% of U.S. meat production. Veal accounts for only 0.3% of U.S. meat production, and lamb and mutton account for only 0.4% of U.S. meat production.

Demand – U.S. per capita meat consumption in 2008 (latest data) rose by 0.9% to 119.0 pounds per person per year, but that is only slightly above the 2006/7 record low of 117 pounds per person reflecting the trend towards eating more chicken and fish and the availability of meat substitutes. Per capita beef consumption in 2008 was unchanged at 65.0 pounds per person per year, which was about half the record high of 127.5 pounds seen in 1976. Per capita pork consumption in 2008 rose by +4.0% to 53.0 pounds per person per year from he record low of 49.0 pounds posted in 2006. Per capita consumption of veal is negligible at .5 pounds per person and lamb/mutton consumption is also negligible at 1.0 pound per person.

Trade – World red meat exports in 2010 rose +1.9% to 12.814 million metric tons, down from the 2008 record high of 13.637 million metric tons. The world's largest red meat exporters will be the U.S. with 22.3% of world exports in 2010, Brazil with 20.1%, Canada with 12.4%, Australia with 10.9%, and European Union with 10.6%.

World Total Meat Production[4]   In Thousands of Metric Tons

Year	Argentina	Australia	Brazil	Canada	China[4]	European Union	India	Mexico	New Zealand	Russia	South Africa	United States	World Total
2002	2,865	2,496	9,805	3,007	46,450	29,928	----	2,795	635	3,370	770	21,356	142,624
2003	2,950	2,492	9,945	2,934	47,811	30,016	----	2,985	729	3,380	756	21,095	144,451
2004	3,308	2,475	10,575	3,280	49,014	29,998	----	2,964	749	3,315	800	20,574	147,041
2005	3,388	2,487	11,302	3,235	51,234	29,766	----	2,828	711	3,260	826	20,710	150,269
2006	3,310	2,572	11,855	3,077	52,272	29,941	----	2,659	699	3,235	876	21,539	153,454
2007	3,515	2,558	12,293	3,024	49,012	31,046	----	2,752	658	3,280	830	22,059	152,816
2008	3,370	2,507	12,039	3,074	52,337	30,686	----	2,828	695	3,375	826	22,762	156,564
2009	3,600	2,456	12,065	3,044	54,669	30,059	----	2,862	676	3,495	829	22,333	157,904
2010[1]	2,830	2,407	12,315	3,035	55,550	30,120	----	2,892	672	3,570	835	21,880	158,270
2011[2]	2,785	2,396	12,670	2,995	56,950	29,970	----	2,959	658	3,580	835	21,760	160,055

[1] Preliminary.   [2] Forecast.   [3] Data through 2000, includes beef, veal, pork, sheep and goat meat. Beginning 2001, excludes sheep and goat.
[4] Predominately pork production.   *Source: Foreign Agricultural Service, U.S. Department of Agriculture (FAS-USDA)*

Production and Consumption of Red Meats in The United States

	Beef			Veal			Lamb & Mutton			Pork (Excluding Lard)			All Meats		
	Commercial Production	Consumption		Commercial Production	Consumption		Commercial Production	Consumption		Commercial Production	Consumption		Commercial Production	Consumption	
Year		Total	Per Capita		Total	Per Capita		Total	Per Capita		Total	Per Capita		Total	Per Capita
	- Million Pounds -		Lbs.	- Million Pounds -		Lbs.	- Million Pounds -		Lbs.	- Million Pounds -		Lbs.	- Million Pounds -		Lbs.
2001	26,212	27,026	66.0	205	204	1.0	227	368	1.0	19,160	18,492	50.0	45,804	46,089	118.0
2002	27,192	27,877	68.0	205	204	1.0	223	381	1.0	19,685	19,146	52.0	47,305	47,608	121.0
2003	26,339	27,000	65.0	202	204	0.6	203	367	1.0	19,966	19,436	52.0	46,710	47,006	118.0
2004	24,650	27,750	66.0	176	177	0.6	200	373	1.0	20,529	19,437	51.0	45,555	47,737	119.0
2005	24,787	27,754	66.0	165	164	0.6	191	355	1.0	20,705	19,112	50.0	45,848	47,385	117.0
2006	26,256	28,137	65.9	156	155	0.4	190	356	1.1	21,074	19,055	49.4	47,675	47,703	116.8
2007	26,523	28,141	65.2	146	145	0.4	189	385	1.1	21,962	19,763	50.8	48,820	48,434	117.5
2008	26,664	27,303	62.7	152	150	0.4	180	343	1.0	23,367	19,415	49.4	50,362	47,211	113.5
2009[1]	26,068	26,836	61.1	147	147	0.4	177	338	1.0	23,020	19,870	50.1	49,412	47,191	112.6
2010[2]	26,419	26,397	59.6	142	147	0.4	171	320	0.9	18,952	18,639	47.7	49,189	45,937	108.6

[1] Preliminary.   [2] Estimate.   [3] Forecast.   *Source: Economic Research Service, U.S. Department of Agriculture (ERS-USDA)*

Total Red Meat Imports[3] (Carcass Weight Equivalent) of Principal Countries — In Thousands of Metric Tons

Year	Brazil	Canada	European Union	Egypt	Hong Kong	Japan	Rep of Korea	Mexico	Philippines	Russia	Taiwan	United States	World Total
2002	77	431	563	179	308	1,805	606	828	155	1,507	116	1,945	9,940
2003	62	395	593	128	339	1,924	620	752	149	1,416	144	1,901	10,279
2004	52	228	694	174	364	1,903	457	754	185	1,333	134	2,168	10,686
2005	48	290	810	222	351	2,000	595	755	160	1,730	129	2,096	11,503
2006	28	326	842	292	366	1,832	708	829	160	1,774	128	1,848	11,700
2007	30	413	676	293	392	1,896	755	854	179	1,924	120	1,823	12,229
2008	29	424	522	166	464	1,926	725	943	205	2,190	141	1,528	13,094
2009	35	427	535	180	523	1,835	705	1,000	182	1,740	182	1,569	12,207
2010[1]	40	435	520	190	570	1,845	725	1,020	275	1,790	190	1,511	12,523
2011[2]	45	475	520	210	595	1,861	760	1,020	260	1,800	196	1,549	12,905

[1] Preliminary. [2] Forecast. [3] Data through 2000, includes beef, veal, pork, sheep and goat meat. Beginning 2001, excludes sheep and goat.
Source: Foreign Agricultural Service, U.S. Department of Agriculture (FAS-USDA)

Total Red Meat Exports[3] (Carcass Weight Equivalent) of Principal Countries — In Thousands of Metric Tons

Year	Argentina	Australia	Brazil	Canada	China	Denmark	France	India	Ireland	Netherlands	New Zealand	United States	World Total
2002	345	1,424	1,462	1,521	344	1,573	411	475	7	187	1,841	225	10,170
2003	382	1,318	1,765	1,388	433	1,578	432	548	10	227	1,921	282	10,672
2004	616	1,431	2,231	1,575	589	1,665	492	594	10	127	1,198	354	11,373
2005	755	1,444	2,606	1,680	578	1,396	617	577	12	91	1,525	418	12,320
2006	553	1,490	2,723	1,558	629	1,503	681	530	9	24	1,878	461	12,727
2007	535	1,454	2,919	1,490	431	1,426	678	496	9	52	2,075	386	12,732
2008	425	1,455	2,426	1,623	281	1,931	672	533	12	24	2,973	361	13,639
2009	657	1,404	2,303	1,603	270	1,563	609	514	9	27	2,735	376	12,963
2010[1]	301	1,364	2,300	1,690	295	1,860	700	510	6	28	3,063	380	13,305
2011[2]	301	1,365	2,450	1,705	322	1,710	725	496	5	28	3,123	390	13,476

[1] Preliminary. [2] Forecast. [3] Data through 2000, includes beef, veal, pork, sheep and goat meat. Beginning 2001, excludes sheep and goat.
Source: Foreign Agricultural Service, U.S. Department of Agriculture (FAS-USDA)

United States Meat Imports by Type of Product — In Metric Tons

Year	Beef and Veal Fresh	Beef and Veal Frozen	Beef and Veal Other Prepared or Preserved	Lamb, Mutton and Goat, Except Canned	Pork Fresh and Chilled	Pork Frozen	Pork Other Prepared or Preserved	Variety Meats, Fresh or Frozen	Other Livestock Meats NSE	Total
1996	227,874	412,805	66,719	33,009	125,220	58,336	72,650	32,579	13,744	1,042,934
1997	262,985	469,949	63,181	37,848	126,061	65,000	72,903	44,317	14,215	1,156,457
1998	295,820	527,063	68,884	51,630	146,965	70,227	76,230	47,031	13,058	1,296,907
1999	337,899	542,524	82,669	50,209	188,556	77,638	84,207	51,640	13,625	1,428,966
2000	336,117	608,737	73,750	59,968	229,395	91,446	92,672	57,388	14,281	1,563,753
2001	368,529	618,897	73,713	66,785	240,275	84,687	83,724	62,541	16,723	1,615,873
2002	400,484	586,500	84,640	73,863	276,639	90,423	91,379	55,384	19,401	1,678,713
2003	285,772	612,569	85,439	77,546	293,169	107,749	107,964	47,688	21,367	1,639,263
2004	387,758	717,942	92,123	82,930	266,583	109,915	96,840	33,776	55,737	1,843,604
2005[1]	406,431	669,935	96,181	83,957	266,544	93,063	78,594	41,067	25,426	1,761,198

[1] Preliminary. NSE = Not specified elsewhere. *Source: Foreign Agricultural Service, U.S. Department of Agriculture (FAS-USDA)*

United States Meat Exports by Type of Product — In Metric Tons

Year	Beef and Veal Fresh	Beef and Veal Frozen	Beef and Veal Other Prepared or Preserved	Lamb and Mutton, Fresh or Frozen	Pork Fresh and Chilled	Pork Frozen	Pork Other Prepared or Preserved	Variety Meats, Fresh, Chilled or Frozen	Other Meats	Total
1996	273,276	324,329	14,577	2,478	101,975	166,057	32,190	495,343	434,759	1,844,984
1997	316,534	359,460	15,227	2,545	134,706	151,121	31,215	469,789	435,258	1,915,854
1998	346,403	352,050	17,966	2,528	147,006	209,135	37,907	495,643	423,980	2,032,618
1999	370,184	414,458	19,323	2,219	160,910	225,492	40,463	524,325	455,561	2,212,935
2000	395,588	417,538	21,791	2,184	208,055	185,240	36,915	604,738	503,942	2,372,990
2001	393,105	362,972	23,932	2,770	227,807	247,461	44,494	685,063	513,969	2,501,573
2002	407,599	393,836	27,232	3,042	235,547	231,274	69,030	592,185	619,491	2,579,236
2003	430,071	390,543	37,572	2,909	237,129	257,360	69,693	598,726	567,565	2,591,568
2004	114,966	20,458	9,068	3,671	352,173	298,786	74,963	456,480	189,127	1,519,691
2005[1]	173,337	31,714	19,027	4,885	404,601	401,115	75,096	497,346	274,990	1,882,111

[1] Preliminary. *Source: Foreign Agricultural Service, U.S. Department of Agriculture (FAS-USDA)*

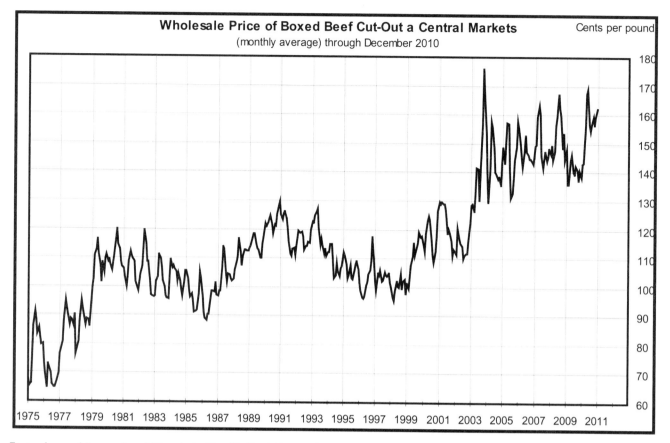

Wholesale Price of Boxed Beef Cut-Out a Central Markets
(monthly average) through December 2010
Cents per pound

Exports and Imports of Meats in the United States (Carcass Weight Equivalent)[3]

	---------- Exports ----------				---------- Imports ----------			
Year	Beef and Veal	Lamb and Mutton	Pork[3]	All Meat	Beef and Veal	Lamb and Mutton	Pork[3]	All Meat
2001	2,269	7	1,539	3,815	3,163	146	951	4,260
2002	2,448	7	1,612	4,067	3,218	160	1,071	4,448
2003	2,518	7	1,717	4,242	3,006	168	1,185	4,359
2004	460	8	2,181	2,649	3,679	181	1,099	4,960
2005	697	9	2,666	3,373	3,599	180	1,024	4,803
2006	1,145	18	2,995	4,158	3,085	190	990	4,265
2007	1,434	9	3,141	4,585	3,052	203	968	4,223
2008	1,887	12	4,667	6,566	2,538	183	832	3,553
2009[1]	1,869	16	4,126	6,011	2,628	171	834	3,633
2010[2]	2,505	17	4,360	6,437	2,660	183	840	3,533

[1] Preliminary.   [2] Estimate.   [3] Includes meat content of minor meats and of mixed products.
Source: Economic Research Service, U.S. Department of Agriculture (FAS-USDA)

Average Wholesale Prices of Meats in the United States   In Cent Per Pound

Year	Composite Retail Price of Beef, Choice, Grade 3	of Pork[3]	Wholesale Value[4] Beef	Pork	Net Farm Value[5] of Pork	Cow Beef Canner & Cutter, Central US	Boxed Beef Cut-out, Choice 1-3, Central US 550-700 Lb.	Pork Carcass Cut-out, U.S., No. 2	Lamb Carcass, Choice-Prime, E. Coast, 55-65 lbs.	Pork[6] Loins, Central US 14-18 lbs.	Skinned Ham, Central US 17-20 lbs.	Pork Bellies, Central US 12-14 lbs.
2001	337.73	269.39	192.12	117.80	81.30	79.50	122.61	66.83	148.96	116.97	64.86	78.61
2002	331.53	265.75	180.02	100.70	61.90	NA	114.42	53.49	151.28	97.98	47.52	69.91
2003	374.62	265.82	222.90	107.40	69.60	NA	143.58	58.87	185.21	100.96	45.48	86.42
2004	406.53	279.16	218.90	127.40	92.10	NA	142.15	73.53	189.08	117.14	64.98	99.35
2005	409.22	282.69	226.10	124.90	88.00	NA	145.78	69.84	209.88	113.22	64.07	81.46
2006	397.02	280.72	228.17	121.38	83.27	NA	146.82	67.62	199.10	104.46	64.04	82.81
2007	415.85	287.03	231.08	121.44	81.98	NA	149.80	67.54	215.96	104.17	57.96	88.97
2008	432.45	293.65	235.04	124.73	82.48	NA	153.17	69.24	226.63	106.63	63.52	69.86
2009[1]	425.98	291.97	217.18	111.19	71.56	NA	140.77	58.13	225.45	92.81	51.34	60.91
2010[2]	439.44	311.36	241.08	141.16	95.68	NA	156.91	81.25	263.02	115.96	76.41	93.63

[1] Preliminary.   [2] Estimate.   [3] Sold as retail cuts (ham, bacon, loin, etc.).   [4] Quantity equivalent to 1 pound of retail cuts.
[5] Portion of gross farm value minus farm by-product allowance.   Source: Economic Research Service, U.S. Department of Agriculture (ERS-USDA)

Average Wholesale Price of Boxed Beef Cut-Out[1], Choice 1-3, at Central US — In Cents Per Pound

Year	Jan.	Feb.	Mar.	Apr.	May	June	July	Aug.	Sept.	Oct.	Nov.	Dec.	Average
2001	129.78	128.87	129.58	128.93	129.03	126.82	118.93	120.20	119.30	115.93	110.95	113.04	122.61
2002	111.99	111.53	120.54	116.61	115.14	114.06	109.88	110.93	111.83	111.64	116.41	122.45	114.42
2003	128.59	128.77	126.35	133.03	141.44	141.16	130.13	139.91	156.64	176.06	167.15	153.71	143.58
2004	138.60	129.29	141.34	157.53	155.70	148.54	140.27	139.33	137.82	138.45	135.64	143.31	142.15
2005	148.93	143.02	150.66	157.34	156.82	140.02	131.19	132.85	137.97	144.30	148.81	157.49	145.78
2006	155.60	149.71	144.94	141.83	147.45	153.09	147.01	146.22	144.69	144.79	143.64	142.92	146.82
2007	149.15	149.54	159.23	163.23	160.20	145.59	141.47	144.51	146.99	144.09	145.39	148.25	149.80
2008	146.41	149.63	144.42	147.47	156.07	159.10	167.33	162.31	159.56	148.03	153.29	144.42	153.17
2009	147.68	136.03	135.91	144.42	146.22	140.22	139.59	142.13	140.94	137.15	140.60	138.35	140.77
2010[2]	142.87	143.22	155.73	167.37	168.80	156.54	154.53	156.67	159.20	156.58	159.25	162.20	156.91

[1] Data through 2004: 550-750 pounds; beginning 2005: 600-900 pounds.   [2] Preliminary.   *Source: Economic Research Service, U.S. Department of Agriculture (ERS-USDA)*

Production (Commercial) of All Red Meats in the United States — In Millions of Pounds (Carcass Weight)

Year	Jan.	Feb.	Mar.	Apr.	May	June	July	Aug.	Sept.	Oct.	Nov.	Dec.	Total
2001	3,935	3,761	3,761	3,506	3,881	3,758	3,643	4,060	3,664	4,264	3,970	3,813	46,016
2002	4,081	3,501	3,677	3,902	4,018	3,813	4,016	4,141	3,873	4,382	3,908	3,859	47,171
2003	4,075	3,496	3,705	3,845	3,944	3,948	4,046	3,913	4,007	4,155	3,524	3,876	46,534
2004	3,713	3,404	3,944	3,713	3,597	3,928	3,708	3,878	3,905	3,921	3,770	3,931	45,412
2005	3,648	3,423	3,879	3,622	3,714	3,963	3,616	4,100	3,933	3,926	3,942	3,954	45,719
2006	3,890	3,485	4,111	3,614	4,048	4,120	3,782	4,245	3,933	4,182	4,136	3,862	47,408
2007	4,091	3,615	4,013	3,753	4,075	4,028	3,940	4,026	3,864	4,614	4,300	4,059	48,378
2008	4,416	3,968	4,090	4,297	4,223	4,050	4,252	4,097	4,273	4,530	3,872	4,162	50,230
2009	4,169	3,825	4,142	4,084	3,919	4,162	4,124	4,077	4,262	4,391	3,963	4,148	49,264
2010[1]	3,918	3,736	4,282	4,013	3,732	4,177	3,956	4,127	4,161	4,265	4,329	4,355	49,050

[1] Preliminary.   *Source: Economic Research Service, U.S. Department of Agriculture (ERS-USDA)*

Cold Storage Holdings of All[2] Meats in the United States, on First of Month — In Millions of Pounds

Year	Jan.	Feb.	Mar.	Apr.	May	June	July	Aug.	Sept.	Oct.	Nov.	Dec.
2001	836.2	907.8	852.6	787.9	771.4	772.5	742.2	717.4	732.6	775.3	849.0	880.9
2002	946.8	982.6	970.7	961.9	996.6	973.0	918.0	912.6	950.7	997.8	1,038.9	997.7
2003	1,011.5	1,015.2	978.2	951.9	926.8	901.5	847.5	825.0	817.3	832.1	836.9	828.1
2004	879.0	953.7	926.9	879.4	883.6	829.3	797.9	807.7	841.9	886.1	889.2	912.6
2005	979.0	965.0	953.2	928.0	908.5	847.0	847.8	850.8	842.9	884.9	900.1	882.1
2006	877.2	1,012.4	987.3	959.8	979.1	940.8	880.9	915.5	918.2	969.4	994.0	1,009.9
2007	946.6	977.3	963.4	943.5	970.3	925.7	919.7	943.5	958.7	991.8	1,003.2	968.4
2008	961.6	1,047.5	1,072.6	1,106.9	1,103.9	1,024.5	983.8	960.5	970.9	1,009.4	1,027.8	1,037.8
2009	1,078.5	1,096.2	1,084.9	1,045.3	1,050.6	1,030.1	1,043.1	1,014.7	980.2	984.0	968.4	936.8
2010[1]	924.9	938.4	941.9	921.8	876.3	837.8	816.1	808.6	803.4	844.7	918.6	925.3

[1] Preliminary.   [2] Includes beef and veal, mutton and lamb, pork and products, rendered pork fat, and miscellaneous meats. Excludes lard.
Source: Economic Research Service, U.S. Department of Agriculture (ERS-USDA)

Cold Storage Holdings of Frozen Beef in the United States, on First of Month — In Millions of Pounds

Year	Jan.	Feb.	Mar.	Apr.	May	June	July	Aug.	Sept.	Oct.	Nov.	Dec.
2001	401.7	410.9	360.2	332.6	315.3	325.1	340.8	351.4	373.2	382.8	395.1	427.6
2002	460.7	455.5	439.0	410.5	405.7	401.8	396.9	416.5	461.8	494.9	525.2	512.6
2003	524.6	482.4	441.9	403.1	389.7	385.1	371.5	368.2	371.0	379.8	375.2	373.8
2004	395.1	434.4	435.0	416.8	421.2	402.8	411.8	427.0	446.0	457.2	452.6	463.3
2005	484.3	453.3	400.2	372.3	329.4	318.2	342.1	385.2	410.6	438.8	439.2	429.9
2006	434.4	465.9	440.6	436.2	441.3	446.3	449.1	479.2	484.5	491.9	485.7	520.3
2007	482.1	470.6	458.9	427.2	417.3	411.5	430.3	467.7	480.9	486.7	488.0	475.3
2008	482.5	450.8	436.5	426.7	416.4	420.4	428.1	430.8	441.2	454.5	471.0	481.6
2009	492.6	462.5	435.5	425.9	410.7	417.9	434.8	444.8	420.1	428.9	427.7	430.9
2010[1]	430.3	426.3	404.5	384.6	369.5	362.8	374.2	388.8	387.4	396.8	414.6	435.2

[1] Preliminary.   *Source: Economic Research Service, U.S. Department of Agriculture (ERS-USDA)*

Mercury

Mercury (symbol Hg) was known to the ancient Hindus and Chinese, and was also found in Egyptian tombs dating back to 1500 BC. The ancient Greeks used mercury in ointments, and the Romans used it in cosmetics. Alchemists thought mercury turned into gold when it hardened.

Mercury, also called quicksilver, is a heavy, silvery, toxic, transitional metal. Mercury is the only common metal that is liquid at room temperatures. When subjected to a pressure of 7,640 atmospheres (7.7 million millibars), mercury becomes a solid. Mercury dissolves in nitric or concentrated sulfuric acid, but is resistant to alkalis. It is a poor conductor of heat. Mercury has superconductivity when cooled to sufficiently low temperatures. It has a freezing point of about –39 degrees Celsius and a boiling point of about 357 degrees Celsius.

Mercury is found in its pure form or combined in small amounts with silvers, but is found most often in the ore cinnabar, a mineral consisting of mercuric sulfide. By heating the cinnabar ore in air until the mercuric sulfide breaks down, pure mercury metal is produced. Mercury forms alloys called amalgams with all common metals except iron and platinum. Most mercury is used for the manufacture of industrial chemicals and for electrical and electronic applications. Other uses for mercury include its use in gold recovery from ores, barometers, diffusion pumps, laboratory instruments, mercury-vapor lamps, pesticides, batteries, and catalysts. A decline in mercury production and usage since the 1970s reflects a trend for using mercury substitutes due to its toxicity.

Prices – The average monthly price of mercury in 2010 rose by +61.8% yr/yr to $997.08 per flask (34.5 kilograms), which is a new record high. In January of 2011 the price rose to $1,325.00 per flask.

Supply – World mine production of mercury in 2010 rose by +2.1% yr/yr to a 13-year high of 1,960 metric tons. The record low of 1,150 metric tons was posted in 2006. The world's largest miners of mercury are China with 71% of world production and Kyrgyzstan with 13%. China's production in 2009 and 2010 was a record high of 1,400 metric tons. China's record low of 190 metric tons was posted only 10 years ago in 2001. Spain is also a large producer but their data has not been available since 2004.

Demand – The breakdown of domestic consumption of mercury by particular categories is no longer available. However, as of 1997 records showed that chlorine and caustic soda accounted for 46% of U.S. mercury consumption, followed by wiring devices and switches (17%), dental equipment (12%), electrical lighting (8%), and measuring control instruments (7%). Substitutes for mercury include lithium and composite ceramic materials.

Trade – U.S. foreign trade in mercury has been relatively small but U.S. imports of mercury in 201- fell -2.9% yr/yr to 200 metric tons but still up from 2007's 7-year low of 67 metric tons. By contrast the U.S.'s record high imports were in 1974 at 1,799 metric tons. U.S. imports were mostly from Chile and Peru. U.S. exports of mercury in 2010 fell by -33.6% to 500 metric tons, but still well up from 2007's 11-year low of 84 metric tons.

World Mine Production of Mercury   In Metric Tons (1 tonne = 29.008216 flasks)

Year	Algeria	China	Finland	Kyrgyzstan	Mexico	Spain	Tajikistan	Russia	Ukraine	United States	World Total
2001	321	190	71	300	15	500	40	50	----	NA	1,500
2002	307	495	51	300	15	727	20	50	NA	NA	1,980
2003	176	610	25	300	15	500	30	50	----	NA	1,730
2004	73	1,140	24	300	15	250	30	50	----	NA	1,900
2005	4	1,100	20	200	6	----	30	50	----	NA	1,520
2006	----	760	20	250	8	----	30	50	----	NA	1,150
2007	----	800	20	250	8	----	30	50	----	NA	1,200
2008	----	800	20	250	21	----	30	50	----	NA	1,320
2009[1]	----	1,400	15	250	21	----	30	50	----	NA	1,920
2010[2]		1,400		250							1,960

[1] Preliminary.   [2] Estimate.   [4] Less than 1/2 unit.   NA = Not available   W = Withheld.   *Source: U.S. Geological Survey (USGS)*

Salient Statistics of Mercury in the United States   In Metric Tons

Year	Producing Mines	Secondary Production Industrial	Secondary Production Government[3]	NDS[4] Shipments	Consumer & Dealer Stocks, Dec. 31	Industrial Demand	Exports	Imports
2002	NA	NA	----	----	40	NA	201	209
2003	NA	NA	----	----	94	72	287	46
2004	NA	NA	----	----	62	91	278	92
2005	NA	NA	----	----	38	40	319	212
2006	NA	NA	----	----	19	38	390	94
2007	NA	NA	----	----	18	31	84	67
2008	NA	NA	----	----	24	NA	732	155
2009[1]	NA	NA	----	----	30	NA	753	206
2010[2]	NA	NA	----	----		NA	500	200

[1] Preliminary.   [2] Estimate.   [3] Secondary mercury shipped from the Department of Energy.   [4] National Defense Stockpile.   NA = Not available.
E = Net exporter.   *Source: U.S. Geological Survey (USGS)*

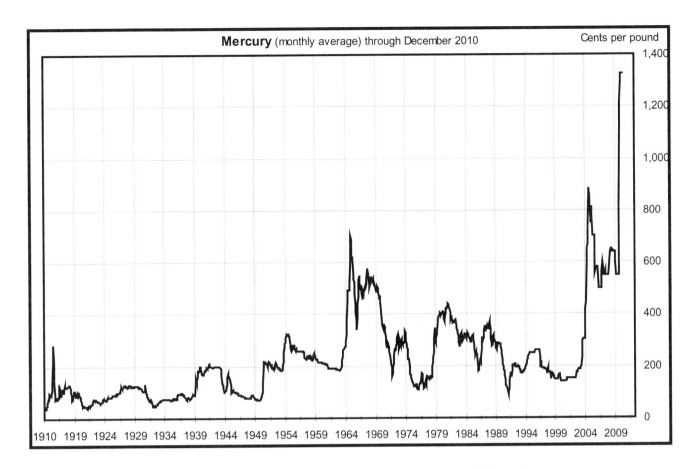

Mercury (monthly average) through December 2010 — Cents per pound

Average Price of Mercury in New York   In Dollars Per Flask of 76 Pounds (34.5 Kilograms)

Year	Jan.	Feb.	Mar.	Apr.	May	June	July	Aug.	Sept.	Oct.	Nov.	Dec.	Average
2001	142.00	142.00	142.00	142.00	142.00	143.71	154.00	154.00	154.00	154.00	154.00	154.00	148.12
2002	154.00	154.00	154.00	154.00	154.00	154.00	154.00	154.00	154.00	154.00	154.00	154.00	154.00
2003	165.43	175.00	175.00	175.00	185.23	187.50	187.50	187.50	187.50	187.50	195.63	200.00	184.07
2004	200.00	256.25	297.61	305.00	305.00	305.00	305.00	305.00	417.05	485.12	649.24	650.00	373.36
2005	678.57	747.50	867.39	873.81	850.00	817.05	759.52	750.00	813.64	730.95	700.00	700.00	774.04
2006	700.00	700.00	691.30	552.50	574.02	582.50	582.50	582.50	582.50	576.59	513.64	500.00	594.84
2007	500.00	500.00	500.00	500.00	500.00	573.81	600.00	600.00	572.50	550.00	550.00	550.00	541.36
2008	550.00	550.00	550.00	550.00	550.00	550.00	550.00	550.00	590.91	600.00	645.00	650.00	573.83
2009	650.00	647.00	640.00	640.00	642.86	640.00	640.00	640.00	603.18	550.00	550.00	550.00	616.09
2010	550.00	550.00	550.00	550.00	828.57	1129.55	1213.64	1293.18	1325.00	1325.00	1325.00	1325.00	997.08

Source: American Metal Market (AMM)

Mercury Consumed in the United States   In Metric Tons

Year	Batteries[3]	Chlorine & Caustic Soda	Catalysts, Misc.	Dental Equip.	Electrical Lighting[3]	General Lab Use	Measuring Control Instrument	Paints	Wiring Devices & Switches[3]	Other Uses	Grand Total
1989	250	379	40	39	31	18	87	192	141	32	1,212
1990	106	247	29	44	33	32	108	14	70	38	720
1991	18	184	26	41	39	30	90	6	71	49	554
1992	13	209	20	42	55	28	80	----	82	92	621
1993	10	180	18	35	38	26	65	----	83	103	558
1994	6	135	25	24	27	24	53	----	79	110	483
1995	----	154	----	32	30	----	43	----	84	93	436
1996[1]	----	136	----	31	29	----	41	----	49	86	372
1997[2]	----	160	----	40	29	----	24	----	57	36	346
	Data No Longer Available										

[1] Preliminary.   [2] Estimate.   W = Withheld proprietary data.   *Source: U.S. Geological Survey (USGS)*

Milk

Evidence of man's use of animal milk as food was discovered in a temple in the Euphrates Valley near Babylon, dating back to 3,000 BC. Humans drink the milk produced from a variety of domesticated mammals, including cows, goats, sheep, camels, reindeer, buffaloes, and llama. In India, half of all milk consumed is from water buffalo. Camels' milk spoils slower than other types of milk in the hot desert, but the vast majority of milk used for commercial production and consumption comes from cows.

Milk directly from a cow in its natural form is called raw milk. Raw milk is processed by spinning it in a centrifuge, homogenizing it to create a consistent texture (i.e., by forcing hot milk under high pressure through small nozzles), and then sterilizing it through pasteurization (i.e., heating to a high temperature for a specified length of time to destroy pathogenic bacteria). Condensed, powdered, and evaporated milk are produced by evaporating some or all of the water content. Whole milk contains 3.5% milk fat. Lower-fat milks include 2% low-fat milk, 1% low- fat milk, and skim milk, which has only 1/2 gram of milk fat per serving.

The Chicago Mercantile Exchange has three different milk futures contracts: Milk Class III which is milk used in the manufacturing of cheese, Milk Class IV which is milk used in the production of butter and all dried milk products, and Nonfat Dry Milk which is used in commercial or consumer cooking or to reconstitute nonfat milk by the consumer. The Milk Class III contract has the largest volume and open interest.

Prices – The average monthly price received by farmers for all milk sold to plants in 2010 rose by +26.9% yr/yr to $16.29 per hundred pounds, down from the 2007 record high of $19.13.

The average monthly price received by farmers for fluid grade milk in 2010 also rose by +26.9% yr/yr to $16.29 per hundred pounds. The average monthly price received by farmers for manufacturing grade milk in 2010 rose by +21.4% to $14.79 per hundred pounds.

Supply – World milk production in 2010 rose +1.5% to 523.247 million metric tons. The biggest producers were the European Union with 27.0% of world production, the U.S. with 17.1%, and India with 22.8%. U.S. 2010 milk production in pounds rose +1.8% yr/yr to 192.726 billion pounds, setting a new record high. The number of dairy cows on U.S. farms has fallen sharply in the past 3 decades from the 12 million seen in 1970. In 2010, there were 9.112 million dairy cows on U.S. farms, down -1.0% yr/yr. Dairy farmers have been able to increase milk production even with fewer cows because of a dramatic increase in milk yield per cow. In 2009, the average cow produced a record 21,151 pounds of milk per year, more than double the 9,751 pounds seen in 1970.

Demand – Per capita consumption of milk in the U.S. fell to a new record low of 206 pounds per year in 2002 (the latest complete data available), down sharply by 26% from 277 pounds in 1977. The utilization breakdown for 2002 shows the largest manufacturing usage categories are cheese (64.504 billion pounds of milk) and creamery butter (30.250 billion pounds).

Trade – U.S. imports of milk in 2009 rose +4.0% yr/yr to 4.058 billion pounds, but still well below the record high of 5.716 billion pounds posted in 2001.

World Fluid Milk Production (Cow's Milk)   In Thousands of Metric Tons

Year	Argentina	Australia	Brazil	China	European Union	India	Japan	Mexico	New Zealand	Russia	Ukraine	United States	World Total
2004	9,250	10,377	23,317	23,684	139,024	88,000	8,329	10,029	15,000	32,000	14,106	77,488	610,515
2005	9,500	10,429	24,250	28,648	139,648	91,500	8,285	10,016	14,500	32,000	13,713	80,255	621,359
2006	10,200	10,395	25,230	33,025	136,281	96,200	8,137	10,214	15,200	31,100	13,175	82,455	626,674
2007	9,550	9,870	26,750	36,334	136,874	102,100	8,007	10,829	15,640	32,200	12,262	84,211	640,783
2008	10,010	9,500	27,820	35,450	137,848	106,000	7,982	11,077	15,141	32,500	11,762	86,174	502,033
2009	10,350	9,326	28,795	29,625	137,720	112,000	7,910	11,036	17,397	32,600	11,610	85,874	504,990
2010[1]	10,600	9,400	29,948	30,328	138,220	117,000	7,790	11,342	16,897	31,740	11,192	87,450	512,708
2011[2]	11,070	9,700	30,846	31,780	138,720	121,500	7,800	11,500	18,642	31,400	10,812	88,690	523,247

[1] Preliminary.   [2] Forecast.   *Source: Foreign Agricultural Service, U.S. Department of Agriculture (FAS-USDA)*

Salient Statistics of Milk in the United States   In Millions of Pounds

Year	Number of Milk Cows on Farms[3] (Thousands)	Production Per Cow[4] (Pounds)	Production Total[4]	Supply Beginning Stocks[5]	Imports	Total Supply	Exports[5]	Domestic Fed to Calves	Domestic Humans	Total Use	All Milk, Whole-sale	Milk, Eligible for Fluid Market	Milk, Manu-facturing Grade	Per Capita Consumption[6] (Fluid Milk in Lbs)
2003	9,083	18,761	170,394	9,891	5,040	185,325	----	964	169,276	170,240	12.52	12.53	11.77	208
2004	9,010	18,958	170,805	8,333	5,278	184,416	3,400	956	169,699	174,055	16.04	16.04	15.41	207
2005	9,040	19,577	176,989	7,154	7,500	191,643	3,300	987	175,788	180,075	15.14	15.14	14.45	206
2006	9,112	19,951	181,798	8,007	7,500	197,305	3,400	943	180,700	185,043	12.91	12.92	12.28	208
2007	9,158	20,266	185,602	9,500	7,200	202,302	5,700	952	184,565	191,217	19.13	19.13	18.18	206
2008	9,315	20,396	189,992	10,356	5,300	205,648	8,700	942	188,917	198,559	18.30	18.28	17.98	204
2009[1]	9,200	20,576	189,320	10,045	5,600	204,965	4,500	898	188,307	193,705	12.84	12.84	12.18	
2010[2]	9,117	21,149	192,819	11,300	4,100	208,219	8,100				16.29	16.29	14.79	

[1] Preliminary.   [2] Estimate.   [3] Average number on farms during year including dry cows, excluding heifers not yet fresh.   [4] Excludes milk sucked by calves.   [5] Government and commercial.   [6] Product pounds of commercial sales and on farm consumption.

Source: Economic Research Service, U.S. Department of Agriculture (ERS-USDA)

Milk-Feed Price Ratio[1] in the United States   In Pounds

Year	Jan.	Feb.	Mar.	Apr.	May	June	July	Aug.	Sept.	Oct.	Nov.	Dec.	Average
2002	3.03	3.00	2.89	2.81	2.64	2.54	2.34	2.27	2.30	2.46	2.44	2.44	2.60
2003	2.40	2.35	2.27	2.25	2.19	2.21	2.60	2.89	3.16	3.23	3.05	2.89	2.62
2004	2.70	2.60	2.80	3.11	3.15	3.12	2.96	2.93	3.22	3.27	3.57	3.67	3.09
2005	3.45	3.50	3.35	3.18	2.93	2.87	2.93	3.08	3.27	3.42	3.45	3.28	3.23
2006	3.17	2.93	2.70	2.48	2.32	2.35	2.33	2.48	2.61	2.53	2.44	2.43	2.56
2007	2.45	2.33	2.39	2.51	2.54	2.88	3.16	3.19	3.19	3.10	3.05	2.85	2.80
2008	2.65	2.24	2.07	1.88	1.81	1.88	1.90	1.81	1.90	2.02	2.01	1.92	2.01
2009	1.60	1.51	1.56	1.59	1.48	1.45	1.57	1.80	2.00	2.11	2.26	2.42	1.78
2010[1]	2.33	2.36	2.19	2.18	2.19	2.28	2.32	2.37	2.38	2.40	2.23	1.98	2.27

[1] Pounds of 16% protein mixed dairy feed equal in value to one pound of whole milk.   [2] Preliminary.   *Source: Economic Research Service, U.S. Department of Agriculture (ERS-USDA)*

Milk Production[2] in the United States   In Millions of Pounds

Year	Jan.	Feb.	Mar.	Apr.	May	June	July	Aug.	Sept.	Oct.	Nov.	Dec.	Total
2002	14,304	13,229	14,864	14,580	15,118	14,317	14,196	14,128	13,467	13,866	13,478	14,211	170,063
2003	14,584	13,441	15,044	14,634	15,003	14,328	14,263	14,015	13,468	13,898	13,470	14,164	170,394
2004	14,402	13,595	14,762	14,519	15,012	14,293	14,405	14,215	13,619	14,070	13,610	14,303	170,805
2005	14,614	13,530	15,206	15,047	15,697	15,087	14,978	14,896	14,260	14,611	14,209	14,854	176,989
2006	15,343	14,238	15,966	15,538	16,068	15,324	15,168	15,061	14,481	14,857	14,523	15,231	181,798
2007	15,605	14,321	16,132	15,763	16,180	15,476	15,714	15,525	14,871	15,370	15,013	15,632	185,602
2008	15,976	15,176	16,458	16,125	16,707	15,942	15,995	15,757	15,129	15,615	15,212	15,900	189,992
2009	16,135	14,754	16,485	16,148	16,805	15,935	16,018	15,737	15,038	15,420	15,070	15,775	189,320
2010[1]	16,020	14,758	16,614	16,416	17,040	16,353	16,436	16,094	15,540	15,900	15,498	16,150	192,819

[1] Preliminary.   [2] Excludes milk sucked by calves.   *Source: Economic Research Service, U.S. Department of Agriculture (ERS-USDA)*

Milk Cows[2] in the United States   In Thousands of Head

Year	Jan.	Feb.	Mar.	Apr.	May	June	July	Aug.	Sept.	Oct.	Nov.	Dec.	Total
2002	9,117	9,109	9,110	9,132	9,149	9,166	9,158	9,157	9,145	9,147	9,146	9,150	9,139
2003	9,147	9,145	9,141	9,125	9,104	9,097	9,087	9,072	9,061	9,034	9,005	8,994	9,083
2004	8,985	8,993	9,002	8,999	8,991	9,014	9,053	9,060	9,066	9,060	9,056	9,063	9,040
2005	9,000	8,996	9,009	9,030	9,042	9,050	9,053	9,060	9,107	9,107	9,111	9,126	9,112
2006	9,081	9,088	9,106	9,116	9,129	9,139	9,119	9,114	9,107	9,181	9,196	9,217	9,158
2007	9,135	9,136	9,142	9,132	9,138	9,144	9,153	9,159	9,166	9,181	9,196	9,217	9,158
2008	9,276	9,287	9,295	9,307	9,318	9,321	9,335	9,331	9,323	9,324	9,333	9,334	9,315
2009	9,312	9,289	9,283	9,282	9,270	9,228	9,191	9,162	9,123	9,094	9,085	9,082	9,200
2010[1]	9,089	9,092	9,099	9,108	9,119	9,129	9,135	9,123	9,121	9,123	9,125	9,141	9,117

[1] Preliminary.   [2] Includes dry cows, excludes heifers not yet fresh.   *Source: Economic Research Service, U.S. Department of Agriculture (ERS-USDA)*

Milk Per Cow[2] in the United States   In Pounds

Year	Jan.	Feb.	Mar.	Apr.	May	June	July	Aug.	Sept.	Oct.	Nov.	Dec.	Total
2002	1,569	1,452	1,632	1,597	1,652	1,562	1,550	1,543	1,473	1,516	1,474	1,553	18,608
2003	1,594	1,470	1,646	1,604	1,648	1,575	1,570	1,545	1,486	1,538	1,496	1,575	18,761
2004	1,603	1,512	1,640	1,613	1,670	1,586	1,596	1,574	1,509	1,559	1,509	1,587	18,958
2005	1,624	1,504	1,688	1,666	1,735	1,668	1,656	1,643	1,572	1,613	1,569	1,639	19,577
2006	1,690	1,567	1,753	1,705	1,760	1,676	1,663	1,653	1,590	1,631	1,594	1,669	19,951
2007	1,708	1,567	1,765	1,726	1,771	1,692	1,717	1,695	1,622	1,674	1,633	1,696	20,266
2008	1,722	1,634	1,771	1,733	1,793	1,710	1,713	1,689	1,623	1,675	1,630	1,703	20,396
2009	1,733	1,588	1,776	1,740	1,812	1,726	1,744	1,718	1,649	1,695	1,658	1,737	20,576
2010[1]	1,763	1,623	1,826	1,802	1,869	1,791	1,799	1,764	1,704	1,743	1,698	1,767	21,149

[1] Preliminary.   [2] Excludes milk sucked by calves.   *Source: Economic Research Service, U.S. Department of Agriculture (ERS-USDA)*

Average Price Received by Farmers for All Milk (Sold to Plants)   In Dollars Per Hundred Pounds (Cwt.)

Year	Jan.	Feb.	Mar.	Apr.	May	June	July	Aug.	Sept.	Oct.	Nov.	Dec.	Average
2002	13.40	13.10	12.70	12.50	12.10	11.50	11.10	11.30	11.60	12.10	11.90	11.90	12.10
2003	11.70	11.40	11.00	11.00	11.00	11.00	12.10	13.30	14.50	15.00	14.40	13.80	12.52
2004	13.20	13.60	15.40	18.10	19.30	18.20	16.10	14.90	15.50	15.60	16.20	16.40	16.04
2005	15.90	15.50	15.60	15.20	14.70	14.40	14.80	14.80	15.30	15.60	15.10	14.80	15.14
2006	14.50	13.50	12.60	12.10	11.90	11.90	11.70	12.00	13.00	13.60	13.90	14.20	12.91
2007	14.50	14.90	15.60	16.60	18.00	20.20	21.60	21.60	21.80	21.40	21.90	21.50	19.13
2008	20.50	19.10	18.10	18.00	18.30	19.30	19.30	18.40	18.20	17.80	17.10	15.50	18.30
2009	13.30	11.60	11.80	11.90	11.60	11.30	11.30	12.10	13.00	14.30	15.40	16.50	12.84
2010[1]	16.10	15.90	14.80	14.60	15.10	15.50	16.00	16.70	17.70	18.50	17.90	16.70	16.29

[1] Preliminary.   *Source: Economic Research Service, U.S. Department of Agriculture (ERS-USDA)*

Molybdenum

Molybdenum (symbol Mo) is a silvery-white, hard, malleable, metallic element. Molybdenum melts at about 2610 degrees Celsius and boils at about 4640 degrees Celsius. Swedish chemist Carl Wilhelm Scheele discovered molybdenum in 1778.

Molybdenum occurs in nature in the form of molybdenite and wulfenite. Contributing to the growth of plants, it is an important trace element in soils. Approximately 70% of the world supply of molybdenum is obtained as a by-product of copper mining. -Molybdenum is chiefly used as an alloy to strengthen steel and resist corrosion. It is used for structural work, aircraft parts, and forged automobile parts because it withstands high temperatures and pressures and adds strength. Other uses include lubricants, a refractory metal in chemical applications, electron tubing, and as a catalyst.

Prices – The average monthly U.S. merchant price of molybdic oxide in 2010 rose by +40.1% yr/yr to $15.85 per pound. That was still far below the 2005 record high of $32.70 per pound but over six times higher than the 2001 record low of $2.37.

Supply – World production of molybdenum in 2010 rose by +5.9% yr/yr to a record high of 234,000 metric tons.

The 17-year low of 122,000 metric tons was seen in 2002. The world's largest producers of molybdenum are China with 40% of world production in 2010, the U.S. with 24%, and Chili with 17%.

U.S. production of molybdenum concentrate in 2010 rose +17.2% yr/yr to 56,000 metric tons, well above the 27-year low of 32,300 metric tons posted in 2002.

U.S. production of molybdenum primary products in 2008 (latest data) rose +7.4% to 33,400 metric tons, with 31,800 metric tons of that production in molybdic oxide and 1,640 metric tons in molybdenum metal powder.

Demand – U.S. consumption of molybdenum concentrate in 2010 rose by +57.4% yr/yr to 48,000 metric tons, remaining well above the 14-year low of 21,200 metric tons posted in 2002. U.S. consumption of molybdenum concentrate has more than doubled over the last 13 years. U.S. consumption of molybdenum primary products in 2009 fell by -0.5% yr/yr to 19,000 metric tons.

Trade – U.S. imports of molybdenum concentrate for consumption in 2008 (latest data) fell by 17.7% yr/yr to 10,200 metric tons, but still well above the 14-year low of 4,710 metric tons posted in 2002.

World Mine Production of Molybdenum   In Metric Tons (Contained Molybdenum)

Year	Armenia	Canada[3]	Chile	China	Iran	Kazakhstan	Mexico	Mongolia	Peru	Russia	United States	Uzbekisten	World Total
2004	2,950	9,519	41,883	38,500	1,800	230	3,730	1,141	14,246	2,900	41,500	500	159,000
2005	3,000	7,935	48,041	40,000	2,476	230	4,246	1,188	17,325	3,000	58,000	575	186,000
2006	3,900	7,842	43,278	43,900	2,500	250	2,516	1,404	17,209	3,100	59,800	600	187,000
2007	4,080	12,000	44,912	59,800	2,600	400	6,159	1,300	16,737	3,300	57,000	600	209,000
2008	4,250	7,720	33,700	81,000	3,800	400	7,810	2,000	16,700	3,600	55,900	500	218,000
2009[1]	4,150	8,840	34,900	93,500	3,700	380	7,800	3,000	12,300	3,800	47,800	550	221,000
2010[2]	4,200	9,100	39,000	94,000	3,700	400	8,000	3,000	12,000	3,800	56,000	550	234,000

[1] Preliminary.   [2] Estimate.   [3] Shipments.   *Source: U.S. Geological Survey (USGS)*

Salient Statistics of Molybdenum in the United States   In Metric Tons (Contained Molybdenum)

Year	Concentrate Production	Total Shipments (Including Exports)	Value Million $	For Exports	Consumption	Imports For Consumption	Stocks Dec. 31[3]	Grand Total	Primary Products[4] Net Production Molybdic Oxide[5]	Molybdenum Metal Powder	Avg Price Value $ / Kg.[6]	Shipments To Domestic Destinations	Oxide for Exports, Gross Weight	Consumption	Producer Stocks, Dec. 31
2003	33,500	33,600	324.0	----	27,500	5,190	2,520	11,800	11,000	760	11.75	30,100	2,580	16,400	2,760
2004	41,500	42,000	1,420.0	----	38,700	8,780	2,610	24,300	23,400	868	36.73	39,300	5,280	17,400	2,840
2005	58,000	57,900	NA	----	46,600	11,900	3,620	29,800	28,700	1,050	70.11	46,700	14,600	18,900	3,770
2006	59,800	60,100	NA	----	44,400	10,900	2,120	30,600	29,000	1,620	54.62	51,000	11,600	19,000	3,210
2007	57,000	57,100	NA	----	40,900	12,400	2,630	31,100	29,500	1,620	66.79	48,700	14,900	21,000	3,140
2008[1]	55,900	57,800	NA	----	36,400	10,200	1,760	33,400	31,800	1,640	62.99	51,200	16,700	20,900	3,850
2009[2]	47,800				30,500						25.84			19,000	

[1] Preliminary.   [2] Estimate.   [3] At mines & at plants making molybdenum products.   [4] Comprises ferromolybdenum, molybdic oxide, & molybdenum salts & metal.   [5] Includes molybdic oxide briquets, molybdic acid, molybdenum trioxide, all other.   [6] U.S. producer price per kilogram of molybdenum oxide contained in technical-grade molybdic oxide.   W = Withheld proprietary data.   E = Net exporter.   *Source: U.S. Geological Survey (USGS)*

US Merchant Price of Molybdic Oxide   In Dollars Per Pound

Year	Jan.	Feb.	Mar.	Apr.	May	June	July	Aug.	Sept.	Oct.	Nov.	Dec.	Average
2004	7.63	8.15	8.93	13.11	14.00	15.03	15.75	16.70	18.27	19.50	22.66	27.50	15.60
2005	33.00	30.15	33.59	34.79	36.41	38.32	32.79	30.00	31.93	32.33	30.33	28.72	32.70
2006	23.70	24.54	23.12	22.93	24.82	26.31	26.01	25.60	26.96	26.02	25.41	25.50	25.08
2007	25.22	25.53	27.77	28.52	30.05	33.71	32.23	31.39	23.00	32.00	32.80	32.63	29.57
2008	32.74	32.88	32.88	32.88	32.88	32.88	32.88	33.17	33.75	33.75	15.58	10.62	29.74
2009	9.78	9.61	9.03	8.55	9.08	10.34	11.56	17.35	15.24	13.22	10.86	11.15	11.31
2010	14.04	15.91	17.68	17.89	17.34	14.60	14.13	15.57	16.20	15.20	15.65	16.03	15.85

Source: American Metal Market (AMM)

Nickel

Nickel (symbol Ni) is a hard, malleable, ductile metal that has a silvery tinge that can take on a high polish. Nickel is somewhat ferromagnetic and is a fair conductor of heat and electricity. Nickel is primarily used in the production of stainless steel and other corrosion-resistant alloys. Nickel is used in coins to replace silver, in rechargeable batteries, and in electronic circuitry. Nickel plating techniques, like electro-less coating or single-slurry coating, are employed in such applications as turbine blades, helicopter rotors, extrusion dies, and rolled steel strip.

Nickel futures and options trade at the London Metal Exchange (LME). The nickel futures contract calls for the delivery of 6 metric tons of primary nickel with at least 99.80% purity in the form of full plate, cut cathodes, pellets or briquettes. The contract is priced in terms of U.S. dollars per metric ton.

Prices – Nickel started the year at about $17,800 per metric ton and rose rapidly to a high of $27,600 per metric ton in May. From there the price fell sharply to a low of $17,945 per metric ton in June. The price then rose steadily to finish the year at about $24,600 per metric ton. The price continued to rise into 2011 to post a high of about $29,000 per metric ton in March.

Supply – World mine production of nickel in 2010 rose +10.7% yr/yr to 1.550 million metric tons, but still below the 2007 record high production of 1.680 million metric tons. The current levels are more than double the production seen in 1970. The world's largest mine producers of nickel in 2009 were Russia (with 17% of world production), Indonesia (15%), Canada (10%), Australia (9%), and New Caledonia (9%). In 2008 (latest data available) U.S. secondary nickel production fell -13.8% to 85,260 metric tons but still well up from the 6-year low of 81,200 metric tons in 2001.

Demand – U.S. consumption of nickel in 2008 (latest data available) rose +7.6% to 128,000 metric tons, but still below from the 2006 record high of 208,000 metric tons. The primary U.S. nickel consumption use is for stainless and heat-resisting steels, which accounted for 88% of U.S. consumption in 2008. Other consumption uses were super alloys (18%), nickel alloys (17%), electro-plating anodes (7%), alloy steels (6%), copper base alloys (4%), and chemicals (1%).

Trade – The U.S. relied on imports for 43% of its nickel consumption in 2010, down from 64% in 1998. U.S. imports of primary and secondary nickel in 2010 rose +43.1% to 168,300 metric tons, up from the 2009 record low of 117,600 metric tons. U.S. exports of primary and secondary nickel in 2009 fell -10.3% to 87,000 metric tons.

World Mine Production of Nickel   In Metric Tons (Contained Nickel)

Year	Australia[3]	Botswana	Brazil	Canada	China	Republic	Greece	Indonesia	New Cal-edonia	Philip-pines	Russia	South Africa	Total
2004	186,800	35,163	44,928	186,694	75,600	46,000	21,700	136,000	118,279	16,973	268,545	39,851	1,370,000
2005	188,900	39,305	74,198	199,932	72,700	53,124	23,210	135,000	111,939	30,717	277,177	42,392	1,470,000
2006	185,000	38,000	82,492	232,948	82,100	47,516	21,670	157,000	102,986	72,947	276,985	41,599	1,570,000
2007	184,900	38,000	58,317	254,915	67,000	47,125	21,190	229,000	125,364	91,367	279,773	37,917	1,680,000
2008	199,200	38,000	58,500	259,588	72,000	31,300	21,100	192,600	102,583	83,895	266,807	31,675	1,600,000
2009[1]	165,000	28,600	54,100	137,000	79,400	----	14,000	203,000	92,800	137,000	262,000	34,600	1,400,000
2010[2]	139,000	32,400	66,200	155,000	77,000	3,100		232,000	138,000	156,000	265,000	41,800	1,550,000

[1] Preliminary.   [2] Estimate.   [3] Content of nickel sulfate and concentrates.   *Source: U.S. Geological Survey (USGS)*

Salient Statistics of Nickel in the United States   In Metric Tons (Contained Nickel)

Year	Net Import Reliance As a % of Apparent Con-sumption	Production - Plant[4]	Secon-dary[5]	Alloy Sheets	Cast Iron	Copper Base Alloys	Electro-plating Anodes	Nickel Alloys	Stainless & Heat Resisting Steels	Super Alloys	Chem-icals	Ap-parent Con-sumption	Stocks, Dec. 31 At Con-sumer Plants	Stocks, Dec. 31 At Pro-ducer Plants	Primary & Secondary Exports	Primary & Secondary Imports	Avg. Price LME $/Lb.
2003	45	----	100,800	3,730	591	5,200	11,400	14,600	114,000	13,400	2,400	165,000	11,680	8,040	53,630	136,500	4.37
2004	49	----	99,700	3,770	306	5,990	11,900	15,400	115,000	15,700	6,270	183,000	11,380	6,580	56,300	154,800	6.27
2005	48	----	98,520	4,020	179	6,090	11,300	18,800	131,000	18,000	2,030	196,000	12,920	5,940	63,230	158,500	6.69
2006	50	----	103,400	4,170	201	7,010	10,700	19,600	136,000	20,000	1,930	208,000	14,070	6,450	67,350	173,300	11.00
2007	17	----	98,900	7,130	212	5,720	10,300	17,900	127,000	22,000	2,880	119,000	19,050	5,690	116,100	141,200	16.88
2008[2]	33	----	85,260	7,080	224	4,890	9,030	21,500	113,000	22,600	844	128,000	19,150	5,860	106,200	149,100	9.57
2009[3]	22												16,600	6,150	97,020	117,600	6.65

[1] Exclusive of scrap.   [2] Preliminary.   [3]/ Estimate.   [4] Smelter & refinery.   [5] From purchased scrap (ferrous & nonferrous).
W = Withheld proprietary data.   NA = Not available.   *Source: U.S. Geological Survey (USGS)*

Average Price of Nickel[1] in the United States   In Cents Per Pound

Year	Jan.	Feb.	Mar.	Apr.	May	June	July	Aug.	Sept.	Oct.	Nov.	Dec.	Average
2006	705.36	718.05	716.83	854.01	994.34	996.93	1,273.06	1,461.61	1,424.67	1,545.18	1,511.97	1,629.01	1,152.59
2007	1,734.23	1,930.47	2,172.62	2,378.64	2,476.96	2,002.41	1,618.56	1,342.03	1,425.77	1,489.95	1,477.33	1,254.00	1,775.25
2008	1,328.12	1,341.80	1,475.21	1,376.29	1,243.11	1,094.23	986.01	929.79	870.45	612.68	551.36	501.41	1,025.87
2009	575.83	535.25	501.88	567.31	610.15	720.34	766.47	950.67	860.98	912.94	862.14	850.66	726.22
2010	929.69	958.30	1,124.71	1,290.79	1,130.91	1,006.54	1,041.32	1,109.42	1,153.47	1,186.36	1,133.19	1,174.23	1,103.24

[1] Plating material, briquettes.   *Source: American Metal Market (AMM)*

Oats

Oats are seeds or grains of a genus of plants that thrive in cool, moist climates. There are about 25 species of oats that grow worldwide in the cooler temperate regions. The oldest known cultivated oats were found inside caves in Switzerland and are believed to be from the Bronze Age. Oats are usually sown in early spring and harvested in mid to late summer, but in southern regions of the northern hemisphere, they may be sown in the fall. Oats are used in many processed foods such as flour, livestock feed, and furfural, a chemical used as a solvent in various refining industries. The oat crop year begins in June and ends in May. Oat futures and options are traded on the Chicago Board of Trade (CBOT).

Prices – Oat prices on the CBOT weekly nearest futures chart showed weakness in early 2010 and hit a low of $1.89 per bushel in May 2010. However, oat prices then staged a sharp rally through the remainder of the year, finally closing 2010 up 42% at $3.94 per bushel.

Regarding cash prices, the average monthly price received by farmers for oats in the U.S. in the first eight months of the 2010-11 marketing year (June/May) rose +43.7% yr/yr to $3.21 per bushel.

Supply – World oat production in 2010-11 fell -14.5% yr/yr to 20.102 million metric tons, a new record low. World annual oat production in the past three decades has dropped very sharply from levels above 50 million metric tons in the early 1970s. The world's largest oat producers

are the European Union with 37.8% of world production in 2010-11, Turkey 15.9%, Canada with 11.4%, Australia with 8.7%, and Russia with 5.9%.

U.S. oat production in the 2010-11 marketing year fell 12.8% yr/yr to 81.190 million bushels, which is a new record low. U.S. oat production has fallen sharply from levels mostly above 1 billion bushels seen from the early 1900s into the early 1960s. U.S. farmers harvested only 1.263 million acres of oats in 2010-11, which was down –8.4% from the previous year and posted a new record low. That is down from the almost 40 million acres harvested back in the 1950s. The oat yield in 2010-11 fell -4.7% to 64.3 bushels per acre. Oat stocks in the U.S. as of September 2010 were down –8.9% yr/yr to a 116.972 million bushels. The largest U.S. oat-producing states in 2010 were the states of Minnesota (with 14% of U.S. production), Wisconsin (12.1%), South Dakota (9.3%), North Dakota (7.9%), Pennsylvania (5.8%), and Iowa (5.3%).

Demand – U.S. usage of oats in 2010-11 rose 1.2% yr/yr to 194.000 million bushels, up from 2008-09 record low of 186.380 million bushels. Regarding U.S. usage of oats in 2010-11, 59.3% was for feed and residual, 34.7% for food, alcohol and industrial, 4.5% for seed, and 1.5% for exports.

Trade – U.S. exports of oats rose 38.8% to a mere 3.0 million bushels in 2010-11. U.S. imports of oats in 2010-11 fell -5.2% yr/yr to 90.0 million bushels, down from the 2007 record high of 123.29 million bushels.

World Production of Oats   In Thousands of Metric Tons

Crop Year	Argentina	Australia	Belarus	Brazil	Canada	China	European Union	Norway	Turkey	Ukraine	United States	Russia	World Total
2001-02	645	1,434	530	342	2,691	790	8,491	330	7,700	265	1,116	1,707	27,290
2002-03	488	957	575	299	2,911	493	9,680	279	5,700	290	943	1,684	25,472
2003-04	332	2,018	500	435	3,377	654	9,019	333	5,200	270	925	2,096	26,374
2004-05	536	1,283	770	460	3,467	600	9,146	367	4,950	270	1,000	1,679	25,728
2005-06	350	1,690	600	522	3,283	700	7,968	279	4,550	270	800	1,667	23,932
2006-07	400	748	550	406	3,852	400	7,768	248	4,900	210	700	1,357	22,817
2007-08	472	1,502	600	238	4,696	350	8,634	276	5,400	200	550	1,313	25,506
2008-09[1]	291	1,160	600	239	4,273	300	8,935	328	5,800	200	950	1,294	25,537
2009-10[2]	182	1,180	800	253	2,906	410	8,505	245	5,400	210	730	1,351	23,520
2010-11[3]	350	1,750	700	370	2,298	420	7,598	245	3,200	210	500	1,178	20,102

[1] Preliminary.   [2] Estimate.   [3] Forecast.   Source: Foreign Agricultural Service, U.S. Department of Agriculture (FAS-USDA)

Official Oats Crop Production Reports in the United States   In Thousands of Bushels

Year	July 1	Aug. 1	Sept. 1	Oct. 1	Dec. 1	Final	Year	July 1	Aug. 1	Sept. 1	Oct. 1	Dec. 1	Final
1999	----	162,096	----	----	----	145,628	2005	131,314	127,819	----	----	----	114,878
2000	151,380	152,745	----	----	----	149,165	2006	110,322	107,423	----	----	----	93,522
2001	132,150	135,445	----	----	----	117,024	2007	100,921	98,341	----	----	----	90,430
2002	147,584	142,580	----	----	----	116,002	2008	92,872	89,897	----	----	----	89,135
2003	147,895	151,345	----	----	----	144,383	2009	91,277	91,960	----	----	----	93,081
2004	121,860	127,950	----	----	----	115,695	2010[1]	87,726	87,239	----	----	----	81,190

[1] Preliminary.   Source: National Agricultural Statistics Service, U.S. Department of Agriculture (NASS-USDA)

Oat Stocks in the United States   In Thousands of Bushels

Year	On Farms Mar. 1	June 1	Sept. 1	Dec. 1	Off Farms Mar. 1	June 1	Sept. 1	Dec. 1	Total Stocks Mar. 1	June 1	Sept. 1	Dec. 1
2001	55,800	32,050	74,800	58,100	54,128	40,677	41,592	56,117	109,928	72,727	116,392	114,217
2002	40,200	28,650	70,500	52,500	53,158	34,552	41,212	51,284	93,358	63,202	111,712	103,784
2003	35,000	20,600	82,100	64,400	47,879	29,233	49,637	54,900	82,879	49,833	131,737	119,300
2004	45,600	27,500	74,300	60,400	49,414	37,348	41,458	44,513	95,014	64,848	115,758	104,913
2005	43,500	25,350	71,700	60,100	38,946	32,592	41,803	35,617	82,446	57,942	113,503	95,717
2006	42,200	25,190	60,800	53,000	32,673	27,376	39,284	45,889	74,873	52,566	100,084	98,889
2007	33,900	18,400	53,650	43,100	37,158	32,198	34,710	51,331	71,058	50,598	88,360	94,431
2008	31,000	16,100	52,800	42,600	47,988	50,674	66,296	72,322	78,988	66,774	119,096	114,922
2009	30,200	17,480	54,500	43,000	65,250	66,619	73,875	67,629	95,450	84,099	128,375	110,629
2010[1]	30,900	17,600	46,250	34,100	67,091	62,716	70,722	66,976	97,991	80,316	116,972	101,076

[1] Preliminary.   Source: National Agricultural Statistics Service, U.S. Department of Agriculture (NASS-USDA)

Supply and Utilization of Oats in the United States   In Millions of Bushels

Crop Year Beginning June 1	Acreage Planted	Harvested	Yield Per Acre (Bushels)	Pro-duction	Imports	Total Supply	Feed & Residual	Food, Alcohol & Industrial	Seed	Exports	Total Use	Ending Stocks	Farm Price	Findley Loan Rate	Target Price
2001-02	4,403	1,905	61.4	117.0	96.0	286.3	148.3	59.2	12.8	2.8	223.1	63.2	1.59	1.21	NA
2002-03	4,995	2,058	56.4	116.0	95.1	274.3	149.9	60.2	11.8	2.6	224.5	49.8	1.81	1.35	1.40
2003-04	4,597	2,220	65.0	144.4	89.7	284.0	143.7	62.4	10.5	2.5	219.1	64.9	1.48	1.35	1.40
2004-05	4,085	1,787	64.7	115.7	90.3	270.9	136.3	63.0	11.0	2.7	212.9	57.9	1.48	1.33	1.44
2005-06	4,246	1,823	63.0	114.9	91.2	264.0	135.7	62.9	10.8	2.1	211.4	52.6	1.63	1.33	1.44
2006-07	4,168	1,566	59.8	93.5	106.2	252.3	124.9	64.5	9.7	2.6	201.7	50.6	1.87	1.33	1.44
2007-08	3,763	1,504	60.1	90.4	123.3	264.3	120.2	66.0	8.5	2.9	197.5	66.8	2.63	1.33	1.44
2008-09	3,247	1,400	63.7	89.1	114.6	270.5	108.1	66.1	8.9	3.3	186.4	84.1	3.15	1.33	1.44
2009-10[1]	3,404	1,379	67.5	93.1	94.9	272.1	115.0	66.2	8.3	2.2	191.7	80.3	2.02	1.33	1.44
2010-11[2]	3,138	1,263	64.3	81.2	90.0	257.6	115.0	67.2	8.8	3.0	194.0	63.6	2.10-2.70	1.33	1.44

[1] Preliminary.   [2] Forecast.   [3] Less than 500,000 bushels.   NA = Not available.
Source: Economic Research Service, U.S. Department of Agiculture (ERS-USDA)

Production of Oats in the United States, by States   In Thousands of Bushels

Year	Illinois	Iowa	Michigan	Minne-sota	Nebraska	New York	North Dakota	Ohio	Penn-slyvania	South Dakota	Texas	Wisconsin	Total
2001	3,200	9,100	3,520	12,600	3,660	5,520	14,880	6,205	7,475	7,800	7,200	12,480	117,024
2002	3,285	13,300	4,160	14,840	2,365	4,160	12,600	3,355	7,015	5,400	6,160	15,000	116,002
2003	4,450	10,790	5,250	18,815	6,570	4,410	21,240	3,960	6,490	15,640	6,300	15,410	144,383
2004	2,450	10,080	4,420	13,300	3,400	3,250	14,080	3,150	6,050	13,940	6,400	13,650	115,695
2005	3,160	9,875	4,575	12,710	4,380	4,050	14,160	3,600	6,050	12,960	4,730	13,760	114,878
2006	3,080	8,360	4,030	11,200	2,025	4,958	4,920	4,125	7,040	5,415	3,700	14,490	93,522
2007	1,488	4,757	3,080	10,800	2,135	3,480	15,340	3,100	4,480	9,360	4,000	10,720	90,430
2008	2,100	4,875	3,960	11,900	2,450	4,224	6,630	3,500	4,640	8,760	5,000	11,780	89,135
2009	1,625	6,175	3,465	12,070	2,070	4,620	11,220	3,375	4,880	6,570	2,820	13,260	93,081
2010[1]	1,950	4,340	4,080	11,385	1,700	3,886	6,405	3,500	4,720	7,560	4,160	9,860	81,190

[1] Preliminary.   Source: National Agricultural Statistics Service, U.S. Department of Agriculture (NASS-USDA)

Average Cash Price of No. 2 Heavy White Oats in Toledo   In Dollars Per Bushel

Year	Jan.	Feb.	Mar.	Apr.	May	June	July	Aug.	Sept.	Oct.	Nov.	Dec.	Average
1996-97	NQ	2.45	2.34	2.19	2.02	1.96	1.96	1.99	2.16	2.26	2.12	2.08	2.14
1997-98	2.12	1.79	1.84	1.80	1.77	NQ	NQ	NQ	NQ	NQ	NQ	NQ	1.86
1998-99	NQ	NQ	NQ	NQ	NQ	NQ	NQ	NQ	NQ	NQ	NQ	NQ	NQ
1999-00	NQ	NQ	NQ	NQ	NQ	NQ	NQ	NQ	NQ	NQ	NQ	NQ	NQ
2000-01	NQ	NQ	NQ	NQ	NQ	NQ	NQ	NQ	NQ	NQ	NQ	NQ	NQ
2001-02	NQ	NQ	NQ	NQ	NQ	NQ	NQ	NQ	NQ	NQ	NQ	NQ	NQ
2002-03	NQ	NQ	NQ	NQ	NQ	NQ	NQ	NQ	NQ	NQ	NQ	NQ	NQ
2003-04	NQ	NQ	NQ	NQ	NQ	NQ	NQ	NQ	NQ	NQ	NQ	NQ	NQ
2004-05	NQ	NQ	NQ	NQ	NQ	NQ	NQ	NQ	NQ	NQ	NQ	NQ	NQ
2005-06[1]	NQ	NQ	NQ										

[1] Preliminary.   NQ = No quotes.   Source: Economic Research Service, U.S. Department of Agriculture (ERS-USDA)

OATS

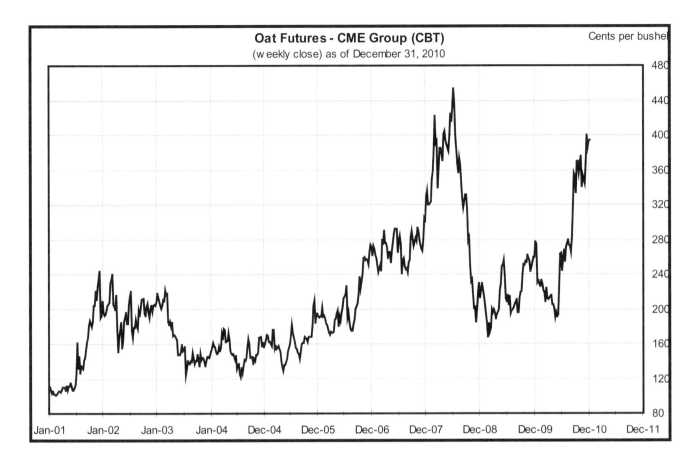

Volume of Trading in Oats Futures in Chicago   In Contracts

Year	Jan.	Feb.	Mar.	Apr.	May	June	July	Aug.	Sept.	Oct.	Nov.	Dec.	Total
2001	26,377	38,040	24,903	41,482	20,516	41,926	50,440	22,883	31,252	50,580	53,578	38,877	440,854
2002	41,516	46,435	30,662	51,889	32,386	39,229	35,217	29,647	23,968	32,847	35,412	15,932	415,140
2003	26,149	31,892	27,766	26,022	20,442	24,113	23,230	21,562	26,658	33,621	30,273	27,170	318,898
2004	33,743	34,605	55,216	49,746	38,951	35,356	25,451	31,023	32,322	25,443	33,942	20,650	416,448
2005	26,439	35,921	36,808	35,199	24,696	33,748	28,353	26,134	17,708	27,080	32,687	26,766	351,539
2006	25,667	40,534	30,437	35,799	39,362	42,812	35,751	30,790	25,700	43,724	51,304	25,435	427,315
2007	42,231	41,327	41,259	46,054	31,288	43,157	32,977	30,240	24,565	29,484	48,488	21,671	432,741
2008	44,184	61,469	44,478	47,918	37,813	52,116	27,923	32,074	19,009	31,829	23,978	18,797	441,588
2009	17,494	34,259	19,035	34,277	25,365	41,961	19,370	24,801	20,076	29,720	29,328	18,619	314,305
2010	31,060	32,283	23,890	37,409	21,363	54,174	26,097	23,735	22,430	25,743	30,649	15,754	344,587

Contract size = 5,000 bu.   *Source: CME Group; Chicago Board of Trade (CBT)*

Average Open Interest of Oats in Chicago   In Contracts

Year	Jan.	Feb.	Mar.	Apr.	May	June	July	Aug.	Sept.	Oct.	Nov.	Dec.
2001	14,093	15,060	14,873	14,962	14,875	13,695	11,861	11,707	10,059	12,111	14,453	12,142
2002	12,640	13,137	11,833	10,976	9,047	10,381	10,230	10,970	9,881	9,550	9,134	6,008
2003	6,929	6,715	5,945	6,135	5,833	5,640	5,811	5,958	6,261	6,194	6,268	5,122
2004	6,284	6,314	10,018	12,988	11,903	11,339	10,293	9,153	6,669	7,010	7,753	6,724
2005	7,691	8,482	7,346	8,110	7,746	7,686	7,779	6,721	5,847	6,914	7,565	9,385
2006	10,200	11,697	10,960	10,961	13,529	14,128	13,965	11,620	11,178	13,483	14,714	13,818
2007	16,176	18,406	19,178	19,255	18,061	17,909	14,824	13,387	14,158	14,251	13,223	10,914
2008	13,696	14,812	14,764	15,097	15,957	16,802	16,667	15,027	14,740	15,495	15,108	16,848
2009	16,519	16,927	14,367	15,142	13,304	14,380	13,805	13,649	13,684	13,526	13,593	11,976
2010	12,601	13,869	15,662	17,612	17,244	16,838	10,329	10,956	11,664	13,477	13,452	11,707

Contract size = 5,000 bu.   *Source: CME Group; Chicago Board of Trade (CBT)*

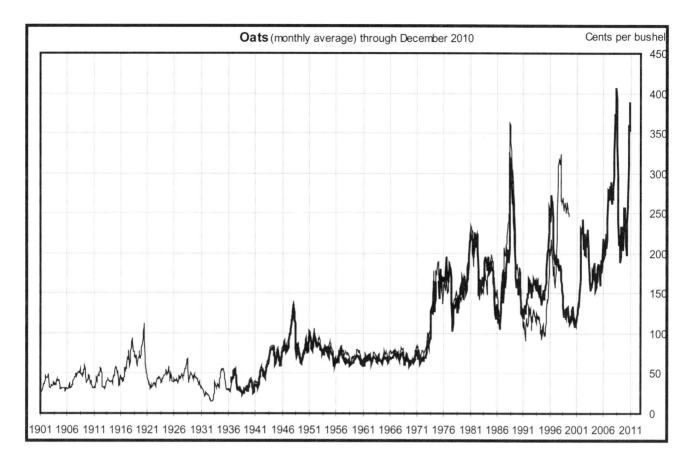

Average Cash Price of No. 2 Heavy White Oats in Minneapolis   In Dollars Per Bushel

Year	Jan.	Feb.	Mar.	Apr.	May	June	July	Aug.	Sept.	Oct.	Nov.	Dec.	Average
2001-02	.83	.95	1.08	1.04	1.29	1.41	1.48	1.41	1.47	1.51	1.31	1.29	1.26
2002-03	1.40	1.24	1.23	1.36	1.36	1.33	1.36	1.44	1.28	1.28	1.22	1.08	1.30
2003-04	1.05	NQ	.98	1.01	1.00	.99	1.04	.99	1.14	1.08	1.22	1.08	1.05
2004-05	1.04	.96	.99	1.11	1.01	1.04	1.13	1.18	1.15	1.16	1.13	.99	1.07
2005-06	.99	1.20	1.12	1.09	1.16	1.16	1.37	1.33	1.29	1.23	1.25	1.33	1.21
2006-07	1.38	1.41	1.29	1.36	1.52	1.69	1.76	1.74	1.66	1.78	1.76	1.73	1.59
2007-08	1.81	1.68	1.63	1.67	NQ	1.74	2.43	2.02	2.28	3.18	2.35	2.47	2.12
2008-09	2.54	2.60	NQ	NQ	NQ	1.33	1.33	1.36	1.18	1.23	1.26	1.45	1.59
2009-10	1.46	1.35	1.33	1.27	1.46	1.60	1.60	1.53	1.43	1.37	1.31	1.19	1.41
2010-11[1]	1.49	1.49	1.68	1.96	2.23	2.21	2.43	2.45					1.99

[1] Preliminary.   NQ = No qoute.   *Source: Economic Research Service, U.S. Department of Agriculture (ERS-USDA)*

Average Price Received by Farmers for Oats in the United States   In Dollars Per Bushel

Year	Jan.	Feb.	Mar.	Apr.	May	June	July	Aug.	Sept.	Oct.	Nov.	Dec.	Average
2001-02	1.38	1.32	1.25	1.39	1.64	1.79	1.92	1.93	1.91	1.99	1.99	1.99	1.71
2002-03	1.95	1.69	1.67	1.80	1.80	1.91	1.95	2.04	2.11	2.08	1.98	1.95	1.91
2003-04	1.83	1.46	1.39	1.39	1.44	1.29	1.58	1.48	1.58	1.60	1.63	1.70	1.53
2004-05	1.61	1.36	1.32	1.42	1.45	1.51	1.60	1.64	1.67	1.73	1.65	1.64	1.55
2005-06	1.75	1.59	1.49	1.54	1.59	1.64	1.73	1.73	1.82	1.82	1.75	1.85	1.69
2006-07	1.90	1.78	1.67	1.70	1.77	2.05	2.01	2.20	2.35	2.40	2.46	2.49	2.07
2007-08	2.54	2.32	2.24	2.47	2.45	2.63	2.69	2.88	3.19	3.43	3.47	3.63	2.83
2008-09	3.56	3.44	3.16	3.29	3.26	3.00	3.12	2.77	2.69	2.77	2.37	2.64	3.01
2009-10	2.37	2.03	1.86	1.82	2.03	2.02	2.22	2.19	2.10	2.28	2.25	2.19	2.11
2010-11[1]	2.08	2.10	2.09	2.29	2.37	3.02	2.96	2.29	2.31				2.39

[1] Preliminary.   *Source: National Agricultural Statistics Service, U.S. Department of Agriculture (NASS-USDA)*

Olive Oil

Olive oil is derived from the fruit of the olive tree and originated in the Mediterranean area. Olives designated for oil are picked before ripening in the fall. Olive picking is usually done by hand. The olives are then weighed and washed in cold water. The olives, along with their oil-rich pits, are then crushed and kneaded until a homogeneous paste is formed. The paste is spread by hand onto metal plates, which are then stacked and pressed hydraulically to yield a liquid. The liquid is then centrifuged to separate the oil. It takes 1,300 to 2,000 olives to produce 1 quart of olive oil. The best olive oil is still produced from the first pressing, which is usually performed within 24 to 72 hours after harvest and is called extra virgin olive oil.

Supply – World production of olive oil (pressed oil) in the marketing year 2009-10 (latest data) rose +8.5% to 3.130 million metric tons, which was a new record high. The world's largest producers of olive oil in 2009-10 were Spain (with 42.8% of world production), Italy (18.8%),

Greece (10.9%), Syria (5.2%), Tunisia (5.0%), and Turkey (5.0%). Production levels in the various countries vary considerable from year-to-year depending on various weather and crop conditions.

Demand – World consumption of olive oil in the 2009-10 marketing year rose +1.3% yr/yr to a new record high of 3.115 million metric tons. The U.S. is the world's largest consumer of olive oil with 8.8% of world consumption in 2009-010. The U.S. consumption of olive oil set a new record high of 273,000 metric tons.

Trade – World olive oil imports in 2009-10 fell -4.2% to 740,000 metric tons. The U.S. was the world's largest importer in 2009-10 with 275,000 metric tons, representing 37.2% of world imports. World olive oil exports in 2009-10 fell -0.6% to 730,000 metric tons. The world's largest exporters were Italy (with 26.0% of world exports), Spain (19.9%), Tunisia (19.2%), and Turkey (7.5%).

World Production of Olive Oil (Pressed Oil) In Thousands of Metric Tons

Crop Year	Algeria	Argentina	Greece	Italy	Jordan	Libya	Morocco	Portugal	Spain	Syria	Tunisia	Turkey	World Total
2001-02	25.5	10.0	388.3	500.0	16.0	7.0	66.0	36.7	1,468.0	104.0	40.0	71.0	2,791.1
2002-03	15.0	11.0	449.0	620.0	30.0	6.5	48.5	31.9	949.4	184.5	76.0	187.0	2,698.0
2003-04	69.5	13.5	332.0	470.0	21.0	6.5	110.0	38.2	1,566.0	121.5	296.0	80.0	3,178.1
2004-05	33.5	18.0	470.0	785.0	49.0	12.5	54.0	46.7	1,034.0	195.0	139.5	157.0	3,077.6
2005-06	32.0	23.0	455.5	635.0	23.0	9.0	81.0	35.5	887.0	110.0	236.5	119.0	2,714.1
2006-07	21.5	16.5	398.0	532.0	39.0	11.0	81.0	51.3	1,139.0	171.5	182.5	174.5	2,924.2
2007-08[1]	24.0	27.0	353.2	553.0	22.5	13.0	92.0	39.3	1,280.0	111.0	183.0	79.0	2,881.4
2008-09[2]	59.0	23.0	329.0	586.0	20.0	15.0	92.0	53.0	1,130.0	142.0	162.0	140.0	2,885.0
2009-10[3]	50.0	22.0	340.0	590.0	28.0	15.0	102.0	54.0	1,340.0	163.0	158.0	157.0	3,130.5

[1] Preliminary. [2] Estimate. [3] Forecast. *Source: The Oil World*

World Imports and Exports of Olive Oil (Pressed Oil) In Thousands of Metric Tons

Crop Year	Imports							Exports					
	Australia	Brazil	Italy	Japan	Spain	United States	World Total	Greece	Italy	Spain	Tunisia	Turkey	World Total
2001-02	26.4	24.0	50.8	31.2	6.6	218.0	491.6	9.4	199.0	116.8	33.0	37.3	470.0
2002-03	32.0	21.1	70.1	31.4	16.6	220.1	536.5	10.4	197.3	118.4	42.9	60.8	532.9
2003-04	30.5	23.2	178.2	33.1	49.1	244.8	721.6	9.3	199.9	123.0	197.0	55.9	725.9
2004-05	28.9	25.7	154.6	32.8	40.7	248.7	719.1	8.9	217.0	125.1	128.3	88.4	734.2
2005-06	32.7	26.0	136.6	30.2	51.1	242.0	700.9	9.8	203.6	114.6	123.3	56.0	686.1
2006-07	42.1	36.6	154.1	32.0	71.3	262.5	801.6	17.8	208.6	148.5	220.7	47.2	804.2
2007-08[1]	27.8	42.9	119.4	30.4	41.8	264.5	738.0	12.0	197.9	158.8	187.4	18.3	740.2
2008-09[2]	29.0	41.4	82.6	33.3	12.1	276.6	710.0	13.7	196.6	179.5	152.2	27.9	726.0
2009-10[3]	30.0	45.0	105.0	32.0	30.0	275.0	740.0	17.0	190.0	145.0	140.0	55.0	730.0

[1] Preliminary. [2] Estimate. [3] Forecast. *Source: The Oil World*

World Consumption and Ending Stocks of Olive Oil (Pressed Oil) In Thousands of Metric Tons

Crop Year	Consumption							Ending Stocks					
	Brazil	Morocco	Syria	Tunisia	Turkey	United States	World Total	European Union	Morocco	Syria	Tunisia	Turkey	World Total
2001-02	24.0	61.1	111.6	38.4	73.7	211.5	2,750.6	709.0	25.3	86.5	3.0	12.0	895.4
2002-03	21.1	64.2	117.7	31.7	91.6	218.7	2,797.3	535.0	19.0	130.9	4.6	47.0	799.6
2003-04	23.2	69.8	133.4	59.2	61.8	225.3	2,924.9	791.0	35.0	95.0	45.0	10.0	1,048.6
2004-05	25.7	62.4	142.8	40.9	65.7	235.9	2,918.6	964.7	11.0	105.0	42.0	13.0	1,219.1
2005-06	26.0	60.4	117.8	46.2	68.1	232.7	2,868.8	862.7	3.0	55.0	110.0	8.0	1,079.2
2006-07	36.6	69.8	128.3	26.8	90.3	244.2	2,999.6	781.7	16.0	43.0	48.0	45.0	1,001.2
2007-08[1]	42.9	76.9	105.2	27.1	97.8	258.7	3,050.5	718.0	28.0	5.0	19.0	8.0	829.9
2008-09[2]	41.4	89.5	107.4	22.8	100.2	265.8	3,075.7	468.1	40.0	5.0	10.0	20.0	623.2
2009-10[3]	45.0	97.0	110.0	23.0	104.1	273.0	3,115.0	509.6	35.0	8.0	8.0	18.0	648.7

[1] Preliminary. [2] Estimate. [3] Forecast. *Source: The Oil World*

Onions

Onions are the bulbs of plants in the lily family. Onions can be eaten raw, cooked, pickled, used as a flavoring or seasoning, or dehydrated. Onions rank in the top 10 vegetables produced in the U.S. in terms of dollar value. Since 1629, onions have been cultivated in the U.S., but are believed to be indigenous to Asia.

The two main types of onions produced in the U.S. are yellow and white onions. Yellow varieties comprise approximately 75% of all onions grown for bulb production in the U.S. Onions that are planted as a winter crop in warm areas are milder in taste and odor than onions planted during the summer in cooler regions.

Prices – Onion prices in 2010 averaged $25.42 per hundred pounds, up 108.3% from $12.20 in 2009. Monthly onion prices were weak in early 2010 at a low of $11.90 per hundred pounds in March, moved up to a high of $60.40 in April, but then faded to end the year at $13.00 per hundred pounds.

Supply – U.S. production in 2010 fell -3.1% to 7.321 billion pounds, still below the 2004 record high of 8.307 billion pounds. The farm value of the U.S. production crop in 2010 rose +9.6% to $1.154 million, down from the 2006 record high of $1.084 billion. U.S. farmers harvested a 17-year low of 149.670 acres in 2010, down −0.9% yr/yr. The yield per acre in 2010 was 489 pounds per acre.

Demand – U.S. per capita consumption of onions in 2010 remained unchanged at 21.3 pounds.

Trade – U.S. exports of fresh onions in 2009 totaled 561 million pounds, and imports totaled 681 million pounds.

Salient Statistics of Onions in the United States

Crop Year	Harvested Acres	Yield Per Acre	Production 1,000 Cwt.	Price Per Cwt.	Farm Value $1,000	Jan. 1 Pack Frozen	Anual Pack Frozen	Imports Canned	Exports (Fresh)	Imports (Fresh)	Per Capita[3] Utilization -- Lbs., Farm Weight -- All	Fresh
2004	169,150	491	83,065	9.06	671,626	38.6	218.2	10.5	620.1	689.3	23.4	21.9
2005	165,220	445	73,504	12.40	848,798	39.9		22.9	667.2	659.2	22.0	20.9
2006	163,780	444	73,066	16.10	1,084,099	48.1			658.8	643.2	21.7	19.9
2007	160,080	497	79,638	11.10	816,061	44.9			550.8	902.5	22.6	21.6
2008	153,490	489	75,120	11.90	834,386	39.4			612.0	714.2	22.4	20.9
2009[1]	151,060	500	75,566	15.00	1,053,812	36.2			561.2	681.6	21.6	19.7
2010[2]	149,670	489	73,213	21.60	1,154,527	39.0					21.3	20.0

[1] Preliminary.　[2] Forecast.　[3] Includes fresh and processing.　*Source: Economic Research Service, U.S. Department of Agiculture (ERS-USDA)*

Production of Onions in the United States　In Thousands of Hundredweight (Cwt.)

Crop Year	Arizona	California (Spring)	Texas	Total (All)	California (Summer)	Colorado	Idaho	Michigan	Minnesota	Mexico	New York	Oregon, Malheur	Texas	Total (All)	Grand Total
2004	800	3,586	3,875	12,031	13,200	5,500	8,008	986	----	----	5,200	8,658	----	71,034	83,065
2005	920	3,800	4,650	11,575	12,240	4,180	6,080	754	----	----	3,808	7,360	----	61,929	73,504
2006	490	3,279	4,104	11,128	13,515	3,800	5,076	650	----	----	4,224	6,084	----	62,049	73,177
2007	495	3,015	3,120	9,870	12,325	3,157	6,825	988	----	----	3,780	9,828	----	69,768	79,638
2008	660	2,860	2,403	9,498	13,303	2,850	6,192	1,008	----	----	4,141	8,662	----	65,622	75,120
2009	576	2,460	3,003	8,559	14,287	2,706	6,512	1,330	----	----	4,275	7,840	----	66,998	75,557
2010[1]		2,542	2,838	7,656	13,050	2,691	6,750	964	----	----	3,672	7,548	----	64,246	71,902

[1] Preliminary.　*Source: Agricultural Statistics Board, U.S. Department of Agiculture (ASB-USDA)*

Cold Storage Stocks of Frozen[2] Onions in the United States, on First of Month　In Thousands of Pounds

Year	Jan.	Feb.	Mar.	Apr.	May	June	July	Aug.	Sept.	Oct.	Nov.	Dec.
2005	39,865	40,428	44,191	48,695	50,579	47,418	45,605	47,231	44,834	40,718	43,751	45,690
2006	48,106	52,207	55,141	54,638	54,276	53,331	45,724	43,707	47,176	47,636	50,175	48,731
2007	44,919	42,027	45,810	46,244	40,350	32,240	34,663	30,966	36,734	39,096	37,653	37,929
2008	39,438	40,120	43,487	44,181	39,503	42,726	45,115	41,242	42,324	42,786	41,006	40,102
2009	36,192	35,247	34,714	32,696	32,860	33,258	31,005	31,252	34,647	36,935	40,862	42,488
2010[1]	38,967	38,348	35,231	29,333	26,484	25,109	25,119	23,805	30,594	32,146	29,197	30,444

[1] Preliminary.　*Source: National Agricultural Statistics Service, U.S. Department of Agiculture (NASS-USDA)*

Average Price Received by Growers for Onions in the United States　In Dollars Per Hundred Pounds (Cwt.)

Year	Jan.	Feb.	Mar.	Apr.	May	June	July	Aug.	Sept.	Oct.	Nov.	Dec.	Season Average
2005	6.29	5.61	6.13	18.20	19.70	17.80	14.00	11.10	13.10	12.90	14.00	12.30	12.40
2006	11.70	8.04	7.45	15.10	15.60	17.00	16.80	13.70	12.30	10.90	11.10	16.60	16.10
2007	22.10	26.20	35.00	55.20	24.20	24.60	15.40	10.80	5.57	4.47	4.70	4.39	11.10
2008	4.13	3.15	2.53	10.60	23.90	17.60	13.10	8.52	10.50	10.70	10.50	13.40	11.90
2009	9.47	8.44	6.99	18.40	13.40	18.00	10.80	8.56	9.27	8.19	7.93	7.83	15.00
2010[1]	11.20	15.00	40.00	60.40	43.90	29.20	21.40	15.30	17.90	16.60	18.70	12.00	21.60

[1] Preliminary.　*Source: Economic Research Service, U.S. Department of Agiculture (ERS-USDA)*

Oranges and Orange Juice

The orange tree is a semi-tropical, non-deciduous tree, and the fruit is technically a hesperidium, a kind of berry. The three major varieties of oranges include the sweet orange, the sour orange, and the mandarin orange (or tangerine). In the U.S., only sweet oranges are grown commercially. Those include Hamlin, Jaffa, navel, Pineapple, blood orange, and Valencia. Sour oranges are mainly used in marmalade and in liqueurs such as triple sec and curacao.

Frozen Concentrated Orange Juice (FCOJ) was developed in 1945, which led to oranges becoming the main fruit crop in the U.S. The world's largest producer of orange juice is Brazil, followed by Florida. Two to four medium-sized oranges will produce about 1 cup of juice, and modern mechanical extractors can remove the juice from 400 to 700 oranges per minute. Before juice extraction, orange oil is recovered from the peel. Approximately 50% of the orange weight is juice, the remainder is peel, pulp, and seeds, which are dried to produce nutritious cattle feed.

The U.S. marketing year for oranges begins December 1 of the first year shown (e.g., the 2005-06 marketing year extends from December 1, 2005 to November 30, 2006). Orange juice futures prices are subject to upward spikes during the U.S. hurricane season (officially June 1 to November 30), and the Florida freeze season (late-November through March).

Frozen concentrated orange juice future and options are traded on the ICE Futures U.S. (ICE) exchange. The ICE orange juice futures contract calls for the delivery of 15,000 pounds of orange solids and is priced in terms of cents per pound.

Prices – ICE orange juice futures prices in early 2010 extended the uptrend that started in February 2009 at a 6-1/2 year low of 64.60 cents. FCOJ prices climbed to a 3-year high of 153.65 cents in March 2010 and then moved sideways into Q4 of 2010. FCOJ prices rallied into the end of the year and posted a 3-1/2 year high of 175.85 cents in December 2010, finishing the year up +39% at 172.35 cents. The rally in 2010 was driven mainly by the drop in Florida orange acreage in 2009 to a 24-year low as farmers cut down orange trees to stop the spread of greening disease. In addition, the 2009/10 Florida orange crop plunged by -18% y/y to a 23-year low of 133.6 million boxes.

Supply – World production of oranges in the 2010-11 marketing year rose +4.1% y/y to 51.379 million metric tons, down from the 2008-09 record high of 51.751 million metric tons. The world's largest producers of oranges in 2010-11 were Brazil with 33.4% of world production, followed by the U.S. (15.5%), and Mexico (8.0%).

U.S. production of oranges in 2010-11 (latest data) fell -7.8% y/y to 194.200 million boxes (1 box equals 90 lbs.) Florida's production in 2010-11 fell -17.8% y/y to 133.600 million boxes and California's production rose +26.9% to 59.000 million boxes.

World Production of Oranges In Thousands of Metric Tons

Year	Argentina	Australia	Brazil	Egypt	Greece	Italy	Mexico	Morocco	South Africa	Spain	Turkey	United States	World Total
2001-02	780	633	18,360	1,696	1,076	1,724	4,020	720	1,263	2,822	1,250	11,290	49,828
2002-03	700	407	15,382	1,734	1,145	1,723	3,734	800	1,148	2,950	1,250	10,527	45,829
2003-04	750	453	19,054	1,740	550	1,835	3,901	705	1,113	3,052	1,250	11,734	50,805
2004-05	770	547	16,565	1,775	764	2,105	4,000	813	1,038	2,691	1,300	8,419	45,493
2005-06	840	470	17,993	1,800	1,017	2,261	4,157	784	1,167	2,376	1,445	8,212	47,453
2006-07	990	419	18,482	1,830	----	----	4,248	721	1,412	----	1,536	6,917	49,331
2007-08	940	403	16,850	2,759	----	----	4,297	732	1,526	----	1,427	9,141	51,327
2008-09[1]	900	430	17,014	3,500	----	----	4,193	790	1,445	----	1,430	8,281	51,751
2009-10[2]	750	380	15,300	3,570	----	----	3,600	823	1,600	----	1,690	7,440	49,360
2010-11[3]	900	430	17,135	3,645	----	----	4,100	905	1,650	----	1,710	7,974	51,379

[1] Preliminary. [2] Estimate. [3] Forecast. NA = Not available. *Source: Foreign Agricultural Service, U.S. Department of Agriculture (FAS-USDA)*

Salient Statistics of Oranges & Orange Juice in the United States

	Production[4]				Florida Crop Processed					Frozen Concentrated Orange Juice - Florida			
Year	California	Florida	Total U.S.	Farm Price $ Per Box	Farm Value Million $	Frozen Concentrates	Chilled Products	Total Processed	Yield Per Box Gallons[5]	Carry-in	Pack	Total Supply	Total Season Movement
	Million Boxes				Million $	Million Boxes				In Millions of Gallons (42 Deg. Brix)			
2000-01	54.5	223.3	280.9	5.88	1,682.8	124.1	89.6	215.9	1.6	112.6	245.2	357.8	226.0
2001-02	51.5	230.0	283.8	6.37	1,846.2	136.0	85.9	223.2	1.6	128.3	253.2	381.5	249.9
2002-03	62.0	203.0	267.0	5.80	1,564.7	102.1	92.5	196.0	1.5	120.2	203.3	323.5	200.1
2003-04	50.5	242.0	294.6	5.88	1,774.5	139.7	93.4	233.6	1.6	124.0	249.7	373.7	213.8
2004-05	64.5	149.8	216.5	6.68	1,475.4	54.3	88.5	143.9	1.6	151.8	86.3	238.1	175.2
2005-06	61.0	147.7	210.8	8.60	1,829.9	51.9	88.7	141.7	1.6	107.8	85.2	193.0	160.8
2006-07	46.0	129.0	177.3	12.56	2,216.5	48.0	74.5	123.4	1.6	67.2	79.6	146.8	149.2
2007-08[1]	62.0	170.2	234.4	9.36	2,198.8	80.8	84.7	165.5	1.7	52.1	135.6	187.7	137.7
2008-09[2]	46.5	162.5	210.7	9.22	1,970.1	72.5	82.6	156.2	1.7	108.1	121.5	229.6	143.9
2009-10[3]	59.0	133.6	194.2	9.96	1,935.0	52.7	74.9	128.2	1.6	118.0	82.3	200.3	130.4

[1] Preliminary. [2] Estimate. [3] Forecast. 4/ Fruit ripened on trees, but destroyed prior to picking not included. [5] 42 deg. Brix equivalent.
Source: Economic Research Service, U.S. Department of Agriculture (ERS-USDA); Florida Department of Citrus

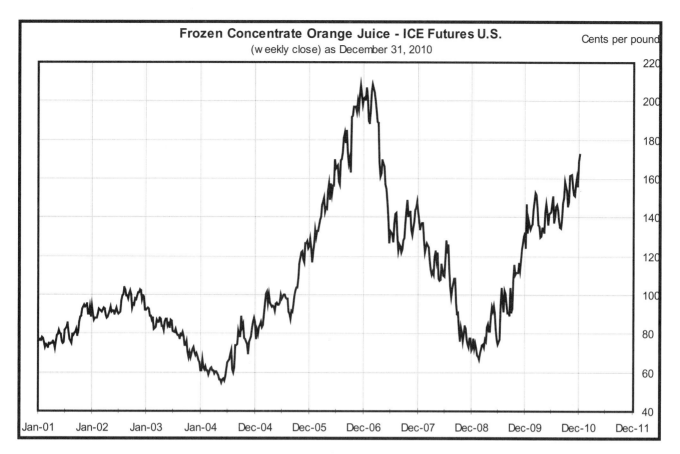

Frozen Concentrate Orange Juice - ICE Futures U.S.
(weekly close) as December 31, 2010

Cents per pound

Average Open Interest of Frozen Concentrated Orange Juice Futures in New York   In Contracts

Year	Jan.	Feb.	Mar.	Apr.	May	June	July	Aug.	Sept.	Oct.	Nov.	Dec.
2001	28,852	28,011	28,073	27,794	24,199	24,428	22,591	22,073	17,789	18,026	21,506	19,275
2002	15,716	16,593	18,515	22,328	23,498	26,581	28,137	33,206	27,323	23,758	22,651	23,461
2003	25,080	26,588	22,707	21,466	20,634	23,794	25,467	26,518	27,788	30,767	31,575	36,336
2004	36,079	35,325	32,806	36,112	34,704	42,299	39,970	38,259	39,877	38,990	33,342	36,072
2005	33,821	33,619	30,008	32,523	26,171	28,730	32,221	29,034	23,603	28,602	34,966	35,795
2006	30,485	35,479	36,603	36,617	34,418	29,180	27,169	29,872	29,515	30,852	29,873	28,342
2007	29,484	28,370	32,312	29,430	28,830	31,917	30,457	29,540	28,335	29,599	26,608	27,412
2008	24,919	26,603	29,806	32,831	32,102	33,136	28,353	31,133	29,112	31,060	28,254	28,802
2009	27,889	28,234	26,905	27,982	29,370	31,608	30,602	31,281	28,806	30,805	29,677	34,210
2010	35,442	34,435	35,991	31,854	29,524	29,143	26,424	27,037	27,400	29,340	28,707	29,996

Contract size = 15,000 lbs.   *Source: ICE Futures U.S. (ICE)*

Volume of Trading of Frozen Concentrated Orange Juice Futures in New York   In Contracts

Year	Jan.	Feb.	Mar.	Apr.	May	June	July	Aug.	Sept.	Oct.	Nov.	Dec.	Total
2001	46,655	66,561	27,994	63,012	38,447	66,773	40,870	64,860	22,246	68,364	23,376	48,338	577,496
2002	31,709	50,898	30,316	58,644	37,283	52,238	45,316	78,111	36,053	71,635	24,111	61,443	577,757
2003	45,945	63,224	23,926	70,846	35,791	64,209	27,056	73,792	40,782	87,055	42,084	78,005	652,715
2004	52,908	86,600	41,941	99,532	45,741	123,815	105,220	118,021	65,655	89,064	56,502	85,438	970,437
2005	54,140	85,349	57,557	87,595	40,785	94,913	61,610	92,195	46,868	117,355	50,098	113,574	902,039
2006	65,978	98,034	82,293	92,312	73,517	87,429	63,429	84,160	50,871	95,955	54,975	74,743	923,696
2007	70,773	84,076	63,417	87,759	59,937	84,150	50,721	78,502	48,392	103,218	45,539	69,308	845,792
2008	57,421	78,860	52,166	80,331	43,942	70,780	51,859	67,402	41,353	78,327	29,013	59,058	710,512
2009	28,514	63,757	31,766	67,156	30,396	81,964	56,197	65,286	40,276	86,071	28,426	77,186	656,995
2010	55,002	62,671	42,726	73,654	36,599	63,734	37,098	64,224	50,953	72,996	34,959	96,967	691,583

Contract size = 15,000 lbs.   *Source: ICE Futures U.S. (ICE)*

ORANGES AND ORANGE JUICE

Cold Storage Stocks of Orange Juice Concentrate[2] in the U.S., on First of Month   In Millions of Pounds

Year	Jan.	Feb.	Mar.	Apr.	May	June	July	Aug.	Sept.	Oct.	Nov.	Dec.
2001	1,382.0	1,610.8	1,825.1	1,735.5	1,872.2	2,061.8	2,035.6	1,913.2	1,691.1	1,537.7	1,398.9	1,406.7
2002	1,571.7	1,721.3	1,770.9	1,794.4	1,886.0	1,982.8	1,934.0	1,870.9	1,680.9	1,543.6	1,409.6	1,471.2
2003	1,673.6	1,851.9	1,833.4	1,856.6	1,936.8	2,102.6	2,021.2	1,848.9	1,672.2	1,529.9	1,335.6	1,428.5
2004	1,585.8	1,613.0	1,646.1	1,790.5	1,987.6	2,128.7	2,075.7	1,953.4	1,823.3	1,644.2	1,516.8	1,458.0
2005	1,468.8	1,553.8	1,578.9	1,578.2	1,652.4	1,668.1	1,548.8	1,501.6	1,397.3	1,243.3	1,139.9	1,027.5
2006	1,044.7	1,065.9	1,076.8	1,005.7	1,087.5	1,157.7	1,104.1	1,002.6	888.8	776.0	714.3	650.3
2007	678.2	726.0	751.1	825.1	901.5	960.7	909.7	849.1	761.2	620.4	582.2	563.7
2008	682.5	837.8	942.4	1,031.9	1,210.6	1,442.7	1,514.9	1,424.9	1,319.4	1,199.7	1,086.0	1,034.6
2009	1,088.0	1,193.2	1,261.2	1,291.4	1,415.4	1,497.2	1,519.7	1,404.3	1,316.7	1,252.2	1,150.3	1,127.2
2010[1]	1,185.2	1,289.7	1,300.4	1,305.1	1,377.6	1,434.2	1,353.1	1,235.7	1,133.9	1,036.8	903.6	795.3

[1] Preliminary.   [2] Adjusted to 42.0 degrees Brix equivalent (9.896 pounds per gallon).   Source: Agricultural Statistics Board, U.S. Department of Agriculture (ASB-USDA)

Producer Price Index of Frozen Orange Juice Concentrate   1982 = 100

Year	Jan.	Feb.	Mar.	Apr.	May	June	July	Aug.	Sept.	Oct.	Nov.	Dec.	Average
2001	98.9	99.2	98.3	96.8	96.8	97.4	97.3	97.2	97.3	97.3	99.6	102.5	98.2
2002	103.0	102.9	103.1	102.9	102.8	103.2	103.2	103.5	107.4	107.4	109.7	110.2	104.9
2003	110.2	110.2	110.7	110.4	108.5	109.4	109.1	108.9	107.1	106.6	105.1	103.0	108.3
2004	103.4	103.2	102.7	101.6	101.6	101.6	98.9	98.9	98.9	98.9	103.3	103.3	101.4
2005	103.3	103.3	105.0	109.0	109.0	109.0	109.3	109.3	108.1	107.9	108.4	126.4	109.0
2006	138.3	142.1	150.1	160.9	161.0	164.1	172.3	174.8	185.4	197.6	208.9	208.7	172.0
2007	198.1	191.7	198.5	179.6	187.7	184.1	173.6	171.5	152.9	159.3	162.6	168.2	177.3
2008	168.0	166.6	160.0	159.2	159.3	159.6	126.0	121.8	121.4	116.8	115.2	124.3	141.5
2009	124.6	124.4	124.4	117.6	125.0	118.0	118.0	119.8	119.1	119.0	119.0	128.8	121.5
2010[1]	141.3	141.1	141.5	144.5	144.5	144.5	144.7	145.0	150.0	150.4	150.4	150.6	145.7

[1] Preliminary.   NA = Not avaliable.   Source: Bureau of Labor Statistics, U.S. Department of Labor (BLS)

Average Price Received by Farmers for Oranges (Equivalent On-Tree) in the U.S.   In Dollars Per Box

Year	Jan.	Feb.	Mar.	Apr.	May	June	July	Aug.	Sept.	Oct.	Nov.	Dec.	Average
2001	2.85	3.20	4.93	4.84	4.64	4.47	4.63	5.01	6.20	4.99	2.90	3.20	4.32
2002	3.75	4.05	4.64	4.65	4.47	4.00	4.06	6.61	5.33	5.18	3.11	3.23	4.42
2003	3.00	3.14	4.17	4.43	4.43	4.41	3.91	4.27	2.80	2.78	2.32	2.55	3.52
2004	2.45	3.02	3.68	3.68	3.60	4.13	8.85	8.49	15.85	20.87	5.34	3.27	6.94
2005	3.39	3.69	4.84	4.80	5.11	5.43	6.55	4.90	4.29	4.04	5.90	4.46	4.78
2006	5.16	5.27	5.78	6.44	7.13	7.05	6.56	12.03	17.96	13.89	6.95	7.28	8.46
2007	8.25	8.11	10.58	10.62	11.12	11.07	8.95	8.81	7.84	9.60	8.14	5.80	9.07
2008	5.77	5.83	6.20	6.40	7.01	6.75	5.79	4.78	5.92	5.57	7.53	5.39	6.08
2009	5.74	6.04	7.08	6.54	6.61	7.04	7.38	8.58	W	W	11.61	6.13	7.28
2010[1]	6.41	6.78	7.35	7.34	7.65	8.10	8.67	7.49	7.12	6.68	11.22	6.69	7.63

[1] Preliminary.   Source: Economic Research Service, U.S. Department of Agriculture (ERS-USDA)

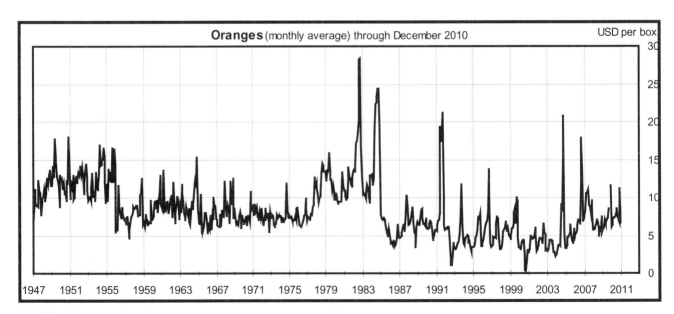

Oranges (monthly average) through December 2010   USD per box

188

Palm Oil

Palm oil is an edible vegetable oil produced from the flesh of the fruit of the oil palm tree. The oil palm tree is a tropical palm tree that is a native of the west coast of Africa and is different from the coconut palm tree. The fruit of the oil palm tree is reddish, about the size of a large plum, and grows in large bunches. A single seed, the palm kernel, is contained in each fruit. Oil is extracted from both the pulp of the fruit (becoming palm oil) and the kernel (palm kernel oil). About 1 metric ton of palm kernel oil is obtained for every 10 metric tons of palm oil.

Palm oil is commercially used in soap, ointments, cosmetics, detergents, and machinery lubricants. It is also used worldwide as cooking oil, shortening, and margarine. Palm kernel oil is a lighter oil and is used exclusively for food use. Crude palm oil and crude palm kernel oil are traded on the Kuala Lumpur Commodity Exchange.

Prices – The monthly average wholesale price of palm oil (CIF, bulk, U.S. ports) in 2009 (latest data) fell by -29.6% yr/yr to 33.88 cents per pound, down from the 2008 record high of 48.09 cents per pound.

Supply – World production of palm oil in the 2010-11 marketing year rose by +4.6% to 447.972 million metric tons. World palm oil production has grown by over twenty times the production level of 1.922 million metric tons seen back in 1970. Indonesia and Malaysia are the world's two major global producers of palm oil. Indonesian production rose +7.3% to a record high of 23.600 million metric tons in 2010-11 and Indonesian production accounted for 49.2% of world production. Malaysian production in 2010-11 rose +1.3% to a record high of 18.000 million metric tons and Malaysian production accounted for 37.5% of world production. Other smaller global producers include Thailand with 3.1% of world production, Nigeria with 1.8%, and Columbia with 1.7%.

Demand – U.S. total disappearance of palm oil in 2010-11 rose +0.1% yr/yr to 1.125 million metric tons which was a new record high.

Trade – World palm oil exports in 2009-10 rose by +3.8% to 36.970 million metric tons, which was a new record high. The world's largest exporters are Malaysia with a 44.6% share of world exports and Indonesia also with a 46.3% share. World palm oil imports in 2009-10 rose +2.7% to 36.890 million metric tons. The world's largest importers are China with a 17.8% share of world imports and India also with a 18.0% share.

World Production of Palm Oil   In Thousands of Metric Tons

Crop Year	Brazil	Came-roon	Colombia	Costa Rica	Ecuador	Ghana	Indonesia	Ivory Coast	Malaysia	Nigeria	Papua New Guinea	Thailand	World Total
2001-02	118	138	518	128	230	108	9,200	260	11,858	760	329	780	25,312
2002-03	129	144	540	155	265	120	10,300	234	13,180	770	316	640	27,683
2003-04	142	147	614	180	270	120	11,970	308	13,420	780	326	840	30,049
2004-05	160	150	655	173	315	120	13,560	298	15,194	790	345	820	33,498
2005-06	170	150	700	181	320	120	15,560	236	15,485	800	350	784	35,784
2006-07	190	165	755	189	410	120	16,600	281	15,290	810	361	1,170	37,329
2007-08	205	165	780	202	405	120	18,000	289	17,567	820	448	1,050	41,084
2008-09[1]	230	182	795	210	440	120	20,500	290	17,259	850	451	1,540	43,992
2009-10[2]	240	190	770	225	430	120	22,000	300	17,763	850	487	1,345	45,862
2010-11[3]	265	190	820	225	460	120	23,600	300	18,000	850	500	1,500	47,972

[1] Preliminary.   [2] Estimate.   [3] Forecast.   *Source: The Oil World*

World Trade of Palm Oil   In Thousands of Metric Tons

	Imports							Exports					
Crop Year	China	Germany	India	Nether-lands	Pakistan	United Kingdom	Total	Hong Kong	Indonesia	Malaysia	Guinea	Sing-apore	Total
2000-01	2,147	497	3,856	907	1,191	607	17,356	180	4,617	10,707	334	228	17,340
2001-02	2,600	592	3,233	1,101	1,333	721	18,590	302	6,094	10,758	332	217	18,917
2002-03	3,167	562	4,110	1,132	1,442	776	21,467	209	7,167	12,133	329	253	21,531
2003-04	3,570	646	3,574	1,174	1,405	819	23,459	154	8,706	12,186	336	227	23,474
2004-05	4,319	766	3,342	1,438	1,683	869	26,328	59	9,862	13,585	322	223	26,152
2005-06	5,182	662	2,820	1,589	1,728	885	28,069	14	11,590	13,718	317	206	28,107
2006-07	5,543	711	3,664	1,710	1,743	734	29,400	27	12,465	13,768	406	185	29,610
2007-08[1]	5,559	654	5,019	2,011	1,769	595	32,645	11	14,100	15,041	385	199	32,820
2008-09[2]	6,297	975	6,875	2,048	1,794	516	35,930	19	16,209	15,990	494	198	35,630
2009-10[3]	6,560	950	6,650	1,977	1,890	534	36,890	10	17,100	16,500	465	210	36,970

[1] Preliminary.   [2] Estimate.   [3] Forecast.   *Source: The Oil World*

PALM OIL

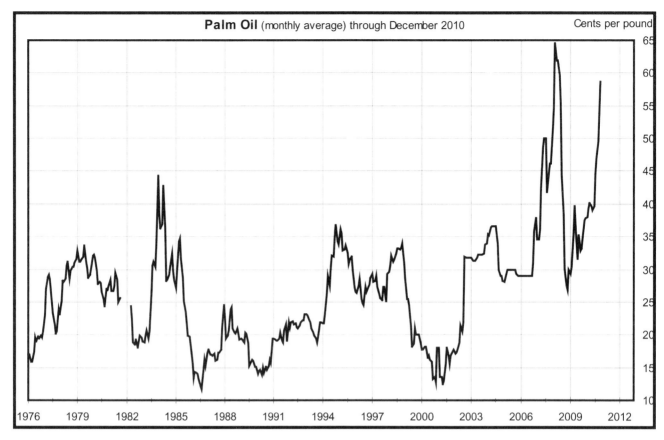

Palm Oil (monthly average) through December 2010 — Cents per pound

Supply and Distribution of Palm Oil in the United States   In Thousands of Metric Tons

Crop Year Beginning Oct. 1	Stocks Oct. 1	Imports	Total Supply	Edible Products	Inedible Products	Total End Products	Total Disap-pearance	Exports	U.S. Import Value[4]	Malaysia, F.O.B., RBD	Palm Kernel Oil, Malaysia, C.I.F Rotterdam
				------ In Millions of Pounds ------					**------ U.S. $ Per Metric Ton ------**		
2001-02	27.5	217.2	244.7	W	22.6	75.1	214.4	6.2	----	359	379
2002-03	24.1	174.4	198.5	W	W	76.7	168.5	8.1	----	428	439
2003-04	22.1	281.5	303.6	51.9	37.5	67.9	226.4	13.1	----	489	619
2004-05	64.0	349.0	413.0	62.3	W	62.3	319.4	17.2	----	420	638
2005-06	76.4	603.8	680.2	436.4	W	436.4	555.6	30.6	----	452	583
2006-07	94.0	702.0	796.0	568.5	W	568.5	796.0	42.0	----	685	768
2007-08	91.0	1,043.0	1,134.0	789.3	W	789.3	1,043.0	22.0	----	1053	1248
2008-09[1]	73.0	1,109.0	1,182.0	973.6	W	973.6	1,109.0	20.0	----	628	662
2009-10[2]	130.0	1,124.0	1,254.0	1,140.8	W	1,140.8	1,124.0	18.0	----	779	871
2010-11[3]	150.0	1,125.0	1,275.0	1,116.7	W	1,116.7	1,125.0	16.0			

[1] Preliminary.   [2] Estimate.   [3] Forecast.   [4] Market value in the foreign country, excluding import duties, ocean freight and marine insurance.
W = Withheld.   *Sources: The Oil World; Economic Research Service, U.S. Department of Agriculture (ERS-USDA)*

Average Wholesale Palm Oil Prices, CIF, Bulk, U.S. Ports   In Cents Per Pound

Year	Jan.	Feb.	Mar.	Apr.	May	June	July	Aug.	Sept.	Oct.	Nov.	Dec.	Average
2001	18.05	18.05	13.50	13.50	12.50	13.00	15.50	18.00	16.75	15.60	16.85	17.45	15.73
2002	17.75	17.06	17.30	17.75	18.85	21.44	20.50	21.85	32.00	31.75	31.75	31.75	23.31
2003	31.75	31.75	31.35	31.25	31.25	31.75	32.25	32.25	32.25	32.25	32.44	33.75	32.02
2004	34.00	35.38	35.25	36.40	36.50	36.50	36.50	36.50	34.00	30.00	29.00	29.00	34.09
2005	28.20	28.00	28.67	30.00	30.00	30.00	30.00	30.00	30.00	30.00	29.25	29.00	29.43
2006	29.00	29.00	29.00	29.00	29.00	29.00	29.00	29.00	29.00	29.00	31.00	35.75	29.73
2007	38.00	34.50	34.50	36.00	42.38	48.63	50.00	NA	41.67	43.19	46.20	46.20	41.93
2008	51.48	54.66	64.63	61.96	61.90	59.70	55.41	44.43	38.52	30.11	27.41	26.91	48.09
2009	29.98	29.32	30.32	35.46	39.86	36.45	31.40	35.39	32.90	33.24	34.66	37.53	33.88
2010	37.83	37.91	39.35	40.11	39.60	38.97	39.64	44.57	47.00	49.55	54.00	58.60	43.93

Source: Economic Research Service, U.S. Department of Agriculture (ERS-USDA)

Paper

The earliest known paper that is still in existence was made from cotton rags around 150 AD. Around 800 AD, paper made its appearance in Egypt but was not manufactured there until 900 AD. The Moors introduced the use of paper to Europe, and around 1150, the first papermaking mill was established in Spain, followed by England in 1495, and the U.S. in 1690.

During the 17th and 18th centuries, the increased usage of paper created a shortage of cotton rags, which were the only source for papermaking. The solution to this problem lead to the introduction of the ground-wood process of pulp-making in 1840 and the first chemical pulp process 10 years later.

Today, the paper and paperboard industries, including newsprint, are sensitive to the economic cycle. As the economy strengthens, paper use increases, and vice versa.

Prices – The average monthly index price (1982 = 100) for paperboard in 2010 rose +8.8% yr/yr to 225.3, making a new record high. The average monthly producer price index of standard newsprint paper in 201- fell by -0.2% to 126.1, down from the 12-year high of 151.8 posted in 2006.

Supply – U.S. production of paper and paperboard in 2009 (latest data) fell -10.1% yr/yr to 72.084 million metric tons. The U.S. is the world's largest producer of paper and paperboard by far, followed by Germany with 21.124 million metric tons and Canada with 12.842 million metric tons.

U.S. production of newsprint fell by −2.4% yr/yr to a record low of 414.6 metric tons per month in 2005 which is the latest data available. U.S. production of newsprint is second in the world, after Canada, which had production of 657.167 metric tons per month in 2005.

Production of Paper and Paperboard by Selected Countries   In Thousands of Metric Tons

Year	Austria	Canada	Finland	France	Germany	Italy	Nether-lands	Norway	Russia/3	Spain	Sweden	United Kingdom	United States
2004	4,852	20,462	14,036	10,255	20,391	9,667	3,459	2,294	6,830	5,526	11,589	6,442	82,084
2005	4,950	19,498	12,391	10,332	21,679	9,999	3,471	2,223	7,126	5,697	11,775	6,241	83,697
2006	5,213	18,189	14,189	10,006	22,656	10,008	3,367	2,109	7,434	6,898	12,066	5,454	84,317
2007	5,199	17,367	14,334	9,871	23,317	10,112	3,224	2,010	7,581	6,713	11,511	5,228	83,916
2008	5,153	15,789	13,126	9,398	22,825	9,467	2,977	1,900	7,700	6,414	11,663	4,983	80,178
2009[1]	4,622	12,842	10,602	8,369	21,124	8,477	2,609	1,594	7,373	6,477	11,000	4,346	72,084

[1] Preliminary.   Source: Food and Agriculture Organization of the United Nations (FAO-UN)

Production of Newsprint by Selected Countires (Monthly Average)   In Thousands of Metric Tons

Year	Australia	Brazil	Canada	China	Finland	France	Germany	India	Japan	Rep. of Korea	Russia/3	Sweden	United States
2005	NA	11.1	657.2	284.1	47.9	92.8	226.0	74.7	310.0	135.9	165.3	213.0	414.6
2006	NA	11.3	NA	334.0	NA	91.6	225.9	85.1	314.3	137.9	166.1	211.4	NA
2007	NA	11.6	NA	382.4	NA	90.6	218.6	85.8	317.0	138.8	159.8	214.1	NA
2008	NA	11.8	NA	387.1	NA	90.3	227.9	95.5	306.7	133.3	165.6	210.3	NA
2009[1]	NA	NA	NA	403.6	NA	NA	207.3	80.7	287.9	124.8	167.2	200.6	NA
2010[2]	NA	NA	NA	380.1	NA	NA	211.4	76.8	283.4	131.8	163.8	202.6	NA

[1] Preliminary.   [2] Estimate.   NA = Not available.   Source: United Nations

Index Price of Paperboard   (1982 = 100)

Year	Jan.	Feb.	Mar.	Apr.	May	June	July	Aug.	Sept.	Oct.	Nov.	Dec.	Average
2004	157.8	157.4	157.5	162.2	165.5	170.0	175.2	178.5	179.2	179.4	180.1	179.3	170.2
2005	179.7	180.0	180.1	180.7	180.9	176.6	174.6	168.5	168.5	168.6	174.1	173.9	175.5
2006	175.3	184.0	184.3	184.3	193.7	196.7	196.8	197.2	197.5	197.7	198.4	197.5	192.0
2007	198.0	198.1	198.2	199.0	198.8	198.7	199.0	199.1	203.1	209.5	209.2	209.4	201.7
2008	209.7	209.8	209.7	209.7	209.7	210.3	211.5	226.0	229.5	230.0	229.6	229.1	217.9
2009	224.6	221.3	216.7	211.8	205.3	203.0	202.8	202.0	202.4	199.1	198.8	197.9	207.1
2010[1]	198.0	210.3	212.6	214.5	229.2	231.4	232.2	232.3	236.3	234.2	234.2	234.2	225.0

[1] Preliminary.   Source: Bureau of Labor Statistics, U.S. Department of Commerce (BLS) (0914)

Producer Price Index of Standard Newsprint   (1982 = 100)

Year	Jan.	Feb.	Mar.	Apr.	May	June	July	Aug.	Sept.	Oct.	Nov.	Dec.	Average
2004	116.5	116.7	118.8	122.4	125.0	126.0	125.6	125.7	125.8	129.5	129.8	132.4	124.5
2005	130.3	131.9	131.6	132.8	133.2	135.9	138.8	141.4	152.2	143.5	144.9	145.6	138.5
2006	148.8	148.0	150.5	149.8	152.0	153.7	154.3	153.3	153.9	153.7	151.9	151.3	151.8
2007	150.3	146.1	145.0	143.1	127.9	127.5	125.8	124.1	122.5	121.8	121.1	124.4	131.6
2008	125.8	129.6	133.4	136.2	142.7	146.5	151.0	156.1	158.6	162.4	167.6	166.1	148.0
2009	162.3	158.9	153.0	141.1	129.6	120.3	107.5	105.3	105.5	107.7	111.0	114.6	126.4
2010[1]	116.5	116.9	118.3	114.8	122.3	124.8	128.6	129.5	132.5	133.5	136.1	136.3	125.8

[1] Preliminary.   Source: Bureau of Labor Statistics, U.S. Department of Commerce (BLS) (0913-02)

Peanuts and Peanut Oil

Peanuts are the edible seeds of a plant from the pea family. Although called a nut, the peanut is actually a legume. Ancient South American Inca Indians were the first to grind peanuts to make peanut butter. Peanuts originated in Brazil and were later brought to the U.S. via Africa. The first major use of peanuts was as feed for pigs. It wasn't until the Civil War that peanuts were used as human food when both Northern and Southern troops used the peanut as a food source during hard times. In 1903, Dr. George Washington Carver, a talented botanist who is considered the "father of commercial peanuts," introduced peanuts as a rotation crop in cotton-growing areas. Carver discovered over 300 uses for the peanut including shaving cream, leather dye, coffee, ink, cheese, and shampoo.

Peanuts come in many varieties, but there are four basic types grown in the U.S.: Runner, Spanish, Valencia, and Virginia. Over half of Runner peanuts are used to make peanut butter. Spanish peanuts are primarily used to make candies and peanut oil. Valencia peanuts are the sweetest of the four types. Virginia peanuts are mainly roasted and sold in and out of the shell.

Peanut oil is extracted from shelled and crushed peanuts through hydraulic pressing, expelled pressing, or solvent extraction. Crude peanut oil is used as a flavoring agent, salad oil, and cooking oil. Refined, bleached and deodorized peanut oil is used for cooking and in margarines and shortenings. The by-product called press cake is used for cattle feed along with the tops of the plants after the pods are removed. The dry shells can be burned as fuel.

Prices – The average monthly price received by farmers for peanuts (in the shell) in the first six months of the 2010-11 marketing year (Aug/July) rose +1.2% to 21.9 cents per pound. The record high is 34.7 cents posted in 1990-91. The average monthly price of peanut oil in the 2010-11 marketing year (through December 2011) rose +23.7% yr/yr to 75.94 cents per pound, down from the 2007-08 record high of 100.92 per pound. The average monthly price of peanut meal (50% Southeast Mills) fell by –8.0% yr/yr in 2006-07 (through February 2007, which is the latest data available) to a record low of $98.40 per short ton.

Supply – World peanut production in 2009-10 (latest data) fell by -9.8% to 30.805 million metric tons, down from the 2008-09 record high of 34.151 million metric tons. The world's largest peanut producers are China with 41% of world production, India with 16%, U.S. with 5%, and Nigeria with 5%. U.S. peanut production in the 2010-11 marketing year rose by +12.6% to 4.155 billion pounds, down from the 2008-09 record high of 5.148 billion pounds.

U.S. farmers harvested 1.255 million acres of peanuts in 2010-11, up +16.3% yr/yr. That was down from the 16-year high harvest of 1.629 million acres in 2005-06. U.S. peanut yield in 2010-11 fell -3.2% yr/yr to 3,311 pounds per acre, down from 2008-09 record high. The largest peanut producing states in the U.S. in 2010 are Georgia (with 47.5% of U.S. production), Texas (14.1%), Alabama (11.6%), Florida 11.0%), and North Carolina (5.8%). U.S. crude peanut oil production in 2010 rose +6.8% to 153.647 million pounds, which was only about 40% of the record high level of 358,195 million pounds posted in 1996.

Demand – U.S. disposition of peanuts in 2009-10 rose by +2.6% yr/yr to 4.255 billion pounds. Of that disposition, 62.4% of the peanuts went for food, 17.0% for exports, 10.7% for crushing into peanut oil, and 9.9% for seed, loss and residual. The most popular type of peanut grown in the U.S. is the Runner peanut with 87.8% of U.S. production in 2009-10. This was followed by the Virginia peanut with 10.6% of production and the Spanish peanut far behind with only 1.7% of production. Peanut butter is a primary use for Runner and Virginia peanuts. It accounts for 55.8% of Runner peanut usage and 64.2% of Virginia peanut usage. In a poor third place, only about 5% of Spanish peanuts are used for peanut butter. Snack peanuts is also a key usage category and accounts for 37.7% of Spanish peanut usage, 17.6% of Virginia peanut usage, and 27.6% of Runner peanut usage. Candy accounts for 38.2% of Spanish peanut usage, 17.4% of Runner peanut usage, and 8.7% of Virginia peanut usage.

Trade – U.S. exports of peanuts in 2009-10 rose +17.0% yr/yr to 7225 million pounds. U.S. imports of peanuts fell by –30.2% yr/yr in 2009-10 to 60 million pounds.

World Production of Peanuts (in the Shell)   In Thousands of Metric Tons

Crop Year	Argentina	Burma	China	India	Indonesia	Nigeria	Senegal	South Africa	Sudan	Thailand	United States	Zaire	World Total
2001-02	517	731	14,415	368	7,600	1,033	1,490	903	120	370	107	1,940	33,816
2002-03	316	756	14,818	355	5,400	1,086	1,510	260	60	370	112	1,506	30,862
2003-04	420	878	13,420	360	7,700	1,130	1,510	445	115	370	113	1,880	32,834
2004-05	585	916	14,340	364	7,000	1,150	1,520	573	85	370	114	1,945	33,606
2005-06	510	931	14,340	365	6,300	1,170	1,520	703	93	370	114	2,209	33,239
2006-07	775	1,023	12,887	370	5,385	1,200	1,520	460	77	850	117	1,571	31,032
2007-08	800	1,000	13,027	370	6,800	1,150	1,550	331	118	850	114	1,666	32,591
2008-09	860	1,000	14,286	370	6,250	1,250	1,550	450	128	850	115	2,342	34,471
2009-10[1]	836	1,000	14,708	370	4,900	1,250	1,550	625	130	850	115	1,675	32,979
2010-11[2]	850	1,000	15,100	370	6,000	1,250	1,550	625	120	850	115	1,885	34,705

[1] Preliminary.   [2] Estimate.   *Source: Foreign Agricultural Service, U.S. Department of Agriculture (FAS-USDA)*

Salient Statistics of Peanuts in the United States

Crop Year Beginning Aug. 1	Acreage Planted	Acreage Harvested for Nuts	Average Yield Per Acre In Lbs.	Pro-duction (1,000 Lbs)	Season Farm Price (Cents Lb.)	Farm Value (Million Dollars)	Exports Unshelled	Exports Shelled	Imports Unshelled	Imports Shelled
	------- 1,000 Acres ------						---------- In Thousands of Pounds ----------			
2001-02	1,541.2	1,411.9	3,029	4,276,704	23.4	1,000.5	699,700	----	202,808	----
2002-03	1,353.0	1,291.7	2,571	3,321,040	18.2	599.7	489,900	----	75,372	----
2003-04	1,344.0	1,312.0	3,159	4,144,150	19.3	799.4	515,900	----	38,088	----
2004-05	1,430.0	1,394.0	3,076	4,288,200	18.9	813.6	491,000	----	36,863	----
2005-06	1,657.0	1,629.0	2,989	4,869,860	17.3	843.4	491,000	----	32,100	----
2006-07	1,243.0	1,210.0	2,863	3,464,250	17.7	612.8	603,000	----	61,000	----
2007-08	1,230.0	1,195.0	3,130	3,740,650	20.5	758.6	750,000	----	73,000	----
2008-09	1,534.0	1,507.0	3,426	5,162,400	23.0	1,193.6	727,000	----	86,000	----
2009-10[1]	1,116.0	1,079.0	3,421	3,691,650	21.0-22.6	793.1	725,000	----	60,000	----
2010-11[2]	1,288.0	1,255.0	3,311	4,155,600		901.3				

[1] Preliminary.   [2] Estimate.   Source: Economic Research Service, U.S. Department of Agriculture (ERS-USDA)

Supply and Disposition of Peanuts (Farmer's Stock Basis) & Support Program in the United States

Crop Year Beginning Aug. 1	Pro-duction	Imports	Stocks Aug. 1	Total	Exports	Crushed for Oil	Seed, Loss & Residual	Food	Total Disap-pearance	Support Price	Addi-tional	Quantity (Mil. Lbs.)	% of Pro-duction
	--------------- Supply ---------------				---------------- Disposition ----------------					------- Government Support Program -------			
												Amount Put Under Support	
	--------------------------- In Millions of Pounds ---------------------------									--- Cents Per Lb. ---			
2002-03	3,321	75	1,476	4,873	490	857	410	2,241	3,998	----	----	----	----
2003-04	4,144	38	875	5,057	516	536	429	2,456	3,936	36.00	----	1,657	80.0
2004-05	4,288	37	1,121	5,446	491	393	547	2,600	4,031	36.00	----	1,948	91.4
2005-06	4,870	32	1,415	6,317	491	542	501	2,616	4,150	36.00	----	2,300	96.1
2006-07	3,464	61	2,167	5,692	603	513	471	2,585	4,172	36.00	----	1,694	97.9
2007-08	3,741	73	1,520	5,265	750	496	471	2,517	4,234	36.00	----	1,363	74.2
2008-09	5,162	86	1,031	6,280	727	445	407	2,571	4,150	36.00	----	2,073	80.5
2009-10[1]	3,692	72	2,130	5,894	592	435	569	2,675	4,271	36.00	----	1,674	90.7
2010-11[2]	4,156	60	1,829	6,044	600	500	432	2,844	4,376				

[1] Preliminary.   [2] Estimate.   Source: Economic Research Service, U.S. Department of Agriculture (ERS-USDA)

Production of Peanuts (Harvested for Nuts) in the United States, by States   In Thousands of Pounds

Crop Year	Alabama	Florida	Georgia	New Mexico	North Carolina	Oklahoma	South Carolina	Texas	Virginia	Total
2001	532,325	250,100	1,711,620	67,044	356,475	197,890	30,600	895,900	234,750	4,276,704
2002	379,800	197,800	1,313,000	54,000	210,000	159,600	19,140	868,000	119,700	3,321,040
2003	508,750	345,000	1,863,000	45,900	320,000	98,000	57,800	810,000	95,700	4,144,150
2004	557,200	364,000	1,817,800	59,500	367,500	102,300	112,200	803,700	104,000	4,288,200
2005	613,250	410,400	2,130,000	66,500	288,000	107,910	168,000	975,000	66,000	4,869,860
2006	407,500	300,000	1,598,500	43,200	268,800	62,700	168,000	514,750	54,400	3,464,250
2007	400,350	321,300	1,622,400	32,000	261,000	57,800	173,600	691,900	52,500	3,740,650
2008	675,500	448,000	2,329,000	25,600	358,900	63,000	265,200	834,900	80,400	5,162,400
2009	495,000	336,000	1,797,800	21,700	244,200	42,900	148,800	506,850	44,400	3,691,650
2010[1]	481,000	459,000	1,975,800	32,000	240,800	67,200	217,600	586,800	32,400	4,155,600

[1] Preliminary.   Source: Agricultural Statistics Board, U.S. Department of Agriculture (ASB-USDA)

Supply and Reported Uses of Shelled Peanuts and Products in the United States   In Thousands of Pounds

Crop Year Beginning Aug. 1	Shelled Peanuts Stocks, Aug. 1 — Edible	Oil Stock[2]	Shelled Peanuts Production — Edible	Oil Stock[2]	Candy[3]	Snack[4]	Sandwich Spread	Butter[5]	Other Products	Total	Shelled Peanuts Crushed[6]	Crude Oil Pro-duction	Cake & Meal Production
					--------------------- Reported Used (Shelled Peanuts - Raw Basis) ---------------------								
					----------- Edible Grades Used In -----------								
2001-02	680,850	16,648	2,090,776	485,092	349,729	360,916	----	818,927	17,284	1,546,856	521,173	230,791	296,874
2002-03	504,186	24,231	1,983,016	611,627	354,232	344,913	----	828,529	24,379	1,552,053	644,194	285,685	356,888
2003-04	603,529	17,686	2,439,231	390,893	365,983	414,588	----	901,637	15,930	1,698,138	402,958	172,977	226,995
2004-05	621,190	17,686	2,357,314	246,663	389,696	450,781	----	938,514	22,547	1,801,538	295,769	126,249	172,668
2005-06	501,868	15,305	2,411,471	357,600	376,777	454,324	----	974,223	12,092	1,817,416	407,817	181,085	232,868
2006-07	510,097	21,499	2,415,495	347,243	373,684	415,131	----	993,445	9,397	1,791,657	385,375	166,450	223,537
2007-08	528,918	33,401	2,291,603	319,186	320,467	425,166	----	1,012,263	10,676	1,768,572	372,980	158,144	211,733
2008-09	431,593	39,508	2,442,345	253,778	316,275	367,478	----	1,102,698	9,840	1,796,291	334,296	142,666	190,748
2009-10[1]	554,295	35,498	2,457,434	280,888	315,595	352,963	----	1,191,821	15,840	1,876,219	326,779	139,903	185,452

[1] Preliminary.   [2] Includes straight run oil stock peanuts.   [3] Includes peanut butter made by manufacturers for own use in candy.   [4] Formerly titled "Salted Peanuts."   [5] Includes peanut butter made by manufacturers for own use in cookies and sandwiches, but excludes peanut butter used in candy.
[6] All crushings regardless of grade.   Source: National Agricultural Statistics Service, U.S. Department of Agriculture (NASS-USDA)

PEANUTS AND PEANUT OIL

Shelled Peanuts (Raw Basis) Used in Primary Products, by Type   In Thousands of Pounds

Crop Year Beginning Aug. 1	Virginia				Runner				Spanish			
	Candy[2]	Peanuts	Butter[3]	Total	Candy[2]	Peanuts	Butter[3]	Total	Candy[2]	Peanuts	Butter[3]	Total
2000-01	19,101	100,650	102,050	225,072	320,304	247,739	643,229	1,227,156	16,205	13,127	7,960	38,135
2001-02	26,640	97,046	106,573	233,356	303,668	250,079	702,454	1,269,776	19,421	13,791	9,900	43,724
2002-03	26,930	75,100	77,018	183,226	312,192	257,259	734,844	1,323,846	15,110	12,555	16,667	44,981
2003-04	23,580	68,257	88,053	181,559	328,560	333,198	805,852	1,481,457	13,843	13,133	7,732	35,122
2004-05	25,466	70,216	112,027	209,411	349,437	367,671	824,876	1,562,692	14,793	12,894	1,611	29,435
2005-06	25,738	81,617	123,402	231,893	335,748	361,176	849,176	1,557,025	15,291	11,531	W	28,498
2006-07	29,542	75,858	113,689	220,196	329,806	328,167	869,014	1,535,250	14,335	11,104	W	36,211
2007-08	27,909	71,059	125,497	225,445	279,564	344,551	878,026	1,511,807	12,994	9,556	W	31,321
2008-09	26,342	52,925	110,737	191,770	276,212	303,730	981,546	1,569,531	13,721	10,823	W	34,990
2009-10[1]	17,361	50,812	W	198,497	286,277	290,358	1,056,699	1,646,454	11,957	11,793	W	31,269

[1] Preliminary.   [2] Includes peanut butter made by manufacturers for own use in candy.   [3] Includes peanut butter made by manufacturers for own use in cookies and sandwiches, but excludes peanut butter used in candy.
Source: National Agricultural Statistics Service, U.S. Department of Agriculture (NASS-USDA)

Production, Consumption, Stocks and Foreign Trade of Peanut Oil in the United States   In Millions of Pounds

Crop Year Beginning Aug. 1	Production		Consumption		Stocks, Dec. 31		Imports for Consumption	Exports
	Crude	Refined	In Refining	In End Products	Crude	Refined		
2001-02	278.5	179.1	291.9	282.5	8.2	1.7	----	----
2002-03	267.7	166.3	W	277.6	52.9	3.5	----	----
2003-04	180.7	115.8	W	203.8	23.0	1.8	----	----
2004-05	135.7	91.0	W	181.9	40.3	2.4	----	----
2005-06	188.0	119.9	W	152.1	15.4	3.7	----	----
2006-07	173.8	115.1	W	W	35.5	5.6	----	----
2007-08	168.7	111.2	W	W	14.1	1.8	----	----
2008-09	150.8	99.9	W	W	17.6	3.0	----	----
2009-10[1]	146.3	96.6	W	W	18.1	2.1	----	----
2010-11[2]	180.0	119.0	W	W				

[1] Preliminary.   [2] Forecast.   W = Withheld.   *Source: Bureau of the Census, U.S. Department of Commerce*

Production of Crude Peanut Oil in the United States   In Millions of Pounds

Year	Jan.	Feb.	Mar.	Apr.	May	June	July	Aug.	Sept.	Oct.	Nov.	Dec.	Total
2001	17.3	15.7	20.1	15.3	12.4	19.1	16.3	16.7	12.9	17.1	13.8	25.6	202.4
2002	24.8	25.5	32.8	28.5	33.8	24.3	22.6	27.7	27.2	26.5	24.9	20.2	319.0
2003	21.7	16.6	19.4	20.5	20.0	23.2	19.8	17.3	18.3	24.1	15.6	13.2	229.6
2004	12.6	15.7	13.0	14.7	11.8	13.7	10.7	9.8	5.8	10.0	11.9	12.6	142.4
2005	14.4	13.1	9.9	11.3	13.3	14.6	8.9	14.5	11.3	15.3	16.4	17.7	160.8
2006	W	16.5	W	15.6	18.1	15.6	15.7	19.7	16.2	18.0	14.4	10.1	159.8
2007	14.3	12.8	14.3	14.9	9.7	15.2	14.1	17.7	19.0	17.3	12.0	14.0	175.3
2008	14.9	6.0	14.3	14.2	13.8	12.6	13.0	11.8	14.6	17.8	12.4	13.9	159.2
2009	13.8	6.8	14.1	12.2	11.9	12.2	9.4	10.9	12.5	15.1	13.6	11.5	143.8
2010[1]	16.0	10.7	12.1	10.0	13.8	7.8	12.3	12.8	13.9	W	15.7	15.7	153.6

[1] Preliminary.   W = Withheld.   *Source: Bureau of the Census, U.S. Department of Commerce*

Average Price of Peanut Meal 50% Southeast Mills   In Dollars Per Short Ton

Year	Jan.	Feb.	Mar.	Apr.	May	June	July	Aug.	Sept.	Oct.	Nov.	Dec.	Average
2001-02	115.00	111.25	100.00	102.50	100.00	105.00	110.00	105.00	NA	130.00	135.00	136.88	113.69
2002-03	NA	130.00	122.50	118.50	114.25	124.00	125.00	135.00	135.00	135.75	130.00	130.00	127.27
2003-04	147.10	161.00	163.25	163.35	168.75	200.40	226.00	237.50	204.00	199.33	143.33	133.00	178.92
2004-05	100.38	99.25	93.50	93.25	99.25	112.00	122.75	137.25	145.25	140.83	132.50	109.00	115.43
2005-06	105.50	102.50	100.88	NA	114.50	113.50	113.17	113.33	107.13	107.50	100.00	98.75	106.98
2006-07	98.50	98.50	98.00	98.50	98.50	NA	NA	NA	NA	NA	NA	NA	98.40
2007-08	NA	NA	NA	NA	NA	NA	NA	NA	NA	NA	NA	NA	NA
2008-09	NA	NA	NA	NA	NA	NA	NA	NA	NA	NA	NA	NA	NA
2009-10	NA	NA	NA	NA	NA	NA	NA	NA	NA	NA	NA	NA	NA
2010-11[1]	NA	NA	NA	NA	NA	NA	NA	NA	NA	NA	NA	NA	NA

[1] Preliminary.   NA = Not available.   *Source: Agricultural Marketing Service, U.S. Department of Agriculture (AMS-USDA)*

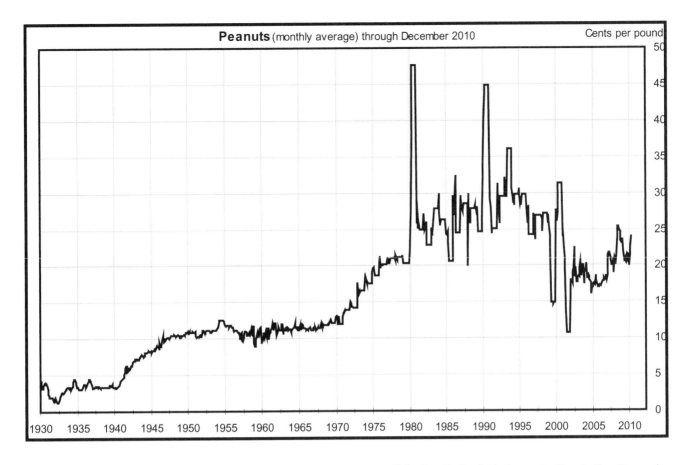

Peanuts (monthly average) through December 2010 — Cents per pound

Average Price Received by Farmers for Peanuts (in the Shell) in the United States   In Cents Per Pound

Year	Jan.	Feb.	Mar.	Apr.	May	June	July	Aug.	Sept.	Oct.	Nov.	Dec.	Average[1]
2001-02	24.1	24.9	22.8	21.0	19.5	13.5	10.7	NQ	NQ	NQ	NQ	NQ	19.5
2002-03	NQ	17.9	17.9	18.0	17.5	19.1	19.6	22.6	18.4	19.6	17.7	NQ	18.8
2003-04	NQ	18.3	18.5	18.4	19.6	20.6	18.9	18.6	19.8	20.6	20.3	17.4	19.2
2004-05	19.0	19.2	20.1	20.3	18.3	18.9	18.6	18.5	18.0	17.8	17.6	16.0	18.5
2005-06	17.0	17.0	17.4	17.5	17.4	17.3	18.6	16.9	17.4	17.3	17.0	17.0	17.3
2006-07	17.0	17.3	17.2	17.2	17.6	17.8	17.8	17.8	18.3	17.9	18.1	18.7	17.7
2007-08	18.0	18.6	21.4	21.7	21.3	21.6	21.0	20.7	20.0	20.4	20.1	21.1	20.5
2008-09	18.9	21.0	20.6	20.1	21.7	23.9	25.3	25.4	25.2	24.8	24.7	23.4	22.9
2009-10	23.1	23.3	23.7	21.7	21.7	20.7	21.0	20.6	20.3	20.6	21.6	21.5	21.7
2010-11[2]	20.7	20.0	21.4	22.3	24.0	22.9	23.1						22.1

[1] Weighted average by sales.   [2] Preliminarily.   NQ = No quote.   *Source: National Agricultural Statistics Service, U.S. Department of Agriculture (NASS-USDA)*

Average Price of Domestic Crude Peanut Oil (in Tanks) F.O.B. Southeast Mills   In Cents Per Pound

Year	Jan.	Feb.	Mar.	Apr.	May	June	July	Aug.	Sept.	Oct.	Nov.	Dec.	Average
2001-02	36.25	37.00	37.00	35.00	28.00	27.50	27.00	27.00	30.00	34.00	35.20	36.25	32.52
2002-03	NA	42.00	43.67	45.75	46.00	47.00	50.25	52.75	56.60	58.25	60.00	60.67	51.18
2003-04	61.60	63.25	64.50	65.00	61.67	60.00	60.00	56.50	NA	56.00	53.75	55.00	59.75
2004-05	55.00	55.00	55.67	56.00	55.00	50.00	50.00	53.25	52.50	52.38	52.25	50.06	53.09
2005-06	45.50	45.50	45.00	42.50	42.50	42.50	42.50	42.50	43.75	45.00	47.30	49.25	44.48
2006-07	52.67	52.50	50.00	49.25	46.25	48.20	52.63	55.63	62.56	69.63	70.00	73.00	56.86
2007-08	76.75	93.20	98.50	97.33	99.00	100.00	104.38	104.80	107.00	110.00	110.00	110.00	100.91
2008-09	97.00	90.00	85.25	79.10	75.00	62.50	58.75	56.60	57.00	60.70	62.00	54.00	69.83
2009-10	51.20	52.00	52.20	59.00	59.50	58.75	63.60	67.63	67.75	67.80	68.38	68.81	61.39
2010-11[1]	71.40	75.13	77.90	79.33									75.94

[1] Preliminary.   NA = Not available.   *Source: Agricultural Marketing Service, U.S. Department of Agriculture (AMS-USDA)*

Pepper

The pepper plant is a perennial climbing shrub that originated in India and Sri Lanka. Pepper is considered the world's most important spice and has been used to flavor foods for over 3,000 years. Pepper was once considered so valuable that it was used to ransom Rome from Attila the Hun. Black pepper alone accounts for nearly 35% of the world's spice trade. Unlike many other popular herbs and spices, pepper can only be cultivated in tropical climates. The pepper plant produces a berry called a peppercorn. Both black and white pepper are obtained from the same plant. The colors of pepper are determined by the maturity of the berry at harvest and by different processing methods.

Black pepper is picked when the berries are still green and immature. The peppercorns are then dried in the sun until they turn black. White pepper is picked when the berries are fully ripe and bright red. The red peppercorns are then soaked, washed to remove the skin of the berry, and dried to produce a white to yellowish-white peppercorn. Black pepper has a slightly hotter flavor and stronger aroma than white pepper. Piperine, an alkaloid of pyridine, is the active ingredient in pepper that makes it hot.

Black pepper oil is obtained from crushed berries using solvent extraction. Black pepper oil is used in the treatment of pain, chills, flu, muscular aches, and in some perfumes. It is also helpful in promoting digestion in the colon.

The world's key pepper varieties are known by their place of origin. Popular types of pepper include Lampong Black and Muntok White from Indonesia, Brazilian Black, and Malabar Black and Tellicherry from India.

Prices – The average monthly price for black pepper in 2007 (latest data available) rose sharply by +55.8% to 161.8 cents per pound, way up from the 14-year low of 75.6 cents per pound in 2004. The average monthly price for white pepper in 2007 (latest data) rose sharply by +40.9% to 216.4 cents per pound, but that was still only 61% of the record high of 356.5 cents seen in 1998.

Trade – The world's largest exporters of pepper in 2008 (latest data available) were Vietnam (with 90,300 metric tons of exports), Indonesia (52,407), India (39,645), Brazil (36,728), and Malaysia (13,592). U.S. imports of black pepper in 2008 (latest data) fell -2.6% yr/yr to 49,625 metric tons. The primary source of U.S. imports of black pepper in 2008 was Indonesia which accounted for 41% of U.S. imports, followed by India with 20%, and Brazil with 17%. Imports from Malaysia have dropped by over 95% since 2003. U.S. imports of white pepper in 2008 rose by +25.1% yr/yr to 6,960 metric tons. The primary source of U.S. imports of white pepper was Indonesia, which accounted for 69% of U.S. imports, followed by Malaysia with 5%, Brazil with 1%, and China with 1%.

World Exports of Pepper (Black and White) and Prices in the United States — In Metric Tons

| | Exports (In Metric Tons) | | | | | | | | New York Spot Prices (Cents Per Pound) | | | | |
| | | | | | | | | | Indonesian | | Indian | | |
Year	Brazil	India	Indo-nesia	Mada-gascar	Malaysia	Mexico	Sri Lanka	Vietnam	Lampong Black	Muntok White	Brazilian Black	Malabar Black	Telli-cherry[2]
1999	19,617	35,635	36,293	619	21,804	4,026	3,754	34,800	254.5	334.9	254.5	254.5	296.3
2000	20,469	19,125	47,502	588	23,684	4,534	4,855	36,400	228.1	227.1	228.1	228.1	282.6
2001	36,975	19,641	53,432	811	25,537	4,658	2,161	57,000	116.2	132.6	116.2	116.2	179.3
2002	38,230	21,066	63,214	880	22,840	4,344	7,915	78,400	92.9	120.6	92.9	92.9	127.8
2003	38,972	15,319	51,546	863	18,346	3,861	7,740	73,900	85.8	139.3	85.8	85.8	128.8
2004	43,003	15,429	32,364	1,243	19,788	5,785	4,852	111,000	75.6	120.9	75.6	75.6	118.8
2005	38,424	21,470	34,531	1,229	18,097	15,415	8,131	109,000	76.0	116.0	76.0	76.0	109.9
2006	42,200	35,499	36,953	1,776	16,610	6,593	7,596	115,000	103.9	153.5	103.9	103.9	136.4
2007	38,679	47,464	38,447	1,892	15,165	4,081	6,940	83,000	161.8	216.4	161.8	161.8	
2008[1]	36,728	39,645	52,407	1,209	13,592	5,376	6,237	90,300					

[1] Preliminary. [2] Extra bold. NA = not avaliable. *Source: Foreign Agricultural Service, U.S. Department of Agriculture (FAS-USDA)*

United States Imports of Unground Pepper from Specified Countries — In Metric Tons

| | Black Pepper | | | | | | | White Pepper | | | | | |
Year	Brazil	India	Indonesia	Malaysia	Sing-apore	Sri Lanka	Total	Brazil	China	Indonesia	Malaysia	Sing-apore	Total
1999	7,093	24,931	8,429	2,392	525	441	47,591	32	451	5,202	420	342	6,789
2000	7,853	10,981	15,713	4,148	306	516	43,539	15	210	6,345	185	215	7,311
2001	11,699	7,998	19,606	2,957	508	279	48,749	48	7	5,807	120	161	6,365
2002	11,300	7,407	13,638	3,213	110	564	50,155	18	73	6,559	103	219	7,207
2003	13,792	4,950	16,370	1,416	163	504	51,124	198	180	4,567	224	904	6,758
2004	15,606	2,039	13,210	97	25	187	50,925	472	98	4,034	192	422	7,290
2005	13,935	3,828	13,502	144	50	269	52,152	460	73	4,134	192	300	7,248
2006	15,622	7,272	12,941	249	90	342	55,523	615	106	3,809	419	344	7,805
2007	14,148	14,763	14,201	162	75	281	50,934	122	121	3,991	520	140	5,564
2008[1]	8,224	9,699	20,180	35	126	665	49,626	88	82	4,783	381	36	6,960

[1] Preliminary. *Source: Foreign Agricultural Service, U.S. Department of Agriculture (FAS-USDA)*

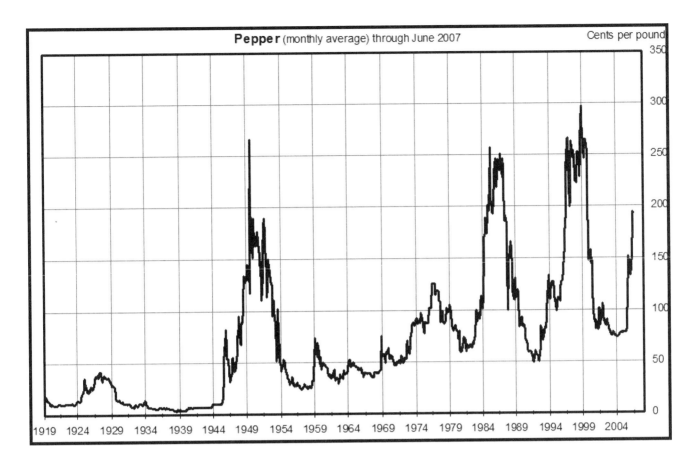

Pepper (monthly average) through June 2007 — Cents per pound

Average Black Pepper in New York (Brazilian)   In Cents Per Pound

Year	Jan.	Feb.	Mar.	Apr.	May	June	July	Aug.	Sept.	Oct.	Nov.	Dec.	Average
1998	199.4	205.5	243.8	262.8	262.8	247.5	253.0	253.8	246.3	243.0	231.3	225.0	239.5
1999	222.5	225.8	252.5	248.0	252.5	250.0	229.0	249.3	263.8	282.0	297.5	281.0	254.5
2000	260.0	256.3	246.0	260.0	265.0	265.0	263.8	252.5	205.0	167.5	147.5	149.0	228.1
2001	157.5	146.3	144.0	150.0	143.8	123.0	97.3	87.0	90.0	89.3	81.6	85.3	116.2
2002	85.0	80.0	81.4	100.5	101.0	92.0	84.8	86.8	93.5	103.5	106.0	100.8	92.9
2003	93.8	89.0	88.5	85.5	83.8	89.0	90.0	86.6	83.5	81.6	80.0	78.0	85.8
2004	78.0	75.5	75.5	75.4	77.3	78.0	76.8	75.0	75.0	74.2	73.3	73.0	75.6
2005	73.0	73.0	73.8	75.2	75.5	77.0	77.0	77.0	77.6	78.0	77.0	77.4	76.0
2006	78.0	78.0	77.8	78.5	80.0	80.4	89.0	112.7	146.0	152.0	139.5	134.3	103.9
2007	132.5	136.0	137.2	177.5	194.5	193.0							161.8

NA = Not available.   *Source: Foreign Agricultural Service, U.S. Department of Agriculture (FAS-USDA)*

Average White Pepper in New York (Indonesian)[1]   In Cents Per Pound

Year	Jan.	Feb.	Mar.	Apr.	May	June	July	Aug.	Sept.	Oct.	Nov.	Dec.	Average
1998	348.0	346.3	362.5	390.0	393.0	358.8	354.0	356.3	348.8	340.0	340.0	340.0	356.5
1999	361.3	355.0	365.0	355.0	352.5	335.0	310.0	313.8	325.0	327.0	316.3	303.0	334.9
2000	295.0	293.8	264.0	253.8	246.3	242.0	226.3	227.5	205.0	171.3	150.0	150.0	227.1
2001	159.0	151.3	144.0	133.8	130.0	127.0	122.5	129.6	128.0	125.5	120.0	120.0	132.6
2002	111.3	100.3	95.6	108.8	108.0	105.0	104.5	118.8	130.0	154.0	157.5	153.0	120.6
2003	152.4	148.8	150.0	150.0	142.6	133.0	133.0	138.2	137.5	133.6	127.5	125.0	139.3
2004	118.0	118.0	125.8	130.0	130.0	125.0	127.0	120.5	119.0	113.8	109.5	114.6	120.9
2005	119.0	118.0	118.0	116.4	115.0	115.0	115.0	115.0	115.2	115.0	115.0	115.0	116.0
2006	115.0	117.5	125.0	125.0	125.0	126.2	145.0	160.0	210.0	212.5	192.5	188.8	153.5
2007	191.3	195.0	197.0	225.0	245.0	245.0							216.4

[1] Muntok White.   *Source: Foreign Agricultural Service, U.S. Department of Agriculture (FAS-USDA)*

Petroleum

Crude oil is petroleum that is acquired directly from the ground. Crude oil was formed millions of years ago from the remains of tiny aquatic plants and animals that lived in ancient seas. Ancient societies such as the Persians, 10th century Sumatrans, and pre-Columbian Indians believed that crude oil had medicinal benefits. Around 4,000 BC in Mesopotamia, bitumen, a tarry crude, was used as caulking for ships, as a setting for jewels and mosaics, and as an adhesive to secure weapon handles. The walls of Babylon and the famed pyramids were held together with bitumen, and Egyptians used it for embalming. During the 19th century in America, an oil find was often met with dismay. Pioneers who dug wells to find water or brine, were disappointed when they struck oil. It wasn't until 1854, with the invention of the kerosene lamp, that the first large-scale demand for petroleum emerged. Crude oil is a relatively abundant commodity. The world has produced approximately 650 billion barrels of oil, but another trillion barrels of proved reserves have yet to be extracted. Crude oil was the world's first trillion-dollar industry and accounts for the single largest product in world trade.

Futures and options on crude oil trade at the New York Mercantile Exchange (Nymex) and at the International Petroleum Exchange in London (IPE). The Nymex trades two main types of crude oil: light sweet crude oil and Brent crude oil. The light sweet futures contract calls for the delivery of 1,000 barrels of crude oil in Cushing, Oklahoma. Light sweet crude is preferred by refiners because of its low sulfur content and relatively high yield of high-value products such as gasoline, diesel fuel, heating oil, and jet fuel. The Brent blend crude is based on a light, sweet North Sea crude oil. Brent blend crude production is approximately 500,000 barrels per day, and is shipped from Sullom Voe in the Shetland Islands.

Prices – NYMEX West Texas Intermediate (WTI) crude oil prices on a nearest-futures basis traded near $80 per barrel in the first half of 2010 with a slight upward bent as the global economy strengthened and posted a 1-1/2 year high of $87.15 per barrel in May 2010. Crude oil prices then plummeted to a 1-year low of $64.24 per barrel in late-May 2010 as the European sovereign-debt crisis intensified. Crude prices recovered and moved higher into the year-end and in December 2010 posted a 2-1/4 year high of $92.06 per barrel, finishing the year 15% higher

at $91.38. The explosion of British Petroleum's leased Deepwater Horizon drilling-rig over its Macondo well in the Gulf of Mexico in April 2010 led to the largest oil spill in U.S. history and prompted a temporary halt in all deep-sea drilling in the Gulf of Mexico as the U.S. government toughed drilling regulations. This was a long-term bullish development and highlights the difficulty the oil industry will have in economically developing reserves and meeting demand in coming years. Crude oil prices remained generally strong in 2010 despite adequate inventories during the year. Crude oil and gasoline prices rallied in early 2011 on widespread protest movements throughout North Africa and the Middle East that resulted in new governments in Tunisia and Egypt. Crude oil prices rallied to a 2-1/2 year high of $106.95 per barrel in March 2011 as a civil war in Libya, Africa's third-biggest oil producer, cut its normal crude output of 1.6 million bpd by more than half.

Supply – World crude oil production in 2010 rose +1.6% yr/yr to 73.497 million barrels per day, which was a new record high. The world's largest oil producers in 2008 were Russia (with 12.7% of world production in 2006), Saudi Arabia (12.6%), the United States (6.7%), Iran (5.5%), China (5.1%), and Mexico (3.8%). U.S. crude oil production in 2010 rose +2.5% yr/yr to 5.495 million barrels per day. Alaskan production in 2010 fell −7.3% yr/yr to 598,000 barrels per day, the lowest level since 1977 and only 34% of the peak level of 2.017 million barrels per day seen in 1988.

Demand – U.S. demand for crude oil in 2010 rose +2.3% yr/yr to 14.671 million barrels per day, below the 2004 record high of 15.475. Most of that demand went for U.S. refinery production of products such as gasoline fuel, diesel fuel, aviation fuel, heating oil, kerosene, asphalt, and lubricants.

Trade – The U.S. is highly dependent on imports of crude oil to meet its energy needs. U.S. imports in 2010 rose +1.4% yr/yr to 9.141 million barrels per day, down from the 2005 record high of 10.126. U.S. imports of petroleum products in 2010 fell −6.8% to 1.977 million barrels per day, imports of distillate fuel oil fell -1.8% yr/yr to 221,000 barrels per day, and imports of residual fuel oil rose +15.1% yr/yr to 381,000 barrels per day.

World Production of Crude Petroleum   In Thousands of Barrels Per Day

Year	Canada	China	Indonesia	Iran	Kuwait	Mexico	Nigeria	Russia/3	Saudi Arabia	United Kingdom	United States	Venezuela	World Total
2001	2,029	3,300	1,340	3,724	1,998	3,127	2,256	6,917	8,031	2,282	5,801	3,010	68,099
2002	2,171	3,390	1,249	3,444	1,894	3,177	2,118	7,408	7,634	2,292	5,746	2,604	67,158
2003	2,306	3,409	1,155	3,743	2,136	3,371	2,275	8,132	8,775	2,093	5,681	2,335	69,433
2004	2,398	3,485	1,096	4,001	2,376	3,383	2,329	8,805	9,101	1,845	5,419	2,557	72,476
2005	2,369	3,609	1,067	4,139	2,529	3,334	2,627	9,043	9,550	1,649	5,178	2,565	73,718
2006	2,525	3,673	1,019	4,028	2,535	3,256	2,440	9,247	9,152	1,490	5,102	2,511	73,430
2007	2,628	3,729	964	3,912	2,464	3,076	2,350	9,437	8,722	1,498	5,064	2,433	72,988
2008	2,579	3,790	972	4,050	2,586	2,792	2,165	9,357	9,261	1,391	4,950	2,394	73,671
2009[1]	2,579	3,799	946	4,037	2,350	2,601	2,208	9,495	8,250	1,328	5,361	2,239	72,314
2010[2]	2,590	4,053	944	4,084	2,350	2,582	2,446	9,689	8,442	1,233	5,492	2,127	73,497

Includes lease condensate.   [1] Preliminary.   [2] Estimate.   *Source: Energy Information Administration, U.S. Department of Energy (EIA-DOE)*

Refiner Sales Prices of Residual Fuel Oil   In Cents Per Gallon

Year	Jan.	Feb.	Mar.	Apr.	May	June	July	Aug.	Sept.	Oct.	Nov.	Dec.	Average
2005	86.9	90.8	98.0	106.6	112.2	111.8	116.8	129.2	138.4	142.7	134.3	134.6	116.9
2006	134.6	137.8	136.0	139.7	143.5	148.1	145.1	145.1	132.4	120.1	117.6	119.9	135.0
2007	117.2	121.4	122.1	125.8	135.9	142.1	153.9	158.4	161.0	166.1	183.2	194.8	148.5
2008	203.9	200.4	204.8	222.1	234.9	265.8	294.5	300.5	266.6	216.6	165.4	121.1	224.7
2009	116.4	120.0	118.3	117.4	121.3	144.0	148.8	164.1	168.9	171.7	173.9	181.3	145.5
2010[1]	185.2	186.2	186.2	188.7	189.8	187.4	185.8	189.5	188.3	191.3			187.8

Sulfur 1% or less, excluding taxes.   [1] Preliminary.   *Source: Energy Information Administration, U.S. Department of Energy (EIA-DOE)*

Refiner Sales Prices of No. 2 Fuel Oil   In Cents Per Gallon

Year	Jan.	Feb.	Mar.	Apr.	May	June	July	Aug.	Sept.	Oct.	Nov.	Dec.	Average
2005	131.4	134.4	153.5	155.9	144.4	159.1	164.7	178.4	199.3	207.1	175.2	172.4	164.7
2006	175.6	171.1	179.1	197.2	201.3	198.4	200.6	206.1	179.7	172.2	169.9	175.3	185.5
2007	161.2	172.9	178.1	191.0	194.9	201.4	207.1	202.1	213.3	226.0	256.9	257.0	205.2
2008	256.4	260.7	297.7	319.5	353.6	376.2	380.2	328.7	300.3	240.0	194.7	157.9	288.8
2009	154.8	142.7	135.8	139.7	146.8	174.4	165.8	180.4	177.4	191.8	200.4	198.9	167.4
2010[1]	207.5	198.6	210.0	221.4	212.9	203.7	200.1	204.1	209.3	222.1			209.0

Excluding taxes.   [1] Preliminary.   *Source: Energy Information Administration, U.S. Department of Energy (EIA-DOE)*

Refiner Sales Prices of No. 2 Diesel Fuel   In Cents Per Gallon

Year	Jan.	Feb.	Mar.	Apr.	May	June	July	Aug.	Sept.	Oct.	Nov.	Dec.	Average
2005	130.6	139.1	158.8	163.8	152.2	167.0	171.5	189.8	212.7	232.3	182.6	175.5	173.0
2006	181.0	180.6	190.1	212.2	218.7	218.7	225.0	234.3	191.3	182.7	186.8	188.6	200.8
2007	169.5	182.4	197.9	211.6	210.1	214.7	222.0	219.3	232.2	242.6	269.8	259.9	219.3
2008	258.0	273.8	315.8	335.6	371.2	385.9	387.6	333.8	316.0	251.4	195.5	146.9	297.6
2009	148.0	132.6	131.5	145.6	153.1	182.8	174.5	193.7	184.8	197.8	203.7	199.7	170.7
2010[1]	207.8	202.5	216.3	231.2	217.7	212.0	209.8	216.1	219.0	232.5			216.5

Excluding taxes.   [1] Preliminary.   *Source: Energy Information Administration, U.S. Department of Energy (EIA-DOE)*

Refiner Sales Prices of Kerosine-Type Jet Fuel   In Cents Per Gallon

Year	Jan.	Feb.	Mar.	Apr.	May	June	July	Aug.	Sept.	Oct.	Nov.	Dec.	Average
2005	131.7	138.3	158.2	165.5	155.8	165.0	171.2	184.7	206.9	233.5	181.4	173.8	172.2
2006	182.4	182.5	186.2	203.2	213.2	213.3	217.4	221.4	194.7	181.5	177.8	190.6	197.0
2007	172.7	176.6	184.6	202.1	207.9	211.4	216.7	215.1	225.6	235.3	265.6	265.5	214.9
2008	266.5	267.4	310.6	331.5	364.2	391.2	397.8	339.3	327.8	256.9	197.4	147.0	299.8
2009	147.2	135.2	126.6	142.5	146.0	178.0	175.9	189.4	182.2	191.7	206.0	201.2	168.5
2010[1]	212.1	199.9	212.9	224.7	218.6	209.4	210.0	213.8	213.1	226.3			214.1

Excluding taxes.   [1] Preliminary.   *Source: Energy Information Administration, U.S. Department of Energy (EIA-DOE)*

Refiner Sales Prices of Propane[2]   In Cents Per Gallon

Year	Jan.	Feb.	Mar.	Apr.	May	June	July	Aug.	Sept.	Oct.	Nov.	Dec.	Average
2005	NA	NA	NA	86.0	82.0	83.0	86.0	93.2	108.2	111.6	103.3	106.8	95.6
2006	104.4	97.5	96.7	102.3	102.9	106.7	110.8	111.3	103.2	100.3	101.3	103.3	103.4
2007	99.5	103.3	104.9	106.7	111.2	109.4	115.9	116.7	124.8	135.1	147.1	146.1	118.4
2008	151.9	146.9	149.5	157.1	167.5	176.1	183.3	166.7	156.5	124.2	100.5	91.6	147.7
2009	97.4	89.0	80.5	71.9	72.8	83.8	76.0	83.7	92.3	100.4	108.8	117.8	89.5
2010[1]	133.2	132.4	117.9	114.4	109.8	104.9	101.2	108.4	115.1	125.3			116.3

[1] Preliminary.   [2] Consumer Grade, Excluding taxes.   *Source: Energy Information Administration, U.S. Department of Energy (EIA-DOE)*

Supply and Disposition of Crude Oil in the United States   In Thousands of Barrels Per Day

	-------- Supply --------						Stock		Disposition		Ending Stocks		
	-- Field Production --		----- Imports -----			Unaccounted for Crude Oil	---- Withdrawal[3] ----		Refinery				Other
	Total Domestic	Alskan	Total	SPR[2]	Other		SPR[2]	Other	Inputs	Exports	Total	SPR[2]	Primary
Year	----------------- In Thousands of Barrels Per Day -----------------										----- In Millions of Barrels -----		
2003	5,681	974	9,665	0	9,665	54	108	-24	15,304	12	907	638	269
2004	5,419	908	10,088	77	10,010	143	102	46	15,475	27	961	676	286
2005	5,178	864	10,126	52	10,074	76	25	104	15,220	32	1,008	685	324
2006	5,102	741	10,118	8	10,089	8	11	-37	15,242	25	1,001	689	312
2007	5,064	722	10,031	7					15,156	27	983	697	286
2008	4,950	683	9,783	19					14,648	29	1,028	702	326
2009	5,361	645	9,013	56					14,336	44	1,052	727	325
2010[1]	5,495	598	9,216	NA					14,671	43	1,084	727	357

[1] Preliminary.   [2] Strategic Petroleum Reserve.   [3] A negative number indicates a decrease in stocks and a positive number indicates an increase.
Source: Energy Information Administration, U.S. Department of Energy (EIA-DOE)

PETROLEUM

Crude Petroleum Refinery Operations Ratio[2] in the United States   In Percent of Capacity

Year	Jan.	Feb.	Mar.	Apr.	May	June	July	Aug.	Sept.	Oct.	Nov.	Dec.	Average
2001	90.2	90.5	89.4	94.9	96.4	95.6	93.9	93.3	92.2	92.0	92.2	90.2	92.6
2002	87.7	86.6	87.9	93.0	91.5	93.1	93.5	92.9	90.4	87.5	92.6	91.1	90.7
2003	87.2	87.4	90.5	94.1	95.8	94.7	94.0	95.0	93.1	92.4	93.6	93.0	92.6
2004	89.1	88.8	88.5	92.5	95.6	97.5	96.8	97.1	90.1	90.2	94.4	95.0	93.0
2005	91.3	90.6	90.8	92.8	94.2	97.1	94.2	92.7	83.6	81.3	89.3	89.4	90.6
2006	87.0	86.5	85.8	88.0	91.2	93.0	92.5	93.2	93.0	87.9	88.0	90.6	89.7
2007	88.2	84.7	87.1	88.1	89.7	88.5	91.2	90.8	88.9	87.4	88.9	88.7	88.5
2008	85.8	85.0	83.2	86.2	88.8	89.5	88.8	87.1	74.6	85.3	85.8	83.9	85.3
2009	82.3	81.5	81.5	82.7	84.0	86.0	84.2	84.1	84.9	81.5	81.1	81.3	82.9
2010[1]	80.0	81.2	83.1	88.6	88.0	90.2	90.9	88.9	86.5	82.2	86.0	88.4	86.2

[1] Preliminary.   [2] Based on the ration of the daily average crude runs to stills to the rated capacity of refineries per day.   *Source: Energy Information Administration, U.S. Department of Energy (EIA-DOE)*

Crude Oil Refinery Inputs in the United States   In Thousands of Barrels Per Day

Year	Jan.	Feb.	Mar.	Apr.	May	June	July	Aug.	Sept.	Oct.	Nov.	Dec.	Average
2001	14,789	14,813	14,649	15,536	15,763	15,650	15,369	15,259	15,005	15,002	15,001	14,688	15,128
2002	14,487	14,306	14,526	15,325	15,301	15,397	15,430	15,338	14,861	14,303	15,155	14,900	14,947
2003	14,338	14,381	14,933	15,575	15,910	15,620	15,546	15,693	15,446	15,342	15,455	15,345	15,304
2004	14,782	14,706	14,787	15,541	15,992	16,240	16,142	16,142	14,980	14,941	15,664	15,750	15,472
2005	15,254	15,142	15,214	15,494	15,905	16,401	15,850	15,664	13,986	13,646	15,032	15,046	15,220
2006	14,805	14,581	14,582	14,928	15,516	15,843	15,702	15,792	15,739	15,008	15,009	15,354	15,238
2007	14,992	14,435	14,840	15,045	15,380	15,248	15,671	15,685	15,226	14,933	15,151	15,202	15,151
2008	14,804	14,625	14,364	14,799	15,263	15,417	15,255	14,947	12,759	14,552	14,606	14,352	14,645
2009	14,146	14,134	14,118	14,382	14,483	14,850	14,636	14,593	14,710	14,095	13,898	13,983	14,336
2010[1]	13,671	13,967	14,302	15,120	15,219	15,389	15,518	15,110	14,741	13,999	14,315	14,944	14,691

[1] Preliminary.   *Source: Energy Information Administration, U.S. Department of Energy (EIA-DOE)*

Production of Major Refined Petroleum Products in Continental United States   In Millions of Barrels

Year	Asphalt	Aviation Gasoline	Fuel Oil Distillate	Fuel Oil Residual	Gasoline	Jet Fuel	Kerosene	Natural Gas Plant Liquids	Lubricants	Liquified Gasses Total	Liquified Gasses at L.P.G.[2]	Liquified Gasses AT L.P.G.[3]
2001	177.3	6.5	1,348.4	262.8	2,913	558.2	26.7	680.3	64.1	810.1	569.1	241.0
2002	179.9	6.4	1,309.8	218.8	2,983	552.3	20.8	686.5	63.3	822.5	576.8	245.7
2003	181.0	5.8	1,355.5	241.8	2,992	543.1	20.4	626.7	60.6	766.1	526.4	239.6
2004	185.6	6.2	1,397.6	238.0	3,013	566.3	23.2	662.7	62.0	797.2	561.3	235.9
2005	186.0	6.1	1,441.4	227.9	3,014	561.5	23.6	623.9	60.8	736.9	527.2	209.8
2006	184.8	6.6	1,478.1	231.5	3,036	540.4	17.3	633.4	66.8	757.6	537.8	219.9
2007	166.1	6.0	1,507.7	244.4	3,045	528.6	12.7	648.3	65.1	789.0	552.8	236.2
2008	150.9	5.5	1,569.5	227.1	3,072	539.5	12.0	651.9	63.2	786.1	556.2	229.9
2009	131.0	5.0	1,476.7	218.6	3,199	510.2	6.9	688.5	55.4	821.1	591.3	229.8
2010[1]	132.1	5.4	1,384.7	200.8	3,298	519.7	7.2	730.4	47.6	869.3	631.7	237.6

[1] Preliminary.   [2] Gas processing plants.   [3] Refineries.   *Source: Energy Information Administration, U.S. Department of Energy (EIA-DOE)*

Stocks of Petroleum and Products in the United States on January 1   In Millions of Barrels

Year	Crude Petroleum	Strategic Reserve	Total	Asphalt	Aviation Gasoline	Fuel Oil Distillate	Fuel Oil Residual	Finished Gasoline	Jet Fuel	Kerosene	Gasses[2]	Lubricants	Motor Gasoline Total	Motor Gasoline Finished[3]
2002	862.2	550.2	445.6	20.6	1.5	144.5	41.0	161.5	42.0	5.4	120.9	13.8	214	161
2003	876.7	599.1	425.1	21.3	1.4	134.1	31.3	161.9	39.2	5.5	105.7	12.0	199	162
2004	906.3	638.4	413.1	19.3	1.2	136.8	37.8	146.8	38.7	5.6	94.4	10.0	----	147
2005	961.9	675.6	405.6	22.1	1.3	126.0	42.4	143.1	40.2	4.9	111.0	10.4	----	143
2006	1,007.8	684.5	403.6	21.0	1.2	136.0	37.3	134.8	41.8	5.1	117.6	9.7	----	135
2007	998.4	688.6	405.9	28.8	1.4	143.7	42.4	118.3	39.1	3.4	125.2	12.4	----	118
2008	982.8	696.9	374.3	22.2	1.2	133.5	38.6	110.0	39.5	2.8	105.5	10.6	----	110
2009	1,026.1	701.8	367.8	20.3	1.2	145.9	36.2	98.2	38.2	2.2	126.9	10.7	----	98
2010	1,051.8	726.6	375.1	17.9	1.0	164.7	37.8	85.9	43.4	2.5	113.2	8.9	----	86
2011[1]	1,058.5	726.5	357.4	19.9	1.1	164.5	41.3	63.4	43.2	2.4	121.3	8.2	----	63

[1] Preliminary.   [2] Includes ethane & ethylene at plants and refineries.   [3] Includes oxygenated.
Source: Energy Information Administration, U.S. Department of Energy (EIA-DOE)

Stocks of Crude Petroleum in the United States, on First of Month   In Millions of Barrels

Year	Jan.	Feb.	Mar.	Apr.	May	June	July	Aug.	Sept.	Oct.	Nov.	Dec.
2001	836.0	824.1	850.8	872.9	871.6	851.5	856.6	851.7	854.0	858.4	859.5	862.2
2002	874.9	887.3	895.0	891.4	898.3	894.0	882.8	878.5	857.9	881.1	884.0	876.7
2003	873.3	870.3	880.8	891.0	888.6	893.1	897.3	897.8	911.0	925.5	914.8	907.3
2004	912.8	931.2	949.5	961.5	965.8	967.2	960.1	947.6	943.2	957.0	961.0	961.3
2005	965.7	984.2	1,008.0	1,029.5	1,030.1	1,024.3	1,017.2	1,010.3	1,000.0	1,007.4	1,008.1	1,008.2
2006	1,006.8	1,027.4	1,028.8	1,035.5	1,029.2	1,024.6	1,019.4	1,020.7	1,020.6	1,027.9	1,023.1	1,000.9
2007	1,013.2	1,006.2	1,019.5	1,031.4	1,043.6	1,044.3	1,027.0	1,011.0	1,003.9	1,001.4	995.0	983.0
2008	994.6	1,001.1	1,015.0	1,021.2	1,007.9	1,001.7	1,002.4	1,009.7	1,006.4	1,014.5	1,023.4	1,027.7
2009	1,055.1	1,063.1	1,079.7	1,089.7	1,081.2	1,071.2	1,069.5	1,059.7	1,060.1	1,057.6	1,063.0	1,051.8
2010[1]	1,060.5	1,066.7	1,082.0	1,087.3	1,085.0	1,089.3	1,081.7	1,082.0	1,086.6	1,092.4	1,077.1	1,058.5

[1] Preliminary.   Source: Energy Information Administration; U.S. Department of Energy

Production of Crude Petroleum in the United States   In Thousands of Barrels Per Day

Year	Jan.	Feb.	Mar.	Apr.	May	June	July	Aug.	Sept.	Oct.	Nov.	Dec.	Average
2001	5,799	5,780	5,880	5,863	5,829	5,766	5,749	5,725	5,709	5,746	5,881	5,887	5,801
2002	5,848	5,871	5,883	5,859	5,924	5,915	5,770	5,811	5,411	5,363	5,597	5,699	5,746
2003	5,785	5,791	5,817	5,774	5,733	5,701	5,526	5,595	5,683	5,635	5,560	5,579	5,681
2004	5,570	5,556	5,607	5,527	5,548	5,398	5,458	5,333	5,062	5,156	5,396	5,413	5,419
2005	5,441	5,494	5,601	5,556	5,581	5,460	5,240	5,218	4,204	4,534	4,837	4,984	5,179
2006	5,106	5,045	5,045	5,128	5,161	5,160	5,102	5,059	5,037	5,106	5,105	5,166	5,102
2007	5,123	5,125	5,106	5,189	5,197	5,096	5,024	4,914	4,884	5,043	5,017	5,056	5,065
2008	5,100	5,122	5,151	5,117	5,102	5,098	5,133	4,894	3,930	4,669	5,024	5,056	4,950
2009	5,154	5,260	5,227	5,273	5,379	5,281	5,402	5,418	5,547	5,501	5,427	5,451	5,360
2010[1]	5,433	5,465	5,502	5,496	5,468	5,465	5,406	5,506	5,567	5,616	5,581	5,592	5,508

[1] Preliminary.   Source: Energy Information Administration, U.S. Department of Energy (EIA-DOE)

U.S. Foreign Trade of Petroleum and Products   In Thousands of Barrels Per Day

	---------------- Exports ----------------			-- Imports --				
Year	Total[2]	Petroleum Products	Crude	Petroleum Products	Distillate Fuel Oil	Residual Fuel Oil	Net Imports[3]
2001	971	951	9,328	2,543	344	295	10,900
2002	984	975	9,140	2,390	267	249	10,546
2003	1,027	1,014	9,665	2,599	333	327	11,237
2004	1,048	1,021	10,088	3,057	325	426	12,097
2005	1,165	1,133	10,126	3,588	329	530	12,549
2006	1,317	1,292	10,118	3,517	365	350	12,390
2007	1,433	1,405	10,031	2,761	304	372	12,035
2008	1,802	1,773	9,783	2,570	213	349	11,113
2009	2,024	1,980	9,013	2,122	225	331	9,667
2010[1]	2,250	2,209	9,141	1,977	221	381	9,470

[1] Preliminary.   [2] Includes crude oil.   [3] Equals imports minus exports.
Source: Energy Information Administration, U.S. Department of Energy (EIA-DOE)

Domestic First Purchase Price of Crude Petroleum at Wells[1]   In Dollars Per Barrel

Year	Jan.	Feb.	Mar.	Apr.	May	June	July	Aug.	Sept.	Oct.	Nov.	Dec.	Average
2001	24.58	25.27	23.02	23.41	24.06	23.43	22.94	23.08	22.37	18.73	16.49	15.54	21.84
2002	15.89	16.92	20.04	22.14	23.51	22.59	23.51	24.76	26.08	25.29	23.38	25.29	22.51
2003	28.35	31.85	30.09	25.46	24.96	26.83	27.53	27.94	25.23	26.52	27.21	28.54	27.54
2004	30.35	31.21	32.86	33.23	36.07	34.53	36.54	40.10	40.62	46.28	42.81	38.22	36.90
2005	40.18	42.19	47.56	47.26	44.03	49.83	53.35	58.90	59.64	56.99	53.20	53.24	50.53
2006	57.85	55.69	55.59	62.51	64.31	64.36	67.72	67.21	59.36	53.26	52.42	55.03	59.61
2007	49.32	52.94	54.95	58.20	58.90	62.35	69.23	67.78	73.16	79.32	87.16	85.29	66.55
2008	87.06	89.41	98.44	106.64	118.55	127.47	128.08	112.83	98.50	73.22	53.67	36.80	94.22
2009	35.00	34.14	42.46	45.22	52.69	63.08	60.43	65.28	65.27	69.82	71.99	70.42	56.32
2010[2]	72.89	72.74	75.77	78.80	70.90	70.77	71.37	72.07	71.23	76.02			73.26

[1] Buyers posted prices.   [2] Preliminary.   Source: Energy Information Administration, U.S. Department of Energy (EIA-DOE)

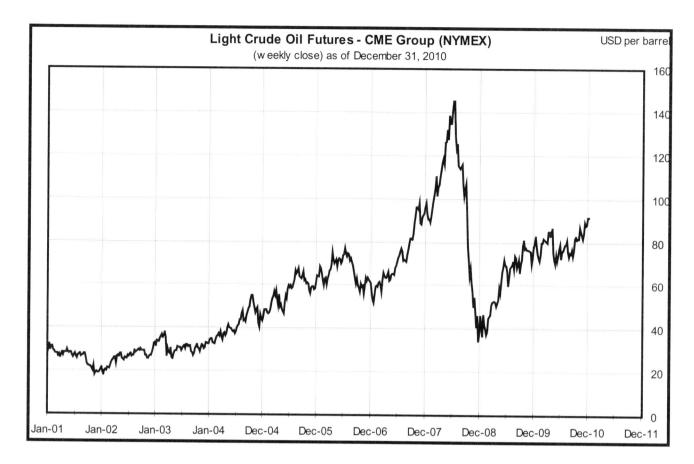

Light Crude Oil Futures - CME Group (NYMEX)
(weekly close) as of December 31, 2010

USD per barrel

Volume of Trading of Crude Oil Futures in New York   In Thousands of Contracts

Year	Jan.	Feb.	Mar.	Apr.	May	June	July	Aug.	Sept.	Oct.	Nov.	Dec.	Total
2001	3,035	2,855	3,449	3,312	3,469	3,572	3,170	3,316	2,773	2,913	3,210	2,455	37,531
2002	3,481	3,150	3,790	4,315	4,317	3,429	3,466	3,883	3,939	4,397	3,478	4,034	45,679
2003	4,553	4,039	4,151	3,355	3,329	3,534	3,401	3,732	3,826	4,248	3,624	3,646	45,437
2004	4,118	3,887	4,495	4,326	4,250	4,633	4,063	4,987	4,711	4,794	4,510	4,108	52,883
2005	4,352	4,032	5,721	5,404	5,045	5,326	4,629	6,091	5,252	5,022	4,488	4,288	59,650
2006	5,482	5,594	5,937	5,285	5,861	5,134	4,500	5,409	6,067	7,492	7,555	6,739	71,053
2007	10,367	9,092	10,069	9,287	9,487	9,862	9,656	10,647	10,670	12,390	11,307	8,692	121,526
2008	10,815	10,100	12,577	11,066	13,497	12,453	11,321	10,589	11,554	11,638	8,662	9,910	134,183
2009	11,369	11,411	11,340	10,106	9,939	11,367	11,924	11,823	11,462	13,179	11,600	11,906	137,428
2010	10,894	12,772	13,298	17,433	17,591	14,458	11,427	14,494	16,018	14,423	13,429	12,416	168,652

Contract size = 1,000 bbl.   *Source: CME Group; New York Mercantile Exchange (NYMEX)*

Average Open Interest of Crude Oil Futures in New York   In Thousands of Contracts

Year	Jan.	Feb.	Mar.	Apr.	May	June	July	Aug.	Sept.	Oct.	Nov.	Dec.
2001	432.9	437.2	432.6	419.9	443.0	462.3	451.0	461.9	435.0	430.8	435.2	436.3
2002	448.1	454.2	497.4	488.1	512.4	474.1	457.0	454.2	505.5	528.5	482.2	531.1
2003	608.3	641.0	568.5	495.5	478.9	494.1	517.5	542.6	507.2	532.0	550.4	580.6
2004	647.7	656.9	673.5	690.0	722.5	705.1	692.9	705.6	684.8	717.0	705.2	676.3
2005	707.9	745.2	829.2	833.8	799.0	785.4	820.1	901.6	870.6	848.7	832.3	841.3
2006	903.5	927.5	954.2	1,000.4	1,055.7	1,016.2	1,068.7	1,164.0	1,181.8	1,168.7	1,176.6	1,200.0
2007	1,284.9	1,281.7	1,314.3	1,328.0	1,390.4	1,431.6	1,523.6	1,477.4	1,483.3	1,447.1	1,451.8	1,362.3
2008	1,393.5	1,384.6	1,428.5	1,393.8	1,396.5	1,351.8	1,277.9	1,224.1	1,171.2	1,076.8	1,139.7	1,160.9
2009	1,232.4	1,223.3	1,190.2	1,163.0	1,159.6	1,180.5	1,170.7	1,176.0	1,174.2	1,231.2	1,207.8	1,200.4
2010	1,303.5	1,304.8	1,324.1	1,375.8	1,416.3	1,307.3	1,252.7	1,262.3	1,338.2	1,419.1	1,414.1	1,380.0

Contract size = 1,000 bbl.   *Source: CME Group; New York Mercantile Exchange (NYMEX)*

Plastics

Plastics are moldable, chemically fabricated materials produced mostly from fossil fuels, such as oil, coal, or natural gas. The word plastic is derived from the Greek *plastikos*, meaning "to mold," and the Latin *plasticus*, meaning "capable of molding." Leo Baekeland created the first commercially successful thermosetting synthetic resin in 1909. More than 50 families of plastics have since been produced.

All plastics can be divided into either thermoplastics or thermosetting plastics. The difference is the way in which they respond to heat. Thermoplastics can be repeatedly softened by heat and hardened by cooling. Thermosetting plastics harden permanently after being heated once.

Prices – The average monthly producer price index (1982=100) of plastic resins and materials in the U.S. in 2010 rose +11.0% yr/yr to 211.8, not far from the 2008 record high of 215.0. The average monthly producer price index of thermoplastic resins in the U.S. in 2010 rose +13.2% yr/yr to 213.2, not far from the 2008 record high of 215.9. The average monthly producer price index of thermosetting resins in the U.S. in 2010 fell 0.5% to 216.3, down from the 2008 record high of 223.5.

Supply – Total U.S. plastics production in 2008 (latest data available) fell – 12.3% yr/yr to 101.546, down from the 2007 record high of 115.793 billion pounds. U.S. plastics production has more than doubled in the past two decades. By sector, the thermoplastics sector is by far the largest, with 2008 production falling -11.7% yr/yr to 81.980 billion pounds and accounting for 81% of total U.S. plastic production. Production in the thermosetting plastic sector (polyester unsaturated, phenolic, and epoxy) fell 14.9% yr/yr in 2008 to 7.614 billion pounds and accounted for 7% of total U.S. plastics production. The category of "other plastics" fell -14.7% to 11.952 billion pounds and accounted for 12% of total U.S. plastics production.

Demand – Total usage of plastic resins by important markets in 2008 (latest data available) in the U.S. fell by -10.0% to 74.156 billion pounds. The breakdown by market shows that the largest single consumption category is "Packaging" with 2.097 billion pounds of usage in 2008, accounting for 32% of total U.S. consumption. After packaging, the largest categories are "Consumer and Industrial" (21% of U.S. consumption), and "Building and Construction" (17% of U.S. consumption).

Trade – U.S. exports of plastics in 2008 (latest data available) fell -3.1% yr/yr to 11.962 billion pounds, down from the 2008 record high of 12.346 billion pounds. U.S. exports accounted for 16% of U.S. supply disappearance in 2005.

Plastics Production by Resin in the United States — In Millions of Pounds

| | ----------- Thermosets ------------- | | | | --------------------------------- Thermoplastics --------------------------- | | | | | | | | | | |
Year	Polyester Unsaturated	Phenolic	Epoxy	Total Thermosets	Thermoplastic Polyester	Polyvinyl Chloride	Polystyrene	Polypropylene	Nylon	Low Density Polyethylene[1]	High Density Polyethylene	Total Thermoplastics	Total Selected Plastics	Other Plastics	Total Plastics
2000	3,149	3,965	669	7,783	7,239	14,364	6,676	15,583	1,395	19,588	16,439	84,553	92,336	13,604	105,940
2001	3,021	3,894	597	7,512	6,972	14,626	6,223	16,135	1,159	18,389	15,195	81,726	89,238	12,720	101,958
2002	3,197	4,076	620	7,893	7,480	15,250	6,768	17,084	1,284	19,515	16,190	86,762	94,655	13,607	108,262
2003	3,152	4,015	587	7,754	7,950	14,938	6,478	17,497	1,306	18,915	15,906	86,071	93,825	12,641	106,466
2004	3,294	4,200	658	8,152	8,632	15,883	6,765	18,523	1,357	20,390	17,519	92,317	100,469	13,471	113,940
2005	3,359	4,689	609	8,657	7,749	15,259	6,293	17,965	1,252	19,736	16,155	87,524	96,181	13,595	109,776
2006	3,430	4,809	624	8,863	8,290	14,919	6,269	18,775	1,270	20,926	17,645	91,204	100,067	13,970	114,037
2007	3,471	4,838	642	8,951	8,745	14,606	6,015	19,445	1,295	21,511	18,222	92,835	101,786	14,007	115,793
2008	2,798	4,233	583	15,091	8,159	12,789	5,220	16,768	1,148	19,061	16,247	86,455	89,594	11,952	101,546
2009			535	12,687		12,754	4,865	16,623	943	19,793	16,956	85,983	98,670		98,670

[1] Includes LDPE and LLDPE.   *Source: American Plastics Council (APC)*

Total Resin Sales and Captive Use by Important Markets — In Millions of Pounds (Dry Weight Basis)

Year	Adhesive, Inks & Coatings	Building & Construction	Consumer & Industrial	Electrical & Electronics	Exports	Furniture & Furnishings	Industrial & Machinary	Packaging	Transportation	Other	Total
2000	1,167	14,439	16,487	2,787	9,771	3,572	1,084	20,941	4,389	3,003	77,640
2001	1,143	13,988	16,510	2,501	9,295	3,226	968	22,847	4,207	2,705	77,390
2002	1,165	14,729	17,649	3,037	10,048	3,507	998	24,170	4,738	2,283	82,324
2003	1,170	14,495	17,571	2,862	9,009	3,361	962	24,087	4,732	2,021	80,270
2004	1,196	15,676	18,714	3,096	9,900	3,458	1,042	25,952	4,899	2,168	86,101
2005	1,160	15,483	17,400	2,917	9,790	3,406	1,087	25,144	4,711	2,133	83,231
2006	1,113	15,429	17,735	2,661	9,957	3,332	1,004	26,161	4,558	2,019	83,970
2007	1,069	14,289	17,193	1,980	12,346	3,091	943	26,527	3,312	1,604	82,354
2008	937	12,313	15,461	1,755	11,962	2,671	834	24,097	2,751	1,375	74,156
2009	835	11,139	14,862	1,495	14,738	2,008	657	23,391	1,941	1,004	72,071

[1] Included in other.   *Source: American Plastics Council (APC)*

PLASTICS

Average Producer Price Index of Plastic Resins and Materials (066) in the United States (1982 = 100)

Year	Jan.	Feb.	Mar.	Apr.	May	June	July	Aug.	Sept.	Oct.	Nov.	Dec.	Average
2001	137.8	139.3	141.4	141.9	139.9	137.6	135.1	131.3	126.8	128.3	126.6	123.9	134.2
2002	122.0	121.3	123.1	125.4	128.0	130.1	135.3	136.4	136.7	138.2	137.0	135.3	130.7
2003	137.2	141.8	149.6	153.2	152.4	149.2	144.9	143.6	144.9	146.2	145.8	144.0	146.1
2004	146.2	150.4	151.4	154.8	156.5	159.6	161.1	164.9	170.6	175.6	181.4	185.2	163.1
2005	190.3	190.8	192.1	192.3	190.3	186.3	185.0	183.4	188.2	203.9	208.6	205.2	193.0
2006	203.9	200.0	198.9	194.3	195.9	198.5	199.2	202.3	202.4	200.0	196.2	189.1	198.4
2007	187.6	185.5	187.0	192.1	193.8	196.9	198.6	198.7	198.0	199.3	205.9	207.5	195.9
2008	209.7	209.6	210.8	212.1	216.4	219.1	229.2	233.3	227.1	222.3	200.3	190.3	215.0
2009	184.6	190.1	188.6	183.5	185.9	185.9	194.4	194.5	196.4	194.5	194.5	196.8	190.8
2010[1]	195.0	206.4	208.2	222.4	213.1	208.1	212.7	211.1	210.7	215.0	221.8	214.0	211.5

[1] Preliminary.   Source: Bureau of Labor Statistics, U.S. Department of Commerce (BLS)

Average Producer Price Index of Thermoplastic Resins (0662) in the United States (1982 = 100)

Year	Jan.	Feb.	Mar.	Apr.	May	June	July	Aug.	Sept.	Oct.	Nov.	Dec.	Average
2001	136.3	138.0	140.2	140.8	138.4	135.7	133.1	128.6	123.4	125.7	123.9	120.8	132.1
2002	118.4	117.8	120.3	123.8	126.2	128.6	135.0	135.9	136.2	137.6	136.1	133.8	129.1
2003	136.3	142.2	151.4	155.8	153.6	149.5	144.3	142.8	144.7	146.3	146.2	143.9	146.4
2004	146.7	151.9	152.6	156.4	157.5	160.9	162.3	165.5	171.3	176.6	182.3	186.9	164.2
2005	193.2	193.8	195.3	194.9	192.0	187.0	185.4	183.7	189.3	208.4	213.7	209.4	195.5
2006	207.9	202.8	201.5	195.6	197.6	201.1	201.6	205.1	205.0	201.6	196.8	188.1	200.4
2007	186.0	183.4	185.3	190.7	193.0	196.2	198.2	198.4	197.6	199.3	206.6	208.2	195.2
2008	209.9	209.9	211.5	213.2	218.4	221.2	232.4	236.5	229.0	223.5	197.6	187.1	215.9
2009	179.3	187.1	185.9	180.3	183.1	183.2	193.2	192.9	194.5	192.2	192.8	194.9	188.3
2010[1]	193.2	206.8	208.8	225.7	214.9	208.8	214.3	212.6	212.1	217.2	225.3	215.9	213.0

[1] Preliminary.   Source: Bureau of Labor Statistics, U.S. Department of Commerce (BLS)

Average Producer Price Index of Thermosetting Resins (0663) in the United States (1982 = 100)

Year	Jan.	Feb.	Mar.	Apr.	May	June	July	Aug.	Sept.	Oct.	Nov.	Dec.	Average
2001	152.1	152.9	154.5	154.4	154.2	154.2	152.3	151.3	150.4	148.2	146.3	146.1	151.4
2002	146.2	144.6	143.8	141.2	144.1	145.5	145.8	147.6	148.4	150.3	150.3	150.6	146.5
2003	150.4	149.7	151.7	152.0	156.8	157.9	157.1	156.4	155.7	155.6	153.8	153.9	154.2
2004	154.0	154.2	155.9	158.3	162.2	164.3	166.4	173.2	179.0	183.0	189.3	189.8	169.1
2005	189.9	190.3	190.5	193.5	195.8	195.8	195.5	194.6	196.1	197.5	199.9	200.2	195.0
2006	200.0	200.8	200.8	201.7	201.6	200.5	202.1	203.6	204.2	206.3	206.6	206.3	202.9
2007	207.8	208.3	207.8	211.7	210.0	212.6	212.3	212.4	211.9	211.6	214.7	216.8	211.5
2008	221.4	220.7	220.0	219.0	218.5	220.3	224.8	229.3	229.8	229.6	228.3	220.7	223.5
2009	226.7	219.3	216.2	213.5	213.9	213.7	213.5	215.5	219.7	220.0	216.2	220.0	217.4
2010[1]	218.0	216.8	217.1	216.7	216.1	217.2	216.3	215.2	215.3	215.4	215.3	216.2	216.3

[1] Preliminary.   Source: Bureau of Labor Statistics, U.S. Department of Commerce (BLS)

Average Producer Price Index of Styrene Plastics Materials (0662-06) in the United States (1982 = 100)

Year	Jan.	Feb.	Mar.	Apr.	May	June	July	Aug.	Sept.	Oct.	Nov.	Dec.	Average
1995	129.0	127.0	132.5	134.7	135.9	137.5	135.1	133.2	132.1	130.1	127.9	126.1	131.8
1996	125.7	123.5	125.0	118.3	120.1	122.7	123.4	123.3	123.6	122.8	122.0	120.9	122.6
1997	120.6	123.1	123.0	121.6	121.6	121.6	122.7	117.7	118.0	116.5	113.5	113.7	119.5
1998	113.3	113.9	115.5	114.9	114.1	112.8	111.3	111.2	107.6	107.9	107.1	106.3	111.3
1999	103.5	102.4	103.5	104.7	103.0	102.3	103.1	101.5	101.4	99.8	99.4	100.5	102.1
2000	103.0	104.3	110.5	113.0	116.2	116.9	118.5	116.5	115.0	114.1	112.1	110.4	112.5
2001	110.5	109.2	107.9	108.0	101.8	99.9	97.6	95.7	87.3	89.4	90.0	85.4	98.6
2002	85.7	85.8	87.9	88.5	90.4	91.7	93.7	100.6	100.5	108.9	108.1	103.9	95.5
2003[1]	102.9	110.2	119.5	127.2	126.7	119.1	118.0	113.3	112.8	113.6	113.7	111.6	115.7
2004[1]	Data no longer available												

[1] Preliminary.   Source: Bureau of Labor Statistics, U.S. Department of Commerce (BLS)

204

Platinum-Group Metals

Platinum is a relatively rare, chemically inert metallic element that is more valuable than gold. Platinum is a grayish-white metal that has a high fusing point, is malleable and ductile, and has a high electrical resistance. Chemically, platinum is relatively inert and resists attack by air, water, single acids, and ordinary reagents. Platinum is the most important of the six-metal group, which also includes ruthenium, rhodium, palladium, osmium, and iridium. The word "platinum" is derived from the Spanish word platina meaning silver.

Platinum is one of the world's rarest metals with new mine production totaling only about 5 million troy ounces a year. All the platinum mined to date would fit in the average-size living room. Platinum is mined all over the world with supplies concentrated in South Africa. South Africa accounts for nearly 80% of world supply, followed by Russia, and North America.

Because platinum will never tarnish, lose its rich white luster, or even wear down after many years, it is prized by the jewelry industry. The international jewelry industry is the largest consumer sector for platinum, accounting for 51% of total platinum demand. In Europe and the U.S., the normal purity of platinum is 95%. Ten tons of ore must be mined and a five-month process is needed to produce one ounce of pure platinum.

The second major consumer sector for platinum is for auto catalysts, with 21% of total platinum demand. Catalysts in autos are used to convert most of vehicle emissions into less harmful carbon dioxide, nitrogen, and water vapor. Platinum is also used in the production of hard disk drive coatings, fiber optic cables, infra-red detectors, fertilizers, explosives, petrol additives, platinum-tipped spark plugs, glassmaking equipment, biodegradable elements for household detergents, dental restorations, and in anti-cancer drugs.

Palladium is very similar to platinum and is part of the same general metals group. Palladium is mined with platinum, but it is somewhat more common because it is also a by-product of nickel mining. The primary use for palladium is in the use of automotive catalysts, with that sector accounting for about 63% of total palladium demand. Other uses for palladium include electronic equipment (21%), dental alloys (12%), and jewelry (4%).

Rhodium, another member of the platinum group, is also used in the automotive industry in pollution control devices. To some extent palladium has replaced rhodium. Iridium is used to process catalysts and it has also found use in some auto catalysts. Iridium and ruthenium are used in the production of polyvinyl chloride. As the prices of these metals change, there is some substitution. Therefore, strength of platinum prices relative to palladium should lead to the substitution of palladium for platinum in catalytic converters.

Platinum futures and options and palladium futures are traded on the New York Mercantile Exchange (NYMEX). Platinum and palladium futures are traded on the Tokyo Commodity Exchange (TOCOM). The NYMEX platinum futures contract calls for the delivery of 50 troy ounces of platinum (0.9995 fineness) and the contract trades in terms of dollars and cents per troy ounce. The NYMEX palladium futures contract calls for the delivery of 50 troy ounces of palladium (0.9995 fineness) and the contract is priced in terms of dollars and cents per troy ounce.

Prices – NYMEX platinum futures prices started the year 2010 at about $1,506 per troy ounce and, except for a slight dip in May, moved steadily higher all year to finally end the year at about $1,809 per troy ounce.

NYMEX palladium futures prices started the year 2010 at about $410 per troy ounce and moved steadily higher all year to finally end the year at about $820 per troy ounce.

Supply – World mine production of platinum in 2010 rose by +1.1% yr/yr to 183,000 kilograms, but still below the record high of 217,000 kilograms in 2006. South Africa is the world's largest producer of platinum by far with 75% of world production in 2010, followed by Russia (13%), Canada (3%) and the U.S. (2%). World mine production of palladium in 2010 rose +2.6% to 197,000 kilograms, which was still below the record high production level of 222,000 in 2006. The world's largest palladium producers are Russia with 44% of world production in 2010, South Africa with 37%, the U.S. with 6%, and Canada with 5%. World production of platinum group metals other than platinum and palladium in 2009 (latest data available) fell by -2.1% yr/yr to 70,800 kilograms, down from the 2007 record high of 79,600 kilograms.

U.S. mine production of platinum in 2010 fell by -8.6% yr/yr to 3,500 kilograms, further below the record high of 4,390 kilograms posted in 2002. U.S. mine production of palladium in 2010 fell by -8.7% yr/yr to 11,600 kilograms, further below the record high of 14,800 kilograms posted in 2002. U.S. refinery production of scrap platinum and palladium in 2008, latest data available, fell 7.9% to 15,050 kilograms, still up from the 2005 record low of 11,580 kilograms but still well below the 13-year high of 24,790 kilograms in 2001.

Demand – The total of platinum-group metals sold to consuming industries in the U.S. in 2004 (the latest data available) rose +7.1% to 91,434 kilograms. The two main U.S. industries that use platinum are the auto industry, which accounts for about 74% of U.S. platinum usage, and the jewelry industry, which accounts for about 26% of U.S. platinum usage.

Trade – U.S. imports of refined platinum and palladium in 2010 for consumption fell -11.2% yr/yr to 254,514 kilograms. U.S. exports of refined platinum and palladium rose by +16.8% to 59,400 kilograms, but still well below the record high of 103,590 kilograms in 2006. The U.S. relied on imports for 94% of its platinum and palladium consumption in 2010.

PLATINUM-GROUP METALS

World Mine Production of Platinum   In Kilograms

Year	Australia	Canada	Colombia[3]	Finland	Japan	Russia	Serbia/Montenegro	Africa	United States	Zimbabwe	World Total
2001	174	7,733	674	510	791	27,000	5	130,307	3,610	519	172,000
2002	200	9,202	661	508	762	27,000	5	132,897	4,390	2,306	178,000
2003	225	6,990	828	461	770	28,000	1	148,348	4,170	4,270	195,000
2004	200	1,000	1,209	705	750	28,000	----	153,239	4,040	4,438	194,000
2005	111	6,075	1,082	800	760	29,000	3	163,711	3,920	4,834	211,000
2006	209	7,500	1,438	800	760	29,000	2	168,125	4,290	4,998	217,000
2007	142	7,000	1,526	800	770	27,000	2	160,940	3,860	5,306	208,000
2008	200	7,000	1,500	800	770	23,000	2	146,140	3,580	5,642	189,000
2009[1]	200	4,600	1,500	800	780	21,000	2	140,819	3,830	7,230	181,000
2010[2]		5,500	1,000			24,000		138,000	3,500	8,800	183,000

[1] Preliminary.   [2] Estimate.   [3] Placer platinum.   W = Withheld.   *Source: U.S. Geological Survey (USGS)*

World Mine Production of Palladium and Other Group Metals   In Kilograms

	--- Palladium ---										------ Other Group Metals ------		
Year	Australia	Canada	Finland	Japan	Russia	Serbia/Montenegro	Africa	United States	Zimbabwe	Total	Russia	South Africa	World Total
2001	828	8,972	----	4,805	96,000	25	62,601	12,100	371	187,000	14,500	37,005	52,300
2002	810	12,210	----	5,618	96,000	25	63,758	14,800	1,943	196,000	14,500	39,986	57,900
2003	820	12,808	----	5,500	97,000	8	70,946	14,000	3,449	207,000	15,000	46,856	64,400
2004	800	12,000	----	5,300	97,000	19	76,403	13,700	3,564	211,000	15,000	46,759	66,600
2005	550	10,415	----	5,400	97,400	19	82,961	13,300	3,879	216,000	15,500	56,309	77,700
2006	750	10,493	----	5,400	98,400	15	86,265	14,400	4,022	222,000	15,600	53,138	74,600
2007	600	10,900	----	5,500	96,800	15	83,643	12,800	4,180	219,000	14,500	59,449	79,600
2008	700	10,000	----	5,500	87,700	15	75,537	11,900	4,386	199,000	12,500	53,999	72,300
2009[1]	600	6,500	----	5,600	83,200	15	75,118	12,700	5,680	192,000	11,900	55,454	70,800
2010[2]		9,400			87,000		73,000	11,600	6,600	197,000			

[1] Preliminary.   [2] Estimate.   *Source: U.S. Geological Survey (USGS)*

Platinum Group Metals Sold to Consuming Industries in the United States   In Kilograms

	-- Automotive --		--- Chemical ---		---- Electrical ----		---- Dental & Medical ----		-- Jewelry & Decorative --		--- Petroleum ---		----- All Platinum Group Metals -----			
Year	Platinum	Other[3]	Platinum	Other[3]	Platinum	Other[3]	Platinum	Other[3]	Platinum	Other[3]	Platinum	Other[3]	Platinum	Palladium	Other[3]	Total
1996	28,550	19,282	2,115	2,457	4,541	17,665	778	6,285	1,493	1,493	3,514	902	44,489	45,157	----	89,646
1997	28,923	20,402	2,239	2,426	4,945	19,997	840	6,376	2,115	1,617	3,390	871	46,184	50,227	----	96,411
1998	29,483	26,528	2,301	2,488	5,194	20,215	902	6,376	2,333	1,617	3,390	809	47,396	61,827	----	109,223
1999	31,100	29,390	2,364	2,519	5,443	21,148	933	6,065	3,110	1,679	3,514	778	50,310	65,248	----	115,558
2000	32,344	31,100	2,457	2,139	5,691	19,282	964	3,732	3,670	1,400	3,639	660	52,808	61,889	----	114,697
2001	33,411	34,832	2,644	715	5,909	17,354	995	3,670	4,043	1,431	4,199	715	55,399	62,293	----	117,692
2002	17,727	19,904	3,110	2,333	2,955	6,531	1,244	6,687	9,641		1,400		33,433	28,768	----	62,200
2003[1]	27,524	37,476	2,955	2,177	2,644	6,687	778	6,998	9,641		1,244		37,476	47,894	----	85,370
2004[2]	24,880	44,940	2,799	2,644	2,799	6,376	622	7,309	9,019		1,089		33,588	57,846	----	91,434

[1] Preliminary.   [2] Estimate.   [3] Includes Palladium, iridium, osmium, rhodium, and ruthenium.
Sources: U.S. Geological Survey (USGS); American Metal Market (AMM)

Salient Statistics of Platinum and Allied Metals[3] in the United States   In Kilograms

	Net Import Reliance as a % of Apparent Consumption	----- Mine Production -----		Refinery Production (Secondary) Refined	Refiner, Importer & Dealer -------- Stocks as of Dec. 31 ---------				----- Imports -----		----- Exports -----		Apparent Con-sumptio
Year		Platinum	Palladium		Total Refined	Platinum	Palladium	Other[4]	Total	Refined	Total	Refined	Total	
2001	66	3,610	12,100	24,790	24,790	3,680	16,300	784	20,764	267,957	----	67,334	----	----
2002	93	4,390	14,800	20,900	20,900	649	5,870	784	7,303	222,356	----	70,943	----	----
2003	91	4,170	14,000	24,250	24,250	649	1,170	562	2,381	223,653	----	45,124	----	----
2004	92	4,040	13,700	22,180	22,180	649	568	501	1,718	248,705	----	52,897	----	----
2005	93	3,920	13,300	11,580	11,580	261	----	189	450	284,849	----	49,395	----	----
2006	90	4,290	14,400	12,530	12,530	261	----	111	372	287,756	----	103,590	----	----
2007	91	3,860	12,800	16,340	16,340	261	----	18	279	362,733	----	81,100	----	----
2008	89	3,580	11,900	15,050	15,050	261	----	18	279	334,961	----	50,430	----	----
2009[1]	95	3,830	12,700							286,688	----	50,870	----	----
2010[2]	94	3,500	11,600							254,514	----	59,400	----	----

[1] Preliminary.   [2] Estimate.   [3] Includes platinum, palladium, iridium, osmium, rhodium, and ruthenium.   [4] Includes iridium, osmium, rhodium, and ruthenium.   W = Withheld.   *Source: U.S. Geological Survey (USGS)*

206

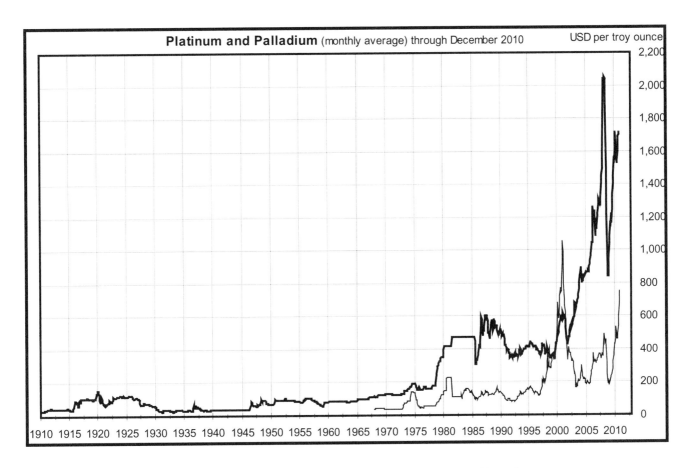

Platinum and Palladium (monthly average) through December 2010   USD per troy ounce

Average Merchant's Price of Platinum in the United States   In Dollars Per Troy Ounce

Year	Jan.	Feb.	Mar.	Apr.	May	June	July	Aug.	Sept.	Oct.	Nov.	Dec.	Average
2001	623.43	453.56	566.67	589.63	611.07	588.91	643.88	457.37	453.50	437.43	427.25	450.24	531.93
2002	471.52	470.68	511.95	539.20	533.66	554.70	526.32	545.48	556.05	580.11	588.15	594.89	539.39
2003	633.09	684.47	677.05	627.19	651.43	664.19	684.68	695.12	707.90	734.91	762.78	810.48	691.78
2004	855.95	849.53	902.78	884.76	814.05	810.59	813.48	851.91	851.05	843.76	856.15	854.55	849.05
2005	861.80	867.40	870.23	867.71	869.00	883.23	876.60	901.04	918.10	933.76	964.00	9,890.48	1,641.95
2006	1,032.48	1,045.16	1,044.39	1,105.00	1,264.05	1,192.73	1,233.03	1,236.74	1,183.30	1,085.32	1,183.73	1,124.79	1,144.23
2007	1,151.90	1,206.47	1,222.77	1,280.90	1,306.50	1,289.14	1,307.38	1,267.30	1,313.00	1,413.87	1,449.45	1,492.47	1,308.43
2008	1,585.09	2,002.55	2,043.65	1,991.32	2,053.57	2,042.24	1,904.68	1,492.52	1,221.71	917.13	841.22	842.40	1,578.17
2009	949.76	1,037.26	1,084.59	1,169.57	1,134.45	1,220.41	1,163.82	1,248.24	1,294.71	1,335.86	1,401.26	1,447.20	1,207.26
2010	1,567.15	1,525.63	1,602.65	1,718.33	1,633.45	1,556.77	1,530.57	1,543.82	1,598.57	1,692.29	1,702.35	1,715.19	1,615.56

Source: American Metal Market (AMM)

Average Dealer Price[1] of Palladium in the United States   In Dollars Per Troy Ounce

Year	Jan.	Feb.	Mar.	Apr.	May	June	July	Aug.	Sept.	Oct.	Nov.	Dec.	Average
2001	1,054.10	984.37	792.68	699.15	663.41	619.67	525.90	459.83	444.47	340.52	333.14	405.95	610.27
2002	412.62	377.79	377.15	372.50	360.00	339.20	325.41	327.55	330.50	319.09	289.20	243.57	339.55
2003	258.41	255.68	226.38	164.76	169.00	181.76	175.27	185.76	214.29	203.74	200.17	200.86	203.01
2004	220.70	237.95	272.43	299.57	249.57	231.32	222.95	217.55	213.95	220.43	215.85	193.00	232.94
2005	188.45	184.15	200.09	200.76	191.38	188.50	186.95	188.13	191.19	209.71	246.35	266.24	203.49
2006	275.95	291.58	312.70	355.74	372.82	319.36	320.21	332.57	324.40	315.18	326.91	328.00	322.95
2007	339.81	344.26	352.27	370.35	369.50	370.76	368.67	344.61	337.63	368.70	366.75	355.42	357.39
2008	376.95	473.65	490.35	449.05	438.29	453.57	428.27	318.29	250.19	193.30	212.61	178.00	355.21
2009	189.81	207.63	203.73	228.29	230.45	247.18	250.64	278.38	295.86	324.45	354.84	376.60	265.66
2010	437.15	429.16	464.48	535.33	495.05	465.18	459.86	493.45	543.24	596.33	687.75	760.29	530.61

[1] Based on wholesale quantities, prompt delivery.   Source: American Metal Market (AMM)

Platinum Futures - CME Group (NYMEX)
(weekly close) as of December 31, 2010
USD Per Troy Ounce

Volume of Trading of Platinum Futures in New York   In Contracts

Year	Jan.	Feb.	Mar.	Apr.	May	June	July	Aug.	Sept.	Oct.	Nov.	Dec.	Total
2001	19,278	12,885	31,617	14,961	15,714	23,245	14,494	12,477	17,040	9,957	11,401	22,890	205,969
2002	12,848	13,807	24,434	11,066	12,294	27,176	14,198	18,583	29,762	11,834	9,878	33,891	219,771
2003	15,545	15,157	38,170	13,472	18,968	30,961	10,852	11,878	37,686	19,275	14,040	42,301	268,305
2004	16,337	15,574	42,249	29,228	13,125	28,495	15,598	18,180	34,076	24,393	18,606	39,834	295,695
2005	15,410	20,253	41,297	16,267	20,135	55,588	25,132	26,604	52,535	21,827	30,447	50,684	376,179
2006	20,604	27,572	42,804	17,215	34,684	45,985	16,220	21,428	44,000	21,182	46,754	34,671	373,119
2007	20,534	26,975	59,099	26,457	35,525	66,968	35,371	35,975	58,091	34,100	36,126	66,324	501,545
2008	54,479	71,978	84,901	41,283	54,476	66,398	43,127	47,539	74,165	38,107	30,011	69,079	675,543
2009	31,090	35,199	82,949	30,849	34,962	104,413	46,045	48,650	134,462	55,865	63,896	134,504	802,884
2010	85,446	83,630	176,594	91,365	133,781	144,344	71,314	74,099	188,874	99,204	151,998	185,858	1,486,507

Contract size = 50 oz.   *Source: CME Group; New York Mercantile Exchange (NYMEX)*

Average Open Interest of Platinum Futures in New York   In Contracts

Year	Jan.	Feb.	Mar.	Apr.	May	June	July	Aug.	Sept.	Oct.	Nov.	Dec.
2001	8,449	7,311	6,855	6,715	7,436	5,751	6,210	5,996	5,646	5,395	6,102	6,033
2002	6,587	6,213	7,121	6,823	6,031	6,901	5,516	6,405	6,930	7,211	7,406	8,388
2003	8,694	8,132	8,034	6,322	6,599	6,847	7,450	8,556	8,794	8,489	9,421	9,373
2004	8,210	7,379	8,879	7,698	5,555	5,590	5,376	6,282	6,091	6,092	7,208	7,184
2005	6,800	7,486	8,047	8,132	8,496	10,109	8,497	11,729	12,478	13,024	12,377	11,327
2006	10,625	9,995	8,407	9,486	9,681	8,265	8,575	9,889	9,076	7,276	8,332	8,186
2007	8,810	10,752	11,154	13,413	15,173	15,033	16,641	12,347	12,341	15,199	14,427	15,404
2008	17,912	15,770	12,966	12,977	15,869	15,821	14,198	12,325	13,904	15,111	16,530	17,267
2009	18,300	20,041	20,388	20,506	21,045	23,755	21,952	25,303	28,571	31,236	33,730	33,542
2010	34,160	34,637	36,720	37,368	33,840	30,242	28,369	31,026	35,528	38,402	36,959	37,115

Contract size = 50 oz.   *Source: CME Group; New York Mercantile Exchange (NYMEX)*

Palladium Futures - CME Group (NYMEX)
(weekly close) as of December 31, 2010
USD Per Troy Ounce

Volume of Trading of Palladium Futures in New York In Contracts

Year	Jan.	Feb.	Mar.	Apr.	May	June	July	Aug.	Sept.	Oct.	Nov.	Dec.	Total
2001	2,171	6,090	1,397	1,121	3,325	1,013	1,173	3,221	523	1,255	3,261	1,375	25,925
2002	1,275	3,372	1,538	1,527	6,126	2,166	2,154	8,971	1,452	1,710	8,118	2,644	41,053
2003	4,200	7,266	3,256	3,971	8,420	3,430	4,221	28,895	10,690	15,036	41,269	16,429	267,552
2004	17,093	41,036	20,508	30,214	27,343	11,433	7,606	28,895	17,747	21,680	50,643	24,403	321,923
2005	7,728	43,268	16,979	13,316	46,112	13,594	17,185	49,268	17,747	21,680	50,643	24,403	321,923
2006	28,447	59,279	32,573	23,135	64,863	25,857	13,464	41,123	16,222	14,351	47,797	11,005	378,116
2007	23,636	62,815	14,987	25,166	69,089	16,322	15,072	65,106	16,975	26,385	52,411	13,029	400,993
2008	26,954	105,845	49,411	24,750	66,939	18,934	26,245	53,692	25,253	28,627	43,879	13,299	483,828
2009	14,284	41,726	14,509	17,332	51,635	23,403	25,689	57,502	25,393	29,401	71,228	28,719	400,821
2010	48,438	90,368	48,314	58,104	134,435	45,840	45,847	87,366	55,399	69,623	156,495	61,355	901,584

Contract size = 100 oz.   *Source: CME Group; New York Mercantile Exchange (NYMEX)*

Average Open Interest of Palladium Futures in New York In Contracts

Year	Jan.	Feb.	Mar.	Apr.	May	June	July	Aug.	Sept.	Oct.	Nov.	Dec.
2001	1,828	1,666	1,525	1,577	1,613	1,385	1,420	1,318	1,383	1,286	1,477	1,244
2002	1,217	1,208	1,042	1,199	1,554	1,806	2,103	2,298	1,878	1,976	1,977	2,025
2003	2,000	2,039	1,948	1,997	2,315	2,609	2,680	3,605	5,184	5,533	6,096	6,737
2004	9,119	11,878	11,465	11,039	8,828	7,861	8,055	8,688	8,933	9,965	11,192	12,188
2005	12,824	13,821	12,946	13,116	13,345	13,527	13,794	14,465	13,340	13,488	14,676	14,477
2006	14,353	16,632	15,426	17,783	18,002	14,251	14,087	13,166	11,247	11,836	12,511	11,210
2007	13,794	16,132	15,587	18,126	19,682	18,288	18,152	18,035	16,062	16,286	17,194	14,820
2008	18,184	20,999	20,227	19,571	19,197	17,106	15,223	13,821	14,294	14,656	13,435	12,688
2009	12,442	12,596	12,230	14,237	15,594	16,288	17,150	20,669	21,877	21,881	22,650	22,692
2010	23,356	22,566	22,944	23,905	23,152	21,271	19,732	19,808	23,036	24,706	24,747	23,089

Contract size = 100 oz.   *Source: CME Group; New York Mercantile Exchange (NYMEX)*

Pork Bellies

Pork bellies are the cut of meat from a hog from which bacon is produced. A hog has two belly slabs, generally weighing 8-18 pounds each, depending on the hog's commercial slaughter weight. Total hog slaughter weights average around 255 pounds, equal to a dressed carcass weight of about 190 pounds. Bellies account for about 12% of a hog's live weight, but represent a larger 14% of the total cutout value of the realized pork products. Pork bellies can be frozen and stored for up to a year before processing. The pork belly futures contract at the Chicago Mercantile Exchange calls for the physical delivery of 40,000 pounds of frozen pork bellies, which have been slaughtered at USDA federally inspected slaughtering plants. Each deliverable belly typically weighs 12-14 pounds each.

There are definite seasonal patterns in pork belly prices. Bellies are storable and the movement into cold storage builds early in the calendar year, peaking about mid-year. Net withdrawals from storage then carry stocks to a low around October. The cycle then starts again. Retail bacon demand also follows a time worn trend, peaking in the summer and tapering off to a low during the winter months. While demand patterns would suggest the highest prices in the summer and the lowest in the winter, just the opposite is not unusual. Such contra-seasonal price moves can be partially attributed to supply logistics, notably the availability of frozen storage stocks deliverable against futures at CME exchange-approved warehouses. When stocks prove either too large or small, the underlying demand variables for bacon can be relegated to the backburner as a market-moving factor. The fact that no contract months are traded between August and the following February adds to the late fall futures price distortion.

Belly prices (cash and futures) are sensitive to the inventory in cold storage and to the weekly net movement in and out of storage, which affords some insight to demand, although a better measure is the weekly quantity of bellies being sliced into bacon. Higher retail prices tend to encourage placing more supply into storage because of lower retail bacon demand. Bacon is not a necessary foodstuff so demand can be buoyed by favorable consumer disposable income. However, dietary standards have changed dramatically in recent years and do not favor the consumption of high fat and salt content food, such as bacon. In addition, alternatives to pork bacon have emerged in recent years such as turkey bacon, which has lower fat and calorie content.

Prices – Pork belly futures prices rallied sharply during 2010 as farmers cut hog herds and pork belly supplies plummeted. In August 2010, pork belly supplies in cold storage tumbled -79% y/y to the lowest ever for the month, which helped propel pork belly prices to an all-time nearest-futures high of 145.50 cents per pound, the highest since pork belly futures trading began in 1961. Pork belly prices ended 2010 at 106.50 cents per pound, up 21% for the year.

Supply – The average monthly level of frozen pork belly storage stocks in 2010 fell by -38.9% to 37.353 million pounds, down from the 2008 10-year high of 60.932 million pounds. As of December 2010, there were 37.696 million pounds of pork bellies in storage.

Average Retail Price of Bacon, Sliced   In Dollars Per Pound

Year	Jan.	Feb.	Mar.	Apr.	May	June	July	Aug.	Sept.	Oct.	Nov.	Dec.	Average
2001	2.99	3.07	3.16	3.11	3.26	3.25	3.32	3.47	3.49	3.34	3.30	3.30	3.25
2002	3.27	3.32	3.27	3.26	3.18	3.19	3.23	3.27	3.16	3.24	3.21	3.24	3.24
2003	3.20	3.28	3.22	3.29	3.09	3.14	3.16	3.23	3.22	3.16	3.23	3.18	3.20
2004	3.16	3.19	3.13	3.20	3.33	3.42	3.47	3.62	3.59	3.61	3.44	3.37	3.38
2005	3.37	3.40	3.36	3.33	3.56	3.46	3.48	3.44	3.40	3.33	3.26	3.33	3.39
2006	3.36	3.39	3.40	3.34	3.31	3.40	3.51	3.56	3.55	3.61	3.44	3.46	3.44
2007	3.51	3.57	3.46	3.50	3.65	3.66	3.72	3.80	3.78	3.88	3.66	3.69	3.66
2008	3.65	3.62	3.62	3.55	3.64	3.66	3.61	3.84	3.73	3.75	3.60	3.67	3.66
2009	3.73	3.62	3.59	3.58	3.66	3.62	3.64	3.59	3.59	3.60	3.50	3.57	3.61
2010[1]	3.63	3.64	3.67	3.64	3.86	4.05	4.21	4.35	4.57	4.77	4.70	4.16	4.11

[1] Preliminary.   Source: Economic Research Service, U.S. Department of Agriculture (ERS-USDA)

Frozen Pork Belly Storage Stocks in the United States, on First of Month   In Thousands of Pounds

Year	Jan.	Feb.	Mar.	Apr.	May	June	July	Aug.	Sept.	Oct.	Nov.	Dec.
2001	47,099	50,145	47,154	45,440	43,878	46,029	39,552	24,996	12,754	8,960	28,216	36,297
2002	44,301	50,849	57,569	60,721	63,293	62,269	51,019	29,925	14,250	9,452	10,354	18,059
2003	28,254	35,354	38,278	42,971	48,542	45,870	43,504	32,075	17,900	10,180	21,135	33,073
2004	49,017	63,095	57,123	50,126	48,363	41,366	37,185	23,383	15,230	11,344	15,970	33,955
2005	56,026	61,528	72,324	77,718	88,367	80,033	66,775	45,254	16,175	8,094	9,421	22,490
2006	40,707	54,902	58,861	61,628	62,665	58,803	46,056	30,506	11,962	10,199	15,597	30,553
2007	41,917	46,227	46,643	55,160	61,796	57,294	47,214	31,619	21,410	17,050	20,356	34,328
2008	54,746	70,647	79,282	98,896	100,189	87,428	74,372	57,964	31,878	21,270	21,696	33,490
2009	51,593	69,166	75,668	72,940	79,543	78,801	76,333	60,238	48,958	38,481	37,127	44,638
2010[1]	56,764	53,584	55,552	58,762	49,656	44,201	35,369	21,380	7,202	4,817	23,248	37,696

[1] Preliminary.   Source: National Agricultural Statistics Service, U.S. Department of Agriculture (NASS-USDA)

Weekly Pork Belly Storage Movement

Week Ending	------------- Stocks[1] in Thousands of Pounds ----------------				Week Ending	------------- Stocks[1] in Thousands of Pounds ----------------			
	In	Out	On Hand	Net Movement		In	Out	On Hand	Net Movement
Jan 03, 2009	3,737	-8	40,167	3,729	Jan 02, 2010	2,057	-84	37,083	1,973
Jan 10, 2009	3,686	-448	43,405	3,238	Jan 09, 2010	953	-647	37,389	306
Jan 17, 2009	4,841	-156	48,090	4,685	Jan 16, 2010	930	-1,542	36,777	-612
Jan 24, 2009	3,585	-239	51,607	3,517	Jan 23, 2010	1,384	-3,558	34,603	-2,174
Jan 31, 2009	2,943	-127	54,423	2,816	Jan 30, 2010	1,102	-2,200	33,505	-1,089
Feb 07, 2009	1,561	-159	55,825	1,402	Feb 06, 2010	335	-820	33,020	-485
Feb 14, 2009	827	-191	56,461	636	Feb 13, 2010	622	-923	32,719	-301
Feb 21, 2009	1,448	-367	57,541	1,081	Feb 20, 2010	624	-324	33,019	300
Feb 28, 2009	812	-156	58,197	656	Feb 27, 2010	1,047	-83	33,983	964
Mar 07, 2009	859	-112	58,943	747	Mar 06, 2010	1,170	-1,739	34,705	-569
Mar 14, 2009	224	0	59,167	224	Mar 13, 2010	736	-571	35,112	165
Mar 21, 2009	307	0	59,474	307	Mar 20, 2010	563	-246	35,429	317
Mar 28, 2009	83	-575	58,982	-492	Mar 27, 2010	736	-551	35,614	185
Apr 04, 2009	631	-542	59,071	89	Apr 03, 2010	1,389	-364	36,639	1,025
Apr 11, 2009	1,098	-438	59,730	660	Apr 10, 2010	964	-444	37,159	520
Apr 18, 2009	1,731	0	61,461	1,731	Apr 17, 2010	856	-1,901	36,114	-1,045
Apr 25, 2009	1,315	0	62,776	1,315	Apr 24, 2010			34,258	-1,856
May 02, 2009	955	0	63,731	955	May 01, 2010	756	-3,451	31,563	-2,695
May 09, 2009	204	0	63,935	204	May 08, 2010	0	-1,581	29,982	-1,581
May 16, 2009	0	0	63,935	0	May 15, 2010	212	-887	29,307	-675
May 23, 2009	84	-1,650	62,369	-1,566	May 22, 2010	82	-775	28,614	-693
May 30, 2009	13	-369	62,013	-356	May 29, 2010	359	-414	28,559	-55
Jun 06, 2009	7	-960	61,060	-953	Jun 05, 2010	337	-1,304	27,592	-967
Jun 13, 2009	1,572	-1,439	61,194	133	Jun 12, 2010	209	-1,407	26,394	-1,198
Jun 20, 2009	1,025	-1,222	60,997	-197	Jun 19, 2010	446	-1,527	25,313	-1,081
Jun 27, 2009	286	-1,829	59,298	-1,543	Jun 26, 2010	284	-1,923	23,674	-1,639
Jul 04, 2009	693	-1,780	58,211	-1,087	Jul 03, 2010	0	-1,177	22,497	-1,177
Jul 11, 2009	385	-3,419	55,177	-3,034	Jul 10, 2010	127	-1,470	21,154	-1,343
Jul 18, 2009	0	-3,028	52,149	-3,028	Jul 17, 2010	41	-3,375	17,820	-3,334
Jul 25, 2009	15	-5,207	46,957	-5,192	Jul 24, 2010	122	-3,833	14,109	-3,711
Aug 01, 2009	562	-4,439	43,080	-3,877	Jul 31, 2010	195	-2,841	11,463	-2,646
Aug 08, 2009	160	-4,071	39,169	-3,911	Aug 07, 2010	243	-3,496	8,210	-3,253
Aug 15, 2009	1,447	-5,401	35,215	-3,954	Aug 14, 2010	42	-2,943	5,309	-2,901
Aug 22, 2009	2,475	-3,712	33,978	-1,237	Aug 21, 2010	77	-2,445	2,941	-2,368
Aug 29, 2009	1,535	-4,428	31,085	-2,893	Aug 28, 2010	0	-1,471	1,470	-1,471
Sep 05, 2009	1,242	-3,578	28,749	-2,336	Sep 04, 2010	0	-1,046	424	-1,046
Sep 12, 2009	391	-1,943	27,198	-1,552	Sep 11, 2010	0	-415	9	-415
Sep 19, 2009	886	-3,315	24,768	-2,429	Sep 18, 2010	0	-5	4	-5
Sep 26, 2009	366	-1,174	23,960	-808	Sep 25, 2010	0	-2	2	-2
Oct 03, 2009	245	-1,184	23,915	-939	Oct 02, 2010	0	0	2	0
Oct 10, 2009	144	-1,190	22,869	-1,046	Oct 09, 2010	1,189	0	1,191	1,189
Oct 17, 2009	781	-881	22,769	-100	Oct 16, 2010	3,448	0	4,639	3,448
Oct 24, 2009	866	-1,030	22,605	-164	Oct 23, 2010	3,695	0	8,334	3,695
Oct 31, 2009	1,291	-906	22,990	385	Oct 30, 2010	4,985	0	13,319	4,985
Nov 07, 2009	1,717	-728	23,283	989	Nov 06, 2010	4,698	0	18,017	4,698
Nov 14, 2009	1,308	-721	23,870	587	Nov 13, 2010	6,032	-4	24,045	6,028
Nov 21, 2009	3,101	-649	26,322	2,452	Nov 20, 2010	5,185	0	29,230	5,185
Nov 28, 2009	3,137	-293	28,044	2,844	Nov 27, 2010	5,748	0	34,978	5,748
Dec 05, 2009	2,087	-201	29,930	1,886	Dec 04, 2010	5,592	-75	40,495	5,517
Dec 12, 2009	2,339	-622	31,647	1,717	Dec 11, 2010	5,669	-783	45,381	4,886
Dec 19, 2009	2,381	-1,002	33,026	1,379	Dec 18, 2010	6,586	-958	51,009	5,628
Dec 26, 2009	2,466	-382	35,110	2,084	Dec 25, 2010	6,661	-544	57,126	6,117

[1] 59 Chicago and Outside Combined Chicago Mercantile Exchange approved warehouses.   *Source: Chicago Mercantile Exchange (CME)*

PORK BELLIES

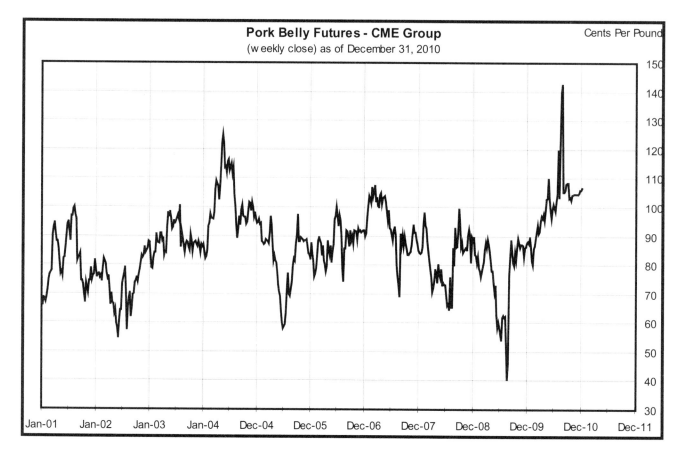

Pork Belly Futures - CME Group
(weekly close) as of December 31, 2010

Cents Per Pound

Average Open Interest of Pork Belly Futures in Chicago   In Contracts

Year	Jan.	Feb.	Mar.	Apr.	May	June	July	Aug.	Sept.	Oct.	Nov.	Dec.
2001	2,719	2,908	2,935	3,138	2,808	2,354	2,526	2,579	2,695	2,321	2,441	2,451
2002	2,574	2,768	2,879	3,271	3,224	2,821	1,885	986	1,116	1,329	2,020	2,548
2003	2,842	2,805	2,915	3,082	3,383	3,410	2,858	1,632	1,899	1,885	2,075	2,484
2004	2,431	3,213	3,491	3,998	3,880	3,158	2,675	1,473	1,399	1,200	1,491	1,900
2005	2,013	3,010	2,858	2,891	3,743	3,725	2,507	1,599	1,143	1,451	1,323	1,868
2006	2,273	2,407	1,949	2,146	2,049	1,938	1,812	1,006	782	907	1,039	1,069
2007	1,257	1,520	1,391	1,259	1,256	1,369	1,146	851	941	1,532	1,911	1,850
2008	2,047	1,718	1,763	2,051	1,976	2,219	1,816	702	704	805	1,140	1,164
2009	1,192	1,291	1,090	894	860	865	667	573	657	642	595	565
2010	475	404	317	268	198	124	48	18	11	10	6	4

Contract size = 40,000 lbs.   *Source: Chicago Mercantile Exchange (CME)*

Volume of Trading of Pork Belly Futures in Chicago   In Contracts

Year	Jan.	Feb.	Mar.	Apr.	May	June	July	Aug.	Sept.	Oct.	Nov.	Dec.	Total
2001	15,861	16,200	16,675	18,274	18,708	16,989	20,187	18,823	12,719	12,905	15,984	13,034	196,359
2002	16,495	16,650	14,279	17,758	13,648	15,764	16,773	7,490	6,857	8,107	8,659	9,574	152,054
2003	13,635	13,956	13,137	18,279	18,112	16,993	19,540	9,967	7,909	10,235	8,542	11,024	161,329
2004	11,519	14,738	17,699	18,412	17,366	15,136	16,012	10,518	9,410	5,713	7,643	7,783	151,949
2005	7,736	13,995	10,767	13,713	11,020	15,226	12,869	11,275	5,099	9,370	6,438	6,910	124,418
2006	10,806	12,890	11,682	13,183	10,342	12,616	9,842	9,634	4,885	4,375	4,568	2,741	107,564
2007	7,767	7,117	6,102	6,200	6,072	6,369	6,965	5,873	3,296	4,006	5,140	3,502	68,409
2008	6,159	5,741	5,396	6,289	4,695	5,608	7,993	4,163	2,377	2,463	2,060	3,761	56,705
2009	3,559	3,340	3,400	2,716	2,538	3,610	2,369	1,614	1,211	1,431	776	1,288	27,852
2010	1,170	1,174	892	659	352	292	115	53	5	2	6	2	4,722

Contract size = 40,000 lbs.   *Source: Chicago Mercantile Exchange (CME)*

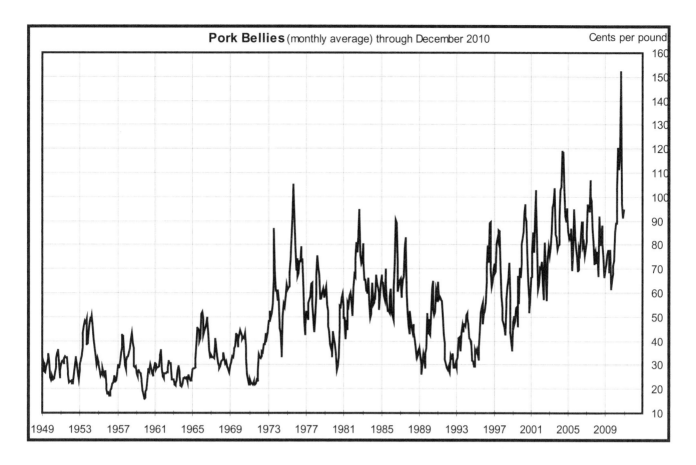

Pork Bellies (monthly average) through December 2010 — Cents per pound

Average Price of Pork Bellies (12-14 lbs.), Central, U.S.   In Cents Per Pound

Year	Jan.	Feb.	Mar.	Apr.	May	June	July	Aug.	Sept.	Oct.	Nov.	Dec.	Average
2001	66.61	66.68	78.04	85.80	77.91	91.50	102.42	98.39	81.91	61.30	63.68	69.13	78.61
2002	70.87	70.75	72.55	63.48	58.65	65.90	81.06	67.98	57.05	76.24	75.50	78.92	69.91
2003	78.02	79.54	85.80	84.94	96.58	97.05	102.37	85.65	83.15	84.46	78.53	81.00	86.42
2004	79.78	90.76	103.67	109.15	117.53	113.00	118.22	99.92	92.00	88.90	91.50	87.81	99.35
2005	78.00	82.13	84.20	78.13	87.31	68.73	77.48	94.00	89.67	84.07	78.82	75.00	81.46
2006	75.00	71.83	78.67	78.83	87.00	101.25	94.29	90.67	82.56	75.44	78.64	79.50	82.81
2007	86.25	96.08	93.25	93.47	106.30	101.06	99.83	86.58	80.42	71.58	75.69	77.08	88.97
2008	75.56	78.94	67.26	61.08	79.00	64.54	78.75	74.17	63.50	77.00	57.25	61.25	69.86
2009	69.88	71.00	65.25	77.50	57.00	50.00	80.36	42.25	45.83	47.33	60.50	64.00	60.91
2010[1]	82.00	73.50	89.00	NA	NA	NA	73.50	122.50	88.00	76.67	143.00	94.50	93.63

[1] Preliminary.   *Source: Economic Research Service, U.S. Department of Agriculture (ERS-USDA)*

Average Price of Pork Loins (12-14 lbs.)[2], Central, U.S.   In Cents Per Pound

Year	Jan.	Feb.	Mar.	Apr.	May	June	July	Aug.	Sept.	Oct.	Nov.	Dec.	Average
2001	110.80	114.32	128.53	117.98	130.72	132.33	126.41	121.22	116.21	108.69	97.87	98.50	116.97
2002	106.95	105.73	100.08	94.13	101.71	104.80	108.64	97.85	87.17	93.04	82.60	93.03	97.98
2003	91.83	95.75	92.43	96.90	108.93	126.51	102.50	104.85	111.38	97.71	89.06	93.72	100.96
2004	111.98	117.30	110.00	115.48	140.65	130.30	121.36	116.93	119.22	110.00	102.92	109.50	117.14
2005	116.08	114.83	115.88	115.03	133.45	115.62	115.03	119.82	111.31	103.78	96.72	101.12	113.22
2006	95.00	96.21	101.31	107.25	112.77	124.61	114.95	109.35	99.58	99.27	92.02	101.15	104.46
2007	100.96	112.08	101.04	108.99	121.61	113.58	111.78	111.66	100.18	93.41	88.25	86.46	104.17
2008	87.70	90.22	90.33	108.10	130.43	115.19	117.11	128.86	114.54	111.10	92.88	93.10	106.63
2009	94.96	94.83	90.46	92.10	97.73	91.58	101.03	90.33	89.08	85.98	82.63	103.03	92.81
2010[1]	110.94	104.08	108.14	122.64	137.62	114.17	118.47	132.73	120.09	110.36	104.06	108.22	115.96

[1] Preliminary.   *Source: Economic Research Service, U.S. Department of Agriculture (ERS-USDA)*

Potatoes

The potato is a member of the nightshade family. The leaves of the potato plant are poisonous and a potato will begin to turn green if left too long in the light. This green skin contains solanine, a substance that can cause the potato to taste bitter and even cause illness in humans.

In Peru, the Inca Indians were the first to cultivate potatoes around 200 BC. The Indians developed potato crops because their staple diet of corn would not grow above an altitude of 3,350 meters. In 1536, after conquering the Incas, the Spanish Conquistadors brought potatoes back to Europe. At first, Europeans did not accept the potato because it was not mentioned in the Bible and was therefore considered an "evil" food. But after Marie Antoinette wore a crown of potato flowers, it finally became a popular food. In 1897, during the Alaskan Klondike gold rush, potatoes were so valued for their vitamin C content that miners traded gold for potatoes. The potato became the first vegetable to be grown in outer space in October 1995.

The potato is a highly nutritious, fat-free, cholesterol-free and sodium-free food, and is an important dietary staple in over 130 countries. A medium-sized potato contains only 100 calories. Potatoes are an excellent source of vitamin C and provide B vitamins as well as potassium, copper, magnesium, and iron. According to the U.S. Department of Agriculture, "a diet of whole milk and potatoes would supply almost all of the food elements necessary for the maintenance of the human body."

Potatoes are one of the largest vegetable crops grown in the U.S., and are grown in all fifty states. The U.S. ranks about 4th in world potato production. The top three types of potatoes grown extensively in the U.S. are white, red, and Russets (Russets account for about two-thirds the U.S. crop). Potatoes in the U.S. are harvested in all four seasons, but the vast majority of the crop is harvested in fall. Potatoes harvested in the winter, spring and summer are used mainly to supplement fresh supplies of fall-harvested potatoes and are also important to the processing industries. The four principal categories for U.S. potato exports are frozen, potato chips, fresh, and dehydrated. Fries account for approximately 95% of U.S. frozen potato exports.

Prices – The average monthly price received for potatoes by U.S. farmers in 2010 rose +10.9% to $8.87 per hundred pounds, a new record high.

Supply –The total potato crop in 2009 (latest data) rose by +3.5% to 42.969 billion pounds, but still well below the record high of 50.936 billion pounds posted in 2000. The fall crop in 2009 (latest data) rose by +3.9% to 39.350 billion pounds and it accounted for 92% of the total crop. Stocks of the fall crop (as of Dec 1, 2008) were 24.330 billion pounds. In 2009 (lastest data), the spring crop rose +5.9% to 2.132 billion pounds, the summer crop rose +4.8% to 1.447 billion pounds, and the winter crop fell -15.7% to 213.20 million billion pounds.

The largest producing states for the fall 2010 crop were Idaho (with 31.7% of the crop), Washington (22.7%), Wisconsin (6.7%), North Dakota (6.1%), and Colorado (6.0%). For the spring crop, the largest producing states were California with 44.1% of the crop and Florida with 32% of the crop. Farmers harvested 1.010 million acres in 2010, down -3.0% a new record low The yield per harvested acre in 2010 fell -4.6% to 39,500 pounds per acre.

Demand – Total utilization of potatoes in 2009 (latest data available) rose +3.9% yr/yr to 43.131 billion pounds, above from last years record low of 41.505 billion pounds. The breakdown shows that the largest consumption category for potatoes is frozen French fries with 32.1% of total consumption, followed closely by table stock (26.7%), dehydration (10.3%), and chips and shoestrings (9.9%). U.S. per capita consumption of potatoes in 2010 fell -0.2% to 116.8 pounds, well below the record high of 145.0 pounds per capita seen in 1996.

Trade – U.S. exports of potatoes in 2008 (latest data available) fell by -0.1% to 615.135 million pounds. U.S. exports hit a record high of 647.119 million pounds in 2002. U.S. imports in 2008 rose +16.1% to 1,072.017 million pounds, which was a new record high.

Salient Statistics of Potatoes in the United States

Crop Year	Planted	Harvested	Yield Per Harvested Acre Cwt.	Total Production	Seed & Feed	Shrinkage & Loss	Sold[2]	Farm Price ($ Cwt.)	Production[3]	sales	Stocks Jan. 1 (1,000 Cwt)	Exports (Fresh)	Imports	Fresh	Total
	----- Acreage -----				---- Used Where Grown ----			---- Value of ----					- Foreign Trade[4] -	Consumption[4] Per Capita	
	--- 1,000 Acres ---			-------- In Thousands of Cwt. --------					---- Million $ ----			-- Millions of Lbs. --		-- In Pounds --	
2001	1,247	1,221	358	437,673	5,386	31,227	401,060	6.99	3,056	2,803	224,680	579,361	487,889	46.6	138.5
2002	1,300	1,266	362	458,171	5,622	30,905	421,644	6.67	3,045	2,812	231,490	647,120	621,461	44.3	131.9
2003	1,273	1,249	367	457,814	5,543	35,294	416,977	5.88	2,677	2,455	233,590	541,775	635,007	46.8	137.9
2004	1,193	1,167	391	456,041	4,796	37,408	413,839	5.65	2,565	2,336	236,700	433,712	575,374	45.8	134.6
2005	1,109	1,087	390	423,926	4,791	28,519	390,616	7.04	2,982	2,750	220,500	586,226	631,252	41.3	125.4
2006	1,139	1,120	393	440,698	4,750	29,639	406,309	7.31	3,209	2,970	225,800	600,715	611,229	38.6	123.7
2007	1,142	1,122	396	444,873	4,105	29,561	411,209	7.51	3,340	3,089	232,300	615,784	923,574	38.7	124.4
2008	1,060	1,047	396	415,053	4,138	26,438	384,478	9.09	3,770	3,494	213,200	616,290	1,071,973	37.8	118.3
2009	1,068	1,041	414	431,318	4,535	29,122	397,661	8.19	3,521	3,256	234,300	682,190	794,611	36.4	113.1
2010[1]	1,021	1,004	395	397,077	3,929	26,176	366,972	8.79	3,489		204,500	808,354	762,925	35.6	112.8

[1] Preliminary. [2] For all purposes, including food, seed processing & livestock feed. [3] Farm weight basis, excluding canned and frozen potatoes.
[4] Calendar year. *Source: Economic Research Service, U.S. Department of Agriculture (ERS-USDA)*

Cold Storage Stocks of All Frozen Potatoes in the United States, on First of Month   In Millions of Pounds

Year	Jan.	Feb.	Mar.	Apr.	May	June	July	Aug.	Sept.	Oct.	Nov.	Dec.
2001	1,189.7	1,228.6	1,254.7	1,220.9	1,280.4	1,270.3	1,355.0	1,282.6	1,197.5	1,323.8	1,338.5	1,297.4
2002	1,239.8	1,274.2	1,271.5	1,271.4	1,222.7	1,182.3	1,223.5	1,106.6	1,040.6	1,141.4	1,252.2	1,214.4
2003	1,131.2	1,173.1	1,211.0	1,217.4	1,150.5	1,106.6	1,181.8	1,130.4	1,070.4	1,151.7	1,248.0	1,232.8
2004	1,120.4	1,167.3	1,207.4	1,192.5	1,158.7	1,185.9	1,128.7	1,117.1	1,127.0	1,178.6	1,274.9	1,219.3
2005	1,074.8	1,168.8	1,152.8	1,093.7	1,174.3	1,178.1	1,190.5	1,154.9	1,121.3	1,180.4	1,200.0	1,122.5
2006	1,051.1	1,076.2	1,147.0	1,158.9	1,176.6	1,104.9	1,108.1	996.4	964.1	1,009.6	1,066.6	1,052.1
2007	954.8	1,041.3	1,063.6	1,116.2	1,102.2	1,070.7	1,078.2	991.8	1,000.4	1,080.0	1,133.8	1,078.4
2008	1,012.4	1,089.1	1,117.5	1,087.7	1,134.4	1,074.9	1,190.0	1,107.5	1,126.7	1,180.8	1,200.5	1,212.1
2009	1,098.6	1,171.0	1,192.1	1,226.8	1,221.4	1,203.2	1,245.1	1,187.5	1,094.8	1,130.2	1,162.9	1,108.1
2010[1]	1,043.8	1,091.3	1,113.6	1,100.5	1,093.7	1,077.3	1,141.9	1,063.9	1,036.3	1,070.1	1,122.9	1,127.5

[1] Preliminary.   Source: Agricultural Statistics Board, U.S. Department of Agriculture (ASB-USDA)

Potato Crop Production Estimates, Stocks and Disappearance in the United States   In Millions of Cwt.

	Crop Production Estimates			Total Storage Stocks[2]							Fall Crop 1,000 Cwt.				
	Total Crop			Fall Crop			Following Year				Production	Disappearance (Sold)	Stocks Dec. 1	Average Price ($/Cwt.)	Value of Sales ($1,000)
Year	Oct. 1	Nov. 1	Dec. 1	Oct. 1	Nov. 1	Dec. 1	Jan. 1	Feb. 1	Mar. 1	Apr. 1	May 1				
2001	----	441.8	----	----	400.7	258.8	224.7	192.1	158.6	120.0	81.2	387,033	358,954	258,750	6.54	2,349,036
2002	----	459.7	----	----	415.0	264.5	231.5	199.0	165.2	125.8	83.0	407,085	378,796	264,485	5.89	2,232,627
2003	----	459.2	----	----	413.5	267.9	233.6	200.2	166.3	126.1	85.0	203,566	371,755	267,900	5.22	1,943,986
2004	----	450.2	----	----	407.8	271.1	236.7	203.5	168.0	128.9	88.6	404,017	369,781	271,100	5.12	1,877,912
2005	----	421.3	----	----	382.2	253.8	220.5	189.1	155.5	115.7	75.9	375,118	351,083	253,800	6.53	2,290,850
2006	----	434.8	----	----	390.9	258.9	225.8	192.2	159.5	120.9	79.1	389,527	365,863	258,900	6.67	2,442,474
2007	----	448.0	----	----	408.3	265.5	232.3	199.3	163.4	125.5	84.0	406,800	374,617	265,500	7.04	2,636,885
2008	----	415.1	----	----	373.5	243.7	213.2	183.9	152.7	115.8	78.1	378,588	349,580	243,700	8.49	2,967,871
2009	----	429.7	----	----	391.5	265.8	234.3	203.5	169.7	128.7	89.6	393,544	361,316	265,800	7.62	2,751,550
2010[1]	----	399.2	----	----	361.4	234.7	204.5	175.7				360,727		234,700	8.38	

[1] Preliminary.   [2] Held by growers and local dealers in the fall producing areas.
Source: Agricultural Statistics Board, U.S. Department of Agriculture (ASB-USDA)

Production of Potatoes by Seasonal Groups in the United States   In Thousands of Cwt.

	Winter	Spring			Summer			Fall								
Year	Total	California	Florida	Total	Mexico	Virgina	Total	Colorado	Idaho	Maine	Minnesota	North Dakota	Oregan	Washington	Wisconsin	Total
2001	4,115	6,045	7,970	21,814	770	1,386	18,209	21,357	120,200	16,430	18,425	26,400	20,730	94,400	31,955	387,033
2002	4,206	7,695	7,883	22,452	736	1,386	17,932	27,885	133,385	16,960	18,810	23,460	24,936	92,340	30,750	407,085
2003	4,027	8,360	8,008	24,433	532	1,550	18,766	23,652	123,180	17,030	22,330	27,440	20,991	93,150	32,800	203,566
2004	4,818	8,313	7,678	22,663	340	1,200	18,307	23,791	131,970	19,065	18,920	26,765	19,775	93,810	30,450	404,017
2005	4,892	6,116	6,527	18,724	----	1,029	17,567	22,910	118,288	15,455	17,630	20,500	22,023	95,480	27,880	375,118
2006	4,495	6,044	6,441	19,766	----	1,512	18,166	22,686	128,915	17,980	20,400	25,480	18,533	89,900	29,370	389,527
2007	2,258	6,123	7,807	19,817	----	1,134	15,997	20,981	130,010	16,668	21,560	23,660	20,294	100,800	28,160	406,800
2008	2,530	6,930	7,952	20,132	----	1,254	13,805	21,907	116,475	14,769	20,400	22,680	18,674	93,000	25,730	378,588
2009	2,132	7,175	7,700	21,321	----	1,416	14,321	22,080	132,500	15,263	20,700	19,125	21,460	87,230	28,980	393,544
2010[1]	NA	10,935	7,950	24,820	----	952	11,530	21,528	114,440	15,892	17,010	22,000	20,058	81,740	24,293	360,727

[1] Preliminary.   Source: Agricultural Statistics Board, U.S. Department of Agriculture (ASB-USDA)

Utilization of Potatoes in the United States   In Thousands of Cwt.

	Sales											Non-Sales			
				For Processing					Other Sales			Used on			
Crop Year	Table Stock	Chips, Shoestrings	Dehydration	Frozen French Fries	Other Frozen Products	Canned Potatoes	Other Canned Products[2]	Starch & Flour	Livestock Feed	Seed	Total Sales	Farms Where Grown	Shrinkage & Loss	Total Non-Sales	Total
2000	139,590	52,405	54,332	146,869	26,723	2,368	2,709	1,966	14,265	23,345	464,572	3,792	43,685	48,972	513,544
2001	122,552	54,080	40,759	126,711	23,598	2,590	1,722	1,015	3,496	24,537	401,060	4,088	31,227	36,613	437,673
2002	131,889	51,640	51,357	124,875	28,951	2,744	2,089	1,050	3,044	24,005	421,644	4,144	30,905	36,527	458,171
2003	133,143	52,790	48,418	126,515	23,870	3,086	1,168	1,379	2,005	24,603	416,977	4,000	35,294	40,837	457,814
2004	130,418	50,068	48,541	131,592	23,003	2,843	984	1,531	1,942	22,915	413,837	3,601	37,408	42,204	456,041
2005	114,123	52,294	43,387	126,429	25,376	2,174	958	1,622	1,999	22,254	390,616	3,595	28,519	33,310	423,926
2006	113,335	64,377	48,809	126,083	24,229	1,957	930	1,369	1,610	23,610	406,309	3,520	29,639	34,389	440,698
2007	110,860	54,343	49,021	139,624	26,571	2,504	800	4,029	1,160	22,297	411,209	2,986	29,561	33,666	444,875
2008	109,351	50,988	40,646	134,123	19,519	2,070	790	5,288	803	20,900	384,478	3,315	26,438	30,576	415,055
2009[1]	115,083	42,886	44,401	138,353	20,968	1,979	746	6,493	6,533	20,219	397,661	3,346	29,122	33,657	431,318

[1] Preliminary.   [2] Hash, stews and soups.   Source: Agricultural Statistics Board, U.S. Department of Agriculture (ASB-USDA)

POTATOES

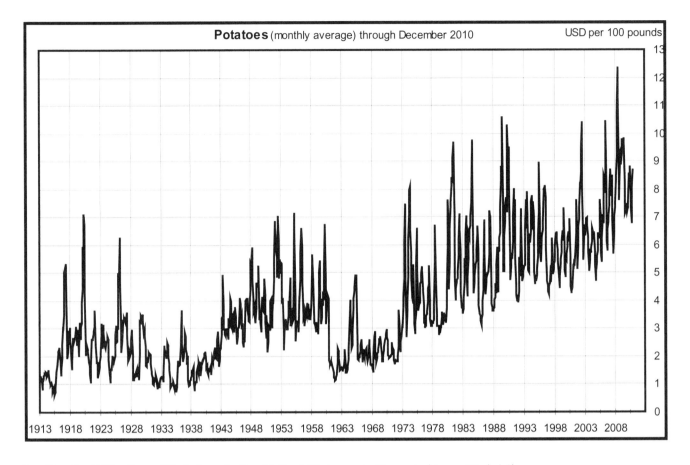

Potatoes (monthly average) through December 2010 — USD per 100 pounds

Per Capita Utilization of Potatoes in the United States   In Pounds (Farm Weight)

Year	Total	Fresh	Freezing	Chips & Shoe-string	Dehy-drating	Canning	Total Processing
2001	138.5	46.6	58.2	17.4	14.8	1.6	91.9
2002	131.9	44.3	55.2	16.3	14.7	1.4	87.6
2003	137.9	46.8	57.1	17.2	15.5	1.4	91.2
2004	134.6	45.8	57.4	16.4	13.8	1.2	88.8
2005	125.4	41.3	54.4	16.1	12.8	0.9	84.1
2006	123.7	38.6	53.3	18.6	12.4	0.8	85.1
2007	124.4	38.7	53.2	18.6	13.0	0.9	85.7
2008	118.3	37.8	51.5	15.6	12.4	1.0	80.5
2009[1]	117.7	37.4	51.2	16.1	12.1	0.9	80.4
2010[2]	117.2	37.0	51.0	16.1	12.4	0.8	80.2

[1] Preliminary.   [2] Forecast.   *Source: Agricultural Statistics Board, U.S. Department of Agriculture (ASB-USDA)*

Average Price Received by Farmers for Potatoes in the U.S.   In Dollars Per Hundred Pounds (Cwt.)

Year	Jan.	Feb.	Mar.	Apr.	May	June	July	Aug.	Sept.	Oct.	Nov.	Dec.	Season Average
2001	4.56	5.26	5.12	5.47	5.24	5.75	6.46	7.61	6.04	5.15	5.96	6.66	6.99
2002	6.90	7.34	8.26	8.00	8.62	9.39	10.40	8.00	6.14	5.44	6.38	6.67	6.67
2003	6.67	6.33	6.87	6.94	6.96	6.68	6.30	5.75	5.24	5.03	5.46	5.77	5.88
2004	5.75	5.87	6.09	6.62	6.47	6.16	6.46	5.77	5.32	4.70	5.02	5.36	5.65
2005	5.59	5.79	6.44	6.20	6.23	6.29	7.63	7.02	5.69	5.37	6.26	6.83	7.04
2006	7.07	6.76	8.50	8.35	7.83	8.41	10.46	8.23	6.12	5.76	6.59	6.79	7.31
2007	7.06	7.42	7.93	8.71	7.95	7.75	8.48	6.85	5.81	5.68	6.47	7.02	7.51
2008	7.33	7.51	8.37	8.45	9.16	10.78	12.33	11.33	8.65	7.60	8.77	9.30	9.09
2009	9.40	8.87	9.27	9.81	9.62	9.48	9.81	9.61	8.27	7.11	7.22	7.47	8.19
2010[1]	7.17	7.34	7.42	8.42	8.57	8.25	8.83	7.78	7.35	6.77	8.06	8.69	8.79

[1] Preliminary.   *Source: Agricultural Statistics Board, U.S. Department of Agriculture (ASB-USDA)*

Potatoes Processed[1] in the United States, Eight States   In Thousands of Cwt.

States	Storage Season	to Dec. 1	to Jan. 1	to Feb. 1	to Mar. 1	to Apr. 1	to May 1	to June 1	Entire Season
Idaho and Oregon-Malheur Co.	2002-03	28,380	34,860	41,200	48,600	56,240	63,840	71,280	85,390
	2003-04	24,310	30,730	36,260	43,640	49,570	56,380	63,770	77,530
	2004-05	24,360	30,840	36,820	44,610	51,000	58,090	65,800	84,600
	2005-06	22,840	29,300	35,970	43,300	50,820	57,830	65,030	77,360
	2006-07	27,090	34,070	41,350	49,840	56,650	63,680	71,220	85,630
	2007-08	26,230	33,250	40,310	48,660	55,460	63,000	70,700	88,030
	2008-09	22,380	28,980	35,430	42,150	49,030	55,570	62,940	77,340
	2009-10	23,110	29,180	35,170	42,050	49,200	56,100	62,930	79,400
	2010-11	21,040	26,840	32,700					
Maine[2]	2002-03	2,230	2,715	3,345	3,905	4,505	5,225	5,905	7,835
	2003-04	1,590	2,085	2,720	3,420	4,095	4,740	5,400	7,270
	2004-05	1,540	1,970	2,600	3,135	3,700	4,340	4,910	6,590
	2005-06	1,365	1,880	2,485	3,090	3,800	4,450	5,130	6,825
	2006-07	1,755	2,360	2,910	3,465	4,185	4,810	5,470	7,560
	2007-08	1,700	2,170	2,815	3,440	3,990	4,670	5,240	7,550
	2008-09	1,635	2,240	2,895	3,515	4,005	4,795	5,540	7,545
	2009-10	1,575	2,060	2,680	3,265	3,915	4,550	5,260	7,160
	2010-11	1,915	2,460	3,090					
Washington & Oregon-Other	2002-03	33,680	39,490	44,190	51,920	58,710	64,300	71,480	79,110
	2003-04	32,670	38,520	43,610	51,210	58,500	64,160	72,350	79,800
	2004-05	32,305	38,130	43,570	50,730	57,140	63,855	71,355	78,680
	2005-06	30,310	35,895	40,545	48,290	55,320	61,855	69,360	78,550
	2006-07	30,980	37,060	41,290	49,930	56,690	63,170	70,410	77,355
	2007-08	30,595	36,940	42,350	50,165	57,160	67,690	72,380	82,770
	2008-09	32,560	38,050	42,795	49,865	56,350	62,635	70,625	81,260
	2009-10	25,395	31,245	36,530	43,780	50,130	56,700	64,805	75,690
	2010-11	27,670	33,570	38,815					
Other States[3]	2002-03	12,675	15,530	18,735	21,780	24,810	27,405	30,655	38,700
	2003-04	13,835	16,505	19,590	22,685	25,920	29,480	32,845	42,160
	2004-05	12,490	15,000	17,965	20,910	24,150	27,480	30,945	41,175
	2005-06	11,055	14,070	17,005	19,895	22,520	25,270	27,740	35,535
	2006-07	14,355	17,800	21,415	24,690	28,205	31,560	35,040	43,565
	2007-08	15,040	17,535	20,755	23,900	26,650	29,710	32,600	39,430
	2008-09	12,480	15,120	18,165	21,030	24,025	26,515	29,590	37,285
	2009-10	10,865	13,565	16,305	18,995	21,600	24,355	27,375	34,240
	2010-11	11,660	14,605	17,255					
Total	2002-03	76,965	92,595	107,470	126,205	144,265	160,770	179,320	211,035
	2003-04	72,405	87,840	102,180	120,955	138,085	154,760	174,365	206,760
	2004-05	70,695	85,940	100,955	119,385	135,990	153,765	173,010	211,045
	2005-06	65,570	81,145	96,005	114,575	132,460	149,405	167,260	198,270
	2006-07	74,210	91,320	107,895	127,050	145,760	163,250	182,170	214,225
	2007-08	73,565	89,895	106,230	126,165	143,260	165,070	180,920	217,780
	2008-09	68,975	84,280	99,155	116,400	133,220	149,285	168,420	203,005
	2009-10	60,945	76,050	90,685	108,090	124,845	141,705	160,370	196,490
	2010-11	62,285	77,475	91,860					
Dehydrated[4]	2002-03	15,675	19,660	23,710	27,950	31,915	36,105	40,455	48,940
	2003-04	14,250	18,440	22,050	26,090	30,290	34,630	39,070	47,750
	2004-05	14,525	18,540	21,875	25,970	30,020	33,685	38,505	47,805
	2005-06	11,920	15,655	19,225	22,765	26,605	30,065	34,130	41,625
	2006-07	14,590	19,250	23,635	27,885	32,210	36,480	40,915	49,375
	2007-08	12,815	16,785	21,040	25,350	29,500	33,650	37,975	46,660
	2008-09	10,675	14,490	18,335	21,465	24,875	28,195	31,870	39,345
	2009-10	10,985	14,035	17,150	19,895	23,155	26,630	30,045	38,915
	2010-11	7,845	10,795	13,640					

[1] Total quantity received and used for processing regardless of the State in which the potatoes were produced. Amount excludes quantities used for potato chips in Maine, Michigan and Wisconsin.   [2] Includes Maine grown potatoes only.   [3] Colorado, Minnesota, , Nevada, North Dakota and Wisconsin.
[4] Dehydrated products except starch and flour. Included in above totals. Includes CO, ID, NV, ND, OR, WA, and WI.
Source: National Agricultural Statistics Service, U.S. Department of Agriculture (NASS-USDA)

Rayon and Other Synthetic Fibers

World Cellulosic Fiber Production   In Thousands of Metric Tons

Year	Brazil	Bulgaria	China	CIS	Czech Republic	India	Indo-nesia	Japan	Mexico	Taiwan	Thailand	United States	World Total
2001	28.7	12.2	608.6	64.4	7.6	251.9	205.0	107.1	22.6	127.4	65.0	103.0	2,083
2002	34.2	5.6	682.1	72.9	7.3	285.7	214.0	68.1	16.8	114.2	71.1	80.7	2,125
2003	47.2	5.2	800.2	78.8	9.1	283.0	223.0	68.3	8.4	121.5	73.8	75.3	2,249
2004	46.8	5.0	966.1	77.2	9.2	311.5	234.0	67.1	8.4	134.9	79.4	66.8	2,465
2005	40.1	5.0	1,056.0	46.6	9.5	295.4	245.0	66.6	3.8	114.5	78.2	49.1	2,483
2006	34.3	5.0	1,179.0	29.2	9.4	309.5	280.0	65.1	----	132.3	80.2	27.2	2,635
2007	39.7	5.0	1,360.2	27.9	9.3	345.4	325.0	71.5	----	136.3	95.4	25.3	2,914
2008	15.9	5.0	1,206.8	9.2	5.9	301.0	282.0	69.1	----	105.5	80.2	22.8	2,545
2009[1]	30.3	4.6	1,401.1	4.5	9.0	327.1	295.0	54.5	----	115.4	104.0	17.1	2,763
2010[2]	42.0	6.0	2,010.0	16.3	13.0	340.6	407.0	96.0	----	150.0	142.0	25.0	3,765

[1] Preliminary.   [2] Producing capacity.   *Source: Fiber Economics Bureau, Inc. (FEB)*

World Noncellulosic Fiber Production (Except Olefin)   In Thousands of Metric Tons

Year	Brazil	China	India	Indonesia	Japan	Rep. of Korea	Mexico	Pakistan	Taiwan	Thailand	Turkey	United States	World Total
2001	288.8	7,322.9	1,570.2	1,190.6	1,239.5	2,471.9	536.4	528.4	2,977.5	784.5	669.2	2,687.6	26,243
2002	293.1	8,849.4	1,695.3	1,132.8	1,129.1	2,455.7	509.6	581.5	3,091.3	852.6	728.1	2,805.0	28,052
2003	314.2	10,456.0	1,792.0	1,144.2	1,030.3	2,418.0	474.9	646.8	3,060.9	872.5	766.9	2,719.5	29,450
2004	330.9	12,474.1	1,904.2	1,064.5	989.2	2,194.3	474.9	659.3	2,965.0	905.9	849.5	2,858.2	31,429
2005	255.6	16,097.9	1,849.2	1,072.0	955.4	1,697.4	390.6	565.2	2,587.8	920.7	792.0	2,680.1	33,511
2006	274.2	18,383.1	2,263.9	1,100.7	923.9	1,484.6	271.0	550.7	2,292.4	869.9	788.8	2,479.3	35,261
2007	275.8	21,356.5	2,652.6	1,148.2	901.1	1,540.2	252.6	558.1	2,345.1	831.0	740.1	2,311.8	38,403
2008	282.4	21,681.1	2,669.4	1,116.3	771.1	1,354.9	195.5	528.8	1,947.3	842.3	580.0	1,908.4	37,023
2009[1]	265.4	23,129.8	2,977.8	1,110.8	569.6	1,300.5	177.4	526.0	1,899.4	842.3	551.0	1,614.8	37,771
2010[2]	331.4	31,151.0	4,221.0	1,399.0	981.2	1,673.0	268.0	746.0	2,162.1	1,051.0	805.0	2,182.6	50,861

[1] Preliminary.   [2] Producing capacity.   *Source: Fiber Economics Bureau, Inc. (FEB)*

World Production of Synthetic Fibers   In Thousands of Metric Tons

Year	Acrylic & Mod-acrylic	Nylon & Aramid	Polyester	Other	Yarn & Monofil-aments	Staple & Tow & Fiberfill	Total	Europe	Japan	Other Americas	United States	Total	China	USSR	Cigarette Tow Production
2001	2,562	3,784	19,563	335	14,968	11,276	26,243	701	273	93	1,016	67	32	2,431	590
2002	2,713	3,941	21,048	350	15,993	12,059	28,052	718	251	96	1,222	90	34	2,661	612
2003	2,707	3,951	22,365	427	16,853	12,597	29,450	724	250	100	1,307	120	37	2,790	633
2004	2,824	3,976	24,136	492	17,957	13,472	31,429	740	250	104	1,363	150	40	2,903	651
2005	2,698	3,893	26,410	510	19,293	14,218	33,511								665
2006	2,525	3,953	28,200	583	20,712	14,549	35,261								680
2007	2,407	3,954	31,406	636	23,027	15,375	38,403								679
2008	1,837	3,596	30,991	600	22,620	14,402	37,023								699
2009[1]	1,938	3,305	31,937	592	23,104	14,667	37,771								740
2010[2]	2,641	4,800	42,568	852	31,046	19,815	50,861								

--------- Noncellulosic Fiber Production (Except Olefin) -----------; *-------------- By Fibers ----------------*; *------- World Total --------*; *----------------------- Glass Fiber Production -----------------------*

[1] Preliminary.   [2] Producing capacity.   [3] Alginate, azion, spandex, saran, etc.   *Source: Fiber Economics Bureau, Inc. (FEB)*

Artificial (Cellulosic) Fiber Distribution in the United States   In Millions of Pounds

Year	Domestic	Exports	Total	Imports	Domestic Con-sumption	Domestic	Exports	Total	Imports	Domestic Con-sumption	Glass Fiber Ship-ments
2001	54.3	33.7	88.0	14.5	68.8	117.2	35.5	152.7	33.9	151.2	----
2002	41.2	33.2	74.4	12.7	53.9	91.1	12.6	103.7	56.2	147.4	----
2003	32.5	35.5	68.0	11.7	44.2	86.7	13.1	99.8	44.5	131.2	----
2004	26.7	38.7	65.4	12.2	38.9	77.4	9.9	87.2	63.9	141.3	----
2005	22.6	41.4	64.0	9.3	31.9	40.2	8.1	48.2	91.0	131.2	----
2006	22.4	37.6	60.0	7.7	30.1	----	8.9	8.9	141.4	141.4	----
2007	18.7	41.1	59.8	17.0	35.7	----	5.4	5.4	200.7	200.7	----
2008	15.4	44.5	59.9	11.8	27.2	----	6.8	6.8	179.8	179.8	----
2009	12.7	43.2	55.9	7.4	20.1	----	3.5	3.5	168.3	168.3	----
2010[1]	13.9	46.1	60.0	10.8	24.7	----	3.1	3.1	164.6	164.6	----

----------------------- Yan & Monofilament ----------------------; *-------------------------- Staple & Tow ----------------------*; *-------------- Producers' Shipments ---------------*

[1] Preliminary.   *Source: Fiber Economice Bureau, Inc.*

Man-Made Fiber Production in the United States   In Millions of Pounds

| | - Artificial (Cellulosic) Fibers - | | | Synthetic (Noncellulosic) Fibers | | | | | | | | | | | |
| | - Rayon & Acetate - | | | Yarn & Monofilament | | | | Staple & Tow | | | | | | | |
Year	Filament Yarn & Monofilament	Staple & Tow	Total Cellulosic	Nylon	Polyester	Olefin	Total Yarn	Nylon	Polyester	Acrylic & Modacrylic	Olefin	Total Staple	Total Noncellulosic Fibers	Total Manufactured Fibers	Total Glass Fiber
2002	----	104	104	1,772	1,218	2,331	5,321	681	2,050	340	749	3,820	9,141	----	2,759
2003	----	100	100	1,762	1,145	2,349	5,255	697	1,886	270	680	3,533	8,788	----	2,789
2004	----	----	----	1,837	1,242	2,383	5,462	680	2,064	240	676	3,660	9,123	----	----
2005	----	----	----	1,788	1,111	2,395	5,295	598	2,019	140	699	3,455	8,750	----	----
2006	----	----	----	1,739	1,072	2,223	5,034	515	1,864	----	622	3,001	8,035	----	----
2007	----	----	----	1,636	1,017	2,266	4,918	429	1,719	----	588	2,736	7,654	----	----
2008	----	----	----	1,348	915	1,915	4,178	266	1,423	----	487	2,177	6,355	----	----
2009[1]	----	----	----	1,127	837	1,622	3,586	178	1,163	----	410	1,752	5,338	----	----
2010[2]	----	----	----	1,268	1,088	1,855	4,211	90	1,310	----	431	1,831	6,042	----	----

[1] Preliminary.   [2] Estimate.   *Source: Fiber Economics Bureau, Inc. (FEB)*

Domestic Distribution of Synthetic (Noncellulosic) Fibers in the United States   In Millions of Pounds

	Yarn & Monofilament								Staple & Tow								
	Producers' Shipments							Domestic Consumption	Producers' Shipments								Domestic Consumption
	Domestic								Domestic								
Year	Nylon	Polyester	Olefin	Total	Exports	Total	Imports		Nylon	Polyester	Acrylic & Modacrylic	Olefin	Total	Exports	Total	Imports	
2002	1,668	1,139	2,289	5,092	189	5,281	765	5,856	637	1,823	255	723	3,438	353	3,791	875	4,312
2003	1,666	1,088	2,318	5,061	179	5,240	766	5,827	673	1,688	211	635	3,206	246	3,452	829	4,035
2004	1,722	1,119	2,347	5,167	249	5,416	785	5,952	658	1,788	200	641	3,287	296	3,583	766	4,053
2005	1,688	1,014	2,369	5,053	197	5,250	849	5,903	582	1,765	122	650	3,120	292	3,411	914	4,034
2006	1,589	914	2,198	4,664	211	4,875	819	5,482	492	1,624	----	596	2,713	268	2,981	1,007	3,719
2007	1,526	928	2,219	4,672	199	4,871	739	5,411	407	1,506	----	549	2,461	256	2,717	1,029	3,490
2008	1,336	841	1,921	4,098	144	4,242	692	4,790	252	1,279	----	448	1,979	184	2,163	1,038	3,017
2009	1,120	781	1,621	3,522	82	3,603	568	4,090	150	1,080	----	363	1,594	135	1,728	841	2,435
2010[1]	1,232	1,002	1,852	4,086	104	4,190	670	4,755	57	1,157	----	390	1,604	169	1,773	969	2,573

[1] Preliminary.   *Source: Fiber Economics Bureau, Inc. (FEB)*

Mill Consumption of Fiber & Products and Per Capita Consumption in the United States   In Millions of Pounds

| | Cellulosic Fibers | | | | Noncellulosic Fibers | | | Total Manufactured Fibers[2] | | | | | Per Capita[4] Mill Consumption (Lbs.) | | | | |
Year	Yarn & Monofilament	Staple & Tow	Net Waste	Total Cellulosic	Noncellulosic	Net Waste	Total Noncellulosic		Cotton	Wool	Other Fibers[3]	Grand Total	Manmade Fibers	Cotton	Wool	Other Fibers[3]	Total
2001	69	151	2.4	222	9,556	193	9,749	9,971	3,983	87	168.1	1,210	43.5	33.1	1.4	2.1	80.0
2002	54	147	1.8	203	10,173	190	10,363	10,566	3,576	56	110.3	14,308	47.7	34.3	1.3	2.2	85.5
2003	44	131	1.3	177	9,873	177	10,050	10,226	3,210	43	106.3	13,586	48.5	34.8	1.4	2.7	87.4
2004	39	141	1.5	182	10,025	144	10,169	10,351	3,126	44	123.4	13,644	48.7	35.1	1.4	3.4	88.7
2005	32	131	2.0	165	9,954	136	10,090	10,255	3,005	36	141.3	13,437	49.8	37.7	1.4	3.1	92.0
2006	30	141	2.9	174	9,240	73	9,312	9,487	2,729	34	106.7	12,357	48.5	38.3	1.4	2.9	91.1
2007	36	201	2.8	239	8,901	77	8,978	9,218	2,624	26	101.1	11,969	47.6	38.5	1.4	2.6	90.1
2008	27	180	2.9	210	7,807	59	7,866	8,076	2,093	30	96.6	10,296	43.4	32.8	1.3	2.4	79.8
2009[1]	20	168	0.6	189	6,583	23	6,606	6,795	1,580	25	84.2	8,484	38.5	29.0	1.1	1.8	70.4

[1] Preliminary.   [2] Excludes Glass Fiber.   [3] Includes silk, linen, jute and sisal & others.   [4] Mill consumption plus inports less exports of semimanufactured and unmanufactured products.   *Source: Fiber Economics Bureau, Inc. (FEB)*

Producer Price Index of Grey Synthetic Broadwovens   (1982 = 100)

Year	Jan.	Feb.	Mar.	Apr.	May	June	July	Aug.	Sept.	Oct.	Nov.	Dec.	Average
2001	110.1	111.3	111.8	111.9	109.2	110.1	107.8	108.8	109.2	107.7	107.7	107.5	109.4
2002	106.7	106.4	108.0	108.5	107.7	108.2	107.3	108.1	108.0	107.2	107.3	108.4	107.7
2003	108.2	108.2	107.6	107.7	110.1	106.0	105.7	107.1	106.7	106.0	106.6	107.7	107.3
2004	107.3	106.9	106.2	107.4	108.9	109.0	107.5	106.2	106.3	106.3	106.2	106.2	107.0
2005	108.5	108.8	109.1	110.5	110.2	110.0	110.7	110.9	110.8	112.4	113.3	116.2	111.0
2006	118.2	119.5	119.8	119.2	119.4	119.4	119.5	120.4	119.1	119.5	119.0	118.1	119.3
2007	117.8	118.8	118.9	119.1	119.6	119.8	120.3	121.5	122.9	122.7	123.0	122.9	120.6
2008	122.9	123.0	122.8	123.0	123.3	123.3	123.6	121.8	122.0	121.2	122.0	120.1	122.4
2009	121.7	122.6	122.6	125.9	125.8	127.5	127.2	124.3	124.2	124.3	124.7	125.0	124.7
2010[1]	124.9	125.1	125.2	125.9	125.2	127.3	127.8	127.5	127.5	123.4	127.9	130.4	126.5

[1] Preliminary.   *Source: Bureau of Labor Statistics, U.S. Department of Commerce (BLS) (0337-03)*

Rice

Rice is a grain that is cultivated on every continent except Antarctica and is the primary food for half the people in the world. Rice cultivation probably originated as early as 10,000 BC in Asia. Rice is grown at varying altitudes (sea level to about 3,000 meters), in varying climates (tropical to temperate), and on dry to flooded land. The growth duration of rice plants is 3-6 months, depending on variety and growing conditions. Rice is harvested by hand in developing countries or by combines in industrialized countries. Asian countries produce about 90% of rice grown worldwide. Rough rice futures and options are traded on the Chicago Board of Trade (CBOT).

Prices – Rough rice prices on the CBOT nearest futures chart showed weakness in early 2010 and fell to a 4-year low of $9.36 per hundred pounds in June 2010. However, rice prices then staged a recovery rally through the remainder of 2010 to close the year down only 4% at $13.995 per hundred pounds.

Regarding cash prices, the average monthly price of rice received by farmers in the U.S. in the first six months of the 2010-11 marketing year (i.e., August 2010 through July 2011) fell by 14.8% yr/yr to $11.92 per hundred pounds (cwt.).

Supply – World rice production in the 2010-11 marketing year rose +2.4% to 676.259 million metric tons, which is a new record high. The world's largest rice producers were China with 29.4% of world production in 2010-11, India with 21.0%, Indonesia with 8.7%, Bangladesh with 7.2%, Vietnam with 5.9%, and Thailand with 4.6%. U.S. production of rice in 2010-11 rose +10.6% yr/yr to 243.104 million cwt (hundred pounds), a new record high.

Demand – World utilization of rice in 2010-11 rose +2.6% to a record high of 446.466 million metric tons. U.S. rice consumption in 2010-11 rose +5.2% yr/yr to 129.0 million cwt (hundred pounds), a new record high.

Trade – World exports of rice in 2010-11 fell -0.5% yr/yr to a new record high of 30.569 metric tons. The world's largest rice exporters are Thailand with 32.7% of world exports, Vietnam with 19.6%, Pakistan with 8.7%, the U.S. with 11.7%, and India with 7.9%. U.S. rice imports in 2010-11 fell -5.3% yr/yr to 18.0 million cwt (hundred pounds), but still below the 2007-08 record high of 23.9 million cwt. U.S. rice exports in 2009-10 rose by +5.3% yr/yr to 116.0 million cwt.

World Rice Supply and Distribution In Thousands of Metric Tons

| | ---------------------------------- Imports ------------------------------------- | | | | | | | ----------- Utilization ------------ | | | ---------- Ending Stocks ---------- | | |
Crop Year	Brazil	Indo-nesia	European Union	Iran	Nigeria	Saudi Arabia	Total	China	India	Total	China	India	Total
2005-06	750	539	1,124	1,500	1,650	1,357	26,548	128,000	85,088	412,981	36,783	10,520	76,215
2006-07	732	2,000	1,340	1,500	1,500	958	28,282	127,200	86,700	418,622	35,915	11,430	74,757
2007-08	422	350	1,568	1,550	1,800	961	29,443	127,450	90,466	426,307	38,015	13,000	80,284
2008-09[1]	675	250	1,339	1,470	1,750	1,166	27,189	133,000	91,090	435,223	38,899	19,000	91,486
2009-10[2]	725	1,150	1,242	1,150	1,750	1,072	27,918	134,320	85,730	435,336	40,896	20,500	94,261
2010-11[3]	500	1,750	1,350	1,200	1,900	1,069	30,031	136,000	91,000	446,466	43,996	21,600	98,775

[1] Preliminary.   [2] Estimate.   [3] Forecast.   *Source: Foreign Agricultural Service, U.S. Department of Agriculture (FAS-USDA)*

World Production of Rough Rice In Thousands of Metric Tons

Year	Bang-ladesh	Brazil	Burma	China	India	Indo-nesia	Japan	Korea	Pakistan	Philip-pines	Thailand	Vietnam	World Total
2005-06	43,141	11,579	18,000	180,591	137,699	54,200	11,342	6,435	8,321	15,109	27,576	34,503	623,831
2006-07	43,504	11,316	18,276	181,714	140,039	54,729	10,695	6,306	8,176	15,516	27,652	34,730	627,004
2007-08	43,204	12,057	18,500	186,034	145,050	57,364	10,893	5,962	8,551	16,633	30,000	36,932	647,195
2008-09[1]	46,505	12,603	17,500	191,900	148,785	59,395	11,029	6,545	10,351	17,071	30,076	38,904	670,525
2009-10[2]	46,505	11,260	18,271	195,100	133,708	57,276	10,592	6,643	10,201	15,511	30,697	39,966	660,613
2010-11[3]	48,455	12,794	18,103	199,000	141,764	58,594	10,604	5,811	7,501	16,429	30,833	39,973	676,259

[1] Preliminary.   [2] Estimate.   [3] Forecast.   *Source: Foreign Agricultural Service, U.S. Department of Agriculture (FAS-USDA)*

World Exports of Rice (Milled Basis) In Thousands of Metric Tons

Year	Argentina	Australia	Burma	China	European Union	Guyana	India	Pakistan	Thailand	Uruguay	Vietnam	United States	World Total
2005-06	485	326	47	1,216	161	170	4,688	3,664	7,376	834	4,705	3,623	29,684
2006-07	452	166	31	1,340	148	190	5,740	2,839	9,557	734	4,522	2,886	31,395
2007-08	443	36	541	969	152	254	4,654	2,982	10,011	778	4,649	3,305	31,237
2008-09[1]	554	15	1,052	783	140	185	2,090	2,910	8,570	987	5,950	3,004	28,912
2009-10[2]	430	40	445	619	228	244	1,900	4,000	9,000	700	6,734	3,466	30,724
2010-11[3]	700	350	200	600	180	275	2,400	2,650	10,000	950	6,000	3,565	30,569

[1] Preliminary.   [2] Estimate.   [3] Forecast.   *Source: Foreign Agricultural Service, U.S. Department of Agriculture (FAS-USDA)*

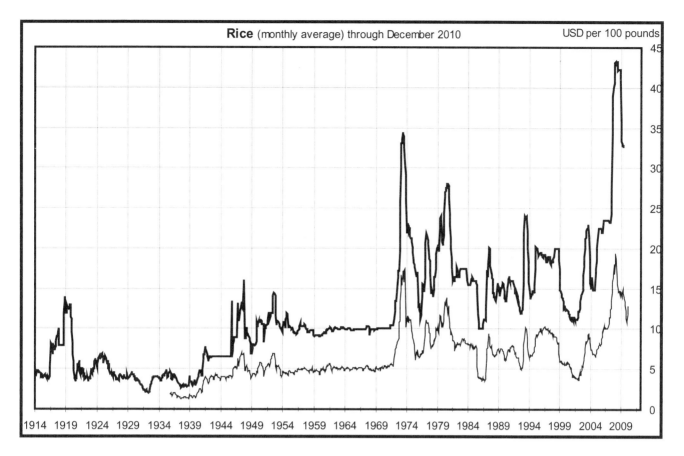

Rice (monthly average) through December 2010   USD per 100 pounds

Average Wholesale Price of Rice No. 2 (Medium)[1] Southwest Louisiana   In Dollars Per Cwt. Bagged

Year	Jan.	Feb.	Mar.	Apr.	May	June	July	Aug.	Sept.	Oct.	Nov.	Dec.	Average
2000-01	13.00	12.34	12.48	12.41	12.38	12.38	12.25	12.00	11.82	11.53	11.25	11.25	12.09
2001-02	11.06	11.50	11.50	11.50	11.08	11.50	11.50	11.43	10.94	11.13	11.13	11.13	11.28
2002-03	11.13	11.50	12.25	12.25	12.25	12.63	13.50	14.05	14.25	14.44	14.50	14.88	13.13
2003-04	16.75	17.70	19.00	19.95	21.25	21.38	22.30	22.46	22.50	23.00	21.50	21.50	20.77
2004-05	18.60	15.69	15.23	15.13	15.13	16.31	14.88	14.88	14.88	14.88	14.88	14.94	15.45
2005-06	17.00	17.50	18.45	20.13	21.38	22.50	22.50	22.50	22.50	22.50	22.50	22.35	20.98
2006-07	21.94	22.00	22.00	23.50	23.50	23.50	23.50	23.50	23.50	23.50	23.50	23.50	23.12
2007-08	23.50	23.50	23.30	23.25	23.25	23.25	24.31	27.45	34.00	39.00	40.00	40.00	28.73
2008-09	40.63	43.10	43.25	43.06	42.88	43.25	43.25	42.15	42.25	42.25	42.25	42.25	42.55
2009-10[2]	41.05	35.75	33.25	33.05	32.75	32.75	32.63						34.46

[1] U.S. No. 2 -- broken not to exceed 4%.   [2] Preliminary.   *Source: Economic Research Service, U.S. Department of Agriculture (ERS-USDA)*

Average Price Received by Farmers for Rice (Rough) in the United States   In Dollars Per Hundred Pounds (Cwt.)

Year	Jan.	Feb.	Mar.	Apr.	May	June	July	Aug.	Sept.	Oct.	Nov.	Dec.	Average[2]
2001-02	5.10	4.78	4.36	4.08	4.07	4.30	4.16	3.99	3.94	3.98	3.92	3.81	4.21
2002-03	3.71	3.94	3.69	3.70	4.13	4.66	4.24	4.31	4.61	4.84	5.43	5.31	4.38
2003-04	5.47	6.18	6.44	6.99	7.57	8.57	8.23	8.45	8.65	9.30	9.37	8.79	7.83
2004-05	8.96	8.47	7.60	7.36	7.37	7.39	6.90	6.97	6.98	6.98	6.96	6.82	7.40
2005-06	6.58	6.76	6.99	7.46	7.49	7.80	8.02	8.05	8.16	8.03	8.41	8.18	7.66
2006-07	8.81	9.03	9.65	10.10	9.91	10.40	10.10	10.00	10.20	10.00	10.00	10.10	9.86
2007-08	10.10	10.30	10.70	11.40	11.50	12.40	12.60	13.60	14.60	15.90	16.50	16.80	13.03
2008-09	18.10	16.90	18.10	19.40	18.60	18.20	16.00	15.60	15.00	14.60	14.70	14.20	16.62
2009-10	14.70	14.60	14.30	14.00	14.40	15.00	14.80	14.00	13.80	13.50	12.90	12.30	14.03
2010-11[1]	11.30	10.80	11.10	11.80	12.80	12.90	13.90						12.09

[1] Preliminary.   [2] Weighted average by sales.   *Source: Economic Research Service, U.S. Department of Agriculture (ERS-USDA)*

RICE

Salient Statistics of Rice, Rough & Milled (Rough Equivalent) in the United States   In Millions of Cwt.

Crop Year Beginning Aug. 1	Supply				Disappearance						Government Support Program						
					Domestic							Put Under Price Support	Loan Rate ($ Per Cwt.)			
	Stocks Aug. 1	Pro-duction	Imports	Total Supply	Food	Brewers	Seed	Total	Resi-dual	Exports	Total Disap-pearance	CCC Stocks July 31		Rough[3]			Milled Long
														Long	Med-ium	All Classes	
2005-06	37.9	223.2	17.1	277.8	114.4	[4]	3.5	117.9	[4]	116.8	234.7	0	----	6.66	6.04	6.50	10.54
2006-07	43.1	193.7	20.6	258.3	123.2	[4]	3.4	126.6	[4]	92.3	218.9	0	----	6.64	6.07	6.50	10.52
2007-08	39.4	198.4	23.9	261.7	121.8	[4]	3.7	125.5	[4]	106.6	232.1	0	----	6.57	6.37	6.50	10.12
2008-09	29.6	203.7	19.2	252.6	122.5	[4]	3.9	126.4	[4]	95.6	222.0	0	----	6.54	6.52	6.50	10.00
2009-10[1]	30.6	219.9	19.0	269.4	118.1	[4]	4.5	122.6	[4]	110.2	232.7	0	----	6.63	6.52	6.50	9.94
2010-11[2]	36.7	243.1	18.0	297.8				129.0		116.0	245.0	0	----				

[1] Preliminary.   [2] Forecast.   [3] Loan rate for each class of rice is the sum of the whole kernels' loan rate weighted by its milling yield (average 56%) and the broken kernels' loan rate weighted by its milling yield (average 12%).   [4] Included in Food.
Source: Economic Research Service, U.S. Department of Agriculture (ERS-USDA)

Acreage, Yield, Production and Prices of Rice in the United States

Crop Year Beginning Aug. 1	Acreage Harvested 1,000 Acres			Yield Per Harvested Acre (In Lbs.)			Production 1,000 Cwt.			Value of Pro-duction ($1,000)	Wholesale Prices $ Per Cwt.		Milled Rice, Average C.I.F. Rotterdam		
	Southern States	Cali-fornia	United States	Cali-fornia	United States	Southern States	Cali-fornia	United States		Arkan-sas[2]	Hous-ton[2]	U.S. No. 2[4] $ Per Metric Ton	Thai "A"[5]	Thai "B"[5]
2005-06	2,838	526	3,364	7,380	6,636	184,399	38,836	223,235	1,741,721	20.52	17.53	293	----	NA
2006-07	2,298	523	2,821	7,660	6,868	153,696	40,040	193,736	1,990,783	22.18	21.10			
2007-08	2,215	533	2,748	8,220	7,185	154,704	43,684	198,388	2,600,871	29.92	29.58			
2008-09	2,459	517	2,976	8,320	6,846	160,703	43,030	203,733	3,603,460	45.05	33.01			
2009-10	2,547	556	3,103	8,600	7,085	172,046	47,804	219,850	3,209,236	33.24	26.67			
2010-11[1]	3,062	553	3,615	8,020	6,725	198,778	44,326	243,104	3,074,990					

[1] Preliminary.   [2] F.O.B. mills, Arkansas, medium.   [3] Houston, Texas (long grain).   [4] Milled, 4%, container, FAS.
[5] SWR, 100%, bulk.   NA = Not available.   *Source: Economic Research Service, U.S. Department of Agriculture (ERS-USDA)*

U.S. Exports of Milled Rice, by Country of Destination   In Thousands of Metric Tons

Trade Year Beginning October	Canada	Haiti	Iran	Ivory Coast	Jamaica	Mexico	Nether-lands	Peru	Saudi Arabia	South Africa	Switzer-land	United Kingdom	Total
2004-05	230.8	299.1	0	32.6	48.2	725.8	44.8	45.7	101.4	.6	18.0	130.9	4,248
2005-06	236.9	340.3	0	25.0	53.5	822.3	38.2	1.7	93.4	.0	12.4	118.0	4,014
2006-07	243.9	279.3	0	0	42.6	810.2	4.0	.1	96.8	.7	.2	37.6	3,306
2007-08	251.5	314.1	0	15.0	56.4	783.0	6.2	2.9	150.0	20.2	1.0	63.5	3,899
2008-09	207.8	239.7	31.7	15.3	26.4	790.9	6.9	.3	129.8	.7	1.3	57.1	3,388
2009-10[1]	220.0	336.1	.0	.4	28.3	829.9	4.4	3.2	116.1	1.2	.5	65.4	4,265

[1] Preliminary.   *Source: Economic Research Service, U.S. Department of Agriculture (ERS-USDA)*

U.S. Rice Exports by Export Program   In Thousands of Metric Tons

Year	PL 480	Section 416	CCC Credit Pro-grams[2]	CCC African Relief Exports	EEP[3]	Export Pro-grams[4]	Exports Outside Specified Export Programs	Total U.S. Rice Exports	% Export Programs as a Share of Total Exports
2004	124	0	----	0	0	239	3,460	3,699	6
2005	128	0	----	0	0	159	4,099	4,258	4
2006	59	0	----	0	0	107	3,917	4,024	3
2007	103	0	----	0	0	142	3,174	3,316	4
2008	65	0	----	0	0	91	3,818	3,909	2
2009[1]	44	0	----	0	0	54	3,358	3,411	2

[1] Preliminary.   [2] May not completely reflect exports made under these programs.   [3] Sales not shipments.   [4] Adjusted for estimated overlap between CCC export credit and EEP shipments.   *Source: Economice Research Service, U.S. Department of Agriculture (ERS-USDA)*

Production of Rice (Rough) in the United States, by Type and Variety   In Thousands of Cwt.

Year	Long Grain	Medium Grain	Short Grain	Total	Year	Long Grain	Medium Grain	Short Grain	Total
2001	167,555	46,105	1,610	215,270	2006	146,214	43,802	3,720	193,736
2002	157,243	52,201	1,516	210,960	2007	143,235	51,063	4,090	198,388
2003	149,011	48,180	2,706	199,897	2008	153,257	47,166	3,310	203,733
2004	170,445	58,689	3,228	230,818	2009	152,725	63,291	3,834	219,850
2005	177,527	42,408	3,300	223,235	2010[1]	183,296	57,144	2,664	243,104

[1] Preliminary.   *Source: National Agricultural Statistics Service, U.S. Department of Agriculture (NASS-USDA)*

Rubber

Rubber is a natural or synthetic substance characterized by elasticity, water repellence, and electrical resistance. Pre-Columbian Native South Americans discovered many uses for rubber such as containers, balls, shoes, and waterproofing for fabrics such as coats and capes. The Spaniards tried to duplicate these products for many years but were unsuccessful. The first commercial application of rubber began in 1791 when Samuel Peal patented a method of waterproofing cloth by treating it with a solution of rubber and turpentine. In 1839, Charles Goodyear revolutionized the rubber industry with his discovery of a process called vulcanization, which involves combining rubber and sulfur and heating the mixture.

Natural rubber is obtained from latex, a milky white fluid, from the Hevea Brasiliensis tree. The latex is gathered by cutting a chevron shape through the bark of the rubber tree. The latex is collected in a small cup, with approximately 1 fluid ounce per cutting. The cuttings are usually done every other day until the cuttings reach the ground. The tree is then allowed to renew itself before a new tapping is started. The collected latex is strained, diluted with water, and treated with acid to bind the rubber particles together. The rubber is then pressed between rollers to consolidate the rubber into slabs or thin sheets and is air-dried or smoke-dried for shipment.

During World War II, natural rubber supplies from the Far East were cut off, and the rubber shortage accelerated the development of synthetic rubber in the U.S.. Synthetic rubber is produced by chemical reactions, condensation or polymerization, of certain unsaturated hydrocarbons. Synthetic rubber is made of raw material derived from petroleum, coal, oil, natural gas, and acetylene and is almost identical to natural rubber in chemical and physical properties.

Natural rubber and Rubber Index futures are traded on the Osaka Mercantile Exchange (OME). The OME's natural rubber contract is based on the RSS3 ribbed smoked sheet No. 3. The OME's Rubber Index Futures Contract is based on a composite of 8 component grades from 6 rubber markets in the world. Rubber futures are also traded on the Shanghai Futures Exchange (SHFE) and the Tokyo Commodity Exchange (TOCOM).

Prices – The average monthly price for spot crude rubber (No.1 smoked sheets, ribbed, plantation rubber), basis in New York, in 2010 (for two months annualized) was up by +80.7% to a record high of 175.93 cents per pound. A 3-decade low of 33.88 cents per pound was seen as recently as 2001 during that recessionary year.

Supply – World production of natural rubber in 2010 rose +6.1% to 10.291 million metric tons. The world's largest producers of natural rubber in 2010 were Thailand with 27.5% of world production, Indonesia (27.5%), Malaysia (9.1%), India (8.3%), Vietnam (7.3%), and China (6.3%).

In 2010, world production of synthetic rubber rose by +14.2% to 14.002 million metric tons. The world's largest producers of synthetic rubber in 2010 were the U.S. with 16.6% of world production, Japan (11.3%), Russia (8.2%), and Germany (6.7%). U.S. production of synthetic rubber in 2010 rose +18.3% to 2.322 million metric tons up from the 14-year low of 2.064 million metric tons posted in 2001. U.S. production of car and truck tires in 2007 (latest data) fell –6.8% to 186.000 million tires.

Demand – World consumption of natural rubber in 2010 rose by +14.4% to 10.671 million metric tons. The largest consumers of natural rubber in 2010 were the U.S. with 8.5% of consumption, Japan with 6.9%, and France, Germany, and the UK with a combined 6.0%. The world's consumption of natural rubber has tripled since 1970. World consumption of synthetic rubber in 2010 rose by +15.2% to 13.751 million metric tons. The largest consumers of synthetic rubber in 2010 were the U.S. with 12.6% of consumption, Japan with 7.1%, and France, Germany, and the UK with a combined 7.2%. The world's consumption of synthetic rubber has more than doubled since 1970.

U.S. consumption of natural rubber in 2010 rose by +32.2% to 908,200 thousand metric tons. U.S. consumption of natural rubber has more than doubled since 1970. U.S. consumption of synthetic rubber in 2010 rose +19.6% to 1.731 million metric tons. The U.S. consumption of synthetic rubber has remained about the same as it was in 1970.

Trade – World exports of natural rubber in 2010 rose +10.4% to a record 7.083 million metric tons. The world's largest exporters of natural rubber in 2010 were Thailand with 37.9% of world exports and Indonesia with 33.6% of world exports. U.S. imports of natural rubber in 2010 rose +4.7% to 989,493 thousand metric tons. U.S. exports of synthetic rubber in 2010 rose +19.2% to 1.163 million metric tons, below the 2007 record high of 1.317 million metric tons.

U.S. Imports of Natural Rubber (Includes Latex & Guayule)   In Thousands of Metric Tons

Year	Jan.	Feb.	Mar.	Apr.	May	June	July	Aug.	Sept.	Oct.	Nov.	Dec.	Total
2001	89.9	70.9	97.4	81.3	82.7	65.2	102.6	111.1	71.4	94.1	70.5	64.7	1,001.8
2002	106.5	73.2	80.3	92.4	109.2	91.2	109.8	191.8	82.6	96.3	100.9	79.1	1,213.3
2003	106.8	88.3	112.8	105.9	94.7	100.9	99.0	71.5	104.7	80.7	69.1	85.8	1,120.3
2004	116.8	77.5	103.2	97.3	113.3	92.8	86.4	83.3	86.7	125.9	71.9	102.8	1,158.1
2005	100.4	102.7	97.7	116.1	81.3	96.3	84.7	95.8	111.8	92.9	85.2	104.1	1,169.1
2006	113.9	72.5	99.7	81.1	119.2	70.0	73.4	98.0	59.4	84.9	81.6	58.0	1,011.7
2007	86.5	69.5	103.1	91.6	64.1	114.2	74.9	85.0	91.3	82.4	83.9	82.4	1,028.9
2008	75.0	97.3	66.1	115.8	90.2	79.1	97.1	100.7	95.2	78.9	78.4	78.6	1,052.3
2009	84.5	52.3	73.3	48.9	51.7	31.1	61.0	48.5	52.1	64.8	65.0	71.6	704.8
2010[1]	78.0	77.0	94.7	87.6	69.7	70.5	80.4	77.1	77.6	73.4	69.8	89.2	945.0

[1] Preliminary.   Source: International Rubber Study Group (IRSG)

RUBBER

World Production[1] of Rubber   In Thousands of Metric Tons

Year	China	India	Indonesia	Malaysia	Sri Lanka	Thailand	Vietnam	World Total Natural	Germany	Japan	United States	Russia	World Total Synthetic
2001	478.0	631.5	1,607.3	882.1	86.2	2,319.5	312.6	7,332	828.4	1,465.5	2,062.1	919.2	10,483
2002	527.0	640.8	1,630.0	889.8	90.5	2,615.1	331.4	7,326	869.2	1,522.0	2,164.4	919.0	10,877
2003	565.0	708.0	1,792.2	985.6	92.0	2,876.0	363.5	8,006	888.0	1,577.4	2,222.3	1,070.0	11,338
2004	573.0	742.6	2,066.2	1,168.7	94.7	2,984.3	419.0	8,744	905.0	1,616.1	2,288.9	1,116.1	11,977
2005	510.0	771.5	2,271.0	1,126.0	104.4	2,937.2	481.6	8,907	855.0	1,626.9	2,312.2	1,146.0	12,073
2006	533.0	853.3	2,637.0	1,283.6	109.2	3,137.0	555.4	9,827	865.0	1,607.0	2,569.4	1,219.0	12,629
2007	590.0	811.1	2,755.2	1,199.6	117.5	3,056.0	605.8	9,890	803.0	1,654.6	2,658.0	1,209.9	13,376
2008	560.0	881.3	2,751.0	1,072.4	129.2	3,089.8	660.0	10,128	791.0	1,651.0	2,275.3	1,173.1	12,741
2009	644.0	820.3	2,440.0	856.2	137.0	3,164.4	723.7	9,702	743.0	1,303.2	1,962.0	971.1	12,261
2010[2]	650.0	851.0	2,828.7	939.0	150.0	3,072.0	750.0	10,291	935.0	1,578.0	2,322.0	1,153.6	14,002

[1] Including rubber in the form of latex.   [2] Preliminary.   *Source: International Rubber Study Group (IRSG)*

World Consumption of Natural and Synthetic Rubber   In Thousands of Metric Tons

Year	Brazil	France	Germany	Japan	United Kingdom	United States	Total Natural	France	Germany	Japan	United Kingdom	United States	Total Synthetic
2001	215.9	282.0	246.0	729.2	98.0	974.1	7,333	464.5	613.0	1,085.1	167.0	1,839.5	10,253
2002	233.4	230.6	247.0	749.0	76.0	1,110.8	7,556	469.3	612.0	1,096.0	210.0	1,895.0	10,874
2003	255.5	218.1	258.1	784.2	90.9	1,078.5	7,937	493.2	615.0	1,110.7	203.9	1,926.4	11,350
2004	284.9	230.1	242.3	814.8	86.3	1,143.6	8,716	420.1	624.5	1,146.3	213.5	1,906.8	11,861
2005	301.8	230.0	258.9	857.4	82.3	1,159.2	9,206	354.9	635.0	1,156.0	222.3	2,002.1	11,871
2006	294.3	219.6	268.9	873.7	67.7	1,003.1	9,690	310.8	635.0	1,170.8	200.6	2,000.8	12,668
2007	344.9	220.1	281.7	887.4	90.8	1,018.4	10,176	316.0	599.0	1,162.2	168.7	1,890.3	13,243
2008	357.2	199.6	246.9	877.9	76.8	1,041.0	10,171	316.0	586.0	1,137.6	148.6	1,694.9	12,616
2009	279.4	108.9	174.6	635.6	42.7	687.1	9,325	236.8	417.0	831.9	133.3	1,447.7	11,941
2010[1]	374.0	136.1	289.2	739.4	54.9	908.1	10,671	305.5	555.0	980.0	142.9	1,731.9	13,751

[1] Preliminary.   *Source: International Rubber Study Group (IRSG)*

World Stocks[1] of Natural & Synthetic Rubber (by Countries) on January 1   In Thousands of Metric Tons

Year	Total Synthetic	Africa	Indo-nesia	Malaysia	Sri Lanka	Thailand	Vietnam	Total Natural	Brazil	India	Japan	United States	Total
1999	1,116	25.3	30	234.2	18.6	209.5	30.0	750	13.0	194.0	58.0	70.4	406
2000	1,103	28.2	33	236.6	18.6	250.9	32.0	929	34.0	215.1	79.1	46.0	475
2001	1,159	11.8	50	151.1	18.7	188.6	15.0	568	40.0	203.3	95.2	44.6	484
2002	1,139	11.4	30	138.3	19.0	214.9	12.0	527	40.0	225.5	46.9	42.6	427
2003	1,161	11.1	20	135.6	19.0	198.5	14.0	460	40.0	151.7	65.0	42.1	299
2004	1,127	10.8	10	162.6	19.0	204.1	19.0	459	40.0	123.3	73.0	40.6	277
2005	1,015	12.0	20	195.0	19.0	234.4	38.0	549	40.0	122.9	58.1	40.6	262
2006	1,004	11.3	60	164.1	19.0	206.1	2.0	497	40.0	114.5	49.3	40.6	244
2007	943	10.7	60	188.0	18.7	251.9	19.0	570	40.0	140.9	60.4	40.6	282
2008[1]	1,223	10.7	60	155.9	18.7	232.0	16.0	516	40.0	195.9	20.4	40.6	297

[1] Preliminary.   *Source: International Rubber Study Group (IRSG)*

Net Exports of Natural Rubber from Producing Areas   In Thousands of Metric Tons

Year	Cambodia	Guatemala[4]	Indo-nesia	Liberia	Malaysia	Nigeria	Sri Lanka	Thailand	Vietnam	Other Africa[2]	Other Asia[3]	Total
2001	38.0	33.0	1,496.9	71.7	345.2	30.0	32.0	2,042.1	270.0	212.4	85.5	5,193
2002	44.3	40.1	1,502.2	109.0	887.0	24.0	36.1	2,354.4	454.8	199.8	91.0	5,158
2003	36.3	41.0	1,660.5	107.0	946.5	22.0	35.2	2,573.5	432.3	211.8	101.2	5,646
2004	32.4	52.9	1,875.1	114.5	1,106.1	29.0	40.3	2,637.1	513.4	220.0	91.9	6,183
2005	28.3	54.6	2,025.1	111.0	1,143.3	25.0	31.6	2,632.4	554.1	250.7	97.3	6,392
2006	25.4	55.4	2,290.3	93.5	1,285.2	24.0	45.8	2,771.6	703.6	275.4	92.8	7,019
2007	24.8	68.7	2,415.7	120.8	1,212.9	24.5	49.5	2,703.8	715.6	292.2	106.5	6,945
2008	14.5	73.4	2,297.3	84.8	1,154.5	25.9	46.2	2,675.3	659.3	321.2	112.0	6,838
2009	36.4	77.6	2,061.3	59.5	1,087.7	31.7	53.7	2,726.2	731.4	330.7	101.7	6,415
2010[1]	45.9	75.9	2,380.1	62.1	1,249.5	43.3	50.3	2,683.0	783.7	359.2	734.6	7,083

[1] Preliminary.   [2] Includes Cameroon, Cote d'Ivoire, Gabon, Ghana and Zaire.   [3] Includes Myanmar, Papua New Guinea and the Philippines.
Source: International Rubber Study Group (IRSG)

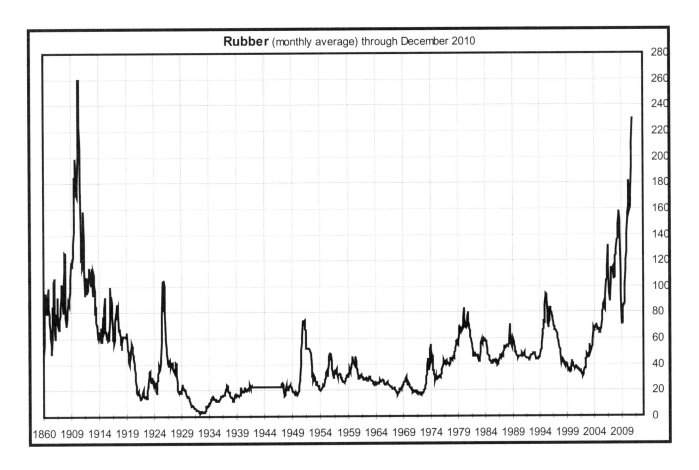

Rubber (monthly average) through December 2010

Average Spot Crude Rubber Prices (Smoked Sheets[1]) in New York   In Cents Per Pound

Year	Jan.	Feb.	Mar.	Apr.	May	June	July	Aug.	Sept.	Oct.	Nov.	Dec.	Average
2003	47.95	49.25	54.96	52.04	49.32	51.76	51.99	53.71	57.61	65.88	67.63	65.20	55.61
2004	65.63	67.28	68.09	68.84	70.40	69.90	68.10	66.50	66.39	67.30	66.80	63.90	67.43
2005	64.20	66.18	66.80	66.70	68.07	73.75	80.50	82.34	85.51	87.90	83.75	81.99	75.64
2006	93.04	104.01	104.48	105.20	115.03	131.74	124.01	114.94	95.17	94.77	87.95	88.53	104.91
2007	104.90	113.90	109.86	112.81	114.76	111.72	105.30	106.90	106.49	113.29	123.08	123.85	112.24
2008	127.94	134.87	135.39	136.24	147.26	156.21	158.67	150.99	143.99	110.66	95.41	70.38	130.67
2009	77.06	75.16	73.44	83.31	86.10	85.06	86.81	101.20	112.81	120.12	126.69	140.60	97.36
2010	151.99	155.74	162.04	180.86	169.91	168.31	158.61	161.69	170.35	191.84	210.61	229.20	175.93

[1] No. 1, ribbed, plantation rubber.   *Source: International Rubber Study Group (IRSG)*

Natural Rubber Prices in London

Year	Jan.	Feb.	Mar.	Apr.	May	June	July	Aug.	Sept.	Oct.	Nov.	Dec.	Average
Buyers' Price RSS 1 (CIF)		In British Pounds per Metric Ton											
2006	2,051.1	2,293.1	2,303.3	2,319.2	2,536.0	2,904.3	2,734.0	2,533.9	2,098.2	2,089.4	1,938.9	1,951.7	2,312.8
2007	2,312.7	2,511.1	2,421.9	2,487.0	2,530.1	2,463.0	2,321.5	2,356.8	2,347.6	2,497.5	2,713.5	2,730.4	2,474.4
2008	2,820.6	2,973.3	2,984.9	3,003.5	3,246.6	3,443.7	3,498.1	3,328.7	3,174.4	2,439.6	2,103.5	1,551.6	2,880.7
2009	1,698.9	1,656.9	1,619.1	1,836.7	1,898.1	1,875.2	1,913.9	2,231.1	2,487.0	2,648.2	2,793.1	3,099.6	2,146.5
2010	3,350.8	3,433.4	3,572.4	3,987.2	3,745.9	3,710.5	3,496.7	3,564.7	3,755.6	4,229.3	4,643.2	5,052.9	3,878.6
Buyers' Prices RSS 3 (CIF)		In Euro per Metric Ton											
2006	1,657.1	1,840.3	1,846.7	1,864.2	2,016.0	2,267.5	2,112.0	1,839.5	1,487.3	1,511.1	1,327.8	1,356.6	1,760.5
2007	1,652.3	1,800.8	1,741.9	1,766.8	1,765.0	1,721.8	1,558.0	1,607.0	1,621.5	1,707.2	1,761.8	1,776.2	1,706.7
2008	1,850.6	1,948.5	1,860.5	1,849.1	2,010.9	2,119.8	2,092.4	2,030.8	2,064.1	1,549.6	1,373.0	952.0	1,808.4
2009	1,178.7	1,197.0	1,138.5	1,273.8	1,286.7	1,246.9	1,284.8	1,487.6	1,530.2	1,629.3	1,749.6	1,963.6	1,413.9
2010	2,223.6	2,337.4	2,492.1	2,958.1	2,923.8	2,908.9	2,635.9	2,615.5	2,749.2	2,889.4	3,206.0	3,634.3	2,797.9
Sellers' Prices SMR 20 (CIF)		In Euro per Metric Ton											
2006	1,564.6	1,727.5	1,704.7	1,694.2	1,788.7	1,952.6	1,949.4	1,797.4	1,490.4	1,475.6	1,313.3	1,294.3	1,646.1
2007	1,547.5	1,688.5	1,599.0	1,541.6	1,678.7	1,622.3	1,532.3	1,565.7	1,679.5	1,654.6	1,691.0	1,723.6	1,627.0
2008	1,790.5	1,902.9	1,795.7	1,782.2	1,959.4	2,089.9	2,087.0	2,014.6	2,030.8	1,510.0	1,357.5	947.4	1,772.3
2009	1,121.2	1,066.4	1,029.7	1,174.9	1,196.2	1,143.5	1,182.9	1,342.8	1,465.6	1,580.3	1,713.8	1,957.9	1,331.3
2010	2,174.5	2,306.4	2,386.7	2,510.5	2,338.6	2,438.6	2,343.1	2,484.0	2,633.1	2,834.6	3,162.4	3,592.3	2,600.4

Source: International Rubber Study Group (IRSG)

RUBBER

Consumption of Natural Rubber in the United States   In Thousands of Metric Tons

Year	Jan.	Feb.	Mar.	Apr.	May	June	July	Aug.	Sept.	Oct.	Nov.	Dec.	Total
2001	85.5	69.4	94.1	80.2	75.1	64.1	101.2	109.3	70.0	92.4	69.4	63.4	974.1
2002	104.9	71.3	79.2	90.4	106.3	92.3	108.7	109.7	81.2	94.7	83.1	89.0	1,110.8
2003	104.2	86.3	106.9	100.1	91.2	97.7	94.6	67.5	101.3	69.9	72.5	86.3	1,078.5
2004	116.0	76.5	101.5	96.5	112.5	92.5	87.5	82.0	86.0	120.0	71.0	101.8	1,143.8
2005	99.8	101.9	97.1	115.5	80.9	95.7	84.5	91.7	113.5	92.2	82.7	103.7	1,159.2
2006	113.3	71.8	98.9	80.5	115.6	72.5	72.4	97.3	58.7	83.0	82.0	57.2	1,003.2
2007	86.1	67.7	102.1	90.7	63.4	113.3	74.3	83.8	90.6	81.8	80.3	84.3	1,018.4
2008	74.1	96.6	65.3	115.0	89.0	77.8	96.3	99.5	94.0	78.0	77.8	77.6	1,041.0
2009	82.3	51.4	71.7	47.7	50.1	29.2	59.7	46.9	50.6	63.1	63.7	70.6	687.0
2010[1]	76.5	76.0	76.0	86.0	68.0	68.6	78.6	75.4	75.6	71.8	68.1	87.6	908.2

[1] Preliminary.   Source: International Rubber Study Group (IRSG)

Stocks of Natural Rubber in the United States, on First of Month   In Thousands of Metric Tons

Year	Jan.	Feb.	Mar.	Apr.	May	June	July	Aug.	Sept.	Oct.	Nov.	Dec.
1998	57.2	61.2	65.5	63.5	60.9	66.7	53.6	57.9	54.7	58.3	58.9	66.5
1999	70.4	68.0	66.0	64.0	62.0	60.0	58.0	56.0	54.0	52.0	50.0	48.0
2000	46.0	63.4	41.6	45.7	39.6	40.5	46.6	32.5	48.7	47.9	51.1	50.3
2001	46.6	44.3	44.0	43.8	43.6	43.4	43.1	43.0	42.9	42.8	42.8	42.6
2002	42.6	42.5	42.4	42.4	42.8	42.6	42.5	42.4	42.4	42.3	42.3	42.2
2003	42.1	42.0	41.9	41.8	41.5	41.7	41.6	41.5	41.4	40.2	40.9	40.7
2004	40.6	40.8	40.9	40.9	40.9	40.9	40.9	40.9	40.9	40.9	40.9	40.9
2005	40.6	40.6	40.6	40.6	40.6	40.6	40.6	40.6	40.6	40.6	40.6	40.6
2006	40.6	40.6	40.6	40.6	40.6	40.6	40.6	40.6	40.6	40.6	40.6	40.6
2007[1]	40.6	40.6	40.6	40.6	40.6	40.6	40.6	40.6	40.6	40.6	40.6	40.6

[1] Preliminary.   Source: International Rubber Study Group (IRSG)

Stocks of Synthetic Rubber in the United States, on First of Month   In Thousands of Metric Tons

Year	Jan.	Feb.	Mar.	Apr.	May	June	July	Aug.	Sept.	Oct.	Nov.	Dec.
1998	377.7	382.2	375.7	379.5	387.5	402.8	394.6	406.8	394.2	398.7	395.7	396.5
1999	409.3	404.0	404.0	406.0	399.0	420.0	410.0	419.0	413.0	390.0	391.0	389.0
2000	406.0	416.0	413.0	402.0	405.0	416.0	409.0	418.0	400.0	412.0	407.0	419.0
2001	433.0	451.0	467.0	4,559.0	448.0	433.0	426.0	420.0	394.0	400.0	394.0	379.0
2002	392.0	377.0	379.0	393.0	398.0	384.0	385.0	381.0	364.0	375.0	364.0	358.0
2003	390.0	325.0	330.0	325.0	336.0	336.0	332.0	332.0	331.0	328.0	317.0	338.0
2004	343.0	347.0	335.0	315.0	310.0	300.0	300.0	290.0	280.0	280.0	280.0	270.0
2005	260.0	255.0	240.0	240.0	235.0	235.0	240.0	245.0	245.0	245.0	245.0	245.0
2006	248.0	240.0	225.0	215.0	210.0	210.0	210.0	210.0	210.0	210.0	210.0	210.0
2007[1]	210.0	210.0	210.0	210.0	210.0	210.0	210.0	210.0	210.0	210.0	210.0	210.0

[1] Preliminary.   Source: International Rubber Study Group (IRSG)

Production of Synthetic Rubber in the United States   In Thousands of Metric Tons

Year	Jan.	Feb.	Mar.	Apr.	May	June	July	Aug.	Sept.	Oct.	Nov.	Dec.	Total
2001	203.0	188.6	184.3	172.1	175.5	162.3	166.7	164.7	174.3	178.6	155.1	139.2	2,064
2002	176.1	171.9	192.3	190.6	187.0	184.6	183.5	177.3	175.1	175.0	160.4	176.4	2,150
2003	185.6	180.9	193.6	179.8	182.9	166.3	174.2	172.9	188.4	189.7	192.0	185.6	2,192
2004	208.3	199.0	203.5	193.5	187.1	183.5	183.5	184.1	193.5	198.5	202.1	188.5	2,325
2005	206.9	204.8	209.4	202.7	196.9	188.9	187.3	193.7	182.7	185.8	206.9	199.8	2,366
2006	212.9	213.7	212.9	210.2	227.5	217.8	218.1	218.2	218.5	218.3	220.4	214.9	2,603
2007	224.3	223.1	222.6	222.6	227.4	227.8	227.9	227.5	228.4	227.5	224.0	225.0	2,708
2008	220.9	216.3	209.2	211.1	210.9	205.8	200.7	191.1	176.6	170.0	155.8	146.0	2,314
2009	116.5	136.8	146.7	151.1	165.9	176.2	180.9	185.6	190.5	184.9	166.9	160.0	1,962
2010[1]	165.0	185.0	180.0	185.0	195.0	202.0	198.0	200.2	204.8	212.0	204.0	191.0	2,322

[1] Preliminary.   Source: International Rubber Study Group (IRSG)

Consumption of Synthetic Rubber in the United States   In Thousands of Metric Tons

Year	Jan.	Feb.	Mar.	Apr.	May	June	July	Aug.	Sept.	Oct.	Nov.	Dec.	Total
2001	170.8	149.6	166.8	153.3	159.8	148.6	156.4	173.0	145.7	162.7	140.8	112.0	1,840
2002	155.5	146.8	153.0	165.8	173.4	160.4	161.5	169.3	154.8	166.7	148.2	139.6	1,895
2003	166.1	156.4	167.7	157.8	162.0	163.0	163.3	152.3	159.0	175.6	147.3	155.9	1,926
2004	170.0	166.2	176.0	156.5	152.2	141.9	158.8	149.2	152.9	155.0	170.0	158.1	1,907
2005	174.7	184.0	180.6	171.5	156.8	147.9	145.2	148.9	153.7	161.2	166.8	163.3	1,955
2006	173.7	182.7	178.0	170.7	172.2	167.4	157.7	158.1	161.5	161.5	160.9	156.6	2,001
2007	157.8	155.0	155.6	164.6	163.8	166.1	165.6	160.4	166.6	163.6	163.0	158.4	1,941
2008	149.8	145.9	150.1	146.0	148.8	154.6	151.6	150.4	142.2	136.0	133.5	125.2	1,734
2009	118.9	108.7	105.8	114.7	111.0	116.7	112.3	142.5	151.3	133.8	122.7	109.3	1,448
2010[1]	118.6	131.9	143.8	131.6	154.3	158.9	152.5	150.5	162.4	154.7	142.8	129.9	1,732

[1] Preliminary.   Source: International Rubber Study Group (IRSG)

U.S. Exports of Synthetic Rubber   In Thousands of Metric Tons

Year	Jan.	Feb.	Mar.	Apr.	May	June	July	Aug.	Sept.	Oct.	Nov.	Dec.	Total
2001	74.6	67.3	76.4	78.2	75.1	69.6	70.6	71.6	68.1	70.7	62.4	59.4	844.4
2002	67.9	71.6	69.5	74.9	78.5	73.6	74.5	72.8	70.9	73.1	70.8	66.3	864.4
2003	73.1	70.1	80.1	85.2	78.4	75.3	74.4	72.4	73.9	83.7	74.5	79.3	920.4
2004	82.0	87.3	97.0	90.9	96.8	92.6	88.9	91.6	94.8	89.0	87.0	81.6	1,079.5
2005	86.3	89.6	91.8	98.4	98.3	96.9	91.5	100.4	76.4	87.0	101.3	87.5	1,105.4
2006	103.4	97.3	106.7	103.2	109.2	106.8	110.0	112.5	101.3	103.3	97.8	98.5	1,250.0
2007	110.5	108.6	118.0	107.8	116.0	109.7	108.8	112.9	106.3	111.7	104.1	102.1	1,316.5
2008	110.6	113.4	101.4	114.2	111.8	100.9	103.0	101.4	79.9	93.5	69.9	56.5	1,156.5
2009	56.2	59.6	71.3	79.2	84.0	92.2	97.4	88.3	87.7	92.5	83.5	84.0	975.9
2010[1]	85.6	95.4	93.5	102.4	100.7	99.4	95.0	99.7	92.5	99.8	102.7	96.9	1,163.6

[1] Preliminary.   Source: International Rubber Study Group (IRSG)

Production of Tyres (Car and Truck) in the United States   In Thousands of Units

Year	First Quarter	Second Quarter	Third Quarter	Fourth Quarter	Total	Year	First Quarter	Second Quarter	Third Quarter	Fourth Quarter	Total
1988	54,677	52,986	51,195	52,493	211,351	1998	----	----	----	----	270,905
1989	56,716	56,626	50,086	49,444	212,870	1999	----	----	----	----	267,652
1990	55,915	53,856	51,163	49,729	210,663	2000	----	----	----	----	276,765
1991	51,296	52,796	49,183	51,115	202,391	2001	65,367	62,809	62,366	56,106	255,700
1992	57,890	57,319	57,554	57,487	230,250	2002	62,937	64,362	60,524	58,241	246,064
1993	61,809	60,752	57,702	57,184	237,447	2003	62,686	59,311	58,441	55,565	236,003
1994	63,586	63,331	57,018	59,442	243,696	2004	60,272	59,774	58,389	54,824	233,259
1995	63,800	63,800	63,800	63,754	255,521	2005	57,377	58,832	54,920	52,074	223,203
1996	64,000	64,000	64,000	63,700	255,723	2006[1]	56,787	53,452	49,612	39,636	199,487
1997	----	----	----	----	263,860	2007[2]	46,600	44,500	45,700	49,200	186,000

[1] Preliminary.   [2] Estimate.   Source: International Rubber Study Group (IRSG)

U.S. Foreign Trade of Tyres (Car and Truck)   In Thousands of Units

Year	Imports First Quarter	Second Quarter	Third Quarter	Fourth Quarter	Total	Exports First Quarter	Second Quarter	Third Quarter	Fourth Quarter	Total
1998	17,046	17,728	18,016	19,346	72,124	12,840	10,678	10,018	10,372	43,923
1999	19,471	22,295	22,194	23,784	87,768	9,874	9,580	10,480	10,537	40,945
2000	24,200	24,698	23,561	22,123	94,019	11,200	10,200	10,200	10,100	44,164
2001	19,563	22,251	22,072	20,956	84,842	10,087	10,362	11,004	10,691	42,144
2002	21,554	25,831	24,868	24,950	97,203	10,438	10,379	10,167	10,380	41,363
2003	26,310	28,557	28,472	27,536	110,875	9,293	2,648	10,263	10,794	32,998
2004	28,996	31,998	30,788	32,707	124,489	10,272	10,902	10,108	10,299	41,581
2005	32,704	36,924	34,391	33,584	137,603	9,808	10,071	10,659	10,570	41,108
2006[1]	34,562	36,863	34,638	36,136	142,199	9,021	9,328	9,388	9,236	36,973
2007[2]	35,984	39,428	38,778	38,273	152,463	8,922	9,360	9,539	9,417	37,238

[1] Preliminary.   [2] Estimate.   Source: International Rubber Study Group (IRSG)

Rye

Rye is a cereal grain and a member of the grass family. Hardy varieties of rye have been developed for winter planting. Rye is most widely grown in northern Europe and Asia. In the U.S., rye is used as an animal feed and as an ingredient in bread and some whiskeys. Bread using rye was developed in northern Europe in the Middle Ages where bakers developed dark, hearty bread consisting of rye, oat and barley flours. Those were crops that grew more readily in the wet and damp climate of northern Europe, as opposed to wheat which fares better in the warmer and drier climates in central Europe. Modern rye bread is made with a mixture of white and rye flours. Coarsely ground rye flour is also used in pumpernickel bread and helps provide the dark color and course texture, along with molasses. The major producing states are North and South Dakota, Oklahoma, and Georgia. The crop year runs from June to May.

Supply – World rye production in 2010-11 marketing year fell by -31.1% yr/yr to 11.943 million metric tons, down from the 2006-07 record low of 12.402 million metric tons. The world's largest producers of rye are the European Union with 64.9% of world production in 2010-11, followed by Russia with 13.8%, Belarus with 10.0%, and the Ukraine with 3.8%. U.S. production of rye accounted for only 1.6% of world production.

U.S. production of rye in 2010 rose +6.3% to 7.431 million bushels but that was far below the production levels of over 20 million bushels seen from the late 1800s through the 1960s. U.S. production of rye fell off in the 1970s, and fell to a record low of 6.488 million bushels in 2002.

U.S. acreage harvested with rye in 2009-10 rose +5.2% to 265,000 acres. U.S. farmers in the late 1800s through the 1960s typically harvested more than 1 million acres of rye, showing how domestic planting of rye has dropped off sharply in the past several decades. Rye yield in 2010-11 rose +0.7% to 28.0 bushels per acre, and that is still well below the record high of 33.1 bushels per acre posted in 1984-85. Modern rye production yields are, however, more than double the levels in the teens seen prior to the 1960s when yields started to rise.

Demand – Total U.S. domestic usage of rye in 2009-10 (latest data) rose +2.6% yr/yr to 11.802 million bushels. The breakdown of domestic usage shows that 28% of rye in 2009-10 was used for food, 25.4% by industry, 25.4% as seed, and 21.2% as feed and residual.

Trade – World exports of rye in the 2010-11 marketing year rose +76.4% yr/yr to 605.000 metric tons, up from the record low of 270,000 metric tons last year. The largest exporters were Canada and the European Union, each with exports of 125,000 metric tons. World imports of rye rose +115.1% to 527,000 metric tons. U.S. imports of rye in 2010-11 rose +5.6% yr/yr to 114,000 metric tons.

World Production of Rye   In Thousands of Metric Tons

Crop Year	Argentina	Australia	Belarus	Canada	European Union	Kazakhstan	Romania	Russia	Switzerland	Turkey	Ukraine	United States	World Total
2001-02	81	20	1,294	228	11,956	43	----	6,600	20	220	1,822	175	22,529
2002-03	80	20	1,600	134	9,255	106	----	7,150	20	255	1,511	165	20,366
2003-04	37	20	1,200	327	6,972	42	----	4,200	20	240	625	219	13,976
2004-05	89	20	1,400	398	10,031	20	----	2,850	20	270	1,600	210	17,007
2005-06	55	20	1,150	330	7,688	24	----	3,600	20	270	1,050	191	14,493
2006-07	55	20	1,200	383	6,541	30	----	3,000	20	271	600	183	12,380
2007-08	77	20	1,300	252	7,679	68	----	3,900	20	265	550	160	14,392
2008-09[1]	55	20	1,500	316	9,262	40	----	4,500	20	250	1,050	203	17,326
2009-10[2]	55	20	1,700	280	9,388	75	----	4,300	20	270	950	178	17,323
2010-11[3]	45	20	1,200	216	7,747	50	----	1,650	20	270	450	189	11,943

[1] Preliminary. [2] Estimate. [3] Forecast.   Source: Foreign Agricultural Service, U.S. Department of Agriculture (FAS-USDA)

World Imports and Exports of Rye   In Thousands of Metric Tons

Year	European Union	Japan	Rep. of Korea	Turkey	Russia	United States	World Total	Belarus	Canada	European Union	Russia	United States	World Total
	---- Imports ----							---- Exports ----					
2001-02	307	335	121	20	7	126	1,056	30	66	647	4	5	1,046
2002-03	436	414	31	14	----	156	1,356	110	53	669	291	3	1,414
2003-04	99	341	114	43	6	83	845	60	173	506	156	1	907
2004-05	----	261	8	59	172	143	783	50	122	574	----	4	854
2005-06	9	279	7	2	49	139	620	50	132	359	----	----	610
2006-07	25	258	8	18	32	150	583	50	208	424	26	2	712
2007-08	98	83	6	13	----	179	415	75	191	76	119	6	470
2008-09[1]	9	57	7	8	----	100	212	50	76	114	16	8	270
2009-10[2]	----	103	5	----	----	108	245	50	124	99	12	2	343
2010-11[3]	10	65	5	5	300	114	527	250	125	100	----	5	605

[1] Preliminary. [2] Estimate. [3] Forecast.   Source: Foreign Agricultural Service, U.S. Department of Agriculture (FAS-USDA)

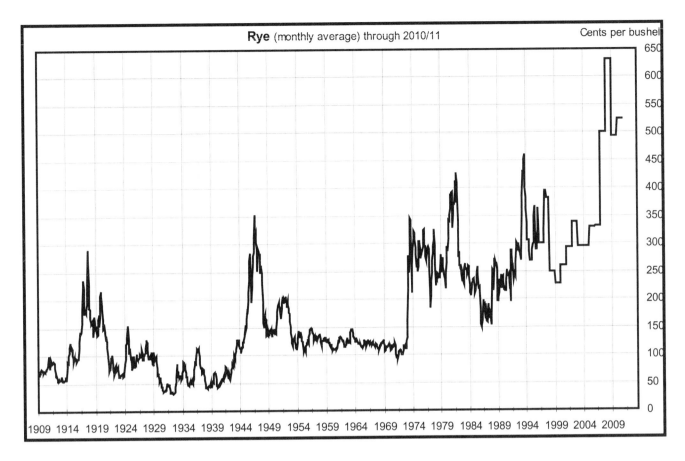

Rye (monthly average) through 2010/11   Cents per bushel

Production of Rye in the United States   In Thousands of Bushels

Year	Georgia	Kansas	Mich-igan	Minne-sota	Neb-raska	Dakota	Okla-homa	Penn-ylvania	Carolina	Dakota	Texas	Wis-consin	Total
2001	875	2	2	2	2	340	1,150	2	2	350	2	2	6,971
2002	560	2	2	2	2	210	1,300	2	2	270	2	2	6,488
2003	800	2	2	2	2	750	1,540	2	2	672	2	2	8,634
2004	600	2	2	2	2	780	1,620	2	2	649	2	2	8,255
2005	810	2	2	2	2	2	1,400	2	2	2	2	2	7,537
2006	650	2	2	2	2	2	1,040	2	2	2	2	2	7,193
2007	800	2	2	2	2	2	1,080	2	2	2	2	2	6,311
2008	1,200	2	2	2	2	2	1,045	2	2	2	2	2	7,979
2009	525	2	2	2	2	2	560	2	2	2	2	2	6,993
2010[1]	960	2	2	2	2	2	1,500	2	2	2	2	2	7,431

[1] Preliminary.   [2] Estimates not published beginning in 2000.   *Source: Agricultural Statistics Board, U.S. Department of Agriculture (ASB-USDA)*

Salient Statistics of Rye in the United States   In Thousands of Bushels

Crop Year Beginning June 1	Supply Stocks June 1	Supply Pro-duction	Supply Imports	Total Supply	Domestic Use Food	Domestic Use Industry	Domestic Use Seed	Domestic Use Feed & Residual	Domestic Use Total	Exports	Total Disap-pearance	Acreage Planted 1,000 Acres	Acreage Harvested for Grain 1,000 Acres	Yield Per Acre Harvested (Bushels)
2001-02	1,190	6,971	4,945	13,106	3,300	3,000	3,000	2,970	12,270	193	12,463	1,328	255	27.3
2002-03	568	6,488	6,140	13,196	3,300	3,000	3,000	3,329	12,629	122	12,751	1,355	263	24.8
2003-04	445	8,634	3,286	12,365	3,300	3,000	3,000	2,425	11,725	60	11,771	1,348	319	27.1
2004-05	594	8,255	5,626	14,475	3,300	3,000	3,000	4,237	13,537	145	13,682	1,380	300	27.5
2005-06	793	7,537	5,481	13,811	3,300	3,000	3,000	3,791	13,091	14	13,105	1,433	279	27.0
2006-07	706	7,193	5,899	13,798	3,300	3,000	3,000	3,947	13,247	70	13,317	1,396	274	26.3
2007-08	481	6,311	7,064	13,856	3,300	3,000	3,000	3,909	13,209	251	13,460	1,334	252	25.0
2008-09[1]	396	7,979	3,953	12,328	3,300	3,000	3,000	2,203	11,503	316	11,819	1,260	269	29.7
2009-10[2]	509	6,993	4,251	11,753	3,300	3,000	3,000	1,448	10,748	73	10,821	1,241	252	27.8
2010-11[3]	932	7,431	4,500	12,863	3,300	3,000	3,000	2,413	11,713	200	11,913	1,211	265	28.0

[1] Preliminary.   [2] Estimate.   [3] Forecast   *Source: Economic Research Service, U.S. Department of Agriculture (ERS-USDA)*

Salt

Salt, also known as sodium chloride, is a chemical compound that is an essential element in the diet of humans, animals, and even many plants. Since prehistoric times, salt has been used to preserve foods and was commonly used in the religious rites of the Greeks, Romans, Hebrews, and Christians. Salt, in the form of salt cakes, served as money in ancient Ethiopia and Tibet. As long ago as 1450 BC, Egyptian art shows records of salt production.

The simplest method of obtaining salt is through the evaporation of salt water from areas near oceans or seas. In most regions, rock salt is obtained from underground mining or by wells sunk into deposits. Salt is soluble in water, is slightly soluble in alcohol, but is insoluble in concentrated hydrochloric acid. In its crystalline form, salt is transparent and colorless, shining with an ice-like luster.

Prices – Salt prices in 2010 (FOB mine, vacuum and open pan) fell -4.9% yr/yr to $170.00 per ton, below last year's record high at $178.67.

Supply – World production of salt in 2010 fell -3.6% yr/yr to 270.000 million metric tons. The world's largest salt producers were China with 22.2% and the U.S. with 16.7% of world production in 2010. U.S. salt production in 2010 fell -2.2% yr/yr to 45.000 million metric tons.

Demand – U.S. consumption of salt in 2010 rose +4.6% to 59.000 million metric tons, down from the 2008 record high of 60.500 million metric tons.

Trade – The U.S. relied on imports for 24% of its salt consumption in 2010, down from the record high of 23% in 2004. U.S. imports of salt for consumption in 2010 rose +2.0% yr/yr to 15.000 million metric tons, a new record high. U.S. exports of salt in 2010 fell by -31.0% to 1.000 million metric tons, with the bulk of those exports going to Canada.

World Production of All Salt   In Thousands of Metric Tons

Year	Australia	Canada	China	France	Germany	India	Italy	Mexico	Poland	Spain	United Kingdom	United States	World Total
2003	10,256	13,718	32,424	6,673	16,424	15,000	2,922	7,547	4,660	3,963	5,900	43,700	225,000
2004	11,088	14,096	37,101	6,910	18,838	15,000	2,876	8,566	5,142	3,993	5,800	46,500	235,000
2005	12,444	13,643	46,610	6,730	19,333	15,500	3,476	9,508	4,023	4,550	5,800	45,200	249,000
2006	11,424	14,389	56,630	8,718	19,846	15,500	3,438	8,371	4,029	4,303	5,800	44,500	259,000
2007	10,855	11,862	59,760	6,140	18,806	16,000	2,214	8,400	3,522	4,350	5,800	44,600	259,000
2008	11,160	14,386	59,520	6,100	15,519	16,000	2,200	8,809	3,518	4,350	5,800	48,100	264,000
2009[1]	11,000	14,566	58,450	6,100	15,100	16,500	2,200	7,445	3,520	4,350	5,800	46,100	276,000
2010[2]	11,500	14,000	60,000	6,000	16,500	15,800		8,800	4,400	4,600	5,800	45,000	270,000

[1] Preliminary.   [2] Estimate.   *Source: U.S. Geological Survey (USGS)*

Salient Statistics of the Salt Industry in the United States   In Thousands of Metric Tons

Year	Net Import Reliance As a % of Apparent Consumption	Average Value FOB Mine Vacuum & Open Pan ($ Per Ton)	Production Total	Production Open & Vacuum Pan	Production Solar	Production Rock	Production Brine	Sold or Used, Producers Open & Vacuum Pan	Sold or Used, Producers Rock	Sold or Used, Producers Brine	Total Salt	Value[3] Million $	Imports for Consumption	Exports Total	Exports To Canada	Apparent Consumption
2003	17	124.24	43,700	4,070	3,330	16,300	20,000	4,010	14,100	20,000	41,100	1,130.0	12,900	718	585	53,200
2004	23	128.39	46,500	4,100	3,520	18,300	20,500	4,040	17,400	20,500	45,000	1,270.0	11,900	1,110	971	55,800
2005	20	130.75	45,100	4,170	3,430	17,700	19,900	3,970	18,100	19,800	45,000	1,310.0	12,100	879	686	56,200
2006	17	145.90	44,400	4,450	3,640	16,500	19,800	4,300	13,500	19,800	40,600	1,310.0	9,490	973	775	49,100
2007	15	154.95	44,500	4,420	3,650	16,800	19,700	4,310	18,400	19,600	45,500	1,520.0	8,640	833	588	53,300
2008	21	158.59	48,000	4,200	4,070	20,900	18,900	4,120	21,100	18,800	47,400	1,690.0	13,800	1,030	896	60,200
2009[1]	24	178.67	46,000	4,030	3,880	20,300	17,800	3,960	18,200	17,800	43,100	1,750.0	14,700	1,450	1,360	56,400
2010[2]	24	170.00	45,000								45,000		15,000	1,000		59,000

[1] Preliminary.   [2] Estimate.   [3] Values are f.o.b. mine or refinery & do not include cost of cooperage or containers.   *Source: U.S. Geological Survey (USGS)*

Salt Sold or Used by Producers in the U.S. by Classes & Consumers or Uses   In Thousands of Metric Tons

Year	Chemical[2]	Tanning Leather	Textile & Dyeing[3]	Meat Packers[3]	Canning	Baking	Agricultural Distribution	Feed Dealers	Feed Manufacturers	Rubber	Oil	Paper & Pulp	Metal Processing	Water Treatment	Grocery Stores	Water Conditioning Distrib.	Ice Control and/or Stabilization
2002	19,500	79	154	395	230	215	245	1,040	507	61	2,010	93	118	662	781	525	13,300
2003	20,100	71	151	374	231	210	215	1,090	460	67	2,210	88	126	777	802	537	18,500
2004	20,400	56	145	385	225	209	242	1,090	451	69	2,350	86	112	858	794	514	18,000
2005	19,700	55	149	398	211	204	227	1,140	477	65	2,210	81	107	1,140	803	511	21,000
2006	18,400	50	121	380	208	203	211	1,090	502	66	2,150	72	49	952	770	489	12,400
2007	21,500	41	98	305	198	149	385	1,160	457	6	211	61	36	1,030	943	522	20,800
2008	18,600	37	78	283	190	144	436	1,260	405	6	286	77	42	1,330	992	464	22,600
2009[1]	17,900	32	48	271	215	324	357	1,310	377	5	314	58	24	1,010	812	469	16,900

[1] Preliminary.   [2] Chloralkali producers and other chemical.   *Source: U.S. Geological Survey (USGS)*

Sheep and Lambs

Sheep and lambs are raised for both their wool and meat. In countries that have high wool production, there is also demand for sheep and lamb meat due to the easy availability. Production levels have declined in New Zealand and Australia, but that has been counteracted by a substantial increase in China.

Prices – The average monthly price received by farmers for lambs in the U.S. in 2010 rose by +24.9% to 124.67 cents per pound, a new record high. The average monthly price received by U.S. farmers for sheep in 2010 rose by +54.5% to a 50.45 cents per pound, a new record high. The average monthly wholesale price of slaughter lambs (choice) at San Angelo, Texas in 2010 rose by +29.1% to 116.81 cents per pound, a new record high.

Supply – World sheep and goat numbers in 2009 (latest data) fell by -0.6% to 1.939 billion head, just below the 2008 record high of 1.940 billion head. The world's largest producers of sheep and goats are China with 14.5% of world production in 2009, India (9.9%), Australia (3.8%), and New Zealand (1.7%). The number of sheep and lambs on U.S. farms in 2010 (Jan 1) fell –1.6% to 5.530 million head. The U.S. states with the most sheep and lambs were Texas (with 15.9% of the U.S. total), California (11.0%), Wyoming (6.6%), Colorado (6.7%), and South Dakota (5.0%).

World Sheep and Goat Numbers in Specified Countries on January 1   In Thousands of Head

Year	Argen-tina	Australia	China	India	Kazak-hstan	New Zealand	Romania	Russia	South Africa	Spain	Turkey	United Kingdom	World Total
2000	17,052	120,457	279,461	182,980	9,657	42,443	8,679	14,751	35,257	26,592	38,030	42,341	1,805,616
2001	16,887	113,040	279,667	183,918	9,981	40,173	8,195	14,773	35,350	27,276	35,693	36,792	1,793,794
2002	16,400	108,916	276,413	184,864	10,479	39,725	7,776	15,327	32,452	26,860	33,994	35,909	1,794,239
2003	16,650	101,782	282,565	185,827	11,273	39,707	7,945	16,051	32,178	26,650	31,954	35,939	1,820,037
2004	16,650	104,127	293,239	186,789	12,247	39,424	8,125	17,030	31,732	25,743	32,203	35,937	1,868,746
2005	16,650	104,525	304,169	187,760	13,409	40,035	8,086	17,771	31,690	25,654	31,811	35,345	1,918,281
2006	16,600	94,778	298,119	188,739	14,335	40,253	8,298	18,213	31,383	25,408	31,822	34,820	1,931,982
2007	16,700	88,711	283,880	189,725	15,350	38,572	8,405	19,675	31,347	25,086	32,260	34,041	1,942,504
2008[1]	16,700	82,938	285,813	190,721	16,080	34,184	9,334	21,503	31,623	22,912	31,749	33,226	1,950,708
2009[2]	16,700	72,740	281,015	191,726	16,770	32,466	9,780	21,770	31,347	21,983	29,568	30,878	1,939,243

[1] Preliminary.   [2] Forecast.   Source: Food and Agricultural Organization of the United Nations (FAO-UN)

Salient Statistics of Sheep & Lambs in the United States (Average Live Weight)   In Thousands of Head

	- Inventory, Jan. 1 -				--- Marketings[3] ---		---------- Slaughter ----------					Production (Live Weight)	Farm Value Jan. 1	
Year	Without New Crop Lambs	With New Crop Lambs	Lamb Crop	Total Supply	Sheep	Lambs	Farm	Com-mercial	Total[4]	Net Exports	Total Disap-pearance	(Mil. Lbs.)		Total
2001	6,965	6,965	4,495	11,460	711	4,795	68	3,222	3,290	299	4,303	495.6	690.5	100.0
2002	6,685	6,685	4,357	11,042	855	4,794	66	3,286	3,352	266	4,380	485.1	614.5	92.0
2003	6,300	6,321	4,140	10,461	828	4,387	67	2,979	3,046	105	3,804	470.1	656.6	104.0
2004	6,105	6,105	4,096	10,201	695	4,184	65	2,839	2,904			464.0	720.4	119.0
2005	6,135	6,135	4,117	10,252	669	4,200	64	2,698	2,762			473.3	798.2	13.0
2006	6,230	6,230	3,950	10,180	692	4,196	69	2,699	2,768			463.1	872.4	141.0
2007	6,165	6,273	3,895	10,168	780	3,927	85	2,694	2,778			473.1	818.5	134.0
2008	5,950	6,055	3,710	9,765	737	3,652	92	2,556	2,647			417.0	823.4	138.0
2009[1]	5,747	5,855	3,690	9,545	615	3,507	95	2,516	2,611			413.1	765.2	133.0
2010[2]	5,620	5,620	3,600	9,220									762.3	135.0

[1] Preliminary.   [2] Estimate.   [3] Excludes interfarm sales.   [4] Includes all commercial and farm.
Source: Economic Research Service, U.S. Department of Agriculture (ERS-USDA)

Sheep and Lambs[3] on Farms in the United States on January 1   In Thousands of Head

Year	Cali-fornia	Colo-rado	Idaho	Iowa	Minne-sota	Mon-tana	Mexico	Ohio	Dakota	Texas	Utah	Wyo-ming	Total
2003	730	380	260	255	145	310	175	150	380	1,040	310	460	6,300
2004	680	360	260	250	140	300	160	140	370	1,100	265	430	6,105
2005	670	365	270	245	145	305	145	142	375	1,070	270	450	6,135
2006	650	390	260	235	155	295	155	141	385	1,090	280	450	6,230
2007	610	400	260	235	150	290	130	141	380	1,050	295	460	6,165
2008	620	420	235	225	145	270	130	125	340	960	280	425	5,950
2009	660	410	210	200	140	255	120	130	305	870	290	420	5,747
2010[1]	610	370	220	210	130	245	120	128	325	830	290	375	5,620
2011[2]	610	370	235	200	130	230	110	129	275	880	280	365	5,530

[1] Preliminary.   [2] Estimate.   [3] Includes sheep & lambs on feed for market and stock sheep & lambs.   Source: Economic Research Service, U.S. Department of Agriculture (ERS-USDA)

SHEEP AND LAMBS

Average Wholesale Price of Slaughter Lambs (Choice[2]) at San Angelo Texas — In Dollars Per Hundred Pounds (Cwt.)

Year	Jan.	Feb.	Mar.	Apr.	May	June	July	Aug.	Sept.	Oct.	Nov.	Dec.	Average
2002	65.85	70.00	64.00	65.15	64.06	68.75	75.83	74.35	73.69	76.20	83.00	86.88	72.31
2003	89.25	90.25	96.25	88.13	95.75	97.25	87.88	85.81	91.44	91.31	91.00	96.17	91.71
2004	99.44	99.94	102.50	92.31	97.50	101.37	97.50	91.12	92.25	91.75	95.58	99.12	96.70
2005	107.25	109.69	101.37	99.37	96.94	99.50	95.00	92.14	91.56	93.00	93.33	94.00	97.76
2006	86.75	76.87	67.47	60.60	68.16	70.94	74.00	84.00	85.30	85.18	85.40	83.00	77.31
2007	81.00	82.27	84.50	85.25	84.20	77.40	86.38	86.19	89.44	84.90	84.83	92.92	84.94
2008	86.63	88.82	83.25	74.70	77.75	86.75	88.81	88.13	89.54	85.55	85.46	95.83	85.94
2009	88.74	89.25	92.75	89.38	95.23	93.91	88.00	88.88	88.17	89.50	89.66	92.25	90.48
2010[1]	95.04	106.63	109.95	112.00	104.47	102.05	109.17	112.15	125.38	129.69	138.50	156.67	116.81

[1] Preliminary.   Source: Economic Research Service, U.S. Department of Agriculture (ERS-USDA)

Federally Inspected Slaughter of Sheep & Lambs in the United States — In Thousands of Head

Year	Jan.	Feb.	Mar.	Apr.	May	June	July	Aug.	Sept.	Oct.	Nov.	Dec.	Total
2002	244	244	311	263	267	216	241	246	259	284	255	262	3,092
2003	227	211	252	280	209	216	225	226	241	251	223	246	2,805
2004	207	199	295	238	175	220	207	219	231	228	228	229	2,676
2005	195	204	268	208	198	210	188	216	219	217	213	219	2,555
2006	210	193	240	234	215	200	191	213	205	223	212	212	2,547
2007	204	194	267	203	205	188	191	212	197	232	223	212	2,529
2008	202	202	219	207	195	181	193	186	207	209	180	213	2,393
2009	179	169	210	213	167	185	189	187	207	201	200	217	2,323
2010[1]	173	167	249	175	167	194	178	185	186	185	201	200	2,261

[1] Preliminary.   Source: Economic Research Service, U.S. Department of Agriculture (ERS-USDA)

Cold Storage Holdings of Lamb and Mutton in the United States, on First of Month — In Thousands of Pounds

Year	Jan.	Feb.	Mar.	Apr.	May	June	July	Aug.	Sept.	Oct.	Nov.	Dec.
2002	11,905	13,110	11,269	10,528	13,172	12,938	13,553	14,215	14,458	11,961	12,004	9,255
2003	7,124	6,232	4,063	3,900	5,016	5,838	5,427	5,929	5,855	6,210	4,485	4,883
2004	3,795	3,671	3,355	3,164	3,251	3,504	3,872	3,376	3,878	4,179	4,166	3,715
2005	3,497	7,549	7,585	7,650	8,739	9,719	9,362	11,756	11,790	10,942	10,137	9,332
2006	9,967	15,730	15,777	15,454	15,247	15,215	15,126	15,254	15,353	15,228	15,452	15,862
2007	15,769	15,640	15,570	15,996	18,206	16,644	15,410	13,811	15,692	14,734	13,944	13,096
2008	12,918	15,177	18,157	17,118	17,783	18,411	19,598	19,723	21,147	20,796	21,331	21,659
2009	21,001	19,469	18,279	19,274	19,801	19,694	21,568	20,062	19,045	17,426	15,301	15,052
2010[1]	14,519	11,759	12,922	16,313	16,453	20,448	22,972	22,059	19,859	18,046	16,189	16,500

[1] Preliminary.   Source: Economic Research Service, U.S. Department of Agriculture (ERS-USDA)

Average Price Received by Farmers for Sheep in the United States — In Dollars Per Hundred Pounds (Cwt.)

Year	Jan.	Feb.	Mar.	Apr.	May	June	July	Aug.	Sept.	Oct.	Nov.	Dec.	Average
2002	36.20	34.30	31.80	26.00	25.30	23.50	25.60	25.60	24.50	25.60	31.30	38.70	29.03
2003	41.30	44.00	40.90	31.10	31.30	29.40	28.60	29.20	32.50	35.00	40.50	45.10	35.74
2004	43.80	40.80	36.70	36.70	36.00	31.30	37.10	37.30	41.20	40.40	41.40	44.60	38.94
2005	53.50	52.40	49.00	45.10	43.70	41.20	41.00	43.00	43.70	43.60	46.20	49.30	45.98
2006	47.70	45.90	40.10	35.20	32.50	28.20	27.60	27.90	32.20	31.40	30.30	34.80	34.48
2007	37.10	37.30	36.60	34.20	30.80	28.20	29.20	28.30	26.70	25.50	27.10	30.20	30.93
2008	31.90	29.90	28.70	28.40	25.40	24.50	26.10	26.60	24.50	21.70	27.30	32.90	27.33
2009	31.40	31.90	32.10	34.70	31.70	28.90	29.60	31.30	29.70	29.80	36.30	44.40	32.65
2010[1]	52.40	54.80	51.80	48.70	46.10	43.30	43.80	47.80	48.10	48.50	54.20	65.70	50.43

[1] Preliminary.   Source: Economic Research Service, U.S. Department of Agriculture (ERS-USDA)

Average Price Received by Farmers for Lambs in the United States — In Dollars Per Hundred Pounds (Cwt.)

Year	Jan.	Feb.	Mar.	Apr.	May	June	July	Aug.	Sept.	Oct.	Nov.	Dec.	Average
2002	65.50	67.80	66.70	64.70	64.40	72.90	75.60	75.30	76.30	79.60	84.00	87.20	73.33
2003	92.00	92.40	97.10	93.70	97.60	89.30	89.40	88.60	95.10	96.80	99.70	97.70	94.12
2004	104.00	106.00	103.00	100.00	103.00	105.00	101.00	97.90	100.00	97.70	99.90	101.00	101.54
2005	114.00	114.00	114.00	114.00	114.00	114.00	110.00	109.00	110.00	108.00	107.00	100.00	110.67
2006	96.10	97.80	92.10	87.20	88.90	92.10	93.40	95.40	98.30	98.50	95.60	94.00	94.12
2007	96.50	94.80	95.50	97.10	97.10	96.80	98.70	97.90	99.00	97.00	97.10	98.40	97.16
2008	97.50	96.50	97.40	99.40	101.00	102.00	103.00	99.90	99.40	97.40	100.00	101.00	99.54
2009	100.00	100.00	100.00	101.00	102.00	104.00	102.00	97.10	98.10	96.80	97.70	98.70	99.78
2010[1]	102.00	106.00	115.00	119.00	123.00	120.00	123.00	127.00	135.00	138.00	142.00	146.00	124.67

[1] Preliminary.   Source: Economic Research Service, U.S. Department of Agriculture (ERS-USDA)

Silk

Silk is a fine, tough, elastic fiber produced by caterpillars, commonly called silkworms. Silk is one of the oldest known textile fibers. Chinese tradition credits Lady Hsi-Ling-Shih, wife of the Emperor Huang Ti, with the discovery of the silkworm and the invention of the first silk reel. Dating to around 3000 BC, a group of ribbons, threads, and woven fragments was found in China. Also found, along the lower Yangzi River, were 7,000 year-old spinning tools, silk thread, and fabric fragments.

Silk filament was first woven into cloth in Ancient China. The Chinese successfully guarded this secret until 300AD, when Japan, and later India, learned the secret. In 550 AD, two Nestorian monks were sent to China to steal mulberry seeds and silkworm eggs, which they hid in their walking staffs, and then brought them back to Rome. By the 17th century, France was the silk center of the West. Unfortunately, the silkworm did not flourish in the English climate, nor has it ever flourished in the U.S.

Sericulture is the term for the raising of silkworms. The blind, flightless moth, Bombyx mori, lays more than 500 tiny eggs. After hatching, the tiny worms eat chopped mulberry leaves continuously until they are ready to spin their cocoons. After gathering the complete cocoons, the first step in silk manufacturing is to kill the insects inside the cocoons with heat. The cocoons are then placed in boiling water to loosen the gummy substance, sericin, holding the filament together. The filament is unwound, and then rewound in a process called reeling. Each cocoon's silk filament is between 600 and 900 meters long. Four different types of silk thread may be produced: organzine, crepe, tram, and thrown singles. During the last 30 years, in spite of the use of man-made fibers, world silk production has doubled.

Raw silk is traded on the Kansai Agricultural Commodities Exchange (KANEX) in Japan. Dried cocoons are traded on the Chuba Commodity Exchange (CCE). Raw silk and dried cocoons are traded on the Yokohama Commodity Exchange.

Supply – World production of silk in 2008, the latest reporting year, rose +0.6% to 170.079 metric tons, which was a record high and sharply above the 14-year low of 79,458 posted in 1997. China is the world's largest producer of silk by far with 65.8% of world production in 2008. Other key producers include India with 10.9% of world production, Vietnam (7.6%), and Turkmenistan (2.6%).

Trade – In 2008, the latest reporting year, the world's largest exporters of silk were China with 90.1% of world exports, Japan with 0.1%, and North Korea with 0.9%. In 2008, the world's largest importers of silk were India (with 52.7% of world imports), Italy (6.5%), Japan (5.9%), and South Korea (4.5%).

World Production of Raw Silk   In Metric Tons

Year	Brazil	China	India	Iran	Japan	North Korea	Rep. of Korea	Kyrgyzstan	Thailand	Turkmenistan	Uzbekistan	Viet Nam	World Total
1999	1,554	70,201	15,544	800	650	150	29	80	1,000	5,000	923	780	97,213
2000	1,389	78,201	15,214	840	650	150	15	67	955	4,700	1,100	7,153	110,996
2001	1,554	94,201	15,857	900	559	150	6	76	1,510	5,000	1,260	10,866	132,496
2002	1,620	100,101	17,347	900	391	200	4	96	1,550	4,500	1,200	12,124	140,551
2003	1,700	95,761	16,319	900	287	320	3	50	1,550	4,500	1,200	11,582	134,816
2004	1,750	104,801	15,742	900	250	350	3	17	1,600	4,500	1,200	12,323	145,930
2005	1,200	111,951	16,500	900	220	350	3	50	1,600	4,500	1,200	13,000	154,043
2006	1,250	111,951	17,305	900	220	350	3	50	1,600	4,500	1,200	13,000	154,924
2007[1]	1,250	111,951	18,475	900	220	350	3	50	1,600	4,500	1,200	13,000	156,094
2008[2]	1,300	111,951	18,475	900	220	350	3	50	1,600	4,500	1,200	13,000	156,144

[1] Preliminary.   [2] Estimate.   NA = Not avaliable.   *Source: Food and Agricultural Organization of the United Nations (FAO-UN)*

World Trade of Silk by Selected Countries   In Metric Tons

	---------------------------------- Imports ----------------------------------						---------------------------------- Exports ----------------------------------					
Year	France	Hong Kong	India	Italy	Japan	Rep. of Korea	World Total	Brazil	China	Hong Kong	Japan	Rep. of Korea	World Total
1999	287	1,059	5,018	2,695	2,596	2,107	18,957	----	12,089	1,048	3	130	35,041
2000	323	561	4,713	3,177	2,581	1,769	17,267	3	12,531	676	9	120	15,183
2001	327	175	6,809	2,760	1,893	1,582	16,410	23	11,266	186	2	90	13,003
2002	262	38	9,054	2,363	2,025	1,845	18,548	4	14,702	102	2	170	16,117
2003	147	67	9,258	2,219	1,949	1,648	18,439	2	13,931	31	96	296	15,866
2004	181	3	7,948	1,983	1,581	1,338	16,607	7	11,288	20	688	227	14,324
2005	262	14	8,383	1,974	1,406	1,359	18,114	36	10,972	11	202	219	13,699
2006	212	3	5,565	2,146	1,295	1,095	14,945	4	6,712	4	11	223	10,011
2007	150	2	7,922	1,463	791	989	15,338	18	13,756	2	10	277	15,699
2008[1]	191	0	8,392	1,040	932	724	15,926	13	13,431	0	16	137	14,906

[1] Preliminary.   *Source: Food and Agricultural Organization of the United Nations (FAO-UN)*

Silver

Silver is a white, lustrous metallic element that conducts heat and electricity better than any other metal. In ancient times, many silver deposits were on or near the earth's surface. Before 2,500 BC, silver mines were worked in Asia Minor. Around 700 BC, ancient Greeks stamped a turtle on their first silver coins. Silver assumed a key role in the U.S. monetary system in 1792 when Congress based the currency on the silver dollar. However, the U.S. discontinued the use of silver in coinage in 1965. Today Mexico is the only country that uses silver in its circulating coinage.

Silver is the most malleable and ductile of all metals, with the exception of gold. Silver melts at about 962 degrees Celsius and boils at about 2212 degrees Celsius. Silver is not very chemically active, although tarnishing occurs when sulfur and sulfides attack silver, forming silver sulfide on the surface of the metal. Because silver is too soft in its pure form, a hardening agent, usually copper, is mixed into the silver. Copper is usually used as the hardening agent because it does not discolor the silver. The term "sterling silver" refers to silver that contains at least 925 parts of silver per thousand (92.5%) to 75 parts of copper (7.5%).

Silver is usually found combined with other elements in minerals and ores. In the U.S., silver is mined in conjunction with lead, copper, and zinc. In the U.S., Nevada, Idaho, Alaska, and Arizona are the leading silver-producing states. For industrial purposes, silver is used for photography, electrical appliances, glass, and as an antibacterial agent for the health industry.

Silver futures and options are traded on the New York Mercantile Exchange (NYMEX), the NYSE-LIFEE exchange, and the London Metal Exchange (LME). Silver futures are traded on the Tokyo Commodity Exchange (TOCOM). The Nymex silver futures contract calls for the delivery of 5,000 troy ounces of silver (0.999 fineness) and is priced in terms of dollars and cents per troy ounce.

Prices – Nymex silver futures prices traded basically sideways in the first half of 2010. The European sovereign debt crisis during spring 2010 caused increased safe-haven demand for precious metals, but that was offset for silver to some extent by weaker European and U.S. economic growth and reduced industrial demand for silver. Silver then staged a sharp rally into year-end to a 30-year nearest-futures high of $30.975 per troy ounce. Silver prices continued to gain in the early part of 2011 and rose to a 32-year high of $36.73 per troy ounce in March 2011. Bullish factors in 2010 included (1) worries about inflation with the central banks of the U.S., England, and Japan all engaging in quantitative easing, (2) an escalation of the Middle East crisis which prompted a surge of safe-haven buying of precious metals, and (3) the global economic recovery which strengthened in 2010 and boosted industrial demand for silver.

Supply – World mine production of silver in 2010 rose +1.8% yr/yr to a new record high of 22,200 metric tons, continuing to show some improvement after flat production figures in 2000-03. The world's largest silver producers in 2010 were Peru with 18.0% of world production, China (13.5%), Mexico (15.8%), Chile (6.8%), Australia (7.7%), and the U.S. (5.8%). U.S. production of refined silver in 2010 (through August, annualized) rose by +12.7% to 6,023 metric tons, a new record high.

Demand – U.S. consumption of silver in 2009 (latest data available) fell −11.8% yr/yr to 164.4 million troy ounces. The largest consumption of silver is for electrical contacts and conductors with 31.9% of total usage, followed by coinage (20.6%), photographic materials (13.4%), jewelry (7.1%), and brazing alloys and solders (3.2%). The world's largest consuming nation of silver for industrial purposes is the U.S. with 20% of world consumption in 2004 (latest data), followed by Japan (16%), India (10%), and Italy (7%).

Trade – U.S. exports of refined silver in 2006 (latest data available) rose +423.2% yr/yr to 50.797 billion troy ounces, which about half of the record high of 99.022 million troy ounces seen in 1997. The major destinations for U.S. silver exports are UK (74.7%), Canada (10.7%), and Switzerland (4.2%). U.S. imports of silver ore and concentrates in 2005 (latest available data) fell −80.5% yr/yr to 14,000 troy ounces. U.S. imports of refined silver bullion in 2005 (latest data available rose +11.2% yr/yr to 134.387 million troy ounces in 2005. The bulk of those imports came from Mexico (65.908 million troy ounces), Canada (41.474 million troy ounces), and Peru (20.319 million troy ounces).

World Mine Production of Silver   In Thousands of Kilograms (Metric Ton)

Year	Australia	Bolivia	Canada[3]	Chile	China	Kazak-hstan	Mexico	Peru	Poland	Russia	Sweden	United States	World Total[2]
2001	1,970	411	1,320	1,349	1,910	982	2,760	2,571	1,194	380	306	1,740	18,700
2002	2,077	450	1,408	1,210	2,200	893	2,727	2,870	1,229	400	294	1,350	18,800
2003	1,868	465	1,310	1,313	2,400	827	2,569	2,921	1,237	700	307	1,240	18,800
2004	2,224	407	1,337	1,360	2,450	733	2,569	3,060	1,419	1,277	293	1,250	20,000
2005	2,417	420	1,124	1,400	2,500	832	2,894	3,206	1,293	1,350	310	1,230	20,800
2006	1,727	472	995	1,607	2,600	830	2,970	3,471	1,242	1,250	268	1,160	20,300
2007	1,879	525	860	1,936	2,700	800	3,135	3,494	1,215	1,200	270	1,260	21,100
2008	1,926	1,114	728	1,405	2,800	700	3,236	3,686	1,193	1,300	265	1,250	21,300
2009[1]	1,630	1,300	600	1,300	2,900		3,550	3,850	1,200	1,400		1,250	21,800
2010[2]	1,700	1,360	700	1,500	3,000		3,500	4,000	1,200	1,400		1,280	22,200

[1] Preliminary.   [2] Estimate.   [3] Shipments.   *Source: U.S. Geological Survey (USGS)*

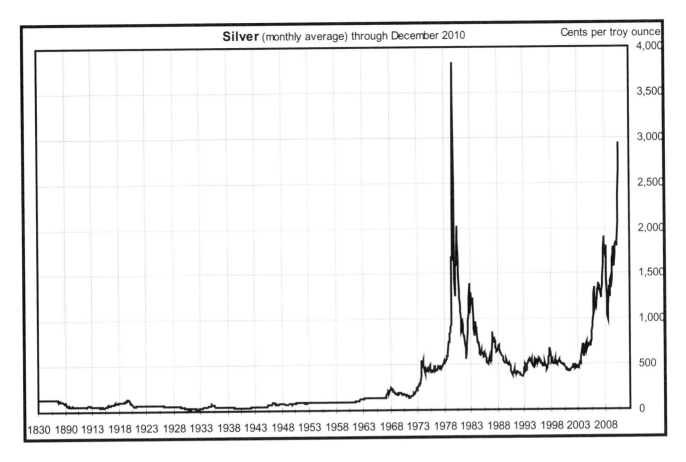

Silver (monthly average) through December 2010 — Cents per troy ounce

Average Price of Silver in New York (Handy & Harman) In Cents Per Troy Ounce (.999 Fine)

Year	Jan.	Feb.	Mar.	Apr.	May	June	July	Aug.	Sept.	Oct.	Nov.	Dec.	Average
2001	470.19	457.34	439.93	439.25	443.59	436.79	425.45	420.72	441.09	441.87	412.35	437.98	438.88
2002	450.17	444.79	457.00	460.50	473.55	492.13	494.57	456.16	458.93	442.28	453.87	465.78	462.39
2003	485.62	468.11	454.74	453.40	475.29	455.62	486.48	502.90	520.62	503.91	520.64	565.33	491.06
2004	637.13	647.71	729.48	708.57	589.19	588.38	637.55	670.98	641.93	717.55	751.43	712.43	669.36
2005	665.45	709.18	728.50	715.74	705.29	733.64	704.40	702.72	719.33	769.90	786.35	865.88	733.87
2006	918.48	952.13	1,037.52	1,263.71	1,337.84	1,077.41	1,121.24	1,225.39	1,159.93	1,161.55	1,298.45	1,329.83	1,156.96
2007	1,286.63	1,394.58	1,316.27	1,373.23	1,319.27	1,315.48	1,295.21	1,233.22	1,292.92	1,372.17	1,467.15	1,431.24	1,341.45
2008	1,605.90	1,766.63	1,921.60	1,751.57	1,704.90	1,703.95	1,806.41	1,457.81	1,219.33	1,042.72	986.78	1,031.66	1,499.94
2009	1,139.90	1,343.68	1,311.50	1,252.02	1,411.30	1,465.93	1,338.64	1,443.05	1,648.74	1,726.34	1,787.68	1,765.68	1,469.54
2010	1,775.05	1,587.21	1,717.11	1,816.83	1,841.90	1,853.43	1,793.98	1,849.25	2,061.12	2,346.86	2,657.20	2,933.00	2,019.41

Source: American Metal Market (AMM)

Average Price of Silver in London (Spot Fix) In Pence Per Troy Ounce (.999 Fine)

Year	Jan.	Feb.	Mar.	Apr.	May	June	July	Aug.	Sept.	Oct.	Nov.	Dec.	Average
2001	315.87	312.57	304.50	304.36	310.19	309.54	300.97	277.97	297.93	289.21	286.92	306.25	302.43
2002	315.08	310.55	318.27	316.61	322.58	329.32	316.07	295.93	292.38	282.49	286.93	291.52	306.48
2003	297.21	289.23	287.39	285.06	292.05	272.79	295.53	313.01	320.30	298.01	306.53	320.48	298.13
2004	347.36	339.49	395.67	391.14	327.03	320.36	342.32	368.78	356.35	392.94	402.52	368.43	362.70
2005	354.28	375.57	382.74	377.48	380.46	403.56	402.10	391.55	397.90	436.23	453.10	496.09	404.26
2006	519.94	544.76	594.70	714.36	715.69	584.44	607.69	647.19	615.09	618.97	678.96	677.31	626.59
2007	656.95	712.03	675.74	690.95	665.15	662.06	636.65	613.19	639.99	670.90	708.45	709.65	670.14
2008	815.50	899.50	960.24	883.98	867.12	866.05	907.89	772.57	677.51	617.03	645.37	693.86	800.55
2009	787.02	931.98	923.81	850.16	912.88	894.99	816.90	872.89	1,010.76	1,065.91	1,076.27	1,087.91	935.96
2010	1,098.45	1,016.07	1,140.22	1,184.58	1,256.63	1,255.90	1,172.41	1,181.47	1,323.37	1,479.95	1,665.70		1,252.25

Source: American Metal Market (AMM)

SILVER

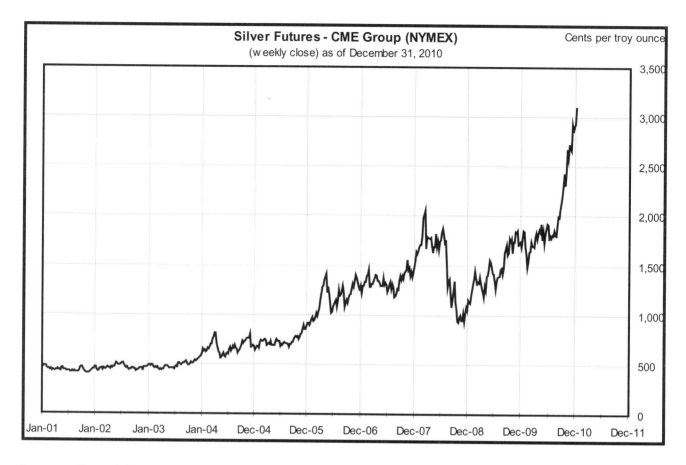

Silver Futures - CME Group (NYMEX)
(weekly close) as of December 31, 2010

Cents per troy ounce

Average Open Interest of Silver Futures in New York (COMEX)   In Contracts

Year	Jan.	Feb.	Mar.	Apr.	May	June	July	Aug.	Sept.	Oct.	Nov.	Dec.
2001	69,408	72,798	74,337	71,589	67,328	67,429	75,019	75,830	65,533	66,530	74,228	66,903
2002	67,442	65,355	67,405	76,158	82,525	100,837	94,731	82,349	80,511	89,094	85,434	78,174
2003	98,561	94,472	84,485	87,445	85,232	80,001	91,544	108,118	110,423	92,216	101,303	103,007
2004	109,860	113,764	117,848	113,172	90,493	87,201	89,062	97,844	85,245	108,762	121,221	107,136
2005	97,744	98,644	101,200	103,562	104,680	124,317	124,521	121,133	117,121	135,335	146,409	136,502
2006	131,767	129,928	132,140	137,121	110,400	110,631	98,733	110,635	102,159	105,167	114,132	105,741
2007	105,692	122,515	113,749	118,275	109,070	120,179	117,817	118,292	110,958	123,781	144,897	146,891
2008	174,969	182,076	157,971	143,333	123,649	128,645	136,866	131,931	110,333	97,927	91,983	84,986
2009	87,525	96,902	92,756	93,855	95,420	106,283	99,018	103,076	122,052	133,409	137,261	124,797
2010	126,921	118,619	112,234	123,849	122,547	129,561	118,619	126,117	145,022	153,013	148,547	133,596

Contract size = 5,000 oz.   *Source: CME Group; New York Mercantile Exchange (NYMEX), COMEX Division*

Volume of Trading of Silver Futures in New York (COMEX)   In Contracts

Year	Jan.	Feb.	Mar.	Apr.	May	June	July	Aug.	Sept.	Oct.	Nov.	Dec.	Total
2001	175,026	302,035	155,658	252,486	204,552	281,846	112,956	267,711	160,329	210,266	266,077	180,256	2,569,198
2002	265,773	271,293	163,898	325,889	243,475	389,798	281,214	296,579	164,537	209,249	292,861	230,998	3,135,564
2003	291,120	409,737	216,660	315,240	251,096	352,729	407,931	442,762	335,508	373,493	464,244	250,835	4,111,355
2004	385,058	544,939	408,447	671,204	278,703	425,501	316,264	427,973	281,737	364,158	541,366	360,775	5,006,125
2005	285,449	513,617	370,338	485,832	392,156	621,647	334,903	600,961	455,033	424,972	652,917	398,526	5,536,351
2006	495,649	624,491	562,330	807,269	513,822	508,746	255,777	452,551	268,393	244,152	424,771	275,112	5,433,063
2007	364,565	589,332	479,896	635,023	417,343	680,612	404,108	783,999	469,459	581,062	1,018,495	393,243	6,817,137
2008	719,308	989,601	881,776	912,952	580,959	859,976	722,663	953,123	792,072	594,307	578,009	332,437	8,917,183
2009	415,581	652,240	433,757	575,714	418,399	869,113	476,592	842,904	657,029	809,637	1,159,284	680,278	7,990,528
2010	755,863	1,065,168	750,170	994,814	936,865	1,079,348	642,826	978,609	757,106	1,314,164	2,282,155	1,269,578	12,826,666

Contract size = 5,000 oz.   *Source: CME Group; New York Mercantile Exchange (NYMEX), COMEX Division*

Mine Production of Recoverable Silver in the United States   In Metric Tons

Year	Arizona	Cali-fornia	Colo-rado	Idaho	Missouri	Montana	Nevada	New Mexico	South Dakota	Wash-ington	Other States	Total
2001	W	8	3	W	W	W	544	W	W	W	1,180	1,740
2002	W	3	W	W	W	W	424	W	W	W	927	1,350
2003	W	1	W	W	W	W	322	W	W	W	916	1,240
2004	W	1	W	W	W	W	302	W	W	W	943	1,250
2005	W	W	W	W	W	W	276	W	W	W	949	1,230
2006	W	W	W	W	W	W	260	W	W	W	895	1,160
2007	W	W	W	W	W	W	243	W	W	W	1,040	1,280
2008	W	W	W	W	W	W	235	W	W	W	1,020	1,250
2009	W	W	W	W	W	W	203	W	W	W	1,040	1,250
2010[1]	W	W	W	W	W	W	204	W	W	W	1,050	1,250

[1] Preliminary.   W = Withheld proprietary data; included in "Other States".   *Source: U.S. Geological Survey (USGS)*

Consumption of Silver in the United States, by End Use   In Millions of Troy Ounces

Year	Brazing Alloys & Solders	Catalysts	Batteries	Mirrors	Electrical Contacts & Con-ductors	Photo-graphic Materials	Silver-plate	Jewerly	Sterling Ware	Total Net Industrial Con-sumption	Coinage	Total Con-sumption
2000	8.7	6.3	5.2	2.6	51.5	70.2	4.5	6.1	5.6	178.8	13.4	192.2
2001	8.3	6.1	5.3	2.5	34.1	65.5	4.0	4.9	4.6	157.3	12.3	169.6
2002	8.4	NA	NA	NA	37.6	64.8	[3]	13.7	[3]	161.7	15.3	177.0
2003	7.9	NA	NA	NA	39.5	58.9	[3]	15.1	[3]	160.8	14.5	175.3
2004	7.3	NA	NA	NA	47.4	55.2	[3]	15.4	[3]	164.8	15.5	180.3
2005	7.7	NA	NA	NA	52.1	56.4	[3]	15.7	[3]	172.8	16.6	189.4
2006	7.2	NA	NA	NA	55.0	46.4	[3]	15.0	[3]	168.2	17.6	185.8
2007	7.7	NA	NA	NA	57.7	35.9	[3]	14.2	[3]	164.2	16.0	180.2
2008	7.2	NA	NA	NA	61.4	29.3	[3]	13.0	[3]	161.0	25.4	186.4
2009[1]	5.2	NA	NA	NA	52.4	22.0	[3]	11.6	[3]	130.5	33.9	164.4

[1] Preliminary.   [3] Included in Jewelry beginning 2002.   NA = Not available.   *Source: American Metal Market*

Commodity Exchange, Inc. (COMEX) Warehouse of Stocks of Silver   In Thousands of Troy Ounces

Year	Jan.	Feb.	Mar.	Apr.	May	June	July	Aug.	Sept.	Oct.	Nov.	Dec.
2001	93,983	93,195	98,659	96,694	95,745	96,090	98,700	100,494	102,770	101,538	103,982	105,235
2002	104,547	102,395	100,983	102,540	104,526	107,766	105,938	105,563	108,090	107,495	107,440	107,090
2003	107,394	107,610	109,153	108,521	108,168	105,092	107,222	105,406	104,862	106,283	118,238	124,498
2004	124,271	124,181	123,195	122,087	122,687	118,442	118,369	116,253	109,311	107,789	104,624	102,831
2005	103,590	102,390	101,494	103,627	103,995	104,257	104,719	109,467	115,588	116,687	116,257	117,608
2006	119,974	124,793	127,898	125,763	123,627	108,443	102,268	102,086	103,634	105,451	105,313	107,770
2007	111,071	113,970	117,637	126,433	131,343	130,497	139,935	132,106	133,057	133,474	133,891	134,533
2008	130,072	135,414	135,037	135,881	133,512	134,896	135,959	138,061	137,821	135,719	130,204	127,170
2009	NA	123,902	124,121	123,615	119,910	120,879	118,519	117,818	117,796	116,159	116,159	112,494
2010	110,588	110,588	110,588	115,786	116,178	119,452	114,015	110,244	110,765	111,075	107,785	107,393

Source: CME Group; New York Mercantile Exchange (NYMEX), COMEX Division

Production[2] of Refined Silver in the United States, from All Sources   In Metric Tons

Year	Jan.	Feb.	Mar.	Apr.	May	June	July	Aug.	Sept.	Oct.	Nov.	Dec.	Total
2001	405	343	405	360	360	331	395	380	338	403	442	383	4,545
2002	544	387	465	532	509	398	398	419	473	437	394	485	5,441
2003	483	426	320	412	357	431	430	373	361	809	363	471	5,235
2004	407	418	460	337	361	177	175	351	433	255	390	678	4,442
2005	402	505	515	568	450	558	556	440	356	376	485	439	5,650
2006	506	434	500	445	381	554	489	431	349	387	209	305	4,990
2007	401	405	445	436	476	452	335	438	290	388	267	339	4,671
2008	325	360	394	460	401	417	420	428	460	445	422	393	4,925
2009	456	182	270	326	337	394	363	495	535	676	530	778	5,342
2010[1]	553	504	794	499	506	353	381	533	438	458	547		6,072

[1] Preliminary.   [2] Includes U.S. mine production of recoverable silver plus imports of refined silver.   *Source: U.S. Geological Survey (USGS)*

SILVER

U.S. Exports of Refined Silver to Selected Countries   In Thousands of Troy Ounces

Year	Canada	France	Germany	Hong Kong	Japan	Sing-apore	Rep of Korea	Switzer-land	United Arab Emirates	United Kingdom	Uruguay	Other Countries	Total
1999	2,180	2	1	----	585	37	31	624	4,244	7,716	180	4,205	19,804
2000	1,906	22	2	----	3,504	1	----	727	----	3,311	109	2,634	12,217
2001	1,598	----	----	11	1,202	2	----	354	----	20,029	105	7,659	30,960
2002	466	----	1	4	466	10	----	727	----	14,532	----	11,990	28,196
2003	524	3	----	3	17	2	16	630	----	3,086	----	2,534	6,816
2004	7,009	1	3	24	585	166	1	2,321	----	3	108	2,125	12,346
2005	3,729	----	25	3	1	95	18	2,829	----	1,145	563	1,302	9,709
2006	5,433	----	874	----	547	120	----	2,154	2	37,937	----	3,730	50,797
2007	3,762	3	1,537	1,804	801	103	25	990	----	1,061	498	12,790	23,373
2008[1]	4,051	13	1,283	5	2,115	131	1,424	527	----	1,929	437	8,597	20,512

[1] Preliminary.   [2] Included in "Other Countries", if any.   NA = Not available.   *Source: American Bureau of Metal Statistics, Inc. (ABMS)*

U.S. Imports of Silver From Selected Countries   In Thousands of Troy Ounces

Year	Canada	Mexico	Other Countries	Total	Canada	Chile	Mexico	Peru	Uruguay	Other Countries	Total
1999	11	334	2	347	43,403	1,048	33,115	5,433	----	2,521	85,519
2000	46	----	----	46	38,902	225	44,689	2,787	----	35,899	122,502
2001	243	----	----	243	44,046	2,054	41,152	5,498	----	1,771	94,521
2002	149	1,813	----	1,961	48,868	2,331	67,837	6,430	----	6,350	131,815
2003	82	----	----	82	41,795	1,987	62,050	18,261	----	12,223	136,316
2004	71	----	----	71	37,616	2,042	59,156	17,297	----	4,774	120,884
2005	14	----	----	14	41,474	2,514	65,908	20,319	----	4,173	134,387
2006	----	----	----	----	47,261	1,106	73,945	13,214	----	2,077	137,602
2007	----	----	12	12	34,722	1,206	78,125	18,358	----	2,942	135,352
2008[1]	----	----	1	1	25,109	2,234	76,196	16,075	----	4,485	124,099

[1] Preliminary.   [2] Included in "Other Countries", if any.   NA = Not available.   *Source: American Bureau of Metal Statistics, Inc. (ABMS)*

World Silver Consumption   In Millions of Troy Ounces

	Industrial Uses										Coinage							
Year	Canada	France	Germany	India	Italy	Japan	Mexico	United Kingdom	United States	World Total	Austria	Canada	France	Germany	Mexico	United States	Total Coinage	World Total
1995	2.0	30.0	43.6	101.3	49.5	112.7	16.9	31.6	148.7	752.7	.5	.7	1.2	2.4	.6	9.0	24.7	777.4
1996	2.0	26.9	41.0	122.2	51.7	112.1	20.3	33.8	155.0	785.8	.5	.7	.3	4.6	.5	7.1	23.3	809.1
1997	2.2	28.3	42.3	122.9	56.1	119.9	23.3	34.9	166.3	828.2	.4	.6	.3	3.7	.4	6.5	28.5	856.7
1998	2.3	28.4	38.4	114.7	55.9	112.8	21.7	38.6	162.6	801.2	.3	1.1	.3	10.0	.2	7.0	27.8	829.0
1999	2.1	26.6	35.1	121.5	61.8	122.5	21.3	39.3	175.2	838.7	.3	1.4	.3	7.0	.4	10.7	29.2	867.8
2000	2.0	28.8	31.8	131.0	65.1	135.0	16.6	42.7	179.1	871.8	.3	1.0	.4	8.8	.6	13.4	32.1	904.0
2001	2.0	28.7	32.4	154.0	58.2	119.3	15.9	45.9	157.3	836.5	.3	.9	.4	8.1	1.1	12.3	30.5	867.0
2002	2.1	27.1	29.4	122.5	56.0	118.7	17.0	43.1	161.6	807.0	.4	1.0	.5	6.0	1.1	15.3	31.6	838.6
2003	2.2	25.6	29.4	122.5	55.0	115.9	18.7	44.1	160.8	817.5	.4	.3	.5	10.3	1.1	14.5	35.8	853.4
2004[2]	2.1	12.0	30.7	79.2	54.8	125.1	18.6	52.2	164.8	807.0	.5	1.3	.5	10.3	.9	15.5	41.1	836.6

[2] Preliminary.   NA = Not available.   *Source: The Silver Institute*

Soybean Meal

Soybean meal is produced through processing and separating soybeans into oil and meal components. By weight, soybean meal accounts for about 35% of the weight of raw soybeans (at 13% moisture). If the soybeans are of particularly good quality, then the processor can get more meal weight by including more hulls in the meal while still meeting the 48% protein minimum. Soybean meal can be further processed into soy flour and isolated soy protein, but the bulk of soybean meal is used as animal feed for poultry, hogs and cattle. Soybean meal accounts for about two-thirds of the world's high-protein animal feed, followed by cottonseed and rapeseed meal, which together account for less than 20%. Soybean meal consumption has been moving to record highs in recent years. The soybean meal marketing year begins in October and ends in September. Soybean meal futures and options are traded on the Chicago Board of Trade (CBOT). The CBOT soybean meal futures contract calls for the delivery of 100 tons of soybean meal produced by conditioning ground soybeans and reducing the oil content of the conditioned product and having a minimum of 48.0% protein, minimum of 0.5% fat, maximum of 3.5% fiber, and maximum of 12.0% moisture.

Soybean crush – The term soybean "crush" refers to both the physical processing of soybeans and also to the dollar-value premium received for processing soybeans into their component products of meal and oil. The conventional model says that processing 60 pounds (one bushel) of soybeans produces 11 pounds of soybean oil, 44 pounds of 48% protein soybean meal, 3 pounds of hulls, and 1 pound of waste. The Gross Processing Margin (GPM) or crush equals (0.22 times Soybean Meal Prices in dollars per ton) + (11 times Soybean Oil prices in cents/pound) – Soybean prices in $/bushel. A higher crush value will occur when the price of the meal and oil products are strong relative to soybeans, e.g., because of supply disruptions or because of an increase in demand for the products. When the crush value is high, companies will have a strong incentive to buy raw soybeans and boost the output of the products. That supply increase should eventually bring the crush value back into line with the long-term equilibrium.

Prices – Soybean meal futures prices at the Chicago Board of Trade in 2010 showed weakness early in the year and fell to a 2-year low of $249.6 per ton in February 2010. However, soybean meal prices then staged a solid rally through the remainder of the year to close 2010 up 18% at $370.3 per ton.

Regarding cash prices, the average price of soybean meal (48% solvent) in Decatur, Illinois in the 2010-11 marketing year (i.e., October 2010 to September 2011) through December of 2010, averaged $338.54 per short ton, up by +8.8% yr/yr.

Supply – World soybean meal production in 2010-11 rose +7.4% yr/yr to a new record high of 177.555 million metric tons. The world's largest soybean meal producers are China with 25.8% of world production in 2010-11, the US with 20.2%, Brazil with 15.1%, and the European Union with 6.0%. U.S. production of soybean meal in 2010-11 fell -5.2% yr/yr to 39.533 million short tons, but that was still below the 2006-07 record high of 43.054. U.S. soybean meal stocks in 2010-11 (Oct 1) rose +28.5% yr/yr to 302,000 short tons, down further from the 2007-08 8-year high of 343,000 short tons.

Demand – World consumption of soybean meal in 2010-11 rose +8.9% yr/yr to a new record high of 174.916 million metric tons. The U.S. accounted for 15.8% of that consumption and the European Union accounted for 19.0%. U.S. consumption of soybean meal in 2010-11 fell -0.4% yr/yr to 27.669 million metric tons.

Trade – World exports of soybean meal in 2010-11 rose +6.8% to 59.457 million metric tons. Brazil accounted for 22.9% of world exports and the U.S. accounted for 14.0%. World imports of soybean meal in 2010-11 rose +8.6% yr/yr to 57.103 million metric tons. U.S. exports of soybean meal in 2010-11 fell -17.7% yr/yr to 9.200 million short tons. U.S. imports of soybean meal in 2010-11 rose +3.1% yr/yr to 165,000 short tons, remaining well below the record high of 285,000 short tons seen in 2003-04.

World Supply and Distribution of Soybean Meal   In Thousands of Metric Tons

Crop Year Beginning Oct. 1	Production Brazil	China	European Union	United States	Total	Exports Brazil	United States	Total	Imports European Union	Total	Consumption European Union	United States	Total	Ending Stocks Brazil	United States	Total
2001-02	19,407	16,300	14,042	36,552	125,034	11,862	7,271	41,810	19,961	40,410	33,406	29,545	123,507	1,560	218	5,693
2002-03	21,449	21,000	12,950	34,649	130,265	13,657	5,728	43,070	20,545	42,470	33,335	29,096	130,047	1,647	200	5,311
2003-04	22,360	20,190	11,084	32,953	129,032	14,792	4,690	46,085	22,012	44,893	32,729	28,531	127,554	1,801	191	5,597
2004-05	22,740	24,026	11,300	36,936	138,568	14,256	6,659	47,701	21,910	45,915	32,680	30,446	136,539	1,577	156	5,840
2005-06	21,920	27,296	10,760	37,416	146,556	12,895	7,301	52,519	22,829	51,165	32,875	30,114	145,218	1,469	285	5,824
2006-07	24,110	28,465	11,550	39,037	154,245	12,715	7,987	55,321	22,213	52,547	33,228	31,166	151,233	1,913	311	6,062
2007-08	24,890	31,280	11,715	38,359	159,096	12,138	8,384	56,602	24,074	54,069	35,169	30,148	156,413	2,588	266	6,212
2008-09	24,700	32,475	10,131	35,473	151,597	13,109	7,708	52,731	20,980	51,131	31,579	27,898	151,798	1,844	213	4,411
2009-10[1]	26,090	38,644	9,880	37,830	165,280	12,985	10,137	55,667	20,730	52,557	30,138	27,777	160,645	2,200	274	5,936
2010-11[2]	26,740	45,778	10,714	35,864	177,555	13,640	8,346	59,457	23,250	57,103	33,256	27,669	174,916	2,045	272	6,221

[1] Preliminary.   [2] Forecast.   *Source: Foreign Agricultural Service, U.S. Department of Agriculture (FAS-USDA)*

Soybean Meal Futures - CME Group (CBT)
(weekly close) as of December 31, 2010
USD per ton

Volume of Trading of Soybean Meal Futures in Chicago   In Thousands of Contracts

Year	Jan.	Feb.	Mar.	Apr.	May	June	July	Aug.	Sept.	Oct.	Nov.	Dec.	Total
2001	530.2	431.8	470.6	485.1	584.4	625.1	710.0	630.9	491.4	652.9	659.3	472.1	6,743.8
2002	610.3	398.3	424.7	618.9	567.2	664.7	806.4	673.7	581.2	613.7	657.8	557.7	7,174.5
2003	639.6	551.4	527.7	676.7	599.6	749.8	772.1	692.8	677.2	896.4	700.7	674.3	8,158.4
2004	648.7	767.1	740.7	819.6	795.8	821.6	873.2	638.9	547.3	559.7	703.5	653.2	8,569.2
2005	658.7	857.6	713.4	661.8	571.3	1,025.0	632.8	693.4	602.9	497.9	694.0	715.8	8,324.6
2006	506.9	605.0	575.3	785.6	716.8	976.1	801.5	819.1	807.7	906.1	1,064.2	785.7	9,350.0
2007	768.9	1,018.8	822.1	985.7	798.9	1,217.3	1,107.9	1,025.1	1,028.6	1,016.4	1,218.8	1,204.7	12,213.3
2008	1,260.6	1,235.1	1,240.4	1,257.7	922.5	1,359.0	1,258.6	1,074.5	1,069.3	1,020.3	837.1	818.9	13,354.2
2009	909.2	988.7	841.7	1,195.1	1,071.4	1,390.1	1,146.6	1,071.8	974.6	1,012.1	1,222.7	1,056.6	12,880.8
2010	994.1	1,134.5	1,330.1	1,264.3	850.7	1,349.0	1,134.2	1,057.8	1,136.4	1,054.7	1,590.7	1,156.3	14,052.8

Contract size = 100 tons.   *Source: CME Group; Chicago Board of Trade (CBT)*

Average Open Interest of Soybean Meal Futures in Chicago   In Contracts

Year	Jan.	Feb.	Mar.	Apr.	May	June	July	Aug.	Sept.	Oct.	Nov.	Dec.
2001	111,880	108,047	107,253	116,888	119,644	135,046	134,982	129,536	123,644	121,845	145,996	147,576
2002	146,674	137,425	134,880	130,138	132,376	143,956	142,728	132,996	137,799	131,249	137,836	140,902
2003	154,821	168,036	157,670	163,532	163,096	154,985	152,121	146,582	153,505	169,709	170,707	176,191
2004	183,462	186,137	185,647	175,069	162,284	149,584	135,675	134,987	133,045	137,447	152,846	147,307
2005	154,984	165,403	146,326	133,578	129,372	149,882	122,088	109,976	121,833	135,970	140,102	140,959
2006	127,922	132,833	147,837	172,905	181,823	182,940	196,236	230,082	236,351	206,002	216,854	206,762
2007	201,214	227,905	213,708	216,258	212,398	217,576	210,612	201,339	219,046	225,683	248,277	251,133
2008	234,286	234,695	225,607	218,126	199,422	216,039	208,444	178,191	163,511	152,968	138,111	124,898
2009	118,930	121,722	110,580	123,445	160,515	190,481	174,733	167,301	155,388	150,639	159,393	165,141
2010	170,924	198,651	200,438	196,464	177,726	187,838	197,981	200,131	208,773	195,256	201,589	194,033

Contract size = 100 tons.   *Source: CME Group; Chicago Board of Trade (CBT)*

Supply and Distribution of Soybean Meal in the United States   In Thousands of Short Tons

Crop Year Beginning Oct. 1	----------------- Supply -----------------			--------------- Distribution ---------------			----------------- Dollars Per Metric Ton -----------------			
	For Stocks Oct. 1	Pro-duction	Total Supply	Domestic	Exports	Total	Decatur 48% Protein Solvent	Decatur 44% Protein Solvent	Brazil FOB 45-46% Protein	Rotter-dam CIF
2001-02	383	40,292	40,818	33,070	7,508	40,578	167.73	180	174	174
2002-03	240	38,194	38,600	32,361	6,019	38,380	181.57	200	163	197
2003-04	220	36,324	36,830	31,449	5,170	36,619	256.05	282	211	273
2004-05	211	40,715	41,073	33,559	7,343	40,902	182.90	202	172	231
2005-06	172	41,244	41,557	33,195	8,048	41,243	174.17	192	176	215
2006-07	314	43,054	43,524	34,374	8,804	43,178	205.44	226	199	276
2007-08	343	42,284	42,768	33,232	9,242	42,474	335.94	370	337	469
2008-09[1]	294	39,102	39,484	30,752	8,497	39,249	331.17	365	333	401
2009-10[2]	235	41,700	42,095	30,619	11,175	41,794	311.27	343	327	391
2010-11[3]	302	39,533	40,000	30,500	9,200	39,700	340-380			

[1] Preliminary.   [2] Estimate.   [3] Forecast.   Source: Economic Research Service, U.S. Department of Agriculture (ERS-USDA)

U.S. Exports of Soybean Cake & Meal by Country of Destination   In Thousands of Metric Tons

Year	Algeria	Australia	Canada	Dominican Republic	Italy	Japan	Mexico	Nether-lands	Philip-pines	Russia	Spain	Vene-zuela	Total
2001	183.7	190.2	1,023.4	369.5	132.6	297.3	268.1	195.3	720.4	113.7	86.0	136.1	7,290
2002	266.5	294.1	1,100.2	358.7	34.1	157.2	435.1	78.4	756.6	121.3	----	59.8	6,703
2003	184.7	383.9	1,056.4	317.5	0.0	329.0	693.7	10.2	238.5	60.7	0.0	190.5	5,582
2004	176.2	209.2	1,140.6	156.9	0.5	220.3	824.1	2.0	299.0	18.2	0.1	193.4	4,937
2005	63.0	74.9	1,155.9	264.2	0.2	523.4	1,356.3	10.1	442.0	16.8	5.0	112.5	6,352
2006	18.4	54.3	1,390.4	423.6	1.3	481.1	1,705.7	6.5	519.4	31.1	----	27.9	7,479
2007	39.5	1.2	1,467.4	448.7	0.1	451.3	1,638.4	8.2	626.9	31.8	0.6	49.3	7,922
2008	50.1	45.3	1,365.0	368.5	58.5	385.8	1,447.3	36.8	551.2	27.3	0.0	545.0	7,996
2009	----	121.9	1,154.3	362.4	48.5	366.3	1,323.0	0.2	803.4	20.0	90.0	487.1	8,791
2010[1]	----	208.0	1,068.0	384.4	28.1	403.0	1,381.7	0.8	860.0	22.0	50.6	571.0	9,331

[1] Preliminary.   Source: Foreign Agricultural Service, U.S. Department of Agriculture (FAS-USDA)

Production of Soybean Cake & Meal[2] in the United States   In Thousands of Short Tons

Year	Oct.	Nov.	Dec.	Jan.	Feb.	Mar.	Apr.	May	June	July	Aug.	Sept.	Total	Yield in lbs.
2001-02	3,534.4	3,538.7	3,655.3	3,703.1	3,313.2	3,589.7	3,315.7	3,344.2	3,194.1	3,085.4	3,106.7	2,911.3	40,292	44.27
2002-03	3,499.3	3,424.7	3,526.8	3,358.4	3,048.4	3,360.1	2,994.7	3,072.4	2,873.4	3,064.4	2,966.6	3,023.5	38,213	43.90
2003-04	3,462.1	3,465.9	3,483.7	3,479.3	3,144.9	3,092.4	2,682.4	2,792.4	2,616.2	2,752.2	2,480.2	2,872.6	36,324	44.32
2004-05	3,685.2	3,584.2	3,567.9	3,553.6	3,293.3	3,547.6	3,328.0	3,396.8	3,160.9	3,320.4	3,122.1	3,157.0	40,717	44.26
2005-06	3,700.9	3,562.3	3,518.0	3,589.5	3,215.3	3,504.0	3,212.6	3,474.6	3,250.9	3,507.8	3,351.7	3,354.5	41,242	43.83
2006-07	3,823.2	3,671.9	3,733.0	3,697.5	3,257.2	3,721.5	3,444.5	3,627.3	3,532.6	3,572.4	3,474.6	3,498.2	43,054	44.03
2007-08	3,869.5	3,709.4	3,887.5	3,791.2	3,473.7	3,701.1	3,500.6	3,633.8	3,352.3	3,316.3	3,052.4	2,996.3	42,284	43.95
2008-09	3,519.4	3,413.5	3,346.0	3,439.8	3,203.7	3,425.4	3,335.2	3,502.8	3,323.2	3,066.7	2,844.9	2,683.5	39,104	43.93
2009-10	3,845.7	3,976.5	4,076.1	3,932.5	3,635.5	3,680.0	3,214.0	3,144.5	3,049.2	3,056.1	3,030.6	3,059.7	41,700	43.81
2010-11[1]	3,738.2	3,714.2	3,675.2										44,510	

[1] Preliminary.   [2] At oil mills; including millfeed and lecithin.   Sources: Economic Research Service, U.S. Department of Agriculture (ERS-USDA)

Stocks (at Oil Mills)[2] of Soybean Cake & Meal in the United States, on First of Month   In Thousands of Short Tons

Year	Jan.	Feb.	Mar.	Apr.	May	June	July	Aug.	Sept.	Oct.	Nov.	Dec.
2001-02	383.3	305.5	302.9	393.7	289.7	272.0	336.5	253.8	212.7	343.3	202.4	256.5
2002-03	240.0	285.2	371.7	337.0	299.1	259.5	335.7	263.5	311.8	271.6	228.4	266.9
2003-04	219.9	317.8	432.4	280.7	328.9	415.8	375.0	338.6	465.5	314.9	344.6	196.3
2004-05	210.7	357.7	286.8	271.3	340.9	310.4	248.0	307.5	349.0	244.8	362.3	238.3
2005-06	171.8	316.1	304.9	338.0	326.6	301.6	286.5	415.4	303.5	266.2	372.6	225.8
2006-07	313.8	388.4	373.6	468.9	372.4	289.4	329.9	328.6	279.0	316.8	314.9	231.9
2007-08	343.0	305.1	295.5	421.6	287.4	331.3	395.4	339.9	433.0	424.3	297.4	415.2
2008-09	293.8	372.0	599.1	413.9	448.0	437.2	360.9	421.8	577.6	426.3	328.4	316.3
2009-10	234.7	446.2	627.4	568.8	630.5	702.4	361.7	296.2	467.7	341.1	425.0	272.5
2010-11[1]	301.6	516.5	484.4									

[1] Preliminary.   [2] Including millfeed and lecithin.   Sources: Economic Research Service, U.S. Department of Agriculture (ERS-USDA)

SOYBEAN MEAL

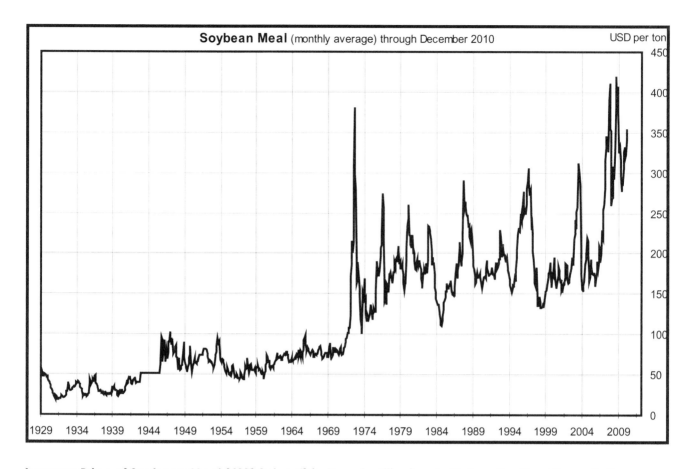

Average Price of Soybean Meal (48% Solvent) in Decatur Illinois   In Dollars Per Short Ton -- Bulk

Year	Jan.	Feb.	Mar.	Apr.	May	June	July	Aug.	Sept.	Oct.	Nov.	Dec.	Average
2001-02	165.45	166.10	154.18	158.01	153.11	160.49	161.57	164.28	170.33	187.45	186.25	185.45	167.72
2002-03	168.20	163.20	163.60	167.40	176.80	175.40	182.10	195.40	191.90	187.30	189.70	217.95	181.58
2003-04	225.20	242.00	231.54	252.15	257.39	301.14	311.83	300.69	285.81	284.05	205.34	175.51	256.05
2004-05	155.37	153.90	161.60	167.34	167.95	187.96	193.19	198.68	219.28	215.75	198.43	175.40	182.90
2005-06	166.22	170.32	193.17	183.64	176.73	175.07	174.64	175.77	176.83	168.97	159.76	168.87	174.17
2006-07	177.71	190.67	180.63	190.36	208.81	205.26	189.37	198.66	229.70	222.05	217.63	254.41	205.44
2007-08	260.55	280.76	314.78	331.28	345.87	331.57	329.94	325.48	390.72	412.25	355.35	352.70	335.94
2008-09	260.66	267.37	268.24	306.85	297.42	292.22	324.27	380.37	418.47	373.18	405.27	379.68	331.17
2009-10	325.69	328.18	333.93	314.23	295.79	277.61	291.21	287.85	305.78	325.56	331.76	317.65	311.27
2010-11	321.92	341.78	351.93										338.54

Source: Economic Research Service, U.S. Department of Agriculture (ERS-USDA)

Average Price of Soybean Meal (44% Solvent) in Decatur Illinois   In Dollars Per Short Ton -- Bulk

Year	Jan.	Feb.	Mar.	Apr.	May	June	July	Aug.	Sept.	Oct.	Nov.	Dec.	Average
1992-93	168.6	170.9	176.4	175.6	167.5	172.4	175.6	181.7	181.3	217.6	206.9	186.5	181.8
1993-94	180.6	195.7	192.5	185.9	184.4	182.0	176.4	191.1	183.0	168.1	165.6	162.5	180.7
1994-95	156.4	150.9	145.4	145.1	149.4	145.7	151.0	148.1	149.1	160.1	157.5	171.8	152.5
1995-96	183.4	194.1	213.6	220.5	216.7	215.7	237.9	232.3	227.9	242.3	251.1	265.5	225.1
1996-97	238.0	242.7	240.9	240.7	253.6	270.4	277.7	296.0	275.9	261.5	261.6	265.7	260.4
1997-98	216.0	231.6	214.9	193.1	182.1	165.3	152.8	150.3	157.8	173.3	135.7	126.9	175.0
1998-99	129.4	139.3	139.6	131.0	124.4	127.2	128.6	127.0	131.7	125.7	135.9	144.1	132.0
1999-00	147.2	148.1	145.4	155.0	163.6	166.6	168.1	180.1	170.2	156.8	151.4	166.9	160.0
2000-01	166.0	173.7	187.9	175.6	158.3	149.1	149.7	155.6	163.1	183.9	170.6	163.5	166.4
2001-02	157.7	157.2	146.6	Disc.	Disc.	Disc.	Disc.	Disc.	Disc.	Disc.	Disc.	Disc.	153.8

Source: Economic Research Service, U.S. Department of Agriculture (ERS-USDA)

Soybean Oil

Soybean oil is the natural oil extracted from whole soybeans. Typically, about 19% of a soybean's weight can be extracted as crude soybean oil. The oil content of U.S. soybeans correlates directly with the temperatures and amount of sunshine during the soybean pod-filling stages. Edible products produced with soybean oil include cooking and salad oils, shortening, and margarine. Soybean oil is the most widely used cooking oil in the U.S. It accounts for 80% of margarine production and for more than 75% of total U.S. consumer vegetable fat and oil consumption. Soy oil is cholesterol-free and high in polyunsaturated fat. Soy oil is also used to produce inedible products such as paints, varnish, resins, and plastics. Of the edible vegetable oils, soy oil is the world's largest at about 32%, followed by palm oil and rapeseed oil. Soybean oil futures and options are traded on the Chicago Board of Trade (CBOT).

Prices – Soybean oil futures prices at the Chicago Board of Trade in 2010 traded sideways early in the year. However, soybean oil futures prices then rallied sharply during the remainder of the year to close 2010 up 43% at 57.74 cents per pound.

Regarding cash prices, for the year 2010-11 (through December 2010), the average monthly price of crude domestic soybean oil (in tank cars) in Decatur (F.O.B.) rose sharply by +37.0% yr/yr to 49.25 cents per pound.

Supply – World production of soybean oil in 2010-11 rose +8.0% yr/yr to a new record high of 41.874 million metric tons. The U.S. accounts for 20.6% of world soybean oil production, while Brazil accounts for 15.8%, and the European Union accounts for 5.8%. U.S. production of soybean oil in 2010-11 fell -3.1% yr/yr to 19.000 billion pounds.

Demand – World consumption of soybean oil in 2010-11 rose +9.2% yr/yr to a new record high of 41.804 million metric tons. The U.S. accounted for 18.6% of world consumption, while Brazil accounted for 12.4%, India for 6.9% and the European Union for 6.4%,. U.S. consumption of soybean oil in 2010-11 rose +7.8% yr/yr to 17.100 billion pounds.

Trade – World exports of soybean oil in 2010-11 rose +5.8% yr/yr to 9.567 million metric tons. U.S. exports of soybean oil in 2010-11 fell 16.6% yr/yr to 2.800 billion pounds, down from last years record high of 3.357 billion pounds.

World Supply and Demand of Soybean Oil   In Thousands of Metric Tons

Crop Year Beginning Oct. 1	Production Brazil	Production European Union	Production United States	Production Total	Exports Brazil	Exports United States	Exports Total	Imports India	Imports Total	Consumption Brazil	Consumption European Union	Consumption India	Consumption United States	Consumption Total	End Stocks[3] United States	End Stocks[3] Total
2001-02	4,700	3,198	8,572	28,922	1,775	1,143	8,226	1,479	7,672	2,949	2,291	2,231	7,635	28,270	1,070	3,197
2002-03	5,205	2,950	8,360	30,511	2,394	1,027	8,796	1,197	8,267	2,925	2,304	1,910	7,748	30,262	676	2,917
2003-04	5,588	2,531	7,748	30,298	2,718	425	8,698	906	8,386	2,959	2,112	1,942	7,650	30,296	488	2,607
2004-05	5,630	2,575	8,782	32,529	2,414	600	9,088	2,026	8,883	3,060	2,210	2,737	7,911	31,819	771	3,112
2005-06	5,430	2,460	9,248	34,790	2,466	523	9,764	1,727	9,090	3,113	2,915	3,000	8,147	33,741	1,365	3,487
2006-07	5,970	2,640	9,294	36,446	2,462	851	10,565	1,447	9,919	3,395	3,368	2,500	8,426	35,467	1,399	3,820
2007-08	6,160	2,667	9,335	37,715	2,388	1,320	10,918	733	10,425	3,955	3,377	2,330	8,317	37,752	1,127	3,290
2008-09	6,120	2,314	8,503	35,743	1,909	995	9,097	1,060	9,078	4,276	2,779	2,300	7,378	36,069	1,298	2,945
2009-10[1]	6,460	2,252	8,897	38,762	1,449	1,523	9,046	1,598	8,682	4,965	2,400	2,810	7,195	38,295	1,523	3,048
2010-11[2]	6,620	2,448	8,618	41,874	1,540	1,270	9,567	1,300	9,211	5,165	2,666	2,870	7,756	41,804	1,167	2,762

[1] Preliminary.   [2] Forecast.   [3] End of season.   *Source: Foreign Agricultural Service, U.S. Department of Agriculture (FAS-USDA)*

Supply and Distribution of Soybean Oil in the United States   In Millions of Pounds

Crop Year Beginning Oct. 1	Pro-duction	Imports	Stocks Oct. 1	Exports	Total Domestic	Food Short-ening	Food Mar-garine	Food Cooking & Salad Oils	Food Other Edible	Food Total Food	Non-Food Paint & Varnish	Non-Food Resins & Plastics	Total Non-Food	Total Disap-pearance
2001-02	18,898	46	2,767	2,519	16,833	8,234	1,298	7,373	125	17,030	60	85	519	19,352
2002-03	18,430	46	2,359	2,261	17,085	8,566	1,212	7,886	119	17,783	64	88	520	19,346
2003-04	17,080	306	1,489	936	16,864	8,304	1,138	7,933	NA	17,375	71	100	623	17,800
2004-05	19,360	26	1,076	1,324	17,439	7,938	1,227	7,790	NA	16,955	81	81	747	18,763
2005-06	20,387	35	1,699	1,153	17,959	7,799	848	8,657	NA	17,304	117	85	1,866	19,112
2006-07	20,489	37	3,010	1,877	18,574	6,225	961	8,708	NA	15,894	63	98	3,445	20,451
2007-08	20,580	65	3,085	2,911	18,335	5,271	902	9,612	NA	15,785	33	108	3,466	21,246
2008-09	18,745	90	2,485	2,193	16,265	4,445	W	10,321	NA	14,766	W	106	2,182	18,459
2009-10[1]	19,614	103	2,861	3,357	15,862	3,883	W	9,339	NA	13,222	W	W	3,166	19,219
2010-11[2]	19,000	115	3,358	2,800	17,100									19,900

[1] Preliminary .   [2] Forecast.   *Source: Economic Research Service, U.S. Department of Agriculture (ERS-USDA)*

SOYBEAN OIL

Stocks of Crude Soybean Oil in the United States, at End of Month

Year	Oct	Nov	Dec	Jan	Feb	Mar	Apr	May	June	July	Aug	Sept
2004-05	1,019.5	1,013.1	1,111.1	1,348.2	1,425.3	1,588.7	1,560.0	1,658.1	1,622.4	1,715.6	1,525.2	1,505.9
2005-06	1,641.0	1,706.5	2,029.6	2,247.4	2,392.2	2,433.1	2,454.7	2,576.8	2,605.3	2,762.9	2,740.2	2,703.5
2006-07	2,680.0	2,719.5	2,700.0	2,739.4	2,853.0	2,974.9	2,897.9	2,928.5	2,962.3	2,816.3	2,666.4	2,558.1
2007-08	2,701.1	2,736.4	2,713.9	2,860.0	2,713.1	2,714.6	2,573.4	2,633.8	2,554.7	2,482.8	2,265.2	2,200.4
2008-09	2,084.0	2,197.8	2,346.7	2,625.6	2,739.6	2,816.2	2,868.5	2,931.6	3,125.9	3,031.2	2,741.3	2,495.8
2009-10	2,452.0	2,611.1	2,836.9	2,933.3	2,992.2	2,995.7	3,094.6	3,186.0	3,249.6	3,266.2	3,029.6	3,080.0
2010-11[1]	2,957.7	2,994.3	3,162.9									

Crop year beginning October 1. [1] Preliminary. *Source: Bureau of the Census, U.S. Department of Commerce*

Stocks of Refined Soybean Oil in the United States, at End of Month   In Millions of Pounds

Year	Oct	Nov	Dec	Jan	Feb	Mar	Apr	May	June	July	Aug	Sept
2004-05	235.8	178.4	200.3	212.6	222.0	222.7	243.4	236.6	216.2	273.8	200.7	193.6
2005-06	254.1	178.9	199.4	251.3	281.2	285.0	300.8	308.2	313.9	343.2	320.9	315.3
2006-07	334.7	355.6	381.7	442.4	427.7	386.5	403.5	382.4	397.9	408.2	380.0	346.1
2007-08	352.1	319.3	364.8	374.5	362.5	360.7	344.1	344.7	338.8	300.8	286.3	282.3
2008-09	307.3	337.6	298.5	282.7	283.1	284.8	294.3	302.8	291.4	298.9	268.8	246.5
2009-10	260.7	275.1	273.5	283.7	294.7	265.9	258.9	279.1	303.3	278.5	253.1	278.4
2010-11[1]	272.2	301.4	310.6									

Crop year beginning October 1. [1] Preliminary. *Source: Bureau of the Census, U.S. Department of Commerce*

U.S. Exports of Soybean Oil[1], by Country of Destination   In Metric Tons

Crop Year Beginning Oct. 1	Canada	Ecuador	Ethiopia	Haiti	India	Mexico	Morocco	Pakistan	Panama	Peru	Turkey	Vene-zuela	Total
2000-01	54,909	9,849	5,224	5,793	54,062	72,456	0	62,999	4,558	60,606	0	577	635,493
2001-02	87,047	0	2,225	9,452	88,529	161,760	39,439	59,999	12,616	37,677	85,199	635	1,142,755
2002-03	124,667	0	11,997	1,997	42,727	188,993	26,517	38,215	2,241	20,349	26,500	311	1,026,638
2003-04	96,450	10	3,665	1,298	14,561	97,099	15,518	17	2,834	25,097	0	169	424,554
2004-05	68,162	0	1,529	4,375	29,385	162,913	6,579	15,506	7,247	15,459	21	6,063	600,399
2005-06	76,342	2	3,270	3,972	23,031	108,515	21,951	12,000	1,546	19,588	4,032	38	523,153
2006-07	80,068	3	550	1,962	14,301	151,641	60,347	2	3,409	5,940	16	26,806	851,221
2007-08	90,361	3,009	2,141	14,138	11	269,249	107,323	0	6,817	183	73	82,035	1,320,430
2008-09	41,500	0	840	19,127	146,086	173,041	110,249	0	1,715	37,061	2,598	54,438	994,927
2009-10[2]	40,818	0	720	24,616	162,342	211,043	231,996	6,795	5,151	92,004	54	52,702	1,522,501

[1] Crude & Refined oil combined as such.   [2] Preliminary.   *Source: Foreign Agricultural Service, U.S. Department of Agriculture (FAS-USDA)*

Production of Crude Soybean Oil in the United States   In Millions of Pounds

Year	Oct.	Nov.	Dec.	Jan.	Feb.	Mar.	Apr.	May	June	July	Aug.	Sept.	Total
2002-03	1,692.6	1,631.5	1,696.0	1,612.8	1,473.6	1,633.3	1,447.5	1,491.7	1,391.0	1,482.4	1,440.4	1,445.2	18,438
2003-04	1,630.8	1,610.6	1,604.6	1,618.3	1,462.4	1,461.4	1,260.3	1,314.6	1,236.0	1,304.0	1,185.9	1,391.7	17,081
2004-05	1,759.6	1,688.0	1,682.3	1,680.2	1,564.1	1,686.4	1,579.6	1,620.1	1,497.3	1,586.7	1,484.4	1,531.1	19,360
2005-06	1,828.6	1,756.7	1,717.3	1,765.2	1,594.8	1,746.5	1,586.3	1,709.3	1,608.7	1,737.6	1,657.7	1,684.1	20,393
2006-07	1,829.5	1,725.0	1,771.0	1,747.2	1,548.3	1,766.9	1,626.3	1,729.9	1,693.5	1,710.7	1,662.8	1,678.0	20,489
2007-08	1,868.6	1,805.4	1,879.4	1,845.2	1,687.7	1,827.8	1,707.0	1,756.4	1,632.8	1,616.4	1,507.5	1,445.5	20,580
2008-09	1,715.9	1,622.9	1,597.0	1,615.1	1,536.1	1,636.0	1,596.0	1,683.2	1,604.3	1,469.2	1,369.4	1,299.9	18,745
2009-10	1,825.2	1,854.0	1,898.3	1,845.0	1,690.1	1,728.8	1,519.2	1,481.6	1,438.8	1,440.5	1,418.4	1,474.4	19,614
2010-11[1]	1,790.5	1,771.2	1,739.4	1,722.9									21,072

Crop year beginning October 1. [1] Preliminary. *Source: Bureau of the Census, U.S. Department of Commerce*

Production of Refined Soybean Oil in the United States   In Millions of Pounds

Year	Oct.	Nov.	Dec.	Jan.	Feb.	Mar.	Apr.	May	June	July	Aug.	Sept.	Total
2002-03	1,451.2	1,367.2	1,262.2	1,224.5	1,181.0	1,308.2	1,238.6	1,378.8	1,316.1	1,293.8	1,290.5	1,334.8	15,647
2003-04	1,393.0	1,350.9	1,226.6	1,205.6	1,196.0	1,330.6	1,210.3	1,267.4	1,195.9	1,246.8	1,268.8	1,306.3	15,198
2004-05	1,377.6	1,331.1	1,243.2	1,243.4	1,188.1	1,321.6	1,324.5	1,287.4	1,253.6	1,295.9	1,324.1	1,324.7	15,515
2005-06	1,389.3	1,307.4	1,245.2	1,273.9	1,132.9	1,409.3	1,326.6	1,361.5	1,352.9	1,329.1	1,399.7	1,400.0	15,928
2006-07	1,477.9	1,309.3	1,303.9	1,269.3	1,165.2	1,361.0	1,361.8	1,409.8	1,340.8	1,457.5	1,404.0	1,421.0	16,281
2007-08	1,468.6	1,372.3	1,359.7	1,350.5	1,259.6	1,400.0	1,346.2	1,277.0	1,257.6	1,354.7	1,371.8	1,314.7	16,133
2008-09	1,388.0	1,248.3	1,102.6	1,121.7	1,088.2	1,200.0	1,185.0	1,210.7	1,139.9	1,239.8	1,200.8	1,227.8	14,353
2009-10	1,377.3	1,294.4	1,193.2	1,148.4	1,122.9	1,245.1	1,121.4	1,133.4	1,104.9	1,135.9	1,141.4	1,154.9	14,173
2010-11[1]	1,269.0	1,211.7	1,125.6										14,426

Crop year beginning October 1. [1] Preliminary. *Source: Bureau of the Census, U.S. Department of Commerce*

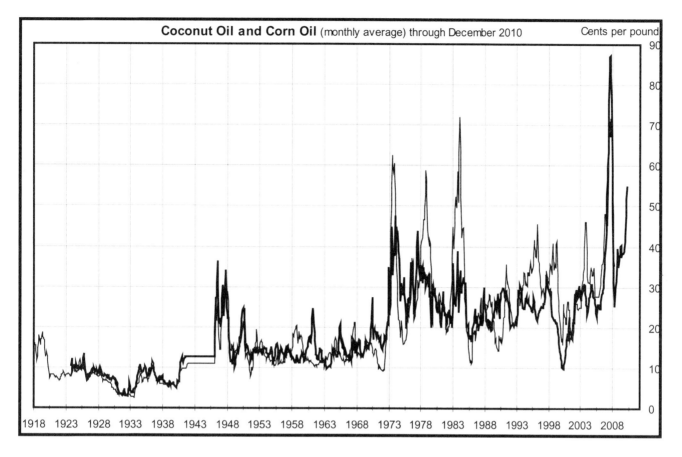

Coconut Oil and Corn Oil (monthly average) through December 2010 — Cents per pound

Consumption of Soybean Oil in End Products in the United States — In Millions of Pounds

Year	Jan.	Feb.	Mar.	Apr.	May	June	July	Aug.	Sept.	Oct.	Nov.	Dec.	Total
2001	1,065.9	1,151.7	1,308.8	1,202.4	1,224.2	1,261.6	1,307.6	1,557.5	1,411.0	1,687.3	1,624.0	1,485.8	16,288
2002	1,461.5	1,395.3	1,568.0	1,505.1	1,549.7	1,492.4	1,490.5	1,545.5	1,543.7	1,710.2	1,587.2	1,458.8	18,308
2003	1,418.1	1,347.4	1,490.0	1,494.9	1,552.6	1,493.1	1,509.5	1,483.5	1,577.7	1,660.7	1,544.2	1,451.4	18,023
2004	1,388.1	1,417.6	1,555.2	1,468.0	1,506.7	1,421.1	1,429.2	1,473.6	1,483.2	1,558.3	1,533.7	1,368.9	17,604
2005	1,365.4	1,609.2	1,609.2	1,587.2	1,589.5	1,496.2	1,523.3	1,570.4	1,527.2	1,589.6	1,546.9	1,416.2	18,430
2006	1,505.2	1,368.8	1,661.4	1,561.1	1,634.9	1,653.2	1,575.5	1,746.2	1,727.9	1,775.6	1,638.6	1,571.5	19,420
2007	1,547.3	1,357.8	1,624.8	1,586.7	1,728.6	1,640.3	1,812.9	1,793.1	1,699.5	1,757.8	1,618.9	1,548.4	19,716
2008	1,623.6	1,476.9	1,625.3	1,580.9	1,510.8	1,528.4	1,589.8	1,624.2	1,559.2	1,662.7	1,500.3	1,348.5	18,630
2009	1,251.8	1,245.9	1,346.9	1,282.5	1,275.3	1,283.6	1,357.4	1,374.8	1,397.9	1,606.5	1,468.2	1,377.4	16,268
2010[1]	1,231.8	1,227.6	1,350.0	1,215.6	1,183.4	1,232.8	1,229.6	1,274.4	1,262.6	1,342.1	1,293.8	1,206.1	15,050

[1] Preliminary.   Source: Bureau of the Census, U.S. Department of Commerce

U.S. Exports of Soybean Oil (Crude and Refined) — In Millions of Pounds

Year	Jan.	Feb.	Mar.	Apr.	May	June	July	Aug.	Sept.	Oct.	Nov.	Dec.	Total
2001	130.4	184.5	142.4	105.8	51.2	109.9	89.1	96.3	70.6	233.9	138.6	164.8	1,518
2002	249.9	446.7	233.3	233.3	87.3	345.4	180.8	95.3	109.8	113.5	194.9	210.2	2,501
2003	277.5	319.1	273.9	211.6	109.5	96.6	234.5	116.0	105.9	152.5	111.3	133.2	2,142
2004	71.2	62.8	73.5	38.8	44.0	39.3	53.9	68.8	86.8	59.9	184.5	239.5	1,023
2005	77.0	217.2	74.6	74.8	71.9	68.5	52.4	137.3	65.9	76.3	154.1	107.8	1,178
2006	71.3	67.0	178.2	96.8	53.8	82.0	89.4	64.7	111.8	167.1	120.3	276.7	1,379
2007	176.4	118.2	75.2	102.7	121.3	123.5	202.0	202.3	190.8	132.9	198.0	391.3	2,035
2008	157.7	509.9	385.5	427.1	163.4	171.7	125.5	183.8	64.2	138.1	102.3	119.9	2,549
2009	96.3	145.9	161.3	350.4	277.9	86.5	247.6	302.9	164.3	332.1	241.0	379.3	2,786
2010[1]	513.4	399.0	408.0	147.8	76.6	128.9	179.1	365.6	174.5	440.3	432.5	395.4	3,661

[1] Preliminary.   Source: Bureau of the Census, U.S. Department of Commerce

SOYBEAN OIL

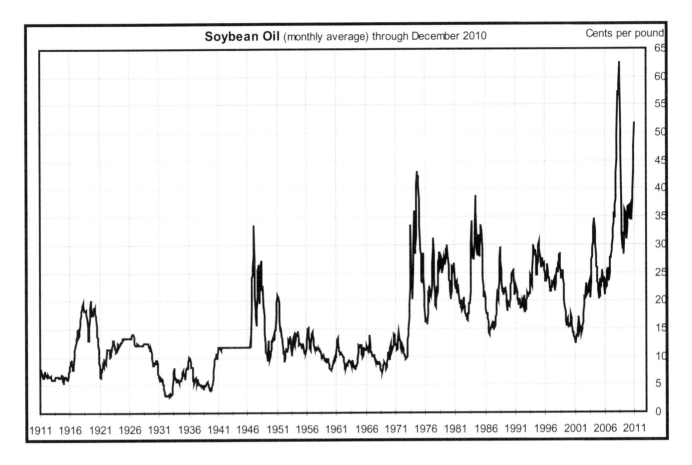

Soybean Oil (monthly average) through December 2010 — Cents per pound

Stocks of Soybean Oil (Crude and Refined) at Factories and Warehouses in the U.S. In Millions of Pounds

Year	Oct.	Nov.	Dec.	Jan.	Feb.	Mar.	Apr.	May	June	July	Aug.	Sept.
2001-02	2,877.2	2,724.9	2,787.4	2,868.1	3,038.5	2,896.4	2,952.7	2,856.8	2,943.2	2,735.9	2,529.7	2,521.7
2002-03	2,358.6	2,280.1	2,326.1	2,398.0	2,395.7	2,271.9	2,244.6	2,120.2	2,053.9	1,928.5	1,794.2	1,654.4
2003-04	1,490.6	1,411.8	1,530.4	1,579.9	1,945.6	1,988.0	1,855.9	1,644.1	1,651.6	1,514.0	1,412.0	1,180.6
2004-05	1,075.6	1,269.4	1,191.2	1,311.1	1,560.1	1,646.8	1,812.7	1,797.1	1,888.7	1,838.0	1,988.8	1,727.0
2005-06	1,699.0	1,883.5	1,851.8	2,190.5	2,498.7	2,673.4	2,718.1	2,755.4	2,885.0	2,919.2	3,106.1	3,061.2
2006-07	3,009.8	3,012.3	3,081.9	3,090.6	3,356.7	3,477.7	3,558.4	3,500.0	3,468.7	3,549.8	3,399.6	3,200.4
2007-08	3,085.2	3,224.9	3,235.2	3,277.0	3,408.0	3,278.3	3,083.5	2,925.8	2,989.0	2,906.0	2,793.2	2,567.4
2008-09	2,484.6	2,388.5	2,519.0	2,629.6	2,992.3	3,124.1	3,191.6	3,279.4	3,338.8	3,530.3	3,448.9	3,134.0
2009-10	2,860.5	2,809.4	2,990.5	3,150.5	3,217.0	3,286.9	3,261.7	3,353.5	3,465.1	3,552.9	3,544.7	3,282.6
2010-11[1]	3,358.4	3,229.9	3,295.7									

On First of Month.   [1] Preliminary.   *Source: Economic Research Service, U.S. Department of Agriculture (ERS-USDA)*

Average Price of Crude Domestic Soybean Oil (in Tank Cars) F.O.B. Decatur In Cents Per Pound

Year	Oct.	Nov.	Dec.	Jan.	Feb.	Mar.	Apr.	May	June	July	Aug.	Sept.	Average
2001-02	14.38	15.23	15.10	14.82	14.15	14.75	15.31	15.98	17.69	19.12	20.61	20.32	16.46
2002-03	20.75	23.00	22.60	21.50	21.20	21.56	22.40	23.17	22.90	21.80	20.40	23.20	22.04
2003-04	27.40	27.76	29.54	30.34	33.05	34.66	34.19	32.68	30.07	28.05	25.98	25.87	29.97
2004-05	23.23	22.95	21.79	20.46	20.70	23.60	23.09	23.38	24.70	25.46	23.59	23.19	23.01
2005-06	24.26	22.52	21.00	21.63	22.21	23.21	22.98	24.76	24.20	25.86	24.80	23.54	23.41
2006-07	24.80	27.64	27.63	28.00	28.94	29.74	31.06	32.90	34.01	35.74	34.87	36.89	31.02
2007-08	38.10	42.68	45.16	49.77	56.68	57.27	56.58	58.27	62.43	60.54	50.78	46.09	52.03
2008-09	35.50	31.55	29.30	32.16	28.93	28.23	32.76	36.06	35.66	31.08	33.69	30.96	32.16
2009-10	33.15	36.59	36.81	34.88	34.69	36.39	37.11	35.41	34.47	35.07	37.57	39.21	35.95
2010-11[1]	44.02	47.62	51.51	53.84									49.25

[1] Preliminary.   *Source: Economic Research Service, U.S. Department of Agriculture (ERS-USDA)*

Soybean Oil Futures - CME Group (CBT)
(weekly close) as of December 31, 2010

Cents per pound

Volume of Trading of Soybean Oil Futures in Chicago   In Thousands of Contracts

Year	Jan.	Feb.	Mar.	Apr.	May	June	July	Aug.	Sept.	Oct.	Nov.	Dec.	Total
2001	327.6	458.4	416.7	443.5	403.1	541.2	751.3	612.3	447.4	551.0	579.5	502.3	6,034.3
2002	474.8	497.4	468.9	497.0	526.9	588.4	701.5	648.9	529.4	549.9	705.4	628.0	6,816.5
2003	522.9	540.6	473.7	618.5	520.0	740.5	761.5	594.7	636.5	733.4	656.5	618.5	7,417.3
2004	521.3	722.6	736.2	760.2	631.2	642.9	657.5	549.5	565.4	552.9	654.3	599.3	7,593.3
2005	475.1	799.9	579.6	636.3	565.5	852.3	548.3	637.1	594.8	607.1	672.8	707.4	7,676.1
2006	531.9	611.2	597.6	866.4	688.6	1,024.5	801.2	816.7	729.0	939.3	1,003.3	878.8	9,488.5
2007	784.1	1,091.9	765.0	1,218.3	805.3	1,476.9	1,113.7	1,092.0	947.7	1,213.6	1,324.4	1,337.9	13,170.9
2008	1,294.7	1,541.4	1,291.0	1,551.1	1,107.0	1,467.6	1,624.2	1,386.9	1,441.7	1,414.4	1,252.4	1,455.9	16,828.4
2009	1,211.9	1,518.5	1,189.8	1,429.7	1,202.9	1,993.4	1,543.9	1,400.4	1,217.9	1,342.1	1,527.1	1,554.4	17,132.1
2010	1,184.3	1,787.0	1,414.2	1,924.2	1,224.4	2,198.2	1,721.4	1,646.8	1,561.7	1,588.9	2,297.3	2,242.9	20,791.2

Contract size = 60,000 lbs.   Source: CME Group; Chicago Board of Trade (CBT)

Average Open Interest of Soybean Oil Futures in Chicago   In Contracts

Year	Jan.	Feb.	Mar.	Apr.	May	June	July	Aug.	Sept.	Oct.	Nov.	Dec.
2001	134,677	133,497	123,770	128,360	142,877	151,713	162,395	166,318	159,467	164,521	167,803	154,589
2002	149,103	158,157	149,913	136,198	128,707	129,480	135,762	143,144	146,759	139,626	169,978	155,871
2003	143,607	140,272	131,323	142,123	147,584	143,218	147,610	157,066	141,596	161,556	183,747	191,176
2004	198,361	212,204	186,745	159,478	141,772	136,887	135,649	142,574	132,936	147,046	154,316	151,800
2005	159,229	174,091	161,971	145,808	135,515	155,962	147,542	132,351	139,489	165,634	175,229	186,760
2006	171,317	183,717	192,643	204,132	244,580	241,962	276,251	269,208	259,464	256,153	279,091	273,375
2007	256,800	283,761	285,436	312,454	301,566	309,109	294,005	285,255	277,219	276,874	306,390	298,906
2008	289,892	292,918	287,995	275,016	253,974	259,416	258,412	254,496	256,621	257,226	252,077	220,725
2009	204,502	211,632	206,299	208,101	217,198	246,451	245,978	239,386	217,068	229,387	248,176	229,970
2010	219,042	283,115	282,973	290,577	299,379	319,098	284,484	292,426	290,685	325,697	358,850	347,185

Contract size = 60,000 lbs.   Source: CME Group; Chicago Board of Trade (CBT)

Soybeans

Soybean is the common name for the annual leguminous plant and its seed. The soybean is a member of the oilseed family and is not considered a grain. The soybean seeds are contained in pods and are nearly spherical in shape. The seeds are usually light yellow in color. The seeds contain 20% oil and 40% protein. Soybeans were an ancient food crop in China, Japan, and Korea and were only introduced to the U.S. in the early 1800s. Today, soybeans are the second largest crop produced in the U.S. behind corn. Soybean production in the U.S. is concentrated in the Midwest and the lower Mississippi Valley. Soybean crops in the U.S. are planted in May or June and are harvested in autumn. Soybean plants usually reach maturity 100-150 days after planting depending on growing conditions.

Soybeans are used to produce a wide variety of food products. The key value of soybeans lies in the relatively high protein content, which makes it an excellent source of protein without many of the negative factors of animal meat. Popular soy-based food products include whole soybeans (roasted for snacks or used in sauces, stews and soups), soy oil for cooking and baking, soy flour, protein concentrates, isolated soy protein (which contains up to 92% protein), soy milk and baby formula (as an alternative to dairy products), soy yogurt, soy cheese, soy nut butter, soy sprouts, tofu and tofu products (soybean curd), soy sauce (which is produced by a fermentation process), and meat alternatives (hamburgers, breakfast sausage, etc).

The primary market for soybean futures is at the Chicago Board of Trade. The CBOT's soybean contract calls for the delivery of 5,000 bushels of No. 2 yellow soybeans (at contract par), No. 1 yellow soybeans (at 6 cents per bushel above the contract price), or No. 3 yellow soybeans (at a 6 cents under the contract price). Soybean futures are also traded at exchanges in Brazil, Argentina, China, and Tokyo.

Prices – Soybean futures prices fell to a 2-year low of $8.79 per bushel in October 2009 but then traded sideways to higher the first half of 2010. Soybean prices were dampened during the first half of 2010 after the USDA in May 2010 projected a 92% y/y increase in 2010/11 U.S. soybean carry-over to a 4-year high of 360 million bushels along with an increase in global soybean carry-over to a record 66.99 MMT. As the summer crop progressed, beneficial weather prompted the USDA to forecast a U.S. soybean crop of 3.345 billion bushels, the second largest in history. Despite expectations for ample global supplies and a bumper U.S. soybean crop, prices rallied into year-end and finished 2010 on a 2-1/4 year high of $13.94 per bushel, up +34% for the year. Strong Chinese demand was the main bullish factor in 2010 after Chinese imports of U.S. soybeans rose to a record 54.8 MMT, up 29% y/y, which prompted the USDA in December 2010 to hike its 2011 U.S. soybean export forecast to a record 1.59 billion bushels. Strength in soybean prices continued into 2011 after January China soybean imports rose +26% y/y to 5.14 MMT. This voracious demand, along with persistent dollar weakness, lifted soybean prices to a 2-1/2 year high of

$14.56 per bushel in February 2011. For 2011, the USDA is projecting an +0.8% y/y increase in U.S. soybean planted acreage to a record 78 million acres, although this remains to be seen as record cotton prices may prompt some farmers to plant more cotton. The US soybean stocks/use ratio for 2010/11 is tight at 4.2%, but with expected bumper crops from Argentina and Brazil, the two largest soybean producers after the U.S., the world stocks/use ratio is near average at 22.8%.

Supply – World soybean production during the 2010-11 marketing year (Sep-Aug) fell by -1.5% yr/yr to 256.102 million metric tons. World soybean production has more than quadrupled from the 62 million metric ton level seen in 1980. The world's largest soybean producers were the U.S. with 35.4% of world production in 2010-11, Brazil (26.7%), Argentina (19.3%), China (5.6%), and India (3.7%). China's soybean production has roughly doubled since 1980. Brazil's production has risen just over four times since 1980.

U.S. soybean production in 2010-11 rose by +1.7% yr/yr to a new record high of 3.375 billion bushels. U.S. farmers harvested a record high of 76.616 million acres of soybeans in 2010-11, which is up +0.3% yr/yr. The average yield in 2010-11 is down -1.1% yr/yr to 43.5 bushels per acre, just under the record high of 44.0 bushels per acre. U.S. ending stocks for the 2010-11 marketing year (September 1), rose by +9.2% to 150.9 million bushels, still above the 3-decade low of 112.4 million bushels seen in 2004-05.

Demand – Total U.S. distribution in 2010-11 fell -0.2% to 3.355 billion bushels. The distribution tables for U.S. soybeans for the 2010-11 marketing year show that 49.3% of U.S. soybean usage went for crushing into soybean oil and meal, 47.4% for exports, and 3.3% for seed and residual. The quantity of U.S. soybeans that went for crushing fell -5.5% yr/yr in 2010-11 to 1.655 billion bushels. The world soybean crush rose +7.5% yr/yr in 2010-11 to a new record high of 225.161 million metric tons, which was about double the level seen in 1993-94.

Trade – World exports of soybeans in 2010-11 rose +6.3% yr/yr to a new record high of 98.648 million metric tons. The world's largest soybean exporters in 2010-11 were the U.S. with 43.9% of world exports, Brazil with 32.7% of world exports, and Argentina with 11.8% of world exports. U.S. soybean exports in 2010-11 rose +5.9% yr/yr to a new record high of 43.273 million metric tons. Brazil's soybean exports have more than doubled in the past decade and Canada's exports have almost tripled.

World imports in 2010-11 rose +9.6% yr/yr to a new record high of 95.869 million metric tons. The world's largest importers of soybeans in 2010-11 were China with 59.5% of world imports, the European Union with 14.6%, Japan with 3.6%, and Mexico with 3.8%. China's imports in 2010-11 rose +13.2% yr/yr to a record level of 57.000 million metric tons, which is far from negligible levels prior to 1994.

World Production of Soybeans In Thousands of Metric Tons

Crop Year[4]	Argentina	Bolivia	Brazil	Canada	China	India	Indonesia	Mexico	Paraguay	Thailand	United States	Russia	World Total
2001-02	30,000	1,245	43,500	1,635	15,410	5,400	870	66	3,547	270	78,672	350	184,815
2002-03	35,500	1,650	52,000	2,336	16,510	4,000	780	89	4,500	250	75,010	423	196,869
2003-04	33,000	1,850	51,000	2,263	15,394	6,800	820	125	3,911	220	66,783	393	186,638
2004-05	39,000	2,027	53,000	3,042	17,400	5,850	825	132	4,040	217	85,019	555	215,777
2005-06	40,500	2,060	57,000	3,156	16,350	7,000	832	185	3,640	226	83,507	689	220,665
2006-07	48,800	1,650	59,000	3,466	15,967	7,690	815	80	5,856	210	87,001	807	237,126
2007-08	46,200	1,050	61,000	2,696	14,000	9,470	780	88	6,900	210	72,859	652	221,006
2008-09[1]	32,000	1,600	57,800	3,336	15,540	9,100	800	153	4,000	180	80,749	744	211,964
2009-10[2]	54,500	1,665	69,000	3,507	14,700	9,000	700	105	7,200	170	91,417	942	259,990
2010-11[3]	49,500	1,580	68,500	4,345	14,400	9,600	740	105	7,500	180	90,610	1,150	256,102

[1] Preliminary. [2] Estimate. [3] Forecast. [4] Spilt year includes Northern Hemisphere crops harvested in the late months of the first year shown combined with Southern Hemisphere crops harvested in the early months of the following year. *Sources: Oil World; Foreign Agricultural Service, U.S. Department of Agriculture (FAS-USDA)*

World Crushings and Ending Stocks of Soybeans In Thousands of Metric Tons

Crop Year	Argentina	Brazil	China	European Union	India	Japan	Mexico	Taiwan	United States	World Total	Brazil	United States	World Total
	Crushings										Ending Stocks		
2001-02	20,859	24,693	20,250	17,819	4,625	3,885	4,610	2,187	46,259	158,014	12,593	5,663	35,768
2002-03	23,533	27,168	26,540	16,480	3,375	4,217	4,335	2,135	43,948	165,189	16,636	4,853	43,214
2003-04	25,040	29,323	25,439	14,084	5,580	3,536	3,889	2,046	41,632	164,211	15,507	3,059	38,110
2004-05	27,313	29,344	30,362	14,350	4,530	3,149	3,729	2,013	46,160	175,256	16,658	6,960	48,150
2005-06	31,888	28,285	34,500	13,670	6,940	2,820	3,823	2,190	47,324	186,138	16,641	12,229	53,376
2006-07	33,586	31,110	35,970	14,670	6,485	2,925	3,900	2,161	49,198	196,075	18,189	15,617	63,129
2007-08	34,607	32,117	39,518	14,870	8,400	2,890	3,620	1,965	49,081	202,749	18,898	5,580	52,912
2008-09[1]	31,243	31,868	41,035	12,860	7,200	2,497	3,465	1,917	45,230	192,911	12,037	3,761	44,071
2009-10[2]	34,123	33,670	48,830	12,510	7,090	2,505	3,510	2,150	47,669	209,512	16,063	4,106	60,170
2010-11[3]	39,000	34,500	57,800	13,600	8,200	2,472	3,670	2,225	45,042	225,161	14,938	3,820	58,209

[1] Preliminary. [2] Estimate. [3] Forecast. *Sources: Oil World; Foreign Agricultural Service, U.S. Department of Agriculture (FAS-USDA)*

World Imports and Exports of Soybeans In Thousands of Metric Tons

Crop Year	China	European Union	Japan	Rep. of Korea	Mexico	Taiwan	World Total	Argentina	Brazil	Canada	Paraguay	United States	World Total
	Imports							Exports					
2001-02	10,385	18,675	5,023	1,434	4,510	2,578	54,385	5,960	14,504	502	2,289	28,948	52,899
2002-03	21,417	16,943	5,087	1,516	4,230	2,351	62,914	8,624	19,629	726	3,070	28,423	61,242
2003-04	16,933	14,675	4,688	1,368	3,797	2,218	53,999	6,741	20,417	914	2,667	24,128	56,042
2004-05	25,802	14,539	4,295	1,240	3,640	2,256	63,472	9,568	20,137	1,124	2,950	29,860	64,820
2005-06	28,317	13,937	3,962	1,190	3,667	2,498	64,129	7,249	25,911	1,326	2,011	25,579	63,432
2006-07	28,726	15,291	4,094	1,231	3,844	2,436	69,066	9,560	23,485	1,683	3,907	30,386	70,861
2007-08	37,816	15,123	4,014	1,232	3,584	2,148	78,129	13,839	25,364	1,753	4,585	31,538	78,774
2008-09[1]	41,098	13,213	3,396	1,167	3,327	2,216	77,175	5,590	29,987	2,017	2,234	34,817	76,851
2009-10[2]	50,338	12,609	3,402	1,197	3,450	2,469	87,439	13,088	28,578	2,247	5,350	40,852	92,783
2010-11[3]	57,000	14,000	3,450	1,260	3,600	2,500	95,869	11,600	32,300	2,625	5,635	43,273	98,648

[1] Preliminary. [2] Estimate. [3] Forecast. *Sources: Oil World; Foreign Agricultural Service, U.S. Department of Agriculture (FAS-USDA)*

Supply and Distribution of Soybeans in the United States In Millions of Bushels

Crop Year Beginning Sept. 1	Farms	Mills, Elevators[3]	Total	Production	Total Supply	Crushings	Exports	Seed, Feed & Residual Use	Total Distribution
	Supply — Stocks, Sept. 1					Distribution			
2001-02	83.5	164.2	247.7	2,890.7	3,141.0	1,700.0	1,064.0	169.0	2,933.0
2002-03	62.7	145.3	208.0	2,756.1	2,969.0	1,615.0	1,044.0	131.0	2,791.0
2003-04	58.0	120.3	178.3	2,453.7	2,638.0	1,530.0	887.0	109.0	2,525.0
2004-05	29.4	83.0	112.4	3,123.7	3,242.0	1,696.0	1,097.0	193.0	2,986.0
2005-06	99.7	156.0	255.7	3,063.2	3,322.0	1,739.0	940.0	194.0	2,873.0
2006-07	176.3	273.0	449.3	3,188.2	3,655.0	1,808.0	1,116.0	157.0	3,081.0
2007-08	143.0	430.8	573.8	2,675.8	3,261.0	1,803.0	1,159.0	94.0	3,056.0
2008-09	47.0	158.0	205.0	2,967.0	3,185.0	1,662.0	1,279.0	106.0	3,047.0
2009-10[1]	35.1	103.1	138.2	3,359.0	3,512.0	1,752.0	1,501.0	108.0	3,361.0
2010-11[2]	35.4	115.5	150.9	3,329.3	3,495.0	1,655.0	1,590.0	110.0	3,355.0

[1] Preliminary. [2] Estimate. [3] Also warehouses. *Source: Economic Research Service, U.S. Department of Agriculture (ERS-USDA)*

SOYBEANS

Salient Statistics & Official Crop Production Reports of Soybeans in the United States   In Millions of Bushels

Year	Planted	Acreage Harvested	Yield Per Acre (Bu.)	Farm Price ($/Bu.)	Farm Value (Million Dollars)	Yield of Oil (Lbs. Per Bushel Crushed)	Yield of Meal (Lbs. Per Bushel Crushed)	Aug. 1	Sept. 1	Oct. 1	Nov. 1	Dec. 1	Final
	---- 1,000 Acres ----									Crop Production Reports — In Thousands of Bushels			
2001-02	74,075	72,975	39.6	4.38	12,606	11.14	44.27	2,867,474	2,833,511	2,907,042	2,922,914	----	2,890,682
2002-03	73,963	72,497	38.0	5.64	15,253	11.39	43.90	2,628,387	2,655,819	2,653,798	2,689,691	----	2,756,147
2003-04	73,404	72,476	33.9	7.95	18,014	11.20	44.32	2,862,039	2,642,644	2,468,390	2,451,759	----	2,453,665
2004-05	75,208	73,958	42.2	5.90	17,895	11.33	44.26	2,876,627	2,835,989	3,106,861	3,150,441	----	3,123,686
2005-06	72,032	71,251	43.0	5.63	17,269	11.64	43.83	2,791,133	2,856,449	2,967,075	3,043,116	----	3,063,237
2006-07	75,522	74,602	42.9	6.67	20,468	11.34	44.03	2,927,634	3,092,970	3,188,576	3,203,908	----	3,188,247
2007-08	64,741	64,146	41.7	11.02	26,974	11.54	43.95	2,625,274	2,618,796	2,598,046	2,594,275	----	2,675,822
2008-09	75,718	74,681	39.7	10.13	29,458	11.36	43.93	2,972,577	2,933,888	2,983,023	2,920,589	----	2,967,007
2009-10[1]	77,451	76,372	44.0	9.61	32,145	11.12	43.81	3,199,172	3,245,292	3,250,113	3,319,270	----	3,359,011
2010-11[2]	77,404	76,616	43.5	11.10	38,915			3,433,370	3,482,899	3,408,211	3,375,067	----	3,329,341

[1] Preliminary.   [2] Forecast.   NA = Not available.   Source: National Agricultural Statistics Service, U.S. Department of Agriculture (NASS-USDA)

Stocks of Soybeans in the United States   In Thousands of Bushels

Year	On Farms Mar. 1	On Farms June 1	On Farms Sept. 1	On Farms Dec. 1	Off Farms Mar. 1	Off Farms June 1	Off Farms Sept. 1	Off Farms Dec. 1	Total Stocks Mar. 1	Total Stocks June 1	Total Stocks Sept. 1	Total Stocks Dec. 1
2001	780,000	365,000	83,500	1,240,000	623,908	343,180	164,247	1,035,713	1,403,908	708,180	247,747	2,275,713
2002	687,000	301,200	62,700	1,170,000	648,987	383,721	145,320	943,641	1,335,987	684,921	208,020	2,113,641
2003	636,500	272,500	58,000	820,000	565,528	329,862	120,329	868,653	1,201,028	602,362	178,329	1,688,653
2004	355,900	110,000	29,400	1,300,000	549,947	300,604	83,014	1,004,640	905,847	410,604	112,414	2,304,640
2005	795,000	356,100	99,700	1,345,000	586,364	343,174	156,038	1,157,098	1,381,364	699,274	255,738	2,502,098
2006	872,000	495,500	176,300	1,461,000	797,206	495,199	273,026	1,240,366	1,669,206	990,699	449,326	2,701,366
2007	910,000	500,000	143,000	1,100,000	876,887	592,185	430,810	1,231,860	1,786,887	1,092,185	573,810	2,331,860
2008	593,000	226,600	47,000	1,189,000	840,982	449,543	158,034	1,086,432	1,433,982	676,143	205,034	2,275,432
2009	656,500	226,300	35,100	1,229,500	645,289	369,859	103,098	1,109,050	1,301,789	596,159	138,198	2,338,550
2010[1]	609,200	232,600	35,400	1,091,000	660,868	338,523	115,485	1,185,860	1,270,068	571,123	150,885	2,276,860

[1] Preliminary.   Source: National Agricultural Statistics Service, U.S. Department of Agriculture (NASS-USDA)

Commercial Stocks of Soybeans in the United States, on First of Month   In Millions of Bushels

Year	Jan.	Feb.	Mar.	Apr.	May	June	July	Aug.	Sept.	Oct.	Nov.	Dec.
2001	34.5	28.8	25.2	22.5	16.3	15.0	12.9	13.4	11.9	9.6	34.7	38.2
2002	29.6	27.0	22.2	21.0	18.4	15.4	14.4	10.2	4.6	8.4	26.9	28.4
2003	25.9	13.2	13.9	12.8	9.7	9.4	11.7	7.6	4.5	7.0	33.0	36.7
2004	35.5	26.2	26.0	19.4	15.7	13.5	8.0	5.9	4.4	10.8	31.1	32.9
2005	26.5	21.5	19.5	16.0	14.8	12.1	11.5	8.8	5.4	17.0	36.7	36.1
2006	36.8	30.2	26.1	25.7	17.6	20.5	14.6	14.5	14.5	19.0	40.1	43.7
2007	42.0	36.5	37.3	34.3	29.7	27.4	26.6	24.6	25.5	32.0	54.0	61.3
2008	51.1	45.5	41.8	36.3	28.2	25.6	19.2	14.8	11.4	19.6	40.5	46.1
2009	44.6	36.8	27.0	15.6	13.9	11.8	10.0	5.8	5.9	24.7	40.5	44.3
2010	30.0	28.5	20.1	22.3	10.8	8.0	8.2	4.5	3.3	19.2	45.0	32.0

Source: Livestock Division, U.S. Department of Agriculture (LD-USDA)

Stocks of Soybeans at Mills in the United States, on First of Month   In Millions of Bushels

Year	Sept.	Oct.	Nov.	Dec.	Jan.	Feb.	Mar.	Apr.	May	June	July	Aug.
2000-01	52.1	56.8	179.4	166.8	137.8	143.3	127.0	120.6	94.9	86.1	79.3	69.0
2001-02	69.0	41.3	152.8	137.1	121.4	129.6	128.2	112.9	104.2	88.2	67.9	65.4
2002-03	46.4	36.3	114.5	113.5	106.0	109.2	102.9	91.5	91.6	76.0	64.9	55.6
2003-04	35.3	31.9	129.9	121.0	121.7	125.6	124.5	134.3	114.8	91.2	76.0	61.4
2004-05	37.0	74.8	114.1	113.1	100.3	85.6	88.1	88.8	70.9	59.2	66.1	51.7
2005-06	43.7	66.2	158.3	129.7	114.1	117.4	108.0	90.0	69.5	64.0	63.1	51.5
2006-07	52.7	48.7	124.7	132.4	127.0	133.0	121.8	123.8	113.8	102.0	103.5	99.1
2007-08	92.6	101.6	157.2	139.5	117.9	135.5	122.0	104.4	100.8	78.9	74.8	73.7
2008-09	53.3	50.1	130.4	121.7	116.4	103.4	99.8	100.5	98.8	82.5	89.6	75.0
2009-10[1]	45.2	31.5	99.2	129.6	108.0	101.6	95.3	96.8	80.5	62.7	66.6	63.5

[1] Preliminary.   Source: Economic Research Service, U.S. Department of Agriculture (ERS-USDA)

Production of Soybeans for Beans in the United States, by State   In Millions of Bushels

Year	Arkan-sas	Illinois	Indiana	Iowa	Ken-tucky	Mich-igan	Minn-esota	Miss-issippi	Missouri	Neb-raska	Ohio	Tenn-essee	Total
2001-02	91.2	477.9	273.9	480.5	48.8	63.9	266.4	37.0	186.2	223.0	187.8	35.4	2,890.7
2002-03	96.5	453.7	239.5	499.2	42.6	78.5	308.9	43.8	170.0	176.3	151.0	34.7	2,756.1
2003-04	111.3	379.6	204.1	342.9	53.9	54.7	238.4	55.8	146.0	182.3	164.8	47.0	2,453.7
2004-05	122.9	495.0	284.3	497.4	57.2	75.2	232.7	61.5	223.2	218.5	207.7	48.4	3,123.7
2005-06	102.0	439.4	263.6	525.0	53.3	76.6	306.0	58.0	181.7	235.3	201.6	41.8	3,063.2
2006-07	107.5	482.4	284.0	510.1	60.3	89.6	319.0	42.9	191.2	250.5	217.1	44.1	3,188.2
2007-08	101.5	360.2	220.3	448.8	30.3	70.7	267.3	58.3	175.1	196.4	199.3	19.2	2,675.8
2008-09	123.5	428.6	244.4	449.7	47.6	69.9	264.9	78.4	191.1	226.0	161.3	49.6	2,967.0
2009-10	122.6	430.1	266.6	486.0	68.2	79.6	284.8	77.1	230.6	259.4	222.0	68.9	3,359.0
2010-11[1]	110.3	466.1	258.5	496.2	47.3	88.7	329.0	76.2	210.4	267.8	220.3	43.7	3,329.3

[1] Preliminary.   Source: Agricultural Statistics Board, U.S. Department of Agriculture (ASB-USDA)

U. S. Exports of Soybeans   In Millions of Bushels

Year	Sept.	Oct.	Nov.	Dec.	Jan.	Feb.	Mar.	Apr.	May	June	July	Aug.	Total
2001-02	31.7	158.9	158.0	133.2	157.2	132.0	63.8	46.0	45.6	43.2	56.0	38.0	1,063.7
2002-03	30.9	136.7	152.8	114.7	159.3	151.5	92.1	66.4	35.9	31.9	37.9	34.3	1,044.4
2003-04	34.0	165.3	186.4	143.2	109.3	82.6	69.9	28.7	19.1	20.2	14.8	10.8	884.2
2004-05	47.2	177.7	181.0	155.0	121.9	123.2	96.4	65.2	49.6	35.2	20.0	30.3	1,102.7
2005-06	32.3	143.1	140.1	83.1	111.8	111.3	95.6	43.4	46.5	39.0	47.6	51.0	944.8
2006-07	64.9	182.6	126.4	122.7	147.2	126.5	96.9	71.1	41.9	48.9	37.9	49.6	1,116.5
2007-08	62.0	138.6	127.4	146.0	146.1	139.2	114.8	72.7	56.2	58.7	51.2	45.9	1,158.8
2008-09	34.3	179.3	173.3	170.9	152.9	159.1	101.6	82.0	60.0	60.5	49.9	55.4	1,279.3
2009-10	39.1	198.0	298.8	225.9	226.4	171.5	131.5	54.0	32.0	28.2	37.2	58.3	1,501.1
2010-11[1]	72.8	289.5	258.0	195.8	185.3								2,481.2

[1] Preliminary.   Source: Economic Research Service, U.S. Department of Agriculture (ERS-USDA)

Spread Between Value of Products and Soybean Price in the United States   In Cents Per Bushel

Year	Sept.	Oct.	Nov.	Dec.	Jan.	Feb.	Mar.	Apr.	May	June	July	Aug.	Average
2000-01	81	76	77	89	85	59	65	72	67	81	96	92	78
2001-02	102	108	106	83	86	65	65	65	57	63	64	89	79
2002-03	77	73	52	60	53	52	61	53	62	59	72	74	62
2003-04	117	88	94	81	84	81	96	96	85	97	150	127	99
2004-05	132	95	70	66	75	76	67	78	69	75	73	82	79
2005-06	100	102	70	91	90	83	94	102	107	104	106	110	97
2006-07	126	105	81	74	73	72	80	64	78	113	110	88	89
2007-08	90	83	100	109	105	103	114	114	84	105	122	114	103
2008-09	195	95	68	72	59	61	61	77	109	106	92	156	95
2009-10[1]	192	123	127	115	104	103	76	88	85	113	89	93	109

[1] Preliminary.   Source: Economic Research Service, U.S. Department of Agriculture (ERS-USDA)

Soybean Crushed (Factory Consumption) in the United States   In Millions of Bushels

Year	Jan.	Feb.	Mar.	Apr.	May	June	July	Aug.	Sept.	Oct.	Nov.	Dec.	Total
2001-02	128.2	150.2	149.1	153.4	155.1	139.0	149.8	139.2	140.6	134.6	129.8	130.6	1,700
2002-03	122.3	149.5	145.7	150.2	142.7	129.2	142.8	127.0	129.8	121.4	129.3	125.1	1,615
2003-04	127.6	146.2	145.6	145.8	146.0	131.4	129.6	112.5	117.5	109.4	115.3	103.0	1,530
2004-05	121.0	155.3	151.1	150.0	148.6	137.6	148.5	139.4	142.8	132.0	139.5	130.3	1,696
2005-06	133.2	157.7	151.5	148.4	152.4	136.3	149.5	135.5	146.2	137.4	148.5	142.1	1,739
2006-07	142.4	161.7	155.1	157.4	155.5	136.9	156.1	145.0	152.1	148.9	150.4	146.2	1,808
2007-08	147.3	163.7	156.3	164.1	160.5	146.5	156.0	147.5	152.6	141.0	139.3	128.6	1,803
2008-09	125.7	150.0	144.7	141.3	145.2	135.4	144.4	140.3	146.2	140.1	128.8	119.8	1,662
2009-10	113.3	163.5	168.7	173.1	167.2	153.9	156.1	136.5	133.0	129.2	129.4	128.1	1,752
2010-11[1]	130.4	157.2	155.1	153.1									1,787

[1] Preliminary.   Source: Economic Research Service, U.S. Department of Agriculture (ERS-USDA)

SOYBEANS

Soybean Futures - CME Group (CBT)
(weekly close) as of December 31, 2010

Cents per bushel

Volume of Trading of Soybean Futures in Chicago   In Thousands of Contracts

Year	Jan.	Feb.	Mar.	Apr.	May	June	July	Aug.	Sept.	Oct.	Nov.	Dec.	Total
2001	935.0	947.4	843.1	916.3	909.5	1,155.6	1,508.1	1,122.0	648.7	1,356.1	964.7	844.1	12,150
2002	1,078.8	899.9	1,065.7	1,238.6	1,048.3	1,311.8	1,762.2	1,346.4	1,002.9	1,486.1	1,070.9	1,163.5	14,475
2003	1,267.3	1,222.9	997.1	1,588.9	1,368.2	1,723.4	1,385.7	1,193.5	1,308.5	2,416.3	1,535.4	1,538.5	17,546
2004	1,509.7	1,879.6	1,957.2	2,036.2	1,593.2	1,601.7	1,551.3	1,107.6	1,052.8	1,635.3	1,395.3	1,526.1	18,846
2005	1,398.6	2,085.8	1,959.9	1,656.5	1,454.6	2,577.3	1,675.4	1,487.2	1,069.1	1,765.0	1,241.5	1,845.1	20,216
2006	1,503.4	1,889.1	1,501.2	1,916.6	1,682.6	2,443.2	1,798.2	1,638.5	1,420.2	2,884.7	2,017.4	1,952.6	22,648
2007	1,976.3	2,620.6	2,251.0	2,641.2	2,107.2	3,461.3	2,734.6	2,323.7	2,315.2	3,680.4	2,521.3	3,093.5	31,726
2008	3,528.7	3,746.2	2,895.0	3,786.1	2,272.2	3,731.2	3,134.9	2,454.4	2,615.1	3,719.0	1,910.5	2,579.7	36,373
2009	2,773.7	2,892.5	2,576.2	3,638.9	2,635.5	3,439.7	2,845.7	2,417.6	2,348.2	3,996.4	2,820.8	3,373.7	35,759
2010	2,659.0	3,392.5	2,932.8	3,414.4	2,078.2	2,946.5	2,546.1	2,266.1	2,553.0	4,660.2	3,455.9	4,029.3	36,934

Contract size = 5,000 bu.   *Source: CME Group; Chicago Board of Trade (CBT)*

Average Open Interest of Soybean Futures in Chicago   In Contracts

Year	Jan.	Feb.	Mar.	Apr.	May	June	July	Aug.	Sept.	Oct.	Nov.	Dec.
2001	160,730	164,017	148,190	156,781	137,227	153,190	181,194	165,630	167,677	195,366	175,522	173,116
2002	156,898	169,242	169,882	164,388	156,548	188,692	220,758	201,494	201,808	210,033	208,099	213,868
2003	201,536	217,680	226,421	251,314	230,325	222,185	190,206	190,533	232,030	265,088	241,320	252,874
2004	258,708	267,482	263,737	262,919	222,310	199,108	172,194	171,791	190,006	242,654	228,700	241,972
2005	244,197	266,745	295,324	268,081	252,582	313,724	278,738	256,853	249,030	285,070	275,308	290,370
2006	315,640	359,379	354,211	374,507	375,124	371,155	336,000	348,321	361,643	384,069	394,259	414,374
2007	416,459	478,579	474,466	470,517	465,303	549,655	536,595	495,302	526,913	580,446	586,635	582,502
2008	563,927	598,278	543,451	506,423	458,047	489,069	446,006	388,939	364,679	348,438	312,905	304,252
2009	297,316	313,704	292,160	358,857	415,599	454,846	410,718	401,752	428,320	461,463	438,531	464,281
2010	446,212	465,666	434,272	477,138	459,342	462,796	470,087	514,703	553,196	633,086	624,213	643,091

Contract size = 5,000 bu.   *Source: CME Group; Chicago Board of Trade (CBT)*

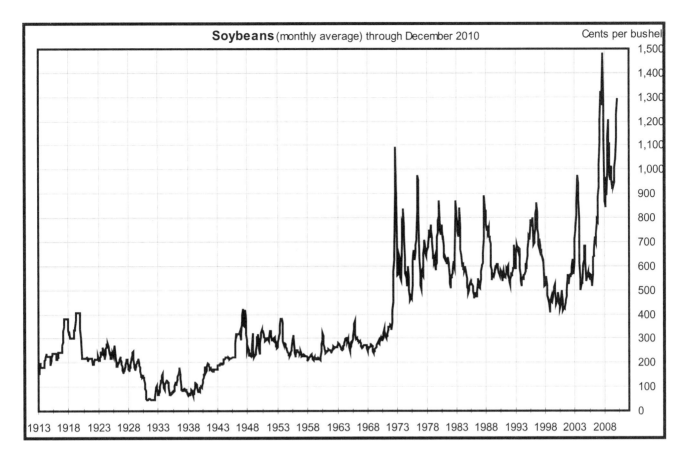

Soybeans (monthly average) through December 2010 — Cents per bushel

Average Cash Price of No. 1 Yellow Soybeans at Illinois Processor   In Cents Per Bushel

Year	Jan.	Feb.	Mar.	Apr.	May	June	July	Aug.	Sept.	Oct.	Nov.	Dec.	Average
2000-01	484	468	483	506	477	457	451	441	457	474	517	510	477
2001-02	469	430	441	438	437	440	464	471	492	519	575	567	479
2002-03	579	541	575	566	570	590	580	611	640	635	601	589	590
2003-04	639	729	763	772	823	872	975	992	958	890	809	641	822
2004-05	562	519	534	545	539	544	628	622	644	701	703	639	598
2005-06	565	553	574	592	576	575	569	562	581	576	577	542	570
2006-07	535	580	661	657	683	735	730	718	749	792	801	804	704
2007-08	907	944	1,032	1,123	1,216	1,335	1,312	1,292	1,324	1,499	1,516	1,288	1,232
2008-09	1,140	903	893	868	991	938	917	1,025	1,166	1,237	1,096	1,136	1,026
2009-10[1]	1,012	978	1,009	1,033	984	944	949	975	955	955	1,030	1,066	991

[1] Preliminary.   *Source: Economic Research Service, U.S. Department of Agriculture (ERS-USDA)*

Average Price Received by Farmers for Soybeans in the United States   In Dollars Per Bushel

Year	Jan.	Feb.	Mar.	Apr.	May	June	July	Aug.	Sept.	Oct.	Nov.	Dec.	Average
2001-02	4.53	4.09	4.16	4.20	4.22	4.22	4.38	4.47	4.64	4.88	5.35	5.53	4.38
2002-03	5.39	5.20	5.46	5.46	5.51	5.55	5.59	5.82	6.07	6.09	5.82	5.68	5.64
2003-04	6.06	6.60	7.05	7.17	7.35	8.28	9.28	9.62	9.56	9.08	8.46	6.83	7.95
2004-05	5.83	5.56	5.36	5.45	5.57	5.42	5.95	6.03	6.21	6.58	6.65	6.15	5.90
2005-06	5.77	5.67	5.62	5.78	5.87	5.67	5.57	5.52	5.68	5.62	5.61	5.23	5.63
2006-07	5.23	5.52	6.08	6.18	6.37	6.87	6.95	6.88	7.12	7.51	7.56	7.72	6.67
2007-08	8.15	8.36	9.42	10.00	9.95	11.70	11.40	12.00	12.10	13.10	13.30	12.80	11.02
2008-09	10.80	9.95	9.39	9.24	9.97	9.54	9.12	9.79	10.70	11.40	10.80	10.80	10.13
2009-10	9.75	9.43	9.53	9.80	9.79	9.41	9.39	9.47	9.41	9.45	9.79	10.10	9.61
2010-11[1]	9.98	10.20	11.10	11.60	11.60	12.10							11.10

[1] Preliminary.   *Source: Economic Research Service, U.S. Department of Agriculture (ERS-USDA)*

Stock Index Futures - U.S.

A stock index simply represents a basket of underlying stocks. Indices can be either price-weighted or capitalization-weighted. In a price-weighted index, such as the Dow Jones Industrials Average, the individual stock prices are simply added up and then divided by a divisor, meaning that stocks with higher prices have a higher weighting in the index value. In a capitalization-weighted index, such as the Standard and Poor's 500 index, the weighting of each stock corresponds to the size of the company as determined by its capitalization (i.e., the total dollar value of its stock). Stock indices cover a variety of different sectors. For example, the Dow Jones Industrials Average contains 30 blue-chip stocks that represent the industrial sector. The S&P 500 index includes 500 of the largest blue-chip U.S. companies. The NYSE index includes all the stocks that are traded at the New York Stock Exchange. The Nasdaq 100 includes the largest 100 companies that are traded on the Nasdaq Exchange. The most popular U.S. stock index futures contract is the S&P 500 at the Chicago Mercantile Exchange (CME).

Prices – The S&P 500 index in 2010 extended the recovery rally that began in 2009 and closed the year up 12.8%, adding to the 23.5% rally seen in 2009. The S&P 500 continued to rally in early 2011 to a 2-1/2 year high of 1344.07 in February, which represented an overall 102% rally from the 14-year low of 666.79 posted in March 2009.

The U.S. stock market was able to double in value from the March 2009 through early 2011 because of the recovery in the U.S. and global economy and the remarkable recovery in earnings growth. That recovery was driven by an extraordinarily easy monetary policy from the Federal Reserve, which kept its federal funds rate target near zero during 2010 and also engaged in a massive new $600 billion quantitative easing program in November 2010.

The U.S. recession, which officially ended in June 2009, showed six straight quarters of growth through 2010. U.S. GDP took a dip to +1.7% in Q2-2010 due to the fall-out from the European debt crisis, but then picked up to +2.6% in Q3-2010 and to +3.2% in Q4-2010.

Strong growth in the developing world also helped to boost U.S. economic growth and corporate earnings. China's economy accelerated in late 2009 and early 2010 with GDP growth of +11.9% in Q1-2010, easing just mildly to +9.8% by Q4-2010. U.S. exports bottomed out in April 2009 and then rose steadily by a total of 31% by December 2010.

U.S. corporations did a remarkably good job of preserving earnings during the recession and then quickly expanding earnings once the recession was over. U.S. corporations preserved margins by slashing employee headcounts and improving productivity. Many corporations also focused on sales in the developing world, where growth was much stronger. By keeping costs down, corporations were able to boost earnings far beyond revenue growth. Bank earnings were devastated by the financial crisis, but managed to bounce back in 2010.

Earnings growth for the S&P 500 companies was negative for nine consecutive quarters from Q3-2007 through Q3-2009. However, earnings growth turned positive in Q4-2009 and was then positive for the next five quarters through Q4-2010, showing growth for all of 2010 of 30.7% y/y. As of early 2011, the S&P 500 was trading at a very reasonable price-to-earnings ratio based on forward-looking earnings of 13.5, which was below the 5-year average of 14.9 as well as the 10-year average of 16.7. The reasonable valuation level leaves room on the upside for further gains in stock prices once earnings growth and the economic recovery gain better traction.

Average Value of Dow Jones Industrials Index (30 Stocks)

Year	Jan.	Feb.	Mar.	Apr.	May	June	July	Aug.	Sept.	Oct.	Nov.	Dec.	Average
2001	10,682.7	10,774.6	10,081.3	10,234.5	11,005.0	10,767.2	10,444.5	10,314.7	9,042.6	9,220.8	9,721.8	9,979.9	10,189.1
2002	9,923.8	9,891.1	10,501.0	10,165.2	10,080.5	9,492.4	8,616.5	8,685.5	8,160.2	8,048.1	8,625.7	8,526.7	9,226.4
2003	8,474.4	7,916.2	7,977.7	8,332.1	8,623.4	9,098.1	9,154.5	9,284.8	9,492.5	9,683.6	9,762.2	10,124.7	8,993.7
2004	10,540.1	10,601.5	10,323.7	10,419.9	10,083.8	10,364.9	10,152.1	10,032.8	10,204.6	10,001.6	10,411.8	10,673.4	10,317.5
2005	10,539.5	10,723.8	10,682.1	10,283.2	10,377.2	10,486.6	10,545.4	10,554.3	10,532.5	10,324.3	10,695.3	10,827.8	10,547.7
2006	10,872.5	10,971.2	11,144.5	11,234.7	11,333.9	10,998.0	11,032.5	11,257.4	11,533.6	11,963.1	12,185.2	12,377.6	11,408.7
2007	12,512.9	12,631.5	12,268.5	12,754.8	13,407.8	13,480.2	13,677.9	13,239.7	13,557.7	13,901.3	13,200.5	13,406.9	13,170.0
2008	12,537.4	12,419.6	12,193.9	12,656.6	12,812.5	12,056.7	11,322.4	11,530.8	11,114.1	9,176.7	8,614.6	8,595.6	11,252.6
2009	8,396.2	7,690.5	7,235.5	7,992.1	8,398.4	8,593.0	8,679.8	9,375.1	9,635.0	9,857.3	10,227.6	10,433.4	8,876.1
2010	10,471.2	1,021.5	10,677.5	11,052.2	10,500.2	10,159.3	10,222.2	10,350.4	10,598.1	11,044.5	11,198.6	11,465.3	9,896.7

Source: New York Stock Exchange (NYSE)

Average Value of Dow Jones Transportation Index (20 Stocks)

Year	Jan.	Feb.	Mar.	Apr.	May	June	July	Aug.	Sept.	Oct.	Nov.	Dec.	Average
2001	3,029.9	3,010.2	2,792.5	2,776.6	2,908.2	2,770.4	2,887.3	2,852.1	2,344.8	2,217.3	2,404.6	2,603.0	2,716.4
2002	2,735.3	2,719.1	2,942.9	2,776.0	2,734.8	2,702.2	2,432.1	2,318.5	2,216.0	2,216.6	2,321.6	2,331.7	2,537.2
2003	2,297.3	2,102.5	2,094.6	2,278.7	2,429.9	2,459.6	2,554.5	2,617.3	2,744.7	2,841.3	2,920.0	2,969.3	2,525.8
2004	3,021.0	2,889.4	2,838.3	2,941.1	2,877.1	3,069.0	3,099.8	3,065.8	3,205.1	3,372.6	3,589.4	3,750.0	3,143.2
2005	3,587.0	3,614.5	3,779.4	3,527.8	3,548.8	3,542.1	3,663.1	3,726.1	3,637.0	3,673.1	4,051.7	4,152.1	3,708.6
2006	4,224.5	4,362.5	4,519.5	4,679.6	4,761.4	4,663.1	4,636.1	4,291.1	4,363.3	4,654.7	4,761.6	4,660.0	4,548.1
2007	4,752.2	5,024.6	4,817.3	5,059.2	5,174.8	5,137.2	5,258.8	4,889.0	4,812.7	4,891.2	4,605.9	4,686.4	4,925.8
2008	4,348.7	4,720.0	4,641.9	4,996.9	5,304.5	5,166.7	4,899.2	5,057.0	4,889.3	3,815.4	3,518.5	3,369.2	4,560.6
2009	3,238.3	2,857.3	2,499.9	2,986.8	3,163.7	3,266.6	3,321.5	3,697.2	3,863.1	3,844.4	3,915.2	4,117.2	3,397.6
2010	4,119.6	3,971.7	4,308.5	4,597.7	4,427.6	4,259.5	4,217.9	4,280.6	4,439.9	4,670.6	4,846.8	5,067.4	4,434.0

Source: New York Stock Exchange (NYSE)

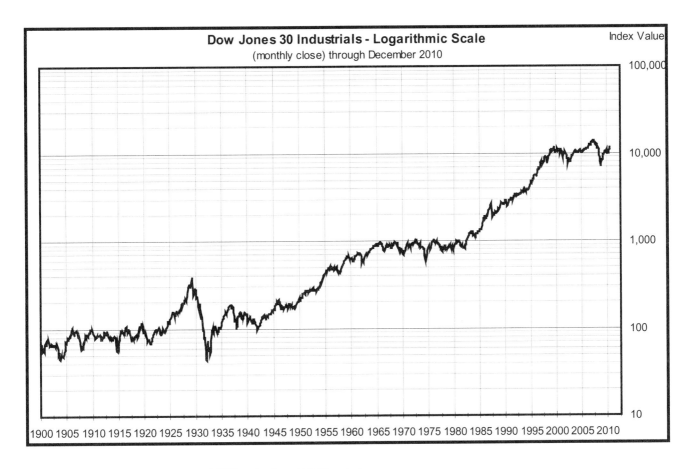

Average Value of Dow Jones Utilities Index (15 Stocks)

Year	Jan.	Feb.	Mar.	Apr.	May	June	July	Aug.	Sept.	Oct.	Nov.	Dec.	Average
2001	360.9	385.1	375.7	387.0	388.9	367.2	356.8	345.4	321.3	308.8	291.4	284.0	347.7
2002	290.7	279.6	298.4	305.1	297.3	276.1	235.5	241.0	221.7	189.2	200.4	208.5	253.6
2003	217.7	199.5	203.3	215.9	232.3	250.4	240.3	236.8	246.5	253.1	249.2	258.4	233.6
2004	268.8	272.2	278.2	275.6	268.4	275.4	278.8	285.3	293.3	303.3	324.9	327.8	287.7
2005	331.9	351.5	356.3	364.5	364.4	376.3	392.5	397.4	422.7	401.3	395.3	409.0	380.2
2006	416.7	408.2	401.7	392.1	401.0	409.2	424.1	436.9	430.1	439.8	449.1	458.5	422.3
2007	449.9	474.1	486.1	516.9	526.2	498.2	502.3	489.0	499.5	514.0	523.5	540.9	501.7
2008	518.8	499.0	480.3	506.2	516.7	519.1	500.8	472.4	446.3	370.1	368.1	362.7	463.4
2009	371.3	356.3	315.8	331.6	339.3	350.6	361.4	373.3	376.0	375.6	373.4	398.9	360.3
2010	393.8	371.9	378.1	384.3	372.7	366.9	379.8	389.8	396.6	404.8	400.5	400.8	386.7

Source: New York Stock Exchange (NYSE)

Average Value of Standard & Poor's 500 Index

Year	Jan.	Feb.	Mar.	Apr.	May	June	July	Aug.	Sept.	Oct.	Nov.	Dec.	Average
2001	1,335.6	1,305.8	1,185.9	1,189.8	1,270.4	1,238.8	1,204.5	1,178.5	1,047.6	1,076.6	1,129.7	1,144.9	1,192.3
2002	1,140.2	1,100.7	1,153.8	1,112.0	1,079.3	1,014.1	903.6	912.6	867.8	854.6	909.9	899.2	995.6
2003	895.8	837.6	846.6	890.0	936.0	988.0	992.5	989.5	1,019.4	1,038.7	1,049.9	1,080.6	963.7
2004	1,132.5	1,143.4	1,124.0	1,133.1	1,102.8	1,132.8	1,105.9	1,088.9	1,117.7	1,118.1	1,168.9	1,199.2	1,130.6
2005	1,181.4	1,199.6	1,194.9	1,164.4	1,178.3	1,202.3	1,222.2	1,224.3	1,225.9	1,192.0	1,237.3	1,262.1	1,207.1
2006	1,278.7	1,276.7	1,293.7	1,302.2	1,290.0	1,253.1	1,260.2	1,287.2	1,317.8	1,363.3	1,388.6	1,416.4	1,310.7
2007	1,424.2	1,444.8	1,407.0	1,463.7	1,511.1	1,514.5	1,520.7	1,454.6	1,497.1	1,539.7	1,463.4	1,479.2	1,476.7
2008	1,378.8	1,354.9	1,316.9	1,370.5	1,403.2	1,341.3	1,257.3	1,281.5	1,217.0	968.8	883.0	877.4	1,220.9
2009	865.6	805.2	757.1	848.2	902.4	926.1	935.8	1,009.7	1,044.6	1,067.7	1,088.1	1,110.4	946.7
2010	1,123.6	1,089.2	1,152.1	1,197.3	1,125.1	1,083.4	1,079.8	1,087.3	1,122.1	1,171.6	1,198.9	1,241.5	1,139.3

Source: Index and Option Market (IOM), division of the Chicago Mercantile Exchange (CME)

STOCK INDEX FUTURES - U.S.

Composite Index of Leading Indicators (1992 = 100)

Year	Jan.	Feb.	Mar.	Apr.	May	June	July	Aug.	Sept.	Oct.	Nov.	Dec.	Average
2001	84.9	84.5	84.2	84.1	84.5	84.6	84.8	84.9	84.2	84.3	85.3	86.6	84.7
2002	87.1	87.7	88.0	88.1	89.0	89.0	89.1	89.3	89.3	89.4	90.2	90.5	88.9
2003	90.6	90.5	90.6	91.1	92.5	93.1	93.8	94.3	95.0	95.8	96.4	96.9	93.4
2004	97.5	97.8	99.1	99.3	100.0	100.2	100.6	100.6	100.8	100.7	101.4	102.0	100.0
2005	101.8	102.2	101.7	101.8	102.1	103.1	102.9	103.1	102.4	103.3	104.2	104.2	102.7
2006	104.7	104.4	104.6	104.4	103.7	103.9	103.7	103.3	103.7	103.9	103.8	104.4	104.0
2007	104.0	103.7	104.1	103.9	104.0	103.9	104.6	103.6	103.7	103.2	102.8	102.6	103.7
2008	102.1	101.9	101.9	102.0	101.9	101.9	101.2	100.3	100.3	99.4	99.0	98.8	100.9
2009	98.8	98.3	98.1	99.2	100.6	101.3	102.5	103.1	104.2	104.7	105.8	106.2	101.9
2010[1]	106.7	107.2	108.6	108.6	109.0	108.8	109.0	109.1	109.7	110.1	111.3	112.4	109.2

[1] Preliminary.   Source: The Conference Board

Consumer Confidence, The Conference Board (2004 = 100)

Year	Jan.	Feb.	Mar.	Apr.	May	June	July	Aug.	Sept.	Oct.	Nov.	Dec.	Average
2001	115.7	109.3	116.9	109.9	116.1	118.9	116.3	114.0	97.0	85.3	84.9	94.6	106.6
2002	97.8	95.0	110.7	108.5	110.3	106.3	97.4	94.5	93.7	79.6	84.9	80.7	96.6
2003	78.8	64.8	61.4	81.0	83.6	83.5	77.0	81.7	77.0	81.7	92.5	94.8	79.8
2004	97.7	88.5	88.5	93.0	93.1	102.8	105.7	98.7	96.7	92.9	92.6	102.7	96.1
2005	105.1	104.4	103.0	97.5	103.1	106.2	103.6	105.5	87.5	85.2	98.3	103.8	100.3
2006	106.8	102.7	107.5	109.8	104.7	105.4	107.0	100.2	105.9	105.1	105.3	110.0	105.9
2007	110.2	111.2	108.2	106.3	108.5	105.3	111.9	105.6	99.5	95.2	87.8	90.6	103.4
2008	87.3	76.4	65.9	62.8	58.1	51.0	51.9	58.5	61.4	38.8	44.7	38.6	58.0
2009	37.4	25.3	26.9	40.8	54.8	49.3	47.4	54.5	53.4	48.7	50.6	53.6	45.2
2010[1]	56.5	46.4	52.3	57.7	62.7	54.3	51.0	53.2	48.6	49.9	54.1		53.3

[1] Preliminary.   Source: The Conference Board (TCB) Copyrighted.

Capacity Utilization Rates (Total Industry)   In Percent

Year	Jan.	Feb.	Mar.	Apr.	May	June	July	Aug.	Sept.	Oct.	Nov.	Dec.	Average
2001	79.1	78.4	77.9	77.5	76.8	76.1	75.6	75.1	74.7	74.2	73.6	73.5	76.0
2002	73.8	73.7	74.1	74.4	74.7	75.3	75.0	75.1	75.2	75.0	75.3	75.0	74.7
2003	75.6	75.9	75.8	75.2	75.3	75.4	75.7	75.7	76.1	76.2	76.8	76.8	75.9
2004	77.0	77.4	77.0	77.4	78.0	77.3	77.8	78.0	78.0	78.7	78.9	79.4	77.9
2005	79.8	80.3	80.2	80.2	80.4	80.5	80.4	80.4	78.7	79.5	80.3	80.6	80.1
2006	80.6	80.5	80.6	80.8	80.6	80.9	81.0	81.0	80.8	80.6	80.3	81.0	80.7
2007	80.6	81.3	81.3	81.7	81.6	81.3	81.4	81.3	81.5	80.9	81.2	81.2	81.3
2008	80.9	80.7	80.5	79.8	79.4	79.0	79.0	77.9	74.8	75.4	74.5	72.9	77.9
2009	71.3	70.7	69.6	69.0	68.3	68.2	69.1	70.0	70.5	70.7	71.1	71.6	70.0
2010[1]	72.3	72.4	72.8	73.2	74.2	74.2	74.9	75.0	75.2	75.2	75.4	76.2	74.3

[1] Preliminary.   Source: Bureau of Economic Analysis, U.S. Department of Commerce (BEA)

Manufacturers New Orders, Durable Goods   In Billions of Constant Dollars

Year	Jan.	Feb.	Mar.	Apr.	May	June	July	Aug.	Sept.	Oct.	Nov.	Dec.	Average
2001	177.97	180.84	182.68	172.53	179.28	176.65	170.40	170.85	163.39	171.74	163.56	166.47	173.03
2002	160.41	169.56	168.58	167.83	171.05	163.47	172.97	175.40	165.66	167.16	168.29	162.14	167.71
2003	167.99	172.81	172.32	170.11	171.05	172.06	173.23	171.84	177.34	182.49	180.66	179.94	174.32
2004	173.08	176.78	189.63	182.38	181.44	182.10	184.43	182.28	185.48	182.81	191.45	189.91	183.48
2005	191.51	194.49	190.03	192.89	205.79	208.03	194.75	202.18	202.15	208.13	218.57	217.09	202.13
2006	201.56	212.24	220.83	212.32	212.51	217.89	208.21	207.36	229.79	211.79	220.20	223.94	214.89
2007	222.27	226.60	233.70	240.17	235.30	236.83	244.26	237.56	233.17	234.94	237.29	247.76	235.82
2008	230.27	228.98	229.28	226.20	225.95	227.10	224.17	212.52	212.06	193.86	186.76	176.93	214.51
2009	162.84	165.19	160.50	163.06	167.07	164.35	176.53	171.93	177.50	177.47	177.06	178.64	170.18
2010[1]	187.48	188.35	188.53	194.02	192.62	192.33	194.70	193.20	202.58	196.23	196.05	191.59	193.14

[1] Preliminary.   Source: Bureau of Economic Analysis, U.S. Department of Commerce (BEA)

Corporate Profits After Tax -- Quarterly   In Billions of Dollars

Year	First Quarter	Second Quarter	Third Quarter	Fourth Quarter	Total	Year	First Quarter	Second Quarter	Third Quarter	Fourth Quarter	Total
1999	593.2	592.9	582.1	602.5	592.7	2005	1,003.1	1,033.3	1,051.6	1,086.8	1,043.7
2000	566.2	558.6	560.0	531.8	554.2	2006	1,130.2	1,122.6	1,158.5	1,128.8	1,135.0
2001	558.3	595.6	569.9	599.6	580.9	2007	1,041.4	1,097.4	1,070.0	1,052.0	1,065.2
2002	651.1	666.0	676.0	726.3	679.9	2008	1,019.6	986.0	1,037.5	774.6	954.4
2003	685.9	723.1	745.5	781.6	734.0	2009	916.2	955.3	1,041.8	1,099.2	1,003.1
2004	909.6	928.7	971.8	953.3	940.9	2010[1]	1,163.3	1,208.5	1,210.7		1,194.2

[1] Preliminary.   Source: Bureau of Economic Analysis, U.S. Department of Commerce (BEA)

Change in Manufacturing and Trade Inventories   In Billions of Dollars

Year	Jan.	Feb.	Mar.	Apr.	May	June	July	Aug.	Sept.	Oct.	Nov.	Dec.	Average
2001	1.7	-40.5	-73.0	-36.6	-38.9	-105.1	-68.2	-34.2	-75.3	-200.6	-139.2	-78.7	-65.2
2002	-0.9	-31.5	-47.8	-20.1	33.6	27.8	78.5	3.5	-106.8	18.5	33.0	-86.0	17.6
2003	-118.4	-60.3	-18.3	0.1	111.8	89.5	24.1	-39.4	78.7	54.4	57.5	45.7	17.6
2004	16.6	108.5	107.0	101.2	88.6	153.5	139.9	373.6	-12.2	54.3	166.0	29.5	72.8
2005	130.5	84.6	60.3	40.0	218.4	-5.7	-66.0	57.9	272.9	81.3	78.8	305.6	54.5
2006	85.9	-49.7	129.5	82.7	169.3	169.3	92.2	93.2	65.9	22.9	28.3	4.2	85.2
2007	37.8	43.6	-17.0	59.5	68.1	55.0	75.6	62.7	87.7	23.8	53.3	96.3	53.4
2008	169.4	78.5	35.6	81.4	66.2	133.3	202.6	34.8	-64.9	-99.6		-250.0	35.2
2009	-170.2	-188.5	-232.1	-197.4	-196.7	-218.1	-159.1	-232.5	-46.8	59.8	75.6	-14.9	-126.7
2010[1]	27.9	102.1	106.0	62.2	24.8	75.0	185.5	140.7	218.4	127.7	36.4		100.6

[1] Preliminary.   *Source: Bureau of Economic Analysis, U.S. Department of Commerce (BEA)*

Productivity: Index of Output per Hour, All Persons, Nonfarm Business -- Quarterly   (1992 = 100)

Year	First Quarter	Second Quarter	Third Quarter	Fourth Quarter	Total	Year	First Quarter	Second Quarter	Third Quarter	Fourth Quarter	Total
1999	82.3	82.4	83.0	84.5	83.0	2005	99.8	99.6	100.3	100.3	100.0
2000	84.1	86.0	86.1	86.9	85.8	2006	100.9	101.0	100.5	101.2	100.9
2001	86.6	88.2	88.7	90.0	88.4	2007	101.3	101.9	103.0	103.9	102.5
2002	91.9	92.0	92.9	92.8	92.4	2008	103.5	103.8	103.5	103.5	103.6
2003	93.6	94.8	97.1	97.4	95.7	2009	104.3	106.5	108.3	109.9	107.2
2004	97.6	98.5	98.7	98.8	98.4	2010[1]	110.9	110.4	111.0	111.8	111.0

[1] Preliminary.   *Source: Bureau of Economic Analysis, U.S. Department of Commerce (BEA)*

Civilian Unemployment Rate

Year	Jan.	Feb.	Mar.	Apr.	May	June	July	Aug.	Sept.	Oct.	Nov.	Dec.	Average
2001	4.2	4.2	4.3	4.5	4.4	4.5	4.5	4.9	4.9	5.4	5.7	5.8	4.8
2002	5.6	5.5	5.7	6.0	5.8	5.9	5.9	5.7	5.6	5.7	6.0	6.0	5.8
2003	5.7	5.8	5.8	6.0	6.1	6.4	6.2	6.1	6.1	6.0	5.9	5.7	6.0
2004	5.6	5.6	5.7	5.6	5.6	5.6	5.5	5.4	5.4	5.5	5.4	5.4	5.5
2005	5.2	5.4	5.1	5.1	5.1	5.0	5.0	4.9	5.1	4.9	5.0	4.9	5.1
2006	4.7	4.8	4.7	4.7	4.6	4.6	4.8	4.7	4.6	4.4	4.5	4.5	4.6
2007	4.6	4.5	4.4	4.5	4.5	4.6	4.7	4.7	4.7	4.8	4.7	5.0	4.6
2008	5.0	4.8	5.1	5.0	5.4	5.5	5.8	6.1	6.2	6.6	6.9	7.4	5.8
2009	7.7	8.2	8.6	8.9	9.4	9.5	9.4	9.7	9.8	10.1	10.0	10.0	9.3
2010[1]	9.7	9.7	9.7	9.8	9.6	9.5	9.5	9.6	9.6	9.7	9.8	9.4	9.6

[1] Preliminary.   *Source: Bureau of Economic Analysis, U.S. Department of Commerce (BEA)*

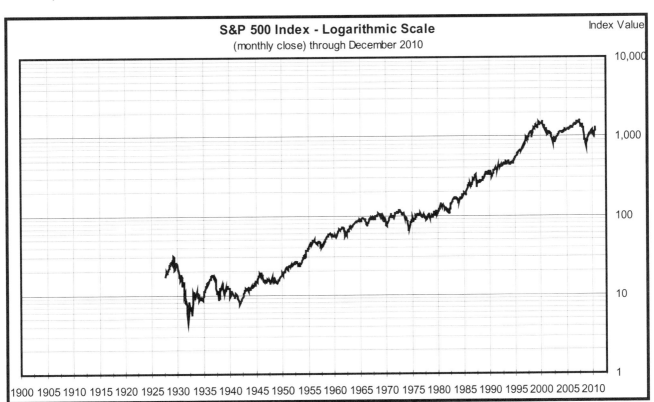

S&P 500 Index - Logarithmic Scale
(monthly close) through December 2010

Index Value

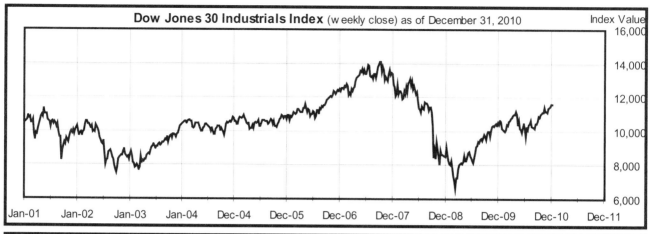

Dow Jones 30 Industrials Index (weekly close) as of December 31, 2010

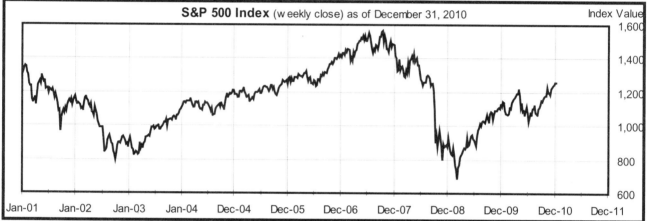

S&P 500 Index (weekly close) as of December 31, 2010

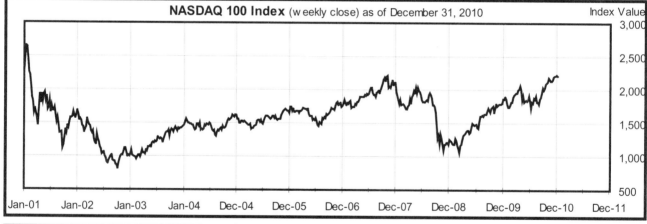

NASDAQ 100 Index (weekly close) as of December 31, 2010

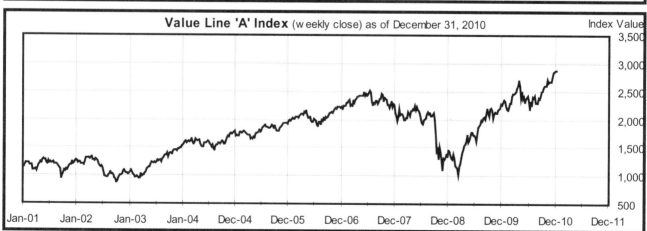

Value Line 'A' Index (weekly close) as of December 31, 2010

Volume of Trading of S&P 500 Stock Index Futures in Chicago   In Thousands of Contracts

Year	Jan.	Feb.	Mar.	Apr.	May	June	July	Aug.	Sept.	Oct.	Nov.	Dec.	Total
2001	1,552.0	1,630.8	2,780.9	1,624.2	1,653.0	2,154.4	1,319.7	1,597.5	2,571.2	1,798.3	1,691.7	2,124.2	22,498
2002	1,459.2	1,677.0	2,251.4	1,472.8	1,584.6	2,720.9	2,205.7	1,615.1	2,943.1	1,930.5	1,374.3	2,465.0	23,700
2003	1,442.8	1,343.0	2,900.2	1,256.8	1,415.6	2,782.4	1,222.9	1,079.4	2,411.7	1,118.1	921.3	2,281.5	20,175
2004	944.8	838.6	2,487.0	880.3	937.7	2,135.8	837.4	964.6	2,076.5	866.3	1,105.3	2,101.3	16,176
2005	764.5	873.6	2,330.2	916.2	891.6	2,090.1	618.4	979.1	2,090.2	902.1	880.2	2,041.4	15,377
2006	711.3	772.9	2,198.8	607.5	1,122.0	2,321.6	726.3	890.8	1,883.1	686.3	935.6	1,988.6	14,845
2007	696.3	765.0	2,341.9	614.6	937.9	2,237.8	803.4	1,546.1	1,941.4	854.5	1,130.8	1,967.9	15,838
2008	1,187.3	907.8	2,374.7	761.0	768.2	1,978.9	921.9	729.7	2,491.2	1,588.1	942.0	2,112.2	16,763
2009	674.4	744.3	2,026.3	555.3	534.7	1,637.5	453.5	427.3	1,338.3	473.3	384.6	1,186.4	10,436
2010	403.6	432.0	1,084.5	363.5	650.7	1,195.3	412.7	433.1	1,027.9	296.8	415.8	974.1	7,690

Contract value = $250.   *Source: Index and Option Market (IOM), division of the Chicago Mercantile Exchange (CME)*

Average Open Interest of S&P 500 Stock Index Futures in Chicago   In Contracts

Year	Jan.	Feb.	Mar.	Apr.	May	June	July	Aug.	Sept.	Oct.	Nov.	Dec.
2001	488,284	495,621	517,666	498,594	490,148	505,063	485,839	501,281	556,737	529,730	550,201	551,175
2002	495,352	519,023	542,358	513,048	542,839	592,888	594,727	621,558	644,806	607,848	631,224	647,022
2003	596,064	619,738	658,749	622,917	643,030	691,003	611,564	611,578	631,509	582,111	589,392	633,997
2004	612,911	614,843	624,209	595,593	587,717	604,154	586,760	597,581	632,050	636,566	686,531	714,420
2005	678,739	686,413	719,141	681,149	697,818	700,618	656,266	653,430	669,849	642,704	657,097	681,868
2006	655,483	668,113	682,218	653,044	664,790	670,449	625,142	634,579	634,817	609,410	640,481	679,221
2007	634,075	639,584	654,891	634,576	662,438	652,951	602,222	643,716	663,165	595,908	623,469	623,631
2008	566,839	602,738	607,396	560,088	559,320	558,810	551,609	565,810	578,027	627,531	633,531	603,664
2009	518,589	583,132	566,284	439,705	467,060	456,209	391,596	393,499	400,489	386,593	398,242	379,761
2010	334,063	379,277	384,532	320,130	323,367	354,304	308,220	320,409	327,551	314,245	352,215	341,358

Contract value = $250.   *Source: Index and Option Market (IOM), division of the Chicago Mercantile Exchange (CME)*

Volume of Trading of E-mini S&P 500 Index Futures in Chicago   In Thousands of Contracts

Year	Jan.	Feb.	Mar.	Apr.	May	June	July	Aug.	Sept.	Oct.	Nov.	Dec.	Total
2001	2,226	2,231	3,191	3,067	2,931	2,905	2,925	3,478	3,601	5,255	4,021	3,289	39,119
2002	4,933	5,337	5,609	7,165	7,564	9,772	14,277	11,200	11,765	17,175	11,054	9,892	115,742
2003	13,584	12,631	15,820	13,520	12,846	15,040	14,854	10,860	15,354	14,558	11,002	11,108	161,177
2004	13,087	11,355	18,033	14,993	15,889	12,428	14,361	12,921	12,755	14,636	13,705	13,039	167,203
2005	15,447	12,561	18,478	20,182	16,591	17,371	14,400	17,759	18,786	22,929	16,088	16,503	207,096
2006	18,716	16,095	21,357	18,174	24,750	30,359	21,629	19,107	21,986	22,377	23,616	19,760	257,927
2007	21,632	22,507	37,944	20,399	26,266	39,351	35,295	55,547	37,578	38,649	46,727	33,454	415,348
2008	55,257	40,368	56,108	38,472	36,217	49,724	53,375	36,400	76,696	84,259	56,426	50,587	633,889
2009	45,814	49,498	69,321	49,293	46,060	48,779	42,273	38,448	46,864	46,352	36,951	36,662	556,314
2010	40,765	42,986	46,644	43,563	64,388	61,258	44,454	42,196	46,366	41,921	45,468	35,320	555,329

Contract value = $50.   *Source: Index and Option Market (IOM), division of the Chicago Mercantile Exchange (CME)*

Average Open Interest of E-mini S&P 500 Index Futures in Chicago   In Thousands of Contracts

Year	Jan.	Feb.	Mar.	Apr.	May	June	July	Aug.	Sept.	Oct.	Nov.	Dec.
2001	55.5	68.5	79.9	91.9	110.8	91.6	97.1	126.2	152.3	134.7	224.8	178.7
2002	86.3	120.1	140.0	156.4	225.6	246.3	291.7	349.0	319.3	312.9	419.0	385.2
2003	265.2	356.6	490.0	567.6	741.8	718.5	399.5	492.5	513.4	460.9	467.7	525.3
2004	510.5	576.4	643.1	545.4	579.9	645.8	603.8	698.0	693.5	708.4	979.9	969.3
2005	827.3	901.7	1,013.6	943.3	1,014.9	986.8	932.6	1,060.8	1,110.1	1,042.2	1,166.4	1,211.3
2006	1,149.2	1,194.6	1,334.1	1,211.3	1,402.5	1,525.3	1,371.2	1,512.3	1,582.4	1,549.5	1,754.4	1,810.9
2007	1,625.6	1,825.1	2,037.4	1,943.7	2,088.7	2,060.5	1,735.6	2,105.4	2,151.5	1,972.4	2,095.4	2,172.5
2008	2,208.2	2,418.8	2,442.6	2,076.5	2,180.8	2,311.5	2,405.0	2,467.2	2,566.1	2,987.6	3,114.1	2,942.0
2009	2,512.9	2,896.4	3,123.3	2,489.2	2,680.4	2,690.2	2,429.6	2,622.9	2,582.3	2,397.1	2,593.6	2,688.5
2010	2,510.1	2,808.4	2,866.0	2,468.7	2,680.5	2,937.2	2,797.2	2,839.5	2,872.0	2,668.2	2,810.5	2,826.7

Contract value = $50.   *Source: Index and Option Market (IOM), division of the Chicago Mercantile Exchange (CME)*

STOCK INDEX FUTURES - U.S.

Volume of Trading of NASDAQ 100 Index Futures in Chicago   In Contracts

Year	Jan.	Feb.	Mar.	Apr.	May	June	July	Aug.	Sept.	Oct.	Nov.	Dec.	Total
2001	422,811	416,445	650,488	498,026	487,334	542,305	369,731	369,845	474,133	516,469	391,042	434,690	5,573,319
2002	380,076	367,561	436,495	378,294	443,579	529,496	454,630	334,242	466,898	367,750	315,925	428,341	4,903,287
2003	360,307	301,454	487,916	301,395	330,640	519,597	350,514	251,058	488,363	322,898	259,960	447,119	4,421,221
2004	271,404	268,590	591,556	321,242	297,320	427,805	286,693	245,050	433,251	286,048	226,853	356,171	4,011,983
2005	254,437	198,956	375,435	217,304	170,882	281,483	125,500	159,789	289,113	200,952	155,141	253,066	2,682,058
2006	186,649	162,841	295,163	113,885	169,399	305,557	132,661	149,906	256,605	136,433	140,407	220,364	2,269,870
2007	122,055	111,962	255,491	73,881	97,857	226,877	94,964	124,717	178,645	112,930	121,891	162,108	1,683,378
2008	137,810	90,886	188,815	72,775	80,472	192,723	103,965	83,158	171,532	125,975	58,023	101,279	1,407,413
2009	61,110	61,943	119,432	47,289	53,465	76,479	46,606	55,012	84,170	45,122	48,519	57,772	756,919
2010	50,060	37,696	55,326	34,026	44,200	47,702	28,137	32,035	46,609	24,746	57,965	49,322	507,824

Contract value = $100.   *Source: Index and Option Market (IOM), division of the Chicago Mercantile Exchange (CME)*

Average Open Interest of NASDAQ 100 Index Futures in Chicago   In Contracts

Year	Jan.	Feb.	Mar.	Apr.	May	June	July	Aug.	Sept.	Oct.	Nov.	Dec.
2001	46,582	49,495	59,916	56,328	49,337	54,394	50,854	55,234	61,665	51,977	61,196	67,769
2002	49,992	52,883	52,617	51,157	65,219	73,151	60,625	67,760	84,317	72,229	77,451	76,660
2003	71,219	79,905	87,252	71,636	77,717	88,914	80,002	83,940	91,685	75,191	85,651	86,480
2004	73,805	74,892	89,874	81,220	80,905	83,282	69,818	71,711	84,355	74,161	83,675	87,172
2005	72,299	81,327	78,387	56,668	57,116	56,836	49,357	53,270	61,369	60,918	59,754	63,712
2006	61,254	62,994	69,322	60,603	65,224	65,908	54,289	57,585	54,235	53,832	68,347	61,397
2007	47,832	51,655	55,782	50,905	59,586	63,132	63,492	67,870	64,324	50,761	53,292	50,372
2008	42,272	52,260	51,385	31,738	37,017	34,864	28,456	30,588	27,761	27,770	31,473	29,459
2009	23,558	29,607	29,090	21,525	24,228	21,913	17,299	21,266	22,113	19,389	21,267	18,502
2010	15,446	28,890	20,717	17,115	23,509	19,880	12,821	18,414	18,068	22,008	29,505	19,916

Contract value = $100.   *Source: Index and Option Market (IOM), division of the Chicago Mercantile Exchange (CME)*

Volume of Trading of E-mini NASDAQ 100 Index Futures in Chicago   In Thousands of Contracts

Year	Jan.	Feb.	Mar.	Apr.	May	June	July	Aug.	Sept.	Oct.	Nov.	Dec.	Total
2001	1,845	1,942	2,603	2,873	2,908	2,969	2,529	2,568	2,387	3,935	3,151	2,595	32,304
2002	3,719	3,649	3,652	4,227	4,625	4,713	5,789	4,225	4,337	6,252	4,812	4,490	54,491
2003	5,200	4,620	5,749	5,132	5,075	6,323	6,369	4,816	7,095	6,601	5,254	5,655	67,889
2004	6,157	5,640	8,011	6,387	6,749	5,646	7,139	6,123	6,476	7,322	5,844	5,675	77,169
2005	7,174	6,149	7,336	7,256	5,735	6,233	4,895	5,171	5,624	6,583	5,288	5,008	72,453
2006	6,628	5,803	7,479	5,459	7,386	8,258	6,741	6,315	7,074	6,769	6,333	5,696	79,940
2007	7,122	6,685	8,700	4,976	7,069	8,426	8,122	10,558	6,856	8,916	11,147	6,733	95,309
2008	11,604	8,072	9,677	6,988	7,042	9,912	10,151	7,607	11,523	12,287	7,300	6,571	108,734
2009	5,713	6,789	8,800	6,383	6,241	6,722	6,243	5,959	6,808	7,048	5,686	5,579	77,972
2010	6,712	6,180	6,448	5,938	8,666	8,055	6,905	6,619	7,366	6,249	5,997	4,505	79,638

Contract value = $20.   *Source: Index and Option Market (IOM), division of the Chicago Mercantile Exchange (CME)*

Average Open Interest of E-mini NASDAQ 100 Index Futures in Chicago   In Contracts

Year	Jan.	Feb.	Mar.	Apr.	May	June	July	Aug.	Sept.	Oct.	Nov.	Dec.
2001	45,370	65,061	79,962	78,094	90,822	95,236	90,803	131,259	132,349	75,686	115,350	124,023
2002	78,070	94,150	98,159	100,849	153,348	176,394	130,337	171,043	162,133	110,952	154,104	155,987
2003	169,160	227,905	258,023	196,739	240,759	257,390	262,564	316,032	287,936	214,659	279,379	244,333
2004	205,078	251,011	251,486	257,573	304,034	261,067	213,080	256,749	299,794	279,170	374,750	384,492
2005	339,077	419,715	382,805	310,664	331,447	290,759	270,134	325,508	307,007	365,277	382,667	371,388
2006	351,240	361,807	345,533	309,746	381,178	427,387	386,930	421,179	437,975	457,275	498,584	433,456
2007	360,663	354,765	423,270	396,080	463,422	454,010	418,512	429,654	451,180	415,073	439,054	408,021
2008	347,374	410,404	424,513	320,046	377,029	358,774	316,037	333,976	336,525	379,643	359,028	302,534
2009	245,830	281,273	302,750	256,064	286,754	284,962	272,424	332,576	341,802	321,653	329,991	338,692
2010	338,217	402,622	362,520	329,709	353,999	353,720	316,651	349,380	397,910	441,782	442,146	401,214

Contract value = $20.   *Source: Index and Option Market (IOM), division of the Chicago Mercantile Exchange (CME)*

Volume of Trading of S&P 400 Midcap Stock Index Futures in Chicago In Contracts

Year	Jan.	Feb.	Mar.	Apr.	May	June	July	Aug.	Sept.	Oct.	Nov.	Dec.	Total
2001	21,527	19,884	58,286	18,061	19,258	50,331	22,029	23,805	50,706	23,741	19,591	51,641	378,860
2002	22,322	22,814	43,819	23,019	22,484	51,775	30,607	23,075	52,375	25,593	21,262	48,105	387,250
2003	18,827	18,392	44,454	15,841	15,194	40,603	15,153	12,082	43,112	15,253	13,109	50,797	302,817
2004	13,647	10,361	46,214	13,921	13,078	45,940	12,602	13,582	36,701	7,923	9,824	36,971	260,764
2005	6,486	5,736	36,685	5,130	7,235	39,025	4,603	7,699	42,503	5,736	4,988	39,232	205,058
2006	5,668	3,739	34,668	3,671	4,619	31,924	2,656	3,311	23,289	3,718	6,409	29,596	153,268
2007	2,854	3,205	26,948	3,716	3,937	22,210	3,906	4,271	17,518	3,610	10,570	15,395	118,140
2008	5,581	3,286	14,864	2,796	3,124	15,896	4,670	3,369	19,246	6,432	4,397	13,563	97,224
2009	2,330	4,802	11,017	4,668	1,707	10,037	1,642	1,822	8,854	3,229	2,285	6,967	59,360
2010	1,852	3,043	5,412	1,019	3,956	6,944	1,580	2,582	4,072	2,330	1,117	4,560	38,467

Contract value = $500.   *Source: Index and Option Market (IOM), division of the Chicago Mercantile Exchange (CME)*

Average Open Interest of S&P 400 Midcap Stock Index Futures in Chicago In Contracts

Year	Jan.	Feb.	Mar.	Apr.	May	June	July	Aug.	Sept.	Oct.	Nov.	Dec.
2001	15,246	15,461	17,235	16,953	15,623	16,606	16,334	16,132	16,718	15,109	15,307	15,337
2002	13,691	14,109	14,954	14,340	16,402	16,611	15,121	16,213	17,006	14,695	15,394	16,432
2003	13,793	13,498	14,530	13,120	13,353	13,986	13,123	13,029	13,726	14,014	15,465	17,446
2004	15,911	15,988	16,554	15,870	15,819	17,148	13,939	13,600	14,213	13,339	14,046	14,755
2005	13,078	13,313	14,861	11,812	11,832	13,811	12,380	12,420	14,477	12,890	12,955	13,822
2006	12,168	11,940	12,409	10,999	10,892	10,447	9,307	9,687	9,194	8,442	9,884	9,794
2007	7,793	8,143	8,267	7,972	9,187	8,425	6,729	6,671	6,951	6,166	8,580	8,839
2008	6,501	7,622	7,512	4,254	5,358	5,700	4,578	5,756	6,847	6,601	6,766	5,761
2009	3,785	4,755	5,227	4,433	4,580	3,781	2,481	2,887	2,847	2,586	2,273	2,437
2010	1,552	2,791	2,274	1,549	2,580	3,250	2,268	2,799	2,334	2,418	3,389	2,539

Contract value = $500.   *Source: Index and Option Market (IOM), division of the Chicago Mercantile Exchange (CME)*

Volume of Trading of Dow Jones Industrials Index Futures in Chicago In Contracts

Year	Jan.	Feb.	Mar.	Apr.	May	June	July	Aug.	Sept.	Oct.	Nov.	Dec.	Total
2001	275,814	310,088	594,326	411,767	377,620	389,919	320,335	410,927	573,479	520,885	375,793	329,898	4,890,851
2002	409,009	472,893	538,804	467,571	456,210	616,754	811,518	539,507	639,154	699,005	427,235	407,665	6,485,325
2003	452,579	426,198	559,372	428,972	410,967	473,432	368,277	286,508	367,845	218,394	157,726	266,032	4,416,302
2004	224,713	207,423	362,668	203,745	208,229	246,564	183,469	149,931	230,829	169,627	152,412	237,528	2,577,138
2005	149,353	107,824	226,113	157,010	124,999	192,165	96,885	121,793	188,541	133,636	108,737	180,349	1,787,405
2006	119,593	111,738	220,880	106,325	152,340	272,494	108,053	97,964	237,988	121,736	111,993	258,743	1,919,847
2007	97,032	97,537	231,466	76,661	127,981	197,380	101,710	119,985	135,432	95,101	91,014	112,518	1,483,817
2008	105,901	82,432	135,860	71,571	51,097	121,220	122,305	76,031	170,465	99,607	53,397	57,771	1,147,657
2009	32,235	36,568	54,497	35,502	32,590	50,874	27,114	17,541	47,003	18,659	13,769	29,232	395,584
2010	13,279	11,251	23,512	14,352	14,189	28,257	9,843	10,761	18,012	9,749	10,888	24,016	188,109

Contract value = $10.   *Source: Chicago Board of Trade (CBT)*

Average Open Interest of Dow Jones Industrials Index Futures in Chicago In Contracts

Year	Jan.	Feb.	Mar.	Apr.	May	June	July	Aug.	Sept.	Oct.	Nov.	Dec.
2001	21,830	23,423	28,340	32,497	33,767	29,357	26,792	33,015	35,451	31,997	30,598	27,018
2002	23,862	35,588	37,582	28,714	32,810	34,482	32,412	32,272	34,665	31,923	34,045	31,892
2003	27,032	30,429	34,371	31,160	34,936	46,641	42,790	43,974	41,747	34,066	37,835	39,727
2004	34,656	44,306	50,172	44,494	45,304	46,641	42,790	42,042	45,940	41,250	43,662	53,469
2005	47,754	48,665	48,423	40,068	41,367	36,909	29,042	30,921	37,232	36,378	37,588	43,819
2006	39,641	39,943	43,595	43,351	45,756	53,833	56,451	58,799	60,497	61,996	63,061	69,927
2007	67,567	72,788	54,933	41,615	48,211	42,631	33,406	37,757	35,894	30,936	35,735	34,375
2008	27,564	32,212	33,736	29,240	31,425	32,987	31,175	34,663	36,423	26,685	27,638	23,708
2009	14,401	22,146	19,045	10,306	15,681	18,781	10,880	11,614	12,693	13,764	16,046	12,915
2010	12,142	13,855	10,785	7,616	11,884	10,945	7,250	8,945	7,325	5,155	7,631	7,591

Contract value = $10.   *Source: Chicago Board of Trade (CBT)*

Stock Index Futures - WorldWide

World stocks – World stock markets in 2010 extended the sharp recovery rally that began in 2009, ending the 3-year bear market that lasted from mid-2007 to March 2009. The MSCI World Index, a benchmark for large companies based in 23 developed countries, rallied by +9.6% in 2010, adding to the +27.0% rally seen in 2009. From the low of 796.24 in March 2009 to the 2-1/2 year high of 1365.07 in early 2011, the MSCI World index rallied by a total of 71% and retraced 64% of the 2007/09 bear market.

The MSCI World index posted a sharp recovery rally in 2009-10 as the global economy recovered and the chances of a depression receded. The global economy in 2010 grew by 3.9% in 2010, according to the World Bank, returning to positive growth after a -1.1% decline in GDP growth in 2009. The global recovery was driven by epic-scale liquidity injections by the Federal Reserve and the other major global banks and by a quick economic recovery in the developing world. Chinese GDP growth in 2010 improved to 10.3% from the 8-year low of 9.2% seen in 2009. India's GDP in 2010 improved to +8.6% from +8.0% in 2009. Eurozone GDP growth improved to +1.7% in 2010 after the sharp -4.1% decline seen in 2009. Global corporate earnings quickly recovered after the recession and hit new record highs. Profits were generated by cost cutting and productivity growth as well as by strong growth in revenue.

Looking ahead, the MSCI World Index as of early 2011 was trading at a reasonable price-to-earnings ratio of 12.8 based on forward-looking earnings. This reasonable valuation level should leave room for stock price gains in coming years as the global economy normalizes and as earnings growth becomes more visible and stable.

Small-Capitalization Stocks – The MSCI World Small-Cap Index, which tracks companies with market caps between $200 million and $1.5 billion, rose by +24.3% in 2010, adding to the +41.7% rally seen in 2009. The index showed two consecutive years of positive growth after the -42.1% plunge seen in 2008 that was caused by the global financial crisis and recession. The rise in the MSCI World Small-Cap Index in 2009 of +24.3% was 14.8 percentage points better than the +9.6% gain in the large-cap MSCI World Index. The out-performance of small-caps in 2010 was similar to the 14.7 percentage point outperformance seen in 2009, illustrating how well small caps have done during the 2009/10 recovery rally.

World Industry Groups – The MSCI industry sectors in 2010 produced the following ranked annual returns: Consumer Discretionary +22.8%, Industrials +21.3%, Materials +19.4%, Consumer Staples +10.1%, Energy +9.5%, Information Technology +9.5%, Telecom +5.3%, Financials +2.3%, Health Care +0.4%, and Utilities -4.5%. The sectors most sensitive to the business cycle did well in 2010 as the economy recovered, with Consumer Discretionary, Industrials and Materials performing the best. Meanwhile, the defensive sectors did poorly in 2010 as stock investors shifted their focus to more aggressive plays. Specifically, the worst performing sectors were Health Care (+0.4%) and Utilities (-4.5%). Financials also did poorly at +2.3% in 2010 as the banks ran into heavier regulation that will throttle their growth and profits.

Emerging markets – Emerging stock markets rallied sharply again in 2010 as investors focused on the stronger economic growth being seen in the emerging world. The MSCI Emerging Markets Free Index, which tracks companies based in 26 emerging countries, rallied by +16.4% in 2010, adding to the very sharp +74.5% rally seen in 2009.

G7 – In 2010, only four of the G7 stock markets saw rallies, as opposed to 2009 when all of the G7 stock markets rose sharply by between +19% and +31%. The ranked returns for the G7 stock markets for 2010 are as follows: German DAX index +16.1%, Canadian Toronto Composite +14.4%, U.S. S&P 500 +12.8%, UK FTSE 100 +9.0%, Japanese Nikkei 225 -3.0%, French CAC40 -3.3%, and Italian MIB -13.2%.

North America – In North America, Mexico's Bolsa Index ended 2010 up +20.0%, outperforming the U.S. and Canadian stock markets for the tenth straight year. The Mexican Bolsa index has now posted double-digit gains in seven of the last eight years (2010 +20.0%, 2009 +43.5%, 2008 −24.2%, 2007 +11.7%, 2006 +48.6%, 2005 +37.8%, 2004 +46.9%, 2003 +43.5%). The Toronto Composite index rallied by +14.4% in 2010, beating the +12.8% gain in the S&P 500 index. The Toronto index has now outperformed the S&P 500 for seven consecutive years.

Latin America – The large Latin America stock markets showed generally strong gains in 2010 following the extraordinary gains seen in 2009 as investors continued to focus on emerging markets: Peru's Lima General Index +65.0%, Argentina's Merval Index +51.8%, Chile's Stock Market Select Index +37.6%, Columbia's General Index +33.6%, Venezuela's Stock Market Index +18.6%, Ecuador's Guayaqui Bolsa Index +16.9%, Jamaica's Stock Exchange Index +2.3%, Brazil's Bovespa Index +1.0%, and Costa Rica's Stock Market Index −16.7%.

Europe – European stocks in 2010 were mixed due to the two-speed recovery where Germany and France showed decent economic growth, but the peripheral countries lagged. The Dow Jones Stoxx 50 index closed unchanged on the year in 2010 following the +24.1% rally seen in 2009. The big European countries saw mixed returns in 2010: German DAX index +16.1%, UK FTSE 100 index +9.0%, French CAC 40 index -3.3%, Italian MIB index -13.2%, and Spanish IBEX 35 index -17.4%.

Asia – The Asian stock markets in 2010 showed a mixed performance after the sharp double-digit gains seen in 2009. The MSCI Far East Index in 2010 rose by 16.6% in 2010, adding to the +12.8% gain seen in 2009. Asia came out of the global financial crisis in much better shape than the U.S. or Europe but there was nevertheless some profit-taking and some localized problems in specific countries. China's Shanghai Composite Index in 2010 fell by -14.3%, correcting downward after the sharp 80.0% rally seen in 2009. Japan closed -3.0% in a lackluster year after the 19.0% gain seen in 2009. The ranked closes for the Asian stock markets in 2010 were as follows: Indonesia's Jakarta Composite Index +46.1%, Thailand's Stock Exchange index +40.6%, Philippines' Composite index +37.6%, Pakistan's 100 Index +28.1%, South Korea's Composite Index +21.9%, Malaysia's Kuala Lumpur Composite index +19.3%, India's Mumbai Sensex 30 index +17.4%, Singapore's Straights Times Index +10.1%, Taiwan's TAIEX Index of +9.6%, Hong Kong's Hang Seng +5.3%, New Zealand's Exchange 50 Index +2.4%, Australia's All-Ordinaries Index -0.7%, Vietnam's Stock Index -2.0%, Japan's Nikkei 225 Index -3.0%, and China's Shanghai Composite Index -14.3%.

Year	Jan.	Feb.	Mar.	Apr.	May	June	July	Aug.	Sept.	Oct.	Nov.	Dec.	Average
United States													
2004	340.0	344.2	338.5	332.8	336.9	342.9	331.2	331.9	335.0	339.7	352.8	364.3	340.9
2005	355.1	361.8	354.9	347.7	358.2	358.1	371.0	366.8	369.4	362.8	375.6	375.2	363.1
2006	384.8	385.0	389.2	394.0	381.8	381.8	383.8	391.9	401.5	414.2	421.0	426.3	396.3
2007	432.3	422.9	427.1	445.6	460.1	451.9	437.4	443.1	458.9	465.7	445.2	441.4	444.3
2008	414.4	400.0	397.6	416.5	420.9	384.8	381.0	385.6	350.6	291.2	269.4	271.5	365.3
2009	248.3	221.0	239.8	262.4	276.3	276.3	296.8	306.8	317.7	311.5	329.3	335.2	285.1
2010	322.8	332.0	351.5	356.7	327.5	309.8	331.1	315.4	343.0	355.7	354.9	378.0	339.9
Canada													
2004	249.1	256.9	251.0	241.0	246.0	249.8	247.2	244.9	253.4	259.3	264.0	270.3	252.7
2005	269.0	282.6	281.0	273.9	280.8	289.5	304.7	311.9	321.9	303.5	316.4	329.5	297.1
2006	349.2	341.7	354.0	356.7	343.3	339.4	345.8	352.9	343.8	360.8	372.8	377.3	353.1
2007	381.0	381.3	384.8	392.2	410.9	406.5	405.4	399.3	412.1	427.5	400.1	404.3	400.5
2008	384.5	397.0	390.2	407.4	430.1	422.9	397.3	402.5	343.5	285.4	271.0	262.7	366.2
2009	254.2	237.4	254.9	272.6	303.1	303.3	315.3	317.7	333.1	318.9	334.6	343.3	299.0
2010	324.3	339.9	351.9	356.9	343.8	330.1	342.4	348.2	361.5	370.5	378.6	392.9	353.4
France													
2004	200.2	205.0	199.5	202.2	201.9	205.4	200.7	197.8	200.3	204.0	206.5	210.2	202.8
2005	215.3	221.6	223.8	215.2	226.7	232.7	244.9	242.1	253.1	244.1	251.3	259.4	235.9
2006	272.2	275.1	287.3	285.5	271.3	273.2	275.6	284.2	288.9	294.3	293.1	304.9	283.8
2007	308.6	303.5	310.0	327.9	335.9	333.2	316.4	311.6	314.5	321.8	312.0	308.9	317.0
2008	267.9	263.6	259.0	274.9	275.9	244.0	241.7	246.6	221.9	191.9	179.5	177.1	237.0
2009	163.6	148.7	154.5	173.9	180.3	172.8	188.5	201.0	208.8	198.5	202.5	216.6	184.1
2010	205.8	204.1	218.7	210.0	193.0	189.4	200.5	192.1	204.4	210.9	198.7	209.3	203.1
Germany													
2004	240.0	237.6	228.0	235.6	231.9	239.6	230.3	223.8	230.2	234.1	243.9	251.6	235.6
2005	251.6	257.2	257.1	247.4	263.7	271.2	288.9	285.6	298.2	291.4	307.1	319.8	278.3
2006	335.5	342.7	353.0	355.3	336.6	336.0	335.9	346.4	355.0	370.6	373.0	390.0	352.5
2007	401.4	397.0	409.0	438.0	466.1	473.4	448.4	451.6	464.8	474.1	465.3	477.0	447.2
2008	405.1	399.0	386.4	410.8	419.6	379.5	383.1	379.7	344.8	294.9	276.1	284.4	363.6
2009	256.5	227.3	241.5	282.0	292.1	284.3	315.3	323.1	335.5	320.2	332.6	352.2	296.9
2010	331.6	331.0	363.8	362.8	352.6	352.7	363.5	350.3	368.3	390.3	395.5	408.8	364.3
Italy													
2004	201.3	203.3	199.4	204.9	200.5	206.5	202.1	199.1	206.4	212.2	218.6	229.6	207.0
2005	234.9	237.8	241.0	230.5	237.0	241.1	251.9	249.5	261.7	242.9	252.5	261.4	245.2
2006	271.8	282.9	286.3	285.5	269.9	271.5	274.1	283.7	287.2	296.4	304.2	310.9	285.4
2007	317.4	310.9	317.2	331.5	329.5	319.9	307.4	304.6	302.4	307.0	291.2	286.7	310.5
2008	252.1	251.6	236.2	251.1	249.8	221.0	213.6	217.1	190.3	158.0	151.0	146.8	211.6
2009	139.5	121.7	123.5	148.7	154.9	149.1	158.5	169.1	178.2	171.6	168.3	177.1	155.0
2010	168.9	163.2	177.2	169.7	153.6	151.4	162.2	153.3	160.8	168.0	153.6	163.2	162.1
Japan													
2004	37.4	38.3	40.6	40.8	39.0	41.1	39.3	38.4	37.5	37.4	37.8	39.9	39.0
2005	39.5	40.7	40.5	38.2	39.1	40.2	41.3	43.1	47.1	47.2	51.6	55.9	43.7
2006	57.8	56.2	59.2	58.6	53.7	53.8	53.6	56.0	55.9	56.9	56.5	59.8	56.5
2007	60.3	61.1	60.0	60.4	62.0	62.9	59.8	57.5	58.2	58.1	54.4	53.1	59.0
2008	47.2	47.2	43.5	48.0	49.7	46.8	46.4	45.4	39.1	29.8	29.5	30.7	41.9
2009	27.7	26.3	28.1	30.6	33.0	34.5	35.9	36.4	35.2	34.8	32.4	36.6	32.6
2010	35.4	35.1	38.5	38.4	33.9	32.5	33.1	30.6	32.5	31.9	34.5	35.5	34.3
United Kingdom													
2004	202.0	207.2	202.9	206.7	203.4	205.9	202.5	204.5	209.8	212.2	216.6	222.7	208.0
2005	225.5	230.5	227.0	221.4	229.4	236.5	244.3	245.6	253.6	246.1	253.2	263.0	239.7
2006	270.5	273.1	281.6	284.0	269.4	274.1	277.5	277.8	281.8	290.1	288.2	297.6	280.5
2007	296.7	295.4	303.3	310.0	317.7	314.5	303.8	301.2	306.4	319.1	303.1	303.6	306.2
2008	277.1	278.3	270.4	286.4	284.7	263.8	254.0	265.0	229.4	201.7	197.1	204.1	251.0
2009	192.0	178.3	183.3	200.7	208.1	200.6	217.4	232.8	243.4	238.8	244.7	255.0	216.3
2010	245.8	252.8	268.8	264.5	246.9	235.0	250.8	249.1	264.9	271.2	264.3	282.9	258.1

Not Seasonally Adjusted.   Source: Economic and Statistics Administration, U.S. Department of Commerce (ESA)

STOCK INDEX FUTURES - WORLDWIDE

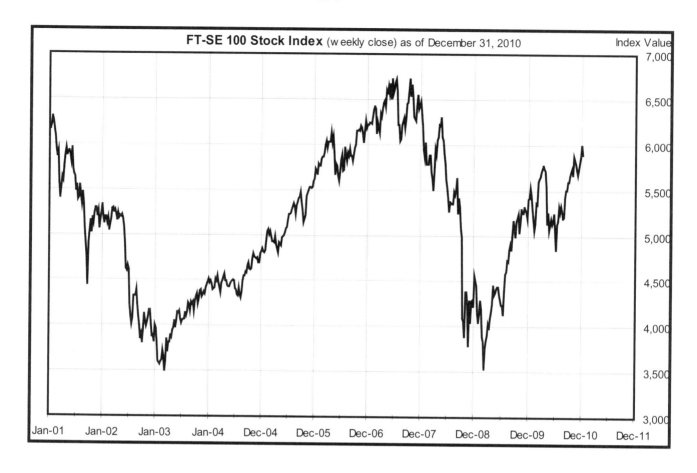

FT-SE 100 Stock Index (weekly close) as of December 31, 2010

Index Value

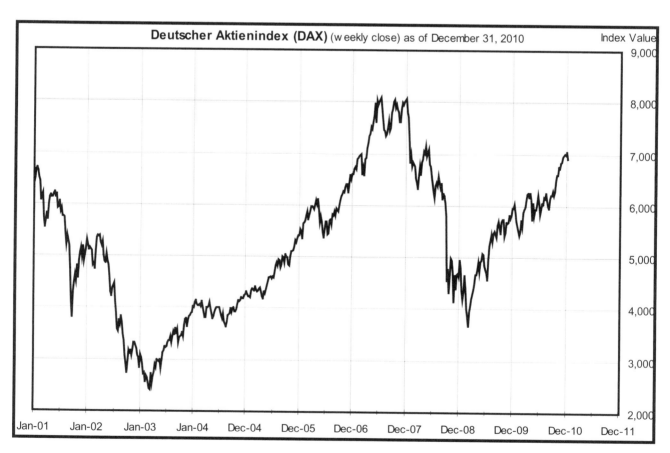

Deutscher Aktienindex (DAX) (weekly close) as of December 31, 2010

Index Value

Toronto 300 Stock Index (weekly close) as of December 31, 2010

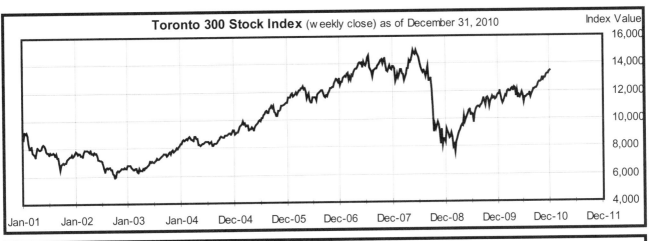

Index Value

CAC-40 Stock Index (weekly close) as of December 31, 2010

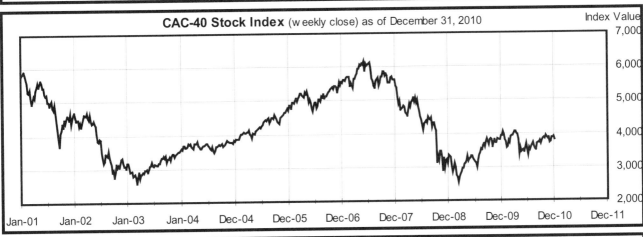

Index Value

Hang Seng Stock Index (weekly close) as of December 31, 2010

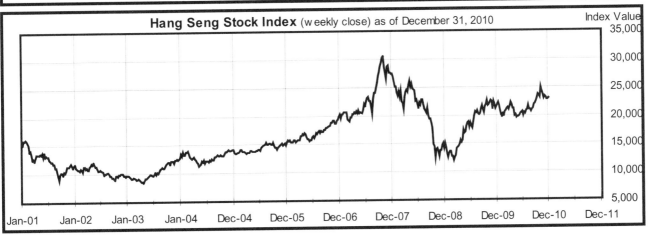

Index Value

Nikkei 225 Stock Index (weekly close) as of December 31, 2010

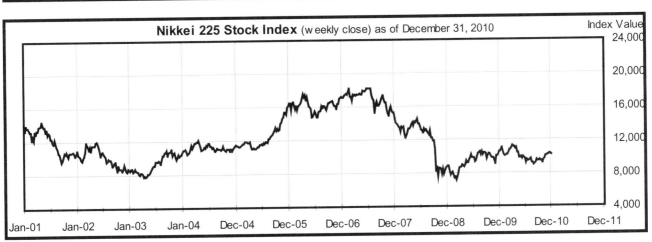

Index Value

Sugar

The white crystalline substance called "sugar" is the organic chemical compound sucrose, one of several related compounds all known as sugars. These include glucose, dextrose, fructose, and lactose. All sugars are members of the larger group of compounds called carbohydrates and are characterized by a sweet taste. Sucrose is considered a double sugar because it is composed of one molecule of glucose and one molecule of fructose. While sucrose is common in many plants, it occurs in the highest concentration in sugarcane (Saccharum officinarum) and sugar beets (Beta vulgaris). Sugarcane is about 7 to 18 percent sugar by weight while sugar beets are 8 to 22 percent.

Sugarcane is a member of the grass family and is a perennial. Sugarcane is cultivated in tropical and subtropical regions around the world roughly between the Tropics of Cancer and Capricorn. It grows best in hot, wet climates where there is heavy rainfall followed by a dry season. The largest cane producers are Florida, Louisiana, Texas, and Hawaii. On a commercial basis, sugarcane is not grown from seeds but from cuttings or pieces of the stalk.

Sugar beets, which are produced in temperate or colder climates, are annuals grown from seeds. Sugar beets do best with moderate temperatures and evenly distributed rainfall. The beets are planted in the spring and harvested in the fall. The sugar is contained in the root of the beet, but the sugars from beets and cane are identical. Sugar beet production takes place mostly in Europe, the U.S., China, and Japan. The largest sugar beet producing states are Minnesota, Idaho, North Dakota, and Michigan. Sugar beets are refined to yield white sugar and very little raw sugar is produced.

Sugar beets and sugarcane are produced in over 100 countries around the world. Of all the sugar produced, about 25 percent is processed from sugar beets and the remaining 75% is from sugar cane. The trend has been that production of sugar from cane is increasing relative to that produced from beets. The significance of this in that sugarcane is a perennial plant while the sugar beet is an annual, and due to the longer production cycle, sugarcane production and the sugar processed from that cane, may not be quite as responsive to changes in price.

Sugar futures are traded on the Bolsa de Mercadorias & Futuros (BM&F), Kansai Commodities Exchange (KANEX), the Tokyo Grain Exchange (TGE), the NYSE-LIFFE exchange in London, and the ICE Futures U.S. (ICE) exchange. Options are traded on the BM&F, the TGE, the NYSE-LIFFE and the ICE.

Raw sugar is traded on the ICE Futures U.S. (ICE) exchange while white sugar is traded on the NYSE-LIFFE exchange in London. The most actively traded contract is the No. 11 (World) sugar contract at the ICE. The No. 11 contract calls for the delivery of 112,000 pounds (50 long tons) of raw cane centrifugal sugar from any of 28 foreign countries of origin and the United States. The ICE also trades the No. 16 sugar contract (Domestic), which calls for the delivery of raw centrifugal cane sugar in the United States. Futures on white sugar are traded on the NYSE-

LIFFE and call for the delivery of 50 metric tons of white beet sugar, cane crystal sugar, or refined sugar of any origin from the crop current at the time of delivery.

Prices – World sugar prices on the ICE No.11 sugar nearest-futures chart fell sharply the first half of 2010 and fell to a 1-3/4 year low of 13.00 cents per pound in May 2010. Sugar prices fell after (1) the USDA forecasted a +7.9% increase in the 2010-11 global sugar crop, and (2) speculation mounted that India would become a net exporter of sugar for the first time in 3 years. Sugar prices then rallied into year-end and posted a 30-year high of 34.77 cents per pound in December 2010, closing the year up 19% at 32.12 cents pre pound. Sugar prices rallied further in early 2011 and climbed to a fresh 30-year high of 36.08 cents per pound in March 2011. Bullish factors included (1) reduced sugar output in Australia, the world's third-largest sugar exporter, after floods and cyclones cut its output to a 9-year low of 3.58 MMT and may reduce its sugar output for the next 2-3 years due to the loss of sugarcane plants, and (2) tight sugar supplies in Brazil and India due to adverse weather from a La Nina weather pattern, and (3) the forecast by the International Sugar Organization for a 1.7% increase in global sugar demand that would cut the inventory-to-consumption ratio to a 20-year low of 32%.

Supply – World production of centrifugal (raw) sugar in the 2010-11 marketing year (Oct 1 to Sep 30) rose +5.5% to 161.899 million metric tons, further down from the 2006-07 record high of 164.196 million metric tons. The world's largest sugar producers in 2010-11 were Brazil with 24.3% of world production, India with 15.9%, and the European Union with 9.1%. U.S. centrifugal sugar production in 2010-11 rose +44.9% to 2.000 million metric tons. World ending stocks in 2010-11 rose +1.2% to 26.457 million metric tons. The stocks/consumption ratio fell -1.4% in 2010-11 to 16,700 metric tons. U.S. production of cane sugar in 2010-11 fell -2.4% to 3.310 million short tons and beet sugar production rose +4.9% yr/yr to 4.800 million short tons.

Demand – World domestic consumption of centrifugal (raw) sugar in 2010-11 rose by +2.7% yr/yr to 158.202 million metric tons, a new record high. U.S. domestic disappearance (consumption) of sugar in 2010-11 fell by -1.0% yr/yr to 11.210 million short tons. U.S. per capita sugar consumption in 2008-09 (latest data) rose +5.9% to 65.79 pounds per year, which is only about two-thirds of the levels seen in the early 1970s.

Trade – World exports of centrifugal sugar in 2010-11 rose slightly to 51.824 million metric tons, a new record high. The world's largest sugar exporter was Brazil, where exports in 2010-11 rose +10.5% to 26.850 million metric tons, which accounted for 51.8% of total world exports. The next largest exporters are Thailand with 9.1% of world exports and Australia with 7.2%. U.S. sugar exports in 2010-11 fell -28.8% yr/yr to 150,000 short tons, but that is down from the 15-year high of 4221,000 seen in 2006-07. U.S. sugar imports in 2010-11 fell -30.1% yr/yr to 2.058 million short tons, down from the 2-decade high of 3.443 in 2005-06.

World Production, Supply & Stocks/Consumption Ratio of Sugar   In 1000's of Metric Tons (Raw Value)

Marketing Year	Beginning Stocks	Production	Imports	Total Supply	Exports	Domestic Consumption	Ending Stocks	Stocks As a % of Consumption
2001-02	39,871	134,398	39,693	213,962	42,332	134,343	36,644	27.3
2002-03	36,644	148,552	41,714	226,910	47,205	138,017	40,639	29.4
2003-04	40,639	142,487	41,226	224,352	46,535	138,898	38,096	27.4
2004-05	38,096	140,674	45,418	224,188	46,930	142,396	33,930	23.8
2005-06	33,930	144,550	44,757	223,237	49,864	141,824	30,779	21.7
2006-07	30,779	164,196	43,504	238,479	51,439	150,411	34,492	22.9
2007-08	34,492	163,087	45,487	243,066	51,535	151,413	39,330	26.0
2008-09[1]	39,330	143,932	47,287	230,549	48,880	152,856	27,946	18.3
2009-10[2]	27,946	153,459	51,409	232,814	51,807	154,096	26,146	17.0
2010-11[3]	26,146	161,899	49,159	237,204	51,824	158,202	26,457	16.7

[1] Preliminary.   [2] Estimate.   [3] Forecast.   *Source: Foreign Agricultural Service, U.S. Department of Agriculture (FAS-USDA)*

World Production of Sugar (Centrifugal Sugar-Raw Value)   In Thousands of Metric Tons

Year	Australia	Brazil	China	Cuba	European Union	India	Indonesia	Mexico	Pakistan	Thailand	United States	Ukraine	World Total
2001-02	4,662	20,400	8,305	3,700	16,153	20,475	1,725	5,169	3,453	6,397	1,790	7,167	134,398
2002-03	5,461	23,810	11,380	2,250	18,675	22,140	1,755	5,229	3,944	7,286	1,550	7,644	148,552
2003-04	5,178	26,400	10,734	2,550	17,132	15,150	1,730	5,330	4,047	7,010	1,580	7,847	142,487
2004-05	5,388	28,175	9,826	1,350	21,648	14,170	2,050	6,149	2,937	5,187	2,054	7,146	140,674
2005-06	5,297	26,850	9,446	1,240	21,373	21,140	2,100	5,604	2,597	4,835	2,054	6,713	144,550
2006-07	5,212	31,450	12,855	1,200	17,757	30,780	1,900	5,633	3,615	6,720	2,850	7,662	164,196
2007-08	4,939	31,600	15,898	1,420	15,614	28,630	2,000	5,852	4,163	7,820	2,020	7,396	163,087
2008-09[1]	4,814	31,850	13,317	1,340	14,014	15,950	2,053	5,260	3,512	7,200	1,710	6,833	143,932
2009-10[2]	4,600	36,400	11,500	1,100	16,830	20,538	1,910	5,115	3,420	6,930	1,380	7,208	153,459
2010-11[3]	4,800	39,400	12,670	1,100	14,800	25,700	1,911	5,450	3,270	6,870	2,000	7,607	161,899

[1] Preliminary.   [2] Estimate.   [3] Forecast.   *Source: Foreign Agricultural Service, U.S. Department of Agriculture (FAS-USDA)*

World Stocks of Centrifugal Sugar at Beginning of Marketing Year   In Thousands of Metric Tons (Raw Value)

Year	Australia	Brazil	China	Cuba	European Union	India	Indonesia	Iran	Mexico	Philippines	Russia	United States	World Total
2001-02	634	860	1,004	350	3,420	11,985	1,415	207	1,548	322	3,100	1,978	39,871
2002-03	507	210	869	360	2,717	11,670	1,385	167	1,172	239	2,130	1,386	36,644
2003-04	662	270	2,021	267	3,581	12,150	1,340	267	1,194	277	1,050	1,515	40,639
2004-05	543	1,030	2,323	275	4,699	8,485	1,170	402	1,237	405	440	1,721	38,096
2005-06	343	585	1,757	215	5,339	4,365	1,120	542	2,045	239	580	1,208	33,930
2006-07	291	-285	703	210	5,088	4,175	1,170	932	1,294	253	470	1,540	30,779
2007-08	402	-485	1,401	203	2,720	9,850	570	1,492	1,718	262	440	1,632	34,492
2008-09[1]	400	215	3,965	333	3,130	9,150	590	1,297	1,975	547	550	1,510	39,330
2009-10[2]	487	-1,135	3,784	343	2,232	3,510	340	637	624	322	481	1,392	27,946
2010-11[3]	313	-835	1,900	140	2,375	4,653	450	637	973	244	380	1,454	26,146

[1] Preliminary.   [2] Estimate.   [3] Forecast.   *Source: Foreign Agricultural Service, U.S. Department of Agriculture (FAS-USDA)*

Centrifugal Sugar (Raw Value) Imported into Selected Countries   In Thousands of Metric Tons

Year	Algeria	Canada	China	European Union	Indonesia	Iran	Japan	Rep. of Korea	Malaysia	Nigeria	Russia	United States	World Total
2001-02	1,015	1,235	1,375	2,025	1,600	1,010	1,407	1,590	1,385	775	4,850	1,393	39,693
2002-03	1,094	1,329	842	2,150	1,600	955	1,483	1,590	1,406	1,000	4,000	1,569	41,714
2003-04	1,185	1,323	1,235	1,900	1,500	760	1,442	1,682	1,484	1,150	3,670	1,591	41,226
2004-05	1,153	1,274	1,360	2,549	1,450	865	1,328	1,652	1,459	1,150	4,300	1,905	45,418
2005-06	1,130	1,445	1,234	2,630	1,800	1,450	1,385	1,669	1,414	1,200	2,900	3,124	44,757
2006-07	1,110	1,294	1,465	3,530	1,800	1,740	1,405	1,518	1,670	1,240	2,950	1,887	43,504
2007-08	1,105	1,417	972	2,948	2,420	855	1,440	1,648	1,390	1,485	3,100	2,377	45,487
2008-09[1]	1,240	1,350	1,077	3,180	2,197	960	1,452	1,550	1,430	1,250	2,150	2,796	47,287
2009-10[2]	1,200	1,300	1,500	2,620	2,600	1,350	1,342	1,600	1,520	1,400	2,380	2,943	51,409
2010-11[3]	1,375	1,300	1,800	3,575	2,910	1,293	1,355	1,600	1,515	1,525	3,050	2,058	49,159

[1] Preliminary.   [2] Estimate.   [3] Forecast.   *Source: Foreign Agricultural Service, U.S. Department of Agriculture (FAS-USDA)*

SUGAR

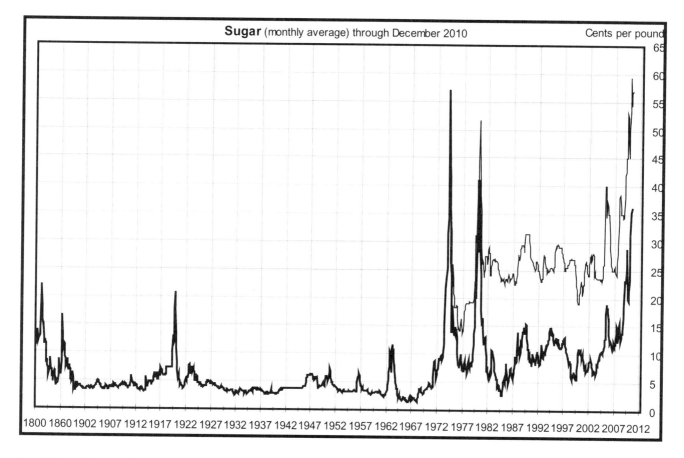

Sugar (monthly average) through December 2010 — Cents per pound

1800 1860 1902 1907 1912 1917 1922 1927 1932 1937 1942 1947 1952 1957 1962 1967 1972 1977 1982 1987 1992 1997 2002 2007 2012

Centrifugal Sugar (Raw Value) Exported From Selected Countries — In Thousands of Metric Tons

Year	Australia	Brazil	Colombia	Cuba	Dominican Republic	European Union	Guate-mala	India	Mauritius	South Africa	Swazi-land	Thailand	World Total
2001-02	3,594	11,600	1,085	3,070	185	4,793	1,310	1,130	628	1,235	208	4,157	42,332
2002-03	4,114	14,000	1,306	1,798	185	5,600	1,335	1,410	542	1,296	278	5,280	47,205
2003-04	4,157	15,240	1,200	1,942	185	4,900	1,335	250	587	1,025	285	4,860	46,535
2004-05	4,447	18,020	1,231	770	185	6,028	1,386	40	581	1,010	298	3,115	46,930
2005-06	4,208	17,090	988	730	251	8,345	1,391	1,510	548	1,230	320	2,242	49,864
2006-07	3,860	20,850	942	705	225	2,439	1,500	2,680	505	1,267	358	4,705	51,439
2007-08	3,700	19,500	661	800	217	1,656	1,333	5,830	455	1,154	350	4,914	51,535
2008-09[1]	3,522	21,550	585	750	217	1,332	1,654	176	470	1,185	350	5,295	48,880
2009-10[2]	3,600	24,300	730	725	244	2,407	1,654	5	500	830	350	5,900	51,807
2010-11[3]	3,750	26,850	740	500	202	1,460	1,680	20	500	800	360	4,700	51,824

[1] Preliminary. [2] Estimate. [3] Forecast. *Source: Foreign Agricultural Service, U.S. Department of Agriculture (FAS-USDA)*

Average Wholesale Price of Refined Beet Sugar[2]--Midwest Market — In Cents Per Pound

Year	Jan.	Feb.	Mar.	Apr.	May	June	July	Aug.	Sept.	Oct.	Nov.	Dec.	Average
2001	23.13	22.75	22.00	20.50	21.38	21.90	22.50	22.50	24.63	25.75	26.20	26.50	23.31
2002	26.75	26.00	25.95	24.63	24.50	24.00	24.00	25.40	26.25	26.75	27.40	27.88	25.79
2003	27.80	26.50	27.13	27.63	28.00	28.00	27.63	25.50	24.00	24.70	23.94	23.63	26.21
2004	23.70	23.50	23.50	23.50	23.50	23.50	23.50	23.50	23.50	23.50	23.38	23.20	23.48
2005	23.50	23.50	23.25	23.80	24.75	25.88	26.00	26.75	40.10	40.00	40.00	36.90	29.54
2006	34.50	36.50	37.10	36.38	35.00	35.00	35.00	34.50	31.20	28.75	27.19	26.10	33.10
2007	25.50	25.00	24.90	25.00	25.00	25.00	25.38	25.60	25.38	25.00	24.50	24.50	25.06
2008	24.13	26.40	28.00	28.00	29.60	33.25	38.00	38.40	38.50	36.20	35.00	35.00	32.54
2009	35.00	35.00	35.00	34.25	34.40	35.50	35.40	38.00	42.00	42.60	45.00	45.00	38.10
2010[1]	50.50	53.00	52.25	48.20	45.00	50.00	53.40	59.50	59.00	54.40	56.50	57.00	53.23

[1] Preliminary. [2] These are f.o.b. basis prices in bulk, not delivered prices. *Source: Economic Research Service, U.S. Department of Agriculture (ERS-)*

Average Price of World Raw Sugar[1]   In Cents Per Pound

Year	Jan.	Feb.	Mar.	Apr.	May	June	July	Aug.	Sept.	Oct.	Nov.	Dec.	Average
2001	10.63	10.26	9.64	9.27	9.96	9.80	9.48	8.77	8.60	7.15	7.80	8.02	9.12
2002	7.96	6.81	7.27	7.12	7.33	7.07	8.02	7.86	8.54	8.84	8.87	8.81	7.88
2003	8.56	9.14	8.50	7.92	7.41	6.85	7.18	7.30	6.70	6.74	6.83	6.95	7.51
2004	6.42	7.01	8.23	8.21	8.08	8.41	9.19	8.99	9.10	9.84	9.65	10.19	8.61
2005	10.33	10.51	10.57	10.19	10.23	10.45	10.89	11.09	11.59	12.40	12.86	15.09	11.35
2006	17.27	18.93	18.01	18.21	17.83	16.19	16.61	13.58	12.42	12.09	12.38	12.47	15.50
2007	11.85	11.63	11.44	10.85	10.78	11.05	12.18	11.66	11.61	11.86	11.83	12.47	11.60
2008	13.75	15.16	14.60	13.68	12.23	13.29	14.90	15.58	14.74	12.99	12.87	12.31	13.84
2009	13.09	13.90	13.83	14.43	16.89	16.94	18.57	22.37	23.11	23.22	22.96	25.28	18.72
2010[2]	28.94	27.29	21.36	19.87	19.59	21.24	23.42	25.09	31.19	34.80	35.44	36.10	27.03

[1] Contract No. 11, f.o.b. stowed Caribbean port, including Brazil, bulk spot price.   [2] Preliminary.   *Source: Economic Research Service, U.S. Department of Agriculture (ERS-USDA)*

Average Price of Raw Sugar in New York (C.I.F., Duty/Free Paid, Contract #12 & #14)   In Cents Per Pound

Year	Jan.	Feb.	Mar.	Apr.	May	June	July	Aug.	Sept.	Oct.	Nov.	Dec.	Average
2001	20.81	21.18	21.40	21.51	21.19	21.04	20.64	21.10	20.87	20.90	21.19	21.43	21.11
2002	21.03	20.69	19.92	19.73	19.52	19.93	20.86	20.91	21.65	21.94	22.22	22.03	20.87
2003	21.62	21.91	22.14	21.87	21.80	21.62	21.32	21.26	21.34	20.92	20.91	20.37	21.42
2004	20.54	20.57	20.86	20.88	20.69	20.03	20.14	20.10	20.47	20.31	20.40	20.55	20.46
2005	20.57	20.36	20.54	21.21	21.96	21.89	21.94	20.49	21.10	21.71	21.83	21.74	21.28
2006	23.61	24.05	23.10	23.56	23.48	23.32	22.44	21.38	21.27	20.22	19.66	19.59	22.14
2007	20.03	20.59	20.85	20.91	21.27	21.33	22.72	21.80	21.42	20.56	20.25	20.12	20.99
2008	20.24	20.21	20.65	20.54	20.83	21.80	23.76	23.15	23.10	21.46	19.83	20.00	21.30
2009	20.15	19.83	19.75	21.58	21.64	22.47	23.02	26.18	28.91	30.48	31.86	33.30	24.93
2010[1]	39.36	40.13	35.11	30.86	30.89	32.73	33.66	34.24	38.17	39.30	38.84	38.35	35.97

[1] Preliminary.   *Source: Economic Research Service, U.S. Department of Agriculture (ERS-USDA)*

Supply and Utilization of Sugar (Cane and Beet) in the United States   In Thousands of Short Tons (Raw Value)

	Supply								Utilization					
	Production			Offshore Receipts						Net Changes in Invisible Stocks	Refining Loss Adjustment	Domestic Disappearance		
Year	Cane	Beet	Total	Foreign	Terri-tories	Total	Beginning Stocks	Total Supply	Total Use	Exports			In Poly-hydric Alcohol[4]	Total	Per Capita Pounds
2001-02	3,985	3,915	7,900	1,535	0	1,535	2,180	11,615	10,087	137	-24	0	33	9,785	64.5
2002-03	3,964	4,462	8,426	1,730	0	1,730	1,528	11,684	10,014	142	161	0	24	9,504	63.3
2003-04	3,957	4,692	8,649	1,750	0	1,750	1,670	12,070	10,172	288	23	0	41	9,678	61.0
2004-05	3,265	4,611	7,876	2,100	0	2,100	1,897	11,873	10,542	259	94	0	48	10,019	61.7
2005-06	2,955	4,444	7,399	3,443	0	3,443	1,332	12,174	10,476	203	-67	0	51	10,184	63.2
2006-07	3,438	5,008	8,445	2,080	0	2,080	1,698	12,223	10,424	422	-132	0	53	9,913	62.5
2007-08	3,431	4,721	8,152	2,620	0	2,620	1,799	12,571	10,907	203	0	0	61	10,501	62.1
2008-09[1]	3,317	4,214	7,531	3,082	0	3,082	1,664	12,277	10,743	136	0	0	46	10,441	65.8
2009-10[2]	3,392	4,575	7,968	3,320	0	3,320	1,534	12,822	11,318	211	0	0	35	10,917	
2010-11[3]	3,310	4,800	8,110	3,006	0	3,006	1,503	12,619	11,210	150	0	0	40	10,875	

[1] Preliminary.   [2] Estimate.   [3] Forecast.   [4] Includes feed use.   *Source: Economic Research Service, U.S. Department of Agriculture (ERS-USDA)*

Sugar Cane for Sugar & Seed and Production of Cane Sugar and Molasses in the United States

			Production					Farm Value		Sugar Production				
	Acreage Harvested (1,000 Acres)	Yield of Cane Per Havested Acre Net Tons	for Sugar	for Seed	Total	Sugar Yield Per Acre (Short Tons)	Farm Price ($ Per Ton)	of Cane Used for Sugar	of Cane Used for Sugar & Seed	Raw Value Total (1,000 Tons)	Per Ton of Cane (In Lbs.)	Refined Basis (1,000 Tons)	Molasses Made Edible	Total[3]
Year			1,000 Tons					1,000 Dollars					1,000 Gallons	
2001	1,027.8	33.7	32,775	1,812	34,587	4.10	29.0	951,813	1,003,046	----	----	----	----	----
2002	1,023.2	34.7	33,903	1,650	35,553	4.07	28.4	961,896	1,007,142	----	----	----	----	----
2003	992.3	34.1	31,942	1,916	33,858	4.26	29.5	943,646	998,269	----	----	----	----	----
2004	938.2	30.9	27,243	1,770	29,013	3.71	28.3	771,734	821,118	----	----	----	----	----
2005	921.9	28.9	24,728	1,878	26,606	3.49	28.4	701,920	754,529	----	----	----	----	----
2006	897.7	32.9	27,962	1,602	29,564	4.05	30.4	849,157	897,601	----	----	----	----	----
2007	879.6	34.1	28,273	1,696	29,969	4.17	29.4	831,218	880,616	----	----	----	----	----
2008	868.0	31.8	26,131	1,472	27,603	4.03	29.5	771,134	814,479	----	----	----	----	----
2009[1]	873.9	34.8	28,484	1,938	30,432	4.17	34.8	NA	1,056,613					
2010[2]	882.2	31.8	26,420	1,667	28,087	3.87								

[1] Preliminary.   [2] Estimate.   [3] Excludes edible molasses.   *Source: Economic Research Service, U.S. Department of Agriculture (ERS-USDA)*

SUGAR

U.S. Sugar Beets, Beet Sugar, Pulp & Molasses Produced from Sugar Beets and Raw Sugar Spot Prices

Year of Harvest	Acreage Planted (1,000 Acres)	Acreage Harvested (1,000 Acres)	Yield Per Harvested Acre (Sh. Tons)	Production (1,000 Tons)	Sugar Yield Per Acre (Sh. Tons)	Price[3] (Dollars)	Farm Value (1,000 $)	Equivalent Raw Value[4] (1,000 Short Tons)	Refined Basis	World[5] Refined #5 (Cents/Pound)	CSCE #11 World (Cents/Pound)	CSCE N.Y. Duty Paid (Cents/Pound)	Wholesale List Price HFCS (42%) Midwest
2001	1,371	1,243	20.7	25,764	3.15	39.80	1,025,306	3,914	----	11.29	9.12	21.11	11.90
2002	1,427	1,361	20.4	27,707	3.28	39.60	1,097,329	4,462	----	10.35	7.88	20.87	13.05
2003	1,365	1,348	22.8	30,710	3.48	41.40	1,270,026	4,692	----	9.74	7.51	21.42	13.24
2004	1,346	1,307	23.0	30,021	3.53	36.90	1,109,272	4,611	----	10.87	8.61	20.46	13.20
2005	1,300	1,243	22.1	27,433	3.58	43.50	1,193,151	4,444	----	13.19	11.35	21.28	13.58
2006	1,366	1,304	26.1	34,064	3.84	44.20	1,506,985	5,008	----	19.01	15.50	22.14	17.03
2007	1,269	1,247	25.5	31,834	3.79	42.00	1,337,173	4,721	----	14.00	11.60	20.99	21.22
2008	1,091	1,005	26.8	26,881	4.15	48.10	1,294,144	4,166	----	15.96	13.84	21.30	24.50
2009[1]	1,186	1,149	25.7	29,563	3.98	50.40	1,499,676	4,575		22.13	18.72	24.93	25.88
2010[2]	1,171	1,156	27.6	31,945	4.15			4,800			27.03	35.97	

[1] Preliminary. [2] Estimate. [3] Includes support payments, but excludes Gov't. sugar beet payments. [4] Refined sugar multiplied by factor of 1.07.
[5] F.O.B. Europe. *Source: Economic Research Service, U.S. Department of Agriculture (ERS-USDA)*

Sugar Deliveries and Stocks in the United States   In Thousands of Short Tons (Raw Value)

Year	Quota Allocation	Actual Imports	Cane Sugar Refineries Deliveries	Beet Sugar Factories Deliveries	Importers of Direct Consumption Sugar	Mainland Cane Sugar Mills[3]	Total Deliveries	Total Domestic Consumption	Stocks Jan. 1 Cane Sugar Refineries	Stocks Jan. 1 Beet Sugar Factories	Stocks Jan. 1 CCC	Stocks Jan. 1 Refiners' Raw	Stocks Jan. 1 Mainland Cane Mills	Stocks Jan. 1 Total
2001	----	----	5,172	4,680	58	----	9,911	10,075	262	1,500	767	274	1,533	4,337
2002	----	----	5,407	4,291	109	----	9,808	9,994	288	1,472	634	351	1,781	4,525
2003	----	----	5,232	4,219	60	----	9,511	9,713	298	1,300	246	299	1,289	3,432
2004	----	----	4,989	4,668	64	----	9,722	9,901	326	1,817	0	286	1,659	4,088
2005	----	----	5,136	4,710	197	----	10,043	10,212	368	1,753	28	245	1,635	4,029
2006	----	----	5,230	4,195	577	----	10,002	10,162	328	1,429	0	217	1,382	3,357
2007	----	----	5,123	4,707	116	----	9,946	10,173	452	1,792	0	358	1,437	4,039
2008	----	----	5,075	4,867	773	----	10,715	10,900	400	1,806	0	304	1,500	4,009
2009[1]	----	----	5,493	4,324	667	----	10,485	10,657	440	1,464	0	468	1,612	3,984
2010[2]	----	----	5,619	4,517	673	----	10,809	11,049	484	1,456	0	346	1,274	3,559

[1] Preliminary. [2] Estimate. [3] Sugar for direct consumption only. [4] Refined. *Source: Economic Research Service, U.S. Department of Agriculture (ERS-USDA)*

Sugar, Refined--Deliveries to End User in the United States   In Thousands of Short Tons

Year	Bakery & Cereal Products	Beverages	Confectionery[2]	Hotels, Restar. & Institutions	Ice Cream & Dairy Products	Canned, Bottled & Frozen Foods	All Other Food Uses	Retail Grocers[3]	Wholesale Grocers[4]	Non-food Uses	Non-Industrial Uses	Industrial Uses	Total Deliveries
2001	2,273	158	1,316	59	484	310	800	1,255	2,250	74	3,920	5,411	9,331
2002	2,075	189	1,223	53	529	297	725	1,322	2,406	99	4,076	5,128	9,203
2003	2,108	214	1,130	52	548	303	632	1,279	2,387	99	4,214	4,886	9,100
2004	2,180	242	1,125	76	603	315	697	1,267	2,398	91	4,071	5,252	9,323
2005	2,297	237	1,131	115	587	336	606	1,262	2,401	92	4,026	5,286	9,312
2006	2,231	228	1,069	88	553	335	535	1,204	2,389	107	3,856	5,056	8,912
2007	2,399	312	1,110	74	609	360	569	1,211	2,411	102	3,888	5,460	9,348
2008	2,312	341	1,108	115	612	427	676	1,212	2,317	97	3,835	5,572	9,407
2009	2,286	351	1,085	127	587	427	573	1,241	2,360	84	3,907	5,393	9,300
2010[1]	2,400	422	1,070	124	583	391	609	1,270	2,471	111	4,079	5,587	9,666

[1] Preliminary. [2] And related products. [3] Chain stores, supermarkets. [4] Jobbers, sugar dealers.
Source: Economic Research Service, U.S. Department of Agriculture (ERS-USDA)

Deliveries[1] of All Sugar by Primary Distributors in the United States, by Quarters   In Thousands of Short Tons

Year	First Quarter	Second Quarter	Third Quarter	Fourth Quarter	Total	Year	First Quarter	Second Quarter	Third Quarter	Fourth Quarter	Total
1999	2,208	2,553	2,655	2,580	9,996	2005	2,335	2,471	2,666	2,571	10,043
2000	2,318	2,484	2,611	2,564	9,977	2006	2,436	2,487	2,690	2,389	10,002
2001	2,370	2,486	2,580	2,474	9,911	2007	2,307	2,535	2,682	2,422	9,946
2002	2,227	2,439	2,645	2,497	9,808	2008	2,489	2,676	2,807	2,743	10,715
2003	2,183	2,360	2,464	2,504	9,511	2009	2,387	2,602	2,780	2,715	10,485
2004	2,286	2,368	2,520	2,547	9,722	2010[2]	2,503	2,691	3,005	2,609	10,809

[1] Includes for domestic consumption and for export. [2] Preliminary. *Source: Economic Research Service, U.S. Department of Agriculture (ERS-USDA)*

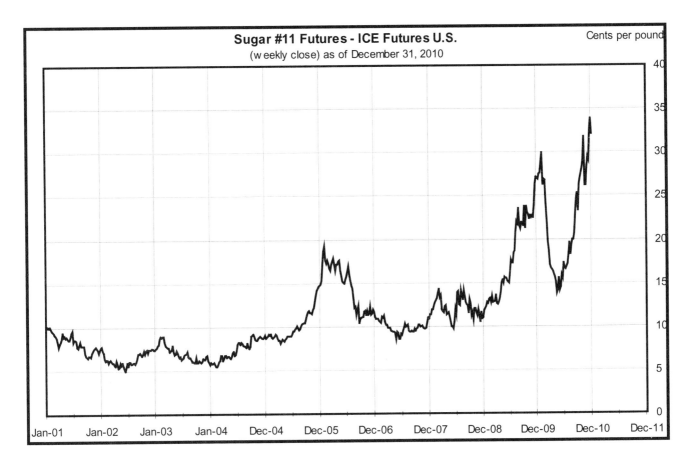

Sugar #11 Futures - ICE Futures U.S.
(weekly close) as of December 31, 2010

Cents per pound

Volume of Trading of World Sugar #11 Futures in New York   In Contracts

Year	Jan.	Feb.	Mar.	Apr.	May	June	July	Aug.	Sept.	Oct.	Nov.	Dec.	Total
2001	410.5	545.5	380.6	567.9	427.0	515.6	356.5	419.1	447.3	348.9	414.0	317.4	5,150
2002	568.8	629.5	417.3	693.6	412.2	610.3	529.5	381.0	756.0	402.8	432.1	340.6	6,174
2003	566.0	797.6	443.8	729.5	489.2	719.8	535.9	545.9	760.2	475.3	403.1	674.4	7,141
2004	513.6	1,018.7	1,181.1	993.7	617.3	1,100.6	614.6	679.5	1,248.7	626.5	539.5	632.7	9,767
2005	981.5	1,279.3	957.1	1,258.6	657.6	1,366.8	779.2	1,198.3	1,803.5	915.8	816.6	992.8	13,007
2006	1,444.2	1,601.2	1,092.2	1,467.4	1,147.7	1,459.1	825.0	1,278.6	1,746.7	1,095.7	918.7	1,024.0	15,101
2007	1,322.9	2,189.7	1,659.6	2,023.2	1,819.5	2,679.8	1,559.7	1,326.6	2,175.7	1,565.3	1,452.1	1,489.7	21,264
2008	3,566.7	3,280.8	2,237.7	2,889.5	1,941.8	3,067.4	1,820.2	1,721.4	2,540.9	1,629.9	1,085.5	1,238.1	27,020
2009	1,624.6	2,040.3	1,867.0	2,995.5	2,229.3	3,359.1	1,741.5	2,833.2	3,219.5	1,824.3	1,576.4	1,989.5	27,300
2010	2,348.9	2,986.5	2,772.9	2,754.5	1,730.0	2,936.0	1,840.3	2,184.6	3,366.7	1,978.1	2,629.3	1,524.7	29,053

Contract size = 112,000 lbs.   *Source: ICE Futures U.S. (ICE)*

Average Open Interest of World Sugar #11 Futures in New York   In Contracts

Year	Jan.	Feb.	Mar.	Apr.	May	June	July	Aug.	Sept.	Oct.	Nov.	Dec.
2001	157,478	158,192	158,448	167,555	131,640	126,426	112,483	128,181	139,915	146,058	163,358	170,710
2002	184,096	205,138	194,541	187,415	157,738	158,276	149,202	170,667	202,144	207,456	207,598	217,904
2003	244,036	265,758	220,971	192,497	170,867	184,257	180,898	196,857	195,200	185,917	200,605	207,995
2004	246,347	269,863	268,250	275,423	267,362	282,842	300,961	309,436	292,917	322,079	304,462	332,803
2005	375,713	391,006	357,056	352,521	355,922	366,568	404,141	473,757	468,737	464,829	478,097	523,820
2006	526,575	501,074	462,871	474,241	490,201	453,021	457,301	479,420	493,931	447,817	503,364	563,844
2007	632,783	695,426	652,346	686,648	738,708	695,249	674,318	667,523	656,128	681,403	763,910	835,526
2008	1,035,301	1,013,324	973,541	939,615	915,325	885,082	809,433	804,956	774,839	664,164	636,078	644,852
2009	664,303	656,033	644,829	681,177	703,355	764,799	735,556	838,638	821,646	770,085	772,808	813,238
2010	842,463	830,888	745,170	667,291	656,182	635,744	587,509	627,022	651,093	585,353	584,909	592,044

Contract size = 112,000 lbs.   *Source: ICE Futures U.S. (ICE)*

Sulfur

Sulfur (symbol S) is an odorless, tasteless, light yellow, nonmetallic element. As early as 2000 BC, Egyptians used sulfur compounds to bleach fabric. The Chinese used sulfur as an essential component when they developed gunpowder in the 13th century.

Sulfur is widely found in both its free and combined states. Free sulfur is found mixed with gypsum and pumice stone in volcanic regions. Sulfur dioxide is an air pollutant released from the combustion of fossil fuels. The most important use of sulfur is the production of sulfur compounds. Sulfur is used in skin ointments, matches, dyes, gunpowder, and phosphoric acid.

Supply – World production of all forms of sulfur in 2009 rose +2.2% yr/yr to a new record high production of 70.300 million metric tons. The world's largest producers of sulfur are the U.S with 14% of world production, Canada with 13%, China with 12%, and Russia with 10%. U.S.

production of sulfur in 2009 rose by +3.7% yr/yr to 9.800 million metric tons. That was up from the 37-year low of 9.060 in 2006.

Demand – U.S. consumption of all forms of sulfur fell by -22.1% in 2009 to 10.200 million metric tons, but still above the 2-decade low of 10.900 million metric tons seen in 2001. U.S. consumption of elemental sulfur in 2010 rose +14.3% to 10.600 million metric tons. U.S. consumption of sulfuric acid fell by -7.8% yr/yr in 2008 (latest data) to 7.680 million metric tons.

Trade – U.S. exports of recovered sulfur in 2010 (latest data available) was unchanged from 2009 at 1.430 million metric tons, further up from the 15-year low of 635,000 metric tons in 2006. U.S. imports of recovered sulfur in 2010 rose by +69.4% yr/yr to 2.880 million metric tons, but still below the 2008 record high of 3.000 million metric tons.

World Production of Sulfur (All Forms) In Thousands of Metric Tons

Year	Canada	China	France	Germany	Iraq	Japan	Mexico	Poland	Russia	Saudi Arabia	Spain	United States	World Total
2003	9,028	6,500	1,420	2,362	----	3,232	1,591	1,231	6,720	2,180	651	9,600	64,100
2004	9,101	7,150	1,405	2,094	----	3,158	1,825	1,290	6,920	2,249	651	10,100	66,400
2005	8,974	7,710	1,372	2,185	----	3,256	1,767	1,280	6,950	2,717	616	9,500	67,200
2006	9,082	7,760	1,366	2,286	----	3,293	1,724	1,310	6,950	2,907	601	9,060	67,000
2007	8,789	8,460	1,306	2,237	----	3,216	1,576	1,350	7,050	3,089	601	9,100	67,500
2008	9,278	8,610	1,310	2,309	----	3,270	1,741	1,280	7,170	3,163	601	9,450	68,800
2009[1]	6,940	9,370	1,310	3,760	----	3,350	1,700	730	7,070	3,200	637	9,780	67,900
2010[2]	7,000	9,400	1,300	3,800		3,400	1,700	750	7,100	3,200	640	9,900	68,000

[1] Preliminary.   [2] Estimate.   *Source: U.S. Geological Survey (USGS)*

Salient Statistics of Sulfur in the United States   In Thousands of Metric Tons (Sulfur Content)

Year	Native Sulfur[3] Frasch	Recovered Petroleum & Cole	Natural Gas	Total	Total Elemental Sulfur	By-product Sulfuric Acid[4]	Other Sulf. Acid Com-pounds	Imports Sulfuric Acid[4]	Exports Sulfuric Acid[4]	Producer Stocks, Dec. 31[5]	Apparent Con-sumption (All Forms)	Frasch	Recovered	Average Total
2003	----	6,970	1,950	8,970	683	----	9,650	908	205	206	11,900	----	----	28.70
2004	----	7,390	1,990	9,380	739	----	10,100	2,400	204	185	12,800	----	----	32.62
2005	----	6,940	1,850	8,790	711	----	9,500	2,680	338	160	12,400	----	----	30.88
2006	----	6,960	1,440	8,390	674	----	9,060	2,430	248	221	12,000	----	----	32.85
2007	----	7,000	1,280	8,280	817	----	9,100	2,600	336	187	11,900	----	----	36.49
2008	----	7,380	1,320	8,690	753	----	9,450	3,440	261	211	13,100	----	----	245.12
2009[1]	----	7,840	1,220	9,030	750	----	9,780	1,270	254	239	10,400	----	----	1.68
2010[2]	----			9,100	800	----	9,900	1,500	188	220	12,000	----	----	40.00

Sulfur Consumption & Foreign Trade of the United States   In Thousands of Metric Tons (Sulfur Content)

Year	Native Sulfur (Frasch)	Rec-overed Sulfur	Total Elemental Form	Pulpmills & Paper Products	Inorganic Chem-icals[3]	Synthetic Rubber & Plastic	Phosph-atic Fertilizers	Petro-leum Refining[4]	Frasch	Exports Re-covered	Exports Value $1,000	Imports Re-covered	Imports Value $1,000
2003	W	10,900	10,900	10,100	225	71	82	6,660	140	----	840	54,400	---- 2,870	70,600
2004	W	11,300	11,300	9,290	272	154	70	6,870	248	----	949	63,300	---- 2,850	76,800
2005	W	10,900	10,900	9,680	267	312	64	7,000	188	----	684	55,200	---- 2,820	70,500
2006	W	10,600	10,600	8,750	246	426	250	6,220	262	----	635	43,800	---- 2,950	70,400
2007	W	10,300	10,300	8,330	245	245	117	6,280	264	----	922	84,800	---- 2,930	79,400
2008	W	10,700	10,700	7,680	187	293	69	5,690	244	----	952	272,000	---- 3,000	753,000
2009	W	9,270	9,270							----	1,420		---- 1,690	
2010[1]	W	10,600	10,600							----	1,200		---- 2,800	

[1] Preliminary.   [2] Sulfur equivalent.   [3] Including inorganic pigments, paints & allied products, and other inorganic chemicals & products.
[4] Including other petroleum and coal products.   W = Withheld proprietary data.   NA = Not available.   *Source: U.S. Geological Survey (USGS)*

Sunflowerseed, Meal and Oil

Sunflowers are native to South and North America, but are now grown almost worldwide. Sunflower-seed oil accounts for approximately 14% of the world production of seed oils. Sunflower varieties that are commercially grown contain from 39% to 49% oil in the seed. Sunflower crops produce about 50 bushels of seed per acre on average, which yields approximately 50 gallons of oil.

Sunflower-seed oil accounts for around 80% of the value of the sunflower crop. Refined sunflower-seed oil is edible and used primarily as a salad and cooking oil and in margarine. Crude sunflower-seed oil is used industrially for making soaps, candles, varnishes, and detergents. Sunflower-seed oil contains 93% of the energy of U.S. No. 2 diesel fuel and is being explored as a potential alternate fuel source in diesel engines. Sunflower meal is used in livestock feed and when fed to poultry, increases the yield of eggs. Sunflower seeds are also used for birdfeed and as a snack for humans.

Prices – The average monthly price received by U.S. farmers for sunflower seeds in the first five months of the 2010-11 marketing year (Sep/Aug) rose +32.3% to $20.16 per hundred pounds, below the 2007-08 record high of $23.08 per hundred pounds.

Supply – World sunflower-seed production in the 2008-09 marketing year (latest data available) rose +14.2% yr/yr to 33.198 million metric tons. The world's largest sunflower-seed producers are Russia with 18.1% of world production, Argentina with 9.2%, China with 5.5%, U.S with 4.1%, and France and India both with a little less than 5%.

U.S. production of sunflower seeds in 2010-11 fell by -9.9% yr/yr to 1.241 million metric tons, but that still less than half the record production level of 3.309 million metric tons posted in 1979-80. U.S. farmers harvested 1.873 million acres of sunflowers in 2010-11, down -4.1% yr/yr, further down from the 9-year high of 2.610 million acres posted in 2005-06. U.S sunflower yield in 2010-11 was down -6.0% to 14.60 hundred pounds per acre, below last year's record high of 15.54 hundred pounds per acre.

Demand – Total U.S. disappearance of sunflower seeds in 2010-11 fell -9.1% yr/yr to 1.335 million metric tons, of which 50.6% went to crushing for oil and meal, 34% went to non-oil and seed use, and 10.8% went to exports.

Trade – World sunflower-seed exports in 2009-10 fell -36.7% yr/yr to 1.440 million metric tons. The world's largest exporters are Russia which accounted for 20.4% of world exports in 2009-10 and the U.S. which accounted for 11.1% of world exports.

World Production of Sunflowerseed   In Thousands of Metric Tons

Crop Year	Argentina	Bulgaria	China	France	Hungary	India	Romania	Africa	Spain	Turkey	States	USSR	Total
2000-01	2,970	425	1,954	1,833	484	646	721	638	848	630	1,608	7,824	23,099
2001-02	3,730	405	1,478	1,584	632	726	824	929	871	530	1,551	5,468	21,302
2002-03	3,350	645	1,946	1,497	777	1,060	1,003	643	757	830	1,112	7,836	23,985
2003-04	2,990	789	1,743	1,530	992	1,160	1,506	648	763	560	1,209	10,179	26,984
2004-05	3,730	1,030	1,700	1,462	1,186	1,350	1,220	620	785	640	930	8,830	26,461
2005-06	3,840	830	1,928	1,510	1,108	1,490	1,180	520	381	780	1,720	12,132	30,572
2006-07	3,190	1,060	1,803	1,440	1,100	1,450	1,390	300	607	820	997	12,697	30,389
2007-08	4,620	635	1,670	1,311	950	1,460	700	872	733	670	1,309	10,889	29,322
2008-09[1]	3,200	1,036	1,750	1,598	1,550	1,150	1,170	801	873	850	1,553	15,037	34,697
2009-10[2]	2,300	1,214	1,650	1,704	1,266	1,000	1,102	502	876	790	1,377	13,885	31,312

[1] Preliminary.   [2] Forecast.   *Source: Economic Research Service, U.S. Department of Agriculture (ERS-USDA)*

World Imports and Exports of Sunflowerseed   In Thousands of Metric Tons

Crop Year	France	Germany	Netherlands	Spain	Turkey	World Total	Argentina	France	Hungary	Former USSR	United States	Uraguay	World Total
			Imports							Exports			
2000-01	174	193	413	368	322	2,460	94	11	6	1,865	153	21	2,462
2001-02	43	58	180	172	164	1,202	342	24	14	186	176	130	1,184
2002-03	62	65	148	151	287	1,462	232	3	19	577	123	223	1,586
2003-04	202	60	167	218	630	2,287	45	25	14	1,374	138	127	2,307
2004-05	5	71	24	188	518	1,302	99	20	52	131	117	134	1,187
2005-06	28	63	90	235	391	1,516	45	9	31	664	156	59	1,548
2006-07	49	73	64	233	495	1,954	63	5	42	606	156	13	1,922
2007-08	9	74	55	64	529	1,334	41	5	51	130	168	38	1,332
2008-09[1]	180	77	77	107	477	2,159	64	5	32	1,071	159	----	2,276
2009-10[2]	10	45	54	52	480	1,520	47	7	27	293	160	22	1,440

[1] Preliminary.   [2] Forecast.   *Source: Economic Research Service, U.S. Department of Agriculture (ERS-USDA)*

SUNFLOWERSEED, MEAL AND OIL

Sunflowerseed Statistics in the United States   In Thousands of Metric Tons

Crop Year Beginning Sept. 1	Acres Harvested (1,000)	Harvested Yield Per CWT	Farm Price ($/Metric Ton)	Value of Pro-duction (Million $)	Stocks, Sept. 1	Production	Imports	Total Supply	Crush	Exports	Non-Oil Use & Seed	Total Disap-pearance
2003-04	2,197	12.13	267	316.2	199	1,209	90	1,498	627	170	538	1,335
2004-05	1,711	11.98	302	272.7	163	930	44	1,137	276	140	631	1,047
2005-06	2,610	15.40	267	487.7	90	1,822	39	1,952	566	178	852	1,596
2006-07	1,770	12.11	320	308.8	356	972	112	1,440	659	182	463	1,303
2007-08	2,012	14.26	478	614.7	137	1,301	87	1,526	683	200	523	1,405
2008-09	2,396	14.29	481	704.1	120	1,553	70	1,743	661	184	675	1,520
2009-10[1]	1,954	15.54	333	459.0	223	1,377	46	1,646	776	179	514	1,469
2010-11[2]	1,874	14.60	472	582.4	177	1,241	27	1,445	676	159	500	1,335

[1] Preliminary.   [2] Forecast.   Source: Economic Research Service, U.S. Department of Agriculture (ERS-USDA)

World Production of Sunflowerseed Oil and Meal   In Thousands of Metric Tons

	Sunflowerseed Oil						Sunflowerseed Meal						
Year	Argen-tina	France	Spain	Turkey	Ex-USSR	World Total	Argen-tina	France	Spain	Turkey	United States	Ex-USSR	World Total
2002-03	1,368	487	454	385	2,928	8,653	1,342	599	527	489	173	2,851	9,832
2003-04	1,204	565	459	486	3,394	9,551	1,184	734	534	616	305	3,385	10,982
2004-05	1,507	416	457	451	3,292	9,441	1,509	508	531	572	138	3,432	10,850
2005-06	1,631	400	421	464	4,634	11,057	1,653	494	490	589	299	4,536	12,347
2006-07	1,315	453	411	496	5,004	11,321	1,407	556	478	629	325	4,993	12,794
2007-08	1,575	443	357	459	4,108	10,197	1,609	484	415	604	342	4,242	11,608
2008-09[1]	1,484	573	444	486	5,833	12,869	1,531	651	516	616	349	5,779	14,329
2009-10=[2]	1,099	576	456	486	5,503	11,812	1,116	690	530	625	356	5,541	13,279

[1] Preliminary.   [2] Forecast.   Source: Economic Research Service, U.S. Department of Agriculture (ERS-USDA)

Sunflower Oil Statistics in the United States   In Thousands of Metric Tons

Crop Year Beginning Sept. 1	Stocks, Oct. 1	Production	Imports	Total Supply	Exports	Domestic Use	Total Disap-pearance	Price $ Per Metric Ton (Crude Mpls.)
2003-04	12	264	12	287	107	162	269	736
2004-05	18	116	34	168	57	102	158	938
2005-06	10	238	26	273	95	154	249	893
2006-07	25	277	71	372	77	268	345	1,242
2007-08	27	287	47	361	77	272	349	1,978
2008-09	12	297	30	339	91	198	289	1,170
2009-10[1]	50	331	22	403	98	267	365	1,163
2010-11[2]	38	284	14	336	82	227	309	

[1] Preliminary.   [2] Forecast.   Source: Economic Research Service, U.S. Department of Agriculture (ERS-USDA)

Sunflower Meal Statistics in the United States   In Thousands of Metric Tons

Crop Year Beginning Sept. 1	Stocks, Oct. 1	Production	Imports	Total Supply	Exports	Domestic Use	Total Disap-pearance	Price USD Per Metric Ton 28% Protein
2003-04	5	301	20	326	12	309	326	125
2004-05	5	133	0	138	3	130	138	91
2005-06	5	272	5	282	6	271	282	88
2006-07	5	316	20	341	13	323	341	114
2007-08	5	328	0	333	17	311	333	183
2008-09	5	335	0	340	7	328	340	172
2009-10[1]	5	374	0	379	6	368	379	164
2010-11[2]	5	327	0	332	14	313	332	

[1] Preliminary.   [2] Forecast.   Source: Economic Research Service, U.S. Department of Agriculture (ERS-USDA)

Average Price Received by Farmers for Sunflower[2] in the United States   In Dollars Per Hundred Pounds (Cwt.)

Year	Jan.	Feb.	Mar.	Apr.	May	June	July	Aug.	Sept.	Oct.	Nov.	Dec.	Average
2005-06	13.20	12.80	12.20	12.20	11.40	11.20	11.50	11.90	11.80	12.30	12.00	12.40	12.08
2006-07	11.70	12.10	12.50	13.60	13.80	14.90	15.60	15.90	16.60	17.00	18.20	18.40	15.03
2007-08	17.70	17.80	18.30	19.20	19.10	24.20	25.90	24.50	27.40	28.10	28.40	26.40	23.08
2008-09	28.20	25.30	23.10	22.80	22.10	22.60	22.10	20.20	21.50	18.40	17.70	20.60	22.05
2009-10	13.90	16.20	14.20	14.80	15.50	16.70	15.80	16.00	14.90	15.00	15.40	14.30	15.23
2010-11[1]	17.30	20.80	19.10	20.60	21.90	25.20							20.82

[1] Preliminary.   [2] KS, MN, ND and SD average.   Source: Economic Research Service, U.S. Department of Agriculture (ERS-USDA)

Tall Oil

Tall oil is a product of the paper and pulping industry. Crude tall oil is the major byproduct of the kraft or sulfate processing of pinewood. Crude tall oil starts as tall oil soap which is separated from recovered black liquor in the kraft pulping process. The tall oil soap is acidified to yield crude tall oil. The resulting tall oil is then fractionated to produce fatty acids, rosin, and pitch. Crude tall oil contains 40-50 percent fatty acids such as oleic and linoleic acids; 5-10 percent sterols, alcohols, and other neutral components. The demand is for the tall oil rosin and fatty acids which are used to produce adhesives, coatings, and ink resins. The products find use in lubricants, soaps, linoleum, flotation and waterproofing agents, paints, varnishes, and drying oils.

Since tall oil and its production are derived from the paper and pulping industry, the amount of tall oil produced is related in part to the pulp industry and in part to the U.S. economy.

Consumption of Tall Oil in Inedible Products in the United States   In Millions of Pounds

Year	Jan.	Feb.	Mar.	Apr.	May	June	July	Aug.	Sept.	Oct.	Nov.	Dec.	Total
2002	93.4	132.9	115.0	121.3	109.3	121.6	128.5	130.2	121.5	141.9	115.5	118.6	1,450
2003	136.1	119.9	136.9	126.3	121.7	121.9	119.3	111.6	131.4	124.1	104.9	120.1	1,474
2004	126.8	109.4	136.1	123.7	135.7	160.5	166.9	140.8	125.3	124.6	129.4	110.7	1,590
2005	134.9	115.4	124.5	97.3	144.4	128.3	125.0	127.5	115.6	137.0	120.3	118.2	1,488
2006	120.4	112.1	135.8	120.2	153.2	131.0	140.6	144.3	134.3	129.6	134.8	133.2	1,590
2007	130.9	126.6	117.7	127.0	130.7	128.7	131.2	129.9	128.5	131.1	128.6	123.8	1,535
2008	135.8	131.8	127.4	130.8	144.0	145.9	144.5	151.0	141.2	148.5	127.6	103.7	1,632
2009	117.1	102.4	103.6	96.2	110.3	110.0	115.0	129.3	115.9	125.8	123.5	107.0	1,356
2010[1]	110.1	127.9	135.3	135.6	146.1	121.2	147.0	142.0	136.4	135.9	131.0	119.1	1,588

[1] Preliminary.   *Source: Bureau of the Census, U.S. Department of Commerce*

Production of Crude Tall Oil in the United States   In Millions of Pounds

Year	Oct.	Nov.	Dec.	Jan.	Feb.	Mar.	Apr.	May	June	July	Aug.	Sept.	Total
2002-03	102.5	87.3	101.8	108.7	89.8	111.5	108.3	99.6	91.8	109.2	100.8	97.1	1,208.6
2003-04	102.1	87.9	109.0	113.7	96.1	112.1	102.8	106.8	99.2	94.4	108.9	104.1	1,236.9
2004-05	88.1	93.7	99.6	110.0	97.9	109.4	107.3	109.8	101.5	101.0	101.0	98.9	1,218.1
2005-06	95.5	92.1	100.3	103.9	103.4	108.1	110.4	117.6	101.4	104.6	109.7	99.7	1,246.8
2006-07	104.8	103.7	108.5	107.5	105.0	104.5	121.5	125.5	98.1	108.5	122.2	107.9	1,317.7
2007-08	100.0	99.7	107.2	113.6	112.1	115.9	117.2	112.9	103.2	102.8	107.4	105.0	1,297.0
2008-09	107.6	100.7	87.0	90.3	93.0	107.2	105.9	104.7	103.1	94.0	106.6	102.2	1,202.2
2009-10	105.8	102.0	102.8	106.0	104.2	115.8	117.2	119.7	120.2	113.2	106.2	111.5	1,324.6
2010-11[1]	113.3	109.8	104.5										1,310.3

[1] Preliminary.   *Source: Bureau of the Census, U.S. Department of Commerce*

Stocks of Crude Tall Oil in the United States, on First of Month   In Millions of Pounds

Year	Oct.	Nov.	Dec.	Jan.	Feb.	Mar.	Apr.	May	June	July	Aug.	Sept.
2002-03	160.2	154.1	155.7	160.5	176.0	167.4	156.3	173.4	163.7	180.3	199.3	209.5
2003-04	210.7	207.3	203.0	210.2	209.6	216.3	205.3	207.1	194.1	190.5	196.1	162.2
2004-05	174.1	140.3	124.4	95.0	109.9	108.8	134.0	132.1	130.5	126.3	122.0	121.8
2005-06	107.5	97.3	83.4	81.5	102.8	118.7	82.6	88.3	94.7	93.9	82.0	92.7
2006-07	73.9	61.7	72.1	75.7	97.8	83.4	115.7	132.5	156.1	162.5	164.3	198.4
2007-08	186.8	185.6	168.5	177.0	176.3	162.9	156.3	187.7	182.2	145.1	137.8	138.6
2008-09	135.7	110.8	95.7	110.8	102.2	112.5	116.2	135.3	134.3	138.3	126.2	108.8
2009-10	98.3	85.9	104.2	87.2	108.9	84.9	126.8	103.0	113.6	111.6	112.0	101.6
2010-11[1]	113.0	111.3	89.0	86.3								

[1] Preliminary.   *Source: Bureau of the Census, U.S. Department of Commerce*

Stocks of Refined Tall Oil in the United States, on First of Month   In Millions of Pounds

Year	Oct.	Nov.	Dec.	Jan.	Feb.	Mar.	Apr.	May	June	July	Aug.	Sept.
2002-03	13.3	16.5	18.7	20.1	20.1	18.6	20.4	19.7	15.8	14.5	13.5	13.9
2003-04	13.1	20.1	19.6	19.9	19.2	13.7	14.3	12.7	16.3	14.2	16.6	17.7
2004-05	14.8	16.6	16.9	17.0	15.2	20.4	16.0	18.2	16.9	17.2	14.5	17.5
2005-06	18.7	28.1	26.9	32.9	28.5	W	6.1	5.3	6.6	4.5	5.9	6.9
2006-07	7.7	7.5	5.3	5.3	5.8	7.3	7.5	7.3	7.9	9.2	6.6	4.2
2007-08	5.9	6.7	5.2	6.4	6.0	7.5	6.8	7.3	6.5	5.4	5.3	8.2
2008-09	6.6	5.0	6.6	5.2	5.3	4.1	5.0	4.3	3.8	6.0	4.1	5.6
2009-10	5.2	7.4	7.4	6.9	5.2	6.0	5.3	5.5	5.9	4.7	4.4	6.1
2010-11[1]	6.4	5.5	3.5	5.3								

[1] Preliminary.   W = Withheld proprietary data.   *Source: Bureau of the Census, U.S. Department of Commerce*

Tallow and Greases

Tallow and grease are derived from processing (rendering) the fat of cattle. Tallow is used to produce both edible and inedible products. Edible tallow products include margarine, cooking oil, and baking products. Inedible tallow products include soap, candles, and lubricants. Production of tallow and greases is directly related to the number of cattle produced. Those countries that are the leading cattle producers are also the largest producers of tallow. The American Fats and Oils Association provides specifications for a variety of different types of tallow and grease, including edible tallow, lard (edible), top white tallow, all beef packer tallow, extra fancy tallow, fancy tallow, bleachable fancy tallow, prime tallow, choice white grease, and yellow grease. The specifications include such characteristics as the melting point, color, density, moisture content, insoluble impurities, and others.

Prices – The monthly average price of tallow (inedible, No. 1 Packers-Prime, delivered Chicago) in 2010 rose +32.5% yr/yr to 33.35 cents per pound, not far from the 2008 record high of 34.18 cents per pound. The wholesale price of inedible tallow in 2010 rose +27.3% yr/yr to 35.05 cents per pound, down from the 2008 record high of 38.02 cents per pound.

Supply – World production of tallow and greases (edible and inedible) in 2009 (latest data), fell by -0.7% yr/yr to 8.355 million metric tons, down from the 2007 record high of 8.544 million metric tons. The world's largest producer of tallow and greases by far is the U.S. with 43.5% of world production, followed by Brazil with 7.0%, Australia with 5.8%, and Canada with 3.4%.

U.S. production of edible tallow in 2008 (lastest data) fell –0.6% yr/yr to 1.779 billion pounds, down from the 2002 record high of 1.974. U.S. production of inedible tallow and greases in 2010 fell -0.4% yr/yr to 5.854 billion pounds, which was well below the record high of 7.156 billion pounds posted in 2002.

Demand – U.S. consumption of inedible tallow and greases in 2010 fell 10.6% yr/yr to 1.582 billion pounds, of which virtually all went for animal feed. U.S. consumption of edible tallow in 2008 (latest data) rose +1.4% yr/yr to 1.423 billion pounds, down from the 2006 record high of 1.583 billion pounds. U.S. per capita consumption of edible tallow in 2007 (latest data) fell –28.2% to 2.8 pounds per person per year, down from the 2000 and 2004 record high of 4.0 pounds.

Trade – U.S. exports of inedible tallow and grease in 2010 rose +6.0 yr/yr to 349.35 million pounds, and accounted for 5.7% of total U.S. supply. U.S. exports of edible tallow in 2008 (latest data) rose +2.0% yr/yr to 396 million pounds, and accounted for 27.8% of U.S. supply.

World Production of Tallow and Greases (Edible and Inedible) In Thousands of Metric Tons

Year	Argentina	Australia	Brazil	Canada	France	Germany	Korea	Nether-lands	New Zealand	Russia	United Kingdom	United States	World Total
2000	161	503	430	293	151	132	17	171	170	178	148	3,948	8,202
2001	142	507	446	296	140	126	15	151	173	171	115	3,503	7,689
2002	147	469	474	305	154	124	14	125	162	178	123	3,826	8,062
2003	154	456	493	289	164	121	15	121	174	183	120	3,707	8,015
2004	178	486	528	343	166	124	15	113	192	181	124	3,714	8,247
2005	184	493	554	339	171	121	15	106	168	175	128	3,797	8,389
2006	181	503	574	314	183	124	16	107	187	177	135	3,808	8,490
2007	194	501	589	306	177	128	16	116	184	183	140	3,818	8,544
2008[1]	188	499	574	292	178	131	16	122	189	186	138	3,695	8,416
2009[2]	205	484	586	282	166	131	16	123	182	188	138	3,634	8,355

[1] Preliminary. [2] Forecast. *Source: Foreign Agricultural Service, U.S. Department of Agriculture (FAS-USDA)*

Salient Statistics of Tallow and Greases (Inedible) in the United States In Millions of Pounds

	--------------------- Supply ---------------------			---------------- Consumption ----------------				Wholesale Prices, Cents Per Lb. ------	
Year	Production	Stocks, Jan. 1	Total	Exports	Soap	Feed	Total	Edible, (Loose) Chicago	Inedible, Chicago No. 1
2001	6,870	347	7,217	616	107	2,834	2,843	13.7	12.0
2002	7,156	327	7,482	384	W	2,886	2,886	14.8	13.5
2003	6,246	240	6,486	307	W	2,434	2,434	20.3	18.3
2004	6,173	282	6,455	336	W	2,536	2,536	19.8	18.0
2005	6,204	281	6,485	276	W	2,456	2,456	19.0	17.5
2006	6,460	309	6,769	331	W	2,585	2,585	18.6	16.9
2007	6,369	291	6,661	361	W	2,385	2,385	30.7	27.8
2008	6,224	350	6,573	319	W	2,095	2,095	38.0	34.2
2009[1]	5,878	315	6,193	330	W	1,770	1,770	27.5	25.2
2010[2]	5,887	286	6,173	348	W	1,564	1,564	35.1	33.3

[1] Preliminary. [2] Forecast. *Source: Foreign Agricultural Service, U.S. Department of Agriculture (FAS-USDA)*

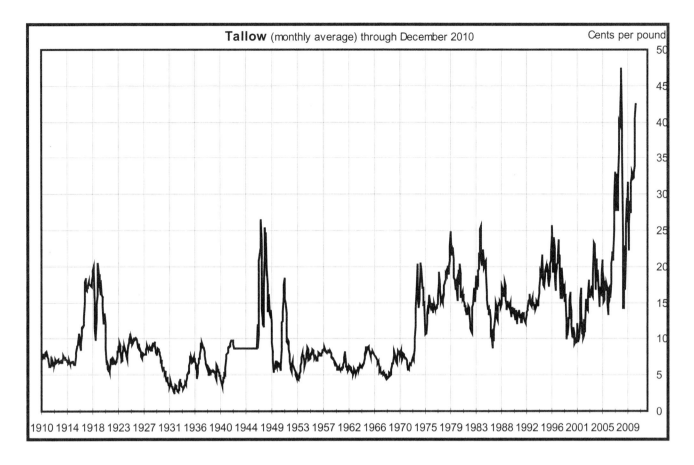

Tallow (monthly average) through December 2010 — Cents per pound

Supply and Disappearance of Edible Tallow in the United States   In Millions of Pounds, Rendered Basis

| | ---------- Supply ---------- | | | | | ---------- Disappearance ---------- | | | |
Year	Stocks, Jan. 1	Production	Total Supply	Domestic Disap- pearance	Exports	Total Disap- pearance	Direct Use	Baking or Frying Fats	Per Capita (Lbs.)
2000	33	1,825	1,866	1,581	248	1,829	1,125	283	4.0
2001	37	1,792	1,859	1,455	364	1,819	869	W	3.0
2002	40	1,974	2,023	1,486	511	1,998	974	W	3.4
2003	25	1,966	1,996	1,552	420	1,972	1,108	W	3.8
2004	24	1,818	1,842	1,565	255	1,820	1,163	W	4.0
2005	22	1,813	1,836	1,518	293	1,811	1,116	W	3.8
2006	25	1,861	1,893	1,583	275	1,858	1,160	W	3.9
2007	35	1,789	1,831	1,404	388	1,792	889	W	2.9
2008[1]	39	1,779	1,848	1,634	185	1,819	872	W	2.9
2009[2]	30	1,851	1,916	1,735	162	1,897	652	W	2.1

[1] Preliminary.   [2] Forecast.   W = Withheld.   *Sources: Economic Research Service, U.S. Department of Agriculture (ERS-USDA); Bureau of the Census, U.S. Department of Commerce*

Average Wholesale Price of Tallow, Inedible, No. 1 Packers (Prime), Delivered, Chicago   In Cents Per Pound

Year	Jan.	Feb.	Mar.	Apr.	May	June	July	Aug.	Sept.	Oct.	Nov.	Dec.	Average
2001	12.17	9.46	9.62	10.26	10.19	12.35	15.44	16.83	13.75	11.24	10.60	12.34	12.02
2002	10.00	10.54	12.64	11.06	11.59	15.47	14.80	14.00	14.23	13.98	15.91	18.08	13.53
2003	17.13	15.65	16.60	16.54	16.48	17.30	16.08	15.85	18.70	22.78	23.37	23.08	18.30
2004	23.23	16.72	17.80	21.05	18.01	18.08	19.55	16.92	17.20	14.33	15.61	16.97	17.96
2005	16.20	16.03	18.73	20.95	19.38	18.23	15.11	15.31	17.54	17.40	17.96	16.67	17.46
2006	17.52	17.05	14.98	13.47	14.77	15.27	17.05	17.35	15.59	17.71	20.42	21.46	16.89
2007	22.02	20.78	21.74	25.04	29.16	33.08	32.58	27.67	30.14	31.29	32.87	27.64	27.83
2008	32.19	36.08	40.03	39.66	40.02	45.36	47.55	40.14	36.17	24.39	14.29	14.23	34.18
2009	22.86	19.57	16.72	21.83	25.80	29.53	26.17	31.75	30.44	22.27	25.89	29.09	25.16
2010[1]	28.37	27.42	31.57	32.74	33.08	32.73	32.15	32.28	32.93	33.88	40.52	42.50	33.35

[1] Preliminary.   *Sources: Economic Research Service, U.S. Department of Agriculture (ERS-USDA)*

Tea

Tea is the common name for a family of mostly woody flowering plants. The tea family contains about 600 species placed in 28 genera and they are distributed throughout the tropical and subtropical areas, with most species occurring in eastern Asia and South America. The tea plant is native to Southeast Asia. There are more than 3,000 varieties of tea, each with its own distinct character, and each is generally named for the area in which it is grown. Tea may have been consumed in China as long ago as 2700 BC and certainly since 1000 BC. In 2737 BC, the Chinese Emperor Shen Nung, according to Chinese mythology, was a scholar and herbalist. While his servant boiled drinking water, a leaf from the wild tea tree he was sitting under dropped into the water and Shen Nung decided to try the brew. Today, half the world's population drinks tea. Tea is the world's most popular beverage next to water.

Tea is a healthful drink and contains antioxidants, fluoride, niacin, folic acid, and as much vitamin C as a lemon. The average 5 oz. cup of brewed tea contains approximately 40 to 60 milligrams of caffeine (compared to 80 to 115 mg in brewed coffee). Decaffeinated tea has been available since the 1980s. Herbal tea contains no true tea leaves but is actually brewed from a collection of herbs and spices.

Tea grows mainly between the tropic of Cancer and the tropic of Capricorn, requiring 40 to 50 inches of rain per year and a temperature ideally between 50 to 86 degrees Fahrenheit. In order to rejuvenate the bush and keep it at a convenient height for the pickers to access, the bushes must be pruned every four to five years. A tea bush can produce tea for 50 to 70 years, but after 50 years, the yield is reduced.

The two key factors in determining different varieties of tea are the production process (sorting, withering, rolling, fermentation, and drying methods) and the growing conditions (geographical region, growing altitude, and soil type). Black tea, often referred to as fully fermented tea, is produced by allowing picked tea leaves to wither and ferment for up to 24 hours. After fermenting, the leaves are fired, which stops oxidation. Green tea, or unfermented tea, is produced by immediately and completely drying the leaves and omitting the oxidization process, thus allowing the tea to remain green in color.

Supply – World production of tea in 2009 (latest available data) fell -0.2% to 3.885 million metric tons, down from the 2007 record high of 3.947 million metric tons. The world's largest producers of tea in 2009 were China (with 33.9% of world production), India (25%), Sri Lanka (7.5%), Kenya (8.1%), Turkey (5.1%), and Indonesia (4.1%).

Trade – U.S. tea imports in 2010 (annualized through May) rose +9.6% to 216,578 metric tons, creating a new record high. World tea imports in 2006 (latest data available) rose +2.4% to 1.471 million metric tons. The world's largest tea importers were Russia (with 12% of total world imports), the United Kingdom (11%), Pakistan (9%), and the U.S. (7%). World exports of tea in 2008 (latest data available) rose +10.8% to 1.895 million metric tons. The world's largest exporters were Kenya (with 20.9% of world exports), Sri Lanka (16.8%), China (15.8%), India (10.7%), Indonesia (5.1%), Vietnam (5.5%), and Argentina (4.1%).

World Tea Production, in Major Producing Countries   In Metric Tons

Year	Argentina	Bangladesh	China	India	Indonesia	Iran	Japan	Kenya	Malawi	Sri Lanka	Turkey	Ex-USSR[2]	World Total
2003	69,866	57,500	788,815	838,000	169,818	63,650	91,900	293,670	41,693	303,230	153,800	26,271	3,225,416
2004	70,389	57,580	855,422	878,000	171,200	40,250	100,700	324,600	50,090	308,090	201,663	22,288	3,427,455
2005	67,871	57,580	953,660	893,000	177,700	59,180	100,000	328,500	38,000	317,200	217,540	24,752	3,627,197
2006	72,129	58,000	1,047,345	928,000	146,858	46,500	91,800	310,580	45,009	310,800	201,866	8,405	3,671,466
2007	76,000	58,500	1,183,002	949,220	150,224	49,680	94,100	369,600	48,140	305,220	206,160	8,614	3,947,527
2008	76,000	59,000	1,257,384	805,180	150,851	42,348	96,500	345,800	48,140	318,700	198,046	6,543	3,894,029
2009[1]	76,000		1,317,384		160,000		86,000	314,100		290,000	198,601	1,077	3,885,302

[1] Preliminary.   [2] Mostly Georgia and Azerbaijan.   *Sources: Foreign Agricultural Service, U.S. Department of Agriculture (FAS-USDA); Food and Agriculture Organization of the United Nations (FAO-UN)*

World Exports of Tea from Producing Countries   In Metric Tons

Year	Argentina	Bangladesh	Brazil	China	India	Indonesia	Kenya	Malawi	Papua New Guinea	Sri Lanka	Vietnam	Zimbabwe	Total
2002	57,643	3,964	3,979	254,875	181,617	100,185	288,300	42,596	5,200	290,500	77,000	18,855	1,580,485
2003	59,062	7,348	4,209	262,663	174,246	88,176	293,751	36,924	6,600	297,003	58,600	13,355	1,529,678
2004	67,819	10,635	3,593	282,643	174,728	98,572	284,309	46,200	8,100	298,909	104,000	14,968	1,634,565
2005	68,270	12,560	3,407	288,814	159,121	102,294	347,971	44,600	6,900	307,793	88,000	4,825	1,718,521
2006	72,056	7,842	3,238	288,625	181,326	95,339	325,066	27,503	6,600	204,240	105,000	11,532	1,629,468
2007[1]	75,767	5,269	3,298	292,199	193,459	83,659	374,329	54,397	6,400	190,203	114,000	6,840	1,711,464
2008[2]	77,426	8,259	3,034	299,789	203,207	96,210	396,641	30,435	5,937	318,329	104,700	6,979	1,895,807

[1] Preliminary.   [2] Estimate.   *Source: Food and Agriculture Organization of the United Nations (FAO-UN)*

Imports of Tea in the United States   In Metric Tons

Year	Jan.	Feb.	Mar.	Apr.	May	June	July	Aug.	Sept.	Oct.	Nov.	Dec.	Total
2005	16,728	13,977	17,877	20,502	16,696	18,445	15,714	14,146	12,775	14,376	11,276	11,750	184,261
2006	15,278	14,469	17,148	18,533	21,840	20,057	15,683	16,378	14,650	11,836	15,432	12,547	193,851
2007	14,094	12,830	17,312	19,165	18,657	20,707	16,623	15,829	16,136	14,475	14,636	13,969	194,434
2008	15,685	17,751	19,648	21,127	19,540	18,409	17,657	16,418	17,221	16,783	14,357	13,363	207,957
2009	15,467	14,748	19,286	18,148	19,208	18,670	17,093	18,668	17,550	13,216	13,428	12,185	197,667
2010[1]	14,764	15,676	18,915	20,420	20,952	19,851	19,865	19,113	18,788	15,722	14,464	13,771	212,301

[1] Preliminary.   *Source: Foreign Agricultural Service, U.S. Department of Agriculture (FAS-USDA)*

Tin

Tin (symbol Sn) is a silvery-white, lustrous gray metallic element. Tin is soft, pliable and has a highly crystalline structure. When a tin bar is bent or broken, a crackling sound called a "tin cry" is produced due to the breaking of the tin crystals. People have been using tin for at least 5,500 years. Tin has been found in the tombs of ancient Egyptians. In ancient times, tin and lead were considered different forms of the same metal. Tin was exported to Europe in large quantities from Cornwall, England, during the Roman period, from approximately 2100 BC to 1500 BC. Cornwall was one of the world's leading sources of tin for much of its known history and into the late 1800s.

The principal ore of tin is the mineral cassiterite, which is found in Malaya, Bolivia, Indonesia, Thailand, and Nigeria. About 80% of the world's tin deposits occur in unconsolidated placer deposits in riverbeds and valleys, or on the sea floor, with only about 20% occurring as primary hard-rock lodes. Tin deposits are generally small and are almost always found closely allied to the granite from which it originates. Tin is also recovered as a by-product of mining tungsten, tantalum, and lead. After extraction, tin ore is ground and washed to remove impurities, roasted to oxidize the sulfides of iron and copper, washed a second time, and then reduced by carbon in a reverberatory furnace. Electrolysis may also be used to purify tin.

Pure tin, rarely used by itself, was used as currency in the form of tin blocks and was considered legal tender for taxes in Phuket, Thailand, until 1932. Tin is used in the manufacture of coatings for steel containers used to preserve food and beverages. Tin is also used in solder alloys, electroplating, ceramics, and in plastic. The world's major tin research and development laboratory, ITRI Ltd, is funded by companies that produce and consume tin. The focus of the research efforts have been on possible new uses for tin that would take advantage of tin's relative non-toxicity to replace other metals in various products. Some of the replacements could be lead-free solders, antimony-free flame-retardant chemicals, and lead-free shotgun pellets. No tin is currently mined in the U.S.

Tin futures and options trade on the London Metal Exchange (LME). Tin has traded on the LME since 1877 and the standard tin contract began in 1912. The futures contract calls for the delivery of 5 metric tons of tin ingots of at least 99.85% purity. The contract trades in terms of U.S. dollars per metric ton.

Prices – The average monthly price of tin (straights) in New York in 2010 rose by +49.8% yr/yr to $12.50 per pound, which is a new record high. The 2010 price of $12.50 is more than four times the 3-decade low of $2.83 per pound seen as recently as 2002. The average monthly price of ex-dock tin in New York in 2010 rose +49.3% yr/yr to $9.51 per pound, and the price rose to $12.74 per pound in January of 2011.

Supply – World mine production of tin in 2009 rose by +2.7% yr/yr to 307,000 metric tons, but still below the 2007 record high of 326,000 metric tons. The world's largest mine producers of tin are China with 37% of world production in 2009, Indonesia with 33%, and Peru with 12%.

World smelter production of tin fell -5.2% in 2008 (latest data available) to 307,000 metric tons, down from the 2007 record high of 324,000 metric tons. The world's largest producers of smelted tin are China with 43% of world production in 2008, Indonesia with 23%, and Malaysia with 7%. The U.S. does not mine tin, and therefore supply consists only of scrap and imports. U.S. tin recovery in 2009 fell -7.3% to a record low of 6,200 metric tons.

Demand – U.S. consumption of tin (pig) in 2010 rose +3.8% to 32,305 metric tons (annualized through September), up from the 2009 record low of 31,330 metric tons. The breakdown of U.S. consumption of tin by finished products in 2008 (latest data) shows that the largest consuming industry of tin is solder (with 33% of consumption), followed by tin plate (23%), chemicals (20%), and bronze and brass (9%).

Trade – The U.S. relied on imports for 80% of its tin consumption in 2009. U.S. imports of unwrought tin metal in 2009 (latest data) fell 9.1% to 33,000 metric tons, which is an 15-year low. The largest sources of U.S. imports in 2009 were Peru (61% of total imports), Bolivia (19%), Indonesia (10%), China (4%), and Brazil (3%). U.S. exports of tin in 2009 fell -67.7% yr/yr to 3,170 metric tons.

World Mine Production of Tin   In Metric Tons (Contained Tin)

Year	Australia	Bolivia	Brazil	China	Indonesia	Malaysia	Nigeria	Peru	Portugal	Russia	Thailand	United Kingdom	World Total
2001	9,602	12,352	13,016	95,000	61,862	4,972	2,870	38,182	1,174	2,000	1,950	----	246,000
2002	7,017	15,242	12,063	62,000	88,142	4,215	790	38,815	574	1,300	1,130	----	235,000
2003	3,864	16,755	12,217	102,000	71,694	3,359	1,800	40,202	218	2,000	793	----	261,000
2004	1,196	17,569	12,202	118,000	65,772	2,745	1,000	67,675	220	2,500	586	----	302,000
2005	2,819	18,640	11,739	126,000	78,404	2,857	1,300	42,145	243	3,000	158	----	297,000
2006	1,478	17,669	9,528	126,000	80,933	2,398	1,400	38,470	25	3,000	190	----	290,000
2007	2,071	15,972	12,596	146,000	66,137	2,263	1,500	39,019	25	2,500	120	----	303,000
2008	1,783	17,319	11,600	110,000	96,000	2,200	1,500	39,037	40	1,500	120	----	299,000
2009[1]	1,400	19,000	13,000	115,000	55,000	2,380	----	37,500	30	1,200	120	----	260,000
2010[2]	2,000	16,000	12,000	115,000	60,000	2,000	----	38,000	100	1,000	100	----	261,000

[1] Preliminary.   [2] Estimate.   *Source: U.S. Geological Survey (USGS)*

TIN

World Smelter Production of Primary Tin   In Metric Tons

Year	Australia	Bolivia	Brazil	China	Indo-nesia	Japan	Malaysia	Mexico	Russia	South Africa	Spain	Thailand	World Total
1999	600	11,166	12,787	90,800	49,105	568	28,913	1,262	4,500	----	50	17,306	249,000
2000	775	9,353	13,825	112,000	46,432	593	26,228	1,204	4,800	----	----	17,076	272,000
2001	1,171	11,292	12,168	105,000	53,470	668	30,417	1,789	4,569	----	----	22,387	272,000
2002	791	10,976	11,675	82,000	67,455	659	30,887	1,748	4,615	----	----	17,548	266,000
2003	597	12,836	10,761	98,000	66,284	662	18,250	1,769	4,100	----	----	15,400	270,000
2004	467	13,627	11,512	115,000	49,872	707	33,914	25	4,570	----	----	20,800	295,000
2005	594	13,841	8,986	122,000	65,300	754	36,924	17	5,000	----	----	31,600	324,000
2006	572	14,100	8,780	132,000	65,357	854	22,850	25	4,980	----	----	27,540	319,000
2007	118	12,251	9,987	149,000	64,127	879	25,263	25	3,800	----	----	20,400	324,000
2008[1]	----	12,000	9,600	129,000	70,000	890	23,000	15	2,000	----	----	20,000	307,000

[1] Preliminary.   *Source: U.S. Geological Survey (USGS)*

United States Foreign Trade of Tin   In Metric Tons

| | | ----- Concentrates[2] (Ore) ----- | | | -------------------------- Imports for Consumption ------------------------- | | | | | | | | |
| | | | | | | ------------------------------------ Unwrought Tin Metal ------------------------------------ | | | | | | | |
Year	Exports (Metal)	Total All Ore	Bolivia	Peru	Total All Metal	Bolivia	Brazil	China	Indo-nesia	Malaysia	Singa-pore	Thailand	Kingdom
2001	4,350	----	----	----	37,500	6,040	5,510	6,360	3,880	674	145	----	118
2002	2,940	----	----	----	42,200	6,150	4,840	7,600	3,340	122	----	----	2
2003	3,690	----	----	----	37,100	5,720	3,000	4,340	3,070	490	----	----	143
2004	3,650	----	----	----	47,600	5,060	4,330	5,310	4,660	6,600	----	500	97
2005	4,330	----	----	----	37,500	5,400	2,150	4,510	5,220	1,530	194	45	67
2006	5,490	----	----	----	43,300	8,160	1,300	4,440	4,600	245	1,090	210	1,370
2007	6,410	----	----	----	34,600	4,340	2,600	4,230	1,680	14	1,730	15	881
2008	9,800	----	----	----	36,300	4,980	1,570	2,380	2,000	1,740	706	1,670	225
2009	3,170	----	----	----	33,000	6,300	1,050	1,210	3,220	169	451	15	----
2010[1]	8,400	----	----	----	32,500	5,700	75	727	3,470	4,480	996	905	----

[1] Preliminary.   [2] Tin content.   *Source: U.S. Geological Survey (USGS)*

Consumption (Total) of Tin (Pig) in the United States   In Metric Tons

Year	Jan.	Feb.	Mar.	Apr.	May	June	July	Aug.	Sept.	Oct.	Nov.	Dec.	Total
2001	4,252	4,185	4,095	4,141	4,148	4,128	4,055	4,163	4,153	4,197	4,129	3,974	49,620
2002	3,965	3,866	3,868	3,819	4,087	3,887	3,887	3,842	3,835	3,966	3,822	3,811	46,655
2003	3,814	3,808	3,851	3,891	3,701	3,814	3,841	3,850	3,803	3,816	3,764	3,887	45,840
2004	3,851	3,632	3,887	3,837	3,874	4,001	3,844	3,871	3,850	3,870	3,947	3,772	46,236
2005	4,097	3,990	4,027	3,874	3,825	3,918	3,806	3,900	3,824	3,833	3,849	3,699	46,642
2006	3,877	3,694	3,508	3,439	3,447	3,580	3,475	3,420	3,456	3,442	3,407	3,356	42,101
2007	3,381	3,342	3,601	3,365	3,716	3,811	3,585	4,070	3,910	3,734	3,586	3,628	43,729
2008	2,653	2,626	2,630	2,693	2,639	2,641	2,665	2,697	2,687	2,607	2,662	2,653	31,853
2009	2,642	2,546	2,610	2,573	2,525	2,521	2,630	2,552	2,626	2,646	2,675	2,564	31,110
2010[1]	2,678	2,673	2,689	2,698	2,666	2,655	2,706	2,740	2,724	2,730	2,619		32,267

[1] Preliminary.   *Source: U.S. Geological Survey (USGS)*

Tin Stocks (Pig-Industrial) in the United States, on First of Month   In Metric Tons

Year	Jan.	Feb.	Mar.	Apr.	May	June	July	Aug.	Sept.	Oct.	Nov.	Dec.
2001	8,140	8,330	8,360	8,460	8,270	8,640	8,760	8,760	8,920	9,030	7,630	7,470
2002	7,700	7,320	7,020	6,990	6,870	6,600	6,540	6,590	6,670	7,130	6,880	6,950
2003	7,280	6,980	6,690	6,640	6,390	6,400	6,380	6,420	6,250	6,180	6,190	6,340
2004	6,520	6,010	6,130	6,280	5,850	6,000	5,900	6,290	6,110	6,030	5,900	6,410
2005	6,140	5,260	5,570	5,420	5,770	5,400	5,670	5,830	5,540	5,350	5,330	5,410
2006	5,400	5,380	5,330	5,350	5,400	5,380	5,420	5,400	5,740	5,650	5,650	5,830
2007	5,700	5,970	6,030	6,030	5,860	5,570	5,270	5,270	5,260	5,310	5,920	6,000
2008	6,140	8,070	8,280	8,020	8,000	7,970	7,930	7,960	7,980	7,960	7,990	7,940
2009	7,970	7,890	7,660	7,640	7,620	7,640	7,570	7,630	7,590	7,540	7,520	7,470
2010[1]	7,450	7,030	7,080	7,060	7,080	7,180	7,270	7,220	7,130	7,060	7,090	7,100

[1] Preliminary.   *Source: U.S. Geological Survey (USGS)*

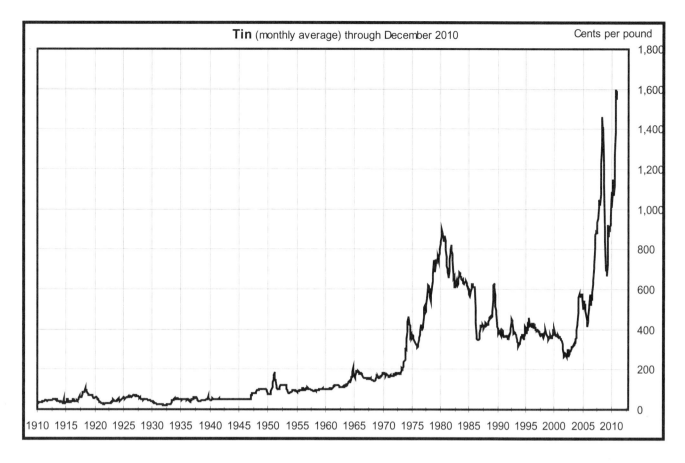

Tin (monthly average) through December 2010   Cents per pound

Average Price of Ex-Dock Tin in New York[1]   In Cents Per Pound

Year	Jan.	Feb.	Mar.	Apr.	May	June	July	Aug.	Sept.	Oct.	Nov.	Dec.	Average
2001	249.32	246.91	243.14	238.33	238.53	231.14	210.17	188.42	179.53	181.38	194.77	195.90	216.46
2002	189.23	183.23	187.65	195.36	201.95	208.01	211.51	188.36	193.79	206.67	205.94	206.63	199.15
2003	212.68	217.98	219.58	217.90	225.40	223.69	225.81	229.58	233.59	248.22	252.93	285.40	232.73
2004	305.34	313.55	357.66	418.57	449.29	438.72	439.24	437.68	438.91	436.80	439.24	414.16	407.43
2005	376.37	393.05	408.41	395.40	394.68	367.81	347.78	347.96	331.01	313.73	300.96	323.43	358.38
2006	338.27	373.87	378.76	420.35	420.53	376.76	400.64	404.26	428.83	461.66	475.57	524.69	417.02
2007	535.46	604.14	648.82	656.53	661.04	659.63	689.99	705.01	700.45	748.39	777.74	756.89	678.67
2008	760.82	800.60	917.15	1,001.99	1,108.30	1,027.62	1,070.50	930.65	850.83	672.97	646.77	532.54	860.06
2009	539.32	523.68	508.12	554.44	646.09	702.56	657.47	694.15	695.88	701.13	698.44	721.79	636.92
2010	823.31	764.25	818.62	870.50	821.34	809.88	851.80	967.17	1,057.81	1,223.59	1,191.80	1,211.71	950.98

Source: American Metal Market (AMM)

Average Price of Tin (Straights) in New York   In Cents Per Pound

Year	Jan.	Feb.	Mar.	Apr.	May	June	July	Aug.	Sept.	Oct.	Nov.	Dec.	Average
2001	356.37	352.87	348.19	341.59	340.61	329.68	302.57	276.55	263.17	264.88	281.23	279.46	311.43
2002	271.59	263.91	270.54	280.98	288.74	296.02	299.39	269.30	277.60	293.79	292.40	292.95	283.10
2003	304.44	312.32	314.52	312.26	321.92	319.67	322.10	327.16	332.21	350.90	356.46	396.46	330.87
2004	422.33	433.50	485.99	557.29	575.39	570.99	565.68	568.14	572.72	573.79	577.07	550.97	537.82
2005	500.93	519.61	539.30	522.71	522.18	492.64	467.71	466.67	444.80	426.36	411.23	440.30	479.54
2006	464.54	509.45	519.31	574.53	575.57	517.52	548.29	552.06	583.57	623.07	644.19	705.62	568.14
2007	719.05	811.07	873.03	883.74	886.54	884.67	931.50	954.26	949.21	1,012.46	1,049.78	1,025.36	915.06
2008	1,025.05	1,071.97	1,224.20	1,325.79	1,461.85	1,357.22	1,410.60	1,229.27	1,124.02	887.70	841.86	694.41	1,137.83
2009	711.20	686.02	664.21	724.55	841.83	920.39	862.04	902.14	899.35	911.42	922.75	964.64	834.21
2010	1,090.89	1,011.26	1,082.71	1,149.23	1,084.11	1,067.12	1,117.84	1,268.74	1,386.44	1,597.89	1,552.75	1,588.29	1,249.77

Source: U.S. Geological Survey (USGS)

TIN

Tin Plate Production & Tin Recovered in the United States   In Metric Tons

Year	Tinplate Waste Gross Weight	Tinplate (All Forms) Gross Weight	Tin Content (Met. Ton)	Tin per Tonne of Plate (Kilograms)	Tin Metal	Bronze & Brass	Solder	Type Metal	Babbitt	Anti-monial Lead	Chemical Com-pounds	Misc.[2]	Grand Total
					---- Tin Recovered from Scrap by Form of Recovery ----								
2000	119,000	1,320,000	8,800	6.7	----	----	----	----	----	----	----	----	----
2001	97,800	2,000,000	7,800	3.9	----	----	----	----	----	----	----	----	----
2002	45,900	2,450,000	7,750	3.2	----	----	----	----	----	----	----	----	----
2003	W	2,500,000	7,750	3.1	----	----	----	----	----	----	----	----	----
2004	W	2,550,000	7,700	3.0	----	----	----	----	----	----	----	----	----
2005	W	2,270,000	7,670	3.4	----	----	----	----	----	----	----	----	----
2006	56,400	2,130,000	6,810	3.2	----	----	----	----	----	----	----	----	----
2007	58,900	1,780,000	7,010	3.9	----	----	----	----	----	----	----	----	----
2008	30,900	2,280,000	6,690	2.9	----	----	----	----	----	----	----	----	----
2009[1]	14,500	1,150,000	6,200	5.4	----	----	----	----	----	----	----	----	----

[1] Preliminary.   [2] Includes foil, terne metal, cable lead, and items indicated by symbol "W".   W = Withheld.   NA = Not available.
Source: U.S. Geological Survey (USGS)

Consumption of Primary and Secondary Tin in the United States   In Metric Tons

Year	Net Import Reliance as a % of Apparent Consumption	Stocks, Jan. 1[2]	Primary	Secondary	Scrap	Total	Available Supply	Stocks, Dec. 31 (Total Available Less Total Processed)	Total Pro-cessed	Consumed in Manu-facturing Products
			---- Net Receipts ----							
1999	85	9,290	40,500	2,790	6,360	49,700	58,900	11,900	47,000	46,900
2000	86	8,910	41,400	2,990	6,050	50,400	59,300	12,200	47,100	47,000
2001	88	8,830	34,500	2,180	4,770	41,400	50,200	8,220	42,000	41,900
2002	79	8,500	34,200	1,610	4,230	40,100	48,600	8,550	40,000	39,800
2003	89	8,220	32,400	1,380	3,440	37,300	45,500	7,770	37,700	37,400
2004	92	7,680	40,800	4,160	4,350	49,300	57,000	11,800	45,200	44,700
2005	78	8,060	32,500	5,790	3,840	42,200	50,200	9,120	41,000	40,600
2006	80	7,640	29,900	5,040	4,100	39,000	46,600	8,520	38,100	37,700
2007	72	7,230	25,600	4,950	3,030	33,600	40,800	8,980	31,700	31,100
2008[1]	70	8,760	22,700	4,300	2,410	29,400	38,200	8,460	29,600	29,200

[1] Preliminary.   [2] Includes tin in transit in the U.S.   NA = Not available.   *Source: U.S. Geological Survey (USGS)*

Consumption of Tin in the United States, by Finished Products   In Metric Tons (Contained Tin)

Year	Tin-plate[2]	Solder	Babbitt	Bronze & Brass	Tinning	Chem-icals[3]	Tin Powder	Bar Tin & Anodes	White Metal	Other	Total	Total Primary	Total Secondary
1999	9,150	18,700	1,610	3,410	905	8,220	W	721	943	3,220	46,900	38,000	8,890
2000	8,800	18,800	1,660	3,360	1,200	8,040	W	714	1,260	3,210	47,000	38,100	8,940
2001	7,800	17,000	770	3,430	1,070	7,590	W	570	1,390	2,230	41,900	34,200	7,630
2002	7,750	13,800	1,310	3,040	679	8,400	W	617	1,320	2,920	39,800	34,000	5,830
2003	7,790	10,600	2,570	2,600	833	8,720	W	852	1,220	2,180	37,400	32,900	4,510
2004	7,700	19,000	728	3,070	798	9,120	W	680	937	2,630	44,700	36,700	7,990
2005	7,250	16,700	554	3,200	790	8,360	W	709	W	3,030	40,600	31,400	9,170
2006	7,110	12,800	484	3,300	696	9,290	W	698	W	1,040	37,700	29,200	8,480
2007	7,010	10,400	604	2,800	451	6,070	W	788	W	1,120	31,100	23,700	7,490
2008[1]	6,840	5,110	592	2,460	395	5,440	W	767	W	5,370	29,200	22,900	6,250

[1] Preliminary.   [2] Includes small quantity of secondary pig tin and tin acquired in chemicals.   [3] Including tin oxide.
W = Withheld proprietary data.   *Source: U.S. Geological Survey (USGS)*

Titanium

Titanium (symbol Ti) is a silver-white, metallic element used primarily to make light, strong alloys. It ranks ninth in abundance among the elements in the crust of the earth but is never found in the pure state. It occurs as an oxide in various minerals. It was first discovered in 1791 by Rev. William Gregor and was first isolated as a basic element in 1910. Titanium was named after the mythological Greek god Titan for its strength.

Titanium is extremely brittle when cold, but is malleable and ductile at a low red heat, and thus easily fabricated. Due to its strength, low weight, and resistance to corrosion, titanium is used in metallic alloys and as a substitute for aluminum. It is used extensively in the aerospace industry, in desalinization plants, construction, medical implants, paints, pigments, and lacquers.

Prices – The price of the mineral ilmenite, a primary source of titanium, in 2008 rose about +27.4% to $99 per metric ton. The price of titanium metal sponge in 2007 (latest data) traded in the range of $6.33 to $7.06 per pound versus $5.87 to $12.84 in 2006. The price of titanium dioxide pigments (Anatase) in 2005 (latest data available) traded in the range of $.95-$1.00 per pound versus 90-95 cents per pound in 2004.

Supply – World production of titanium ilmenite concentrates in 2008 (latest data) fell -2.2% yr/yr to 6.790 million metric tons, down from the 2007 record high of 6.790 million metric tons. The world's largest producers of titanium ilmenite concentrates are Australia with 32% of world production in 2008, China (16%), Norway (13%), India (11%), and Vietnam (8%). World production of titanium rutile concentrates in 2008 (latest data) rose +2.4% yr/yr to 608,000 metric tons, which is a new record high. The world's largest producers are Australia with 51% of world production in 2008 followed by South Africa with 20% and Sierra Leone with 16%.

Demand – U.S. consumption of titanium dioxide pigment in 2010 rose +4.0% yr/yr to 786,000 metric tons, but still down from 2004's record high of 1.170 million metric tons. U.S. consumption of ilmenite in 2005 (latest data available) fell –12.8% to 1.290 million metric tons, down from 2004's 8-year high of 1.480 million metric tons. U.S. consumption of rutile in 2005 (latest data available) fell 4.7% yr/yr to a 7-year low of 424,000 metric tons.

Trade – U.S. imports of titanium dioxide pigment in 2010 rose by +12.6% yr/yr to 197,000 metric tons, but still below the 2005 record high of 341,000 metric tons. U.S. imports of ilmenite in 2005 (latest data) rose +17.3% yr/yr to 822,000 metric tons.

World Produciton of Titanium Illmenite Concentrates   In Thousands of Metric Tons

Year	Australia[2]	Brazil	China	Egypt	India	Malaysia	Norway	Ukraine	United States	Vietnam	World Total	-- Titaniferous Slag[4] --- Canada	Africa
1999	2,008	96	180	130	378	128	600	537	W	91	4,150	950	1,168
2000	2,173	123	250	125	380	125	750	436	400	174	4,940	910	1,090
2001	2,047	165	300	125	430	130	750	485	500	180	5,130	1,010	1,025
2002	1,956	177	750	125	460	106	750	512	400	170	5,400	900	973
2003	2,063	218	800	125	562	95	840	421	500	314	5,950	873	1,010
2004	1,965	75	840	----	621	61	860	370	500	550	5,850	863	1,020
2005	2,080	75	900	----	686	38	860	375	500	523	6,050	860	1,020
2006	2,508	87	1,000	----	690	46	850	470	500	605	6,790	930	1,230
2007	2,503	92	1,100	----	700	59	850	500	400	550	6,940	960	1,295
2008[1]	2,199	90	1,100	----	720	50	910	500	300	550	6,790	1,000	1,230

[1] Preliminary.   [2] Includes leucoxene.   [3] Approximately 10% of total production is ilmenite. Beginning in 1988, 25% of Norway's ilmenite production was used to produce slag containing 75% TiO2.   NA = Not available.   *Source: U.S. Geological Survey (USGS)*

Salient Statistics of Titanium in the United States   In Metric Tons

Year	--- Titanium Dioxide Pigment --- Production	Imports[3]	Apparent Consumption	Ilmenite Imports[3]	Consumption	Titanium Slag Imports[3]	Consumption	Rutile[4] Imports[3]	Consumption	Exports of Titanium Products Ores & Concentrates	Scrap	Dioxide & Pigments	Ingots, Billets, Etc.
2001	1,330,000	209,000	1,100,000	1,060,000	1,180,000	594,000	----	325,000	483,000	7,800	7,500	349,000	3,260
2002	1,410,000	231,000	1,110,000	840,000	1,300,000	445,000	----	390,000	487,000	3,810	6,000	485,000	3,460
2003	1,420,000	240,000	1,070,000	804,000	1,300,000	409,000	----	427,000	489,000	10,300	5,320	518,000	3,960
2004	1,540,000	264,000	1,170,000	701,000	1,480,000	457,000	----	360,000	445,000	8,690	9,760	576,000	4,990
2005	1,310,000	341,000	1,130,000	822,000	1,290,000	667,000	----	366,000	424,000	20,900	20,600	486,000	6,350
2006	1,370,000	288,000	1,080,000	187,000		693,000		355,000		32,800	10,800	513,000	7,900
2007	1,440,000	221,000	979,000	246,000		749,000		463,800		9,730	9,510	564,000	8,670
2008	1,350,000	183,000	800,000	433,000		461,000		487,000		14,900	8,180	668,000	10,500
2009[1]	1,230,000	175,000	756,000										
2010[2]	1,400,000	197,000	786,000										

[1] Preliminary.   [2] Estimate.   [3] For consumption.   [4] Natural and synthetic.   W = Withheld.   *Source: U.S. Geological Survey (USGS)*

TITANIUM

World Production of Titanium Rutile Concentrates   In Metric Tons

Year	Australia	Brazil	India	Sierra Leone	South Africa	Sri Lanka	Thailand	Ukraine	World Total
2003	173,000	2,450	18,000	----	108,000	----	----	60,000	384,000
2004	162,000	2,500	19,600	----	110,000	----	----	60,000	354,000
2005	177,000	2,500	20,100	----	115,000	----	----	60,000	374,000
2006	232,000	2,500	21,000	73,802	123,000	----	----	60,000	512,000
2007	312,000	2,500	21,000	82,527	114,000	----	----	60,000	594,000
2008	325,000	2,500	21,000	78,908	121,000	----	----	57,000	608,000
2009	266,000	3,000	20,000	61,000	127,000	11,000	----	57,000	550,000
2010[1]	280,000	3,000	20,000	67,000	130,000	12,000	----	57,000	580,000

[1] Preliminary.   NA = Not available.   *Source: U.S. Geological Survey (USGS)*

World Production of Titanium Sponge Metal & U.S. Consumption of Titanium Concentrates

	Production of Titanium (In Metric Tons) Sponge Metal[2]						U.S. Consumption of Titanium Concentrates, by Products (In Metric Tons) Ilmenite (TiO$_2$ Content)			Rutile (TiO$_2$ Content)			
Year	China	Japan	Russia	United Kingdom	United States	Total	Pigments	Misc.	Total	Welding Rod Coatings	Pigments	Misc.	Total
2001	----	----	----	----	----	----	1,160,000	15,400	1,180,000	----	455,000	28,500	483,000
2002	----	----	----	----	----	----	1,280,000	16,000	1,300,000	----	464,000	22,900	487,000
2003	----	----	----	----	----	----	1,280,000	16,700	1,300,000	----	466,000	22,500	489,000
2004	----	----	----	----	----	----	1,460,000	19,300	1,480,000	----	418,000	26,700	445,000
2005	----	----	----	----	----	----	1,260,000	34,000	1,390,000	----	394,000	30,000	424,000
2006	----	----	----	----	----	----	NA	NA	1,510,000	----	----	----	----
2007	----	----	----	----	----	----	NA	NA	1,600,000	----	----	----	----
2008[1]	----	----	----	----	----	----	NA	NA	1,420,000	----	----	----	----

[1] Preliminary.   [2] Unconsolidated metal in various forms.   [4] Included in Pigments.   NA = Not available.   W = Withheld.
Source: U.S. Geological Survey (USGS)

Average Prices of Titanium in the United States

Year	Ilmenite FOB Australian Ports[2]	Slag, 85% TiO2 FOB Richards Bay, South Africa	Rutile Large Lots Bulk, FOB U.S. East Coast[3]	Rutile Bagged FOB Australian Ports	Avg. Price of Grade A Titanium Sponge, FOB Shipping Point	Titanium Metal Sponge	Titanium Dioxide Pigments FOB US Plants Anatase	Titanium Dioxide Pigments FOB US Plants Rutile
	----- Dollars Per Metric Ton -----					----- Dollars Per Pound -----		
2001	$90 - $110	$419.00	$450 - $500	$475 - $565	----	$3.58	$0.92 - $0.94	$1.00 - $1.09
2002	$85 - $100	$445.00	$430 - $470	$400 - $540	----	$3.64	$0.85 - $0.95	$0.85 - $0.95
2003	$80 - $100	$401.00	$415 - $445	$430 - $540	----	$2.72 - $3.95	$0.85 - $0.95	$0.85 - $0.90
2004	$81.00	$347 - $466	$455.00	$550 - $650	----	$3.55 - $6.44	$0.90 - $0.95	$0.90 - $0.95
2005	$80.00	$390 - $555	$470.00	$550 - $650	----	$3.46 - $12.22	$0.95 - $1.00	$0.95 - $1.00
2006	$80.00	$402 - $454	$475.00	$570 - $700	----	$5.87 - $12.84	----	----
2007[1]	$107.00	$418 - $457	$594.00					
2008[2]	$99.00	$404 - $505	$500.00					

[1] Preliminary.   [2] Estimate.   NA = Not available.   *Source: U.S. Geological Survey (USGS)*

Average Price of Titanium[1] in United States   In Dollars Per Pound

Year	Jan.	Feb.	Mar.	Apr.	May	June	July	Aug.	Sept.	Oct.	Nov.	Dec.	Average
2005	10.60	11.25	11.25	15.44	17.25	20.25	20.25	20.33	22.00	22.00	22.00	22.13	17.90
2006	24.75	24.75	25.53	26.10	27.50	27.58	27.75	27.75	27.75	27.75	27.75	27.75	26.89
2007	27.21	26.50	26.50	25.69	25.32	24.50	24.50	22.15	21.50	20.63	18.90	17.79	23.43
2008	16.62	16.00	15.60	15.50	15.50	15.14	14.95	14.50	14.50	14.50	13.56	13.17	14.96
2009	12.93	12.50	10.50	9.93	9.20	9.00	9.00	9.00	8.92	8.75	8.75	8.75	9.77
2010	8.75	8.75	8.92	9.13	10.10	10.70	11.00	11.00	11.00	11.00	11.43	11.50	10.27

[1] Ingot, 6Al - 4V.   NA = Not available.   *Source: American Metal Market (AMM)*

Average Price of Titanium[1] in United States   In Dollars Per Pound

Year	Jan.	Feb.	Mar.	Apr.	May	June	July	Aug.	Sept.	Oct.	Nov.	Dec.	Average
2005	19.81	22.25	22.25	22.51	27.75	27.75	27.75	27.75	29.39	33.50	33.50	33.50	27.31
2006	33.50	33.50	40.54	42.50	42.50	43.14	44.50	44.50	44.50	44.50	44.50	44.50	41.89
2007	44.50	44.50	44.50	40.45	39.50	39.50	39.50	39.50	39.50	37.76	37.50	37.50	40.35
2008	36.74	35.50	35.50	35.50	35.50	35.50	35.50	35.50	34.55	33.00	33.00	33.00	34.90
2009	31.20	31.00	31.00	29.76	29.00	29.00	29.00	29.00	29.00	27.10	26.50	26.50	29.01
2010	26.50	25.55	24.50	25.50	26.50	26.50	28.50	28.50	28.50	28.50	30.20	30.50	27.48

[1] Plate, Alloy.   NA = Not available.   *Source: American Metal Market (AMM)*

Tobacco

Tobacco is a member of the nightshade family. It is commercially grown for its leaves and stems, which are rolled into cigars, shredded for use in cigarettes and pipes, processed for chewing, or ground into snuff. Christopher Columbus introduced tobacco cultivation and use to Spain after observing natives from the Americas smoking loosely rolled tobacco-stuffed tobacco leaves.

Tobacco is cured, or dried, after harvesting and then aged to improve its flavor. The four common methods of curing are: air cured, fire cured, sun cured, and flue cured. Flue curing is the fastest method of curing and requires only about a week compared with up to 10 weeks for other methods. Cured tobacco is tied into small bundles of about 20 leaves and aged one to three years.

Virginia tobacco is by far the most popular type used in pipe tobacco since it is the mildest of all blending tobaccos. Approximately 60% of the U.S. tobacco crop is Virginia-type tobacco. Burley tobacco is the next most popular tobacco. It is air-cured, burns slowly and provides a relatively cool smoke. Other tobacco varieties include Perique, Kentucky, Oriental, and Latakia.

Prices – U.S. tobacco farm prices in 2009 (latest data) fell -0.9% to 184.2 cents per pound. That is, however, below the record high of 198.4 cents per pound posted in 2004.

Supply – World production of tobacco in 2009 (latest data available) rose by +2.8% yr/yr to a nine year high of 6.911 million metric tons. The world's largest producers of tobacco are China with 43.4% of world production, followed at a distance by Brazil (with 12.5% of world production), India (8%), and the U.S. (5.4%). U.S. production in 2009 rose by +2.8% yr/yr to 373,440 metric tons, where it was down by more than half from the 2-decade high of 810,750 metric tons posted in 1997. Tobacco in the U.S. is grown primarily in the Mid-Atlantic States and they account for the vast majority of U.S. production. Specifically, the largest tobacco producing states in the U.S. are North Carolina (with 49.0% of U.S. production in 2010), Kentucky (25.3%), Tennessee (6.4%), Virginia (6.3%), South Carolina (5.0%), and Georgia (3.8%).

Flue-cured tobacco (type 11-14) is the most popular tobacco type grown in the U.S. and U.S. production in 2009 (latest data) rose by +5.2% yr/yr to 525.400 million pounds. The second most popular type is burley tobacco (type 31), which saw U.S. production in 2009 rose +6.6% to 214.896

million pounds.

Total U.S. production of tobacco in 2010 fell -12.5% yr/yr to 719.786 million pounds, which is less than half of the 2-decade high of 1.787 billion pounds posted in 1997. U.S. farmers have sharply reduced the planting acreage for tobacco. In 2010, harvested tobacco acreage fell by 4.7% yr/yr to 337.450 acres, which is up from the 2005 record low of 297,080 but still far below the 25-year high of 836,230 posted in 1997. Yield in 2010 fell -8.2% to 2,133, down from a 15-year high of 2,325 pounds per acre in 2009. The farm value of the U.S. tobacco crop in 2009 rose by +1.8% yr/yr to $1.515 billion.

U.S. marketings of flue-cured tobacco (Types 11-14) in the 2006-07 (latest data) marketing year rose by +18.5% yr/yr to 453.8 million pounds. U.S. marketings of burley tobacco (Type 31) in the 2006-07 marketing year rose by +6.9% yr/yr to 217.4 million pounds.

U.S. production of cigarettes in 2006 (latest data) rose by +1.5% to 496.4 billion cigarettes, which was still down sharply from the record high of 754.5 million posted in 1996. U.S. production of cigars rose by +8.2% yr/yr to 3.977 billion in 2006. U.S. production of chewing tobacco in 2006 fell by 3.1% to 38.0 million pounds, which was a record low.

Demand – U.S. per capita consumption of tobacco products in 2006 (latest data) was unchanged at 3.69 pounds per person but there appears to be a shifting from cigarettes to cigars. The 3.69 pounds per capita consumption of tobacco in 2006 is less than half the record high of 9.68 pounds per person that occurred at the beginning of the series in 1970. Per capita cigarette consumption in 2006 fell 1.5% yr/yr to 1,691 cigarettes per person, which was a record low. Per capita consumption of cigars in 2006 rose +1.9% yr/yr to a record high of 47.80 cigars per person. Per capita consumption of loose smoking tobacco in 2006 fell –6.3% yr/yr to 0.15 pounds.

Trade – U.S. tobacco exports in 2004 (latest data available) rose +3.5% yr/yr to 354.0 million pounds, rebounding further from the record low of 325.8 million pounds seen in 2002. Meanwhile, U.S. tobacco imports in 2004 fell –10.9% yr/yr to 561.7 million pounds from the 11-year high of 630.1 million pounds see in 2003. The U.S. exported 111.3 billion cigarettes and 180 million cigars in 2006.

World Production of Leaf Tobacco   In Metric Tons

Year	Brazil	Canada	China	Greece	India	Indo-nesia	Italy	Japan	Pakistan	Turkey	United States	Zim-babwe	World Total
2000	578,451	53,010	2,563,854	136,593	520,000	146,100	129,937	60,803	107,700	200,280	477,753	227,726	6,690,627
2001	568,505	58,606	2,358,842	142,000	340,000	201,900	130,487	60,600	85,100	144,786	449,643	195,905	6,152,414
2002	670,309	54,550	2,454,105	133,000	550,000	194,500	122,231	58,200	94,500	152,856	395,134	178,408	6,510,985
2003	656,200	46,338	2,262,658	136,000	490,000	200,875	124,985	50,662	88,200	112,158	364,035	102,683	6,025,557
2004	921,281	42,430	2,411,490	133,937	549,900	165,108	117,882	52,659	86,200	133,913	400,012	78,312	6,532,593
2005	889,426	43,000	2,685,743	124,351	549,100	153,470	115,983	46,800	100,500	135,247	292,574	83,230	6,739,799
2006	900,381	43,000	2,746,193	37,405	552,200	146,265	96,600	37,700	112,592	98,137	330,169	44,451	6,617,071
2007	908,679	44,000	2,397,152	29,370	520,000	164,851	110,000	37,800	103,240	74,584	357,273	79,000	6,264,243
2008[1]	851,058	44,000	2,836,725	28,000	520,000	169,668	110,000	38,500	107,765	93,403	363,103	79,000	6,724,338
2009[2]	862,355		3,001,725	28,000				36,600		85,000	373,440		6,911,395

[1] Preliminary.   [2] Estimate.   *Source: Food and Agriculture Organization of the United Nations (FAO-UN)*

TOBACCO

Production and Consumption of Tobacco Products in the United States

			--- Chewing Tobacco ---			Smoking			-------- Consumption[5] of Per Capita[6] --------						
	Cigar-ettes	Cigars[3]	Plug	Twist	Loose-leaf	Total Tobacco	Snuff[4]	Cigar-ettes	Cigars[3]	Cigar-ettes	Cigars[3]	Smoking Tobacco	Chewing Tobacco	Total Products
Year	- Billions -	- Millions -	---------------- In Millions of Pounds ----------------					----- Number -----		---------------- In Pounds ----------------				
2000	593.2	2,825	2.6	0.8	46.0	49.4	13.6	69.5	2,049	38.0	3.40	.62	.13	.48	4.10
2001	562.8	3,741	2.4	0.8	43.9	47.1	12.8	70.9	2,051	41.2	3.50	.68	.15	.47	4.30
2002	484.3	3,816	2.2	0.8	41.5	44.5	15.5	72.7	1,982	41.8	3.40	.68	.16	.43	4.16
2003	499.4	4,017	1.7	0.7	39.2	41.6	17.8	73.8	1,890	44.5	3.20	.73	.16	.40	3.97
2004	492.7	4,342	1.7	0.7	37.0	39.3	16.1	79.3	1,814	47.9	3.10	.79	.15	.37	3.87
2005	498.7	3,674	1.4	0.6	37.2	39.2	17.4	86.7	1,716	46.9	2.90	.77	.16	.36	3.69
2006	483.7	4,256	1.3	0.6	36.4	38.3	16.5	81.8	1,691	47.8	2.90	.78	.15	.37	3.69
2007	449.7	4,797	1.2	0.5	35.1	36.8									
2008[1]	396.1	4,984	1.1	0.5	30.9	32.5									
2009[2]	338.1	8,232	0.9	0.5	28.0	29.3									

[1] Preliminary. [2] Estimate. [3] Large cigars and cigarillos. [4] Includes loose-leaf. [5] Consumption of tax-paid tobacco products. Unstemmed rocessing weight. [6] 18 years and older. NA = Not available. *Source: Economic Research Service, U.S. Department of Agriculture (ERS-USDA)*

Production of Tobacco in the United States, by States   In Thousands of Pounds

Year	Florida	Georgia	Indiana	Kentucky	Maryland	North Carolina	Ohio	Pennsyl-vania	South Carolina	Tenn-essee	Virginia	Wisconsin	Total
2001	11,700	64,206	9,450	254,653	3,300	386,920	11,956	6,166	78,400	86,893	63,415	3,619	991,223
2002	11,960	53,000	7,800	222,991	1,800	347,920	9,625	6,815	59,475	71,331	64,407	3,817	871,122
2003	11,000	59,400	8,190	225,042	1,595	299,995	8,745	7,880	63,000	65,632	38,818	4,255	802,560
2004	9,800	46,690	8,610	235,003	1,870	350,560	10,976	8,100	63,450	65,381	67,285	3,541	881,875
2005	5,500	27,760	----	174,260	----	278,900	6,732	10,700	39,900	51,670	40,351	----	645,015
2006	2,860	30,090	----	186,780	----	330,580	7,000	16,790	48,300	49,135	47,322	----	727,897
2007	----	39,775	----	197,040	----	383,420	7,175	18,310	46,125	38,636	46,142	----	787,653
2008	----	33,600	----	205,850	----	390,360	6,970	17,630	39,900	52,380	45,970	----	800,504
2009	----	28,014	----	206,900	----	423,856	6,800	18,660	38,850	49,960	46,530	----	822,581
2010[1]	----	27,360	----	181,760	----	352,625	5,125	19,965	36,000	45,740	45,400	----	719,786

[1] Preliminary. *Source: Agricultural Statistics Board, U.S. Department of Agriculture (ASB-USDA)*

Salient Statistics of Tobacco in the United States

	Acres		Pro-			---- Tobacco ---- (June - July)		------------ U.S. Exports of ------------				Stocks of Tobacco[5] ---------- Various Types ------------			
Year	Harvested 1,000 Acres	Yield Per Acre Pounds	duction Million Pounds	Farm Price cents Lb.	Farm Value Million $	Exports[2] - Million Pounds -	Imports[3]	Cigar-ettes ----- In Millions -----	Cigars & Cheroots	All Tobacco	Smoking Tobacco[4]	All Tobacco	Fire Cured[6]	Cigar Filler[7]	Mary-land
												---------------- In Millions of Pounds ----------------			
2001	432.3	2,293	991	195.7	1,940	386.7	568.0	133,900	124	411	118.2	1,893	93.8	12.1	13.4
2002	427.3	2,039	871	193.6	1,687	325.8	549.7	127,400	123	338	144.0	1,738	99.5	12.3	9.7
2003	411.2	1,952	803	196.7	1,576	342.1	630.1	121,500	130	343	121.2	1,584	100.5	10.7	8.2
2004	408.1	2,161	882	198.4	1,750	354.0	561.7	118,700	171	361	45.4	1,529	101.5	9.7	7.2
2005	297.1	2,171	645	164.2	1,059			113,300	301			1,455		9.9	5.0
2006	339.0	2,144	728	166.5	1,211			111,317	180			1,167		10.8	0.8
2007	356.0	2,213	788	169.3	1,329										
2008	354.5	2,258	801	185.9	1,488										
2009	354.0	2,323	823	183.7	1,511										
2010[1]	337.5	2,133	720	177.1	1,275										

[1] Preliminary. [2] Domestic. [3] For consumption. [4] In bulk. [5] Flue-cured and cigar wrapper, year beginning July 1; for all other types, October 1. [6] Kentucky-Tennessee types 22-23. [7] Types 41-46. *Source: Economic Research Service, U.S. Department of Agriculture (ERS-USDA)*

Tobacco Production in the United States, by Types   In Thousands of Pounds (Farm-Sale Weight)

Year	11-14	21	22	23	31	32	35-36	37	41	41-61	51	54	55	61
2001	579,091	2,202	30,720	12,377	334,066	5,346	13,949	154	4,120	13,318	3,822	3,042	577	1,757
2002	514,385	1,471	23,292	10,145	293,537	4,205	10,570	116	4,410	13,401	4,021	3,151	666	1,153
2003	456,690	839	23,504	10,165	281,698	4,195	11,230	84	5,280	14,155	3,386	3,472	783	1,234
2004	521,535	1,345	24,800	11,006	292,172	5,830	11,798	124	4,140	13,265	3,767	2,744	797	1,915
2005	380,850	----	----	----	203,383	3,000	----	----	2,860	8,621	4,117	----	----	----
2006	447,190	----	----	----	217,255	2,090	----	----	2,600	8,265	4,434	----	----	----
2007	503,760	----	----	----	216,087	2,420	----	----	4,140	11,442	5,473	----	----	1,829
2008	499,220	----	----	----	201,530	3,780	----	----	3,960	8,444	3,076	----	----	1,408
2009	525,414	----	----	----	214,896	4,830	----	----	4,400	7,411	1,872	----	----	1,139
2010[1]	453,085	----	----	----	187,570	4,950	----	----	4,935	10,746	4,692	----	----	1,119

[1] Preliminary. *Source: Agricultural Statistics Board, U.S. Department of Agriculture (ASB-USDA)*

U.S. Exports of Unmanufactured Tobacco   In Millions of Pounds (Declared Weight)

Year	Australia	Belgium-Luxem.	Denmark	France	Germany	Italy	Japan	Nether-lands	Sweden	Switzer-land	Thailand	United Kingdom	Total U.S. Exports
2001	3.4	49.7	12.2	11.5	94.8	6.2	51.6	21.6	3.6	14.4	7.7	1.6	410.7
2002	4.5	29.4	13.6	10.3	59.5	8.6	49.6	10.3	1.2	27.3	12.6	6.0	338.2
2003	6.3	61.7	13.5	8.8	55.8	7.6	42.4	9.8	1.6	34.8	3.6	4.8	343.3
2004	3.6	27.4	10.2	16.3	53.5	6.6	34.6	15.8	.6	9.4	8.5	4.0	360.9
2005	2.9	12.7	8.4	10.7	55.3	5.8	21.7	25.4	.7	15.6	4.1	3.2	339.0
2006	4.9	16.8	8.4	7.5	81.2	3.2	3.9	37.0	.7	38.5	3.0	1.1	397.6
2007	3.5	18.0	9.7	13.2	63.1	.7	4.0	24.0	.3	41.7	1.8	.0	411.5
2008	1.3	3.9	6.5	7.0	39.2	.0	.0	46.3	.3	69.3	3.0	.1	372.3
2009	6.4	3.6	6.4	7.7	23.9	.4	.0	37.7	.3	59.1	2.8	.1	380.3
2010[1]	5.2	44.6	4.5	8.3	20.8	.6	.0	44.7	.4	34.7	3.0	1.1	393.9

[1] Preliminary.   *Source: Economic Research Service, U.S. Department of Agriculture (ERS-USDA)*

U.S. Salient Statistics for Flue-Cured Tobacco (Types 11-14) in the United States   In Millions of Pounds

Year	Acres Harvested 1,000	Yield Per Acre Pounds	Mar-ketings	Stocks Oct. 1	Total Supply	Exports	Domestic Disap-pearance	Total Disap-pearance	Farm Price cents/Lb.	Placed Under Gov't Loan (Mil. Lb.)	Price Support Level (cents/) Lb.	Loan Stocks Nov. 30	Loan Stocks Uncom-mitted
2001-02	238.1	2,432	544	1,036	1,581	276	389	665	185.7	15.0	166.0	93.2	65.0
2002-03	245.6	2,094	565	916	1,481	220	423	643	182.0	24.8	165.6	17.8	12.8
2003-04	233.4	1,957	508	838	1,345	216	307	522	185.1	59.8	166.3	70.6	68.7
2004-05	228.4	2,283	499	823	1,322	189	338	526	184.5	94.9	169.0	108.2	128.5
2005-06	174.5	2,182	383	796	1,179	258	317	575	147.4	----	----	79.0	----
2006-07	213.1	2,095	455	604	1,058	270	248	518	149.6				
2007-08	223.0	2,259							152.7				
2008-09	223.0	2,239							175.7				
2009-10[1]	223.8	2,348							175.4				
2010-11[2]	210.9	2,148											

[1] Preliminary.   [2] Estimate.   NA = Not available.   *Source: Economic Research Service, U.S. Department of Agriculture (ERS-USDA)*

Salient Statistics for Burley Tobacco (Type 31) in the United States   In Millions of Pounds

Year	Acres Harvested 1,000	Yield Per Acre Pounds	Mar-ketings	Stocks Oct. 1	Total Supply	Exports	Domestic Disap-pearance	Total Disap-pearance	Farm Price cents/Lb.	Gross Sales[3]	Price Support Level cents/Lb.	Loan Stocks Nov. 30	Loan Stocks Uncom-mitted
2001-02	167.6	2,033	344	689	1,033	140	245	385	197.3	258.5	182.6	119.3	74.8
2002-03	157.7	1,861	300	648	948	149	221	370	197.4	217.7	183.5	124.2	46.1
2003-04	152.3	1,850	272	578	1,850	174	136	310	197.7	197.3	184.9	91.7	26.5
2004-05	153.2	1,908	280	540	820	228	100	328	199.4	202.3	187.3	115.1	8.5
2005-06	100.2	2,031	203	493	696	208	84	293	156.4	----	----	78.7	----
2006-07	103.6	2,095	225	403	628	190	56	246	163.8				
2007-08	106.3	2,033							160.1				
2008-09	97.5	2,067							166.9				
2009-10[1]	101.9	2,109							170.9				
2010-11[2]	97.6	1,922											

[1] Preliminary.   [2] Estimate.   [3] Before Christmas holidays.   NA = Not available.
Source: Economic Research Service, U.S. Department of Agriculture (ERS-USDA)

Exports of Tobacco from the United States (Quantity and Value)   In Metric Tons

	Unmanufactured							
Year	Flue-Cured	Value 1,000 USD	Burley	Value 1,000 USD	Total	Value 1,000 USD	Manu-factured	Value 1,000 USD
2001	89,930	660,924	42,464	361,567	186,302	1,268,839	104,282	422,979
2002	73,125	532,713	40,170	334,621	153,427	1,049,709	110,092	376,814
2003	70,669	519,732	41,876	346,504	155,722	1,038,073	102,351	370,618
2004	67,183	490,547	58,764	373,001	163,693	1,044,440	60,770	350,410
2005	62,779	420,532	61,606	412,588	153,762	989,588	19,364	297,511
2006	88,020	569,431	63,214	409,272	180,368	1,141,374	22,261	353,863
2007	82,093	541,816	75,905	498,168	186,643	1,207,945	17,552	362,192
2008	100,848	730,677	44,506	342,732	168,885	1,238,047	25,474	339,712
2009[1]	86,429	660,678	37,395	301,497	172,504	1,159,991	4,654	300,982
2010[2]	85,723		32,687		178,675		4,930	302,015

[1] Preliminary.   [2] Forecast.   *Source: Foreign Agricultural Service, U.S. Department of Agriculture (FAS-USDA)*

Tung Oil

Tung oil is a yellow drying oil produced from the seed of the tung tree. The seeds or nuts of the tung tree are harvested and pressed to yield tung oil. Tung oil is used mostly as an industrial lubricant and drying agent, and is the most powerful drying agent known. It is also used in paints and varnishes, soaps, inks, and electrical insulators. Tung oil is poisonous, containing glycerol esters of unsaturated fats. The oil is also used as a substitute for linseed oil in paints, varnishes, and linoleum, and as a waterproofing agent.

Prices – The price of tung oil in 2009 (latest data) fell by -5.0% yr/yr to 135.80 cents per pound, down from last year's record high of 143.03 cents per pound.

Demand – U.S. consumption of tung oil has fallen sharply over the past decade. In 2008 (latest data annualized) U.S. consumption rose by +1.8% yr/yr to 1.314 million pounds but that 2008 consumption level was only about 7% of 1996's 18-year high of 21.645 million pounds.

Trade – World imports of tung oil in 2009 (latest data) fell –11.0% yr/yr to 14,913 metric tons. U.S. imports of tung oil in 2009 fell by -4.6% to 1,670 metric tons. The world's largest importers of tung oil are South Korea with 13.7% of world imports, Taiwan with 10.9%, Japan with 7.9%, the U.S. with 11.2%, and the Netherlands with 9.3%. The world's largest exporter of tung oil by far is China with 8,913 metric tons of exports in 2009, accounting for 59.7% of total world exports.

World Tung Oil Trade   In Metric Tons

	-- Imports --							-------------------------- Exports --------------------------				
Year	Germany	Hong Kong	Japan	Nether- lands	Rep. of Korea	Taiwan	United States	World Total	Argen- tina	China	Hong Kong	Para- guay	World Total
2003	303	306	2,023	1,687	6,396	3,974	4,287	27,419	2,299	19,509	323	2,479	25,951
2004	100	207	1,900	1,778	5,486	3,529	2,975	24,961	1,299	18,850	240	3,626	25,501
2005	43	154	2,067	2,376	3,769	2,938	1,866	22,476	1,035	16,563	171	4,306	23,459
2006	478	104	1,984	2,342	1,828	2,891	2,076	20,183	733	14,668	104	2,876	19,539
2007	1,307	120	1,858	2,119	2,685	2,021	1,630	18,899	956	13,313	100	2,085	18,542
2008[1]	1,251	120	1,937	1,693	1,894	1,884	1,750	16,762	364	12,245	100	2,148	16,351
2009[2]	1,290	90	1,178	1,394	2,036	1,621	1,670	14,913	262	8,913	70	3,024	14,925

[1] Preliminary.   [2] Estimate.   *Source: The Oil World*

Consumption of Tung Oil in Inedible Products in the United States   In Thousands of Pounds

Year	Jan.	Feb.	Mar.	Apr.	May	June	July	Aug.	Sept.	Oct.	Nov.	Dec.	Total
2004	428	400	350	402	264	324	338	310	186	186	101	109	3,398
2005	128	110	144	151	371	127	161	189	92	171	146	110	1,900
2006	174	175	138	103	128	193	198	114	198	134	136	75	1,766
2007	170	81	108	104	176	117	153	83	68	92	75	64	1,291
2008	W	W	141	91	98	W	108	W	W	W	W	W	1,314
2009	W	W	W	W	W	W	W	W	W	W	W	W	W
2010[1]	W	W	W	W	W	W	W	W	W	W	W	W	W

[1] Preliminary.   W = Withheld.   *Source: Bureau of the Census, U.S. Department of Commerce*

Stocks of Tung Oil at Factories & Warehouses in the United States, on First of Month   In Thousands of Pounds

Year	Jan.	Feb.	Mar.	Apr.	May	June	July	Aug.	Sept.	Oct.	Nov.	Dec.
2004	W	W	W	519	229	209	226	137	91	161	121	117
2005	90	128	107	182	130	141	134	122	114	93	116	70
2006	109	99	98	124	81	116	128	85	128	125	76	98
2007	109	135	109	92	66	110	117	153	101	100	36	59
2008	82	87	94	63	29	79	50	78	86	73	W	W
2009	W	W	W	W	W	W	W	W	W	W	W	W
2010[1]	W	W	W	W	W	W	W	W	W	W	W	W

[1] Preliminary.   W = Withheld.   *Source: Bureau of the Census, U.S. Department of Commerce*

Average Price of Tung Oil (Imported, Drums) F.O.B. in New York   In Cents Per Pound

Year	Jan.	Feb.	Mar.	Apr.	May	June	July	Aug.	Sept.	Oct.	Nov.	Dec.	Average
2004	85.00	85.00	85.00	85.00	85.00	85.00	85.00	85.00	85.00	85.00	85.00	90.00	85.42
2005	92.50	95.00	97.50	97.50	97.50	97.50	97.50	102.50	105.00	105.00	97.50	95.00	98.33
2006	95.00	95.00	95.00	95.00	95.00	93.75	90.00	90.00	89.00	89.00	89.00	89.00	92.06
2007	85.40	84.33	87.00	85.00	85.00	85.00	85.00	NA	90.00	99.50	100.00	100.71	89.72
2008	107.62	110.79	126.00	130.00	130.00	135.14	139.86	147.62	164.29	175.00	175.00	175.00	143.03
2009	170.00	151.32	135.00	133.33	130.00	130.00	130.00	130.00	130.00	130.00	130.00	130.00	135.80
2010[1]	130.00	130.00	130.00	130.00	130.00	130.00	130.00	130.00	NA	NA	NA	NA	130.00

[1] Preliminary.   *Source: Economic Research Service, U.S. Department of Agriculture (ERS-USDA)*

Tungsten

Tungsten (symbol W) is a grayish-white, lustrous, metallic element. The atomic symbol for tungsten is W because of its former name of Wolfram. Tungsten has the highest melting point of any metal at about 3410 degrees Celsius and boils at about 5660 degrees Celsius. In 1781, the Swedish chemist Carl Wilhelm Scheele discovered tungsten.

Tungsten is never found in nature but is instead found in the minerals wolframite, scheelite, huebnertite, and ferberite. Tungsten has excellent corrosion resistance qualities and is resistant to most mineral acids. Tungsten is used as filaments in incandescent lamps, electron and television tubes, alloys of steel, spark plugs, electrical contact points, cutting tools, and in the chemical and tanning industries.

Prices – The average monthly price of tungsten at U.S. ports in 2010 rose by +5.6% yr/yr to $194.78 per short ton, but still below the 2006 record high of $265.68 per short ton. In January 2011 the price rose further to $263.45 per short ton.

Supply – World concentrate production of tungsten in 2009 rose by +3.8% yr/yr to 58,000 metric tons. That was down from the 2004 record high of 66,600 metric tons. The world's largest producer of tungsten by far is China with 47,000 metric tons of production in 2009, which was 81% of total world production. Russia is the next largest producer at 4% with only a miniscule production of only 2,400 metric tons.

Trade – The U.S. in 2009 relied on imports for 63% of its tungsten consumption. U.S. imports for consumption in 2009 fell by -4.8% yr/yr to 3,800 metric tons. U.S. exports in 2009 were negligible at 16 metric tons.

World Concentrate Production of Tungsten   In Metric Tons (Contained Tungsten[3])

Year	Austria	Bolivia	Brazil	Burma	Canada	China	Mongolia	Korea	Portugal	Russia	Rwanda	Thailand	Total
2003	1,381	441	30	96	3,636	36,200	40	600	715	3,600	69	216	47,200
2004	1,335	403	262	107	----	59,900	77	280	746	2,800	90	187	66,600
2005	1,280	531	577	168	384	51,200	78	650	816	2,800	318	345	59,600
2006	1,153	868	525	197	1,983	45,000	85	900	780	2,800	820	303	56,600
2007	1,117	1,107	537	183	2,305	41,000	245	250	846	3,300	1,534	477	54,500
2008	1,122	1,148	540	200	2,277	43,500	142	350	850	3,000	975	600	55,900
2009[1]	900	1,000	----	----	2,000	51,000	----	----	900	2,500	----	----	61,300
2010[2]	1,000	1,100	----	----	300	52,000	----	----	950	2,500	----	----	61,000

[1] Preliminary.   [2] Estimate.   [3] Conversion Factors: WO_3 to W, multiply by 0.7931; 60% WO_3 to W, multiply by 0.4758.
Source: U.S. Geological Survey (USGS)

Salient Statistics of Tungsten in the United States   In Metric Tons (Contained Tungsten)

Year	Net Import Reliance as a % Apparent Consumption	Total Con-sumption	Tool	Stainless & Heat Assisting	Alloy Steel[3]	Super-alloys	Cutting & Wear Resistant Materials	Products Made From Metal Powder	Miscel-laneous	Chemical and Ceramic	Exports	Imports for Con-sumption	Con-sumers	Pro-ducers
2003	63	W	W	312	W	W	5,210	W	----	129	20	4,690	W	W
2004	73	W	W	259	W	W	6,020	W	----	130	43	2,310	W	W
2005	68	W	W	280	W	W	6,020	W	----	130	52	2,080	W	W
2006	67	W	W	292	W	W	6,710	W	----	118	130	2,290	W	W
2007	67	W	W	282	W	W	6,090	W	----	89	109	3,880	W	W
2008	60	W	W	283	W	W	6,650	W	----	80	496	3,990	W	W
2009[1]	68	W									38	3,590	W	W
2010[2]	68	W									400	3,000	W	W

Column headings: Consumption of Tungsten Products by End Uses; Steel sub-group (Tool, Stainless & Heat Assisting, Alloy Steel[3]); Stocks, Dec. 31 -- Concentrates -- (Consumers, Producers).

[1] Preliminary.   [2] Estimate.   [3] Other than tool.   [4] Included with stainless & heat assisting.   W = Withheld.
Source: U.S. Geological Survey (USGS)

Average Price of Tungsten at U.S. Ports (Including Duty)   In Dollars Per Short Ton

Year	Jan.	Feb.	Mar.	Apr.	May	June	July	Aug.	Sept.	Oct.	Nov.	Dec.	Average
2003	60.25	61.55	63.00	63.00	63.00	63.00	63.00	63.00	63.00	63.00	63.00	63.00	62.65
2004	63.00	63.00	66.83	89.77	92.50	92.50	88.95	86.09	87.00	89.86	92.00	93.83	83.78
2005	97.08	109.32	134.13	178.21	272.26	277.61	275.25	237.28	232.50	244.05	255.00	255.00	213.97
2006	255.00	265.66	282.50	275.00	266.36	265.00	265.00	265.00	266.13	267.50	262.00	253.00	265.68
2007	252.50	256.71	261.36	262.50	262.50	262.50	262.50	261.63	252.50	252.50	252.50	252.50	257.68
2008	252.50	252.50	252.50	252.50	252.50	252.50	252.50	252.50	252.50	252.50	252.50	252.50	252.50
2009	252.50	215.00	205.00	205.00	165.00	165.00	165.00	165.00	165.00	165.00	166.58	180.00	184.51
2010	173.95	175.00	175.65	177.50	177.50	177.50	175.12	169.46	217.50	238.21	240.00	240.00	194.78

U.S. Spot Quotations, 65% WO_3, Basis C.I.F.   *Source: U.S. Geological Survey (USGS)*

Turkeys

During the past three decades, the turkey industry has experienced tremendous growth in the U.S. Turkey production has more than tripled since 1970, with a current value of over $7 billion. Turkey was not a popular dish in Europe until a roast turkey was eaten on June 27, 1570, at the wedding feast of Charles XI of France and Elizabeth of Austria. The King was so impressed with the birds that the turkey subsequently became a popular dish at banquets held by French nobility.

The most popular turkey product continues to be the whole bird, with heavy demand at Thanksgiving and Christmas. The primary breeders maintain and develop the quality stock, concentrating on growth and conformation in males and fecundity in females, as well as characteristics important to general health and welfare. Turkey producers include large companies that produce turkeys all year round, and relatively small companies and farmers who produce turkeys primarily for the seasonal Thanksgiving market.

Prices – The average monthly price received by farmers for turkeys in the U.S. in 2010 rose by +22.6% yr/yr to 61.2 cents per pound, making a new record high.

The monthly average retail price of turkeys (whole frozen) in the U.S. in 2010 rose by +5.8% yr/yr to a record high of 147.7 cents per pound. Turkey prices have more than tripled from the low 40-cent area seen in the early 1970s.

Supply – World production of turkeys in 2010 rose by +1.9% yr/yr to 5.156 million metric tons. World production of turkeys has grown by more than two and one-half times since 1980 when production was a mere 2.090 million metric tons. The U.S. is the largest producer of turkeys in the world by far with 2.607 million metric tons of production in 2010, which is 50.6% of world production. The value of U.S. turkey production in the U.S. in 2009 (latest data) was $5.588 billion.

Demand – World consumption of turkeys in 2010 rose by +2.2% to 5.048 million metric tons. U.S. turkey consumption of 2.381 million metric tons in 2010 which accounted for 47.2% of world consumption. U.S. per capita consumption of turkeys in 2010 is forecasted to fall -0.6% yr/yr to 16.6 pounds per person per year. U.S. per capital consumption of turkeys has been in the range of 16-18 pounds since 1990, but the USDA is projecting that per capita consumption will drop somewhat.

Production and Consumption of Turkey Meat, by Selected Countries   In Thousands of Metric Tons (RTC)

| | | | Production | | | | | | | | Consumption | | | | |
Year	Brazil	Canada	European Union	Mexico	Russia	United States	World Total	Brazil	Canada	European Union	Mexico	Russia	United States	World Total
2002	220	147	2,105	13	9	2,557	5,063	130	142	1,932	146	174	2,316	4,952
2003	272	148	2,028	14	12	2,529	5,015	160	137	1,939	167	126	2,301	4,956
2004	315	145	2,032	13	15	2,441	4,974	179	139	1,966	152	112	2,272	4,882
2005	360	155	1,919	14	17	2,464	4,942	199	143	1,888	194	124	2,246	4,862
2006	353	163	1,858	14	19	2,543	4,963	197	144	1,841	197	110	2,295	4,867
2007	458	170	1,790	15	25	2,664	5,138	281	150	1,769	211	100	2,401	5,017
2008	465	180	1,830	15	37	2,796	5,335	261	163	1,835	212	102	2,431	5,092
2009	466	167	1,795	11	40	2,535	5,027	302	151	1,801	155	84	2,360	4,919
2010[1]	485	165	1,815	13	45	2,484	5,021	321	148	1,820	158	70	2,266	4,848
2011[2]	510	167	1,795	15	55	2,489	5,045	345	154	1,805	165	65	2,238	4,837

[1] Preliminary.   [2] Forecast.   *Source: Foreign Agricultural Service, U.S. Department of Agriculture (FAS-USDA)*

Salient Statistics of Turkeys in the United States

| | | | Liveweight | | Value of Production | Production | Ready-to-Cook Basis | | | Consumption | Production Costs | | Wholesale Ready-to-Cook | |
| Year | Poults Placed[3] | Number Raised[4] | Produced | Price cents | of Production | | Beginning Stocks | Exports | Total | Per Capita | Feed | Total | Production | 3-Region Weighted |
	--- In Thousands ----		Mil Lbs	Per Lb.	Million $ ---------		In Millions of Pounds ---------			Lbs.	- Liveweight Basis -		Costs	Avg Price[5]
2000	298,094	269,969	6,942.8	40.7	2,828.5	5,334	254	445	4,903	17.4	19.98	33.68	58.40	68.06
2001	301,721	272,059	7,154.8	39.0	2,796.8	5,489	241	487	5,004	17.5	20.55	34.25	59.11	63.63
2002	296,877	275,477	7,494.9	36.5	2,732.5	5,638	241	439	5,108	17.7	20.85	34.55	59.48	61.09
2003	289,542	274,048	7,487.3	36.1	2,699.7	5,576	333	484	5,074	17.4	22.59	36.29	61.66	60.41
2004	277,717	263,207	7,278.4	42.0	3,054.3	5,383	354	442	5,003	17.0	----	----	----	----
2005	293,683	252,053	7,096.0	44.9	3,182.8	5,432	288	570	4,952	16.7	----	----	----	----
2006	293,137	262,460	7,463.9	47.9	3,573.7	5,607	206	547	5,060	16.9	----	----	----	----
2007	308,402	266,828	7,566.3	52.3	3,954.5	5,873	218	547	5,294	17.5	----	----	----	----
2008[1]	297,590	273,088	7,922.1	56.5	4,477.1	6,165	261	676	5,361	17.6	----	----	----	----
2009[2]	273,904	247,359	7,104.0	50.0	3,573.6	5,588	396	535	5,201	16.9	----	----	----	----

[1] Preliminary.   [2] Estimate.   [3] Poults placed for slaughter by hatcheries.   [4] Turkeys place August 1-July 31.   [5] Regions include central, eastern and western. Central region receives twice the weight of the other regions in calculating the average.
Source: Economic Research Service, U.S. Department of Agriculture (ERS-USDA)

Turkey-Feed Price Ratio in the United States   In Pounds[2]

Year	Jan.	Feb.	Mar.	Apr.	May	June	July	Aug.	Sept.	Oct.	Nov.	Dec.	Average
2001	7.3	7.5	7.7	8.0	8.1	8.3	7.9	7.8	8.3	9.6	9.6	8.1	8.2
2002	7.2	7.2	6.8	6.8	7.3	7.3	6.9	6.3	6.0	6.1	6.5	6.4	6.7
2003	5.7	5.7	5.9	5.9	5.7	5.8	5.9	5.7	6.0	6.3	6.3	5.7	5.9
2004	5.1	4.6	4.5	4.5	4.8	5.2	5.8	7.0	7.9	8.4	8.7	8.2	6.2
2005	6.9	6.9	6.6	6.7	6.9	7.0	7.3	8.0	9.0	9.5	10.0	9.5	7.9
2006	7.0	6.9	6.9	7.3	7.1	7.6	7.7	8.5	9.1	9.6	9.4	5.9	7.8
2007	5.6	5.3	5.5	5.8	5.9	6.1	6.6	6.7	6.6	6.4	6.1	4.9	6.0
2008	4.1	3.6	4.0	4.0	4.3	4.3	4.5	4.7	5.4	5.9	5.6	4.4	4.6
2009	4.1	4.6	4.8	4.7	4.7	4.8	5.1	5.2	5.3	5.6	5.7	5.6	5.0
2010[1]	4.8	5.3	5.6	5.9	6.2	6.9	6.9	6.7	6.6	6.8	6.4	5.6	6.1

[1] Preliminary.   [2] Pounds of feed equal in value to one pound of turkey, liveweight.   *Source: Economic Research Service, U.S. Department of Agriculture (ERS-USDA)*

Average Price Received by Farmers for Turkeys in the United States (Liveweight)   In Cents Per Pound

Year	Jan.	Feb.	Mar.	Apr.	May	June	July	Aug.	Sept.	Oct.	Nov.	Dec.	Average
2001	36.6	36.3	37.1	37.6	38.2	38.3	38.5	38.7	40.5	44.2	44.5	38.7	39.1
2002	34.1	34.1	32.9	32.9	35.8	37.2	38.6	38.2	37.2	37.2	39.8	38.7	36.4
2003	34.6	34.5	35.1	35.6	34.9	34.9	33.6	32.7	36.2	39.1	41.2	38.2	35.9
2004	34.9	35.0	36.6	38.4	40.1	41.7	43.3	45.1	46.2	48.1	48.7	45.9	42.0
2005	39.3	38.0	38.1	38.8	40.7	42.1	44.6	46.5	50.3	52.5	54.5	53.9	44.9
2006	40.8	39.6	40.3	42.5	43.3	45.4	45.9	48.6	53.3	62.7	66.3	42.7	47.6
2007	40.8	42.4	44.3	46.8	48.3	52.0	55.5	57.2	60.4	61.5	61.6	52.6	52.0
2008	44.8	47.5	52.9	55.1	58.1	59.8	60.9	63.2	66.4	64.6	58.6	44.5	56.4
2009	43.8	46.5	47.1	47.6	50.1	52.5	52.0	51.1	48.5	52.1	54.1	53.7	49.9
2010[1]	46.5	49.1	52.2	53.7	56.1	61.7	64.7	66.8	69.0	73.4	73.6	67.7	61.2

[1] Preliminary.   *Source: Economic Research Service, U.S. Department of Agriculture (ERS-USDA)*

Average Wholesale Price of Turkeys[1] (Hens, 8-16 Lbs.) in New York   In Cents Per Pound

Year	Jan.	Feb.	Mar.	Apr.	May	June	July	Aug.	Sept.	Oct.	Nov.	Dec.	Average
2001	61.50	61.18	62.38	63.45	65.65	66.00	66.10	66.38	68.81	72.86	73.48	67.71	66.29
2002	60.86	60.03	59.00	59.52	63.52	65.68	66.52	66.56	67.15	67.75	69.79	66.96	64.45
2003	61.04	61.13	61.24	61.43	60.36	60.12	58.18	57.74	61.52	66.08	69.33	66.85	62.09
2004	62.13	61.61	62.62	64.52	66.41	68.95	71.21	73.32	74.69	76.89	78.29	76.05	69.72
2005	67.63	65.34	64.68	65.86	67.69	69.50	72.56	75.98	80.90	82.40	85.75	82.60	73.41
2006	68.29	65.84	67.67	69.75	71.27	72.95	74.95	78.70	84.40	95.83	99.51	74.20	76.95
2007	67.63	69.84	71.66	74.45	76.98	82.12	86.89	89.70	93.12	95.20	94.71	82.47	82.06
2008	73.74	76.40	82.20	85.99	89.19	91.45	92.91	96.85	99.62	97.27	87.44	74.88	87.33
2009	71.20	74.32	75.22	76.59	78.71	82.00	82.68	81.33	80.26	82.52	84.96	83.95	79.48
2010[2]	76.50	78.72	82.64	83.90	86.45	93.38	98.68	102.45	105.81	111.03	109.29	101.16	94.17

[1] Ready-to-cook.   [2] Preliminary.   *Source: Economic Research Service, U.S. Department of Agriculture (ERS-USDA)*

Certified Federally Inspected Turkey Slaughter in the U.S. (Ready-to-Cook Weights)   In Millions of Pounds

Year	Jan.	Feb.	Mar.	Apr.	May	June	July	Aug.	Sept.	Oct.	Nov.	Dec.	Total
2001	458.3	405.9	458.7	425.1	485.1	460.7	465.1	481.7	409.2	536.2	477.7	413.2	5,477
2002	477.2	442.1	447.8	487.2	496.7	448.0	474.7	475.9	439.4	519.0	488.2	457.9	5,654
2003	473.6	427.1	464.6	471.1	475.8	478.0	483.9	449.3	453.6	522.8	450.3	436.1	5,586
2004	435.5	389.0	466.6	445.2	445.1	462.8	455.4	462.2	451.2	461.5	479.6	434.4	5,389
2005	439.0	396.3	459.4	439.7	456.3	485.8	427.5	483.7	450.6	479.1	478.2	434.4	5,430
2006	443.0	412.4	487.9	430.3	492.8	504.4	453.5	493.6	456.5	535.8	499.7	423.5	5,633
2007	479.0	442.7	478.8	459.6	507.5	495.7	502.0	517.3	456.4	577.8	520.3	457.3	5,894
2008	544.6	504.0	484.5	515.9	517.9	519.7	544.1	503.8	511.5	570.1	507.9	488.2	6,212
2009	465.5	441.6	467.7	472.2	448.8	490.7	482.3	460.7	463.8	504.4	475.3	453.2	5,626
2010[1]	421.1	423.3	488.0	452.8	437.5	487.0	463.9	478.2	464.1	521.7	518.0	458.6	5,614

[1] Preliminary.   *Source: Economic Research Service, U.S. Department of Agriculture (ERS-USDA)*

TURKEYS

Per Capita Consumption of Turkeys in the United States   In Pounds

Year	First Quarter	Second Quarter	Third Quarter	Fourth Quarter	Total	Year	First Quarter	Second Quarter	Third Quarter	Fourth Quarter	Total
2000	3.7	4.2	4.4	5.5	17.8	2006	3.5	3.9	4.3	5.2	16.9
2001	3.9	3.8	4.3	5.6	17.5	2007	3.8	4.1	4.2	5.5	17.5
2002	3.5	3.9	4.4	5.9	17.7	2008	4.0	4.1	4.3	5.3	17.6
2003	3.6	3.9	4.6	5.3	17.4	2009	3.7	3.9	4.0	5.3	16.9
2004	3.6	4.0	4.5	5.0	17.0	2010[1]	3.5	3.6	4.1	5.2	16.4
2005	3.6	3.9	4.2	5.1	16.7	2011[2]	3.5	3.7	3.7		15.8

[1] Preliminary.   [2] Estimate.   *Source: Economic Research Service, U.S. Department of Agriculture (ERS-USDA)*

Storage Stocks of Turkeys (Frozen) in the United States on First of Month   In Millions of Pounds

Year	Jan.	Feb.	Mar.	Apr.	May	June	July	Aug.	Sept.	Oct.	Nov.	Dec.
2001	241.3	291.4	333.5	355.8	392.6	456.0	506.7	534.2	545.3	542.0	497.9	260.0
2002	240.5	327.1	413.2	457.6	515.2	578.2	644.1	706.2	685.6	672.4	624.9	334.3
2003	333.0	451.9	492.7	549.3	573.5	658.8	718.2	722.5	706.5	647.5	582.7	350.7
2004	354.0	420.5	471.7	504.6	548.8	571.1	597.6	599.6	600.2	527.4	472.3	294.9
2005	288.4	332.9	379.4	414.2	440.1	465.9	506.3	518.9	523.1	477.8	417.6	194.7
2006	206.2	260.5	315.7	377.7	423.7	466.5	507.5	512.2	500.3	464.2	404.2	214.5
2007	218.4	293.4	312.9	346.8	360.2	398.0	448.4	503.5	524.4	504.9	417.0	206.9
2008	260.6	327.6	416.7	428.1	491.3	522.4	562.7	620.7	629.2	621.5	578.0	360.4
2009	396.1	446.2	462.4	513.4	571.7	585.7	594.7	641.1	653.5	613.9	517.5	244.5
2010[1]	261.8	302.1	342.4	379.7	422.1	461.8	507.2	501.5	502.2	473.7	410.2	174.1

[1] Preliminary.   Source: Economic Research Service, U.S. Department of Agriculture (ERS-USDA)

Average Retail Price of Turkeys (Whole frozen) in the United States   In Cents Per Pound

Year	Jan.	Feb.	Mar.	Apr.	May	June	July	Aug.	Sept.	Oct.	Nov.	Dec.	Average
2001	108.8	112.5	112.7	109.7	109.4	110.9	111.0	113.5	116.2	114.6	98.0	99.5	109.7
2002	102.2	105.1	106.6	104.0	102.5	107.3	108.0	106.8	106.6	111.7	103.8	98.8	105.3
2003	106.6	105.8	105.5	100.1	106.0	110.6	113.4	116.2	116.7	111.2	100.6	105.4	108.2
2004	108.4	109.4	113.4	108.4	109.0	111.7	112.9	114.2	108.8	112.3	99.6	100.3	109.0
2005	105.8	106.3	106.1	105.8	106.9	108.0	106.6	106.3	112.1	113.7	102.3	106.6	107.2
2006	106.9	119.7	120.9	111.1	108.4	112.8	113.0	110.6	115.1	114.9	97.3	99.1	110.8
2007	110.3	113.6	107.9	108.1	114.6	122.3	122.2	122.9	121.6	124.1	111.3	101.0	115.0
2008	120.7	123.0	115.1	117.0	125.8	123.8	127.0	128.8	132.0	122.2	130.9	133.2	125.0
2009	136.5	136.9	134.7	135.4	136.6	141.0	144.5	146.1	145.4	148.0	133.6	136.5	139.6
2010[1]	139.8	137.5	142.5	147.9	146.4	147.4	155.4	152.1	156.6	167.7	140.7	138.0	147.7

[1] Preliminary.   *Source: Economic Research Service, U.S. Department of Agriculture (ERS-USDA)*

Average Retail-to-Consumer Price Spread of Turkeys (Whole) in the United States   In Cents Per Pound

Year	Jan.	Feb.	Mar.	Apr.	May	June	July	Aug.	Sept.	Oct.	Nov.	Dec.	Average
2001	39.5	43.3	42.5	39.1	37.7	38.7	38.6	40.5	41.0	35.6	18.7	27.0	36.9
2002	34.2	37.9	40.7	38.3	32.9	35.9	35.9	34.9	35.4	40.2	29.8	24.6	35.1
2003	38.4	37.6	36.8	31.2	38.1	42.9	47.1	50.0	47.2	37.8	25.1	33.2	38.8
2004	39.4	40.4	42.5	35.0	33.5	33.9	33.3	32.5	25.7	26.9	14.0	18.0	31.3
2005	31.3	33.4	33.3	31.5	30.9	29.4	25.6	22.4	24.1	22.9	8.7	16.8	25.9
2006	29.4	44.5	44.8	32.8	28.6	30.8	29.6	22.9	21.5	9.3	-11.3	15.9	24.9
2007	33.7	34.3	27.2	25.2	28.7	30.9	26.5	24.6	19.7	20.0	7.4	9.8	24.0
2008	38.0	37.5	23.7	21.6	27.3	23.4	25.1	23.0	23.4	18.0	33.9	48.8	28.6
2009						51.0	53.9	56.0	56.2	56.3	39.4	43.7	50.9
2010[1]	55.6	50.6	51.9	55.5	52.2			42.8	42.9	49.3	22.7	28.8	45.2

[1] Preliminary.   *Source: Economic Research Service, U.S. Department of Agriculture (ERS-USDA)*

Uranium

Uranium (symbol U) is a chemically reactive, radioactive, steel-gray, metallic element and is the main fuel used in nuclear reactors. Uranium is the heaviest of all the natural elements. Traces of uranium have been found in archeological artifacts dating back to 79 AD. Uranium was discovered in pitchblende by German chemist Martin Heinrich Klaproth in 1789. Klaproth named it uranium after the recently discovered planet Uranus. French physicist Antoine Henri Becquerel discovered the radioactive properties of uranium in 1896 when he produced an image on a photographic plate covered with a light-absorbing substance. Following Becquerel's experiments, investigations of radioactivity led to the discovery of radium and to new concepts of atomic organization.

The principal use for uranium is fuel in nuclear power plants. Demand for uranium concentrates is directly linked to the level of electricity generated by nuclear power plants. Uranium ores are widely distributed throughout the world and are primarily found in Canada, DRC (formerly Zaire), and the U.S.. Uranium is obtained from primary mine production and secondary sources. Two Canadian companies are the primary producers of uranium from deposits in the Athabasca Basin of northern Saskatchewan. Specifically, the companies Cameco accounted for 19% of global mine production in 2000 and Cogema Resources accounted for 15% of world production. Secondary sources of uranium include excess inventories from utilities and other fuel cycle participants, used reactor fuel, and dismantled Russian nuclear weapons.

Prices – The average price of delivered uranium in 2009 (the latest data available) fell by -0.04% yr/yr to $45.86 per pound, down slightly from the 2008 record high of $45.88 per pound. The 2001 price of $10.15 was the record low for the data series that goes back to 1981.

Supply – World production of uranium oxide (U308) concentrate in 2003 (the latest data available) rose +7.3% yr/yr to a 13-year high of 56,552 short tons, up from 2002's production of 52,709 short tons. The world's largest uranium producers in 2003 were Canada with 17,050 short tons of production in 2003 (30% of world production), the U.S. with 10,200 short tons of production (18% of world production), and Australia with 9,326 short tons of production (16% of world production).

U.S. uranium production in 2003 rose +64.4% yr/yr to a 20-year high of 10,200 short tons, up sharply from the record low of 1,315 short tons in 2001. U.S. production had reached a peak of 21,850 short tons in 1980 and production had fallen steadily to the record low in 2001, which was only 6% of the record level of production. In the last two years production has increased significantly.

Trade – U.S. imports of uranium in 2008 (latest data available) rose +5.6% yr/yr to 57.100 million pounds. The record high of 66.100 million pounds was posted in 2004. The U.S. is being forced to import more uranium as domestic production steadily declines. U.S. exports of uranium in 2008 rose +16.2% yr/yr to 17.200 million pounds, which if still below the record high of 20.500 million pounds posted in 2005.

World Production of Uranium Oxide (U₃O₈) Concentrate   In Short Tons (Uranium Content)

Year	Australia	Canada	China	Czech Rep. & Slovakia	France	Gabon	Germany	Namibia	Niger	South Africa	United States	Ex-USSR	World Total
1994	3,050	11,950	----	----	1,700	750	----	2,500	3,800	2,250	1,950	----	41,750
1995	4,900	13,600	----	----	1,250	800	----	2,600	3,750	1,850	3,050	----	43,050
1996	6,450	15,250	----	----	1,200	750	----	3,150	4,300	2,200	3,150	----	46,650
1997	7,150	15,650	----	----	940	600	----	3,770	4,500	1,065	2,900	----	46,550
1998	6,350	14,200	----	----	660	950	----	3,590	4,850	1,250	2,435	----	44,110
1999	7,875	10,680	----	----	450	380	----	3,495	3,790	1,195	2,325	----	39,640
2000	9,830	13,875	655	795	525	----	45	2,430	3,270	1,305	1,890	655	43,475
2001	10,035	16,270	650	595	195	----	----	2,910	3,795	1,135	1,315	1,050	47,395
2002[1]	10,857	17,153	W	0	----	W	W	1,082	W	764	6,206	W	52,709
2003[2]	9,326	17,050	W	W	----	0	0	1,034	0	1,438	10,200	W	56,552

[1] Preliminary.   [2] Estimate.   W = Withheld.   *Source: American Bureau of Metal Statistics, Inc. (ABMS)*

Commercial and U.S. Government Stocks of Uranium, End of Year   In Millions of Pounds U₃O₈ Equivalent

Year	Utility — Natural Uranium	Utility — Enriched Uranium[1]	Domestic Supplier — Natural Uranium	Domestic Supplier — Enriched Uranium[1]	Total Commercial Stocks	DOE Owned & USEC Held — Natural Uranium	DOE Owned & USEC Held — Enriched Uranium[1]
2000	36.0	18.9	12.6	43.8	111.3	53.1	----
2001	34.4	21.2	9.2	39.0	103.8	53.1	----
2002	31.0	22.4	15.0	32.9	102.1	51.8	----
2003	22.7	23.0	[2]	39.9	85.5	W	W
2004	27.9	29.8	[2]	37.5	95.2	W	W
2005	45.3	19.4	[2]	29.1	93.8	W	W
2006	54.3	23.2	[2]	29.1	106.6	W	W
2007	55.9	25.3	[2]	31.2	112.4	W	W
2008	58.8	24.2	[2]	27.0	110.0	W	W
2009	55.8	27.7	[2]	26.8	110.3	W	W

[1] Includes amount reported as UF₆ at enrichment suppliers.   [2] Included in Enriched beginning 2003.   DOE = Department of Energy
USEC = U.S. Energy Commission   *Source: Energy Information Administration, U.S. Department of Energy (EIA-DOE)*

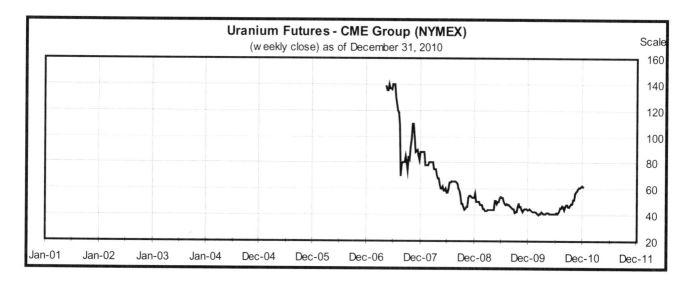

Uranium Futures - CME Group (NYMEX)
(weekly close) as of December 31, 2010

Reported Average Price Settlements for Purchases by U.S. Utilities and Domestic Suppliers In Dollars Per Pound

Year of Delivery	Contract Price	Market Price[1]	Price & Cost Floor	Total	Contract & Market	Year of Delivery	Contract Price	Market Price[1]	Price & Cost Floor	Total	Contract & Market
	---------- Averages of Reported Prices ----------						---------- Averages of Reported Prices ----------				
2000	12.31	9.11	----	11.04	----	2005	----	----	----	14.36	----
2001	11.72	8.04	----	10.15	----	2006	----	----	----	18.61	----
2002	10.73	9.79	----	10.36	----	2007	----	----	----	32.78	----
2003	----	----	----	10.81	----	2008	----	----	----	45.88	----
2004	----	----	----	12.61	----	2009	----	----	----	45.86	----

[1] No floor.   Note: Price excludes uranium delivered under litigation settlements. Price is given in year-of-delivery dollars.   *Source: Energy Information Administration, U.S. Department of Energy (EIA-DOE)*

Uranium Industry Statistics in the United States   In Millions of Pounds U_3O_8

Year	Production Mine	Concent-rate	Concent-rate Ship-ments	Exploration	Mining	Milling	Pro-cessing	Total[1]	Deliveries to U.S. Utilities[2]	Avg Price Delivered Uranium $/lb U_3O_8	Imports	Avg Price Delivered Uranium Imports $/lb U_3O_8	Exports
2003	2.2	2.000	1.600	W	W	W	W	321			53.0	10.59	13.2
2004	2.5	2.300	2.300	18	108	W	W	420					
2005	3.0	2.700	2.700	79	149	142	154	648					
2006	4.7	4.100	3.800	188	121	W	W	755					
2007	4.5	4.500	4.000	375	378	107	216	1,231					

[1] From suppliers under domestic purchases.   *Source: Energy Information Administration, U.S. Department of Energy (EIA-DOE)*

Volume of Trading of Uranium Futures in New York   In Contracts

Year	Jan.	Feb.	Mar.	Apr.	May	June	July	Aug.	Sept.	Oct.	Nov.	Dec.	Total
2007	----	----	----	----	220	50	38	372	164	116	250	58	1,268
2008	157	22	719	617	511	14	1,617	10	7,553	2,000	30	41	13,291
2009	408	40	1,400	16	1	600	1,300	400	403	0	1,581	0	6,149
2010	152	2	101	2,031	4,024	1,743	4,728	330	750	2,933	7,619	1,684	26,097

Contract size = 250 pounds of U308.   *Source: CME Group; New York Mercantile Exchange (NYMEX)*

Average Open Interest of Uranium Futures in New York   In Contracts

Year	Jan.	Feb.	Mar.	Apr.	May	June	July	Aug.	Sept.	Oct.	Nov.	Dec.
2007	----	----	----	----	68	81	95	362	463	460	675	696
2008	552	508	1,158	1,479	1,949	1,912	2,200	2,206	2,644	2,604	2,544	2,343
2009	1,951	1,951	2,651	2,666	2,665	2,865	3,465	3,865	3,568	3,568	3,395	3,395
2010	3,277	3,279	2,980	4,710	8,013	9,753	11,742	11,649	12,274	13,534	15,154	15,622

Contract size = 250 pounds of U308.   *Source: CME Group; New York Mercantile Exchange (NYMEX)*

Vanadium

Vanadium (symbol V) is a silvery-white, soft, ductile, metallic element. Discovered in 1801, but mistaken for chromium, vanadium was rediscovered in 1830 by Swedish chemist Nils Sefstrom, who named the element in honor of the Scandinavian goddess Vanadis.

Never found in the pure state, vanadium is found in about 65 different minerals such as carnotite, roscoelite, vanadinite, and patronite, as well as in phosphate rock, certain iron ores, some crude oils, and meteorites. Vanadium is one of the hardest of all metals. It melts at about 1890 degrees Celsius and boils at about 3380 degrees Celsius.

Vanadium has good structural strength and is used as an alloying agent with iron, steel, and titanium. It is used in aerospace applications, transmission gears, photography, as a reducing agent, and as a drying agent in various paints.

Prices – The price of vanadium in 2009 fell sharply by -59.3% to $6.00 per pound and moving further below the record high of $16.28 per pound in 2005.

Supply – Virtually all (99%) of vanadium is produced from ores, concentrates, and slag, with the remainder coming from petroleum residues, ash, and spent catalysts.

World production in 2009 from ore, concentrates and slag fell -4.1% to 53,500 metric tons. World production of all vanadium in 2008 (latest data available) fell -4.1% yr/yr to 54,100 metric tons.

The world's largest producer of vanadium from ores, concentrates and slag is China with 21,000 metric tons of production in 2009 which was 39% of total world production. The two other major producers are South Africa with 17,000 metric tons of production in 2009, which was 32% of world production, and Russia with 14,500 metric tons of production which was 27% of world production. Production in Russia and South Africa has been relatively stable in recent years, while China's production grew sharply in the late 1990s. China's production level of 21,000 metric tons in 2009 is a new record high and almost four times the levels seen in the early 1990s.

Trade – U.S. exports of vanadium in 2009 were in the forms of oxides & hydroxides (270 metric tons, -74.0% yr/yr), ferro-vanadium (740 metric tons, +163.4%), and vanadium pent-oxide, anhydride (360 metric tons, +44.6%). U.S. imports of vanadium in 2009 were in the forms of vanadium pent-oxide, anhydride (1,120 metric tons, -69.7% yr/yr); ferro-vanadium (353 metric tons, -87.0% yr/yr); ore, slag and residues (791 metric tons), -23.9% yr/yr; and oxides & hydroxides (25 metric tons, -82.6% yr/yr).

World Production of Vanadium — In Metric Tons (Contained Vanadium)

							From Petroleum Residues Ash, Spent Catalysts			
	-------------------------- From Ores, Concentrates and Slag ----------------------------						----------- Ash, Spent Catalysts -----------			World
Year	Australia	China[3]	Kazak-hstan	Russia	South Africa	Total[4]	Japan[5]	United States[6]	Total	Total
2005	100	17,000	1,000	15,100	22,604	55,800	560	----	560	56,400
2006	----	17,500	1,000	15,100	23,780	57,400	560	----	560	57,900
2007	----	19,000	1,000	14,500	23,486	58,000	560	----	560	58,500
2008	----	20,000	1,000	14,500	20,295	55,800	560	----	560	56,400
2009[1]	----	21,000	1,000	14,500	17,000	53,500	560	----	560	54,100
2010[2]	----	23,000	1,000	14,000	18,000	56,000				

[1] Preliminary. [2] Estimate. [3] In vanadiferous slag product. [4] Excludes U.S. production. [5] In vanadium pentoxide product. [6] In vanadium pentoxide and ferrovanadium products. Source: U.S. Geological Survey (USGS)

Salient Statistics of Vanadium in the United States — In Metric Tons (Contained Vanadium)

	Con-sumer & Producer Stocks, Dec. 31	-------- Vanadium Consumption by Uses in the U.S. ---------								-------- Exports ---------			---------------- Imports ----------------			
Year		Tool Steel	Cast Irons	High Strength, Low Alloy	Stainless & Heat Resisting	Super-alloys	Carbon	Full Alloy	Total	Average $ Per Lb. V₂O₅	Vanadium Pent-oxide Anhydride	Oxides & Hydr-oxides	Ferro-Vana-dium	Ores, Slag, Residues	Vanadium Pent-oxide Anhydride	Oxides & Hydr-oxides	Ferro-Vana-dium
2005	371	402	W	974	60	36	1,170	1,010	3,910	16.28	254	899	505	1,070	1,370	186	712
2006	330	323	W	1,020	61	40	1,210	1,030	4,030	7.86	341	832	389	637	1,920	129	685
2007	323	379	W	1,560	61	44	1,190	1,380	4,970	7.40	327	626	154	1,000	2,390	42	1,440
2008	334	152	W	W	116	39	1,010	2,030	5,170	12.92	249	1,040	281	1,040	3,700	144	2,720
2009[1]	309	417	W	1,540	119	13	610	1,880	5,000	5.43	401	506	672	791	1,120	25	353
2010[2]	154	W	W	W	120	5	663	1,970	5,100	6.40	180	810	460	490	2,500	12	1,080

[1] Preliminary. [2] Estimate. W = Withheld. Source: U.S. Geological Survey (USGS)

Average Price of Vanadium Pentoxide — In Dollars Per Pound

Year	Jan.	Feb.	Mar.	Apr.	May	June	July	Aug.	Sept.	Oct.	Nov.	Dec.	Average
2005	9.65	10.24	13.75	15.00	20.36	26.16	19.96	11.63	11.10	13.74	13.75	11.00	14.70
2006	8.73	9.11	8.78	7.92	8.15	8.08	7.40	7.07	7.85	7.70	7.27	6.70	7.90
2007	6.21	6.34	7.22	8.10	7.98	7.67	7.48	7.36	7.64	7.74	7.67	7.40	7.40
2008	8.03	13.11	15.80	14.60	15.85	17.61	15.65	16.39	15.23	12.83	9.85	8.66	13.63
2009	6.50	6.05	5.66	4.75	3.73	4.78	5.25	6.11	6.93	6.69	6.13	6.13	5.73
2010	6.97	7.25	7.72	8.00	7.85	6.96	6.23	6.41	6.75	6.63	6.63	6.63	7.00

Source: American Metal Market (AMM)

Vegetables

Vegetables are the edible products of herbaceous plants, which are plants with soft stems. Vegetables are grouped according to the edible part of each plant including leaves (e.g., lettuce), stalks (celery), roots (carrot), tubers (potato), bulbs (onion), fruits (tomato), seeds (pea), and flowers (broccoli). Each of these groups contributes to the human diet in its own way. Fleshy roots are high in energy value and good sources of the vitamin B group, seeds are relatively high in carbohydrates and proteins, while leaves, stalks, and fruits are excellent sources of minerals, vitamins, water, and roughage. Vegetables are an important food for the maintenance of health and prevention of disease. Higher intakes of vegetables have been shown to lower the risks of cancer and coronary heart disease.

Vegetables are best consumed fresh in their raw state in order to derive the maximum benefits from their nutrients. While canned and frozen vegetables are often thought to be inferior to fresh vegetables, they are sometimes nutritionally superior to fresh produce because they are usually processed immediately after harvest when nutrient content is at its peak. When cooking vegetables, aluminum utensils should not be used, because aluminum is a soft metal that is affected by food acids and alkalis. Scientific evidence shows that tiny particles of aluminum from foods cooked in aluminum utensils enter the stomach and can injure the sensitive lining of the stomach.

Prices – The monthly average index of fresh vegetable prices received by growers in the U.S. in 2010 rose by +14.6% to 194.1, a new record high.

Demand – The leading vegetable in terms of U.S. per capita consumption in 2010 was the potato with 121.0 pounds of consumption. Runner-up vegetables were tomatoes (92.8 pounds), sweet corn (24.6 pounds), lettuce (30.4 pounds), and onions (22.6 pounds). Total U.S. per capita vegetable consumption in 2010 fell -0.1% to 296.8 pounds.

Index of Prices Received by Growers for Commercial Vegetables[2] in the United States   (1990-92=100)

Year	Jan.	Feb.	Mar.	Apr.	May	June	July	Aug.	Sept.	Oct.	Nov.	Dec.	Average
2005	93	117	165	181	135	138	112	118	127	113	113	152	130
2006	128	115	133	151	156	131	119	152	160	123	119	150	136
2007	177	165	192	181	144	133	126	146	155	196	139	138	158
2008	138	118	134	162	154	153	143	143	174	178	154	155	151
2009	173	139	151	176	141	155	135	140	135	167	216	208	161
2010[1]	157	150	215	203	187	164	161	162	156	151	191	166	172

[1] Preliminary.   [2] Includes fresh and processing vegetables.   Not seasonally adjusted.   *Source: National Agricultural Statistics Service, U.S. Department of Agriculture (NASS-USDA)*

Index of Prices Received by Growers for Fresh Vegetables in the United States   (1990-92=100)

Year	Jan.	Feb.	Mar.	Apr.	May	June	July	Aug.	Sept.	Oct.	Nov.	Dec.	Average
2005	122.0	152.8	168.5	174.7	144.2	160.0	126.8	132.3	153.3	144.0	163.1	200.8	153.5
2006	207.6	138.8	137.6	174.4	147.9	128.7	134.1	179.5	193.1	167.7	138.3	178.4	160.5
2007	175.3	190.3	222.4	222.5	142.1	145.4	146.0	137.8	162.7	218.3	177.4	204.5	178.7
2008	200.2	158.3	194.1	179.3	170.7	191.7	168.3	146.1	158.7	185.1	200.3	155.9	175.7
2009	179.8	163.6	167.4	182.3	134.1	182.5	149.8	144.3	140.4	180.6	197.8	210.4	169.4
2010[1]	178.6	190.6	310.4	274.1	215.4	158.6	177.1	157.3	171.2	153.7	156.0	186.7	194.1

[1] Preliminary.   Not seasonally adjusted.   *Source: National Agricultural Statistics Service, U.S. Department of Agriculture (NASS-USDA)*

Producer Price Index of Canned[2] Processed Vegetables in the United States   (1982 = 100)

Year	Jan.	Feb.	Mar.	Apr.	May	June	July	Aug.	Sept.	Oct.	Nov.	Dec.	Average
2005	135.7	135.9	136.1	136.3	137.6	137.6	137.7	137.7	137.5	137.7	137.6	138.0	137.1
2006	138.0	136.8	137.1	137.3	138.8	140.2	140.0	140.5	141.4	141.5	142.2	142.2	139.7
2007	142.8	142.9	143.1	143.3	143.5	143.6	143.1	143.1	144.0	143.9	144.2	144.6	143.5
2008	147.8	148.4	149.6	151.2	150.2	151.3	153.3	158.6	162.5	163.0	164.2	167.8	155.7
2009	168.9	169.0	170.5	170.7	171.0	171.1	171.3	170.9	170.6	170.7	169.9	169.2	170.3
2010[1]	169.8	167.3	167.2	167.0	166.7	166.0	164.1	164.6	161.6	161.1	162.2	161.5	164.9

[1] Preliminary.   [2] Includes canned vegetables and juices, including hominy and mushrooms.   Not seasonally adjusted.   *Source: Bureau of Labor Statistics, U.S. Department of Labor (BLS)*

Producer Price Index of Frozen Processed Vegetables in the United States   (1982 = 100)

Year	Jan.	Feb.	Mar.	Apr.	May	June	July	Aug.	Sept.	Oct.	Nov.	Dec.	Average
2005	137.3	137.3	137.4	137.5	137.5	137.4	137.2	136.8	136.6	136.7	136.1	136.4	137.0
2006	137.3	137.7	138.7	138.6	138.8	139.5	139.4	139.3	139.9	142.0	142.7	142.6	139.7
2007	144.0	144.0	144.0	145.2	145.9	146.7	148.2	149.3	149.9	151.5	152.5	153.2	147.9
2008	153.3	153.8	155.6	156.5	156.7	157.1	158.8	161.1	163.9	170.6	172.7	177.9	161.5
2009	176.5	178.1	178.5	178.1	178.1	178.5	178.1	177.4	179.3	180.3	180.4	180.1	178.6
2010[1]	179.9	180.3	180.8	180.2	180.5	180.3	179.6	179.8	179.0	174.9	175.3	175.5	178.8

[1] Preliminary.   Not seasonally adjusted.   *Source: Bureau of Labor Statistics, U.S. Department of Labor (BLS)*

Per Capita Use of Selected Commercially Produced Fresh and Processing Vegetables and Melons in the United States   In Pounds, farm weight basis

Crop	2002	2003	2004	2005	2006	2007	2008	2009	2010[10]	2011[11]
Asparagus, All	1.2	1.3	1.4	1.4	1.4	1.4	1.5	1.5	1.6	1.6
Fresh	1.0	1.0	1.1	1.1	1.1	1.2	1.2	1.3	1.3	1.4
Canning	0.2	0.2	0.2	0.2	0.2	0.1	0.2	0.2	0.2	0.1
Freezing	0.1	0.1	0.1	0.1	0.1	0.1	0.1	0.1	0.1	0.1
Snap beans, All	7.2	7.5	7.6	7.6	7.8	7.8	7.4	7.1	7.2	7.1
Fresh	2.1	2.0	1.9	1.8	2.1	2.2	2.0	1.6	1.6	1.9
Canning	3.4	3.7	3.7	4.0	3.9	3.5	3.3	3.6	3.7	3.3
Freezing	1.8	1.9	1.9	1.8	1.9	2.1	2.1	1.9	1.9	1.9
Broccoli, All [1]	7.5	7.9	8.0	8.1	8.0	8.3	8.7	8.6	8.5	8.6
Fresh	5.4	5.4	5.3	5.3	5.8	5.6	6.0	6.1	6.0	6.1
Freezing	2.1	2.6	2.7	2.7	2.3	2.7	2.7	2.5	2.5	2.5
Cabbage, All	9.5	8.5	9.1	9.0	9.0	9.0	9.0	8.2	7.9	8.2
Fresh	8.3	7.4	8.0	7.8	7.8	8.0	8.1	7.3	7.1	7.3
Canning (kraut)	1.2	1.1	1.1	1.2	1.2	1.0	0.9	0.9	0.8	0.8
Carrots, All [2]	11.5	11.9	11.8	11.8	11.2	10.5	10.6	9.6	10.1	10.0
Fresh	8.4	8.8	8.7	8.7	8.1	8.1	8.1	7.4	7.9	7.7
Canning	1.0	1.1	1.1	1.1	1.0	0.9	1.0	0.8	0.9	0.7
Freezing	2.1	2.0	2.0	2.0	2.1	1.5	1.5	1.4	1.4	1.5
Cauliflower, All [1]	1.7	1.9	1.9	2.1	2.1	2.0	2.0	1.9	1.9	1.7
Fresh	1.4	1.6	1.6	1.8	1.7	1.7	1.6	1.5	1.5	1.4
Freezing	0.3	0.4	0.4	0.4	0.4	0.4	0.4	0.4	0.4	0.4
Celery	6.3	6.3	6.2	5.9	6.1	6.3	6.2	6.1	6.0	6.2
Sweet Corn, All [3]	26.1	26.5	26.2	26.7	26.1	26.1	24.3	25.5	26.0	24.6
Fresh	9.0	9.2	9.0	8.7	8.3	9.2	9.1	9.0	9.1	9.1
Canning	7.8	8.3	8.2	8.6	8.4	6.9	6.7	7.6	7.4	6.8
Freezing	9.3	9.0	9.1	9.5	9.4	10.0	8.4	8.8	9.6	8.6
Cucumbers, All	12.0	10.6	11.3	10.0	9.1	10.2	9.9	11.6	10.7	10.1
Fresh	6.6	6.2	6.4	6.2	6.2	6.4	6.4	6.6	6.7	7.1
Pickling	5.4	4.5	4.9	3.8	3.0	3.7	3.5	5.0	4.0	3.0
Melons	27.9	27.1	25.4	25.6	26.9	26.4	26.7	26.8	27.1	25.8
Watermelon	14.0	13.5	13.0	13.6	15.1	14.4	15.6	15.3	15.6	15.1
Cantaloupe	11.1	10.8	9.8	9.6	9.3	9.6	8.9	9.3	9.3	8.5
Honeydew	2.2	2.2	2.1	1.9	1.9	1.8	1.7	1.6	1.7	1.6
Lettuce, All	32.1	33.1	33.2	30.6	32.0	29.9	27.3	28.1	28.2	27.1
Head lettuce	22.5	22.2	21.3	20.9	20.1	18.4	16.9	17.1	17.1	16.1
Romaine & Leaf	9.6	10.8	12.0	9.7	12.0	11.5	10.4	11.0	11.2	10.9
Onions, All	20.4	21.4	23.4	22.0	21.7	22.6	22.4	21.6	21.3	21.3
Fresh	19.3	19.5	21.9	20.9	19.9	21.6	20.9	19.7	20.0	19.7
Dehydrating	1.1	1.8	1.5	1.1	1.8	1.0	1.5	1.9	1.3	1.5
Green Peas, All [4]	2.8	3.1	2.8	2.7	2.7	3.0	2.9	2.9	3.0	2.7
Canning	1.1	1.3	1.2	1.0	1.1	1.1	1.1	1.2	1.2	1.1
Freezing	1.7	1.8	1.6	1.6	1.6	1.8	1.8	1.7	1.7	1.6
Peppers, All	14.1	14.0	14.8	15.3	15.8	15.2	15.8	16.0	15.4	16.6
Bell Peppers, All	8.3	8.4	8.6	9.2	9.5	9.4	9.6	9.4	9.0	10.0
Chile Peppers, All	5.8	5.6	6.1	6.1	6.4	5.9	6.2	6.6	6.4	6.6
Tomatoes, All	89.7	89.3	90.5	93.9	84.3	87.9	85.6	89.5	90.8	93.8
Fresh	20.3	19.4	20.0	20.2	19.8	19.2	18.5	19.3	18.7	21.6
Canning	69.4	69.9	70.5	73.7	64.5	68.7	67.1	70.2	72.2	72.2
Other, Fresh [5]	18.3	18.7	19.4	20.1	20.0	19.1	18.7	17.8	18.5	18.6
Other, Canning [6]	2.3	2.3	2.7	2.9	2.6	2.6	2.5	2.3	2.4	2.4
Other, Freezing [7]	4.3	3.9	3.8	4.1	4.1	4.1	4.0	4.3	4.3	4.1
Subtotal, All [8]	294.9	295.3	299.6	299.5	290.8	292.3	285.4	289.3	290.9	290.2
Fresh	174.6	173.9	176.8	173.7	175.1	174.2	170.3	168.0	168.6	171.0
Canning	97.5	98.0	99.7	102.6	92.1	94.4	92.5	98.4	99.2	97.1
Freezing	21.7	21.6	21.5	22.1	21.8	22.6	21.1	21.0	21.8	20.6
Potatoes, All	131.9	137.9	134.6	125.4	123.7	124.4	118.3	113.1	112.8	109.9
Fresh	44.3	46.8	45.8	41.3	38.6	38.7	37.8	36.4	35.6	33.6
Processing	87.6	91.2	88.8	84.1	85.1	85.7	80.5	76.7	77.2	76.3
Sweet Potatoes	3.8	4.7	4.6	4.5	4.6	5.1	5.0	5.3	6.3	6.2
Mushrooms	4.1	4.1	4.2	3.9	4.0	3.9	3.6	3.6	3.7	3.6
Dry Peas & Lentils [9]	0.8	0.6	0.7	0.8	1.2	0.7	0.4	0.8	0.8	0.7
Dry Edible Beans	6.8	6.7	6.0	6.1	6.2	6.7	6.6	6.1	7.0	6.8
Total, All Items	442.2	449.3	449.6	440.2	430.5	433.0	419.2	418.2	421.4	417.5

[1] All production for processing broccoli and cauliflower is for freezing.   [2] Industry allocation suggests that 27 percent of processing carrot production is for canning and 73 percent is for freezing.   [3] On-cob basis.   [4] In-shell basis.   [5] Includes artichokes, brussels sprouts, eggplant, endive/escarole, garlic, radishes, green limas, squash, and spinach. In 2000, okra, pumpkins, kale, collards, turnip greens and mustard greens added.   [6] Includes beets, green limas (1992-2003), spinach, and miscellaneous imports (1990-2001).   [7] Includes green limas, spinach, and miscellaneous freezing vegetables.   [8] Fresh, canning, and freezing data do not sum to the total because onions for dehydrating are included in the total.   [9] Production from new areas in upper midwest added in 1998. A portion of this is likely for feed use.   [10] Preliminary.   [11] Forecast.   NA = Not available.   Source: Economic Research Service, U.S. Department of Agriculture (ERS-USDA)

VEGETABLES

Average Price Received by Growers for Broccoli in the United States   In Dollars Per Cwt

Year	Jan.	Feb.	Mar.	Apr.	May	June	July	Aug.	Sept.	Oct.	Nov.	Dec.	Season Average
2003	25.20	40.90	28.10	27.10	29.70	24.60	27.00	29.80	49.10	38.90	48.00	40.00	32.70
2004	33.60	28.50	21.60	24.00	27.20	28.70	24.20	29.70	57.00	43.90	44.20	45.40	33.20
2005	22.60	33.30	42.60	39.80	22.40	39.70	22.40	30.50	27.70	22.40	20.90	34.10	28.50
2006	32.50	23.80	27.60	32.40	29.00	51.10	26.20	56.90	39.40	24.60	27.50	53.10	33.70
2007	69.80	25.40	27.60	36.90	26.70	24.80	28.80	38.20	41.80	61.00	38.10	40.70	36.70
2008	47.90	24.40	30.80	52.10	25.20	29.60	26.70	26.60	41.10	57.50	41.20	33.70	36.20
2009	44.60	29.50	46.90	41.90	32.80	31.00	26.50	29.70	31.60	64.60	57.10	53.50	39.80
2010[1]	26.50	26.70	49.50	35.40	43.50	34.50	29.30	25.70	33.30	30.40	55.40	66.60	35.40

[1]Preliminary.   *Source: National Agricultural Statistics Service, U.S. Department of Agriculture (NASS-USDA)*

Average Price Received by Growers for Carrots in the United States   In Dollars Per Cwt

Year	Jan.	Feb.	Mar.	Apr.	May	June	July	Aug.	Sept.	Oct.	Nov.	Dec.	Season Average
2003	19.30	19.10	18.70	19.40	19.90	20.00	19.90	20.50	19.80	19.10	21.60	24.30	19.00
2004	24.50	24.90	24.60	24.20	24.90	22.50	20.20	18.00	16.70	16.40	17.20	18.00	20.20
2005	20.30	21.00	21.00	21.10	21.20	21.30	21.80	21.40	20.00	21.40	23.10	22.00	20.90
2006	21.40	21.50	21.50	21.50	20.80	21.40	21.50	22.40	19.30	19.80	20.20	19.10	20.60
2007	21.00	28.10	28.30	29.60	32.00	25.90	19.70	17.10	16.10	15.80	15.80	16.20	22.10
2008	16.20	25.90	25.90	25.50	32.00	25.60	25.60	25.60	25.30	25.20	24.70	25.20	24.50
2009	25.20	25.20	25.20	25.20	25.50	25.80	25.60	24.00	25.20	25.30	27.20	27.80	25.20
2010[1]	28.50	23.90	27.50	27.40	27.40	26.20	27.10	27.10	26.70	26.80	27.60	33.00	26.20

[1]Preliminary.   *Source: National Agricultural Statistics Service, U.S. Department of Agriculture (NASS-USDA)*

Average Price Received by Growers for Cauliflower in the United States   In Dollars Per Cwt

Year	Jan.	Feb.	Mar.	Apr.	May	June	July	Aug.	Sept.	Oct.	Nov.	Dec.	Season Average
2003	24.60	30.70	30.80	20.70	39.50	46.30	27.60	25.30	40.30	25.80	57.00	75.50	35.10
2004	27.30	42.20	24.20	23.50	28.80	46.20	27.60	26.30	31.10	32.20	43.80	54.40	30.80
2005	27.70	38.20	50.60	36.70	29.70	38.10	25.60	31.50	28.50	19.70	25.50	43.90	30.30
2006	33.10	26.40	31.40	32.80	29.00	51.10	26.20	56.90	39.40	24.60	34.80	41.60	32.30
2007	45.70	29.40	51.40	51.60	24.90	30.00	22.30	27.90	27.20	46.20	26.60	52.40	34.40
2008	51.80	30.00	41.70	63.80	24.90	53.90	38.20	43.20	29.50	48.50	29.50	43.90	40.70
2009	68.20	30.00	51.30	41.40	46.60	43.50	41.70	31.90	26.90	58.10	54.40	47.10	44.30
2010[1]	33.20	36.70	50.30	58.20	68.60	32.90	31.20	26.30	27.70	31.50	51.90	66.40	39.60

[1]Preliminary.   *Source: National Agricultural Statistics Service, U.S. Department of Agriculture (NASS-USDA)*

Average Price Received by Growers for Celery in the United States   In Dollars Per Cwt

Year	Jan.	Feb.	Mar.	Apr.	May	June	July	Aug.	Sept.	Oct.	Nov.	Dec.	Season Average
2003	8.29	11.80	12.60	17.00	11.00	9.34	12.80	11.90	13.30	15.90	23.40	14.50	13.40
2004	20.80	24.40	13.90	15.60	15.00	13.80	12.00	10.00	11.90	15.10	18.10	13.40	14.80
2005	12.90	22.90	28.40	20.80	15.50	9.62	10.00	10.80	12.80	12.20	13.10	10.70	13.90
2006	9.64	10.80	14.90	16.60	12.70	17.80	21.00	23.30	27.70	27.10	22.00	20.20	18.20
2007	33.90	58.90	31.90	18.80	18.30	11.60	11.60	9.64	13.80	13.30	18.60	13.50	20.40
2008	16.20	13.20	13.40	14.00	37.40	30.10	22.10	12.40	11.90	17.10	16.90	20.30	18.50
2009	35.10	29.70	15.00	17.40	17.40	11.70	11.30	11.40	12.00	20.90	21.10	38.80	20.10
2010[1]	37.40	21.60	25.70	22.90	20.00	15.80	15.90	14.30	14.60	14.70	14.30	20.20	19.70

[1]Preliminary.   *Source: National Agricultural Statistics Service, U.S. Department of Agriculture (NASS-USDA)*

Average Price Received by Growers for Sweet Corn in the United States   In Dollars Per Cwt

Year	Jan.	Feb.	Mar.	Apr.	May	June	July	Aug.	Sept.	Oct.	Nov.	Dec.	Season Average
2003	29.00	24.00	18.90	14.90	16.60	23.20	21.30	20.10	19.70	23.70	30.70	22.60	19.30
2004	30.80	20.70	20.20	17.60	18.10	22.80	21.80	22.90	24.10	33.50	46.70	36.80	20.80
2005	21.30	28.60	26.10	21.50	18.10	22.60	22.20	20.30	24.70	25.50	37.30	21.20	22.10
2006	36.50	35.00	34.00	27.20	15.40	21.60	21.10	22.70	25.90	21.20	20.00	14.40	23.00
2007	27.40	23.60	30.20	25.60	21.40	17.30	22.20	22.80	23.20	21.40	20.60	34.10	22.70
2008	30.80	23.00	28.60	20.50	21.90	19.90	28.50	27.20	27.10	23.70	30.80	22.20	25.90
2009	24.90	46.40	59.30	32.50	20.80	25.40	34.60	26.40	23.70	23.30	19.80	19.40	29.30
2010[1]	37.80	58.50	69.30	37.60	20.50	16.30	19.60	23.10	25.40	28.00	20.30	31.60	25.70

[1]Preliminary.   *Source: National Agricultural Statistics Service, U.S. Department of Agriculture (NASS-USDA)*

Average Price Received by Growers for Head Lettuce in the United States In Dollars Per Cwt

Year	Jan.	Feb.	Mar.	Apr.	May	June	July	Aug.	Sept.	Oct.	Nov.	Dec.	Season Average
2001	13.60	22.80	15.10	21.60	18.80	12.10	16.40	26.90	26.20	11.50	10.90	10.00	17.90
2002	26.20	44.10	86.40	14.10	10.20	10.60	11.30	14.60	14.30	13.50	11.90	30.00	21.10
2003	12.10	11.80	9.64	12.50	21.20	32.20	11.90	21.50	23.90	26.30	31.70	21.30	18.10
2004	15.40	19.80	10.40	14.80	10.50	13.30	10.70	17.10	15.20	24.10	14.90	15.70	16.90
2005	11.50	11.70	27.90	30.10	13.90	17.30	11.00	13.50	12.70	12.40	9.81	16.60	15.50
2006	10.50	12.00	19.10	22.40	33.70	11.80	12.20	20.70	16.30	11.80	12.50	22.40	16.90
2007	20.80	15.50	29.70	17.80	13.60	17.80	17.30	23.10	29.20	44.40	17.40	16.00	21.70
2008	17.60	13.40	14.70	21.60	15.50	17.70	17.30	17.20	31.90	32.90	18.80	23.50	20.10
2009	28.50	17.80	19.40	27.70	18.20	18.90	16.90	16.70	16.60	27.20	49.60	38.70	22.40
2010[1]	17.30	14.10	21.20	19.00	24.30	25.70	26.00	23.30	17.20	20.20	35.50	17.50	23.80

[1]Preliminary.   Source: National Agricultural Statistics Service, U.S. Department of Agriculture (NASS-USDA)

Average Price Received by Growers for Tomatoes in the United States In Dollars Per Cwt

Year	Jan.	Feb.	Mar.	Apr.	May	June	July	Aug.	Sept.	Oct.	Nov.	Dec.	Season Average
2001	43.80	29.10	56.40	19.00	37.80	28.50	27.40	27.60	23.50	28.60	28.50	25.00	30.00
2002	40.50	26.60	38.50	34.30	29.60	33.00	28.50	25.80	23.70	27.60	40.10	38.00	31.60
2003	47.20	31.70	53.30	30.00	23.70	45.70	37.60	41.00	35.70	30.10	30.50	29.10	37.40
2004	34.50	36.30	42.20	44.20	32.20	21.70	23.40	37.80	38.20	67.90	89.00	47.10	37.60
2005	15.40	40.90	40.70	65.10	49.40	40.00	28.00	26.10	46.10	37.30	36.50	96.80	41.80
2006	79.20	46.50	24.80	34.40	23.30	30.90	25.10	27.80	79.80	53.20	28.10	24.80	43.70
2007	35.60	31.20	26.30	52.60	35.60	29.60	26.70	28.60	33.10	41.60	58.70	81.20	34.80
2008	58.20	45.50	66.10	47.40	48.20	56.80	40.90	29.40	25.60	33.80	64.90	37.90	45.50
2009	29.30	32.70	41.50	45.40	33.20	67.20	31.70	35.90	34.40	40.20	73.70	65.00	40.40
2010[1]	58.90	84.60	114.00	97.80	48.30	24.80	34.30	37.60	40.40	32.40	35.00	37.30	48.10

[1]Preliminary.   Source: National Agricultural Statistics Service, U.S. Department of Agriculture (NASS-USDA)

Frozen Vegetables: January 1 and July 1 Cold Storage Holdings in the United States In Thousands of Pounds

Crop	2006 July 1	2007 Jan. 1	July 1	2008 Jan. 1	July 1	2009 Jan. 1	July 1	2010 Jan. 1	July 1	2011[1] Jan. 1
Asparagus	11,929	6,178	9,952	5,409	9,964	7,368	12,279	9,057	11,127	7,630
Limas, Fordhook	2,368	6,543	2,619	7,442	2,209	3,676	960	2,973	2,622	7,255
Limas, Baby	21,851	41,849	18,367	40,364	16,213	41,020	20,264	58,390	31,238	49,100
Green Beans, Reg. Cut	24,377	183,610	72,177	183,696	70,854	211,997	95,706	176,371	70,842	166,011
Green Beans, Fr. Style	8,388	27,433	9,303	32,284	12,675	29,298	13,140	25,325	13,169	19,028
Broccoli, Spears	32,699	27,628	23,878	24,078	33,587	36,649	37,560	29,456	35,163	20,851
Broccoli, Chopped & Cut	61,769	46,855	40,715	36,422	49,873	45,513	24,864	41,547	48,760	34,885
Brussels sprouts	10,243	21,650	11,535	21,491	10,392	21,049	12,898	20,789	13,813	17,845
Carrots, Diced	64,540	117,159	53,574	128,121	68,556	156,398	95,309	165,191	94,385	159,405
Carrots, Other	97,528	127,449	51,911	142,063	85,955	150,459	99,242	155,247	86,154	150,944
Cauliflower	18,694	38,196	17,768	36,694	20,334	27,564	16,266	27,066	19,977	23,524
Corn, Cut	188,556	475,671	161,547	461,503	172,494	463,724	202,653	584,048	305,686	571,012
Corn, Cob	71,738	281,694	69,152	256,464	78,251	264,562	98,389	252,108	102,824	249,387
Mixed vegetables	50,856	51,925	43,342	43,868	46,341	47,729	54,394	50,129	46,561	38,245
Okra	26,363	31,507	16,638	23,720	21,505	24,115	21,470	29,030	14,933	21,457
Onion Rings	7,532	7,533	8,136	7,428	5,925	6,628	4,306	3,456	5,382	4,955
Onions, Other	38,192	37,386	26,527	32,010	39,190	29,564	26,699	35,511	19,737	32,549
Blackeye Peas	4,080	4,784	3,136	4,394	2,815	2,737	1,519	3,653	2,757	2,764
Green Peas	222,513	230,351	241,116	232,647	198,133	255,471	252,937	275,625	298,995	276,587
Peas and Carrots Mixed	5,422	4,946	4,654	5,090	4,756	5,109	5,258	6,075	7,096	5,992
Spinach	107,607	52,674	70,443	47,467	80,320	42,505	87,057	47,993	96,542	52,103
Squash, Summer/Zucchini	50,704	64,255	49,275	62,534	46,531	56,537	40,733	52,275	39,685	64,783
Southern greens	17,546	14,826	10,741	12,833	14,231	12,632	16,551	11,621	16,742	13,507
Other Vegetables	238,391	323,249	220,569	373,370	275,882	423,684	293,501	408,829	280,686	360,009
Total	1,413,886	2,225,351	1,237,075	2,221,392	1,366,986	2,365,988	1,563,955	2,471,765	1,664,876	2,354,112
Potatoes, French Fries	877,400	758,254	871,947	820,461	947,666	874,095	1,011,186	847,238	899,847	820,872
Potatoes, Other Frozen	230,710	196,566	206,261	191,894	242,365	224,485	233,941	196,607	242,099	198,033
Potatoes, Total	1,108,110	954,820	1,078,208	1,012,355	1,190,031	1,098,580	1,245,127	1,043,845	1,141,946	1,018,905
Grand Total	2,521,996	3,180,171	2,315,283	3,233,747	2,557,017	3,464,568	2,809,082	3,515,610	2,806,822	3,373,017

Wheat

Wheat is a cereal grass, but before cultivation it was a wild grass. It has been grown in temperate regions and cultivated for food since prehistoric times. Wheat is believed to have originated in southwestern Asia. Archeological research indicates that wheat was grown as a crop in the Nile Valley about 5,000 BC. Wheat is not native to the U.S. and was first grown here in 1602 near the Massachusetts coast. The common types of wheat grown in the U.S. are spring and winter wheat. Wheat planted in the spring for summer or autumn harvest is mostly red wheat. Wheat planted in the fall or winter for spring harvest is mostly white wheat. Winter wheat accounts for nearly three-fourths of total U.S. production. Wheat is used mainly as a human food and supplies about 20% of the food calories for the world's population. The primary use for wheat is flour, but it is also used for brewing and distilling, and for making oil, gluten, straw for livestock bedding, livestock feed, hay or silage, newsprint, and other products.

Wheat futures and options are traded on the Mercado a Termino de Buenos Aires (MATBA), Sydney Futures Exchange (SFE), JSE Securities Exchange of South Africa, National Commodity & Derivatives Exchange of India, NYSE-LIFFE exchange in London and Paris, Budapest Stock Exchange (BSE), the Chicago Board of Trade (CBOT), the Kansas City Board of Trade (KCBT), and the Minneapolis Grain Exchange (MGE). The Chicago Board of Trade's wheat futures contract calls for the delivery of soft red wheat (No. 1 and 2), hard red winter wheat (No. 1 and 2), dark northern spring wheat (No. 1 and 2), No.1 northern spring at 3 cents/bushel premium, or No. 2 northern spring at par.

Prices – CBOT wheat prices on the nearest-futures chart traded sideways to lower during the first half of 2010 and posted a 1-1/2 year low of $4.25 a bushel in May 2010. Wheat prices then exploded higher to a 2-year high of $8.41 a bushel in August 2010 after the worst drought in Russia and Eastern Europe since record keeping began 130 years ago prompted Russia to ban grain exports for the rest of the year. Wheat prices quickly fell $2 a bushel into November 2010, though, after the USDA forecast that 2010/11 global wheat production would fall by only about 1%, which would boost U.S. carry-over to a 23-year high and global 2010/11 carry-over to a 9-year high. Wheat prices rebounded in December and finished 2010 up 47% at $7.94 a bushel. Wheat prices started 2011 on a firm note and posted a 2-1/2 year high of $8.93 a bushel after the United Nations FAO warned that a severe drought in China may cause the world's largest wheat producer to import large quantities of wheat. Foreign demand for U.S. wheat supplies strengthened toward the end of 2010 due to scant European and Russian supplies and quality issues for Canadian and Australian supplies because of flooding. 2011 U.S. winter-wheat plantings rose 9.8% y/y to 40.99 million acres and the U.S. wheat supply situation remains above average with the U.S. stocks-to-use ratio at 34%, but the global stocks-to-use ratio of 27% is tighter and is near the decade average.

Supply – World wheat production in the 2010-11 marketing year fell -5.5% to 645.408 million metric tons, down from 2008-09 record high. The world's largest wheat producers were the European Union with 21.2% of world production in 2010-11, China (17.7%), India (12.5%), the U.S. (9.3%), Russia (6.4%), and Australia (3.9%). China's wheat production in 2010-11 fell -0.5% yr/yr to 114.500 million metric tons, but is still well below its record high of 123.289 million metric tons seen in 1997-98. Australia's wheat production rose +14.0% yr/yr to 25.000 million metric tons in 2010-11, but still well below its record high of 26.132 million metric tons in 2003-04. The world land area harvested with wheat in 2010-11 fell -2.0% yr/yr to 222.2 million hectares (1 hectare equals 10,000 square meters or 2.471 acres), remaining above the 209.6 million hectares in 2003-04, which was the smallest wheat harvest area since 1970-71. World wheat yield in 2010-11 fell -3.7% to 2.90 metric tons per acre, down from the 2008-09 record high of 3.04 metric tons per hectare.

U.S. wheat production in 2010-11 fell -0.4% yr/yr to 2.208 billion bushels, well below the record U.S. wheat crop of 2.785 billion bushels seen in 1981-82. The U.S. winter wheat crop in 2010 fell -2.6% yr/yr to 1.485 billion bushels, which was well below the record winter wheat crop of 2.097 billion bushels seen in 1981. U.S. production of durum wheat in 2010 fell -1.7% yr/yr to 107.180 million bushels. U.S. production of other spring wheat in 2010 rose +5.4% yr/yr to 615.975 million bushels. The largest U.S. producing states of winter wheat in 2010 were Kansas with 24.2% of U.S. production, Texas with 8.6%, Oklahoma with 8.1%, and Washington with 7.9%. U.S. farmers planted 53.603 million acres of wheat in 2010, which was down -9.4% yr/yr. U.S. wheat yield in 2010-11 was 46.4 bushels per acre, making a new record high. Ending stocks for U.S. wheat for 2010-11 were at 818.0 million bushels, down 16.2% yr/yr.

Demand – World wheat utilization in 2010-11 rose +1.9% yr/yr to a record high of 662,7 million metric tons. U.S. consumption of wheat in 2010-11 rose +3.4% yr/yr to 1.176 billion bushels, which was below the record high of 1.381 billion bushels seen in 1998-99. The consumption breakdown shows that 79.1% of U.S. wheat consumption in 2010-11 went for food, 14.5% for feed and residuals, and 6.5% for seed.

Trade – World trade in wheat in 2010-11 fell -6.7% yr/yr to 125.3 million metric tons, down from 2008-09 record high of 143.2 million metric tons. U.S. exports of wheat in 2010-11 rose +47.6% yr/yr to 1.3 billion bushes, and remained below the record of 1.771 billion bushels of exports seen in 1981-82. U.S. imports of wheat in 2010-11 fell -7.6% to 110.0 million bushels, down from the 2006-07 record high of 121.9 million bushels.

World Production of Wheat   In Thousands of Metric Tons

Crop Year	Argen-tina	Australia	Canada	China	European Union	India	Iran	Kazak-hstan	Pakistan	Russia	Turkey	United States	World Total
2001-02	15,700	24,299	20,568	93,873	123,353	69,680	9,459	12,707	19,024	46,900	15,500	53,001	583,473
2002-03	12,700	10,132	16,198	90,290	132,579	71,810	12,450	12,700	18,227	50,550	16,800	43,705	568,578
2003-04	15,100	26,132	23,049	86,490	110,578	65,100	13,440	11,537	19,183	34,100	16,800	63,805	554,806
2004-05	16,900	21,905	24,796	91,952	146,886	72,150	14,568	9,937	19,500	45,400	18,500	58,698	626,680
2005-06	13,800	25,173	25,748	97,445	132,356	68,640	14,308	11,198	21,612	47,700	18,500	57,243	619,222
2006-07	16,300	10,822	25,265	108,466	124,870	69,350	14,500	13,460	21,277	44,900	17,500	49,217	596,115
2007-08	18,600	13,569	20,054	109,298	120,133	75,810	15,000	16,467	23,295	49,400	15,500	55,821	611,202
2008-09[1]	11,000	21,420	28,611	112,464	151,122	78,570	10,000	12,538	20,959	63,700	16,800	68,016	684,155
2009-10[2]	11,000	21,923	26,848	115,120	138,051	80,680	12,000	17,052	24,033	61,700	18,450	60,366	682,654
2010-11[3]	14,000	25,000	23,167	114,500	136,528	80,710	14,400	9,700	23,900	41,500	17,000	60,103	645,408

[1] Preliminary.   [2] Estimate.   [3] Forecast.   *Source: Foreign Agricultural Service, U.S. Department of Agriculture (FAS-USDA)*

World Supply and Demand of Wheat   In Millions of Metric Tons/Hectares

Year	Area Harvested	Yield	Production	World Trade	Utilization Total	Ending Stocks	Stocks as a % of Utilization
2001-02	215.6	2.71	583.5	108.0	587.1	204.4	34.8
2002-03	215.1	2.64	568.6	106.8	602.1	168.6	28.0
2003-04	209.9	2.64	554.8	103.6	580.9	134.1	23.1
2004-05	217.6	2.88	626.7	113.9	605.6	153.2	25.3
2005-06	219.7	2.82	619.2	114.1	616.7	150.3	24.4
2006-07	213.3	2.79	596.1	115.6	618.3	130.3	21.1
2007-08	217.9	2.81	611.2	116.4	613.3	124.8	20.3
2008-09[1]	225.3	3.04	684.2	143.2	635.0	167.2	26.3
2009-10[2]	226.7	3.01	682.7	134.3	650.3	197.6	30.4
2010-11[3]	222.2	2.90	645.4	125.3	662.7	177.8	26.8

[1] Preliminary.   [2] Estimate.   [3] Forecast.   *Source: Foreign Agricultural Service, U.S. Department of Agriculture (FAS-USDA)*

Salient Statistics of Wheat in the United States

Year	Planting Intentions	Winter	Spring	All	Average All Yield Per Acre in Bushels	Value of Production $1,000	Domestic Exports[2]	Imports[3]	Flour	Cereal
		---------- Acreage Harvested ----------					------ Foreign Trade[5] ------		Per Capita[4] ------- Consumption -------	
		--------- 1,000 Acres ---------				--- In Millions of Bushels ---		---------- In Pounds ----------	
2001-02	59,597	31,295	17,338	48,633	40.2	5,440,217	962.3	107.6	141.0	3.8
2002-03	60,318	29,742	16,166	45,824	35.0	5,637,416	850.2	77.4	136.8	3.7
2003-04	62,141	36,753	16,310	53,063	44.2	7,929,039	1,158.3	63.0	136.7	3.7
2004-05	59,674	34,462	15,537	49,999	43.2	7,283,324	1,065.9	70.6	134.5	3.6
2005-06	57,229	33,794	16,325	50,119	42.0	7,171,441	1,002.8	81.4	134.3	3.6
2006-07	57,344	31,117	16,769	46,810	38.7	7,694,734	908.5	121.9	135.7	----
2007-08	60,460	35,938	15,061	50,999	40.5	13,289,326	1,262.6	112.6	138.1	----
2008-09	63,193	39,608	16,091	55,699	44.9	16,625,759	1,015.4	127.0	136.5	----
2009-10	59,168	34,510	15,383	49,893	44.5	10,654,115	881.0	119.0	134.7	----
2010-11[1]	53,603	31,749	15,888	47,657	46.4	12,992,156	1,300.0	110.0		

[1] Preliminary.   [2] Includes flour milled from imported wheat.   [3] Total wheat, flour & other products.   [4] Civilian only.   [5] Year beginning June.
Source: Economic Research Service, U.S. Department of Agriculture (ERS-USDA)

Supply and Distribution of Wheat in the United States   In Millions of Bushels

Crop Year Beginning June 1	On Farms	Mills, Elevators[3]	Total Stocks	Production	Imports[4]	Total Supply	Food	Seed	Feed & Residual[5]	Total	Exports[4]	Total Disap-pearance
	--------- Stocks, June 1 ---------											
2001-02	197.3	678.9	876.2	1,957.0	107.6	2,931.2	926.4	83.4	182.0	1,191.8	962.3	2,154.1
2002-03	216.8	560.3	777.1	1,605.9	77.4	2,460.4	918.6	84.4	115.7	1,118.7	850.2	1,968.9
2003-04	132.1	359.3	491.4	2,344.8	63.0	2,898.9	911.9	79.7	202.5	1,194.1	1,158.3	2,352.4
2004-05	131.9	414.6	546.4	2,158.2	70.6	2,773.8	909.6	77.6	180.6	1,167.8	1,065.9	2,233.7
2005-06	161.3	378.8	540.1	2,104.7	81.4	2,724.8	917.1	77.1	156.6	1,150.8	1,002.8	2,153.6
2006-07	111.0	460.2	571.2	1,812.0	121.9	2,501.5	937.9	81.9	117.1	1,136.8	908.5	2,045.3
2007-08	73.2	383.0	456.2	2,051.1	112.6	2,619.9	947.9	87.6	16.0	1,051.4	1,262.6	2,314.1
2008-09	25.6	280.2	305.8	2,499.2	127.0	2,932.0	926.8	78.0	255.2	1,260.0	1,015.4	2,275.4
2009-10[1]	140.7	515.8	656.5	2,218.1	119.0	2,993.0	917.0	69.0	150.0	1,137.0	881.0	2,017.5
2010-11[2]	209.9	765.7	975.6	2,208.4	110.0	3,294.0	930.0	76.0	170.0	1,176.0	1,300.0	2,476.0

[1] Preliminary.   [2] Estimate.   [3] Also warehouses and all off-farm storage not otherwise designated, including flour mills.   [4] Imports & exports are for wheat, including flour & other products in terms of wheat.   [5] Mostly feed use.
Source: Economic Research Service, U.S. Department of Agriculture (ERS-USDA)

WHEAT

Year	Hard Spring Stocks June 1	Hard Spring Pro-duction	Hard Spring Exports[3]	Durum[2] Stocks June 1	Durum[2] Pro-duction	Durum[2] Exports[3]	Hard Winter Stocks June 1	Hard Winter Pro-duction	Hard Winter Exports[3]	Soft Red Winter Stocks June 1	Soft Red Winter Pro-duction	Soft Red Winter Exports[3]	White Stocks June 1	White Pro-duction	White Exports[3]
2001-02	210	476	216	45	84	50	411	767	349	135	400	199	75	232	147
2002-03	230	351	259	33	80	32	363	620	309	78	321	105	73	233	148
2003-04	145	500	272	28	97	44	188	1,071	512	55	380	140	75	297	192
2004-05	157	525	314	26	90	31	227	856	388	64	380	122	72	306	207
2005-06	159	467	282	38	101	47	193	930	430	88	309	76	63	298	175
2006-07	132	432	250	40	53	35	215	682	281	106	390	146	78	254	197
2007-08	117	450	305	21	72	42	165	956	538	109	352	209	44	221	170
2008-09	68	512	210	8	84	24	138	1,035	447	55	614	199	37	255	136
2009-10	142	548	214	25	109	44	254	920	370	171	404	109	64	237	143
2010-11[1]	234	570	375	35	107	45	385	1,018	605	242	238	95	80	275	180

[1] Preliminary. [2] Includes "Red Durum." [3] Includes four made from U.S. wheat & shipments to territories.
Source: Economic Research Service, U.S. Department of Agriculture (ERS-USDA)

Seeded Acreage, Yield and Production of all Wheat in the United States

Year	Seed Acreage - 1,000 Acres Winter	Seed Acreage - 1,000 Acres Other Spring	Seed Acreage - 1,000 Acres Durum	Seed Acreage - 1,000 Acres All	Yield Per Harvested Acre (Bushels) Winter	Yield Per Harvested Acre (Bushels) Other Spring	Yield Per Harvested Acre (Bushels) Durum	Yield Per Harvested Acre (Bushels) All	Production (Million Bushels) Winter	Production (Million Bushels) Other Spring	Production (Million Bushels) Durum	Production (Million Bushels) All
2001	41,078	15,609	2,910	59,597	43.5	35.2	30.0	40.2	1,361.5	512.0	83.6	1,957.0
2002	41,766	15,639	2,913	60,318	38.2	29.1	29.5	35.0	1,137.0	388.9	80.0	1,605.9
2003	45,384	13,842	2,915	62,141	46.7	39.5	33.7	44.2	1,716.7	531.4	96.6	2,344.8
2004	43,350	13,763	2,561	59,674	43.5	43.2	38.0	43.2	1,499.4	568.9	89.9	2,158.2
2005	40,433	14,036	2,760	57,229	44.4	37.1	37.2	42.0	1,499.1	504.5	101.1	2,104.7
2006	40,575	14,899	1,870	57,344	41.7	33.2	29.5	38.7	1,298.1	460.5	53.5	1,812.0
2007	45,012	13,292	2,156	60,460	41.7	37.1	34.1	40.2	1,499.2	479.6	72.2	2,051.1
2008	46,307	14,165	2,721	63,193	47.1	40.5	32.6	44.9	1,867.3	548.0	83.8	2,499.2
2009	43,346	13,268	2,554	59,168	44.2	45.1	44.9	44.5	1,524.6	584.4	109.0	2,218.1
2010[1]	37,335	13,698	2,570	53,603	46.8	46.1	42.4	46.4	1,485.2	616.0	107.2	2,208.4

[1] Preliminary. *Source: Economic Research Service, U.S. Department of Agriculture (ERS-USDA)*

Production of Winter Wheat in the United States, by State   In Thousands of Bushels

Year	Colorado	Idaho	Illinois	Kansas	Missouri	Montana	Neb-raska	Ohio	Okla-homa	Oregon	Texas	Wash-ington	Total
2001	66,000	51,830	43,920	328,000	41,040	19,140	59,200	60,300	122,100	28,000	108,800	106,750	1,361,479
2002	36,300	48,510	30,870	270,600	33,440	21,840	50,160	50,220	103,600	29,820	78,300	104,400	1,137,001
2003	77,000	57,600	52,650	480,000	53,070	67,340	83,720	68,000	179,400	47,940	96,600	117,000	1,716,721
2004	45,900	63,000	53,100	314,500	48,360	66,830	61,050	55,180	164,500	47,580	108,500	117,250	1,499,434
2005	52,800	66,430	36,600	380,000	29,160	94,500	68,640	58,930	128,000	47,580	96,000	120,600	1,499,129
2006	39,900	54,670	60,970	291,200	49,140	82,560	61,200	65,280	81,600	38,690	33,600	118,800	1,298,081
2007	91,650	51,830	48,950	283,800	37,840	83,220	84,280	44,530	98,000	38,160	140,600	104,780	1,499,241
2008	57,000	60,000	73,600	356,000	55,680	94,380	73,480	74,120	166,500	44,950	99,000	96,320	1,867,333
2009	98,000	56,700	45,920	369,600	34,310	89,540	76,800	70,560	77,000	42,000	61,250	96,760	1,524,608
2010[1]	105,750	58,220	16,520	360,000	12,600	93,600	64,070	45,750	120,900	54,270	127,500	117,990	1,485,236

[1] Preliminary. *Source: Crop Reporting Board, U.S. Department of Agriculture (CRB-USDA)*

Official Winter Wheat Crop Production Reports in the United States   In Thousands of Bushels

Crop Year	May 1	June 1	July 1	August 1	September 1	Current December	Final
2001-02	1,341,381	1,321,126	1,366,192	1,385,048	----	----	1,361,479
2002-03	1,300,726	1,237,671	1,178,320	1,158,710	----	----	1,137,001
2003-04	1,563,314	1,626,376	1,715,912	1,712,150	----	----	1,716,721
2004-05	1,550,395	1,530,742	1,469,735	1,489,408	----	----	1,499,434
2005-06	1,590,862	1,545,971	1,525,302	1,520,848	----	----	1,499,129
2006-07	1,322,831	1,263,766	1,280,005	1,283,134	----	----	1,298,081
2007-08	1,615,613	1,609,679	1,561,907	1,537,262	----	----	1,499,241
2008-09	1,777,532	1,817,364	1,864,245	1,874,857	----	----	1,867,333
2009-10	1,502,074	1,491,769	1,524,771	1,537,348	----	----	1,524,608
2010-11[1]	1,458,350	1,482,364	1,505,493	1,522,902	----	----	1,485,236

[1] Preliminary. *Source: Crop Reporting Board, U.S. Department of Agriculture (CRB-USDA)*

Production of All Spring Wheat in the United States, by State   In Thousands of Bushels

Year	Arizona	California	Montana	North Dakota	South Dakota	Total	Idaho	Minnesota	Montana	North Dakota	Oregon	South Dakota	Washington	Total
				Durum Wheat						Other Spring Wheat				
2001	7,917	8,505	11,880	54,600	576	83,556	33,320	79,200	65,550	234,600	4,650	64,350	25,830	512,008
2002	8,928	9,000	12,995	48,750	147	79,960	29,900	61,200	75,900	165,200	4,680	24,000	25,370	388,917
2003	11,500	11,500	14,490	58,410	621	96,637	27,060	104,400	60,500	252,800	5,600	56,280	22,345	531,402
2004	9,603	9,000	17,985	52,800	450	89,893	38,710	88,550	88,350	243,950	8,400	71,910	26,250	568,918
2005	7,900	6,555	16,380	68,250	260	101,105	32,400	70,930	81,600	224,400	5,980	67,600	18,700	504,456
2006	7,400	6,435	6,715	31,500	90	53,475	34,310	77,550	63,800	212,350	5,750	42,600	21,250	460,480
2007	8,364	8,000	11,400	43,070	175	72,224	30,600	79,200	55,200	234,000	5,520	52,260	20,562	479,623
2008	14,602	15,225	10,830	42,250	190	83,827	37,440	100,800	59,520	246,400	7,650	68,400	22,470	548,004
2009	12,400	17,000	16,585	61,230	207	109,042	40,810	82,150	70,500	289,800	6,858	64,680	26,325	584,411
2010[1]	9,085	11,550	18,020	66,750	555	107,180	47,970	85,250	103,740	277,200	9,316	59,220	29,900	615,975

[1] Preliminary.   Source: Crop Reporting Board, U.S. Department of Agriculture (CRB-USDA)

Grindings of Wheat by Mills in the United States   In Millions of Bushels -- of 60 Pounds Each

Year	Jan.	Feb.	Mar.	Apr.	May	June	July	Aug.	Sept.	Oct.	Nov.	Dec.	Total
2001-02	-----	230.2	-----	-----	238.7	-----	-----	217.0	-----	-----	217.6	-----	903.6
2002-03	-----	230.3	-----	-----	224.4	-----	-----	215.8	-----	-----	217.4	-----	888.0
2003-04	-----	231.8	-----	-----	224.2	-----	-----	214.7	-----	-----	214.5	-----	885.2
2004-05	-----	224.8	-----	-----	222.1	-----	-----	214.9	-----	-----	216.5	-----	878.3
2005-06	-----	229.3	-----	-----	223.4	-----	-----	216.1	-----	-----	217.1	-----	885.9
2006-07	-----	233.3	-----	-----	228.0	-----	-----	222.0	-----	-----	226.1	-----	909.5
2007-08	-----	239.3	-----	-----	236.3	-----	-----	223.2	-----	-----	224.3	-----	923.1
2008-09	-----	235.2	-----	-----	225.3	-----	-----	217.6	-----	-----	221.2	-----	899.3
2009-10	-----	232.7	-----	-----	224.6	-----	-----	220.8	-----	-----	217.5	-----	895.5
2010-11[1]	-----	234.6	-----	-----	226.7	-----	-----	-----	-----	-----	-----	-----	922.5

[1] Preliminary.   Source: Bureau of the Census, U.S. Department of Commerce

Stocks of Wheat in the United States   In Millions of Bushels

Year	Mar. 1	June 1	Sept. 1	Dec. 1	Mar. 1	June 1	Sept. 1	Dec. 1	Mar. 1	June 1	Sept. 1	Dec. 1
		On Farms				Off Farms				Total Stocks		
2001	384.8	197.3	696.9	517.9	953.6	678.9	1,459.0	1,105.6	1,338.4	876.2	2,155.8	1,623.5
2002	338.5	216.8	580.2	384.8	871.3	560.3	1,170.8	935.1	1,209.8	777.1	1,751.0	1,319.9
2003	236.3	132.1	687.3	491.9	670.3	359.3	1,351.7	1,028.4	906.6	491.4	2,039.0	1,520.3
2004	257.9	131.9	790.6	531.0	762.7	414.6	1,147.8	899.3	1,020.6	546.4	1,938.4	1,430.3
2005	304.7	161.3	721.4	513.0	679.7	378.8	1,201.9	916.4	984.4	540.1	1,923.3	1,429.4
2006	256.0	111.0	572.0	403.3	716.2	460.2	1,178.5	911.4	972.2	571.2	1,750.5	1,314.7
2007	192.5	73.2	495.0	289.5	664.3	383.0	1,221.9	842.4	856.7	456.2	1,716.9	1,131.9
2008	92.0	25.6	635.7	454.0	617.3	280.2	1,222.2	968.1	709.3	305.8	1,857.9	1,422.1
2009	280.4	140.7	836.0	558.8	759.7	515.8	1,373.3	1,222.9	1,040.1	656.5	2,209.3	1,781.7
2010[1]	348.3	209.9	812.1	550.0	1,008.1	765.7	1,637.5	1,377.8	1,356.4	975.6	2,449.6	1,927.8

[1] Preliminary.   Source: National Agricultural Statistics Service, U.S. Department of Agriculture (NASS-USDA)

Wheat Supply and Distribution in Canada, Australia and Argentina   In Millions of Metric Tons

Crop Year	Stocks Aug. 1	New Crop	Total Supply	Domestic	Exports[3]	Stocks Oct. 1	New Crop	Total Supply	Domestic	Exports[3]	Stocks Dec. 1	New Crop	Total Supply	Domestic	Exports[3]
	Canada (Year Beginning Aug. 1)	Supply		Disappearance		Australia (Year Beginning Oct. 1)	Supply		Disappearance		Argentina (Year Beginning Dec. 1)	Supply		Disappearance	
2001-02	9.7	20.6	30.3	7.7	16.3	5.5	24.3	29.8	5.4	16.4	.6	15.5	16.1	4.9	10.1
2002-03	6.5	16.2	22.7	8.0	9.4	8.0	10.1	18.1	6.1	9.1	1.1	12.7	13.8	5.3	6.8
2003-04	5.7	23.0	28.7	7.2	15.8	3.2	26.1	29.3	6.0	18.0	1.3	15.1	16.4	5.4	9.5
2004-05	6.0	24.8	30.8	8.2	14.9	5.4	21.9	27.3	6.0	14.7	1.6	16.9	18.5	5.4	11.9
2005-06	7.9	25.7	33.6	8.2	16.0	6.7	25.2	31.9	6.6	16.0	1.3	13.8	15.1	5.1	9.6
2006-07	9.7	25.3	35.0	9.0	19.4	9.4	10.8	20.2	7.6	8.7	.4	16.3	16.7	5.4	10.7
2007-08	6.9	20.1	27.0	6.8	16.1	4.0	13.6	17.6	6.5	7.5	.6	18.6	19.2	5.7	11.2
2008-09	4.4	28.6	33.0	8.0	18.8	3.7	21.4	25.1	6.9	14.7	2.4	11.0	13.4	5.3	6.8
2009-10[1]	6.5	26.8	33.3	7.0	19.0	3.6	21.9	25.5	6.7	14.8	1.3	11.0	12.3	5.8	5.1
2010-11[2]	7.8	23.2	31.0	8.2	17.5	4.1	26.0	30.1	9.0	13.5	1.4	15.0	16.4	5.9	8.5

[1] Preliminary.   [2] Forecast.   [3] Including flour.   Source: Foreign Agricultural Service, U.S. Department of Agriculture (FAS-USDA)

WHEAT

Quarterly Supply and Disappearance of Wheat in the United States   In Millions of Bushels

Crop Year Beginning June 1	Supply — Beginning Stocks	Pro-duction	Imports[3]	Total Supply	Domestic Use — Food	Seed	Feed & Residual	Total	Exports[3]	Total Disap-pearance	Ending Stocks — Gov't Owned[4]	Privately Owned[5]	Total Stocks
2000-01	949.7	2,228.2	89.8	3,267.7	949.6	79.5	300.4	1,329.5	1,062.0	2,391.6	97.0	779.2	876.2
June-Aug.	949.7	2,228.2	20.4	3,198.3	238.8	1.1	317.9	557.8	287.8	845.6	108.9	2,243.8	2,352.7
Sept.-Nov.	2,352.7	----	25.1	2,377.8	253.0	49.8	-24.5	278.4	293.3	571.6	102.9	1,703.2	1,806.1
Dec.-Feb.	1,806.1	----	21.4	1,827.5	228.2	3.5	11.4	243.1	246.1	489.1	104.4	1,234.0	1,338.4
Mar.-May	1,338.4	----	22.9	1,361.3	229.7	25.2	-4.5	250.3	234.8	485.1	97.0	779.2	876.2
2001-02	876.2	1,947.5	107.6	2,931.2	926.4	83.4	182.0	1,191.8	962.3	2,154.1	99.0	678.1	777.1
June-Aug.	876.2	1,947.5	25.7	2,849.3	233.8	3.5	237.9	475.2	218.3	693.5	97.7	2,058.1	2,155.8
Sept.-Nov.	2,155.8	----	29.0	2,184.9	245.1	51.6	-23.1	273.6	287.8	561.4	96.9	1,526.6	1,623.5
Dec.-Feb.	1,623.5	----	27.6	1,651.0	221.1	2.0	-6.6	216.5	224.7	441.2	96.9	1,112.9	1,209.8
Mar.-May	1,209.8	----	25.2	1,235.0	226.4	26.3	-26.2	226.4	231.5	457.9	99.0	678.1	777.1
2002-03	777.1	1,605.9	77.4	2,460.4	918.6	84.4	115.7	1,118.7	850.2	1,968.9	66.4	425.0	491.4
June-Aug.	777.1	1,605.9	26.7	2,409.6	233.2	2.7	184.5	420.4	240.2	660.7	91.4	1,657.6	1,749.0
Sept.-Nov.	1,749.0	----	23.1	1,772.1	237.8	54.6	-74.7	217.7	234.5	454.2	80.9	1,239.0	1,319.9
Dec.-Feb.	1,319.9	----	12.7	1,332.6	218.9	3.1	14.1	236.1	189.8	425.9	74.1	832.5	906.6
Mar.-May	906.6	----	14.9	921.6	228.4	23.9	-8.2	244.5	185.7	430.2	66.4	425.0	491.4
2003-04	491.4	2,344.8	63.1	2,899.3	911.9	79.6	202.9	1,194.4	1,158.1	2,352.5	60.9	485.5	546.4
June-Aug.	491.4	2,344.8	15.7	2,851.9	230.5	2.1	315.3	547.9	264.9	812.8	60.3	1,978.7	2,039.0
Sept.-Nov.	2,039.0	----	17.8	2,056.7	239.6	53.3	-61.9	231.0	305.4	536.4	60.4	1,459.6	1,520.3
Dec.-Feb.	1,520.3	----	12.9	1,533.2	215.9	2.2	3.1	221.2	291.4	512.6	60.0	960.6	1,020.6
Mar.-May	1,020.6	----	16.7	1,037.3	225.9	22.0	-53.6	194.3	296.4	490.7	60.9	485.5	546.4
2004-05	546.4	2,158.2	70.6	2,775.2	904.6	78.9	188.9	1,172.4	1,062.9	2,235.3	54.0	486.1	540.1
June-Aug.	546.4	2,158.2	17.4	2,722.1	227.5	4.1	265.2	496.8	286.8	783.6	61.9	1,876.5	1,938.4
Sept.-Nov.	1,938.4	----	18.7	1,957.1	235.6	48.2	-57.0	226.8	300.0	526.8	61.7	1,369.0	1,430.3
Dec.-Feb.	1,430.3	----	17.8	1,448.1	216.3	2.4	7.7	226.4	237.4	463.8	55.9	928.5	984.4
Mar.-May	984.4	----	16.7	1,001.1	225.2	24.2	-27.0	222.4	238.7	461.1	54.5	485.6	540.1
2005-06	2,105.0	2,104.7	81.0	4,290.7	914.0	78.0	154.0	1,146.0	1,009.0	2,155.0			571.0
June-Aug.	540.1	2,104.7	19.0	2,663.0	231.0	2.0	263.0	496.0	244.0	740.0	48.3	1,875.0	1,923.0
Sept.-Nov.	1,923.0	----	20.0	1,944.0	238.0	51.0	-61.0	228.0	286.0	514.0	44.1	1,385.4	1,429.0
Dec.-Feb.	1,429.0	----	20.0	1,450.0	219.0	1.0	1.0	221.0	257.0	478.0			972.0
Mar.-May	972.0	----	22.0	995.0	226.0	24.0	-49.0	201.0	222.0	423.0			571.0
2006-07	571.0	1,808.0	121.0	2,500.0	937.0	81.0	117.0	1,135.0	908.0	2,043.0			456.0
June-Aug.	571.0	1,808.0	26.0	2,406.0	235.0	2.0	205.0	442.0	214.0	656.0			1,751.0
Sept.-Nov.	1,751.0	----	29.0	1,780.0	243.0	56.0	-47.0	252.0	212.0	464.0			1,315.0
Dec.-Feb.	1,315.0	----	32.0	1,346.0	225.0	1.0	28.0	254.0	235.0	489.0			857.0
Mar.-May	857.0	----	34.0	891.0	234.0	22.0	-69.0	187.0	247.0	434.0			456.0
2007-08	456.0	2,051.0	112.0	2,619.0	947.0	88.0	16.0	1,051.0	1,262.0	2,313.0			306.0
June-Aug.	456.0	2,051.0	30.0	2,538.0	240.0	1.0	257.0	498.0	323.0	821.0			1,717.0
Sept.-Nov.	1,717.0	----	21.0	1,738.0	245.0	60.0	-120.0	185.0	421.0	606.0			1,132.0
Dec.-Feb.	1,132.0	----	24.0	1,156.0	227.0	2.0	-42.0	187.0	261.0	448.0			709.0
Mar.-May	709.0	----	37.0	746.0	235.0	25.0	-79.0	181.0	257.0	438.0			306.0
2008-09	306.0	2,499.0	127.0	2,932.0	924.0	75.0	256.0	1,255.0	1,016.0	2,271.0			657.0
June-Aug.	306.0	2,499.0	28.0	2,833.0	236.0	2.0	393.0	631.0	345.0	976.0			1,858.0
Sept.-Nov.	1,858.0	----	28.0	1,886.0	238.0	54.0	-124.0	168.0	295.0	463.0			1,422.0
Dec.-Feb.	1,422.0	----	36.0	1,459.0	219.0	1.0	28.0	248.0	170.0	418.0			1,040.0
Mar.-May	1,040.0	----	35.0	1,075.0	231.0	18.0	-41.0	208.0	206.0	414.0			657.0
2009-10[1]	657.0	2,218.0	119.0	2,994.0	917.0	69.0	150.0	1,136.0	881.0	2,017.0			976.0
June-Aug.	657.0	2,218.0	28.0	2,902.0	231.0	1.0	261.0	493.0	200.0	693.0			2,209.0
Sept.-Nov.	2,209.0	----	24.0	2,234.0	237.0	46.0	-83.0	200.0	252.0	452.0			1,782.0
Dec.-Feb.	1,782.0	----	30.0	1,812.0	221.0	1.0	31.0	253.0	202.0	455.0			1,356.0
Mar.-May	1,356.0	----	37.0	1,393.0	228.0	21.0	-59.0	190.0	227.0	417.0			976.0
2010-11[2]	976.0	2,208.0	104.0	3,288.0	930.0	76.0	170.0	1,176.0	1,158.0	2,334.0			818.0
June-Aug.	976.0	2,208.0	28.0	3,212.0	234.0	2.0	262.0	498.0	265.0	763.0			2,450.0
Sept.-Nov.	2,450.0	----	24.0	2,473.0	245.0	52.0	-65.0	232.0	314.0	546.0			1,928.0

[1] Preliminary.   [2] Forecast.   [3] Imports & exports include flour and other products expressed in wheat equivalent.   [4] Uncommitted, Government only.
[5] Includes total loans.   [6] Includes alcoholic beverages.   *Source: Economic Research Service, U.S. Department of Agriculture (ERS-USDA)*

Wheat Government Loan Program Data in the United States   Loan Rates--Cents Per Bushel

Crop Year Beginning June 1	National Average[3]	Target Rate[4]	Corn Belt (Soft Red Winter)	Central & Southern Plains (Hard Winter)	Northern Plains (Spring & Durum)	Pacific Northwest (White)	Placed Under Loan	% of Production	Acquired by CCC Under Program	Total Stocks May 31	Total CCC Stocks May 31	CCC Loans	Farmer-Owned Reserve	"Free"
										In Millions of Bushels				
2000-01	258	NA	253	257	258	271	181	8.1	27	876	97	42	0	779
2001-02	258	NA	NA	NA	NA	NA	197	10.1	17	777	99	78	0	678
2002-03	280	386	NA	NA	NA	NA	120	7.5	2	491	66	55	0	425
2003-04	280	386	NA	NA	NA	NA	186	7.9	3	546	61	37	0	485
2004-05	275	392	NA	NA	NA	NA	178	8.3	10	540	55	58	0	486
2005-06	275	392	NA	NA	NA	NA	170	8.1	1	571	43	NA	0	528
2006-07	275	392	NA	NA	NA	NA	94	5.2	0	456	41	NA	0	437
2007-08	275	392	NA	NA	NA	NA				306	NA	NA	NA	NA
2008-09[1]	275		NA	NA	NA	NA				657	NA	NA	NA	NA
2009-10[2]			NA	NA	NA	NA				976	NA	NA	NA	NA

[1] Preliminary.   [2] Estimate.   [3] The national average loan rate at the farm as a percentage of the parity-priced wheat at the beginning of the marketing year.   [4] 1996-97 through 2001-02 marketing year, target prices not applicable.   NA = Not avaliable.
Source: Agricultural Marketing Service, U.S. Department of Agriculture (AMS-USDA)

Exports of Wheat (Only)[2] from the United States   In Thousands of Bushels

Year	June	July	Aug.	Sept.	Oct.	Nov.	Dec.	Jan.	Feb.	Mar.	Apr.	May	Total
2001-02	59,190	64,911	89,582	86,941	94,598	99,800	81,369	72,114	63,446	78,070	84,211	58,449	932,681
2002-03	63,219	78,013	92,345	73,606	78,866	75,678	69,485	62,769	48,618	65,990	55,764	59,438	823,791
2003-04	54,665	88,042	115,869	125,312	101,168	76,222	79,811	109,607	94,480	96,685	102,588	91,917	1,136,366
2004-05	80,599	97,962	103,222	119,965	92,634	83,947	81,718	77,349	73,131	76,612	81,885	75,575	1,044,599
2005-06	64,553	90,760	83,173	102,761	103,423	77,164	91,531	84,659	71,175	74,420	69,050	72,209	984,878
2006-07	63,115	67,846	78,225	76,431	70,752	60,595	72,226	84,629	75,412	76,512	75,130	85,565	886,438
2007-08	73,088	80,285	153,223	149,168	158,064	116,504	82,343	87,539	84,414	92,251	82,781	79,725	1,239,385
2008-09	77,176	119,492	141,173	117,332	93,462	75,311	54,389	56,634	55,825	75,580	61,048	65,884	993,306
2009-10	63,851	58,627	68,321	100,213	77,627	68,117	54,438	65,060	76,522	73,780	76,958	68,473	851,987
2010-11[1]	74,400	80,546	104,145	130,529	86,525	92,159							1,136,608

[1] Preliminary.   [2] Grains.   *Source: Economic Research Service, U.S. Department of Agriculture (ERS-USDA)*

United States Wheat and Wheat Flour Imports and Exports   In Thousands of Bushels

Crop Year Beginning June 1	Suitable for Milling	Wheat Unfit for Human Consump.	Grain	Flour & Products[2]	Total	P.L. 480	Foreign Donations Sec. 416	Aid[3]	Total concessional	CCC Export Credit	Export Enhancement Program	Total U.S. Wheat
	Wheat		Wheat Equivalent						In Thousands of Metric Tons			
2003-04	37,156	----	37,156	25,871	63,026	1,211	20	----	1,628	3,791	0	31,179
2004-05	44,499	----	44,499	26,071	70,570	1,867	12	----	2,139	2,554	0	26,505
2005-06	54,073	----	54,073	27,281	81,354	969	17	----	1,191	1,052	0	25,005
2006-07	92,928	----	92,928	21,752	121,870	767	0	----	961	1,008	0	29,636
2007-08	85,806	----	85,806	26,702	112,631	734	12	----	841	1,360	0	32,847
2008-09[1]	101,964	----	101,964	22,356	126,970	722	12	----	965	2,691	0	22,545
2009-10[1]	93,003	----	93,003	29,227	118,595							

[1] Preliminary.   [2] Includes macaroni, semolina & similar products.   [3] Shipment mostly under the Commodity Import Program, financed with foreign aid funds.   NA = Not available.   *Source: Economic Research Service, U.S. Department of Agriculture (ERS-USDA)*

Comparative Average Cash Wheat Prices   In Dollars Per Bushel

Crop Year June to May	Received by U.S. Farmers	No. 2 Soft Red Winter, Chicago	No 1 Hard Red Ordinary Protein, Kansas City	No 2 Soft Red Winter, St. Louis	No 1 Dark Northern Spring 14%	No 1 Hard Amber Durum	No 1 Soft White, Portland, Oregon	No 2 Western White Pacific Northwest	No 2 Soft White, Standard Toledo	Australian Standard White	Canada Vancouver No 1 CWRS 13 1/2%	Argentina F.O.B. B.A.	U.S. Gulf No 2 Hard Winter	Rotterdam C.I.F. U.S. No 2 Hard Winter
					-- Minneapolis --					Export Prices[2] (U.S. $ Per Metric Ton)				
2003-04	3.40	3.66	4.03	3.73	4.39	5.31	3.95	4.24	3.59	182	188	161	156	204
2004-05	3.40	3.01	3.99	3.40	4.66	----	3.93	4.04	3.08	177	202	127	151	213
2005-06	3.42	3.13	4.45	3.20	4.98	----	3.57	4.35	3.15	191	204	140	168	224
2006-07	4.26	3.98	5.38	4.11	5.41	----	4.87	5.48	3.85	230	230	192	204	257
2007-08	6.48	7.71	9.11	7.43	10.81	13.08	9.97	8.68	8.06	294	447	298	340	321
2008-09	6.78	5.04	7.03	4.86	8.53	----	6.25	6.62	4.98	217	350	244	292	----
2009-10	4.87	4.39	5.24	3.88	6.96	----	4.91	5.00	4.31	209	280	227	213	----
2010-11[1]	5.50-5.80	5.96	6.53	6.16	8.21		5.98	4.63	5.93	246	327	269		

[1] Preliminary.   [2] Calendar year.   NA = Not available.   *Source: Economic Research Service, U.S. Department of Agriculture (ERS-USDA)*

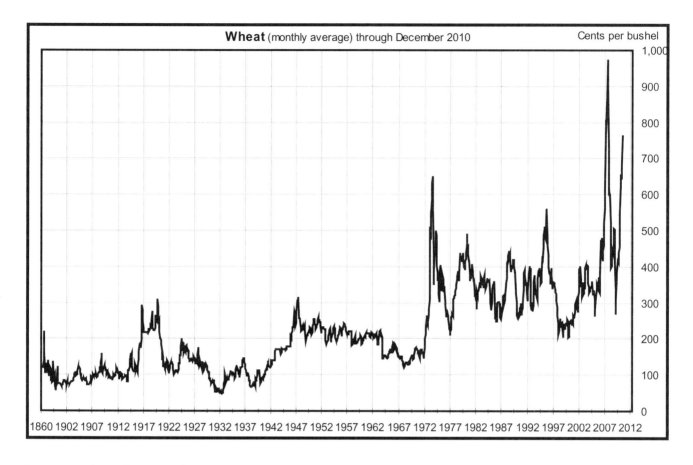

Wheat (monthly average) through December 2010   Cents per bushel

Average Price of No. 2 Soft Red Winter (30 Days) Wheat in Chicago   In Dollars Per Bushel

Year	June	July	Aug.	Sept.	Oct.	Nov.	Dec.	Jan.	Feb.	Mar.	Apr.	May	Average
2001-02	2.40	2.56	2.57	2.57	2.68	2.75	2.83	2.96	2.74	2.76	2.75	2.73	2.69
2002-03	2.81	3.19	3.42	3.92	3.89	3.85	3.53	3.32	3.44	3.14	3.08	3.25	3.40
2003-04	3.11	3.23	3.63	3.46	3.42	3.87	3.92	3.90	3.84	3.85	3.92	3.73	3.66
2004-05	3.46	3.26	2.92	2.97	2.82	2.79	2.88	2.93	2.95	3.28	2.92	2.96	3.01
2005-06	3.09	3.22	3.04	2.93	2.99	2.83	2.98	3.11	3.34	3.29	3.21	3.54	3.13
2006-07	3.26	3.43	3.20	3.39	4.40	4.35	4.49	4.19	4.20	4.07	4.25	4.50	3.98
2007-08	5.25	5.52	6.24	7.98	7.89	7.57	8.69	8.55	10.12	10.40	7.72	6.59	7.71
2008-09	7.20	6.87	6.77	5.45	3.76	3.68	4.01	4.62	4.28	4.40	4.43	4.96	5.04
2009-10	4.96	4.45	4.18	3.70	4.01	4.53	4.67	4.55	4.37	4.38	4.43	4.49	4.39
2010-11[1]	4.26	5.38	6.29	6.43	5.97	6.20	7.20						5.96

[1] Preliminary.   Source: Economic Research Service, U.S. Department of Agriculture (ERS-USDA)

Average Price Received by Farmers for Wheat in the United States   In Dollars Per Bushel

Year	June	July	Aug.	Sept.	Oct.	Nov.	Dec.	Jan.	Feb.	Mar.	Apr.	May	Average
2001-02	2.74	2.70	2.73	2.85	2.87	2.87	2.88	2.87	2.83	2.87	2.83	2.81	2.82
2002-03	2.92	3.21	3.63	4.21	4.38	4.25	4.06	3.89	3.70	3.55	3.37	3.33	3.71
2003-04	3.08	2.95	3.35	3.39	3.44	3.61	3.68	3.68	3.77	3.83	3.88	3.82	3.54
2004-05	3.55	3.37	3.27	3.36	3.43	3.46	3.40	3.43	3.36	3.42	3.35	3.31	3.39
2005-06	3.23	3.20	3.24	3.36	3.43	3.45	3.53	3.52	3.66	3.79	3.81	4.09	3.53
2006-07	3.98	3.88	3.91	4.06	4.59	4.59	4.52	4.53	4.71	4.75	4.89	4.88	4.44
2007-08	5.03	5.17	5.64	6.76	7.65	7.39	7.71	7.96	10.10	10.50	10.10	8.87	7.74
2008-09	7.62	7.15	7.61	7.43	6.65	6.29	5.95	6.20	5.79	5.71	5.75	5.84	6.50
2009-10	5.72	5.17	4.85	4.48	4.47	4.79	4.87	4.90	4.73	4.70	4.42	4.33	4.79
2010-11[1]	4.17	4.50	5.44	5.83	5.87	6.13	6.45	6.71	8.56				5.96

[1] Preliminary.   Source: Economic Research Service, U.S. Department of Agriculture (ERS-USDA)

Average Price of No. 1 Hard Red Winter (Ordinary Protein) Wheat in Kansas City   In Dollars Per Bushel

Year	June	July	Aug.	Sept.	Oct.	Nov.	Dec.	Jan.	Feb.	Mar.	Apr.	May	Average
2001-02	3.32	3.20	3.15	3.18	3.28	3.37	3.26	3.29	3.25	3.23	3.24	3.21	3.25
2002-03	3.55	3.92	4.29	5.04	5.10	4.76	4.40	4.06	4.08	3.80	3.79	3.87	4.22
2003-04	3.63	3.34	3.87	3.74	3.79	4.21	4.31	4.32	4.25	4.30	4.35	4.28	4.03
2004-05	4.13	3.97	3.73	4.01	3.95	4.22	4.22	4.14	4.00	4.00	3.76	3.80	3.99
2005-06	3.87	3.83	3.96	4.30	4.57	4.53	4.52	4.46	4.72	4.62	4.86	5.21	4.45
2006-07	5.25	5.27	5.00	5.16	5.62	5.61	5.49	5.29	5.39	5.40	5.52	5.54	5.38
2007-08	6.22	6.28	6.84	8.52	8.89	8.62	9.80	9.97	12.28	12.29	10.29	9.33	9.11
2008-09	9.19	8.68	8.64	7.52	6.17	6.21	6.06	6.59	6.21	6.23	6.10	6.70	7.03
2009-10	6.63	5.58	5.15	4.56	5.06	5.58	5.37	5.24	5.10	4.99	4.86	4.78	5.24
2010-11[1]	4.50	5.26	6.76	7.01	7.04	7.13	8.04						6.53

[1] Preliminary.   *Source: Economic Research Service, U.S. Department of Agriculture (ERS-USDA)*

Average Price of No. 1 Dark Northern Spring (14% Protein) Wheat in Minneapolis   In Dollars Per Bushel

Year	June	July	Aug.	Sept.	Oct.	Nov.	Dec.	Jan.	Feb.	Mar.	Apr.	May	Average
2001-02	3.81	3.72	3.54	3.52	3.71	3.69	3.59	3.55	3.51	3.51	3.55	3.59	3.61
2002-03	3.64	4.03	4.37	5.24	5.20	4.99	4.47	4.34	4.52	4.36	4.22	4.20	4.47
2003-04	4.12	4.00	4.15	4.03	4.31	4.59	4.43	4.44	4.64	4.63	4.69	4.69	4.39
2004-05	4.56	4.31	4.12	4.68	4.87	5.14	4.93	5.01	4.13	4.79	4.69	4.69	4.66
2005-06	5.03	4.71	4.83	4.80	5.11	5.11	5.28	4.87	4.90	4.83	4.94	5.31	4.98
2006-07	5.59	5.65	4.94	4.86	5.36	5.55	5.44	5.27	5.40	5.55	5.65	5.64	5.41
2007-08	6.19	6.60	6.88	8.20	9.27	9.39	11.06	12.59	19.00	15.60	12.93	12.06	10.81
2008-09	11.46	11.46	9.87	8.51	7.37	6.80	7.78	8.02	7.64	7.57	7.72	8.13	8.53
2009-10	7.96	6.82	6.17	6.30	6.36	7.29	6.79	7.39	7.57	7.48	6.88	6.55	6.96
2010-11[1]	6.90	6.89	7.92	8.35	8.61	8.67	10.14						8.21

[1] Preliminary.   *Source: Economic Research Service, U.S. Department of Agriculture (ERS-USDA)*

Average Farm Prices of Winter Wheat in the United States   In Dollars Per Bushel

Year	June	July	Aug.	Sept.	Oct.	Nov.	Dec.	Jan.	Feb.	Mar.	Apr.	May	Average
2003-04	2.94	2.89	3.28	3.31	3.37	3.56	3.62	3.66	3.67	3.76	3.79	3.72	3.46
2004-05	3.46	3.31	3.19	3.26	3.34	3.39	3.34	3.28	3.27	3.32	3.27	3.23	3.31
2005-06	3.15	3.15	3.16	3.28	3.34	3.27	3.45	3.45	3.59	3.82	3.74	4.06	3.46
2006-07	3.95	3.82	3.77	4.03	4.63	4.67	4.53	4.53	4.67	4.67	4.87	4.77	4.41
2007-08	5.00	5.13	5.66	6.89	7.55	7.31	7.70	7.75	9.17	9.96	9.62	8.17	7.49
2008-09	7.51	7.10	7.30	6.99	6.03	5.65	5.40	5.70	5.26	5.27	5.26	5.52	6.08
2009-10	5.47	5.02	4.67	4.20	4.27	4.60	4.68	4.57	4.53	4.45	4.19	4.21	4.57
2010-11[1]	4.05	4.47	5.48	5.80	5.80	6.00	6.40	6.37	8.13				5.83

[1] Preliminary.   *Source: Economic Research Service, U.S. Department of Agriculture (ERS-USDA)*

Average Farm Prices of Durum Wheat in the United States   In Dollars Per Bushel

Year	June	July	Aug.	Sept.	Oct.	Nov.	Dec.	Jan.	Feb.	Mar.	Apr.	May	Average
2003-04	3.99	3.85	3.78	3.95	3.89	3.95	3.95	3.96	4.08	4.14	4.19	4.21	4.00
2004-05	4.35	4.09	3.86	3.89	3.87	3.79	3.67	3.64	3.72	3.70	3.63	3.67	3.82
2005-06	3.67	3.72	3.35	3.38	3.39	3.28	3.37	3.29	3.34	3.39	3.41	3.94	3.46
2006-07	3.81	3.83	4.09	4.07	4.55	4.62	4.53	4.71	5.16	5.32	5.46	5.39	4.63
2007-08	5.49	6.69	7.00	8.98	11.70	11.70	11.50	13.10	14.10	15.40	14.30	13.50	11.12
2008-09	8.48	11.70	12.60	11.90	11.50	8.93	8.40	8.26	7.53	7.40	7.18	7.05	9.24
2009-10	6.83	7.57	4.95	4.86	4.59	4.91	4.94	4.94	4.61	4.57	4.23	4.28	5.11
2010-11[1]	4.75	4.43	4.70	4.97	6.04	6.07	6.07	7.07	9.39				5.94

[1] Preliminary.   *Source: Economic Research Service, U.S. Department of Agriculture (ERS-USDA)*

Average Farm Prices of Other Spring Wheat in the United States   In Dollars Per Bushel

Year	June	July	Aug.	Sept.	Oct.	Nov.	Dec.	Jan.	Feb.	Mar.	Apr.	May	Average
2003-04	3.45	3.31	3.42	3.42	3.53	3.68	3.72	3.67	3.84	3.90	3.94	4.01	3.66
2004-05	3.83	3.55	3.38	3.48	3.50	3.57	3.48	3.61	3.49	3.51	3.39	3.37	3.51
2005-06	3.51	3.45	3.43	3.51	3.61	3.71	3.68	3.70	3.83	3.85	3.95	4.18	3.70
2006-07	4.18	4.41	4.11	4.11	4.48	4.48	4.74	4.51	4.73	4.73	4.87	4.98	4.53
2007-08	5.17	5.43	5.53	6.26	6.99	7.00	7.39	8.01	11.20	10.90	10.50	10.70	7.92
2008-09	10.10	9.52	8.18	7.76	7.20	7.10	6.89	7.02	6.61	6.50	6.49	6.76	7.51
2009-10	6.66	5.96	5.54	4.85	5.00	5.19	5.18	5.30	5.04	5.04	4.89	4.61	5.27
2010-11[1]	4.62	4.73	5.48	6.00	6.15	6.36	6.57	7.13	9.09				6.24

[1] Preliminary.   *Source: Economic Research Service, U.S. Department of Agriculture (ERS-USDA)*

WHEAT

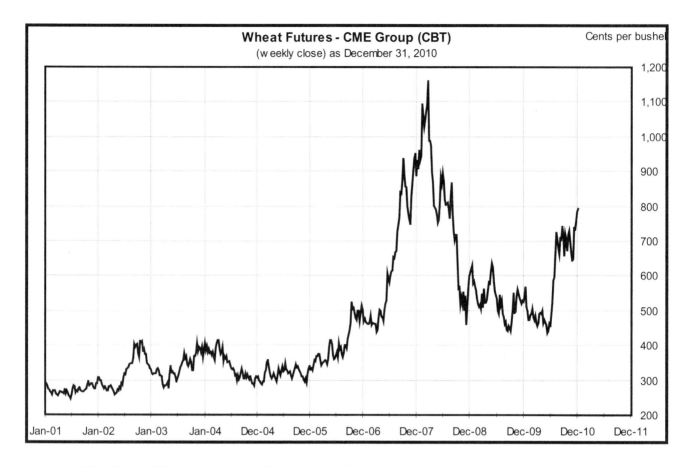

Wheat Futures - CME Group (CBT)
(weekly close) as December 31, 2010

Cents per bushel

Volume of Trading of Wheat Futures in Chicago   In Thousands of Contracts

Year	Jan.	Feb.	Mar.	Apr.	May	June	July	Aug.	Sept.	Oct.	Nov.	Dec.	Total
2001	551.8	595.3	536.1	580.0	537.8	720.4	695.3	600.3	385.9	629.5	614.7	354.3	6,801.5
2002	603.0	593.1	501.1	563.1	419.3	689.8	586.4	651.6	682.9	609.4	594.4	378.8	6,872.9
2003	438.0	526.0	411.0	496.8	638.6	661.8	585.1	689.6	536.5	778.9	739.8	465.4	6,967.4
2004	656.9	771.7	783.1	786.2	606.1	786.5	501.7	747.4	520.9	478.7	913.7	402.3	7,955.2
2005	613.0	1,053.6	827.8	937.5	694.7	1,088.0	690.3	1,024.8	660.0	717.4	1,164.5	642.4	10,114.1
2006	889.2	1,421.3	1,059.6	1,300.0	1,511.6	1,617.1	1,067.4	1,659.9	1,365.9	1,938.1	1,613.7	781.2	16,224.9
2007	1,346.2	1,506.0	1,148.0	2,082.5	1,170.5	2,343.7	1,514.4	2,111.3	1,320.3	1,648.4	2,109.7	1,281.8	19,582.7
2008	1,861.3	2,527.7	1,398.7	1,558.6	1,121.6	2,185.7	1,314.2	2,093.6	1,228.1	1,139.0	1,644.5	939.0	19,011.9
2009	986.9	1,505.7	1,213.8	1,747.8	1,300.1	2,350.9	1,298.1	1,926.4	1,040.0	1,451.2	1,952.5	904.2	17,677.5
2010	1,297.9	1,936.2	1,289.8	2,029.8	1,392.3	2,547.3	2,394.8	3,386.6	1,501.6	1,527.8	2,383.2	1,402.9	23,090.3

Contract size = 5,000 bu.   *Source: CME Group; Chicago Board of Trade (CBT)*

Average Open Interest of Wheat Futures in Chicago   In Contracts

Year	Jan.	Feb.	Mar.	Apr.	May	June	July	Aug.	Sept.	Oct.	Nov.	Dec.
2001	145,802	146,927	137,377	138,876	134,051	151,951	142,399	143,574	136,514	126,772	113,456	104,975
2002	118,192	118,484	112,469	112,870	96,050	98,047	118,041	131,303	129,913	114,544	101,354	82,934
2003	92,679	99,882	95,464	99,500	97,750	96,230	92,484	119,817	110,703	109,449	125,335	120,376
2004	130,101	137,459	141,239	155,383	127,086	135,322	154,623	166,422	154,431	156,290	172,064	182,402
2005	201,297	223,108	218,153	208,149	207,407	223,014	239,219	256,533	276,741	297,319	301,838	298,523
2006	320,974	380,405	389,284	385,698	466,013	491,343	473,749	459,650	455,755	476,906	435,059	426,976
2007	453,140	441,924	405,383	377,162	363,297	401,509	411,971	404,940	379,871	407,669	414,509	423,198
2008	443,193	440,137	400,426	375,845	362,835	359,429	332,360	331,301	294,696	279,041	283,832	250,914
2009	268,513	297,116	291,831	309,503	302,088	335,407	317,024	327,977	320,607	331,678	355,414	353,774
2010	388,660	431,434	427,821	457,548	469,103	490,351	477,461	504,547	487,184	516,982	507,512	480,059

Contract size = 5,000 bu.   *Source: CME Group; Chicago Board of Trade (CBT)*

Commercial Stocks of Domestic Wheat[1] in the United States, on First of Month In Millions of Bushels

Year	July	Aug.	Sept.	Oct.	Nov.	Dec.	Jan.	Feb.	Mar.	Apr.	May	June
2001-02	271.0	296.6	318.7	321.9	291.9	251.8	224.5	224.6	217.2	195.6	177.3	176.0
2002-03	193.9	207.7	237.2	241.0	237.7	218.8	195.1	179.7	158.3	133.1	107.2	93.8
2003-04	133.3	171.9	212.0	226.3	220.7	198.1	145.0	126.3	113.1	94.0	89.6	85.4
2004-05	118.3	147.6	174.3	173.5	161.6	137.8	129.8	122.5	113.4	103.8	92.2	88.8
2005-06	127.5	138.6	159.9	163.5	158.5	147.8	137.9	130.9	128.8	122.9	116.7	126.2
2006-07	154.3	172.5	190.3	170.9	166.8	159.5	154.7	146.7	136.3	129.3	116.6	99.2
2007-08	108.6	155.9	173.1	185.7	164.8	151.2	148.3	138.9	123.5	112.3	87.1	78.7
2008-09	98.2	150.4	176.4	214.5	212.9	179.7	167.8	135.9	126.1	124.9	119.5	115.0
2009-10	152.4	198.2	221.3	224.5	219.8	208.8	199.8	192.9	184.1	177.1	181.2	174.8
2010-11	229.8	237.4	247.3	242.3	235.4	229.5	222.6	234.4				

[1] Domestic wheat in storage in public and private elevators in 39 markets and wheat afloat in vessels or barges at lake and seaboard ports, the first Saturday of the month.   *Source: Livestock Division, U.S. Department of Agriculture (LD-USDA)*

Stocks of Wheat Flour Held by Mills in the United States   In Thousands of Sacks--100 Pounds

Year	Jan. 1	April 1	July 1	Oct. 1	Year	Jan. 1	April 1	July 1	Oct. 1
1999	7,544	5,920	5,697	4,265	2005	5,085	4,268	4,637	4,781
2000	5,099	5,217	5,062	5,244	2006	5,211	5,775	5,576	5,587
2001	5,241	5,506	5,178	5,393	2007	5,919	5,884	5,587	6,188
2002	5,377	5,164	4,632	4,184	2008	6,374	6,219	6,157	6,719
2003	4,265	4,707	4,622	4,554	2009	5,831	5,561	5,607	5,430
2004	4,764	4,666	4,700	4,868	2010[1]	5,407	5,644	5,586	5,507

[1] Preliminary.   *Source: Bureau of the Census, U.S. Department of Commerce*

Average Producer Price Index of Wheat Flour (Spring[2])   June 1983 = 100

Year	Jan.	Feb.	Mar.	Apr.	May	June	July	Aug.	Sept.	Oct.	Nov.	Dec.	Average
2001	104.7	105.1	106.2	105.7	106.9	108.2	107.9	106.8	107.4	110.0	109.5	108.8	107.3
2002	109.6	109.6	110.6	106.5	108.2	108.8	112.6	115.5	120.9	123.0	119.3	116.6	113.4
2003	119.4	121.6	120.2	120.3	122.6	121.6	119.2	122.2	120.4	117.2	121.1	122.4	120.7
2004	123.5	125.1	123.9	124.0	127.6	126.4	125.2	121.0	128.5	127.2	130.2	128.5	125.9
2005	128.5	130.4	130.8	127.6	129.6	130.8	130.3	129.7	130.6	131.4	133.6	131.8	130.4
2006	130.2	134.2	132.8	139.4	142.2	144.2	148.5	141.6	144.2	151.9	151.8	147.5	142.4
2007	144.8	144.6	148.2	153.2	154.3	161.9	167.4	174.0	196.2	209.4	207.1	229.5	174.2
2008	239.6	278.9	293.6	262.8	248.1	246.5	228.5	229.5	214.6	194.8	190.8	181.5	234.1
2009	187.4	185.3	186.5	183.4	185.0	196.2	176.4	171.1	165.2	168.0	169.2	168.5	178.5
2010[1]	167.2	168.1	163.7	162.5	167.1	161.7	169.7	190.5	190.6	190.1	203.7	207.9	178.6

[1] Preliminary.   [2] Standard patent.   *Source: Bureau of Labor Statistics, U.S. Department of Commerce (BLS) (0212-0301)*

World Wheat Flour Production (Monthly Average)   In Thousands of Metric Tons

Year	Australia	France	Germany	Hungary	India	Japan	Kazak-hstan	Rep. of Korea	Mexico	Poland	Russia	Turkey	United Kingdom
2001	NA	NA	403.1	72.4	197.2	387.2	116.5	142.8	221.1	126.8	866.6	145.2	374.0
2002	NA	473.9	415.3	67.6	211.6	389.4	143.4	151.2	218.3	135.2	797.3	139.6	369.0
2003	NA	467.3	424.4	70.7	234.1	391.0	144.2	149.3	220.6	143.1	821.4	159.8	365.0
2004	NA	465.8	441.8	67.6	238.5	390.1	145.2	157.6	217.4	135.2	799.5	176.8	370.0
2005	NA	464.5	437.9	67.3	205.4	384.6	197.6	153.1	239.1	207.3	765.8	299.0	368.0
2006	NA	472.3	444.2	62.2	180.3	384.6	207.9	154.2	243.8	211.9	776.1	290.0	366.0
2007	NA	478.2	437.7	59.7	181.1	387.8	224.6	146.7	243.8	124.3	757.0	310.0	NA
2008	NA	477.8	453.0	57.6	178.6	387.3	242.0	140.1	244.7	109.8	762.4	327.4	NA
2009[1]	NA	449.5	429.1	59.2	195.1	379.9	255.0	150.7	249.9	143.2	779.8	349.6	NA
2010[2]	NA	464.5	451.2		202.6	396.9		159.2	256.3	122.8	736.7	367.7	NA

[1] Preliminary.   [2] Estimate.   NA = Not available.   *Source: United Nations (UN)*

309

WHEAT

Production of Wheat Flour in the United States   In Millions of Sacks--100 Pounds Each

Year	July	Aug.	Sept.	Oct.	Nov.	Dec.	Jan.	Feb.	Mar.	Apr.	May	June	Total
2001-02	-----	102.1	-----	-----	105.8	-----	-----	96.0	-----	-----	96.3	-----	400.2
2002-03	-----	102.1	-----	-----	100.3	-----	-----	95.9	-----	-----	96.8	-----	395.0
2003-04	-----	103.1	-----	-----	100.5	-----	-----	96.6	-----	-----	96.8	-----	396.9
2004-05	-----	100.9	-----	-----	99.7	-----	-----	95.9	-----	-----	96.2	-----	392.7
2005-06	-----	102.5	-----	-----	100.3	-----	-----	98.1	-----	-----	98.0	-----	398.9
2006-07	-----	104.9	-----	-----	102.5	-----	-----	100.3	-----	-----	102.5	-----	410.1
2007-08	-----	109.0	-----	-----	107.1	-----	-----	101.4	-----	-----	102.5	-----	420.0
2008-09	-----	108.2	-----	-----	104.2	-----	-----	100.7	-----	-----	102.9	-----	416.0
2009-10	-----	107.4	-----	-----	103.7	-----	-----	102.3	-----	-----	100.6	-----	414.0
2010-11[1]	-----	108.5	-----	-----	104.7	-----	-----		-----	-----		-----	426.5

[1] Preliminary.   *Source: Bureau of the Census, U.S. Department of Commerce*

United States Wheat Flour Exports (Grain Equivalent[2])   In Thousands of Bushels

Year	June	July	Aug.	Sept.	Oct.	Nov.	Dec.	Jan.	Feb.	Mar.	Apr.	May	Total
2001-02	1,412	661	1,990	1,005	3,226	2,534	2,479	2,207	3,294	2,301	2,802	2,759	26,670
2002-03	1,474	1,547	753	1,373	2,437	2,854	4,645	1,049	884	1,146	1,083	541	19,786
2003-04	824	1,074	3,444	1,087	765	1,295	1,673	1,789	1,342	1,020	732	1,386	16,431
2004-05	742	1,220	885	770	834	1,005	1,347	955	617	756	722	781	10,634
2005-06	859	686	839	720	840	871	734	572	620	937	1,188	966	9,832
2006-07	720	488	780	610	532	754	756	786	999	941	1,425	2,711	11,502
2007-08	1,467	1,220	1,277	1,135	1,758	2,515	1,960	1,224	1,544	1,328	1,114	1,126	17,668
2008-09	1,417	1,052	1,093	1,053	856	1,055	958	969	858	750	687	793	11,541
2009-10	865	1,515	1,704	1,473	2,255	1,609	1,194	1,231	1,722	2,525	1,652	1,993	19,738
2010-11[1]	1,158	915	898	1,005	1,727	988							13,382

[1] Preliminary.   [2] Includes meal, groats and durum.   *Source: Economic Research Service, U.S. Department of Agriculture (ERS-USDA)*

Supply and Distribution of Wheat Flour in the United States

Year	Wheat Ground -- 1,000 Bu. --	Milfeed Production - 1,000 Tons -	Flour Production[3]	Flour & Product Imports[2]	Total Supply In 1,000 Cwt.	Exports Flour	Exports Products	Domestic Disappearance	Total Population July 1 -- Millions --	Per Capita Disappearance -- Pounds --
2000	944,868	7,374	421,270	9,666	430,936	16,005	1,693	413,239	282.4	146.3
2001	914,036	7,273	404,521	10,130	414,651	10,507	1,695	402,449	285.3	141.0
2002	889,412	6,893	394,700	11,291	405,991	9,226	2,683	394,082	288.1	136.8
2003	889,188	7,029	396,215	11,145	407,360	5,768	3,953	397,639	290.8	136.7
2004	876,047	6,764	393,925	10,726	404,651	5,152	4,662	394,837	293.5	134.5
2005	884,101	6,826	394,973	11,262	406,235	3,747	4,741	397,748	296.2	134.3
2006	894,527	6,916	403,391	11,740	415,131	3,412	5,867	405,852	299.1	135.7
2007	923,756	7,103	418,836	11,511	430,347	6,707	6,486	417,155	302.0	138.1
2008	907,979	6,753	416,283	10,822	427,105	4,925	6,179	416,001	304.8	136.5
2009[1]	896,060	6,460	414,658	10,313	424,971	5,911	5,338	413,722	307.5	134.6

[1] Preliminary.   [2] Commercial production of wheat flour, whole wheat, industrial and durum flour and farina reported by Bureau of Census.
Source: Economic Research Service, U.S. Department of Agriculture (ERS-USDA)

Wheat and Flour Price Relationships at Milling Centers in the United States   In Dollars

	At Kansas City					At Minneapolis				
	Cost of Wheat to Produce 100 lb. Flour[1]	Wholesale Price of Bakery Flour 100 lb. Flour[2]	By-Products Obtained 100 lb. Flour[3]	Total Products Actual	Over Cost of Wheat	Cost of Wheat to Produce 100 lb. Flour[1]	Wholesale Price of Bakery Flour 100 lb. Flour[2]	By-Products Obtained 100 lb. Flour[3]	Total Products Actual	Over Cost of Wheat
Year										
2003-04	9.43	10.58	1.36	11.95	2.52	9.98	10.67	1.15	11.82	1.84
2004-05	9.33	10.88	.95	11.83	2.50	10.62	11.31	.94	12.25	1.62
2005-06	10.38	11.73	1.03	12.76	2.38	11.35	12.25	.93	13.19	1.84
2006-07	12.41	13.27	1.57	14.85	2.44	12.33	12.92	1.50	14.41	2.08
2007-08	22.67	22.83	2.00	24.83	2.16	24.66	24.94	2.03	26.98	2.32
2008-09	17.14	17.60	2.18	19.77	2.63	19.44	19.18	2.15	21.33	1.89
2009-10	13.29	14.13	1.51	15.64	2.35	16.16	15.90	1.55	17.45	1.29
2010-11	15.90	16.21	1.82	18.03	2.14	18.67	17.65	1.86	19.51	.84
June-Aug.	14.27	15.30	1.18	16.48	2.21	17.18	16.75	1.35	18.10	.92
Sept.-Nov.	17.52	17.12	2.46	19.58	2.06	20.16	18.55	2.37	20.92	.75

[1] Based on 73% extraction rate, cost of 2.28 bushels: At Kansas City, No. 1 hard winter 13% protein; and at Minneapolis, No. 1 dark northern spring, 14% protein.   [2] quoted as mid-month bakers' standard patent at Kansas City and spring standard patent at Minneapolis, bulk basis.   [3] Assumed 50-50 millfeed distribution between bran and shorts or middlings, bulk basis.   *Source: Agricultural Marketing Service, U.S. Department of Agriculture*

Wool

Wool is light, warm, absorbs moisture, and is resistant to fire. Wool is also used for insulation in houses, for carpets and furnishing, and for bedding. Sheep are sheared once a year and produce about 4.3 kg of "greasy" wool per year.

Greasy wool is wool that has not been washed or cleaned. Wool fineness is determined by fiber diameter, which is measured in microns (one millionth of a meter). Fine wool is softer, lightweight, and produces fine clothing. Merino sheep produce the finest wool.

Wool futures and options are traded on the Sydney Futures Exchange (SFE), where there are futures and options contracts on greasy wool, and futures on fine wool and broad wool. All three futures contracts call for the delivery of merino combing wool. Wool yarn futures are traded on the Chubu Commodity Exchange (CCE), the Osaka Mercantile Exchange (OME) and the Tokyo Commodity Exchange (TOCOM).

Prices – Average monthly wool prices at U.S. mills in 2010 (through November) rose by +45.7% yr/yr to $3.20 per pound, a new record high. Wool prices in 2009 were about double the 3-decade low of $1.09 posted in 2000. The value of U.S. wool production in 2010 rose +45.0% to $35.288 million, a new record high.

Supply – World production of wool has been falling in the past decade due to the increased use of polyester fabrics. Greasy wool world production in 2009, the latest reporting year for the data series, fell -1.8% yr/yr to 2.080 million metric tons. The world's largest producers of greasy wool in 2009 were Australia with 17.8% of world production, followed by China (17.7%), and New Zealand (10%).

U.S. wool production of 10,000 metric tons in 2009 accounted for only 0.7% of world production. U.S. production of wool goods rose +18.4% yr/yr in 2009 (9 months annualized) to 5.6 million yards, up from last year's record low of 4.8 million yards. That was less that 4% of the record high of 222.5 million yards of wool goods production seen in 1969. The U.S. sheep herd in 2010 rose +0.5% to 4.215 million sheep, up from last year's record low of 4.195 million sheep.

Demand – U.S. consumption of apparel wool has dropped sharply, along with production, and it fell 13.5% yr/yr to a record low of 13.333 million pounds in 2006, which is latest data available. The breakdown of U.S. mill consumption in 2003, the latest data available, showed that wool usage for carpets was 6.017 million pounds, which was a new record low. Wool usage for apparel production in 2003 was 43.869 million pounds, up +21.8%, up from the 2002 record low of 36.015 million pounds.

Trade – U.S. exports of domestic wool in 2006 (latest data) rose +45.2% yr/yr to 18.000 million pounds. U.S. imports in 2006 rose +17.8% to 7.324 million pounds.

World Production of Wool, Greasy   In Metric Tons

Year	Argen-tina	Australia	China	Kazak-hstan	New Zealand	Pakistan	Rom-ania	Russia	South Africa	United Kingdom	United States	Uruguay	World Total
2000	58,000	671,000	292,502	22,924	257,200	38,900	17,997	39,241	52,671	64,000	21,070	57,218	2,318,945
2001	56,000	657,000	298,254	23,612	236,661	39,200	16,880	39,210	48,649	55,000	19,510	56,744	2,264,128
2002	65,000	587,274	307,588	24,818	228,300	39,400	16,659	41,428	47,502	60,000	18,633	39,376	2,183,196
2003	72,000	551,107	338,058	26,782	229,600	39,700	16,879	44,586	44,156	60,000	17,326	34,922	2,189,461
2004	60,000	509,473	373,902	28,499	217,700	39,900	17,505	47,111	44,156	60,000	17,046	37,271	2,179,460
2005	60,000	519,660	393,172	30,444	215,500	40,000	17,600	48,033	45,000	60,000	16,865	42,009	2,225,729
2006	60,000	486,726	388,777	32,389	224,700	40,100	19,378	50,276	45,000	60,000	16,284	46,709	2,202,990
2007	60,000	450,529	363,470	34,200	217,900	40,600	21,025	52,022	45,000	62,000	15,750	45,570	2,151,662
2008[1]	60,000	407,881	367,687	35,200	217,900	41,000	17,700	53,491	45,000	62,000	14,952	45,000	2,117,390
2009[2]	60,000	370,601		36,400				54,658			13,999		2,080,190

[1] Preliminary.   [2] Estimate.   NA = Not avaliable.   *Source: Food and Agriculture Organization of the United Nations (FAO-UN)*

Production of Wool Goods[2] in the United States   In Millions of Yards

Year	First Quarter	Second Quarter	Third Quarter	Fourth Quarter	Total	Year	First Quarter	Second Quarter	Third Quarter	Fourth Quarter	Total
2001	20.8	12.4	11.0	9.0	53.2	2006	4.1	3.9	2.8	2.8	13.7
2002	7.4	8.6	6.2	5.5	27.7	2007	2.6	2.5	2.2	2.1	9.5
2003	6.5	6.4	5.2	4.9	23.0	2008	2.3	2.1	1.7	1.5	7.5
2004	5.5	5.9	4.2	4.2	19.8	2009	1.4	1.2	1.0	1.1	4.8
2005	4.9	6.9	4.2	4.3	20.3	2010[1]	1.5	1.5	1.2		5.6

[1] Preliminary.   [2] Woolen and worsted woven goods, except woven felts.   *Source: Bureau of the Census, U.S. Department of Commerce*

Consumption of Apparel Wool[2] in the United States   In Millions of Pounds--Clean Basis

Year	First Quarter	Second Quarter	Third Quarter	Fourth Quarter	Total	Year	First Quarter	Second Quarter	Third Quarter	Fourth Quarter	Total
1997	33.1	33.8	30.6	32.8	130.4	2002	11.0	10.5	6.5	W	36.0
1998	29.3	29.6	21.9	17.5	98.4	2003	W	W	W	W	W
1999	17.3	16.8	15.8	13.6	63.5	2004	W	W	W	W	W
2000	17.4	16.1	14.6	13.9	63.0	2005	2.3	5.2	3.9	4.0	15.4
2001	17.0	13.5	11.6	10.9	53.0	2006[1]	3.7	3.8	2.8	3.0	13.3

[1] Preliminary.   [2] Woolen and worsted woven goods, except woven felts.   W = Withheld.   Source: Bureau of the Census, U.S. Department of Commerce

WOOL

Salient Statistics of Wool in the United States

Year	Sheep & Lambs Shorn[4] -1,000's-	Weight per Fleece -In Lbs.-	Shorn Wool Production 1,000 Lbs.	Price per Lb.	Value of Production -$1,000-	Shorn Wool Support Cents Per Lb.	Shorn Payment Rate	Total Wool Production	Domestic Production	Domestic Wool Exports	Dutiable Imports for Consumption[3] (48's & Finer)	Total New Supply[2]	Duty Free Raw Imports (Not Finer than 46's)	Mill Apparel	Consumption Carpet
								\-\-\- In Thousands of Pounds \-\-\-							
2002	5,476	7.50	41,322	53.0	21,876	100	40.0	41,078	21,689	8,461	10,526	37,913	14,159	36,015	6,891
2003	5,074	7.50	38,229	73.0	28,126	100	40.0	38,197	20,168	11,067	4,986	29,836	15,749	43,869	6,017
2004	5,073	7.40	37,622	80.0	29,921	100	40.0	37,581	19,843	11,168	6,204	31,334	16,455	NA	NA
2005	5,072	7.30	37,232	71.0	26,272	100	40.0	37,182	19,632	12,573	6,220	25,434	12,156	NA	NA
2006	4,852	7.40	36,019	68.0	24,510	100	40.0	35,899	18,955	17,998	7,324	18,210	9,929	NA	NA
2007	4,657	7.50	34,723	87.0	30,242	100	40.0	34,723	18,334	17,077	5,245	15,527	9,025	NA	NA
2008	4,434	7.43	32,963	99.0	32,486	100	40.0	32,963	17,404	10,307	4,551	20,279	8,631	NA	NA
2009	4,195	7.40	38,060	79.0	24,337	100	40.0				3,306				
2010[1]	4,215	7.30	30,600	115.0	35,288										

[1] Preliminary.   [2] Production minus exports plus imports; stocks not taken into consideration.   [3] Apparel wool includes all dutiable wool; carpet wool includes all duty-free wool.   [4] Includes sheep shorn at commercial feeding yards.
Source: Economic Research Service, U.S. Department of Agriculture (ERS-USDA)

Shorn Wool Prices   In Dollars Per Pound

Year	US Farm Price Shorn Wool Greasy Basis[1] -- cents/Lb --	Australian Offering Price, Clean[2] — Grade 70's type 61	Grade 64's type 63	Grade 62's type 64	Grade 60/62's type 64A	Grade 58's-56's 433-34	Market Indicator[3] Cents/Kg.	Graded Territory Shorn Wool, Clean Basis[4] — 62's Staple 3"& up	60's Staple 3"& up	58's Staple 3 1/4"& up	56's Staple 3 1/4"& up	54's Staple 3 1/2"& up
		\-\-\- In Dollars Per Pound \-\-\-						In Dollars Per Pound				
2001	36.0	2.42	1.66	1.69	1.60	1.54	841	1.21	.91	.77	.66	.65
2002	53.0	2.87	2.68	2.70	2.63	2.55	1,051	1.90	1.41	1.40	1.19	1.02
2003	73.0	3.23	3.14	3.16	3.02	2.81	821	2.41	1.73	1.79	1.48	1.24
2004	80.0	3.21	2.75	2.89	2.49	2.33	NA	2.35	1.59	1.74	1.50	1.25
2005	71.0	2.99	2.57	2.65	2.42	2.23	NA	1.86	1.46	1.39	1.41	1.03
2006	68.0	3.17	2.65	2.75	2.47	2.26	NA	1.79	1.45	1.30	1.00	.94
2007	87.0	4.41	3.73	3.90	3.31	2.77	NA	2.65	2.24	1.82	1.32	1.04
2008	99.0	4.35	3.47	3.59	3.19	2.71	NA	3.09	2.45	2.25	1.82	1.20
2009	79.0	3.48	3.02	3.08	2.86	2.46	NA	2.27	1.89	1.73	1.36	1.34

[1] Annual weighted average.   [2] F.O.B. Australian Wool Corporation South Carolina warehouse in bond.   [3] Index of prices of all wool sold in Australia for the crop year July-June.   [4] Wool principally produced in Texas and the Rocky Mountain States.
Source: Economic Research Service, U.S. Department of Agriculture (ERS-USDA)

Average Wool Prices[1] --Australian-- 64's, Type 62, Duty Paid--U.S. Mills   In Cents Per Pound

Year	Jan.	Feb.	Mar.	Apr.	May	June	July	Aug.	Sept.	Oct.	Nov.	Dec.	Average
2001	160	168	164	158	164	166	167	172	169	159	166	183	166
2002	218	243	250	251	249	259	255	254	268	312	322	328	267
2003	344	346	326	333	296	326	316	308	306	292	285	290	314
2004	304	294	288	281	261	275	277	263	255	255	270	271	275
2005	273	271	268	242	265	266	270	259	252	244	233	236	257
2006	243	256	259	251	258	254	260	260	258	260	308	315	265
2007	352	344	355	367	381	380	378	359	364	393	405	400	373
2008	416	411	407	404	378	376	386	346	317	257	226	239	347
2009	229	223	230	250	287	295	295	318	339	379	386	392	302
2010	423	404	412	404	381	379	381	381	390	419	450	479	409

[1] Raw, clean basis.   *Source: Economic Research Service, U.S. Department of Agriculture (ERS-USDA)*

Average Wool Prices --Domestic[1]-- Graded Territory, 64's, Staple 2 3/4 & Up--U.S. Mills   In Cents Per Pound

Year	Jan.	Feb.	Mar.	Apr.	May	June	July	Aug.	Sept.	Oct.	Nov.	Dec.	Average
2001	95	100	108	129	137	125	127	122	126	130	122	127	121
2002	134	150	170	181	189	200	200	200	198	204	223	233	190
2003	236	260	258	250	223	234	239	243	243	243	232	233	241
2004	233	239	240	240	235	229	233	236	240	236	230	230	235
2005	215	207	200	185	185	185	179	186	195	181	168	140	186
2006	NQ	NQ	162	183	173	171	165	165	165	NQ	212	220	180
2007	186	242	245	279	311	295	285	270	276	NQ	NQ	NQ	265
2008	290	318	319	325	285	295	305	NQ	NQ	NQ	NQ	NQ	305
2009	NQ	NQ	NQ	157	215	226	228	223	NQ	270	NQ	NQ	220
2010	NQ	NQ	310	337	341	313	300	NQ	NQ	NQ	NQ	334	323

[1] Raw, shorn, clean basis.   NQ = No quote.   *Source: Economic Research Service, U.S. Department of Agriculture (ERS-USDA)*

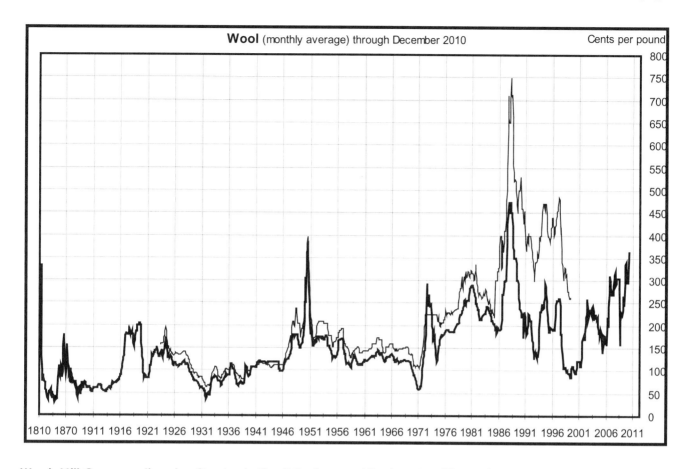

Wool (monthly average) through December 2010 — Cents per pound

Wool: Mill Consumption, by Grades in the U.S., Scoured Basis   In Millions of Pounds

| | ---- Apparel Class[1] ---- | | | | | | | |
| | -- Woolen System -- | | | -- Worsted System -- | | | | |
Year	60's & Finer	Coarser Than 60's	Total	60's & Finer	Coarser Than 60's	Total	All Total	Carpet Wool[2]
1998	31,258	15,079	46,337	42,243	9,793	52,036	98,373	16,331
1999	18,379	10,772	29,151	27,429	6,955	34,384	63,535	13,950
2000	18,503	13,432	31,935	21,732	8,374	30,106	62,041	15,205
2001	16,062	9,849	25,911	NA	NA	27,058	52,969	13,310
2002	9,627	8,482	18,109	NA	NA	17,906	36,015	6,891
2003	6,681	5,309	11,990	NA	NA	31,879	43,869	6,017
2004	NA	NA	NA	NA	NA	NA	NA	NA
2005	NA	NA	NA	NA	NA	NA	NA	NA
2006[3]	NA	NA	NA	NA	NA	NA	NA	NA
2007[4]	NA	NA	NA	NA	NA	NA	NA	NA

[1] Domestic & duty-paid foreign.   [2] Duty-free foreign.   [3] Preliminary.   [4] Estimate.   NA = Not available.   *Source: Economic Research Service, U.S. Department of Agriculture (ERS-USDA)*

United States Imports[2] of Unmanufactured Wool (Clean Yield)   In Millions of Pounds

Year	Jan.	Feb.	Mar.	Apr.	May	June	July	Aug.	Sept.	Oct.	Nov.	Dec.	Total
2001	4.9	4.3	4.3	1.5	2.9	2.8	4.0	1.9	2.0	2.8	1.3	1.3	34.1
2002	1.9	1.8	2.6	2.4	2.3	1.5	1.6	1.2	1.9	2.4	2.1	3.1	24.6
2003	2.5	2.8	2.3	2.2	2.1	1.8	1.2	1.1	0.8	1.6	1.1	1.2	20.8
2004	1.3	1.5	2.1	1.8	1.4	2.8	1.6	1.9	2.7	2.4	1.9	1.2	22.7
2005	2.3	1.1	2.0	1.5	1.5	2.0	1.5	1.4	1.0	1.7	1.5	1.0	18.4
2006	1.9	1.0	1.8	1.5	1.3	1.6	0.9	1.5	1.2	1.5	1.6	1.6	17.3
2007	1.3	1.1	1.4	1.4	1.4	1.3	1.1	0.9	0.8	1.3	1.3	1.0	14.3
2008	1.8	0.9	1.4	1.1	1.3	1.1	1.3	0.8	1.2	1.0	0.7	0.7	13.2
2009	1.1	1.0	1.0	0.8	0.5	0.7	0.8	0.8	0.4	0.8	0.6	0.6	9.4
2010[1]	0.7	0.3	0.7	0.8	0.4	0.6	1.2	0.7	0.7	0.6	0.6	0.4	7.6

[1] Preliminary.   [2] Data are imports for consumption.   *Source: Economic Research Service, U.S. Department of Agriculture (ERS-USDA)*

Zinc

Zinc (symbol Zn) is a bluish-while metallic element that is the 24th most abundant element in the earth's crust. Zinc is never found in its pure state but rather in zinc oxide, zinc silicate, zinc carbonate, zinc sulfide, and in minerals such as zincite, hemimorphite, smithsonite, franklinite, and sphalerite. Zinc is utilized as a protective coating for other metals, such as iron and steel, in a process known as galvanizing. Zinc is used as an alloy with copper to make brass and also as an alloy with aluminum and magnesium. There are, however, a number of substitutes for zinc in chemicals, electronics, and pigments. For example, with aluminum, steel and plastics can substitute for galvanized sheets. Aluminum alloys can also replace brass. Zinc is used as the negative electrode in dry cell (flashlight) batteries and also in the zinc-mercuric-oxide battery cell, which is the round, flat battery typically used in watches, cameras, and other electronic devices. Zinc is also used in medicine as an antiseptic ointment.

Zinc futures and options are traded on the London Metals Exchange (LME). The LME zinc futures contract calls for the delivery of 25 metric tons of at least 99.995% purity zinc ingots (slabs and plates). The contract trades in terms of U.S. dollars per metric ton. Zinc first started trading on the LME in 1915.

Prices – Zinc prices in 2010 rose 31.0% to a monthly average of 102.05 cents per pound, but still below the 2006 record high of 158.44 cents per pound.

Supply – World smelter production of zinc in 2010 rose +7.1% to a record high of 12.000 million metric tons. The world's largest producer of zinc in 2010 is China with 29% of world smelter production, followed by Australia with 12% (in 2008), Canada with 6%, the U.S. with 6%, and Mexico with 5%. China's production of 2.8 million metric tons in 2009 was more than five times its production level of 550,000 metric tons seen in 1990. Australia's latest production data was from 2008 when it produced 579,000 metric tons.

U.S. smelter production in 2010 fell -2.2% to 720,000 metric tons. U.S. mine production of recoverable zinc in 2010 rose +2.4% yr/yr to 725,300 metric tons. U.S. production in 2009 (latest data) of slab zinc on a primary basis fell -20.0% yr/yr to 100,000 metric tons, while secondary production fell -28.6% yr/yr to 115,000 metric tons.

Demand – U.S. consumption of slab zinc in 2009 (latest data) fell by -7.8% yr/yr to an 18-year low of 920,000 metric tons. U.S. consumption of all classes of zinc fell by -16.4% yr/yr in 2007 (latest data) to 1.170 million metric tons, which was a new 16-year low. U.S. consumption of slab zinc by fabricators in 2010 fell by -5.8% yr/yr to a record low of 213,000 metric tons.

The breakdown of consumption by industries for 2008 (latest data) showed that 61% of slab zinc consumption was for galvanizers, 25 for brass products, and the rest for other miscellaneous industries. The consumption breakdown by grades for 2008 showed that 45% was for special high grade, 24% for prime western, 18% for re-melt and other, and 14% for high grade. Within that grade breakdown, Prime Western consumption has fallen by nearly half since 2000.

Trade – The U.S. in 2009 relied on imports for 76% of its consumption of zinc, up sharply from the 35% average seen in the 1990s. U.S. imports for consumption of slab zinc fell by -3.4 yr/yr to 700,000 metric tons in 2009, while imports of zinc ore rose +19.0% yr/yr to 75,000 metric tons. The dollar value of U.S. zinc imports in 2008 fell by -38.5% yr/yr to $1.902 billion, down from the 2007 record high $3.091 billion. The breakdown of imports in 2008 shows that most zinc is imported as blocks, pigs and slabs (725,000 metric tons); followed by ores (63,200 metric tons); dust, powder and flakes (28,500 metric tons); waste and scrap (17,000 metric tons); dross, ashes and fume (13,200 metric tons); and sheets, plates and other (3,330 metric tons).

Salient Statistics of Zinc in the United States   In Metric Tons

Year	Slab Zinc Production Primary	Slab Zinc Production Secondary	Mine Production Recovered	Imports for Consumption Slab Zinc	Imports for Consumption Ore (Zinc Content)	Exports Slab Zinc	Exports Ore (Zinc Content)	Consumption Slab Zinc	Consumed as Ore	Consumption All Classes[3]	Net Import Reliance As a % of Apparent Consumption	High-Grade, Price -Cents/Lb.-
2000	228,000	143,000	805,000	915,000	52,800	2,770	523,000	1,330,000	----	1,630,000	60	55.61
2001	203,000	108,000	799,000	813,000	84,000	1,180	696,000	1,150,000	----	1,420,000	60	43.96
2002	182,000	113,000	754,000	874,000	122,000	1,160	822,000	1,170,000	----	1,420,000	60	38.64
2003	187,000	150,000	768,000	792,000	164,000	1,680	841,000	1,120,000	----	1,390,000	58	40.63
2004	194,000	156,000	739,000	868,000	231,000	3,300	745,000	1,190,000	----	1,430,000	72	52.47
2005	195,000	156,000	748,000	700,000	156,000	784	786,000	1,080,000	----	1,290,000	67	67.11
2006	113,000	156,000	727,000	895,000	383,000	2,530	825,000	1,190,000	----	1,400,000	78	158.89
2007	121,000	157,000	803,000	758,000	271,000	8,070	816,000	1,040,000	----	1,170,000	74	154.40
2008[1]	125,000	161,000	778,000	725,000	63,200	3,250	725,000	1,010,000	----		73	88.93
2009[2]	94,000	109,000	736,000	686,000	74,200	2,960	785,000	893,000	----		76	77.91

[1] Preliminary.   [2] Estimate.   [3] Based on apparent consumption of slab zinc plus zinc content of ores and concentrates and secondary materials used to make zinc dust and chemicals.   *Source: U.S. Geological Survey (USGS)*

World Smelter Production of Zinc[3] In Thousands of Metric Tons

Year	Australia	Belgium	Canada	China	France	Germany	Italy	Japan	Kazak-hstan	Mexico	Spain	United States	World Total
2001	558.5	259.3	661.2	2,040.0	347.0	358.3	177.8	684.1	277.1	303.8	418.0	311.0	9,320
2002	573.0	260.0	793.4	2,100.0	350.0	378.6	176.0	673.9	286.3	302.1	488.0	362.0	9,840
2003	613.0	244.0	761.2	2,320.0	268.0	388.1	123.0	686.1	316.7	320.4	519.0	351.0	10,100
2004	538.0	263.0	805.4	2,720.0	268.4	382.0	118.0	667.2	357.1	316.9	524.8	350.0	10,600
2005	463.3	257.0	724.0	2,780.0	267.5	344.9	121.0	675.2	364.8	327.2	506.2	351.0	10,300
2006	469.0	251.0	824.5	3,170.0	127.8	342.6	109.0	654.2	364.8	279.7	507.4	269.0	10,800
2007	508.0	241.0	802.1	3,740.0	129.1	294.7	109.0	638.7	358.2	321.9	494.1	278.0	11,400
2008	505.0	251.0	764.3	4,000.0	117.9	292.3	100.0	632.6	365.6	305.4	456.1	286.0	11,700
2009[1]	531.0	26.0	685.5	4,360.0	161.0	159.0	1,000.0	643.0	328.8	300.0	500.8	203.0	11,400
2010[2]			670.0	3,500.0					480.0	550.0		220.0	12,000

[1] Preliminary. [2] Estimate. [3] Secondary metal included. *Source: U.S. Geological Survey (USGS)*

Consumption (Reported) of Slab Zinc in the United States, by Industries and Grades In Metric Tons

Year	Total	Galvanizers	Brass Products	Zinc-Base Alloy[3]	Zinc Oxide	Other	Special High Grade	High Grade	Remelt and Other	Prime Western
2000	640,000	293,000	82,800	123,000	[4]	NA	332,000	60,600	41,500	206,000
2001	543,000	281,000	74,400	91,200	[4]	NA	294,000	54,000	30,300	165,000
2002	496,000	265,000	86,800	103,000	[4]	NA	294,000	61,400	28,000	113,000
2003	506,000	264,000	87,400	113,000	[4]	NA	310,000	60,000	27,600	109,000
2004	510,000	248,000	96,700	W	[4]	NA	321,000	58,800	33,600	96,200
2005	486,000	238,000	83,900	W	[4]	NA	316,000	62,100	40,300	68,000
2006	504,000	259,000	42,300	W	[4]	203,000	315,000	69,100	73,900	75,400
2007	484,000	304,000	39,700	W	[4]	141,000	242,000	80,700	92,700	69,000
2008[1]	433,000	262,000	107,000	23,200	[4]	40,600	195,000	60,400	75,800	102,000
2009[2]	306,000	226,000	45,500	17,900	[4]	17,200	170,000	46,600	55,000	34,600

[1] Preliminary. [2] Estimated. [3] Die casters. [4] Included in other. W = Withheld. NA = Not applicable. *Source: U.S. Geological Survey (USGS)*

United States Foreign Trade of Zinc In Metric Tons

Year	Ores[3]	Blocks, Pigs, Slabs	Sheets, Plates, Other	Waste & Scrap	Dross, Ashes, Fume	Dust, Powder & Flakes	Total Value $1,000	Blocks, Pigs, Anodes Un-wrought	Un-wrought Alloys	Sheets, Plates & Strips	Angles, Bars, Rods, etc.	Waste & Scrap	Dust (Blue Powder)	Zinc Ore & Con-centrates
1999	74,600	1,060,000	22,600	26,600	20,000	21,300	1,133,890	----	----	----	----	28,200	5,050	531,000
2000	52,800	915,000	9,380	36,500	15,500	26,700	1,272,750	----	----	----	----	36,100	4,830	523,000
2001	84,000	813,000	7,240	39,300	12,000	26,700	937,110	----	----	----	----	44,000	4,690	696,000
2002	122,000	874,000	1,640	31,200	15,500	30,900	887,785	----	----	----	----	47,700	5,660	822,000
2003	164,000	792,000	1,790	10,300	14,100	27,400	839,705	----	----	----	----	50,200	6,550	841,000
2004	231,000	868,000	2,500	10,800	16,100	24,800	1,142,733	----	----	----	----	53,900	7,640	745,000
2005	156,000	700,000	3,630	9,580	15,800	23,400	1,198,040	----	----	----	----	56,000	9,310	786,000
2006	383,000	895,000	2,050	14,200	31,100	30,100	2,771,580	2,530	19,900	3,780	11,200	83,800	16,400	825,000
2007[1]	271,000	758,000	2,160	21,800	18,600	31,300	3,090,910	8,070	22,500	4,310	26,700	102,000	19,400	816,000
2008[2]	63,200	725,000	3,330	17,000	13,200	28,500	1,901,830	3,250	8,550	4,970	28,100	91,000	13,000	725,000

[1] Preliminary. [2] Estimate. [3] Zinc content. *Source: U.S. Geological Survey (USGS)*

Mine Production of Recoverable Zinc in the United States In Thousands of Metric Tons

Year	Jan.	Feb.	Mar.	Apr.	May	June	July	Aug.	Sept.	Oct.	Nov.	Dec.	Total
2001	68.4	60.5	62.2	65.2	66.9	66.1	66.7	67.6	60.9	67.1	54.0	55.4	799.0
2002	61.3	60.4	67.8	55.2	63.4	63.8	66.0	67.2	54.4	68.3	61.3	65.5	754.6
2003	65.2	60.2	62.7	54.0	65.2	64.0	64.5	59.6	63.3	58.6	61.0	60.5	738.8
2004	60.4	55.3	57.9	58.5	56.1	59.0	60.8	62.0	61.6	61.6	56.8	56.5	706.5
2005	53.6	56.0	64.1	56.7	53.3	64.6	64.5	68.9	61.8	64.4	51.2	62.3	721.4
2006	58.1	51.4	61.5	54.2	54.3	59.8	64.7	62.3	65.8	66.3	51.5	47.4	697.3
2007	60.3	55.8	63.5	56.6	61.2	64.1	63.1	69.5	61.3	64.6	53.9	69.6	743.5
2008	72.4	67.3	72.1	65.6	67.8	72.5	72.4	61.6	58.7	52.2	52.8	64.7	780.1
2009	69.3	54.0	55.2	58.4	56.1	58.6	57.0	62.1	60.5	65.2	49.9	62.1	708.4
2010[1]	59.4	56.5	63.5	61.6	62.6	57.4	64.8	60.3	60.0	66.0	50.0	63.2	725.3

[1] Preliminary. *Source: U.S. Geological Survey (USGS)*

ZINC

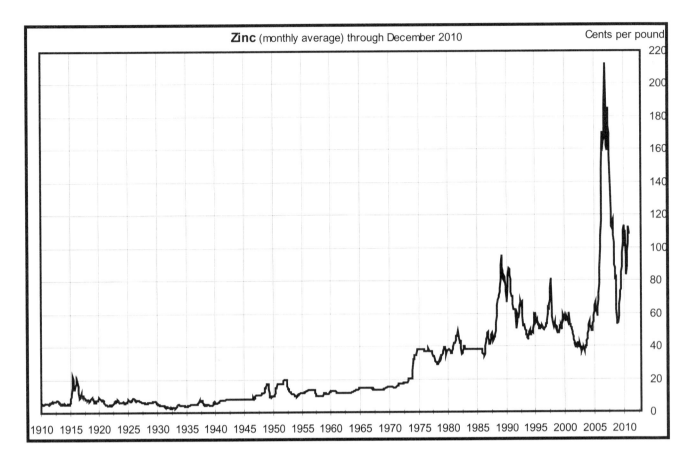

Zinc (monthly average) through December 2010 — Cents per pound

Consumption of Slab Zinc by Fabricators in the United States   In Thousands of Metric Tons

Year	Jan.	Feb.	Mar.	Apr.	May	June	July	Aug.	Sept.	Oct.	Nov.	Dec.	Total
2001	45.4	43.5	44.1	42.7	43.6	38.2	30.6	39.2	37.7	35.7	32.1	27.3	543.0
2002	31.2	31.3	30.4	33.1	34.9	34.4	34.3	35.8	36.1	36.1	32.7	33.3	403.6
2003	33.1	33.1	34.4	35.2	34.7	38.2	34.2	35.5	36.8	36.8	35.3	36.4	423.7
2004	35.1	36.2	36.6	36.7	35.9	37.0	33.7	33.6	33.8	34.6	34.3	33.4	420.9
2005	33.6	33.9	34.1	33.5	33.8	34.1	31.3	33.7	34.8	34.7	33.8	34.1	405.4
2006	34.8	34.5	34.8	34.0	33.1	34.2	32.4	33.4	31.4	32.8	32.0	32.4	399.8
2007	33.0	23.1	22.3	23.1	22.7	23.5	22.3	22.7	23.2	23.4	23.4	17.4	280.1
2008	19.7	19.8	21.0	18.6	24.8	23.3	21.5	21.5	22.1	20.2	19.5	19.4	251.4
2009	18.8	20.5	17.4	16.5	17.3	17.3	17.8	20.2	21.0	20.3	18.6	20.4	226.1
2010[1]	19.7	19.1	20.4	20.8	18.3	18.8	19.1	18.3	16.4	14.9	14.0	13.2	213.0

[1] Preliminary.   Source: U.S. Geological Survey (USGS)

Average Price of Zinc, Prime Western Slab (Delivered U.S. Basis)   In Cents Per Pound

Year	Jan.	Feb.	Mar.	Apr.	May	June	July	Aug.	Sept.	Oct.	Nov.	Dec.	Average
2001	51.82	51.29	50.55	48.95	47.54	45.56	43.62	42.53	41.14	39.53	39.99	39.25	45.15
2002	40.98	39.97	42.15	41.66	39.97	39.70	41.01	38.91	39.26	39.08	36.99	38.52	39.64
2003	38.88	38.46	38.48	36.99	37.86	38.57	40.30	39.77	39.84	43.44	44.11	47.60	40.36
2004	49.61	53.31	54.63	51.89	51.88	51.53	49.85	49.31	49.37	53.36	54.61	58.32	52.31
2005	61.10	64.57	66.59	63.55	60.70	61.97	58.26	62.76	67.73	72.10	77.60	87.45	67.03
2006	100.02	106.57	116.10	147.28	170.57	158.11	163.89	164.23	166.56	185.80	210.32	211.82	158.44
2007	183.91	161.21	158.81	171.08	184.68	173.23	169.81	155.93	139.28	140.84	122.63	112.65	156.17
2008	111.49	115.37	117.27	107.07	102.59	89.16	87.44	81.53	81.83	62.25	55.26	53.22	88.71
2009	57.28	53.96	57.96	65.19	69.91	73.34	74.38	85.30	88.25	97.11	102.32	109.97	77.91
2010	113.30	100.72	106.15	110.33	93.02	83.34	88.25	97.11	102.16	112.55	109.67	108.04	102.05

Source: American Metal Market (AMM)